LONDON LABOUR

AND THE LONDON POOR

BY

HENRY MAYHEW

WITH A NEW INTRODUCTION BY
JOHN D. ROSENBERG
Professor of English, Columbia University

IN FOUR VOLUMES
VOLUME I
The London Street-Folk (partial)

British Library Cataloguing-in-Publication Data
A catalogue record for this book is available from
the British Library

HENRY MAYHEW.

[*From a Daguerreotype by* BEARD.]

INTRODUCTION
TO THE DOVER EDITION

THIS reprint of the definitive edition of *London Labour and the London Poor* restores to our literature, after nearly a century of neglect, one of the most remarkable books of the nineteenth century. The tangled history of the text and the biography of its author remain to be written, but it is clear that the pages that follow constitute the first and possibly the greatest sociological study in English.

Of Henry Mayhew himself (1812-87), the little that is known is highly perplexing. Although extraordinary gifts of observation and articulation are everywhere present in *London Labour and the London Poor*, Mayhew dissipated most of his literary energies in writing witless farces, tawdry jest-books, moralizing biographies, and assorted ephemera. Only once—in 1841, when he acted as co-founder and editor of the then radical *Punch*—did Mayhew move clearly in the direction of his masterpiece. For the most part, one senses in Mayhew's failed schemes and rootless shiftings from place to place a quality of high-class vagabondage, a Bohemian irresponsibility curiously akin to that of the street vendors and scavengers whose lives he so richly records. In 1847, for example, this biographer of the frugal Ben Franklin narrowly escaped imprisonment for bankruptcy, and his associates, who readily acknowledged his genius, as readily deplored his "indolence" and inconstancy of purpose. Yet Mayhew walked hundreds of miles of London streets and painstakingly gathered thousands of pages of testimony in order to write his book. However wayward he may have been, he produced in *London Labour and the London Poor* an indictment of mid-century economic barbarism as compassionate and searingly accurate as Engels' classic *The Condition of the Working-Class in England*. His very detachment from conventional Victorian proprieties and his constantly shifting curiosity, like his frequent changes of residence—in short, his mobile and subversive posture within Victorian society—equipped him to portray those disestablished citizens whom Her Majesty's census-taker chose totally to ignore.

London Labour and the London Poor first appeared as a series of articles in the *Morning Chronicle* in 1849-50. The work was interrupted by litigation two years later and was at length completed in four volumes in 1861-62. The image of London that emerges from Mayhew's pages is that of a vast, ingeniously balanced mechanism in which each class subsists on the drippings and droppings of the stratum above, all the way from the rich, whom we scarcely glimpse, down to the deformed and starving, whom we see groping for bits of salvageable bone or decaying vegetables in the markets. Such extreme conditions bred weird extremities of adaptation, a remarkably diverse yet cohesive subculture of poverty. Ragged, fantastic armies, each with its distinctive jargon and implements, roamed the streets: "pure-finders" with bucket and glove, picking up dog dung and selling it to tanners; rag-gatherers, themselves dressed in the rotted cloth they salvage, armed with pointed sticks; bent, slime-soiled "mud-larks," groping at low tide in the ooze of the Thames for bits of coal, chips of wood, or copper nails dropped from the sheathing of barges, a regiment of three hundred who subsisted on average earnings of *threepence a day*. Describing the life of a boy who began mud-larking at the age of eleven, Mayhew writes (Vol. II, p. 157):

He worked every day, with 20 or 30 boys, who might all be seen at daybreak with their trowsers tucked up, groping about, and picking out the pieces of coal from the mud on the banks of the Thames. He went into the river up to his knees, and in searching the mud he often ran pieces of glass and long nails into his feet. When this was the case, he went home and dressed the wounds, but returned to the river-side directly, "for should the tide come up," he added, "without my having found something, why I must starve till next low tide." In the very cold weather he and his other shoeless companions used to stand in the hot water that ran down the river side from some of the steam-factories, to warm their frozen feet.

The remarkable first-person narrative that follows this excerpt, like hundreds of others in *London Labour and the London Poor*, recalls Mayhew's claim in his Preface that his is the first book "to publish the history of a people, from the lips of the people themselves—giving a literal description of their labour, their earnings, their trials, and their sufferings, in their own 'unvarnished' language." Mayhew invented "oral history" a century before the term was coined. He is also the explorer, as he puts it, of a class of whom "the public had less knowledge than of the most distant tribes." The rapid, wrenching industrialization of England (London's population trebled between 1800 and 1850) was breeding a new species of humanity, a rootless generation entirely environed by brick, smoke, work, and want. Mayhew devised new techniques for penetrating the uncharted regions of the disaffected and for recording their experience. With the incredible energy of the Victorians, this "indolent" journalist uncovered and codified data on the modern proletariat that whole municipal and federal agencies are only now beginning to assemble. Michael Harrington's *The Other America*, Danilo Dolci's *Inquest at Palermo*, Kenneth B. Clark's *Dark Ghetto*, Oscar Lewis' *La Vida: A Puerto Rican Family in the Culture of Poverty* are all in one way or another the offspring of *London Labour and the London Poor*.

The very virtues which make Mayhew's achievement so original have impeded its proper recognition. It is difficult to praise a book which fits into no established category. More than any other work I know, *London Labour and the London Poor* strains that flimsy boundary separating fact from art, life from literature. As Thackeray wrote, Mayhew provides us with "a picture of human life so wonderful, so awful, so piteous and pathetic, so exciting and terrible, that readers of romances own they never read anything like to it."

Consider, for example, this excerpt from the narrative of a "running-patterer," a man who hawks and at times invents accounts of murders, disasters, and the like (Vol. I, pp. 223-24):

There's nothing beats a stunning good murder, after all. Why there was Rush [a homicidal farmer]—I lived on him for a month or more. When I commenced with Rush, I was 14s. in debt for rent, and in less than fourteen days I astonished the wise men in the east by paying my landlord all I owed him. . . . Why I went down to Norwich expressly to work the execution. I worked my way down there with *"a sorrowful lamentation"* of his own composing, which I'd got written by the blind man expressly for the occasion. On the morning of the execution we beat all the regular newspapers out of the field; for we had the full, true, and particular account down, you see, by our own express, and that can beat anything that ever they can publish; for we gets it printed several days afore it comes off, and goes and stands with it right under the drop; and many's the penny I've turned away when I've been asked for an account of the whole business *before* it happened.

The patterer is indistinguishable from a character out of Dickens. Although he is a bonafide "case-history," he belongs as much to literature as to journalism, criminology, or sociology. Reading *London Labour and the London Poor*, with its brave abundance of life, its vast scope yet minuteness of detail, its celebration of the intricate, dense, eccentric texture of Victorian London, its moral outrage and grotesque wit, brings one closer to the feel of Dickens than to anything else in our literature. To pass from Mayhew's case-histories to Dickens' inventions is merely to cross sides of the same street; only the point of view shifts, not the landscape. Knowledge of Mayhew persuades us that Dickens the comic-caricaturist is in essence a great *realist*, just as reading Dickens persuades us that Mayhew was not merely a fine reporter but also a superb artist.

Mayhew's artistry manifests itself above all in the shaping of his characters' monologues. As a dramatizer of character through speech, Mayhew is as superior to the tape recorder as Hamlet is to the ordinary run of Danish princes. He does not distort, but he edits, shapes, and intensifies, until we are stunned by the slang beauty and inventiveness of the spoken voices he recreates. His years of editorial experience, his nose for animal effluvia, his ear for quirks of speech, his novelist's eye for significant detail ("the girl with her basket of walnuts lifts her *brown-stained fingers* [italics mine] to her mouth, as she screams, 'Fine warnuts!' sixteen a penny, fine war-r-nuts.")—all found the richest possible field for exercise in the inventively vociferous streets of London. The bardic speech of much Victorian verse is further from true poetry than the idiom of Mayhew's costermongers and peep-showmen.

The analogy with poetry suggests that Mayhew should be credited with evolving a new art form, a kind of dramatic monologue in prose. Just as the speaker in a Browning monologue is always talking *to* someone, the silent auditor actually functioning as a second character, so the speaker in a Mayhew interview is never merely a disembodied voice talking into a recording machine. Mayhew is always there, a pleasantly neutral, transparent presence into which we gradually fit our own image, until we feel uncannily that we have ourselves gained entry into some bare hovel and are overhearing the life-story of a street vendor. The monologues are not interrupted by the formality of direct questions, but the *implied* questioner is always present, as in these sentences spoken by a woefully ignorant seller of crabs (Vol. I, p. 22):

I don't know what the Pope is. Is he [in] any trade? It's nothing to me, when he's
no customer of mine. I have nothing to say about nobody that ain't no customers.
My crabs is caught in the sea, in course. I gets them at Billingsgate. I never saw the
sea, but it's salt-water, I know. I can't say whereabouts it lays. I believe it's in the
hands of Billingsgate salesmen—all of it? I've heard of shipwrecks at sea, caused by
drownding, in course. . . .

The few selections from *London Labour and the London Poor* which have appeared
in recent years reproduce a fair sampling of such monologues but drastically alter
the quality of the book. They provide the reader with a gallery of picturesque portraits but tear from the fabric of the work the larger social background that gives
it coherence and authority. Mayhew, for example, was obsessed with statistics, and
in his innumerable tables he portrays the workings of London as a macro-organism,
ingesting so many tons of solid or liquid matter and passing it out, so many tons
or gallons per borough, onto the streets and into the sewers, the very drains providing the subject of an elaborate chart analyzing "The Soluble Matter in Different
Specimens of Street Drainage Water."

Despite the monstrous suffering it depicts, *London Labour and the London Poor*
also possesses the minute and circumstantial gaiety of a Dutch painting. To savor
this curiously mixed quality, the reader might compare Mayhew's account (Vol. III,
p. 428) of five hundred vagrants, their bare limbs blue from the snow, seeking
entrance to the Asylum for the Houseless Poor, with the narrative (Vol. III, pp.
219-20) of the "Exhibitor of Birds and Mice," whose canaries ride in a chariot
drawn by a goldfinch and whose mice "dance the tight-rope on their hind legs, with
balance-poles in their mouths." Whether reporting the careers of mice or of men,
Mayhew is always exhaustive, conveying that superabundance of detail we associate
with actual life. The massive intricacy of *London Labour and the London Poor*
mirrors unerringly the labyrinthine vitality of London itself.

New York, 1967   JOHN D. ROSENBERG

A NOTE ON THE TEXT

The investigations which were to become *London Labour and the London Poor*
began with Mayhew's exposé, published in the *Morning Chronicle* of 24 September
1849, of the slums of Jacob's Island. He persuaded the editors of the *Chronicle* to
follow up the initial article with a full-scale survey of poverty throughout England,
with Mayhew himself serving as "The Metropolitan Correspondent." Within a year
he had published some seventy-five letters, but, dissatisfied over editorial tampering
with his copy, he resigned from the paper late in 1850, and in the following year the
entire *Chronicle* series came to a halt. In 1851 Mayhew resumed his labors independently, publishing his investigations in a twopenny weekly under the title of
London Labour and the London Poor, bound copies of which were published in book
form in 1851-52. Characteristically, he ran into legal difficulties with his printer,
and the weekly series ceased in 1852.

Mayhew made an abortive attempt to revive the project in 1856, but it did not see fruition until 1861, when Griffin, Bohn and Company gathered into four volumes the various fragments of Mayhew's grand design. The first two volumes are largely reprints of the earlier edition of 1851-52. Volume III consists of some of the original *Morning Chronicle* letters, together with interviews of street-entertainers which Mayhew compiled in 1856. Volume IV is largely the work of three other investigators, Bracebridge Hemyng, John Binny, and Andrew Halliday, but contains a prefatory article by the Rev. William Tuckniss and an Introduction by Mayhew, who also collaborated with Hemyng on part of the section on prostitutes. Two chapters from Volumes II and III—"Crossing-Sweepers" and "A Night at Rat-Killing"—were probably written by Mayhew's brother Augustus. A second, cheap edition of *London Labour and the London Poor* appeared in 1865; the present text, however, is reprinted from the definitive 1861-62 edition of Griffin, Bohn and Company.

A useful summary of Mayhew's life appears in the introduction to John L. Bradley's brief *Selections from London Labour and the London Poor*. Peter Quennell's edition of excerpts contains, in the volume entitled *London's Underworld* and dealing with prostitutes and criminals, a perceptive preface suggesting how long in advance of us the Victorians themselves were aware of "The Other Victorians." Anne Humpherys is currently writing what promises to be the first authoritative study of Mayhew and of *London Labour and the London Poor*.

LONDON LABOUR

AND THE

LONDON POOR;

A

CYCLOPÆDIA OF THE CONDITION AND EARNINGS

OF

THOSE THAT *WILL* WORK,
THOSE THAT *CANNOT* WORK, AND
THOSE THAT *WILL NOT* WORK.

BY

HENRY MAYHEW.

THE LONDON STREET-FOLK;

COMPRISING,

STREET SELLERS.	STREET PERFORMERS.
STREET BUYERS.	STREET ARTIZANS.
STREET FINDERS.	STREET LABOURERS.

WITH NUMEROUS ILLUSTRATIONS FROM PHOTOGRAPHS.

VOLUME I.

THIS BOOK IS DEDICATED TO DOUGLAS JERROLD, WHOM, KNOWING MOST INTIMATELY, THE AUTHOR HAS LEARNT TO LOVE AND HONOUR MOST PROFOUNDLY.

CONTENTS

OF

VOLUME I.

~~~~~~~~~~~~~~~~~~~~~~~~~~~

THE STREET-FOLK.

LIST OF ILLUSTRATIONS

PREFACE.

THE present volume is the first of an intended series, which it is hoped will form, when complete, a cyclopædia of the industry, the want, and the vice of the great Metropolis.

It is believed that the book is curious for many reasons :

It surely may be considered curious as being the first attempt to publish the history of a people, from the lips of the people themselves—giving a literal description of their labour, their earnings, their trials, and their sufferings, in their own "unvarnished" language; and to pourtray the condition of their homes and their families by personal observation of the places, and direct communion with the individuals.

It may be considered curious also as being the first commission of inquiry into the state of the people, undertaken by a private individual, and the first "blue book" ever published in twopenny numbers.

It is curious, moreover, as supplying information concerning a large body of persons, of whom the public had less knowledge than of the most distant tribes of the earth—the government population returns not even numbering them among the inhabitants of the kingdom ; and as adducing facts so extraordinary, that the traveller in the undiscovered country of the poor must, like Bruce, until his stories are corroborated by after investigators, be content to lie under the imputation of telling such tales, as travellers are generally supposed to delight in.

Be the faults of the present volume what they may, assuredly they are rather short-comings than exaggerations, for in every instance the author and his coadjutors have sought to understate, and most assuredly never to exceed the truth. For the omissions, the author would merely remind the reader of the entire novelty of the task—there being no other similar work in the language by which to guide or check his inquiries. When the following leaves are turned over, and the two or three pages of information derived from books contrasted with the hundreds of pages of facts obtained by positive observation and investigation, surely some allowance will be made for the details which may still be left for others to supply. Within the last two years some thousands of the humbler classes of society must have been seen and visited with the especial view of noticing their condition and learning their histories ; and it is but right that the truthfulness of the poor generally should be made known ; for though checks have been usually adopted, the people have been mostly found to be astonishingly correct in their statements,—so much so indeed, that the attempts at deception are certainly the exceptions rather than the rule. Those persons who, from an ignorance of the simplicity of the honest poor, might be inclined to think otherwise, have, in order to be convinced of the justice of the above remarks, only to consult the details given in the present volume, and to perceive the extraordinary agreement in the statements of all the vast number of individuals who have been seen at different times, and who cannot possibly have been supposed to have been acting in concert. The larger statistics, such as those of the quantities of fish and fruit, &c., sold in London, have been collected from tradesmen connected with the several markets, or from the wholesale merchants belonging to the trade specified—gentlemen to whose courtesy and co-operation I am indebted for much valuable information, and whose names, were I at liberty to publish them, would be an indisputable guarantee for the facts advanced. The other statistics have been obtained in the same manner—the best authorities having been invariably consulted on the subject treated of.

It is right that I should make special mention of the assistance I have received in the compilation of the present volume from Mr. Henry Wood and Mr. Richard Knight (late of the City Mission), gentlemen who have been engaged with me from nearly the commencement of my inquiries, and to whose hearty co-operation both myself and the public are indebted for a large increase of knowledge. Mr. Wood, indeed, has contributed so large a proportion of the contents of the present volume that he may fairly be considered as one of its authors.

The subject of the Street-Folk will still require another volume, in order to complete it in that comprehensive manner in which I am desirous of executing the modern history of this and every other portion of the people. There still remain —the *Street-Buyers*, the *Street-Finders*, the *Street-Performers*, the *Street-Artizans*, and the *Street-Labourers*, to be done, among the several classes of street-people; and the *Street Jews*, the *Street Italians and Foreigners*, and the *Street Mechanics*, to be treated of as varieties of the order. The present volume refers more particularly to the *Street-Sellers*, and includes special accounts of the *Costermongers* and the *Patterers* (the two broadly-marked varieties of street tradesmen), the *Street Irish*, the *Female Street-Sellers*, and the *Children Street-Sellers* of the metropolis.

My earnest hope is that the book may serve to give the rich a more intimate knowledge of the sufferings, and the frequent heroism under those sufferings, of the poor—that it may teach those who are beyond temptation to look with charity on the frailties of their less fortunate brethren—and cause those who are in " high places," and those of whom much is expected, to bestir themselves to improve the condition of a class of people whose misery, ignorance, and vice, amidst all the immense wealth and great knowledge of " the first city in the world," is, to say the very least, a national disgrace to us.

LONDON LABOUR

AND THE LONDON POOR

LONDON LABOUR

AND

THE LONDON POOR.

THE STREET-FOLK.

OF WANDERING TRIBES IN GENERAL.

OF the thousand millions of human beings that are said to constitute the population of the entire globe, there are—socially, morally, and perhaps even physically considered—but two distinct and broadly marked races, viz., the wanderers and the settlers—the vagabond and the citizen—the nomadic and the civilized tribes. Between these two extremes, however, ethnologists recognize a mediate variety, partaking of the attributes of both. There is not only the race of hunters and manufacturers—those who live by shooting and fishing, and those who live by producing—but, say they, there are also the herdsmen, or those who live by tending and feeding, what they consume.

Each of these classes has its peculiar and distinctive physical as well as moral characteristics. "There are in mankind," says Dr. Pritchard, "three principal varieties in the form of the head and other physical characters. Among the rudest tribes of men—the hunters and savage inhabitants of forests, dependent for their supply of food on the accidental produce of the soil and the chase—a form of head is prevalent which is mostly distinguished by the term "*prognathous,*" indicating a prolongation or extension forward of the jaws. A second shape of the head belongs principally to such races as wander with their herds and flocks over vast plains; these nations have broad lozenge-shaped faces (owing to the great development of the cheek bones), and pyramidal skulls. The most civilized races, on the other hand—those who live by the arts of cultivated life,—have a shape of the head which differs from both of those above mentioned. The characteristic form of the skull among these nations may be termed oval or elliptical."

These three forms of head, however, clearly admit of being reduced to two broadly-marked varieties, according as the bones of the face or those of the skull are more highly developed. A greater relative development of the jaws and cheek bones, says the author of the "Natural History of Man," indicates a more ample extension of the organs subservient to sensation and the animal faculties. Such a configuration is adapted to the wandering tribes; whereas, the greater relative development of the bones of the skull—indicating as it does a greater expansion of the brain, and consequently of the intellectual faculties—is especially adapted to the civilized races or settlers, who depend mainly on their knowledge of the powers and properties of things for the necessaries and comforts of life.

Moreover it would appear, that not only are all races divisible into wanderers and settlers, but that each civilized or settled tribe has generally some wandering horde intermingled with, and in a measure preying upon, it.

According to Dr. Andrew Smith, who has recently made extensive observations in South Africa, almost every tribe of people who have submitted themselves to social laws, recognizing the rights of property and reciprocal social duties, and thus acquiring wealth and forming themselves into a respectable caste, are surrounded by hordes of vagabonds and outcasts from their own community. Such are the Bushmen and *Sonquas* of the Hottentot race—the term "*sonqua*" meaning literally *pauper*. But a similar condition in society produces similar results in regard to other races; and the Kafirs have their Bushmen as well as the Hottentots—these are called *Fingoes*—a word signifying wanderers, beggars, or outcasts. The Lappes seem to have borne a somewhat similar relation to the Finns; that is to say, they appear to have been a wild and predatory tribe who sought the desert like the Arabian Bedouins, while the Finns cultivated the soil like the industrious Fellahs.

But a phenomenon still more deserving of

notice, is the difference of speech between the Bushmen and the Hottentots. The people of some hordes, Dr. Andrew Smith assures us, vary their speech designedly, and adopt new words, with the intent of rendering their ideas unintelligible to all but the members of their own community. For this last custom a peculiar name exists, which is called "*cuze-cat.*" This is considered as greatly advantageous in assisting concealment of their designs.

Here, then, we have a series of facts of the utmost social importance. (1) There are two distinct races of men, viz. : — the wandering and the civilized tribes ; (2) to each of these tribes a different form of head is peculiar, the wandering races being remarkable for the development of the bones of the face, as the jaws, cheek-bones, &c., and the civilized for the development of those of the head ; (3) to each civilized tribe there is generally a wandering horde attached ; (4) such wandering hordes have frequently a different language from the more civilized portion of the community, and that adopted with the intent of concealing their designs and exploits from them.

It is curious that no one has as yet applied the above facts to the explanation of certain anomalies in the present state of society among ourselves. That we, like the Kafirs, Fellahs, and Finns, are surrounded by wandering hordes —the " Sonquas " and the " Fingoes " of this country—paupers, beggars, and outcasts, possessing nothing but what they acquire by depredation from the industrious, provident, and civilized portion of the community ;—that the heads of these nomades are remarkable for the greater development of the jaws and cheekbones rather than those of the head.;—and that they have a secret language of their own—an English " *cuze-cat* " or " slang " as it is called—for the concealment of their designs : these are points of coincidence so striking that, when placed before the mind, make us marvel that the analogy should have remained thus long unnoticed.

The resemblance once discovered, however, becomes of great service in enabling us to use the moral characteristics of the nomade races of other countries, as a means of comprehending the more readily those of the vagabonds and outcasts of our own. Let us therefore, before entering upon the subject in hand, briefly run over the distinctive, moral, and intellectual features of the wandering tribes in general.

The nomad then is distinguished from the civilized man by his repugnance to regular and continuous labour—by his want of providence in laying up a store for the future—by his inability to perceive consequences ever so slightly removed from immediate apprehension —by his passion for stupefying herbs and roots, and, when possible, for intoxicating fermented liquors—by his extraordinary powers of enduring privation—by his comparative insensibility to pain—by an immoderate love of gaming, frequently risking his own personal liberty upon a single cast—by his love of libidinous dances—

by the pleasure he experiences in witnessing the suffering of sentient creatures—by his delight in warfare and all perilous sports—by his desire for vengeance—by the looseness of his notions as to property — by the absence of chastity among his women, and his disregard of female honour—and lastly, by his vague sense of religion — his rude idea of a Creator, and utter absence of all appreciation of the mercy of the Divine Spirit.

Strange to say, despite its privations, its dangers, and its hardships, those who have once adopted the savage and wandering mode of life, rarely abandon it. There are countless examples of white men adopting all the usages of the Indian hunter, but there is scarcely one example of the Indian hunter or trapper adopting the steady and regular habits of civilized life ; indeed, the various missionaries who have visited nomade races have found their labours utterly unavailing, so long as a wandering life continued, and have succeeded in bestowing the elements of civilization, only on those compelled by circumstances to adopt a settled habitation.

Of the Wandering Tribes of this Country.

The nomadic races of England are of many distinct kinds—from the habitual vagrant— half-beggar, half-thief—sleeping in barns, tents, and casual wards—to the mechanic on tramp, obtaining his bed and supper from the trade societies in the different towns, on his way to seek work. Between these two extremes there are several mediate varieties — consisting of pedlars, showmen, harvest-men, and all that large class who live by either selling, showing, or doing something through the country. These are, so to speak, the rural nomads—not confining their wanderings to any one particular locality, but ranging often from one end of the land to the other. Besides these, there are the urban and suburban wanderers, or those who follow some itinerant occupation in and round about the large towns. Such are, in the metropolis more particularly, the pickpockets — the beggars — the prostitutes — the street-sellers—the street-performers—the cabmen—the coachmen—the watermen—the sailors and such like. In each of these classes— according as they partake more or less of the purely vagabond, doing nothing whatsoever for their living, but moving from place to place preying upon the earnings of the more industrious portion of the community, so will the attributes of the nomade tribes be found to be more or less marked in them. Whether it be that in the mere act of wandering, there is a greater determination of blood to the surface of the body, and consequently a less quantity sent to the brain, the muscles being thus nourished at the expense of the mind, I leave physiologists to say. But certainly be the physical cause what it may, we must all allow that in each of the classes above-mentioned, there is a greater development of the animal than of the intellectual or moral nature of man, and that they are all more or less distinguished for their high cheek-bones and protruding jaws—for their use of a slang language—for their lax ideas of property—for their general improvidence—their repugnance to continuous labour—their disregard of female honour—their love of cruelty—their pugnacity—and their utter want of religion.

OF THE LONDON STREET-FOLK.

THOSE who obtain their living in the streets of the metropolis are a very large and varied class; indeed, the means resorted to in order " to pick up a crust," as the people call it, in the public thoroughfares (and such in many instances it *literally* is,) are so multifarious that the mind is long baffled in its attempts to reduce them to scientific order or classification.

It would appear, however, that the street-people may be all arranged under six distinct genera or kinds.

These are severally:

I. STREET-SELLERS.
II. STREET-BUYERS.
III. STREET-FINDERS.
IV. STREET-PERFORMERS, ARTISTS, AND SHOWMEN.
V. STREET-ARTIZANS, or WORKING PEDLARS; and
VI. STREET-LABOURERS.

The first of these divisions—the STREET-SELLERS—includes many varieties; viz.—

1. *The Street-sellers of Fish, &c.*—"wet," "dry," and shell-fish—and poultry, game, and cheese.

2. *The Street-sellers of Vegetables,* fruit (both "green" and "dry"), flowers, trees, shrubs, seeds, and roots, and "green stuff" (as watercresses, chickweed and grun'sel, and turf).

3. *The Street-sellers of Eatables and Drinkables,*—including the vendors of fried fish, hot eels, pickled whelks, sheep's trotters, ham sandwiches, peas'-soup, hot green peas, penny pies, plum " duff," meat-puddings, baked potatoes, spice-cakes, muffins and crumpets, Chelsea buns, sweetmeats, brandy-balls, cough drops, and cat and dog's meat—such constituting the principal eatables sold in the street; while under the head of street-drinkables may be specified tea and coffee, ginger-beer, lemonade, hot wine, new milk from the cow, asses milk, curds and whey, and occasionally water.

4. *The Street-sellers of Stationery, Literature, and the Fine Arts*—among whom are comprised the flying stationers, or standing and running patterers; the long-song-sellers; the wall-song-sellers (or "pinners-up," as they are technically termed); the ballad sellers; the vendors of play-bills, second editions of newspapers, back numbers of periodicals and old books, almanacks, pocket books, memorandum books, note paper, sealing-wax, pens, pencils, stenographic cards, valentines, engravings, manuscript music, images, and gelatine poetry cards.

5. *The Street-sellers of Manufactured Articles,* which class comprises a large number of individuals, as, (*a*) the vendors of chemical articles of manufacture—viz., blacking, lucifers, corn-salves, grease-removing compositions, plating-balls, poison for rats, crackers, detonating-balls, and cigar-lights. (*b*) The vendors of metal articles of manufacture—razors and pen-knives, tea-trays, dog-collars, and key-rings, hardware, bird-cages, small coins, medals, jewellery, tinware, tools, card-counters, red-herring-toasters, trivets, gridirons, and Dutch ovens. (*c*) The vendors of china and stone articles of manufacture—as cups and saucers, jugs, vases, chimney ornaments, and stone fruit. (*d*) The vendors of linen, cotton, and silken articles of manufacture—as sheeting, table-covers, cotton, tapes and thread, boot and stay-laces, haberdashery, pretended smuggled goods, shirt-buttons, etc., etc.; and (*e*) the vendors of miscellaneous articles of manufacture—as cigars, pipes, and snuff-boxes, spectacles, combs, "lots," rhubarb, sponges, wash-leather, paper-hangings, dolls, Bristol toys, sawdust, and pin-cushions.

6. *The Street-sellers of Second-hand Articles,* of whom there are again four separate classes; as (*a*) those who sell old metal articles—viz. old knives and forks, keys, tin-ware, tools, and marine stores generally; (*b*) those who sell old linen articles—as old sheeting for towels; (*c*) those who sell old glass and crockery—including bottles, old pans and pitchers, old looking glasses, &c.; and (*d*) those who sell old miscellaneous articles—as old shoes, old clothes, old saucepan lids, &c., &c.

7. *The Street-sellers of Live Animals*—including the dealers in dogs, squirrels, birds, gold and silver fish, and tortoises.

8. *The Street-sellers of Mineral Productions and Curiosities*—as red and white sand, silver sand, coals, coke, salt, spar ornaments, and shells.

These, so far as my experience goes, exhaust the whole class of street-sellers, and they appear to constitute nearly three-fourths of the entire number of individuals obtaining a subsistence in the streets of London.

The next class are the STREET-BUYERS, under which denomination come the purchasers of hare-skins, old clothes, old umbrellas, bottles, glass, broken metal, rags, waste paper, and dripping.

After these we have the STREET-FINDERS, or those who, as I said before, literally " pick up " their living in the public thoroughfares. They are the "pure" pickers, or those who live by gathering dogs'-dung; the cigar-end finders, or "hard-ups," as they are called, who collect the refuse pieces of smoked cigars from the gutters, and having dried them, sell them as tobacco to the very poor; the dredgermen or coal-finders; the mud-larks; the bone-grubbers; and the sewer-hunters.

Under the fourth division, or that of the STREET-PERFORMERS, ARTISTS, AND SHOWMEN, are likewise many distinct callings.

1. *The Street-Performers,* who admit of being classified into (*a*) mountebanks—or those who enact puppet-shows, as Punch and Judy, the fan-

toccini, and the Chinese shades. (b) The street-performers of feats of strength and dexterity—as "acrobats" or posturers, "equilibrists" or balancers, stiff and bending tumblers, jugglers, conjurors, sword-swallowers, "salamanders" or fire-eaters, swordsmen, etc. (c) The street-performers with trained animals — as dancing dogs, performing monkeys, trained birds and mice, cats and hares, sapient pigs, dancing bears, and tame camels. (d) The street-actors—as clowns, "Billy Barlows," "Jim Crows," and others.

2. The Street Showmen, including shows of (a) extraordinary persons—as giants, dwarfs, Albinoes, spotted boys, and pig-faced ladies. (b) Extraordinary animals—as alligators, calves, horses and pigs with six legs or two heads, industrious fleas, and happy families. (c) Philosophic instruments—as the microscope, telescope, thaumascope. (d) Measuring-machines — as weighing, lifting, measuring, and striking machines; and (e) miscellaneous shows—such as peep-shows, glass ships, mechanical figures, wax-work shows, pugilistic shows, and fortune-telling apparatus.

3. The Street-Artists—as black profile-cutters, blind paper-cutters, "screevers" or draughtsmen in coloured chalks on the pavement, writers without hands, and readers without eyes.

4. The Street Dancers—as street Scotch girls, sailors, slack and tight rope dancers, dancers on stilts, and comic dancers.

5. The Street Musicians—as the street bands (English and German), players of the guitar, harp, bagpipes, hurdy-gurdy, dulcimer, musical bells, cornet, tom-tom, &c.

6. The Street Singers, as the singers of glees, ballads, comic songs, nigger melodies, psalms, serenaders, reciters, and improvisatori.

7. The Proprietors of Street Games, as swings, highflyers, roundabouts, puff-and-darts, rifle shooting, down the dolly, spin-'em-rounds, prick the garter, thimble-rig, etc.

Then comes the Fifth Division of the Street-Folk, viz., the STREET-ARTIZANS, or WORKING PEDLARS;

These may be severally arranged into three distinct groups—(1) Those who make things in the streets; (2) Those who mend things in the streets; and (3) Those who make things at home and sell them in the streets.

1. Of those who make things in the streets there are the following varieties: (a) the metal workers—such as toasting-fork makers, pin makers, engravers, tobacco-stopper makers. (b) The textile-workers—stocking-weavers, cabbage-net makers, night-cap knitters, doll-dress knitters. (c) The miscellaneous workers,—the wooden spoon makers, the leather brace and garter makers, the printers, and the glass-blowers.

2. Those who mend things in the streets, consist of broken china and glass menders, clock menders, umbrella menders, kettle menders, chair menders, grease removers, hat cleaners, razor and knife grinders, glaziers, travelling bell hangers, and knife cleaners.

3. Those who make things at home and sell them in the streets, are (a) the wood workers—as the makers of clothes-pegs, clothes-props, skewers, needle-cases, foot-stools and clothes-horses, chairs and tables, tea-caddies, writing-desks, drawers, work-boxes, dressing-cases, pails and tubs. (b) The trunk, hat, and bonnet-box makers, and the cane and rush basket makers. (c) The toy makers—such as Chinese roarers, children's windmills, flying birds and fishes, feathered cocks, black velvet cats and sweeps, paper houses, cardboard carriages, little copper pans and kettles, tiny tin fireplaces, children's watches, Dutch dolls, buy-a-brooms, and gutta-percha heads. (d) The apparel makers—viz., the makers of women's caps, boys and men's cloth caps, night-caps, straw bonnets, children's dresses, watch-pockets, bonnet shapes, silk bonnets, and gaiters. (e) The metal workers,—as the makers of fire-guards, bird-cages, the wire workers. (f) The miscellaneous workers—or makers of ornaments for stoves, chimney ornaments, artificial flowers in pots and in nose-gays, plaster-of-Paris night-shades, brooms, brushes, mats, rugs, hearthstones, firewood, rush matting, and hassocks,

Of the last division, or STREET-LABOURERS, there are four classes:

1. The Cleansers—such as scavengers, nightmen, flushermen, chimney-sweeps, dustmen, crossing-sweepers, "street-orderlies," labourers to sweeping-machines and to watering-carts.

2. The Lighters and Waterers—or the turncocks and the lamplighters.

3. The Street-Advertisers — viz., the billstickers, bill-deliverers, boardmen, men to advertising vans, and wall and pavement stencillers.

4. The Street-Servants—as horse holders, linkmen, coach-hirers, street-porters, shoe-blacks.

OF THE NUMBER OF COSTERMONGERS AND OTHER STREET-FOLK.

THE number of costermongers, — that is to say, of those street-sellers attending the London "green" and "fish markets,"—appears to be, from the best data at my command, now 30,000 men, women, and children. The census of 1841 gives only 2,045 "hawkers, hucksters, and pedlars," in the metropolis, and no costermongers or street-sellers, or street-performers at all. This number is absurdly small, and its absurdity is accounted for by the fact that not one in twenty of the costermongers, or of the people with whom they lodged, troubled themselves to fill up the census returns—the majority of them being unable to read and write, and others distrustful of the purpose for which the returns were wanted.

The costermongering class extends itself yearly; and it is computed that for the last five years it has increased considerably faster than the general metropolitan population. This increase is derived partly from all the children of costermongers following the father's trade, but chiefly from working men, such as the servants of greengrocers or of innkeepers, when out of employ, "taking to a coster's barrow" for a livelihood; and the same being done by mechanics and labourers out of work. At the time of the famine in Ireland, it is calculated, that the number of Irish obtaining a living in the London streets must have been at least doubled.

The great discrepancy between the government returns and the accounts of the costermongers themselves, concerning the number of people obtaining a living by the sale of fish, fruit, and vegetables, in the streets of London, caused me to institute an inquiry at the several metropolitan markets concerning the number of street-sellers attending them : the following is the result :

During the summer months and fruit season, the average number of costermongers attending Covent-garden market is about 2,500 per market-day. In the strawberry season there are nearly double as many, there being, at that time, a large number of Jews who come to buy; during that period, on a Saturday morning, from the commencement to the close of the market, as many as 4,000 costers have been reckoned purchasing at Covent-garden. Through the winter season, however, the number of costermongers does not exceed upon the average 1,000 per market morning. About one-tenth of the fruit and vegetables of the least expensive kind sold at this market is purchased by the costers. Some of the better class of costers, who have their regular customers, are very particular as to the quality of the articles they buy; but others are not so particular ; so long as they can get things cheap, I am informed, they do not care much about the quality. The Irish more especially look out for damaged articles, which they buy at a low price. One of my informants told me that the costers were the best customers to the growers, inasmuch as when the market is flagging on account of the weather, they (the costers) wait and make their purchases. On other occasions, such as fine mornings, the costers purchase as early as others. There is no trust given to them—to use the words of one of my informants, they are such slippery customers ; here to-day and gone to-morrow.

At Leadenhall market, during the winter months, there are from 70 to 100 costermongers general attendants; but during the summer not much more than one-half that number make their appearance. Their purchases consist of warren - rabbits, poultry, and game, of which about one-eighth of the whole amount brought to this market is bought by them. When the market is slack, and during the summer, when there is "no great call" for game, etc., the costers attending Leadenhall-market turn their hand to crockery, fruit, and fish.

The costermongers frequenting Spitalfields-market average all the year through from 700 to 1,000 each market-day. They come from all parts, as far as Edmonton, Edgeware, and Tottenham ; Highgate, Hampstead, and even from Greenwich and Lewisham. Full one-third of

the produce of this market is purchased by them.

The number of costermongers attending the Borough-market is about 250 during the fruit season, after which time they decrease to about 200 per market morning. About one-sixth of the produce that comes into this market is purchased by the costermongers. One gentleman informed me, that the salesmen might shut up their shops were it not for these men. "In fact," said another, "I don't know what would become of the fruit without them."

The costers at Billingsgate-market, daily, number from 3,000 to 4,000 in winter, and about 2,500 in summer. A leading salesman told me that he would rather have an order from a costermonger than a fishmonger; for the one paid ready money, while the other required credit. The same gentleman assured me, that the costermongers bought excellent fish, and that very largely. They themselves aver that they purchase half the fish brought to Billingsgate—some fish trades being entirely in their hands. I ascertained, however, from the authorities at Billingsgate, and from experienced salesmen, that of the quantity of fish conveyed to that great mart, the costermongers bought one-third ; another third was sent into the country ; and another disposed of to the fishmongers, and to such hotel-keepers, or other large purchasers, as resorted to Billingsgate.

The salesmen at the several markets all agreed in stating that no trust was given to the costermongers. "Trust them !" exclaimed one, "O, certainly, as far as I can see them."

Now, adding the above figures together, we have the subjoined sum for the gross number of

COSTERMONGERS ATTENDING THE LONDON MARKETS.

Billingsgate-market	3,500
Covent-garden	4,000
Spitalfields	1,000
Borough	250
Leadenhall	100
	9,350

Besides these, I am credibly informed, that it may be assumed there are full 1,000 men who are unable to attend market, owing to the dissipation of the previous night; another 1,000 are absent owing to their having "stock on hand," and so requiring no fresh purchases ; and further, it may be estimated that there are at least 2,000 boys in London at work for costers, at half profits, and who consequently have no occasion to visit the markets. Hence, putting these numbers together, we arrive at the conclusion that there are in London upwards of 13,000 street-sellers, dealing in fish, fruit, vegetables, game, and poultry alone. To be on the safe side, however, let us assume the number of London costermongers to be 12,000, and that one-half of these are married and have two children (which from all accounts appears to be about the proportion); and then we have 30,000 for the sum total of men, women, and children dependent on " costermongering " for their subsistence.

Large as this number may seem, still I am satisfied it is rather within than beyond the truth. In order to convince myself of its accuracy, I caused it to be checked in several ways. In the first place, a survey was made as to the number of stalls in the streets of London—forty-six miles of the principal thoroughfares were travelled over, and an account taken of the " standings." Thus it was found that there were upon an average upwards of fourteen stalls to the mile, of which five-sixths were fish and fruit-stalls. Now, according to the Metropolitan Police Returns, there are 2,000 miles of street throughout London, and calculating that the stalls through the whole of the metropolis run upon an average only four to the mile, we shall thus find that there are 8,000 stalls altogether in London; of these we may reckon that at least 6,000 are fish and fruit-stalls. I am informed, on the best authority, that twice as many costers " go rounds" as have standings; hence we come to the conclusion that there are 18,000 itinerant and stationary street-sellers of fish, vegetables, and fruit, in the metropolis; and reckoning the same proportion of wives and children as before, we have thus 45,000 men, women, and children, obtaining a living in this manner. Further, " to make assurance doubly sure," the street-markets throughout London were severally visited, and the number of street-sellers at each taken down on the spot. These gave a grand total of 3,801, of which number two-thirds were dealers in fish, fruit, and vegetables; and reckoning that twice as many costers again were on their rounds, we thus make the total number of London costermongers to be 11,403, or calculating men, women, and children, 34,209. It would appear, therefore, that if we estimate the gross number of individuals subsisting on the sale of fish, fruit, and vegetables, in the streets of London, at between thirty and forty thousand, we shall not be very wide of the truth.

But, great as is this number, still the costermongers are only a portion of the street-folk. Besides, there are, as we have seen, many other large classes obtaining their livelihood in the streets. The street musicians, for instance, are said to number 1,000, and the old clothesmen the same. There are supposed to be at the least 500 sellers of water-cresses; 200 coffee-stalls; 300 cats-meat men; 250 ballad-singers; 200 play-bill sellers; from 800 to 1,000 bone-grubbers and mud-larks; 1,000 crossing-sweepers; another thousand chimney-sweeps, and the same number of turncocks and lamp-lighters; all of whom, together with the street-performers and showmen, tinkers, chair, umbrella, and clock-menders, sellers of bonnet-boxes, toys, stationery, songs, last dying-speeches, tubs, pails, mats, crockery, blacking, lucifers, corn-salves, clothes-pegs, brooms, sweetmeats, razors, dog-collars, dogs, birds, coals, sand,—scavengers, dustmen, and others, make up, it may be fairly assumed,

full thirty thousand adults, so that, reckoning men, women, and children, we may truly say that there are upwards of fifty thousand individuals, or about a fortieth-part of the entire population of the metropolis getting their living in the streets.

Now of all modes of obtaining subsistence, that of street-selling is the most precarious. Continued wet weather deprives those who depend for their bread upon the number of people frequenting the public thoroughfares of all means of living; and it is painful to think of the hundreds belonging to this class in the metropolis who are reduced to starvation by three or four days successive rain. Moreover, in the winter, the street-sellers of fruit and vegetables are cut off from the ordinary means of gaining their livelihood, and, consequently, they have to suffer the greatest privations at a time when the severity of the season demands the greatest amount of physical comforts. To expect that the increased earnings of the summer should be put aside as a provision against the deficiencies of the winter, is to expect that a precarious occupation should beget provident habits, which is against the nature of things, for it is always in those callings which are the most uncertain, that the greatest amount of improvidence and intemperance are found to exist. It is not the well-fed man, be it observed, but the starving one that is in danger of surfeiting himself.

Moreover, when the religious, moral, and intellectual degradation of the great majority of these fifty thousand people is impressed upon us, it becomes positively appalling to contemplate the vast amount of vice, ignorance and want, existing in these days in the very heart of our land. The public have but to read the following plain unvarnished account of the habits, amusements, dealings, education, politics, and religion of the London costermongers in the nineteenth century, and then to say whether they think it safe—even if it be thought fit—to allow men, women, and children to continue in such a state.

OF THE VARIETIES OF STREET-FOLK IN GENERAL, AND COSTERMONGERS IN PARTICULAR.

AMONG the street-folk there are many distinct characters of people—people differing as widely from each in tastes, habits, thoughts and creed, as one nation from another. Of these the costermongers form by far the largest and certainly the mostly broadly marked class. They appear to be a distinct race—perhaps, originally, of Irish extraction—seldom associating with any other of the street-folks, and being all known to each other. The " patterers," or the men who cry the last dying-speeches, &c. in the street, and those who help off their wares by long harrangues in the public thoroughfares, are again a separate class. These, to use their own term, are " the aristocracy of the street-sellers," despising the costers for their ignorance, and boasting that they live by their intellect. The public, they say, do not expect to receive from them an equivalent for their money — they pay to hear them talk. Compared with the costermongers, the patterers are generally an educated class, and among them are some classical scholars, one clergyman, and many sons of gentlemen. They appear to be the counterparts of the old mountebanks or street-doctors. As a body they seem far less improvable than the costers, being more "knowing" and less impulsive. The street-performers differ again from those; these appear to possess many of the characteristics of the lower class of actors, viz., a strong desire to excite admiration, an indisposition to pursue any settled occupation, a love of the tap-room, though more for the society and display than for the drink connected with it, a great fondness for finery and predilection for the performance of dexterous or dangerous feats. Then there are the street mechanics, or artizans— quiet, melancholy, struggling men, who, unable to find any regular employment at their own trade, have made up a few things, and taken to hawk them in the streets, as the last shift of independence. Another distinct class of street-folk are the blind people (mostly musicians in a rude way), who, after the loss of their eyesight, have sought to keep themselves from the workhouse by some little excuse for alms-seeking. These, so far as my experience goes, appear to be a far more deserving class than is usually supposed—their affliction, in most cases, seems to have chastened them and to have given a peculiar religious cast to their thoughts.

Such are the several varieties of street-folk, intellectually considered—looked at in a national point of view, they likewise include many distinct people. Among them are to be found the Irish fruit-sellers; the Jew clothesmen; the Italian organ boys, French singing women, the German brass bands, the Dutch buy-a-broom girls, the Highland bagpipe players, and the Indian crossing-sweepers—all of whom I here shall treat of in due order.

The costermongering class or order has also its many varieties. These appear to be in the following proportions:—One-half of the entire class are costermongers proper, that is to say, the calling with them is hereditary, and perhaps has been so for many generations; while the other half is composed of three-eighths Irish, and one-eighth mechanics, tradesmen, and Jews.

Under the term "costermonger" is here included only such "street-sellers" as deal in fish, fruit, and vegetables, purchasing their goods at the wholesale "green" and fish markets. Of these some carry on their business at the same stationary stall or "standing" in the street, while others go on "rounds." The itinerant costermongers, as contradistinguished from the stationary street-fishmongers and greengrocers, have in many instances regular rounds, which they go daily, and which extend from two to ten miles. The longest are those which embrace a suburban

part; the shortest are through streets thickly peopled by the poor, where duly to "work" a single street consumes, in some instances, an hour. There are also "chance" rounds. Men "working" these carry their wares to any part in which they hope to find customers. The costermongers, moreover, diversify their labours by occasionally going on a country round, travelling on these excursions, in all directions, from thirty to ninety and even a hundred miles from the metropolis. Some, again, confine their callings chiefly to the neighbouring races and fairs.

Of all the characteristics attending these diversities of traders, I shall treat severally. I may here premise, that the regular or "thorough-bred costermongers," repudiate the numerous persons who sell only nuts or oranges in the streets, whether at a fixed stall, or any given locality, or who hawk them through the thoroughfares or parks. They repudiate also a number of Jews, who confine their street-trading to the sale of "coker-nuts" on Sundays, vended from large barrows. Nor do they rank with themselves the individuals who sell tea and coffee in the streets, or such condiments as peas-soup, sweetmeats, spice-cakes, and the like; those articles not being purchased at the markets. I often heard all such classes called "the illegitimates."

OF COSTERMONGERING MECHANICS.

"FROM the numbers of mechanics," said one smart costermonger to me, "that I know of in my own district, I should say there's now more than 1,000 costers in London that were once mechanics or labourers. They are driven to it as a last resource, when they can't get work at their trade. They don't do well, at least four out of five, or three out of four don't. They're not up to the dodges of the business. They go to market with fear, and don't know how to venture a bargain if one offers. They're inferior salesmen too, and if they have fish left that won't keep, it's a dead loss to them, for they aren't up to the trick of selling it cheap at a distance where the coster ain't known; or of quitting it to another, for candle-light sale, cheap, to the Irish or to the 'lushingtons,' that haven't a proper taste for fish. Some of these poor fellows lose every penny. They're mostly middle-aged when they begin costering. They'll generally commence with oranges or herrings. We pity them. We say, ' Poor fellows! they'll find it out by-and-bye.' It's awful to see some poor women, too, trying to pick up a living in the streets by selling nuts or oranges. It's awful to see them, for they can't set about it right; besides that, there's too many before they start. They don't find a living, *it's only another way of starving.*"

ANCIENT CALLING OF COSTERMONGERS.

THE earliest record of London cries is, according to Mr. Charles Knight, in Lydgate's poem of "London Lyckpeny," which is as old as the days of Henry V., or about 430 years back. Among Lydgate's cries are enumerated "Strawberries ripe and cherries in the rise;" the *rise* being a twig to which the cherries were tied, as at present. Lydgate, however, only indicates costermongers, but does not mention them by name.

It is not my intention, as my inquiries are directed to the *present* condition of the costermongers, to dwell on this part of the question, but some historical notice of so numerous a body is indispensable. I shall confine myself therefore to show from the elder dramatists, how the costermongers flourished in the days of Elizabeth and James I.

"Virtue," says Shakespeare, "is of so little regard in these *coster-monger times,* that true valour is turned bear-herd." Costermonger times are as old as any trading times of which our history tells; indeed, the stationary costermonger of our own day is a legitimate descendant of the tradesmen of the elden time, who stood by their shops with their open casements, loudly inviting buyers by praises of their wares, and by direct questions of "What d'ye buy? What d'ye lack?"

Ben Jonson makes his *Morose,* who hated all noises, and sought for a silent wife, enter "upon divers treaties with the fish-wives and orange-women," to moderate their clamour; but *Morose,* above all other noisy people, "cannot endure a costard-monger; he swoons if he hear one."

In Ford's "Sun's Darling" I find the following: "Upon my life he means to turn costermonger, and is projecting how to forestall the market. I shall cry pippins rarely."

In Beaumont and Fletcher's "Scornful Lady" is the following:

"Pray, sister, do not laugh; you'll anger him,
And then he'll rail like a rude costermonger."

Dr. Johnson, gives the derivation of costard-monger (the orthography he uses), as derived from the sale of apples or costards, "round and bulky like the head;" and he cites Burton as an authority: "Many country vicars," writes Burton, "are driven to shifts, and if our great patrons hold us to such conditions, they will make us *costard-mongers,* graziers, or sell ale."

"The costard-monger," says Mr. Charles Knight, in his "London," "was originally an apple-seller, whence his name, and, from the mention of him in the old dramatists, he appears to have been frequently an Irishman."

In Ireland the word "costermonger" is almost unknown.

OF THE OBSOLETE CRIES OF THE COSTERMONGERS.

A brief account of the cries once prevalent among the street-sellers will show somewhat significantly the change in the diet or regalements of those who purchase their food in the street. Some of the articles are not vended in the public thoroughfares now, while others are still sold, but in different forms.

"Hot sheep's feet," for instance, were cried in the streets in the time of Henry V.; they are now sold *cold,* at the doors of the lower-priced theatres, and at the larger public-houses. Among the street cries, the following were common prior to the wars of the Roses: "Ribs of beef," — "Hot peascod," — and "Pepper and saffron." These certainly indicate a different street diet from that of the present time.

The following are more modern, running from Elizabeth's days down to our own. "Pippins," and, in the times of Charles II., and subsequently, oranges were sometimes cried as "Orange pips,"—"Fair lemons and oranges; oranges and citrons,"—"New Wall-fleet oysters," ["*fresh*"] fish was formerly cried as "new,"]—"New-river water," [I may here mention that water-carriers still ply their trade in parts of Hampstead,] — "Rosemary and lavender," — "Small coals," [a cry rendered almost poetical by the character, career, and pitiful end, through a practical joke, of Tom Britton, the "small-coal man,"] — "Pretty pins, pretty women,"—"Lilly-white vinegar," —"Hot wardens" (pears)—"Hot codlings,"—and lastly the greasy-looking beverage which Charles Lamb's experience of London at early morning satisfied him was of all preparations the most grateful to the stomach of the then existing climbing-boys — viz., "Sa-loop." I may state, for the information of my younger readers, that saloop (spelt also "salep" and "salop") was prepared, as a powder, from the root of the *Orchis mascula,* or Red-handed Orchis, a plant which grows luxuriantly in our meadows and pastures, flowering in the spring, though never cultivated to any extent in this country; that required for the purposes of commerce was imported from India. The saloop-stalls were superseded by the modern coffee-stalls.

There were many other cries, now obsolete, but what I have cited were the most common.

OF THE COSTERMONGERS "ECONOMICALLY" CONSIDERED.

POLITICAL economy teaches us that, between the two great classes of producers and consumers, stand the distributors — or dealers — saving time, trouble, and inconvenience to, the one in disposing of, and to the other in purchasing, their commodities.

But the distributor was not always a part and parcel of the economical arrangements of the State. In olden times, the producer and consumer were brought into immediate contact, at markets and fairs, holden at certain intervals. The inconvenience of this mode of operation, however, was soon felt; and the pedlar, or wandering distributor, sprang up as a means of carrying the commodities to those who were unable to attend the public markets at the appointed time. Still the pedlar or wandering distributor was not without *his* disadvantages. He only came at certain periods, and commodities were occasionally required in the interim. Hence the shopkeeper, or stationary distributor, was called into existence, so that the consumer might obtain any commodity of the producer at any time he pleased. Hence we see that the pedlar is the primitive tradesman, and that the one is contradistinguished from the other by the fact, that the pedlar carries the goods to the consumer, whereas, in the case of the shopkeeper, the consumer goes after the goods. In country districts, remote from towns and villages, the pedlar is not yet wholly superseded; "but a dealer who has a fixed abode, and fixed customers, is so much more to be depended on," says Mr. Stewart Mill, "that consumers prefer resorting to him if he is conveniently accessible, and dealers, therefore, find their advantage in establishing themselves in every locality where there are sufficient customers near at hand to afford them a remuneration." Hence the pedlar is now chiefly confined to the poorer districts, and is consequently distinguished from the stationary tradesman by the character and means of his customers, as well as by the amount of capital and extent of his dealings. The shopkeeper supplies principally the noblemen and gentry with the necessaries and luxuries of life, but the pedlar or hawker is the purveyor in general to the poor. He brings the greengrocery, the fruit, the fish, the water-cresses, the shrimps, the pies and puddings, the sweetmeats, the pine-apples, the stationery, the linendrapery, and the jewellery, such as it is, to the very door of the working classes; indeed, the poor man's food and clothing are mainly supplied to him in this manner. Hence the class of travelling tradesmen are important, not only as forming a large portion of the poor themselves, but as being the persons through whom the working people obtain a considerable part of their provisions and raiment.

But the itinerant tradesman or street-seller is still further distinguished from the regular fixed dealer—the *stall*keeper from the *shop*keeper—the *street*-wareman from the *warehouse*man, by the arts they respectively employ to attract custom. The street-seller cries his goods aloud at the head of his barrow; the enterprising tradesman distributes bills at the door of his shop. The one appeals to the ear, the other to the eye. The cutting costermonger has a drum and two boys to excite attention to his stock; the spirited shopkeeper has a column of advertisements in the morning newspapers. They are but different means of attaining the same end.

THE LONDON STREET MARKETS ON A SATURDAY NIGHT.

THE street sellers are to be seen in the greatest numbers at the London street markets on a Saturday night. Here, and in the shops immediately adjoining, the working-classes generally purchase their Sunday's dinner; and after pay-time on Saturday night, or early on Sunday morning, the crowd in the New-cut, and the Brill in particular, is almost impassable. Indeed, the scene in these parts has more of the character of a fair than a market. There are hundreds of stalls, and every stall has its one or two lights; either it is

illuminated by the intense white light of the new self-generating gas-lamp, or else it is brightened up by the red smoky flame of the old-fashioned grease lamp. One man shows off his yellow haddock with a candle stuck in a bundle of firewood; his neighbour makes a candlestick of a huge turnip, and the tallow gutters over its sides; whilst the boy shouting "Eight a penny, stunning pears!" has rolled his dip in a thick coat of brown paper, that flares away with the candle. Some stalls are crimson with the fire shining through the holes beneath the baked chestnut stove; others have handsome octohedral lamps, while a few have a candle shining through a sieve: these, with the sparkling ground-glass globes of the tea-dealers' shops, and the butchers' gaslights streaming and fluttering in the wind, like flags of flame, pour forth such a flood of light, that at a distance the atmosphere immediately above the spot is as lurid as if the street were on fire.

The pavement and the road are crowded with purchasers and street-sellers. The housewife in her thick shawl, with the market-basket on her arm, walks slowly on, stopping now to look at the stall of caps, and now to cheapen a bunch of greens. Little boys, holding three or four onions in their hand, creep between the people, wriggling their way through every interstice, and asking for custom in whining tones, as if seeking charity. Then the tumult of the thousand different cries of the eager dealers, all shouting at the top of their voices, at one and the same time, is almost bewildering. "So-old again," roars one. "Chestnuts all 'ot, a penny a score," bawls another. "An 'aypenny a skin, blacking," squeaks a boy. "Buy, buy, buy, buy, buy—bu-u-uy!" cries the butcher. "Half-quire of paper for a penny," bellows the street stationer. "An 'aypenny a lot ing-uns." "Twopence a pound grapes." "Three a penny Yarmouth bloaters." "Who'll buy a bonnet for fourpence?" "Pick 'em out cheap here! three pair for a halfpenny, bootlaces." "Now's your time! beautiful whelks, a penny a lot." "Here's ha'p'orths," shouts the perambulating confectioner. "Come and look at 'em! here's toasters!" bellows one with a Yarmouth bloater stuck on a toasting-fork. "Penny a lot, fine russets," calls the apple woman: and so the Babel goes on.

One man stands with his red-edged mats hanging over his back and chest, like a herald's coat; and the girl with her basket of walnuts lifts her brown-stained fingers to her mouth, as she screams, "Fine warnuts! sixteen a penny, fine war-r-nuts." A bootmaker, to "ensure custom," has illuminated his shop-front with a line of gas, and in its full glare stands a blind beggar, his eyes turned up so as to show only "the whites," and mumbling some begging rhymes, that are drowned in the shrill notes of the bamboo-flute-player next to him. The boy's sharp cry, the woman's cracked voice, the gruff, hoarse shout of the man, are all mingled together. Sometimes an Irishman is heard with his "fine ating apples;" or else the jingling music of an unseen organ breaks out, as the trio of street singers rest between the verses. Then the sights, as you elbow your way through the crowd, are equally multifarious. Here is a stall glittering with new tin saucepans; there another, bright with its blue and yellow crockery, and sparkling with white glass. Now you come to a row of old shoes arranged along the pavement; now to a stand of gaudy tea-trays; then to a shop with red handkerchiefs and blue checked shirts, fluttering backwards and forwards, and a counter built up outside on the kerb, behind which are boys beseeching custom. At the door of a tea-shop, with its hundred white globes of light, stands a man delivering bills, thanking the public for past favours, and "defying competition." Here, alongside the road, are some half-dozen headless tailors' dummies, dressed in Chesterfields and fustian jackets, each labelled, "Look at the prices," or "Observe the quality." After this is a butcher's shop, crimson and white with meat piled up to the first-floor, in front of which the butcher himself, in his blue coat, walks up and down, sharpening his knife on the steel that hangs to his waist. A little further on stands the clean family, begging; the father with his head down as if in shame, and a box of lucifers held forth in his hand—the boys in newly-washed pinafores, and the tidily got-up mother with a child at her breast. This stall is green and white with bunches of turnips—that red with apples, the next yellow with onions, and another purple with pickling cabbages. One minute you pass a man with an umbrella turned inside up and full of prints; the next, you hear one with a peepshow of Mazeppa, and Paul Jones the pirate, describing the pictures to the boys looking in at the little round windows. Then is heard the sharp snap of the percussion-cap from the crowd of lads firing at the target for nuts; and the moment afterwards, you see either a black man half-clad in white, and shivering in the cold with tracts in his hand, or else you hear the sounds of music from "Frazier's Circus," on the other side of the road, and the man outside the door of the penny concert, beseeching you to "Be in time—be in time!" as Mr. Somebody is just about to sing his favourite song of the "Knife Grinder." Such, indeed, is the riot, the struggle, and the scramble for a living, that the confusion and uproar of the New-cut on Saturday night have a bewildering and saddening effect upon the thoughtful mind.

Each salesman tries his utmost to sell his wares, tempting the passers-by with his bargains. The boy with his stock of herbs offers "a double 'andful of fine parsley for a penny;" the man with the donkey-cart filled with turnips has three lads to shout for him to their utmost, with their "Ho! ho! hi-i-i! What do you think of this here? A penny a bunch—hurrah for free trade! Here's your turnips!" Until

it is seen and heard, we have no sense of the scramble that is going on throughout London for a living. The same scene takes place at the Brill—the same in Leather-lane—the same in Tottenham-court-road—the same in Whitecross-street; go to whatever corner of the metropolis you please, either on a Saturday night or a Sunday morning, and there is the same shouting and the same struggling to get the penny profit out of the poor man's Sunday's dinner.

Since the above description was written, the New Cut has lost much of its noisy and brilliant glory. In consequence of a New Police regulation, "stands" or "pitches" have been forbidden, and each coster, on a market night, is now obliged, under pain of the lock-up house, to carry his tray, or keep moving with his barrow. The gay stalls have been replaced by deal boards, some sodden with wet fish, others stained purple with blackberries, or brown with walnut-peel; and the bright lamps are almost totally superseded by the dim, guttering candle. Even if the pole under the tray or "shallow" is seen resting on the ground, the policeman on duty is obliged to interfere.

The mob of purchasers has diminished one-half; and instead of the road being filled with customers and trucks, the pavement and kerb-stones are scarcely crowded.

THE SUNDAY MORNING MARKETS.

NEARLY every poor man's market does its Sunday trade. For a few hours on the Sabbath morning, the noise, bustle, and scramble of the Saturday night are repeated, and but for this opportunity many a poor family would pass a dinnerless Sunday. The system of paying the mechanic late on the Saturday night—and more particularly of paying a man his wages in a public-house—when he is tired with his day's work lures him to the tavern, and there the hours fly quickly enough beside the warm tap-room fire, so that by the time the wife comes for her husband's wages, she finds a large portion of them gone in drink, and the streets half cleared, so that the Sunday market is the only chance of getting the Sunday's dinner.

Of all these Sunday-morning markets, the Brill, perhaps, furnishes the busiest scene; so that it may be taken as a type of the whole.

The streets in the neighbourhood are quiet and empty. The shops are closed with their different-coloured shutters, and the people round about are dressed in the shiney cloth of the holiday suit. There are no "cabs," and but few omnibuses to disturb the rest, and men walk in the road as safely as on the footpath.

As you enter the Brill the market sounds are scarcely heard. But at each step the low hum grows gradually into the noisy shouting, until at last the different cries become distinct, and the hubbub, din, and confusion of a thousand voices bellowing at once again fill the air. The road and footpath are crowded, as on the over-night; the men are standing in groups, smoking and talking; whilst the women run to and fro, some with the white round turnips showing out of their filled aprons, others with cabbages under their arms, and a piece of red meat dangling from their hands. Only a few of the shops are closed , but the butcher's and the coal-shed are filled with customers, and from the door of the shut-up baker's, the women come streaming forth with bags of flour in their hands, while men sally from the halfpenny barber's smoothing their clean-shaved chins. Walnuts, blacking, apples, onions, braces, combs, turnips, herrings, pens, and corn-plaster, are all bellowed out at the same time. Labourers and mechanics, still unshorn and undressed, hang about with their hands in their pockets, some with their pet terriers under their arms. The pavement is green with the refuse leaves of vegetables, and round a cabbage - barrow the women stand turning over the bunches, as the man shouts, " Where you like, only a penny." Boys are running home with the breakfast herring held in a piece of paper, and the side-pocket of the apple-man's stuff coat hangs down with the weight of the halfpence stored within it. Presently the tolling of the neighbouring church bells breaks forth. Then the bustle doubles itself, the cries grow louder, the confusion greater. Women run about and push their way through the throng, scolding the saunterers, for in half an hour the market will close. In a little time the butcher puts up his shutters, and leaves the door still open ; the policemen in their clean gloves come round and drive the street-sellers before them, and as the clock strikes eleven the market finishes, and the Sunday's rest begins.

The following is a list of the street-markets, and the number of costers usually attending :—

MARKETS ON THE SURREY SIDE.

New-cut, Lambeth	300	Bermondsey	107
Lambeth-walk	104	Union-street, Borough	29
Walworth-road	22	Great Suffolk-street	46
Camberwell	15	Blackfriars-road	58
Newington	45		
Kent-street, Borough	38		664

MARKETS ON THE MIDDLESEX SIDE.

Brill and Chapel-st., Somers' Town	300	Leather-lane	150
Camden Town	50	St. John's-street	47
Hampstead-rd. and Tottenham-ct.-rd.	333	Old-street (St. Luke's)	46
		Whitecross - street, Cripplegate	150
St. George's Market, Oxford-street	177	Islington	79
		City-road	49
Marylebone	37	Shoreditch	100
Edgeware-road	78	Bethnal-green	100
Crawford-street	145	Whitechapel	258
Knightsbridge	46	Mile End	105
Pimlico	32	Commercial-rd. (East)	114
Tothill-st. & Broad-way, Westminster	119	Limehouse	88
		Ratcliffe Highway	122
Drury-lane	22	Rosemary-lane	119
Clare-street	139		
Exmouth-street and Aylesbury- street, Clerkenwell	142		3137

We find, from the foregoing list of markets, held in the various thoroughfares of the metropolis, that there are 10 on the Surrey side and 27 on the Middlesex side of the Thames. The total number of hucksters attending these markets is 3801, giving an average of 102 to each market.

HABITS AND AMUSEMENTS OF COSTERMONGERS.

I find it impossible to separate these two headings ; for the habits of the costermonger are not domestic. His busy life is past in the markets or the streets, and as his leisure is devoted to the beer-shop, the dancing-room, or the theatre, we must look for his habits to his demeanour at those places. Home has few attractions to a man whose life is a street-life. Even those who are influenced by family ties and affections, prefer to " home"—indeed that word is rarely mentioned among them — the conversation, warmth, and merriment of the beer-shop, where they can take their ease among their " mates." Excitement or amusement are indispensable to uneducated men. Of beer-shops resorted to by costermongers, and principally supported by them, it is computed that there are 400 in London.

Those who meet first in the beer-shop talk over the state of trade and of the markets, while the later comers enter at once into what may be styled the serious business of the evening—amusement.

Business topics are discussed in a most peculiar style. One man takes the pipe from his mouth and says, " Bill made a doogheno hit this morning." " Jem," says another, to a man just entering, " you'll stand a top o' reeb ?" " On," answers Jem, " I've had a trosseno tol, and have been doing dab." For an explanation of what may be obscure in this dialogue, I must refer my readers to my remarks concerning the language of the class. If any strangers are present, the conversation is still further clothed in slang, so as to be unintelligible even to the partially initiated. The evident puzzlement of any listener is of course gratifying to the costermonger's vanity, for he feels that he possesses a knowledge peculiarly his own.

Among the in-door amusements of the costermonger is card-playing, at which many of them are adepts. The usual games are all-fours, all-fives, cribbage, and put. Whist is known to a few, but is never played, being considered dull and slow. Of short whist they have not heard ; " but," said one, whom I questioned on the subject, " if it's come into fashion, it'll soon be among us." The play is usually for beer, but the game is rendered exciting by bets both among the players and the lookers-on. " I'll back Jem for a yanepatine," says one. " Jack for a gen," cries another. A penny is the lowest sum laid, and five shillings generally is the highest, but a shilling is not often exceeded. " We play fair among ourselves," said a costermonger to me— " aye, fairer than the aristocrats—but we'll take in anybody else." Where it is known that the landlord will not supply cards, " a sporting coster" carries a pack or two with him. The cards played with have rarely been stamped ;

they are generally dirty, and sometimes almost illegible, from long handling and spilled beer. Some men will sit patiently for hours at these games, and they watch the dealing round of the dingy cards intently, and without the attempt—common among politer gamesters—to appear indifferent, though they bear their losses well. In a full room of card-players, the groups are all shrouded in tobacco-smoke, and from them are heard constant sounds—according to the games they are engaged in—of "I'm low, and Ped's high." "Tip and me's game." "Fifteen four and a flush of five." I may remark it is curious that costermongers, who can neither read nor write, and who have no knowledge of the multiplication table, are skilful in all the intricacies and calculations of cribbage. There is not much quarrelling over the cards, unless strangers play with them, and then the costermongers all take part one with another, fairly or unfairly.

It has been said that there is a close resemblance between many of the characteristics of a very high class, socially, and a very low class. Those who remember the disclosures on a trial a few years back, as to how men of rank and wealth passed their leisure in card-playing—many of their lives being one continued leisure—can judge how far the analogy holds when the card-passion of the costermongers is described.

"Shove-halfpenny" is another game played by them; so is "Three up." Three halfpennies are thrown up, and when they fall all "heads" or all "tails," it is a mark; and the man who gets the greatest number of marks out of a given amount—three, or five, or more—wins. "Three-up" is played fairly among the costermongers; but is most frequently resorted to when strangers are present to "make a pitch,"—which is, in plain words, to cheat any stranger who is rash enough to bet upon them. "This is the way, sir," said an adept to me; "bless you, I can make them fall as I please. If I'm playing with Jo, and a stranger bets with Jo, why, of course, I make Jo win." This adept illustrated his skill to me by throwing up three halfpennies, and, five times out of six, they fell upon the floor, whether he threw them nearly to the ceiling or merely to his shoulder, all heads or all tails. The halfpence were the proper current coins—indeed, they were my own; and the result is gained by a peculiar position of the coins on the fingers, and a peculiar jerk in the throwing. There was an amusing manifestation of the pride of art in the way in which my obliging informant displayed his skill.

"Skittles" is another favourite amusement, and the costermongers class themselves among the best players in London. The game is always for beer, but betting goes on.

A fondness for "sparring" and "boxing" lingers among the rude members of some classes of the working men, such as the tanners. With the great majority of the costermongers this fondness is still as dominant as it was among the "higher classes," when boxers were the pets of princes and nobles. The sparring among the

costers is not for money, but for beer and "a lark"—a convenient word covering much mischief. Two out of every ten landlords, whose houses are patronised by these lovers of "the art of self-defence," supply gloves. Some charge 2*d.* a night for their use; others only 1*d.* The sparring seldom continues long, sometimes not above a quarter of an hour; for the costermongers, though excited for a while, weary of sports in which they cannot personally participate, and in the beer-shops only two spar at a time, though fifty or sixty may be present. The shortness of the duration of this pastime may be one reason why it seldom leads to quarrelling. The stake is usually a "top of reeb," and the winner is the man who gives the first "noser;" a *bloody* nose however is required to show that the blow was veritably a noser. The costermongers boast of their skill in pugilism as well as at skittles. "We are all handy with our fists," said one man, "and are matches, aye, and more than matches, for anybody but reg'lar boxers. We've stuck to the ring, too, and gone reg'lar to the fights, more than any other men."

"Twopenny-hops" are much resorted to by the costermongers, men and women, boys and girls. At these dances decorum is sometimes, but not often, violated. "The women," I was told by one man, "doesn't show their necks as I've seen the ladies do in them there pictures of high life in the shop-winders, or on the stage. Their Sunday gowns, which is their dancing gowns, ain't made that way." At these "hops" the clog-hornpipe is often danced, and sometimes a collection is made to ensure the performance of a first-rate professor of that dance; sometimes, and more frequently, it is volunteered gratuitously. The other dances are jigs, "flash jigs"—hornpipes in fetters—a dance rendered popular by the success of the acted "Jack Sheppard"—polkas, and country-dances, the last-mentioned being generally demanded by the women. Waltzes are as yet unknown to them. Sometimes they do the "pipe-dance." For this a number of tobacco-pipes, about a dozen, are laid close together on the floor, and the dancer places the toe of his boot between the different pipes, keeping time with the music. Two of the pipes are arranged as a cross, and the toe has to be inserted between each of the angles, without breaking them. The numbers present at these "hops" vary from 30 to 100 of both sexes, their ages being from 14 to 45, and the female sex being slightly predominant as to the proportion of those in attendance. At these "hops" there is nothing of the leisurely style of dancing—half a glide and half a skip—but vigorous, laborious capering. The hours are from half-past eight to twelve, sometimes to one or two in the morning, and never later than two, as the costermongers are early risers. There is sometimes a good deal of drinking; some of the young girls being often pressed to drink, and frequently yielding to the temptation. From 1*l.* to 7*l.* is spent in drink at a hop; the youngest men or lads present spend the most, especially in that act of costermonger

THE LONDON COSTERMONGER.

"Here Pertaters! Kearots and Turnups! fine Brockello-o-o!"

[From a Daguerreotype by BEARD.]

politeness—" treating the gals." The music is always a fiddle, sometimes with the addition of a harp and a cornopean. The band is provided by the costermongers, to whom the assembly is confined ; but during the present and the last year, when the costers' earnings have been less than the average, the landlord has provided the harp, whenever that instrument has added to the charms of the fiddle. Of one use to which these " hops " are put I have given an account, under the head of " Marriage."

The other amusements of this class of the community are the theatre and the penny concert, and their visits are almost entirely confined to the galleries of the theatres on the Surrey-side —the Surrey, the Victoria, the Bower Saloon, and (but less frequently) Astley's. Three times a week is an average attendance at theatres and dances by the more prosperous costermongers. The most intelligent man I met with among them gave me the following account. He classes himself with the many, but his tastes are really those of an educated man :—" Love and murder suits us best, sir ; but within these few years I think there's a great deal more liking for deep tragedies among us. They set men a thinking ; but then we all consider them too long. Of *Hamlet* we can make neither end nor side ; and nine out of ten of us—ay, far more than that—would like it to be confined to the ghost scenes, and the funeral, and the killing off at the last. *Macbeth* would be better liked, if it was only the witches and the fighting. The high words in a tragedy we call jaw-breakers, and say we can't tumble to that barrikin. We always stay to the last, because we've paid for it all, or very few costers would see a tragedy out if any money was returned to those leaving after two or three acts. We are fond of music. Nigger music was very much liked among us, but it's stale now. Flash songs are liked, and sailors' songs, and patriotic songs. Most costers—indeed, I can't call to mind an exception—listen very quietly to songs that they don't in the least understand. We have among us translations of the patriotic French songs. ' Mourir pour la patrie' is very popular, and so is the ' Marseillaise.' A song to take hold of us must have a good chorus." " They like something, sir, that is worth hearing," said one of my informants, " such as the ' Soldier's Dream,' ' The Dream of Napoleon,' or ' I 'ad a dream— an 'appy dream.' "

The songs in ridicule of Marshal Haynau, and in laudation of Barclay and Perkin's draymen, were and are very popular among the costers ; but none are more popular than Paul Jones— " A noble commander, Paul Jones was his name." Among them the chorus of " Britons never shall be slaves," is often rendered " Britons always shall be slaves." The most popular of all songs with the class, however, is " Duck-legged Dick," of which I give the first verse.

" Duck-legged Dick had a donkey,
    And his lush loved much for to swill,
One day he got rather lumpy,
    And got sent seven days to the mill.

His donkey was taken to the green-yard,
    A fate which he never deserved.
Oh ! it was such a regular mean yard,
    That alas ! the poor moke got starved.
Oh ! bad luck can't be prevented,
    Fortune she smiles or she frowns,
He 's best off that's contented,
    To mix, sirs, the ups and the downs."

Their sports, are enjoyed the more, if they are dangerous and require both courage and dexterity to succeed in them. They prefer, if crossing a bridge, to climb over the parapet, and walk along on the stone coping. When a house is building, rows of coster lads will climb up the long ladders, leaning against the unslated roof, and then slide down again, each one resting on the other's shoulders. A peep show with a battle scene is sure of its coster audience, and a favourite pastime is fighting with cheap theatrical swords. They are, however, true to each other, and should a coster, who is the hero of his court, fall ill and go to a hospital, the whole of the inhabitants of his quarter will visit him on the Sunday, and take him presents of various articles so that " he may live well."

Among the men, rat-killing is a favourite sport. They will enter an old stable, fasten the door and then turn out the rats. Or they will find out some unfrequented yard, and at night time build up a pit with apple-case boards, and lighting up their lamps, enjoy the sport. Nearly every coster is fond of dogs. Some fancy them greatly, and are proud of making them fight. If when out working, they see a handsome stray, whether he is a " toy " or " sporting " dog, they whip him up—many of the class not being *very* particular whether the animals are stray or not.

Their dog fights are both cruel and frequent. It is not uncommon to see a lad walking with the trembling legs of a dog shivering under a bloody handkerchief, that covers the bitten and wounded body of an animal that has been figuring at some " match." These fights take place on the sly—the tap-room or back-yard of a beershop, being generally chosen for the purpose. A few men are let into the secret, and they attend to bet upon the winner, the police being carefully kept from the spot.

Pigeons are " fancied " to a large extent, and are kept in lath cages on the roofs of the houses. The lads look upon a visit to the Redhouse, Battersea, where the pigeon-shooting takes place, as a great treat. They stand without the hoarding that encloses the ground, and watch for the wounded pigeons to fall, when a violent scramble takes place among them, each bird being valued at 3d. or 4d. So popular has this sport become, that some boys take dogs with them trained to retrieve the birds, and two Lambeth costers attend regularly after their morning's work with their guns, to shoot those that escape the ' shots' within.

A good pugilist is looked up to with great admiration by the costers, and fighting is considered to be a necessary part of a boy's education. Among them cowardice in any shape is despised as being degrading and loathsome, indeed the man who would avoid a fight, is scouted by the whole of the court he lives in. Hence it is important for a lad and even a girl to know how to "work their fists well"—as expert boxing is called among them. If a coster man or woman is struck they are obliged to fight. When a quarrel takes place between two boys, a ring is formed, and the men urge them on to have it out, for they hold that it is a wrong thing to stop a battle, as it causes bad blood for life; whereas, if the lads fight it out they shake hands and forget all about it. Everybody practises fighting, and the man who has the largest and hardest muscle is spoken of in terms of the highest commendation. It is often said in admiration of such a man that "he could muzzle half a dozen bobbies before breakfast."

To serve out a policeman is the bravest act by which a costermonger can distinguish himself. Some lads have been imprisoned upwards of a dozen times for this offence; and are consequently looked upon by their companions as martyrs. When they leave prison for such an act, a subscription is often got up for their benefit. In their continual warfare with the force, they resemble many savage nations, from the cunning and treachery they use. The lads endeavour to take the unsuspecting "crusher" by surprise, and often crouch at the entrance of a court until a policeman passes, when a stone or a brick is hurled at him, and the youngster immediately disappears. Their love of revenge too, is extreme — their hatred being in no way mitigated by time; they will wait for months, following a policeman who has offended or wronged them, anxiously looking out for an opportunity of paying back the injury. One boy, I was told, vowed vengeance against a member of the force, and for six months never allowed the man to escape his notice. At length, one night, he saw the policeman in a row outside a public-house, and running into the crowd kicked him savagely, shouting at the same time: "Now, you b——, I've got you at last." When the boy heard that his persecutor was injured for life, his joy was very great, and he declared the twelvemonth's imprisonment he was sentenced to for the offence to be "dirt cheap." The whole of the court where the lad resided sympathized with the boy, and vowed to a man, that had he escaped, they would have subscribed a pad or two of dry herrings, to send him into the country until the affair had blown over, for he had shown himself a "plucky one."

It is called "plucky" to bear pain without complaining. To flinch from expected suffering is scorned, and he who does so is sneered at and told to wear a gown, as being more fit to be a woman. To show a disregard for pain, a lad, when without money, will say to his pal, "Give us a penny, and you may have a punch at my nose." They also delight in tattooing their chests and arms with anchors,

and figures of different kinds. During the whole of this painful operation, the boy will not flinch, but laugh and joke with his admiring companions, as if perfectly at ease.

GAMBLING OF COSTERMONGERS.

IT would be difficult to find in the whole of this numerous class, a youngster who is not—what may be safely called—a desperate gambler. At the age of fourteen this love of play first comes upon the lad, and from that time until he is thirty or so, not a Sunday passes but he is at his stand on the gambling ground. Even if he has no money to stake, he will loll away the morning looking on, and so borrow excitement from the successes of others. Every attempt made by the police, to check this ruinous system, has been unavailing, and has rather given a gloss of daring courage to the sport, that tends to render it doubly attractive.

If a costermonger has an hour to spare, his first thought is to gamble away the time. He does not care what he plays for, so long as he can have a chance of winning something. Whilst waiting for a market to open, his delight is to find out some pieman and toss him for his stock, though, by so doing, he risks his market-money and only chance of living, to win that which he will give away to the first friend he meets. For the whole week the boy will work untiringly, spurred on by the thought of the money to be won on the Sunday. Nothing will damp his ardour for gambling, the most continued ill-fortune making him even more reckless than if he were the luckiest man alive.

Many a lad who had gone down to the gambling ground, with a good warm coat upon his back and his pocket well filled from the Saturday night's market, will leave it at evening penniless and coatless, having lost all his earnings, stock-money, and the better part of his clothing. Some of the boys, when desperate with "bad luck," borrow to the utmost limit of their credit; then they mortgage their "king's-man" or neck-tie, and they will even change their cord trousers, if better than those of the winner, so as to have one more chance at the turn of fortune. The coldest winter's day will not stop the Sunday's gathering on the river-side, for the heat of play warms them in spite of the sharp wind blowing down the Thames. If the weather be wet, so that the half-pence stick to the ground, they find out some railway-arch or else a beer-shop, and having filled the tap-room with their numbers, they muffle the table with handkerchiefs, and play secretly. When the game is very exciting, they will even forget their hunger, and continue to gamble until it is too dark to see, before they think of eating. One man told me, that when he was working the races with lemonade, he had often seen in the centre of a group, composed of costers, thimble-riggers and showmen, as much as 100l. on the ground at one time, in gold and silver. A friend of his, who had gone down in company with him, with a pony-truck of toys, lost in less than an hour his earnings, truck, stock of goods, and great-coat. Vowing to have his revenge next time, he took his boy on his back, and started off on the tramp to London, there to borrow sufficient money to bring down a fresh lot of goods on the morrow, and then gamble away his earnings as before.

It is perfectly immaterial to the coster with whom he plays, whether it be a lad from the Lambeth potteries, or a thief from the Westminster slums. Very often, too, the gamblers of one costermonger district, will visit those of another, and work what is called "a plant" in this way. One of the visitors will go before hand, and, joining a group of gamblers, commence tossing. When sufficient time has elapsed to remove all suspicion of companionship, his mate will come up and commence betting on each of his pals' throws with those standing round. By a curious quickness of hand, a coster can make the toss tell favourably for his wagering friend, who meets him after the play is over in the evening, and shares the spoil.

The spots generally chosen for the Sunday's sport are in secret places, half-hidden from the eye of the passers, where a scout can give quick notice of the approach of the police: in the fields about King's-cross, or near any unfinished railway buildings. The Mint, St. George's-fields, Blackfriars'-road, Bethnal-green, and Marylebone, are all favourite resorts. Between Lambeth and Chelsea, the shingle on the left side of the Thames, is spotted with small rings of lads, half-hidden behind the barges. One boy (of the party) is always on the look out, and even if a stranger should advance, the cry is given of "Namous" or "Kool Eslop." Instantly the money is whipped-up and pocketed, and the boys stand chattering and laughing together. It is never difficult for a coster to find out where the gambling parties are, for he has only to stop the first lad he meets, and ask him where the "erht pu" or "three up" is going on, to discover their whereabouts.

If during the game a cry of "Police!" should be given by the looker-out, instantly a rush at the money is made by any one in the group, the costers preferring that a stranger should have the money rather than the policeman. There is also a custom among them, that the ruined player should be started again by a gift of 2d. in every shilling lost, or, if the loss is heavy, a present of four or five shillings is made; neither is it considered at all dishonourable for the party winning to leave with the full bloom of success upon him.

That the description of one of these Sunday scenes might be more truthful, a visit was paid to a gambling-ring close to ——. Although not twenty yards distant from the steam-boat pier, yet the little party was so concealed among the the coal-barges, that not a head could be seen. The spot chosen was close to a small narrow court, leading from the street to the water-side, and here the lad on the look-out was stationed. There were about thirty young fellows, some

tall strapping youths, in the costers' cable-cord costume,—others, mere boys, in rags, from the potteries, with their clothes stained with clay. The party was hidden from the river by the black dredger-boats on the beach; and it was so arranged, that should the alarm be given, they might leap into the coal-barges, and hide until the intruder had retired. Seated on some oars stretched across two craft, was a mortar-stained bricklayer, keeping a look-out towards the river, and acting as a sort of umpire in all disputes. The two that were tossing had been playing together since early morning; and it was easy to tell which was the loser, by the anxious-looking eye and compressed lip. He was quarrelsome too; and if the crowd pressed upon him, he would jerk his elbow back savagely, saying, "I wish to C——t you'd stand backer." The winner, a short man, in a mud-stained canvas jacket, and a week's yellow beard on his chin, never spake a word beyond his "heads," or "tails;" but his cheeks were red, and the pipe in his mouth was unlit, though he puffed at it.

In their hands they each held a long row of halfpence, extending to the wrist, and topped by shillings and half-crowns. Nearly every one round had coppers in his hands, and bets were made and taken as rapidly as they could be spoken. "I lost a sov. last night in less than no time," said one man, who, with his hands in his pockets, was looking on; "never mind—I musn't have no wenson this week, and try again next Sunday."

The boy who was losing was adopting every means to "bring back his luck again." Before crying, he would toss up a halfpenny three times, to see what he should call. At last, with an oath, he pushed aside the boys round him, and shifted his place, to see what that would do; it had a good effect, for he won toss after toss in a curiously fortunate way, and then it was strange to watch his mouth gradually relax and his brows unknit. His opponent was a little startled, and passing his fingers through his dusty hair, said, with a stupid laugh, "Well, I never see the likes." The betting also began to shift. "Sixpence Ned wins!" cried three or four; "Sixpence he loses!" answered another; "Done!" and up went the halfpence. "Half-a-crown Joe loses!"—"Here you are," answered Joe, but he lost again. "I'll try you a 'gen'" (shilling) said a coster; "And a 'rouf yenap'" (fourpence), added the other. "Say a 'exes'" (sixpence).—"Done!" and the betting continued, till the ground was spotted with silver and halfpence.

"That's ten bob he's won in five minutes," said Joe (the loser), looking round with a forced smile; but Ned (the winner) never spake a word, even when he gave any change to his antagonist; and if he took a bet, he only nodded to the one that offered it, and threw down his money. Once, when he picked up more than a sovereign from the ground, that he had won in one throw, a washed sweep, with a black rim round his neck, said, "There's a hog!" but

there wasn't even a smile at the joke. At last
Joe began to feel angry, and stamping his foot
till the water squirted up from the beach, cried,
"It's no use; luck's set in him—he'd muck a
thousand!" and so he shifted his ground, and
betted all round on the chance of better fortune
attending the movement. He lost again, and
some one bantering said, "You'll win the shine-
rag, Joe," meaning that he would be "cracked
up," or ruined, if he continued.

When one o'clock struck, a lad left, saying,
he was "going to get an inside lining" (dinner).
The sweep asked him what he was going to
have. "A two-and-half plate, and a ha'p'orth
of smash" (a plate of soup and a ha'p'orth of
mashed potatoes), replied the lad, bounding into
the court. Nobody else seemed to care for his
dinner, for all stayed to watch the gamblers.

Every now and then some one would go up
the court to see if the lad watching for the
police was keeping a good look-out; but the
boy never deserted his post, for fear of losing
his threepence. If he had, such is the wish to
protect the players felt by every lad, that even
whilst at dinner, one of them, if he saw a policeman pass, would spring up and rush to the
gambling ring to give notice.

When the tall youth, "Ned," had won nearly
all the silver of the group, he suddenly jerked
his gains into his coat-pocket, and saying, "I've
done," walked off, and was out of sight in an
instant. The surprise of the loser and all
around was extreme. They looked at the court
where he had disappeared, then at one another,
and at last burst out into one expression of
disgust. "There's a scurf!" said one; "He's
a regular scab," cried another; and a coster
declared that he was "a trosseno, and no mistake." For although it is held to be fair for
the winner to go whenever he wishes, yet such
conduct is never relished by the losers.

It was then determined that "they would
have him to rights" the next time he came to
gamble; for every one would set at him, and
win his money, and then "turn up," as he had
done.

The party was then broken up, the players
separating to wait for the new-comers that would
be sure to pour in after dinner.

"Vic. Gallery."

On a good attractive night, the rush of costers
to the threepenny gallery of the Coburg (better
known as "the Vic") is peculiar and almost
awful.

The long zig-zag staircase that leads to the
pay box is crowded to suffocation at least an
hour before the theatre is opened; but, on the
occasion of a piece with a good murder in it,
the crowd will frequently collect as early as
three o'clock in the afternoon. Lads stand
upon the broad wooden bannisters about 50 feet
from the ground, and jump on each others'
backs, or adopt any expedient they can think of
to obtain a good place.

The walls of the well-staircase having a

remarkably fine echo, and the wooden floor of
the steps serving as a sounding board, the
shouting, whistling, and quarrelling of the
impatient young costers is increased tenfold.
If, as sometimes happens, a song with a chorus
is started, the ears positively ache with the din,
and when the chant has finished it seems as
though a sudden silence had fallen on the
people. To the centre of the road, and all round
the door, the mob is in a ferment of excitement; and no sooner is the money-taker at his
post than the most frightful rush takes place,
every one heaving with his shoulder at the back
of the person immediately in front of him.
The girls shriek, men shout, and a nervous fear
is felt lest the massive staircase should fall in
with the weight of the throng, as it lately did
with the most terrible results. If a hat
tumbles from the top of the staircase, a hundred
hands snatch at it as it descends. When it is
caught a voice roars above the tumult, "All
right, Bill, I've got it"—for they all seem to
know one another—"Keep us a pitch and I'll
bring it."

To any one unaccustomed to be pressed flat
it would be impossible to enter with the mob.
To see the sight in the gallery it is better to
wait until the first piece is over. The ham-
sandwich men and pig-trotter women will give
you notice when the time is come, for with the
first clatter of the descending footsteps they
commence their cries.

There are few grown-up men that go to the
"Vic" gallery. The generality of the visitors
are lads from about twelve to three-and-twenty,
and though a few black-faced sweeps or whitey-
brown dustmen may be among the throng, the
gallery audience consists mainly of costermongers. Young girls, too, are very plentiful, only
one-third of whom now take their babies, owing
to the new regulation of charging half-price for
infants. At the foot of the staircase stands a
group of boys begging for the return checks,
which they sell again for 1½d. or 1d., according
to the lateness of the hour.

At each step up the well-staircase the warmth
and stench increase, until by the time one
reaches the gallery doorway, a furnace-heat
rushes out through the entrance that seems to
force you backwards, whilst the odour positively
prevents respiration. The mob on the landing,
standing on tiptoe and closely wedged together,
resists any civil attempt at gaining a glimpse of
the stage, and yet a coster lad will rush up,
elbow his way into the crowd, then jump up on
to the shoulders of those before him, and suddenly disappear into the body of the gallery.

The gallery at "the Vic" is one of the
largest in London. It will hold from 1500 to
2000 people, and runs back to so great a
distance, that the end of it is lost in shadow,
excepting where the little gas-jets, against the
wall, light up the two or three faces around
them. When the gallery is well packed, it is
usual to see piles of boys on each others
shoulders at the back, while on the partition

boards, dividing off the slips, lads will pitch themselves, despite the spikes.

As you look up the vast slanting mass of heads from the upper boxes, each one appears on the move. The huge black heap, dotted with faces, and spotted with white shirt sleeves, almost pains the eye to look at, and should a clapping of hands commence, the twinkling nearly blinds you. It is the fashion with the mob to take off their coats; and the cross-braces on the backs of some, and the bare shoulders peeping out of the ragged shirts of others, are the only variety to be found. The bonnets of the "ladies" are hung over the iron railing in front, their numbers nearly hiding the panels, and one of the amusements of the lads in the back seats consists in pitching orange peel or nutshells into them, a good aim being rewarded with a shout of laughter.

When the orchestra begins playing, before "the gods" have settled into their seats, it is impossible to hear a note of music. The puffed-out cheeks of the trumpeters, and the raised drumsticks tell you that the overture has commenced, but no tune is to be heard. An occasional burst of the full band being caught by gushes, as if a high wind were raging. Recognitions take place every moment, and "Bill Smith" is called to in a loud voice from one side, and a shout in answer from the other asks "What's up?" Or family secrets are revealed, and "Bob Triller" is asked where "Sal" is, and replies amid a roar of laughter, that she is "a-larning the pynanney."

By-and-by a youngster, who has come in late, jumps up over the shoulders at the door, and doubling himself into a ball, rolls down over the heads in front, leaving a trail of commotion for each one as he passes aims a blow at the fellow. Presently a fight is sure to begin, and then every one rises from his seat whistling and shouting; three or four pairs of arms fall to, the audience waving their hands till the moving mass seems like microscopic eels in paste. But the commotion ceases suddenly on the rising of the curtain, and then the cries of "Silence!" "Ord-a-a-r!" "Ord-a-a-r!" make more noise than ever.

The "Vic" gallery is not to be moved by touching sentiment. They prefer vigorous exercise to any emotional speech. "The Child of the Storm's" declaration that she would share her father's "death or imprisonment as her duty," had no effect at all, compared with the split in the hornpipe. The shrill whistling and brayvos that followed the tar's performance showed how highly it was relished, and one "god" went so far as to ask "how it was done." The comic actor kicking a dozen Polish peasants was encored, but the grand banquet of the Czar of all the Russias only produced merriment, and a request that he would "give them a bit" was made directly the Emperor took the willow-patterned plate in his hand. All affecting situations were sure to be interrupted by cries of "orda-a-r;" and the lady begging

for her father's life was told to "speak up old gal;" though when the heroine of the "dummestic dreamer" (as they call it) told the general of all the Cossack forces "not to be a fool," the uproar of approbation grew greater than ever,—and when the lady turned up her swan's-down cuffs, and seizing four Russian soldiers shook them successively by the collar, then the enthusiasm knew no bounds, and the cries of "Bray-vo Vincent! Go it my tulip!" resounded from every throat. Altogether the gallery audience do not seem to be of a gentle nature. One poor little lad shouted out in a crying tone, "that he couldn't see," and instantly a dozen voices demanded "that he should be thrown over."

Whilst the pieces are going on, brown, flat bottles are frequently raised to the mouth, and between the acts a man with a tin can, glittering in the gas-light, goes round crying, "Port-a-a-a-r! who's for port-a-a-a-r." As the heat increased the faces grew bright red, every bonnet was taken off, and ladies could be seen wiping the perspiration from their cheeks with the play-bills.

No delay between the pieces will be allowed, and should the interval appear too long, some one will shout out—referring to the curtain—"Pull up that there winder blind!" or they will call to the orchestra, saying, "Now then you catgut-scrapers! Let's have a ha'purth of liveliness." Neither will they suffer a play to proceed until they have a good view of the stage, and "Higher the blue," is constantly shouted, when the sky is too low, or "Light up the moon," when the transparency is rather dim.

The dances and comic songs, between the pieces, are liked better than any' .ing else. A highland fling is certain to be repeated, and a stamping of feet will accompany the tune, and a shrill whistling, keep time through the entire performance.

But the grand hit of the evening is always when a song is sung to which the entire gallery can join in chorus. Then a deep silence prevails all through the stanzas. Should any burst in before his time, a shout of "orda-a-r" is raised, and the intruder put down by a thousand indignant cries. At the proper time, however, the throats of the mob burst forth in all their strength. The most deafening noise breaks out suddenly, while the cat-calls keep up the tune, and an imitation of a dozen Mr. Punches squeak out the words. Some actors at the minor theatres make a great point of this, and in the bill upon the night of my visit, under the title of "There's a good time coming, boys," there was printed, "assisted by the most numerous and effective chorus in the metropolis—" meaning the whole of the gallery. The singer himself started the mob, saying, "Now then, the Exeter Hall touch if you please gentlemen," and beat time with his hand, parodying M. Jullien with his *baton.* An "angcore" on such occasions is always demanded, and, despite a few murmurs of "change it to 'Duck-legged Dick,'" invariably insisted on.

THE POLITICS OF COSTERMONGERS.— POLICEMEN.

THE notion of the police is so intimately blended with what may be called the politics of the costermongers that I give them together.

The politics of these people are detailed in a few words—they are nearly all Chartists. "You might say, sir," remarked one of my informants, "that they *all* were Chartists, but as its better you should rather be under than over the mark, say *nearly* all." Their ignorance, and their being impulsive, makes them a dangerous class. I am assured that in every district where the costermongers are congregated, one or two of the body, more intelligent than the others, have great influence over them; and these leading men are all Chartists, and being industrious and not unprosperous persons, their pecuniary and intellectual superiority cause them to be regarded as oracles. One of these men said to me : "The costers think that working-men know best, and so they have confidence in us. I like to make men discontented, and I will make them discontented while the present system continues, because it's all for the middle and the moneyed classes, and nothing, in the way of rights, for the poor. People fancy when all's quiet that all's stagnating. Propagandism is going on for all that. It's when all's quiet that the seed's a growing. Republicans and Socialists are pressing their doctrines."

The costermongers have very vague notions of an aristocracy ; they call the more prosperous of their own body "aristocrats." Their notions of an aristocracy of birth or wealth seem to be formed on their opinion of the rich, or reputed rich salesmen with whom they deal ; and the result is anything but favourable to the nobility.

Concerning free-trade, nothing, I am told, can check the costermongers' fervour for a cheap loaf. A Chartist costermonger told me that he knew numbers of costers who were keen Chartists without understanding anything about the six points.

The costermongers frequently attend political meetings, going there in bodies of from six to twelve. Some of them, I learned, could not understand why Chartist leaders exhorted them to peace and quietness, when they might as well fight it out with the police at once. The costers boast, moreover, that they stick more together in any "row" than any other class. It is considered by them a reflection on the character of the thieves that they are seldom true to one another.

It is a matter of marvel to many of this class that people can live without working. The ignorant costers have no knowledge of "property," or "income," and conclude that the non-workers all live out of the taxes. Of the taxes generally they judge from their knowledge that

tobacco, which they account a necessary of life, pays 3*s.* per lb. duty.

As regards the police, the hatred of a costermonger to a "peeler" is intense, and with their opinion of the police, all the more ignorant unite that of the governing power. "Can you wonder at it, sir," said a costermonger to me, "that I hate the police ? They drive us about, we must move on, we can't stand here, and we can't pitch there. But if we're cracked up, that is if we're forced to go into the Union (I've known it both at Clerkenwell and the City of London workhouses,) why the parish gives us money to buy a barrow, or a shallow, or to hire them, and leave the house and start for ourselves : and what's the use of that, if the police won't let us sell our goods?—Which is right, the parish or the police?"

To thwart the police in any measure the costermongers readily aid one another. One very common procedure, if the policeman has seized a barrow, is to whip off a wheel, while the officers have gone for assistance ; for a large and loaded barrow requires two men to convey it to the green-yard. This is done with great dexterity ; and the next step is to dispose of the stock to any passing costers, or to any "standing" in the neighbourhood, and it is honestly accounted for. The policemen, on their return, find an empty, and unwheelable barrow, which they must carry off by main strength, amid the jeers of the populace.

I am assured that in case of a political riot every "coster" would seize his policeman.

MARRIAGE AND CONCUBINAGE OF COSTERMONGERS.

ONLY one-tenth—at the outside one-tenth—of the couples living together and carrying on the costermongering trade, are married. In Clerkenwell parish, however, where the number of married couples is about a fifth of the whole, this difference is easily accounted for, as in Advent and Easter the incumbent of that parish marries poor couples without a fee. Of the rights of "legitimate" or "illegitimate" children the costermongers understand nothing, and account it a mere waste of money and time to go through the ceremony of wedlock when a pair can live together, and be quite as well regarded by their fellows, without it. The married women associate with the unmarried mothers of families without the slightest scruple. There is no honour attached to the marriage state, and no shame to concubinage. Neither are the unmarried women less faithful to their "partners" than the married ; but I understand that, of the two classes, the unmarried betray the most jealousy.

As regards the fidelity of these women I was assured that, "in anything like good times," they were rigidly faithful to their husbands or paramours ; but that, in the worst pinch of poverty, a departure from this fidelity—if it provided a few meals or a fire—was not considered at all heinous. An old costermonger, who had been mixed up with other callings, and whose prejudices were certainly not in favour of his present trade, said to me, " What I call the working girls, sir, are as industrious and as faithful a set as can well be. I'm satisfied that they're more faithful to their mates than other poor working women. I never knew one of these working girls do wrong that way. They're strong, hearty, healthy girls, and keep clean rooms. Why, there's numbers of men leave their stock-money with their women, just taking out two or three shillings to gamble with and get drunk upon. They sometimes take a little drop themselves, the women do, and get beaten by their husbands for it, and hardest beaten if the man's drunk himself. They're sometimes beaten for other things too, or for nothing at all. But they seem to like the men better for their beating them. I never could make that out." Notwithstanding this fidelity, it appears that the "larking and joking" of the young, and sometimes of the middle-aged people, among themselves, is anything but delicate. The unmarried separate as seldom as the married. The fidelity characterizing the women does not belong to the men.

The dancing-rooms are the places where matches are made up. There the boys go to look out for "mates," and sometimes a match is struck up the first night of meeting, and the couple live together forthwith. The girls at these dances are all the daughters of costermongers, or of persons pursuing some other course of street life. Unions take place when the lad is but 14. Two or three out of 100 have their female helpmates at that early age; but the female is generally a couple of years older than her partner. Nearly all the costermongers form such alliances as I have described, when both parties are under twenty. One reason why these alliances are contracted at early ages is, that when a boy has assisted his father, or any one engaging him, in the business of a costermonger, he knows that he can borrow money, and hire a shallow or a barrow—or he may have saved 5s.—" and then if the father vexes him or snubs him," said one of my informants, "he'll tell his father to go to h—l, and he and his gal will start on their own account."

Most of the costermongers have numerous families, but not those who contract alliances very young. The women continue working down to the day of their confinement.

" Chance children," as they are called, or children unrecognised by any father, are rare among the young women of the costermongers.

RELIGION OF COSTERMONGERS.

AN intelligent and trustworthy man, until very recently actively engaged in costermongering, computed that not 3 in 100 costermongers had ever been in the interior of a church, or any place of worship, or knew what was meant by Christianity. The same person gave me the following account, which was confirmed by others: " The costers have no religion at all, and very little notion, or none at all, of what religion or

a future state is. Of all things they hate tracts. They hate them because the people leaving them never give them anything, and as they can't read the tract—not one in forty—they're vexed to be bothered with it. And really what is the use of giving people reading before you've taught them to read? Now, they respect the City Missionaries, because they read to them—and the costers will listen to reading when they don't understand it—and because they visit the sick, and sometimes give oranges and such like to them and the children. I've known a City Missionary buy a shilling's worth of oranges of a coster, and give them away to the sick and the children—most of them belonging to the costermongers—down the court, and that made him respected there. I think the City Missionaries have done good. But I'm satisfied that if the costers had to profess themselves of some religion to-morrow, they would all become Roman Catholics, every one of them. This is the reason:—London costers live very often in the same courts and streets as the poor Irish, and if the Irish are sick, be sure there comes to them the priest, the Sisters of Charity —they *are* good women—and some other ladies. Many a man that's not a Catholic, has rotted and died without any good person near him. Why, I lived a good while in Lambeth, and there wasn't one coster in 100, I'm satisfied, knew so much as the rector's name,—though Mr. Dalton's a very good man. But the reason I was telling you of, sir, is that the costers reckon *that* religion's the best that gives the most in charity, and they think the Catholics do this. I'm not a Catholic myself, but I believe every word of the Bible, and have the greater belief that it's the word of God because it teaches democracy. The Irish in the courts get sadly chaffed by the others about their priests,—but they'll die for the priest. Religion is a regular puzzle to the costers. They see people come out of church and chapel, and as they're mostly well dressed, and there's very few of their own sort among the church-goers, the costers somehow mix up being religious with being respectable, and so they have a queer sort of feeling about it. It's a mystery to them. It's shocking when you come to think of it. They'll listen to any preacher that goes among them; and then a few will say—I've heard it often —' A b—y fool, why don't he let people go to h-ll their own way?' There's another thing that makes the costers think so well of the Catholics. If a Catholic coster—there's only very few of them—is 'cracked up' (penniless), he's often started again, and the others have a notion that it's through some chapel-fund. I don't know whether it is so or not, but I know the cracked-up men are started again, if they're Catholics. It's still the stranger that the regular costermongers, who are nearly all Londoners, should have such respect for the Roman Catholics, when they have such a hatred of the Irish, whom they look upon as intruders and underminers."—" If a missionary came among us with plenty of money," said another coster-monger, "he might make us all Christians or Turks, or anything he liked." Neither the Latter-day Saints, nor any similar sect, have made converts among the costermongers.

OF THE UNEDUCATED STATE OF COSTERMONGERS.

I HAVE stated elsewhere, that only about one in ten of the regular costermongers is able to read. The want of education among both men and women is deplorable, and I tested it in several instances. The following statement, however, from one of the body, is no more to be taken as representing the ignorance of the class gene-rally, than are the clear and discriminating accounts I received from intelligent coster-mongers to be taken as representing the intelli-gence of the body.

The man with whom I conversed, and from whom I received the following statement, seemed about thirty. He was certainly not ill-looking, but with a heavy cast of countenance, his light blue eyes having little expression. His state-ments, or opinions, I need hardly explain, were given both spontaneously in the course of con-versation, and in answer to my questions. I give them almost verbatim, omitting oaths and slang:

"Well, times is bad, sir," he said, "but it's a deadish time. I don't do so well at present as in middlish times, I think. When I served the Prince of Naples, not far from here (I presume that he alluded to the Prince of Capua), I did better and times was better. That was five years ago, but I can't say to a year or two. He was a good customer, and was wery fond of peaches. I used to sell them to him, at 12s. the plasket when they was new. The plasket held a dozen, and cost me 6s. at Covent-garden—more sometimes; but I didn't charge him more when they did. His footman was a black man, and a ignorant man quite, and his housekeeper was a English-woman. He was the Prince o' Naples, was my customer; but I don't know what he was like, for I never saw him. I've heard that he was the brother of the king of Naples. I can't say where Naples is, but if you was to ask at Euston-square, they'll tell you the fare there and the time to go it in. It may be in France for anything I know may Naples, or in Ireland. Why don't you ask at the square? I went to Croydon once by rail, and slept all the way without stirring, and so you may to Naples for anything I know. I never heard of the Pope being a neighbour of the King of Naples. Do you mean living next door to him? But I don't know nothing of the King of Naples, only the prince. I don't know what the Pope is. Is he any trade? It's nothing to me, when he's no customer of mine. I have nothing to say about nobody that ain't no customers. My crabs is caught in the sea, in course. I gets them at Billingsgate. I never saw the sea, but it's salt-water, I know. I

can't say whereabouts it lays. I believe it's in the hands of the Billingsgate salesmen—all of it? I've heard of shipwrecks at sea, caused by drownding, in course. I never heard that the Prince of Naples was ever at sea. I like to talk about him, he was such a customer when he lived near here." (Here he repeated his account of the supply of peaches to his Royal Highness.) "I never was in France, no, sir, never. I don't know the way. Do you think I could do better there? I never was in the Republic there. What's it like? Bona-parte? O, yes; I've heard of him. He was at Waterloo. I didn't know he'd been alive now and in France, as you ask me about him. I don't think you're larking, sir. Did I hear of the French taking possession of Naples, and Bonaparte making his brother-in-law king? Well, I didn't, but it may be true, because I served the Prince of Naples, what *was* the brother of the king. I never heard whether the Prince was the king's older brother or his younger. I wish he may turn out his older if there's property coming to him, as the oldest has the first turn; at least so I've heard—first come, first served. I've worked the streets and the courts at all times. I've worked them by moonlight, but you couldn't see the moonlight where it was busy. I can't say how far the moon's off us. It's nothing to me, but I've seen it a good bit higher than St. Paul's. I don't know nothing about the sun. Why do you ask? It must be nearer than the moon for it's warmer,—and if they're both fire, that shows it. It's like the tap-room grate and that bit of a gas-light; to compare the two is. What was St. Paul's that the moon was above? A church, sir; so I've heard. I never was in a church. O, yes, I've heard of God; he made heaven and earth; I never heard of his making the sea; that's another thing, and you can best learn about that at Billingsgate. (He seemed to think that the sea was an appur-tenance of Billingsgate.) Jesus Christ? Yes. I've heard of him. Our Redeemer? Well, I only wish I could redeem my Sunday togs from my uncle's."

Another costermonger, in answer to inquiries, said: "I 'spose you think us 'riginal coves that you ask. We're not like Methusalem, or some such swell's name, (I presume that Malthus was meant) as wanted to murder children afore they was born, as I once heerd lectured about—we're nothing like that."

Another on being questioned, and on being told that the information was wanted for the press, replied: "The press? I'll have nothing to say to it. We are oppressed enough already."

That a class numbering 30,000 should be per-mitted to remain in a state of almost brutish ignorance is a national disgrace. If the London costers belong especially to the "dangerous classes," the danger of such a body is assuredly an evil of our own creation; for the gratitude of the poor creatures to any one who seeks to give them the least knowledge is almost pathetic.

LANGUAGE OF COSTERMONGERS.

THE slang language of the costermongers is not very remarkable for originality of construction ; it possesses no humour : but they boast that it is known only to themselves; it is far beyond the Irish, they say, and puzzles the Jews. The *root* of the costermonger tongue, so to speak, is to give the words spelt backward, or rather pronounced rudely backward,—for in my present chapter the language has, I believe, been reduced to orthography for the first time. With this backward pronunciation, which is very arbitrary, are mixed words reducible to no rule and seldom referrable to any origin, thus complicating the mystery of this unwritten tongue ; while any syllable is added to a proper slang word, at the discretion of the speaker.

Slang is acquired very rapidly, and some costermongers will converse in it by the hour. The women use it sparingly ; the girls more than the women ; the men more than the girls ; and the boys most of all. The most ignorant of all these classes deal most in slang and boast of their cleverness and proficiency in it. In their conversations among themselves, the following are invariably the terms used in money matters. A rude back-spelling may generally be traced :

Flatch	Halfpenny.
Yenep	Penny.
Owt-yenep . . .	Twopence.
Erth-yenep	Threepence.
Rouf-yenep	Fourpence.
Ewif-yenep . . .	Fivepence.
Exis-yenep	Sixpence.
Neves-yenep . . .	Sevenpence.
Teaich-yenep . . .	Eightpence.
Enine-yenep . . .	Ninepence.
Net-yenep	Tenpence.
Leven	Elevenpence.
Gen	Twelvepence.
Yenep-flatch . . .	Three half-pence.

and so on through the penny-halfpennies.

It was explained to me by a costermonger, who had introduced some new words into the slang, that " leven " was allowed so closely to resemble the proper word, because elevenpence was almost an unknown sum to costermongers, the transition—weights and measures notwithstanding—being immediate from 10*d.* to 1*s.*

" Gen " is a shilling and the numismatic sequence is pursued with the gens, as regards shillings, as with the " yeneps " as regards pence. The blending of the two is also according to the same system as " Owt-gen, teaich-yenep " two-and-eightpence. The exception to the uniformity of the " gen " enumeration is in the sum of 8*s.*, which instead of " teaich-gen " is " teaich-guy :" a deviation with ample precedents in all civilised tongues.

As regards the larger coins the translation into slang is not reducible into rule. The following are the costermonger coins of the higher value :

Couter	Sovereign.
Half-Couter, or *Net-gen*. . . . . }	Half-sovereign.
Ewif-gen	Crown.
Flatch-ynork . . .	Half-crown.

The costermongers still further complicate their slang by a mode of multiplication. They thus say, " Erth Ewif-gens" or 3 times 5*s.*, which means of course 15*s.*

Speaking of this language, a costermonger said to me : " The Irish can't tumble to it anyhow ; the Jews can tumble better, but we're *their* masters. Some of the young salesmen at Billingsgate understand us,—but only at Billingsgate ; and they think they're uncommon clever, but they're not quite up to the mark. The police don't understand us at all. It would be a pity if they did."

I give a few more phrases :

A doogheno or dab- heno ? . . . . }	{ Is it a good or bad market ?
A regular trosseno . .	A regular bad one.
On	No.
Say	Yes.
Tumble to your bar- rikin . . . . }	Understand you.
Top o' reeb	Pot of beer.
Doing dab	Doing badly.
Cool him	Look at him.

The latter phrase is used when one costermonger warns another of the approach of a policeman " who might order him to move on, or be otherwise unpleasant." " Cool " (look) is exclaimed, or " Cool him " (look at him). One costermonger told me as a great joke that a very stout policeman, who was then new to the duty, was when in a violent state of perspiration, much offended by a costermonger saying " Cool him."

Cool the esclop . . .	Look at the police.
Cool the namesclop .	{ Look at the policeman.
Cool ta the dillo nemo .	{ Look at the old woman ;

said of any woman, young or old, who, according to costermonger notions, is " giving herself airs."

This language seems confined, in its general use, to the immediate objects of the costermonger's care ; but is, among the more acute members of the fraternity, greatly extended, and is capable of indefinite extension.

The costermongers oaths, I may conclude, are all in the vernacular ; nor are any of the common salutes, such as " How d'you do ?" or " Good-night " known to their slang.

Kennetseeno	Stinking ;

(applied principally to the quality of fish.)

Flatch kanurd . .	Half-drunk.
Flash it	Show it ;

(in cases of bargains offered.)

On doog	No good.

Cross chap	A thief.
Showfulls	Bad money;

(seldom in the hands of costermongers.)

I'm on to the deb . .	I'm going to bed.
Do the tightner . .	Go to dinner.
Nommus	Be off.
Tol	Lot, Stock, or Share.

Many costermongers, " but principally—perhaps entirely,"—I was told, " those who had not been regular born and bred to the trade, but had taken to it when cracked up in their own," do not trouble themselves to acquire any knowledge of slang. It is not indispensable for the carrying on of their business; the grand object, however, seems to be, to shield their bargainings at market, or their conversation among themselves touching their day's work and profits, from the knowledge of any Irish or uninitiated fellow-traders.

The simple principle of costermonger slang—that of pronouncing backward, may cause its acquirement to be regarded by the educated as a matter of ease. But it is a curious fact that lads who become costermongers' boys, without previous association with the class, acquire a very ready command of the language, and this though they are not only unable to spell, but don't "know a letter in a book." I saw one lad, whose parents had, until five or six months back, resided in the country. The lad himself was fourteen ; he told me he had not been " a costermongering" more than three months, and prided himself on his mastery over slang. To test his ability, I asked him the coster's word for " hippopotamus;" he answered, with tolerable readiness, "musatoppop." I then asked him for the like rendering of " equestrian" (one of Astley's bills having caught my eye). He replied, but not quite so readily, " nirtseque." The last test to which I subjected him was " good-naturedly;" and though I induced him to repeat the word twice, I could not, on any of the three renderings, distinguish any precise sound beyond an indistinct gabbling, concluded emphatically with " doog:"—" good " being a word with which all these traders are familiar. It must be remembered, that the words I demanded were remote from the young costermonger's vocabulary, if not from his understanding.

Before I left this boy, he poured forth a minute or more's gibberish, of which, from its rapid utterance, I could distinguish nothing ; but I found from his after explanation, that it was a request to me to make a further purchase of his walnuts.

This slang is utterly devoid of any applicability to humour. It gives no new fact, or approach to a fact, for philologists. One superior genius among the costers, who has invented words for them, told me that he had no system for coining his term. He gave to the known words some terminating syllable, or, as he called it, " a new turn, just," to use his own words, " as if he chorussed them, with a tol-de-rol."

The intelligence communicated in this slang is, in a great measure, communicated, as in other slang, as much by the inflection of the voice, the emphasis, the tone, the look, the shrug, the nod, the wink, as by the words spoken.

Of the Nicknames of Costermongers.

Like many rude, and almost all wandering communities, the costermongers, like the cabmen and pickpockets, are hardly ever known by their real names ; even the honest men among them are distinguished by some strange appellation. Indeed, they are all known one to another by nicknames, which they acquire either by some mode of dress, some remark that has ensured costermonger applause, some peculiarity in trading, or some defect or singularity in personal appearance. Men are known as " Rotten Herrings," " Spuddy" (a seller of bad potatoes, until beaten by the Irish for his bad wares,) "Curly" (a man with a curly head), " Foreigner" (a man who had been in the Spanish-Legion), " Brassy" (a very saucy person), " Gaffy" (once a performer), " The One-eyed Buffer," " Jawbreaker," " Pine-apple Jack," " Cast-iron Poll " (her head having been struck with a pot without injury to her), " Whilky," " Blackwall Poll " (a woman generally having two black eyes), " Lushy Bet," " Dirty Sall" (the costermongers generally objecting to dirtywomen), and " Dancing Sue."

Of the Education of Costermongers' Children.

I have used the heading of " Education," but perhaps to say " non-education," would be more suitable. Very few indeed of the costermongers' children are sent even to the Ragged Schools ; and if they are, from all I could learn, it is done more that the mother may be saved the trouble of tending them at home, than from any desire that the children shall acquire useful knowledge. Both boys and girls are sent out by their parents in the evening to sell nuts, oranges, &c., at the doors of the theatres, or in any public place, or " round the houses" (a stated circuit from their place of abode). This trade they pursue eagerly for the sake of " bunts," though some carry home the money they take, very honestly. The costermongers are kind to their children, "perhaps in a rough way, and the women make regular pets of them very often." One experienced man told me, that he had seen a poor costermonger's wife—one of the few who could read—instructing her children in reading ; but such instances were very rare. The education of these children is such only as the streets afford ; and the streets teach them, for the most part—and in greater or lesser degrees,—acuteness—a precocious acuteness—in all that concerns their immediate wants, business, or gratifications ; a patient endurance of cold and hunger ; a desire to obtain money without working for it ; a craving for the excitement of gambling ; an inordinate love of amusement ; and an irrepressible repugnance to any settled in-door industry.

The Literature of Costermongers.

We have now had an inkling of the London costermonger's notions upon politics and religion. We have seen the brutified state in which he is allowed by society to remain, though possessing the same faculties and susceptibilities as ourselves—the same power to perceive and admire the forms of truth, beauty, and goodness, as even the very highest in the state. We have witnessed how, instinct with all the elements of manhood and beasthood, the qualities of the beast are principally developed in him, while those of the man are stunted in their growth. It now remains for us to look into some other matters concerning this curious class of people, and, first, of their literature:

It may appear anomalous to speak of the literature of an uneducated body, but even the costermongers have their tastes for books. They are very fond of hearing any one read aloud to them, and listen very attentively. One man often reads the Sunday paper of the beer-shop to them, and on a fine summer's evening a costermonger, or any neighbour who has the advantage of being "a schollard," reads aloud to them in the courts they inhabit. What they love best to listen to—and, indeed, what they are most eager for—are Reynolds's periodicals, especially the "Mysteries of the Court." "They've got tired of Lloyd's blood-stained stories," said one man, who was in the habit of reading to them, "and I'm satisfied that, of all London, Reynolds is the most popular man among them. They stuck to him in Trafalgar-square, and would again. They all say he's 'a trump,' and Feargus O'Connor's another trump with them.'"

One intelligent man considered that the spirit of curiosity manifested by costermongers, as regards the information or excitement derived from hearing stories read, augured well for the improvability of the class.

Another intelligent costermonger, who had recently read some of the cheap periodicals to ten or twelve men, women, and boys, all costermongers, gave me an account of the comments made by his auditors. They had assembled, after their day's work or their rounds, for the purpose of hearing my informant read the last number of some of the penny publications.

"The costermongers," said my informant, "are very fond of illustrations. I have known a man, what couldn't read, buy a periodical what had an illustration, a little out of the common way perhaps, just that he might learn from some one, who could read, what it was all about. They have all heard of Cruikshank, and they think everything funny is by him—funny scenes in a play and all. His 'Bottle' was very much admired. I heard one man say it was very prime, and showed what 'lush' did, but I saw the same man," added my informant, "drunk three hours afterwards. Look you here, sir," he continued, turning over a periodical, for he had the number with him, "here's a portrait of 'Catherine of Russia.' 'Tell us all about her,' said one man to

me last night; read it; what was she?' When I had read it," my informant continued, "another man, to whom I showed it, said, 'Don't the cove as did that know a deal?' for they fancy—at least, a many do—that one man writes a whole periodical, or a whole newspaper. Now here," proceeded my friend, "you see's an engraving of a man hung up, burning over a fire, and some costers would go mad if they couldn't learn what he'd been doing, who he was, and all about him. 'But about the picture?' they would say, and this is a very common question put by them whenever they see an engraving.

"Here's one of the passages that took their fancy wonderfully," my informant observed:

'With glowing cheeks, flashing eyes, and palpitating bosom, Venetia Trelawney rushed back into the refreshment-room, where she threw herself into one of the arm-chairs already noticed. But scarcely had she thus sunk down upon the flocculent cushion, when a sharp click, as of some mechanism giving way, met her ears; and at the same instant her wrists were caught in manacles which sprang out of the arms of the treacherous chair, while two steel bands started from the richly-carved back and grasped her shoulders. A shriek burst from her lips—she struggled violently, but all to no purpose: for she was a captive—and powerless!

'We should observe that the manacles and the steel bands which had thus fastened upon her, were covered with velvet, so that they inflicted no positive injury upon her, nor even produced the slightest abrasion of her fair and polished skin.'

Here all my audience," said the man to me, "broke out with—'Aye! that's the way the harristocrats hooks it. There's nothing o' that sort among us; the rich has all that barrikin to themselves.' 'Yes, that's the b—— way the taxes goes in,' shouted a woman.

"Anything about the police sets them a talking at once. This did when I read it:

'The Ebenezers still continued their fierce struggle, and, from the noise they made, seemed as if they were tearing each other to pieces, to the wild roar of a chorus of profane swearing. The alarm, as Bloomfield had predicted, was soon raised, and some two or three policemen, with their bull's-eyes, and still more effective truncheons, speedily restored order.'

'The blessed crushers is everywhere,' shouted one. 'I wish I'd been there to have had a shy at the eslops,' said another. And then a man sung out: 'O, don't I like the Bobbys?'

"If there's any foreign language which can't be explained, I've seen the costers," my informant went on, "annoyed at it—quite annoyed. Another time I read part of one of Lloyd's numbers to them—but they like something spicier. One article in them—here it is—finishes in this way:

"The social habits and costumes of the Magyar *noblesse* have almost all the characteristics of the corresponding class in Ireland. This word *noblesse* is one of wide signification in Hungary; and one may with great truth say of this strange nation, that '*qui n'est point noble n'est rien.*'"

'I can't tumble to that barrikin,' said a young fellow; 'it's a jaw-breaker. But if this here—what d' ye call it, you talk about—was like the Irish, why they was a rum lot.' 'Noblesse,' said a man that's considered a clever fellow, from having once learned his letters, though he can't read or write. ' Noblesse!' Blessed if I know what he's up to.' Here there was a regular laugh."

From other quarters I learned that some of the costermongers who were able to read, or loved to listen to reading, purchased their literature in a very commercial spirit, frequently buying the periodical which is the largest in size, because when " they've got the reading out of it," as they say, " it's worth a halfpenny for the barrow."

Tracts they will rarely listen to, but if any persevering man *will* read tracts, and state that he does it for their benefit and improvement, they listen without rudeness, though often with evident unwillingness. " Sermons or tracts," said one of their body to me, " gives them the 'orrors." Costermongers purchase, and not unfrequently, the first number of a penny periodical, " to see what it's like."

The tales of robbery and bloodshed, of heroic, eloquent, and gentlemanly highwaymen, or of gipsies turning out to be nobles, now interest the costermongers but little, although they found great delight in such stories a few years back. Works relating to Courts, potentates, or "harristocrats," are the most relished by these rude people.

OF THE HONESTY OF COSTERMONGERS.

I heard on all hands that the costers never steal from one another, and never wink at any one stealing from a neighbouring stall. Any stall-keeper will leave his stall untended to get his dinner, his neighbour acting for him ; sometimes he will leave it to enjoy a game at skittles. It was computed for me, that property worth 10,000*l.* belonging to costers is daily left exposed in the streets or at the markets, almost entirely unwatched, the policeman or market-keeper only passing at intervals. And yet thefts are rarely heard of, and when heard of are not attributable to costermongers, but to regular thieves. The way in which the sum of 10,000*l.* was arrived at, is this : " In Hooper-street, Lambeth," said my informant, "there are thirty barrows and carts exposed on an evening, left in the street, with nobody to see to them; left there all night. That is only one street. Each barrow and board would be worth, on the average, 2*l.* 5*s.*, and that would be 75*l.* In the other bye-streets and courts off the New-cut are six times as many, Hooper-street having the most. This would give 525*l.* in all, left unwatched of a night. There are, throughout London, twelve more districts besides the New-cut—at least twelve districts—and, calculating the same amount in these, we have, altogether, 6,300*l.* worth of barrows. Taking in other bye-streets, we may safely reckon it at 4,000 barrows; for the numbers I have given in the thirteen places are 2,520, and 1,480 added is moderate. At least half of those which are in use next day, are left unwatched ; more, I have no doubt, but say half. The stock of these 2,000 will average 10*s.* each, or 1,000*l.*; and the barrows will be worth 4,500*l.*; in all 5,500*l.*, and

the property exposed on the stalls and the markets will be double in amount, or 11,000*l.* in value, every day, but say 10,000*l.*

" Besides, sir," I was told, " the thieves won't rob the costers so often as they will the shopkeepers. It's easier to steal from a butcher's or bacon-seller's open window than from a costermonger's stall or barrow, because the shopkeeper's eye can't be always on his goods. But there's always some one to give an eye to a coster's property. At Billingsgate the thieves will rob the salesmen far readier than they will us. They know we'd take it out of them readier if they were caught. It's Lynch law with us. We never give them in charge."

The costermongers' boys will, I am informed, cheat their employers, but they do not steal from them. The costers' donkey stables have seldom either lock or latch, and sometimes oysters, and other things which the donkey will not molest, are left there, but are never stolen.

OF THE CONVEYANCES OF THE COSTERMONGERS AND OTHER STREET-SELLERS.

WE now come to consider the matters relating more particularly to the commercial life of the costermonger.

All who pass along the thoroughfares of the Metropolis, bestowing more than a cursory glance upon the many phases of its busy street life, must be struck with astonishment to observe the various modes of conveyance, used by those who resort to the public thoroughfares for a livelihood. From the more provident costermonger's pony and donkey cart, to the old rusty iron tray slung round the neck by the vendor of blacking, and down to the little grey-eyed Irish boy with his lucifer-matches, in the last remains of a willow hand-basket—the shape and variety of the means resorted to by the costermongers and other street-sellers, for carrying about their goods, are almost as manifold as the articles they vend.

The pony—or donkey — carts (and the latter is by far the more usual beast of draught), of the prosperous costermongers are of three kinds:—the first is of an oblong shape, with a rail behind, upon which is placed a tray filled with bunches of greens, turnips, celery, &c., whilst other commodities are laid in the bed of the cart. Another kind is the common square cart without springs, which is so constructed that the sides, as well as the front and back, will let down and form shelves whereon the stock may be arranged to advantage. The third sort of pony-cart is one of home manufacture, consisting of the framework of a body without sides, or front, or hind part. Sometimes a coster's barrow is formed into a donkey cart merely by fastening, with cord, two rough poles to the handles. All these several kinds of carts are used for the conveyance of either fruit, vegetables, or fish; but besides those, there is the salt and mustard vendor's cart, with and without the tilt or covering, and a square piece of tin (stuck into a block of salt), on which is painted "salt 3 lbs. a penny," and "mustard a penny an ounce" Then there is the poultry cart, with the wild-ducks, and rabbits dangling at its sides, and with two uprights and a cross-stick, upon which are suspended birds, &c., slung across in couples.

The above conveyances are all of small dimensions, the barrows being generally about five feet long and three wide, while the carts are mostly about four feet square.

Every kind of harness is used; some is well blacked and greased and glittering with brass, others are almost as grey with dust as the donkey itself. Some of the jackasses are gaudily caparisoned in an old carriage-harness, which fits it like a man's coat on a boy's back, while the plated silver ornaments are pink, with the copper showing through; others have rope traces and belly-bands, and not a few indulge in old cotton handkerchiefs for pads.

The next conveyance (which, indeed, is the most general) is the costermonger's hand-barrow. These are very light in their make, with springs terminating at the axle. Some have rails behind for the arrangement of their goods; others have not. Some have side rails, whilst others have only the frame-work. The shape of these barrows is oblong, and sloped from the hind-part towards the front; the bottom of the bed is not boarded, but consists of narrow strips of wood nailed athwart and across. When the coster is hawking his fish, or vending his green stuff, he provides himself with a wooden tray, which is placed upon his barrow. Those who cannot afford a tray get some pieces of board and fasten them together, these answering their purpose as well. Pine-apple and pine-apple rock barrows are not unfrequently seen with small bright coloured flags at the four corners, fluttering in the wind.

The knife-cleaner's barrow, which has lately appeared in the streets, must not be passed over here. It consists of a huge sentry-box, with a door, and is fixed upon two small wheels, being propelled in the same way as a wheel-barrow. In the interior is one of Kent's Patent Knife-cleaning Machines, worked by turning a handle. Then there are the cat and dog's-meat barrows. These, however, are merely common wheelbarrows, with a board in front and a ledge or shelf, formed by a piece of board nailed across the top of the barrow, to answer the purpose of a cutting-board. Lastly, there is the hearth-stone barrow, piled up with hearth-stone, Bath-brick, and lumps of whiting.

Another mode of conveying the goods through the streets, is by baskets of various kinds; as the sieve or head basket; the square and oval "shallow," fastened in front of the fruit-woman with a strap round the waist; the hand-basket; and the "prickle." The sieve, or head-basket, is a round willow basket, containing about one-third of a bushel. The square and oval shallows are willow baskets, about four inches deep, and thirty inches long, by eighteen broad. The hand-basket is the common oval basket, with

a handle across to hang upon the arm; the latter are generally used by the Irish for onions and apples. The prickle is a brown willow basket, in which walnuts are imported into this country from the Continent; they are about thirty inches deep, and in bulk rather larger than a gallon measure; they are used only by the vendors of walnuts.

Such are the principal forms of the costermongers' conveyances; but besides carts, barrows, and baskets, there are many other means adopted by the London street-sellers for carrying their goods from one part of the metropolis to another. The principal of these are cans, trays, boxes, and poles.

The baked potato-cans sometimes are square and sometimes oval; they are made with and without legs, a lid fastened on with hinges, and have a small charcoal fire fixed at the bottom of the can, so as to keep the potatoes hot, while there is a pipe at top to let off the steam. On one side of the can is a little compartment for the salt, and another on the other side for the butter. The hot pie-can is a square tin can, standing upon four legs, with a door in front, and three partitions inside; a fire is kept in the bottom, and the pies arranged in order upon the iron plates or shelves. When the pies at the bottom are sufficiently hot they are taken out, and placed on the upper shelf, whilst those above are removed to the lower compartments, by which means all the pies are kept "hot and hot."

The muffin and crumpet-boy carries his articles in a basket, covered outside with oil-cloth and inside with green-baize, either at his back, or slung over his arm, and rings his bell as he walks.

The blacking boy, congreve-match and water-cress girl, use a rusty tray, spread over with their "goods," and suspended to the neck by a piece of string.

The vendors of corn-salve, plating balls, soap for removing grease spots, paper, steel pens, envelopes, &c., carry their commodities in front of them in boxes, suspended round the neck by a narrow leather strap.

Rabbits and game are sometimes carried in baskets, and at other times tied together and slung over a pole upon the shoulder. Hat and bonnet-boxes are likewise conveyed upon a pole.

Door-mats, baskets and "duffer's" packs, wood pails, brushes, brooms, clothes-props, clothes-lines and string, and grid-irons, Dutch-ovens, skewers and fire-shovels, are carried across the shoulder.

OF THE "SMITHFIELD RACES."

HAVING set forth the costermonger's usual mode of conveying his goods through the streets of London, I shall now give the reader a description of the place and scene where and when he purchases his donkeys.

When a costermonger wishes to sell or buy a donkey, he goes to Smithfield-market on a Friday afternoon. On this day, between the hours of one and five, there is a kind of fair held, attended solely by costermongers, for whose convenience a long paved slip of ground, about eighty feet in length, has been set apart. The animals for sale are trotted up and down this—the "race-course," as it is called—and on each side of it stand the spectators and purchasers, crowding among the stalls of peas-soup, hot eels, and other street delicacies.

Every thing necessary for the starting of a costermonger's barrow can be had in Smithfield on a Friday,—from the barrow itself to the weights—from the donkey to the whip. The animals can be purchased at prices ranging from 5s. to 3l. On a brisk market-day as many as two hundred donkeys have been sold. The barrows for sale are kept apart from the steeds, but harness to any amount can be found everywhere, in all degrees of excellence, from the bright japanned cart saddle with its new red pads, to the old mouldy trace covered with buckle marks. Wheels of every size and colour, and springs in every stage of rust, are hawked about on all sides. To the usual noise and shouting of a Saturday night's market is added the shrill squealing of distant pigs, the lowing of the passing oxen, the bleating of sheep, and the braying of donkeys. The paved road all down the "race-course" is level and soft, with the mud trodden down between the stones. The policeman on duty there wears huge fishermen's or flushermen's boots, reaching to their thighs; and the trouser ends of the costers' corduroys are black and sodden with wet dirt. Every variety of odour fills the air; you pass from the stable smell that hangs about the donkeys, into an atmosphere of apples and fried fish, near the eating-stalls, while a few paces further on you are nearly choked with the stench of goats. The crowd of black hats, thickly dotted with red and yellow plush caps, reels about; and the "hi-hi-i-i" of the donkey-runners sounds on all sides. Sometimes a curly-headed bull, with a fierce red eye, on its way to or from the adjacent cattle-market, comes trotting down the road, making all the visitors rush suddenly to the railings, for fear—as a coster near me said—of "being taught the hornpipe."

The donkeys standing for sale are ranged in a long line on both sides of the "race-course," their white velvetty noses resting on the wooden rail they are tied to. Many of them wear their blinkers and head harness, and others are ornamented with ribbons, fastened in their halters. The lookers-on lean against this railing, and chat with the boys at the donkeys' heads, or with the men who stand behind them, and keep continually hitting and shouting at the poor still beasts to make them prance. Sometimes a party of two or three will be seen closely examining one of these "Jerusalem ponys," passing their hands down its legs, or looking quietly on, while the proprietor's ash stick descends on the patient brute's back, making a dull hollow sound. As you walk in front of the long line of donkeys, the lads seize the animals by their nostrils, and show their large teeth, asking if you "want a hass, sir," and all warranting the creature to be "five years old next buff-day." Dealers are quarrelling among themselves, downcrying each other's goods. "A hearty man," shouted one proprietor, pointing to his rival's stock, "could eat three sich donkeys as yourn at a meal."

One fellow, standing behind his steed, shouts as he strikes, "Here's the real Brittannia mettle;" whilst another asks, "Who's for the Pride of the Market?" and then proceeds to flip "the pride" with his whip, till she clears away the mob with her kickings. Here, standing by its mother, will be a shaggy little colt, with a group of ragged boys fondling it, and lifting it in their arms from the ground.

During all this the shouts of the drivers and runners fill the air, as they rush past each other n the race-course. Now a tall fellow, dragging a donkey after him, runs by crying, as he charges in amongst the mob, "Hulloa! Hulloa! hi! hi!' his mate, with his long coat-tails flying in the wind, hurrying after and roaring, between his blows, "Keem-up!"

On nearly every post are hung traces or bridles; and in one place, on the occasion of my visit, stood an old collar with a donkey nibbling at the straw that had burst out. Some of the lads, in smock-frocks, walk about with cart-saddles on their heads, and crowds gather round the trucks, piled up with a black heap of harness studded with brass. Those without trays have spread out old sacks on the ground, on which are laid axle-trees, bound-up springs, and battered carriage-lamps. There are plenty of rusty nails and iron bolts to be had, if a barrow should want mending; and if the handles are broken, an old cab-shaft can be bought cheap, to repair them.

In another "race-course," opposite to the donkeys,—the ponies are sold. These make a curious collection, each one showing what was his last master's whim. One has its legs and belly shorn of its hair, another has its mane and tail cut close, and some have switch tails, muddy at the end from their length. A big-hipped black nag, with red tinsel-like spots on its back, had its ears cut close, and another curly-haired brute that was wet and steaming with having been shown off, had two huge letters burnt into its hind-quarters. Here the clattering of the hoofs and the smacking of whips added to the din; and one poor brute, with red empty eye-holes, and carrying its head high up—as a blind man does—sent out showers of sparks from its hoofs as it spluttered over the stones, at each blow it received. Occasionally, in one part of the pony market, there may be seen a crowd gathered round a nag, that some one swears has been stolen from him.

Raised up over the heads of the mob are bundles of whips, and men push their way past, with their arms full of yellow-handled curry-combs; whilst, amongst other cries, is heard that of "Sticks ½d. each! sticks—real smarters."

At one end of the market the barrows for sale

are kept piled up one on another, or filled with old wheels, and some with white unpainted wood, showing where they have been repaired. Men are here seen thumping the wooden trays, and trying the strength of the springs by leaning on them; and here, too, stood, on the occasion of my visit, a ragged coster lad trying to sell his scales, now the cherry-season had past.

On all sides the refreshment-barrows are surrounded by customers. The whelk-man peppers his lots, and shouts, "A lumping penn'orth for a ha'penny;" and a lad in a smock-frock carries two full pails of milk, slopping it as he walks, and crying, "Ha'penny a mug-full, new milk from the ke-ow!" The only quiet people to be seen are round the peas-soup stall, with their cups in their hands; and there is a huge crowd covering in the hot-eel stand, with the steam rising up in the centre. Baskets of sliced cake, apples, nuts, and pine-apple rock, block up the pathway; and long wicker baskets of live fowls hem you in, round which are grouped the costers, handling and blowing apart the feathers on the breast.

OF THE DONKEYS OF THE COSTERMONGERS.

THE costermongers· almost universally treat their donkeys with kindness. Many a costermonger will resent the ill-treatment of a donkey, as he would a personal indignity. These animals are often not only favourites, but pets, having their share of the costermonger's dinner when bread forms a portion of it, or pudding, or anything suited to the palate of the brute. Those well-used, manifest fondness for their masters, and are easily manageable; it is, however, difficult to get an ass, whose master goes regular rounds, away from its stable for any second labour during the day, unless it has fed and slept in the interval. The usual fare of a donkey is a peck of chaff, which costs 1*d.*, a quart of oats and a quart of beans, each averaging 1½*d.*, and sometimes a pennyworth of hay, being an expenditure of 4*d.* or 5*d.* a day; but some give double this quantity in a prosperous time. Only one meal a day is given. Many costermongers told me, that their donkeys lived well when they themselves lived well.

"It's all nonsense to call donkeys stupid," said one costermonger to me; "them's stupid that calls them so: they're sensible. Not long since I worked Guildford with my donkey-cart and a boy. Jack (the donkey) was slow and heavy in coming back, until we got in sight of the lights at Vauxhall-gate, and then he trotted on like one o'clock, he did indeed! just as if he smelt it was London besides seeing it, and knew he was at home. He had a famous appetite in the country, and the fresh grass did him good. I gave a country lad·2*d.* to mind him in a green lane there. I wanted my own boy to do so, but he said, 'I'll see you further first.' A London boy hates being by himself in a lone country part. He's afraid of being burked; he is indeed. One can't quarrel with a lad when

he's away with one in the country; he's very useful. I feed my donkey well. I sometimes give him a carrot for a luxury, but carrots are dear now. He's fond of mashed potatoes, and has many a good mash when I can buy them at 4lb. a penny."

"There was a friend of mine," said another man, "had great trouble about his donkey a few months back. I saw part of it, and knew all about it. He was doing a little work on a Sunday morning at Wandsworth, and the poor thing fell down dead. He was very fond of his donkey and kind to it, and the donkey was very fond of him. He thought he wouldn't leave the poor creature he'd had a good while, and had been out with in all weathers, by the road side; so he dropped all notion of doing business, and with help got the poor dead thing into his cart; its head lolloping over the end of the cart, and its poor eyes staring at nothing. He thought he'd drag it home and bury it somewheres. It wasn't for the value he dragged it, for what's a dead donkey worth? There was a few persons about him, and they was all quiet and seemed sorry for the poor fellow and for his donkey; but the church-bells struck up, and up came a 'crusher,' and took the man up, and next day he was fined 10*s.*, I can't exactly say for what. He never saw no more of the animal, and lost his stock as well as his donkey."

OF THE COSTERMONGERS' CAPITAL.

THE costermongers, though living by buying and selling, are seldom or never capitalists. It is estimated that not more than one-fourth of the entire body trade upon their own property. Some borrow their stock money, others borrow the stock itself, others again borrow the donkey-carts, barrows, or baskets, in which their stock is carried round, whilst others borrow even the weights and measures by which it is meted out.

The reader, however uninformed he may be as to the price the poor usually have to pay for any loans they may require, doubtlessly need not be told that the remuneration exacted for the use of the above-named commodities is not merely confined to the legal 5*l.* per centum per annum; still many of even the most "knowing" will hardly be able to credit the fact that the ordinary rate of interest in the costermongers' money-market amounts to 20 per cent. per week, or no less than 1040*l.* a year, for every 100*l.* advanced.

But the iniquity of this usury in the present instance is felt, not so much by the costermongers themselves, as by the poor people whom they serve; for, of course, the enormous rate of interest must be paid out of the profits on the goods they sell, and consequently added to the price, so that coupling this overcharge with the customary short allowance—in either weight or measure, as the case may be—we can readily perceive how cruelly the poor are defrauded, and how they not only get often too little for what they do, but have as often to pay too much for what they buy.

Premising thus much, I shall now proceed to describe the terms upon which the barrow, the cart, the basket, the weights, the measures, the stock-money, or the stock, is usually advanced to the needy costermongers by their more thrifty brethren.

The hire of a barrow is 3*d.* a day, or 1*s.* a week, for the six winter months; and 4*d.* a day, or 1*s.* 6*d.* a week, for the six summer months. Some are to be had rather lower in the summer, but never for less than 4*d.*—sometimes for not less than 6*d.* on a Saturday, when not unfrequently every barrow in London is hired. No security and no deposit is required, but the lender satisfies himself that the borrower is really what he represents himself to be. I am informed that 5,000 hired barrows are now in the hands of the London costermongers, at an average rental of 3*l.* 5*s.* each, or 16,250*l.* a year. One man lets out 120 yearly, at a return (dropping the 5*s.*) of 360*l.*; while the cost of a good barrow, new, is 2*l.* 12*s.*, and in the autumn and winter they may be bought new, or "as good as new," at 30*s.* each; so that reckoning each to cost this barrow-letter 2*l.* each, he receives 360*l.* rent or interest —exactly 150 per cent. per annum for property which originally cost but 240*l.*, and property which is still as good for the ensuing year's business as for the past. One man has rented a barrow for eight years, during which period he has paid 26*l.* for what in the first instance did not cost more than twice as many shillings, and which he must return if he discontinues its use. " I know men well to do," said an intelligent costermonger, "who have paid 1*s.* and 1*s.* 6*d.* a week for a barrow for three, four, and five years; and they can't be made to understand that it's rather high rent for what might cost 40*s.* at first. They can't see they are losers. One barrow-lender sends his son out, mostly on a Sunday, collecting his rents (for barrows), but he's not a hard man." Some of the lenders complain that their customers pay them irregularly and cheat them often, and that in consequence they must charge high; while the "borrowers" declare that it is very seldom indeed that a man "shirks" the rent for his barrow, generally believing that he has made an advantageous bargain, and feeling the want of his vehicle, if he lose it temporarily. Let the lenders, however, be deceived by many, still, it is evident, that the rent charged for barrows is most exorbitant, by the fact, that all who take to the business become men of considerable property in a few years.

Donkey-carts are rarely hired. "If there's 2,000 donkey and pony-carts in London, more or less, not 200 of them's borrowed; out of barrows five to two is borrowed." A donkey-cart costs from 2*l.* to 10*l.*; 3*l.* 10*s.* being an average price. The hire is 2*s.* or 2*s.* 6*d.* a week. The harness costs 2*l.* 10*s.* new, but is bought, nineteen times out of twenty, second-hand, at from 2*s.* 6*d.* to 20*s.* The donkeys themselves are not let out on hire, though a costermonger may let out his donkey to another in the trade

when he does not require its services; the usual sum paid for the hire of a donkey is 2*s.* 6*d.* or 3*s.* per week. The cost price of a pony varies from 5*l.* to 13*l.*; that of a donkey from 1*l.* to 3*l.* There may be six donkeys, or more, in costermonger use, to one pony. Some traffic almost weekly in these animals, liking the excitement of such business.

The repairs to barrows, carts, and harness are almost always effected by the costermongers themselves.

"Shallows" (baskets) which cost 1*s.* and 1*s.* 6*d.*, are let out at 1*d.* a day; but not five in 100 of those in use are borrowed, as their low price places them at the costermonger's command. A pewter quart-pot, for measuring onions, &c., is let out at 2*d.* a day, its cost being 2*s.* Scales are 2*d.*, and a set of weights 1*d.* a day.

Another common mode of usury is in the lending of stock-money. This is lent by the costermongers who have saved the means for such use of their funds, and by beer-shop keepers. The money-lending costermongers are the most methodical in their usury— 1,040*l.* per cent. per annum, as was before stated, being the rate of interest usually charged. It is seldom that a lower sum than 10*s.* is borrowed, and never a higher sum than 2*l.* When a stranger applies for a loan, the money-lender satisfies himself as I have described of the barrow-lender. He charges 2*d.* a day for a loan of 2*s.* 6*d.*; 3*d.* a day for 5*s.*; 6*d.* a day for 10*s.*; and 1*s.* a day for 1*l.* If the daily payments are rendered regularly, at a month's end the terms are reduced to 6*d.* a week for 5*s.*; 1*s.* for 10*s.*; and 2*s.* for 1*l.* "That's reckoned an extraordinary small interest," was said to me, " only 4*d.* a day for a pound." The average may be 3*s.* a week for the loan of 20*s.*; it being only to a few that a larger sum than 20*s.* is lent. " I paid 2*s.* a week for 1*l.* for a whole year," said one man, " or 5*l.* 4*s.* for the use of a pound, and then I was liable to repay the 1*l.*" The principal, however, is seldom repaid; nor does the lender seem to expect it, though he will occasionally demand it. One money-lender is considered to have a floating capital of 150*l.* invested in loans to costermongers. If he receive 2*s.* per week per 1*l.* for but twenty-six weeks in the year (and he often receives it for the fifty-two weeks)—his 150*l.* brings him in 390*l.* a year.

Sometimes a loan is effected only for a day, generally a Saturday, as much as 2*s.* 6*d.* being sometimes given for the use of 5*s.*; the 5*s.* being of course repaid in the evening.

The money-lenders are subject to at least twice the extent of loss to which the barrow-lender is exposed, as it is far oftener that money is squandered (on which of course no interest can be paid) than that a barrow is disposed of.

The money-lenders, (from the following statement, made to me by one who was in the habit of borrowing,) pursue their business in a not very dissimilar manner to that imputed to those who advance larger sums:—" If I want to borrow in a hurry," said my informant, " as I may hear of a good bargain, I run to my neighbour L——'s, and he first says he hasn't 20s. to lend, and his wife's by, and she says she hasn't 2s. in her pocket, and so I can't be accommodated. Then he says if I must have the money he'll have to pawn his watch,—or to borrow it of Mr. ——, (an innkeeper) who would charge a deal of interest, for he wasn't paid all he lent two months back, and 1s. would be expected to be spent in drink—though L—— don't drink—or he must try if his sister would trust him, but she was sick and wanted all her money—or perhaps his barrow-merchant would lend him 10s., if he'd undertake to return 15s. at night; and it ends by my thinking I've done pretty well if I can get 1l. for 5s. interest, for a day's use of it."

The beer-shop keepers lend on far easier terms, perhaps at half the interest exacted by the others, and without any regular system of charges; but they look sharp after the repayment, and expect a considerable outlay in beer, and will only lend to good customers; they however have even lent money without interest.

"In the depth of last winter," said a man of good character to me, "I borrowed 5s. The beer-shop keeper wouldn't lend; he'll rather lend to men doing well and drinking. But I borrowed it at 6d. a day interest, and that 6d. a day I paid exactly four weeks, Sundays and all; and that was 15s. in thirty days for the use of 5s. I was half starving all the time, and then I had a slice of luck, and paid the 5s. back slap, and got out of it."

Many shopkeepers lend money to the stall-keepers, whom they know from standing near their premises, and that without interest. They generally lend, however, to the women, as they think the men want to get drunk with it. "Indeed, if it wasn't for the women," said a costermonger to me, "half of us might go to the Union."

Another mode of usurious lending or trading is, as I said before, to provide the costermonger —not with the stock-money—but with the stock itself. This mode also is highly profitable to the usurer, who is usually a costermonger, but sometimes a greengrocer. A stock of fruit, fish, or vegetables, with a barrow for its conveyance, is entrusted to a street-seller, the usual way being to "let him have a sovereign's worth." The value of this, however, at the market cost, rarely exceeds 14s., still the man entrusted with it must carry 20s. to his creditor, or he will hardly be trusted a second time. The man who trades with the stock is not required to pay the 20s. on the first day of the transaction, as he may not have realised so much, but he must pay some of it, generally 10s., and must pay the remainder the next day or the money-lender will decline any subsequent dealings.

It may be thought, as no security is given, and as the costermongering barrow, stock, or money-lender never goes to law for the recovery of any debt or goods, that the per centage is not so very exorbitant after all. But I ascer-

tained that not once in twenty times was the money lender exposed to any loss by the non-payment of his usurious interest, while his profits are enormous. The borrower knows that if he fail in his payment, the lender will acquaint the other members of his fraternity, so that no future loan will be attainable, and the costermonger's business may be at an end. One borrower told me that the re-payment of his loan of 2l., borrowed two years ago at 4s. a week, had this autumn been reduced to 2s. 6d. a week: "He's a decent man I pay now," he said; "he has twice forgiven me a month at a time when the weather was very bad and the times as bad as the weather. Before I borrowed of him I had dealings with ——. He *was* a scurf. If I missed a week, and told him I would make it up next week, 'That won't do,' he'd say, 'I'll turn you up. I'll take d——d good care to stop you. *I'll* have you to rights.' If I hadn't satisfied him, as I did at last, I could never have got credit again; never." I am informed that most of the money-lenders, if a man has paid for a year or so, will now "drop it for a month or so in a very hard-up time, and go on again." There is no I.O.U. or any memorandum given to the usurer. "There's never a slip of paper about it, sir," I was told.

I may add that a very intelligent man from whom I derived information, said to me concerning costermongers never going to law to recover money owing to them, nor indeed for any purpose: "If any one steals anything from me—and that, as far as I know, never happened but once in ten years—and I catch him, I take it out of him on the spot. I give him a jolly good hiding and there's an end of it. I know very well, sir, that costers are ignorant men, but in my opinion" (laughing) "our never going to law shows" that in *that* point we are in advance of the aristocrats. I never heard of a coster in a law court, unless he was in trouble (charged with some offence)—for assaulting a crusher, or anybody he had quarrelled with, or something of that kind."

The barrow-lender, when not regularly paid, sends some one, or goes himself, and carries away the barrow.

My personal experience with this peculiar class justifies me in saying that they are far less dishonest than they are usually believed to be, and much more honest than their wandering habits, their want of education and "principle" would lead even the most charitable to suppose. Since I have exhibited an interest in the sufferings and privations of these neglected people, I have, as the reader may readily imagine, had many applications for assistance, and without vanity, I believe I may say, that as far as my limited resources would permit, I have striven to extricate the street-sellers from the grasp of the usurer. Some to whom I have *lent* small sums (for gifts only degrade struggling honest men into the apathy of beggars) have taken the money with many a protestation that they would repay it in certain weekly instalments, which they themselves proposed, but still have never made their appearance before me a second time—it may be from dishonesty and it may be from inability and shame—others, however, and they are not a few, have religiously kept faith with me, calling punctually to pay back a sixpence or a shilling as the precariousness of their calling would permit, and doing this, though they knew that I abjured all claims upon them but through their honour, and was, indeed, in most cases, ignorant where to find them, even if my inclination led me to seek or enforce a return of the loan. One case of this kind shows so high a sense of honour among a class, generally considered to rank among the most dishonourable, that, even at the risk of being thought egotistical, I will mention it here:—" Two young men, street-sellers, called upon me and begged hard for the loan of a little stock-money. They made needle-cases and hawked them from door to door at the east end of the town, and had not the means of buying the wood. I agreed to let them have ten shillings between them; this they promised to repay at a shilling a week. They were utter strangers to me; nevertheless, at the end of the first week one shilling of the sum was duly returned. The second week, however, brought no shilling, nor did the third, nor the fourth, by which time I got to look upon the money as lost; but at the end of the fifth week one of the men called with his sixpence, and told me how he should have been with me before but his mate had promised each week to meet him with his sixpence, and each week disappointed him; so he had come on alone. I thanked him, and the next week he came again; so he did the next, and the next after that. On the latter occasion he told me that in five more weeks he should have paid off his half of the amount advanced, and that then, as he had come with the other man, he would begin paying off *his* share as well!"

Those who are unacquainted with the character of the people may feel inclined to doubt the trustworthiness of the class, but it is an extraordinary fact that but few of the costermongers fail to repay the money advanced to them, even at the present ruinous rate of interest. The poor, it is my belief, have not yet been sufficiently tried in this respect;—pawnbrokers, loan-offices, tally-shops, dolly-shops, are the only parties who will trust them—but, as a startling proof of the good faith of the humbler classes generally, it may be stated that Mrs. Chisholm (the lady who has exerted herself so benevolently in the cause of emigration) has lent out, at different times, as much as 160,000*l.* that has been entrusted to her for the use of the "lower orders," and that the whole of this large amount has been returned—*with the exception of 12l.!*

I myself have often given a sovereign to professed thieves to get "changed," and never knew one to make off with the money. Depend upon it, if we would really improve,

we must begin by elevating instead of degrading.

OF THE "SLANG" WEIGHTS AND MEASURES.

ALL counterfeit weights and measures, the costermongers call by the appropriate name of "slang." "There are not half so many slangs as there was eighteen months ago," said a 'general dealer' to me. "You see, sir, the letters in the *Morning Chronicle* set people a talking, and some altered their way of business. Some was very angry at what was said in the articles on the street-sellers, and swore that costers was gentlemen, and that they'd smash the men's noses that had told you, sir, if they knew who they were. There's plenty of costers wouldn't use slangs at all, if people would give a fair price; but you see the boys *will* try it on for their bunts, and how is a man to sell fine cherries at 4*d.* a pound that cost him 3½*d.*, when there's a kid alongside of him a selling his 'tol' at 2*d.* a pound, and singing it out as bold as brass? So the men slangs it, and cries ' 2*d.* a pound,' and gives half-pound, as the boy does; which brings it to the same thing. We doesn't 'dulterate our goods like the tradesmen—that is, the regular hands doesn't. It wouldn't be easy, as you say, to 'dulterate cabbages or oysters; but we deals fair to all that's fair to us,—and that's more than many a tradesman does, for all their juries."

The slang quart is a pint and a half. It is made precisely like the proper quart; and the maker, I was told, " knows well enough what it's for, as it's charged, new, 6*d.* more than a true quart measure; but it's nothing to him, as he says, what it's for, so long as he gets his price." The slang quart is let out at 2*d.* a day—1*d.* extra being charged " for the risk." The slang pint holds in some cases three-fourths of the just quantity, having a very thick bottom ; others hold only half a pint, having a false bottom half-way up. These are used chiefly in measuring nuts, of which the proper quantity is hardly ever given to the purchaser; " but, then," it was often said, or implied to me, the "price is all the lower, and people just brings it on themselves, by wanting things for next to nothing ; so it's all right ; it's people's own faults." The hire of the slang pint is 2*d.* per day.

The scales used are almost all true, but the weights are often beaten out flat to look large, and are 4, 5, 6, or even 7 oz. deficient in a pound, and in the same relative proportion with other weights. The charge is 2*d.*, 3*d.*, and 4*d.* a day for a pair of scales and a set of slang weights.

The wooden measures—such as pecks, half pecks, and quarter pecks—are not let out slang, but the bottoms are taken out by the costers, and put in again half an inch or so higher up. " I call this," said a humorous dealer to me, "slop-work, or the cutting-system."

One candid costermonger expressed his perfect contempt of slangs, as fit only for bunglers, as *he* could always " work slang " with a true measure. " Why, I can cheat any man," he said. " I can manage to measure mussels so as you'd think you got a lot over, but there's a lot under measure, for I holds them up with my fingers and keep crying, ' Mussels! full measure, live mussels!' I can do the same with peas. I delight to do it with stingy aristocrats. We don't work slang in the City. People know what they're a buying on there. There's plenty of us would pay for an inspector of weights; I would. We might do fair without an inspector, and make as much if we only agreed one with another."

In conclusion, it is but just I should add that there seems to be a strong disposition on the part of the more enlightened of the class to adopt the use of fair weights and measures; and that even among the less scrupulous portion of the body, short allowance seems to be given chiefly from a desire to be *even* with a " scaly customer." The coster makes it a rule never to refuse an offer, and if people *will* give him less than what he considers his proper price, why—he gives them less than their proper quantity. As a proof of the growing honesty among this class, many of the better disposed have recently formed themselves into a society, the members of which are (one and all) pledged not only to deal fairly with their customers, but to compel all other street-sellers to do the same. With a view of distinguishing themselves to the public, they have come to the resolution of wearing a medal, on which shall be engraved a particular number, so that should any imposition be practised by any of their body, the public will have the opportunity of complaining to the Committee of the Association, and having the individual (if guilty) immediately expelled from the society.

OF HALF PROFITS.

BESIDES the modes of trading on borrowed capital above described, there is still another means of obtaining stock prevalent among the London costermongers. It is a common practice with some of the more provident costermongers, who buy more largely—for the sake of buying cheaply—than is required for the supply of their own customers, to place goods in the hands of young men who are unable to buy goods on their own account, " on half profits," as it is called. The man adopting this means of doing a more extensive business, says to any poor fellow willing to work on those terms, " Here's a barrow of vegetables to carry round, and the profit on them will be 2s.; you sell them, and half is for yourself." The man sells them accordingly; if however he fail to realize the 2s. anticipated profit, his employer must still be paid 1s., even if the " seller " prove that only 13d. was cleared; so that the costermonger capitalist, as he may be described, is always, to use the words of one of my informants, " on the profitable side of the hedge."

Boys are less frequently employed on half-

profits than young men; and I am assured that instances of these young men wronging their employers are hardly ever known.

OF THE BOYS OF THE COSTERMONGERS, AND THEIR BUNTS.

BUT there are still other " agents " among the costermongers, and these are the " boys " deputed to sell a man's goods for a certain sum, all over that amount being the boys' profit or " bunts." Almost every costermonger who trades through the streets with his barrow is accompanied by a boy. The ages of these lads vary from ten to sixteen, there are few above sixteen, for the lads think it is then high time for them to start on their own account. These boys are useful to the man in " calling," their shrill voices being often more audible than the loudest pitch of an adult's lungs. Many persons, moreover, I am assured, prefer buying of a boy, believing that if the lad did not succeed in selling his goods he would be knocked about when he got home; others think that they are safer in a boy's hands, and less likely to be cheated; these, however, are equally mistaken notions. The boys also are useful in pushing at the barrow, or in drawing it along by tugging at a rope in front. Some of them are the sons of the costermongers; some go round to the costermongers' abodes and say: " Will you want me to-morrow?" " Shall I come and give you a lift?" The parents of the lads thus at large are, when they *have* parents, either unable to support them, or, if able, prefer putting their money to other uses, (such as drinking); and so the lads have to look out for themselves, or, as they say, " pick up a few halfpence and a bit of grub as we can." Such lads, however, are the smallest class of costermongering youths; and are sometimes called " cas'alty boys," or " nippers."

The boys—and nearly the whole of them—soon become very quick, and grow masters of slang, in from six weeks to two or three months. " I suppose," said one man familiar with their character, " they'd learn French as soon, if they was thrown into the way of it. They must learn slang to live, and as they have to wait at markets every now and then, from one hour to six, they associate one with another and carry on conversations in slang about the " penny gaffs" (theatres), criticising the actors; or may be they toss the pieman, if they've got any ha'pence, or else they chaff the passers by. The older ones may talk about their sweethearts; but they always speak of them by the name of ' nammow' (girls).

" The boys are severe critics too (continued my informant). I heard one say to another; ' What do you think of Johnny Millicent's new step?' for they always recognise a new step, or they discuss the female dancer's legs, and not very decently. At other times the boys discuss the merits or demerits of their masters, as to who feeds them best. I have heard one say, ' O, aint Bob stingy? We have bread and cheese!' Another added; ' *We* have steak and beer, and I've the use of Bill's, (the master's) 'baccy box.'"

Some of these lads are paid by the day, generally from 2d. or 3d. and their food, and as much fruit as they think fit to eat, as by that they soon get sick of it. They generally carry home fruit in their pockets for their playmates, or brothers, or sisters ; the costermongers allow this, if they are satisfied that the pocketing is not for sale. Some lads are engaged by the week, having from 1s. to 1s. 6d., and their food when out with their employer. Their lodging is found only in a few cases, and then they sleep in the same room with their master and mistress. Of master or mistress, however, they never speak, but of Jack and Bet. They behave respectfully to the women, who are generally kind to them. They soon desert a very surly or stingy master ; though such a fellow could get fifty boys next day if he wanted them, but not lads used to the trade, for to these he's well known by their talk one with another, and they soon tell a man his character very plainly—"very plainly indeed, sir, and to his face too," said one.

Some of these boys are well beaten by their employers ; this they put up with readily enough, if they experience kindness at the hands of the man's wife; for, as I said before, parties that have never thought of marriage, if they live together, call one another husbands and wives.

In "working the country" these lads are put on the same footing as their masters, with whom they eat, drink, and sleep; but they do not gamble with them. A few, however, go out and tempt country boys to gamble, and—as an almost inevitable consequence—to lose. "Some of the boys," said one who had seen it often, "will keep a number of countrymen in a beer-shop in a roar for the hour, while the countrymen ply them with beer, and some of the street-lads can drink a good deal. I've known three bits of boys order a pot of beer each, one after the other, each paying his share, and a quartern of gin each after that—drunk neat ; they don't understand water. Drink doesn't seem to affect them as it does men. I don't know why." "Some coster-mongers," said another informant, "have been known, when they've taken a fancy to a boy— I know of two—to dress him out like themselves, silk handkerchiefs and all ; for if they didn't find them silk handkerchiefs, the boys would soon get them out of their ' bunts.' They like silk handkerchiefs, for if they lose all their money gambling, they can then pledge their handker-chiefs."

I have mentioned the term "bunts." Bunts is the money made by the boys in this manner :— If a costermonger, after having sold a sufficiency, has 2s. or 3s. worth of goods left, and is anxious to get home, he says to the boy, "Work these streets, and bring me 2s. 6d. for the tol," (lot) which the costermonger knows by his eye—for he seldom measures or counts—is easily worth that money. The lad then proceeds to sell the things entrusted to him, and often shows great ingenuity in so doing. If, for instance, turnips

be tied up in penny bunches, the lad will open some of them, so as to spread them out to nearly twice their previous size, and if any one ask if that be a penn'orth, he will say, "Here's a larger for 1½d., marm," and so palm off a penny bunch at 1½d. Out of each bunch of onions he takes one or two, and makes an extra bunch. All that the lad can make in this way over the half-crown is his own, and called "bunts." Boys have made from 6d. to 1s. 6d. "bunts," and this day after day. Many of them will, in the course of their traffic, beg old boots or shoes, that they meet with better sort of people, and so "work it to rights," as they call it among themselves ; servants often give them cast-off clothes. It is seldom that a boy carries home less than the stipulated sum. The above is what is understood as "fair bunts."

"Unfair bunts" is what the lad may make unknown to his master ; as, if a customer call from the area for goods cried at 2d., the lad may get 2½d., by pretending what he had carried was a superior sort to that called at 2d.,—or by any similar trick.

"I have known some civil and industrious boys," said a costermonger to me, "get to save a few shillings, and in six months start with a shallow, and so rise to a donkey-cart. The greatest drawback to struggling boys is their sleeping in low lodging-houses, where they are frequently robbed, or trepanned to part with their money, or else they get corrupted."

Some men employ from four to twelve boys, sending them out with shallows and barrows, the boys bringing home the proceeds. The men who send lads out in this way, count the things, and can tell to a penny what can be realised on them. They neither pay nor treat the boys well, I am told, and are looked upon by the other costermongers as extortioners, or unfair dealers, making money by trading on poor lads' necessi-ties, who serve them to avoid starvation. These men are called "Scurfs." If the boys working for them make bunts, or are suspected of making bunts, there is generally "a row" about it.

The bunts is for the most part the gambling money, as well as the money for the "penny gaff," the "twopenny hop," the tobacco, and the pudding money of the boys. "More would save their wages and their bunts," was said to me on good authority, "but they have no place to keep their money in, and don't under-stand anything about savings banks. Many of these lads are looked on with suspicion by the police, and treated like suspected folks; but in my opinion they are not thieves, or they wouldn't work so hard ; for a thief's is a much easier life than a costermonger's."

When a boy begins business on his own ac-count, or "sets up," as they call it, he purchases a shallow, which costs at least 1s., and a half hundred of herrings, 1s. 6d. By the sale of the herrings he will clear 1s., going the round he has been accustomed to, and then trade on the 2s. 6d. Or, if it be fruit time, he will trade in

apples until master of 5s., and then "take to
a barrow," at 3d. a day hire. By this system
the ranks of the costermongers are not only
recruited but increased. There is one grand
characteristic of these lads; I heard on all hands
they are, every one of them, what the costers call
—" wide awake."

There are I am assured from 200 to 300
costers, who, in the busier times of the year,
send out four youths or lads each on an
average. The young men thus sent out generally live with the costermonger, paying 7s.
a week for board, lodging and washing. These
youths, I was told by one who knew them
well, were people who " didn't care to work for
themselves, because they couldn't keep their
money together ; it would soon all go ; and they
must keep it together for their masters. They
are not fed badly, but then they make 'bunts'
sometimes, and it goes for grub when they're
out, so they eat less at home."

Of the Juvenile Trading of the Costermongers.

My inquiries among the costermongers induced
one of their number to address me by letter.
My correspondent—a well-informed and well-
educated man—describes himself as " being
one of those that have been unfortunately thrust
into that precarious way of obtaining a living,
not by choice but circumstances." The writer
then proceeds to say : " No person but those
actually connected with the streets can tell the
exertion, anxiety, and difficulties we have to
undergo ; and I know for a fact it induces a
great many to drink that would not do so,
only to give them a stimulant to bear up
against the troubles that they have to contend
with ; and so it ultimately becomes habitual.
I could point out many instances of the kind.
My chief object in addressing you is to give my
humble suggestion as to the best means of alleviating our present position in society, and
establishing us in the eyes of the public as a
respectable body of men, honestly endeavouring
to support our families, without becoming
chargeable to the parish, and to show that we
are not all the degraded class we are at present
thought to be, subject to the derision of every
passer by, and all looked upon as extortioners
and the confederates of thieves. It is grievous
to see children, as soon as they are able to speak,
thrust into the streets to sell, and in many instances, I am sorry to state, to support their
parents. Kind sir, picture to yourself a group
of those children mixing together indiscriminately—the good with the bad—all uneducated—
and without that parental care which is so essen-
tial for youth—and judge for yourself the result :
the lads in some instances take to thieving,
(this being easier for a living), and the girls to
prostitution ; and so they pass the greater part of
their time in gaol, or get transported. Even
those who are honestly disposed cannot have a
chance of bettering their condition, in consequence of their being uneducated, so that they

often turn out brutal husbands and bad fathers.
Surely, sir, Government could abolish in a
measure this juvenile trading, so conducive to
crime and so injurious to the shopkeeper, who
is highly rated. How is it possible, if children
congregate around his door with the very articles
he may deal in, that he can meet the demands for rates and taxes ; whereas the
educated man, brought by want to sell in the
streets, would not do so, but keep himself
apart from the shopkeeper, and not merit
his enmity, and the interference of the police,
which he necessarily claims. I have procured
an existence (with a few years' exception) in the
streets for the last twenty-five years as a general
salesman of perishable and imperishable articles,
and should be most happy to see anything done
for the benefit of my class. This juvenile trading
I consider the root of the evil ; after the removal
of this, the costermongers might, by classifying
and co-operation, render themselves comparatively happy, in their position, and become
acknowledged members of society."

Another costermonger, in conversing with me
concerning these young traders, said, that many
of them would ape the vices of men : mere
urchins would simulate drunkenness, or boast,
with many an exaggeration, of their drinking
feats. They can get as much as they please at
the public-houses ; and this too, I may add,
despite the 43rd clause in the Police Act, which
enacts, that " every person, licensed to deal in
exciseable liquors within the said (Metropolitan
Police) District, who shall knowingly supply any
sort of distilled exciseable liquor to be drunk
upon the premises, to any boy or girl, apparently
under the age of sixteen years, shall be liable to
a penalty of not more than 20s. ;" and upon a
second conviction to 40s. penalty ; and on a
third to 5l.

Of the Education of the " Coster-Lads."

Among the costers the term education is (as I
have already intimated) merely understood as
meaning a complete knowledge of the art of
" buying in the cheapest market and selling in
the dearest." There are few lads whose training
extends beyond this. The father is the tutor,
who takes the boy to the different markets,
instructs him in the art of buying, and when
the youth is perfect on this point, the parent's
duty is supposed to have been performed.
Nearly all these boys are remarkable for their
precocious sharpness. To use the words of one
of the class, "these young ones are as sharp
as terriers, and learns every dodge of business
in less than half no time. There's one I knows
about three feet high, that's up to the business
as clever as a man of thirty. Though he's only
twelve years old he'll chaff down a peeler so
uncommon severe, that the only way to stop
him is to take him in charge !"

It is idle to imagine that these lads, possessed
of a mental acuteness almost wonderful, will
not educate themselves in vice, if we neglect

to train them to virtue. At their youthful age, the power of acquiring knowledge is the strongest, and some kind of education is continually going on. If they are not taught by others, they will form their own characters—developing habits of dissipation, and educing all the grossest passions of their natures, and learning to indulge in the gratification of every appetite without the least restraint.

As soon as a boy is old enough to shout well and loudly, his father takes him into the streets. Some of these youths are not above seven years of age, and it is calculated that not more than one in a hundred has ever been to a school of any kind. The boy walks with the barrow, or guides the donkey, shouting by turns with the father, who, when the goods are sold, will as a reward, let him ride home on the tray. The lad attends all markets with his father, who teaches him his business and shows him his tricks of trade; "for," said a coster, "a governor in our line leaves the knowledge of all his dodges to his son, jist as the rich coves do their tin."

The life of a coster-boy is a very hard one. In summer he will have to be up by four o'clock in the morning, and in winter he is never in bed after six. When he has returned from market, it is generally his duty to wash the goods and help dress the barrow. About nine he begins his day's work, shouting whilst the father pushes; and as very often the man has lost his voice, this share of the labour is left entirely to him. When a coster has regular customers, the vegetables or fish are all sold by twelve o'clock, and in many coster families the lad is then packed off with fruit to hawk in the streets. When the work is over, the father will perhaps take the boy to a public-house with him, and give him part of his beer. Sometimes a child of four or five is taken to the tap-room, especially if he be pretty and the father proud of him. "I have seen," said a coster to me, "a baby of five year old reeling drunk in a tap-room. His governor did it for the lark of the thing, to see him chuck hisself about—sillyfied like."

The love of gambling soon seizes upon the coster boy. Youths of about twelve or so will as soon as they can get away from work go to a public-house and play cribbage for pints of beer, or for a pint a corner. They generally continue playing till about midnight, and rarely—except on a Sunday—keep it up all night.

It ordinarily happens that when a lad is about thirteen, he quarrels with his father, and gets turned away from home. Then he is forced to start for himself. He knows where he can borrow stock-money and get his barrow, for he is as well acquainted with the markets as the oldest hand at the business, and children may often be seen in the streets under-selling their parents. "How's it possible," said a woman, "for people to live when there's their own son at the end of the court a-calling his goods as cheap again as we can afford to sell ourn."

If the boy is lucky in trade, his next want is to get a girl to keep home for him. I was assured, that it is not at all uncommon for a lad of fifteen to be living with a girl of the same age, as man and wife. It creates no disgust among his class, but seems rather to give him a position among such people. Their courtship does not take long when once the mate has been fixed upon. The girl is invited to "raffles," and treated to "twopenny hops," and half-pints of beer. Perhaps a silk neck handkerchief—a "King's-man" is given as a present; though some of the lads will, when the arrangement has been made, take the gift back again and wear it themselves. The boys are very jealous, and if once made angry behave with great brutality to the offending girl. A young fellow of about sixteen told me, as he seemed to grow angry at the very thought, "If I seed my gal a talking to another chap I'd fetch her sich a punch of the nose as should plaguy quick stop the whole business." Another lad informed me, with a knowing look, "that the gals—it was a rum thing now he come to think on it—axully liked a feller for walloping them. As long as the bruises hurted, she was always thinking on the cove as gived 'em her." After a time, if the girl continues faithful, the young coster may marry her; but this is rarely the case, and many live with their girls until they have grown to be men, or perhaps they may quarrel the very first year, and have a fight and part.

These boys hate any continuous work. So strong is this objection to continuity that they cannot even remain selling the same article for more than a week together. Moreover none of them can be got to keep stalls. They must be perpetually on the move—or to use their own words "they like a roving life." They all of them delight in dressing "flash" as they call it. If a "governor" was to try and "palm off" his old cord jacket upon the lad that worked with him, the boy wouldn't take it. "Its too big and seedy for me," he'd say, "and I aint going to have your leavings." They try to dress like the men, with large pockets in their cord jackets and plenty of them. Their trowsers too must fit tight at the knee, and their boots they like as good as possible. A good "King's-man," a plush skull cap, and a seam down the trowsers are the great points of ambition with the coster boys. A lad about fourteen informed me that "brass buttons, like a huntman's, with foxes' heads on em, looked stunning flash, and the gals liked em." As for the hair, they say it ought to be long in front, and done in "figure-six" curls, or twisted back to the ear "Newgate-knocker style." "But the worst of hair is," they add, "that it is always getting cut off in quod, all along of muzzling the bobbies."

The whole of the coster-boys are fond of good living. I was told that when a lad started

THE COSTER-GIRL.

"Apples! An 'aypenny a lot, Apples!"

[*From a Daguerreotype by* BEARD.]

for himself, he would for the first week or so live almost entirely on cakes and nuts. When settled in business they always manage to have what they call "a relish" for breakfast and tea, "a couple of herrings, or a bit of bacon, or what not." Many of them never dine except- ing on the Sunday—the pony and donkey pro- prietors being the only costers whose incomes will permit them to indulge in a "fourpenny plate of meat at a cook's shop." The whole of the boys too are extremely fond of pudding, and should the "plum duff" at an eating- house contain an unusual quantity of plums, the news soon spreads, and the boys then endeavour to work that way so as to obtain a slice. While waiting for a market, the lads will very often spend a shilling in the cakes and three cornered puffs sold by the Jews. The owners toss for them, and so enable the young coster to indulge his two favourite passions at the same time—his love of pastry, and his love of gambling. The Jews crisp butter biscuits also rank very high with the boys, who declare that they "slip down like soapsuds down a gully hole." In fact it is curious to notice how perfectly unrestrained are the passions and appetites of these youths. The only thoughts that trouble them are for their girls, their eating and their gambling— beyond the love of self they have no tie that binds them to existence.

THE LIFE OF A COSTER-LAD.

ONE lad that I spoke to gave me as much of his history as he could remember. He was a tall stout boy, about sixteen years old, with a face utterly vacant. His two heavy lead- coloured eyes stared unmeaningly at me, and, beyond a constant anxiety to keep his front lock curled on his cheek, he did not exhibit the slightest trace of feeling. He sank into his seat heavily and of a heap, and when once settled down he remained motionless, with his mouth open and his hands on his knees—almost as if paralyzed. He was dressed in all the slang beauty of his class, with a bright red handker- chief and unexceptionable boots.

"My father" he told me in a thick unim- passioned voice, "was a waggoner, and worked the country roads. There was two on us at home with mother, and we used to play along with the boys of our court, in Golding-lane, at buttons and marbles. I recollects nothing more than this—only the big boys used to cheat like bricks and thump us if we grumbled—that's all I recollects of my infancy, as you calls it. Father I've heard tell died when I was three and brother only a year old. It was worse luck for us!—Mother was so easy with us. I once went to school for a couple of weeks, but the cove used to fetch me a wipe over the knuckles with his stick, and as I wasn't going to stand that there, why you see I aint no great schol- lard. We did as we liked with mother, she was so precious easy, and I never learned any- thing but playing buttons and making leaden

'bonces,' that's all," (here the youth laughed slightly.) " Mother used to be up and out very early washing in families — anything for a living. She was a good mother to us. We was left at home with the key of the room and some bread and butter for dinner. Afore she got into work—and it was a goodish long time— we was shocking hard up, and she pawned nigh everything. Sometimes, when we had'nt no grub at all, the other lads, perhaps, would give us some of their bread and butter, but often our stomachs used to ache with the hunger, and we would cry when we was werry far gone. She used to be at work from six in the morning till ten o'clock at night, which was a long time for a child's belly to hold out again, and when it was dark we would go and lie down on the bed and try and sleep until she came home with the food. I was eight year old then.

"A man as know'd mother, said to her, 'Your boy's got nothing to do, let him come along with me and yarn a few ha'pence,' and so I became a coster. He gave me 4d. a morning and my breakfast. I worked with him about three year, until I learnt the markets, and then I and brother got baskets of our own, and used to keep mother. One day with another, the two on us together could make 2s. 6d. by selling greens of a morning, and going round to the publics with nuts of a evening, till about ten o'clock at night. Mother used to have a bit of fried meat or a stew ready for us when we got home, and by using up the stock as we couldn't sell, we used to manage pretty tidy. When I was fourteen I took up with a girl. She lived in the same house as we did, and I used to walk out of a night with her and give her half-pints of beer at the publics. She were about thirteen, and used to dress werry nice, though she weren't above middling pretty. Now I'm working for another man as gives me a shilling a week, victuals, washing, and lodging, just as if I was one of the family.

" On a Sunday I goes out selling, and all I yarns I keeps. As for going to church, why, I can't afford it,—besides, to tell the truth, I don't like it well enough. Plays, too, ain't in my line much; I'd sooner go to a dance—its more livelier. The 'penny gaffs' is rather more in my style; the songs are out and out, and makes our gals laugh. The smuttier the better, I thinks; bless you! the gals likes it as much as we do. If we lads ever has a quarrel, why, we fights for it. I* I was to let a cove off once, he'd do it agair ; but I never give a lad a chance, so long as I can get anigh him. I never heard about Christianity, but if a cove was to fetch me a lick of the head, I'd give it him again, whether he was a big 'un or a little 'un. I'd precious soon see a henemy of mine shot afore I'd forgive him,—where's the use ? Do I understand what behaving to your neigh- bour is?—In coorse I do. If a feller as lives next me wanted a basket of mine as I wasn't using, why, he might have it ; if I was working it though, I'd see him further! I can understand that all as lives in a court is neighbours; but as for policemen, they're nothing to me, and I should like to pay 'em all off well. No; I never heerd about this here creation you speaks about. In coorse God Almighty made the world, and the poor bricklayers' labourers built the houses arterwards—that's *my* opinion; but I can't say, for I've never been in no schools, only always hard at work, and knows nothing about it. I have heerd a little about our Saviour, — they seem to say he were a goodish kind of a man; but if he says as how a cove's to forgive a feller as hits you, I should say he know'd nothing about it. In coorse the gals the lads goes and lives with thinks our walloping 'em wery cruel of us, but we don't. Why don't we ? — why, because we don't. Before father died, I used sometimes to say my prayers, but after that mother was too busy getting a living to mind about my praying. Yes, I knows!—in the Lord's prayer they says, 'Forgive us our trespasses, as we forgives them as trespasses agin us.' It's a very good thing, in coorse, but no costers can't do it."

Of the "Penny Gaff."

In many of the thoroughfares of London there are shops which have been turned into a kind of temporary theatre (admission one penny), where dancing and singing take place every night. Rude pictures of the performers are arranged outside, to give the front a gaudy and attractive look, and at night-time coloured lamps and transparencies are displayed to draw an audience. These places are called by the costers "Penny Gaffs;" and on a Monday night as many as six performances will take place, each one having its two hundred visitors.

It is impossible to contemplate the ignorance and immorality of so numerous a class as that of the costermongers, without wishing to discover the cause of their degradation. Let any one curious on this point visit one of these penny shows, and he will wonder that *any* trace of virtue and honesty should remain among the people. Here the stage, instead of being the means for illustrating a moral precept, is turned into a platform to teach the cruelest debauchery. The audience is usually composed of children so young, that these dens become the school-rooms where the guiding morals of a life are picked up; and so precocious are the little things, that the girl of nine will, from constant attendance at such places, have learnt to understand the filthiest sayings, and laugh at them as loudly as the grown-up lads around her. What notions can the young female form of marriage and chastity, when the penny theatre rings with applause at the performance of a scene whose sole point turns upon the pantomimic imitation of the unrestrained indulgence of the most corrupt appetites of our nature ? How can the lad learn to check his hot passions and think honesty and virtue admirable, when the shouts around him impart a glory to a descriptive song so painfully corrupt, that it can only have been made tolerable by the most habitual excess ? The men who preside over these infamous places know too well the failings of their audiences. They know that these poor children require no nicely-turned joke to make the evening pass merrily, and that the filth they utter needs no double meaning to veil its obscenity. The show that will provide the most unrestrained debauchery will have the most crowded benches; and to gain this point, things are acted and spoken that it is criminal even to allude to.

Not wishing to believe in the description which some of the more intelligent of the costermongers had given of these places, it was thought better to visit one of them, so that all exaggeration might be avoided. One of the least offensive of the exhibitions was fixed upon. The "penny gaff" chosen was situated in a broad street near Smithfield; and for a great distance off, the jingling sound of music was heard, and the gas-light streamed out into the thick night air as from a dark lantern, glittering on the windows of the houses opposite, and lighting up the faces of the mob in the road, as on an illumination night. The front of a large shop had been entirely removed, and the entrance was decorated with paintings of the "comic singers," in their most "humourous" attitudes. On a table against the wall was perched the band, playing what the costers call "dancing tunes" with great effect, for the hole at the money-taker's box was blocked up with hands tendering the penny. The crowd without was so numerous, that a policeman was in attendance to preserve order, and push the boys off the pavement—the music having the effect of drawing them insensibly towards the festooned green-baize curtain.

The shop itself had been turned into a waiting-room, and was crowded even to the top of the stairs leading to the gallery on the first floor. The ceiling of this "lobby" was painted blue, and spotted with whitewash clouds, to represent the heavens; the boards of the trap-door, and the laths that showed through the holes in the plaster, being all of the same colour. A notice was here posted, over the canvass door leading into the theatre, to the effect that "Ladies and Gentlemen to the front places must pay Twopence."

The visitors, with a few exceptions, were all boys and girls, whose ages seemed to vary from eight to twenty years. Some of the girls—though their figures showed them to be mere children—were dressed in showy cotton-velvet polkas, and wore dowdy feathers in their crushed bonnets. They stood laughing and joking with the lads, in an unconcerned, impudent manner, that was almost appalling. Some of them, when tired of waiting, chose their partners, and commenced dancing grotesquely, to the admiration of the lookers-on, who expressed their approbation in obscene terms, that, far from disgusting the poor little women, were received as compliments, and acknowledged with smiles and coarse repartees. The boys clustered together, smoking their pipes, and laughing at each other's anecdotes, or else jingling halfpence in time with the tune, while they whistled an accompaniment to it. Presently one of the performers, with a gilt crown on his well greased locks, descended from the staircase, his fleshings covered by a dingy dressing-gown, and mixed with the mob, shaking hands with old acquaintances. The " comic singer," too, made his appearance among the throng—the huge bow to his cravat, which nearly covered his waistcoat, and the red end to his nose, exciting neither merriment nor surprise.

To discover the kind of entertainment, a lad near me and my companion was asked " if there was any flash dancing." With a knowing wink the boy answered, " Lots ! show their legs and all, prime ! " and immediately the boy followed up his information by a request for a " yennep" to get a "tib of occabot." After waiting in the lobby some considerable time, the performance inside was concluded, and the audience came pouring out through the canvass door. -As they had to pass singly, I noticed them particularly. Above three - fourths of them were women and girls, the rest consisting chiefly of mere boys — for out of about two hundred persons I counted only eighteen men. Forward they came, bringing an overpowering stench with them, laughing and yelling as they pushed their way through the waiting-room. One woman carrying a sickly child with a bulging forehead, was reeling drunk, the saliva running down her mouth as she stared about her with a heavy fixed eye. Two boys were pushing her from side to side, while the poor infant slept, breathing heavily, as if stupified, through the din. Lads jumping on girls' shoulders, and girls laughing hysterically from being tickled by the youths behind them, every one shouting and jumping, presented a mad scene of frightful enjoyment.

When these had left, a rush for places by those in waiting began, that set at defiance the blows and strugglings of a lady in spangles who endeavoured to preserve order and take the checks. As time was a great object with the proprietor, the entertainment within began directly the first seat was taken, so that the lads without, rendered furious by the rattling of the piano within, made the canvass partition bulge in and out, with the strugglings of those seeking admission, like a sail in a flagging wind.

To form the theatre, the first floor had been removed ; the whitewashed beams however still stretched from wall to wall. The lower room had evidently been the warehouse, while the upper apartment had been the sitting-room, for the paper was still on the walls. A gallery, with a canvass front, had been hurriedly built up, and it was so fragile that the boards bent under the weight of those above. The bricks in the warehouse were smeared over with red paint, and had a few black curtains daubed upon them. The coster-youths require no very

great scenic embellishment, and indeed the stage—which was about eight feet square—could admit of none. Two jets of gas, like those outside a butcher's shop, were placed on each side of the proscenium, and proved very handy for the gentlemen whose pipes required lighting. The band inside the " theatre " could not compare with the band without. An old grand piano, whose canvass - covered top extended the entire length of the stage, sent forth its wiry notes under the be-ringed fingers of a " professor Wilkinsini," while another professional, with his head resting on his violin, played vigorously, as he stared unconcernedly at the noisy audience.

Singing and dancing formed the whole of the hours' performance, and, of the two, the singing was preferred. A young girl, of about fourteen years of age, danced with more energy than grace, and seemed to be well-known to the spectators, who cheered her on by her Christian name. When the dance was concluded, the proprietor of the establishment threw down a penny from the gallery, in the hopes that others might be moved to similar acts of generosity ; but no one followed up the offering, so the young lady hunted after the money and departed. The " comic singer," in a battered hat and the huge bow to his cravat, was received with deafening shouts. Several songs were named by the costers, but the " funny gentleman " merely requested them " to hold their jaws," and putting on a " knowing" look, sang a song, the whole point of which consisted in the mere utterance of some filthy word at the end of each stanza. Nothing, however, could have been more successful. The lads stamped their feet with delight ; the girls screamed with enjoyment. Once or twice a young shrill laugh would anticipate the fun—as if the words were well known—or the boys would forestall the point by shouting it out before the proper time. When the song was ended the house was in a delirium of applause. The canvass front to the gallery was beaten with sticks, drum-like, and sent down showers of white powder on the heads in the pit. Another song followed, and the actor knowing on what his success depended, lost no opportunity of increasing his laurels. The most obscene thoughts, the most disgusting scenes were coolly described, making a poor child near me wipe away the tears that rolled down her eyes with the enjoyment of the poison. There were three or four of these songs sung in the course of the evening, each one being encored, and then changed. One written about " Pine-apple rock," was the grand treat of the night, and offered greater scope to the rhyming powers of the author than any of the others. In this, not a single chance had been missed ; ingenuity had been exerted to its utmost lest an obscene thought should be passed by, and it was absolutely awful to behold the relish with which the young ones jumped to the hideous meaning of the verses.

There was one scene yet to come, that was perfect in its wickedness. A ballet began between a man dressed up as a woman, and a country clown. The most disgusting attitudes were struck, the most immoral acts represented, without one dissenting voice. If there had been any feat of agility, any grimacing, or, in fact, anything with which the laughter of the uneducated classes is usually associated, the applause might have been accounted for; but here were two ruffians degrading themselves each time they stirred a limb, and forcing into the brains of the childish audience before them thoughts that must embitter a lifetime, and descend from father to child like some bodily infirmity.

When I had left, I spoke to a better class costermonger on this saddening subject. "Well, sir, it is frightful," he said, "but the boys *will* have their amusements. If their amusements is bad they don't care; they only wants to laugh, and this here kind of work does it. Give 'em better singing and better dancing, and they'd go, if the price was as cheap as this is. I've seen, when a decent concert was given at a penny, as many as four thousand costers present, behaving themselves as quietly and decently as possible. Their wives and children was with 'em, and no audience was better conducted. It's all stuff talking about them preferring this sort of thing. Give 'em good things at the same price, and I *know* they will like the good, better than the bad."

My own experience with this neglected class goes to prove, that if we would really lift them out of the moral mire in which they are wallowing, the first step must be to provide them with *wholesome* amusements. The misfortune, however, is, that when we seek to elevate the character of the people, we give them such mere dry abstract truths and dogmas to digest, that the uneducated mind turns with abhorrence from them. We forget how we ourselves were originally won by our *emotions* to the consideration of such subjects. We do not remember how our own tastes have been formed, nor do we, in our zeal, stay to reflect how the tastes of a people generally are created; and, consequently, we cannot perceive that a habit of enjoying any matter whatsoever can only be induced in the mind by linking with it some æsthetic affection. The heart is the mainspring of the intellect, and the feelings the real educers and educators of the thoughts. As games with the young destroy the fatigue of muscular exercise, so do the sympathies stir the mind to action without any sense of effort. It is because "serious" people generally object to enlist the emotions in the education of the poor, and look upon the delight which arises in the mind from the mere perception of the beauty of sound, motion, form, and colour—or from the apt association of harmonious or incongruous ideas—or from the sympathetic operation of the affections; it is because, I say, the zealous portion of society look upon these matters as "*vanity*," that the amusements of the working-classes are left to venal traders to provide. Hence, in the low-priced entertainments which necessarily appeal to the poorer, and, therefore, to the least educated of the people, the proprietors, instead of trying to develop in them the purer sources of delight, seek only to gratify their audience in the coarsest manner, by appealing to their most brutal appetites. And thus the emotions, which the great Architect of the human mind gave us as the means of quickening our imaginations and refining our sentiments, are made the instruments of crushing every operation of the intellect and debasing our natures. It is idle and unfeeling to believe that the great majority of a people whose days are passed in excessive toil, and whose homes are mostly of an uninviting character, will forego *all* amusements, and consent to pass their evenings by their *no* firesides, reading tracts or singing hymns. It is folly to fancy that the mind, spent with the irksomeness of compelled labour, and depressed, perhaps, with the struggle to live by that labour after all, will not, when the work is over, seek out some place where at least it can forget its troubles or fatigues in the temporary pleasure begotten by some mental or physical stimulant. It is because we exact too much of the poor—because we, as it were, strive to make true knowledge and true beauty as forbidding as possible to the uneducated and unrefined, that they fly to their penny gaffs, their twopenny-hops, their beer-shops, and their gambling-grounds for pleasures which we deny them, and which we, in our arrogance, believe it is possible for them to do without.

The experiment so successfully tried at Liverpool of furnishing music of an enlivening and yet elevating character at the same price as the concerts of the lowest grade, shows that the people may be won to delight in beauty instead of beastiality, and teaches us again that it is *our* fault to allow them to be as they are and not their's to remain so. All men are compound animals, with many inlets of pleasure to their brains, and if one avenue be closed against them, why it but forces them to seek delight through another. So far from the perception of beauty inducing habits of gross enjoyment as "serious" people generally imagine, a moment's reflection will tell us that these very habits are only the necessary consequences of the non-development of the æsthetic faculty; for the two assuredly cannot co-exist. To cultivate the sense of the beautiful is necessarily to inculcate a detestation of the sensual. Moreover, it is impossible for the mind to be accustomed to the contemplation of what is admirable without continually mounting to higher and higher forms of it—from the beauty of nature to that of thought—from thought to feeling, from feeling to action, and lastly to the fountain of all goodness—the great munificent Creator of the sea, the mountains, and the flowers—the stars, the sunshine, and the rainbow—the fancy, the reason, the love and the heroism of man and womankind—the instincts of the beasts—the glory of the angels—and the mercy of Christ.

OF THE COSTER-GIRLS.

THE costermongers, taken as a body, entertain the most imperfect idea of the sanctity of marriage. To their undeveloped minds it merely consists in the fact of a man and woman living together, and sharing the gains they may each earn by selling in the street. The father and mother of the girl look upon it as a convenient means of shifting the support of their child over to another's exertions; and so thoroughly do they believe this to be the end and aim of matrimony, that the expense of a church ceremony is considered as a useless waste of money, and the new pair are received by their companions as cordially as if every form of law and religion had been complied with.

The notions of morality among these people agree strangely, as I have said, with those of many savage tribes—indeed, it would be curious if it were otherwise. They are a part of the Nomades of England, neither knowing nor caring for the enjoyments of home. The hearth, which is so sacred a symbol to all civilized races as being the spot where the virtues of each succeeding generation are taught and encouraged, has no charms to them. The tap-room is the father's chief abiding place; whilst to the mother the house is only a better kind of *tent*. She is away at the stall, or hawking her goods from morning till night, while the children are left to play away the day in the court or alley, and pick their morals out of the gutter. So long as the limbs gain strength the parent cares for nothing else. As the young ones grow up, their only notions of wrong are formed by what the policeman will permit them to do. If we, who have known from babyhood the kindly influences of a home, require, before we are thrust out into the world to get a living for ourselves, that our perceptions of good and evil should be quickened and brightened (the same as our perceptions of truth and falsity) by the experience and counsel of those who are wiser and better than ourselves,—if, indeed, it needed a special creation and example to teach the best and strongest of us the law of right, how bitterly must the children of the street-folk require tuition, training, and advice, when from their very cradles (if, indeed, they ever knew such luxuries) they are doomed to witness in their parents, whom they naturally believe to be their superiors, habits of life in which passion is the sole rule of action, and where every appetite of our animal nature is indulged in without the least restraint.

I say thus much because I am anxious to make others feel, as I do myself, that *we* are the culpable parties in these matters. That they poor things should do as they do is but human nature—but that *we* should allow them to remain thus destitute of every blessing vouchsafed to ourselves—that we should willingly sha*e what we enjoy with our brethren at the Antipodes, and yet leave those who are nearer and who, therefore, should be dearer to

us, *to* want even the commonest moral necessaries is a paradox that gives to the zeal of our Christianity a strong savour of the chicanery of Cant.

The costermongers strongly resemble the North American Indians in their conduct to their wives. They can understand that it is the duty of the woman to contribute to the happiness of the man, but cannot feel that there is a reciprocal duty from the man to the woman. The wife is considered as an inexpensive servant, and the disobedience of a wish is punished with blows. She must work early and late, and to the husband must be given the proceeds of her labour. Often when the man is in one of his drunken fits—which sometimes last two or three days continuously—she must by her sole exertions find food for herself and him too. To live in peace with him, there must be no murmuring, no tiring under work, no fancied cause for jealousy—for if there be, she is either beaten into submission or cast adrift to begin life again—as another's leavings.

The story of one coster girl's life may be taken as a type of the many. When quite young she is placed out to nurse with some neighbour, the mother—if a fond one—visiting the child at certain periods of the day, for the purpose of feeding it, or sometimes, knowing the round she has to make, having the infant brought to her at certain places, to be " suckled." As soon as it is old enough to go alone, the court is its play-ground, the gutter its school-room, and under the care of an elder sister the little one passes the day, among children whose mothers like her own are too busy out in the streets helping to get the food, to be able to mind the family at home. When the girl is strong enough, she in her turn is made to assist the mother by keeping guard over the younger children, or, if there be none, she is lent out to carry about a baby, and so made to add to the family income by gaining her sixpence weekly. Her time is from the earliest years fully occupied; indeed, her parents cannot afford to keep her without doing and getting *something*. Very few of the children receive the least education. " The parents," I am told, " never give their minds to learning, for they say, ' What's the use of it? *that* won't yarn a gal a living.' " Everything is sacrificed—as, indeed, under the circumstances it must be—in the struggle to live—aye! and to live *merely*. Mind, heart, soul, are all absorbed in the belly. The rudest form of animal life, physiologists tell us, is simply a locomotive stomach. Verily, it would appear as if our social state had a tendency to make the highest animal sink into the lowest.

At about seven years of age the girls first go into the streets to sell. A shallow-basket is given to them, with about two shillings for stock-money, and they hawk, according to the time of year, either oranges, apples, or violets; some begin their street education with the sale of water-cresses. The money earned by this means is strictly given to the parents. Sometimes—

though rarely—a girl who has been unfortunate during the day will not dare to return home at night, and then she will sleep under some dry arch or about some market, until the morrow's gains shall ensure her a safe reception and shelter in her father's room.

The life of the coster-girls is as severe as that of the boys. Between four and five in the morning they have to leave home for the markets, and sell in the streets until about nine. Those that have more kindly parents, return then to breakfast, but many are obliged to earn the morning's meal for themselves. After breakfast, they generally remain in the streets until about ten o'clock at night; many having nothing during all that time but one meal of bread and butter and coffee, to enable them to support the fatigue of walking from street to street with the heavy basket on their heads. In the course of a day, some girls eat as much as a pound of bread, and very seldom get any meat, unless it be on a Sunday.

There are many poor families that, without the aid of these girls, would be forced into the workhouse. They are generally of an affectionate disposition, and some will perform acts of marvellous heroism to keep together the little home. It is not at all unusual for mere children of fifteen to walk their eight or ten miles a day, carrying a basket of nearly two hundred weight on their heads. A journey to Woolwich and back, or to the towns near London, is often undertaken to earn the 1s. 6d. their parents are anxiously waiting for at home.

Very few of these girls are married to the men they afterwards live with. Their courtship is usually a very short one; for, as one told me, " the life is such a hard one, that a girl is ready to get rid of a *little* of the labour at any price." The coster-lads see the girls at market, and if one of them be pretty, and a boy take a fancy to her, he will make her bargains for her, and carry her basket home. Sometimes a coster working his rounds will feel a liking for a wench selling her goods in the street, and will leave his barrow to go and talk with her. A girl seldom takes up with a lad before she is sixteen, though some of them, when barely fifteen or even fourteen, will pair off. They court for a time, going to raffles and "gaffs" together, and then the affair is arranged. The girl tells her parents "she's going to keep company with so-and-so," packs up what things she has, and goes at once, without a word of remonstrance from either father or mother. A furnished room, at about 4s. a week, is taken, and the young couple begin life The lad goes out as usual with his barrow, and the girl goes out with her basket, often working harder for her lover than she had done for her parents. They go to market together, and at about nine o'clock her day's selling begins. Very often she will take out with her in the morning what food she requires during the day, and never return home until eleven o'clock at night.

The men generally behave very cruelly to the girls they live with. They are as faithful to them as if they were married, but they are jealous in the extreme. To see a man talking to their girl is sufficient to ensure the poor thing a beating. They sometimes ill-treat them horribly—most unmercifully indeed—nevertheless the girls say they cannot help loving them still, and continue working for them, as if they experienced only kindness at their hands. Some of the men are gentler and more considerate in their treatment of them, but by far the larger portion are harsh and merciless. Often when the Saturday night's earnings of the two have been large, the man will take the entire money, and as soon as the Sunday's dinner is over, commence drinking hard, and continue drunk for two or three days together, until the funds are entirely exhausted. The women never gamble; they say, " it gives them no excitement." They prefer, if they have a spare moment in the evening, sitting near the fire making up and patching their clothes. " Ah, sir," said a girl to me, " a neat gown does a deal with a man; he always likes a girl best when everybody else likes her too." On a Sunday they clean their room for the week and go for a treat, if they can persuade their young man to take them out in the afternoon, either to Chalk Farm or Battersea Fields —" where there's plenty of life."

After a girl has once grown accustomed to a street-life, it is almost impossible to wean her from it. The muscular irritability begotten by continued wandering makes her unable to rest for any time in one place, and she soon, if put to any *settled* occupation, gets to crave for the severe exercise she formerly enjoyed. The least restraint will make her sigh after the perfect liberty of the coster's " roving life." As an instance of this I may relate a fact that has occurred within the last six months. A gentleman of high literary repute, struck with the heroic strugglings of a coster Irish girl to maintain her mother, took her to his house, with a view of teaching her the duties of a servant. At first the transition was a painful one to the poor thing. Having travelled barefoot through the streets since a mere child, the pressure of shoes was intolerable to her, and in the evening or whenever a few minutes' rest could be obtained, the boots were taken off, for with them on she could enjoy no ease. The perfect change of life, and the novelty of being in a new place, reconciled her for some time to the loss of her liberty. But no sooner did she hear from her friends, that sprats were again in the market, than, as if there were some magical influence in the fish, she at once requested to be freed from the confinement, and permitted to return to her old calling.

Such is the history of the lower class of girls, though this lower class, I regret to say, constitutes by far the greater portion of the whole. Still I would not for a moment have it inferred that *all* are bad. There are many young girls getting their living, or rather helping to get the living of others in the streets, whose goodness, considering the temptations and hardships besetting such an occupation, approximates to the marvellous. As a type of the more prudent class of coster girls, I would cite the following narrative received from the lips of a young woman in answer to a series of questions.

THE LIFE OF A COSTER GIRL.

I wished to have obtained a statement from the girl whose portrait is here given, but she was afraid to give the slightest information about the habits of her companions, lest they should recognize her by the engraving and persecute her for the revelations she might make. After disappointing me some dozen times, I was forced to seek out some other coster girl. The one I fixed upon was a fine-grown young woman of eighteen. She had a habit of curtsying to every question that was put to her. Her plaid shawl was tied over the breast, and her cotton-velvet bonnet was crushed in with carrying her basket. She seemed dreadfully puzzled where to put her hands, at one time tucking them under her shawl, warming them at the fire, or measuring the length of her apron, and when she answered a question she invariably addressed the fireplace. Her voice was husky from shouting apples.

" My mother has been in the streets selling all her lifetime. Her uncle learnt her the markets and she learnt me. When business grew bad she said to me, ' Now you shall take care on the stall, and I'll go and work out charing.' The way she learnt me the markets was to judge of the weight of the baskets of apples, and then said she, ' Always bate 'em down, a'most a half.' I always liked the street-life very well, that was if I was selling. I have mostly kept a stall myself, but I've known gals as walk about with apples, as have told me that the weight of the baskets is sich that the neck cricks, and when the load is took off, its just as if you'd a stiff neck, and the head feels as light as a feather. The gals begins working very early at our work ; the parents makes them go out when a'most babies. There's a little gal, I'm sure she an't more than half-past seven, that stands selling water-cresses next my stall, and mother was saying, ' Only look there, how that little one has to get her living afore she a'most knows what a penn'orth means.'

" There 's six on us in family, and father and mother makes eight. Father used to do odd jobs with the gas-pipes in the streets, and when work was slack we had very hard times of it. Mother always liked being with us at home, and used to manage to keep us employed out of mischief—she'd give us an old gown to make into pinafores for the children and such like! She's been very good to us, has mother, and so's father. She always liked to hear us read to her whilst she was washing or such like! and then we big ones had to learn the little ones. But when father's work got slack, if she had no

employment charing, she'd say, ' Now I'll go and buy a bushel of apples,' and then she'd turn out and get a penny that way. I suppose by sitting at the stall from nine in the morning till the shops shuts up—say ten o'clock at night, I can earn about 1s. 6d. a day. It's all according to the apples—whether they're good or not—what we makes. If I'm unlucky, mother will say, ' Well, I'll go out to-morrow and see what I can do ;' and if I've done well, she'll say ' Come you're a good hand at it ; you've done famous.' Yes, mother's very fair that way. Ah! there's many a gal I knows whose back has to suffer if she don't sell her stock well ; but, thank God! I never get more than a blowing up. My parents is very fair to me.

" I dare say there ain't ten out of a hundred gals what's living with men, what's been married Church of England fashion. I know plenty myself, but I don't, indeed, think it right. It seems to me that the gals is fools to be 'ticed away, but, in coorse, they needn't go without they likes. This is why I don't think it's right. Perhaps a man will have a few words with his gal, and he'll say, ' Oh! I ain't obligated to keep her !' and he'll turn her out : and then where's that poor gal to go ? Now, there's a gal I knows as came to me no later than this here week, and she had a dreadful swole face and a awful black eye ; and I says, ' Who's done that ?' and she says, says she,' Why, Jack'—just in that way ; and then she says, says she, ' I'm going to take a warrant out to-morrow.' Well, he gets the warrant that same night, but she never appears again him, for fear of getting more beating. That don't seem to me to be like married people ought to be. Besides, if parties is married, they ought to bend to each other ; and they won't, for sartain, if they're only living together. A man as is married is obligated to keep his wife if they quarrels or not ; and he says to himself, says he, ' Well, I may as well live happy, like.' But if he can turn a poor gal off, as soon as he tires of her, he begins to have noises with her, and then gets quit of her altogether. Again, the men takes the money of the gals, and in coorse ought to treat 'em well —which they don't. This is another reason : when the gal is in the family way, the lads mostly sends them to the workhouse to lay in, and only goes sometimes to take them a bit of tea and shuggar ; but, in coorse, married men wouldn't behave in such likes to their poor wives. After a quarrel, too, a lad goes and takes up with another young gal, and that isn't pleasant for the first one. The first step to ruin is them places of ' penny gaffs,' for they hears things there as oughtn't to be said to young gals. Besides, the lads is very insinivating, and after leaving them places will give a gal a drop of beer, and make her half tipsy, and then they makes their arrangements. I've often heerd the boys boasting of having ruined gals, for all the world as if they was the first noblemen in the land.

" It would be a good thing if these sort of goings on could be stopped. It's half the parents' fault; for if a gal can't get a living, they turns her out into the streets, and then what's to become of her? I'm sure the gals, if they was married, would be happier, because they couldn't be beat worse. And if they was married, they'd get a nice home about 'em; whereas, if they's only living together, they takes a furnished room. I'm sure, too, that it's a bad plan; for I've heerd the gals themselves say, 'Ah! I wish I'd never seed Jack' (or Tom, or whatever it is); 'I'm sure I'd never be half so bad but for him.'

"Only last night father was talking about religion. We often talks about religion. Father has told me that God made the world, and I've heerd him talk about the first man and woman as was made and lived—it must be more than a hundred years ago—but I don't like to speak on what I don't know. Father, too, has told me about our Saviour what was nailed on a cross to suffer for such poor people as we is. Father has told us, too, about his giving a great many poor people a penny loaf and a bit of fish each, which proves him to have been a very kind gentleman. The Ten Commandments was made by him, I've heerd say, and he performed them too among other miracles. Yes! this is part of what our Saviour tells us. We are to forgive everybody, and do nobody no injury. I don't think I could forgive an enemy if she injured me very much; I'm sure I don't know why I couldn't, unless it is that I'm poor, and never learnt to do it. If a gal stole my shawl and didn't return it back or give me the value on it, I couldn't forgive her; but if she told me she lost it off her back, I shouldn't be so hard on her. We poor gals ain't very religious, but we are better than the men. We all of us thanks God for everything—even for a fine day; as for sprats, we always says they're God's blessing for the poor, and thinks it hard of the Lord Mayor not to let 'em come in afore the ninth of November, just because he wants to dine off them—which he always do. Yes, we knows for certain that they eats plenty of sprats at the Lord Mayor's 'blanket.' They say in the Bible that the world was made in six days: the beasts, the birds, the fish, and all—and sprats was among them in coorse. There was only one house at that time as was made, and that was the Ark for Adam and Eve and their family. It seems very wonderful indeed how all this world was done so quick. I should have thought that England alone would have took double the time; shouldn't you, sir? But then it says in the Bible, God Almighty's a just and true God, and in coorse time would be nothing to him. When a good person is dying, we says, 'The Lord has called upon him, and he must go,' but I can't think what it means, unless it is that an angel comes—like when we're a-dreaming—and tells the party he's wanted in heaven. I know where heaven is; it's above the clouds, and they're placed there to prevent us seeing into it. That's where all the good people go, but I'm afeerd,"—she continued solemnly—

"there's very few costers among the angels— 'specially those as deceives poor gals.

"No, I don't think this world could well go on for ever. There's a great deal of ground in it, certainly, and it seems very strong at present; but they say there's to be a flood on the earth, and earthquakes, and that will destroy it. The earthquake ought to have took place some time ago, as people tells me, but I never heerd any more about it. If we cheats in the streets, I know we shan't go to Heaven; but it's very hard upon us, for if we didn't cheat we couldn't live, profits is so bad. It's the same with the shops, and I suppose the young men there won't go to Heaven neither; but if people won't give the money, both costers and tradesmen must cheat, and that's very hard. Why, look at apples! customers want them for less than they cost us, and so we are forced to shove in bad ones as well as good ones; and if we're to suffer for that, it does seem to me dreadful cruel."

Curious and extravagant as this statement may perhaps appear to the uninitiated, nevertheless it is here given as it was spoken; and it was spoken with an earnestness that proved the poor girl looked upon it as a subject, the solemnity of which forced her to be truthful.

Of Costermongers and Thieves.

Concerning the connection of these two classes I had the following account from a costermonger: "I've known the coster trade for twelve years, and never knew thieves go out a costering as a cloak; they may have done so, but I very much doubt it. Thieves go for an idle life, and costermongering don't suit them. Our chaps don't care a d—n who they associate with,—if they're thieves they meet 'em all the same, or anything that way. But costers buy what they call 'a gift,'—may-be it's a watch or coat wot's been stolen—from any that has it to sell. A man will say: 'If you've a few shillings, you may make a good thing of it. Why this identical watch is only twenty shillings, and it's worth fifty;' so if the coster has money, he buys. Thieves will get 3d. where a mechanic or a coster will earn ½d., and the most ignorant of our people has a queer sort of respect for thieves, because of the money they make. Poverty's as much despised among costers as among other people. People that's badly off among us are called 'cursed.' In bad weather it's common for costers to 'curse themselves,' as they call having no trade. 'Well, I'm cursed,' they say when they can make no money. It's a common thing among them to shout after any one they don't like, that's reduced, 'Well, ain't you cursed?'" The costers, I am credibly informed, gamble a great deal with the wealthier class of thieves, and win of them the greater part of the money they get.

Of the more provident Costermongers.

Concerning this head, I give the statement of a man whose information I found fully con-

firmed:—" We are not such a degraded set as
some believe; sir, but a living doesn't tumble
into a man's mouth, now a days. A good
many of us costers rises into greengrocers and
coal-sheds, and still carries on their rounds as
costers, all the same. Why, in Lock's-fields,
I could show you twenty such, and you'd find
them very decent men, sir—very. There's one
man I know, that's risen that way, who is worth
hundreds of pounds, and keeps his horse and
cart like a gentleman. They rises to be voters,
and they all vote liberal. Some marry the better
kind of servants, — such servant-maids as
would'nt marry a rag and bottle shop, but
doesn't object to a coal shed. It's mostly
younger men that manages this. As far as I
have observed, these costers, after they has
settled and got to be housekeepers, don't turn
their backs on their old mates. They'd have a
nice life of it if they did—yes! a very nice life."

OF THE HOMES OF THE COSTERMONGERS.

THE costermongers usually reside in the courts
and alleys in the neighbourhood of the different
street-markets. They themselves designate the
locality where, so to speak, a colony of their
people has been established, a "coster district,"
and the entire metropolis is thus parcelled out,
almost as systematically as if for the purposes
of registration. These costermonger districts
are as follows, and are here placed in the order
of the numerical importance of the residents :

The New Cut (Lambeth).	Ratcliffe Highway.
Whitecross-street.	Lisson-grove.
Leather-lane.	Petticoat and Rosemary-
The Brill, Somers' Town.	lane.
Whitechapel.	Marylebone-lane.
Camberwell.	Oxford-street.
Walworth.	Rotherhithe.
Peckham.	Deptford.
Bermondsey.	Dockhead.
The Broadway, West-	Greenwich.
minster.	Commercial-road (East).
Shoreditch.	Pop'ar.
Paddington and Edge-	Limehouse.
ware Road.	Bethnal-green.
Tottenham-court Road.	Hackney-road.
Drury-lane.	Kingsland.
Old-street Road.	Camden Town.
Clare Market.	

The homes of the costermongers in these
places, may be divided into three classes ; firstly,
those who, by having a regular trade or by prudent economy, are enabled to live in comparative ease and plenty ; secondly, those who, from
having a large family or by imprudent expenditure, are, as it were, struggling with the world ;
and thirdly, those who for want of stock-money,
or ill success in trade are nearly destitute.

The first home I visited was that of an old
woman, who with the assistance of her son and
girls, contrived to live in a most praiseworthy
and comfortable manner. She and all her
family were teetotallers, and may be taken as a
fair type of the thriving costermonger.

As I ascended a dark flight of stairs, a savory
smell of stew grew stronger at each step I
mounted. The woman lived in a large airy
room on the first floor ("the drawing-room")

as she told me laughing at her own joke), well
lighted by a clean window, and I found her
laying out the savory smelling dinner looking
most temptingly clean. The floor was as white
as if it had been newly planed, the coke fire
was bright and warm, making the lid of the
tin saucepan on it rattle up and down as the
steam rushed out. The wall over the fire-place
was patched up to the ceiling with little square
pictures of saints, and on the mantel-piece,
between a row of bright tumblers and wine
glasses filled with odds and ends, stood glazed
crockeryware images of Prince Albert and M.
Jullien. Against the walls, which were papered
with "hangings" of four different patterns and
colours, were hung several warm shawls, and in
the band-box, which stood on the stained chest
of drawers, you could tell that the Sunday
bonnet was stowed safely away from the dust.
A turn-up bedstead thrown back, and covered
with a many-coloured patch-work quilt, stood
opposite to a long dresser with its mugs and
cups dangling from the hooks, and the clean
blue plates and dishes ranged in order at the
back. There were a few bushel baskets piled
up in one corner, " but the apples smelt so," she
said, " they left them in a stable at night."

By the fire sat the woman's daughter, a
pretty meek-faced gray-eyed girl of sixteen,
who "was home nursing" for a cold. "Steve"
(her boy) I was informed, was out working.
With his help, the woman assured me, she could
live very comfortably—" God be praised ! " and
when he got the barrow he was promised, she
gave me to understand, that their riches were to
increase past reckoning. Her girl too was to be
off at work as soon as sprats came in. "Its on
Lord Mayor's-day they comes in," said a neighbour who had rushed up to see the strange
gentleman, "they says he has 'em on his table,
but I never seed 'em. They never gives us the
pieces, no not even the heads," and every one
laughed to their utmost. The good old dame
was in high spirits, her dark eyes sparkling as
she spoke about her "Steve." The daughter in
a little time lost her bashfulness, and informed
me "that one of the Polish refugees was
a-courting Mrs. M —— , who had given him a
pair of black eyes."

On taking my leave I was told by the mother
that their silver gilt Dutch clock—with its glass
face and blackleaded weights—"was the best
one in London, and might be relied on with the
greatest safety."

As a specimen of the dwellings of the struggling costers, the following may be cited :

The man, a tall, thick-built, almost good-
looking fellow, with a large fur cap on his head,
lived with his family in a front kitchen, and
as there were, with his mother-in-law, five
persons, and only one bed, I was somewhat
puzzled to know where they could all sleep.
The barrow standing on the railings over the
window, half shut out the light, and when any
one passed there was a momentary shadow
thrown over the room, and a loud rattling of the

iron gratings above that completely prevented all conversation. When I entered, the mother-in-law was reading aloud one of the threepenny papers to her son, who lolled on the bed, that with its curtains nearly filled the room. There was the usual attempt to make the fireside comfortable. The stone sides had been well whitened, and the mantel-piece decorated with its small tin trays, tumblers, and a piece of looking-glass. A cat with a kitten were seated on the hearth-rug in front. "They keeps the varmint away," said the woman, stroking the "puss," "and gives a look of home." By the drawers were piled up four bushel baskets, and in a dark corner near the bed stood a tall measure full of apples that scented the room. Over the head, on a string that stretched from wall to wall, dangled a couple of newly-washed shirts, and by the window were two stone barrels, for lemonade, when the coster visited the fairs and races.

Whilst we were talking, the man's little girl came home. For a poor man's child she was dressed to perfection; her pinafore was clean, her face shone with soap, and her tidy cotton print gown had clearly been newly put on that morning. She brought news that "Janey" was coming home from auntey's, and instantly a pink cotton dress was placed by the mother-in-law before the fire to air. (It appeared that Janey was out at service, and came home once a week to see her parents and take back a clean frock.) Although these people were living, so to speak, in a cellar, still every endeavour had been made to give the home a look of comfort. The window, with its paper-patched panes, had a clean calico blind. The side-table was dressed up with yellow jugs and cups and saucers, and the band-boxes had been stowed away on the flat top of the bedstead. All the chairs, which were old fashioned mahogany ones, had sound backs and bottoms.

Of the third class, or the very poor, I chose the following "type" out of the many others that presented themselves. The family here lived in a small slanting-roofed house, partly stripped of its tiles. More than one half of the small leaden squares of the first-floor window were covered with brown paper, puffing out and crackling in the wind, while through the greater part of the others were thrust out ball-shaped bundles of rags, to keep out the breeze. The panes that did remain were of all shapes and sizes, and at a distance had the appearance of yellow glass, they were so stained with dirt. I opened a door with a number chalked on it, and groped my way up a broken tottering staircase.

It took me some time after I had entered the apartment before I could get accustomed to the smoke, that came pouring into the room from the chimney. The place was filled with it, curling in the light, and making every thing so indistinct that I could with difficulty see the white mugs ranged in the corner-cupboard, not three yards from me. When the wind was in the north, or when it rained, it was always that way, I was told, "but otherwise," said an old

dame about sixty, with long grisly hair spreading over her black shawl, "it is pretty good for that."

On a mattrass, on the floor, lay a pale-faced girl—"eighteen years old last twelfth-cake day" —her drawn-up form showing in the patch-work counterpane that covered her. She had just been confined, and the child had died! A little straw, stuffed into an old tick, was all she had to lie upon, and even that had been given up to her by the mother until she was well enough to work again. To shield her from the light of the window, a cloak had been fastened up slantingly across the panes; and on a string that ran along the wall was tied, amongst the bonnets, a clean nightcap—"against the doctor came," as the mother, curtsying, informed me. By the side of the bed, almost hidden in the dark shade, was a pile of sieve baskets, crowned by the flat shallow that the mother "worked" with.

The room was about nine feet square, and furnished a home for three women. The ceiling slanted like that of a garret, and was the colour of old leather, excepting a few rough white patches, where the tenants had rudely mended it. The white light was easily seen through the laths, and in one corner a large patch of the paper looped down from the wall. One night the family had been startled from their sleep by a large mass of mortar—just where the roof bulged in—falling into the room. "We never want rain water," the woman told me, "for we can catch plenty just over the chimney-place."

They had made a carpet out of three or four old mats. They were "obligated to it, for fear of dropping anything through the boards into the donkey stables in the parlour underneath. But we only pay ninepence a week rent," said the old woman, "and mustn't grumble."

The only ornament in the place was on the mantel-piece—an old earthenware sugar-basin, well silvered over, that had been given by the eldest girl when she died, as a remembrance to her mother. Two cracked tea-cups, on their inverted saucers, stood on each side, and dressed up the fire-side into something like tidiness. The chair I sat on was by far the best out of the three in the room, and that had no back, and only half its quantity of straw.

The parish, the old woman told me, allowed her 1s. a week and two loaves. But the doctor ordered her girl to take sago and milk, and she was many a time sorely puzzled to get it. The neighbours helped her a good deal, and often sent her part of their unsold greens;—even if it was only the outer leaves of the cabbages, she was thankful for them. Her other girl—a big-boned wench, with a red shawl crossed over her bosom, and her black hair parted on one side— did all she could, and so they lived on. "As long as they kept out of the 'big house' (the workhouse) she would not complain."

I never yet beheld so much destitution borne with so much content. Verily the acted philosophy of the poor is a thing to make those who write and preach about it hide their heads.

THE OYSTER STALL.

"Penny a lot, Oysters! Penny a lot!"

[*From a Daguerreotype by* BEARD.]

OF THE DRESS OF THE COSTERMONGERS.

FROM the homes of the costermongers we pass
to a consideration of their dress.

The costermonger's ordinary costume partakes
of the durability of the warehouseman's, with the
quaintness of that of the stable-boy. A well-
to-do " coster," when dressed for the day's
work, usually wears a small cloth cap, a little
on one side. A close-fitting worsted tie-up
skull-cap, is very fashionable, just now, among
the class, and ringlets at the temples are looked
up to as the height of elegance. Hats they
never wear—excepting on Sunday—on account
of their baskets being frequently carried on
their heads. Coats are seldom indulged in;
their waistcoats, which are of a broad-ribbed
corduroy, with fustian back and sleeves, being
made as long as a groom's, and buttoned
up nearly to the throat. If the corduroy
be of a light sandy colour, then plain brass, or
sporting buttons, with raised fox's or stag's heads
upon them—or else black bone-buttons, with a
flower-pattern—ornament the front; but if the
cord be of a dark rat-skin hue, then mother-of-
pearl buttons are preferred. Two large pockets
—sometimes four—with huge flaps or lappels,
like those in a shooting-coat, are commonly
worn. If the costermonger be driving a good
trade and have his set of regular customer i, he
will sport a blue cloth jacket, similar in cut to
the cord above described; but this is
looked upon as an extravagance of the highest
order, for the slime and scales of the fish stick to
the sleeves and shoulders of the garment, so as
to spoil the appearance of it in a short time. The
fashionable stuff for trousers, at the present, is a
dark-coloured " cable cord," and they are made
to fit tightly at the knee and swell gradually
until they reach the boot, which they nearly
cover. Velveteen is now seldom worn, and knee-
breeches are quite out of date. Those who deal
wholly in fish wear a blue serge apron, either
hanging down or tucked up round their waist.
The costermonger, however, prides himself most
of all upon his neckerchief and boots. Men, women, boys and girls, all have a passion for these
articles. The man who does not wear his silk
neckerchief—his " King's-man " as it is called
—is known to be in desperate circumstances;
the inference being that it has gone to supply
the morning's stock-money. A yellow flower
on a green ground, or a red and blue pattern, is
at present greatly in vogue. The women wear
their kerchiefs tucked-in under their gowns,
and the men have theirs wrapped loosely round
the neck, with the ends hanging over their
waistcoats. Even if a costermonger has two or
three silk handkerchiefs by him already, he seldom hesitates to buy another, when tempted
with a bright showy pattern hanging from a
Field-lane door-post.

The costermonger's love of a good strong boot
is a singular prejudice that runs throughout the
whole class. From the father to the youngest
child, all will be found well shod. So strong is

their predilection in this respect, that a costermonger may be immediately known by a glance
at his feet. He will part with everything rather
than his boots, and to wear a pair of second-
hand ones, or "translators" (as they are called), is
felt as a bitter degradation by them all. Among
the men, this pride has risen to such a pitch,
that many will have their upper-leathers tastily
ornamented, and it is not uncommon to see the
younger men of this class with a heart or a
thistle, surrounded by a wreath of roses, worked
below the instep, on their boots. The general
costume of the women or girls is a black
velveteen or straw bonnet, with a few ribbons or
flowers, and almost always a net cap fitting
closely to the cheek. The silk " King's-man "
covering their shoulders, is sometimes tucked
into the neck of the printed cotton-gown, and
sometimes the ends are brought down outside
to the apron-strings. Silk dresses are never
worn by them—they rather despise such articles. The petticoats are worn short, ending at
the ankles, just high enough to show the
whole of the much-admired boots. Coloured,
or " illustrated shirts," as they are called, are
especially objected to by the men.

On the Sunday no costermonger will, if he
can possibly avoid it, wheel a barrow. If a
shilling be an especial object to him, he may,
perhaps, take his shallow and head-basket as
far as Chalk-farm, or some neighbouring resort;
but even then he objects strongly to the Sun-
day-trading. They leave this to the Jews and
Irish, who are always willing to earn a penny—
as they say.

The prosperous coster *will* have his holiday
on the Sunday, and, if possible, his Sunday suit
as well—which usually consists of a rough
beaver hat, brown Petersham, with velvet
facings of the same colour, and cloth trousers,
with stripes down the side. The women, generally, manage to keep by them a cotton gown
of a bright showy pattern, and a new shawl.
As one of the craft said to me—" Costers likes
to see their gals and wives look lady-like when
they takes them out." Such of the costers as
are not in a flourishing way of business, seldom make any alteration in their dress on the
Sunday.

There are but five tailors in London who
make the garb proper to costermongers ; one of
these is considered somewhat " slop," or as a
coster called him, a " springer-up."

This springer-up is blamed by some of the
costermongers, who condemn him for employing women at reduced wages. A whole court of
costermongers, I was assured, would withdraw
their custom from a tradesman, if one of their
body, who had influence among them, showed
that the tradesman was unjust to his workpeople.
The tailor in question issues bills after the following fashion. I give one verbatim, merely
withholding the address for obvious reasons :

" ONCE TRY YOU'LL COME AGAIN.
Slap-up Tog and out-and-out Kicksies Builder.
Mr. —— nabs the chance of putting his cus-

tomers awake, that he has just made his escape from Russia, not forgetting to clap his mawleys upon some of the right sort of Ducks, to make single and double backed Slops for gentlemen in black, when on his return home he was stunned to find one of the top manufacturers of Manchester had cut his lucky and stepped off to the Swan Stream, leaving behind him a valuable stock of Moleskins, Cords, Velveteens, Plushes, Swandowns, &c., and I having some ready in my kick, grabbed the chance, and stepped home with my swag, and am now safe landed at my crib. I can turn out toggery of every description very slap up, at the following low prices for

Ready Gilt—Tick being no go.

Upper Benjamins, built on a downey plan, a monarch to half a finnuff. Slap up Velveteen Togs, lined with the same, 1 pound 1 quarter and a peg. Moleskin ditto, any colour, lined with the same, 1 couter. A pair of Kerseymere Kicksies, any colour, built very slap up, with the artful dodge, a canary. Pair of stout Cord ditto, built in the ' Melton Mowbray' style, half a sov. Pair of very good broad Cord ditto, made very saucy, 9 bob and a kick. Pair of long sleeve Moleskin, all colours, built hanky-spanky, with a double fakement down the side and artful buttons at bottom, half a monarch. Pair of stout ditto, built very serious, 9 times. Pair of out-and-out fancy sleeve Kicksies, cut to drop down on the trotters, 2 bulls. Waist Togs, cut long, with moleskin back and sleeves, 10 peg. Blue Cloth ditto, cut slap, with pearl buttons, 14 peg. Mud Pipes, Knee Caps, and Trotter Cases, built very low.

" A decent allowance made to Seedy Swells, Tea Kettle Purgers, Head Robbers, and Flunkeys out of Collar.

" N.B. Gentlemen finding their own Broady can be accommodated."

Of the Diet and Drink of Costermongers.

It is less easy to describe the diet of costermongers than it is to describe that of many other of the labouring classes, for their diet, so to speak, is an " out-door diet." They breakfast at a coffee-stall, and (if all their means have been expended in purchasing their stock, and none of it be yet sold) they expend on the meal only 1*d.*, reserved for the purpose. For this sum they can procure a small cup of coffee, and two " thin " (that is to say two thin slices of bread and butter). For dinner— which on a week-day is hardly ever eaten at the costermonger's abode—they buy "block ornaments," as they call the small, dark-coloured pieces of meat exposed on the cheap butchers' blocks or counters. These they cook in a tap-room; half a pound costing 2*d.* If time be an object, the coster buys a hot pie or two; preferring fruit-pies when in season, and next to them meat-pies. " We never eat eel-pies," said one man to me, " because we know they're often made of large dead eels.

We, of all people, are not to be had that way. But the haristocrats eats 'em and never knows the difference." I did not hear that these men had any repugnance to meat-pies ; but the use of the dead eel happens to come within the immediate knowledge of the costermongers, who are, indeed, its purveyors. Saveloys, with a pint of beer, or a glass of "short" (neat gin) is with them another common week-day dinner. The costers make all possible purchases of street-dealers, and pride themselves in thus "sticking to their own." On Sunday, the costermonger, when not "cracked up," enjoys a good dinner at his own abode. This is always a joint—most frequently a shoulder or half-shoulder of mutton—and invariably with "lots of good taturs baked along with it." In the quality of their potatoes these people are generally particular.

The costermonger's usual beverage is beer, and many of them drink hard, having no other way of spending their leisure but in drinking and gambling. It is not unusual in "a good time," for a costermonger to spend 12*s.* out of every 20*s.* in beer and pleasure.

I ought to add, that the " single fellows," instead of living on "block ornaments" and the like, live, when doing well, on the best fare, at the "spiciest" cook-shops on their rounds, or in the neighbourhood of their residence.

There are some families of costermongers who have persevered in carrying out the principles of teetotalism. One man thought there might be 200 individuals, including men, women, and children, who practised total abstinence from intoxicating drinks. These parties are nearly all somewhat better off than their drinking companions. The number of teetotallers amongst the costers, however, was more numerous three or four years back.

Of the Cries, Rounds, and Days of Costermongers.

I shall now proceed to treat of the London costermongers' mode of doing business.

In the first place all the goods they sell are cried or "hawked," and the cries of the costermongers in the present day are as varied as the articles they sell. The principal ones, uttered in a sort of cadence, are now, "Ni-ew mackerel, 6 a shilling." ("I've got a good jacketing many a Sunday morning," said one dealer, "for waking people up with crying mackerel, but I've said, ' I must live while you sleep.' ") " Buy a pair of live soles, 3 pair for 6*d.*"—or, with a barrow, "Soles, 1*d.* a pair, 1*d.* a pair ;" " Plaice alive, alive, cheap ;" " Buy a pound crab, cheap ;" " Pine-apples, ½*d.* a slice ;" " Mussels a penny a quart ;" " Oysters, a penny a lot ;" " Salmon alive, 6*d.* a pound ;" " Cod alive, 2*d.* a pound ;" " Real Yarmouth bloaters, 2 a penny ;" " New herrings alive, 16 a groat " (this is the loudest cry of any) ; " Penny a bunch turnips " (the same with greens, cabbages, &c.); " All new nuts, 1*d.* half-pint ;" " Oranges, 2 a penny ;" " All large and alive-O, new sprats, O, 1*d.* a plate ;"

"Wi-ild Hampshire rabbits, 2 a shilling;" "Cherry ripe, 2d. a pound;" "Fine ripe plums, 1d. a pint;" "Ing-uns, a penny a quart;" "Eels, 3lbs. a shilling—large live eels 3lbs. a shilling."

The continual calling in the streets is very distressing to the voice. One man told me that it had broken his, and that very often while out he lost his voice altogether. "They seem to have no breath," the men say, "after calling for a little while." The repeated shouting brings on a hoarseness, which is one of the peculiar characteristics of hawkers in general. The costers mostly go out with a boy to cry their goods for them. If they have two or three halloo-ing together, it makes more noise than one, and the boys can shout better and louder than the men. The more noise they can make in a place the better they find their trade. Street-selling has been so bad lately that many have been obliged to have a drum for their bloaters, "to drum the fish off," as they call it.

In the second place, the costermongers, as I said before, have mostly their little bit of a "round;" that is, they go only to certain places; and if they don't sell their goods they "work back" the same way again. If they visit a respectable quarter, they confine themselves to the mews near the gentlemen's houses. They generally prefer the poorer neighbourhoods. They go down or through almost all the courts and alleys—and avoid the better kind of streets, unless with lobsters, rabbits, or onions. If they have anything inferior, they visit the low Irish districts—for the Irish people, they say, want only quantity, and care nothing about quality—*that* they don't study. But if they have any-thing they wish to make a price of, they seek out the mews, and try to get it off among the gentlemen's coachmen, for *they* will have what is good; or else they go among the residences of mechanics,—for their wives, they say, like good-living as well as the coachmen. Some costers, on the other hand, go chance rounds.

Concerning the busiest days of the week for the coster's trade, they say Wednesdays and Fridays are the best, because they are regular fish days. These two days are considered to be those on which the poorer classes generally run short of money. Wednesday night is called "draw night" among some mechanics and labourers —that is, they then get a portion of their wages in advance, and on Friday they run short as well as on the Wednesday, and have to make shift for their dinners. With the few halfpence they have left, they are glad to pick up anything cheap, and the street-fishmonger never refuses an offer. Besides, he can supply them with a cheaper dinner than any other person. In the season the poor generally dine upon herrings. The poorer classes live mostly on fish, and the "dropped" and "rough" fish is bought chiefly for the poor. The fish-huckster has no respect for persons, however; one assured me that if Prince Halbert was to stop him in the street to buy a pair of soles of him, he'd as soon sell him a "rough pair as any

other man—indeed, I'd take in my own father," he added, "if he wanted to deal with me." Saturday is the worst day of all for fish, for then the poor people have scarcely anything at all to spend; Saturday night, however, the street-seller takes more money than at any other time in the week.

OF THE COSTERMONGERS ON THEIR COUNTRY ROUNDS.

SOME costermongers go what they term "country rounds" and they speak of their country ex-peditions as if they were summer excursions of mere pleasure. They are generally variations from a life growing monotonous. It was com-puted for me that at present three out of every twenty costermongers "take a turn in the coun-try" at least once a year. Before the prevalence of railways twice as many of these men carried their speculations in fish, fruit, or vegetables to a country mart. Some did so well that they never returned to London. Two for instance, after a country round, settled at Salisbury; they are now regular shopkeepers, "and very respect-able, too," was said to me, "for I believe they are both pretty tidy off for money; and are growing rich." The railway communication supplies the local-dealer with fish, vegetables, or any perishable article, with such rapidity and cheapness that the London itinerant's occupation in the towns and villages about the metropolis is now half gone.

In the following statement by a costermonger, the mode of life on a country round, is detailed with something of an assumption of metropolitan superiority.

"It was fine times, sir, ten year back, aye, and five year back, in the country, and it ain't so bad now, if a man's known. It depends on that now far more than it did, and on a man's knowing how to work a village. Why, I can tell you if it wasn't for such as me, there's many a man working on a farm would never taste such a nice thing as a fresh herring—never, sir. It's a feast at a poor country labourer's place, when he springs six-penn'orth of fresh herrings, some for supper, and some in salt for next day. I've taken a shillings'-worth to a farmer's door of a darkish night in a cold autumn, and they'd a warm and good dish for supper, and looked on me as a sort of friend. We carry them relishes from London; and they like London relishes, for we know how to set them off. I've fresh herringed a whole village near Guildford, first thing in the morning. I've drummed round Guildford too, and done well. I've waked up Kingston with herrings. I've been as welcome as anything to the soldiers in the barracks at Brentwood, and Romford, and Maidstone with my fresh herrings; for they're good customers. In two days I've made 2l. out of 10s. worth of fresh herrings, bought at Billingsgate. I always lodge at a public-house in the country; so do all of us, for the publicans are customers. We are well received at the public-houses; some of us go there for the handiness of the 'lush.' I've done pretty well with red herrings in the country. A barrel holds (say) 800. We sell the barrels at 6*d.* a piece, and the old women fight after them. They pitch and tar them, to make water-barrels. More of us would settle in the country, only there's no life there."

The most frequented round is from Lambeth to Wandsworth, Kingston, Richmond, Guildford, and Farnham. The costermonger is then " sold out," as he calls it,—he has disposed of his stock, and returns by the way which is most lightly tolled, no matter if the saving of 1*d.* or 2*d.* entail some miles extra travelling. " It cost me 15*d.* for tolls from Guildford for an empty cart and donkey," said a costermonger just up from the country.

Another round is to Croydon, Reigate, and the neighbourhoods; another to Edgeware, Kilburn, Watford, and Barnet; another to Maidstone; but the costermonger, if he starts trading at a distance, as he now does frequently, has his barrow and goods sent down by railway to such towns as Maidstone, so he saves the delay and cost of a donkey-cart. A "mate" sees to the transmission of the goods from London, the owner walking to Maidstone to be in readiness to " work" them immediately he receives them. " The railway's an ease and a saving," I was told; " I've got a stock sent for 2*s.*, and a donkey's keep would cost that for the time it would be in travelling. There's 5,000 of us, I think, might get a living in the country, if we stuck to it entirely."

If the country enterprise be a failure, the men sometimes abandon it in " a pet," sell their goods at any loss, and walk home, generally getting drunk as the first step to their return. Some have been known to pawn their barrow on the road for drink. This they call " doing queer."

In summer the costermongers carry plums, peas, new potatoes, cucumbers, and quantities of pickling vegetables, especially green walnuts, to the country. In winter their commodities are onions, fresh and red herrings, and sprats. " I don't know how it is," said one man to me, " but we sell ing-uns and all sorts of fruits and vegetables, cheaper than they can buy them where they're grown; and green walnuts, too, when you'd think they had only to be knocked off a tree."

Another costermonger told me that, in the country, he and his mates attended every dance or other amusement, " if it wasn't too respectable." Another said: " If I'm idle in the country on a Sunday, I never go to church. I never was in a church; I don't know why, for my silk handkerchief's worth more than one of their smock-frocks, and is quite as respectable."

Some costermongers confine their exertions to the fairs and races, and many of them are connected with the gipsies, who are said to be the usual receivers of the stolen handkerchiefs at such places.

Of the Earnings of Costermongers.

THE earnings of the costermonger—the next subject of inquiry that, in due order, presents itself—vary as much as in more fashionable callings, for he is greatly dependent on the season, though he may be little affected by London being full or empty.

Concurrent testimony supplied me with the following estimate of their earnings. I cite the average earnings (apart from any charges or drawbacks), of the most staple commodities:

In January and February the costers generally sell fish. In these months the wealthier of the street fishmongers, or those who can always command "money to go to market," enjoy a kind of monopoly. The wintry season renders the supply of fish dearer and less regular, so that the poorer dealers cannot buy "at first hand," and sometimes cannot be supplied at all; while the others monopolise the fish, more or less, and will not sell it to any of the other street-dealers until a profit has been realised out of their own regular customers, and the demand partially satisfied. " Why, I've known one man sell 10*l.* worth of fish — most of it mackarel — at his stall in Whitecross-street," said a costermonger to me, " and all in one snowy day, in last January. It was very stormy at that time, and fish came in unregular, and he got a haul. I've known him sell 2*l.* worth in an hour, and once 2*l.* 10*s.* worth, for I then helped at his stall. If people has dinner parties they must have fish, and gentlemen's servants came to buy. The *average* earnings however of those that "go rounds" in these months are computed not to exceed 8*s.* a week; Monday and Saturday being days of little trade in fish.

" March is dreadful," said an itinerant fish seller to me; " we don't average, I'm satisfied, more nor 4*s.* a week. I've had my barrow idle for a week sometimes — at home every day, though it had to be paid for, all the same. At the latter end of March, if it's fine, it's 1*s.* a week better, because there's flower roots in— ' all a-growing,' you know, sir. And that lasts until April, and we then make above 6*s.* a week. I've heard people say when I've cried 'all a-growing' on a fine-ish day, 'Aye, now summer's a-coming.' I wish you may get it, says I to myself; for I've studied the seasons."

In May the costermonger's profit is greater. He vends fresh fish—of which there is a greater supply and a greater demand, and the fine and often not very hot weather insures its freshness— and he sells dried herrings and "roots" (as they are called) such as wall-flowers and stocks. The average earnings then are from 10*s.* to 12*s.* a week.

In June, new potatoes, peas, and beans tempt the costermongers' customers, and then his earnings rise to 1*l.* a week. In addition to this 1*l.*, if the season allow, a costermonger at the end of the week, I was told by an experienced hand, " will earn an extra 10*s.* if he has anything of a round," " Why, I've cleared thirty shillings myself," he added, " on a Saturday night."

In July cherries are the principal article of traffic, and then the profit varies from 4*s.* to 8*s.*

a day, weather permitting, or 30s. a week on a low average. On my inquiry if they did not sell fish in that month, the answer was, "No, sir; we pitch fish to the ——; we stick to cherries, strawberries, raspberries, and ripe currants and gooseberries. Potatoes is getting good and cheap then, and so is peas. Many a round's worth a crown every day of the week."

In August, the chief trading is in Orleans plums, green-gages, apples and pears, and in this month the earnings are from 5s. to 6s. a day. [I may here remark that the costermongers care little to deal in either vegetables or fish, "when the fruit's in," but they usually carry a certain supply of vegetables all the year round, for those customers who require them.]

In September apples are vended, and about 2s. 6d. a day made.

In October "the weather gets cold," I was told, "and the apples gets fewer, and the day's work's over at four; we then deals most in fish, such as soles; there's a good bit done in oysters, and we may make 1s. or 1s. 6d. a day, but it's uncertain."

In November fish and vegetables are the chief commodities, and then from 1s. to 1s. 6d. a day is made; but in the latter part of the month an extra 6d. or 1s. a day may be cleared, as sprats come in and sell well when newly introduced.

In December the trade is still principally in fish, and 12d. or 18d. a day is the costermonger's earnings. Towards the close of the month he makes rather more, as he deals in new oranges and lemons, holly, ivy, &c., and in Christmas week he makes 3s. or 4s. a day.

These calculations give an average of about 14s. 6d. a week, when a man pursues his trade regularly. One man calculated it for me at 15s. average the year through—that is supposing, of course, that the larger earnings of the summer are carefully put by to eke out the winter's income. This, I need hardly say, is never done. Prudence is a virtue, which is comparatively unknown to the London costermongers. They have no knowledge of savings'-banks; and to expect that they themselves should keep their money by them untouched for months (even if they had the means of so doing) is simply to expect impossibilities—to look for the continued withstanding of temptation among a class who are unused to the least moral or prudential restraint.

Some costers, I am told, make upwards of 30s. a week all the year round; but allowing for cessations in the street-trade, through bad weather, neglect, ill-health, or casualty of any kind, and taking the more prosperous costers with the less successful—the English with the Irish—the men with the women—perhaps 10s. a week may be a fair average of the earnings of the entire body the year through.

These earnings, I am assured, were five years ago at least 25 per cent higher; some said they made half as much again: "I can't make it out how it is," said one man, "but I remember that I could go out and sell twelve bushel of

fruit in a day, when sugar was dear, and now, when sugar's cheap, I can't sell three bushel on the same round. Perhaps we want thinning."

Such is the state of the working-classes; say all the costers, they have little or no money to spend. "Why, I can assure you," declared one of the parties from whom I obtained much important information, "there's my missis—she sits at the corner of the street with fruit. Eight years ago she would have taken 8s. out of that street on a Saturday, and last Saturday week she had one bushel of apples, which cost 1s. 6d. She was out from ten in the morning till ten at night, and all she took that day was 1s. 7½d. Go to whoever you will, you will hear much upon the same thing." Another told me, "The costers are often obliged to sell the things for what they gave for them. The people haven't got money to lay out with them—they tell us so; and if they are poor we must be poor too. If we can't get a profit upon what goods we buy with our stock-money, let it be our own or anybody's else, we are compelled to live upon it, and when that's broken into, we must either go to the workhouse or starve. If we go to the workhouse, they'll give us a piece of dry bread, and abuse us worse than dogs." Indeed, the whole course of my narratives shows how the costers generally— though far from universally—complain of the depressed state of their trade. The following statement was given to me by a man who, for twelve years, had been a stall-keeper in a street-market. It shows to what causes he (and I found others express similar opinions) attributes the depression:—

" I never knew things so bad as at present— never! I had six prime cod-fish, weighing 15lbs. to 20lbs. each, yesterday and the day before, and had to take two home with me last night, and lost money on the others—besides all my time, and trouble, and expense. I had 100 herrings, too, that cost 3s.—prime quality, and I only sold ten out of them in a whole day. I had two pads of soles, sir, and lost 4s.—that is one pad—by them. I took only 4s. the first day I laid in this stock, and only 2s. 6d. the next; I then had to sell for anything I could get, and throw some away. Yet, people say mine's a lazy, easy life. I think the fall off is owing to meat being so cheap, 'cause people buy that rather than my goods, as they think there's more stay in it. I'm afeard things will get worse too." (He then added by way of *sequitur*, though it is difficult to follow the reasoning,) "If this here is free-trade, then to h— with it, I say!"

OF THE CAPITAL AND INCOME OF THE COSTERMONGERS.

I shall now pass, from the consideration of the individual earnings, to the income and capital of the entire body. Great pains have been taken to ensure exactitude on these points, and the following calculations are certainly below the mark. In order to be within due bounds, I will take the costermongers, exclusive of their wives and families, at 10,000, whereas it won'd appear that their numbers are upwards of 11,000.

1,000 carts, at 3*l.* 3*s.* each.	£3,150
[Donkeys, and occasionally ponies, are harnessed to barrows.]	
5,000 barrows, at 2*l.* each . . .	10,000
1,500 donkeys, at 1*l.* 5*s.* each . . .	1,875
[One intelligent man thought there were 2,000 donkeys, but I account that in excess.]	
200 ponies, at 5*l.* each	1,000
[Some of these ponies, among the very first-class men, are worth 20*l.*: one was sold by a coster for 30*l.*]	
1,700 sets of harness, at 5*s.* each . .	425
[All calculated as worn and second-hand.]	
4,000 baskets (or shallows), at 1*s.* each	200
3,500 stalls or standings, at 5*s.* each .	875
[The stall and barrow men have generally baskets to be used when required.]	
10,000 weights, scales, and measures, at 2*s.* 6*d.* each	1,250
[It is difficult to estimate this item with exactitude. Many averaged the value at 3*s.* 4*d.*]	
Stock-money for 10,000 costers, at 10*s.* each.	5,000
Total capital . . . £24,135	

Upwards of 24,000*l.*, then, at the most moderate computation, represents the value of the animals, vehicles, and stock, belonging to the costermongers in the streets of London.

The keep of the donkeys is not here mixed up with their value, and I have elsewhere spoken of it.

The whole course of my narrative shows that the bulk of the property in the street goods, and in the appliances for their sale, is in the hands of usurers as well as of the costers. The following account shows the sum paid yearly by the London costermongers for the hire, rent, or interest (I have heard each word applied) of their barrows, weights, baskets, and stock:

Hire of 3,000 barrows, at 1*s.* 3*d.* a week £14,000	
Hire of 600 weights, scales, &c., at 1*s.* 6*d.* a week for 2, and 6*d.* a week for 10 months	1,020
Hire of 100 baskets, &c., at 6*d.* a week	6,500
Interest on 2,500*l.* stock-money, at 125*l.* per week	6,500
[Calculating at 1*s.* interest weekly for 20*s.*]	
Total paid for hire and interest £22,550	

Concerning the income of the entire body of costermongers in the metropolis, I estimate the earnings of the 10,000 costermongers, taking the average of the year, at 10*s.* weekly. My own observation, the result of my inquiries, confirmed by the opinion of some of the most intelligent of the costermongers, induce me to adopt this amount. It must be remembered, that if some costermongers do make 30*s.* a week through the year, others will not earn a fourth of it, and hence many of the complaints and sufferings of the class. Then there is the draw-

back in the sum paid for "hire," "interest," &c., by numbers of these people; so that it appears to me, that if we assume the income of the entire body—including Irish and English—to be 15*s.* a week per head in the summer, and 5*s.* a week each in the winter, as the two extremes, or a mean of 10*s.* a week all the year through, we shall not be far out either way. The aggregate earnings of the London costermongers, at this rate, are 5,000*l.* per week, or 260,000*l.* yearly. Reckoning that 30,000 individuals have to be supported out of this sum, it gives an average of 3*s.* 4*d.* a week per head.

But it is important to ascertain not only the earnings or aggregate amount of profit made by the London costermongers in the course of the year, but likewise their receipts, or aggregate amount of "takings," and thus to arrive at the gross sum of money annually laid out by the poorer classes of the metropolis in the matter of fish, fruit, and vegetables alone. Assuming that the average profits of the costermongers are at the rate of 25 per cent. (and this, I am satisfied, is a high estimate — for we should remember, that though cent. per cent. may be frequently obtained, still their "goods," being of a "perishable" nature, are as frequently lost or sold off at a "tremendous sacrifice"); assuming then, I say, that the *average* profits of the entire 10,000 individuals are 25 per cent on the cost-price of their stock, and that the aggregate amount of their profits or earnings is upwards of 260,000*l.*, it follows that the gross sum of money laid out with the London costers in the course of the twelvemonth is between 1,250,000*l.* and 1,500,000*l.* sterling—a sum so enormous as almost to make us believe that the tales of individual want are matters of pure fiction. Large, however, as the amount appears in the mass, still, if distributed among the families of the working men and the poorer class of Londoners, it will be found that it allows but the merest pittance per head per week for the consumption of those articles, which may be fairly said to constitute the staple commodities of the dinners and "desserts!" of the poor.

Of the Providence and Improvidence of Costermongers.

The costermongers, like all wandering tribes, have generally no foresight; only an exceptional few are provident—and these are mostly the more intelligent of the class—though some of the very ignorant do occasionally save. The providence of the more intelligent costermonger enables him in some few cases to become "a settled man," as I have before pointed out. He perhaps gets to be the proprietor of a coal-shed, with a greengrocery and potato business attached to it; and with the usual trade in oysters and ginger-beer. He may too, sometimes, have a sum of money in the savings'-bank, or he may invest it in the purchase of a lease of the premises he occupies, or expend it in furnishing the rooms of his house to let them out to single-men lodgers; or he may become an usurer, and lend out his money to his less provident brethren at 1040*l.* per cent. per annum ; or he may purchase largely at the markets, and engage youths to sell his surplus stock at half profits.

The provident costermonger, who has thus " got on in the world," is rarely speculative. He can hardly be induced to become a member of a "building" or "freehold land" society, for instance. He has been accustomed to an almost *immediate* return for his outlays, and distrusts any remote or contingent profit. A regular costermonger – or any one who has been a regular costermonger, in whatever trade he may be afterwards engaged—generally dies intestate, let his property be what it may ; but there is seldom any dispute as to the disposition of his effects : the widow takes possession of them, as a matter of course. If there be grown-up children, they may be estranged from home, and not trouble their heads about the matter ; or, if not estranged, an amicable arrangement is usually come to. The costermongers' dread of all courts of law, or of anything connected with the law, is only second to their hatred of the police.

The more ignorant costermonger, on the other hand, if he be of a saving turn, and have no great passion for strong drink or gaming, is often afraid to resort to the simple modes of investment which I have mentioned. He will rather keep money in his pocket; for, though it does not fructify there, at least it is safe. But this is only when provided with a donkey or pony "what suits ;" when not so provided, he will " suit himself" forthwith. If, however, he have saved a little money, and have a craving after gambling or amusements, he is sure at last to squander it that way. Such a man, without any craving for drink or gaming, will often continue to pay usuriously for the hire of his barrow, not suspecting that he is purchasing it over and over and over again, in his weekly payments. To suggest to him that he might place his money in a bank, is to satisfy him that he would be "had" in some way or other, as he believes all banks and public institutions to be connected with government, and the taxes, and the police. Were any one to advise a man of this class—and it must be remembered that I am speaking of the *ignorant* costers — to invest a spare 50*l.* (supposing he possessed it) in the "three per cents.," it would but provoke a snappish remark that he knew nothing about them, and would have nothing to do with them ; for he would be satisfied that there was " some cheatery at the bottom." If he could be made to understand what is meant by 3*l.* per centum per annum, he would be sure to be indignant at the robbery of giving only 7½*d.* for the use of 1*l.* for a whole year !

I may state, in conclusion, that a costermonger of the class I have been describing, mostly objects to give change for a five-pound note; he will sooner give credit—when he knows "the party" —than change, even if he have it. If, however, he feels compelled, rather than offend a regular customer, to take the note, he will not rest until he has obtained sovereigns for it at a neighbouring innkeeper's, or from some tradesman to whom he is known. " Sovereigns," said one man, and not a very ignorant man, to me, "is something to lay hold on ; a note ain't."

Moreover, should one of the more ignorant, having tastes for the beer-shop, &c., meet with "a great haul," or save 5*l.* by some continuous industry (which he will most likely set down as "luck"), he will spend it idly or recklessly in dissipation and amusement, regardless of the coming winter, whatever he may have suffered during the past. Nor, though they know, from the bitterest experience, that their earnings in the winter are not half those of the rest of the year, and that they are incapacitated from pursuing their trade in bad weather, do they endeavour to make the extra gains of their best time mitigate the want of the worst.

OF THE COSTERMONGERS IN BAD WEATHER AND DURING THE CHOLERA.

" THREE wet days," I was told by a clergyman, who is now engaged in selling stenographic cards in the streets, " will bring the greater part of 30,000 street-people to the brink of starvation." This statement, terrible as it is, is not exaggerated. The average number of wet days every year in London is, according to the records of the Royal Society, 161—that is to say, rain falls in the metropolis more than three days in each week, and very nearly every other day throughout the year. How precarious a means of living then must street-selling be !

When a costermonger cannot pursue his outdoor labour, he leaves it to the women and children to "work the public-houses," while he spends his time in the beer-shop. Here he gambles away his stock-money oft enough, "if the cards or the luck runs again him ;" or else he has to dip into his stock-money to support himself and his family. He must then borrow fresh capital at any rate of interest to begin again, and he begins on a small scale. If it be in the cheap and busy seasons, he may buy a pad of soles for 2*s.* 6*d.*, and clear 5*s.* on them, and that " sets him a-going again, and then he gets his silk handkerchief out of pawn, and goes as usual to market."

The sufferings of the costermongers during the prevalence of the cholera in 1849, were intense. Their customers generally relinquished the consumption of potatoes, greens, fruit, and fish ; indeed, of almost every article on the consumption of which the costermongers depend for his daily bread. Many were driven to apply to the parish ; " many had relief and many hadn't," I was told. Two young men, within the knowledge of one of my informants, became professional thieves, after enduring much destitution. It does not appear that the costermongers manifested any personal dread of the visitation of the cholera, or thought that their lives were imperilled : " We weren't a bit afraid," said one of them, " and, perhaps, that was the reason so few costers died of the cholera. I knew them all in Lambeth, I think, and I knew only one die of it, and he drank hard. Poor Waxy! he was a good fellow enough, and was well known in the Cut. But it was a terrible time for us, sir. It seems to me now like a shocking dream. Fish I could'nt sell a bit of ; the people had a perfect dread of it — all but the poor Irish, and there was no making a crust out of them. *They* had no dread of fish, however ; indeed, they reckon it a religious sort of living, living on fish,—but they *will* have ·· dirt cheap. We were in terrible distress all that time."

Of the Costermongers' Raffles.

In their relief of the sick, if relief it is to be called, the costermongers resort to an exciting means ; something is raffled, and the proceeds given to the sufferer. This mode is common to other working-classes; it partakes of the excitement of gambling, and is encouraged by the landlords of the houses to which the people resort. The landlord displays the terms of the raffle in his bar a few days before the occurrence, which is always in the evening. The raffle is not confined to the sick, but when any one of the class is in distress—that is to say, without stock-money, and unable to borrow it, —a raffle for some article of his is called at a public-house in the neighbourhood. Cards are printed, and distributed among his mates. The article, let it be whatever it may—perhaps a handkerchief— is put up at 6d. a member, and from twenty to forty members are got, according as the man is liked by his "mates," or as he has assisted others similarly situated. The paper of every raffle is kept by the party calling it, and before he puts his name down to a raffle for another party, he refers to the list of subscribers to *his* raffle, in order to see if the person ever assisted him. Raffles are very " critical things, the pint pots fly about wonderful sometimes"— to use the words of one of my informants. The party calling the raffle is expected to take the chair, if he can write down the subscribers' names. One who had been chairman at one of these meetings assured me that on a particular occasion, having called a " general dealer" to order, the party very nearly split his head open with a quart measure. If the hucksters know that the person calling the raffle is " down," and that it is necessity that has made him call it, they will not allow the property put up to be thrown for. " If you was to go to the raffle to-night, sir," said one of them to me, many months ago, before I became known to the class, " they'd say to one another directly you come in, ' Who's this here swell ? What's he want ? ' And they'd think you were a ' cad,' or else a spy, come from the police. But they'd treat you civilly, I'm sure. Some very likely would fancy you was a fast kind of a gentleman, come there for a lark. But you need have no fear, though the pint pots *does* fly about sometimes."

Of the Markets and Trade Rights of the Costerongers, and of the laws affecting them.

The next point of consideration is what are the legal regulations under which the several descriptions of hawkers and pedlars are allowed to pursue their occupations.

The laws concerning hawkers and pedlars, (50 Geo. III., c. 41, and 6 Geo. IV., c. 80,) treat of them as identical callings. The "hawker," however, is, strictly speaking, one who sells wares by *crying* them in the streets of towns, while the *pedlar* travels *on foot* through the country with his wares, not publicly proclaiming them, but visiting the houses on his way to solicit private custom. Until the commencement of the present century—before the increased facilities for conveyance—the pedlars were a numerous body in the country. The majority of them were Scotchmen and some amassed considerable wealth. Railways, however, have now reduced the numbers to insignificance.

Hawkers and pedlars are required to pay 4l. yearly for a license, and an additional 4l. for every horse or ass employed in the conveyance of wares. The hawking or exposing for sale of fish, fruit, or victuals, does not require a license ; and further, it is lawful for any one " being the maker of any home manufacture," to expose it for sale in any fair or market, without a warrant. Neither does anything in either of the two acts in question prohibit " any tinker, cooper, glazier, plumber, harness-mender, or other person, from going about and carrying the materials proper to their business."

The right of the costermongers, then, to "hawk" their wares through the streets is plainly inferred by the above acts; that is to say, nothing in them extends to prohibit persons "going about," unlicensed, and at their own discretion, and selling fish, vegetables, fruit, or provisions generally.

The law acknowledges none of the street "markets." These congregations are, indeed, in antagonism to the municipal laws of London, which provide that no market, or public place where provisions are sold, shall be held within seven miles of the city. The law, though it permits butchers and other provisionmongers to hire stalls and standings in the flesh and other markets, recognised by custom or usage, gives no such permission as to street-trading.

The right to sell provisions from stands in the streets of the metropolis, it appears, is merely permissive. The regulation observed is this : where the costermongers or other street-dealers have been in the habit of standing to sell their goods, they are not to be disturbed by the police unless on complaint of an adjacent shopkeeper or other inhabitant. If such a person shows that the costermonger, whose stand is near his premises, is by his improper conduct a nuisance, or that, by his clamour or any peculiarity in his mode of business, he causes a crowd to gather and obstruct the thoroughfare, the policeman's duty is to remove him. If the complaint from the inhabitants against the street-sellers be at all general the policemen of the beat report it to the authorities, taking no steps until they receive instructions.

It is somewhat anomalous, however, that the law now recognises—inferentially it is true—the right of costermongers to carry about their goods for sale. Formerly the stands were sometimes tolerated, but not the itinerancy.

The enactments of the Common-council from the time of Elizabeth are stringent against itinerant traders of all descriptions, but stringent to no purpose of prevention. In 1607, a Common-council enactment sets forth, that "many People of badd and lewde Condicon daylie resorte from the most Parte of this Realme to the said Cyttie, Suburbes, and Places adjoininge, procuringe themselves small Habytacons, namely, one Chamber-Roome for a poore Forreynor and his Familye, in a small Cottage with some other as poore as himself in the Cyttie, Suburbes, or Places adjacente, to the great Increase and Pestringe of this Cyttie with poore People; many of them proovinge Shifters, lyvinge by Cozeninge, Stealinge, and Imbeazellinge of Mens Gooddes as Opportunitye may serve them, remoovinge from Place to Place accordinglye; many Tymes runninge away, forsakinge their Wives and Children, leavinge them to the Charge of the said Cyttie, and the Hospitalles of the same."

It was towards this class of men who, by their resort to the capital, recruited the numbers of the street-sellers and public porters and others that the jealousy of the Corporation was directed. The city shop-keepers, three centuries ago, complained vehemently and continuously of the injuries inflicted on their trade by itinerant dealers, complaints which led to bootless enactments. In Elizabeth's reign the Court of Common Council declared that the streets of the city should be used, as in ancient times, for the common highway, and not for the traffic of hucksters, pedlars, and hagglers. But this traffic increased, and in 1632 another enactment was accounted necessary. Oyster-wives, herb-wives, tripe-wives, and all such "unruly people," were threatened with the full pains and penalties of the outraged law if they persevered in the prosecution of their callings, which are stigmatised as "a way whereby to live a more easie life than by labour." In 1694 the street-sellers were menaced with the punishments then deemed suitable for arrant rogues and sturdy beggars—whipping; and that remedy to be applied alike to males and females!

The tenor of these Vagrant Laws not being generally known, I here transcribe them, as another proof of the "wisdom" and mercy of our "ancestors" in "the good old times!"

In the year 1530 the English Parliament enacted, that, while the impotent poor should receive licenses from the justices of the peace to beg within certain limits, all men and *women*,

"being whole and mighty in body, and able to labour," if found vagrant and unable to give an account as to how they obtained their living, should be apprehended by the constables, tied to the tail of a cart *naked*, and beaten with whips through the nearest market-town, or hamlet, "till their bodies be bloody by reason of such whipping!" Five years afterwards it was added, that, if the individual had been once already whipped, he or she should not only be whipped again, but "also shall have the upper part of the gristle of his ear clean cut off, so as it may appear for a perpetual token hereafter that he hath been a contemner of the good order of the commonwealth." And finally, in 1562, it was directed that any person convicted of being a vagabond should, after being grievously whipped, be burnt through the gristle of the right ear "with a hot iron of the compass of an inch about," unless some person should agree to take him as a servant—of course without wages —for a year; then, that if he twice ran away from such master, he should be adjudged a felon; and that if he ran away a third time, he should "suffer pains of death and loss of land and goods as a felon, without benefit of clergy or sanctuary."

The only acts now in force which regulate the government of the streets, so to speak, are those best known as Michael Angelo Taylor's Act, and the 2 & 3 Vic., best known as the Police Act.

Of the Removals of Costermongers from the Streets.

Such are the laws concerning street trading: let us now see the effect of them.

Within these three months, or little more, there have been many removals of the costermongers from their customary standings in the streets. This, as I have stated, is never done, unless the shopkeepers represent to the police that the costermongers are an injury and a nuisance to them in the prosecution of their respective trades. The costermongers, for the most part, know nothing of the representation of the shopkeepers, so that perhaps the first intimation that they must "quit" comes from the policemen, who thus incur the full odium of the measure, the majority of the street people esteeming it a mere arbitrary act on the part of the members of the force.

The first removal, recently, took place in Leather-lane, Holborn, between three and four months back. It was effected in consequence of representations from the shopkeepers of the neighbourhood. But the removal was of a brief continuance. "Leather-lane," I was told, "looked like a desert compared to what it was. People that had lived there for years hardly knew their own street; and those that had complained, might twiddle their thumbs in their shops for want of something better to do."

The reason, or one reason, why the shopkeepers' trade is co-existent with that of the street-sellers was explained to me in this way by a tradesman perfectly familiar with the subject. "The poorer women, the wives of mechanics or small tradesmen, who have to prepare dinners for their husbands, like, as they call it, 'to make one errand do.' If the wife buys fish or vegetables in the street, as is generally done, she will, at the same time, buy her piece of bacon or cheese at the cheesemonger's, her small quantity of tea and sugar at the grocer's, her fire-wood at the oilman's, or her pound of beef or liver at the butcher's. In all the street-markets there are plenty of such tradesmen, supplying necessaries not vended in the streets, and so one errand is sufficient to provide for the wants of the family. Such customers—that is, such as have been used to buy in the streets—will *not* be driven to buy at the shops. They can't be persuaded that they can buy as cheap at the shops; and besides they are apt to think shopkeepers are rich and street-sellers poor, and that they may as well encourage the poor. So if one street-market is abolished, they'll go to another, or buy of the itinerant costermongers, and they'll get their bits of groceries and the like at the shops in the neighbourhood of the other street-market, even if they have a walk for it; and thus everybody's injured by removing markets, except a few, and they are those at the nearest markets that's not disturbed."

In Leather-lane the shopkeepers speedily retrieved what many soon came to consider the false step (as regards their interests) which they had taken, and in a fortnight or so, they managed, by further representations to the police authorities, and by agreement with the street-sellers, that the street-market people should return. In little more than a fortnight from that time, Leather-lane, Holborn, resumed its wonted busy aspect.

In Lambeth the case at present is different. The men, women, and children, between two and three months back, were all driven by the police from their standings. These removals were made, I am assured, in consequence of representations to the police from the parishioners, not of Lambeth, but of the adjoining parish of Christchurch, Blackfriars-road, who described the market as an injury and a hindrance to their business. The costermongers, etc., were consequently driven from the spot.

A highly respectable tradesman in "the Cut" told me, that he and all his brother shopkeepers had found their receipts diminished a quarter, or an eighth at least, by the removal; and as in all populous neighbourhoods profits were small, this falling off was a very serious matter to them.

In "the Cut" and its immediate neighbourhood, are tradesmen who supply street-dealers with the articles they trade in,—such as cheap stationery, laces, children's shoes, braces, and toys. They, of course, have been seriously affected by the removal; but the pinch has fallen sorest upon the street-sellers themselves. These people depend a good deal one upon another, as they make mutual purchases; now, as they have neither stalls nor means, such a source of profit is abolished.

"It is hard on such as me," said a fruit-seller to me, "to be driven away, for nothing that I've done wrong as I knows of, and not let me make a living, as I've been brought up to. I can't get no work at any of the markets. I've tried Billingsgate and the Borough hard, but there is so many poor men trying for a crust, they're fit to knock a new-comer's head off, though if they did, it wouldn't be much matter. I had 9s. 6d. stock-money, and I sold the apples and a few pears I had for 3s. 9d., and that 13s. 3d. I've been spinning out since I lost my pitch. That's done now, and I haven't had two meals a day for a week and more—and them not to call meals—only bread and coffee, or bread and a drink of beer. I tried to get a round of customers, but all the rounds was full, and I'm a very bad walker, and a weak man too. My wife's gone to try the country—I don't know where she is now. I suppose I shall lose my lodging this week, and then I must see what 'the great house' will say to me. Perhaps they'll give me nothing, but take me in, and that's hard on a man as don't want to be a pauper."

Another man told me that he now paid 3s. a week for privilege to stand with two stalls on a space opposite the entrance into the National Baths, New Cut; and that he and his wife, who had stood for eleven years in the neighbourhood, without a complaint against them, could hardly get a crust.

One man, with a fruit-stall, assured me that nine months ago he would not have taken 20l. for his pitch, and now he was a "regular bankrupt." I asked a girl, who stood beside the kerb with her load in front strapped round her loins, whether her tray was heavy to carry. "After eight hours at it," she answered, "it swaggers me, like drink." The person whom I was with brought to me two girls, who, he informed me, had been forced to go upon the streets to gain a living. Their stall on the Saturday night used to have 4l. worth of stock; but trade had grown so bad since the New Police order, that after living on their wares, they had taken to prostitution for a living, rather than go to the "house." The ground in front of the shops has been bought up by the costermongers at any price. Many now give the tradesmen six shillings a week for a stand, and one man pays as much as eight for the right of pitching in front.

The applications for parochial relief, in consequence of these removals, have been fewer than was anticipated. In Lambeth parish, however, about thirty families have been relieved, at a cost of 50l. Strange to say, a quarter, or rather more, of the very applicants for relief had been furnished by the parish with money to start the trade, their expulsion from which had driven them to pauperism.

It consequently becomes a question for serious consideration, whether any particular body of householders should, for their own interest, convenience, or pleasure, have it in their power to deprive so many poor people of their only means of livelihood, and so either force the rate-payers to keep them as paupers, or else drive the women, who object to the imprisonment of the Union, to prostitution, and the men to theft—especially when the very occupation which they are not allowed to pursue, not only does no injury to the neighbourhood, but is, on the contrary, the means of attracting considerable custom to the shops in the locality, and has, moreover, been provided for them by the parish authorities as a means of enabling them to get a living for themselves.

OF THE TRICKS OF COSTERMONGERS.

I shall now treat of the tricks of trade practised by the London costermongers. Of these the costers speak with as little reserve and as little shame as a fine gentleman of his peccadilloes. "I've boiled lots of oranges," chuckled one man, "and sold them to Irish hawkers, as wasn't wide awake, for stunning big uns. The boiling swells the oranges and so makes 'em look finer ones, but it spoils them, for it takes out the juice. People can't find that out though until it's too late. I boiled the oranges only a few minutes, and three or four dozen at a time." Oranges thus prepared will not keep, and any unfortunate Irishwoman, tricked as were my informant's customers, is astonished to find her stock of oranges turn dark-coloured and worthless in forty-eight hours. The fruit is "cooked" in this way for Saturday night and Sunday sale —times at which the demand is the briskest. Some prick the oranges and express the juice, which they sell to the British wine-makers.

Apples cannot be dealt with like oranges, but they are mixed. A cheap red-skinned fruit, known to costers as "gawfs," is rubbed hard, to look bright and feel soft, and is mixed with apples of a superior description. "Gawfs are sweet and sour at once," I was told, "and fit for nothing but mixing." Some foreign apples, from Holland and Belgium, were bought very cheap last March, at no more than 16*d.* a bushel, and on a fine morning as many as fifty boys might be seen rubbing these apples, in Hooper-street, Lambeth. "I've made a crown out of a bushel of 'em on a fine day," said one sharp youth. The larger apples are rubbed sometimes with a piece of woollen cloth, or on the coat skirt, if that appendage form part of the dress of the person applying the friction, but most frequently they are rolled in the palms of the hand. The smaller apples are thrown to and fro in a sack, a lad holding each end. " I wish I knew how the shopkeepers manages *their* fruit," said one youth to me; "I should like to be up to some of their moves; they do manage their things so plummy."

Cherries are capital for mixing, I was assured by practical men. They purchase three sieves of indifferent Dutch, and one sieve of good English cherries, spread the English fruit over the inferior quality, and sell them as the best. Strawberry pottles are often half cabbage leaves, a few tempting strawberries being displayed on the top of the pottle. "Topping up," said a fruit dealer to me, "is the principal thing, and we are perfectly justified in it. You ask any coster that knows the world, and he'll tell you that all the salesmen in the markets tops up. It's only making the best of it." Filberts they bake to make them look brown and ripe. Prunes they boil to give them a plumper and finer appearance. The latter trick, however, is not unusual in the shops.

The more honest costermongers will throw away fish when it is unfit for consumption, less scrupulous dealers, however, only throw away what is utterly unsaleable; but none of them fling away the dead eels, though their prejudice against such dead fish prevents their indulging in eel-pies. The dead eels are mixed with the living, often in the proportion of 20 lb. dead to 5 lb. alive, equal quantities of each being accounted very fair dealing. "And after all," said a street fish dealer to me, "I don't know why dead eels should be objected to; the aristocrats don't object to them. Nearly all fish is dead before it's cooked, and why not eels? Why not eat them when they're sweet, if they're ever so dead, just as you eat fresh herrings? I believe it's only among the poor and among our chaps, that there's this prejudice. Eels die quickly if they're exposed to the sun."

Herrings are made to look fresh and bright by candle-light, by the lights being so disposed "as to give them," I was told, "a good reflection. Why I can make them look splendid; quite a pictur. I can do the same with mackerel, but not so prime as herrings."

There are many other tricks of a similar kind detailed in the course of my narrative. We should remember, however, that *shopkeepers* are not immaculate in this respect.

OF THE STREET-SELLERS OF FISH.

OF THE KIND AND QUANTITIES OF FISH SOLD BY THE LONDON COSTERMONGERS.

HAVING now given the reader a general view of the numbers, characters, habits, tastes, amusements, language, opinions, earnings, and vicissitudes of the London costermongers,—having described their usual style of dress, diet, homes, conveyances, and street-markets,—having explained where their donkeys are bought, or the terms on which they borrow them, their barrows, their stock-money, and occasionally their stock itself,—having shown their ordinary mode of dealing, either in person or by deputy, either at half-profits or by means of boys,—where they go and how they manage on their rounds in town and in the country,—what are the laws affecting them, as well as the operation of those laws upon the rest of the community,—having done all this by way of giving the reader a general knowledge of the street-sellers of fish, fruit, and vegetables,—I now proceed to treat more particularly of each of these classes *seriatim.* Beginning with the street-fishmongers, I shall describe, in due order, the season when, the market where, and the classes of people by whom, the wet-fish, the dry-fish, and the shell-fish are severally sold and purchased in the London streets, together with all other concomitant circumstances.

The facilities of railway conveyance, by means of which fish can be sent from the coast to the capital with much greater rapidity, and therefore be received much fresher than was formerly the case, have brought large supplies to London from places that before contributed no quantity to the market, and so induced, as I heard in all quarters at Billingsgate, an extraordinary lowness of price in this species of diet. This cheap food, through the agency of the costermongers, is conveyed to every poor man's door, both in the thickly-crowded streets where the poor reside—a family at least in a room—in the vicinity of Drury-lane and of Whitechapel, in Westminster, Bethnal-green, and St. Giles's, and through the long miles of the suburbs. For all low-priced fish the poor are the costermongers' best customers, and a fish diet seems becoming almost as common among the ill-paid classes of London, as is a potato diet among the peasants of Ireland. Indeed, now, the fish season of the poor never, or rarely, knows an interruption. If fresh herrings are not in the market, there are sprats ; and if not sprats, there are soles, or whitings, or mackarel, or plaice.

The rooms of the very neediest of our needy metropolitan population, always smell of fish ; most frequently of herrings. So much so, indeed, that to those who, like myself, have been in the habit of visiting their dwellings, the smell of herrings, even in comfortable homes, savours from association, so strongly of squalor and wretchedness, as to be often most oppressive. The volatile oil of the fish seems to hang about the walls and beams of the rooms for ever. Those who have experienced the smell of fish only in a well-ordered kitchen, can form no adequate notion of this stench, in perhaps a dilapidated and ill-drained house, and in a rarely-cleaned room ; and I have many a time heard both husband and wife—one couple especially, who were "sweating" for a gorgeous clothes' emporium—say that they had not time to be clean.

The costermonger supplies the poor with every kind of fish, for he deals, usually, in every kind when it is cheap. Some confine their dealings to such things as shrimps, or periwinkles, but the adhering to one particular article is the exception and not the rule ; while shrimps, lobsters, &c., are rarely bought by the very poor. Of the entire quantity of fish sent to Billingsgate-market, the costermongers, stationary and itinerant, may be said to sell one-third, taking one kind with another.

The fish sent to London is known to Billingsgate salesmen as "red" and "white" fish. The red fish is, as regards the salmon. The other descriptions are known as "white." The costermongers classify the fish they vend as "wet" and "dry." All fresh fish is "wet;" all cured or salted fish, "dry." The fish which is sold "pickled," is known by that appellation, but its street sale is insignificant. The principal fish-staple, so to speak of the street-fishmonger, is soles, which are in supply all, or nearly all, the year. The next are herrings, mackarel, whitings, Dutch eels, and plaice. The trade in plaice and sprats is almost entirely in the hands of the costermongers ; their sale of shrimps is nearer a half than a third of the entire quantity sent to Billingsgate ; but their purchase of cod, or of the best lobsters, or crabs, is far below a third. The costermonger rarely buys turbot, or brill, or even salmon, unless he can retail it at 6d. the pound. When it is at that price, a street salmon-seller told me that the eagerness to buy it was extreme. He had known persons, who appeared to him to be very poor, buy a pound of salmon, "just for a treat once in a way." His best, or rather readiest customers—for at 6d. a pound all classes of the community may be said to be his purchasers—were the shopkeepers of the busier parts, and the occupants of the smaller private houses of the suburbs. During the past year salmon was scarce and dear, and the costermongers bought, comparatively, none of it. In a tolerably cheap season they do not sell more than from a fifteenth to a twentieth of the quantity received at Billingsgate.

In order to be able to arrive at the quantity or weight of the several kinds of fish sold by the costermongers in the streets of London, it is necessary that we should know the entire amount sent to Billingsgate-market, for it is only by estimating the proportion which the street-sale bears to the whole, that we can attain even an approximation to the truth. The following Table gives the results of certain information collected by myself for the first time, I believe, in this country. The facts, as well as the estimated proportions of each kind of fish sold by the costermongers, have been furnished me by the most eminent of the Billingsgate salesmen—gentlemen to whom I am under many obligations for their kindness, consideration, and assistance, at all times and seasons.

TABLE, SHOWING THE QUANTITY, WEIGHT, OR MEASURE OF THE FOL-
LOWING KINDS OF FISH SOLD IN BILLINGSGATE MARKET IN THE
COURSE OF THE YEAR:

Description of Fish.	Number of Fish.	Weight or Measure of Fish.	Proportion sold by Costermongers.
WET FISH.		lbs.	
Salmon and Salmon Trout (29,000 boxes, 14 fish per box)	406,000	3,480,000	One-twentieth.
Live Cod (averaging 10 lbs. each)	400,000	4,000,000	One-fourth.
Soles (averaging ¼ lb. each)	97,520,000	26,880,000	One-fifteenth.
Whiting (averaging 6 oz. each)	17,920,000	6,720,000	One-fourth.
Haddock (averaging 2 lbs. each)	2,470,000	5,040,000	One-tenth.
Plaice (averaging 1 lb. each)	33,600,000	33,600,000	Seven-eighths.
Mackarel (averaging 1 lb. each)	23,520,000	23,520,000	Two-thirds.
Fresh Herrings (250,000 bars., 700 fish per bar.)	175,000,000	42,000,000	One-half.
" (in bulk)	1,050,000,000	252,000,000	Three-fourths.
Sprats	. . . . .	4,000,000	Three-fourths.
Eels from Holland } (6 fish per 1 lb.)	9,797,760	{ 1,505,280	One-fourth.
" England and Ireland		127,680	One-fourth.
Flounders (7,200 quarterns, 36 fish per quartern)	259,200	43,200	All.
Dabs (7,500 quarterns, 36 fish per quartern)	270,000	48,750	All.
DRY FISH.			
Barrelled Cod (15,000 barrels, 50 fish per barrel)	750,000	4,200,000	One-eighth.
Dried Salt Cod (5 lbs. each)	1,600,000	8,000,000	One-tenth.
Smoked Haddock (65,000 bars., 300 fish per bar.)	19,500,000	10,920,000	One-eighth.
Bloaters (265,000 baskets, 150 fish per basket)	147,000,000	10,600,000	One-fourth.
Red Herrings (100,000 bars., 500 fish per bar.)	50,000,000	14,000,000	One-half.
Dried Sprats (9,600 large bundles, 30 fish per bundle)*	288,000	96,000	None.
SHELL FISH.			
Oysters (309,935 bars., 1,600 fish per bar.)	495,896,000	. . . . .	One-fourth.
Lobsters (averaging 1 lb. each fish)	1,200,000	1,200,000	One-twentieth.
Crabs (averaging 1 lb. each fish)	600,000	600,000	One-twelfth.
Shrimps (324 to the pint)	498,428,648	192,295 gals.	One-half.
Whelks (224 to the ½ bus.)	4,943,200	24,300 ½ bus.†	All.
Mussels (1000 to the ½ bus.)	50,400,000	50,400 "	Two-thirds.
Cockles (2,000 to the ½ bus.)	67,392,000	32,400 "	Three-fourths.
Periwinkles (4,000 to the ½ bus.)	304,000,000	76,000 "	Three-fourths.

* Costermongers dry their own sprats.
† The half-bushel measure at Billingsgate is double quantity—or, more correctly, a bushel.

OF THE COSTERMONGERS' FISH SEASON.

THE season for the street-fishmongers begins about October and ends in May.

In October, or a month or two earlier, may-be, they generally deal in fresh herrings, the supply of which lasts up to about the middle or end of November. This is about the best season. The herrings are sold to the poor, upon an average, at twelve a groat, or from 3s. to 4s. the hundred. After or during November, the sprat and plaice season begins. The regular street-fishmonger, however, seldom deals in sprats. He "works" these only when there is no other fish to be got. He generally considers this trade beneath him, and more fit for women than men. Those costers who do sell them dispose of them now by weight at the rate of 1d. to 2d. the pound—a bushel averaging from 40 to 50 pounds. The plaice season

continues to the first or second week in May. During May the casualty season is on, and there is little fish certain from that time till salmon comes in, and this is about the end of the month. The salmon season lasts till about the middle of July. The selling of salmon is a bad trade in the poor districts, but a very good one in the better streets or the suburbs. At this work the street-fishmonger will sometimes earn on a fine day from 5s. to 12s. The losses, however, are very great in this article if the weather prove bad. If kept at all "over" it loses its colour, and turns to a pale red, which is seen immediately the knife goes into the fish. While I was obtaining this information some months back, a man went past the window of the house in which I was seated, with a barrow drawn by a donkey. He was crying, " Fresh cod, oh! 1½d. a pound, cod alive, oh!" My informant called me to the window, saying, " Now, here is what we call rough cod." He told me it was three days old. He thought it was eatable *then*, he said. The eyes were dull and heavy and sunken, and the limp tails of the fish dangled over the ends of the barrow. He said it was a hanging market that day—that is to say, things had been dear, and the costers couldn't pay the price for them. He should fancy, he told me, the man had paid for the fish from 9*d*. to 1*s*. each, which was at the rate of 1*d*. per pound. He was calling them at 1½*d*. He would not take less than this until he had "got his own money in;" and then, probably, if he had one or two of the fish left, he would put up with 1*d*. per pound. The weight he was "working" was 12 oz. to the pound. My inform-ant assured me he knew this, because he had borrowed *his* 12 oz. pound weight that morning. This, with the draught of 2 oz. in the weighing-machine, and the ounce gained by placing the fish at the end of the pan, would bring the actual weight given to 9 oz. per pound, and probably, he said the man had even a lighter pound weight in his barrow ready for a " scaly" customer.

After the street-fishmonger has done his morning's work, he sometimes goes out with his tub of pickled salmon on a barrow or stall, and sells it in saucers at 1*d*. each, or by the piece. This he calls as " fine Newcastle salmon." There is generally a great sale for this at the races ; and if country-people begin with a penny-worth they end with a shillingsworth—a penny-worth, the costers say, makes a fool of the mouth. If they have any on hand, and a little stale, at the end of the week, they sell it at the public-houses to the " Lushingtons," and to them, with plenty of vinegar, it goes down sweet. It is gene-rally bought for 7*s*. a kit, a little bit " pricked ;" but, if good, the price is from 12*s*. to 18*s*. " We're in no ways particular to that," said one candid coster to me. " We don't have the eating on it ourselves, and people a'n't always got their taste, especially when they have been drinking, and we sell a great deal to parties in that way. We think it no sin to cheat 'em of 1*d*. while the pub-licans takes 1*s*."

Towards the middle of June the street-fish-monger looks for mackerel, and he is gene-rally employed in selling this fish up to the end of July. After July the Billingsgate season is said to be finished. From this time to the middle of October, when the herrings return, he is mostly engaged selling dried haddocks and red herrings, and other " cas'alty fish that may come across him." Many of the street-fish-mongers object to deal in periwinkles, or stewed mussels, or boiled whelks, because, being accus-tomed to take their money in sixpences at a time, they do not like, they say, to traffic in halfpenny-worths. The dealers in these articles are gene-rally looked upon as an inferior class.

There are, during the day, two periods for the sale of street-fish—the one (the morning trade) beginning about ten, and lasting till one in the day—and the other (the night trade) lasting from six in the evening up to ten at night. What fish is left in the forenoon is generally disposed of cheap at night. That sold at the latter time is generally used by the working-class for supper, or kept by them with a little salt in a cool place for the next day's dinner, if it will last as long. Several articles are sold by the street-fishmonger chiefly by night. These are oysters, lobsters, pickled salmon, stewed mussels, and the like. The reason why the latter articles sell better by night is, my informant say :, " Because people are lofty-minded, and don't like to be seen eating on 'em in the street in the day-time." Shrimps and winkles are the staple commodities of the afternoon trade, which lasts from three to half-past five in the evening. These articles are generally bought by the working-classes for their tea.

BILLINGSGATE.

To see this market in its busiest costermonger time, the visitor should be there about seven o'clock on a Friday morning. The marke opens at four, but for the first two or three hours, it is attended solely by the regular fishmongers and " bummarees" who have the pick of the best there. As soon as these are gone, the costers' sale begins.

Many of the costers that usually deal in vegetables, buy a little fish on the Friday. It is the fast day of the Irish, and the mechanics' wives run short of money at the end of the week, and so make up their dinners with fish ; for this reason the attendance of costers' bar-rows at Billingsgate on a Friday morning is always very great. As soon as you reach the Monument you see a line of them, with one or two tall fishmonger's carts breaking the uni-formity, and the din of the cries and commotion of the distant market, begins to break on the ear like the buzzing of a hornet's nest. The whole neighbourhood is covered with the hand-barrows, some laden with baskets, others with sacks. Yet as you walk along, a fresh line of costers' barrows are creeping in or being backed into almost im-possible openings ; until at every turning nothing but donkeys and rails are to be seen. The morn-ing air is filled with a kind of seaweedy odour, reminding one of the sea-shore ; and on entering the market, the smell of fish, of whelks, red herrings, sprats, and a hundred others, is almost overpowering.

The wooden barn-looking square where the fish is sold, is soon after six o'clock crowded with shiny cord jackets and greasy caps. Every-body comes to Billingsgate in his worst clothes, and no one knows the length of time a coat can be worn until they have been to a fish sale. Through the bright opening at the end are seen the tangled rigging of the oyster-boats and the red worsted caps of the sailors. Over the hum of voices is heard the shouts of the salesmen, who, with their white aprons, peering above the heads of the mob, stand on their tables, roaring out their prices.

All are bawling together—salesmen and huck-sters of provisions, capes, hardware, and newspapers—till the place is a perfect Babel of competition. "Ha-a-ansome cod! best in the market! All alive! alive! alive O!" "Ye-o-o! Ye-o-o! here's your fine Yarmouth bloaters! Who's the buyer?" "Here you are, governor, splendid whiting! some of the right sort!" "Turbot! turbot! all alive! turbot!" "Glass of nice peppermint! this cold morning a ha'penny a glass!" "Here you are at your own price! Fine soles, O!" "Oy! oy! oy! Now's your time! fine grizzling sprats! all large and no small!" "Hullo! hullo here! beautiful lobsters! good and cheap! fine cock crabs all alive O!" "Five brill and one turbot—have that lot for a pound! Come and look at 'em, governor; you wont see a better sample in the market." "Here, this way! this way for splendid skate! skate O! skate O!" "Had—had —had—had—haddick! all fresh and good!" "Currant and meat puddings! a ha'penny each!" "Now, you mussel-buyers, come along! come along! come along! now's your time for fine fat mussels!" "Here's food for the belly, and clothes for the back, but I sell food for the mind" (shouts the newsvender). "Here's smelt O!" "Here ye are, fine Finney haddick!" "Hot soup! nice peas-soup! a-all hot! hot!" "Ahoy! ahoy here! live plaice! all alive O!" "Now or never! whelk! whelk! whelk!" "Who'll buy brill O! brill O!" "Currant! water-proof capes! sure to keep the wet out! a shilling a piece!" "Eels O! eels O! Alive! alive O!" "Fine flounders, a shilling a lot! Who'll have this prime lot of flounders?" "Shrimps! shrimps! fine shrimps!" "Wink! wink! wink!" "Hi! hi-i! here you are, just eight eels left, only eight!" "O ho! O ho! this way—this way! Fish alive! alive! alive O!"

In the darkness of the shed, the white bellies of the turbots, strung up bow-fashion, shine like mother-of-pearl, while, the lobsters, lying upon them, look intensely scarlet, from the contrast. Brown baskets piled up on one another, and with the herring-scales glittering like spangles all over them, block up the narrow paths. Men in coarse canvas jackets, and bending under huge hampers, push past, shouting "Move on! move on, there!" and women, with the long limp tails of cod-fish dangling from their aprons, elbow their way through the crowd. Round the auction-tables stand groups of men turning over the piles of soles, and throwing them down till they slide about in their slime; some are smelling them, while others are counting the lots. "There, that lot of soles are worth your money," cries the salesman to one of the crowd as he moves on leisurely; "none better in the market. You shall have 'em for a pound and half-a-crown." "Oh!" shouts another salesman, "it's no use to bother him—he's no go." Presently a tall porter, with a black oyster-bag, staggers past, trembling under the weight of his load, his back and shoulders wet with the drippings from the sack. "Shove on one side!" he mutters from between his clenched teeth, as he forces

his way through the mob. Here is a tray of reddish-brown shrimps piled up high, and the owner busy sifting his little fish into another stand, while a doubtful customer stands in front, tasting the flavour of the stock and consulting with his companion in speculation. Little girls carrying matting-bags, that they have brought from Spitalfields, come up, and ask you in a begging voice to buy their baskets; and women with bundles of twigs for stringing herrings, cry out, "Half-penny a bunch!" from all sides. Then there are blue-black piles of small live lobsters, moving about their bound-up claws and long "feelers," one of them occasionally being taken up by a looker-on, and dashed down again, like a stone. Everywhere every one is asking, "What's the price, master?" while shouts of laughter from round the stalls of the salesmen, bantering each other, burst out, occasionally, over the murmuring noise of the crowd. The transparent smelts on the marble-slabs, and the bright herrings, with the lump of transparent ice magnifying their eyes like a lens, are seldom looked at until the market is over, though the hampers and piles of huge maids, dropping slime from the counter, are eagerly examined and bartered for.

One side of the market is set apart for whelks. There they stand in sackfulls, with the yellow shells piled up at the mouth, and one or two of the fish, curling out like corkscrews, placed as a sample. The coster slips one of these from its shell, examines it, pushes it back again, and then passes away, to look well round the market. In one part the stones are covered with herring-barrels, packed closely with dried fish, and yellow heaps of stiff haddock rise up on all sides. Here a man walks up with his knot on his shoulder, waiting for a job to carry fish to the trucks. Boys in ragged clothes, who have slept during the night under a railway-arch, clamour for employment; while the heads of those returning from the oyster-boats, rise slowly up the stone sides of the wharf.

The costermongers have nicknamed the long row of oyster boats moored close alongside the wharf "Oyster-street." On looking down the line of tangled ropes and masts, it seems as though the little boats would sink with the crowds of men and women thronged together on their decks. It is as busy a scene as one can well behold. Each boat has its black sign-board, and salesman in his white apron walking up and down "his shop," and on each deck is a bright pewter pot and tin-covered plate, the remains of the salesman's breakfast. "Who's for Baker's?" "Who's for Archer's?" "Who'll have Alston's?" shout the oyster-merchants, while the red cap of the man in the hold bobs up and down as he rattles the shells about with his spade. These holds are filled with oysters—a gray mass of sand and shell—on which is a bushel measure well piled up in the centre, while some of them have a blue muddy heap of mussels divided off from the "natives." The sailors in their striped guernseys sit on the boat sides smoking their morning's pipe, allowing themselves to be tempted by the Jew boys with cloth caps, old shoes, and silk handkerchiefs. Lads with bundles of whips skip from one boat to another, and, seedy-looking mechanics, with handfuls of tin fancy goods, hover about the salesmen, who are the principal supporters of this trade. The place has somewhat the appearance of a little Holywell-street; for the old clothes' trade is entirely in the hands of the Jew boys, and coats, caps, hats, umbrellas, and old shoes, are shouted out in a rich nasal twang on all sides.

Passing by a man and his wife who were breakfasting on the stone coping, I went to the shore where the watermen ply for passengers to the eel boats. Here I found a crowd of punts, half filled with flounders, and small closely-packed baskets of them ranged along the seats. The lads, who act as jacks-in-the-water, were busy feeling in the mud for the fish that had fallen over board, little caring for the water that dashed over their red swollen feet. Presently a boat, piled up with baskets, shot in, grazing the bottom, and men and women, blue with the cold morning air, stepped out.

The Dutch built eel-boats, with their bulging polished oak sides, were half-hidden in the river mist. They were surrounded by skiffs, that ply from the Surrey and Middlesex shores, and wait whilst the fares buy their fish. The holds of these eel-boats are fitted up with long tanks of muddy water, and the heads of the eels are seen breathing on the surface—a thick brown bubble rising slowly, and floating to the sides. Wooden sabots and large porcelain pipes are ranged round the ledges, and men in tall fur caps with high check bones, and rings in their ears, walk the decks. At the stern of one boat was moored a coffin-shaped barge pierced with holes, and hanging in the water were baskets, shaped like olive jars—both to keep the stock of fish alive and fresh. In the centre of the boat stood the scales,—a tall heavy apparatus, one side fitted up with the conical net-bag to hold the eels, and the other with the weights, and pieces of stone to make up for the extra draught of the water hanging about the fish. When a skiff load of purchasers arrives, the master Dutchman takes his hands from his pockets, lays down his pipe, and seizing a sort of long-handled landing-net scoops from the tank a lot of eels. The purchasers examine them, and try to beat down the price. "You calls them eels do you?" said a man with his bag ready opened. "Yeas," answered the Dutchman without any show of indignation. "Certainly, there is a few among them," continued the customer; and after a little more of this kind of chaffering the bargain is struck.

The visitors to the eel-boats were of all grades; one was a neatly-dressed girl to whom the costers showed the utmost gallantry, calling her "my dear," and helping her up the shining sides of the boat; and many of the men had on their blue serge apron, but these were only where the prices were high. The greatest crowd of customers is in the heavy barge alongside of the Dutch craft. Here a stout sailor in his red woollen shirt, and canvass petticoat, is surrounded by the most miserable and poorest of fish purchasers—the men with their crushed hats, tattered coats, and unshorn chins, and the women with their pads on their bonnets, and brown ragged gowns blowing in the breeze. One, in an old table-cover shawl, was beating her palms together before the unmoved Dutchman, fighting for an abatement, and showing her stock of halfpence. Others were seated round the barge, sorting their lots in their shallows, and sanding the fish till they were quite yellow. Others, again, were crowding round the scales narrowly watching the balance, and then begging for a few dead eels to make up any doubtful weight.

As you walk back from the shore to the market, you see small groups of men and women dividing the lot of fish they have bought together. At one basket, a coster, as you pass, calls to you, and says, "Here, master, just put these three halfpence on these three cod, and obleege a party." The coins are placed, and each one takes the fish his coin is on; and so there is no dispute.

At length nearly all the busy marketing has finished, and the costers hurry to breakfast. At one house, known as "Rodway's Coffee-house," a man can have a meal for 1d.—a mug of hot coffee and two slices of bread and butter, while for two-pence what is elegantly termed "a tightner," that is to say, a most plentiful repast, may be obtained. Here was a large room, with tables all round, and so extremely silent, that the smacking of lips and sipping of coffee were alone heard. Upwards of 1,500 men breakfast here in the course of the morning, many of them taking as many as three such meals. On the counter was a pile of white mugs, and the bright tin cans stood beside the blazing fire, whilst Rodway himself sat at a kind of dresser, cutting up and buttering the bread, with marvellous rapidity. It was a clean, orderly, and excellent establishment, kept by a man, I was told, who had risen from a saloop stall.

Opposite to the Coal Exchange were ranged the stalls and barrows with the street eatables, and the crowds round each showed the effects of the sharp morning air. One—a Jew's—had hot-pies with lids that rose as the gravy was poured in from an oil can; another carried a stone jar of peppermint-water, at ½d. a glass; and the pea-soup stand was hemmed in by boys and men blowing the steam from their cups. Beside these were Jews with cloth caps and knives, and square yellow cakes; one old man, in a corner, stood examining a thread-bare scarf that a cravatless coster had handed to him. Coffee-stalls were in great plenty; and men left their barrows to run up and have "an oyster," or "an 'ot heel." One man here makes his living by selling sheets of old newspapers, at ½d. each, for the costers to dress their trays with. Though seemingly rather out of place, there was a Mosaic jewellery stand; old umbrellas, too, were far from scarce; and one had brought a horse-hair stool for sale.

Everybody was soon busy laying out. their stock. The wrinkled dull-eyed cod was freshened up, the red-headed gurnet placed in rows, the eels prevented from writhing over the basket sides by cabbage-leaves, and the soles paired off like gloves. Then the little trucks began to leave, crawling, as it were, between the legs of the horses in the vans crowding Thames-street, and plunging in between huge waggons, but still appearing safely on the other side; and the 4,000 costers who visit Billingsgate on the Friday morning were shortly scattered throughout the metropolis.

OF THE FORESTALLING OF MARKETS AND THE BILLINGSGATE BUMMAREES.

" FORESTALLING," writes Adam Smith, "is the buying or contracting for any cattle, provisions, or merchandize, on its way to the market (or at market), or dissuading persons from buying their goods there, or persuading them to raise the price, or spreading any false rumour with intent to enhance the value of any article. In the remoter periods of our history several statutes were passed, prohibiting forestalling under severe penalties; but as more enlarged views upon such subjects began to prevail, their impolicy became obvious, and they were consequently repealed in 1772. But forestalling is still punishable by fine and imprisonment; though it be doubtful whether any jury would now convict an individual accused of such practices."

In Billingsgate the "forestallers" or middlemen are known as "bummarees," who, as regards means, are a far superior class to the "hagglers" (the forestallers of the "green" markets). The bummaree is the jobber or speculator on the fish-exchange. Perhaps on every busy morning 100 men buy a quantity of fish, which they account likely to be remunerative, and retail it, or dispose of it in lots to the fishmongers or costermongers. Few if any of these dealers, however, are merely bummarees. A salesman, if he have disposed of the fish consigned to himself, will turn bummaree if any bargain tempt him. Or a fishmonger may purchase twice the quantity he requires for his own trade, in order to procure a cheaper stock, and "bummaree" what he does not require. These speculations in fish are far more hazardous than those in fruit or vegetables, for later in the day a large consignment by railway may reach Billingsgate, and, being thrown upon the market, may reduce the price one half. In the vegetable and fruit markets there is but one arrival. The costermongers are among the best customers of the bummarees.

I asked several parties as to the origin of the word "bummaree," and how long it had been in use. " Why, bless your soul, sir,"

said one Billingsgate labourer, " there always was bummarees, and there always will be; just as Jack there is a ' rough,' and I'm a blessed ' bobber.'" One man assured me it was a French name; another that it was Dutch. A fishmonger, to whom I was indebted for information, told me he thought that the bummaree was originally a bum-boat man, who purchased of the wind-bound smacks at Gravesend or the Nore, and sent the fish up rapidly to the market by land.

I may add, as an instance of the probable gains of the forestallers, in the olden time, that a tradesman whose family had been long connected with Billingsgate, showed me by his predecessors' books and memoranda, that in the depth of winter, when the Thames was perhaps choked with ice, and no supply of fish " got up " to London, any, that might, by management, reach Billingsgate used to command exorbitant prices. To speak only of the present century: March 11th, 1802, a cod fish (8 lbs.) was bought by Messrs. Phillips and Robertson, fishmongers, Bond-street, for 1*l*. 8*s*. February, 1809, a salmon (19 lbs.) was bought by Mr. Phillips at a guinea a pound, 19*l*. 19*s*. for the fish ! March 24th, 1824, three lobsters were sold for a guinea each.

The "haggler," I may here observe, is the bummaree or forestaller or middleman of the green markets; as far as the costermonger's trade is concerned, he deals in fruit and vegetables. Of these trafficers there are fully 200 in Covent-garden-market; from 60 to 70 in the Farringdon; from 40 to 50 in the Borough; from 50 to 60 in Spitalfields; and none in Portman-market; such being the only wholesale green-markets for the purposes of the costermongers. The haggler is a middleman who makes his purchases of the growers when the day is somewhat advanced, and the whole produce conveyed to the market has not been disposed of. The grower will then, rather than be detained in town, sell the whole lot remaining in his cart or wagon to a haggler, who re-sells it to the costers, or to any other customer, from a stand which he hires by the day. The costermongers who are the most provident, either have means or club their resources for a large purchase, often buy early in the morning, and so have the advantage of anticipating their fellows in the street-trade, with the day before them. Those who buy later are the customers of the hagglers, and are street-sellers, whose means do not command an extensive purchase, or who do not care to venture upon one unless it be very cheap. These men speak very bitterly of the hagglers, calling them " cracked-up shopkeepers" and " scurfs," and declaring that but for them the growers must remain, and sell off their produce cheap to the costermongers.

A species of forestalling is now not uncommon, and is on the increase among the costermongers themselves. There are four men, having the command of money, who attend the markets and buy either fish or vegetables largely. One man especially buys almost daily as much fruit and vegetables as will supply thirty street-dealers. He adds 3d. a bushel to the wholesale market price of apples; 6d. to that of pears; 9d. to plums; and 1s. to cherries. A purchaser can thus get a smaller quantity than he can always buy at market, and avails himself of the opportunity.

Moreover, a good many of the more intelligent street-dealers now club together—six of them, for instance—contributing 15s. each, and a quantity of fish is thus bought by one of their body (a smaller contribution suffices to buy vegetables). Perhaps, on an equal partition, each man thus gets for his 15s. as much as might have cost him 20s., had he bought "single-handed." This mode of purchase is also on the increase.

OF "WET" FISH-SELLERS IN THE STREETS.

CONCERNING the sale of "wet" or fresh fish, I had the following account from a trustworthy man, of considerable experience and superior education:

"I have sold 'wet fish' in the streets for more than fourteen years," he said; "before that I was a gentleman, and was brought up a gentleman, if I'm a beggar now. I bought fish largely in the north of England once, and now I must sell it in the streets of London. Never mind talking about that, sir; there's some things won't bear talking about. There's a wonderful difference in the streets since I knew them first; I could make a pound then, where I can hardly make a crown now. People had more money, and less meanness then. I consider that the railways have injured me, and all wet fish-sellers, to a great extent. Fish now, you see, sir, comes in at all hours, so that nobody can calculate on the quantity that will be received—nobody. That's the mischief of it; we are afraid to buy, and miss many a chance of turning a penny. In my time, since railways were in, I've seen cod-fish sold at a guinea in the morning that were a shilling at noon; for either the wind and the tide had served, or else the railway fishing-places were more than commonly supplied, and there was a glut to London. There's no trade requires greater judgment than mine — none whatever. Before the railways—and I never could see the good of them—the fish came in by the tide, and we knew how to buy, for there would be no more till next tide. Now, we don't know. I go to Billingsgate to buy my fish, and am very well known to Mr. —— and Mr. —— (mentioning the names of some well-known salesmen. The Jews are my ruin there now. When I go to Billingsgate, Mr. —— will say, or rather, I will say to him, 'How much for this pad of soles?' He will answer, 'Fourteen shillings.' 'Fourteen shillings!' I say, 'I'll give you seven shillings, — that's the proper amount;' then the Jew boys—none of them twenty that are there—ranged about will begin; and one says, when I bid 7s., 'I'll give 8s;' 'nine,' says another, close on my left; 'ten,' shouts another, on my right, and so they go offering on; at last Mr. —— says to one of them, as grave as a

judge, 'Yours, sir, at 13s,' but it's all gammon. The 13s. buyer isn't a buyer at all, and isn't required to pay a farthing, and never touches the goods. It's all done to keep up the price to poor fishmen, and so to poor buyers that are our customers in the streets. Money makes money, and it don't matter how. Those Jew boys—I dare say they're the same sort as once sold oranges about the streets—are paid, I know 1s. for spending three or four hours that way in the cold and wet. My trade has been injured, too, by the great increase of Irish coster-mongers; for an Irishman will starve out an Englishman any day; besides if a tailor can't live by his trade, he'll take to fish, or fruit and cabbages. The month of May is a fine season for plaice, which is bought very largely by my customers. Plaice are sold at ½d. and 1d. a piece. It is a difficult fish to manage, and in poor neighbourhoods an important one to manage well. The old hands make a profit out of it; new hands a loss. There's not much cod or other wet fish sold to the poor, while plaice is in. "My customers are poor men's wives, —mechanics, I fancy. They want fish at most unreasonable prices. If I could go and pull them off a line flung off Waterloo-bridge, and no other expense, I couldn't supply them as cheap as they expect them. Very cheap fish-sellers lose their customers, through the Billingsgate bummarees, for they have pipes, and blow up the cod-fish, most of all, and puff up their bellies till they are twice the size, but when it comes to table, there's hardly to say any fish at all. The Billingsgate authorities would soon stop it, if they knew all I know. They won't allow any roguery, or any trick, if they only come to hear of it. These bummarees have caused many respectable people to avoid street-buying, and so fair traders like me are injured. I've nothing to complain of about the police. Oft enough, if I could be allowed ten minutes longer on a Saturday night, I could get through all my stock without loss. About a quarter to twelve I begin to halloo away as hard as I can, and there's plenty of customers that lay out never a farthing till that time, and then they can't be served fast enough, so they get their fish cheaper than I do. If any halloos out that way sooner, we must all do the same. Anything rather than keep fish over a warm Sunday. I have kept mine in ice; I haven't opportunity now, but it'll keep in a cool place this time of year. I think there's as many sellers as buyers in the streets, and there's scores of them don't give just weight or measure. I wish there was good moral rules in force, and everybody gave proper weight. I often talk to street-dealers about it. I've given them many a lecture; but they say they only do what plenty of shopkeepers do, and just get fined and go on again, without being a pin the worse thought of. They are abusive sometimes, too; I mean the street-sellers are, because they are ignorant. I have no children, thank God, and my wife helps me in my business. Take the year through, I clear from 10s. to 12s. every week. That's not much to support two people. Some weeks I earn only 4s.,—such as in wet March weather. In others I earn 18s. or 1l. November, December, and January are good months for me. I wouldn't mind if they lasted all the year round. I'm often very badly off indeed—very badly; and the misery of being hard up, sir, is not when you're making a struggle to get out of your trouble; no, nor to raise a meal off herrings that you've given away once, but when your wife and you's sitting by a grate without a fire, and putting the candle out to save it, a planning how to raise money. ' Can we borrow there ? ' ' Can we manage to sell if we can borrow ? ' ' Shall we get from very bad to the parish ? ' Then, perhaps, there's a day lost, and without a bite in our mouths trying to borrow. Let alone a little drop to give a body courage, which perhaps is the only good use of spirit after all. That's the pinch, sir. When the rain you hear outside puts you in mind of drownding ! "

Subjoined is the amount (in round numbers) of wet fish annually disposed of in the metropolis by the street-sellers :

	No. of Fish.	lbs. weight.
Salmon	20,000	175,000
Live-cod	100,000	1,000,000
Soles	6,500,000	1,650,000
Whiting	4,440,000	1,680,000
Haddock	250,000	500,000
Plaice	29,400,000	29,400,000
Mackarel	15,700,000	15,700,000
Herrings	875,000,000	210,000,000
Sprats	,,	3,000,000
Eels, from Holland	400,000	65,000
Flounders	260,000	43,000
Dabs	270,000	48,000
Total quantity of wet fish sold in the streets of London	932,340,000	263,281,000

From the above Table we perceive that the fish, of which the greatest quantity is eaten by the poor, is herrings; of this, compared with plaice there is upwards of thirty times the number consumed. After plaice rank mackerel, and of these the consumption is about one-half less in number than plaice, while the number of soles vended in the streets, is again half of that of mackerel. Then come whiting, which are about two-thirds the number of the soles, while the consumption to the poor of haddock, cod, eels, and salmon, is comparatively insignificant. Of sprats, which is estimated by weight, only one-fifth of the number of pounds are consumed compared with the weight of mackerel. The pounds' weight of herrings sold in the streets, in the course of a year, is upwards of seven times that of plaice, and fourteen times that of mackerel. Altogether more than 260,000,000 pounds, or 116,000 tons weight of wet fish are yearly purchased in the streets of London, for the consumption of the humbler classes. Of this aggregate amount, no less than five-sixths consists of herrings; which, indeed, constitute the great slop diet of the metropolis.

OF SPRAT-SELLING IN THE STREETS.

SPRATS—one of the cheapest and most grateful luxuries of the poor—are generally introduced about the 9th of November. Indeed " Lord Mayor's day" is sometimes called "sprat day." They continue in about ten weeks. They are sold at Billingsgate by the " toss," or "chuck," which is about half a bushel, and weighs from 40lbs. to 50lbs. The price varies from 1s. to 5s. Sprats are, this season, pronounced remarkably fine. "Look at my lot sir," said a street-seller to me ; "they're a heap of new silver," and the bright shiny appearance of the glittering little fish made the comparison not inappropriate. In very few, if in any, instances does a costermonger confine himself to the sale of sprats, unless his means limit him to that one branch of the business. A more prosperous street-fishmonger will sometimes detach the sprats from his stall, and his wife, or one of his children will take charge of them. Only a few sprat-sellers are itinerant, the fish being usually sold by stationary street-sellers at " pitches." One who worked his sprats through the streets, or sold them from a stall as he thought best, gave me the following account. He was dressed in a newish fustian-jacket, buttoned close up his chest, but showing a portion of a clean cotton shirt at the neck, with a bright-coloured coarse handkerchief round it ; the rest of his dress was covered by a white apron. His hair, as far as I could see it under his cloth cap, was carefully brushed, and (it appeared) as carefully oiled. At the first glance I set him down as having been a gentleman's servant. He had a somewhat deferential, though far from cringing manner with him, and seemed to be about twenty-five or twenty-six—he thought he was older, he said, but did not know his age exactly.

"Ah! sir," he began, in a tone according with his look, " sprats is a blessing to the poor. Fresh herrings is a blessing too, and sprats is young herrings, and is a blessing in 'portion" [for so he pronounced what seemed to be a favourite word with him "proportion"]. "It's only four years—yes, four, I'm sure of that— since I walked the streets starving, in the depth of winter, and looked at the sprats, and said, I wish I could fill my belly off you. Sir, I hope it was no great sin, but I could hardly keep my hands from stealing some and eating them raw. If they make me sick, thought I, the police 'll take care of me, and that ' ll be something. While these thoughts was a passing through my mind, I met a man who was a gentleman's coachman ; I knew him a little formerly, and so I stopped him and told him who I was, and that I hadn't had a meal for two days. ' Well, by G—,' said the coachman, ' you look like it, why I shouldn't have known you. Here's a shilling.' And then he went on a little way, and then stopped, and turned back and thrust 3½d. more into my hand, and bolted off. I've never seen him since. But I'm grateful to him in the same 'portion (proportion) as if I had. After I'd had a penn'orth of bread and a penn'orth of cheese, and half-a-pint of beer, I felt a new man, and I went to the party as I'd longed to steal the sprats from, and told him what I'd thought of. I can't say what made me tell him, but it turned out for good. I don't know much about religion, though I can read a little, but may be that had something to do with it." The rest of the man's narrative was—briefly told—as follows. He was the only child of a gentleman's coachman His father had deserted his mother and him, and gone abroad, he believed, with some family. His mother, however, took care of him until her death, which happened " when he was a little turned thirteen, he had heard, but could not remember the year." After that he was " a helper and a jobber in different stables," and " anybody's boy," for a few years, until he got a footman's, or rather footboy's place, which he kept above a year. After that he was in service, in and out of different situations, until the time he specified, when he had been out of place for nearly five weeks, and was starving. His master had got in difficulties, and had gone abroad; so he was left without a character. " Well, sir," he continued, " the man as I wanted to steal the sprats from, says to me, says he, ' Poor fellow ; I know what a hempty belly is myself—come and have a pint.' And over that there pint, he told me, if I could rise 10s. there might be a chance for me in the streets, and he'd show me how to do. He died not very long after that, poor man. Well, after a little bit, I managed to borrow 10s. of Mr. —— (I thought of him all of a sudden). He was butler in a family that I had lived in, and had a charitab'e character, though he was reckoned very proud. But I plucked up a spirit, and told him how I was off, and he said, ' Well, I'll try you,' and he lent me 10s., which I paid him back, little by little, in six or eight weeks ; and so I started in the costermonger line, with the advice of my friend, and I've made from 5s. to 10s., sometimes more, a week, at it ever since. The police don't trouble me much. They is civil to me in 'portion (proportion) as I am civil to them. I never mixed with the costers but when I've met them at market. I stay at a lodging-house, but it's very decent and clean, and I have a bed to myself, at 1s. a week, for I'm a regular man. I'm on sprats now, you see, sir, and you'd wonder, sometimes, to see how keen people looks to them when they're new. They're a blessing to the poor, in 'portion (proportion) of course. Not twenty minutes before you spoke to me, there was two poor women came up—they was sickly-looking, but I don't know what they was —perhaps shirt-makers—and they says to me, says they, ' Show us what a penny plateful is.' 'Sart'nly, ladies,' says I. Then they whispered together, and at last one says, says she, ' We'll have two platefuls.' I told you they was a blessing to the poor, sir—'specially to such as them, as lives all the year round on bread and

tea. But it's not only the poor as buys; others in 'portion (proportion). When they're new they're a treat to everybody. I've sold them to poor working-men, who've said, ' I'll take a treat home to the old 'oman and the kids ; they dotes on sprats.' Gentlemen's servants is very fond of them, and mechanics comes down — such as shoemakers in their leather aprons, and sings out, ' Here, old sprats, give us two penn'orth.' They're *such* a relish. I sell more to men than to women, perhaps, but there's little difference. They're best stewed, sir, I think — if you're fond of sprats — with vinegar and a pick of allspice ; that's my opinion, and, only yesterday, an old cook said I was right. I makes 1s. 6d. to 2s. 6d. a day, and sometimes rather more, on my sprats, and sticks to them as much as I can. I sell about my ' toss ' a day, seldom less. Of course I can make as many penn'orths of it as I please, but there's no custom without one gives middling penn'orths. If a toss costs me 3s., I may make sixty penn'orths of it sometimes— sometimes seventy or more — and sometimes less than sixty. There's many turns over as much as me and more than that. I'm thinking that I'll work the country with a lot ; they'll keep to a second day, when they're fresh to start, 'specially if its frosty weather, too, and then they're better than ever — yes, and a greater treat—scalding hot from the fire, they're the cheapest and best of all suppers in the winter time. I hardly know which way I'll go. If I can get anythink to do among horses in the country, I'll never come back. I've no tie to London."

To show how small a sum of money will enable the struggling striving poor to obtain a living, I may here mention that, in the course of my inquiries among the mudlarks, I casually gave a poor shoeless urchin, who was spoken of by one of the City Missionaries as being a well-disposed youth, 1s. out of the funds that had been entrusted to me to dispense. Trifling as the amount appears, it was the means of keeping his mother, sister, and himself through the winter. It was invested in sprats, and turned over and over again.

I am informed, by the best authorities, that near upon 1000 " tosses" of sprats are sold daily in London streets, while the season lasts. These, sold retail in pennyworths, at very nearly 5s. the toss, give about 150l. a day, or say 1,000l. a week spent on sprats by the poorer classes of the metropolis ; so that, calculating the sprat season to last ten weeks, about 10,000l. would be taken by the costermongers during that time from the sale of this fish alone.

Another return, furnished me by an eminent salesman at Billingsgate, estimates the gross quantity of sprats sold by the London costers in the course of the season at three millions of pounds weight, and this disposed of at the rate of 1d. per pound, gives upwards of 12,000l. for the sum of money spent upon this one kind of fish.

OF SHELL-FISH SELLERS IN THE STREETS.

I had the following account from an experienced man. He lived with his mother, his wife, and four children, in one of the streets near Gray's-inn-lane. The street was inhabited altogether by people of his class, the women looking sharply out when a stranger visited the place. On my first visit to this man's room, his wife, who is near her confinement, was at dinner with her children. The time was ¼ to 12. The meal was tea, and bread with butter very thinly spread over it. On the wife's bread was a small piece of pickled pork, covering about one-eighth of the slice of a quartern loaf cut through. In one corner of the room, which is on the ground-floor, was a scantily-covered bed. A few dingy-looking rags were hanging up to dry in the middle of the room, which was littered with baskets and boxes, mixed up with old furniture, so that it was a difficulty to stir. The room (although the paper, covering the broken panes in the window, was torn and full of holes) was most oppressively close and hot, and there was a fetid smell, difficult to sustain, though it was less noticeable on a subsequent call. I have often had occasion to remark that the poor, especially those who are much subjected to cold in the open air, will sacrifice much for heat. The adjoining room, which had no door, seemed littered like the one where the family were. The walls of the room I was in were discoloured and weather-stained. The only attempt at ornament was over the mantel-shelf, the wall here being papered with red and other gay-coloured papers, that once had been upholsterer's patterns.

On my second visit; the husband was at dinner with the family, on good boiled beef and potatoes. He was a small-featured man, with a head of very curly and long black hair, and both in mien, manners, and dress, resembled the mechanic far more than the costermonger. He said :—

" I've been twenty years and more, perhaps twenty-four, selling shell-fish in the streets. I was a boot-closer when I was young, and have made my 20s. and 30s., and sometimes 40s., and then sometimes not 10s. a week ; but I had an attack of rheumatic-fever, and lost the use of my hands for my trade. The streets hadn't any great name, as far as I knew, then, but as I couldn't work, it was just a choice between street-selling and starving, so I didn't prefer the last. It was reckoned degrading to go into the streets—but I couldn't help that. I was astonished at my success when I first began, and got into the business—that is into the understanding of it—after a week, or two, or three. Why, I made 3l. the first week I knew my trade, properly ; yes, I cleared 3l.! I made, not long after, 5l. a week—but not often. I was giddy and extravagant. Indeed, I was a fool, and spent my money like a fool I could have brought up a family then like a gentleman—I

send them to school as it is—but I hadn't a wife and family then, or it might have been better ; it's a great check on a man, is a family. I began with shell-fish, and sell it still ; very seldom anything else. There's more demand for shells, no doubt, because its far cheaper, but then there's so many more sellers. I don't know why exactly. I suppose it's because poor people go into the streets when they can't live other ways, and some do it because they think it's an idle life ; but it ain't. Where I took 35s. in a day at my stall—and well on to half of it profit—I now take 5s. or 6s., or perhaps 7s., in the day and less profit on that less money. I don't clear 3s. a day now, take the year through. I don't keep acccounts, but I'm certain enough that I average about 15s. a week the year through, and my wife has to help me to make that. She'll mind the stall, while I take a round sometimes. I sell all kinds of shell-fish, but my great dependence is on winkles. I don't do much in lobsters. Very few speculate in them. The price varies very greatly. What's 10s. a score one day may be 25s. the next. I sometimes get a score for 5s. or 6s., but it's a poor trade, for 6d. is the top of the tree, with me, for a price to a seller. I never get more. I sell them to mechanics and tradesmen. I do more in pound crabs. There's a great call for haporths and pennorths of lobster or crab, by children ; that's their claws. I bile them all myself, and buy them alive. I can bile twenty in half an hour, and do it over a grate in a back-yard. Lobsters don't fight or struggle much in the hot water, if they're properly packed. It's very few that knows how to bile a lobster as he should be biled. I wish I knew any way of killing lobsters before biling them. I can't kill them without smashing them to bits, and that won't do at all. I kill my crabs before I bile them. I stick them in the throat with a knife and they're dead in an instant. Some sticks them with a skewer, but they kick a good while with the skewer in them. It's a shame to torture anything when it can be helped. If I didn't kill the crabs they'd shed every leg in the hot water ; they'd come out as bare of claws as this plate. I've known it oft enough, as it is : though I kill them uncommon quick, a crab will be quicker and shed every leg—throw them off in the moment I kill them, but that doesn't happen once in fifty times. Oysters are capital this season, I mean as to quality, but they're not a good sale. I made 3l. a week in oysters, not reckoning anything else, eighteen or twenty years back. It was easy to make money then ; like putting down one sovereign and taking two up. I sold oysters then oft enough at 1d. a piece. Now I sell far finer at three a penny and five for 2d. People can't spend money in shell-fish when they haven't got any. They say that fortune knocks once at every man's door. I wish I'd opened my door when he knocked at it."

This man's wife told me afterwards, that last

winter, after an attack of rheumatism, all their stock-money was exhausted, and her husband sat day by day at home almost out of his mind; for nothing could tempt him to apply to the parish, and " he would never have mentioned his sufferings to me," she said; " he had too much pride." The loan of a few shillings from a poor costermonger enabled the man to go to market again, or he and his family would now have been in the Union.

As to the quantity of shell-fish sold in the streets of London, the returns before-cited give the following results :

Oysters	124,000,000
Lobsters	60,000
Crabs	50,000
Shrimps	770,000 pts.
Whelks	4,950,000
Mussels	1,000,000 qts.
Cockles	750,000 qts.
Periwinkles	3,640,000 pts.

Of Shrimp Selling in the Streets.

Shrimp selling, as I have stated, is one of tho trades to which the street-dealer often con fines himself throughout the year. The sale is about equally divided between the two sexes, but the men do the most business, walking some of them fifteen to twenty miles a day in a " round " of "ten miles there and ten back."

The shrimps vended in the streets are the Yarmouth prawn shrimps, sold at Billingsgate at from 6d. to 10d. a gallon, while the best shrimps (chiefly from Lee, in Essex,) vary in price from 10d. to 2s. 6d. a gallon ; 2s. being a common price. The shrimps are usually mixed by the street-dealers, and they are cried, from stalls or on rounds, " a penny half-pint, fine fresh s'rimps." (I heard them called nothing but " s'rimps" by the street-dealers.) The half-pint, however, is in reality but half that quantity. " It's the same measure as it was thirty years back," I was told, in a tone as if its anti- quity removed all imputation of unfair deal- ing. Some young men " do well on s'rimps," sometimes taking 5s. in an hour on a Saturday evening, " when people get their money, and wants a relish." The females in the shrimp line are the wives, widows, or daughters of costermongers. They are computed to average 1s. 6d. a day profit in fine, and from 9d. to 1s. in bad weather ; and, in snowy, or very severe weather, sometimes nothing at all.

One shrimp-seller, a middle-aged woman, wrapped up in a hybrid sort of cloak, that was half a man's and half a woman's gar- ment, gave me the following account. There was little vulgarity in either her language or manner.

" I was in the s'rimp trade since I was a girl. I don't know how long. I don't know how old I am. I never knew ; but I've two children, one's six and t'other's near eight, both girls ; I've kept count of that as well as I can. My husband sells fish in the street; so did father, but he's dead. We buried him without the help of the parish, as many gets—that's something to say. I've known the trade every way. It never was any good in public-houses. They want such great ha'p'orths there. They'll put up with what isn't very fresh, to be sure, some- times ; and good enough for them too, I say, as spoils their taste with drink." [This was said very bitterly.] " If it wasn't for my hus- band's drinking for a day together now and then we'd do better. He's neither to have nor to hold when he's the worse for liquor; and it's the worse with him, for he's a quiet man when he's his own man. Perhaps I make 9d. a day, per- haps 1s. or more. Sometimes my husband takes my stand, and I go a round. Sometimes, if he gets through his fish, he goes my round. I give good measure, and my pint's the regular s'rimp pint." [It was the half-pint I have described.] " The trade's not so good as it was. People hasn't the money, they tells me so. It's bread before s'rimps, says they. I've heard them say it very cross, if I've wanted hard to sell. Some days I can sell nothing. My children stays with my sister, when me and my old man's out. They don't go to school, but Jane (the sister) learns them to sew. She makes drawers for the slop- sellers, but has very little work, and gets very little for the little she does; she would learn them to read if she knew how. She's married to a pavior, that's away all day. It's a hard life mine, sir. The winter's a coming, and I'm now sometimes numbed with sitting at my stall in the cold. My feet feels like lumps of ice in the winter ; and they're beginning now, as if they weren't my own. Standing 's far harder work than going a round. I sell the best s'rimps. My customers is judges. If I've any s'rimps over on a night, as I often have one or two nights a week, I sells them for half-price to an Irishwoman, and she takes them to the beer-shops, and the coffee-shops. She washes them to look fresh. I don't mind telling that, because people should buy of regular people. It's very few people know how to pick a s'rimp properly. You should take it by the head and the tail and jam them up, and then the shell separates, and the s'rimp comes out beautifully. That's the proper way."

Sometimes the sale on the rounds may be the same as that at the stalls, or 10 or 20 per cent. more or less, according to the weather, as shrimps can be sold by the itinerant dealers better than by the stall-keepers in wet weather, when people prefer buying at their doors. But in hot weather the stall trade is the best, " for people often fancy that the s'rimps is sent out to sell 'cause they'll not keep no longer. It's only among customers as knows you, you can do any good on a round then."

The costermongers sell annually, it ap- pears, about 770,000 pints of shrimps. At 2d. a pint (a very low calculation) the street sale of shrimps amount to upwards of 6,400l. yearly.

ORANGE MART, DUKE'S PLACE.—[*From a Daguerreotype by* BEARD.]

OF OYSTER SELLING IN THE STREETS.

THE trade in oysters is unquestionably one of the oldest with which the London—or rather the English—markets are connected; for oysters from Britain were a luxury in ancient Rome. Oysters are now sold out of the smacks at Billingsgate, and a few at Hungerford. The more expensive kind such as the real Milton, are never bought by the costermongers, but they buy oysters of a "good middling quality." At the commencement of the season these oysters are 14s. a "bushel," but the measure contains from a bushel and a half to two bushels, as it is more or less heaped up. The general price, however, is 9s. or 10s., but they *have* been 16s. and 18s. The "big trade" was unknown until 1848, when the very large shelly oysters, the fish inside being very small, were introduced from the Sussex coast. They were sold in Thames-street and by the Borough-market. Their sale was at first enormous. The costermongers distinguished them by the name of "scuttle-mouths." One coster informant told me that on the Saturdays he not unfrequently, with the help of a boy and a girl, cleared 10s. by selling these oysters in the streets, disposing of four bags. He thus sold, reckoning twenty-one dozen to the bag, 2,016 oysters; and as the price was two for a penny, he took just 4*l.* 4*s.* by the sale of oysters in the streets in one night. With the scuttle-mouths the costermonger takes no trouble: he throws them into a yard, and dashes a few pails of water over them, and then places them on his barrow, or conveys them to his stall. Some of the better class of costermongers, however, lay down their oysters carefully, giving them oatmeal "to fatten on."

In April last, some of the street-sellers of this article established, for the first time, "oyster-rounds." These were carried on by costermongers whose business was over at twelve in the day, or a little later; they bought a bushel of scuttle-mouths (never the others), and, in the afternoon, went a round with them to poor neighbourhoods, until about six, when they took a stand in some frequented street. Going these oyster-rounds is hard work, I am told, and a boy is generally taken to assist. Monday afternoon is the best time for this trade, when 10s. is sometimes taken, and 4s. or 5s. profit made. On other evenings only from 1s. to 5s. is taken—very rarely the larger sum—as the later the day in the week the smaller is the receipt, owing to the wages of the working classes getting gradually exhausted.

The women who sell oysters in the street, and whose dealings are limited, buy either of the costermongers or at the coal-sheds. But nearly all the men buy at Billingsgate, where as small a quantity as a peck can be had.

An old woman, who had "seen better days," but had been reduced to keep an oyster-stall, gave me the following account of her customers. She showed much shrewdness in her conversation, but having known better days, she declined

to enter upon any conversation concerning her former life:—

"As to my customers, sir," she said, "why, indeed, they're all sorts. It's not a very few times that gentlemen (I call them so because they're mostly so civil) will stop—just as it's getting darkish, perhaps,—and look about them, and then come to me and say very quick: 'Two penn'orth for a whet.' Ah! some of 'em will look, may be, like poor parsons down upon their luck, and swallow their oysters as if they was taking poison in a hurry. They'll not touch the bread or butter once in twenty times, but they'll be free with the pepper and vinegar, or, mayhap, they'll say quick and short, 'A crust off that.' I many a time think *that* two penn'orth is a poor gentleman's dinner. It's the same often—but only half as often, or not half—with a poor lady, with a veil that once was black, over a bonnet to match, and shivering through her shawl. She'll have the same. About two penn'orth is the mark still; it's mostly two penn'orth. My son says, it's because that's the price of a glass of gin, and some persons buy oysters instead—but that's only his joke, sir. It's not the vulgar poor that's our chief customers. There's many of them won't touch oysters, and I've heard some of them say: 'The sight on 'em makes me sick; it's like eating snails.' The poor girls that walk the streets often buy; some are brazen and vulgar, and often the finest dressed are the vulgarest; at least, I think so; and of those that come to my oyster stalls, I'm sure it's the case. Some are shy to such as me, who may, perhaps, call their own mothers to their minds, though it aint many of them that is so. One of them always says that she must keep at least a penny for gin after her oysters. One young woman ran away from my stall once after swallowing one oyster out of six that she'd paid for. I don't know why. Ah! there's many things a person like me sees that one may say, 'I don't know why' to; that there is. My heartiest customers, that I serve with the most pleasure, are working people, on a Saturday night. One couple—I think the wife always goes to meet her husband on a Saturday night— has two, or three, or four penn'orth, as happens, and it's pleasant to hear them say, 'Won't you have another, John?' or, 'Do have one or two more, Mary Anne.' I've served them that way two or three years. They've no children, I'm pretty sure, for if I say, 'Take a few home to the little ones,' the wife tosses her head, and says, half vexed and half laughing, 'Such nonsense.' I send out a good many oysters, opened, for people's suppers, and sometimes for supper parties—at least, I suppose so, for there's five or six dozen often ordered. The maid-servants come for them then, and I give them two or three for themselves, and say, jokingly-like, 'It's no use offering you any, perhaps, because you'll have plenty that's left.' They've mostly one answer: 'Don't we wish we may get 'em?' The *very* poor never buy of me, as I told you. A penny buys a loaf, you see, or a ha'porth of bread and a ha'porth of cheese, or a half-pint of beer, with a farthing out. My customers are mostly working people and tradespeople. Ah! sir, I wish the parson of the parish, or any parson, sat with me a fortnight; he'd see what life is then. 'It's different,' a learned man used to say to me—that's long ago—'from what's noticed from the pew or the pulpit.' I've missed the gentleman as used to say that, now many years—I don't know how many. I never knew his name. He was drunk now and then, and used to tell me he was an author. I felt for him. A dozen oysters wasn't much for him. We see a deal of the world, sir—yes, a deal. Some, mostly working people, take quantities of pepper with their oysters in cold weather, and say it's to warm them, and no doubt it does; but frosty weather is very bad oyster weather. The oysters gape and die, and then they are not so much as manure. They are very fine this year. I clear 1s. a day, I think, during the season -at least 1s., taking the fine with the wet days, and the week days with the Sundays, though I'm not out then; but, you see, I'm known about here."

The number of oysters sold by the costermongers amounts to 124,000,000 a year. These, at four a penny, would realise the large sum of 129,650l. We may therefore safely assume that 125,000l. is spent yearly in oysters in the streets of London.

OF PERIWINKLE SELLING IN THE STREETS.

THERE are some street people who, nearly all the year through, sell nothing but periwinkles, and go regular rounds, where they are well known. The "wink" men, as these periwinkle sellers are called, generally live in the lowest parts, and many in lodging-houses. They are forced to live in low localities, they say, because of the smell of the fish, which is objected to. The city district is ordinarily the best for winkle-sellers, for there are not so many cheap shops there as in other parts. The summer is the best season, and the sellers then make, upon the average, 12s. a week clear profit; in the winter, they get upon the average, 5s. a week clear, by selling mussels and whelks—for, as winkles last only from March till October, they are then obliged to do what they can in the whelk and mussel way. "I buy my winks," said one, "at Billingsgate, at 3s. and 4s. the wash. A wash is about a bushel. There's some at 2s., and some sometimes as low as 1s. the wash, but they wouldn't do for me, as I serve very respectable people. If we choose we can boil our winkles at Billingsgate by paying 4d. a week for boiling, and ½d. for salt, to salt them after they are boiled. Tradesmen's families buy them for a relish to their tea. It's reckoned a nice present from a young man to his sweetheart, is winks. Servant girls are pretty good customers, and want them cheaper when they say it's for themselves; but I have only one price."

One man told me he could make as much as 12s. a week—sometimes more and sometimes less.

He made no speeches, but sung—"Winketty-winketty-wink-wink-wink—wink-wink—wick-etty-wicketty-wink—fine fresh winketty-winks wink wink." He was often so sore in the stomach and hoarse with hallooing that he could hardly speak. He had no child, only himself and wife to keep out of his earnings. His room was 2s. a week rent. He managed to get a bit of meat every day, he said, "somehow or 'nother."

Another, more communicative and far more intelligent man, said to me concerning the character of his customers : "They're people I think that like to daddle" (dawdle, I presume) "over their teas or such like; or when a young woman's young man takes tea with her mother and her, then they've winks; and then there's joking, and helping to pick winks, between Thomas and Betsy, while the mother's busy with her tea, or is wiping her specs, 'cause she can't see. Why, sir, I've known it! I was a Thomas that way myself when I was a tradesman. I was a patten-maker once, but pattens is no go now, and hasn't been for fifteen year or more. Old people, I think, that lives by themselves, and has perhaps an annuity or the like of that, and nothing to do perticklar, loves winks, for they likes a pleasant way of making time long over a meal. They're the people as reads a newspaper, when it's a week old, all through. The other buyers, I think, are tradespeople or working-people what wants a relish. But winks is a bad trade now, and so is many that depends on relishes."

One man who "works" the New Cut, has the "best wink business of all." He sells only a little dry fish with his winks, never wet fish, and has "got his name up," for the superiority of that shell-fish — a superiority which he is careful to ensure. He pays 8s. a week for a stand by a grocer's window. On an ordinary afternoon he sells from 7s. to 10s. worth of periwinkles. On a Monday afternoon he often takes 20s.; and on the Sunday afternoon 3l. and 4l. He has two coster lads to help him, and sometimes on a Sunday from twenty to thirty customers about him. He wraps each parcel sold in a neat brown paper bag, which, I am assured, is of itself, an inducement to buy of him. The "unfortunate" women who live in the streets contiguous to the Waterloo, Blackfriars, and Borough-roads, are among his best customers, on Sundays especially. He is rather a public character, getting up dances and the like. "He aint bothered—not he—with ha'p'orths or penn'orths of a Sunday," said a person who had assisted him. "It's the top of the tree with his customers ; 3d. or 6d. at a go." The receipts are one-half profit. I heard from several that he was "the best man for winks a-going."

The quantity of periwinkles disposed of by the London street-sellers is 3,600,000 pints, which, at 1d. per pint, gives the large sum of 15,000l. expended annually in this street luxury. It should be remembered, that a very large consumption of periwinkles takes place in public-houses and suburban tea-gardens.

OF "DRY" FISH SELLING IN THE STREETS.

THE dealing in "dry" or salt fish is never carried on as a totally distinct trade in the streets, but some make it a principal part of their business; and many wet fish-dealers whose "wet fish" is disposed of by noon, sell dry fish in the afternoon. The dry fish, proper, consists of dried mackerel, salt cod—dried or barrelled—smoked or dried haddocks (often called "finnie haddies"), dried or pickled salmon (but salmon is only salted or pickled for the streets when it can be sold cheap), and salt herrings.

A keen-looking, tidily-dressed man, who was at one time a dry fish-seller principally, gave me the following account. For the last two months he has confined himself to another branch of the business, and seemed to feel a sort of pleasure in telling of the "dodges" he once resorted to :

"There's Scotch haddies that never knew anything about Scotland," he said, "for I've made lots of them myself by Tower-street, just a jump or two from the Lambeth station-house. I used to make them on Sundays. I was a wet fish-seller then, and when I couldn't get through my haddocks or my whitings of a Saturday night, I wasn't a-going to give them away to folks that wouldn't take the trouble to lift me out of a gutter if I fell there, so I presarved them. I've made haddies of whitings, and good ones too, and Joe made them of codlings besides. I had a bit of a back-yard to two rooms, one over the other, that I had then, and on a Sunday I set some wet wood a fire, and put it under a great tub. My children used to gut and wash the fish, and I hung them on hooks all round the sides of the tub, and made a bit of a chimney in a corner of the top of the tub, and that way I gave them a jolly good smoking. My wife had a dry fish-stall and sold them, and used to sing out 'Real Scotch haddies,' and tell people how they was from Aberdeen ; I've often been fit to laugh, she did it so clever. I had a way of giving them a yellow colour like the real Scotch, but that's a secret. After they was well smoked they was hung up to dry all round the rooms we lived in, and we often had stunning fires that answered as well to boil crabs and lobsters when they was cheap enough for the streets. I've boiled a mate's crabs and lobsters for 2½*d*. ; it was two boilings and more, and 2½*d*. was reckoned the price of half a quarter of a hundred of coals and the use of the pan. There's more ways than one of making 6*d*., if a man has eyes in his head and keeps them open. Haddocks that wouldn't fetch 1*d*. a piece, nor any money at all of a Saturday night, I've sold—at least she has" (indicating his wife by a motion of his thumb)— "at 2*d*., and 3*d*., and 4*d*. I've bought fish of costers that was over on a Saturday night, to make Scotch haddies of them. I've tried experience" (experiments) "too. Ivy, burnt

under them, gave them, I thought, a nice sort of flavour, rather peppery, for I used always to taste them; but I hate living on fish. Ivy with brown berries on it, as it has about this time o' year, I liked best. Holly wasn't no good. A black-currant bush was, but it's too dear ; and indeed it couldn't be had. I mostly spread wetted fire-wood, as green as could be got, or damp sticks of any kind, over shavings, and kept feeding the fire. Sometimes I burnt sawdust. Somehow, the dry fish trade fell off. People does get so prying and so knowing, there's no doing nothing now for no time, so I dropped the dry fish trade. There's few up to smoking them proper ; they smoke 'em black, as if they was hung up in a chimbley."

Another costermonger gave me the following account :

"I've salted herrings, but the commonest way of salting is by the Jews about Whitechapel. They make real Yarmouth bloaters and all sorts of fish. When I salted herrings, I bought them out of the boats at Billingsgate by the hundred, which is 120 fish. We give them a bit of a clean —hardly anything—then chuck them into a tub of salt, and keep scattering salt over them, and let them lie a few minutes, or sometimes half an hour, and then hang them up to dry. They eat well enough, if they're eaten in time, for they won't keep. I've known three day's old herrings salted, just because there was no sale for them. One Jew sends out six boys crying 'real Yarmouth bloaters.' People buy them in preference, they look so nice and clean and fresh-coloured. It's quite a new trade among the Jews. They didn't do much that way until two years back. I sometimes wish I was a Jew, because they help one another, and start one another with money, and so they thrive where Christians are ruined. I smoked mackerel, too, by thousands ; that's a new trade, and is done the same way as haddocks. Mackerel that won't bring 1*d*. a piece fresh, bring 2*d*. smoked ; they are very nice indeed. I make about 10*s*. or 11*s*. a week by dry fish in the winter months, and about as much by wet,— but I have a tidy connection. Perhaps I make 17*s*. or 18*s*. a week all the year round."

The aggregate quantity of dry fish sold by the London costermongers throughout the year is as follows—the results being deduced from the table before given :

Wet salt cod	93,750
Dry do.	1,000,000
Smoked Haddocks . .	4,875,000
Bloaters	36,750,000
Red-herrings	25,000,000

GROSS VALUE OF THE SEVERAL KINDS OF FISH ANNUALLY SOLD IN THE STREETS OF LONDON.

IT now but remains for me, in order to complete this account of the "street-sellers of fish," to form an estimate of the amount of money annually expended by the labourers and the poorer classes of London upon the different kinds of wet, dry, and shell-fish. This, according to the best authorities, is as follows:

Wet Fish.

	£
175,000 lbs. of salmon, at 6d. per lb.	4,000
1,000,000lbs. of live cod, at 1½d. per lb.	5,000
3,250,000 pairs of soles, at 1½d. per pair	20,000
4,400,000 whiting, at ½d. each . . .	9,000
29,400,000 plaice, at ¾d.	90,000
15,700,000 mackarel, at 6 for 1s. .	130,000
875,000,000 herrings, at 16 a groat .	900,000
3,000,000 lbs. of sprats. at 1d. per lb.	12,000
400,000 lbs. of eels, at 3 lb. for 1s. .	6,000
260,000 flounders, at 1d. per dozen.	100
270,000 dabs, at 1d. per dozen . .	100

Sum total expended yearly in wet fish 1,177,000

Dry Fish.

	£
525,000 lbs. barrelled cod, at 1½d. .	3,000
500,000 lbs. dried salt cod, at 2d. .	4,000
4,875,000 smoked haddock, at 1d. .	20,000
36,750,000 bloaters, at 2 for 1d.. . .	75,000
25,000,000 red herrings, at 4 for 1d. .	25,000

Sum total expended yearly in dry fish 127,000

Shell Fish.

	£
124,000,000 oysters, at 4 a penny .	125,000
60,000 lobsters, at 3d.	750
50,000 crabs, at 2d.	400
770,000 pints of shrimps, at 2d. .	6,000
1,000,000 quarts of mussels, at 1d. .	4,000
750,000 quarts of cockles, at 1d. .	3,000
4,950,000 whelks, at 8 for 1d. . . .	2,500
3,600,000 pints of periwinkles, at 1d.	15,000

Sum total expended yearly in shell-fish 156,650

Adding together the above totals, we have the following result as to the gross money value of the fish purchased yearly in the London streets:

		£
Wet fish	. .	1,177,200
Dry fish	. .	127,000
Shell fish	. .	156,650
Total	.	£1,460,850

Hence we find that there is nearly a million and a half of money annually spent by the poorer classes of the metropolis in fish; a sum so prodigious as almost to discredit every statement of want, even if the amount said to be so expended be believed. The returns from which the above account is made out have been obtained, however, from such unquestionable sources —not from one salesman alone, but checked and corrected by many gentlemen who can have no conceivable motive for exaggeration either one way or the other—that, sceptical as our utter ignorance of the subject must necessarily make

us, still if we will but examine for ourselves, we shall find there is no gainsaying the facts.

Moreover as to the enormity of the amount dispelling all ideas of privation among the industrious portion of the community, we shall also find on examination that assuming the working-men of the metropolis to be 500,000 in number (the Occupation Abstract of 1841, gives 773,560 individuals following *some* employment in London, but these include merchants, employers, shopkeepers, Government-officers and others), and that they, with their wives and children, make up one million individuals, it follows that the sum per head, expended in fish by the poorer classes every week, is a fraction more than 6¾d., or, in other words, not quite one penny a day.

If the diet of a people be a criterion, as has been asserted, of their character, it may be feared that the present extensive fish-diet of the working-people of London, is as indicative of degeneracy of character, as Cobbett insisted must result from the consumption of tea, and " the cursed root," the potato. " The flesh of fish," says Pereira on Diet, " is less satisfying than the flesh of either quadrupeds or birds. As it contains a larger proportion of water (about 80 per cent.), it is obviously less nourishing." Haller tells us he found himself weakened by a fish-diet; and he states that Roman Catholics are generally debilitated during Lent. Pechlin also affirms that a mechanic, nourished merely by fish, has less muscular power than one who lives on the flesh of warm-blooded animals. Jockeys, who *waste themselves* in order to reduce their weight, live principally on fish.

The classes of fish above given, are, when considered in a " dietetical point of view," of two distinct kinds; viz., those which form the staple commodity of the dinners and suppers of the poor, and those which are mere relishes or stimuli to failing, rather than stays to, eager appetites. Under the former head, I include red-herrings, bloaters, and smoked haddocks; such things are not merely provocatives to eat, among the poor, as they are at the breakfast-table of many an over-fed or intemperate man. With the less affluent these salted fish are not a " relish," but a meal.

The shell-fish, however, can only be considered as luxuries. The 150,000l. thus annually expended in the streets, represents the sum laid out in mere relishes or stimuli to sluggish appetites. A very large proportion of this amount, I am inclined to believe, is spent by persons whose stomachs have been disordered by drink. A considerable part of the trade in the minor articles, as winks, shrimps, &c., is carried on in public-houses, while a favourite pitch for an oyster-stall is outside a tavern-door. If, then, so large an amount is laid out in an endeavour to restore the appetite after drinking, how much money must be squandered in destroying it by the same means?

OF THE STREET-SELLERS OF FRUIT AND VEGETABLES.

OF THE KINDS AND QUANTITY OF FRUIT AND VEGETABLES SOLD IN THE STREETS.

THERE are two kinds of fruit sold in the streets —" green fruit" and " dry fruit."

In commerce, all fruit which is edible as it is taken from the tree or the ground, is known as " green." A subdivision of this green fruit is into " fresh" or " tender" fruit, which includes currants, gooseberries, strawberries, and, indeed, all fruits that demand immediate consumption, in contradistinction to such productions as nuts which may be kept without injury for a season. All fruit which is " cured" is known as " dry" fruit. In summer the costers vend " green fruit," and in the winter months, or in the early spring, when the dearness or insufficiency of the supply of green fruit renders it unsuited for their traffic, they resort, but not extensively, to " dry fruit." It is principally, however, when an abundant season, or the impossibility of keeping the dry fruit much longer, has tended to reduce the price of it, that the costlier articles are to be found on the costermonger's barrow.

Fruit is, for the most part, displayed on barrows, by the street-dealers in it. Some who supply the better sort of houses—more especially those in the suburbs—carry such things as apples and plums, in clean round wicker-baskets, holding pecks or half-pecks.

The commoner " green" fruits of home produce are bought by the costermonger in the markets. The foreign green fruit, as pine-apples, melons, grapes, chestnuts, coker-nuts, Brazil-nuts, hazel-nuts, and oranges, are purchased by them at the public sales of the brokers, and of the Jews in Duke's-place. The more intelligent and thrifty of the costers buy at the public sales on the principle of association, as I have elsewhere described. Some costermongers expend as much as 20l. at a time in such green fruit, or dry fruit, as is not immediately perishable, at a public sale, or at a fruit-warehouse, and supply the other costers.

The regular costermongers seldom deal in oranges and chestnuts. If they sell walnuts, they reserve these, they say, for their Sunday afternoon's pastime. The people who carry oranges, chestnuts, or walnuts, or Spanish nuts about the town, are not considered as costermongers, but are generally, though not always, classed, by the regular men, with the watercress-women, the sprat-women, the winkle-dealers, and such others, whom they consider beneath them. The orange season is called by the costermonger the " Irishman's harvest." Indeed, the street trade in oranges and nuts is almost entirely in the

hands of the Irish and their children; and of the children of costermongers. The costers themselves would rather starve—and do starve now and then—than condescend to it. The trade in coker-nuts is carried on greatly by the Jews on Sundays, and by young men and boys who are not on other days employed as street-sellers.

The usual kinds of fruit the regular costers deal in are strawberries, raspberries (plain and stalked), cherries, apricots, plums, green-gages, currants, apples, pears, damsons, green and ripe gooseberries, and pine-apples. They also deal in vegetables, such as turnips, greens, brocoli, carrots, onions, celery, rhubarb, new potatoes, peas, beans (French and scarlet, broad and Windsor), asparagus, vegetable marrow, seakale, spinach, lettuces, small salads, radishes, etc. Their fruit and vegetables they usually buy at Covent-garden, Spitalfields, or the Borough markets. Occasionally they buy some at Farringdon, but this they reckon to be very little better than a "haggler's market,"—a " haggler" being, as I before explained, the middle-man who attends in the fruit and vegetable-markets, and buys of the salesman to sell again to the retail dealer or costermonger.

Concerning the quantity of fruit and vegetables sold in the streets, by the London costermongers. This, as I said, when treating of the street-trade in fish, can only be arrived at by ascertaining the entire quantity sold wholesale at the London markets, and then learning from the best authorities the proportion retailed in the public thoroughfares, Fully to elucidate this matter, both as to the extent of the metropolitan supply of vegetables and fruit, (" foreign" as well as " home-grown," and " green" as well as " dry") and the relative quantity of each, vended through the agency of the costermongers, I caused inquiries to be instituted at all the principal markets and brokers (for not even the vaguest return on the subject had, till then, been prepared), and received from all the gentlemen connected therewith, every assistance and information, as I have here great pleasure in acknowledging.

To carry out my present inquiry, I need not give returns of the articles not sold by the costermongers, nor is it necessary for me to cite any but those dealt in by them generally. Their exceptional sales, such as of mushrooms, cucumbers, &c., are not included here.

The following Table shows the ordinary annual supply of home grown fruit (nearly all produced within a radius of twelve miles from the Bank) to each of the London " green" markets.

A TABLE SHOWING THE QUANTITY OR MEASURE OF THE UNDERMENTIONED HOME-
GROWN FRUITS AND VEGETABLES SOLD THROUGHOUT THE YEAR, WHOLESALE, IN
THE METROPOLITAN "GREEN" MARKETS, WITH THE PROPORTION SOLD RETAIL IN
THE STREETS.

Description of Fruits and Vegetables.	Covent Garden.	Borough.	Spitalfields.	Farringdon.	Portman.	Total.	Proportion sold by Costermongers.
GREEN FRUIT.							
Apples	360,000 bushels	25,000	250,000	35,000	16,000	686,000	One-half.
Pears . . .	230,000 ,,	10,000	83,000	20,000	10,000	353,000	One-half.
Cherries . . .	90,000 doz. lbs.	45,000	15,000	12,000	11,200	173,200	One-half.
Plums*	93,000 bushels	15,500	45,000	3,000	20,000	176,500	One-fifteenth.
Green Gages* .	2,000 ,,	333	1,500	1,000	500	5,333	One-fiftieth.
Damsons* . . .	19,800 ,,	3,150	4,500	9,000	1,200	16,450	One-thirtieth.
Bullace	1,800 ,,	1,620	400	540	540	4,900	One-half.
Gooseberries . .	140,000 ,,	26,200	91,500	12,000	7,000	276,700	Three-fourths.
Currants (Red)* .	70,000 sieves	15,000	75,000	6,000	9,000	171,000	One-half.
Ditto (Black).	45,000 ,,	12,000	45,000	6,000	4,000	108,000	One-eighth.
Ditto (White).	3,800 ,,	3,000	15,000	3,000	2,000	24,000	One-eighth.
Strawberries† . .	638,000 pottles	330,000	396,000	15,000	148,500	1,527,500	One-half.
Raspberries . .	22,500 ,,	3,750	2,500	3,500	3,000	35,250	One-twentieth.
Mulberries . .	17,496 ,,	57,600	7,064	17,281	22,500	121,940	One-fourth.
Hazel Nuts . .	2,700 bushels	1,000	648	5,400	270	9,018	Two-thirds.
Filberts	221,400 lbs.	72,000	43,200	144,000	37,800	518,400	One-thirtieth.
VEGETABLES.							
Potatoes . . .	161,280,000 lbs.	48,384,000	64,512,000	24,192,000	12,096,000	310,464,000	One-fifteenth.
Cabbages‡ . . .	33,600,000 plants	19,200,000	12,000,000	8,400,000	16,472,000	89,672,000	One-third.
Brocoli and Cauli-flowers . . .	} 1,800,000 heads	3,780,000	2,880,000	5,320,000	546,000	14,326,000	One-twentieth.
Turnips . . .	18,800,000 roots	4,800,000	4,800,000	3,500,000	748,000	32,648,000	One-tenth.
Turnip Tops . .	300,000 junks,	500,000	600,000	250,000	200,000	1,850,000	One-third.
Carrots	12,000,000 roots	1,571,000	2,400,000	1,500,000	546,000	16,817,000	One-thirtieth.
Peas	270,000 bushels	50,000	100,000	14,000	4,000	438,000	One-fifteenth.
Beans	100,000 ,,	20,000	10,000	2,400	1,000	133,400	One-fifteenth.
French Beans .	140,000 ,,	9,600	12.000	50,000	9,600	221,100	One-tenth.
Vegetab. Marrows	10,800 dozen	3,240	3,600	432	1,800	19,872	One-third.
Asparagus . . .	12,000 dz. bun.	3,600	1,080	1,440	1,440	19,560	One-fortieth.
Celery	15,000 ,,	4,800	6,000	3,000	6,000	34,800	One-eighth.
Rhubarb . . .	7,200 ,,	48,000	28,800	2,400	4,800	91,200	One-tenth.
Lettuces . . .	734,400 plants	1,080,000	2,073,600	129,000	475,200	4,492,800	One-eighth.
Radishes . . .	6,912 dz. hands	43,200	36,000	18,000	28,800	132,912	One-tenth.
Onions	500,000 bushels	398,000	400,000	9,600	182,000	1,489,600	One-third.
Ditto (Spring) .	36,000 dz. bun.	10,800	21,600	21,600	14,400	94,000	One-fourth.
Cucumbers . .	2,160 bushels	10,800	24,000	12,000	38,400	87,360	One-eighth.
Herbs	7,200 dz. bun.	9,600	9,400	7,800	3,900	32,900	One-tenth.

* The above fruits are not all home grown. The currants, I am informed, are one-fifteenth foreign. The
foreign "tender" fruit being sent to the markets, it is impossible to obtain separate returns.

† A common sale of strawberries in the markets is "rounds." I have, however, given the quantity thus
sold less technically, and in the measures most familiar to the general public.

‡ The cabbages, turnips, &c. are brought in loads to the great wholesale markets, a load varying from 150
to 200 dozen, but being more frequently nearer 200, and not unfrequently to fully that amount. Not to perplex
my reader with too great a multiciplicity of figures in a tabular arrangement, I have given the quantity of
individual articles in a load, without specifying it. In the smaller market (for vegetables) of Portman, the
cabbages, &c., are not conveyed in waggons, as to the other markets, but in carts containing generally sixty
dozens.

The various proportions of the several kinds
of fruit and vegetables sold by the costermongers
are here calculated for *all* the markets, from
returns which have been obtained from each
market separately. To avoid unnecessary detail,
however, these several items are lumped together, and the aggregate proportion above given.

The foregoing Table, however, relates chiefly
to "home grown" supplies. Concerning the
quantity of foreign fruit and vegetables imported into this country, the proportion consumed in London, and the relative amount sold
by the costers, I have obtained the following
returns : —

TABLE, SHOWING THE QUANTITY OR MEASURE OF THE UNDERMENTIONED FOREIGN GREEN FRUITS AND VEGETABLES SOLD WHOLESALE THROUGHOUT THE YEAR IN LONDON, WITH THE PROPORTION SOLD RETAIL IN THE STREETS.

Description.	Quantity sold wholesale in London.	Proportion sold retail in the streets.
FRUIT.		
Apples . . .	39,561 bush.	seven-eighths.
Pears . . .	19,742 „	seven-eighths.
Cherries . .	264,240 lbs.	two-thirds.
Grapes . . .	1,328,190 „	one-fiftieth.
Pine-apples .	200,000 fruit	one-tenth.
Oranges . . .	61,635,146 „	one-fourth.
Lemons . .	15,408,789 „	one-hundredth.
NUTS.		
Spanish Nuts } Barcelona „ }	72,509 bush.	one-third.
Brazil „ . .	11,700 „	one-fourth.
Chestnuts . .	26,250 „	one-fourth.
Walnuts . . .	36,088 „	two-thirds.
"Coker"-nuts .	1,255,000 nuts	one-third.
VEGETABLES.		
Potatoes . . .	79,654,400lbs.	one-half.

Here, then, we have the entire metropolitan supply of the principal vegetables and green fruit (both home grown and foreign), as well as the relative quantity "distributed" throughout London by the costermongers; it now but remains for me, in order to complete the account, to do the same for "the dry fruit."

TABLE, SHOWING THE QUANTITY OF "DRY" FRUIT SOLD WHOLESALE IN LONDON THROUGHOUT THE YEAR, WITH THE PROPORTION SOLD RETAIL IN THE STREETS.

Description.	Quantity sold wholesale in London.	Proportion sold retail in the streets.
Shell Almonds .	12,500 cwt.	half per cent.
Raisins . .	135,000 „	quarter per cent.
Currants . .	250,000 „	none.
Figs . . .	21,700 „	one per cent.
Prunes . .	15,000 „	quarter per cent.

OF THE FRUIT AND VEGETABLE SEASON OF THE COSTERMONGERS.

The strawberry season begins about June, and continues till about the middle of July. From the middle to the end of July the costers "work" raspberries. During July cherries are "in" as well as raspberries; but many costers prefer working raspberries, because "they're a quicker sixpence." After the cherries, they go to work upon plums, which they have about the end of August. Apples and pears come in after the plums in the month of September, and the apples last them all through the winter till the

month of May. The pears last only till Christmas. Currants they work about the latter end of July, or beginning of August.

Concerning the costermonger's vegetable season, it may be said that he "works" greens during the winter months, up to about March; from that time they are getting "leathery," the leaves become foxy, I was told, and they eat tough when boiled. The costers generally do not like dealing either in greens or turnips, "they are such heavy luggage," they say. They would sooner "work" green peas and new potatoes. They say. They would

The costermonger, however, does the best at fruit; but this he cannot work—with the exception of apples—for more than four months in the year. They lose but little from the fruit spoiling. "If it doesn't fetch a good price, it must fetch a bad one," they say; but they are never at a great loss by it. They find the "ladies" their hardest or "scaliest" customers. Whatever price they ask, they declare the "ladies" will try to save the market or "gin" penny out of it, so that they may have "a glass of something short" before they go home.

OF COVENT GARDEN MARKET.

ON a Saturday—the coster's business day—it is computed that as many as 2,000 donkey-barrows, and upwards of 3,000 women with shallows and head-baskets visit this market during the forenoon. About six o'clock in the morning is the best time for viewing the wonderful restlessness of the place, for then not only is the "Garden" itself all bustle and activity, but the buyers and sellers stream to and from it in all directions, filling every street in the vicinity. From Long Acre to the Strand on the one side, and from Bow-street to Bedford-street on the other, the ground has been seized upon by the market-goers. As you glance down any one of the neighbouring streets, the long rows of carts and donkey-barrows seem interminable in the distance. They are of all kinds, from the greengrocer's taxed cart to the coster's barrow—from the showy excursion-van to the rude square donkey-cart and bricklayer's truck. In every street they are ranged down the middle and by the kerb-stones. Along each approach to the market, too, nothing is to be seen, on all sides, but vegetables; the pavement is covered with heaps of them waiting to be carted; the flag-stones are stained green with the leaves trodden under foot; sieves and sacks full of apples and potatoes, and bundles of brocoli and rhubarb, are left unwatched upon almost every door-step; the steps of Covent Garden Theatre are covered with fruit and vegetables; the road is blocked up with mountains of cabbages and turnips; and men and women push past with their arms bowed out by the cauliflowers under them, or the red tips of carrots pointing from their crammed aprons, or else their faces are red with the weight of the loaded head-basket.

The donkey-barrows, from their number and singularity, force you to stop and notice them. Every kind of ingenuity has been exercised to construct harness for the costers' steeds; where a buckle is wanting, tape or string make the fastening secure; traces are made of rope and old chain, and an old sack or cotton handkerchief is folded up as a saddle-pad. Some few of the barrows make a magnificent exception, and are gay with bright brass; while one of the donkeys may be seen dressed in a suit of old plated carriage-harness, decorated with coronets in all directions. At some one of the coster conveyances stands the proprietor, arranging his goods, the dozing animal starting up from its sleep each time a heavy basket is hoisted on the tray. Others, with their green and white and red load neatly arranged, are ready for starting, but the coster is finishing his breakfast at the coffee-stall. On one barrow there may occasionally be seen a solitary sieve of apples, with the horse of some neighbouring cart helping himself to the pippins while the owner is away. The men that take charge of the trucks, whilst the costers visit the market, walk about, with their arms full of whips and sticks. At one corner a donkey has slipped down, and lies on the stones covered with the cabbages and apples that have fallen from the cart.

The market itself presents a beautiful scene. In the clear morning air of an autumn day the whole of the vast square is distinctly seen from one end to the other. The sky is red and golden with the newly-risen sun, and the rays falling on the fresh and vivid colours of the fruit and vegetables, brightens up the picture as with a coat of varnish. There is no shouting, as at other markets, but a low murmuring hum is heard, like the sound of the sea at a distance, and through each entrance to the market the crowd sweeps by. Under the dark Piazza little bright dots of gas-lights are seen burning in the shops; and in the paved square the people pass and cross each other in all directions, hampers clash together, and excepting the carters from the country, every one is on the move. Sometimes a huge column of baskets is seen in the air, and walks away in a marvellously steady manner, or a monster railway van, laden with sieves of fruit, and with the driver perched up on his high seat, jolts heavily over the stones. Cabbages are piled up into stacks as it were. Carts are heaped high with turnips, and bunches of carrots like huge red fingers, are seen in all directions. Flower-girls, with large bundles of violets under their arms, run past, leaving a trail of perfume behind them. Wagons, with their shafts sticking up in the air, are ranged before the salesmen's shops, the high green load railed in with hurdles, and every here and there bunches of turnips are seen flying in the air over the heads of the people. Groups of apple-women, with straw pads on their crushed bonnets, and coarse shawls crossing their bosoms, sit on their porter's knots, chatting in Irish, and smoking short pipes; every passer-by is hailed with the cry of, "Want a baskit, yer honor?" The porter, trembling under the piled-up hamper, trots along the street, with his teeth clenched and shirt wet with the weight, and staggering at every step he takes.

Inside, the market all is bustle and confusion. The people walk along with their eyes fixed on the goods, and frowning with thought. Men in all costumes, from the coster in his corduroy suit to the greengrocer in his blue apron, sweep past. A countryman, in an old straw hat and dusty boots, occasionally draws down the anger of a woman for walking about with his hands in the pockets of his smock-frock, and is asked, "if that is the way to behave on a market-day?" Even the granite pillars cannot stop the crowd, for it separates and rushes past them, like the tide by a bridge pier. At every turn there is a fresh odour to sniff at; either the bitter aromatic perfume of the herbalists' shops breaks upon you, or the scent of oranges, then of apples, and then of onions is caught for an instant as you move along. The brocoli tied up in square packets, the white heads tinged slightly red, as it were, with the sunshine, —the sieves of crimson love-apples, polished like china,—the bundles of white glossy leeks, their roots dangling like fringe, — the celery, with its pinky stalks and bright green tops,— the dark purple pickling-cabbages,—the scarlet carrots,—the white knobs of turnips,—the bright yellow balls of oranges, and the rich brown coats of the chesnuts—attract the eye on every side. Then there are the apple-merchants, with their fruit of all colours, from the pale yellow green to the bright crimson, and the baskets ranged in rows on the pavement before the little shops. Round these the customers stand examining the stock, then whispering together over their bargain, and counting their money. "Give you four shillings for this here lot, master," says a coster, speaking for his three companions. "Four and six is my price," answers the salesman. "Say four, and it's a bargain," continues the man. "I said my price," returns the dealer; "go and look round, and see if you can get 'em cheaper; if not, come back. I only wants what's fair." The men, taking the salesman's advice, move on. The walnut merchant, with the group of women before his shop, peeling the fruit, their fingers stained deep brown, is busy with the Irish purchasers. The onion stores, too, are surrounded by Hibernians, feeling and pressing the gold-coloured roots, whose dry skins crackle as they are handled. Cases of lemons in their white paper jackets, and blue grapes, just seen above the sawdust are ranged about, and in some places the ground is slippery as ice from the refuse leaves and walnut husks scattered over the pavement.

Against the railings of St. Paul's Church are hung baskets and slippers for sale, and near the public-house is a party of countrymen preparing their bunches of pretty coloured grass— brown and glittering, as if it had been bronzed. Between the spikes of the railing are piled up square cakes of green turf for larks; and at the pump, boys, who probably have passed the previous night in the baskets about the market, are washing, and the water dripping from their hair that hangs in points over the face. The kerb-stone is blocked up by a crowd of admiring lads, gathered round the bird-catcher's green stand, and gazing at the larks beating their breasts against their cages. The owner, whose boots are red with the soil of the brick-field, shouts, as he looks carelessly around, " A cock linnet for tuppence," and then hits at the youths who are poking through the bars at the fluttering birds.

Under the Piazza the costers purchase their flowers (in pots) which they exchange in the streets for old clothes. Here is ranged a small garden of flower-pots, the musk and mignonette smelling sweetly, and the scarlet geraniums, with a perfect glow of coloured air about the flowers, standing out in rich contrast with the dark green leaves of the evergreens behind them. "There's myrtles, and larels, and boxes," says one of the men selling them, "and there's a harbora witus, and lauristiners, and that bushy shrub with pink spots is heath." Men and women, selling different articles, walk about under the cover of the colonnade. One has seed-cake, another small-tooth and other combs, others old caps, or pig's feet, and one hawker of knives, razors, and short hatchets, may occasionally be seen driving a bargain with a country-man, who stands passing his thumb over the blade to test its keenness. Between the pillars are the coffee-stalls, with their large tin cans and piles of bread and butter, and protected from the wind by paper screens and sheets thrown over clothes-horses; inside these little parlours, as it were, sit the coffee-drinkers on chairs and benches, some with a bunch of cabbages on their laps, blowing the steam from their saucers, others, with their mouths full, munching away at their slices, as if not a moment could be lost. One or two porters are there besides, seated on their baskets, breakfasting with their knots on their heads.

As you walk away from this busy scene, you meet in every street barrows and costers hurrying home. The pump in the market is now surrounded by a cluster of chattering wenches quarrelling over whose turn it is to water their drooping violets, and on the steps of Covent Garden Theatre are seated the shoeless girls, tying up the halfpenny and penny bundles.

OF "GREEN" FRUIT SELLING IN THE STREETS.

The fruit selling of the streets of London is of a distinct character from that of vegetable or fish selling, inasmuch as fruit is for the most part a luxury, and the others are principally necessaries.

There is no doubt that the consumption of fruit supplies a fair criterion of the condition of the working classes, but the costermongers, as a body of traders, are little observant, so that it is not easy to derive from them much information respecting the classes who are their customers, or as to how their custom is influenced by the circumstances of the times. One man, however, told me that during the last panic he sold hardly anything beyond mere necessaries. Other street-sellers to whom I spoke could not comprehend what a panic meant.

The most intelligent costers whom I conversed with agreed that they now sold less fruit than ever to working people, but perhaps more than ever to the dwellers in the smaller houses in the suburbs, and to shopkeepers who were not in a large way of business. One man sold baking apples, but not above a peck on an average weekly, to women whom he knew to be the wives of working men, for he had heard them say, "Dear me, I didn't think it had been so late, there's hardly time to get the dumplings baked before my husband leaves work for his dinner." The course of my inquiries has shown me—and many employers whom I have conversed with are of a similar opinion—that the well-conducted and skilful artisan, who, in spite of slop competition, continues to enjoy a fair rate of wages, usually makes a prudent choice of a wife, who perhaps has been a servant in a respectable family. Such a wife is probably "used to cooking," and will oft enough make a pie or pudding to eke out the cold meat of the Monday's dinner, or "for a treat for the children." With the mass of the working people, however, it is otherwise. The wife perhaps has been reared to incessant toil with her needle, and does not know how to make even a dumpling. Even if she possess as much knowledge, she may have to labour as well as her husband, and if their joint earnings enable them to have " the added pudding," there is still the trouble of making it; and, after a weary week's work, rest is often a greater enjoyment than a gratification of the palate. Thus something easily prepared, and carried off to the oven, is preferred. The slop-workers of all trades never, I believe, taste either fruit pie or pudding, unless a penny one be bought at a shop or in the street; and even among mechanics who are used to better diet, the pies and puddings, when wages are reduced, or work grows slack, are the first things that are dispensed with. "When the money doesn't come in, sir," one working-man said to me, " we mustn't think of puddings, but of *bread.*"

A costermonger, more observant than the rest, told me that there were some classes to whom he had rarely sold fruit, and whom he had seldom seen buy any. Among these he mentioned sweeps, scavengers, dustmen, nightmen, gas-pipe-layers, and sewer-men, who preferred to any fruit, "something to bite in the mouth, such as a penn'orth of gin." My informant believed that this abstinence from fruit was common to all persons engaged in such offensive trades as fiddle-string making, gut-dressing for whip-makers or sausage-makers, knackers, &c. He was confident of it, as far as his own experience extended. It is, moreover, less common for the women of the town, of the poorer sort, to expend pence in fruit than in such things as whelks, shrimps, or winks, to say nothing of gin. Persons, whose stomachs may be one week jaded to excess, and the next be deprived of a sufficiency of proper food, seek for stimulants, or, as they term it, "relishes."

The fruit-sellers, meaning thereby those who deal principally in fruit in the season, are the more intelligent costermongers. The calculation as to what a bushel of apples, for instance, will make in half or quarter pecks, puzzles the more ignorant, and they buy "second-hand," or of a middle-man, and consequently dearer. The Irish street-sellers do not meddle much with fruit, excepting a few of the very best class of them, and they "do well in it," I was told, "they have such tongue."

The improvement in the quality of the fruit and vegetables now in our markets, and consequently in the necessaries and luxuries of the poorer classes, is very great. Prizes and medals have been deservedly awarded to the skilled and persevering gardeners who have increased the size and heightened the flavour of the pine-apple or the strawberry—who have given a thinner rind to the peach, or a fuller gush of juice to the apricot,—or who have enhanced alike the bloom, the weight, and the size of the fruit of the vine, whether as regards the classic "bunch," or the individual grape. Still these are benefits confined mainly to the rich. But there is another class of growers who have rendered greater services and whose services have been comparatively unnoticed. I allude to those gardeners who have improved or introduced our *every day* vegetables or fruit, such as now form the cheapest and most grateful and healthy enjoyments of the humbler portion of the community. I may instance the introduction of rhubarb, which was comparatively unknown until Mr. Myatt, now of Deptford, cultivated it thirty years ago. He then, for the first time, carried seven bundles of rhubarb into the Borough market. Of these he could sell only three, and he took four back with him. Mr. Myatt could not recollect the price he received for the first rhubarb he ever sold in public, but he told me that the stalks were only about half the substance of those he now produces. People laughed at him for offering "physic pies," but he persevered, and I have shown what the sale of rhubarb now is.

Moreover, the importation of foreign "pines" may be cited as another instance of the increased luxuries of the poor. The trade in this commodity was unknown until the year 1842. At that period Mr. James Wood and Messrs. Claypole and Son, of Liverpool, imported them from the Bahamas, a portion being conveyed to Messrs. Keeling and Hunt, of London. Since that period the trade has gradually increased until, instead of 1000 pines being sent to Liverpool, and a portion of them conveyed to London, as at first, 200,000 pines are now imported to London alone. The fruit is brought over in "trees," stowed in numbers from ten to thirty thousand, in galleries constructed fore and aft in

the vessel, which is so extravagantly fragrant, that it has to be ventilated to abate the odour. But for this importation, and but for the trade having become a part of the costermonger's avocation, hundreds and thousands in London would never have tasted a pine-apple. The quality of the fruit has, I am informed, been greatly improved since its first introduction; the best description of "pines" which Coventgarden can supply having been sent out to graft, to increase the size and flavour of the Bahaman products, and this chiefly for the regalement of the palates of the humbler classes of London. The supply from the Bahamas is considered inexhaustible.

Pine-apples, when they were first introduced, were a rich harvest to the costermonger. They made more money "working" these than any other article. The pines cost them about 4*d*. each, one with the other, good and bad together, and were sold by the costermonger at from 1*s*. to 1*s*. 6*d*. The public were not aware then that the pines they sold were "salt-water touched," and the people bought them as fast as they could be sold, not only by the whole one, but at 1*d*. a slice,—for those who could not afford to give 1*s*. for the novelty, had a slice as a taste for 1*d*. The costermongers used then to have flags flying at the head of their barrows, and gentlefolk would stop them in the streets; indeed, the sale for pines was chiefly among "the gentry." The poorer people—sweeps, dustmen, cabmen — occasionally had pennyworths, "just for the fun of the thing;" but gentlepeople, I was told, used to buy a whole one to take home, so that all the family might have a taste. One costermonger assured me that he had taken 22*s*. a day during the rage for pines, when they first came up.

I have before stated that when the season is in its height the costermonger prefers the vending of fruit to the traffic in either fish or vegetables; those, however, who have regular rounds and "a connection," must supply their customers with vegetables, if not fish, as well as fruit, but the costers prefer to devote themselves principally to fruit. I am unable, therefore, to draw a comparison between what a coster realises in fruit, and what in fish, as the two seasons are not contemporary. The fruit sale is, however, as I have shown in p. 54, the costermonger's harvest.

All the costermongers with whom I conversed represented that the greater cheapness and abundance of fruit had been anything but a benefit to them, nor did the majority seem to know whether fruit was scarcer or more plentiful one year than another, unless in remarkable instances. Of the way in which the introduction of foreign fruit had influenced their trade, they knew nothing. If questioned on the subject, the usual reply was, that things got worse, and people didn't buy so much fruit as they did half-a-dozen years back, and so less was sold. That these men hold such opinions must be accounted for mainly by the increase in their numbers, of which I have before spoken, and from their general ignorance.

The fruit of which there is the readiest sale in the streets is one usually considered among the least useful—cherries. Probably, the greater eagerness on the part of the poorer classes to purchase this fruit arises from its being the first of the fresh "green" kind which our gardens supply for street-sale after the winter and the early spring. An intelligent costermonger suggested other reasons. "Poor people," he said, "like a *quantity* of any fruit, and no fruit is cheaper than cherries at 1*d.* a pound, at which I have sold some hundreds of pounds' weight. I'm satisfied, sir, that if a cherry could be grown that weighed a pound, and was of a finer flavour than ever was known before, poor people would rather have a number of little ones, even if they was less weight and inferior quality. Then boys buy, I think, more cherries than other fruit; because, after they have eaten 'em, they can play at cherry-stones.'"

From all I can learn, the halfpenny-worth of fruit purchased most eagerly by a poor man, or by a child to whom the possession of a halfpenny is a rarity, is cherries. I asked a man "with a good connection," according to his own account, as to who were his customers for cherries. He enumerated ladies and gentlemen; working-people; wagoners and carters (who "slipped them quietly into their pockets," he said); parlour-livers (so he called the occupants of parlours); maid-servants; and soldiers. "Soldiers." I was told, " are very fond of something for a change from their feed, which is about as regular as a prison's."

The currant, and the fruit of the same useful genus, the gooseberry, are sold largely by the costermongers. The price of the currants is 1*d.* or 2*d.* the half-pint, 1*d.* being the more usual charge. Of red currants there is the greatest supply, but the black "go off better." The humbler classes buy a half-pint of the latter for a dumpling, and "they're reckoned," said my informant, "capital for a sore throat, either in jam or a pudding." Gooseberries are also retailed by the half-pint, and are cheaper than currants —perhaps ½*d.* the half-pint is the average street-price. The working-classes do not use ripe gooseberries, as they do ripe currants, for dumplings, but they are sold in greater quantities and may be said to constitute, when first introduced, as other productions do afterwards, the working-people's Sunday dessert. " Only you go on board a cheap steamer to Greenwich, on a fine summer Sunday," observed a street-seller to me, " and you'll see lots of young women with gooseberries in their handkerchiefs in their laps. Servant-maids is very good customers for such things as gooseberries, for they always has a penny to spare." The costers sell green gooseberries for dumplings, and sometimes to the extent of a fourth of the ripe fruit. The price of green gooseberries is generally ½*d.* a pint dearer than the ripe.

When strawberries descend to such a price

as places them at the costermonger's command, the whole fraternity is busily at work, and as the sale can easily be carried on by women and children, the coster's family take part in the sale, offering at the corners of streets the fragrant pottle, with the crimson fruit just showing beneath the green leaves at the top. Of all cries, too, perhaps that of " hoboys" is the most agreeable. Strawberries, however, according to all accounts, are consumed least of all fruits by the poor. "They like something more solid," I was told, "something to bite at, and a penny pottle of strawberries is only like a taste; what's more, too, the really good fruit never finds its way into penny pottles." The coster's best customers are dwellers in the suburbs, who purchase strawberries on a Sunday especially, for dessert, for they think that they get them fresher in that way than by reserving them from the Saturday night, and many are tempted by seeing or hearing them cried in the streets. There is also a good Sunday sale about the steam-wharfs, to people going " on the river," especially when young women and children are members of a party, and likewise in the " clerk districts," as Camden-town and Camberwell. Very few pottles, comparatively, are sold in public-houses; "they don't go well down with the beer at all," I was told. The city people are good customers for street strawberries, conveying them home. Good strawberries are 2*d.* a pottle in the streets when the season is at its height. Inferior are 1*d.* These are the most frequent prices. In raspberries the coster does little, selling them only to such customers as use them for the sake of jam or for pastry. The price is from 6*d.* to 1*s.* 6*d.* the pottle, 9*d.* being the average.

The great staple of the street trade in green fruit is apples. These are first sold by the travelling costers, by the measure, for pies, &c., and to the classes I have described as the makers of pies. The apples, however, are soon vended in penny or halfpenny-worths, and then they are bought by the poor who have a spare penny for the regalement of their children or themselves, and they are eaten without any preparation. Pears are sold to the same classes as are apples. The average price of apples, as sold by the costermonger, is 4*s.* a bushel, and six a penny. The sale in halfpenny and penny-worths is very great. Indeed the costermongers sell about half the apples brought to the markets, and I was told that for one pennyworth of apples bought in a shop forty were bought in the street. Pears are 9*d.* a bushel, generally, dearer than apples, but, numerically, they run more to the bushel.

The costers purchase the French apples at the wharf, close to London-bridge, on the Southwark side. They give 10*s.*, 12*s.*, 18*s.*, or 20*s.* for a case containing four bushels. They generally get from 9*d.* to 1*s.* profit on a bushel of English, but on the French apples they make a clear profit of from 1*s.* 3*d.* to 2*s.* a bushel, and would make more, but the fruit sometimes "turns out damaged." This extra profit is owing to the French giving better measure, their four bushels being about five market bushels, as there is much straw packed up with the English apples, and none with the French.

Plums and damsons are less purchased by the humbler classes than apples, or than any other larger sized fruit which is supplied abundantly.

"If I've worked plums or damsons," said an experienced costermonger, "and have told any woman pricing them: 'They don't look so ripe, but they're all the better for a pie,' she's answered, 'O, a plum pie's too fine for us, and what's more, it takes too much sugar.'" They are sold principally for desserts, and in pennyworths, at 1*d.* the half-pint for good, and ½*d.* for inferior. Green-gages are 50 per cent. higher. Some costers sell a cheap lot of plums to the eating-house keepers, and sell them more readily than they sell apples to the same parties.

West Indian pine-apples are, as regards the street sale, disposed of more in the city than elsewhere. They are bought by clerks and warehousemen, who carry them to their suburban homes. The slices at ½*d.* and 1*d.* are bought principally by boys. The average price of a " good street pine " is 9*d.*

Peaches are an occasional sale with the costermongers', and are disposed of to the same classes as purchase strawberries and pines. The street sale of peaches is not practicable if the price exceed 1*d.* a piece.

Of other fruits, vended largely in the streets, I have spoken under their respective heads.

The returns before cited as to the quantity of home-grown and foreign green fruit sold in London, and the *proportion* disposed of by the costermongers give the following results (in round numbers), as to the absolute quantity of the several kinds of green fruit (oranges and nuts excepted) " distributed " throughout the metropolis by the street-sellers.

343,000	bushels of apples, (home-grown)	
34,560	„ apples, (foreign)	
176,500	„ pears, (home-grown)	
17,235	„ pears, (foreign)	
1,039,200	lbs. of cherries, (home-grown)	
176,160	„ cherries, (foreign)	
11,766	bushels of plums,	
100	„ greengages,	
548	„ damsons,	
2,450	„ bullaces,	
207,525	„ gooseberries,	
85,500	sieves of red currants,	
13,500	„ black currants,	
3,000	„ white currants,	
763,750	pottles of strawberries,	
1,762	„ raspberries,	
30,485	„ mulberries,	
6,012	bushels of hazel nuts,	
17,280	lbs. of filberts,	
26,563	„ grapes,	
20,000	pines.	

OF THE ORANGE AND NUT MARKET.

IN Houndsditch there is a market supported principally by costermongers, who there purchase their oranges, lemons, and nuts. This market is entirely in the hands of the Jews; and although a few tradesmen may attend it to buy grapes, still it derives its chief custom from the street-dealers who say they can make far better bargains with the Israelites, (as they never refuse an offer,) than they can with the Covent-garden salesmen, who generally cling to their prices. This market is known by the name of " Duke's-place," although its proper title is St. James's-place. The nearest road to it is through Duke's-street, and the two titles have been so confounded that at length the mistake has grown into a custom.

Duke's-place—as the costers call it—is a large square yard, with the iron gates of a synagogue in one corner, a dead wall forming one entire side of the court, and a gas-lamp on a circular pavement in the centre. The place looks as if it were devoted to money-making— for it is quiet and dirty. Not a gilt letter is to be seen over a doorway; there is no display of gaudy colour, or sheets of plate-glass, such as we see in a crowded thoroughfare when a customer is to be caught by show. As if the merchants knew their trade was certain, they are content to let the London smoke do their painter's work. On looking at the shops in this quarter, the idea forces itself upon one that they are in the last stage of dilapidation. Never did property in Chancery look more ruinous. Each dwelling seems as though a fire had raged in it, for not a shop in the market has a window to it; and, beyond the few sacks of nuts exposed for sale, they are empty, the walls within being blackened with dirt, and the paint without blistered in the sun, while the door-posts are worn round with the shoulders of the customers, and black as if charred. A few sickly hens wander about, turning over the heaps of dried leaves that the oranges have been sent over in, or roost the time away on the shafts and wheels of the nearest truck. Excepting on certain days, there is little or no business stirring, so that many of the shops have one or two shutters up, as if a death had taken place, and the yard is quiet as an inn of court. At a little distance the warehouses, with their low ceilings, open fronts, and black sides, seem like dark holes or coal-stores ; and, but for the mahogany backs of chairs showing at the first floors, you would scarcely believe the houses to be inhabited, much more to be elegantly furnished as they are. One of the drawing-rooms that I entered here was warm and red with morocco leather, Spanish mahogany, and curtains and Turkey carpets ; while the ormolu chandelier and the gilt frames of the looking-glass and pictures twinkled at every point in the fire-light.

The householders in Duke's-place are all of the Jewish persuasion, and among the costers a saying has sprung up about it. When a man has been out of work for some time, he is said to be " Cursed, like a pig in Duke's-place."

Almost every shop has a Scripture name over it, and even the public-houses are of the Hebrew faith, their signs appealing to the followers of those trades which most abound with Jews. There is the "Jeweller's Arms," patronised greatly of a Sunday morning, when the Israelite jewellers attend to exchange their trinkets and barter amongst themselves. Very often the counter before " the bar" here may be seen covered with golden ornaments, and sparkling with precious stones, amounting in value to thousands of pounds. The landlord of this house is licensed to *manufacture* tobacco and cigars. There is also the " Fishmongers' Arms," the resort of the vendors of fried soles; here, in the evening, a concert takes place, the performers and audience being Jews. The landlord of this house too is licensed to manufacture tobacco and cigars. Entering one of these houses I found a bill announcing a " Bible to be raffled for, the property of ——." And, lastly, there is " Benjamin's Coffee-house," open to old clothesmen; and here, again, the proprietor is a licensed tobacco-manufacturer. These facts are mentioned to show the untiring energy of the Jew when anything is to be gained, and to give an instance of the curious manner in which this people support each other.

Some of the nut and orange shops in Duke's-place it would be impossible to describe. At one sat an old woman, with jet-black hair and a wrinkled face, nursing an infant, and watching over a few matted baskets of nuts ranged on a kind of carpenter's bench placed upon the pavement. The interior of the house was as empty as if it had been to let, excepting a few bits of harness hanging against the wall, and an old salt-box nailed near the gas-lamp, in which sat a hen, "hatching," as I was told. At another was an excessively stout Israelite mother, with crisp negro's hair and long gold earrings, rolling hei child on the table used for sorting the nuts. Here the black walls had been chalked over with scores, and every corner was filled up with sacks and orange-cases. Before one warehouse a family of six, from the father to the infant, were busy washing walnuts in a huge tub with a trap in the side, and around them were ranged measures of the wet fruit. The Jewish women are known to make the fondest parents; and in Duke's-place there certainly was no lack of fondlings. Inside almost every parlour a child was either being nursed or romped with, and some little things were being tossed nearly to the ceiling, and caught, screaming with enjoyment, in the jewelled hands of the delighted mother. At other shops might be seen a circle of three or four women—some old as if grandmothers, grouped admiringly round a hook-nosed infant, tickling it and poking their fingers at it in a frenzy of affection.

The counters of these shops are generally placed in the open streets like stalls, and the shop itself is used as a store to keep the stock in. On these counters are ranged the large matting baskets, some piled up with dark-brown polished chestnuts—shining like a racer's neck—others filled with wedge-shaped Brazil-nuts, and rough hairy cocoa-nuts.- There are heaps, too, of newly-washed walnuts, a few showing their white crumpled kernels as a sample of their excellence. Before every doorway are long pot-bellied boxes of oranges, with the yellow fruit just peeping between the laths on top, and lemons—yet green—are ranged about in their paper jackets to ripen in the air.

In front of one store the paving-stones were soft with the sawdust emptied from the grape-cases, and the floor of the shop itself was whitened with the dry powder. Here stood a man in a long tasselled smoking-cap, puffing with his bellows at the blue bunches on a tray, and about him were the boxes with the paper lids thrown back, and the round sea-green berries just rising above the sawdust as if floating in it. Close by, was a group of dark-eyed women bending over an orange-case, picking out the rotten from the good fruit, while a sallow-complexioned girl was busy with her knife scooping out the damaged parts, until, what with sawdust and orange-peel, the air smelt like the pit of a circus.

Nothing could be seen in this strange place that did not, in some way or another, appertain to Jewish customs. A woman, with a heavy gold chain round her neck, went past, carrying an old green velvet bonnet covered with feathers, and a fur tippet, that she had either recently purchased or was about to sell. Another woman, whose features showed her to be a Gentile, was hurrying toward the slop-shop in the Minories with a richly quilted satin-lined coat done up in her shawl, and the market-basket by her side, as if the money due for the work were to be spent directly for housekeeping.

At the corner of Duke's-street was a stall kept by a Jew, who sold things that are eaten only by the Hebrews. Here in a yellow pie-dish were pieces of stewed apples floating in a thick puce-coloured sauce.

One man that I spoke to told me that he considered his Sunday morning's work a very bad one if he did not sell his five or six hundred bushels of nuts of different kinds. He had taken 150*l.* that day of the street-sellers, and usually sold his 100*l.* worth of goods in a morning. Many others did the same as himself. Here I met with every attention, and was furnished with some valuable statistical information concerning the street-trade.

OF ORANGE AND LEMON SELLING IN THE STREETS.

OF foreign fruits, the oranges and nuts supply by far the greater staple for the street trade, and, therefore, demand a brief, but still a fuller, notice than other articles.

Oranges were first sold in the streets at the

close of Elizabeth's reign. So rapidly had the trade increased, that four years after her death, or in 1607, Ben Jonson classes "orange-wives," for noisiness, with "fish-wives." These women at first carried the oranges in baskets on their heads; barrows were afterwards used; and now trays are usually slung to the shoulders.

Oranges are brought to this country in cases or boxes, containing from 500 to 900 oranges. From official tables, it appears that between 250,000,000 and 300,000,000 of oranges and lemons are now yearly shipped to England. They are sold wholesale, principally at public sales, in lots of eight boxes, the price at such sales varying greatly, according to the supply and the quality. The supply continues to arrive from October to August.

Oranges are bought by the retailers in Duke's-place and in Covent-Garden; but the costermongers nearly all resort to Duke's-place, and the shopkeepers to Covent-Garden. They are sold in baskets of 200 or 300; they are also disposed of by the hundred, a half-hundred being the smallest quantity sold in Duke's-place. These hundreds, however, number 110, containing 10 double "hands," a single hand being 5 oranges. The price in December was 2s. 6d., 3s. 6d., and 4s. the hundred. They are rarely lower than 4s. about Christmas, as there is then a better demand for them. The damaged oranges are known as "specks," and the purchaser runs the risk of specks forming a portion of the contents of a basket, as he is not allowed to empty it for the examination of the fruit: but some salesmen agree to change the specks. A month after Christmas, oranges are generally cheaper, and become dearer again about May, when there is a great demand for the supply of the fairs and races.

Oranges are sold by all classes connected with the fruit, flower, or vegetable trade of the streets. The majority of the street-sellers are, however, women and children, and the great part of these are Irish. It has been computed that, when oranges are "at their best" (generally about Easter), there are 4,000 persons, including stall-keepers, selling oranges in the metropolis and its suburbs; while there are generally 3,000 out of this number "working" oranges—that is, hawking them from street to street: of these, 300 attend at the doors of the theatres, saloons, &c. Many of those "working" the theatres confine their trade to oranges, while the other dealers rarely do so, but unite with them the sale of nuts of some kind. Those who sell only oranges, or only nuts, are mostly children, and of the poorest class. The smallness of the sum required to provide a stock of oranges (a half-hundred being 15d. or 18d.), enables the poor, who cannot raise "stock-money" sufficient to purchase anything else, to trade upon a few oranges.

The regular costers rarely buy oranges until the spring, except, perhaps, for Sunday afternoon sale—though this, as I said before, they mostly object to. In the spring, however, they stock their barrows with oranges. One man told

me that, four or five years back, he had sold in a day 2,000 oranges that he picked up as a bargain. They did not cost him half a farthing each; he said he "cleared 2l. by the spec." At the same period he could earn 5s. or 6s. on a Sunday afternoon by the sale of oranges in the street; but now he could not earn 2s.

A poor Irishwoman, neither squalid in appearance nor ragged in dress, though looking pinched and wretched, gave me the subjoined account; when I saw her, resting with her basket of oranges near Coldbath-fields prison, she told me she almost wished she was inside of it, but for the "childer." Her history was one common to her class —

"I was brought over here, sir, when I was a girl, but my father and mother died two or three years after. I was in service then, and very good service I continued in as a maid-of-all-work, and very kind people I met; yes, indeed, though I was Irish and a Catholic, and they was English Protistants. I saved a little money there, and got married. My husband's a labourer; and when he's in full worruk he can earn 12s. or 14s. a week, for he's a good hand and a harrud-worruking man, and we do middlin' thin. He's out of worruk now, and I'm forced to thry and sill a few oranges to keep a bit of life in us, and my husband minds the childer. Bad as I do, I can do 1d. or 2d. a day profit betther than him, poor man! for he's tall and big, and people thinks, if he goes round with a few oranges, it's just from idleniss; and the Lorrud above knows he'll always worruk whin he can. He goes sometimes whin I'm harrud tired. One of us must stay with the childer, for the youngist is not three and the ildest not five. We don't live, we starruve. We git a few 'taties, and sometimes a plaice. To-day I've not taken 3d. as yit, sir, and it's past three. Oh, no, indeed and indeed, thin, I dont make 9d. a day. We live accordingly, for there's 1s. 3d. a week for rint. I have very little harrut to go into the public-houses to sill oranges, for they begins flying out about the Pope and Cardinal Wiseman, as if I had anything to do with it. And that's another reason why I like my husband to stay at home, and me to go out, because he's a hasty man, and might get into throuble. I don't know what will become of us, if times don't turn."

On calling upon this poor woman on the following day, I found her and her children absent. The husband had got employment at some distance, and she had gone to see if she could not obtain a room 3d. a week cheaper, and lodge near the place of work.

According to the Board of Trade returns, there are nearly two hundred millions of oranges annually imported into this country. About one-third of these are sold wholesale in London, and one-fourth of the latter quantity disposed of retail in the streets. The returns I have procured, touching the London sale, prove that no less than 15,500,000 are sold yearly by the street-sellers. The retail price of these may be said to be, upon an average, 5s. per 110, and this would give us about 35,000l. for the gross sum of money laid out every year, in the streets, in the matter of oranges alone.

The street lemon-trade is now insignificant, lemons having become a more important article of commerce since the law required foreign-bound ships to be provided with lemon-juice. The street-sale is chiefly in the hands of the Jews and the Irish. It does not, however, call for special notice here.

OF NUT SELLING IN THE STREETS.

THE sellers of foreign hazel nuts are principally women and children, but the stall-keepers, and oftentimes the costermongers, sell them with other "goods." The consumption of them is immense, the annual export from Tarragona being little short of 8,000 tons. They are to be found in every poor shop in London, as well as in the large towns; they are generally to be seen on every street-stall, in every country village, at every fair, and on every race-ground. The supply is from Gijon and Tarragona. The Gijon nuts are the "Spanish," or "fresh" nuts. They are sold at public sales, in barrels of three bushels each, the price being from 35s. to 40s. The nuts from Tarragona, whence comes the great supply, are known as "Barcelonas," and they are kiln-dried before they are shipped. Hence the Barcelonas will "keep," and the Spanish will not. The Spanish are coloured with the fumes of sulphur, by the Jews in Duke's-place.

It is somewhat remarkable that nuts supply employment to a number of girls in Spain, and then yield the means of a scanty subsistence to a number of girls (with or without parents) in England.

The prattle and the laughter (according to Inglis) of the Spanish girls who sort, find no parallel however among the London girls who sell the nuts. The appearance of the latter is often wretched. In the winter months they may be seen as if stupified with cold, and with the listlessness, not to say apathy, of those whose diet is poor in quantity and insufficient in amount.

Very few costermongers buy nuts (as hazel nuts are always called) at the public sales—only those whose dealings are of a wholesale character, and they are anything but regular attendants at the sales. The street-sellers derive nearly the whole of their supply from Duke's-place. The principal times of business are Friday afternoons and Sunday mornings. Those who have "capital" buy on the Friday, when they say they can make 10s. go as far as 12s. on the Sunday. The "Barcelonas" are from 4½d. to 6d. a quart to the street-sellers. The cob-nuts, which are the large size, used by the pastry-cooks for mottos, &c., are 2d. and 2½d. the quart, but they are generally destitute of a kernel. A quart contains from 100 to 180 nuts, according to the size. The costermongers buy somewhat largely when nuts are 3d. the quart;

they then, and not unfrequently, stock their barrows with nuts entirely, but 2s. a day is reckoned excellent earnings at this trade. "It's the worst living of all, sir," I was told, "on nuts." The sale in the streets is at the fruit-stalls, in the public-houses, on board the steamers, and at the theatre doors. They are sold by the same class as the oranges, and a stock may be procured for a smaller sum even than is required for oranges. By the outlay of 1s. many an Irishwoman can send out her two or three children with nuts, reserving some for herself. Seven-eighths of the nuts imported are sold, I am assured, in the open air.

Some of the costermongers who are to be found in Battersea-fields, and who attend the fairs and races, get through 5s. worth of nuts in a day, but only exceptionally. These men have a sort of portable shooting-gallery. The customer fires a kind of rifle, loaded with a dart, and according to the number marked on the centre, or on the encircling rings of a board which forms the head of the stall, and which may be struck by the dart, is the number of nuts payable by the stall-keeper for the half-penny "fire."

The Brazil nuts, which are now sold largely in the streets at twelve to sixteen a penny, were not known in this country as an article of commerce before 1824. They are sold by the peck —2s. being the ordinary price—in Duke's-place.

Coker-nuts—as they are now generally called, and indeed "entered" as such at the Custom-house, and so written by Mr. McCulloch, to distinguish them from cocoa, or the berries of the cacâo, used for chocolate, etc.—are brought from the West Indies, both British and Spanish, and Brazil. They are used as dunnage in the sugar ships, being interposed between the hogsheads, to steady them and prevent their being flung about. The coker-nut was introduced into England in 1690. They are sold at public sales and otherwise, and bring from 10s. to 14s. per 100. Coker-nuts are now used at fairs to "top" the sticks.

The costermongers rarely speculate in coker-nuts now, as the boys will not buy them unless cut, and it is almost impossible to tell how the coker-nut will "open." The interior is sold in halfpenny-worths and penny-worths. These nuts are often "worked with a drum." There may be now forty coker-nut men in the street trade, but not one in ten confines himself to the article.

A large proportion of the dry or ripe walnuts sold in the streets is from Bordeaux. They are sold at public sales, in barrels of three bushels each, realising 21s. to 25s. a barrel. They are retailed at from eight to twenty a penny, and are sold by all classes of street-traders.

A little girl, who looked stunted and wretched, and who did not know her age (which might be eleven), told me she was sent out by her mother with six halfpenny-worth of nuts, and she must carry back 6d. or she would be beat. She had no father, and could neither read nor write.

Her mother was an Englishwoman, *she believed,* and sold oranges. She had heard of God; he was "Our Father who art in heaven." She'd heard that said. She did not know the Lord's Prayer; had never heard of it; did not know who the Lord was; perhaps the Lord Mayor, but she had never been before him. She went into public-houses with her nuts, but did not know whether she was ever insulted or not; she did not know what insulted was, but she was never badly used. She often went into tap-rooms with her nuts, just to warm herself. A man once gave her some hot beer, which made her ill. Her mother was kind enough to her, and never beat her but for not taking home 6*d.* She had a younger brother that did as she did. She had bread and potatoes to eat, and sometimes tea, and sometimes herrings. Her mother didn't get tipsy (at first she did not know what was meant by tipsy) *above* once a week.

OF ROASTED. CHESTNUTS AND APPLES.

How long the street-trade in roasted chestnuts has been carried on I find no means of ascertaining precisely, but it is unquestionably one of the oldest of the public traffics. Before potato-cans were introduced, the sale of roasted chestnuts was far greater than it is now.

It is difficult to compute the number of roasted chestnut-sellers at present in the streets. It is probable that they outnumber 1,000, for I noticed that on a cold day almost every street fruit-seller, man or woman, had roasted chestnuts for sale.

Sometimes the chestnuts are roasted in the streets, in a huge iron apparatus, made expressly for the purpose, and capable of cooking perhaps a bushel at a time—but these are to be found solely at the street-markets.

The ordinary street apparatus for roasting chestnuts is simple. A round pan, with a few holes punched in it, costing 3*d.* or 4*d.* in a marine-store shop, has burning charcoal within it, and is surmounted by a second pan, or kind of lid, containing chestnuts, which are thus kept hot. During my inquiry, chestnuts were dear. "People don't care," I was told, "whether chestnuts are three and six, as they are now, or one and six a peck, as I hope they will be afore long; they wants the same pennyworths."

Chestnuts are generally bought wholesale in Duke's-place, on the Sunday mornings, for street sale; but some street-dealers buy them of those costermongers, whose means enable them "to lay in" a quantity. The retail customers are, for the most part, boys and girls, or a few labourers or street people. The usual price is sixteen a penny.

Roasted apples used to be vended in the streets, and often along with roasted chestnuts, but it is a trade which has now almost entirely disappeared, and its disappearance is attributed to the prevalence of potato cans.

I had the following account from a woman, apparently between sixty and seventy, though she said she was only about fifty. What she was in her youth, she said, she neither knew nor cared. At any rate she was unwilling to converse about it. I found her statement as to chestnuts corroborated:—

"The trade's nothing to what it was, sir," she said. "Why when the hackney coaches was in the streets, I've often sold 2*s.* worth of a night at a time, for a relish, to the hackneymen that was waiting their turn over their beer. Six and eight a penny was enough then; now people must have sixteen; though I pays 3*s.* a peck, and to get them at that's a favour. I could make my good 12*s.* a week on roasted chestnuts and apples, and as much on other things in them days, but I'm half-starved now. There'll never be such times again. People didn't want to cut one another's throats in the street business then. O, I don't know anything about how long ago, or what year—years is nothing to me—but I only know that it was so. I got a penny a piece then for my roasted apples, and a halfpenny for sugar to them. I *could* live then. Roasted apples was reckoned good for the tooth-ache in them days, but, people change so, they aren't now. I don't know what I make now in chestnuts and apples, which is all I sells—perhaps 5*s.* a week. My rent's 1*s.* 3*d.* a week. I lives on a bit of fish, or whatever I can get, and that's all about it."

The absolute quantity of oranges, lemons, and nuts sold annually in the London streets is as follows:

Oranges	15,400,000
Lemons	154,000
Spanish and Barcelona nuts	24,000 bushels
Brazil do.	3,000 ,,
Chestnuts	6,500 ,,
Walnuts	24,000 ,,
Coker-nuts	400,000 nuts

OF "DRY" FRUIT SELLING IN THE STREETS.

THE sellers of "dry fruit" cannot be described as a class, for, with the exception of one old couple, none that I know of confine themselves to its sale, but resort to it merely when the season prevents their dealing in "green fruit" or vegetables. I have already specified what in commerce is distinguished as "dry fruit," but its classification among the costers is somewhat narrowed.

The dry-fruit sellers derive their supplies partly from Duke's-place, partly from Pudding-lane, but perhaps principally from the costers concerning whom I have spoken, who buy wholesale at the markets and elsewhere, and who will "clear out a grocer," or buy such figs, &c. as a leading tradesman will not allow to be sent, or offered, to his regular customers, although, perhaps, some of the articles are tolerably good. Or else the dry-fruit men buy a damaged lot of a broker or grocer, and pick out all that is eatable, or rather saleable.

The sale of dry fruit is unpopular among the costermongers. Despite their utmost pains, they cannot give to figs, or raisins, or currants, which may be old and stale, anything of the bloom and plumpness of good fruit, and the price of good fruit is too high for them. Moreover, if the fruit be a "damaged lot," it is almost always discoloured, and the blemish cannot be removed.

It is impossible to give the average price of dry fruit to the costermonger. The quality and the " harvest " affect the price materially in the regular trade.

The rule which I am informed the costermonger, who sometimes " works " a barrow of dried fruit, observes, is this : he will aim at cent. per cent., and, to accomplish it, " slang " weights are not unfrequently used. The stale fruit is sold by the grocers, and the damaged fruit by the warehouses to the costers, at from a half, but much more frequently a fourth to a twentieth of its prime cost. The principal street-purchasers are boys.

A dry-fruit seller gave me the following account:—By " half profits " he meant cent. per cent., or, in other words, that the money he received for his stock was half of it cost price and half profit.

" I sell dry fruit, sir, in February and March, because I must be doing something, and green fruit's not my money then. It's a poor trade. I've sold figs at 1d. a pound, —no, sir, not slang the time I mean—and I could hardly make 1s. a day at it, though it was half profits. Our customers look at them quite particler. ' Let's see the other side of them figs,' the boys 'll say, and then they'll out with—' I say, master, d' you see any green about me?' Dates I can hardly get off at all, no!—not if they was as cheap as potatoes, or cheaper. I've been asked by women if dates was good in dumplings? I've sometimes said ' yes,' though I knew nothing at all about them. They're foreign. I can't say where they're grown. Almonds and raisins goes off best with us. I don't sell them by weight, but makes them up in ha'penny or penny lots. There's two things, you see, and one helps off the other. Raisins is dry grapes, I've heard. I've sold grapes before they was dried, at 1d. and 2d. the pound. I didn't do no good in any of 'em; 1s. a day on 'em was the topper, for all the half profits. I'll not touch 'em again if I aint forced."

There are a few costers who sell tolerable dry fruit, but not to any extent.

The old couple I have alluded to stand all the year round at the corner of a street running into a great city thoroughfare. They are supplied with their fruit, I am told, through the friendliness of a grocer who charges no profit, and sometimes makes a sacrifice for their benefit. As I was told that this old couple would not like inquiries to be made of them, I at once desisted.

There are sometimes twenty costermongers selling nothing but dry fruit, but more frequently only ten, and sometimes only five; while, perhaps, from 300 to 400 sell a few figs, &c., with other things, such as late apples,

the dry fruit being then used "just as a fill up."

According to the returns before given, the gross quantity of dry fruit disposed of yearly in the streets of London may be stated as follows :

7,000 lbs. of shell almonds,
37,800 „ raisins,
24,300 „ figs,
4,200 „ prunes.

OF THE STREET-SALE OF VEGETABLES.

THE seller of fruit in the streets confines his traffic far more closely to fruit, than does the vegetable-dealer to vegetables. Within these three or four years many street-traders sell only fruit the year through; but the purveyor of vegetables now usually sells fish with his cabbages, turnips, cauliflowers, or other garden stuff. The fish that he carries out on his round generally consists of soles, mackerel, or fresh or salt herrings. This combination of the street-green-grocer and street-fishmonger is called a general dealer."

The general dealers are usually accompanied by boys (as I have elsewhere shown), and sometimes by their wives. If a woman be a general dealer, she is mostly to be found at a stall or standing, and not " going a round."

The general dealer " works " everything through the season. He generally begins the year with sprats or plaice : then he deals in soles until the month of May. After this he takes to mackerel, haddocks, or red herrings. Next he trades in strawberries or raspberries. From these he will turn to green and ripe gooseberries ; thence he will go to cherries ; from cherries he will change to red or white currants ; from them to plums or green-gages, and from them again to apples and pears, and damsons. After these he mostly " works " a few vegetables, and continues with them until the fish season begins again. Some general dealers occasionally trade in sweetmeats, but this is not usual, and is looked down upon by the " trade."

" I am a general dealer," said one of the better class ; " my missis is in the same line as myself, and sells everything that I do (barring green stuff.) She follows me always in what I sell. She has a stall, and sits at the corner of the street. I have got three children. The eldest is ten, and goes out with me to call my goods for me. I have had inflammation in the lungs, and when I call my goods for a little while my voice leaves me. My missis is lame. She fell down a cellar, when a child, and injured her hip. Last October twelvemonth I was laid up with cold, which settled on my lungs, and laid me in my bed for a month. My missis kept me all that time. She was ' working' fresh herrings; and if it hadn't been for her we must all have gone into the workhouse. We are doing very badly now. I have no work to do. I have no stock-money to work with, and I object to pay 1s. 6d. a week for the loan of 10s. Once I gave a man 1s. 6d. a week for ten months for the loan of 10s., and that nearly did me up. I have had 8*s.* of the same party since, and paid 1*s.* a week for eight weeks for the loan of it. I consider it most extortionate to have to pay 2*d.* a day for the loan of 8*s.*, and won't do it. When the season gets a bit better I shall borrow a shilling of one friend and a shilling of another, and then muddle on with as much stock-money as I can scrape together. My missis is at home now doing nothing. Last week it's impossible to say what she took, for we're obliged to buy victuals and firing with it as we take it. She can't go out charing on account of her hip. When she is out, and I am out, the children play about in the streets. Only last Saturday week she was obligated to take the shoes off her feet to get the children some victuals. We owe two weeks' rent, and the landlord, though I've lived in the house five years, is as sharp as if I was a stranger."

"Why, sir," said another vegetable-dealer, who was a robust-looking young man, very clean in his person, and dressed in costermonger corduroy, "I can hardly say what my business is worth to me, for I'm no scholard. I was brought up to the business by my mother. I've a middling connection, and perhaps clear 3*s.* a day, every fine day, or 15*s.* or 16*s.* a week; but out of that there's my donkey to keep, which I suppose costs 6*d.* a day, that's seven sixpences off. Wet or fine, she must be fed, in coarse. So must I; but I've only myself to keep at present, and I hire a lad when I want one. I work my own trap. Then things is so uncertain. Why, now, look here, sir. Last Friday, I think it was—but that don't matter, for it often happens—fresh herrings was 4*s.* the 500 in the morning, and 1*s.* 6*d.* at night, so many had come in. I buy at Billingsgate-market, and sometimes of a large shopkeeper, and at Covent-garden and the Borough. If I lay out 7*s.* in a nice lot of cabbages, I may sell them for 10*s.* 6*d.*, or if it isn't a lucky day with me for 8*s.*, or less. Sometimes people won't buy, as if the cholera was in the cabbages. Then turnips isn't such good sale yet, but they may be soon, for winter's best for them. There's more bilings then than there's roastings, I think. People like broth in cold weather. I buy turnips by the 'tally.' A tally's five dozen bunches. There's no confinement of the number to a bunch; it's by their size; I've known twelve, and I've known twice that. I sell three parts of the turnips at 1*d.* a bunch, and the other part at 1½*d.* If I get them at 3*s.* 6*d.* the tally I do well on turnips. I go the same rounds pretty regularly every day, or almost every day. I don't object to wet weather so much, because women don't like to stir out then, and so they'll buy of me as I pass. Carrots I do little in; they're dear, but they'll be cheaper in a month or two. They always are. I don't work on Sundays. If I did, I'd get a jacketing. Our chaps would say: 'Well, you *are* a scurf. *You* have a round; give another man a Sunday chance.' A gentleman once said to me, when I was obligated to work on a Sunday: 'Why don't you leave it off, when you know it ain't right?' 'Well, sir,' said I,

and he spoke very kind to me, 'well, sir, I'm working for my dinner, and if you'll give me 4*s.* or 3*s.* 6*d.*, I'll tumble to your notion and drop it, and I'll give you these here cowcumbers,' (I was working cowcumbers at that time) 'to do what you like with, and they cost me half-a-crown.' In potatoes I don't do a great deal, and it's no great trade. If I did, I should buy at the warehouses in Tooley-street, where they are sold in sacks of 1 cwt.; 150 lbs. and 200 lbs., at 2*s.* 9*d.* and 3*s.* the cwt. I sell mine, tidy good, at 3 pound 2*d.*, and a halfpenny a pound, but as I don't do much, not a bushel a day, I buy at market by the bushel at from 1*s.* 6*d.* to 2*s.* I never uses slangs. I sold three times as many potatoes as I do now four years back. I don't know why, 'cept it be that the rot set people again them, and their taste's gone another way. I sell a few more greens than I did, but not many. Spinach I don't do only a little in it. Celery I'm seldom able to get rid on. It's more women's work. Ing-uns the same."

I may add that I found the class, who confined their business principally to the sale of vegetables, the dullest of all the costermongers. Any man may labour to make 1*s.* 6*d.* of cabbages or turnips, which cost him 1*s.*, when the calculation as to the relative proportion of measures, &c. is beyond his comprehension.

Pursuing the same mode of calculation as has been heretofore adopted, we find that the absolute quantity of vegetables sold in the London streets by the costers is as follows:

20,700,000	lbs. of potatoes (home grown)	
39,800,000	„	(foreign)
23,760,133	cabbages,	
3,264,800	turnips,	
616,666	junks of turnip tops,	
601,000	carrots,	
567,300	brocoli and cauliflowers,	
219,000	bushels of peas,	
8,893	„	beans,
22,110	„	french beans,
25,608	dozens of vegetable marrows,	
489	dozen bundles of asparagus,	
9,120	„	rhubarb,
4,350	„	celery,
561,600	lettuces,	
13,291	dozen hands of radishes,	
499,533	bushels of onions,	
23,600	dozen bunches of spring onions,	
10,920	bushels of cucumbers,	
3,290	dozen bunches of herbs.	

Of the "Aristocratic" Vegetable-Sale.

In designating these dealers I use a word not uncommon among the costermongers. These aristocratic sellers, who are not one in twenty, or perhaps in twenty-five, of the whole body of costermongers, are generally men of superior manners and better dressed than their brethren. The following narrative, given to me by one of the body, shows the nature of the trade:—

"It depends a good deal upon the season and the price, as to what I begin with in the 'haristocratic' way. My rounds are always in the suburbs. I sell neither in the streets, nor squares in town. I like it best where there are detached villas, and best of all where there are kept mistresses. They are the best of all customers to men like me. We talk our customers over among ourselves, and generally know who's who. One way by which we know the kept ladies is, they never sell cast-off clothes, as some ladies do, for new potatoes or early peas. Now, my worst customers, as to price, are the ladies—or gentlemen—they're both of a kidney—what keeps fashionable schools. *They* are the people to drive a bargain, but then they buy largely. Some buy entirely of costermongers. There's one gent. of a school-keeper buys so much and knows so well what o'clock it is, that I'm satisfied he saves many a pound a year by buying of us 'stead of the greengrocers.

"Perhaps I begin the season in the haristocratic way, with early lettuces for salads. I carry my goods in handsome baskets, and sometimes with a boy, or a boy and a girl, to help me. I buy my lettuces by the score (of heads) when first in, at 1s. 6d., and sell them at 1½d. each, which is 1s. profit on a score. I have sold twenty, and I once sold thirty score, that way in a day. The profit on the thirty was 2l. 5s., but out of that I had to pay three boys, for I took three with me, and our expenses was 7s. But you must consider, sir, that this is a precarious trade. Such goods are delicate, and spoil if they don't go off. I give credit sometimes, if anybody I know says he has no change. I never lost nothing

"Then there's grass (asparagus), and that's often good money. I buy all mine at Coventgarden, where it's sold in bundles, according to the earliness of the season, at from 5s. to 1s., containing from six to ten dozen squibs (heads). These you have to take home, untie, cut off the scraggy ends, trim, and scrape, and make them level. Children help me to do this in the court where I live. I give them a few ha'pence, though they're eager enough to do it for nothing but the fun. I've had 10s. worth made ready in half an hour.

"Well, now, sir, about grass, there's not a coster in London, I'm sure, ever tasted it; and how it's eaten puzzles us." [I explained the manner in which asparagus was brought to table.] "That's the ticket, is it, sir? Well, I was once at the Surrey, and there was some macaroni eaten on the stage, and I thought grass was eaten in the same way, perhaps; swallowed like one o'clock," [rather a favourite comparison among the costers.]

"I have the grass—it's always called, when cried in the streets, 'Spar-row gra-ass'—tied up in bundles of a dozen, twelve to a dozen, or one over, and for these I never expect less than 6d. For a three or four dozen lot, in a neat sieve, I ask 2s. 6d., and never take less than 1s. 3d. I once walked thirty-five miles with grass, and have oft enough been thirty miles. I made 7s. or 8s. a day by it, and next day or two perhaps nothing, or may-be had but one customer. I've

sold half-crown lots, on a Saturday night, for a sixpence; and it *was* sold some time back at 2d. a bundle, in the New Cut, to poor people. I dare say some as bought it had been maidservants and understood it. I've raffled 5s. worth of grass in the parlour of a respectable country inn of an evening.

"The costers generally buy new potatoes at 4s. to 5s. the bushel, and cry them at 'threepound-tuppence;' but I've given 7s. a bushel, for choice and early, and sold them at 2d. a pound. It's no great trade, for the bushel may weigh only 50 lb., and at 2d. a pound that's only 8s. 4d. The schools don't buy at all until they're 1d. the pound, and don't buy in any quantity until they're 1s. 6d. the 25 lb. One day a school 'stonished me by giving me 2s. 6d. for 25 lb., which is the general weight of the half bushel. Perhaps the master had taken a drop of something short that morning. The schools are dreadful screws, to be sure.

"Green peas, early ones, I don't buy when they first come in, for then they're very dear, but when they're 4s. or 3s. 6d. a bushel, and that's pretty soon. I can make five pecks of a bushel. Schools don't touch peas 'till they're 2s. a bushel.

"Cowcumbers were an aristocratic sale. Four or five years ago they were looked upon, when first in, and with a beautiful bloom upon them, as the finest possible relish. But the cholera came in 1849, and everybody—'specially the women—thought the cholera was in cowcumbers, and I've known cases, foreign and English, sent from the Borough Market for manure.

"I sell a good many mushrooms. I sometimes can pick up a cheap lot at Covent Garden. I make them up in neat sieves of three dozen to eight dozen according to size, and I have sold them at 4s. the sieve, and made half that on each sieve I sold. They are down to 1s. or 1s. 6d. a sieve very soon.

"Green walnuts for pickling I sell a quantity of. One day I sold 20s. worth—half profit—I got them so cheap, but that was an exception. I sold them cheap too. One lady has bought a bushel and a half at a time. For walnut catsup the refuse of the walnut is used; it's picked up in the court, where I've got children or poor fellows for a few ha'pence or a pint of beer to help me to peel the walnuts."

OF ONION SELLING IN THE STREETS.

THE sale of onions in the streets is immense. They are now sold at the markets at an average of 2s. a bushel. Two years ago they were 1s., and they have been 4s. and up to 7s. the bushel. They are now twisted into "ropes" for street sale. The ropes are of straw, into which the roots are platted, and secured firmly enough, so that the ropes can be hung up; these have superseded the netted onions, formerly sold by the Jew boys. The plaiting, or twisting, is done rapidly by the women, and a straw-bonnet-maker described it to me as somewhat after the mode of her trade, only that the top, or projecting portion of the stem of the onion, was twisted within the straw, instead of its being plaited close and flat together. The trade in rope onions is almost entirely in the hands of the Irish women and girls. There are now, it is said, from 800 to 1000 persons engaged in it. Onion selling can be started on a small amount of capital, from 6*d*. to 1*s*., which is no doubt one inducement for those poor persons to resort to it. The sixpenny ropes, bunches, or strings (I heard each word applied), contain from three to four dozen; the penny bunches, from six to twenty roots, according to size; and the intermediate and higher priced bunches in proportion. Before Christmas, a good many shilling lots are sold. Among the costermongers I heard this useful root — which the learned in such matters have pronounced to be, along with the mushroom, the foundation of every sauce, ancient or modern—called ing-guns, ingans, injens, injyens, inions, innons, almost everything but onions.

An Irishwoman, apparently of thirty-five, but in all probability younger—she did not know her age—gave me the following account. Her face, with its strongly-marked Irish features, was almost purpled from constant exposure to the weather. She was a teetotaller. She was communicative and garrulous, even beyond the average of her countrywomen. She was decently clad, had been in London fifteen years (she thought) having been brought from Ireland, *viâ* Bristol, by her parents (both dead). She herself was a widow, her husband, "a bricklayer" she called him (probably a bricklayer's labourer), having died of the cholera in 1849. I take up her statement from that period :

"Yes, indeed, sir, he died—the heavins be his bed!—and he was prepared by Father M——. We had our thrials togither, but sore's been the cross and heavy the burthin since it plased God to call him. Thin, there's the two childer, Biddy and Ned. They'll be tin and they'll be eight come their next burreth-days, 'plase the Lorrud. They can hilp me now, they can. They sells ing-uns as well. I ropes 'em for 'em. How is ing-uns roped ? Shure, thin—but it's not mocking me your 'onnur is—shure, thin, a gintleman like you, that can write like a horrus a-galloping, and perhaps is as larned as a praste, glory be to God! *must* know how to rope ing-uns! Poor people can do it. Some say it's a sacrit, but that's all a say, or there couldn't be so many ropes a-silling. I buy the sthraw at a sthrawda er's; twopinn'orth at a time; that'll make six or twilve ropes, according to what they are, sixpinny or what. It's as sthraight as it can be grown, the sthraw, that it is indeed. Och, sir, we've had many's the black day, me and the childer, poor things; it's thim I care about, but —God's name be praised!—we've got on somehow. Another poor woman—she's a widdur too, hilp her!—and me has a 2*s*. room for the two of us. We've our siprate furnithur. She has only hersilf, but is fond of the childer, as you or your ady—bliss her! if you've got one—might be, if you was with them. I can read a little mysilf, at laste I could oncte, and I gits them a bit o'

schoolin' now and thin, whin I can, of an evenin mostly. I can't write a letther; I wish I could. Shure, thin, sir, I'll tell you the thruth—we does best on ing-uns. Oranges is nixt, and nuts isn't near so good. The three of us now makes 1*s*. and sometimes 1*s*. 6*d*. a day, and that's grand doin's. We may sill bechuxt us from two to three dozin ropes a day. I'm quick at roping the ing-uns. I never noted how many ropes an hour. I buy them of a thradesman, an honist gintleman, I know, and I see him at mass ivery Sunday, and he gives me as many as he can for 1*s*. or what it is. We has 1*d*., plase God, on ivery 6*d*. ; yis, sir, perhaps more sometimes. I'll not tell your 'onnur a bit of a lie. And so we now get a nice bit o' fish, with a bit of li er on a Sunday. I sell to the thradesmen, and the lodgers of them, about here (Tottenham-court-road), and in many other parruts, for we thravels a dale. The childer always goes the same round. We follows one another. I've sould in the sthreets ever since I've been in this counthry."

The greatest sum of money expended by the poor upon any vegetable (after potatoes) is spent upon onions—99,900*l*. being annually devoted to the purchase of that article. To those who know the habits of the poor, this will appear in no way singular—a piece of bread and an onion being to the English labourer what bread and an apple or a bunch of grapes is to the French peasant—often his dinner.

OF POT-HERBS AND CELERY.

I use the old phrase, *pot-herbs,* for such productions as sage, thyme, mint, parsley, sweet marjoram, fennel, (though the last is rarely sold by the street-people), &c. ; but " herbs" is the usual term. More herbs, such as agrimony, balm (balsam), wormwood, tansy, &c., used to be sold in the streets. These were often used for "teas," medicinally perhaps, except tansy, which, being a strong aromatic, was used to flavour puddings. Wormwood, too, was often bought to throw amongst woollen fabrics, as a protective against the attack of moths.

The street herb-trade is now almost entirely in the hands of Irishwomen, and is generally carried on during the autumn and winter at stalls. With it, is most commonly united the sale of celery. The herbs are sold at the several markets, usually in shilling lots, but a quarter of a shilling lot may be purchased. The Irishwoman pursues a simple method of business. What has cost her 1*s*. she divides into 24 lots, each of 1*d*., or she will sell half of a lot for a halfpenny. An Irishwoman said to me :

"Thrade isn't good, sir ; it falls and it falls. I don't sell so many herrubs or so much ciliry as I did whin mate was higher. Poor people thin, I've often been said it, used to buy bones and bile them for broth with ciliry and the beautiful herrubs. Now they buys a bit of mate and ates it without brothing. It's good one way and it's bad another. Only last Sathurday night my husband—and a good husband he's to me, though he is a London man, for he knows how to mak* a bargain—he bought a bit of mutton, afore the stroke of twilve, in Newgit-markit, at 2½d. the pound. I don't know what parrut it was. I don't understand that, but he does, and tills me how to cook it. He has worruk at the docks, but not very rigular. I think I sill most parrusley. Whin frish herrings is chape, some biles them with parrusley, and some fries them with ing-uns. No, sir; I don't make sixpence a day; not half-a-crown a week, I'm shure. Whin herrubs isn't in—and they're autumn and winther things, and so is ciliry—I sills anything; gooseberries and currints, or anything. If I'd had a family, I couldn't have had a shoe to my futt."

GROSS VALUE OF THE FRUIT AND VEGE-
TABLES SOLD ANNUALLY IN THE LONDON
STREETS.

To complete the present account of the coster-monger's trade, we must now estimate the money value of the fruit and vegetables disposed of by them throughout the year. The money annually spent in fish by the humbler portion of the me-tropolitan population comes to, as we have seen, very nearly one million five hundred thousand pounds sterling—the sum laid out in fruit and vegetables we shall find is but little more than a third of this amount.

GREEN FRUIT.

377,500 bushels of apples, at six a penny or 4s. per bush. (288 to the bushel) . .	£75,500
193,700 bushels of pears, at 5s. per bushel	48,400
1,215,360 lbs. of cherries, at 2d. per lb.	10,000
11,700 bushels of plums, at 1d. per half pint	6,270
100 bushels of greengages, at 1½d. per half pint . .	80
548 bushels of damsons, at 1½d. per half pint	430
2,450 bushels of bullace, at 1½d. per half pint . . .	1,960
207,500 bushels of gooseberries, at 3d. per quart	83,000
85,500 sieves of red currants, at 1d. per pint (three half-sieves to the bushel) .	15,300
13,500 sieves of black currants, at 1d. per pint (three half-sieves to the bushel) .	2,400
3,000 sieves of white currants, at 1d. per pint (three half-sieves to the bushel) .	530
763,750 pottles of strawberries, at 2d. per pottle	6,360
1,760 pottles of raspberries, at 6d. per pottle	40
30,485 pottles of mulberries, at 6d. per pottle	760
6,000 bushels of hazel nuts, at ¾d. per half pint . . .	2,400
17,280 lbs. of filberts, at 3d. per lb.	200
26,563 lbs. of grapes, at 4d. per lb.	440
20,000 pine apples, at 6d. each .	500
15,400,000 oranges, at two for 1d. . .	32,000
154,000 lemons, at two for 1d. . .	320
24,000 bushels of Spanish and Barcelona nuts, at 6d. per quart	19,200
3,000 bushels of Brazil nuts (1500 to the bushel), at fifteen for 1d.	£1,250
6,500 bushels of chestnuts (1500 to the bushel), at fifteen for 1d.	2,700
24,000 bushels of walnuts (1750 to the bushel), at ten for 1d.	17,500
400,000 coker-nuts, at 3d. each .	5,000
Total expended yearly in green fruit	£333,420

DRY FRUIT.

7,000 lbs. of shell almonds, at 20 a penny (320 to the lb.)	£460
37,800 lbs. of raisins, at 2d. per lb.	300
24,300 lbs. of figs, at 2d. per lb. .	200
4,800 lbs. of prunes, at 2d. per lb.	40
Total expended yearly on dry fruit	£1,000

VEGETABLES.

60,500,000 lbs. of potatoes, at 5lbs. for 2d.	£100,800
23,760,000 cabbages, at ¼d. each . .	49,500
3,264,800 turnips, at 1½d. per doz. .	1,700
601,000 carrots, at 2½d. per doz. .	520
567,300 brocoli and cauliflowers, at 1d. per head	2,360
616,666 junks of turnip tops, at 4d. per junk	10,270
219,000 bushels of peas, at 1s. 6d. per bushel	16,420
8,890 bushels of beans, at 1s. 6d. per bushel	660
22,110 bushels of French beans, at 6d. per peck, or 2s. per bushel	2,210
25,608 vegetable marrows, at ½d. each	50
489 dozen bundles of aspara-gus, at 2s. 6d. per bundle (4d. or 6d. a doz. heads)	73)
9,120 dozen bundles of rhubarb, at 2s. 6d. per doz. . .	1,14)
4,350 dozen bundles of celery, at 3d. per bundle . . .	650
561,602 lettuces, at 3 a penny . .	783
13,291 dozen hands of radishes, at 3 bunches for 1d., and 6 bunches to the hand .	1,330
499,530 bushels of onions, at 4s. per bushel	99,900
10,920 bushels of cucumbers, at 1d. each (60 to the bush.)	2,730
3,290 dozen bundles of herbs, at 3d. a bundle . . .	490
Total expended yearly in vegetables	£292,240

Putting the above sums together we have the following aggregate result:—

Expended yearly in green fruit	. .	£333,420
Expended yearly in dry fruit	. . .	1,000
Expended yearly in vegetables	. . .	292,000

Gross sum taken annually by the London costermongers for fruit and vegetables . . . . } £626,420

Then adding the above to the gross amount received by the street-sellers of fish, which we have before seen comes to as much as £1,460,850, we have for the annual income of the London costermongers no less a sum than £2,087,270.

OF THE STATIONARY STREET-SELLERS OF FISH, FRUIT, AND VEGETABLES.

OF THE NUMBER OF STREET STALLS.

THUS far we have dealt only with the itinerant dealers in fish, fruit, or vegetables; but there are still a large class of street-sellers, who obtain a living by the sale of the same articles at some fixed locality in the public thoroughfares; and as these differ from the others in certain points, they demand a short special notice here. First, as to the number of stalls in the streets of London, I caused personal observations to be made; and in a walk of 46 miles, 632 stalls were counted, which is at the rate of very nearly 14 to the mile. This, too, was in bad weather,—was not on a Saturday night,—and at a season when the fruit-sellers all declare that "things is dull." The routes taken in this inquiry were: — No. 1, from Vauxhall to Hatton-garden; No. 2, from Baker-street to Bermondsey; No. 3, from Blackwall to Brompton; No. 4, from the Hackney-road to the Edgeware-road. I give the results.

	F.	FR.	V.	M.	T.
No. 1 . .	9	28	5	7	49
„ 2 . .	37	50	4	14	105
„ 3 . .	90	153	30	40	313
„ 4 . .	75	52	23	15	165
	211	283	62	76	632

F. denotes fish-stalls; Fr. fruit-stalls; V. vegetable-stalls; M. miscellaneous; and T. presents the total:

The miscellaneous stalls include peas-soup, pickled whelks, sweetmeats, toys, tin-ware, elder-wine, and jewellery stands. Of these, the toy-stalls were found to be the most numerous; sweetmeats the next; tin-ware the next; while the elder-wine stalls were least numerous.

Some of the results indicate, curiously enough, the character of the locality. Thus, in Fleet-street there were 3, in the Haymarket 5, in Regent-street 6, and in Piccadilly 14 fruit-stalls, and no fish-stalls — these streets not being resorted to by the poor, to whom fruit is a luxury, but fish a necessity. In the Strand were 17 fruit and 2 fish-stalls; and in Drury-lane were 8 stalls of fish to 6 of fruit. On the other hand, there were in Ratcliffe-high-way, 38 fish and 23 fruit-stalls; in Rosemary-lane, 13 fish and 8 fruit-stalls; in Shoreditch,

28 fish and 13 fruit-stalls; and in Bethnal-green Road (the poorest district of all), 14 of the fish, and but 3 of the fruit stalls. In some places, the numbers were equal, or nearly so; as in the Minories, for instance, the City-road, the New-road, Goodge-street, Tottenham-court Road, and the Camberwell-road; while in Smithfield were 5, and in Cow-cross 2 fish-stalls, and no fruit-stalls at all. In this enumeration the street-markets of Leather-lane, the New Cut, the Brill, &c., are not included.

The result of this survey of the principal London thoroughfares is that in the *mid-route* (viz., from Brompton, along Piccadilly, the Strand, Fleet-street, and so *via* the Commercial-road to Blackwall), there are twice as many stalls as in the great *northern thoroughfare* (that is to say, from the Edgeware-road, along the New-road, to the Hackney-road); the latter route, however, has more than one-third as many stalls as route No. 2, and more than double the number of route No. 1. Hence it appears that the more frequented the thoroughfare, the greater the quantity of street-stalls.

The number of miles of streets contained within the inner police district of the metropolis, are estimated by the authorities at 2,000 (including the city), and assuming that there are on an average only four stalls to the mile throughout London, we have thus a grand total of 8,000 fish, fruit, vegetable, and other stalls dispersed throughout the capital.

Concerning the character of the stalls at the street-markets, the following observations have been made:—At the New-cut there were, before the removals, between the hours of eight and ten on a Saturday evening, ranged along the kerb-stone on the north side of the road, beginning at Broad-wall to Marsh-gate (a distance of nearly half-a-mile), a dense line of "pitches"—at 77 of which were vegetables for sale, at 40 fruit, 25 fish, 22 boots and shoes, 14 eatables, consisting of cakes and pies, hot eels, baked potatoes, and boiled whelks; 10 dealt in nightcaps, lace, ladies' collars, artificial flowers, silk and straw bonnets; 10 in tinware—such as saucepans, tea-kettles, and Dutch-ovens; 9 in crockery and glass, 7 in brooms and brushes, 5 in poultry and rabbits, 6 in paper, books, songs, and almanacs; and about 60 in sundries.

THE IRISH STREET-SELLER.

"Sweet Chany! Two a pinny Or-r-ranges— two a pinny!"

[*From a Daguerreotype by* BEARD.]

OF THE CHARACTER OF THE STREET-STALLS.

THE stalls occupied by costermongers for the sale of fish, fruit, vegetables, &c., are chiefly constructed of a double cross-trestle or moveable frame, or else of two trestles, each with three legs, upon which is laid a long deal board, or tray. Some of the stalls consist merely of a few boards resting upon two baskets, or upon two herring-barrels. The fish-stalls are mostly covered with paper—generally old newspapers or periodicals—but some of the street-fishmongers, instead of using paper to display their fish upon, have introduced a thin marble slab, which gives the stall a cleaner, and, what they consider a high attribute, a "respectable" appearance.

Most of the fruit-stalls are, in the winter time, fitted up with an apparatus for roasting apples and chestnuts; this generally consists of an old saucepan with a fire inside; and the woman who vends them, huddled up in her old faded shawl or cloak, often presents a picturesque appearance, in the early evening, or in a fog, with the gleam of the fire lighting up her half somnolent figure. Within the last two or three years, however, there has been so large a business carried on in roasted chestnuts, that it has become a distinct street-trade, and the vendors have provided themselves with an iron apparatus, large enough to roast nearly half a bushel at a time. At the present time, however, the larger apparatus is less common in the streets, and more frequent in the shops, than in the previous winter.

There are, moreover, peculiar kinds of stalls—such as the hot eels and hot peas-soup stalls, having tin oval pots, with a small chafing-dish containing a charcoal fire underneath each, to keep the eels or soup hot. The early breakfast stall has two capacious tin cans filled with tea or coffee, kept hot by the means before described, and some are lighted up by two or three large oil-lamps; the majority of these stalls, in the winter time, are sheltered from the wind by a screen made out of an old clothes horse covered with tarpaulin. The cough-drop stand, with its distilling apparatus, the tin worm curling nearly the whole length of the tray, has but lately been introduced. The nut-stall is fitted up with a target at the back of it. The ginger-beer stand may be seen in almost every street, with its French-polished mahogany frame and bright polished taps, and its foot-bath-shaped reservoir of water, to cleanse the glasses. The hot elder wine stand, with its bright brass urns, is equally popular.

The sellers of plum-pudding, "cake, a penny a slice," sweetmeats, cough-drops, pin-cushions, jewellery, chimney ornaments, tea and table-spoons, make use of a table covered over, some with old newspapers, or a piece of oil-cloth, upon which are exposed their articles for sale.

Such is the usual character of the street-stalls. There are, however, "stands" or "cans" peculiar to certain branches of the street-trade. The most important of these, such as the baked-potatoe can, and the meat-pie stand, I have before described, p. 27.

The other means adopted by the street-sellers for the exhibition of their various goods at certain "pitches" or fixed localities are as follows. Straw bonnets, boys' caps, women's caps, and prints, are generally arranged for sale in large umbrellas, placed "upside down." Haberdashery, with rolls of ribbons, edgings, and lace, some street-sellers display on a stall; whilst others have a board at the edge of the pavement, and expose their wares upon it as tastefully as they can. Old shoes, patched up and well blacked, ready for the purchaser's feet, and tin ware, are often ranged upon the ground, or, where the stock is small, a stall or table is used.

Many stationary street-sellers use merely baskets, or trays, either supported in their hand, or on their arm, or else they are strapped round their loins, or suspended round their necks. These are mostly fruit-women, watercress, blacking, congreves, sheep's-trotters, and ham-sandwich sellers.

Many stationary street-sellers stand on or near the bridges; others near the steam-packet wharfs or the railway terminuses; a great number of them take their pitch at the entrance to a court, or at the corners of streets; and stall-keepers with oysters stand opposite the doors of public-houses.

It is customary for a street-seller who wants to "pitch" in a new locality to solicit the leave of the housekeeper, opposite whose premises he desires to place his stall. Such leave obtained, no other course is necessary.

OF FRUIT-STALL KEEPERS.

I HAD the following statement from a woman who has "kept a stall" in Marylebone, at the corner of a street, which she calls "my corner," for 38 years. I was referred to her as a curious type of the class of stall-keepers, and on my visit, found her daughter at the "pitch." This daughter had all the eloquence which is attractive in a street-seller, and so, I found, had her mother when she joined us. They are profuse in blessings; and on a bystander observing, when he heard the name of these street-sellers, that a jockey of that name had won the Derby lately, the daughter exclaimed, "To be sure he did; he's my own uncle's relation, and what a lot of money came into the family! Bless God for all things, and bless every body! Walnuts, sir, walnuts, a penny a dozen! Wouldn't give you a bad one for the world, which is a great thing for a poor 'oman for to offer to do." The daughter was dressed in a drab great-coat, which covered her whole person. When I saw the mother, she carried a similar great-coat, as she was on her way to the stall; and she used it as ladies do their muffs, burying her hands in it. The mother's dark-coloured old clothes seemed, to borrow a description from Sir Walter Scott, flung on with a pitchfork. These two women were at first very suspicious, and could not be made to understand my object in questioning them; but after a little while, the mother became not only communicative, but garrulous, conversing—with no small impatience at any interruption—of the doings of the people in her neighbourhood. I was accompanied by an intelligent costermonger, who assured me of his certitude that the old woman's statement was perfectly correct, and I found moreover from other inquiries that it was so.

"Well, sir," she began, "what is it that you want of me? Do I owe you anything? There's half-pay officers about here for no good; what is it you want? Hold your tongue, you young fool," (to her daughter, who was beginning to speak;) "what do you know about it?" [On my satisfying her that I had no desire to injure her, she continued, to say after spitting, a common practice with her class, on a piece of money, "for luck,"] "Certainly, sir, that's very proper and good. Aye, I've seen the world—the town world and the country. I don't know where I was born; never mind about that—it's nothing to nobody. I don't know nothing about my father and mother; but I know that afore I was eleven I went through the country with my missis. She was a smuggler. I didn't know then what smuggling was—bless you, sir, I didn't; I knew no more nor I know who made that lamp-post. I didn't know the taste of the stuff we smuggled for two years—didn't know it from small beer; I've known it well enough since, God knows. My missis made a deal of money that time at Deptford Dockyard. The men wasn't paid and let out till twelve of a night—I hardly mind what night it was, days was so alike then—and they was our customers till one, two, or three in the morning—Sunday morning, for anything I know. I don't know what my missis gained; something jolly, there's not a fear of it. She was kind enough to me. I don't know how long I was with missis. After that I was a hopping, and made my 15s. regular at it, and a haymaking; but I've had a pitch at my corner for thirty-eight year—aye! turned thirty-eight. It's no use asking me what I made at first—I can't tell; but I'm sure I made more than twice as much as my daughter and me makes now, the two of us. I wish people that thinks we're idle now were with me for a day. I'd teach them. I don't—that's the two of us don't—make 15s. a week now, nor the half of it, when all's paid. D—d if I do. The d—d boys take care of that." [Here I had a statement of the boys' tradings, similar to what I have given.] "There's 'Canterbury' has lots of boys, and they bother me. I can tell, and always could, how it is with working men. When mechanics is in good work, their children has halfpennies to spend with me. If they're hard up, there's no halfpennies. The pennies go to a loaf or to buy a candle. I might have saved money once, but had a misfortunate family. My husband? O, never mind about him. D—n him. I've been a widow many years. My son —it's nothing how many children I have—is married; he had the care of an ingine. But

he lost it from ill health. It was in a feather-house, and the flue got down his throat, and coughed him; and so he went into the country, 108 miles off, to his wife's mother. But his wife's mother got her living by wooding, and other ways, and couldn't help him or his wife; so he left, and he's with me now. He has a job sometimes with a greengrocer, at 6d. a day and a bit of grub; a little bit—very. I must shelter him. I couldn't turn him out. If a Turk I knew was in distress, and I had only half a loaf, I'd give him half of that, if he was ever such a Turk—I would, sir! Out of 6d. a day, my son —poor fellow, he's only twenty-seven!—wants a bit of 'baccy and a pint of beer. It 'ud be unnatural to oppose that, wouldn't it, sir? He frets about his wife, that's staying with her mother, 108 miles off; and about his little girl; but I tell him to wait, and he may have more little girls. God knows, they come when they're not wanted a bit. I joke and say all my old sweethearts is dying away. Old Jemmy went off sudden. He lent me money sometimes, but I always paid him. He had a public once, and had some money when he died. I saw him the day afore he died. He was in bed, but wasn't his own man quite; though he spoke sensible enough to me. He said, said he, 'Won't you have half a quartern of rum, as we've often had it?' 'Certainly, Jemmy,' says I, 'I came for that very thing.' Poor fellow! his friends are quarrelling now about what he left. It's 56l. they say, and they'll go to law very likely, and lose every thing. There'll be no such quarrelling when I die, unless it is for the pawn-tickets. I get a meal now, and got a meal afore; but it was a better meal then, sir. Then look at my expenses. I was a customer once. I used to buy, and plenty such did, blue cloth aprons, opposite Drury-lane theatre: the very shop's there still, but I don't know what it is now; I can't call to mind. I gave 2s. 6d. a yard, from twenty to thirty years ago, for an apron, and it took two yards, and I paid 4d. for making it, and so an apron cost 5s. 4d.—that wasn't much thought of in those times. I used to be different off then. I never go to church; I used to go when I was a little child at Sevenoaks. I suppose I was born somewhere thereabouts. I've forgot what the inside of a church is like. There's no costermongers ever go to church, except the rogues of them, that wants to appear good. I buy my fruit at Covent-garden. Apples is now 4s. 6d. a bushel there. I may make twice that in selling them; but a bushel may last me two, three, or four days."

As I have already, under the street-sale of fish, given an account of the oyster stall-keeper, as well as the stationary dealers in sprats, and the principal varieties of wet fish, there is no necessity for me to continue this part of my subject.

We have now, in a measure, finished with the metropolitan costermongers. We have seen that the street-sellers of fish, fruit, and vegetables constitute a large proportion of the London population; the men, women, and children numbering at the least 30,000, and taking as much as 2,000,000*l.* per annum. We have seen, moreover, that these are the principal purveyors of food to the poor, and that consequently they are as important a body of people as they are numerous. Of all classes they *should* be the most honest, since the poor, least of all, can afford to be cheated; and yet it has been shown that the consciences of the London costermongers, generally speaking, are as little developed as their intellects; indeed, the moral and religious state of these men is a foul disgrace to us, laughing to scorn our zeal for the "propagation of the gospel in *foreign* parts," and making our many societies for the civilization of savages on the other side of the globe appear like a "delusion, a mockery, and a snare," when we have so many people sunk in the lowest depths of barbarism round about our very homes. It is well to have Bishops of New Zealand when we have Christianized all *our own* heathen; but with 30,000 individuals, in merely *one* of our cities, utterly creedless, mindless, and principleless, surely it would look more like earnestness on our parts if we created Bishops of the New-Cut, and sent "right reverend fathers" to watch over the "cure of souls" in the Broadway and the Brill. If our sense of duty will not rouse us to do this, at least our regard for our own interests should teach us, that it is not safe to allow this vast dungheap of ignorance and vice to seethe and fester, breeding a social pestilence in the very heart of our land. That the costermongers belong essentially to the dangerous classes none can doubt; and those who know a coster's hatred of a "crusher," will not hesitate to believe that they are, as they themselves confess, one and all ready, upon the least disturbance, to seize and disable their policeman. It would be a marvel indeed if it were otherwise. Denied the right of getting a living by the street authorities, after having, perhaps, been supplied with the means of so doing by the parish authorities—the stock which the one had provided seized and confiscated by the other—law seems to them a mere farce, or at best, but the exercise of an arbitrary and despotic power, against which they consider themselves justified, whenever an opportunity presents itself, of using the same physical force as it brings to bear against them. That they are ignorant and vicious as they are, surely is not their fault. If we were all born with learning and virtue, then might we, with some show of justice, blame the costermongers for their want of both; but seeing that even the most moral and intelligent of us owe the greater part, if not the whole, of our wisdom and goodness to the tuition of others, we must not in the arrogance of our self-conceit condemn these men because they are not like ourselves, when it is evident that we should have been as they are, had not some one done *for* us what we refuse to do for them. We leave them destitute of all perception of beauty, and there-

fore without any means of pleasure but through their appetites, and then we are surprized to find their evenings are passed either in brutalizing themselves with beer, or in gloating over the mimic sensuality of the "penny gaff." Without the least intellectual culture is it likely, moreover, that they should have that perception of antecedents and consequents which enables us to see in the shadows of the past the types of the future—or that power of projecting the mind into the space, as it were, of time, which we in Saxon-English call fore-sight, and in Anglo-Latin pro-vidence—a power so godlike that the latter term is often used by us to express the Godhead itself? Is it possible, then, that men who are as much creatures of the present as the beasts of the field—instinctless animals—should have the least faculty of pre-vision? or rather is it not natural that, following the most precarious of all occupations—one in which the subsistence depends upon the weather of this the most variable climate of any—they should fail to make the affluence of the fine days mitigate the starvation of the rainy ones? or that their appetites, made doubly eager by the privations suffered in their adversity, should be indulged in all kinds of excess in their prosperity—their lives being thus, as it were, a series of alternations between starvation and surfeit?

The fate of children brought up amid the influence of such scenes—with parents starving one week and drunk all the next—turned loose into the streets as soon as they are old enough to run alone—sent out to sell in public-houses almost before they know how to put two half-pence together—their tastes trained to libidinism long before puberty at the penny concert, and their passions inflamed with the unrestrained intercourse of the twopenny hops—the fate of the young, I say, abandoned to the blight of such associations as these, cannot well be otherwise than it is. If the child be father to the man, assuredly it does not require a great effort of imagination to conceive the manhood that such a childhood must necessarily engender.

Some months back Mr. Mayhew, with a view to mitigate what appeared to him to be the chief evils of a street-seller's life, founded " The Friendly Association of London Costermongers," the objects of which were as follows:

1. To establish a Benefit and Provident Fund for insuring to each Member a small weekly allowance in Sickness or Old Age, as well as a certain sum to his family at his death, so that the Costermongers, when incapacitated from labour, may not be forced to seek parochial relief, nor, at their decease, be left to be buried by the parish.

2. To institute a Penny Savings' Bank and Winter Fund, where the smallest deposits will be received and bear interest, so that the Costermongers may be encouraged to lay by even the most trivial sums, not only as a provision for future comfort, but as the means of assisting their poorer brethren with future loans.

3. To form a Small Loan Fund for supplying the more needy Costermongers with Stock-Money, &c., at a fair and legitimate interest, instead of the exorbitant rates that are now charged.

4. To promote the use of full weights and measures by every Member of the Association, as well as a rigid inspection of the scales, &c., of all other Costermongers, so that the honestly disposed Street-sellers may be protected, and the public secured against imposition.

5. To protect the Costermongers from interference when lawfully pursuing their calling, by placing it in their power to employ counsel to defend them, if unjustly prosecuted.

6. To provide harmless, if not rational, amusements at the same cheap rate as the pernicious entertainments now resorted to by the Street-sellers.

7. To adopt means for the gratuitous education of the children of the Costermongers, in the day time, and the men and women themselves in the evening.

This institution remains at present comparatively in abeyance, from the want of funds to complete the preliminary arrangements. Those, however, who may feel inclined to contribute towards its establishment, will please to pay their subscriptions into Messrs. Twinings' Bank, Strand, to the account of Thomas Hughes, Esq. (of 63, Upper Berkeley-street, Portman-square), who has kindly consented to act as Treasurer to the Association.

Of a Public Meeting of Street-sellers.

The Association above described arose out of a meeting of costermongers and other street-folk, which was held, at my instance, on the evening of the 12th of June last, in the National Hall, Holborn. The meeting was announced as one of "street-sellers, street-performers, and street-labourers," but the costermongers were the great majority present. The admission was by ticket, and the tickets, which were of course gratuitous, were distributed by men familiar with all the classes invited to attend. These men found the tickets received by some of the street-people with great distrust; others could not be made to understand why any one should trouble himself on their behoof; others again, cheerfully promised their attendance. Some accused the ticket distributors with having been bribed by the Government or the police, though for what purpose was not stated. Some abused them heartily, and some offered to treat them. At least 1,000 persons were present at the meeting, of whom 731 presented their tickets; the others were admitted, because they were known to the door-keepers, and had either lost their tickets or had not the opportunity to obtain them. The persons to whom cards of admission were given were invited to write their names and callings on the backs, and the cards so received gave the following result. Costermongers, 256; fish-sellers, 28; hucksters, 23; lot-sellers, 18; street-labourers, 16; paper-sellers and workers, 13;

toy-sellers, 11; ginger-beer-sellers, 9; hardware-sellers, 9; general-dealers, 7; street-musicians, 5; street-performers, 5; cakes and pastry-sellers, fried-fish-vendors, and tinkers, each, 4; turf-vendors, street-exhibitors, strolling-players, cat's-meat-men, water-cress-sellers, stay-lace, and cotton-sellers, each, 3; board-carriers, fruit-sellers, street-tradesmen, hawkers, street-green-grocers, shell-fish-vendors, poulterers, mud-larks, wire-workers, ballad-singers, crock-men, and booksellers, each, 2; the cards also gave one each of the following avocations:—fly-cage-makers, fly-paper-sellers, grinders, tripe-sellers, pattern-printers, blind-paper-cutters, lace-collar-sellers, bird-sellers, bird-trainers, pen-sellers, lucifer-merchants, watch-sellers, decorators, and play-bill-sellers. 260 cards were given in without being indorsed with any name or calling.

My object in calling this meeting was to ascertain from the men themselves what were the grievances to which they considered themselves subjected; what were the peculiarities and what the privations of a street-life. Cat-calls, and every description of discordant sound, prevailed, before the commencement of the proceedings, but there was also perfect good-humour. Although it had been announced that all the speakers were to address the meeting from the platform, yet throughout the evening some man or other would occasionally essay to speak from the body of the hall. Some of those present expressed misgivings that the meeting was got up by the Government, or by Sir R. Peel, and that policemen, in disguise, were in attendance. The majority showed an ignorance of the usual forms observed at public meetings, though some manifested a thorough understanding of them. Nor was there much delicacy observed—but, perhaps, about as much as in some assemblages of a different character—in clamouring down any prosy speaker. Many present were without coats (for it was a warm evening), some were without waistcoats, many were in tatters, hats and caps were in infinite varieties of shape and shade, while a few were well and even genteelly dressed. The well dressed street-sellers were nearly all young men, and one of these wore moustachios. After I had explained, amidst frequent questions and interruptions, the purpose for which I had summoned the meeting, and had assured the assembly that, to the best of my knowledge, no policemen were present, I invited free discussion.

It was arranged that some one person should address the meeting as the representative of each particular occupation. An elderly man of small stature and lively intelligent features, stood up to speak on behalf of the "paper-workers," "flying-stationers," and "standing-patterers." He said, that "for twenty-four years he had been a penny-showman, a street-seller, and a patterer." He dwelt upon the difference of a street-life when he was young and at the present time, the difference being between meals and no meals; and complained that though he had been well educated, had friends in a respectable way of life, and had never been accused of any dishonesty, such was the moral brand," of having been connected with a "street life, that it was never got rid of. He more than once alluded to this "moral brand." The question was, he concluded, in what way were they to obtain an honest livelihood, so as to keep their wives and children decently, without being buffeted about like wild beasts in the open streets? This address was characterised by propriety in the delivery, and by the absence of any grammatical inaccuracy, or vulgarity of tone or expression.

A costermonger, a quiet-looking man, tidily clad, said he was the son of a country auctioneer, now dead; and not having been brought up to any trade, he came to London to try his luck. His means were done before he could obtain employment; and he was in a state of starvation. At last he was obliged to apply to the parish. The guardians took him into the workhouse, and offered to pass him home: but as he could do no good there, he refused to go. Whereupon, giving him a pound of bread, he was turned into the streets, and had nowhere to lay his head. In wandering down the New-cut a costermonger questioned him, and then took him into his house and fed him This man kept him for a year and a half; he showed him how to get a living in the street trade; and when he left, gave him 20s. to start with. With this sum he got a good living directly; and he could do so now, were it not for the police, whose conduct, he stated, was sometimes very tyrannical. He had been dragged to the station-house, for standing to serve customers, though he obstructed nobody; the policeman, however, called it an obstruction, and he (the speaker) was fined 2s. 6d.; whereupon, because he had not the half-crown, his barrow and all it contained were taken from him, and he had heard nothing of them since. This almost broke him down. There was no redress for these things, and he thought they ought to be looked into.

This man spoke with considerable energy; and when he had concluded, many costermongers shouted, at the top of their voices, that they could substantiate every word of what he had said.

A young man, of superior appearance, said he was the son of a gentleman who had held a commission as Lieutenant in the 20th Foot, and as Captain in the 34th Infantry, and afterwards became Sub-director of the Bute Docks; in which situation he died, leaving no property. He (the speaker) was a classical scholar; but having no trade, he was compelled, after his father's death, to come to London in search of employment, thinking that his pen and his school acquirements would secure it. But in this expectation he was disappointed,—though for a short period he was earning two guineas a week in copying documents for the House of Commons. That time was past; and he was a street-patterer now through sheer necessity. He could say

from experience that the earnings of that class were no more than from 8s. to 10s. a week. He then declaimed at some length against the interference of the police with the patterers, considering it harsh and unnecessary.

After some noisy and not very relevant discussion concerning the true amount of a street-patterer's earnings, a clergyman of the Established Church, now selling stenographic cards in the street, addressed the meeting. He observed, that in every promiscuous assembly there would always be somebody who might be called unfortunate. Of this number he was one; for when, upon the 5th September, 1831, he preached a funeral sermon before a fashionable congregation, upon Mr. Huskisson's death by a railway accident, he little thought he should ever be bound over in his own recognizances in 10l. for obstructing the metropolitan thoroughfares. He was a native of Hackney, but in early life he went to Scotland, and upon the 24th June, 1832, he obtained the presentation to a small extra-parochial chapel in that country, upon the presentation of the Rev. Dr. Bell. His people embraced Irvingism, and he was obliged to leave; and in January, 1837, he came to the metropolis. His history since that period he need not state. His occupation was well known, and he could confirm what had been stated with regard to the police. The Police Act provided, that all persons selling goods in the streets were to keep five feet off the pavement, the street not being a market. He had always kept with his wares and his cards beyond the prohibited distance of five feet; and for six years and a half he had sold his cards without molesting or being molested. After some severe observations upon the police, he narrated several events in his personal history to account for his present condition, which he attributed to misfortune and the injustice of society. In the course of these explanations he gave an illustration of his classical acquirements, in having detected a grammatical error in a Latin inscription upon the plate of a foundation-stone for a new church in Westminster. He wrote to the incumbent, pointing out the error, and the incumbent asked the beadle who he was. "Oh," said the beadle, "he is a fellow who gets his living in the streets." This was enough. He got no answer to his letter, though he knew the incumbent and his four curates, and had attended his church for seven years. After dwelling on the sufferings of those whose living was gained in the streets, he said, that if persons wished really to know anything of the character or habits of life of the very poor, of whom he was one, the knowledge could only be had from a personal survey of their condition in their own homes. He ended, by expressing his hope that by better treatment, and an earnest attention—moral, social, and religious—to their condition, the poor of the streets might be gathered to the church, and to God.

A "wandering musician" in a Highland garb, worn and dirty, complained at some length of the way in which he was treated by the police.

A hale-looking man, a costermonger, of middle age—who said he had a wife and four children dependent upon him—then spoke. It was a positive fact, he said, notwithstanding their poverty, their hardships, and even their degradation in the eyes of some, that the first markets in London were mainly supported by costermongers. What would the Duke of Bedford's market in Covent-garden be without them? This question elicited loud applause.

Several other persons followed with statements of a similar character, which were listened to with interest; but from their general sameness it is not necessary to repeat them here. After occupying nearly four hours, the proceedings were brought to a close by a vote of thanks, and the "street-sellers, performers, and labourers," separated in a most orderly manner.

OF THE STREET-IRISH.

THE Irish street-sellers are both a numerous and peculiar class of people. It therefore behoves me, for the due completeness of this work, to say a few words upon their numbers, earnings, condition, and mode of life.

The number of Irish street-sellers in the metropolis has increased greatly of late years. One gentleman, who had every means of being well-informed, considered that it was not too much to conclude, that, within these five years, the numbers of the poor Irish people who gain a scanty maintenance, or what is rather a substitute for a maintenance, by trading, or begging, or by carrying on the two avocations simultaneously in the streets of London, had been doubled in number.

I found among the English costermongers a general dislike of the Irish. In fact, next to a policeman, a genuine London costermonger hates an Irishman, considering him an intruder. Whether there be any traditional or hereditary ill-feeling between them, originating from a clannish feeling, I cannot ascertain. The costermongers whom I questioned had no knowledge of the feelings or prejudices of their predecessors, but I am inclined to believe that the prejudice is modern, and has originated in the great influx of Irishmen and women, intermixing, more especially during the last five years, with the costermonger's business. An Irish costermonger, however, is no novelty in the streets of London. "From the mention of the costardmonger," says Mr. Charles Knight, "in the old dramatists, he appears to have been frequently an Irishman."

Of the Irish street-sellers, at present, it is computed that there are, including men, women, and children, upwards of 10,000. Assuming the street-sellers attending the London fish and green markets to be, with their families, 30,000 in number, and 7 in every 20 of these to be Irish, we shall have rather more than the total above given. Of this large body three-fourths sell only fruit, and more especially nuts and oranges; indeed, the orange-season is called the "Irishman's harvest." The others deal in fish, fruit, and vegetables, but these are principally men. Some of the most wretched of the street-

Irish deal in such trifles as lucifer-matches, water-cresses, &c.

I am informed that the great mass of these people have been connected, in some capacity or other, with the culture of the land in Ireland. The mechanics who have sought the metropolis from the sister kingdom have become mixed with their respective handicrafts in England, some of the Irish—though only a few—taking rank with the English skilled labourers. The greater part of the Irish artizans who have arrived within the last five years are to be found among the most degraded of the tailors and shoemakers who work at the East-end for the slop-masters. A large class of the Irish who were agricultural labourers in their country are to be found among the men working for bricklayers, as well as among the dock-labourers and excavators, &c. Wood chopping is an occupation greatly resorted to by the Irish in London. Many of the Irish, however, who are not regularly employed in their respective callings, resort to the streets when they cannot obtain work otherwise.

The Irish women and girls who sell fruit, &c., in the streets, depend almost entirely on that mode of traffic for their subsistence. They are a class not sufficiently taught to avail themselves of the ordinary resources of women in the humbler walk of life. Unskilled at their needles, working for slop employers, even at the commonest shirt-making, is impossible to them. Their ignorance of household work, moreover (for such description of work is unknown in their wretched cabins in many parts of Ireland), incapacitates them in a great measure for such employments as "charing," washing, and ironing, as well as from regular domestic employment. Thus there seems to remain to them but one thing to do—as, indeed, was said to me by one of themselves—viz., "to sell for a ha'pinny the three apples which cost a farruthing."

Very few of these women (nor, indeed, of the men, though rather more of them than the women) can read, and they are mostly all wretchedly poor; but the women present two characteristics which distinguish them from the London coster-women generally—they are chaste, and, unlike the "coster girls," very seldom form any connection without the sanction of the marriage ceremony. They are, moreover, attentive to religious observances.

The majority of the Irish street-sellers of both sexes beg, and often very eloquently, as they carry on their trade ; and I was further assured, that, but for this begging, some of them might starve outright.

The greater proportion of the Irish streetsellers are from Leinster and Munster, and a considerable number come from Connaught.

OF THE CAUSES WHICH HAVE MADE THE IRISH TURN COSTERMONGERS.

NOTWITHSTANDING the prejudices of the English costers, I am of opinion that the Irishmen and women who have become costermongers, belong to a better class than the Irish labourers. The Irishman may readily adapt himself, in a strange place, to labour, though not to trade; but these costers are—or the majority at least are—poor persevering traders enough.

The most intelligent and prosperous of the street-Irish are those who have " risen "—for so I heard it expressed—" into regular costers." The untaught Irishman's capabilities, as I have before remarked, with all his powers of speech and quickness of apprehension, are far less fitted for "buying in the cheapest market and selling in the dearest" than for mere physical employment. Hence those who take to streettrading for a living seldom prosper in it, and three-fourths of the street-Irish confine their dealings to such articles as are easy of sale, like apples, nuts, or oranges, for they are rarely masters of purchasing to advantage, and seem to know little about tale or measure, beyond the most familiar quantities. Compared with an acute costermonger, the mere apple-seller is but as the labourer to the artizan.

One of the principal causes why the Irish costermongers have increased so extensively of late years, is to be found in the fact that the labouring classes, (and of them chiefly the class employed in the culture of land,) have been driven over from "the sister Isle" more thickly for the last four or five years than formerly. Several circumstances have conspired to effect this.—First, they were driven over by the famine, when they could not procure, or began to fear that soon they could not procure, food to eat. Secondly, they were forced to take refuge in this country by the evictions, when their landlords had left them no roof to shelter them in their own. (The shifts, the devices, the plans, to which numbers of these poor creatures had recourse, to raise the means of quitting Ireland for England—or for anywhere—will present a very remarkable chapter at some future period.) Thirdly, though the better class of small farmers who have emigrated from Ireland, in hopes of " bettering themselves," have mostly sought the shores of North America, still some who have reached this country have at last settled into street-sellers. And, fourthly, many who have come over here only for the

harvest have been either induced or compelled to stay.

Another main cause is, that the Irish, as labourers, can seldom obtain work all the year through, and thus the ranks of the Irish streetsellers are recruited every winter by the slackness of certain periodic trades in which they are largely employed—such as hodmen, dockwork, excavating, and the like. They are, therefore, driven by want of employment to the winter sale of oranges and nuts. These circumstances have a doubly malefic effect, as the increase of costers accrues in the winter months, and there are consequently the most sellers when there are the fewest buyers.

Moreover, the cessation of work in the construction of railways, compared with the abundance of employment which attracted so many to this country during the railway mania, has been another fertile cause of there being so many Irish in the London streets.

The prevalence of Irish women and children among street-sellers is easily accounted for—they are, as I said before, unable to do anything else to eke out the means of their husbands or parents. A needle is as useless in their fingers as a pen.

Bitterly as many of these people suffer in this country, grievous and often eloquent as are their statements, I met with *none* who did not manifest repugnance at the suggestion of a return to Ireland. If asked why they objected to return, the response was usually in the form of a question: " Shure thin, sir, and what good could I do there ?" Neither can ? say that I heard any of these people express any love for their country, though they often spoke with great affection of their friends.

From an Irish costermonger, a middle-aged man, with a physiognomy best known as " Irish," and dressed in corduroy trousers, with a loose great-coat, far too big for him, buttoned about him, I had the following statement :

" I had a bit o' land, yer honor, in County Limerick. Well, it wasn't just a farrum, nor what ye would call a garden here, but my father lived and died on it—glory be to God !—and brought up me and my sister on it. It was about an acre, and the taties was well known to be good. But the sore times came, and the taties was afflicted, and the wife and me—I have no childer—hadn't a bite nor a sup, but wather to live on, and an igg or two. I filt the famine a-comin'. I saw people a-feedin' on the wild green things, and as I had not such a bad take, I got Mr. —— (he was the head master's agent) to give me 28s. for possission in quietness, and I sould some poulthry I had—their iggs was a blessin' to keep the life in us—I sould them in Limerick for 3s. 3d.—the poor things—four of them. The furnithur' I sould to the nabors, for somehow about 6s. Its the thruth I'm ay-tellin' of you, sir, and there's 2s. owin' of it still, and will be a perpitual loss. The wife and me walked to Dublin, though we had bether have gone by the 'long say,' but I didn't understand it thin, and we got to Liverpool. Then sorrow's the taste of worruk could I git, beyant oncte 3s. for two days harrud porthering, that broke my back half in two. I was tould I'd do betther in London, and so, glory be to God! I have—perhaps I have. I knew Mr. ——, he porthers at Covent-garden, and I made him out, and hilped him in any long distance of a job. As I'd been used to farrumin' I thought it good raison I should be a costermonger, as they call it here. I can read and write too. And some good Christian—the heavens light him to glory when he's gone!—I don't know who he was—advanced me 10s.—or he gave it me, so to spake, through Father ——," (a Roman Catholic priest.)" We carrun what keeps the life in us. I don't go to markit, but buy of a fair dealin' man —so I count him—though he's harrud sometimes. I can't till how many Irishmen is in the thrade. There's many has been brought down to it by the famin' and the changes. I don't go much among the English street-dalers. They talk like haythens. I never miss mass on a Sunday, and they don't know what the blissed mass manes. I'm almost glad I have no childer, to see how they're raired here. Indeed, sir, they're not raired at all—they run wild. They haven't the fear of God or the saints. They'd hang a praste —glory be to God! they would.''

How the Street-Irish displanted the Street-Jews in the Orange Trade.

The Jews, in the streets, while acting as costermongers, never "worked a barrow," nor dealt in the more ponderous and least profitable articles of the trade, such as turnips and cabbages. They however, had, at one period, the chief possession of a portion of the trade which the "regular hands" do not consider proper costermongering, and which is now chiefly confined to the Irish—viz.: orange selling.

The trade was, not many years ago, confined almost entirely to the Jew boys, who kept aloof from the vagrant lads of the streets, or mixed with them only in the cheap theatres and concert-rooms. A person who had had great experience at what was, till recently, one of the greatest "coaching inns," told me that, speaking within his own recollection and from his own observation, he thought the sale of oranges was not so much in the hands of the Jew lads until about forty years back. The orange monopoly, so to speak, was established by the street-Jews, about 1810, or three or four years previous to that date, when recruiting and local soldiering were at their height, and when a great number of the vagabond or "roving" population, who in one capacity or other now throng the streets, were induced to enlist. The young Jews never entered the ranks of the army. The streets were thus in a measure cleared for them, and the itinerant orange-trade fell almost entirely into their hands. Some of the young Jews gained, I am assured, at least 100l. a year in this traffic.

The numbers of country people who hastened to London on the occasion of the Allied Sovereigns' visit in 1814—many wealthy persons then seeing the capital for the first time—afforded an excellent market to these dealers.

Moreover, the perseverance of the Jew orange boys was not to be overcome; they would follow a man who even looked encouragingly at their wares for a mile or two. The great resort of these Jew dealers—who eschewed night-work generally, and left the theatre-doors to old men and women of all ages—was at the coaching inns; for year by year, after the peace of 1815, the improvement of the roads and the consequent increase of travellers to London, progressed.

About 1825, as nearly as my informant could recollect, these keen young traders began to add the sale of other goods to their oranges, pressing them upon the notice of those who were leaving or visiting London by the different coaches. So much was this the case, that it was a common remark at that time, that no one could reach or leave the metropolis, even for the shortest journey, without being expected to be in urgent want of oranges and lemons, black-lead pencils, sticks of sealing-wax, many-bladed pen-knives, pocket-combs, razors, strops, braces, and sponges. To pursue the sale of the last-mentioned articles—they being found, I presume, to be more profitable—some of the street-Jews began to abandon the sale of oranges and lemons; and it was upon this, that the trade was "taken up" by the wives and children of the Irish bricklayers' labourers, and of other Irish work-people then resident in London. The numbers of Irish in the metropolis at that time began to increase rapidly; for twenty years ago, they resorted numerously to England to gather in the harvest, and those who had been employed in contiguous counties during the autumn, made for London in the winter. " I can't say they were well off, sir," said one man to me, " but they liked bread and herrings, or bread and tea—better than potatoes without bread at home." From 1836 to 1840, I was informed, the Irish gradually superseded the Jews in the fruit traffic about the coaching-houses. One reason for this was, that they were far more eloquent, begging pathetically, and with many benedictions on their listeners. The Jews never begged, I was told; " they were merely traders." Another reason was, that the Irish, men or lads, who had entered into the fruit trade in the coach-yards, would not only sell and beg, but were ready to "lend a hand" to any over-burthened coach-porter. This the Jews never did, and in that way the people of the yard came to encourage the Irish to the prejudice of the Jews. At present, I understand that, with the exception of one or two in the city, no Jews vend oranges in the streets, and that the trade is almost entirely in the hands of the Irish.

Another reason why the Irish could supersede and even undersell the Jews and regular costermongers was this, as I am informed on excellent authority:—Father Mathew, a dozen years back, made temperance societies popular in Ireland. Many of the itinerant Irish, especially the younger classes, were "temperance men." Thus the Irish could live as sparely as the Jew, but they did not, like him, squander any money for the evening's amusement, at the concert or the theatre.

I inquired what might be the number of the Jews plying, so to speak, at the coaching inns, and was assured that it was less numerous than was generally imagined. One man computed it at 300 individuals, all under 21; another at only 200; perhaps the mean, or 250, might be about the mark. The number was naturally considered greater, I was told, because the same set of street traders were seen over and over again. The Jews knew when the coaches were to arrive and when they started, and they would hurry, after availing themselves of a departure, from one inn—the Belle Sauvage, Ludgate-hill, for instance—to take advantage of an arrival at another—say the Saracen's Head, Snow-hill. Thus they appeared everywhere, but were the same individuals.

I inquired to what calling the youthful Jews, thus driven from their partially monopolized street commerce, had devoted themselves, and was told that even when the orange and hawking trade was at the best, the Jews rarely carried it on after they were twenty-two or twenty-three, but that they then resorted to some more wholesale calling, such as the purchase of nuts or foreign grapes, at public sales. At present, I am informed, they are more thickly than ever engaged in these trades, as well as in two new avocations, that have been established within these few years,—the sale of the Bahama pineapples and of the Spanish and Portuguese onions.

About the Royal Exchange, Jew boys still hawk pencils, etc., but the number engaged in this pursuit throughout London is not, as far as I can ascertain, above one-eighth—if an eighth—of what it was even twelve years ago.

Of the Religion of the Street-Irish.

HAVING now given a brief sketch as to how the Irish people have come to form so large a proportion of the London street-sellers, I shall proceed, as I did with the English costermongers, to furnish the reader with a short account of their religious, moral, intellectual, and physical condition, so that he may be able to contrast the habits and circumstances of the one class with those of the other. First, of the religion of the Irish street-folk.

Almost all the street-Irish are Roman Catholics. Of course I can but speak generally; but during my inquiry I met with only two who said they were Protestants, and when I came to converse with them, I found out that they were partly ignorant of, and partly indifferent to, any religion whatever. An Irish Protestant gentleman said to me: "You may depend upon it, if ever you meet any of my poor countrymen who

will not talk to you about religion, they either know or care nothing about it; for the religious spirit runs high in Ireland, and Protestants and Catholics are easily led to converse about their faith."

I found that some of the Irish Roman Catholics—but they had been for many years resident in England, and that among the poorest or vagrant class of the English—had become indifferent to their creed, and did not attend their chapels, unless at the great fasts or festivals, and this they did only occasionally. One old stall-keeper, who had been in London nearly thirty years, said to me: "Ah! God knows, sir, I ought to attend mass every Sunday, but I haven't for a many years, barrin' Christmas-day and such times. But I'll thry and go more rigular, plase God." This man seemed to resent, as a sort of indignity, my question if he ever attended any other place of worship. "Av coorse not!" was the reply.

One Irishman, also a fruit-seller, with a well-stocked barrow, and without the complaint of poverty common among his class, entered keenly into the subject of his religious faith when I introduced it. He was born in Ireland, but had been in England since he was five or six. He was a good-looking, fresh-coloured man, of thirty or upwards, and could read and write well. He spoke without bitterness, though zealously enough. "Perhaps, sir, you are a gintleman connected with the Protistant clargy," he asked, "or a missionary?" On my stating that I had no claim to either character, he resumed: "Will, sir, it don't matter. All the worruld may know my riligion, and I wish all the worruld was of my riligion, and betther min in it than I am; I do, indeed. I'm a Roman Catholic, sir;" [here he made the sign of the cross]; "God be praised for it! O yis, I know all about Cardinal Wiseman. It's the will of God, I feel sure, that he's to be 'stablished here, and it's no use ribillin' against that. I've nothing to say against Protistints. I've heard it said, 'It's best to pray for them.' The street-people that call thimselves Protistants are no riligion at all at all. I serruve Protistant gintlemen and ladies too, and sometimes they talk to me kindly about religion. They're good custhomers, and I have no doubt good people. I can't say what their lot may be in another worruld for not being of the true faith. No, sir, I'll give no opinions—none."

This man gave me a clear account of his belief that the Blessed Virgin (he crossed himself repeatedly as he spoke) was the mother of our Lord Jesus Christ, and was a mediator with our Lord, who was God of heaven and earth—of the duty of praying to the holy saints—of attending mass—(" but the priest," he said, "won't exact too much of a poor man, either about that or about fasting")—of going to confession at Easter and Christmas times, at the least—of receiving the body of Christ, "the rale prisince," in the holy sacrament—of keeping all God's commandments—of purgatory being a purgation of sins—and of heaven and hell.

I found the majority of those I spoke with, at least as earnest in their faith, if they were not as well instructed in it as my informant, who may be cited as an example of the better class of street-sellers.

Another Irishman,—who may be taken as a type of the less informed, and who had been between two and three years in England, having been disappointed in emigrating to America with his wife and two children,—gave me the following account, but not without considering and hesitating. He was a very melancholy looking man, tall and spare, and decently clad. He and his family were living upon 8*d.* a day, which he earned by sweeping a crossing. He had been prevented by ill health from earning 2*l.*, which he could have made, he told me, in harvest time, as a store against winter. He had been a street-seller, and so had his wife; and she would be so again as soon as he could raise 2*s.* to buy her a stock of apples. He said, touching his hat at each holy name,—

" Sure, yis, sir, I'm a Roman Cartholic, and go to mass every Sunday. Jesus Christ? O yis," (hesitating, but proceeding readily after a word of prompting), " he is the Lord our Saviour, and the Son of the Holy Virgin. The blessed saints? Yis, sir, yis. The praste prays for them. I— I mane prays to them. O, yis. I pray to them mysilf ivery night for a blissin', and to rise me out of my misery. No, sir, I can't say I know what the mass is about. I don't know what I'm prayin' for thin, only that it's right. A poor man, that can neither read nor write—I wish I could and I might do betther—can't understand it; it's all in Latin. Iv'e heard about Cardinal Wiseman. It'll do us no good sir; it'll only set people more against us. But it ain't poor min's fault."

As I was anxious to witness the religious zeal that characterizes these people, I obtained permission to follow one of the priests as he made his rounds among his flock. Everywhere the people ran out to meet him. He had just returned to them I found, and the news spread round, and women crowded to their door-steps, and came creeping up from the cellars through the trap-doors, merely to curtsey to him. One old crone, as he passed, cried, "You're a good father, Heaven comfort you," and the boys playing about stood still to watch him. A lad, in a man's tail coat and a shirt-collar that nearly covered in his head—like the paper round a bouquet—was fortunate enough to be noticed, and his eyes sparkled, as he touched his hair at each word he spoke in answer. At a conversation that took place between the priest and a woman who kept a dry fish-stall, the dame excused herself for not having been up to take tea " with his rivirince's mother lately, for thrade had been so bisy, and night was the fullest time." Even as the priest walked along the street, boys running at full speed would pull up to touch their hair, and the stall-women would rise from their baskets; while all noise—even a quarrel—ceased until he had passed by. Still

there was no look of fear in the people. He called them all by their names, and asked after their families, and once or twice the "father" was taken aside and held by the button while some point that required his advice was whispered in his ear.

The religious fervour of the people whom I saw was intense. At one house that I entered, the woman set me marvelling at the strength of her zeal, by showing me how she contrived to have in her sitting-room a sanctuary to pray before every night and morning, and even in the day, "when she felt weary and lonesome." The room was rudely enough furnished, and the only decent table was covered with a new piece of varnished cloth ; still before a rude print of our Saviour there were placed two old plated candlesticks, pink, with the copper shining through; and here it was that she told her beads. In her bed-room, too, was a coloured engraving of the "Blessed Lady," which she never passed without curtseying to.

Of course I detail these matters as mere facts, without desiring to offer any opinion here, either as to the benefit or otherwise of the creed in question. As I had shown how the English costermonger neither had nor knew any religion whatever, it became my duty to give the reader a view of the religion of the Irish street-sellers. In order to be able to do so as truthfully as possible, I placed myself in communication with those parties who were in a position to give me the best information on the subject. The result is given above, in all the simplicity and impartiality of history.

OF THE EDUCATION, LITERATURE, AMUSEMENTS, AND POLITICS OF THE STREET-IRISH.

THESE several heads have often required from me lengthened notices, but as regards the class I am now describing they may be dismissed briefly enough. The majority of the street-Irish whom I saw were unable to read, but I found those who had no knowledge of reading—(and the same remark applies to the English street-sellers as well)—regret their inability, and say, "I wish I could read, sir; I'd be better off now." On the other hand, those who had a knowledge of reading and writing, said frequently enough, "Why, yes, sir, I can read and write, but it's been no good to me," as if they had been disappointed in their expectations as to the benefits attendant upon scholarship. I am inclined to think, however, that a greater anxiety exists among the poor generally, to have some schooling provided for their children, than was the case a few years back. One Irishman attributed this to the increased number of Roman Catholic schools, "for the more schools there are," he said, "the more people think about schooling their children."

The literature, or reading, of she street-Irish is, I believe, confined to Roman Catholic books, such as the "Lives of the Saints," published in a cheap form ; one, and only one, I found with the "Nation" newspaper. The very poor have no leisure to read. During three days spent in visiting the slop-workers at the East end of the town, not so much as the fragment of a leaf of a book was seen.

The amusements of the street-Irish are not those of the English costermongers—though there are exceptions, of course, to the remark. The Irish fathers and mothers do not allow their daughters, even when they possess the means, to resort to the "penny gaffs" or the "twopenny hops," unaccompanied by them. Some of the men frequent the beer-shops, and are inveterate drinkers and smokers too. I did not hear of any amusements popular among, or much resorted to, by the Irishmen, except dancing parties at one another's houses, where they jig and reel furiously. They frequent raffles also, but the article is often never thrown for, and the evening is spent in dancing.

I may here observe—in reference to the statement that Irish parents will not expose their daughters to the risk of what they consider corrupt influences—that when a young Irishwoman *does* break through the pale of chastity, she often becomes, as I was assured, one of the most violent and depraved of, perhaps, *the* most depraved class.

Of politics, I think, the street-Irish understand nothing, and my own observations in this respect were confirmed by a remark made to me by an Irish gentleman: "Their politics are either a dead letter, or the politics of their priests."

THE HOMES OF THE STREET-IRISH.

IN almost all of the poorer districts of London are to be found "nests of Irish"—as they are called—or courts inhabited solely by the Irish costermongers. These people form separate colonies, rarely visiting or mingling with the English costers. It is curious, on walking through one of these settlements, to notice the manner in which the Irish deal among themselves—street-seller buying of street-seller. Even in some of the smallest courts there may be seen stalls of vegetables, dried herrings, or salt cod, thriving, on the associative principle, by mutual support.

The parts of London that are the most thickly populated with Irish lie about Brook-street, Ratcliff-cross, down both sides of the Commercial-road, and in Rosemary-lane, though nearly all the "coster-districts" cited at p. 47, have their Irish settlements—Cromer-street, Saffron-hill and King-street, Drury-lane, for instance, being thickly peopled with the Irish; but the places I have mentioned above are peculiarly distinguished, by being almost entirely peopled by visitors from the sister isle.

The same system of immigration is pursued in London as in America. As soon as the first settler is thriving in his newly chosen country, a certain portion of his or her earnings are carefully hoarded up, until they are sufficient to pay for the removal of another member of

the family to England; then one of the friends left "at home" is sent for; and thus by degrees the entire family is got over, and once more united.

Perhaps there is no quarter of London where the habits and habitations of the Irish can be better seen and studied than in Rosemary-lane, and the little courts and alleys that spring from it on each side. Some of these courts have other courts branching off from them, so that the locality is a perfect labyrinth of "blind alleys;" and when once in the heart of the maze it is difficult to find the path that leads to the main-road. As you walk down "the lane," and peep through the narrow openings between the houses, the place seems like a huge peep-show, with dark holes of gateways to look through, while the court within appears bright with the daylight; and down it are seen rough-headed urchins running with their feet bare through the puddles, and bonnetless girls, huddled in shawls, lolling against the door-posts. Sometimes you see a long narrow alley, with the houses so close together that opposite neighbours are talking from their windows; while the ropes, stretched zig-zag from wall to wall, afford just room enough to dry a blanket or a couple of shirts, that swell out dropsically in the wind.

I visited one of the paved yards round which the Irish live, and found that it had been turned into a complete drying-ground, with shirts, gowns, and petticoats of every description and colour. The buildings at the end were completely hidden by "the things," and the air felt damp and chilly, and smelt of soap-suds. The gutter was filled with dirty gray water emptied from the wash-tubs, and on the top were the thick bubbles floating about under the breath of the boys "playing at boats" with them.

It is the custom with the inhabitants of these courts and alleys to assemble at the entrance with their baskets, and chat and smoke away the morning. Every court entrance has its little group of girls and women, lolling listlessly against the sides, with their heads uncovered, and their luxuriant hair fuzzy as oakum. It is peculiar with the Irish women that—after having been accustomed to their hoods—they seldom wear bonnets, unless on a long journey. Nearly all of them, too, have a thick plaid shawl, which they keep on all the day through, with their hands covered under it. At the mouth of the only thoroughfare deserving of the name of street—for a cart could just go through it—were congregated about thirty men and women, who rented rooms in the houses on each side of the road. Six women, with baskets of dried herrings, were crouching in a line on the kerb-stone with the fish before them; their legs were drawn up so closely to their bodies that the shawl covered the entire figure, and they looked very like the podgy "tomblers" sold by the Italian boys. As all their wares were alike, it was puzzling work to imagine how, without the strongest opposition, they could each obtain a living. The men were dressed in long-tail coats, with one or two brass buttons. One old dame, with a face wrinkled like a dried plum, had her cloak placed over her head like a hood, and the grisly hair hung down in matted hanks about her face, her black eyes shining between the locks like those of a Skye terrier; beside her was another old woman smoking a pipe so short that her nose reached over the bowl.

After looking at the low foreheads and long bulging upper lips of some of the group, it was pleasant to gaze upon the pretty faces of the one or two girls that lolled against the wall. Their black hair, smoothed with grease, and shining almost as if "japanned," and their large gray eyes with the thick dark fringe of lash, seemed out of place among the hard features of their companions. It was only by looking at the short petticoats and large feet you could assure yourself that they belonged to the same class.

In all the houses that I entered were traces of household care and neatness that I had little expected to have seen. The cupboard fastened in the corner of the room, and stocked with mugs and cups, the mantelpiece with its images, and the walls covered with showy-coloured prints of saints and martyrs, gave an air of comfort that strangely disagreed with the reports of the cabins in "ould Ireland." As the doors to the houses were nearly all of them kept open, I could, even whilst walking along, gain some notion of the furniture of the homes. In one house that I visited there was a family of five persons, living on the ground floor and occupying two rooms. The boards were strewn with red sand, and the front apartment had three beds in it, with the printed curtains drawn closely round. In a dark room, at the back, lived the family itself. It was fitted up as a parlour, and crowded to excess with chairs and tables, the very staircase having pictures fastened against the wooden partition. The fire, although it was midday, and a warm autumn morning, served as much for light as for heat, and round it crouched the mother, children, and visitors, bending over the flame as if in the severest winter time. In a room above this were a man and woman lately arrived in England. The woman sat huddled up in a corner smoking, with the husband standing over her in, what appeared at first, a menacing attitude; I was informed, however, that they were only planning for the future. This room was perfectly empty of furniture, and the once white-washed walls were black, excepting the little square patches which showed where the pictures of the former tenants had hung. In another room, I found a home so small and full of furniture, that it was almost a curiosity for domestic management. The bed, with its chintz curtains looped up, filled one end of the apartment, but the mattress of it served as a long bench for the visitors to sit on. The table was so large that it divided the room in two, and if there was one picture there must have been thirty—all of "holy men," with yellow

glories round their heads. The window-ledge was dressed out with crockery, and in a tumbler were placed the beads. The old dame herself was as curious as her room. Her shawl was fastened over her large frilled cap. She had a little "button" of a nose, with the nostrils entering her face like bullet holes. She wore over her gown an old pilot coat, well-stained with fish slime, and her petticoats being short, she had very much the appearance of a Dutch fisherman or stage smuggler.

Her story was affecting—made more so, perhaps, by the emotional manner in which she related it. Nine years ago "the father" of the district—"the Blissed Lady guard him!"— had found her late at night, rolling in the gutter, and the boys pelting her with orange-peel and mud. She was drunk—"the Lorrud pass by her"—and when she came to, she found herself in the chapel, lying before the sanctuary, "under the shadow of the holy cross." Watching over her was the "good father," trying to bring back her consciousness. He spoke to her of her wickedness, and before she left she took the pledge of temperance. From that time she prospered, and the 1s. 6d. the "father" gave her "had God's blissin' in it," for she became the best dressed woman in the court, and in less than three years had 15l. in the savings' bank, "the father—Heaven chirish him"—keeping her book for her, as he did for other poor people. She also joined "the Association of the Blissed Lady," (and bought herself the dress of the order "a beautiful grane vilvit, which she had now, and which same cost her 30s."), and then she was secure against want in old age and sickness. But after nine years prudence and comfort, a brother of hers returned home from the army, with a pension of 1s. a day. He was wild, and persuaded her to break her pledge, and in a short time he got all her savings from her and spent every penny. She could'nt shake him off, "for he was the only kin she had on airth," and "she must love her own flish and bones." Then began her misery. "It plased God to visit her ould limbs with aches and throubles, and her hips swole into the cowld," so that she was at last forced into a hospital, and all that was left of her store was "aten up by sufferin's." This, she assured me, all came about by the "good father's" leaving that parish for another one, but now he had returned to them again, and, with his help and God's blessing, she would yet prosper once more.

Whilst I was in the room, the father entered, and "old Norah," half-divided between joy at seeing him and shame at "being again a beggar," laughed and wept at the same time. She stood wiping her eyes with the shawl, and groaning out blessings on "his rivirince's hid," begging of him not "to scould her for she was a wake woman." The renegade brother was had in to receive a lecture from "his rivirince." A more sottish idiotic face it would be difficult to imagine. He stood with his hands hanging down like the paws of a dog begging, and his two small eyes stared in the face of the priest, as he censured him, without the least expression even of consciousness. Old Norah stood by, groaning like a bagpipe, and writhing while the father spoke to her " own brother," as though every reproach were meant for her.

The one thing that struck me during my visit to this neighbourhood, was the apparent listlessness and lazy appearance of the people. The boys at play were the only beings who seemed to have any life in their actions. The women in their plaid shawls strolled along the pavements, stopping each friend for a chat, or joining some circle, and leaning against the wall as though utterly deficient in energy. The men smoked, with their hands in their pockets, listening to the old crones talking, and only now and then grunting out a reply when a question was directly put to them. And yet it is curious that these people, who here seemed as inactive as negroes, will perform the severest bodily labour, undertaking tasks that the English are almost unfitted for.

To complete this account, I subjoin a brief description of the lodging-houses resorted to by the Irish immigrants on their arrival in this country.

IRISH LODGING-HOUSES FOR IMMIGRANTS.

OFTEN an Irish immigrant, whose object is to settle in London, arrives by the Cork steamer without knowing a single friend to whom he can apply for house-room or assistance of any kind. Sometimes a whole family is landed late at night, worn out by sickness and the terrible fatigues of a three days' deck passage, almost paralysed by exhaustion, and scarcely able to speak English enough to inquire for shelter till morning.

If the immigrants, however, are bound for America, their lot is very different. Then they are consigned to some agent in London, who is always on the wharf at the time the steamer arrives, and takes the strangers to the homes he has prepared for them until the New York packet starts. During the two or three days' necessary stay in London, they are provided for at the agent's expense, and no trouble is experienced by the travellers. A large provision-merchant in the city told me that he often, during the season, had as many as 500 Irish consigned to him by one vessel, so that to lead them to their lodgings was like walking at the head of a regiment of recruits.

The necessities of the immigrants in London have caused several of their countrymen to open lodging-houses in the courts about Rosemary-lane; these men attend the coming in of the Cork steamer, and seek for customers among the poorest of the poor, after the manner of touters to a sea-side hotel.

The immigrants'-houses are of two kinds— clean and dirty. The better class of Irish lodging-houses almost startle one by the comfort and cleanliness of the rooms; for after the descriptions you hear of the state in which the deck passengers are landed from the Irish boats, their clothes stained with the manure of the pigs, and drenched with the spray, you somehow expect to find all the accommodations disgusting and unwholesome. But one in particular, that I visited, had the floor clean, and sprinkled with red sand, while the windows were sound, bright, and transparent. The hobs of the large fire-place were piled up with bright tin pots, and the chimney piece was white and red with the china images ranged upon it. In one corner of the principal apartment there stood two or three boxes still corded up, and with bundles strung to the sides, and against the wall was hung a bunch of blue cloaks, such as the Irishwomen wear. The proprietor of the house, who was dressed in a gray tail-coat and knee-breeches, that had somewhat the effect of a footman's livery, told me that he had received seven lodgers the day before, but six were men, and they were all out seeking for work. In front of the fire sat a woman, bending over it so close that the bright cotton gown she had on smelt of scorching. Her feet were bare, and she held the soles of them near to the bars, curling her toes about with the heat. She was a short, thick-set woman, with a pair of wonderfully muscular arms crossed over her bosom, and her loose rusty hair streaming over her neck. It was in vain that I spoke to her about her journey, for she wouldn't answer me, but kept her round, open eyes fixed on my face with a wild, nervous look, following me about with them everywhere.

Across the room hung a line, with the newly-washed and well-patched clothes of the immigrants hanging to it, and on a side-table were the six yellow basins that had been used for the men's breakfasts. During my visit, the neighbours, having observed a strange gentleman enter, came pouring in, each proferring some fresh bit of news about their newly-arrived countrymen. I was nearly stunned by half-a-dozen voices speaking together, and telling me how the poor people had been four days " at say," so that they were glad to get near the pigs for " warrumth," and instructing me as to the best manner of laying out the sum of money that it was supposed I was about to shower down upon the immigrants.

In one of the worst class of lodging-houses I found ten human beings living together in a small room. The apartment was entirely devoid of all furniture, excepting an old mattrass rolled up against the wall, and a dirty piece of cloth hung across one corner, to screen the women whilst dressing. An old man, the father of five out of the ten, was seated on a tea-chest, mending shoes, and the other men were looking on with their hands in their pockets. Two girls and a woman were huddled together on the floor in front of the fire, talking in Irish. All these people seemed to be utterly devoid of energy, and the men moved about so lazily that I couldn't help asking some of them if they had tried to obtain work. Every one turned to a good-looking young fellow lolling against the wall, as if they expected him to answer for them. " Ah, sure, and that they have," was the reply; " it 's the dooks they have tried, worrus luck." The others appeared struck with the truthfulness of the answer, for they all shook their heads, and said, " Sure an' that's thruth, anyhow." Here my Irish guide ventured an observation, by remarking solemnly, " It's no use tilling a lie;" to which the whole room assented, by exclaiming altogether, " Thrue for you, Norah." The chosen spokesman then told me, " They paid half-a-crown a week for the room, and that was as much as they could earrun, and it was starruve they should if the neighbours didn't hilp them a bit." I asked them if they were better off over here than when in Ireland, but could get no direct answer, for my question only gave rise to a political discussion. " There 's plenty of food over here," said the spokesman, addressing his companions as much as myself, " plenty of 'taties—plenty of mate—plenty of porruk." " But where the use," observed my guide, " if there's no money to buy 'em wid ?" to which the audience muttered, " Thrue for you again, Norah ;" and so it went on, each one pleading poverty in the most eloquent style.

After I had left, the young fellow who had acted as spokesman followed me into the street, and taking me into a corner, told me that he was a " sailor by thrade, but had lost his 'rigisthration-ticket,' or he'd have got a berruth long since, and that it was all for 3s. 6d. he wasn't at say."

Concerning the number of Irish immigrants, I have obtained the following information :

The great influx of the Irish into London was in the year of the famine, 1847-8. This cannot be better shown than by citing the returns of the number of persons admitted into the Asylum for the Houseless Poor, in Playhouse-yard, Cripplegate. These returns I obtained for fourteen years, and the average number of admissions of the applicants from all parts during that time was 8,794 yearly. Of these, the Irish averaged 2,455 yearly, or considerably more than a fourth of the whole number received. The total number of applicants thus sheltered in the fourteen years was 130,625, of which the Irish numbered 34,378. The smallest number of Irish (men, women, and children) admitted, was in 1834-5, about 300 ; in 1846-7, it was as many as 7,576, while in 1847-8, it was 10,756, and in 1848-9, 5,068.

But it was into Liverpool that the tide of immigration flowed the strongest, in the calamitous year of the famine. " Between the 13th Jan, and the 13th Dec., both inclusive," writes Mr. Rushton, the Liverpool magistrate, to Sir G. Grey, on the 21st April last, " 296,231 persons landed in this port (Liverpool) from Ireland. Of this vast number, about 130,000 emigrated to

the United States; some 50,000 were passengers on business; and the remainder (161,231), mere paupers, half-naked and starving, landed, for the most part, during the winter, and became, immediately on landing, applicants for parochial relief. You already know the immediate results of this accumulation of misery in the crowded town of Liverpool; of the cost of relief at once rendered necessary to prevent the thousands of hungry and naked Irish perishing in our streets; and also of the cost of the pestilence which generally follows in the train of famine and misery such as we then had to encounter. . . . . Hundreds of patients perished, notwithstanding all efforts made to save them ; and ten Roman Catholic and one Protestant clergyman, many parochial officers, and many medical men, who devoted themselves to the task of alleviating the sufferings of the wretched, died in the discharge of these high duties."

Great numbers of these people were, at the same time, also conveyed from Ireland to Wales, especially to Newport. They were brought over by coal-vessels as a return cargo—a living ballast —2s. 6d. being the highest fare, and were huddled together like pigs. The manager of the Newport tramp-house has stated concerning these people, " They don't live long, diseased as they are. They are . very remarkable ; they will cat salt by basons-full, and drink a great quantity of water after. I have frequently known those who could not have been hungry eat cabbage-leaves and other refuse from the ash-heap."

It is necessary that I should thus briefly allude to this matter, as there is no doubt that some of these people, making their way to London, soon became street-sellers there, and many of them took to the business subsequently, when there was no employment in harvesting, hop-picking, &c. Of the poor wretches landed at Liverpool, many (Mr. Rushton states) became beggars, and many thieves. Many, there is no doubt, tramped their way to London, sleeping at the " casual wards " of the Unions on their way ; but I believe that of those who had become habituated to the practice of beggary or theft, few or none would follow the occupation of street-selling, as even the half-passive industry of such a calling would be irksome to the apathetic and dishonest.

Of the immigration, direct by the vessels trading from Ireland to London, there are no returns such has have been collected by Mr. Rushton for Liverpool, but the influx is comparatively small, on account of the greater length and cost of the voyage. During the last year I am informed that 15,000 or 16,000 passengers were brought from Ireland to London direct, and, in addition to these, 500 more were brought over from Cork in connection with the arrangements for emigration to the United States, and consigned to the emigration agent here. Of the 15,500 (taking the mean between the two numbers above given) 1,000 emigrated to the United States. It appears, on the authority of Mr. Rushton, that even in the great year of the immigration, more than one-sixth of the passengers from Ireland to Dublin came on business. It may, then, be reasonable to calculate that during last year one-fourth at least of the passengers to London had the same object in view, leaving about 10,000 persons who have either emigrated to British North America, Australia, &c., or have resorted to some mode of subsistence in the metropolis or the adjacent parts. Besides these there are the numbers who make their way up to London, tramping it from the several provincial ports—namely, Liverpool, Bristol, Newport, and Glasgow. Of these I have no means of forming any estimate, or of the proportion who adopt street-selling on their arrival here—all that can be said is, that the influx of Irish into the street-trade every year must be very considerable. I believe, however, that only those who "have friends in the line" resort to street-selling on their arrival in London, though all may make it a resource when other endeavours fail. The great immigration into London is from Cork, the average cost of a deck passage being 5s. The immigrants direct to London from Cork are rarely of the poorest class.

Of the Diet, Drink, and Expense of Living of the Street-Irish.

The diet of the Irish men, women, and children, who obtain a livelihood (or what is so designated) by street-sale in London, has, I am told, in good authority, experienced a change. In the lodging-houses that they resorted to, their breakfast, two or three years ago, was a dish of potatoes—two, three, or four lbs., or more, in weight—for a family. Now half an ounce of coffee (half chicory) costs ½d., and that, with the half or quarter of a loaf, according to the number in family, is almost always their breakfast at the present time. When their constant diet was potatoes, there were frequent squabbles at the lodging-houses—to which many of the poor Irish on their first arrival resort—as to whether the potato-pot or the tea-kettle should have the preference on the fire. A man of superior intelligence, who had been driven to sleep and eat occasionally in lodging-houses, told me of some dialogues he had heard on these occasions:—"It's about three years ago," he said, "since I heard a bitter old Englishwoman say, 'To —— with your 'taty-pot; they're only meat for pigs.' 'Sure, thin,' said a young Irishman—he was a nice 'cute fellow—' sure, thin, ma'am, I should be afther offering you a taste.' I heard that myself, sir. You may have noticed, that when an Irishman doesn't get out of temper, he never loses his politeness, or rather his blarney."

The dinner, or second meal of the day—assuming that there has been a breakfast—ordinarily consists of cheap fish and potatoes. Of the diet of the poor street-Irish I had an account from a little Irishman, then keeping an oyster-stall, though he generally sold fruit. In all such details I have found the

Irish far more communicative than the English. Many a poor untaught Englishman will shrink from speaking of his spare diet, and his trouble to procure that; a reserve, too, much more noticeable among the men than the women. My Irish informant told me he usually had his breakfast at a lodging-house—he preferred a lodging-house, he said, on account of the warmth and the society. Here he boiled half an ounce of coffee, costing a ½d. He purchased of his landlady the fourth of a quartern loaf (1¼d. or 1½d.), for she generally cut a quartern loaf into four for her single men lodgers, such as himself, clearing sometimes a farthing or two thereby. For dinner, my informant boiled at the lodging-house two or three lbs. of potatoes, costing usually 1d. or 1¼d., and fried three, or four herrings, or as many as cost a penny. He sometimes mashed his potatoes, and spread over them the herrings, the fatty portion of which flavoured the potatoes, which were further flavoured by the roes of the herrings being crushed into them. He drank water to this meal, and the cost of the whole was 2d. or 2½d. A neighbouring stall-keeper attended to this man's stock in his absence at dinner, and my informant did the same for him in his turn. For "tea" he expended 1d. on coffee, or 1½d. on tea, being a "cup" of tea, or "half-pint of coffee," at a coffee-shop. Sometimes he had a halfpenny-worth of butter, and with his tea he ate the bread he had saved from his breakfast, and which he had carried in his pocket. He had no butter to his breakfast, he said, for he could not buy less than a pennyworth about where he lodged, and this was too dear for one meal. On a Sunday morning however he generally had butter, sometimes joining with a fellow-lodger for a pennyworth; for his Sunday dinner he had a piece of meat, which cost him 2d. on the Saturday night. Supper he dispensed with, but if he felt much tired he had a half-pint of beer, which was three farthings "in his own jug," before he went to bed, about nine or ten, as he did little or nothing late at night, except on Saturday. He thus spent 4½d. a day for food, and reckoning 2½d. extra for somewhat better fare on a Sunday, his board was 2s. 10d. a week. His earnings he computed at 5s., and thus he had 2s. 2d. weekly for other expenses. Of these there was 1s. for lodging; 2d. or 3d. for washing (but this not every week); ½d. for a Sunday morning's shave; 1d. "for his religion" (as he worded it); and 6d. for "odds and ends," such as thread to mend his clothes, a piece of leather to patch his shoes, worsted to darn his stockings, &c. He was subject to rheumatism, or "he might have saved a trifle of money." Judging by his methodical habits, it was probable he had done so. He had nothing of the eloquence of his countrymen, and seemed indeed of rather a morose turn.

A family boarding together live even cheaper than this man, for more potatoes and less fish fall to the share of the children. A meal too is

not unfrequently saved in this manner:—
If a man, his wife, and two children, all go
out in the streets selling, they breakfast before
starting, and perhaps agree to re-assemble at
four o'clock. Then the wife prepares the dinner
of fish and potatoes, and so tea is dispensed with.
In that case the husband's and wife's board
would be 4d. or 4½d. a day each, the children's
3d. or 3½d. each, and giving 1½d. extra to each
for Sunday, the weekly cost is 10s. 3d. Supposing the husband and wife cleared 5s. a week
each, and the children each 3s., their earnings
would be 16s. The balance is the surplus left
to pay rent, washing, firing, and clothing.

From what I can ascertain, the Irish street-
seller can always live at about half the cost
of the English costermonger; the Englishman
must have butter for his bread, and meat at no
long intervals, for he "hates fish more than
once a week." It is by this spareness of
living, as well as by frequently importunate
and mendacious begging, that the street-Irish
manage to save money.

The diet I have spoken of is *generally*, but
not universally, that of the poor street-Irish;
those who live differently, do not, as a rule,
incur greater expense.

It is difficult to ascertain in what proportion
the Irish street-sellers consume strong drink,
when compared with the consumption of the
English costers; as a poor Irishman, if questioned on that or any subject, will far more
frequently shape his reply to what he thinks will
please his querist and induce a trifle for himself,
than answer according to the truth. The landlord of a large public-house, after inquiring of
his assistants, that his opinions might be checked
by theirs, told me that in one respect there was
a marked difference between the beer-drinking
of the two people. He considered that in the
poor streets near his house there were residing
quite as many Irish street-sellers and labourers
as English, but the instances in which the Irish
conveyed beer to their own rooms, as a portion
of their meals, was not as 1 in 20 compared
with the English: "I have read your work,
sir," he said, "and I know that you are quite
right in saying that the costermongers go for a
good Sunday dinner. I don't know what my
customers are except by their appearance, but I
do know that many are costermongers, and by the
best of all proofs, for I have bought fish, fruit,
and vegetables of them. Well, now, we'll take
a fine Sunday in spring or summer, when times
are pretty good with them; and, perhaps, in the
ten minutes after my doors are opened at one on
the Sunday, there are 100 customers for their
dinner-beer. Nearly three-quarters of these are
working men and their wives, working either in
the streets, or at their indoor trades, such as
tailoring. But among the number, I'm satisfied, there are not more than two Irishmen.
There may be three or four Irishwomen, but one
of my barmen tells me he knows that two of
them—very well-behaved and good-looking
women—are married to Englishmen. In my

opinion the proportion, as to Sunday dinner-
beer, between English and Irish, may be two
or three in 70."

An Irish gentleman and his wife, who are
both well acquainted with the habits and condition of the people in their own country, informed me, that among the classes who,
though earning only scant incomes, could
not well be called "impoverished," the use
of beer, or even of small ale — known, now
or recently—as "Thunder's thruppeny," was
very unfrequent. Even in many "independent" families, only water is drunk at dinner, with punch to follow. This shows the
accuracy of the information I derived from
Mr. —— (the innkeeper), for persons unused to
the drinking of malt liquor in their own country are not likely to resort to it afterwards,
when their means are limited. I was further
informed, that reckoning the teetallers among
the English street-sellers at 300, there are 600
among the Irish,—teetallers too, who, having
taken the pledge, under the sanction of their
priests, and looking upon it as a religious obligation, keep it rigidly.

The Irish street-sellers who frequent the gin-
palaces or public-houses, drink a pot of beer, in
a company of three or four, but far more frequently, a quartern of gin (very seldom whisky)
oftener than do the English. Indeed, from all
I could ascertain, the Irish street-sellers, whether from inferior earnings, their early training,
or the restraints of their priests, drink less beer,
by one-fourth, than their English brethren, but
a larger proportion of gin. "And you must bear
this in mind, sir," I was told by an innkeeper,
"I had rather have twenty poor Englishmen
drunk in my tap-room than a couple of poor
Irishmen. They'll quarrel with anybody—
the Irish will—and sometimes clear the room
by swearing they'll 'use their knives, by Jasus;'
and if there's a scuffle they'll kick like devils,
and scratch, and bite, like women or cats, instead of using their fists. I wish all the drunkards were teetallers, if it were only to be rid
of them."

Whiskey, I was told, would be drunk by the
Irish, in preference to gin, were it not that gin
was about half the price. One old Irish fruit-
seller—who admitted that he was fond of a
glass of gin—told me that he had not tasted
whiskey for fourteen years, "because of the
price." The Irish, moreover, as I have shown,
live on stronger and coarser food than the
English, buying all the rough (bad) fish, for, to
use the words of one of my informants, they
look to quantity more than quality; this may
account for their preferring a stronger and fiercer
stimulant by way of drink.

OF THE RESOURCES OF THE STREET-IRISH
AS REGARDS "STOCK-MONEY," SICKNESS,
BURIALS, &c.

IT is not easy to ascertain from the poor Irish
themselves how they raise their stock-money,
for their command of money is a subject on

which they are not communicative, or, if communicative, not truthful. " My opinion is," said an Irish gentleman to me, " that some of these poor fellows would declare to God that they hadn't the value of a halfpenny, even if you heard the silver chink in their pockets." It is certain that they never, or very rarely, borrow of the usurers like their English brethren.

The more usual custom is, that if a poor Irish street-seller be in want of 5*s.*, it is lent to him by the more prosperous people of his court—bricklayers' labourers, or other working-men—who club 1*s.* a piece. This is always repaid. An Irish bricklayer, when in full work, will trust a needy countryman with some article to pledge, on the understanding that it is to be redeemed and returned when the borrower is able. Sometimes, if a poor Irishwoman need 1*s.* to buy oranges, four others—only less poor than herself, because not utterly penniless — will readily advance 3*d.* each. Money is also advanced to the deserving Irish through the agency of the Roman Catholic priests, who are the medium through whom charitable persons of their own faith exercise good offices. Money, too, there is no doubt, is often advanced out of the priest's own pocket.

On all the kinds of loans with which the poor Irish are aided by their countrymen no interest is ever charged. " I don't like the Irish," said an English costermonger to me; " but they *do* stick to one another far more than we do."

The Irish costers hire barrows and shallows like the English, but, if they " get on " at all, they will possess themselves of their own vehicles much sooner than an English costermonger. A quick-witted Irishman will begin to ponder on his paying 1*s.* 6*d.* a week for the hire of a barrow worth 20*s.*, and he will save and hoard until a pound is at his command to purchase one for himself; while an obtuse English coster (who will yet buy cheaper than an Irishman) will probably pride himself on his cleverness in having got the charge for his barrow reduced, in the third year of its hire, to 1*s.* a week the twelvemonth round !

In cases of sickness the mode of relief adopted is similar to that of the English. A raffle is got up for the benefit of the Irish sufferer, and, if it be a bad case, the subscribers pay their money without caring what trifle they throw for, or whether they throw at all. If sickness continue and such means as raffles cannot be persevered in, there is one resource from which a poor Irishman never shrinks—the parish. He will apply for and accept parochial relief without the least sense of shame, a sense which rarely deserts an Englishman who has been reared apart from paupers. The English costers appear to have a horror of the Union. If the Irishman be taken into the workhouse, his friends do not lose sight of him. In case of his death, they apply for, and generally receive his body, from the parochial authorities, undertaking the

expence of the funeral, when the body is duly " waked." " I think there's a family contract among the Irish," said a costermonger to me; " that's where it is."

The Irish street-folk are, generally speaking, a far more provident body of people than the English street-sellers. To save, the Irish will often sacrifice what many Englishmen consider a necessary, and undergo many a hardship. From all I could ascertain, the saving of an Irish street-seller does not arise from any wish to establish himself more prosperously in his business, but for the attainment of some cherished project, such as emigration. Some of the objects, however, for which these struggling men hoard money, are of the most praiseworthy character. They will treasure up halfpenny after halfpenny, and continue to do so for years, in order to send money to enable their wives and children, and even their brothers and sisters, when in the depth of distress in Ireland, to take shipping for England. They will save to be able to remit money for the relief of their aged parents in Ireland. They will save to defray the expense of their marriage, an expense the English costermonger so frequently dispenses with—but they will *not* save to preserve either themselves or their children from the degradation of a workhouse; indeed they often, with the means of independence secreted on their persons, apply for parish relief, and that principally to save the expenditure of their own money. Even when detected in such an attempt at extortion an Irishman betrays no passion, and hardly manifests any emotion—he has speculated and failed. Not one of them but has a positive genius for begging—both the taste and the faculty for alms-seeking developed to an extraordinary extent.

Of the amount " saved " by the patience of the poor Irishmen, I can form no conjecture.

OF THE HISTORY OF SOME IRISH STREET-SELLERS.

IN order that the following statements might be as truthful as possible, I obtained permission to use the name of a Roman Catholic clergyman, to whom I am indebted for much valuable information touching this part of my subject.

A young woman, of whose age it was not easy to form a conjecture, her features were so embrowned by exposure to the weather, and perhaps when I saw her a little swollen from cold, gave me the following account as to her living. Her tone and manner betrayed indifference to the future, caused perhaps by ignorance,—for uneducated persons I find are apt to look on the future as if it must needs be but a repetition of the present, while the past in many instances is little more than a blank to them. This young woman said, her brogue being little perceptible, though she spoke thickly :

" I live by keepin' this fruit stall. It's a poor livin' when I see how others live. Yes, in thruth, sir, but it's thankful I am for to be able to live at all, at all; troth is it, in these sore times. My father and mother are both did. God be gracious to their sowls! They was evicted. The family of us was. The thatch of the bit o' home was tuk off above our hids, and we were lift to the wide worruld—yis, indeed, sir, and in the open air too. The rint wasn't paid and it couldn't be paid, and so we had to face the wither. It was a sorrowful time. But God was good, and so was the neighbours. And when we saw the praste, he was a frind to us. And we came to this counthry, though I'd always heard it called a black counthry. Sure, an' there's much in it to indhure. There's goin's on it, sir, that the praste, God rewarrud him! wouldn't like to see. There's bad ways. I won't talk about thim, and I'm sure you are too much of a gintlemin to ask me; for if you know Father ——, that shows you are the best of gintlemin, sure. It was the eviction that brought us here. I don't know about where we was just; not in what county; nor parish. I was so young whin we lift the land. I belave I'm now 19, perhaps only 18" (she certainly looked much older, but I have often noticed that of her class). "I can't be more, I think, for sure an its only 5 or 6 years since we left Watherford and come to Bristol. I'm sure it was Watherford, and a beautiful place it is, and I know it was Bristol we come to. We walked all the long way to London. My parints died of the cholera, and I live with mysilf, but my aunt lodges me and sees to me. She sills in the sthreets too. I don't make 7d. a day. I may make 6d. There's a good many young payple I know is now sillin' in the streets because they was evicted in their own counthry. I suppose they had no where ilse to come to. I'm nivir out of a night. I sleep with my aunt, and we keep to oursilves sure. I very sildom taste mate, but perhaps I do oftener than before we was evicted—glory be to God."

One Irish street-seller I saw informed me that she was a "widdy wid three childer." Her husband died about four years since. She had then five children, and was near her confinement with another. Since the death of her husband she had lost three of her children; a boy about twelve years died of stoppage on his lungs, brought on, she said, through being in the streets, and shouting so loud "to get sale of the fruit." She has been in Clare-street, Clare-market, seven years with a fruit stall. In the summer she sells green fruit, which she purchases at Covent-garden. When the nuts, oranges, &c., come in season, she furnishes her stall with that kind of fruit, and continues to sell them until the spring salad comes in. During the spring and summer her weekly average income is about 5s., but the remaining portion of the year her income is not more than 3s. 6d. weekly, so that taking the year through, her average weekly income is about 4s. 3d.; out of this she pays 1s. 6d. a week rent, leaving only 2s. 9d. a week to find necessary comforts for herself and family. For fuel the

children go to the market and gather up the waste walnuts, bring them home and dry them, and these, with a pennyworth of coal and coke, serve to warm their chilled feet and hands. They have no bedstead, but in one corner of a room is a flock bed upon the floor, with an old sheet, blanket, and quilt to cover them at this inclement season. There is neither chair nor table; a stool serves for the chair, and two pieces of board upon some baskets do duty for a table, and an old penny tea-canister for a candlestick. She had parted with every article of furniture to get food for her family. She received nothing from the parish, but depended upon the sale of her fruit for her living.

The Irishmen who are in this trade are also very poor; and I learned that both Irishmen and Irishwomen left the occupation now and then, and took to begging, as a more profitable calling, often going begging this month and fruit-selling the next. This is one of the causes which prompt the London costermongers' dislike of the Irish. "They'll beg themselves into a meal, and work us out of one," said an English coster to me. Some of them are, however, less "poverty-struck" (a word in common use among the costermongers); but these for the most part are men who have been in the trade for some years, and have got regular "pitches."

The woman who gave me the following statement seemed about twenty-two or twenty-three. She was large-boned, and of heavy figure and deportment. Her complexion and features were both coarse, but her voice had a softness, even in its broadest brogue, which is not very frequent among poor Irishwomen. The first sentence she uttered seems to me tersely to embody a deplorable history of the poverty of a day. It was between six and seven in the evening when I saw the poor creature:—

"Sure, thin, sir, it's thrippince I've taken to-day, and tuppince is to pay for my night's lodgin'. I shall do no more good to-night, and shall only stay in the cowld, if I stay in it, for nothing. I'm an orphand, sir," (she three or four times alluded to this circumstance,) "and there's nobody to care for me but God, glory be to his name! I came to London to join my brother, that had come over and did will, and he sint for me, but whin I got here I couldn't find him in it anyhow. I don't know how long that's ago. It may be five years; it may be tin; but" (she added, with the true eloquence of beggary,) "sure, thin, sir, I had no harrut to keep count, if I knew how. My father and mother wasn't able to keep me, nor to keep thimsilves in Ireland, and so I was sint over here. They was counthry payple. I don't know about their landlorrud. They died not long afther I came here. I don't know what they died of, but sure it was of the will of God, and they hadn't much to make them love this worruld; no more have I. Would I like to go back to my own counthry? Will, thin, what would be the use? I sleep at a lodging-house, and it's a dacint place.

It's mostly my own counthrywomen that's in it; that is, in the women's part. I pay 1s. a week, that's 2d. a night, for I'm not charged for Sundays. I live on brid, and 'taties and salt, and a herrin' sometimes. I niver taste beer, and not often tay, but I sit here all day, and I feel the hunger this day and that day. It goes off though, if I have nothin' to ate. I don't know why, but I won't deny the goodness of God to bring such a thing about. I have lived for a day on a pinny, sir: a ha'pinny for brid, and a ha'pinny for a herrin', or two herrin's for a ha'pinny, and 'taties for the place of brid. I've changed apples for a herrin' with a poor man, God rewarrud him. Sometimes I make on to 6d. a day, and sometimes I *have* made 1s. 6d., but I think that I don't make 5d. a day—arrah, no, thin, sir! one day with the other, and I don't worruk on Sunday, not often. If I've no mate to ate, I'd rather riot. I never miss mass on a Sunday. A lady gives me a rag sometimes, but the bitther time's comin'. If I was sick I don't know what I'd do, but I would sind for the praste, and he'd counsil me. I could read a little oncte, but I can't now."

Of the Irish "Refuse"-Sellers.

There still remains to be described one branch of the Irish street-trade which is peculiar to the class—viz., the sale of "refuse," or such fruit and vegetables as are damaged, and suited only to the very poorest purchasers.

In assorting his goods, a fruit-salesman in the markets generally throws to one side the shrivelled, dwarfish, or damaged fruit—called by the street-traders the "specks." If the supply to the markets be large, as in the pride of the season, he will put his several kinds of specks in separate baskets. At other times all kinds are tossed together, and sometimes with an admixture of nuts and walnuts. The Irish women purchase these at a quarter, or within a quarter, of the regular price, paying from 6d. to 1s. a bushel for apples; 9d. to 1s. 6d. for pears; 1s. 6d. to 2s. 6d. for plums. They are then sorted into halfpenny-worths for sale on the stalls. Among the refuse is always a portion of what is called " tidy" fruit, and this occupies the prominent place in the "halfpenny lots"—for they are usually sold at a halfpenny. Sometimes, too, a salesman will throw in among the refuse a little good fruit, if he happen to have it over, either gratuitously or at the refuse price; and this, of course, is always made the most conspicuous on the stalls. Of other fruits, perhaps, only a small portion is damaged, from over-ripeness, or by the aggression of wasps and insects, the remainder being very fine, so that the retail "lots" are generally cheap. The sellers aim at "half profits," or cent. per cent.

The "refuse" trade in fruit—and the refuse-trade is mainly confined to fruit—is principally in the hands of the Irish. The persons carrying it on are nearly all middle-aged and elderly women. I once or twice saw a delicate and pretty-looking girl sitting with the old "re-

fuse" women; but I found that she was not a "regular hand," and only now and then "minded the stall" in her mother's absence. She worked with her needle, I was told.

Of the women who confine themselves to this trade there are never less than twenty, and frequently thirty. Sometimes, when the refuse is very cheap and very abundant, as many as 100 fruit-sellers, women and girls, will sell it in halfpenny-worths, along with better articles. These women also sell refuse dry-fruit, purchased in Duke's-place, but only when they cannot obtain green-fruit, or cannot obtain it sufficiently. All is sold at stalls; as these dealers seem to think that if it were hawked, the police might look too inquisitively at a barrow stocked with refuse. The "refuse-sellers" buy at all the markets. The poorer street-sellers, whose more staple trade is in oranges or nuts, are *occasional* dealers in it.

Perhaps the regular refuse-buyers are not among the *very* poorest class, as their sale is tolerably quick and certain, but with the usual drawbacks of wet weather. They make, I was told, from 4d. to 1s. a day the year round, or perhaps 7d. or 8d. a day, Sunday included. They are all Roman Catholics, and resort to the street-sale after mass. They are mostly widows, or women who have reached middle-age, unmarried: Some are the wives of street-sellers. Two of their best pitches are on Saffron-hill and in Petticoat-lane. It is somewhat curious to witness these women sitting in a line of five or six, and notwithstanding their natural garrulity, hardly exchanging a word one with another. Some of them derive an evident solace from deliberate puffs at a short black pipe.

A stout, healthy-looking woman of this class said:—"Sure thin, sir, I've sat and sould my bit of fruit in this place, or near it, for twinty year and more, as is very well known indeed, is it. I could make twice the money twinty year ago that I can now, for the boys had the ha'pinnies more thin than they has now, more's the pity. The childer is my custhomers, very few beyant—such as has only a ha'pinny now and thin, God hilp them. They'll come a mile from any parrut, to spind it with such as me, for they know it's chape we sill! Yis, indeed, or they'll come with a fardin either, for it's a ha'pinny lot we'll split for them any time. The boys buys most, but they're dridful tazes. It's the patience of the divil must be had to dale wid the likes of thim. They was dridful about the Pope, but they've tired of it now. O, no, it wasn't the boys of my counthry that demaned themselves that way. Well, I make 4d. some days, and 6d. some, and 1s. 6d. some, and I have made 3s. 6d., and I have made nothing. Perhaps I make 5s. or 6s. a week rigular, but I'm established and well-known you see."

The quantity of refuse at the metropolitan "green" markets varies with the different descriptions of fruit. Of apples it averages one-twentieth, and of plums and greengages one-fifteenth, of the entire supply. With pears, cherries, gooseberries, and currants, however, the damaged amounts to one-twelfth, while of strawberries and mulberries it reaches as high as one-tenth of the aggregate quantity sent to market.

The Irish street-sellers, I am informed, buy full two-thirds of all the refuse, the other third being purchased by the lower class of English costermongers—"the illegitimates,"—as they are called. We must not consider the sale of the damaged fruit so great an evil as it would, at the first blush, appear, for it constitutes perhaps the sole luxury of poor children, as well as of the poor themselves, who, were it not for the halfpenny and farthing lots of the refuse-sellers, would doubtlessly never know the taste of such things.

———

Before leaving this part of the subject, it may be as well to say a few words concerning the curious revelations made by the returns from Billingsgate, Covent-garden, and the other London markets, as to the diet of the poor. In the first place, then, it appears that in the matter of fish, herrings constitute the chief article of consumption—no less than 210,000,000 lbs. weight of this fish in a "fresh" state, and 60,000,000 lbs. in a "dried" state, being annually eaten by the humbler classes of the metropolis and the suburbs. Of sprats there are 3,000,000 lbs. weight consumed—and these, with the addition of plaice, are the staple comestibles at the dinners and suppers of the ichthyophagous part of the labouring population of London. One of the reasons for this is doubtless the extraordinary cheapness of these kinds of fish. The sprats are sold at a penny per pound; the herrings at the same rate; and the plaice at a fraction less, perhaps; whereas a pound of butcher's meat, even "pieces," or the "block ornaments," as they are sometimes called, cannot be got for less than twopence-halfpenny or threepence. But the relative cheapness of these two kinds of food can only be tested by the proportionate quantity of nutrition in each. According to Liebig, butcher's meat contains 26 per cent. of solid matter, and 74 per cent. of water; whereas, according to Brande, fish consists of 20 parts of solid matter, and 80 parts water in every 100. Hence it would appear that butcher's meat is five per cent more nutritive than fish—or, in other words, that if the two were equally cheap, the prices, according to the quantity of nutrition in each, should be for fish one penny per pound, and butcher's meat not five farthings; so that even at twopence-halfpenny the pound, meat is more than twice as dear an article of diet as fish.

But it is not only on account of their cheapness that herrings and sprats are consumed in such vast quantities by the labouring people of London. Salmon, eels, herrings, pilchards, and sprats, Dr. Pereira tells us, abound in oil; and oleaginous food, according to Leibig, is an "element of respiration," consisting of nearly 80 per cent. charcoal, which burns away in the lungs, and so contributes to the warmth of the system. Fat, indeed, may be said to act as fuel to the vital fire; and we now know, from observations made upon the average daily consumption of food by 28 soldiers of the Grand Duke of Hesse Darmstadt, in barracks, for a month—which is the same as 840 men for one day—that an adult taking moderate exercise consumes, in the act of respiration, very nearly a pound of charcoal every day, which of course must be supplied in his food. "But persons who take much exercise, or labour hard," says Dr. Pereira, "require more frequent and copious meals than the indolent or sedentary. In the active man the number of respirations is greater than in the inactive, and therefore a more frequent supply of food is required to furnish the increased quantity of carbon and hydrogen to be consumed in the lungs." "A bird deprived of food," says Liebig, "dies on the third day; while a serpent, with its sluggish respiration, can live without food three months, or longer."

Captain Parry, in his account of one of the Polar expeditions (1827), states, that both himself and Mr. Beverley, the surgeon, were of opinion, that, in order to maintain the strength of the men during their harassing journey across the ice, living constantly in the open air, and exposed to the wet and cold for twelve hours a day, an addition was requisite of at least one-third to the quantity of provisions daily issued. So, in the gaol dietaries, the allowance to prisoners sentenced to hard labour for three months is one-third more than the scale for those sentenced to hard labour for three days—the former having 254 ounces, and the latter only 168 ounces of solid food served out to them every week.

But the hard-working poor not only require more food than the non-working rich, but it is mainly because the rich are better fed that they are more lethargic than the poor; for the greater the supply of nutriment to the body, the more inactive does the system become. From experiments made a few years ago at the Zoological Gardens, it was found that, by feeding the animals twice, instead of once, in the twenty-four hours, their habits, as regards exercise, were altered—a fact which readily explains how the fat and overfed are always the least energetic; fat being at once the cause and consequence of inaction. It is well to hear an obese citizen tell a hollow-cheeked man, who begs a penny of him, "to go and work—a lazy scoundrel;" but physiology assures us that the fat tradesman is naturally the laziest of the two. In a word, he is fat because he is lazy, and lazy because he is fat.

The industrious poor, however, not only require more food than the indolent rich, but, getting less, they become more susceptible of cold, and, therefore, more eager for all that tends to promote warmth. I have often had occasion to remark the sacrifices that the ill-fed will make to have "a bit of fire." "He who is well fed," observes Sir John Ross, "resists cold better than the man who is stinted, while starvation from cold follows but too soon a starvation in food. This doubtlessly explains in a great measure the resisting powers of the natives of frozen climates, their consumption of food being enormous, and often incredible." Captain Cochrane, in his "Journey through Russia and Siberian Tartary," tells us that he has repeatedly seen a Yakut or Tongouse devour forty pounds of meat in a day; and one of the Yakuti he speaks of as having consumed, in twenty-four hours, "the hind-quarter of a large ox, twenty pounds of fat, and a proportionate quantity of melted butter for his drink." (Vol. i. p. 255) Much less heat is evolved, physiologists tell us, where there is a deficiency of food. "During the whole of our march," says Sir John Franklin, "we experienced that no quantity of clothing could keep us warm while we fasted; but, on those occasions on which we were enabled to go to bed with full stomachs, we passed the night in a warm and comfortable manner." Hence, it is evident, that in summer a smaller quantity of food suffices to keep up the temperature of the body. I know of no experiments to show the different proportions of aliment required at different seasons of the year. In winter, however, when a greater supply is certainly needed, the labouring man, unfortunately, has less means of obtaining it—nearly all trades slacken as the cold weather comes on, and some, as brick-making, market-gardening, building, &c., then almost entirely cease—so that, were it not for the cheapness of fish, and, moreover, the oleaginous quality of those kinds which are most plentiful in the winter time, the metropolitan poor would be very likely to suffer that "starvation from cold which," in the words of Sir John Ross, "follows but too soon a starvation in food." Hence we can readily understand the remark of the enthusiastic street-seller—"Sprats *is* a blessing to the poor."

The returns as to the other articles of food sold in the streets are equally curious. The 1,500,000*l.* spent yearly in fish, and the comparatively small amount expended on vegetables, viz., 290,000*l.*, is a circumstance which seems to show that the labouring population of London have a greater relish for animal than vegetable diet. "It is quite certain," says Dr. Carpenter, "that the most perfect physical development and the greatest intellectual vigour are to be found among those races in which a mixed diet of animal and vegetable food is the prevalent habit." And yet, in apparent contradiction to the proposition asserted with so much confidence by Dr. Carpenter, we have the following curious fact cited by Mr. Jacob Bentley:—

"It is, indeed, a fact worthy of remark, and one that seems never to have been noticed, that throughout the whole animal creation, in every country and clime of the earth the most useful animals cost nature the least waste to sustain them with food. For in-

stance, all animals that work, live on vegetable or fruit food; and no animal that eats flesh, works. The all-powerful elephant, and the patient, untiring camel in the torrid zone; the horse, the ox, or the donkey in the temperate, and the rein-deer in the frigid zone; obtain all their muscular power for enduring labour, from Nature's simplest productions,—the vegetable kingdom.

"But all the flesh-eating animals, keep the rest of the animated creation in constant dread of them. They seldom eat vegetable food till some other animal has eaten it first, and made it into flesh. Their only use seems to be, to destroy life; their own flesh is unfit for other animals to eat, having been itself made out of flesh, and is most foul and offensive. Great strength, fleetness of foot, usefulness, cleanliness and docility, are then always characteristic of vegetable-eating animals, while all the world dreads flesh-eaters."

Of vegetables we have seen that the greatest quantity consumed by the poor consists of potatoes, of which 60,500,000 lbs. are annually sold in the streets; but ten pounds of potatoes are only equal in nutritive power to one pound of butcher's meat, which contains one-fifth more solid food than fish,—so that a pound of fish may be said to equal eight pounds of potatoes, and thus the 60,000,000 lbs. of vegetable is dietetically equivalent to nearly 7,000,000 lbs. of fish diet. The cost of the potatoes, at five pounds for 2*d.*, is, as we have seen, 100,000*l.*; whereas the cost of the same amount of nutritive matter in the form of fish, at 1*d.* per pound, would have been only 30,000*l.*, or upwards of two-thirds less. The vegetable of which there is the next greatest street sale is onions, upon which 90,000*l.* are annually expended. This has been before accounted for, by saying, that a piece of bread and an onion are to the English labourer what bread and grapes are to the Frenchman—oftentimes a meal. The relish for onions by the poorer classes is not difficult to explain. Onions are strongly stimulating substances, and they owe their peculiar odour and flavour, as well as their pungent and stimulating qualities, to an acrid volatile oil which contains sulphur. This oil becomes absorbed, quickens the circulation, and occasions thirst. The same result takes place with the oil of fish. It not only proves a stimulant to the general system, but we are told that the thirst and uneasy feeling at the stomach, frequently experienced after the use of the richer species of fish, have led to the employment of spirit to this kind of food. Hence, says Dr. Pereira, the vulgar proverb, "Brandy is Latin for Fish." Moreover, the two classes of food are similar in their comparative indigestibility, for the uneducated palates of the poor not only require a more pungent kind of diet, but their stronger stomachs need something that will resist the action of the gastric juice for a considerable time. Hence their love of shell-fish. The small quantity of fruit, too, sold to the poor is a further proof of what is here stated. The amount of the street sale of this luxury is no criterion as to the quantity purchased by the London labourers; for according to all accounts the fruit-buyers in the streets consist mostly of clerks, shopmen, small tradesmen, and the children of mechanics or the lower grade of middle class people. Those who may be said strictly to belong to the poor,—viz. those whose incomes are barely sufficient for their support—seldom purchase fruit. In the first place they have no money to spend on such a mere toothsome extravagance ; and, secondly, they require a stronger and more stimulating, and "*staying*" kind of food. The delights of the palate, we should remember, are studied only when the cravings of the stomach are satisfied, so that those who have strong stomachs have necessarily dull palates, and, therefore, prefer something that " bites in the mouth,"—to use the words of one of my informants — like gin, onions, sprats, or pickled whelks. What the poor term "relishes" are very different things from what the rich style the " delicacies of the season."

I have no means of ascertaining the average number of ounces of solid food consumed by the poorer class of the metropolis. The *whole* of the fish, fruit, and vegetables, sold to the London costermongers, is not disposed of in the London streets—many of the street-sellers going, as we have seen, country excursions with their goods. According to the result of the Government Commissioners of Inquiry, the labourers in the country are unable to procure for themselves and families an average allowance of more than 122 ounces of solid food—principally bread—every week ; hence it has been justly said we may infer that the man consumes, as his share, 140 ounces (134 bread and 6 meat). The gaol dietaries allow 254 ounces, or nearly twice as much to all prisoners, who undergo continuous hard labour. In the construction of these dietaries Sir James Graham—the then Secretary of State—says, in his " Letter to the Chairman of Quarter Sessions " (January 27th, 1843), " I have consulted not only the Prison Inspectors, but medical men of the greatest eminence possessing the advantage of long experience." They are proposed, he adds, " as the *minimum* amount which can be safely afforded to prisoners without the risk of inflicting a punishment not contemplated by law and which it is unjust and cruel to inflict ; namely, loss of health and strength through the inadequacy of the food supplied." Hence it appears not that the thief gets too much, but the honest

working man too little—or, in other words, that the labourer of this country is able to procure, by his industry, only half the quantity of food that is considered by "medical men of the greatest eminence" to be "the *minimum* amount" that can be *safely* afforded for the support of the criminals—a fact which it would be out of place to comment upon here.

One word concerning the incomes of the London costermongers, and I have done. It has been before shown that the gross sum of money *taken* yearly, in the streets, by the sale of fish, fruit, and vegetables, amounts, in round numbers, to two million pounds—a million and a half being expended in fish, and a quarter of a million upon fruit and vegetables respectively. In estimating the yearly receipts of the costermongers, from their average gains, the gross "takings" of the entire body were concluded to be between a million and a quarter and a million and a half sterling—that is to say, each one of the 10,000 street-sellers of fish, fruit, and vegetables, was supposed to clear ten shillings a week all the year through, and to *take* fifty shillings. But, according to the returns furnished me by the salesmen, at the several metropolitan markets, the weekly "*takings*" of the ten thousand men and their families—for often both wife and children sell—cannot be less than four pounds per week all the year round, out of which it would seem that the clear weekly *gains* are about fifteen shillings. (Some costers we have seen take pounds in a day, others—·as the nut and orange-women and children—only a few shillings a week; some, again, make cent. per cent. profit, whilst others are obliged to sell at a loss.) This, from all I can gather, as well as from a comparison of the coster's style of living with other classes whose weekly income is nearly the same, appears to be very close upon the truth.

We may then, I think, safely assert, that the gross yearly receipts of the London costermongers are two millions of money; that their clear annual gain, or income, is 425,000*l.*; and that the capital invested in their business, in the form of donkey‑carts, barrows, baskets, weights, and stock-money, is 25,000*l.*;—half of this being borrowed, for which they pay upwards of 20,000*l.* interest per annum.

OF THE STREET-SELLERS OF GAME, POULTRY (LIVE AND DEAD), RABBITS, BUTTER, CHEESE, AND EGGS.

THE class who sell game and poultry in the public thoroughfares of the metropolis are styled hawkers, both in Leadenhall and Newgate-market. The number of these dealers in London is computed at between 200 and 300. Of course, legally to sell game, a license, which costs 2*l.* 2*s.* yearly, is required ; but the street-seller laughs at the notion of being subjected to a direct tax ; which, indeed, it might be impossible to levy on so "slippery" a class.

The sale of game, even with a license, was not legalised until 1831 ; and, prior to that year, the mere killing of game by an "unqualified" person was an offence entailing heavy penalties. The "qualification" consisted of the possession of a freehold estate of 100*l.* a year, or a leasehold for ninety-nine years of 150*l.* a year! By an Act, passed in the 25th year of George III., it was provided that a certificate (costing 3*l.* 13*s.* 6*d.*) must be taken out by all qualified persons killing game. Since 1831 (1 & 2 William IV., c. 32,) a certificate, without any qualification, is all that is required from the game-killer. Both sexes carry on the trade in game-hawking, but there are more than thrice as many men as women engaged in the business, the weight occasionally carried being beyond a woman's strength. The most customary dress of the game or poultry-hawker is a clean smock-frock covering the whole of his other attire, except the ends of his trousers and his thick boots or shoes. Indeed he often, but less frequently than was the case five years ago, assumes the dress of a country labourer, although he may have been for years a resident in London. About forty years ago, I am informed, it was the custom for countrymen, residing at no great distance, to purchase a stock of chickens or ducks; and, taking their places in a wagon, to bring their birds to London, and hawk them from door to door. Some of these men's smock-frocks were a convenient garb, for they covered the ample pockets of the coat beneath, in which were often a store of partridges, or an occasional pheasant or hare. This game, illegally killed—for it was all poached— was illegally sold by the hawker, and illegally bought by the hotel-keepers and the richer tradesmen. One informant (an old man) was of opinion that the game was rarely offered for sale by these countrymen at the West-end mansions of the aristocracy. "In fact," he said, "I knew one country fellow—though he was sharp enough in his trade of game and poultry-selling—who seemed to think that every fine house, without a shop, and where there were livery servants, must needs be inhabited by a magistrate! But, as the great props of poaching were the rich—for, of course, the poor couldn't buy game—there was, no doubt, a West-end as well as a City trade in it. I have bought game of a country poultry-hawker," continued my informant, "when I lived in the City at the beginning of this century, and generally gave 3s. 6d. a brace for partridges. I have bid it, and the man has left, refusing to take it; and has told me afterwards, and, I dare say, he spoke the truth, that he had sold his partridges at 5s. or 6s. or more. I believe 5s. a brace was no uncommon price in the City. I have given as much as 10s. for a pheasant for a Christmas supper. The hawker, before offering the birds for sale, used to peer about him, though we were alone in my counting-house, and then pull his partridges out of his pockets, and say, 'Sir, do you want any very young chickens?'—for so he called them. Hares he called 'lions;' and they cost often, enough, 5s. each of the hawker. The trade had all the charms and recommendations of a mystery and a risk about it, just like smuggling."

The sale of game in London, however, was not confined to the street-hawkers, who generally derived their stock-in-trade immediately from the poacher. Before the legalisation of the sale, the trade was carried on, under the rose, by the salesmen in Leadenhall-market, and that to an extent of not less than a fifteenth of the sale now

accomplished there. The purveyors for the London game-market—I learned from leading salesmen in Leadenhall—were not then, as now, noble lords and honourable gentlemen, but peasant or farmer poachers, who carried on the business systematically. The guards and coachmen of the stage-coaches were the media of communication, and had charge of the supply to the London market. The purchasers of the game thus supplied to a market, which is mostly the property of the municipality of the City of London, were not only hotel-keepers, who required it for public dinners presided over by princes, peers, and legislators, but the purveyors for the civic banquets—such as the Lord Mayor's ninth of November dinner, at which the Ministers of State always attended.

This street-hawking of *poached* game, as far as I could ascertain from the best-informed quarters, hardly survived the first year of the legalised sale.

The female hawkers of game are almost all the wives of the men so engaged, or are women living with them as their wives. The trade is better, as regards profit, than the costermonger's ordinary pursuits, but only when the season is favourable; it is, however, more uncertain.

There is very rarely a distinction between the hawkers of game and of poultry. A man will carry both, or have game one day and poultry the next, as suits his means, or as the market avails. The street-sellers of cheese are generally costers, while the vendors of butter and eggs are almost extinct.

Game, I may mention, consists of grouse (including black-cocks, and all the varieties of heath or moor-game), partridges, pheasants, bustards, and hares. Snipe, woodcocks, plovers, teal, widgeons, wild ducks, and rabbits are not game, but can only be taken or killed by certificated persons, who are owners or occupiers of the property on which they are found, or who have the necessary permission from such persons as are duly authorised to accord it. Poultry consists of chickens, geese, ducks, and turkeys, while some persons class pigeons as poultry.

Birds are dietetically divided into three classes: (1) the white-fleshed, as the common fowl and the turkey; (2) the dark-fleshed game, as the grouse and the black-cock; and (3) the aquatic (including swimmers and waders), as the goose and the duck; the flesh of the latter is penetrated with fat, and difficult of digestion.

OF THE QUANTITY OF GAME, RABBITS, AND POULTRY, SOLD IN THE STREETS.

IT appears from inquiries that I instituted, and from authentic returns which I procured on the subject, that the following is the quantity of game and poultry sold yearly, as an average, in the markets of the metropolis. I give it exclusive of such birds as wild-ducks, woodcocks, &c., the supply of which depends upon the severity of the winter. I include all wild birds or animals, whether considered game or not, and I use round numbers, but as closely as possible.

During the past Christmas, however, I may observe, that the supply of poultry to the markets has been greater than on any previous occasion. The immensity of the supply was favourable to the hawker's profit, as the glut enabled him to purchase both cheaply and largely. One young poultry-hawker told me that he had cleared *3l.* in the Christmas week, and had spent it all in four days—except *5s.* reserved for stock-money. It was not spent *entirely* in drunkenness, a large portion of it being expended in treats and amusements. So great, indeed, has been the supply of game and poultry this year, that a stranger, unused to the grand scale on which provisions are displayed in ihe great metropolitan marts, on visiting Leadenhall, a week before or after Christmas, might have imagined that the staple food of the London population consisted of turkeys, geese, and chickens. I give, however, an *average* yearly supply:

Description.	Leadenhall.	Newgate.	Total.	Proportion sold in the Streets.
GAME, &c.				
Grouse	45,000	12,000	57,000	One-eleventh.
Partridges	85,000	60,000	145,000	One-seventh.
Pheasants	44,000	20,000	64,000	One-fifth.
Snipes	60,000	47,000	107,000	One-twentieth.
Wild Birds	40,000	20,000	60,000	None.
Plovers	28,000	18,000	46,000	None.
Larks.	213,000	100,000	313,000	None.
Teals	10,000	5,000	15,000	None.
Widgeons	30,000	8,000	38,000	None.
Hares	48,000	55,000	102,000	One-fifth.
Rabbits	680,000	180,000	860,000	Three-fourths.
	1,283,000	524,000	1,807,000	
POULTRY.				
Domestic Fowls	1,266,000	490,000	1,756,000	One-third.
———— (alive)	45,000	15,000	60,000	One-tenth.
Geese	888,000	114,000	1,002,000	One-fifth.
Ducks	235,000	148,000	383,000	One-fourth.
—— (alive)	20,000	20,000	40,000	One-tenth.
Turkeys	69,000	55,000	124,000	One-fourth.
Pigeons	285,000	98,000	383,000	None.
	2,808,000	940,000	3,748,000	
Game, &c. . .	1,283,000	524,000	1,807,000	
	4,091,000	1,464,000	5,555,000	

In the above return wild ducks and woodcocks are not included, because the quantity sent to London is dependent entirely upon the severity of the winter. With the costers wild ducks are a favourite article of trade, and in what those street tradesmen would pronounce a favourable season for wild ducks, which means a very hard winter, the number sold in Londen will, I am told, equal that of pheasants (64,000). The great stock of wild ducks for the London tables is from Holland, where the duck decoys are objects of great care. Less than a fifth of the importation from Holland is from Lincolnshire. These birds, and even the finest and largest, have been sold during a glut at 1s. each. Woodcocks, under similar circumstances, number with plovers (45,000), nearly all of which are "golden plovers;" but of woodcocks the costermongers buy very few: "They're only a mouthful and a half," said one of them, "and don't suit our customers." In severe weather a few ptarmigan are sent to London from Scotland, and in 1841-2 great numbers were sent to the London markets from Norway. One salesman received nearly 10,000 ptarmigan in one day. A portion of these were disposed of to the costers, but the sale was not such as to encourage further importations.

The returns I give show, that, at the two great game and poultry-markets, 5,500,000 birds and animals, wild and tame, are yearly sent to London. To this must be added all that may be consigned direct to metropolitan game-dealers and poulterers, besides what may be sent as presents from the country, &c., so that the London supply may be safely estimated, I am assured, at 6,000,000.

It is difficult to arrive at any very precise computation of the quantity of game and poultry sold by the costers, or rather at the money value (or price) of what they sell. The most experienced salesmen agree, that, as to *quantity*, including everything popularly considered game (and I have so given it in the return), they sell one-third. As regards *value*, however, their purchases fall very short of a third. Of the best qualities of game, and even more especially of poultry, a third of the hawkers may buy a fifteenth, compared with their purchases in the lower-priced kinds. The others buy none of the best qualities. The more "aristocratic" of the poultry-hawkers will, as a rule, only buy, "when they have an order" or a sure sale, the best quality of English turkey-cocks; which cannot be wondered at, seeing that the average price of the English turkey-cock is 12s. One salesman this year sold (at Leadenhall) several turkey-cocks at 30s. each, and one at 3l. The average price of an English turkey-hen is 4s. 6d., and of these the costers buy a few: but their chief trade is in foreign turkey-hens; of which the average price (when of good quality and in good condition) is 3s. The foreign turkey-cocks average half the price of the English (or 6s.). Of Dorking fat chickens, which average 6s. the couple, the hawkers buy none (save as in the case of the turkey-cocks); but of the Irish fowls, which, this season, have averaged 2s. 6d. the couple, they buy largely. On the other hand they buy nearly all the rabbits sent from Scotland, and half of those sent from Ostend, while they "clear the market"—no matter of what the glut may consist—when there *is* a glut. There is another distinction of which the hawker avails himself. The average price of young plump partridges is 2s. 6d. the brace, of old partridges, 2s.; accordingly, the coster buys the old. It is the same with pheasants, the young averaging 7s. the brace, the old 6s.: "And I can sell them best," said one man; "for my customers say they're more tastier-like. I've sold game for twelve years, or more, but I never tasted any of any kind, so I can't say who's right and who's wrong."

The hawkers buy, also, game and poultry which will not "keep" another day. Sometimes they puff out the breast of a chicken with fresh pork fat, which melts as the bird roasts. "It freshens the fowl, I've been told, and improves it," said one man; "and the shopkeepers now and then, does the same. It's a improvement, sir."

In the present season the costers have bought of wild ducks, comparatively, none, and of teal, widgeons, wild birds, and larks, none at all; or so sparely, as to require no notice.

OF THE STREET-PURCHASERS OF GAME AND POULTRY.

As the purchasers of game and poultry are of a different class to the costermongers' ordinary customers, I may devote a few words to them. From all the information that I could acquire, they appear to consist, principally, of those who reside at a distance from any cheap market, and buy a cheap luxury when it is brought to their doors, as well as of those who are "always on the look-out for something toothy, such as the shabby genteels, as they're called, who never gives nothing but a scaly price. They've bargained with me till I was hard held from pitching into them, and over and over again I should, only it would have been fourteen days anyhow. They'll tell me my birds stinks, when they're as sweet as flowers. They'd go to the devil to save three farthings on a partridge." Other buyers are old gourmands, living perhaps on small incomes, or if possessed of ample incomes, but confining themselves to a small expenditure; others, again, are men who like a cheap dinner, and seldom enjoy it, at their own cost, unless it be cheap, and who best of all like "such a thing as a moor bird (grouse)," said one hawker, "which can be eat up to a man's own cheek." This was also the opinion of a poulterer and game-dealer, who sometimes sold "goods" to the hawkers. Of this class of "patrons" many shopkeepers, in all branches of business, have a perfect horror, as they will care nothing for having occupied the tradesmen's time to no purpose.

The game and poultry street-sellers, I am told, soon find out when a customer is bent upon a bargain, and shape their prices accordingly. Although these street-sellers may generally take as their motto the announcement so often seen in the shops of competitive tradesmen, "no reasonable offer refused," they are sometimes so worried in bargaining that they *do* refuse.

In a conversation I had with a "retired" game salesman, he said it might be curious to trace the history of a brace of birds—of grouse, for instance—sold in the streets; and he did it after this manner. They were shot in the Highlands of Scotland by a member of parliament who had gladly left the senate for the moors. They were transferred to a tradesman who lived in or near some Scotch town having railway communication, and with whom "the honourable gentleman," or "the noble lord," had perhaps endeavoured to drive a hard bargain. He (the senator) *must* have a good price for his birds, as he had given a large sum for the moor: and the season was a bad one: the birds were scarce and wild: they would soon be "packed" (be in flocks of twenty or thirty instead of in broods), and then there would be no touching a feather of them. The canny Scot would quietly say that it was early in the season, and the birds never packed so early; that as to price, he could only give what he could get from a London salesman, and he was "nae just free to .enter into any agreement for a fixed price at a'." The honourable gentleman, after much demurring, gives way, feeling perhaps that he cannot well do anything else. In due course the grouse are received in Leadenhall, and unpacked and flung about with as little ceremony as if they had been "slaughtered" by a Whitechapel journeyman butcher, at so much a head. It is a thin market, perhaps, when they come to hand. A dealer, fashionable in the parish of St. George, Hanover-square, has declined to give the price demanded; they were not his money; "he had to give such long credit." A dealer, popular in the ward of Cheap, has also declined to buy, and for the same alleged reason. The salesman, knowing that some of these dealers *must* buy, quietly says that he will take no less, and as he is known to be a man of his word, little is said upon the subject. As the hour arrives at which fashionable game-dealers are compelled to' buy, or disappoint customers who will not brook such disappointment, the market, perhaps, is glutted, owing to a very great consignment by a later railway train. The *Inverness Courier*, or the *North of Scotland Gazette*, are in due course quoted by the London papers, touching the "extraordinary sport" of a party of lords and gentlemen in the Highlands; and the "heads" of game are particularized with a care that would do honour to a *Price Current*. The salesman then disposes rapidly of divers "brace" to the "hawkers," at 1s. or 2s. the brace, and the hawker offers them to hotel-keepers, and shop-keepers, and housekeepers, selling some at 3s. 6d. the brace, some at 3s., at 2s. 6d., at 2s., and at less. "At last," said my informant, "he may sell the finest brace of his basket, which he has held back to get a better price for, at 6d. a-piece, rather than keep them over-night, and that to a woman of the town, whom he may have met reeling home with money in her purse. Thus the products of an honourable gentleman's skilful industry, on which he greatly prided himself, are eaten by the woman and her 'fancy man,' grumblingly enough, for they pronounce the birds inferior to tripe."

The best quarters for the street-sale 'f game and poultry are, I am informed from several sources, either the business parts of the metropolis, or else the houses in the several suburbs which are the furthest from a market or from a business part. The squares, crescents, places, and streets, that do not partake of one or the other of these characteristics, are pronounced "no good."

OF THE EXPERIENCE OF A GAME HAWKER.

THE man who gave me the following information was strong and robust, and had a weather-beaten look. He seemed about fifty. He wore when I saw him a large velveteen jacket, a cloth waistcoat which had been once green, and brown corduroy trousers. No part of his attire, though it seemed old, was patched, his shirt being clean and white. He evidently aimed at the game-keeper style of dress. He affected some humour, and was dogged in his opinions:

" I was a gentleman's footman when I was a young man," he said, "and saw life both in town and country; so I knows what things belongs." [A common phrase among persons of his class to denote their being men of the world.] " I never liked the confinement of ser-vice, and besides the upper servants takes on so. The others puts up with it more than they would, I suppose, because they hopes to be butlers themselves in time. The only decent people in the house I lived in last was master and mis-sus. I won 20l., and got it too, on the Colonel, when he won the Leger. Master was a bit of a turf gentleman, and so we all dabbled—like master like man, you know, sir. I think that was in 1828, but I'm not certain. We came to London not long after Doncaster" [he meant Doncaster races], "something about a lawsuit, and that winter I left service and bought the goodwill of a coffee-shop for 25l. It didn't answer. I wasn't up to the coffee-making, I think; there's a deal of things belongs to it things; so I got out of it, and after that I was in service again, and then I was a boots at an inn. But I couldn't settle to nothing long; I'm of a free spirit, you see. I was hard up at last, and I popped my watch for a sovereign, because a friend of mine—we sometimes drank together of a night—said he could put me in the pigeon and chicken line; that was what he called it, but it meant game. This just suited me, for I'd been out with the poachers when I was a lad, and indeed when I was in service, out of a night on the sly; so I knew they got stiffish prices. My friend got me the pigeons. I believe he cheated me, but he's gone to glory. The next season game was made legal eating. Before that I cleared from 25s. to 40s. a week by selling my 'pigeons.' I carried real pigeons as well, which I said was my own rearing at Gravesend. I sold my game pigeons—there was all sorts of names for them—in the City, and sometimes in the Strand, or Charing-cross, or Covent-garden. I sold to shopkeepers. Oft enough I've been offered so much tea for a hare. I sometimes had a hare in each pocket, but they was very awk-ward carriage; if one was sold, the other sagged so. I very seldom sold them, at that time, at less than 3s. 6d., often 4s. 6d., and sometimes 5s. or more. I once sold a thumping old jack-hare to a draper for 6s.; it was Christmas time, and he thought it was a beauty. I went into the country after that, among my friends, and had a deal of ups and downs in different parts. I was a navvy part of the time, till five or six year back I came to London again, and got into my old trade; but it's quite a different thing now. I hawks grouse, and every thing, quite open. Leadenhall and Newgate is my markets. Six of one and half-a-dozen of t'other. When there's a great arrival of game, after a game battle" (he would so call a *battue*) " and it's-warm weather, that's my time of day, for then I can buy cheap. A muggy day, when it's close and warm, is best of all. I have a tidy bit of connection now in game, and don't touch poultry when I can get game. Grouse is the first thing I get to sell. They are legal eating on the 12th of August, but as there's hundreds of braces sold in London that day, and as they're shot in Scotland and Yorkshire, and other places where there's moors, in course they're killed before it's legal. It's not often I can get them early in the season; not the first week, but I have had three brace two days before they were legal, and sold them at 5*s.* a brace; they cost me 3*s.* 3*d.*, but I was told I was favoured. I got them of a dealer, but that's a secret. I sold a few young partridges with grouse this year at 1*s.* 6*d.* and 1*s.* 9*d.* a piece, allowing 2*d.* or 3*d.* if a brace was taken. They weren't legal eating till the 1st of September, but they was shot by grouse shooters, and when I hawked them I called them quails. Lord, sir, gentlefolks—and I serve a good many, leastways their cooks, and now and then themselves—*they* don't make a fuss about Game Laws; they've too much sense. I've bought grouse quite fresh and fine when there's been a lot, and bad keeping weather, at 1*s.* and 15*d.* each. I've sold them sometimes at 1*s.* 6*d.* and 2*s.* each, and 2*s.* 6*d.* the big ones, but only twice or thrice. If you ask very low at first, people won't buy, only a few good judges, 'cause they think something must be amiss. I once bought a dozen good hares, on a Saturday afternoon, for 10*s.* 6*d.* It was jolly hot, and I could hardly sell them. I got 1*s.* 6*d.* a piece for three of them; 2*s.* for the finest one; 1*s.* 3*d.* for five, no, for four; 1*s.* 10*d.* for two; and I had a deal of trouble to get a landlord to take the last two for 1*s.* 6*d.*, to wipe off a bit of a drink score. I didn't do so bad as it was, but if it hadn't been Saturday, I should have made a good thing of 'em. It's very hard work carrying a dozen hares; and every one of that lot—except two, and *they* was fine leverets—was as cheap as butcher's meat at half-a-crown a piece. I've done middling in partridges this year. I've bought them, but mixed things they was, as low as from 10*d.* to 16*d.* a brace, and have made a profit, big or little as happened, on every one. People that's regular customers I always charge 6*d.* profit in 2*s.* 6*d.* to, and that's far cheaper than they can get served other ways. It's chiefly the game battles that does so much to cheapen partridges or peasants" (so he always called pheasants); "and it's only then I meddles with peasants. They're sold handier than the other birds at the shops, I think. They're legal eating on the 1st of October. Such nonsense! why isn't mutton made legal eating, only just at times, as well? In very hard weather I've done well on wild ducks. They come over here when the weather's a clipper, for you see cold weather suits some birds and kills others. It aint hard weather that's driven them here; the frost has drawed them here, because it's only then they're cheap. I've bought beauties at 1*s.* a piece, and one day I cleared 10*s.* 6*d.* out of twelve brace of them. I've often cleared 6*s.* and 7*s.*—at least as often as there's been a chance. I knew a man that did uncommon well on them; and he once told a parson, or a journeyman parson, I don't know what he was, that if ever *he* prayed it was for a hard winter and lots of wild ducks. I've done a little sometimes in plover, and woodcock, and

snipe, but not so much. I never plays no tricks with *my* birds. I trims them up to look well, certainly. If they won't keep, and won't sell, I sticks them into a landlord I knows, as likes them high, for a quartern or a pot, or anything. It's often impossible to keep them. If they're hard hit it's soon up with them. A sportsman, if he has a good dog—but you'll know that if you've ever been a shooting, sir—may get close upon a covey of young partridges before he springs them, and then give them his one, two, with both barrels, and they're riddled to bits. I may make 18*s.* a week all the year round, because I have a connection. I'm very much respected, I thinks, on my round, for I deal fair; that there, sir, breeds respect, you know. When I can't get game (birds) I can sometimes, indeed often, get hares, and mostly rabbits. I've hawked venson, but did no good—though I cried it at 4*d.* the lb. My best weeks is worth 30*s.* to 35*s.*, my worst is 6*s.* to 10*s.* I'm a good deal in the country, working it. I'm forced to sell fish sometimes. Geese I sometimes join a mate in selling. I don't mix much with the costermongers; in coorse I knows some. I live middling. Do I ever eat my own game if it's high? No, sir, never. I couldn't stand such cag-mag—my stomach couldn't—though I've been a gentleman's servant. Such stuff don't suit nobody but rich people, whose stomach's diseased by over-feeding, and that's been brought up to it, like. I've only myself to keep now. I've had a wife or two, but we parted " (this was said gravely enough); " there was nothing to hinder us. I see them sometimes and treat them."

The quantity of game annually sold in the London streets is as follows :—

Grouse	. . . .	5,000
Partridges	. . .	20,000
Pheasants	. . .	12,000
Snipes	. . . .	5,000
Hares	. . .	20,000

STATEMENT OF TWO POULTRY HAWKERS.

Two brothers, both good-looking and well-spoken young men—one I might characterise as handsome—gave me the following account. I found them unwilling to speak of their youth, and did not press them. I was afterwards informed that their parents died within the same month, and that the family was taken into the workhouse; but the two boys left it in a little time, and before they could benefit by any schooling. Neither of them could read nor write. They left, I believe, with some little sum in hand, *to* " start theirselves." An intelligent costermonger, who was with me when I saw the two brothers, told me that " a costermonger would rather be thought to have come out of prison than out of a workhouse," for his " mates " would say, if they heard he had been locked up, " O, he's only been quodded for pitching into a crusher." The two brothers wore clean smock country frocks over their dress, and made a liberal display of their clean, but coarse, shirts. It was on a Monday that I saw them. What one brother said, the other confirmed: so I use the plural " we."

" We sell poultry and game, but stick most to poultry, which suits our connection best. We buy at Leadenhall. We' re never cheated in the things we buy; indeed, perhaps, we could'nt be. A salesman will say—Mr. H—— will—' Buy, if you like, I can't recommend them. Use your own judgment. They're cheap.' He has only one price, and that's often a low one. We give from 1s. to 1s. 9d. for good chickens, and from 2s. 6d. mostly for geese and turkeys. Pigeons is 1s. 9d. to 3s. a dozen. We aim at 6d. profit on chickens; and 1s., if we can get it, or 6d. if we can do no better, on geese and turkeys. Ducks are the same as chickens. All the year through, we may make 12s. a week a piece. We work together, one on one side of the street and the other on the other. It answers best that way. People find we can't undersell one another. We buy the poultry, whenever we can, undressed, and dress them ourselves; pull the feathers off and make them ready for cooking. We sell cheaper than the shops, or we couldn't sell at all. But you must be known, to do any trade, or people will think your poultry's bad. We work game as well, but mostly poultry. We've been on hares to-day, mostly, and have made about 2s. 6d. a piece, but that's an extra day. Our best customers are tradesmen in a big way, and people in the houses a little way out of town. Working people don't buy of us now. We're going to a penny gaff to-night" (it was then between four and five); " we've no better way of spending our time when our day's work is done."

From the returns before given, the street-sale of poultry amounts yearly to

500,000 fowls.
80,000 ducks.
20,000 geese.
30,000 turkeys.

Of the Street Sale of Live Poultry.

The street trade in live poultry is not considerable, and has become less considerable every year, since the facilities of railway conveyance have induced persons in the suburbs to make their purchases in London rather than of the hawkers. Geese used to be bought very largely by the hawkers in Leadenhall, and were driven in flocks to the country, 500 being a frequent number of a flock. Their sale commenced about six miles from town in all directions, the purchasers being those who, having the necessary convenience, liked to fatten their own Christmas geese, and the birds when bought were small and lean. A few flocks, with 120 or 150 in each, are still disposed of in this way; but the trade is not a fifth of what it was. As this branch of the business is not in the hands of the hawkers, but generally of country poulterers resident in the towns not far from the metropolis, I need but allude to it. A few flocks of ducks are driven in the same way.

The street trade in live poultry continues only for three months—from the latter part of June to the latter part of September. At this period, the hawkers say, as they can't get " dead " they must get " live." During these three months the hawkers sell 500 chickens and 300 ducks weekly, by hawking, or 10,400 in the season of 13 weeks. Occasionally, as many as 50 men and women—the same who hawk dead game and poultry—are concerned in the traffic I am treating of. At other times there are hardly 30, and in some not 20 so employed, for if the weather be temperate, dead poultry is preferred to live by the hawkers. Taking the average of " live " sellers at 25 every week, it gives only a trade of 32 birds each weekly. Some, however, will sell 18 in a day; but others, who occasionally resort to the trade, only a dozen in a week. The birds are sometimes carried in baskets on the hawker's arm, their heads being let through network at the top; but more frequently they are hawked in open wicker-work coops carried on the head. The best live poultry are from Surrey and Sussex; the inferior from Ireland, and perhaps more than three-fourths of that sold by the hawkers is Irish.

The further nature of the trade, and the class of customers, is shown in the following statement, given to me by a middle-aged man, who had been familiar with the trade from his youth.

" Yes, sir," he said, " I've had a turn at live poultry for — let me see — someways between twenty and twenty-five years. The business is a sweater, sir; it's heavy work, but 'live' aint so heavy as 'dead.' There's fewer of them to carry in a round, that's it. Ah! twenty years ago, or better, live poultry was worth following. I did a good bit in it. I've sold 160 fowls and ducks, and more, in a week, and cleared about 4l. But out of that I had to give a man 1s. a day, and his peck, to help me. At that time I sold my ducks and chickens—I worked nothing else—at from 2s. to 3s. 6d. a piece, according to size and quality. Now, if I get from 14d. to 2s. it's not so bad. I sell more, I think, however, over 1s. 6d. than under it, but I'm perticler in my ' live.' I never sold to any but people out of town that had convenience to keep them, and, Lord knows, I've seen ponds I could jump over reckoned prime for ducks. Them that keeps their gardens nice won't buy live poultry. I've seldom sold to the big houses anything like to what I've done to the smaller. The big houses, you see, goes for fancy bantems, such as Sir John Seabright's, or Spanish hens, or a bit of a game cross, or real game—just for ornament, and not for fighting— or for anything that's got its name up. I've known young couples buy fowls to have their breakfast eggs from them. One young lady told me to bring her—that's fifteen year ago, it is so—six couples, that I knew would lay. I told her she'd better have five hens to a cock, and she didn't seem pleased, but I'm sure I don't know why, for I hope I'm always civil. I told her there would be murder if there was a cock to every hen. I supplied her, and made 6s. by the job. I *have* sold

THE WALLFLOWER GIRL.

[*From a Daguerreotype by* BEARD.]

live fowls to the Jews about Whitechapel, on my way to Stratford and Bow, but only when I've bought a bargain and sold one. I don't know nothing how the Jews kills their fowls. Last summer I didn't make 1s. 6d. a day; no, nor more than three half-crowns a week in 'live.' But that's only part of my trade. I don't complain, so it's nothing to nobody what I makes. From Beever (De Beauvoir) Town to Stamford Hill, and on to Tottenham and Edmonton, and turning off Walthamstow way is as good a round as any for live; it is so; but nothing to what it was. Highgate and Hampstead is middling. The t'other side the water isn't good at all."

Fancy chickens, I may add, are never hawked, nor are live pigeons, nor geese, nor turkeys.

The hawkers' sale of live poultry may be taken, at a moderate computation, as 6,500 chickens, and 3,900 ducks.

Of Rabbit Selling in the Streets.

Rabbit-selling cannot be said to be a distinct branch of costermongering, but some street-sellers devote themselves to it more exclusively than to other "goods," and, for five or six months of the year, sell little else. It is not often, though it is sometimes, united with the game or poultry trade, as a stock of rabbits, of a dozen or a dozen and a half, is a sufficient load for one man. The best sale for rabbits is in the suburbs. They are generally carried slung two and two on a long pole, which is supported on the man's shoulders, or on a short one which is carried in the hand. Lately, they have been hawked about hung up on a barrow. The trade is the briskest in the autumn and winter months; but some men carry them, though they do not confine themselves to the traffic in them, all the year round. The following statement shows the nature of the trade.

" I was born and bred a costermonger," he said, " and I've been concerned with everything in the line. I've been mostly ' on rabbits' these five or six years, but I always sold a few, and now sometimes I sell a hare or two, and, if rabbits is too dear, I tumble on to fish. I buy at Leadenhall mainly. I've given from 6s. to 14s. a dozen for my rabbits. The usual price is from 5s. to 8s. a dozen. [I may remark that the costers buy nearly all the Scotch rabbits, at an average of 6s. the dozen; and the Ostend rabbits, which are a shilling or two dearer.] They're Hampshire rabbits; but I don't know where Hampshire is. I know they're from Hampshire, for they're called ' Wild Hampshire rabbits, 1s. a pair.' But still, as you say, that's only a call. I never sell a rabbit at 6d., in course—it costs more. My way in business is to get 2d. profit, and the skin, on every rabbit. If they cost me 8d., I try to get 10d. It's the skins is the profit. The skins now brings me from 1s. to 1s. 9d. a dozen. They're best in frosty weather. The fur's thickest then. It grows best in frost, I suppose. If I sell a dozen, it's a tidy day's work. If I get 2d.

a-piece on them, and the skins at 1s. 3d., it's 3s. 3d., but I dont sell above 5 dozen in a week —that's 16s. 3d. a week, sir, is it? Wet and dark weather is against me. People won't often buy rabbits by candlelight, if they're ever so sweet. Some weeks in spring and summer I can't sell above two dozen rabbits. I have sold two dozen and ten on a Saturday in the country, but then I had a young man to help me. I sell the skins to a warehouse for hatters. My old 'oman works a little fish at a stall sometimes, but she only can in fine weather, for we've a kid that can hardly walk, and it don't do to let it stand out in the cold. Perhaps I may make 10s. to 14s. a week all the year round. I'm paying 1s. a week for 1l. borrowed, and paid 2s. all last year; but I'll pay no more after Christmas. I did better on rabbits four or five year back, because I sold more to working-people and small shopkeepers than I do now. I suppose it's because they're not so well off now as they was then, and, as you say, butchers'-meat may be cheaper now, and tempts them. I do best short ways in the country. Wandsworth way ain't bad. No more is parts of Stoke-Newington and Stamford-hill. St. John's Wood and Hampstead is middling. Hackney's bad. I goes all ways. I dont know what sort of people's my best customers. Two of 'em, I've been told, is banker's clerks, so in course they is rich."

There are 600,000 rabbits sold every year in the streets of London; these, at 7d. a-piece, give 17,500l. thus expended annually in the metropolis.

Of the Street Sale of Butter, Cheese, and Eggs.

All these commodities used to be hawked in the streets, and to a considerable extent. Until, as nearly as I can ascertain, between twenty and thirty years back, butter was brought from Epping, and other neighbouring parts, where good pasture existed, and hawked in the streets of London, usually along with poultry and eggs. This trade is among the more ancient of the street-trades. Steam-vessels and railways, however, have so stocked the markets, that no hawking of butter or eggs, from any agricultural' part, even the nearest to London, would be remunerative now. Eggs are brought in immense quantities from France and Belgium, though thirty, or even twenty years ago the notion having of a good French egg, at a London breakfast-table, would have been laughed at as an absurd attempt at an impossible achievement. The number of eggs now annually imported into this kingdom, is 98,000,000, half of which may be said to be the yearly consumption of London. No butter is now hawked, but sometimes a few " new laid " eggs are carried from a rural part to the nearest metropolitan suburb, and are sold readily enough, if the purveyor be known. Mr. M'Culloch estimates the average consumption of butter, in London, at 6,250,000 lbs. per annum, or 5 oz., weekly, each individual.

The hawking of cheese was never a prominent part of the street-trade. Of late, its sale in the streets, may be described as accidental. A considerable quantity of American cheese was hawked, or more commonly sold at a standing, five or six years ago; unto December last, and for three months preceding, cheese was sold in the streets which had been rejected from Government stores, as it would not "keep" for the period required; but it was good for immediate consumption, for which all street-goods are required. This, and the American cheese, were both sold in the streets at 3*d.* the pound; usually, at fair weights, I am told, for it might not be easy to deceive the poor in a thing of such frequent purchase as "half a quarter or a quarter" (of a pound) of cheese.

The total quantity of foreign cheese consumed, yearly, in the metropolis may be estimated at 25,000,000 lbs. weight, or half of the gross quantity annually imported.

The following statement shows the quantity and sum paid for the game and poultry sold in London streets:

	£
5,000 grouse, at 1*s.* 9*d.* each . . .	437
20,000 partridges, at 1*s.* 6*d.*	1,500
12,000 pheasants, at 3*s.* 6*d.*	2,100
5,000 snipes, at 8*d.*	160
20,000 hares, at 2*s.* 3*d.*	2,250
600,000 rabbits, at 7*d.*	17,500
500,000 fowls, at 1*s.* 6*d.*	37,500
20,000 geese, at 2*s.* 6*d.*	2,500
80,000 ducks, at 1*s.* 6*d.*	6,000
30,000 turkeys, at 3*s.* 6*d.*	5,250
10,000 live fowls and ducks, at 1*s.* 6*d.* . .	750
	£75,953

In this table I do not give the *refuse* game and poultry, bought sometimes for the mere feathers, when "undressed;" neither are the wild ducks nor woodcocks, nor those things of which the costers buy only exceptionally, included. Adding these, it may be said, that with the street sale of butter, cheese, and eggs, 80,000*l.* are annually expended in the streets on this class of articles.

OF THE SELLERS OF TREES, SHRUBS, FLOWERS (CUT AND IN POTS), ROOTS, SEEDS, AND BRANCHES.

THE street-sellers of whom I have now to treat comprise those who deal in trees and shrubs, in flowers (whether in pots, or merely with soil attached to the roots, or cut from the plant as it grows in the garden), and in seeds and branches (as of holly, mistletoe, ivy, yew, laurel, palm, lilac, and may). The "root-sellers" (as the dealers in flowers in pots are mostly called) rank, when in a prosperous business, with the highest "aristocracy" of the street-greengrocers. The condition of a portion of them, may be characterised by a term which is readily understood as "comfortable," that is to say, comparatively comfortable, when the circumstances of other street-sellers are considered. I may here remark, that though there are a great number of Scotchmen connected with horticultural labour in England, but more in the provincial than the metropolitan districts, there is not one Scotchman concerned in the metropolitan street-sale of flowers; nor, indeed, as I have good reason to believe, is there a single Scotchman earning his bread as a costermonger in London. A non-commissioned officer in an infantry regiment, a Scotchman, whom I met with a few months back, in the course of my inquiries concerning street musicians, told me that he thought any of his young countrymen, if hard pushed "to get a crust," would enlist, rather than resort, even under favourable circumstances, to any kind of street-sale in London.

The dealers in trees and shrubs are the same as the root-sellers.

The same may be said, but with some few exceptions, of the seed-sellers.

The street-trade in holly, mistletoe, and all kinds of evergreens known as "Christmas," is in the hands of the coster boys more than the men, while the trade in may, &c., is almost altogether confined to these lads.

The root-sellers do not reside in any particular localities, but there are more of them living in the outskirts than in the thickly populated streets.

The street-sellers of cut flowers present characteristics peculiarly their own. This trade is mostly in the hands of girls, who are of two classes. This traffic ranks with the street sale of water-cresses and congreves, that is to say, among the lowest grades of the street-trade, being pursued only by the very poor, or the very young.

OF THE QUANTITY OF SHRUBS, "ROOTS," FLOWERS, ETC., SOLD IN THE STREETS, AND OF THE BUYERS.

THE returns which I caused to be procured, to show the extent of the business carried on in the metropolitan markets, give the following results as to the quantity of trees, shrubs, flowers, roots, and branches, sold wholesale in London, as well as the proportion retailed in the streets.

TABLE SHOWING THE QUANTITY OF TREES, SHRUBS, FLOWERS, ROOTS,
AND BRANCHES SOLD ANNUALLY, WHOLESALE, AT THE METROPO-
LITAN MARKETS, AND THE PROPORTION RETAILED IN THE STREETS.*

	Covent Garden.		Farringdon.	Total.	Proportion sold to Costers.
TREES AND SHRUBS.					
Firs	400	doz. roots	400	800	One-third.
Laurels	480	,,	480	960	One-third.
Myrtles	1,440	,,	1,120	2,560	One-fourth.
Rhododendrons	288	,,	256	544	One-ninth.
Lilac	192	,,	192	384	One-sixth.
Box	288	,,	192	480	One-sixth.
Heaths (of all kinds)	1,600	,,	1,440	3,040	One-fifth.
Broom and Furze	544	,,	480	1,024	One-fourth.
Laurustinus	400	,,	320	720	One-fourth.
Southernwood (Old Man)	960	,,	480	1,440	One-half.
FLOWERS (IN POTS).					
Roses (Moss)	1,200	doz pots	960	2,160	One-half.
Ditto (China)	1,200	,,	960	2,160	One-half.
Fuchsias	1,200	,,	960	2,160	One-half.
FLOWER ROOTS.					
Primroses	600	doz. roots	400	1,000	One-half.
Polyanthus	720	,,	720	1,440	One-half.
Cowslips	720	,,	480	1,200	One-half.
Daisies	800	,,	600	1,400	One-half.
Wallflowers	960	,,	960	1,920	One-half.
Candytufts	720	,,	480	1,200	One-half.
Daffodils	720	,,	480	1,200	One-half.
Violets	1,200	,,	1,200	2,400	One-third.
Mignonette	2,000	,,	1,800	3,800	One-sixth.
Stocks	1,600	,,	1,280	2,880	One-sixth.
Pinks and Carnations	480	,,	320	800	One-half.
Lilies of the Valley	144	,,	144	288	One-fourth.
Pansies	600	,,	480	1,080	One-fourth.
Lilies and Tulips	152	,,	128	280	One-ninth.
Balsam	320	,,	320	640	One sixth.
Calceolarii	360	,,	240	600	One-ninth.
Musk-plants	5,760	,,	4,800	10,560	One-half.
London Pride	400	,,	320	720	One-third.
Lupins	960	,,	640	1,600	One-third.
China-asters	450	,,	400	850	One-sixth.
Marigolds	5,760	,,	4,800	10,560	One-eighth.
Dahlias	80	,.	80	160	One-ninth.
Heliotrope	800	,,	480	1,280	One-sixth.
Michaelmas Daisies	216	,,	216	432	One-third.
FLOWERS (CUT).					
Violets	1,440	doz. bunches	1,280	2,720	One-half.
Wallflowers	3,200	,,	1,600	4,800	One-half.
Lavender (green and dry)	1,600	,,	1,200	4,120†	One-half.
Pinks	720	,,	600	1,320	One-third.
Mignonette	2,000	,,	1,600	3,600	One-half.
Lilies of the Valley	180	,,	160	340	One-tenth.
Moss Roses	2,000	,,	1,600	3,600	One-third.
China ditto	2,000	,,	1,600	3,600	One-third.
Stocks	800	,,	480	1,280	One-third.
BRANCHES.					
Holly	840	doz. bundles	720	1,640†	One-half.
Mistletoe	800	,,	640	1,560†	One-half.
Ivy and Laurel	360	,,	280	740†	One-half.
Lilac	96	,,	64	150	One-half.
Palm	12	,,	8	28†	One-half.
May	30	,,	20	70†	One-half.

* The numbers here given do not include the shrubs, roots, &c., bought by the hawkers at the nursery gardens.
† These totals include the supplies sent to the other markets.

Perhaps the pleasantest of all cries in early spring is that of "All a-growing—all a-blowing" heard for the first time in the season. It is that of the "root-seller" who has stocked his barrow with primroses, violets, and daisies. Their beauty and fragrance gladden the senses; and the first and, perhaps, unexpected sight of them may prompt hopes of the coming year, such as seem proper to the spring.

Cobbett has insisted, and with unquestioned truth, that a fondness for bees and flowers is among the very best characteristics of the English peasant. I consider it equally unquestionable that a fondness for in-door flowers, is indicative of the good character and healthful tastes, as well as of the domestic and industrious habits, of the city artizan. Among some of the most intelligent and best-conducted of these artizans, I may occasionally have found, on my visits to their homes, neither flowers nor birds, but then I have found books.

United with the fondness for the violet, the wallflower, the rose—is the presence of the quality which has been pronounced the handmaiden of all the virtues — cleanliness. I believe that the bunch of violets, on which a poor woman or her husband has expended 1d., rarely ornaments an unswept hearth. In my investigations, I could not but notice how the presence or absence of flowers, together with other indications of the better tastes, marked the difference between the well-paid and the ill-paid workman. Concerning the tailors, for instance, I had occasion to remark, of the dwellings of these classes:—" In the one, you occasionally find small statues of Shakspere beneath glass shades; in the other, all is dirt and fœtor. The working-tailor's comfortable first-floor at the West-end is redolent with the perfume of the small bunch of violets that stands in a tumbler over the mantel-piece; the sweater's wretched garret is rank with the stench of filth and herrings." The presence of the bunch of flowers of itself tells us of "a better state of things" elevating the workman ; for, amidst the squalid poverty and fustiness of a slopworker's garret, the nostril loses its daintiness of sense, so that even a freshly fragrant wallflower is only so many yellow petals and green leaves.

A love of flowers is also observable among men whose avocations are out of doors, and those whose habits are necessarily those of order and punctuality.

Among this class are such persons as gentlemen's coachmen, who delight in the display of a flower or two in the button-holes of their coats when out of doors, and in small vases in their rooms in their masters' mews. I have even seen the trellis work opposite the windows of cabmen's rooms, which were over stables, with a projecting roof covering the whole, thickly yellow and green with the flowers and leaves of the easily-trained nasturtium and herb "twopence." The omnibus driver occasionally " sports a nosegay "—as he himself might

word it—in his button-hole; and the stage-coachman of old felt he was improperly dressed if a big bunch of flowers were not attached to his coat. Sailors ashore are likewise generally fond of flowers.

A delight in flowers is observable, also, among the workers whose handicraft requires the exercise of taste, and whose eyes are sensible, from the nature of their employment, to the beauty of colour. To this class belong especially the Spitalfields' silk-weavers. At one time the Spitalfields weavers were almost the only botanists in London, and their love of flowers is still strong. I have seen fuchsias gladdening the weaver's eyes by being placed near his loom, their crimson pendants swinging backwards and forwards to the motion of the treadles, while his small back garden has been many-coloured with dahlias. These weavers, too, were at one time highly-successful as growers of tulips.

Those out-door workmen, whose calling is of coarse character, are never known to purchase flowers, which to them are mere trumpery. Perhaps no one of my readers ever saw a flower in the possession of a flusherman, nightman, slaughterer, sweep, gaslayer, gut and tripe-preparer, or such like labourer. *Their* eyes convey to the mind no appreciation of beauty, and the sense of smell is actually dead in them, except the odour may be rank exceedingly.

The fondness for flowers in London is strongest in the women, and, perhaps, strongest in those whose callings are in-door and sedentary. Flowers are to them a companionship.

It remains only for me to state that, in the poorest districts, and among people where there is no sense of refinement or but a small love for natural objects, flowers are little known. Flowers are not bought by the slop-workers, the garret and chamber-masters of Bethnal-green, nor in the poor Irish districts, nor by the City people Indeed, as I have observed, there is not a flower-stand in the city.

It should be remembered that, in poor districts, the first appearance of flowers conveys to the slop-workman only one pleasurable association—that the season of warmth has arrived, and that he will not only escape being chilled with cold, but that he will be delivered from the heavy burden of providing fire and candle.

A pleasant-looking man, with an appearance which the vulgar characterise as "jolly," and with hearty manners, gave me the following account as to the character of his customers. He had known the business since he was a boy, his friends having been in it previously. He said:

"There's one old gentleman a little way out of town, he always gives 1s. for the first violet root that any such as me carries there. I'm often there before any others: 'Ah!' he says, ' here you are ; you've come, like Buonaparte, with your violet.' I don't know exactly what he means. I don't like to ask him you see ; for, though he's civil, he's not what you may call a free sort of man—that's it." [I explained to him that the allusion was to Buonaparte's emblem of the violet, with the interpretation he or his admirers gave to it— "I come in the spring."] "That's it, sir, is it?" he resumed; "well, I'm glad I know, because I don't like to be puzzled. Mine's a puzzling trade, though. Violets have a good sale. I've sold six dozen roots in a day, and only half as many primroses and double-daisies, if half. Everybody likes violets. I've sold some to poor people in town, but they like their roots in pots. They haven't a bit of a garden for 'em. More shame too I say, when they pays such rents. People that sits working all day is very fond of a sweet flower. A gentleman that's always a-writing or a-reading in his office—he's in the timber-trade—buys something of me every time I see him; twice or thrice a week, sometimes. I can't say what he does with them all. Barmaids, though you mightn't think it, sir, is wery tidy customers. So, sometimes, is young women that's in an improper way of life, about Lisson-grove, and in some parts near Oxford-street. They buys all sorts. Perhaps stocks than anything, for they're beautiful roots, and not dear. I've sold real beauties for 2d.—real beauties, but small; 6d. is a fair price; one stock will perfume a house. I tell my customers not to sleep with them in the room; it isn't good for the health. A doctor told me that, and said, 'You ought to give me a fuchsia for my opinion.' That was his joke. Primroses I sell most of—they're not in pots—two or three or four miles out of town, and most if a family's come into a new house, or changed their house, if there's children. The young ones teases the old ones to buy them to set in the garden, and when children gets fairly to work that way, it's a sure sale. If they can't get over father, they'll get over mother. Busy men never buy flowers, as far as I've seen." [' In no thoroughfare in the city, I am assured, is there a flower-stand—a circumstance speaking volumes as to the habits and tastes of the people. Of fruit-stalls and chop-houses there are in the neighbourhood of the Exchange, more than in any other part of London perhaps—the faculty of perceiving the beauty of colour, form, and perfume, as combined in flowers is not common to the man of business. The pleasures of the palate, however, they can all understand.'] "Parsons and doctors are often tidy customers," resumed my informant. "They have a good deal of sitting and reading, I believe. I've heard a parson say to his wife, 'Do, my dear, go and buy a couple of those wallflowers for my study.' I don't do much for working-men; the women's my best customers. There's a shoemaker to be sure comes down sometimes with his old woman to lay out 2d. or 3d. on me; 'Let's have something that smells strong,' he'll say, 'stronger than cobbler's wax; for, though I can't smell that, others can.' I've sold him musks (musk-plants) as often as anything.

"The poor people buy rather largely at times; that is, many of them buy. One day last summer, my old woman and me sold 600 penny pots of mignonette; and all about you saw them—and it was a pleasure to see them—in the poor women's windows. The women are far the best customers. There was the mignonette behind the bits of bars they have, in the shape of gates and such like, in the front of their windows, in the way of preventing the pots falling into the street. Mignonette's the best of all for a sure sale; where can you possibly have a sweeter or a nicer penn'orth, pot and all."

OF THE STREET SALE OF TREES AND SHRUBS.

THE street-trade in trees and shrubs is an appendage of "root-selling," and not an independent avocation. The season of supply at the markets extends over July, August, September, and October, with a smaller trade in the winter and spring months. At the nursery gardens, from the best data I can arrive at, there are about twice as many trees and shrubs purchased as in the markets by the costermongers. Nor is this the only difference. It is the more costly descriptions that are bought at the nursery grounds.

The trees and shrubs are bought at the gardens under precisely the same circumstances as the roots, but the trade is by no means popular with the root-sellers. They regard these heavy, cumbrous goods, as the smarter costers do such things as turnips and potatoes, requiring more room, and yielding less profit. "It breaks a man's heart," said one dealer, "and half kills his beast, going round with a lot of heavy things, that perhaps you can't sell." The street-dealers say they must keep them, "or people will go, where they can get roots, and trees, and everything, all together." In winter, or in early spring, the street-seller goes a round now and then, with evergreens and shrubs alone, and the trade is then less distasteful to him. The trees and shrubs are displayed, when the market-space allows, on a sort of stand near the flower-stand; sometimes they are placed on the ground, along-side the flower-stand, but only when no better display can be made.

The trees and shrubs sold by the costers are mezereons, rhododendrons, savine, laurustinus, acacias (of the smaller genera, some being highly aromatic when in flower), myrtles, guelder-roses (when small), privet, genistas, broom, furze (when small), the cheaper heaths, syringas (small), lilacs (almost always young and for transplanting), southernwood (when large), box (large) dwarf laurels, variegated laurels (called a *cuber* by the street-people), and young fir-trees, &c.

The prices of trees vary far more than flower-roots, because they are dependent upon *size* for value. "Why," said one man, "I've bought roddies, as I calls them (rhododendrons), at 4s. a dozen, but they was scrubby things, and I've bought them at 14s. 6d. I once gave 5s. for two trees of them, which I had ordered, and there was a rare grumbling about the price, though I only charged 7*s.* 6*d.* for the two, which was 1*s.* 3*d.* a piece for carriage, and hard earned too, to carry them near five miles in my cart, almost on purpose, but I thought I was pleasing a good customer. Then there's myrtles, why I can get them at 5*d.* a piece, and at 5*s.*, and a deal more if wanted. You can have myrtles that a hat might be very big for them to grow in, and myrtles that will fill a great window in a fine house. I've bought common heaths at 1*s.* 3*d.* a dozen."

The coster ordinarily confines himself to the cheaper sorts of plants, and rarely meddles with such things as acacias, mezereons, savines, syringas, lilacs, or even myrtles, and with none of these things unless cheap. "Trees, real trees," I was told, "are often as cheap as anything. Them young firs there was 4*s.* 6*d.* a dozen, and a man at market can buy four or six of them if he don't want a dozen."

The customers for trees and shrubs are generally those who inhabit the larger sort of houses, where there is room in the hall or the windows for display; or where there is a garden capacious enough for the implantation of the shrubs. Three-fourths of the trees are sold on a round, and when purchased at a stall the costermonger generally undertakes to deliver them at the purchaser's residence, if not too much out of his way, in his regular rounds. Or he may diverge, and make a round on speculation, purposely. There is as much bartering trees for old clothes, as for roots, and as many, or more, complaints of the hard bargainings of ladies: "I'd rather sell polyanthuses at a farthing a piece profit to poor women, if I could get no more," said one man, "than I'd work among them screws that's so fine in grand caps and so civil. They'd skin a flea for his hide and tallow."

The number of trees and shrubs sold annually, in the streets, are, as near as I can ascertain, as follows—I have added to the quantity purchased by the street-sellers, at the metropolitan markets, the amount bought by them at the principal nursery-gardens in the environs of London:

Firs	. . . . .	9,576	roots
Laurels	. . . .	1,152	„
Myrtles	. . . .	23,040	„
Rhododendrons	.	2,160	„
Lilacs	. . . . .	2,304	„
Box	. . . . .	2,880	„
Heaths	. . . .	21,888	„
Broom	. . . .	2,880	„
Furze	. . . . .	6,912	„
Laurustinus	. .	6,480	„
Southernwood	. .	25,920	„

THE LONDON FLOWER GIRLS.

It is not easy to arrive at any accurate estimate of the number of flower-sellers in the streets of London. The cause of the difficulty lies in the fact that none can be said to devote themselves entirely to the sale of flowers in the street, for the flower-sellers, when oranges are cheap and

good, find their sale of the fruit more certain and profitable than that of flowers, and resort to it accordingly. Another reason is, that a poor costermonger will on a fine summer's day send out his children to sell flowers, while on other days they may be selling watercresses or, perhaps, onions. Sunday is the best day for flower-selling, and one experienced man computed, that in the height and pride of the summer 400 children were selling flowers, on the Sundays, in the streets. Another man thought that number too low an estimate, and contended that it was nearer 800. I found more of the opinion of my last mentioned informant than of the other, but I myself am disposed to think the smaller number nearer the truth. On week days it is computed there are about half the number of flower-sellers that there are on the Sundays. The trade is almost entirely in the hands of children, the girls outnumbering the boys by more than eight to one. The ages of the girls vary from six to twenty; few of the boys are older than twelve, and most of them are under ten.

Of flower-girls there are two classes. Some girls, and they are certainly the smaller class of the two, avail themselves of the sale of flowers in the streets for immoral purposes, or rather, they seek to eke out the small gains of their trade by such practises. They frequent the great thoroughfares, and offer their bouquets to gentlemen, whom on an evening they pursue for a hundred yards or two in such places as the Strand, mixing up a leer with their whine for custom or for charity. Their ages are from fourteen to nineteen or twenty, and sometimes they remain out offering their flowers—or dried lavender when no fresh flowers are to be had— until late at night. They do not care, to make their appearance in the streets until towards evening, and though they solicit the custom of ladies, they rarely follow or importune them. Of this class I shall treat more fully under another head.

The other class of flower-girls is composed of the girls who, wholly or partially, depend upon the sale of flowers for their own support or as an assistance to their parents. Some of them are the children of street-sellers, some are orphans, and some are the daughters of mechanics who are out of employment, and who prefer any course rather than an application to the parish. These girls offer their flowers in the principal streets at the West End, and resort greatly to the suburbs; there are a few, also, in the business thoroughfares. They walk up and down in front of the houses, offering their flowers to any one looking out of the windows, or they stand at any likely place. They are generally very persevering, more especially the younger children, who will run along, barefooted, with their "Please, gentleman, do buy my flowers. Poor little girl!"—" Please, kind lady, buy my violets. O, do! please! Poor little girl! Do buy a bunch, please, kind lady!"

The statement I give, "of two orphan flower-sellers" furnishes another proof, in addition to the many I have already given, of the heroic struggles of the poor, and of the truth of the saying, "What would the poor do without the poor?"

The better class of flower-girls reside in Lisson-grove, in the streets off Drury-lane, in St. Giles's, and in other parts inhabited by the very poor. Some of them live in lodging-houses, the stench and squalor of which are in remarkable contrast to the beauty and fragrance of the flowers they sometimes have to carry thither with them unsold.

OF TWO ORPHAN FLOWER GIRLS.

OF these girls the elder was fifteen and the younger eleven. Both were clad in old, but not torn, dark print frocks, hanging so closely, and yet so loosely, about them as to show the deficiency of under-clothing; they wore old broken black chip bonnets. The older sister (or rather half-sister) had a pair of old worn-out shoes on her feet, the younger was barefoot, but trotted along, in a gait at once quick and feeble—as if the soles of her little feet were impervious, like horn, to the roughness of the road. The elder girl has a modest expression of countenance, with no pretensions to prettiness except in having tolerably good eyes. Her complexion was somewhat muddy, and her features somewhat pinched. The younger child had a round, chubby, and even rosy face, and quite a healthful look. Her portrait is here given.

They lived in one of the streets near Drury-lane. They were inmates of a house, not let out as a lodging-house, in separate beds, but in rooms, and inhabited by street-sellers and street-labourers. The room they occupied was large, and one dim candle lighted it so insufficiently that it seemed to exaggerate the dimensions. The walls were bare and discoloured with damp. The furniture consisted of a crazy table and a few chairs, and in the centre of the room was an old four-post bedstead of the larger size. This bed was occupied nightly by the two sisters and their brother, a lad just turned thirteen. In a sort of recess in a corner of the room was the decency of an old curtain—or something equivalent, for I could hardly see in the dimness—and behind this was, I presume, the bed of the married couple. The three children paid 2s. a week for the room, the tenant an Irishman out of work paying 2s. 9d., but the furniture was his, and his wife aided the children in their trifle of washing, mended their clothes, where such a thing was possible, and such like. The husband was absent at the time of my visit, but the wife seemed of a better stamp, judging by her appearance, and by her refraining from any direct, or even indirect, way of begging, as well as from the "Glory be to Gods!" "the heavens be your honour's bed!" or "it's the thruth I'm telling of you sir," that I so frequently meet with on similar visits.

The elder girl said, in an English accent, not at all garrulously, but merely in answer to my questions: "I sell flowers, sir; we live almost on flowers when they are to be got. I sell, and so does my sister, all kinds, but it's very little use offering any that's not sweet. I think it's the sweetness as sells them. I sell primroses, when they're in, and violets, and wall-flowers, and stocks, and roses of different sorts, and pinks, and carnations, and mixed flowers, and lilies of the valley, and green lavender, and mignonette (but that I do very seldom), and violets again at this time of the year, for we get them both in spring and winter." [They are forced in hot-houses for winter sale, I may remark.] "The best sale of all is, I think, moss-roses, young moss-roses. We do best of all on them. Primroses are good, for people say: 'Well, here's spring again to a certainty.' Gentlemen are our best customers. I've heard that they buy flowers to give to the ladies. Ladies have sometimes said: 'A penny, my poor girl, here's three-halfpence for the bunch.' Or they've given me the price of two bunches for one; so have gentlemen. I never had a rude word said to me by a gentleman in my life. No, sir, neither lady nor gentleman ever gave me 6d. for a bunch of flowers. I never had a sixpence given to me in my life—never. I never go among boys, I know nobody but my brother. My father was a tradesman in Mitchelstown, in the County Cork. I don't know what sort of a tradesman he was. I never saw him. He was a tradesman I've been told. I was born in London. Mother was a chairwoman, and lived very well. None of us ever saw a father." [It was evident that they were illegitimate children, but the land-lady had never seen the mother, and could give me no information.] "We don't know anything about our fathers. We were all 'mother's children.' Mother died seven years ago last Guy Faux day. I've got myself, and my brother and sister a bit of bread ever since, and never had any help but from the neighbours. I never troubled the parish. O, yes, sir, the neighbours are all poor people, very poor, some of them. We've lived with her" (indicating her landlady by a gesture) "these two years, and off and on before that. I can't say how long." "Well, I don't know exactly," said the landlady, "but I've had them with me almost all the time, for four years, as near as I can recollect; perhaps more. I've moved three times, and they always followed me." In answer to my inquiries the landlady assured me that these two poor girls, were never out of doors all the time she had known them after six at night. "We've always good health. We can all read." [Here the three somewhat insisted upon proving to me their proficiency in reading, and having produced a Roman Catholic book, the "Garden of Heaven," they read very well.] "I put myself," continued the girl, "and I put my brother and sister to a Roman Catholic school—and to Ragged schools—but *I* could read before mother died. My brother can write, and I pray to God that he'll do well with it. I buy my flowers at Covent Garden; sometimes, but very seldom, at Farringdon. I pay 1s. for a dozen bunches, whatever flowers are in. Out of every two bunches I can make three, at 1d. a piece. Sometimes one or two over in the dozen, but not so often as I would like. We make the bunches up ourselves. We get the rush to tie them with for nothing. We put their own leaves round these violets (she produced a bunch). The paper for a dozen costs a penny; sometimes only a halfpenny. The two of us doesn't make less than 6d. a day, unless it's very ill luck. But religion teaches us that God will support us, and if we make less we say nothing. We do better on oranges in March or April, I think it is, than on flowers. Oranges keep better than flowers you see, sir. We make 1s. a day, and 9d. a day, on oranges, the two of us. I wish they was in all the year. I generally go St. John's-wood way, and Hampstead and Highgate way with my flowers. I can get them nearly all the year, but oranges is better liked than flowers, I think. I always keep 1s. stock-money, if I can. If it's bad weather, so bad that we can't sell flowers at all, and so if we've had to spend our stock-money for a bit of bread, *she* (the landlady) lends us 1s., if she has one, or she borrows one of a neighbour, if she hasn't, or if the neighbours hasn't it, she borrows it at a dolly-shop" (the illegal pawnshop). "There's 2d. a week to pay for 1s. at a dolly, and perhaps an old rug left for it; if it's very hard weather, the rug must be taken at night time, or we are starved with the cold. It sometimes has to be put into the dolly again next morning, and then there's 2d. to pay for it for the day. We've had a frock in for 6d., and that's a penny a week, and the same for a day. We never pawned anything; we have nothing they would take in at the pawnshop. We live on bread and tea, and sometimes a fresh herring of a night. Sometimes we don't eat a bit all day when we're out; sometimes we take a bit of bread with us, or buy a bit. My sister can't eat taturs; they sicken her. I don't know what emigrating means." [I informed her and she continued]: "No, sir, I wouldn't like to emigrate and leave brother and sister. If they went with me I don't think I should like it, not among strangers. I think our living costs us 2s. a week for the two of us; the rest goes in rent. That's all we make."

The brother earned from 1s. 6d. to 2s. a week, with an occasional meal, as a costermonger's boy. Neither of them ever missed mass on a Sunday.

Of the Life of a Flower Girl.

SOME of these girls are, as I have stated, of an immoral character, and some of them are sent out by their parents to make out a livelihood by prostitution. One of this class, whom I saw, had come out of prison a short time previously. She was not nineteen, and had been sentenced about a twelvemonth before to three months' imprisonment with hard labour, "for heaving her shoe," as she said, "at the Lord Mayor, to get a comfortable lodging, for she was tired of being about the streets." After this she was locked up for breaking the lamps in the street. She alleged that her motive for this was a belief that by committing some such act she might be able to get into an asylum for females. She was sent out into the streets by her father and mother, at the age of nine, to sell flowers. Her father used to supply her with the money to buy the flowers, and she used to take the proceeds of the day's work home to her parents. She used to be out frequently till past midnight, and seldom or never got home before nine. She associated only with flower-girls of loose character. The result may be imagined. She could not state positively that her parents were aware of the manner in which she got the money she took home to them. She supposes that they must have imagined what her practices were. He used to give her no supper if she "didn't bring home a good bit of money." Her father and mother did little or no work all this while. They lived on what she brought home. At thirteen years old she was sent to prison (she stated) "for selling combs in the street" (it was winter, and there were no flowers to be had). She was incarcerated fourteen days, and when liberated she returned to her former practices. The very night that she came home from gaol her father sent her out into the streets again. She continued in this state, her father and mother living upon her, until about twelve months before I received this account from her, when her father turned her out of his house, because she didn't bring home money enough. She then went into Kent, hop-picking, and there fell in with a beggar, who accosted her while she was sitting under a tree. He said, "You have got a very bad pair of shoes on; come with me, and you shall have some better ones." She consented, and walked with him into the village close by, where they stood out in the middle of the streets, and the man began addressing the people, "My kind good Christians, me and my poor wife here is ashamed to appear before you in the state we are in." She remained with this person all the winter, and travelled with him through the country, begging. He was a beggar by trade. In the spring she returned to the flower-selling, but scarcely got any money either by that or other means. At last she grew desperate, and wanted to get back to prison. She broke the lamps outside the Mansion-house, and was sentenced to fourteen days' imprisonment. She had been out of prison nearly three weeks when I saw her, and was in training to go into an asylum. She was sick and tired, she said, of her life.

OF THE STREET SALE OF LAVENDER.

THE sale of green lavender in the streets is carried on by the same class as the sale of flowers, and is, as often as flowers, used for immoral purposes, when an evening or night sale is carried on.

The lavender is sold at the markets in bundles, each containing a dozen branches. It is sold principally to ladies in the suburbs, who purchase it to deposit in drawers and wardrobes; the odour communicated to linen from lavender being, perhaps, more agreeable and more communicable than that from any other flower. Nearly a tenth of the market sale may be disposed of in this way. Some costers sell it cheap to recommend themselves to ladies who are customers, that they may have the better chance for a continuance of those ladies' custom.

The number of lavender-sellers can hardly be given as distinct from that of flower-sellers, because any flower-girl will sell lavender, "when it is in season." The season continues from the beginning of July to the end of September. In the winter months, generally after day-fall, dried lavender is offered for sale; it is bought at the herb-shops. There is, however, an addition to the number of the flower-girls of a few old women, perhaps from twenty to thirty, who vary their street-selling avocations by going from door to door in the suburbs with lavender for sale, but do not stand to offer it in the street.

The street-seller's profit on lavender is now somewhat more than cent. per cent., as the bundle, costing 2½d., brings when tied up in sprigs, at least, 6d. The profit, I am told, was, six or seven years ago, 200 per cent; "but people will have better penn'orths now." I was informed, by a person long familiar with the trade in flowers, that, from twenty to twenty-five years ago, the sale was the best. It was a fashionable amusement for ladies to tie the sprigs of lavender together, compressing the stems very tightly with narrow ribbon of any favourite colour, the heads being less tightly bound, or remaining unbound; the largest stems were in demand for this work. The lavender bundle, when its manufacture was complete, was placed in drawers, or behind books in the shelves of a glazed book-case, so that a most pleasant atmosphere was diffused when the book-case was opened.

CUT FLOWERS.

I now give the quantity of cut flowers sold in the streets. The returns have been derived from nursery-men and market-salesmen. It will be seen how fully these returns corroborate the statement of the poor flower-girl—(p. 135)— "it's very little use offering anything that's not sweet."

I may remark, too, that at the present period, from "the mildness of the season," wallflowers, primroses, violets, and polyanthuses are almost as abundant as in spring sunshine.

Violets	65,280	bunches.
Wallflowers	115,200	,,
Lavender	296,640	,,
Pinks and Carnations	63,360	,,
Moss Roses	172,800	,,
China ditto	172,800	,,
Mignonette	86,400	,,
Lilies of the Valley	1,632	,,
Stocks	20,448	,,
Cut flowers sold yearly in the streets	994,560	,,

OF THE STREET SALE OF FLOWERS IN POTS, ROOTS, ETC.

THE "flower-root sellers"—for I heard them so called to distinguish them from the sellers of "cut flowers"—are among the best-mannered and the best-dressed of all the street-sellers I have met with, but that only as regards a portion of them. Their superiority in this respect may perhaps be in some measure attributable to their dealing with a better class of customers —with persons who, whether poor or rich, exercise healthful tastes.

I may mention, that I found the street-sellers of "roots"—always meaning thereby flower-roots in bloom—more attached to their trade than others of their class.

The roots, sold in the streets, are bought in the markets and at the nursery-gardens; but about three-fourths of those required by the better class of street-dealers are bought at the gardens, as are "cut flowers" occasionally. Hackney is the suburb most resorted to by the root-sellers. The best "pitches" for the sale of roots in the street are situated in the New-road, the City-road, the Hampstead-road, the Edgeware-road, and places of similar character, where there is a constant stream of passers along, who are not too much immersed in business. Above three-fourths of the sale is effected by itinerant costermongers. For this there is one manifest reason: a flower-pot, with the delicate petals of its full-blown moss-rose, perhaps, suffers even from the trifling concussion in the journey of an omnibus, for instance. To carry a heavy flower-pot, even any short distance, cannot be expected, and to take a cab for its conveyance adds greatly to the expense. Hence, flower-roots are generally purchased at the door of the buyer.

For the flowers of commoner or easier culture, the root-seller receives from 1d. to 3d. These are primroses, polyanthuses, cowslips (but in small quantities comparatively), daisies (single and double,—and single or wild, daisies were coming to be more asked for, each 1d.), small early wallflowers, candy-tufts, southernwood (called "lad's love" or "old man" by some), and daffodils, (but daffodils were sometimes dearer than 3d.). The plants that may be said to struggle against frost and snow in a hard season, such as the snowdrop, the crocus, and the mezereon, are rarely sold by the costers; "They come too soon," I was told. The primroses, and the other plants I have enumerated, are sold, for the most part, not in pots, but with soil attached to the roots, so that they may be planted in a garden (as they most frequently are) or in a pot.

Towards the close of May, in an early season, and in the two following months, the root-trade is at its height. Many of the stalls and barrows are then exceedingly beautiful, the barrow often resembling a moving garden. The stall-keepers have sometimes their flowers placed on a series of shelves, one above another, so as to present a small amphitheatre of beautiful and diversified hues; the purest white, as in the lily of the valley, to the deepest crimson, as in the fuschia; the bright or rust-blotted yellow of the wall-flower, to the many hues of the stock. Then there are the pinks and carnations, double and single, with the rich-coloured and heavily scented "clove-pinks;" roses, mignonette, the velvetty pansies (or heart's-ease), the white and orange lilies, calceolarias, balsams (a flower going out of fashion), geraniums (flowers coming again into fashion), musk-plants, London pride (and other saxifrages; the species known, oddly enough, as London pride being a native of wild and mountainous districts, such as botanists call "Alpine habitats,") and the many coloured lupins. Later again come the China-asters, the African marigolds, the dahlias, the poppies, and the common and very aromatic marigold. Later still there are the Michaelmas daisies—the growth of the "All-Hallow'n summer," to which Falstaff was compared.

There is a class of "roots" in which the street-sellers, on account of their general dearness, deal so sparingly, that I cannot class them as a part of the business. Among these are anemones, hyacinths, tulips, ranunculuses, and the orchidaceous tribe. Neither do the street people meddle, unless very exceptionally, with the taller and statelier plants, such as foxgloves, hollyoaks, and sunflowers; these are too difficult of carriage for their purpose. Nor do they sell, unless again as an exception, such flowers as require support—the convolvolus and the sweet-pea, for instance.

The plants I have specified vary in price. Geraniums are sold at from 3*d*. to 5*s*.; pinks at from 3*d*. for the common pink, to 2*s*. for the best single clove, and 4*s*. for the best double; stocks, as they are small and single, to their being large and double, from 3*d*. (and sometimes less) to 2*s*.; dahlias from 6*d*. to 5*s*.; fuschias, from 6*d*. to 4*s*.; rose-bushes from 3*d*. to 1*s*. 6*d*., and sometimes, but not often, much higher; musk-plants, London pride, lupins, &c., are 1*d*. and 2*d*., pots generally included.

To carry on his business efficiently, the root-seller mostly keeps a pony and a cart, to convey his purchases from the garden to his stall or his barrow, and he must have a sheltered and cool shed in which to deposit the flowers which are to be kept over-night for the morrow's business. "It's a great bother, sir," said a root-seller, "a man having to provide a shed for his roots.

It wouldn't do at all to have them in the same room as we sleep in—they'd droop. I have a beautiful big shed, and a snug stall for a donkey in a corner of it; but he won't bear tying up—he'll fight against tying all night, and if he was loose, why in course he'd eat the flowers I put in the shed. The price is nothing to him; he'd eat the Queen's camellias, if he could get at them, if they cost a pound a-piece. So I have a deal of trouble, for I must block him up somehow; but he's a first-rate ass." To carry on a considerable business, the services of a man and his wife are generally required, as well as those of a boy.

The purchases wholesale are generally by the dozen roots, all ready for sale in pots. Mignonette, however, is grown in boxes, and sold by the box at from 5*s*. to 20*s*., according to the size, &c. The costermonger buys, for the large sale to the poor, at a rate which brings the mignonette roots into his possession at something less, perhaps, than a halfpenny each. He then purchases a gross of small common pots, costing him 1½*d*. a dozen, and has to transfer the roots and soil to the pots, and then offer them for sale. The profit thus is about 4*s*. per hundred, but with the drawback of considerable labour and some cost in the conveyance of the boxes. The same method is sometimes pursued with young stocks.

The cheapness of pots, I may mention incidentally, and the more frequent sale of roots in them, has almost entirely swept away the fragment of a pitcher and "the spotless tea-pot," which Cowper mentions as containing the poor man's flowers, that testified an inextinguishable love of rural objects, even in the heart of a city. There are a few such things, however, to be seen still.

Of root-sellers there are, for six months of the year, about 500 in London. Of these, one-fifth devote themselves principally, but none entirely, to the sale of roots; two-fifths sell roots regularly, but only as a portion, and not a larger portion of their business; and the remaining two-fifths are casual dealers in roots, buying them — almost always in the markets—whenever a bargain offers. Seven-eighths of the root-sellers are, I am informed, regular costers, occasionally a gardener's assistant has taken to the street trade in flowers, "but I fancy, sir," said an experienced man to me, "they've very seldom done any good at it. They're always *gardening* at their roots, trimming them, and such like, and they overdo it. They're too careful of their plants; people like to trim them theirselves."

"I did well on fuschias last season," said one of my informants; "I sold them from 6*d*. to 1*s*. 6*d*. The 'Globes' went off well. Geraniums was very fair. The 'Fairy Queens' of them sold faster than any, I think. It's the ladies out of town a little way, and a few in town, that buy them, and buy the fuschias too. They require a good window. The 'Jenny Linds'—they was geraniums and other plants—didn't sell so well as the Fairy Queens, though they was cheaper. Good cloves (pinks) sell to the better sort of houses; so do carnations. Mignonette's everybody's money. Dahlias didn't go off so well. I had very tidy dahlias at 6*d.* and 1*s.*, and some 1*s.* 6*d.* I do a goodish bit in giving flowers for old clothes. I very seldom do it, but to ladies. I deal mostly with them for their husbands' old hats, or boots, or shoes; yes, sir, and their trowsers and waistcoats sometimes—very seldom their coats—and ladies boots and shoes too. There's one pleasant old lady, and her two daughters, they'll talk me over any day. I very seldom indeed trade for ladies' clothes. I have, though. Mostly for something in the shawl way, or wraps of some kind. Why, that lady I was telling you of and her daughters, got me to take togs that didn't bring the prime cost of my roots and expenses. They called them by such fine names, that I was had. Then they was so polite; 'O, my good man,' says one of the young daughters, 'I must have this geranium in 'change.' It was a most big and beautiful Fairy Queen, well worth 4*s.* The tog—I didn't know what they called it—a sort of cloak, fetched short of half-a-crown, and that just with cheaper togs. Some days, if it's very hot, and the stall business isn't good in *very* hot weather, my wife goes a round with me, and does considerable in swopping with ladies. They can't do her as they can me. The same on wet days, if it's not very wet, when I has my roots covered in the cart. Ladies is mostly at home such times, and perhaps they're dull, and likes to go to work at a bargaining. My wife manages them. In good weeks, I can clear 3*l.* in my trade; the two of us can, anyhow. But then there's bad weather, and there's sometimes roots spoiled if they're not cheap, and don't go off—but I'll sell one that cost me 1*s.* for 2*d.* to get rid of it; and there's always the expenses to meet, and the pony to keep, and everything that way. No, sir, I don't make 2*l.* a week for the five months—its nearer five than six—the season lasts; perhaps something near it. The rest of the year I sell fruit, or anything, and may clear 10*s.* or 15*s.* a week, but, some weeks, next to nothing, and the expenses all going on.

"Why, no, sir; I can't say that times is what they was. Where I made 4*l.* on my roots five or six years back, I make only 3*l.* now. But it's no use complaining; there's lots worse off than I am—lots. I've given pennies and twopences to plenty that's seen better days in the streets; it might be their own fault. It is so mostly, but perhaps only partly. I keep a connection together as well as I can. I have a stall; my wife's there generally, and I go a round as well."

One of the principal root-sellers in the streets told me that he not unfrequently sold ten dozen a day, over and above those sold not in pots. As my informant had a superior trade, his business is not to be taken as an average; but, reckoning that he averages six dozen a day for 20 weeks—he said 26—it shows that one man alone sells 8,640 flowers in pots in the season. The prin-

cipal sellers carry on about the same extent of business.

According to similar returns, the number of the several kinds of flowers in pots and flower roots sold annually in the London streets, are as follows:

FLOWERS IN POTS.

Moss-roses	38,880
China-roses	38,880
Fuschias	38,800
Geraniums	12,800
Total number of flowers in pots sold in the streets	123,360

FLOWER-ROOTS.

Primroses	24,000
Polyanthuses	34,560
Cowslips	28,800
Daisies	33,600
Wallflowers	46,080
Candytufts	28,800
Daffodils	28,800
Violets	38,400
Mignonette	30,384
Stocks	23,040
Pinks and Carnations	19,200
Lilies of the Valley	3,456
Pansies	12,960
Lilies	660
Tulips	852
Balsams	7,704
Calceolarias	3,180
Musk Plants	253,440
London Pride	11,520
Lupins	25,596
China-asters	9,156
Marigolds	63,360
Dahlias	852
Heliotrope	13,356
Poppies	1,920
Michaelmas Daisies	6,912
Total number of flower-roots sold in the streets	750,588

OF THE STREET SALE OF SEEDS.

THE street sale of seeds, I am informed, is smaller than it was thirty, or even twenty years back. One reason assigned for this falling off is the superior cheapness of "flowers in pots." At one time, I was informed, the poorer classes who were fond of flowers liked to "grow their own mignonette." I told one of my informants that I had been assured by a trustworthy man, that in one day he had sold 600 penny pots of mignonette: "Not a bit of doubt of it, sir," was the answer, "not a doubt about it; I've heard of more than that sold in a day by a man who set on three hands to help him; and that's just where it is. When a poor woman, or poor man either—but its mostly the women—can buy a mignonette pot, all blooming and smelling for 1*d.*, why she won't bother to buy seeds and set them in a box or a pot and wait for them to come into full blow. Selling seeds in the streets can't be done so well now, sir. Anyhow it ain't done as it was, as I've often heard old folk say." The reason assigned for this is that cottages in many parts—such places as Lisson-grove, Islington, Hoxton, Hackney, or Stepney—where the inhabitants formerly cultivated flowers in their little gardens, are now let out in single apartments, and the gardens—or yards as they mostly are now—were used merely to hang clothes in. The only green thing which remained in some of these gardens, I was told, was horse-radish, a root which it is difficult to extirpate : " And it's just the sort of thing," said one man, "that poor people hasn't no great call for, because they, you see, a'n't not overdone with joints of roast beef, nor rump steaks." In the suburbs where the small gardens are planted with flowers, the cultivators rarely buy seeds of the street-sellers, whose stands are mostly at a distance.

None of the street seed-vendors confine themselves to the sale. One man, whom I saw, told me that last spring he was penniless, after sickness, and a nurseryman, whom he knew, trusted him 5s. worth of seeds, which he continued to sell, trading in nothing else, for three or four weeks, until he was able to buy some flowers in pots. Though the profit is cent. per cent. on most kinds, 1s. 6d. a day is accounted " good earnings, on seeds." On wet days there is no sale, and, indeed, the seeds cannot be exposed in the streets. My informant computed that he cleared 5s. a week. His customers were principally poor women, who liked to sow mignonette in boxes, or in a garden-border, " if it had ever such a little bit of sun," and who resided, he believed, in small, quiet streets, branching off from the thoroughfares. Of flower-seeds, the street-sellers dispose most largely of mignonette, nasturtium, and the various stocks ; and of herbs, the most is done in parsley. One of my informants, however, " did best in grass-seeds," which people bought, he said, " to mend their grass-plots with," sowing them in any bare place, and throwing soil loosely over them. Lupin, larkspur, convolvulus, and Venus's looking-glass had a fair sale.

The street-trade, in seeds, would be less than it is, were it not that the dealers sell it in smaller quantities than the better class of shop-keepers. The street-traders buy their seeds by the quarter of a pound—or any quantity not considered retail—of the nurserymen, who often write the names for the costers on the paper in which the seed has to be inclosed. Seed that costs 4d., the street-seller makes into eight penny lots. " Why, yes, sir," said one man, in answer to my inquiry, " people is often afraid that our seeds ain't honest. If they're not, they're mixed, or they're bad, before they come into our hands. I don't think any of our chaps does anything with them."

Fourteen or fifteen years ago, although seeds, generally, were fifteen to twenty per cent. dearer than they are now, there was twice the demand for them. An average price of good mignonette

seed, he said, was now 1s. the quarter of a pound, and it was then 1s. 2d. to 1s. 6d. The shilling's worth, is made, by the street-seller, into twenty or twenty-four pennyworths. An average price of parsley, and of the cheaper seeds, is less than half that of mignonette. Other seeds, again, are not sold to the street-people by the weight, but are made up in sixpenny and shilling packages. Their extreme lightness prevents their being weighed to a customer. Of this class are, the African marigold, the senecios (groundsel), and the china-aster ; but of these compound flowers, the street-traders sell very few. Poppy-seed used to be in great demand among the street-buyers, but it has ceased to be so. " It's a fine hardy plant, too, sir," I was told, " but somehow, for all its variety in colours, it's gone out of fashion, for fashion runs strong in flowers."

One long-established street-seller, who is well known to supply the best seeds, makes for the five weeks or so of the season more than twice the weekly average of 5s. ; perhaps 12s.; but as he is a shop as well as a stall-keeper, he could not speak very precisely as to the proportionate sale in the street or the shop. This man laughed at the fondness some of his customers manifested for " fine Latin names." " There are some people," he said, " who will buy antirrhinum, and artemisia, and digitalis, and wouldn't hear of snapdragon, or wormwood, or foxglove, though they're the identical plants." The same informant told me that the railways in their approaches to the metropolis had destroyed many small gardens and had, he thought, injured his trade. It was, also, a common thing now for the greengrocers and corn-chandlers to sell garden-seeds, which until these six or eight years they did much less extensively.

Last spring, I was told, there were not more than four persons, in London, selling only seeds. The " root-sellers," of whom I have treated, generally deal in seeds also, but the demand does not extend beyond four or five weeks in the spring, though there was " a straggling trade that way " two or three weeks longer. It was computed for me, that there were fully one hundred persons selling seeds (with other things) in the streets, and that each might average a profit of 5s. weekly, for a month ; giving 200l. expended in seeds, with 100l. profit to the costers. Seeds are rarely hawked as flowers are.

It is impossible to give as minutely detailed an account of the street-sale of seeds as of flowers, as from their diversity in size, weight, quantity in a pennyworth, &c., no calculation can be prepared by weight or measure, only by *value.* Thus, I find it necessary to depart somewhat from the order hitherto observed. One seedsman, acquainted with the street-trade from his dealings with the vendors, was of opinion that the following list and proportions were as nice an approximation as could be arrived at. It was found necessary to give it in proportions of twenty-fifths ; but it must be borne in mind that the *quantity* in $\frac{3}{25}$ths of parsley, for example, is more than double that of $\frac{1}{25}$ths of mignonette. I give, in unison, seeds of about equal sale, whether of the same botanical family or not. Many of the most popular flowers, such as polyanthuses, daisies, violets, and primroses, are not raised from seed, except in the nursery gardens:—

Seeds.	Twenty-fifths.	Value.
Mignonette . . .	Three	£24
Stocks (of all kinds)	Two	16
Marigolds (do.). .	One	8
Convolvulus (do.) .	„	8
Wallflower . . .	„	8
Scarlet-beans and Sweet-peas . .	„	8
China-asters and Venus' looking-glass	„	8
Lupin and Larkspur	„	8
Nasturtium . . .	„	8
Parsley	Two	16
Other Pot-herbs . .	One	8
Mustard and Cress, Lettuce, and the other vegetables .	Two	16
Grass	One	8
Other seeds . . .	Seven	56

Total expended annually on street-seeds . £200

OF CHRISTMASING—LAUREL, IVY, HOLLY, AND MISTLETOE.

IN London a large trade is carried on in "Christmasing," or in the sale of holly and mistletoe, for Christmas sports and decorations. I have appended a table of the quantity of these "branches" sold, nearly 250,000, and of the money expended upon them in the streets. It must be borne in mind, to account for this expenditure for a brief season, that almost every housekeeper will expend something in "Christmasing;" from 2d. to 1s. 6d., and the poor buy a pennyworth, or a halfpennyworth each, and they are the coster's customers. In some houses, which are let off in rooms, floors, or suites of apartments, and not to the poorest class, every room will have the cheery decoration of holly, its bright, and as if *glazed* leaves and red berries, reflecting the light from their own stem. "Then, look," said a gardener to me, "what's spent on a Christmasing the churches! Why, now, properly to Christmas St. Paul's, I say *properly*, mind, would take 50l. worth at least; aye, more, when I think of it, nearer 100l. I hope there'll be no 'No Popery' nonsense against Christmasing this year. I'm always very when anything of that kind's afloat, because it's frequently a hindrance to business." This was said three weeks before Christmas. In London there are upwards of 300,000 inhabited houses. The whole of the evergreen branches sold number 375,000.

Even the ordinary-sized inns, I was informed, displayed holly decorations, costing from 2s. to 10s.; while in the larger inns, where, perhaps, an assembly-room, a concert-room, or a club-room, had to be adorned, along with other apartments, 20s. worth of holly, &c., was a not

uncommon outlay. "Well, then, consider," said another informant, "the plum-puddings! Why, at least there's a hundred thousand of 'em eaten, in London, through the Christmas and the month following. That's nearly one pudding to every twenty of the population, is it, sir? Well, perhaps, that's too much. But, then, there's the great numbers eaten at public dinners and suppers; and there's more plum-pudding clubs at the small grocers and public-houses than there used to be, so, say full a hundred thousand, flinging in any mince-pies that may be decorated with ever-greens. Well, sir, every plum-pudding will have a sprig of holly in him. If it's bought just for the occasion, it may cost 1d., to be really prime and nicely berried. If it's part of a lot, why it won't cost a halfpenny, so reckon it all at a halfpenny. What does that come to? Above 200l. Think of that, then, just for sprigging puddings!"

Mistletoe, I am informed, is in somewhat less demand than it was, though there might be no very perceptible difference. In many houses holly is now used instead of the true plant, for the ancient ceremonies and privileges observed "under the mistletoe bough." The holly is not half the price of the mistletoe, which is one reason; for, though there is not any great disparity of price, wholesale, the holly, which costs 6d. retail, is more than the quantity of mistletoe retailed for 1s. The holly-tree may be grown in any hedge, and ivy may be reared against any wall; while the mistletoe is parasitical of the apple-tree, and, but not to half the extent, of the oak and other trees. It does not grow in the northern counties of England. The purchasers of the mistletoe are, for the most part, the wealthier classes, or, at any rate, I was told, "those who give parties." It is bought, too, by the male servants in large establishments, and more would be so bought, "only so few of the great people, of the most fashionable squares and places, keep their Christmas in town." Half-a-crown is a not uncommon price for a handsome mistletoe bough.

The costermongers buy about a half of the holly, &c., brought to the markets; it is also sold either direct to those requiring evergreens, or to green-grocers and fruiterers who have received orders for it from their customers, or who know it will be wanted. A shilling's worth may be bought in the market, the bundles being divided. Mistletoe, the costers—those having regular customers in the suburbs—receive orders for. "Last December," said a coster to me, "I remember a servant-girl, and she weren't such a girl either, running after me in a regular flutter, to tell me the family had forgot to order 2s. worth of mistletoe of me, to be brought next day. Oh, yes, sir, if it's ordered by, or delivered to, the servant-girls, they generally have a little giggling about it. If I've said : ' What are you laughing at?' they'll mostly say: ' Me! I'm not laughing.' "

The costermongers go into the neighbourhood of London to procure the holly for street-sale. This is chiefly done, I was told, by those who were "cracked up," and some of them laboured at it "days and days." It is, however, a very uncertain trade, as they must generally trespass, and if they are caught trespassing, by the occupier of the land, or any of his servants, they are seldom "given in charge," but their stock of evergreens is not unfrequently taken from them, "and that, sir, that's the cuttingest of all." They do not so freely venture upon the gathering of mistletoe, for to procure it they must trespass in orchards, which is somewhat dangerous work, and they are in constant apprehension of traps, spring-guns, and bull-dogs. Six or seven hundred men or lads, the lads being the most numerous, are thus employed for a week or two before Christmas, and, perhaps, half that number, irregularly at intervals, for a week or two after it. Some of the lads are not known as regular coster-lads, but they are *habitués* of the streets in some capacity. To procure as much holly one day, as will sell for 2s. 6d. the next, is accounted pretty good work, and 7s. 6d. would be thus realised in six days. But 5s. is more frequently the return of six days' labour and sale, though a very few have cleared 10s., and one man, "with uncommon luck," once cleared 20s. in six days. The distance travelled in a short winter's day, is sometimes twenty miles, and, perhaps, the lad or man has not broken his fast, on some days, until the evening, or even the next morning, for had he possessed a few pence he would probably have invested it in oranges or nuts, for street-sale, rather than "go a-gathering Christmas."

One strong-looking lad, of 16 or 17, gave me the following account:—

"It's hard work, is Christmasing; but, when you have neither money nor work, you must do something, and so the holly may come in handy. I live with a elder brother; he helps the masons, and as we had neither of us either work or money, he cut off Tottenham and Edmonton way, and me the t'other side of the water, Mortlake way, as well as I know. We'd both been used to costering, off and on. I was out, I think, ten days altogether, and didn't make 6s. in it. I'd been out two Christmases before. O, yes, I'd forgot. I made 6d. over the 6s., for I had half a pork-pie and a pint of beer, and the landlord took it out in holly. I meant to have made a quarter of pork do, but I was so hungry—and so would you, sir, if you'd been out a-Christmasing—that I had the t'other quarter. It's 2d. a quarter. I did better when I was out afore, but I forget what I made. It's often slow work, for you must wait sometimes 'till no one's looking, and then you must work away like anything. I'd nothing but a sharp knife, I borrowed, and some bits of cord to tie the holly up. You *must* look out sharp, because, you see, sir, a man very likely won't like his holly-tree to be stripped. Wherever there is a berry, we goes for the berries.

They're poison berries, I've heard. Moonlight nights is the thing, sir, when you knows where you are. I never goes for mizzletoe. I hardly knows it when I sees it. The first time I was out, a man got me to go for some in a orchard, and told me how to manage; but I cut my lucky in a minute. Something came over me like. I felt sickish. But what can a poor fellow do? I never lost my Christmas, but a little bit of it at once. Two men took it from me, and said I ought to thank them for letting me off without a jolly good jacketing, as they was gardeners. I believes they was men out a-Christmasing, as I were. It was a dreadful cold time that; and I was wet, and hungry,—and thirsty, too, for all I was so wet,—and I'd to wait a-watching in the wet. I've got something better to do now, and I'll never go a-Christmasing again, if I can help it."

This lad contrived to get back to his lodging, in town, every night, but some of those out Christmasing, stay two or three days and nights in the country, sleeping in barns, out-houses, carts, or under hay-stacks, inclement as the weather may be, when their funds are insufficient to defray the charge of a bed, or a part of one, at a country "dossing-crib" (low lodging-house). They resorted, in considerable numbers, to the casual wards of the workhouses, in Croydon, Greenwich, Reigate, Dartford, &c., when that accommodation was afforded them, concealing their holly for the night.

As in other matters, it may be a surprise to some of my readers to learn in what way the evergreens, used on festive occasions in their homes, may have been procured.

The costermongers who procure their own Christmasing, generally hawk it. A few sell it by the lot to their more prosperous brethren. What the costers purchase in the market, they aim to sell at cent. per cent.

Supposing that 700 men and lads gathered their own holly, &c., and each worked for three weeks (not regarding interruptions), and calculating that, in the time they cleared even 15s. each, it amounts to 575l.

Some of the costermongers deck their carts and barrows, in the general line, with holly at Christmas. Some go out with their carts full of holly, for sale, and may be accompanied by a fiddler, or by a person beating a drum. The cry is, "Holly! Green Holly!"

One of my informants alluded incidentally to the decoration of the churches, and I may observe that they used to be far more profusely decked with Christmas evergreens than at present; so much so, that a lady correspondent in January, 1712, complained to "*Mr. Spectator*" that her church-going was bootless. She was constant at church, to hear divine service and make conquests; but the clerk had so overdone the greens in the church that, for three weeks, Miss Jenny Simper had not even seen the young baronet, whom she dressed at for divine worship, although he pursued his devotions only three pews from hers. The aisle was a pretty shady walk, and each pew was an arbour. The pulpit was so clustered with holly and ivy that the congregation, like Moses, heard the word out of a bush. " Sir Anthony Love's pew in particular," concludes the indignant Miss Simper, "is so well hedged, that all my batteries have no effect. I am obliged to shoot at random among the boughs without taking any manner of aim. Mr. Spectator, unless you'll give orders for removing these greens, I shall grow a very awkward creature at church, and soon have little else to do there but to say my prayers." In a subsequent number, the clerk glorifies himself that he had checked the ogling of Miss Simper. He had heard how the Kentish men evaded the Conqueror by displaying green boughs before them, and so he bethought him of a like device against the love-warfare of this coquettish lady.

Of all the "branches" in the markets, the costers buy one-half. This season, holly has been cheaper than was ever known previously. In some years, its price was double that cited, in some treble, when the December was very frosty.

Of the Sale of May, Palm, etc.

THE sale of the May, the fragrant flower of the hawthorn, a tree indigenous to this country—Wordsworth mentions one which must have been 800 years old—is carried on by the coster boys (principally), but only in a desultory way. The chief supply is brought to London in the carts or barrows of the costers returning from a country expedition. If the costermonger be accompanied by a lad—as he always is if the expedition be of any length—the lad will say to his master, "Bill, let's have some May to take back." The man will almost always consent, and often assist in procuring the thickly green branches with their white or rose-tinted, and *freshly*-smelling flowers. The odour of the hawthorn blossom is peculiar, and some eminent botanist—Dr. Withering if I remember rightly — says it may be best described as "fresh." No flower, perhaps, is blended with more poetical, antiquarian, and beautiful associations than the ever-welcome blossom of the may-tree. One gardener told me that as the hawthorn was in perfection in June instead of May, the name was not proper. But it must be remembered that the name of the flower was given during the old style, which carried our present month of May twelve days into June, and the name would then be more appropriate.

The May is obtained by the costermongers in the same way as the holly, by cutting it from the trees in the hedges. It has sometimes to be cut or broken off stealthily, for persons may no more like their hawthorns to be stripped than their hollies, and an ingenuous lad—as will have been observed—told me of "people's " objections to the unauthorized stripping of their holly-bushes. But there is not a quarter of the difficulty in procuring May that there is in procuring holly at Christmas.

The costermonger, if he has "done tidy " in the country will very probably leave the May at the disposal of his boy ; but a few men, though perhaps little more than twenty, I was told, bring it on their own account. The lads then carry the branches about for sale ; or if a considerable quantity has been brought, dispose of it to other boys or girls, or entrust them with the sale of it, at "half-profits," or any terms agreed upon. Costermongers have been known to bring home "a load of May," and this not unfrequently, at the request, and for the benefit of a "cracked-up" brother-trader, to whom it has been at once delivered gratuitously.

A lad, whom I met with as he was selling holly, told me that he had brought may from the country when he had been there with a coster. He had also gone out of town a few miles to gather it on his own account. " But it ain't no good;" he said ; "you must often go a good way—I never knows anything about how many miles—and if it's very ripe (the word he used) it's soon shaken. There's no sure price. You may get 4d. for a big branch or you must take 1d. I may have made 1s. on a round but hardly ever more. It can't be got near hand. There 's some stunning fine trees at the top of the park there (the Regent's Park) the t'other side of the 'logical Gardens, but there's always a cove looking after them, they say, and both night and day."

Palm, the flower of any of the numerous species of the willow, is sold only on Palm Sunday, and the Saturday preceding. The trade is about equally in the hands of the English and Irish lads, but the English lads have a commercial advantage on the morning of Palm Sunday, when so many of the Irish lads are at chapel. The palm is all gathered by the street-vendors. One costermonger told me that when he was a lad, he had sold palm to a man who had managed to get half-drunk on a Sunday morning, and who told him that he wanted it to show his wife, who very seldom stirred out, that he'd been taking a healthful walk into the country !

Lilac in flower is sold (and procured) in the same way as May, but in small quantities. Very rarely indeed, laburnum; which is too fragile ; or syringa, which, I am told, is hardly saleable in the streets. One informant remembered that forty years ago, when he was a boy, branches of elder-berry flowers were sold in the streets, but the trade has disappeared.

It is very difficult to form a calculation as to the extent of this trade. The best informed give me reason to believe that the sale of all these branches (apart from Christmas) ranges, according to circumstances, from 30*l*. to 50*l*., the cost being the labour of gathering, and the subsistence of the labourer while at the work. This is independent of what the costers buy in the markets.

I now show the quantity of branches forming the street trade :—

Holly	59,040 bunches
Mistletoe . . .	56,160 „
Ivy and Laurel . .	26,640 „
Lilac	5,400 „
Palm	1,008 „
May	2,520 „

| Total number of bunches sold in the streets from market-sale . . | 150,000 |
| Add to quantity from other sources . . | 75,000 |

225,768

The quantity of branches "from other sources" is that gathered by the costers in the way I have described; but it is impossible to obtain a return of it with proper precision: to state it as half of that purchased in the markets is a low average.

I now give the amount paid by street-buyers who indulge in the healthful and innocent tastes of which I have been treating—the fondness for the beautiful and the natural.

CUT FLOWERS.

Bunches of		per bunch		
65,280	Violets	at ½d.	.	£136
115,200	Wallflowers . . .	„ ½d.	.	240
86,400	Mignonette . . .	„ 1d.	.	360
1,632	Lilies of the Valley	„ ½d.	.	3
20,448	Stocks	„ ½d.	.	42
316,800	Pinks and Carnations	„ ½d. each		660
864,000	Moss Roses . . .	„ ½d.	„	1,800
864,000	China ditto . . .	„ ½d.	„	1,800
296,640	Lavender . . .	„ 1d.	„	1,236

Total annually £6,277

FLOWER ROOTS.

		per root		
24,000	Primroses	at ½d.	.	£50
34,560	Polyanthuses . . .	„ 1d.	.	144
28,800	Cowslips	„ ½d.	.	50
33,600	Daisies	„ 1d.	.	140
46,080	Wallflowers	„ 1d.	.	192
28,800	Candy-tufts	„ 1d.	.	120
28,800	Daffodils	„ ½d.	.	60
38,400	Violets	„ ½d.	.	80
30,380	Mignonette	„ ½d.	.	63
23,040	Stocks	„ 1d.	.	96
19,200	Pinks and Carnations	„ 2d.	.	160
3,456	Lilies of the Valley .	„ 1d.	.	14
12,960	Pansies	„ 1d.	.	54
660	Lilies	„ 2d.	.	5
850	Tulips	„ 2d.	.	7
7,704	Balsams	„ 2d.	.	64
3,180	Calceolarias	„ 2d.	.	26
253,440	Musk Plants . . .	„ 1d.		1,056
11,520	London Pride . . .	„ 1d.	.	48
25,595	Lupins	„ 1d.	.	106
9,156	China-asters . . .	„ 1d.	.	38
63,360	Marigolds . . .	„ ½d.	.	132
852	Dahlias	„ 6d.	.	21
13,356	Heliotropes	„ 2d.	.	111
1,920	Poppies	„ 2d.	.	16
6,912	Michaelmas Daisies .	„ ½d.	.	14

Total annually £2,867

BRANCHES.

Bunches of		per bunch		
59,040	Holly	at 3d.	.	£738
56,160	Mistletoe	„ 3d.	.	702
26,640	Ivy and Laurel . .	„ 3d.	.	333
5,400	Lilac	„ 3d.	.	67
1,008	Palm	„ 3d.	.	12
2,520	May	„ 3d.	.	31

Total annually from Markets . . £1,183
Add one-half as shown 591

£2,774

TREES AND SHRUBS.

		each root		
9,576	Firs (roots)	at 3d.	. . . .	£119
1,152	Laurels . .	„ 3d.	. . . .	14
23,040	Myrtles .	„ 4d.	. . . .	384
2,160	Rhododendrons	9d.	. . . .	81
2,304	Lilacs . .	„ 4d	. . . .	38
2,880	Box . . .	„ 2d.	. . . .	24
21,888	Heaths . .	„ 4d.	. . . .	364
2,880	Broom . .	„ 1d.	. . . .	12
6,912	Furze . .	„ 1d.	. . . .	28
6,480	Laurustinus	„ 8d.	. . . .	216
25,920	Southernwood	„ 1d.	. . . .	108

Total annually spent £1,388

FLOWERS IN POTS.

		per pot		
38,880	Moss Roses	at 4d.		£648
38,880	China ditto	„ 2d.	.	324
38,800	Fuschias	„ 3d.	.	485
12,850	Geraniums and Pelargoniums (of all kinds)	3d.	.	210

Total annually £1,667

The returns give the following aggregate amount of street expenditure:—

	£
Trees and shrubs	1,388
Cut Flowers	6,277
Flowers in pots	1,667
Flower roots	2,867
Branches	2,774
Seeds	200

£15,173

From the returns we find that of "cut flowers" the roses retain their old English favouritism, no fewer than 1,628,000 being annually sold in the streets; but locality affects the sale, as some dealers dispose of more violets than roses, because violets are accounted less fragile. The cheapness and hardihood of the musk-plant and marigold, to say nothing of their peculiar odour, has made them the most popular of the "roots," while the myrtle is the favourite among the "trees and shrubs." The heaths, moreover, command an extensive sale, —a sale, I am told, which was unknown, until eight or ten years ago, another instance of the "fashion in flowers," of which an informant has spoken.

STREET-SELLERS OF GREEN STUFF.

UNDER this head I class the street-purveyors of water-cresses, and of the chickweed, groundsel, plantain, and turf required for cage-birds. These purveyors seem to be on the outskirts, as it were, of the costermonger class, and, indeed, the regular costers look down upon them as an inferior caste. The green-stuff trade is carried on by very poor persons, and, generally, by children or old people, some of the old people being lame, or suffering from some infirmity, which, however, does not prevent their walking about with their commodities. To the children and infirm class, however, the turf-cutters supply an exception. The costermongers, as I have intimated, do not resort, and do not let their children resort, to this traffic. If reduced to the last shift, they will sell nuts or oranges in preference. The "old hands" have been " reduced," as a general rule, from other avocations. Their homes are in the localities I have specified as inhabited by the poor.

I was informed by a seller of birds, that he thought fewer birds were kept by poor working-people, and even by working-people who had regular, though, perhaps, diminished earnings, than was the case six or eight years ago. At one time, it was not uncommon for a young man to present his betrothed with a pair of singing-birds in a neat cage; now such a present, as far as my informant's knowledge extended—and he was a sharp intelligent man—was but rarely made. One reason this man had often heard advanced for poor persons not renewing their birds, when lost or dead, is pitiful in its plainness— "they eat too much." I do not know, that, in such a gift as I have mentioned, there was any intention on the part of the lover to typify the beauty of cheerfulness, even in a very close confinement to home. "I can't tell, sir," was said to me, " how it may have been originally, but I never heard such a thing said much about, though there's been joking about the matter, as when would the birds have young ones, and such like. No, sir; I think it was just a fashion." Contrary to the custom in more prosperous establishments, I am satisfied, that, among the labouring classes, birds are more frequently the pets of the men than of the women. My bird-dealing informant cited merely his own experience, but there is no doubt that cage-birds are more extensively kept than ever in London; consequently there is a greater demand for the " green stuff" the birds require.

OF WATERCRESS-SELLING, IN FARRINGDON-MARKET.

THE first coster-cry heard of a morning in the London streets is that of " Fresh wo-orter-creases." Those that sell them have to be on their rounds in time for the mechanics' breakfast, or the day's gains are lost. As the stock-money for this calling need only consist of a few

halfpence, it is followed by the very poorest of the poor; such as young children, who have been deserted by their parents, and whose strength is not equal to any very great labour, or by old men and women, crippled by disease or accident, who in their dread of a workhouse life, linger on with the few pence they earn by street-selling.

As winter draws near, the Farringdon cress-market begins long before daylight. On your way to the City to see this strange sight, the streets are deserted; in the squares the blinds are drawn down before the windows, and the shutters closed, so that the very houses seem asleep. All is so silent that you can hear the rattle of the milkmaids' cans in the neighbouring streets, or the noisy song of three or four drunken voices breaks suddenly upon you, as if the singers had turned a corner, and then dies away in the distance. On the cab-stands, but one or two crazy cabs are left, the horses dozing with their heads down to their knees, and the drawn-up windows covered with the breath of the driver sleeping inside. At the corners of the streets, the bright fires of the coffee-stalls sparkle in the darkness, and as you walk along, the policeman, leaning against some gas-lamp, turns his lantern full upon you, as if in suspicion that one who walks abroad so early could mean no good to householders. At one house there stands a man, with dirty boots and loose hair, as if he had just left some saloon, giving sharp single knocks, and then going into the road and looking up at the bed-rooms, to see if a light appeared in them. As you near the City, you meet, if it be a Monday or Friday morning, droves of sheep and bullocks, tramping quietly along to Smithfield, and carrying a fog of steam with them, while behind, with his hands in his pockets, and his dog panting at his heels, walks the sheep-drover.

At the principal entrance to Farringdon-market there is an open space, running the entire length of the railings in front, and extending from the iron gates at the entrance to the sheds down the centre of the large paved court before the shops. In this open space the cresses are sold, by the salesmen or saleswomen to whom they are consigned, in the hampers they are brought in from the country.

The shops in the market are shut, the gas-lights over the iron gates burn brightly, and every now and then you hear the half-smothered crowing of a cock, shut up in some shed or bird-fancier's shop. Presently a man comes hurrying along, with a can of hot coffee in each hand, and his stall on his head, and when he has arranged his stand by the gates, and placed his white mugs between the railings on the stone wall, he blows at his charcoal fire, making the bright sparks fly about at every puff he gives. By degrees the customers are creeping up, dressed in every style of rags; they shuffle up and down before the gates, stamping to warm their feet, and rubbing their hands together till they grate like sandpaper. Some of the boys have brought large hand-baskets, and carry them with the handles round their necks, covering the head entirely with the wicker-work as with a hood; others have their shallows fastened to their backs with a strap, and one little girl, with the bottom of her gown tattered into a fringe like a blacksmith's apron, stands shivering in a large pair of worn-out Vestris boots, holding in her blue hands a bent and rusty tea-tray. A few poor creatures have made friends with the coffee-man, and are allowed to warm their fingers at the fire under the cans, and as the heat strikes into them, they grow sleepy and yawn.

The market—by the time we reach it—has just begun; one dealer has taken his seat, and sits motionless with cold—for it wants but a month to Christmas—with his hands thrust deep into the pockets of his gray driving coat. Before him is an opened hamper, with a candle fixed in the centre of the bright green cresses, and as it shines through the wicker sides of the basket, it casts curious patterns on the ground—as a night shade does. Two or three customers, with their "shallows" slung over their backs, and their hands poked into the bosoms of their gowns, are bending over the hamper, the light from which tinges their swarthy features, and they rattle their halfpence and speak coaxingly to the dealer, to hurry him in their bargains.

Just as the church clocks are striking five, a stout saleswoman enters the gates, and instantly a country-looking fellow, in a wagoner's cap and smock-frock, arranges the baskets he has brought up to London. The other ladies are soon at their posts, well wrapped up in warm cloaks, over their thick shawls, and sit with their hands under their aprons, talking to the loungers, whom they call by their names. Now the business commences; the customers come in by twos and threes, and walk about, looking at the cresses, and listening to the prices asked. Every hamper is surrounded by a black crowd, bending over till their heads nearly meet, their foreheads and cheeks lighted up by the candle in the centre. The saleswomen's voices are heard above the noise of the mob, sharply answering all objections that may be made to the quality of their goods. "They're rather spotty, mum," says an Irishman, as he examines one of the leaves. "No more spots than a new-born babe, Dennis," answers the lady tartly, and then turns to a new comer. At one basket, a street-seller in an old green cloak, has spread out a rusty shawl to receive her bunches, and by her stands her daughter, in a thin cotton dress, patched like a quilt. "Ah! Mrs. Dolland," cried the saleswoman in a gracious tone, "can you keep yourself warm? it bites the fingers like biling water, it do." At another basket, an old man, with long gray hair streaming over a kind of policeman's cape, is bitterly complaining of the way he has been treated by

another saleswoman. "He bought a lot of her, the other morning, and by daylight they were quite white; for he only made threepence on his best day." "Well, Joe," returns the lady, "you should come to them as knows you, and allers treats you well."

These saleswomen often call to each other from one end of the market to the other. If any quarrel take place at one of the hampers, as frequently it does, the next neighbour is sure to say something. "Pinch him well, Sally," cried one saleswoman to another; "pinch him well; *I* do when I've a chance." "It's no use," was the answer; "I might as well try to pinch a elephant."

One old wrinkled woman, carrying a basket with an oilcloth bottom, was asked by a buxom rosy dealer, "Now, Nancy, what's for you?" But the old dame was surly with the cold, and sneering at the beauty of the saleswoman, answered, "Why don't you go and get a sweetheart; sich as you aint fit for sich as we." This caused angry words, and Nancy was solemnly requested "to draw it mild, like a good soul."

As the morning twilight came on, the paved court was crowded with purchasers. The sheds and shops at the end of the market grew every moment more distinct, and a railway-van, laden with carrots, came rumbling into the yard. The pigeons, too, began to fly on to the sheds, or walk about the paving-stones, and the gas-man came round with his ladder to turn out the lamps. Then every one was pushing about; the children crying, as their naked feet were trodden upon, and the women hurrying off, with their baskets or shawls filled with cresses, and the bunch of rushes in their hands. In one corner of the market, busily tying up their bunches, were three or four girls seated on the stones, with their legs curled up under them, and the ground near them was green with the leaves they had thrown away. A saleswoman, seeing me looking at the group, said to me, "Ah! you should come here of a summer's morning, and then you'd see 'em, sitting tying up, young and old, upwards of a hundred poor things as thick as crows in a ploughed field."

As it grew late, and the crowd had thinned; none but the very poorest of the cress-sellers were left. Many of these had come without money, others had their halfpence tied up carefully in their shawl-ends, as though they dreaded the loss. A sickly-looking boy, of about five, whose head just reached above the hampers, now crept forward, treading with his blue naked feet over the cold stones as a cat does over wet ground. At his elbows and knees, his skin showed in gashes through the rents in his clothes, and he looked so frozen, that the buxom saleswoman called to him, asking if his mother had gone home. The boy knew her well, for without answering her question, he went up to her, and, as he stood shivering on one foot, said, "Give us a few old cresses, Jinney," and in a few minutes was running off with a green bundle under his arm. All of the saleswomen

THE GROUNDSEL MAN.

"Chick-weed and Grun-sell!"

[From a Daguerreotype by BEARD.]

seemed to be of kindly natures, for at another stall an old dame, whose rags seemed to be beyond credit, was paying for some cresses she had long since been trusted with, and excusing herself for the time that had passed since the transaction. As I felt curious on the point of the honesty of the poor, I asked the saleswoman when she was alone, whether they lost much by giving credit. "It couldn't be much," she answered, "if they all of them decamped." But they were generally honest, and paid back, often reminding her of credit given that she herself had forgotten. Whenever she lost anything, it was by the very very poor ones; "though it aint their fault, poor things," she added in a kindly tone, "for when they keeps away from here, it's either the workhouse or the churchyard as stops them."

As you walk home—although the apprentice is knocking at the master's door—the little water-cress girls are crying their goods in every street. Some of them are gathered round the pumps, washing the leaves and piling up the bunches in their baskets, that are tattered and worn as their own clothing; in some of the shallows the holes at the bottom have been laced up or darned together with rope and string, or twigs and split laths have been fastened across; whilst others are lined with oilcloth, or old pieces of sheet-tin. Even by the time the cress-market is over, it is yet so early that the maids are beating the mats in the road, and mechanics, with their tool-baskets swung over their shoulders, are still hurrying to their work. To visit Farringdon-market early on a Monday morning, is the only proper way to judge of the fortitude and courage and perseverance of the poor. As Douglas Jerrold has beautifully said, "there is goodness, like wild honey, hived in strange nooks and corners of the earth." These poor cress-sellers belong to a class so poor that their extreme want alone would almost be an excuse for theft, and they can be trusted paying the few pence they owe even though they hunger for it. It must require no little energy of conscience on the part of the lads to make them resist the temptations around them, and refuse the luring advice of the young thieves they meet at the low lodging-house. And yet they prefer the early rising—the walk to market with naked feet along the cold stones—the pinched meal—and the day's hard labour to earn the few halfpence—to the thief's comparatively easy life. The heroism of the unknown poor is a thing to set even the dullest marvelling, and in no place in all London is the virtue of the humblest—both young and old—so conspicuous as among the watercress-buyers at Farringdon-market.

OF THE STREET-SELLERS OF WATER-CRESS.

THE dealers in water-cresses are generally very old or very young people, and it is a trade greatly in the hands of women. The cause of this is, that the children are sent out by their parents "to get a loaf of bread somehow" (to use the words of an old man in the trade), and the very old take to it because they are unable to do hard labour, and they strive to keep away from the workhouse—("I'd do anything before I'd go there—sweep the crossings, or anything: but I should have had to have gone to the house before, if it hadn't been for my wife. I'm sixty-two," said one who had been sixteen years at the trade). The old people are both men and women. The men have been sometimes one thing, and sometimes another. "I've been a porter myself," said one, "jobbing about in the markets, or wherever I could get a job to do. Then there's one old man goes about selling water-cresses who's been a seafaring man; he's very old, he is—older than what I am, sir. Many a one has been a good mechanic in his younger days, only he's got too old for labour. The old women have, many of them, been laundresses, only they can't now do the work, you see, and so they're glad to pick up a crust anyhow. Nelly, I know, has lost her husband, and she hasn't nothing else but her few creases to keep her. She's as good, honest, hard-working a creature as ever were, for what she can do—poor old soul! The young people are, most of them, girls. There are some boys, but girls are generally put to it by the poor people. There's Mary Macdonald, she's about fourteen. Her father is a bricklayer's labourer. He's an Englishman, and he sends little Mary out to get a halfpenny or two. He gets sometimes a couple of days' work in the week. He don't get more now, I'm sure, and he's got three children to keep out of that; so all on 'em that can work are obligated to do something. The other two children are so small they can't do nothing yet. Then there's Louisa; she's about twelve, and she goes about with creases like I do. I don't think she's got ne'er a father. I know she's a mother alive, and *she* sells creases like her daughter. The mother's about fifty odd, I dare say. The sellers generally go about with an arm-basket, like a greengrocer's at their side, or a 'shallow' in front of them; and plenty of them carry a small tin tray before them, slung round their neck. Ah! it would make your heart ache if you was to go to Farringdon-market early, this cold weather, and see the poor little things there without shoes and stockings, and their feet quite blue with the cold—oh, that they are, and many on 'em don't know how to set one foot before the t'other, poor things' You would say they wanted something give to 'em."

The small tin tray is generally carried by the young children. The cresses are mostly bought in Farringdon-market: "The usual time to go to the market is between five and six in the morning, and from that to seven," said one informant; "myself, I am generally down in the market by five. I was there this morning at five, and bitter cold it was, I give you my word. We poor old people feel it dreadful. Years ago I didn't mind cold, but I feel it now cruel bad, to be sure. Sometimes, when I'm turning up my things, I don't hardly know whether I've got 'em in my hands or not; can't even pick off a dead leaf. But that's nothing to the poor little things without shoes. Why, bless you, I've seen 'em stand and cry two and three together, with the cold. Ah! my heart has ached for 'em over and over again. I've said to 'em, I wonder why your mother sends you out, that I have; and they said they was obligated to try and get a penny for breakfast. We buy the water-cresses by the 'hand.' One hand will make about five halfpenny bundles. There's more call for 'em in the spring of the year than what there is in the winter. Why, they're reckoned good for sweetening the blood in the spring; but, for my own eating, I'd sooner have the crease in the winter than I would have it in the spring of the year. There's an old woman sits in Farringdon-market, of the name of Burrows, that's sot there twenty-four years, and she's been selling out creases to us all that time.

"The sellers goes to market with a few pence. I myself goes down there and lays out sometimes my 4*d.*; that's what I laid out this morning. Sometimes I lay out only 2*d.* and 3*d.*, according as how I has the halfpence in my pocket. Many a one goes down to the market with only three halfpence, and glad to have that to get a halfpenny, or anything, so as to earn a mouthful of bread—a bellyful that they can't get no how. Ah, many a time I walked through the streets, and picked a piece of bread that the servants chucked out of the door—may be to the birds. I've gone and picked it up when I've been right hungry. Thinks I, I can eat that as well as the birds. None of the sellers ever goes down to the market with less than a penny. They won't make less than a pennorth, that's one 'hand,' and if the little thing sells that, she won't earn more than three halfpence out of it. After they have bought the creases they generally take them to the pump to wet them. I generally pump upon mine in Hatton-garden. It's done to make them look nice and fresh all the morning, so that the wind shouldn't make them flag. You see they've been packed all night in the hamper, and they get dry. Some ties them up in ha'porths as they walks along. Many of them sit down on the steps of St. Andrew's Church and make them up into bunches. You'll see plenty of them there of a morning between five and six. Plenty, poor little dear souls, sitting there," said the old man to me. There the hand is parcelled out into five halfpenny bunches. In the summer the dealers often go to market and lay out as much as 1*s.* "On Saturday morning, this time of year, I buys as many as nine hands—there's more call for 'em on Saturday and Sunday morning than on any other days; and we always has to buy on Saturdays what we want for Sundays—there an't no market on that day, sir. At the market sufficient creases are bought by the sellers for the morning and afternoon as well. In the morning some begin crying their creases through

the streets at half-past six, and others about seven. They go to different parts, but there is scarcely a place but what some goes to—there are so many of us now—there's twenty to one to what there used to be. Why, they're so thick down at the market in the summer time, that you might bowl balls along their heads, and all a fighting for the creases. There's a regular scramble, I can assure you, to get at 'em, so as to make a halfpenny out of them. I should think in the spring mornings there's 400 or 500 on 'em down at Farringdon-market all at one time—between four and five in the morning—if not more than that, and as fast as they keep going out, others keep coming in. I think there is more than a thousand, young and old, about the streets in the trade. The working classes are the principal of the customers. The bricklayers, and carpenters, and smiths, and plumbers, leaving work and going home to breakfast at eight o'clock, purchase the chief part of them. A great many are sold down the courts and mews, and bye streets, and very few are got rid of in the squares and the neighbourhood of the more respectable houses. Many are sold in the principal thoroughfares—a large number in the City. There is a man who stands close to the Post-office, at the top of Newgate-street, winter and summer, who sells a great quantity of bunches every morning. This man frequently takes between 4*s.* and 5*s.* of a winter's morning, and about 10*s.* a day in the summer." "Sixteen years ago," said the old man who gave me the principal part of this information, "I could come out and take my 18*s.* of a Saturday morning, and 5*s.* on a Sunday morning as well; but now I think myself very lucky if I can take my 1*s.* 3*d.*, and it's only on two mornings in the week that I can get that." The hucksters of watercresses are generally an honest, industrious, striving class of persons. The young girls are said to be well-behaved, and to be the daughters of poor struggling people. The old men and women are persons striving to save themselves from the workhouse. The old and young people generally travel nine and ten miles in the course of the day. They start off to market at four and five, and are out on their morning rounds from seven till nine, and on their afternoon rounds from half-past two to five in the evening. They travel at the rate of two miles an hour. "If it wasn't for my wife, I must go to the workhouse outright," said the old watercress man. "Ah, I do'nt know what I should do without her, I can assure you. She earns about 1*s.* 3*d.* a day. She takes in a little washing, and keeps a mangle. When I'm at home I turn the mangle for her. The mangle is my own. When my wife's mother was alive she lent us the money to buy it, and as we earnt the money we paid her back so much a week. It is *that* what has kept us together, or else we shouldn't have been as we are. The mangle we give 50*s.* for, and it brings us in now 1*s.* 3*d.* a day with the washing. My wife is younger than I am. She is about thirty-five years old. We have got two children. One is thirteen and the other fifteen. They've both got learning, and are both in situations. I always sent 'em to school. Though I can't neither read nor write myself, I wished to make them some little scholards. I paid a penny a week for 'em at the school. Lady M—— has always given me my Christmas dinner for the last five years, and God bless her for it—that I *do* say indeed."

WATERCRESS GIRL.

The little watercress girl who gave me the following statement, although only eight years of age, had entirely lost all childish ways, and was, indeed, in thoughts and manner, a woman. There was something cruelly pathetic in hearing this infant, so young that her features had scarcely formed themselves, talking of the bitterest struggles of life, with the calm earnestness of one who had endured them all. I did not know how to talk with her. At first I treated her as a child, speaking on childish subjects; so that I might, by being familiar with her, remove all shyness, and get her to narrate her life freely. I asked her about her toys and her games with her companions; but the look of amazement that answered me soon put an end to any attempt at fun on my part. I then talked to her about the parks, and whether she ever went to them. "The parks!" she replied in wonder, "where are they?" I explained to her, telling her that they were large open places with green grass and tall trees, where beautiful carriages drove about, and people walked for pleasure, and children played. Her eyes brightened up a little as I spoke; and she asked, half doubtingly, "Would they let such as me go there—just to look?" All her knowledge seemed to begin and end with watercresses, and what they fetched. She knew no more of London than that part she had seen on her rounds, and believed that no quarter of the town was handsomer or pleasanter than it was at Farringdon-market or at Clerkenwell, where she lived. Her little face, pale and thin with privation, was wrinkled where the dimples ought to have been, and she would sigh frequently. When some hot dinner was offered to her, she would not touch it, because, if she eat too much, "it made her sick," she said; "and she wasn't used to meat, only on a Sunday."

The poor child, although the weather was severe, was dressed in a thin cotton gown, with a threadbare shawl wrapped round her shoulders. She wore no covering to her head, and the long rusty hair stood out in all directions. When she walked she shuffled along, for fear that the large carpet slippers that served her for shoes should slip off her feet.

"I go about the streets with water-creases, crying, 'Four bunches a penny, water-creases.' I am just eight years old—that's all, and I've a big sister, and a brother and a sister younger than I am. On and off, I've been very near a twelvemonth in the streets. Before that, I had to take care of a baby for my aunt. No, it wasn't heavy—it was only two months old; but I minded it for ever such a time—till it could walk. It was a very nice little baby, not a very pretty one; but, if I touched it under the chin, it would laugh. Before I had the baby, I used to help mother, who was in the fur trade; and, if there was any slits in the fur, I'd sew them up. My mother learned me to needle-work and to knit when I was about five. I used to go to school, too; but I wasn't there long. I've forgot all about it now, it's such a time ago; and mother took me away because the master whacked me, though the missus use'n't to never touch me. I didn't like him at all. What do you think? he hit me three times, ever so hard, across the face with his cane, and made me go dancing down stairs; and when mother saw the marks on my cheek, she went to blow him up, but she couldn't see him—he was afraid. That's why I left school.

"The creases is so bad now, that I haven't been out with 'em for three days. They're so cold, people won't buy 'em; for when I goes up to them, they say, 'They'll freeze our bellies.' Besides, in the market, they won't sell a ha'penny handful now—they're ris to a penny and tuppence. In summer there's lots, and 'most as cheap as dirt; but I have to be down at Farringdon-market between four and five, or else I can't get any creases, because everyone almost —especially the Irish—is selling them, and they're picked up so quick. Some of the saleswomen—we never calls 'em ladies—is very kind to us children, and some of them altogether spiteful. The good one will give you a bunch for nothing, when they're cheap; but the others, cruel ones, if you try to bate them a farden less than they ask you, will say, 'Go along with you, you're no good.' I used to go down to market along with another girl, as must be about fourteen, 'cos she does her back hair up. When we've bought a lot, we sits down on a door-step, and ties up the bunches. We never goes home to breakfast till we've sold out; but, if it's very late, then I buys a penn'orth of pudden, which is very nice with gravy. I don't know hardly one of the people, as goes to Farringdon, to talk to; they never speaks to me, so I don't speak to them. We children never play down there, 'cos we're thinking of our living. No; people never pities me in the street—excepting one gentleman, and he says, says he, 'What do you do out so soon in the morning?' but he gave me nothink —he only walked away.

"It's very cold before winter comes on reg'lar—specially getting up of a morning. I gets up in the dark by the light of the lamp in the court. When the snow is on the ground, there's no creases. I bears the cold—you must; so I puts my hands under my shawl, though it hurts 'em to take hold of the creases, especially when we takes 'em to the pump to wash 'em. No; I never see any children crying—it's no use.

"Sometimes I make a great deal of money.

One day I took 1s. 6d., and the creases cost 6d.; but it isn't often I get such luck as that. I oftener makes 3d. or 4d. than 1s.; and then I'm at work, crying, 'Creases, four bunches a penny, creases!' from six in the morning to about ten. What do you mean by mechanics?—I don't know what they are. The shops buys most of me. Some of 'em says, 'Oh! I ain't a-goin' to give a penny for these;' and they want 'em at the same price as I buys 'em at.

"I always give mother my money, she's so very good to me. She don't often beat me; but, when she do, she don't play with me. She's very poor, and goes out cleaning rooms sometimes, now she don't work at the fur. I ain't got no father, he's a father-in-law. No; mother ain't married again—he's a father-in-law. He grinds scissors, and he's very good to me. No; I dont mean by that that he says kind things to me, for he never hardly speaks. When I gets home, after selling creases, I stops at home. I puts the room to rights: mother don't make me do it, I does it myself. I cleans the chairs, though there's only two to clean. I takes a tub and scrubbing-brush and flannel, and scrubs the floor—that's what I do three or four times a week.

"I don't have no dinner. Mother gives me two slices of bread-and-butter and a cup of tea for breakfast, and then I go till tea, and has the same. We has meat of a Sunday, and, of course, I should like to have it every day. Mother has just the same to eat as we has, but she takes more tea—three cups, sometimes. No; I never has no sweet-stuff; I never buy none—I don't like it. Sometimes we has a game of 'honeypots' with the girls in the court, but not often. Me and Carry H—— carries the little 'uns. We plays, too, at 'kiss-in-the-ring.' I knows a good many games, but I don't play at 'em, 'cos going out with creases tires me. On a Friday night, too, I goes to a Jew's house till eleven o'clock on Saturday night. All I has to do is to snuff the candles and poke the fire. You see they keep their Sabbath then, and they won't touch anything; so they gives me my wittals and 1½d., and I does it for 'em. I have a reg'lar good lot to eat. Supper of Friday night, and tea after that, and fried fish of a Saturday morning, and meat for dinner, and tea, and supper, and I like it very well.

"Oh, yes; I've got some toys at home. I've a fire-place, and a box of toys, and a knife and fork, and two little chairs. The Jews gave 'em to me where I go to on a Friday, and that's why I said they was very kind to me. I never had no doll; but I misses little sister—she's only two years old. We don't sleep in the same room; for father and mother sleeps with little sister in the one pair, and me and brother and other sister sleeps in the top room. I always goes to bed at seven, 'cos I has to be up so early.

"I am a capital hand at bargaining—but only at buying watercreases. They can't take me in. If the woman tries to give me a small handful of creases, I says, 'I ain't a goin' to have that for a ha'porth,' and I go to the next basket, and so on, all round. I know the quantities very well. For a penny I ought to have a full market hand, or as much as I could carry in my arms at one time, without spilling. For 3d. I has a lap full, enough to earn about a shilling; and for 6d. I gets as many as crams my basket. I can't read or write, but I knows how many pennies goes to a shilling, why, twelve, of course, but I don't know how many ha'pence there is, though there's two to a penny. When I've bought 3d. of creases, I ties 'em up into as many little bundles as I can. They must look biggish, or the people won't buy them, some puffs them out as much as they'll go. All my money I earns I puts in a club and draws it out to buy clothes with. It's better than spending it in sweet-stuff, for them as has a living to earn. Besides it's like a child to care for sugar-sticks, and not like one who's got a living and vittals to earn. I aint a child, and I shan't be a woman till I'm twenty, but I'm past eight, I am. I don't know nothing about what I earns during the year, I only know how many pennies goes to a shilling, and two ha'pence goes to a penny, and four fardens goes to a penny. I knows, too, how many fardens goes to tuppence — eight. That's as much as I wants to know for the markets."

The market returns I have obtained show the following result of the quantity vended in the streets, and of the receipts by the cress-sellers:—

A TABLE SHOWING THE QUANTITY OF WATER-CRESSES SOLD WHOLESALE THROUGHOUT THE YEAR IN LONDON, WITH THE PROPORTION RETAILED IN THE STREETS.

Market.	Quantity sold wholesale.	Proportion retailed in the Streets.
Covent Garden	1,578,000 bunches	one-eighth.
Farringdon .	12,960,000 ,,	one-half.
Borough . .	180,000 ,,	one-half.
Spitalfields .	180,000 ,,	one-half.
Portman . .	60,000 ,,	one-third.
Total . .	14,958,000 ,,	

From this sale the street cress-sellers receive:—

	Bunches.		Receipts
Farringdon .	6,480,000	⅛d. per bunch	£13,500
Covent Garden	16,450	,,	34
Borough . .	90,000	,,	187
Spitalfields .	90,000	,,	187
Portman . .	20,000	,,	41
			£13,949

The discrepancy in the quantity sold in the respective markets is to be accounted for by the fact, that Farringdon is the water-cress market to which are conveyed the qualities, large-leaved and big-stalked, that suit the street-folk. Of this description of cress they purchase one-half of all that is sold in Farringdon; of the finer, and smaller, and brown-leaved cress sold there, they purchase hardly any. At Covent Garden only the finer sorts of cress are in demand, and, consequently, the itinerants buy only an eighth in that market, and they are not encouraged there. They purchase half the quantity in the Borough, and the same in Spital-fields, and a third at Portman. I have before mentioned that 500 might be taken as the number supported by the sale of "creases;" that is, 500 families, or at least 1,000 individuals. The total amount received is nearly 14,000*l.*, and this apportioned among 1,000 street-sellers, gives a weekly receipt of 5*s.* 5*d.*, with a profit of 3*s.* 3*d.* per individual.

The discrepancy is further accounted for because the other market salesmen buy cresses at Farringdon; but I have given under the head of Farringdon *all* that is sold to those other markets to be disposed to the street-sellers, and the returns from the other markets are of the cresses carried *direct* there, apart from any purchases at Farringdon.

OF GROUNDSEL AND CHICKWEED SELLERS.

ON a former occasion (in the *Morning Chronicle*) I mentioned that I received a letter informing me that a woman, residing in one of the courts about Saffron-hill, was making braces, and receiving only 1*s.* for four dozen of them. I was assured she was a most deserving character, strictly sober, and not receiving parochial relief. "Her husband," my informant added, "was paralysed, and endeavoured to assist his family by gathering green food for birds. They are in deep distress, but their character is irreproachable." I found the couple located up a court, the entrance to which was about as narrow as the opening to a sentry-box, and on each side lolled groups of labourers and costermongers, with short black pipes in their mouths. As I dived into the court, a crowd followed me to see whither I was going. The brace-maker lived on the first floor of a crazy, fœtid house. I ascended the stairs, and the banisters, from which the rails had all been purloined, gave way in my hands. I found the woman, man, and their family busy at their tea-dinner. In a large broken chair, beside the fire-place, was the old paralysed man, dressed in a ragged greasy fustian coat, his beard unshorn, and his hair in the wildest disorder. On the edge of the bed sat a cleanly looking woman, his wife, with a black apron on. Standing by the table was a blue-eyed laughing and shoeless boy, with an old camlet cape pinned over his shoulders. Next him was a girl in a long grey pinafore, with her hair cut close to her head, with the exception of a few locks in front, which hung down over her forehead like a dirty fringe. On a chair near the window stood a basket half full of chickweed and groundsel, and two large cabbages. There was a stuffed linnet on the

mantel-piece and an empty cage hanging outside the window. In front of the window-sill was the small imitation of a gate and palings, so popular among the workpeople. On the table were a loaf, a few mugs of milkless tea, and a small piece of butter in a saucer. I had scarcely entered when the mother began to remove the camlet cape from the boy's shoulders, and to slip a coarse clean pinafore over his head instead. At present I have only to deal with the trade of the husband, who made the following statement:

"I sell chickweed and grunsell, and turfs for larks. That's all I sell, unless it's a few nettles that's ordered. I believe they're for tea, sir. I gets the chickweed at Chalk Farm. I pay nothing for it. I gets it out of the public fields. Every morning about seven I goes for it. The grunsell a gentleman gives me leave to get out of his garden: that's down Battle-bridge way, in the Chalk-road, leading to Holloway. I gets there every morning about nine. I goes there straight. After I have got my chickweed, I generally gathers enough of each to make up a dozen halfpenny bunches. The turfs I buys. A young man calls here with them. I pay 2*d.* a dozen for 'em to him. He gets them himself. Sometimes he cuts 'em at Kilburn Wells; and Notting-hill he goes to sometimes, I believe. He hires a spring barrow, weekly, to take them about. He pays 4*d.* a day, I believe, for the barrow. He sells the turfs to the bird-shops, and to such as me. He sells a few to some private places. I gets the nettles at Highgate. I don't do much in the nettle line—there ain't much call for it. After I've gathered my things I puts them in my basket, and slings 'em at my back, and starts round London. Low Marrabun I goes to always of a Saturday and Wednesday. I goes to St. Pancras on a Tuesday. I visit Clerkenwell, and Russell-square, and round about there, on a Monday. I goes down about Covent-garden and the Strand on a Thursday. I does High Marrabun on a Friday, because I aint able to do so much on that day, for I gathers my stuff on the Friday for Saturday. I find Low Marrabun the best of my beats. I cry 'chickweed and grunsell' as I goes along. I don't say 'for young singing birds.' It is usual, I know, but I never did. I've been at the business about eighteen year. I'm out in usual till about five in the evening. I never stop to eat. I'm walking all the time. I has my breakfast afore I starts, and my tea when I comes home." Here the woman shivered. I turned round and found the fire was quite out. I asked them whether they usually sat without one. The answer was, "We most generally raise a pennyworth, some how, just to boil the kettle with." I inquired whether she was cold, and she assured me she wasn't. "It was the blood," she said, "that ran through her like ice sometimes." "I am a walking ten hours every day—wet or dry," the man continued. "I don't stand nice much about that. I can't go much above one mile and a half an hour, owing to my right side being paralysed. My leg and foot and all is quite dead. I goes with a stick." [The wife brought the stick out from a corner of the room to show me. It was an old peculiarly carved one, with a bird rudely cut out of wood for the handle, and a snake twisting itself up the stick.] " I walk fifteen miles every day of my life, that I do—quite that—excepting Sunday, in course. I generally sell the chickweed and grunsell and turfs, all to the houses, not to the shops. The young man as cut the turf gathers grunsell as well for the shops. They're tradespeople and gentlefolks' houses that I sells to—such as keeps canaries, or goldfinches, or linnets. I charge ½d. a bunch for chickweed and grunsell together. It's the regular charge. The nettles is ordered in certain quantities ; I don't get them unless they're ordered : I sells these in three-penn'orths at a time. Why, Saturday is my best day, and that's the reason why I can't spare time to gather on that day. On Saturday I dare say I gets rid on two dozen bunches of chickweed and grunsell. On the other days, sometimes, I goes out and don't sell above five or six bunches ; at other times I get rid on a dozen ; that I call a tidy day's work for any other day but a Saturday, and some days I don't sell as much as a couple of bunches in the whole day. Wednesday is my next best day after Saturday. On a Wednesday, sometimes, I sell a dozen and a half. In the summer I does much better than in winter. They gives it more to the birds then, and changes it oftener. I've seed a matter of eight or nine people that sell chickweed and grunsell like myself in the fields where I goes to gather it. They mostly all goes to where I do to get mine. They are a great many that sells grunsell about the streets in London, like I do. I dare say there is a hundred, and far more nor that, taking one place with another. I takes my nettles to ladies' houses. They considers the nettles good for the blood, and drinks 'em at tea, mostly in the spring and autumn. In the spring I generally sells three threepenn' orths of 'em a week, and in the autumn about two threepenn'orths. The ladies I sell the nettles to are mostly sickly, but sometimes they aint, and has only a breaking out in the skin, or in their face. The nettles are mostly taken in Low Marrabun. I gathers more than all for Great Titchfield-street. The turfs I sell mostly in London-street, in Marrabun and John-street, and Carburton-street, and Portland-street, and Berners, and all about there. I sells about three dozen of turfs a week. I sells them at three and four a penny. I charges them at three a penny to gentlefolks and four a penny to tradespeople. I pays 2d. a dozen for 'em and so makes from 1d. to 2d. a dozen out of 'em. I does trifling with these in the winter—about two dozen a week, but always three dozen in the summer. Of the chickweed and grunsell I sells from six to seven dozen bunches a week in the summer, and about four or five dozen bunches in the winter. I sells

mostly to regular customers, and a very few to chance ones that meet me in the street. The chance customers come mostly in the summer times. Altogether I should say with my regular and chance customers I make from 4s. to 5s. a week in the summer, and from 3s. to 4s. in the winter. That's as near as I can tell. Last Monday I was out all day, and took 1½d. ; Tuesday I took about 5½d. ; Wednesday I got 9½d.; Thursday I can't hardly recollect, not to tell the truth about it. But oh, dear me, yes I wasn't allowed to go out on that day. We was given to understand nothing was allowed to be sold on that day. They told us it were the Thanksgiving-day. I was obliged to fast on that day. We did have a little in the morning, a trifle, but not near enough. Friday I came home with nigh upon 6d., and Saturday I got 1s., and 3d. after when I went out at night. I goes into Leather-lane every Saturday night, and stands with my basket there, so that altogether, last week I made 3s. 1½d. But that was a slack week with me, owing to my having lost Thursday. If it hadn't been for that I should have made near upon 4s. We felt the loss very severely. Prices have come down dreadful with us. The same bunches as I sell now for ½d. I used to get 1d. for nine or ten years ago. I dare say I could earn then, take one day with another, such a thing as 7s. a week, summer and winter through. There's so many at it now to what there was afore, that it's difficult to get a living, and the ladies are very hard with a body. They tries to beat me down, and particular in the matter of turfs. They tell me they can buy half-a-dozen for 1d., so I'm obligated to let 'em have three or four. There's a many women at the business. I hardly know which is the most, men or women. There's pretty nigh as much of one as the other, I think. I am a bed-sacking weaver by trade. When I worked at it I used to get 15s. a week regularly. But I was struck with paralysis nearly nineteen years ago, and lost the use of all one side, so I was obleeged to turn to summut else. Another grunseller told me on the business, and what he got, and I thought I couldn't do no better. That's a favourite linnet. We had that one stuffed it for me. A young man that I knew stuffed it for me. I was very sorry when the poor thing died. I've got another little linnet up there." " I'm particular fond of little birds," said the wife. " I never was worse off than I am now. I pays 2s. a week rent, and we has, take one time with another, about 3s. for the four of us to subsist upon for the whole seven days ; yes, that, take one time with another, is generally what I do have. We very seldom has any meat. This day week we got a pound of pieces. I gave 4d. for 'em. Everything that will pledge I've got in pawn. I've been obliged to let them go. I can't exactly say how much I've got in pledge, but you can see the tickets." [The wife brought out a tin box full of duplicates. They were for the usual articles—coats, shawls, shirts, sheets,

handkerchiefs, indeed almost every article of
wearing-apparel and bedding. The sums lent
were mostly 6*d.* and 9*d.*, while some ran as high
as 2*s.* The dates of many were last year, and
these had been backed for three months.]
" I've been paying interest for many of the
things there for seven years. I pay for the
backing 2½*d.*, that is 1*d.* for the backing, and
1½*d.* for the three months' interest. I pay 6*d.* a
year interest on every one of the tickets. If its
only 3*d.*, I have to pay ½*d.* a month interest just
the same, but nothing for the ticket when we
put it in." The number of duplicates was 26,
and the gross sum amounted to 1*l.* 4*s.* 8*d.* One
of the duplicates was for 4*d.*; nine were for 6*d.*,
two for 9*d.*, nine were for 1*s.*, two for 1*s.* 6*d.*,
one for 1*s.* 3*d.*, one for 1*s.* 7*d.* and two for 2*s.*
" The greatest comfort I should like to have
would be something more on our beds. We
lay dreadful cold of a night, on account of
being thin clad. I have no petticoats at all.
We have no blankets—of late years I haven't
had any. The warm clothing would be the
greatest blessing I could ask. I'm not at all
discontented at my lot. That wouldn't mend
it. We strive and do the best we can, and may
as well be contented over it. I think its God's
will we should be as we are. Providence is
kind to me, even badly off as we are. I know
it's all for the best."
There are no "pitches," or stands, for the
sale of groundsel in the streets; but, from the
best information I could acquire, there are now
1,000 itinerants selling groundsel, each person
selling, as an average, 18 bunches a day. We
thus have 5,616,000 bunches a year, which, at
½*d.* each, realise 11,700*l.*—about 4*s.* 2*d.* per week
per head of sellers of groundsel. The "oldest
hand" in the trade is the man whose statement
and likeness I give. The sale continues
through the year, but "the groundsel" season
extends from April to September; in those
months 24 bunches, per individual seller, is the
extent of the traffic, in the other months half
that quantity, giving the average of 18 bunches.
The capital required for groundsel-selling is
4*d.* for a brown wicker-basket; leather strap to
sling it from the shoulder, 6*d.*; in all, 10*d.* No
knife is necessary; they pluck the groundsel.
Chickweed is only sold in the summer, and is
most generally mixed with groundsel and plantain. The chickweed and plantain, together, are
but half the sale of groundsel, and that only for
five months, adding, to the total amount, 2,335*l.*
But this adds little to the profits of the regular
itinerants; for, when there is the best demand,
there are the greatest number of sellers, who in
winter seek some other business. The total
amount of "green stuff" expended upon birds,
as supplied by the street-sellers, I give at the
close of my account of the trade of those purveyors.
Many of the groundsel and chickweed-sellers
—for the callings are carried on together—who
are aged men, were formerly brimstone-match
sellers, who " didn't like to take to the lucifers."

On the publication of this account in the
Morning Chronicle, several sums were forwarded
to the office of that journal for the benefit of
this family. These were the means of removing
them to a more comfortable home, of redeeming
their clothing, and in a measure realizing the
wishes of the poor woman.

OF TURF CUTTING AND SELLING.

A man long familiar with this trade, and who
knew almost every member of it individually,
counted for me 36 turf-cutters, to his own knowledge, and was confident that there were 40 turf-
cutters and 60 sellers in London; the addition
of the sellers, however, is but that of 10 women,
who assist their husbands or fathers in the street
sales,—but no women cut turf,—and of 10 men
who sell, but buy of the cutters.
The turf is simply a sod, but it is considered
indispensable that it should contain the leaves
of the "small Dutch clover," (the shamrock of
the Irish), the most common of all the trefoils.
The turf is used almost entirely for the food and
roosting-place of the caged sky-larks. Indeed
one turf-cutter said to me: "It's only people
that don't understand it that gives turf to other
birds, but of course if we're asked about it, we
say it's good for every bird, pigeons and chickens
and all; and very likely it is if they choose to
have it." The principal places for the cutting
of turf are at present Shepherd's Bush, Notting
Hill, the Caledonian Road, Hampstead, Highgate, Hornsey, Peckham, and Battersea. Chalk
Farm was an excellent place, but it is now
exhausted, "fairly flayed" of the shamrocks.
Parts of Camden Town were also fertile in turf,
but they have been built over. Hackney was a
district to which the turf-cutters resorted, but
they are now forbidden to cut sods there. Hampstead Heath used to be another harvest-field for
these turf-purveyors, but they are now prohibited
from "so much as sticking a knife into the
Heath;" but turf-cutting is carried on surreptitiously on all the outskirts of the Heath, for
there used to be a sort of feeling, I was told,
among some real Londoners that Hampstead
Heath yielded the best turf of any place. All
the "commons" and "greens," Paddington,
Camberwell, Kennington, Clapham, Putney, &c.
are also forbidden ground to the turf-cutter.
"O, as to the parks and Primrose Hill itself—
round about it's another thing—nobody," it was
answered to my inquiry, "ever thought of cutting their turf there. The people about, if they
was only visitors, wouldn't stand it, and right
too. I wouldn't, if I wasn't in the turf-cutting
myself."
The places where the turf is principally cut
are the fields, or plots, in the suburbs, in which
may be seen a half-illegible board, inviting the
attention of the class of speculating builders to
an "eligible site" for villas. Some of these
places are open, and have long been open, to
the road; others are protected by a few crazy
rails, and the turf-cutters consider that outside
the rails, or between them and the road, they

have a *right* to cut turf, unless forbidden by the police. The fact is, that they cut it on sufferance; but the policeman never interferes, unless required to do so by the proprietor of the land or his agent. One gentleman, who has the control over a considerable quantity of land "eligible" for building, is very inimical to the pursuits of the turf-cutters, who, of course, return his hostility. One man told me that he was required, late on a Saturday night, some weeks ago, to supply six dozen of turfs to a very respectable shopkeeper, by ten or eleven on the Sunday morning. The shopkeeper had an aristocratic connection, and durst not disappoint his customers in their demands for fresh turf on the Sunday, so that the cutter must supply it. In doing so, he encountered Mr. —— (the gentleman in question), who was exceedingly angry with him: "You d—d poaching thief!" said the gentleman, "if this is the way you pass your Sunday, I'll give you in charge." One turf-cutter, I was informed, had, within these eight years, paid 3*l.* 15*s.* fines for trespassing, besides losing his barrow, &c., on every conviction: "But he's a most outdacious fellor," I was told by one of his mates, "and won't mind spoiling anybody's ground to save hisself a bit of trouble. There's too many that way, which gives us a bad name." Some of the managers of the land to be built upon give the turf-cutters free leave to labour in their vocation; others sell the sods for garden-plots, or use them to set out the gardens to any small houses they may be connected with, and with them the turf-cutters have no chance of turning a sod or a penny.

I accompanied a turf-cutter, to observe the manner of his work. We went to the neighbourhood of Highgate, which we reached a little before nine in the morning. There was nothing very remarkable to be observed, but the scene was not without its interest. Although it was nearly the middle of January, the grass was very green and the weather very mild. There happened to be no one on the ground but my companion and myself, and in some parts of our progress nothing was visible but green fields with their fringe of dark-coloured leafless trees; while in other parts, which were somewhat more elevated, glimpses of the crowded roof of an omnibus, or of a line of fleecy white smoke, showing the existence of a railway, testified to the neighbourhood of a city; but no sound was heard except, now and then, a distant railway whistle. The turf-cutter, after looking carefully about him—the result of habit, for I was told afterwards, by the policeman, that there was no trespass—set rapidly to work. His apparatus was a sharp-pointed table-knife of the ordinary size, which he inserted in the ground, and made it rapidly describe a half-circle; he then as rapidly ran his implement in the opposite half-circle, flung up the sod, and, after slapping it with his knife, cut off the lower part so as to leave it flat—working precisely as does a butcher cutting out a joint or a chop, and reducing the fat. Small holes are thus left in the ground—

of such shape and size as if deep saucers were to be fitted into them—and in the event of a thunder-shower in droughty weather, they become filled with water, and have caused a puzzlement, I am told, to persons taking their quiet walk when the storm had ceased, to comprehend why the rain should be found to gather in little circular pools in some parts, and not in others.

The man I accompanied cut and shaped six of these turfs in about a minute, but he worked without intermission, and rather to show me with what rapidity and precision he could cut, than troubling himself to select what was saleable. After that we diverged in the direction of Hampstead; and in a spot not far from a temporary church, found three turf-cutters at work,—but they worked asunder, and without communication one with another. The turfs, as soon as they are cut and shaped, are thrown into a circular basket, and when the basket is full it is emptied on to the barrow (a costermonger's barrow), which is generally left untended at the nearest point: "We can trust one another, as far as I know," said one turf-man to me, "and nobody else would find it worth while to steal turfs." The largest number of men that my most intelligent informant had ever seen at work in one locality was fourteen, and that was in a field just about to be built over, and "where they have leave." Among the turf-purveyors there is no understanding as to where they are to "cut." Wet weather does not interfere with turf procuring; it merely adds to the weight, and consequently to the toil of drawing the barrow. Snow is rather an advantage to the street-seller, as purchasers are apt to fancy that if the storm continues, turfs will not be obtainable, and so they buy more freely. The turf-man clears the snow from the ground in any known locality—the cold pinching his ungloved hands—and cuts out the turf, "as green," I was told, "as an April sod." The weather most dreaded is that when hoar frost lies long and heavy on the ground, for the turf cut with the rime upon it soon turns black, and is unsaleable. Foggy dark weather is also prejudicial, "for then," one man said, "the days clips it uncommon short, and people won't buy by candlelight, no more will the shops. Birds has gone to sleep then, and them that's fondest on them says, 'We can get fresher turf to-morrow.'" The gatherers cannot work by moonlight; "for the clover leaves then shuts up," I was told by one who said he was a bit of a botanist, "like the lid of a box, and you can't tell them."

One of my informants told me that he cut 25 dozen turfs every Friday (the great working turf-day) of the year on an average (he sometimes cut on that day upwards of 30 dozen); 17 dozen on a Tuesday; and 6 dozen on the other days of the week, more or less, as the demand justified—but 6 dozen was an average. He had also cut a few turfs on a Sunday morning, but only at long intervals, sometimes only thrice a year. Thus one man will cut 2,496 dozen, or 29,952 turfs in a year, not reckoning the product of any Sunday. From the best information I could acquire, there seems no doubt but that one-half of the turf-cutters (20) exert a similar degree of industry to that detailed; and the other 20 procure a moiety of the quantity cut and disposed of by their stronger and more fortunate brethren. This gives an aggregate, for an average year, of 598,560 turfs, or including Sunday turf-cutting, of 600,000. Each turf is about 6 inches diameter at the least; so that the whole extent of turf cut for London birds yearly, if placed side by side, would extend fifty-six miles, or from London to Canterbury.

In wet weather, 6 dozen turfs weigh, on an average, 1 cwt.; in dry weather, 8 dozen weigh no more; if, therefore, we take 7 dozen as the usual hundred-weight, a turf-cutter of the best class carries, in basket-loads, to his barrow, and when his stock is completed, drags into town from the localities I have specified, upwards of 3½ cwt. every Friday, nearly 2½ every Tuesday, and about 7 cwt. in the course of a week; the smaller traders drag half the quantity,—and the total weight of turf disposed of for the cage-birds of London, every year, is 546 tons.

Of the supply of turf, obtained as I have described, at least three-fourths is sold to the bird-shops, who retail it to their customers. The price paid by these shopkeepers to the labourers for their turf trade is 2d. and 2½d. a dozen, but rarely 2½d. They retail it at from 3d. to 6d. a dozen, according to connection and locality. The remainder is sold by the cutters on their rounds from house to house, at two and three a penny.

None of the turf-cutters confine themselves to it. They sell in addition groundsel, chickweed, plaintain, very generally; and a few supply nettles, dandelion, ground-ivy, snails, worms, frogs, and toads. The sellers of groundsel and chickweed are far more numerous, as I have shown, than the turf-cutters—indeed many of them are incapable of cutting turf or of dragging the weight of the turfs.

OF THE EXPERIENCE AND CUSTOMERS OF A TURF-CUTTER.

A short but strongly-built man, of about thirty, with a very English face, and dressed in a smock-frock, wearing also very strong unblacked boots, gave me the following account:—

"My father," he said, "was in the Earl of ——'s service, and I was brought up to stable-work. I was employed in a large coaching inn, in Lancashire, when I was last employed in that way, but about ten years ago a railway line was opened, and the coaching was no go any longer; it hadn't a chance to pay, so the horses and all was sold, and I was discharged with a lot of others. I walked from Manchester to London—for I think most men when they don't know what in the world to do, come to London—and I lived a few months on what little money I had, and what I could pick up in an odd job about horses. I had some expectations when I came up that I might get something to do through my lord, or some of his people—they all knew me: but my lord was abroad, and his establishment wasn't in town, and I had to depend entirely on myself. I was beat out three or four times, and didn't know what to do, but somehow or other I got over it. At last—it's between eight and nine years ago—I was fairly beat out. I was taking a walk—I can't say just now in what way I went, for it was all one which way—but I remember I saw a man cutting turf, and I remembered then that a man that lived near me lived pretty middling by turf-cutting. So I watched how it was done, and then I inquired how I could get into it, and as I'd paid my way I could give reference to show I might be trusted; so I got a barrow on hire, and a basket, and bought a knife for 3d. at a marine-shop, and set to work. At first I only supplied shops, but in a little time I fell into a private round, and that pays better. I've been at it almost every day, I may say, ever since. My best customers are working people that's fond of birds; they're far the best. It's the ready penny with them, and no grumbling. I've lost money by trusting noblemen; of course I blame their servants. You'd be surprised, sir, to hear how often at rich folks' houses, when they've taken their turf or what they want, they'll take credit and say, ' O, I've got no change,' or ' I can't be bothered with ha'pence,' or ' you must call again.' There's one great house in Cavendish-square always takes a month's credit, and pays one month within another (pays the first month as the second is falling due), and not always that very regular. They can't know how poor men has to fight for a bit of bread. Some people are very particular about their turfs, and look very sharp for the small clover leaves. We never have turfs left on hand: in summer we water them to keep them fresh; in wet weather they don't require it; they'll keep without. I think I make on turf 9s. a week all the year round; the summer's half as good again as the winter. Supposing I make 3s. a week on groundsel, and chickweed, and snails, and other things, that's 12s.—but look you here, sir. I pay 3s. 6d. a week for my rent—it's a furnished room—and 1s. 6d. a week for my barrow; that's 5s. off the 12s.; and I've a wife and one little boy. My wife may get a day at least every week at charring; she has 1s. for it and her board. She helps me when she's not out, and if she is out, I sometimes have to hire a lad, so it's no great advantage the shilling a day. I've paid 1s. 6d. a week for my barrow—it's a very good and big one—for four years. Before that I paid 2s. a week. O yes, sir, I know very well, that at 1s. 6d. a week I've paid nearly 14l. for a barrow worth only 2l. 2s.; but I can't help it; I really can't. I've tried my hardest to get money to have one of my own, and to get a few sticks (furniture) of my own too. It's no use trying any more. If I have ever got a few shillings a-head, there's a pair of shoes wanted, or there's something else, or my wife has a fit of sickness, or my little boy has, or something's sure to happen that way, and it all goes. Last winter was a very hard time for people in my way, from hoar frost and fogs. I ran near 3*l.* into debt ; greater part of it for house-rent and my barrow ; the rest was small sums borrowed of shopkeepers that I served. I paid all up in the summer, but I'm now 14*s.* in debt for my barrow ; it always keeps me back ; the man that owns it calls every Sunday morning, but he don't press me, if I haven't money. I would get out of the life if I could, but will anybody take a groom out of the streets ? and I'm not master of anything but grooming. I can read and write. I was brought up a Roman Catholic, and was christened one. I never go to mass now. One gets out of the way of such things, having to fight for a living as I have. It seems like mocking going to chapel, when you're grumbling in your soul."

Of Plantain-Sellers.

Plantain is sold extensively, and is given to canaries, but water-cress is given to those birds more than any other green thing. It is the ripe seed, in a spike, of the "great" and the "ribbed" plantain. The green leaves of the last-mentioned plant used to be in demand as a styptick. Shenstone speaks of "plantain ribbed, that heals the reaper's wound." I believe that it was never sold in the streets of London. The most of the plantain is gathered in the brick-fields, wherever they are found, as the greater plantain, which gives three-fourths of the supply, loves an arid situation. It is sold in hands to he shops, about 60 "heads" going to a " hand," at a price, according to size, &c., from 1*d.* to 4*d.* On a private round, five or six are given for a halfpenny. It is, however, generally gathered and sold with chickweed, and along with chickweed I have shown the quantity used.

The money-value of the several kinds and quantities of "green-stuff" annually purchased in the streets of London is as follows :—

6,696,450 bunches of water-cresses, at ⅓*d.* per bunch		£13,949
5,616,000 „ groundsel, at ⅓*d.*		11,700
1,120,800 „ chickweed and plantain		2,335
660,000 turfs, at 2½*d.* per doz.		520
		28,504

Of the above amount, it may be said that upwards of 14,000*l.* are spent yearly on what may be called the bird-food of London.

OF THE STREET-SELLERS OF EATABLES AND DRINKABLES.

These dealers were, more numerous, even when the metropolitan population was but half its present extent. I heard several causes assigned for this,—such as the higher rate of earnings of the labouring people at that time, as well as the smaller number of shopkeepers who deal in such cheap luxuries as penny pies, and the fewer places of cheap amusement, such as the "penny gaffs." These places, I was told, "run away with the young people's pennies," which were, at one period, expended in the streets.

The class engaged in the manufacture, or in the sale, of these articles, are a more intelligent people than the generality of street-sellers. They have nearly all been mechanics who, from inability to procure employment at their several crafts—from dislike to an irksome and, perhaps, sedentary confinement—or from an overpowering desire "to be their own masters," have sought a livelihood in the streets. The purchase and sale of fish, fruit, or vegetables require no great training or deftness; but to make the dainties, in which street-people are critical, and to sell them at the lowest possible price, certainly requires some previous discipline to produce the skill to combine and the taste to please.

I may here observe, that I found it common enough among these street-sellers to describe themselves and their fraternity not by their names or callings, but by the article in which they deal. This is sometimes ludicrous enough : " Is the man you're asking about a pickled whelk, sir ?" was said to me. In answer to another inquiry, I was told, " Oh, yes, I know him—he's a sweet-stuff." Such ellipses, or abbreviations, are common in all mechanical or commercial callings.

Men and women, and most especially boys, purchase their meals day after day in the streets. The coffee-stall supplies a warm breakfast ; shell-fish of many kinds tempt to a luncheon ; hot-eels or pea-soup, flanked by a potato "all hot," serve for a dinner ; and cakes and tarts, or nuts and oranges, with many varieties of pastry, confectionary, and fruit, woo to indulgence in a dessert ; while for supper there is a sandwich, a meat pudding, or a " trotter."

The street provisions consist of cooked or prepared victuals, which may be divided into solids, pastry, confectionary, and drinkables. The "solids" however, of these three divisions, are such as only regular street-buyers consider to be sufficing for a substantial meal, for it will be seen that the comestibles accounted "good for dinner," are all of a *dainty*, rather than a solid character. Men whose lives, as I have before stated, are alternations of starvation and surfeit, love some easily-swallowed and comfortable food, better than the most approved substantiality of a dinner-table. I was told by a man, who was once foodless for thirty-eight hours, that in looking into the window of a cook-shop—he longed far more for a basin of soup than for a cut from the boiled round, or the roasted ribs, of beef. He felt a gnawing rather than a ravenous desire, and some tasty semi-liquid was the incessant object of his desires.

The solids then, according to street estimation, consist of hot-eels, pickled whelks, oysters, sheep's-trotters, pea-soup, fried fish, ham-sandwiches, hot green peas, kidney puddings, boiled meat puddings, beef, mutton, kidney, and eel pies, and baked potatos. In each of these provisions the street poor find a mid-day or midnight meal.

The pastry and confectionary which tempt the street eaters are tarts of rhubarb, currant, gooseberry, cherry, apple, damson, cranberry, and (so called) mince pies; plum dough and plum-cake; lard, currant, almond and many other varieties of cakes, as well as of tarts; gingerbread-nuts and heart-cakes; Chelsea buns; muffins and crumpets; "sweet stuff" includes the several kinds of rocks, sticks, lozenges, candies, and hard-bakes; the medicinal confectionary of cough-drops and horehound; and, lastly, the more novel and aristocratic luxury of street-ices; and strawberry cream, at 1*d.* a glass, (in Greenwich Park).

The drinkables are tea, coffee, and cocoa; ginger-beer, lemonade, Persian sherbet, and some highly-coloured beverages which have no specific name, but are introduced to the public as " cooling " drinks; hot elder cordial or wine ; peppermint water ; curds and whey ; water (as at Hampstead); rice milk ; and milk in the parks.

At different periods there have been attempts to introduce more substantial viands into the street provision trade, but all within these twenty years have been exceptional and unsuccessful. One man a few years back established a portable cook-shop in Leather-lane, cutting out portions of the joints to be carried away or eaten on the spot, at the buyer's option. But the speculation was a failure. Black puddings used to be sold, until a few years back, smoking from cans, not unlike potato cans, in such places as the New Cut; but the trade in these rather suspicious articles gradually disappeared.

Mr. Albert Smith, who is an acute observer in all such matters, says, in a lively article on the Street Boys of London :

" The kerb is his club, offering all the advantages of one of those institutions without any subscription or ballot. Had he a few pence, he might dine equally well as at Blackwall, and with the same variety of delicacies without going twenty yards from the pillars of St. Clement's churchyard. He might begin with a water *souchée* of eels, varying his first course with pickled whelks, cold fried flounders, or periwinkles. Whitebait, to be sure, he would find a difficulty in procuring, but as the more cunning gourmands do not believe these delicacies to be fish at all, but merely little bits of light pie-crust fried in grease ;—and as moreover, the brown bread and butter is after all the grand attraction,—the boy might soon find a substitute. Then would come the potatos, apparently giving out so much steam that the can which contains them seems in momentary danger of blowing up ; large, hot, mealy fellows, that prove how unfounded were the alarms of the bad-crop-ites; and he might next have a course of boiled feet of some animal or other, which he would be certain to find in front of the gin-shop. Cyder-cups perhaps he would not get; but there would be ' ginger-beer from the fountain, at 1*d.* per glass ;' and instead of mulled claret, he could indulge in hot elder cordial ; whilst for dessert he could calculate upon all the delicacies of the season, from the salads at the corner of Wych-street to the baked apples at Temple Bar. None of these things would cost more than a penny a piece ; some of them would be under that sum ; and since as at Verey's, and some other foreign restaurateurs, there is no objection to your dividing the "portions," the boy might, if he felt inclined to give a dinner to a friend, get off under 6*d.* There would be the digestive advantage too of moving leisurely about from one course to another ; and, above all, there would be no fee to waiters." After alluding to the former glories of some of the street-stands, more especially of the kidney pudding establishments which displayed rude transparencies, one representing the courier of St. Petersburg riding six horses at once for a kidney pudding, Mr. Smith continues,—" But of all these eating-stands the chief favourite with the boy is the potato-can. They collect around it as they would do on 'Change, and there talk over local matters, or discuss the affairs of the adjacent cab-stand, in which they are at times joined by the waterman whom they respect, more so perhaps than the policeman ; certainly more than they do the street-keeper, for him they especially delight to annoy, and they watch any of their fellows eating a potato, with a curiosity and an attention most remarkable, as if no two persons fed in the same manner, and they expected something strange or diverting to happen at every mouthful."

A gentleman, who has taken an artist's interest in all connected with the streets, and has been familiar with their daily and nightly aspect from the commencement of the present century, considers that the great change is not so much in what has ceased to be sold, but in the introduction of fresh articles into street-traffic—such as pine-apples and Brazil-nuts, rhubarb and cucumbers, ham-sandwiches, ginger-beer, &c. The coffee-stall, he represents, has but superseded the saloop-stall (of which I have previously spoken); while the class of street-customers who supported the saloop-dealer now support the purveyor of coffee. The *appearance* of the two stalls, however, seen before daybreak, with their respective customers, on a bleak winter's morning, was very different. Round the saloop-stall was a group—hardly discernible at a little distance in the dimly-lighted streets—the prominent figures being of two callings now extinct—the climbing-boy and the old hackney-coach-man.

The little sweep *would* have his saloop smoking hot—and there was the common appliance of a charcoal grate—regaling himself with the savoury steam until the mess was cool enough for him to swallow; whilst he sought to relieve his naked feet from the numbing effects of the cold by standing now on the right foot and now on the left, and swinging the other to and fro, until a change of posture was necessitated; his white teeth the while gleamed from his sooty visage as he gleefully licked his lips at the warm and oily breakfast.

The old hackney-coachman was wrapped up in a many-caped great coat, drab—when it left the tailor's hands some years before—but then worn and discoloured, and, perhaps, patched or tattered; its weight alone, however, communicated a sort of warmth to the wearer; his legs were closely and artistically "wisped" with hay-bands; and as he kept smiting his chest with his arms, "to keep the cold out," while his saloop was cooling, he would, in no very gentle terms, express his desire to add to its comforting influence the stimulant of a "flash of lightning," a "go of rum," or a "glass of max,"—for so a dram of neat spirit was then called.

The old watchman of that day, too, almost as heavily coated as the hackneyman, would sometimes partake of the street "Saloop-loop-loop! *Sa*-loop!" The woman of the town, in "looped and windowed raggedness," the outcast of the very lowest class, was at the saloop, as she is now and then at the coffee-stall, waiting until daylight drove her to her filthy lodging-house. But the climbing-boy has, happily, left no successor; the hackneyman has been succeeded by the jauntier cabman; and the taciturn old watchman by the lounging and trim policeman.

Another class of street-sellers, no longer to be seen, were the "barrow-women." They sold fruit of all kinds, little else, in very clean white barrows, and their fruit was excellent, and purchased by the wealthier classes. They were, for the most part, Irish women, and some were remarkable for beauty. Their dress was usually a good chintz gown, the skirt being tidily tucked or pinned up behind, "in a way," said one informant, "now sometimes seen on the stage when correctness of costume is cared for." These women were prosperous in their calling, nor was there any imputation on their chastity, as the mothers were almost always wives.

Concerning the bygone street-cries, I had also the following account from the personal observation of an able correspondent:—

"First among the old 'musical cries,' may be cited the 'Tiddy Doll!'—immortalised by Hogarth—then comes the last person, who,

with a fine bass voice, coaxed his customers to buy *sweets* with, 'Quack, quack, quack, quack! Browns, browns, browns! have you got any mouldy browns?' There was a man, too, who sold tripe, &c., in this way, and to some purpose; he was as fine a man as ever stepped, and his deep rich voice would ring through a whole street, 'Dog's-meat! cat's-meat! nice tripe! neat's feet! Come buy my trotters!' The last part would not have disgraced Lablache. He discovered a new way of pickling tripe—got on—made contracts for supplying the Navy during the war, and acquired a large property. One of our most successful artists is his grandson—Then there was that delight of our childhood—the eight o'clock 'Hot spiced gingerbread! hot spiced gingerbread! buy my spiced gingerbread! sm-o-o-king hot!'" Another informant remembered a very popular character (among the boys), whose daily cry was: "Hot spiced gingerbread nuts, nuts, nuts! If *one*'ll warm you, *wha-at*'ll a pound do?—*Wha-a-a-at*'ll a pound do?'" Gingerbread was formerly in much greater demand than it is now.

Of the Street-sellers of Pea-Soup and Hot Eels.

Two of the condiments greatly relished by the chilled labourers and others who regale themselves on street luxuries, are "pea-soup" and "hot eels." Of these tradesmen there may be 500 now in the streets on a Saturday. As the two trades are frequently carried on by the same party, I shall treat of them together. The greatest number of these stands is in Old-street, St. Luke's, about twenty. In warm weather these street-cooks deal only in "hot eels" and whelks; as the whelk trade is sometimes an accompaniment of the others, for then the soup will not sell. These dealers are stationary, having stalls or stands in the street, and the savoury odour from them attracts more hungry-looking gazers and longers than does a cook-shop window. They seldom move about, but generally frequent the same place. A celebrated dealer of this class has a stand in Clare-street, Clare-market, opposite a cat's-meat shop; he has been heard to boast, that he wouldn't sell his hands at the business if he didn't get his 30s. a day, and his 2l. 10s. on a Saturday. Half this amount is considered to be about the truth. This person has mostly all the trade for hot eels in the Clare-market district. There is another "hot eel purveyor" at the end of Windmill-street, Tottenham-court-road, that does a very good trade. It is thought that he makes about 5s. a day at the business, and about 10s. on Saturday. There was, before the removals, a man who came out about five every afternoon, standing in the New-cut, nearly opposite the Victoria Theatre, his "girl" always attending to the stall. He had two or three lamps with "hot eels" painted upon them, and a handsome stall. He was considered to make about 7s. a day by the sale of eels alone, but he dealt in fried fish and pickled whelks as well, and often had a pile of fried fish a foot high. Near the

Bricklayers' Arms, at the junction of the Old and New Kent-roads, a hot-eel man dispenses what a juvenile customer assured me was " as spicy as any in London, as if there was gin in it." But the dealer in Clare-market does the largest trade of all in the hot-eel line. He is " the head man." On one Saturday he was known to sell 100lbs. of eels, and on most Saturdays he will get rid of his four " draughts" of eels (a draught being 20lbs.) He and his son are dressed in Jenny Lind hats, bound with blue velvet, and both dispense the provisions, while the daughter attends to wash the cups. " On a Sunday, anybody," said my informant, " would think him the first nobleman or squire in the land, to see him dressed in his white hat, with black crape round it, and his drab palctot and mother-o'-pearl buttons, and black kid gloves, with the fingers too long for him."

I may add, that even the very poorest, who have only a halfpenny to spend, as well as those with better means, resort to the stylish stalls in preference to the others. The cels are all purchased at Billingsgate early in the morning. The parties themselves, or their sons or daughters, go to Billingsgate, and the watermen row them to the Dutch eel vessels moored off the market. The fare paid to the watermen is 1*d.* for every 10lbs. purchased and brought back in the boat, the passenger being gratis. These dealers generally trade on their own capital ; but when some have been having " a flare up," and have " broke down for stock," to use the words of my informant, they borrow 1*l.*, and pay it back in a week or a fortnight at the outside, and give 2*s.* for the loan of it. The money is usually borrowed of the barrow, truck, and basket-lenders. The amount of capital required for carrying on the business of course depends on the trade done ; but even in a small way, the utensils cost 1*l.* They consist of one fish-kettle and one soup-kettle, holding upon an average three gallons each ; besides these, five basins and five cups and ten spoons are required, also a washhand basin to wash the cups, basins, and spoons in, and a board and tressel on which the whole stand. In a large way, it requires from 3*l.* to 4*l.* to fit up a handsome stall. For this the party would have " two fine kettles," holding about four gallons each, and two patent cast-iron fireplaces (the 1*l.* outfit only admits of the bottoms of two tin saucepans being used as fireplaces, in which charcoal is always burning to keep the eels and soup hot ; the whelks are always eaten cold). The crockery and spoons would be in no way superior. A small dealer requires, over and above this sum, 10*s.* to go to market with and purchase stock, and the large dealer about 30*s.* The class of persons belonging to the business have either been bred to it, or taken to it through being out of work. Some have been disabled during their work, and have resorted to it to save themselves from the workhouse. The price of the hot eels is a halfpenny for five or seven pieces of fish, and three-parts of a cupfull of liquor. The charge for a half-

pint of pea-soup is a halfpenny, and the whelks are sold, according to the size, from a halfpenny each to three or four for the same sum. These are put out in saucers.

The eels are Dutch, and are cleaned and washed, and cut in small pieces of from a half to an inch each. [The daughter of one of my informants was busily engaged, as I derived this information, in the cutting of the fish. She worked at a blood-stained board, with a pile of pieces on one side and a heap of entrails on the other.] The portions so cut are then boiled, and the liquor is thickened with flour and flavoured with chopped parsley and mixed spices. It is kept hot in the streets, and served out, as I have stated, in halfpenny cupfulls, with a small quantity of vinegar and pepper. The best purveyors add a little butter. The street-boys are extravagant in their use of vinegar.

To dress a draught of eels takes three hours—to clean, cut them up, and cook them sufficiently ; and the cost is now 5*s.* 2*d.* (much lower in the summer) for the draught (the 2*d.* being the expense of " shoring"), 8*d.* for 4 lb. of flour to thicken the liquor, 2*d.* for the parsley to flavour it, and 1*s.* 6*d.* for the vinegar, spices, and pepper (about three quarts of vinegar and two ounces of pepper). This quantity, when dressed and seasoned, will fetch in halfpennyworths from 15*s.* to 18*s.* The profit upon this would be from 7*s.* to 9*s.* 6*d.* ; but the cost of the charcoal has to be deducted, as well as the salt used while cooking. These two items amount to about 5*d.*

The pea-soup consists of split peas, celery, and beef bones. Five pints, at 3½*d.* a quart, are used to every three gallons ; the bones cost 2*d.*, carrots 1*d.*, and celery ½*d.*—these cost 1*s.* 0¼*d.* ; and the pepper, salt, and mint, to season it, about 2*d.* This, when served in halfpenny basinfulls, will fetch from 2*s.* 3*d.* to 2*s.* 4*d.*, leaving 1*s.* 1*d.* profit. But from this the expenses of cooking must be taken ; so that the clear gain upon three gallons comes to about 11*d.* In a large trade, three kettles, or twelve gallons, of pea-soup will be disposed of in the day, and about four draughts, or 80 lbs., of hot eels on every day but Saturday,—when the quantity of eels disposed of would be about five draughts, or 100 lbs. weight, and about 15 gallons of pea-soup. Hence the profits of a good business in the hot-eel and pea-soup line united will be from 7*l.* to 7*l.* 10*s.* per week, or more. But there is only one man in London does this amount of business, or rather makes this amount of money. A small business will do about 15 lbs. of eels in the week, including Saturday, and about 12 gallons of soup. Sometimes credit is given for a halfpennyworth, or a pennyworth, at the outside ; but very little is lost from bad debts. Boys who are partaking of the articles will occasionally say to the proprietor of the stall, " Well, master, they *are* nice ; trust us another ha'-p'orth, and I'll pay you when I comes again ;" but they are seldom credited, for the stall-keepers know well they would never see them again. Very often the stock cooked is not disposed of, and then it is brought home and eaten by the family. The pea-soup will seldom keep a night, but what is left the family generally use for supper.

The dealers go out about half-past ten in the morning, and remain out till about ten at night. Monday is the next best day to Saturday. The generality of the customers are boys from 12 to 16 years of age. Newsboys are very partial to hot eels—women prefer the pea-soup. Some of the boys will have as many as six halfpenny cupfulls consecutively on a Saturday night; and some women will have three halfpenny basinsfull of soup. Many persons in the cold weather prefer the hot soup to beer. On wet, raw, chilly days, the soup goes off better than usual, and in fine weather there is a greater demand for the hot eels. One dealer assured me that he once *did* serve two gentlemen's servants with twenty-eight halfpenny cupfulls of hot eels one after another. One servant had sixteen, and the other twelve cupfulls, which they ate all at one standing; and one of these customers was so partial to hot eels, that he used to come twice a day every day for six months after that, and have eight cupfulls each day, four at noon and four in the evening. These two persons were the best customers my informant ever had. Servants, however, are not generally partial to the commodity. Hot eels are not usually taken for dinner, nor is pea-soup, but throughout the whole day, and just at the fancy of the passers-by. There are no shops for the sale of these articles. The dealers keep no accounts of what their receipts and expenditure are.

The best time of the year for the hot eels is from the middle of June to the end of August. On some days during that time a person in a small way of business will clear upon an average 1s. 6d. a day, on other days 1s.; on some days, during the month of August, as much as 2s. 6d. a day. Some cry out " Nice hot eels—nice hot eels!" or "Warm your hands and fill your bellies for a halfpenny." One man used to give his surplus eels, when he considered his sale completed on a night, to the poor creatures refused admission into a workhouse, lending them his charcoal fire for warmth, which was always returned to him. The poor creatures begged cinders, and carried the fire under a railway arch. The general rule, however, is for the dealer to be silent, and merely expose the articles for sale. " I likes better," said one man to me, " to touch up people's noses than their heyes or their hears." There are now in the trade almost more than can get a living at it, and their earnings are less than they were formerly. One party attributed this to the opening of a couple of penny-pie shops in his neighbourhood. Before then he could get 2s. 6d. a day clear, take one day with another; but since the establishment of the business in the penny-pie line he cannot take above 1s. 6d. a day clear. On the day the first of these pie-shops opened, it made as much as 10 lbs., or half a draught of eels, difference to him. There was

a band of music and an illumination at the pie-shop, and it was impossible to stand against *that*. The fashionable dress of the trade is the " Jenny Lind " or " wide-awake " hat, with a broad black ribbon tied round it, and a white apron and sleeves. The dealers usually go to Hampton-court or Greenwich on a fine Sunday. They are partial to the pit of Astley's. One of them told his waterman at Billingsgate the other morning that " he and his good lady had been werry amused with the osses at Hashley's last night."

OF THE EXPERIENCE OF A HOT-EEL AND PEA-SOUP MAN.

" I was a coalheaver," said one of the class to me, as I sat in his attic up a close court, watching his wife "thicken the liquor;" " I was a-going along the plank, from one barge to another, when the swell of some steamers throwed the plank off the ' horse,' and chucked me down, and broke my knee agin the side of the barge. Before that I was yarning upon an average my 20s. to 30s. a week. I was seven months and four days in King's College Hospital after this. I found they was a-doing me no good there, so I come out and went over to Bartholemy's Hospital. I was in there nineteen months altogether, and after that I was a month in Middlesex Hospital, and all on 'em turned me out oncurable. You see, the bone's decayed—four bits of bone have been taken from it. The doctor turned me out three times 'cause I wouldn't have it off. He asked my wife if she would give consent, but neither she nor my daughter would listen to it, so I was turned out on 'em all. How my family lived all this time it's hard to tell. My eldest boy did a little—got 3s. 6d. a week as an errand-boy, and my daughter was in service, and did a little for me; but that was all we had to live upon. There was six children on my hands, and however they *did* manage I can't say. After I came out of the hospital I applied to the parish, and was allowed 2s. 6d. a week and four loaves. But I was anxious to do something, so a master butcher, as I knowed, said he would get me ' a pitch ' (the right to fix a stall), if I thought I could sit at a stall and sell a few things. I told him I thought I could, and would be very thankful for it. Well, I had heard how the man up in the market was making a fortune at the hot-eel and pea-soup line. [A paviour as left his barrow and two shovels with me told me to-day, said the man, by way of parenthesis — 'that he knowed for a fact he was clearing 6l. a week regular.'] So I thought I'd have a touch at the same thing. But you see, I never could rise money enough to get sufficient stock to make a do of it, and never shall, I expect—it don't seem like it, however. I ought to have 5s. to go to market with to-morrow, and I ain't got above 1s. 6d.; and what's that for stock-money, I'd like to know? Well, as I was saying, the master butcher lent me 10s. to start in the line. He was the best friend I ever had. But I've never been able to do anything at it—not to say to get a living." "He can't carry anything now, sir," said his wife, as the old man strove to get the bellows to warm up the large kettle of pea-soup that was on the fire. "Aye, I can't go without my crutch. My daughter goes to Billingsgate for me. I've got nobody else; and she cuts up the eels. If it warn't for her I must give it up altogether, and go into the workhouse outright. I couldn't fetch 'em. I ought to have been out to-night by rights till ten, if I'd had anything to have sold. My wife can't do much; she's troubled with the rheumatics in her head and limbs." "Yes," said the old body, with a sigh, "I'm never well, and never shall be again, I know." "Would you accept on a drop of soup, sir?" asked the man; "you're very welcome, I can assure you. You'll find it very good, sir." I told him I had just dined, and the poor old fellow proceeded with his tale. "Last week I earned clear about 8s., and that's to keep six on us. I didn't pay no rent last week nor yet this, and I don't know when I shall again, if things goes on in this way. The week before there was a fast-day, and I didn't earn above 6s. that week, if I did that. My boy can't go to school. He's got no shoes nor nothing to go in. The girls go to the ragged-school, but we can't send them of a Sunday nowhere." "Other people can go," said one of the young girls nestling round the fire, and with a piece of sacking over her shoulders for a shawl—"them as has got things to go in; but mother don't like to let us go as we are." "She slips her mother's shoes on when she goes out. It would take 1l. to start me well. With that I could go to market, and buy my draught of eels a shilling cheaper, and I could afford to cut my pieces a little bigger; and people where they gets used well comes again—don't you see? I could have sold more eels if I'd had 'em to-day, and soup too. Why, there's four hours of about the best time to-night that I'm losing now 'cause I've nothing to sell. The man in the market can give more than we can. He gives what is called the lumping ha'p'orth—that is, seven or eight pieces; ah, that I daresay he does; indeed, some of the boys has told me he gives as many as eight pieces. And then the more eels you biles up, you see, the richer the liquor is, and in our little tin-pot way it's like biling up a great jint of meat in a hocean of water. In course we can't compete agin the man in the market, and so we're being ruined entirely. The boys very often comes and asks me if I've got a farden's-worth of heads. The woman at Broadway, they tells me, sells 'em at four a farden and a drop of liquor, but we chucks 'em away, there's nothing to eat on them; the boys though will eat anything."

In the hot-eel trade are now 140 vendors, each selling 6 lb. of eels daily at their stands; 60 sell 40 lb. daily; and 100 are itinerant,

selling 5 lb. nightly at the public-houses. The first mentioned take 2s. daily; the second 16s.; and the third 1s. 8d. This gives a street expenditure in the trade in hot eels of 19,448l. for the year.

To start in this business a capital is required after this rate:—stall 6s.; eel-kettle 3s. 6d.; jar 6d.; ladle 4d.; 12 cups 1s.; 12 spoons 1s.; stew-pan 2s.; chafing-dish 6d.; strainer 1s.; 8 cloths 2s. 8d.; a pair sleeves 4d.; apron 4d.; charcoal 2s. (4d. being an average daily consumption); ¼ cwt. coal 3½d.; ½ lb. butter (the weekly average) 4d.; 1 quartern flour 5d.; 4 oz. pepper 4d.; 1 quart vinegar 10d.; 1 lb. salt ½d.; 1 lb. candles for stall 6d.; parsley 3d.; stock-money 10s. In all 1l. 15s. In the course of a year the property which may be described as fixed, as in the stall, &c., and the expenditure daily occurring as for stock, butter, coal, according to the foregoing statement, amounts to 15,750l. The eels purchased for this trade at Billingsgate are 1,166,880 lb., costing, at 3d. per lb., 12,102l.

In the pea-soup trade there are now one half of the whole number of the hot-eel vendors; of whom 100 will sell, each 4 gallons daily; and of the remaining 50 vendors, each will sell upon an average 10 gallons daily. The first mentioned take 3s. daily; and the last 7s. 6d. This gives a street expenditure of 4,050l. during the winter season of five months.

To commence business in the street sale of pea-soup a capital is required after this rate: soup-kettle 4s.; peas 2s.; soup-ladle 6d.; pepper-box 1d.; mint-box 3d.; chafing-dish 6d.; 12 basons 1s.; 12 spoons 1s.; bones, celery, mint, carrots, and onions, 1s. 6d. In all 10s. 10d. The hot-eel trade being in conjunction with the pea-soup, the same stall, candles, towels, sleeves, and aprons, does for both, and the quantity of extra coal and charcoal; pepper and salt given in the summary of hot-eels serves in cooking, &c., both eels and pea-soup.

OF THE STREET-SELLERS OF PICKLED WHELKS.

THE trade in whelks is one of which the costermongers have the undisputed monopoly. The wholesale business is all transacted in Billingsgate, where this shell-fish is bought by the measure (a double peck or gallon), half-measure, or wash. A wash is four measures, and is the most advantageous mode of purchase; "It's so much cheaper by taking that quantity," I was told, "it's as good as having a half-measure in." An average price for the year may be 4s. the wash; "But I've given 21s. for three wash," said one costermonger, and he waxed indignant as he spoke, "one Saturday, when there was a great stock in too, just because there was a fair coming on on Monday, and the whelkmen, who are the biggest rogues in Billingsgate, always have the price up then, and hinder a poor man doing good—they've a great knack of that." A wash weighs about 60 lbs. On rare occasions it has been as low as 2*s*. 6*d*., and even 1*s*. 6*d*.

About one-half of the whelks are sold alive (wholesale), and the other half "cooked" (boiled), some of the salesmen having "convenience for cooking" near the market; but they are all brought to London alive, "or what should be alive." When bought alive, which ensures a better quality, I was told—for "whelks 'll boil after they're dead and gone, you see, sir, as if they was alive and hungry"—the costermonger boils them in the largest sauce-pan at his command for about ten minutes, and then leaves them until they cool. "They never kicks as they boils, like lobsters or crabs," said one whelk dealer, "they takes it quiet. A missionary cove said to me, 'Why don't you kill them first? it's murder.' *They* doesn't suffer; *I've* suffered more with a toothach than the whole of a measure of whelks has in a boiling, that I'm clear upon." The boiling is generally the work of the women. The next process is to place them in a tub, throw boiling water over them, and stir them up for ten or fifteen minutes with a broom-handle. If the quantity be a wash, two broom-handles, usually wielded by the man and his wife, are employed. This is both to clean them and "to make them come out easier to be wormed." The "worming" is equivalent to the removing of the beard of an oyster or mussel. The whelks are wormed one by one. The operator cuts into the fish, rapidly draws out the "worm," and pushes the severed parts together, which closes. The small whelks are not wormed, "because it's not reckoned necessary, and they're sold to poor lads and such like, that's not particular; but nearly all the women, and a good many of the boys, are very particular. They think the worm's poison." The whelks are next shaken in a tub, in cold water, and are then ready for sale. The same process, after the mere boiling, is observed, when the whelks are bought "cooked."

Some whelk-sellers, who wish to display a superior article, engage children for a few half-pence to rub the shell of every whelk, so that it looks clean and even bright.

I find a difficulty, common in the course of this inquiry, of ascertaining precisely the number of whelk-sellers, because the sale is often carried on simultaneously with that of other things, (stewed eels, for instance,) and because it is common for costermongers to sell whelks on a Saturday night only, both at stalls and "round to the public-houses," but only when they are cheap at Billingsgate. On a Saturday night there may be 300 whelk-sellers in the streets, nearly half at stalls, and half, or more, "working the public-houses." But of this number it must be understood that perhaps the wife is at the stall while the husband is on a round, and some whelks are sent out by a man having an extra stock. This, therefore, reduces the number of independent dealers, but not the actual number of sellers. On all other nights

there may be half the number engaged in this traffic, in the streets regularly all the year; and more than half on a Monday, as regards the public-house business, in which little is done between Monday and Saturday nights. But a man will, in some instances, work the public-houses every night (the wife tending the stall), and the more assiduously if the weather be bad or foggy, when a public-house custom is the best. A fair week's earnings in whelks, "when a man's known," is 1*l*.; a bad week is from 5*s*. to 8*s*. I am assured that bad weeks are "as plenty as good, at least, the year round;" and thus the average to the street whelk-sellers, in whelks alone, is about 13*s*. when the trade is carried on daily and regularly, and 5*s*. a week by those who occasionally resort to it; and as the occasional hands are the more numerous, the average may be struck at 7*s*.

The whelks are sold at the stalls at two, three, four, six, and eight a penny, according to size. Four is an average pennyworth for good whelks; the six a penny are small, and the eight a penny very small. The principal place for their sale is in Old-street, City-road. The other principal places are the street-markets, which I have before particularised. The whelks are sold in saucers, generally small and white, and of common ware, and are contained in jars, ready to be "shelled" into any saucer that may have been emptied. Sometimes a small pyramid of shells, surmounted by a candle protected by a shade, attracts the regard of the passer-by. The man doing the best business in London was to be found, before the removals of which I have spoken, in Lambeth-walk, but he has now no fixed locality. His profits, I am informed, were regularly 3*l*. a week; but out of this he had to pay for the assistance of two or sometimes three persons, in washing his whelks, boiling them, &c.; besides that, his wife was as busy as himself. To the quality and cleanliness of his whelks he was very attentive, and would sell no mediocre article if better could be bought. "He deserved all he earned, sir," said another street-dealer to me; "why, in Old-street now they'll have the old original saucers, miserable things, such as they had fifty years back; but the man we're talking of, about two years ago, brought in very pretty plates, quite enterprising things, and they answered well. His example's spreading, but it's slowly." The whelks are eaten with vinegar and pepper.

For sale in the public-houses, the whelks are most frequently carried in jars, and transferred in a saucer to the consumer. "There's often a good sale," said a man familiar with the business, "when a public room's filled. People drinking there always want to eat. They buy whelks, not to fill themselves, but for a relish. A man that's used to the trade will often get off inferior sorts to the lushingtons; he'll have them to rights. Whelks is all the same, good, bad, or middling, when a man's drinking, if they're well seasoned with pepper and vinegar.

Oh yes; any whelk-man will take in a drunken fellow, and he will do it all the same, if he's made up his mind to, get drunk hisself that very night."

The trade is carried on by the regular costers, but of the present number of whelk-sellers, about twenty have been mechanics or servants. The whelk-trade is an evening trade, commencing generally about six, summer and winter, or an hour earlier in winter.

The capital required to start in the whelk-business is: stall, 2s. 6d.; saucers, vinegar-bottle, jar, pepper-castor, and small watering-pan (used only in dusty weather), 2s. 6d.; a pair of stilts (supports for the stall), 1s. 6d.; stock-money, 5s.; pepper and vinegar, 6d., or 12s. in all. If the trade be commenced in a round basket, for public-house sale, 7s. or 8s. only is required, but it is a hazardous experiment for a person unpractised in street business.

OF THE CUSTOMERS, ETC., OF PICKLED WHELK-SELLERS.

AN intelligent man gave me the following account. He had been connected with street-trading from his youth up, and is now about thirty:

"The chief customers for whelks, sir, are working people and poor people, and they prefer them to oysters; I do myself, and I think they're not so much eaten because they're not fashionable like oysters. But I've sold them to first-rate public-houses, and to doctors' shops—more than other shops, I don't know why—and to private houses. Masters have sent out their servant-maids to me for three or four penn'orths for supper. I've offered the maids a whelk, but they won't eat them in the street; I dare say they're afraid their young men may be about, and might think they wasn't ladies if they eat whelks in the street. Boys are the best customers for 'small,' but if you don't look sharp, you'll be done out of three-ha'porth of vinegar to a ha'porth of whelks. I can't make out why they like it so. They're particular enough in their way. If the whelks are thin, as they will be sometimes, the lads will say, 'What a lot of snails you've gathered to-night!' If they're plump and fine, then they'll say, 'Fat 'uns to-night—stunners!' Some people eat whelks for an appetite; they give me one, and more in summer than winter. The women of the town are good customers, at least they are in the Cut and Shoreditch, for I know both. If they have five-penn'orth, when they're treated perhaps, there's always sixpence. They come on the sly sometimes, by themselves, and make what's a meal, I'm satisfied, on whelks, and they'll want credit sometimes. I've given trust to a woman of that sort as far as 2s. 6d. I've lost very little by them; I don't know how much altogether. I keep no account, but carry any credit in my head. Those women's good pay, take it altogether, for they know how hard it is to get a crust, and have a feeling for a poor man, if they haven't for a rich one—that's my opinion, sir. Costermongers in a good time are capital customers; they'll buy five or six penn'orths at a time. The dust's a great injury to the trade in summer time; it dries the whelks up, and they look old. I wish whelks were cheaper at Billingsgate, and I could do more business; and I could do more if I could sell a few minutes after twelve on a Saturday night, when people must leave the public-house. I have sold three wash of a Saturday night, and cleared 15s. on them. I one week made 3l., but I had a few stewed eels to help,—that is, I cleared 2l., and had a pound's worth over on the Saturday night, and sent them to be sold— and they were sold—at Battersea on the Sunday; I never went there myself. I've had twenty people round my stall at one time on a Saturday. Perhaps my earnings on that (and other odd things) may come to 1l. a week, or hardly so much, the year round. I can't say exactly. The shells are no use. Boys have asked me for them 'to make sea-shells of,' they say — to hold them to their ears when they're big, and there's a sound like the sea rolling. Gentlemen have sometimes told me to keep a dozen dozen or twenty dozen, for borders to a garden. I make no charge for them—just what a gentleman may please to give.

The information given shows an outlay of 5,250l. yearly for street whelks, and as the return I have cited shows the money spent in whelks at Billingsgate to be 2,500l., the number of whelks being 4,950,000, the account is correct, as the coster's usual " half-profits " make up the sum expended.

OF THE STREET SELLERS, AND OF THE PREPARATION OF FRIED FISH.

AMONG the cooked food which has for many years formed a portion of the street trade is fried fish. The sellers are about 350, as a maximum and 250 as a minimum, 300 being an average number. The reason of the variation in number is, that on a Saturday night, and occasionally on other nights, especially on Mondays, stall-keepers sell fried fish, and not as an ordinary article of their trade. Some men, too, resort to the trade for a time, when they cannot be employed in any way more profitable or suitable to them. The dealers in this article are, for the most part, old men and boys, though there may be 30 or 40 women who sell it, but only 3 or 4 girls, and they are the daughters of the men in the business as the women are the wives. Among the fried-fish sellers there are not half a dozen Irish people, although fish is so especial a part of the diet of the poor Irish. The men in the calling have been, as regards the great majority, mechanics or servants; none, I was told, had been fishmongers, or their assistants.

The fish fried by street dealers is known as "plaice dabs" and "sole dabs," which are merely plaice and soles, "dab" being a common word for any flat fish. The fish which supplies upwards of one half the quantity fried for the streets is plaice ; the other fishes used are soles, haddocks, whitings, flounders, and herrings, but very sparingly indeed as regards herrings. Soles are used in as large a quantity as the other kinds mentioned altogether. On my inquiry as to the precise quantity of each description fried, the answer from the traders was uniform : " I can't say, sir. I buy whatever's cheapest." The fish is bought at Billingsgate, but some of the street dealers obtain another and even a cheaper commodity than at that great mart. This supply is known in the trade as " friers," and consists of the overplus of a fishmonger's stock, of what he has not sold overnight, and does not care to offer for sale on the following morning, and therefore vends it to the costermongers, whose customers are chiefly among the poor. The friers are sometimes half, and sometimes more than half, of the wholesale price in Billingsgate. Many of the friers are good, but some, I was told, " in any thing like muggy or close weather were very queer fish, very queer indeed," and they are consequently fried with a most liberal allowance of oil, " which will conceal anything."

The fish to be fried is first washed and gutted ; the fins, head, and tail are then cut off, and the trunk is dipped in flour and water, so that in frying, oil being always used, the skin will not be scorched by the, perhaps, too violent action of the fire, but merely browned. Pale rape oil is generally used. The sellers, however, are often twitted with using lamp oil, even when it is dearer than that devoted to the purpose. The fish is cooked in ordinary frying-pans. One tradesman in Cripplegate, formerly a costermonger, has on his premises a commodious oven which he had built for the frying, or rather baking, of fish. He supplies the small shopkeepers who deal in the article (although some prepare it themselves), and sells his fish retail also, but the street-sellers buy little of him, as they are nearly all "their own cooks." Some of the "illegitimates," however, lay in their stock by purchase of the tradesman in question. The fish is cut into portions before it is fried, and the frying occupies about ten minutes. The quantity prepared together is from six to twenty portions, according to the size of the pans ; four dozen portions, or "pieces," as the street people call them, require a quart of oil.

The fried fish-sellers live in some out of the way alley, and not unfrequently in garrets ; for among even the poorest class there are great objections to their being fellow-lodgers, on account of the odour from the frying. Even when the fish is fresh (as it most frequently is), and the oil pure, the odour is rank. In one place I visited, which was, moreover, admirable for cleanliness, it was very rank. The cooks, however, whether husbands or wives—for the women often attend to the pan—when they hear of this disagreeable rankness, answer that it may be so, many people say so ; but for their parts they cannot smell it at all. The garments of the fried-fish sellers are more strongly impregnated with the smell of fish than were those of any " wet " or other fish-sellers whom I met with. Their residences are in some of the labyrinths of courts and alleys that run from Gray's-inn-lane to Leather-lane, and similar places between Fetter and Chancery-lanes. They are to be found, too, in the courts running from Cow-cross, Smithfield ; and from Turnmill-street and Ray-street, Clerkenwell ; also, in the alleys about Bishopsgate-street and the Kingsland-road, and some in the half-ruinous buildings near the Southwark and Borough-roads. None, or very few, of those who are their own cooks, reside at a greater distance than three miles from Billingsgate. A gin-drinking neighbourhood, one coster said, suits best, " for people hasn't their smell so correct there."

The sale is both on rounds and at stalls, the itinerants being twice as numerous as the stationary. The round is usually from public-house to public-house, in populous neighbourhoods. The itinerants generally confine themselves to the trade in fried fish, but the stall-keepers always sell other articles, generally fish of some kind, along with it. The sale in the public-houses is the greatest.

At the neighbouring races and fairs there is a great sale of fried fish. At last Epsom races, I was told, there were at least fifty purveyors of that dainty from London, half of them perhaps being costermongers, who speculated in it merely for the occasion, preparing it themselves. Three men joined in one speculation, expending 8*l.* in fish, and did well, selling at the usual profit of cent. per cent., but with the drawback of considerable expenses. Their customers at the races and fairs are the boys who hold horses or brush clothes, or who sell oranges or nuts, or push at roundabouts, and the costers who are there on business. At Epsom races there was plenty of bread, I was informed, to be picked up on the ground ; it had been flung from the carriages after luncheon, and this, with a piece of fish, supplied a meal or " a relish " to hundreds.

In the public-houses, a slice of bread, 16 or 32 being cut from a quartern loaf—as they are whole or half slices—is sold or offered with the fish for a penny. The cry of the seller is, " fish and bread, a penny." Sometimes for an extra-sized piece, with bread, 2*d.* is obtained, but very seldom, and sometimes two pieces are given for 1½*d.* At the stalls bread is rarely sold with the edible in question.

For the itinerant trade, a neatly painted wooden tray, slung by a leathern strap from the neck, is used : the tray is papered over generally with clean newspapers, and on the paper is spread the shapeless brown lumps of fish. Parsley is often strewn over them, and a salt-box is placed at the discretion of the customer. The trays contain from two to five dozen pieces.

THE BAKED POTATO MAN.

"Baked 'taturs! All 'ot, all 'ot!"

[*From a Daguerreotype by* BEARD]

I understand that no one has a trade greatly in advance of his fellows. The whole body complain of their earnings being far less than was the case four or five years back.

The itinerant fried fish-sellers, when pursuing their avocation, wear generally a jacket of cloth or fustian buttoned round them, but the rest of their attire is hidden by the white sleeves and apron some wear, or by the black calico sleeves and dark woollen aprons worn by others.

The capital required to start properly in the business is:—frying-pan 2s. (second-hand 9d.); tray 2s. 6d. (second-hand 8d.); salt-box 6d. (second-hand 1d.); and stock-money 5s.—in all 10s. A man has gone into the trade, however, with 1s., which he expended in fish and oil, borrowed a frying-pan, borrowed an old tea-board, and so started on his venture.

OF THE EXPERIENCE OF A FRIED FISH-SELLER, AND OF THE CLASS OF CUSTOMERS.

THE man who gave me the following information was well-looking, and might be about 45 or 50. He was poorly dressed, but his old brown surtout fitted him close and well, was jauntily buttoned up to his black satin stock, worn, but of good quality; and, altogether, he had what is understood among a class as "a *betterly* appearance about him." His statement, as well as those of the other vendors of provisions, is curious in its details of public-house vagaries:—

"I've been in the trade," he said, "seventeen years. Before that, I was a gentleman's servant, and I married a servant-maid, and we had a family, and, on that account, couldn't, either of us, get a situation, though we'd good characters. I was out of employ for seven or eight months, and things was beginning to go to the pawn for a living; but at last, when I gave up any hope of getting into a gentleman's service, I raised 10s., and determined to try something else. I was persuaded, by a friend who kept a beer-shop, to sell oysters at his door. I took his advice, and went to Billingsgate for the first time in my life, and bought a peck of oysters for 2s. 6d. I was dressed respectable then—nothing like the mess and dirt I'm in now" [I may observe, that there was no dirt about him]; "and so the salesman laid it on, but I gave him all he asked. I know a deal better now. I'd never been used to open oysters, and I couldn't do it. I cut my fingers with the knife slipping all over them, and had to hire a man to open for me, or the blood from my cut fingers would have run upon the oysters. For all that, I cleared 2s. 6d. on that peck, and I soon got up to the trade, and did well; till, in two or three months, the season got over, and I was advised, by the same friend, to try fried fish. That suited me. I've lived in good families, where there was first-rate men-cooks, and I know what good cooking means. I bought a dozen plaice; I forget what I gave for them, but they were dearer then than now. For all that, I took between 11s. and 12s. the first night—it was Saturday—that I started; and I stuck to it, and took

from 7s. to 10s. every night, with more, of course, on Saturday, and it was half of it profit then. I cleared a good mechanic's earnings at that time —30s. a week and more. Soon after, I was told that, if agreeable, my wife could have a stall with fried fish, opposite a wine-vaults just opened, and she made nearly half as much as I did on my rounds. I served the public-houses, and soon got known. With some landlords I had the privilege of the parlour, and tap-room, and bar, when other tradesmen have been kept out. The landlords will say to me still: ' You can go in, Fishy.' Somehow, I got the name of ' Fishy' then, and I've kept it ever since. There was hospitality in those days. I've gone into a room in a public-house, used by mechanics, and one of them has said: 'I'll stand fish round, gentlemen;' and I've supplied fifteen penn'orths. Perhaps he was a stranger, such a sort of customer, that wanted to be agreeable. Now, it's more likely I hear: 'Jack, lend us a penny to buy a bit of fried;' and then Jack says: ' You be d—d! here, lass, let's have another pint.' The insults and difficulties I've had in the public-house trade is dreadful. I once sold 16d. worth to three rough-looking fellows I'd never seen before, and they seemed hearty, and asked me to drink with them, so I took a pull; but they wouldn't pay me when I asked, and I waited a goodish bit before I did ask. I thought, at first, it was their fun, but I waited from four to seven, and I found it was no fun. I felt upset, and ran out and told the policeman; he said it was only a debt, and he couldn't interfere. So I ran to the station, but the head man there said the same, and told me I should hand over the fish with one hand, and hold out the other hand for my money. So I went back to the public-house, and asked for my money—and there was some mechanics that knew me there then—but I got nothing but '—— you's!' and one of 'em used most dreadful language. At last, one of the mechanics said : ' Muzzle him, Fishy, if he won't pay.' He was far bigger than me, him that was one in debt; but my spirit was up, and I let go at him and gave him a bloody nose, and the next hit I knocked him backwards, I'm sure I don't know how, on to a table; but I fell on him, and he clutched me by the coat-collar—I was respectable dressed then—and half smothered me. He tore the back of my coat, too, and I went home like Jim Crow. The potman and the others parted us, and they made the man give me 1s., and the waiter paid me the other 4d., and said he'd take his chance to get it—but he never got it. Another time I went into a bar, and there was a ball in the house, and one of the ball gents came down and gave my basket a kick without ever a word, and started the fish; and in a scuffle—he was a little fellow, but my master—I had this finger put out of joint—you can see that, sir, still—and was in the hospital a week from an injury to my leg; the tiblin bone was hurt, the doctors said" [the tibia.] "I've had my tray kicked over for a lark in a public-house, and a scramble for my fish, and all gone, and no help and no money for me. The landlords always prevent such things, when they can, and interfere for a poor man; but then it's done sudden, and over in an instant. That sort of thing wasn't the worst. I once had some powdery stuff flung sudden over me at a parlour door. My fish fell off, for I jumped, because I felt blinded, and what became of them I don't know; but I aimed at once for home—it was very late—and had to feel my way almost like a blind man. I can't tell what I suffered. I found it was something black, for I kept rubbing my face with my apron, and could just tell it came away black. I let myself in with my latch, and my wife was in bed, and I told her to get up and look at my face and get some water, and she thought I was joking, as she was half asleep; but when she got up and got a light, and a glass, she screamed, and said I looked such a shiny image; and so I did, as well as I could see, for it was black lead—such as they use for grates—that was flung on me. I washed it off, but it wasn't easy, and my face was sore days after. I had a respectable coat on then, too, which was greatly spoiled, and no remedy at all. I don't know who did it to me. I heard some one say: 'You're served out beautiful' Its men that calls themselves gentlemen that does such things. I know the style of them then—it was eight or ten years ago; they'd heard of Lord ——, and his goings on. That way it's better now, but worse, far, in the way of getting a living. I dare say, if I had dressed in rough corderoys, I shouldn't have been larked at so much, because they might have thought I was a regular coster, and a fighter; but I don't like that sort of thing—I like to be decent and respectable, if I can.

"I've been in the 'fried' trade ever since, except about three months that I tried the sandwiches. I didn't do so well in them, but it was a far easier trade; no carrying heavy weights all the way from Billingsgate: but I went back to the fried. Why now, sir, a good week with me—and I've only myself in the trade now" [he was a widower]—"is to earn 12s., a poor week is 9s.; and there's as many of one as of the other. I'm known to sell the best of fish, and to cook it in the best style. I think half of us, take it round and round for a year, may earn as much as I do, and the other half about half as much. I think so. I might have saved money, but for a family. I've only one at home with me now, and he really *is* a good lad. My customers are public-house people that want a relish or a sort of supper with their beer, not so much to drinkers. I sell to tradesmen, too; 4d. worth for tea or supper. Some of them send to my place, for I'm known. The Great Exhibition can't be any difference to me. I've a regular round. I used to sell a good deal to women of the town, but I don't now. They haven't the money, I believe. Where I took 10s. of them, eight or ten years ago, I now take only 6d. They may go for other sorts of relishes now; I can't say. The worst of my trade is, that people must

have as big penn'orths when fish is dear as when its cheap. I never sold a piece of fish to an Italian boy in my life, though they're Catholics. Indeed, I never saw an Italian boy spend a halfpenny in the streets on anything."

A working-man told me that he often bought fried fish, and accounted it a good to men like himself. He was fond of fried fish to his supper; he couldn't buy half so cheap as the streetsellers, perhaps not a quarter; and, if he could, it would cost him 1d. for dripping to fry the fish in, and he got it ready, and well fried, and generally good, for 1d.

Subsequent inquiries satisfied me that my informant was correct as to his calculations of his fellows' earnings, judging from his own. The price of plaice at Billingsgate is from ½d. to 2d. each, according to size (the fried fish purveyors never calculate by the weight), ¾d. being a fair average. A plaice costing 1d. will now be fried into four pieces, each 1d.; but the addition of bread, cost of oil, &c., reduces the "fried" peoples' profits to rather less than cent. per cent. Soles and the other fish are, moreover, 30 per cent. dearer than plaice. As 150 sellers make as much weekly as my informant, and the other 150 half that amount, we have an average yearly earning of 27l. 6s. in one case, and of 13l. 13s. in the other. Taking only 20l. a year as a medium earning, and adding 90 per cent for profit, the outlay on the fried fish supplied by London street-sellers is 11,400l.

OF THE PREPARATION AND QUANTITY OF SHEEP'S TROTTERS, AND OF THE STREET-SELLERS.

THE sale of sheep's trotters, as a regular street-trade, is confined to London, Liverpool, Newcastle-on-Tyne, and a few more of our greater towns. The "trotter," as it is commonly called, is the boiled foot of the sheep. None of my readers can have formed any commensurate notion of the extent of the sale in London, and to some readers the very existence of such a comestible may be unknown. The great supply now required is readily attained. The wholesale trade is now in the hands of one fellmongering firm, though until within these twenty months or so there were two, and the feet are cut off the sheep-skins by the salesmen in the skin-market, in Bermondsey, and conveyed to the fellmonger's premises in carts and in trucks.

Sheep's trotters, one of my informants could remember, were sold in the streets fifty years ago, but in such small quantities that it could hardly be called a trade. Instead of being prepared wholesale as at present, and then sold out to the retailers, the trotters were then prepared by the individual retailers, or by small traders in tripe and cow-heel. Twenty-five years ago nearly all the sheep's trotters were "lined and prepared," when the skin came into the hands of the fellmonger, for the glue and size makers. Twenty years ago only about one-twentieth of the trotters now prepared for eating were devoted to the same purpose; and it was not until about fifteen years back that the trade began to reach its present magnitude; and for the last twelve years it has been about stationary, but there were never more sold than last year.

From fifteen to twenty years ago glue and size, owing principally to improved modes of manufacture, became cheaper, so that it paid the fellmonger better to dispose of the trotters as an article "cooked" for the poor, than to the glueboiler.

The process of cookery is carried on rapidly at the fellmonger's in question. The feet are first scalded for about half an hour. After that from ten to fifteen boys are employed in scooping out the hoofs, which are sold for manure or to manufacturers of Prussian blue, which is extensively used by painters. Women are then employed, forty being an average number, "to scrape the hair off,"—for hair it is called—quickly, but softly, so that the skin should not be injured, and after that the trotters are boiled for about four hours, and they are then ready for market.

The proprietor of this establishment, after he had obligingly given me the information I required, invited me to walk round his premises unaccompanied, and observe how the business was conducted. The premises are extensive, and are situated, as are nearly all branches of the great trade connected with hides and skins, in Bermondsey. The trotter business is kept distinct from the general fellmongering. Within a long shed are five coppers, each containing, on an average, 250 "sets," a set being the complement of the sheep's feet, four. Two of these coppers, on my visit, were devoted to the scalding, and three to the boiling of the trotters. They looked like what one might imagine to be witches' big caldrons; seething, hissing, boiling, and throwing forth a steam not peculiarly grateful to the nostrils of the uninitiated. Thus there are, weekly, "cooking" in one form or other, the feet of 20,000 sheep for the consumption of the poorer classes, or as a relish for those whose stomachs crave after edibles of this description. At one extremity of this shed are the boys, who work in a place open at the side, but the flues and fires make all parts sufficiently warm. The women have a place to themselves on the opposite side of the yard. The room where they work has forms running along its sides, and each woman has a sort of bench in front of her seat, on which she scrapes the trotters. One of the best of these workwomen can scrape 150 sets, or 600 feet in a day, but the average of the work is 500 sets a week, including women and girls. I saw no girls but what seemed above seventeen or eighteen, and none of the women were old. They were exceedingly merry, laughing and chatting, and appearing to consider that a listener was not of primary consequence, as they talked pretty much altogether. I saw none but what were decently

dressed, some were good-looking, and none seemed sickly.

In this establishment are prepared, weekly, 20,000 sets, or 80,000 feet; a yearly average of 4,160,000 trotters, or the feet of 1,040,000 sheep. Of this quantity the street-folk buy seven-eighths; 3,640,000 trotters yearly, or 70,000 weekly. The number of sheep trotter-sellers may be taken at 300, which gives an average of nearly sixty sets a week per individual.

The wholesale price, at the "trotter yard," is five a penny, which gives an outlay by the street-sellers of 3,031*l.* 11*s.* yearly.

But this is not the whole of the trade. Lamb's trotters are also prepared, but only to one-twentieth of the quantity of sheep's trotters, and that for only three months of the year. These are all sold to the street-sellers. The lamb's foot is usually left appended to the leg and shoulder of lamb. It is weighed with the joint, but the butcher's man or boy will say to the purchaser: "Do you want the foot?" As the answer is usually in the negative, it is at once cut off and forms a "perquisite." There are some half dozen men, journeymen butchers not fully employed, who collect these feet, prepare and sell them to the street-people, but as the lamb's feet are very seldom as fresh as those of the sheep carried direct from the skin market to—so to speak—the great trotter kitchen, the demand for "lamb's" falls off yearly. Last year the sale may be taken at about 14,000 sets, selling, wholesale, at about 46*l.*, the same price as the sheep.

The sellers of trotters, who are stationary at publichouse and theatre doors, and at street corners, and itinerant, but itinerant chiefly from one public house to another are a wretchedly poor class. Three fourths of them are elderly women and children, the great majority being Irish people, and there are more boys than girls in the trade. The capital required to start in the business is very small. A hand basket of the larger size costs 1*s.* 9*d.*, but smaller or second-hand only 1*s.*, and the white cotton cloth on which the trotters are displayed costs 4*d.* or 6*d.*; stock-money need not exceed 1*s.*, so that 3*s.* is all that is required. This is one reason, I heard from several trotter-sellers, why the business is over-peopled.

STATEMENTS OF SHEEP'S TROTTER WOMEN.

FROM one woman, who, I am assured, may be taken as a fair type of the better class of trotter-sellers—some of the women being sottish and addicted to penn'orths of gin beyond their means—I had the following statement. I found her in the top room of a lofty house in Clerkenwell. She was washing when I called, and her son, a crippled boy of 16, with his crutch by his side, was cleaning knives, which he had done for many months for a family in the neighbourhood, who paid for his labour in what the mother pronounced better than money—broken victuals, because they were of such good, wholesome quality. The room, which is of a good size, had its red-brown plaster walls, stained in parts with damp, but a great portion was covered with the cheap engravings " given away with No. 6" (or any other number) of some periodical "of thrilling interest ;" while the narrow mantel-shelf was almost covered with pot figures of dumpy men, red-breeched and blue-coated, and similar ornaments. I have often noted such attempts to subdue, as it were, the grimness of poverty, by the poor who had "seen better days." The mother was tall and spare, and the boy had that look of premature sedateness, his face being of a sickly hue, common to those of quiet dispositions, who have been afflicted from their childhood :—

"I'm the widow of a sawyer, sir," said Mrs. ——, with a very slight brogue, for she was an Irishwoman, "and I've been a widow 18 long years. I'm 54, I believe, but that 18 years seems longer than all the rest of my life together. My husband earned hardly ever less than 30s. a week, sometimes 3l., and I didn't know what pinching was. But I was left destitute with four young children, and had to bring them up as well as I could, by what I could make by washing and charing, and a hard fight it was. One of my children went for a soldier, one's dead, another's married, and that's the youngest there. Ah! poor fellow, what he's gone through! He's had 18 abscesses, one after another, and he has been four times in Bartholomew's. There's only God above to help him when I'm gone. My health broke six years ago, and I couldn't do hard work in washing, and I took to trotter selling, because one of my neighbours was in that way, and told me how to go about it. My son sells trotters too; he always sits at the corner of this street. I go from one public-house to another, and sometimes stand at the door, or sit inside, because I'm known and have leave. But I can't either sit, or stand, or walk long at a time, I'm so rheumatic. No, sir, I can't say I was ever badly insulted in a public-house ; but I only go to those I know. Others may be different. We depend mostly on trotters, but I have a shilling and my meat, for charing, a day in every week. I've tried 'winks and whelks too, 'cause I thought they might be more in my pocket than trotters, but they don't suit a poor woman that's begun a street-trade when she's not very young. And the trotters can be carried on with so little money. It's not so long ago that I've sold three-penn'orth of trotters—that is, him and me has—pretty early in the evening ; I'd bought them at Mr. ——'s, in Bermondsey, in the afternoon, for we can buy three penn'orth, and I walked there again—perhaps it's four miles there and back—and bought another 3d. worth. The first three-pence was all I could rise. It's a long weary way for me to walk, but some walk from Poplar and Limehouse. If I lay out 2s. on the Saturday—there's 15 sets for 1s., that's 60 trotters—they'll carry us on to Monday night, and sometimes, if they'll keep, to Tuesday night. Sometimes I could sell half-a-crown's worth in less time. I have to go to Bermondsey three or four times a week. The trade was far better six years ago, though trotters were dearer then, only 13 sets 1s., then 14, now 15. For some very few, that's very fine and very big, I get a penny a piece ; for some I get 1½d. for two ; the most's ½d. each ; some's four for 1½d. ; and some I have to throw into the dust-hole. The two of us earns 5s. a week on trotters, not more, I'm sure. I sell to people in the public-houses ; some of them may be rather the worse for drink, but not so many ; regular drunkards buys nothing but drink. I've sold them too to steady, respectable gentlemen, that's been passing in the street, who put them in their pockets for supper. My rent's 1s. a week."

I then had some conversation with the poor lad. He told me he had many a bitter night, he told me, from half-past five to twelve, for he knew there was no breakfast for his mother and him if he couldn't sell some trotters. He had a cry sometimes. He didn't know any good it did him, but he couldn't help it. The boys gathered round him sometimes, and teased him, and snatched at his crutch ; and the policeman said that he must make him "move on," as he encouraged the boys about him. He didn't like the boys any more than they were fond of the policemen. He had often sad thoughts as he sat with his trotters before him, when he didn't cry ; he wondered if ever he would be better off ; but what could he do ? He could read, but not write ; he liked to read very well when he had anything to read. His mother and he never missed mass.

Another old woman, very poorly, but rather tidily dressed, gave me the following account, which shows a little of public-house custom :—

"I've seen better days, sir, I have indeed ; I don't like to talk about that, but now I'm only a poor sheep's trotter seller, and I've been one a good many years. I don't know how long, and I don't like to think about it. It's a shocking bad trade, and such insults as we have to put up with. I serve some public-houses, and I stand sometimes at a playhouse-door. I make 3s. or 3s. 6d. a week, and in a very good week 4s., but, then, I sometimes make only 2s. I'm infirm now, God help me! and I can do nothing else. Another old woman and me has a room between us, at 1s. 4d. a week. Mother's the best name I'm called in a public-house, and it ain't a respectable name. 'Here, mother, give us one of your b— trotters,' is often said to me. One customer sometimes says : 'The stuff'll choke me, but that's as good as the Union.' *He* ain't a bad man, though. He sometimes treats me. He'll bait my trotters, but that's his larking way, and then he'll say :

'A pennorth o' gin,
'll make your old body spin.'

It's his own poetry, he says. I don't know what he is, but he's often drunk, poor fellow. Women's far worse to please than men. I've known a woman buy a trotter, put her teeth into it, and then say it wasn't good, and return it. It wasn't paid for when she did so, and because I grumbled, I was abused by her, as if I'd been a Turk. The landlord interfered, and he said, said he, ' I'll not have this poor woman insulted; she's here for the convenience of them as requires trotters, and she's a well-conducted woman, and I'll not have her insulted,' he says, says he, lofty and like a gentleman, sir. ' Why, who's insulting the old b—h?' says the woman, says she. ' Why, you are,' says the landlord, says he, ' and you ought to pay her for her trotter, or how is she to live?' ' What the b— h—ll do I care how she lives,' says the woman, ' its nothing to me, and I won't pay her.' ' Then I will,' says the landlord, says he, ' here's 6d.,' and he wouldn't take the change. After that I soon sold all my trotters, and some gave me double price, when the landlord showed himself such a gentleman, and I went out and bought nine trotters more, another woman's stock, that she was dreading she couldn't sell, and I got through them in no time. It was the best trotter night I ever had. She wasn't a woman of the town as used me so. I have had worse sauce from modest women, as they called themselves, than from the women of the town, for plenty of *them* knows what poverty is, and is civiler, poor things — yes, I'm sure of that, though it's a shocking life— O, shocking! I never go to the playhouse-door but on a fine night. Young men treats their sweethearts to a trotter, for a relish, with a drop of beer between the acts. Wet nights is the best for public-houses. ' They're not salt enough,' has been said to me, oft enough, ' they don't make a man thirsty.' It'll come to the workhouse with me before long, and, perhaps, all the better. It's warm in the public-house, and that draws me to sell my trotters there sometimes. I live on fish and bread a good deal.''

The returns I collected show that there is expended yearly in London streets on trotters, calculating their sale, retail, at ½d. each, 6,500l., but though the regular price is ½d., some trotters are sold at four for 1½d., very few higher than ½d., and some are kept until they are unsaleable, so that the amount may be estimated at 6,000l., a receipt of 7s. 6d. weekly, per individual seller, rather more than one-half of which sum is profit.

OF THE STREET TRADE IN BAKED POTATOES.

THE *baked potato trade*, in the way it is at present carried on, has not been known more than fifteen years in the streets. Before that, potatoes were sometimes roasted as chestnuts are now, but only on a small scale. The trade is more profitable than that in fruit, but continues for but six months of the year.

The potatoes, for street-consumption, are bought of the greengrocers, at the rate of 5s. 6d. the cwt. They are usually a large-sized "fruit," running about two or three to the pound. The kind generally bought is what are called the "French Regent's." French pota-

toes are greatly used now, as they are cheaper than the English. The potatoes are picked, and those of a large size, and with a rough skin, selected from the others, because they are the mealiest. A waxy potato shrivels in the baking. There are usually from 280 to 300 potatoes in the cwt.; these are cleaned by the huckster, and, when dried, taken in baskets, about a quarter cwt. at a time, to the baker's, to be cooked. They are baked in large tins, and require an hour and a half to do them well. The charge for baking is 9d. the cwt., the baker usually finding the tins. They are taken home from the bakehouse in a basket, with a yard and a half of green baize in which they are covered up, and so protected from the cold. The huckster then places them in his can, which consists of a tin with a half-lid; it stands on four legs, and has a large handle to it, while an iron fire-pot is suspended immediately beneath the vessel which is used for holding the potatoes. Directly over the fire-pot is a boiler for hot water. This is concealed within the vessel, and serves to keep the potatoes always hot. Outside the vessel where the potatoes are kept is, at one end, a small compartment for butter and salt, and at the other end another compartment for fresh charcoal. Above the boiler, and beside the lid, is a small pipe for carrying off the steam. These potato-cans are sometimes brightly polished, sometimes painted red, and occasionally brass-mounted. Some of the handsomest are all brass, and some are highly ornamented with brass-mountings. Great pride is taken in the cans. The baked-potato man usually devotes half an hour to polishing them up, and they are mostly kept as bright as silver. The handsomest potato-can is now in Shoreditch. It cost ten guineas, and is of brass mounted with German silver. There are three lamps attached to it, with coloured glass, and of a style to accord with that of the machine; each lamp cost 5s. The expense of an ordinary can, tin and brass-mounted, is about 50s. They are mostly made by a tinman in the Ratcliffe-highway. The usual places for these cans to stand are the principal thoroughfares and street-markets. It is considered by one who has been many years at the business, that there are, taking those who have regular stands and those who are travelling with their cans on their arm, at least two hundred individuals engaged in the trade in London. There are three at the bottom of Farringdon-street, two in Smithfield, and three in Tottenham-court-road (the two places last named are said to be the best ' pitches ' in all London), two in Leather-lane, one on Holborn-hill, one at King's-cross, three at the Brill, Somers-town, three in the New-cut, three in Covent-garden (this is considered to be on market-days the second-best pitch), two at the Elephant and Castle, one at Westminster-bridge, two at the top of Edgeware-road, one in St. Martin's-lane, one in Newport-market, two at the upper end of Oxford-street, one in Clare-market, two in Regent-street, one in Newgate-market, two at the Angel, Islington, three at Shoreditch church, four about Rosemary-lane, two at Whitechapel, two near Spitalfields-market, and more than double the above number wandering about London. Some of the cans have names—as the " Royal Union Jack" (engraved in a brass plate), the " Royal George," the " Prince of Wales," the " Original Baked Potatoes," and the " *Old* Original Baked Potatoes."

The business begins about the middle of August and continues to the latter end of April, or as soon as the potatoes get to any size,— until they are pronounced 'bad.' The season, upon an average, lasts about half the year, and depends much upon the weather. If it is cold and frosty, the trade is brisker than in wet weather; indeed then little is doing. The best hours for business are from half-past ten in the morning till two in the afternoon, and from five in the evening till eleven or twelve at night. The night trade is considered the best. In cold weather the potatoes are frequently bought to warm the hands. Indeed, an eminent divine classed them, in a public speech, among the best of modern improvements, it being a cheap luxury to the poor wayfarer, who was benumbed in the night by cold, and an excellent medium for diffusing warmth into the system, by being held in the gloved hand. Some buy them in the morning for lunch and some for dinner. A newsvender, who had to take a hasty meal in his shop, told me he was "always glad to hear the baked-potato cry, as it made a dinner of what was only a snack without it." The best time at night, is about nine, when the potatoes are purchased for supper.

The customers consist of all classes. Many gentlefolks buy them in the street, and take them home for supper in their pockets; but the working classes are the greatest purchasers. Many boys and girls lay out a halfpenny in a baked potato. Irishmen are particularly fond of them, but they are the worst customers, I am told, as they want the largest potatoes in the can. Women buy a great number of those sold. Some take them home, and some eat them in the street. Three baked potatoes are as much as will satisfy the stoutest appetite. One potato dealer in Smithfield is said to sell about 2½ cwt. of potatoes on a market-day; or, in other words, from 900 to 1,000 potatoes, and to take upwards of 2*l.* One informant told me that he himself had often sold 1½ cwt. of a day, and taken 1*l.* in halfpence. I am informed, that upon an average, taking the good stands with the bad ones throughout London, there are about 1 cwt. of potatoes sold by each baked-potato man—and there are 200 of these throughout the metropolis — making the total quantity of baked potatoes consumed every day 10 tons. The money spent upon these comes to within a few shillings of 125*l.* (calculating 300 potatoes to the cwt., and each of those potatoes to be sold at a halfpenny). Hence, there are 60 tons of

baked potatoes eaten in London streets, and 750*l.* spent upon them every week during the season. Saturdays and Mondays are the best days for the sale of baked potatoes in those parts of London that are not near the markets; but in those in the vicinity of Clare, Newport, Covent-garden, Newgate, Smithfield, and other markets, the trade is briskest on the market-days. The baked-potato men are many of them broken-down tradesmen. Many are labourers who find a difficulty of obtaining employment in the winter time; some are costermongers; some have been artisans; indeed, there are some of all classes among them.

After the baked potato season is over, the generality of the hucksters take to selling strawberries, raspberries, or anything in season. Some go to labouring work. One of my informants, who had been a bricklayer's labourer, said that after the season he always looked out for work among the bricklayers, and this kept him employed until the baked potato season came round again.

" When I first took to it," he said, " I was very badly off. My master had no employment for me, and my brother was ill, and so was my wife's sister, and I had no way of keeping 'em, or myself either. The labouring men are mostly out of work in the winter time, so I spoke to a friend of mine, and he told me how he managed every winter, and advised me to do the same. I took to it, and have stuck to it ever since. The trade was much better then. I could buy a hundred-weight of potatoes for 1*s.* 9*d.* to 2*s.* 3*d.*, and there were fewer to sell them. We generally use to a cwt. of potatoes three-quarters of a pound of butter—tenpenny salt butter is what we buy—a pennyworth of salt, a pennyworth of pepper, and five pennyworth of charcoal. This, with the baking, brings the expenses to just upon 7*s.* 6*d.* per cwt., and for this our receipts will be 12*s.* 6*d.*, thus leaving about 5*s.* per cwt. profit." Hence the average profits of the trade are about 30*s.* a week—" and more to some," said my informant. A man in Smithfield-market, I am credibly informed, clears at the least 3*l.* a week. On the Friday he has a fresh basket of hot potatoes brought to him from the baker's every quarter of an hour. Such is his custom that he has not even time to take money, and his wife stands by his side to do so.

Another potato-vender who shifted his can, he said, " from a public-house where the tap dined at twelve," to another half-a-mile off, where it " dined at one, and so did the parlour," and afterwards to any place he deemed best, gave me the following account of his customers:—

" Such a day as this, sir [Jan. 24], when the fog's like a cloud come down, people looks very shy at my taties, very; they've been more suspicious ever since the taty rot. I thought I should never have rekivered it; never, not the rot. I sell most to mechanics—I was a grocer's porter myself before I was a baked taty—for their dinners, and they're on for good shops where I serves the taps and parlours, and pays me without grumbling, like gentlemen. Gentlemen does grumble though, for I've sold to them at private houses when they've held the door half open as they've called me—aye, and ladies too—and they've said, ' Is *that* all for 2*d.*?' If it 'd been a peck they'd have said the same, I know. Some customers is very pleasant with me, and says I'm a blessing. One always says he'll give me a ton of taties when his ship comes home, 'cause he can always have a hot murphy to his cold saveloy, when tin's short. He's a harness-maker, and the railways has injured him. There's Union-street and there's Pearl-row, and there's Market-street, now,—they're all off the Borough-road—if I go there at ten at night or so, I can sell 3*s.* worth, perhaps, 'cause they know me, and I have another baked taty to help there sometimes. They're women that's not reckoned the best in the world that buys there, but they pay me. I know why I got my name up. I had luck to have good fruit when the rot was about, and they got to know me. I only go twice or thrice a week, fo˖ it's two miles from my regular places. I've trusted them sometimes. They've said to me, as modest as could be, ' Do give me credit, and 'pon my word you shall be paid; there's a dear!' I am paid mostly. Little shopkeepers is fair customers, but I do best for the taps and the parlours. Perhaps I make 12*s.* or 15*s.* a week—I hardly know, for I've only myself and keep no 'count —for the season; money goes one can't tell how, and 'specially if you drinks a drop, as I do sometimes. Foggy weather drives me to it, I'm so worritted ; that is, now and then, you'll mind, sir."

There are, at present, 300 vendors of hot baked potatoes getting their living in the streets of London, each of whom sell, upon an average, ¾ cwt. of potatoes daily. The average takings of each vendor is 6*s.* a day ; and the receipts of the whole number throughout the season (which lasts from the latter end of September till March inclusive), a period of 6 months, is 14,000*l.* A capital is required to start in this trade as, follows :—can, 2*l.* ; knife, 3*d.* ; stock-money, 8*s.* ; charge for baking 100 potatoes, 1*s.* ; charcoal, 4*d.* ; butter, 2*d.* ; salt, 1*d.*, and pepper, 1*d.* ; altogether, 2*l.* 9*s.* 11*d.* The can and knife is the only property described as fixed, stock-money, &c., being daily occurring, amounts to 75*l.* during the season.

Of " Trotting," or " Hawking " Butchers.

These two appellations are, or have been, used somewhat confusedly in the meat trade. Thirty, or forty, or fifty years ago—for each term was mentioned to me—the butcher in question was a man who went "trotting" on his small horse to the mere distant suburbs to sell meat. This was when the suburbs, in any direction, were "not built up to" as they are now, and the appearance of the trotting butcher

might be hailed as saving a walk of a mile, or a mile and a half, to a butcher's shop, for only tradesmen of a smaller capital then opened butcher's shops in the remoter suburbs. For a suburban butcher to send round "for orders" at that period would have occupied too much time, for a distance must be traversed ; and to have gone, or sent, on horseback, would have entailed the keeping or hiring of a horse, which was in those days an expensive matter. One butcher who told me that he had known the trade, man and boy, for nearly fifty years, said : " As to ' trotting,' a small butcher couldn't so well do it, for if 20*l.* was offered for a tidy horse in the war time it would most likely be said, ' I'll get more for it in the cavalry—for it was often called cavalry then—there's better plunder there.' (*Plunder*, I may explain, is a common word in the horse trade to express *profit*.) So it wasn't so easy to get a horse."

The trotting butchers were then men sent or going out from the more frequented parts to supply the suburbs, but in many cases only when a tradesman was "hung up" with meat. They carried from 20 to 100 lb. of meat generally in one basket, resting on the pommel of the saddle, and attached by a long leathern strap to the person of the "trotter." The trade, however, was irregular and, considering the expenses, little remunerative; neither was it extensive, but what might be the extent I could not ascertain. There then sprung up the class of butchers—or rather the class became greatly multiplied—who sent their boys or men on fast trotting horses to take orders from the dwellers in the suburbs, and even in the streets, not suburbs, which were away from the shop thoroughfares, and afterwards to deliver the orders—still travelling on horseback—at the customer's door. This system still continues, but to nothing like its former extent, and as it does not pertain especially to the street-trade I need not dwell upon it at present, nor on the competition that sprung up as to "trotting butcher's ponies,"—in the "matching" of which "against time" sporting men have taken great interest.

Of "trotting" butchers, keeping their own horses, there are now none, but there are still, I am told, about six of the class who contrive, by hiring, or more frequently borrowing, horses of some friendly butcher, to live by trotting. These men are all known, and all call upon known customers—often those whom they have served in their prosperity, for the trotting butcher is a "reduced" man—and are not likely to be succeeded by any in the same line, or— as I heard it called—" ride " of business. These traders not subsisting exactly upon street traffic, or on any adventure depending upon door by door, or street by street, commerce, but upon a *connection* remaining from their having been in business on their own accounts, need no further mention.

The present class of street-traders in raw meat are known to the trade as "hawking" butchers, and they are as thoroughly street-sellers as are the game and poultry "hawkers." Their number, I am assured, is never less than 150, and sometimes 200 or even 250. They have all been butchers, or journeymen butchers, and are broken down in the one case, or unable to obtain work in the other. They then "watch the turn of the markets," as small meat "jobbers," and—as on the Stock Exchange—"invest," when they account the market at the lowest. The meat so purchased is hawked in a large basket carried on the shoulders, if of a weight too great to be sustained in a basket on the arm. The sale is confined almost entirely to public-houses, and those at no great distance from the great meat marts of Newgate, Leadenhall, and Whitechapel. The hawkers do not go to the suburbs. Their principal trade is in pork and veal,—for those joints weigh lighter, and present a larger surface in comparison with the weight, than do beef or mutton. The same may be said of lamb; but of that they do not buy one quarter so much as of pork or veal.

The hawking butcher bought his meat last year at from 2½d. to 5½d. the pound, according to kind and quality. He seldom gave 6d., even years ago, when meat was dearer; for it is difficult—I was told by one of these hawkers—to get more than 6d. per lb. from chance customers, no matter what the market price. "If I ask 7½d. or 7d.," he said, "I'm sure of one answer—'Nonsense!' I never goes no higher nor 6d.'" Sometimes—and especially if he can command credit for two or three days—the hawking butcher will buy the whole carcass of a sheep. If he reside near the market, he may "cut it up" in his own room; but he can generally find the necessary accommodation at some friendly butcher's block. If the weather be "bad for keeping," he will dispose of a portion of the carcass to his brother-hawkers; if cold, he will persevere in hawking the whole himself. He usually, however, buys only a hind or forequarter of mutton, or other meat, except beef, which he buys by the joint, and more sparingly than he buys any other animal food. The hawker generally has his joints weighed before he starts, and can remember the exact pounds and ounces of each, but the purchasers generally weigh them before payment; or, as one hawker expressed it, "They goes to the scales before they come to the tin."

Many of these hawkers drink hard, and, being often men of robust constitution, until the approach of age, can live "hard,"—as regards lodging, especially. One hawker I heard of slept in a slaughter-house, on the bare but clean floor, for nearly two years: "But that was seven years ago, and no butcher would allow it now."

OF THE EXPERIENCE OF A HAWKING BUTCHER.

A middle-aged man, the front of his head being nearly bald, and the few hairs there were to be seen shining strongly and lying flat, as if rubbed with suet or dripping, gave me the following account. He was dressed in the usual blue garb of the butcher:—

"I've hawked, sir—well, perhaps for fifteen years. My father was a journeyman butcher, and I helped him, and so grew up to it. I never had to call regular work, and made it out with hawking. Perhaps I've hawked, take it altogether, nearly three quarters of every year. The other times I've had a turn at slaughtering. But I haven't slaughtered for these three or four years; I've had turns as a butcher's porter, and wish I had more, as it's sure browns, if it's only 1s. 6d.: but there's often a bit of cuttings. I sell most pork of anything in autumn and winter, and most mutton in summer; but the summer isn't much more than half as good as the winter for my trade. When I slaughtered I had 3s. for an ox, 4d. for a sheep, and 1s. for a pig. Calves is slaughtered by the master's people generally. Well, I dare say it *is* cruel the way they slaughter calves; you would think it so, no doubt. I believe they slaughter cheaper now. If I buy cheap—and on a very hot day and a slow market, I have bought a fore, aye, and a hind, quarter of mutton, about two and a half stone each (8 lbs. to the stone), at 2d. a pound; but that's only very, very seldom—when I buy cheap sir, I aim at 2d. a pound over what I give, if not so cheap at 1d., and then its low to my customers. But I cut up the meat, you see, myself, and I carry it. I sell eight times as much to public-houses and eating-houses as anywhere else; most to the publics if they've ordinaries, and a deal for the publics' families' eating, 'cause a landlord knows I wouldn't deceive *him*,—and there's a part of it taken out in drink, of course, and landlords is good judges. Trade was far better years back. I've heard my father and his pals talk about a hawking butcher that twenty years ago was imprisoned falsely, and got a honest lawyer to bring his haction, and had 150*l.* damages for false imprisonment. It was in the Lord Mayor's Court of Equity, I've heard. It was a wrong arrest. I don't understand the particulars of it, but it's true; and the damages was for loss of time and trade. I'm no lawyer myself; not a bit. I have sold the like of a loin of mutton, when it was small, in a tap-room, to make chops for the people there. They'll cook chops and steaks for a pint of beer, at a public; that is, you must order a pint—but I've sold it very seldom. When mutton was dearer it was easier to sell it that way, for I sold cheap; and at one public the mechanics—I hardly know just what they was, something about building—used to gather there at one o'clock and wait for Giblets'; so they called me there. I live a good bit on the cuttings of the meat I hawk, or I chop a meal off if I can manage or afford it, or my wife—(I've only a wife and she earns never less than 2s. a week in washing for a master butcher—I wish I was a master butcher,—and that covers the rent)—

my wife makes it into broth. Take it all the year round, I s'pose I sell three stun a day (24 lb.), and at 1*d.* a pound profit. Not a farthing more go round and round. I don't think the others, altogether, do as much, for I'm known to a many landlords. But some make 3*s.* and 4*s.* a day oft enough. I've made as much myself sometimes. We all aim at 1*d.* a pound profit, but have to take less in hot weather sometimes. Last year 4*d.* the pound has been a haverage price to me for all sorts."

"Dead salesmen," as they are called—that is, the market salesmen of the meat sent so largely from Scotland and elsewhere, ready slaughtered—expressed to me their conviction that my informant's calculation was correct, and might be taken as an average; so did butchers. Thus, then, we find that the hawking butchers, taking their number at 150, sell 747,000 lbs. of meat, producing 12,450*l.* annually, one-fourth being profit; this gives an annual receipt of 83*l.* each, and an annual earning of 20*l.* 15*s.* The capital required to start in this trade is about 20*s.*, which is usually laid out as follows:—A basket for the shoulders, which costs 4*s.* 6*d.*; a leathern strap, 1*s.*; a basket for the arm, 2*s.* 6*d.*; a butcher's knife, 1*s.*; a steel, 1*s.* 6*d.*; a leather belt for the waist to which the knife is slung, 6*d.*; a chopper, 1*s.* 6*d.*; and a saw, 2*s.*; 6*s.* stock-money, though credit is sometimes given.

OF THE STREET-SELLERS OF HAM-SAND-WICHES.

THE ham-sandwich-seller carries his sandwiches on a tray or flat basket, covered with a clean white cloth; he also wears a white apron, and white sleeves. His usual stand is at the doors of the theatres.

The trade was unknown until eleven years ago, when a man who had been unsuccessful in keeping a coffee-shop in Westminster, found it necessary to look out for some mode of living, and he hit upon the plan of vending sandwiches, precisely in the present style, at the theatre doors. The attempt was successful; the man soon took 10*s.* a night, half of which was profit. He "attended" both the great theatres, and was "doing well;" but at five or six weeks' end, competitors appeared in the field, and increased rapidly, and so his sale was affected, people being regardless of his urging that he "was the original ham-sandwich." The capital required to start in the trade was small; a few pounds of ham, a proportion of loaves, and a little mustard was all that was required, and for this 10*s.* was ample. That sum, however, could not be commanded by many who were anxious to deal in sandwiches; and the man who commenced the trade supplied them at 6*d.* a dozen, the charge to the public being 1*d.* a-piece. Some of the men, however, murmured, because they thought that what they thus bought were not equal to those the wholesale sandwich-man offered for sale himself; and his wholesale trade fell off, until now, I am told, he has only two customers among street-sellers.

Ham sandwiches are made from any part of the bacon which may be sufficiently lean, such as "the gammon," which now costs 4*d.* and 5*d.* the pound. It is sometimes, but very rarely, picked up at 3½*d.* When the trade was first started, 7*d.* a pound was paid for the ham, but the sandwiches are now much larger. To make three dozen a pound of meat is required, and four quartern loaves. The "ham" may cost 5*d.*, the bread 1*s.* 8*d.* or 1*s.* 10*d.*, and the mustard 1*d.* The proceeds for this would be 3*s.*, but the trade is very precarious: little can be done in wet weather. If unsold, the sandwiches spoil, for the bread gets dry, and the ham loses its fresh colour; so that those who depend upon this trade are wretchedly poor. A first-rate week is to clear 10*s.*; a good week is put at 7*s.*; and a bad week at 3*s.* 6*d.* On some nights they do not sell a dozen sandwiches. There are half-penny sandwiches, but these are only half the size of those at a penny.

The persons carrying on this trade have been, for the most part, in some kind of service—errand-boys, pot-boys, foot-boys (or pages), or lads engaged about inns. Some few have been mechanics. Their average weekly earnings hardly exceed 5*s.*, but some "get odd jobs" at other things.

"There are now, sir, at the theatres this (the Strand) side the water, and at Ashley's, the Surrey, and the Vic., two dozen and nine sandwiches." So said one of the trade, who counted up his brethren for me. This man calculated also that at the Standard, the saloons, the concert-rooms, and at Limehouse, Mile-end, Bethnal-green-road, and elsewhere, there might be more than as many again as those "working" the theatres—or 70 in all. They are nearly all men, and no boys or girls are now in the trade. The number of these people, when the large theatres were open with the others, was about double what it is now.

The information collected shows that the expenditure in ham-sandwiches, supplied by street-sellers, is 1,820*l.* yearly, and a consumption of 436,800 sandwiches.

To start in the ham-sandwich street-trade requires 2*s.* for a basket, 2*s.* for kettle to boil ham in, 6*d.* for knife and fork, 2*d.* for mustard-pot and spoon, 7*d.* for ½ cwt. of coals, 5*s.* for ham, 1*s.* 3*d.* for bread, 4*d.* for mustard, 9*d.* for basket, cloth, and apron, 4*d.* for over-sleeves—or a capital of 12*s.* 11*d.*

OF THE EXPERIENCE OF A HAM SANDWICH-SELLER.

A young man gave me the following account. His look and manners were subdued; and, though his dress was old and worn, it was clean and unpatched:—

"I hardly remember my father, sir;" he said; "but I believe, if he'd lived, I should have been better off. My mother couldn't keep my brother and me—he's older than me—when we grew to be twelve or thirteen, and we had to shift for ourselves. She works at the stays, and now makes only 3*s.* a week, and we can't help her. I was first in place as a sort of errand-boy, then I was a stationer's boy, and then a news agent's boy. I wasn't wanted any longer, but left with a good character. My brother had gone into the sandwich trade—I hardly know what made him —and he advised me to be a ham sandwich-man, and so I started as one. At first, I made 10*s.*, and 7*s.*, and 8*s.* a week—that's seven years, or so—but things are worse now, and I make 3*s.* 6*d.* some weeks, and 5*s.* others, and 6*s.* is an out-and-outer. My rent's 2*s.* a week, but I haven't my own things. I am so sick of this life, I'd do anything to get out of it; but I don't see a way. Perhaps I might have been more careful when I was first in it; but, really, if you do make 10*s.* a week, you want shoes, or a shirt —so what is 10*s.* after all? I wish I had it now, though. I used to buy my sandwiehes at 6*d.* a dozen, but I found that wouldn't do; and now I buy and boil the stuff, and make them myself. What *did* cost 6*d.*, now only costs me 4*d.* or 4½*d.* I work the theatres this side of the water, chiefly the 'Lympic and the 'Delphi. The best theatre I ever had was the Garding, when it had two galleries, and was dramatic—the operas there wasn't the least good to me. The Lyceum was good, when it was Mr. Keeley's. I hardly know what sort my customers are, but they're those that go to theaytres: shopkeepers and clerks, I think. Gentlemen don't often buy of me. They *have* bought, though. Oh, no, they never give a farthing over; they're more likely to want seven for 6*d.* The women of the town buy of me, when it gets late, for themselves and their fancy men. They're liberal enough when they've money. They sometimes treat a poor fellow in a public-house. In summer I'm often out 'till four in the morning, and then must lie in bed half next day. The 'Delphi was better than it is. I've taken 3*s.* at the first " turn out " (the leaving the theatre for a short time after the first piece), "but the turn-outs at the Garding was better than that. A penny pie-shop has spoiled us at the 'Delphi and at Ashley's. I go out between eight and nine in the evening. People often want more in my sandwiches, though I'm starving on them. ' Oh,' they'll say, ' you've been 'prenticed to Vauxhall, you have.' ' They're 1*s.* there,' says I, ' and no bigger. I haven't Vauxhall prices.' I stand by the night-houses when it's late—not the fashionables. Their customers would'nt look at me; but I've known women, that carried their heads very high, glad to get a sandwich afterwards. Six times I've been upset by drunken fellows, on purpose, I've no doubt, and lost all my stock. Once, a gent. kicked my basket into the dirt, and he was going off—for it was late—but some people by began to make remarks about using a poor fellow that way, so he paid for all, after he had them counted. I am *so* sick of this life, sir. I *do* dread the winter so. I've stood up to the ankles in snow till after midnight, and till I've wished I was snow myself, and could melt like it and have an end. I'd do anything to get away from this, but I can't.

Passion Week's another dreadful time. It drives us to starve, just when we want to get up a little stock-money for Easter. I've been bilked by cabmen, who've taken a sandwich; but, instead of paying for it, have offered to fight me. There's no help. We're knocked about sadly by the police. Time's very heavy on my hands, sometimes, and that's where you feel it. I read a bit, if I can get anything to read, for I was at St. Clement's school; or I walk out to look for a job. On summer-days I sell a trotter or two. But mine's a wretched life, and so is most ham sandwich-men. I've no enjoyment of my youth, and no comfort

" Ah, sir! I live very poorly. A ha'porth or a penn'orth of cheap fish, which I cook myself, is one of my treats—either herrings or plaice—with a 'tatur, perhaps. Then there's a sort of meal, now and then, off the odds and ends of the ham, such as isn't quite viewy enough for the public, along with the odds and ends of the loaves. I can't boil a bit of greens with my ham, 'cause I'm afraid it might rather spoil the colour. I don't slice the ham till it's cold—it cuts easier, and is a better colour then, I think. I wash my aprons, and sleeves, and cloths myself, and iron them too. A man that sometimes makes only 3*s.* 6*d.* a week, and sometimes less, and must pay 2*s.* rent out of that, must look after every. farthing. I've often walked eight miles to see if I could find ham a halfpenny a pound cheaper anywhere. If it was tainted, I know it would be flung in my face. If I was sick there's only the parish for me."

Of the Street-sellers of Bread.

The street-trade in bread is not so extensive as might be expected, from the universality of the consumption. It is confined to Petticoat-lane and the poorer districts in that neighbourhood. A person who has known the East-end of town for nearly fifty years, told me that as long as he could recollect, bread was sold in the streets, but not to the present extent. In 1812 and 1813, when bread was the dearest, there was very little sold in the streets. At that time, and until 1815, the Assize Acts, regulating the bread-trade, were in force, and had been in force in London since 1266. Previously to 1815 bakers were restricted, by these Acts, to the baking of three kinds of bread—wheaten, standard wheaten, and household. The wheaten was made of the best flour, the standard wheaten of the different kinds of flour mixed together, and the household of the coarser and commoner flour. In 1823, however, it was enacted that within the City of London and ten miles round, " it shall be lawful for the bakers to make and sell bread made of wheat, barley, rye, oats, buck-wheat, Indian-corn, peas, beans, rice, or potatoes, or any of them, along with common salt, pure-water, eggs, milk, barm-leaven, potato, or other yeast, and mixed in such proportions as they shall think fit." I mention this because my informant, as well as an old master baker with whom I conversed on the subject, remembered that every now and then, after 1823, but only for two or three years, some speculative trader, both in shops and in the streets, would endeavour to introduce an inferior, but still a wholesome, bread, to his customers, such as an admixture of barley with wheat-flour, but no one—as far as I could learn —persevered in the speculation for more than a week or so. Their attempts were not only unsuccessful but they met with abuse, from street-buyers especially, for endeavouring to palm off " brown" bread as " good enough for poor people." One of my elder informants remembered his father telling him that in 1800 and 1801, George III. had set the example of eating brown bread at his one o'clock dinner, but he was sometimes assailed as he passed in his carriage, with the reproachful epithet of "*Brown* George." This feeling continues, for the poor people, and even the more intelligent working-men, if cockneys, have still a notion that only " white " bread is fit for consumption. Into the question of the relative nutrition of breads, I shall enter when I treat of the bakers.

During a period of about four months in the summer, there are from twenty to thirty men daily selling stale bread. Of these only twelve sell it regularly every day of the year, and they trade chiefly on their own account. Of the others, some are sent out by their masters, receiving from 1s. to 2s. for their labour. Those who sell on their own account, go round to the bakers' shops about Stepney, Mile-end, and Whitechapel, and purchase the stale-bread on hand. It is sold to them at ½d., 1d. and 1½d. per quartern less than the retail shop price; but when the weather is very hot, and the bakers have a large quantity of stale-bread on hand, the street-sellers sometimes get the bread at 2d. a quartern less than the retail price. All the street-sellers of bread have been brought up as bakers. Some have resorted to the street-trade, I am told, when unable to procure work ; others because it is a less toilsome, and sometimes a more profitable means of subsistence, than the labour of an operative baker. It is very rarely that any of the street-traders leave their calling to resume working as journeymen. Some of these traders have baskets containing the bread offered for street-sale; others have barrows, and one has a barrow resembling a costermonger's, with a long basket made to fit upon it. The dress of these vendors is a light coat of cloth or fustian ; corduroy, fustian, or cloth trousers, and a cloth cap or a hat, the whole attire being, what is best understood as " dusty," ingrained as it is with flour.

From one bread-seller, a middle-aged man, with the pale look and habitual stoop of a journeyman baker, I had the following account :

" I've known the street-trade a few years ; I can't say exactly how many. I was a journeyman baker before that, and can't say but what I had pretty regular employment ; but then, sir, what an employment it is ! So much night-work, and the heat of the oven, with the close air, and sleeping on sacks at nights (for you can't leave the place), so that altogether it's a slave's life. A journeyman baker hasn't what can be called a home, for he's so much away at the oven ; he'd better not be a married man, for if his wife isn't very careful there's talk, and there's unhappiness about nothing perhaps. I can't be thought to speak feelingly that way though, for I've been fortunate in a wife. But a journeyman baker's life drives him to drink, almost whether he will or not. A street life's not quite so bad. I was out of work two or three weeks, and I certainly lushed too much, and can't say as I tried very hard to get work, but I had a pound or two in hand, and then I began to think I'd try and sell stale bread in the streets, for it's a healthfuller trade than the other ; so I started, and have been at it ever since, excepting when I work a few days, or weeks, for a master baker ; but he's a relation, and I assist him when he's ill. My customers are all poor persons,—some in rags, and some as decent as their bad earnings 'll let them. No doubt about it, sir, there's poor women buy of me that's wives of mechanics working slop, and that's forced to live on stale bread. Where there's a family of children, stale bread goes so very much further. I think I sell to few but what has families, for a quartern's too much at a time for a single woman. I often hear my customers talk about their children, and say they must make haste, as the poor things are hungry, and they couldn't get them any bread sooner. O, it's a hard fight to live, all Spitalfields and Bethnal-green way, for I know it all. There are first the journeyman bakers over-worked and fretted into drinking, a-making the bread, and then are the poor fellows in all sorts of trade over-worked to get money to buy it. I've had women that looked as if they was ' reduced,' come to me of an evening as soon as it was dusk, and buy stale bread, as if they was ashamed to be seen. Yes, I give credit. Some has a week's credit regular, and pays every Saturday night. I lose very little in trusting. I sometimes have bread over and sell it—rather than hold it over to next day—for half what it cost me. I have given it away to begging people, sooner than keep it to be too stale, and they would get something for it at a lodging-house. The lodging-house keepers never buy of me that I know of. They can buy far cheaper than I can—you understand, sir. Perhaps, altogether, I make about a guinea every week ; wet weather and short days are against me. I don't sell more, I think, on a Saturday than on other nights. The nights are much of a muchness that way."

The average quantity sold by each vendor during the summer months is 150 quarterns daily, usually at 4d., but occasionally at 3d. the quartern. One man informed me that he had sold in one day 350 quarterns, receiving 5l. 16s. 8d. for them.

The number of men (for if there be women they are the men's wives) engaged daily throughout the year in the street-sale of bread is 12.

These sell upon an average 100 quarterns each per day: taking every day in the year 1*l*. 12*s*. each (a few being sold at 3*d*.)

Calculating then the four months' trade in summer at 150 quarterns per day per man, and reckoning 15 men so selling, and each receiving 45*s*. (thus allowing for the threepenny sale); and taking the receipts of the 12 regular traders at 1*l*. 12*s*. per day, we find nearly 9,000*l*. annually expended in the street purchase of 700,000 quartern loaves of bread. The profits of the sellers vary from 1*l*. to 2*l*. a week, according to the extent of their business.

To start in this branch of the street-trade a capital is required according to the following rate: — Stock-money for bread, average 1*l*.; (largest amount required, 5*l*.; smallest, 10*s*.); a basket, 4*s*. 6*d*. Of those who are employed in the summer, one-half have baskets, and the other half bakers' barrows; while of those who attend the year through, 8 have baskets at 4*s*. 6*d*. each, 3 have barrows at 40*s*. each, and one a barrow and the long basket, before mentioned. The barrow costs 30*s*., and the basket 2*l*.

OF THE STREET-SELLERS OF HOT GREEN PEAS.

THE sale of hot green peas in the streets is of great antiquity, that is to say, if the cry of " hot peas-cod," recorded by Lydgate (and formerly alluded to), may be taken as having intimated the sale of the same article. In many parts of the country it is, or was, customary to have " *scaldings* of peas," often held as a sort of rustic feast. The peas were not shelled, but boiled in the pod, and eaten by the pod being dipped in melted butter, with a little pepper, salt, and vinegar, and then drawn through the teeth to extract the peas, the pod being thrown away. The mention of *peas-cod* (or pea-shell) by Lydgate renders it probable that the " scalding" method was that then in use in the streets. None of the street-sellers, however, whom I saw, remembered the peas being vended in any other form than shelled and boiled as at present.

The sellers of green peas have no stands, but carry a round or oval tin pot or pan, with a swing handle; the pan being wrapped round with a thick cloth, to retain the heat. The peas are served out with a ladle, and eaten by the customers, if eaten in the street, out of basins, provided with spoons, by the pea-man. Salt, vinegar, and pepper, are applied from the vendor's store, at the customer's discretion.

There are now four men carrying on this trade. They wear no particular dress, " just what clothes we can get," said one of them. One, who has been in the trade twenty-five years, was formerly an inn-porter ; the other three are ladies' shoemakers in the day-time, and pea-sellers in the evening, or at early morning, in any market. Their average sale is three gallons daily, with a receipt of 7*s*. per man. Seven gallons a day is accounted a large sale ; but the largest of all is at Greenwich fair, when each pea-man will take 35*s*. in a day. Each

vendor has his district. One takes Billingsgate, Rosemary-lane, and its vicinity ; another, the Old Clothes Exchange, Bishopsgate, Shoreditch, and Bethnal-green ; a third, Mile-end and Stepney ; and a fourth, Ratcliffe-highway, Limehouse, and Poplar. Each man resides in his " round," for the convenience of boiling his peas, and introducing them to his customers " hot and hot."

The peas used in this traffic are all the dried field pea, but dried green and whole, and not split, or prepared, as are the yellow peas for soup or puddings. They are purchased at the corn-chandlers' or the seed-shops, the price being 2*s*. the peck (or two gallons.) The peas are soaked before they are boiled, and swell considerably, so that one gallon of the dried peas makes rather more than two gallons of the boiled. The hot green peas are sold in halfpennyworths ; a halfpennyworth being about a quarter of a pint. The cry of the sellers is, " Hot green peas ! all hot, all hot ! Here's your peas hot, hot, hot !"

OF THE EXPERIENCE OF A HOT GREEN PEA SELLER.

THE most experienced man in the trade gave me the following account :—

" Come the 25th of March, sir, and I shall have been 26 years in the business, for I started it on the 25th of March—it's a day easy for to remember, 'cause everybody knows it's quarter-day—in 1825. I was a porter in coaching-inns before ; but there was a mishap, and I had to drop it. I didn't leave 'cause I thought the pea line might be better, but because I must do something, and knew a man in the trade, and all about it. It was a capital trade then, and for a good many years after I was in it. Many a day I've taken a guinea, and, sometimes, 35*s*. ; and I have taken two guineas at Greenwich Fair, but then I worked till one or two in the morning from eleven the day before. Money wasn't so scarce then. Oh, sir, as to what my profit was or is, I never tell. I wouldn't to my own wife ; neither her that's living nor her that's dead." [A person present intimated that the secret might be safely confided to the dead wife, but the pea-seller shook his head.] " Now, one day with another, except Sundays, when I don't work, I may take 7*s*. I always use the dried peas. They pay better than fresh garden-peas would at a groat a peck. People has asked for young green peas, but I've said that I didn't have them. Billingsgate's my best ground. I sell to the costers, and the roughs, and all the parties that has their dinners in the tap-rooms—they has a bit of steak, or a bit of cold meat they've brought with them. There's very little fish eat in Billingsgate, except, perhaps, at the ord'n'ries (ordinaries). I'm looked for as regular as dinner-time. The landlords tell me to give my customers plenty of pepper and salt, to make them thirsty. I go on board the Billingsgate ships, too, and sometimes sell 6*d*. worth to captain and crew. It's a treat, after a rough voyage. Oh, no, sir, I never go on board the Dutch eel-vessels. There's nothing to be got out of scaly fur'ners (foreigners.) I sell to the herring, and mackarel, and oyster-boats when they're up. My great sale is in public-houses, but I sometimes sell 2d. or 3d. worth to private houses. I go out morning, noon, and night; and at night I go my round when people's having a bite of supper, perhaps, in the public-houses. I sell to the women of the town then. Yes, I give them credit. To-night, now (Saturday), I expect to receive 2s. 3d., or near on to it, that I've trusted them this week. They mostly pay me on a Saturday night. I lose very little by them. I'm knocked about in public-houses by the Billingsgate roughs, and I've been bilked by the prigs. I've known at least six people try my trade, and fail in it, and I was glad to see them broke. I sell twice as much in cold weather as in warm."

I ascertained that my informant sold three times as much as the other dealers, who confine their trade principally to an evening round. Reckoning that the chief man of business sells 3 gallons a day (which, at 1d. the quarter-pint, would be 8s., my informant said 7s.), and that the other three together sell the same quantity, we find a street-expenditure on hot green peas of 250l. and a street consumption of 1870 gallons. The peas, costing 2s. the two gallons, are vended for 4s. or 5s., at the least, as they boil into more than double the quantity, and a gallon, retail, is 2s. 8d.; but the addition of vinegar, pepper, &c., may reduce the profit to cent. per cent., while there is the heaping up of every measure retail to reduce the profit. Thus, independent of any consideration as to the labour in boiling, &c. (generally done by the women), the principal man's profit is 21s. a week; that of the others 7s. each weekly.

The capital required to start in the business is—can, 2s. 6d.; vinegar-bottle and pepper-box, 4d.; saucers and spoons, 6d.; stock-money, about 2s.; cloth to wrap over the peas, 4d. (a vendor wearing out a cloth in three months); or an average of 9s. or 10s.

OF CATS' AND DOGS'-MEAT DEALERS.

THE supply of food for cats and dogs is far greater than may be generally thought. "Vy, sir," said one of the dealers to me, "can you tell me 'ow many people's in London?" On my replying, upwards of two millions; "I don't know nothing vatever," said my informant, "about millions, but I think there's a cat to every ten people, aye, and more than that; and so, sir, you can reckon." [I told him this gave a total of 200,000 cats in London; but the number of inhabited houses in the metropolis was 100,000 more than this, and though there was not a cat to every house, still, as many lodgers as well as householders kept cats, I added that I thought the total number of cats in London might be taken at the same number as the inhabited houses, or 300,000 in all.] "There's not near half so many dogs as cats. I must know, for they all knows me, and I sarves about 200 cats

and 70 dogs. Mine's a middling trade, but some does far better. Some cats has a hap'orth a day, some every other day; werry few can afford a penn'orth, but times is inferior. Dogs is better pay when you've a connection among 'em."

The cat and dogs'-meat dealers, or "carriers," as they call themselves, generally purchase the meat at the knackers' (horse-slaughterers') yards. There are upwards of twenty of such yards in London; three or four are in White-chapel, one in Wandsworth, two in Cow-cross —one of the two last mentioned is the largest establishment in London—and there are two about Bermondsey. The proprietors of these yards purchase live and dead horses. They contract for them with large firms, such as brewers, coal-merchants, and large cab and 'bus yards, giving so much per head for their old live and dead horses through the year. The price varies from 2l. to 50s. the carcass. The knackers also have contractors in the country (harness-makers and others), who bring or send up to town for them the live and dead stock of those parts. The dead horses are brought to the yard —two or three upon one cart, and sometimes five. The live ones are tied to the tail of these carts, and behind the tail of each other. Occasionally a string of fourteen or fifteen are brought up, head to tail, at one time. The live horses are purchased merely for slaughtering. If among the lot bought there should chance to be one that is young, but in bad condition, it is placed in the stable, fed up, and then put into the knacker's carts, or sold by them, or let on hire. Occasionally a fine horse has been rescued from death in this manner. One person is known to have bought an animal for 15s., for which he afterwards got 150l. Frequently young horses that will not work in cabs—such as "jibs"—are sold to the horse-slaughterers as useless. They are kept in the yard, and after being well fed, often turn out good horses. The live horses are slaughtered by the persons called "knackers." These men get upon an average 4s. a day. They begin work at twelve at night, because some of the flesh is required to be boiled before six in the morning; indeed, a great part of the meat is delivered to the carriers before that hour. The horse to be slaughtered has his mane clipped as short as possible (on account of the hair, which is valuable). It is then blinded with a piece of old apron smothered in blood, so that it may not see the slaughterman when about to strike. A pole-axe is used, and a cane, to put an immediate end to the animal's sufferings. After the animal is slaughtered, the hide is taken off, and the flesh cut from the bones in large pieces. These pieces are termed, according to the part from which they are cut, hind-quarters, fore-quarters, cram-bones, throats, necks, briskets, backs, ribs, kidney pieces, hearts, tongues, liver and lights. The bones (called "racks" by the knackers) are chopped up and boiled, in order to extract the fat, which is used for greasing common harness, and the wheels of carts and drags, &c. The bones themselves are sold for manure. The pieces of flesh are thrown into large coppers or pans, about nine feet in diameter and four feet deep. Each of these pans will hold about three good-sized horses. Sometimes two large brewers' horses will fill them, and sometimes as many as four "poor" cab-horses may be put into them. The flesh is boiled about an hour and 20 minutes for a "killed" horse, and from two hours to two hours and 20 minutes for a dead horse (a horse dying from age or disease). The flesh, when boiled, is taken from the coppers, laid on the stones, and sprinkled with water to cool it. It is then weighed out in pieces of 112, 56, 28, 21, 14, 7, and 3½ lbs. weight. These are either taken round in a cart to the "carriers," or, at about five, the carriers call at the yard to purchase, and continue doing so till twelve in the day. The price is 14s. per cwt. in winter, and 16s. in summer. The tripe is served out at 12 lb. for 6d. All this is for cats and dogs. The carriers then take the meat round town, wherever their "walk" may lie. They sell it to the public at the rate of 2½d. per lb., and in small pieces, on skewers, at a farthing, a halfpenny, and a penny each. Some carriers will sell as much as a hundred-weight in a day, and about half a hundred-weight is the average quantity disposed of by the carriers in London. Some sell much cheaper than others. These dealers will frequently knock at the doors of persons whom they have seen served by another on the previous day, and show them that they can let them have a larger quantity of meat for the same money. The class of persons belonging to the business are mostly those who have been unable to obtain employment at their trade. Occasionally a person is bred to it, having been engaged as a lad by some carrier to go round with the barrow and assist him in his business. These boys will, after a time, find a "walk" for themselves, beginning first with a basket, and ultimately rising to a barrow. Many of the carriers give light weight to the extent of 2 oz. and 4 oz. in the pound. At one yard alone near upon 100 carriers purchase meat, and there are, upon an average, 150 horses slaughtered there every week. Each slaughter-house may be said to do, one with another, 60 horses per week throughout the year, which, reckoning the London slaughter-houses at 12, gives a total of 720 horses killed every week in the metropolis, or, in round numbers, 37,500 in the course of the year. The London cat and dogs'-meat carriers or sellers—nearly all men—number at the least 1,000.

The slaughtermen are said to reap large fortunes very rapidly—indeed, the carriers say they coin the money. Many of them retire after a few years, and take large farms. One, after 12 years' business, retired with several thousand pounds, and has now three large farms. The carriers are men, women, and boys. Very few women do as well as the men at it. The carriers "are generally sad drunkards." Out of five hundred, it is said three hundred at least spend 1l. a head a week in drink. One party in

the trade told me that he knew a carrier who would often spend 10s. in liquor at one sitting. The profit the carriers make upon the meat is at present only a penny per pound. In the summer time the profit per pound is reduced to a halfpenny, owing to the meat being dearer on account of its scarcity. The carriers give a great deal of credit—indeed, they take but little ready money. On some days they do not come home with more than 2s. One with a middling walk pays for his meat 7s. 6d. per day. For this he has half a hundred-weight. This produces him as much as 11s. 6d., so that his profit is 4s.; which, I am assured, is about a fair average of the earnings of the trade. One carrier is said to have amassed 1,000l. at the business. He usually sold from 1½ to 2 cwt. every morning, so that his profits were generally from 16s. to 1l. per day. But the trade is much worse now. There are so many at it, they say, that there is barely a living for any. A carrier assured me that he seldom went less than 30, and frequently 40 miles, through the streets every day. The best districts are among the houses of tradesmen, mechanics, and labourers. The coachmen in the mews at the back of the squares are very good customers. "The work lays thicker there," said my informant. Old maids are bad, though very plentiful, customers. They cheapen the carriers down so, that they can scarcely live at the business. "They will pay one halfpenny and owe another, and forget that after a day or two." The cats' meat dealers generally complain of their losses from bad debts. Their customers require credit frequently to the extent of 1l. "One party owes me 15s. now," said a carrier to me, "and many 10s.; in fact, very few people pay ready money for the meat."

The carriers frequently serve as much as ten pennyworths to one person in a day. One gentleman has as much as 4 lbs. of meat each morning for two Newfoundland dogs; and there was one woman—a black—who used to have as much as 16 pennyworth every day. This person used to get out on the roof of the house and throw it to the cats on the tiles. By this she brought so many stray cats round about the neighbourhood, that the parties in the vicinity complained; it was quite a nuisance. She *would* have the meat always brought to her before ten in the morning, or else she would send to a shop for it, and between ten and eleven in the morning the noise and cries of the hundreds of stray cats attracted to the spot was "terrible to hear." When the meat was thrown to the cats on the roof, the riot, and confusion, and fighting, was beyond description. "A beer-shop man," I was told, "was obliged to keep five or six dogs to drive the cats from his walls." There was also a mad woman in Islington, who used to have 14 lbs. of meat a day. The party who supplied her had his money often at 2l. and 3l. at a time. She had as many as thirty cats at times in her house. Every stray one that came she would take in and support. The stench was so great that she was obliged to be ejected. The best days for the cats' meat business are Mondays, Tuesdays, and Saturdays. A double quantity of meat is sold on the Saturday; and on that day and Monday and Tuesday the weekly customers generally pay.

"My father was a baker by trade," said a carrier to me, "but through an enlargement of the heart he was obliged to give up working at his trade; leaning over the trough increased his complaint so severely, that he used to fall down, and be obliged to be brought home. This made him take to the cats' and dogs' meat trade, and he brought me up to it. I do pretty comfortably. I have a very good business, having been all my life at it. If it wasn't for the bad debts I should do much better; but some of the people I trust leave the houses, and actually take in a double quantity of meat the day before. I suppose there is at the present moment as much as 20*l.* owing to me that I never expect to see a farthing of."

The generality of the dealers wear a shiny hat, black plush waistcoat and sleeves, a blue apron, corduroy trousers, and a blue and white spotted handkerchief round their necks. Some, indeed, will wear two and three handkerchiefs round their necks, this being fashionable among them. A great many meet every Friday afternoon in the donkey-market, Smithfield, and retire to a public-house adjoining, to spend the evening.

A "cats' meat carrier" who supplied me with information was more comfortably situated than any of the poorer classes that I have yet seen. He lived in the front room of a second floor, in an open and respectable quarter of the town, and his lodgings were the perfection of comfort and cleanliness in an humble sphere. It was late in the evening when I reached the house. I found the "carrier" and his family preparing for supper. In a large morocco leather easy chair sat the cats' meat carrier himself; his "blue apron and black shiny hat" had disappeared, and he wore a "dress" coat and a black satin waistcoat instead. His wife, who was a remarkably pretty woman, and of very attractive manners, wore a "Dolly Varden" cap, placed jauntily at the back of her head, and a drab merino dress. The room was cosily carpeted, and in one corner stood a mahogany "crib" with cane-work sides, in which one of the children was asleep. On the table was a clean white table-cloth, and the room was savoury with the steaks, and mashed potatoes that were cooking on the fire. Indeed, I have never yet seen greater comfort in the abodes of the poor. The cleanliness and wholesomeness of the apartment were the more striking from the unpleasant associations connected with the calling.

It is believed by one who has been engaged at the business for 25 years, that there are from 900 to 1,000 horses, averaging 2 cwt. of meat each—little and big—boiled down every week; so that the quantity of cats' and dogs' meat used throughout London is about 200,000 lbs. per

week, and this, sold at the rate of 2½*d.* per lb., gives 2,000*l.* a week for the money spent in cats' and dogs' meat, or upwards of 100,000*l.* a year, which is at the rate of 100*l.*-worth sold annually by each carrier. The profits of the carriers may be estimated at about 50*l.* each per annum.

The capital required to start in this business varies from 1*l.* to 2*l.* The stock-money needed is between 5*s.* and 10*s.* The barrow and basket, weights and scales, knife and steel, or blackstone, cost about 2*l.* when new, and from 15*s.* to 4*s.* second-hand.

OF THE STREET-SALE OF DRINKABLES.

THE street-sellers of the drinkables, who have now to be considered, belong to the same class as I have described in treating of the sale of street-provisions generally. The buyers are not precisely of the same class, for the street-eatables often supply a meal, but with the exception of the coffee-stalls, and occasionally of the rice-milk, the drinkables are more of a luxury than a meal. Thus the buyers are chiefly those who have "a penny to spare," rather than those who have "a penny to dine upon." I have described the different classes of purchasers of each potable, and perhaps the accounts—as a picture of street-life—are even more curious than those I have given of the purchasers of the eatables—of (literally) the diners *out.*

OF COFFEE-STALL KEEPERS.

THE vending of tea and coffee, in the streets, was little if at all known twenty years ago, saloop being then the beverage supplied from stalls to the late and early wayfarers. Nor was it until after 1842 that the stalls approached to anything like their present number, which is said to be upwards of 300—the majority of the proprietors being women. Prior to 1824, coffee was in little demand, even among the smaller tradesmen or farmers, but in that year the duty having been reduced from 1*s.* to 6*d.* per lb., the consumption throughout the kingdom in the next seven years was nearly trebled, the increase being from 7,933,041 lbs., in 1824, to 22,745,627 lbs., in 1831. In 1842, the duty on coffee, was fixed at 4*d.*, from British possessions, and from foreign countries at 6*d.*

But it was not owing solely to the reduced price of coffee, that the street-vendors of it increased in the year or two subsequent to 1842, at least 100 per cent. The great facilities then offered for a cheap adulteration, by mixing ground chicory with the ground coffee, was an enhancement of the profits, and a greater temptation to embark in the business, as a smaller amount of capital would suffice. Within these two or three years, this cheapness has been still further promoted, by the medium of adulteration, the chicory itself being, in its turn, adulterated by the admixture of baked carrots, and the like saccharine roots, which, of course, are not subjected to any duty, while foreign chicory is charged 6d. per lb. English chicory is not chargeable with duty, and is now cultivated, I am assured, to the yield of between 4,000 and 5,000 tons yearly, and this nearly all used in the adulteration of coffee. Nor is there greater culpability in this trade among street-venders, than among "respectable" shopkeepers; for I was assured, by a leading grocer, that he could not mention twenty shops in the city, of which he could say: "You can go and buy a pound of ground coffee there, and it will not be adulterated." The revelations recently made on this subject by the *Lancet* are a still more convincing proof of the *general* dishonesty of grocers.

The coffee-stall keepers generally stand at the corner of a street. In the fruit and meat markets there are usually two or three coffee-stalls, and one or two in the streets leading to them; in Covent-garden there are no less than four coffee-stalls. Indeed, the stalls abound in all the great thoroughfares, and the most in those not accounted "fashionable" and great "business" routes, but such as are frequented by working people, on their way to their day's labour. The best "pitch" in London is supposed to be at the corner of Duke-street, Oxford-street. The proprietor of that stall is said to take full 30s. of a morning, in halfpence. One stall-keeper, I was informed, when "upon the drink" thinks nothing of spending his 10l. or 15l. in a week. A party assured me that once, when the stall-keeper above mentioned was away "on the spree," he took up his stand there, and got from 4s. to 5s. in the course of ten minutes, at the busy time of the morning.

The coffee-stall usually consists of a spring-barrow, with two, and occasionally four, wheels. Some are made up of tables, and some have a tressel and board. On the top of this are placed two or three, and sometimes four, large tin cans, holding upon an average five gallons each. Beneath each of these cans is a small iron fire-pot, perforated like a rushlight shade, and here charcoal is continually burning, so as to keep the coffee or tea, with which the cans are filled, hot throughout the early part of the morning. The board of the stall has mostly a compartment for bread and butter, cake, and ham sandwiches, and another for the coffee mugs. There is generally a small tub under each of the stalls, in which the mugs and saucers are washed. The "grandest" stall in this line is the one before-mentioned, as standing at the corner of Duke-street, Oxford-street (of which an engraving is here given). It is a large truck on four wheels, and painted a bright green. The cans are four in number, and of bright polished tin, mounted with brass-plates. There are compartments for bread and butter, sandwiches, and cake. It is lighted by three large oil lamps, with bright brass mountings, and covered in with an oil-cloth roof. The coffee-stalls, generally, are lighted by candle-lamps. Some coffee-stalls are covered over with tarpaulin, like a tent, and others screened from the sharp night or morning air by a clothes-horse covered with blankets, and drawn half round the stall.

Some of the stall-keepers make their appearance at twelve at night, and some not till three or four in the morning. Those that come out at midnight, are for the accommodation of the "night-walkers"—"fast gentlemen" and loose girls; and those that come out in the morning, are for the accommodation of the working men. I may add, piteous enough to see a few young and good-looking girls, some without the indelible mark of habitual depravity on their countenances, clustering together for warmth round a coffee-stall, to which a penny expenditure, or the charity of the proprietor, has admitted them. The thieves do not resort to the coffee-stalls, which are so immediately under the eye of the policeman.

The coffee-stall keepers usually sell coffee and tea, and some of them cocoa. They keep hot milk in one of the large cans, and coffee, tea, or cocoa in the others. They supply bread and butter, or currant cake, in slices — ham sandwiches, water-cresses, and boiled eggs. The price is 1d. per mug, or ½d. per half-mug, for coffee, tea, or cocoa; and ½d. a slice the bread and butter or cake. The ham sandwiches are 2d. (or 1d.) each, the boiled eggs 1d., and the water-cresses a halfpenny a bunch. The coffee, tea, cocoa, and sugar they generally purchase by the single pound, at a grocer's. Those who do an extensive trade purchase in larger quantities. The coffee is usually bought in the berry, and ground by themselves. All purchase chicory to mix with it. For the coffee they pay about 1s.; for the tea about 3s.; for the cocoa 6d. per lb.; and for the sugar 3½d. to 4d. For the chicory the price is 6d. (which is the amount of the duty alone on foreign chicory), and it is mixed with the coffee at the rate of 6 ozs. to the pound; many use as much as 9 and 12 ozs. The coffee is made of a dark colour by means of what are called "finings," which consist of burnt sugar — such, as is used for browning soups. Coffee is the article mostly sold at the stalls; indeed, there is scarcely one stall in a hundred that is supplied with tea, and not more than a dozen in all London that furnish cocoa. The stall-keepers usually make the cake themselves. A 4 lb. cake generally consists of half a pound of currants, half a pound of sugar, six ounces of beef dripping, and a quartern of flour. The ham for sandwiches costs 5½d. or 6d. per lb.; and when boiled produces in sandwiches about 2s. per lb. It is usually cut up in slices little thicker than paper. The bread is usually "second bread;" the butter, salt, at about 8d. the pound. Some borrow their barrows, and pay 1s. a week for the hire of them. Many borrow the capital upon which they trade, frequently of their landlord. Some get credit for their grocery—some for their bread. If they borrow, they pay about 20 per cent. per week for the loan. I was told of one man that makes a practice of lending

THE LONDON COFFEE-STALL.

[From a Daguerreotype by BEARD.]

money to the coffee-stall-keepers and other hucksters, at the rate of at least 20 per cent. a week. If the party wishing to borrow a pound or two is unknown to the money-lender, he requires security, and the interest to be paid him weekly. This money-lender, I am informed, has been transported once for receiving stolen property, and would now purchase any amount of plate that might be taken to him.

The class of persons usually belonging to the business have been either cab-men, policemen, labourers, or artisans. Many have been bred to dealing in the streets, and brought up to no other employment, but many have taken to the business owing to the difficulty of obtaining work at their own trade. The generality of them are opposed to one another. I asked one in a small way of business what was the average amount of his profits, and his answer was,—

"I usually buy 10 ounces of coffee a night. That costs, when good, 1s. 0½d. With this I should make five gallons of coffee, such as I sell in the street, which would require 3 quarts of milk, at 3d. per quart, and 1½ lb. of sugar, at 3½d. per lb., there is some at 3d. This would come to 2s. 2¾d.; and, allowing 1½d. for a quarter of a peck of charcoal to keep the coffee hot, it would give 2s. 4d. for the cost of five gallons of coffee. This I should sell out at about 1½d. per pint; so that the five gallons would produce me 5s., or 2s. 8d. clear. I generally get rid of one quartern loaf and 6 oz. of butter with this quantity of coffee, and for this I pay 5d. the loaf and 3d. the butter, making 8d.; and these I make into twenty-eight slices at ½d. per slice; so the whole brings me in 1s. 2d., or about 6d. clear. Added to this, I sell a 4 lb. cake, which costs me 3½d. per lb. 1s. 2d. the entire cake; and this in twenty-eight slices, at 1d. per slice, would yield 2s. 4d., or 1s. 2d. clear; so that altogether my clear gains would be 4s. 4d. upon an expenditure of 2s. 2d.—say 200 per cent."

This is said to be about the usual profit of the trade. Sometimes they give credit. One person assured me he trusted as much as 9½d. that morning, and out of that he was satisfied there was 4d., at least, he should never see. Most of the stalls are stationary, but some are locomotive. Some cans are carried about with yokes, like milk-cans, the mugs being kept in a basket. The best district for the night-trade is the City, and the approaches to the bridges. There are more men and women, I was told, walking along Cheapside, Aldersgate-street, Bishopsgate-street, and Fleet-street. In the latter place a good trade is frequently done between twelve at night and two in the morning. For the morning trade the best districts are the Strand, Oxford-street, City-road, New-road (from one end to the other), the markets, especially Covent Garden, Billingsgate, Newgate, and the Borough. There are no coffee-stalls in Smithfield. The reason is that the drovers, on arriving at the market, are generally tired and cold, and prefer sitting down to their coffee in a warm shop rather than drink it in the open street. The best days for coffee-stalls are market mornings, viz. Tuesday, Thursday, and Saturday. On these days the receipts are generally half as much again as those of the other mornings. The best time of the year for the business is the summer. This is, I am told, because the workpeople and costermongers have more money to spend. Some stall-keepers save sufficient to take a shop, but these are only such as have a "pitch" in the best thoroughfares. One who did a little business informed me that he usually cleared, including Sunday, 14s.—last week his gains were 15s.; the week before that he could not remember. He is very frequently out all night, and does not earn sixpence. This is on wet and cold nights, when there are few people about. His is generally the night-trade. The average weekly earnings of the trade, throughout the year, are said to be 1l. The trade, I am assured by all, is overstocked. They are half too many, they say. "Two of us," to use their own words, "are eating one man's bread." "When coffee in the streets first came up, a man could go and earn," I am told, "his 8s. a night at the very lowest; but now the same class of men cannot earn more than 3s." Some men may earn comparatively a large sum, as much as 38s., or 2l., but the generality of the trade cannot make more than 1l. per week, if so much. The following is the statement of one of the class:—

"I was a mason's labourer, a smith's labourer, a plasterer's labourer, or a bricklayer's labourer. I was, indeed, a labouring man. I could not get employment. I was for six months without any employment. I did not know which way to support my wife and child (I have only one child). Being so long out of employment, I saw no other means of getting a living but out of the streets. I was almost starving before I took to it—that I certainly was. I'm not ashamed of telling anybody that, because it's true, and I sought for a livelihood wherever I could. Many said they wouldn't do such a thing as keep a coffee-stall, but I said I'd do anything to get a bit of bread honestly. Years ago, when I was a boy, I used to go out selling water-cresses, and apples, oranges, and radishes, with a barrow, for my landlord; so I thought, when I was thrown out of employment, I would take to selling coffee in the streets. I went to a tinman, and paid him 10s. 6d. (the last of my savings, after I'd been four or five months out of work) for a can, I didn't care how I got my living so long as I could turn an honest penny. Well; I went on, and knocked about, and couldn't get a pitch anywhere; but at last I heard that an old man, who had been in the habit of standing for many years at the entrance of one of the markets, had fell ill; so, what did I do, but I goes and pops into his pitch, and there I've done better than ever I did afore. I get 20s. now where I got 10s. one time; and if I only had such a thing as 5*l.* or 10*l.*, I might get a good living for life. I cannot do half as much as the man that was there before me. He used to make his coffee down there, and had a can for hot water as well; but I have but one can to keep coffee and all in; and I have to borrow my barrow, and pay 1*s.* a week for it. If I sell my can out, I can't do any more. The struggle to get a living is so great, that, what with one and another in the coffee-trade, it's only those as can get good 'pitches' that can get a crust at it."

As it appears that each coffee-stall keeper on an average, clears 1*l.* a week, and his takings may be said to be at least double that sum, the yearly street expenditure for tea, coffee, &c., amounts to 31,200*l.* The quantity of coffee sold annually in the streets, appears to be about 550,000 gallons.

To commence as a coffee-stall keeper in a moderate manner requires about 5*l.* capital. The truck costs 2*l.*, and the other utensils and materials 3*l.* The expense of the cans is near upon 16*s.* each. The stock-money is a few shillings.

OF THE STREET SALE OF GINGER-BEER, SHERBET, LEMONADE, &c.

THE street-trade in ginger-beer—now a very considerable traffic—was not known to any extent until about thirty years ago. About that time (1822) a man, during a most sultry drought, sold extraordinary quantities of "cool ginger-beer" and of "soda-powders," near the Royal Exchange, clearing, for the three or four weeks the heat continued, 30*s.* a day, or 9*l.* weekly. Soda-water he sold "in powders," the acid and the alkali being mixed in the water of the glass held by the customer, and drunk whilst effervescing. His prices were 2*d.* and 3*d.* a glass for ginger-beer; and 3*d.* and 4*d.* for soda-water, "according to the quality;" though there was in reality no difference whatever in the quality—only in the price. From that time, the numbers pursuing this street avocation increased gradually; they have however fallen off of late years.

The street-sellers who "brew their own beer" generally prepare half a gross (six dozen) at a time. For a "good quality" or the "penny bottle" trade, the following are the ingredients and the mode of preparation:—3 gallons of water; 1 lb. of ginger, 6*d.*; lemon-acid, 2*d.*; essence of cloves, 2*d.*; yeast, 2*d.*; and 1 lb. of raw sugar, 7*d.* This admixture, the yeast being the last ingredient introduced, stands 24 hours, and is then ready for bottling. If the beverage be required in 12 hours, double the quantity of yeast is used. The bottles are filled only "to the ridge," but the liquid and the froth more than fill a full-sized half-pint glass. "Only half froth," I was told, "is reckoned very fair, and it's just the same in the shops." Thus, 72 bottles, each to be sold at 1*d.*, cost—apart from any outlay in utensils, or any consideration of the value of labour—only 1*s.* 7*d.*, and yield, at

1*d.* per bottle, 6*s.* For the cheaper beverage —called "playhouse ginger-beer" in the trade —instead of sugar, molasses from the "private distilleries" is made available. The "private" distilleries are the illicit ones: "'Jiggers,' we call them," said one man; "and I could pass 100 in 10 minutes' walk from where we're talking." Molasses, costing 3*d.* at a jigger's, is sufficient for a half-gross of bottles of ginger-beer; and of the other ingredients only half the quantity is used, the cloves being altogether dispensed with, but the same amount of yeast is generally applied. This quality of "beer" is sold at ½*d.* the glass.

About five years ago "fountains" for the production of ginger-beer became common in the streets. The ginger-beer trade in the open air is only for a summer season, extending from four to seven months, according to the weather, the season last year having been over in about four months. There were then 200 fountains in the streets, all of which, excepting 20 or 30 of the best, were hired of the ginger-beer manufacturers, who drive a profitable trade in them. The average value of a street-fountain, with a handsome frame or stand, which is usually fixed on a wheeled and movable truck, so as one man's strength may be sufficient to propel it, is 7*l.*; and, for the rent of such a fountain, 6*s.* a week is paid when the season is brisk, and 4*s.* when it is slack; but last summer, I am told, 4*s.* 6*d.* was an average. The largest and handsomest ginger-beer fountain in London was—I speak of last summer—in use at the East-end, usually standing in Petticoat-lane, and is the property of a dancing-master. It is made of mahogany, and presents somewhat the form of an upright piano on wheels. It has two pumps, and the brass of the pump-handles and the glass receivers is always kept bright and clean, so that the whole glitters handsomely to the light. Two persons "serve" at this fountain; and on a fine Sunday morning, from six to one, that being the best trading time, they take 7*l.* or 8*l.* in halfpennies—for "the beer" is ½*d.* a glass—and 2*l.* each other day of the week. This machine, as it may be called, is drawn by two ponies, said to be worth 10*l.* a-piece; and the whole cost is pronounced—perhaps with a sufficient exaggeration—to have been 150*l.* There were, in the same neighbourhood, two more fountains on a similar scale, but commoner, each drawn by only one pony instead of the aristocratic "pair."

The ingredients required to feed the "ginger-beer" fountains are of a very cheap description. To supply 10 gallons, 2 quarts of lime-juice (as it is called, but it is, in reality, lemon-juice), costing 3*s.* 6*d.*, are placed in the recess, sometimes with the addition of a pound of sugar (4*d.*); while some, I am assured, put in a smaller quantity of juice, and add two-pennyworth of oil of vitriol, which "brings out the sharpness of the lime-juice." The rest is water. No process of brewing or fermentation is necessary, for the fixed air pumped into the liquid as it is drawn from the fountain, communicates a sufficient briskness or effervescence. "The harder you pumps," said one man who had worked a fountain, "the frothier it comes; and though it seems to fill a big glass—and the glass an't so big for holding as it looks—let it settle, and there's only a quarter of a pint." The hirer of a fountain is required to give security. This is not, as in some sloptrades, a deposit of money; but a householder must, by written agreement, make himself responsible for any damage the fountain may sustain, as well as for its return, or make good the loss: the street ginger-beer seller is alone responsible for the rent of the machine. It is however, only men that are known, who are trusted in this way. Of the fountains thus hired, 50 are usually to be found at the neighbouring fairs and races. As the ginger-beer men carry lime-juice, &c., with them, only water is required to complete the "brewing of the beer" and so conveyance is not difficult.

There is another kind of "ginger-beer," or rather of "small acid tiff," which is sold out of barrels at street-stalls at ½d. the glass. To make 2½ gallons of this, there is used ½lb. tartaric, or other acid, 1s.; ½ lb. alkali (soda), 10d.; ½ lb. lump sugar, bruised fine, 4d.; and yeast 1d. Of these "barrel-men" there are now about one hundred.

Another class of street-sellers obtain their stock of ginger-beer from the manufacturers. One of the largest manufacturers for the street-trade resides near Ratcliffe-highway, and another in the Commercial-road. The charge by the wholesale traders is 8d. the doz., while to a known man, or for ready money, 13 are given to the dozen. The beer, however, is often let out on credit—or in some cases security is given in the same way as for the fountains—and the empty bottles must be duly returned. It is not uncommon for two gross of beer to be let out in this way at a time. For the itinerant trade these are placed on a truck or barrow, fitted up with four shelves, on which are ranged the bottles. These barrows are hired in the same way as the costers' barrows. Some sell their beer at stalls fitted up exclusively for the trade, a kind of tank being let into the centre of the board and filled with water, in which the glasses are rinsed or washed. Underneath the stall there is usually a reserve of the beer, and a keg containing water. Some of the best frequented stalls were in Whitechapel, Old-street-road, City-road, Tottenham-court-road, the New-cut, Elephant and Castle, the Commercial-road, Tower-hill, the Strand, and near Westminster-bridge. The stationary beer business is, for the most part, carried on in the more public streets, such as Holborn and Oxford-street, and in the markets of Covent-garden, Smithfield, and Billingsgate; while the peripatetic trade, which is briskest on the Sundays—when, indeed, some of the stationary hands become itinerant—is more for the suburbs; Victoria-park, Battersea-fields, Hampstead-heath, Primrose-hill, Kennington-common, and Camberwell-green, being approved Sunday haunts.

The London street-sellers of ginger-beer, say the more experienced, may be computed at 3,000—of whom about one-third are women. I heard them frequently estimated at 5,000, and some urged that the number was at least as near 5,000 as 3,000. For my own part I am inclined to believe that half the smaller number would be nearer the truth. Judging by the number of miles of streets throughout the metropolis, and comparing the street-sellers of ginger-beer with the fruit-stall keepers, I am satisfied that in estimating the ginger-beer-sellers at 1,500 we are rather over than under the truth. This body of street-sellers were more numerous five years back by 15 or 20 per cent., but the introduction of the street fountains, and the trade being resorted to by the keepers of coal-sheds and the small shopkeepers—who have frequently a stand with ginger-beer in front of their shops —have reduced the amount of the street-sellers. In 1842, there were 1,200 ginger-beer sellers in the streets who had attached to their stalls or trucks labels, showing that they were members —or assumed to be members—of the Society of Odd Fellows. This was done in hopes of a greater amount of custom from the other members of the Society, but the expectation was not realised—and so the Odd Fellowship of the ginger-beer people disappeared. Of the street-traders 200 work fountains; and of the remaining portion the stationary and the itinerant are about equally divided. Of the whole number, however, not above an eighth confine themselves to the trade, but usually sell with their "pop" some other article of open-air traffic—fruit, sweet-stuff, or shell-fish. There are of the entire number about 350, who, whenever the weather permits, stay out all night with their stands or barrows, and are to be found especially in all the approaches to Covent-garden, and the other markets to which there is a resort during the night or at day-break. These men, I was told by one of their body, worked from eight in the evening to eight or ten next morning, then went to bed, rose at three, and "plenty of 'em then goes to the skittles or to get drunk."

The character of the ginger-beer-sellers does not differ from what I have described as pertaining to the costermonger class, and to street-traders generally. There is the same admixture of the reduced mechanic, the broken-down gentleman's servant, the man of any class in life who cannot brook the confinement and restraint of ordinary in-door labour, and of the man "brought up to the streets." One experienced and trustworthy man told me that from his own knowledge he could count up twenty "classical men," as he styled them, who were in the street ginger-beer-trade, and of these four had been, or were said to have been "parsons," two being of the same name (Mr. S ——); but my informant did not know if they stood in any degree of consanguinity one to another. The women are the wives, daughters, or other connections of the men.

Some of the stalls at which ginger-beer is sold —and it is the same at the coal-sheds and the chandlers' shops—are adorned pictorially. Erected at the end of a stall is often a painting, papered on a board, in which a gentleman, with the bluest of coats, the whitest of trousers, the yellowest of waistcoats, and the largest of guard-chains or eye-glasses, is handing a glass of ginger-beer, frothed up like a pot of stout, and containing, apparently, a pint and a half, to some lady in flowing white robes, or gorgeous in purple or orange.

To commence in this branch of the street business requires, in all 18s. 3d.: six glasses, 2s. 9d.; board, 5s.; tank, 1s.; keg, 1s.; gross of beer, 8s. (this is where the seller is not also the maker); and for towels, &c., 6d.; if however the street-seller brew his own beer, he will require half a gross of bottles, 5s. 6d.; and the ingredients I have enumerated, 1s. 7d.

In addition to the street-sale of ginger-beer is that of other summer-drinks. Of these, the principal is lemonade, the consumption of which is as much as that of all the others together. Indeed, the high-sounding names given to some of these beverages—such as "Nectar" and "Persian Sherbet"—are but other names for lemonade, in a slightly different colour or fashion.

Lemonade is made, by those vendors who deal in the best articles, after the following method: 1 lb. of carbonate of soda, 6d.; 1 lb. of tartaric acid, 1s. 4d. ("at least," said an informant, 'I pay 1s. 4d. at 'Pothecaries Hall, but it can be had at 1s."); 1 lb. of loaf-sugar, 5½d.; essence of lemon, 3d. This admixture is kept, in the form of a powder, in a jar, and water is drawn from what the street-sellers call a "stone-barrel"—which is a stone jar, something like the common-shaped filters, with a tap—and a larger or smaller spoonful of the admixture in a glass of water supplies an effervescing draught for 1d. or ¼d. "There's sometimes shocking roguishness in the trade," said one man, "and there is in a many trades—some uses vitriol!" Lemonade, made after the recipe I have given, is sometimes bottled by the street-sellers, and sold in the same way as ginger-beer. It is bought, also, for street sale of the ginger-beer manufacturers—the profit being the same—but so bought to less than a twentieth of the whole sale. The water in the stone barrel is spring-water, obtained from the nearest pump, and in hot weather obtained frequently, so as to be "served" in as cool a state as possible. Sometimes lemonade powders are used; they are bought at a chemist's, at 1s. 6d. the pound. "Sherbet" is the same admixture, with cream of tartar instead of tartaric acid. "Raspberry" has, sometimes, the addition of a few crusted raspberries, and a colouring of cochineal, with, generally, a greater degree of sweetening than lemonade. "If cochineal is used for colouring," said one man, "it sometimes turns brown in the sun, and the

rasberry don't sell. A little lake's better." "Lemon-juice" is again lemonade, with a slight infusion of saffron to give it a yellow or pale orange colour. "Nectar," in imitation of Soyer's, has more sugar and less acid than the lemonade; spices, such as cinnamon, is used to flavour it, and the colouring is from lake and saffron.

These "cooling drinks" are sold from the powder or the jar, as I have described, from fountains, and from bottles. The fountain sale is not above a tenth of the whole. All is sold in ½d. and 1d. glasses, except the nectar, which is never less than 1d. The customers are the same as those who buy ginger-beer; but one "lemonader" with whom I conversed, seemed inclined to insist that they were a "more respectable class." Boys are good customers—better, perhaps, than for the beer,—as "the colour and the fine names attracts them."

The "cooling drink" season, like that of the ginger-beer, is determined by the weather, and last summer it was only four months. It was computed for me that there were 200 persons, chiefly men, selling solely lemonade, &c., and an additional 300 uniting the sale with that of ginger-beer. One man, whose statement was confirmed by others, told me that on fine days he took 3s. 6d., out of which he cleared 2s. to 2s. 6d.; and he concluded that his brother tradesmen cleared as much every fine day, and so, allowing for wet weather and diminished receipts, made 10s. a week. The receipts, then, for this street luxury—a receipt of 17s. 6d. affording a profit of 10s.—show a street expenditure in such a summer as the last, of 2,800l., by those who do not unite ginger-beer with the trade. Calculating that those who do unite ginger beer with it sell only one-half as much as the others, we find a total outlay of 4,900l. One of the best trades is in the hands of a man who "works" Smithfield, and on the market days clears generally from 6s. to 9s.

The stalls, &c., are of the same character as those of the ginger-beer sellers. The capital required to start is:—stone barrel, with brass tap, 5s. 6d.; stand and trestle, 6s.; 6 tumbler glasses, 2s. 3d.; 2 towels, 6d.; stock money, 2s. 6d.; jar, 2s.; 12 bottles (when used), 3s. 6d.; in all, about a guinea.

In showing the money expended in the ginger-beer trade it must be borne in mind that a large portion of the profits accrues to persons who cannot be properly classed with the regular street-traders. Such is the proprietor of the great fountain of which I have spoken, who is to be classed as a speculative man, ready to embark capital in any way—whether connected with street-traffic or not—likely to be remunerative. The other and large participants in the profits are the wholesale ginger-beer manufacturers, who are also the letters-out of fountains, one of them having generally nine let out at a time. For a street trader to sell three gross of ginger-beer in bottle is now accounted a *good* week, and for that the receipts will be 36s. with a profit in the penny bottle trade, to the seller, if he buy of a manufacturer, of 12s.; if he be his own brewer—reckoning a fair compensation for labour, and for money invested in utensils, and in bottles, &c., of 20s. An ordinary week's sale is two gross, costing the public 24s., with the same proportion of profit in the same trade to the seller. In a *bad* week, or "in a small way to help out other things," not more than one gross is sold.

The fountain trade is the most profitable to the proprietors, whether they send out their machines on their own account, or let them out on hire; but perhaps there are only an eighth of the number not let out on hire. Calculating that a fountain be let out for three successive seasons of twenty weeks each, at only 4s. the week, the gross receipts are 12l. for what on the first day of hire was worth only 7l.; so that the returns from 200 machines let out for the same term, would be 2,400l., or a profit of 1,000l. over and above the worth of the fountain, which having been thus paid for is of course in a succeeding year the means of a clear profit of 4l. I am assured that the weekly average of "a fountain's takings," when in the hands of the regular street-dealers, is 18s.

The barrel traders may be taken as in the average receipt of 6s. a week.

The duration of the season was, last year, only sixteen weeks. Calculating from the best data I could acquire, it appears that for this period 200 street-sellers of ginger-beer in the bottle trade of the penny class take 30s. a week each (thus allowing for the inferior receipts in bad weather); 300 take 20s. each, selling for the most part at ½d. the bottle, and that the remaining 400 "in a small way" take 6s. each; hence we find 11,480l. expended in the bottled ginger-beer of the streets. Adding the receipts from the fountains and the barrels, the barrel season continuing only ten weeks, the total sum expended annually in street ginger-beer is altogether 14,660l. The bottles of ginger-beer sold yearly in the streets will number about 4,798,000, and the total street consumption of the same beverage may be said to be about 250,000 gallons per annum.

OF THE EXPERIENCE AND CUSTOMERS OF A
GINGER-BEER SELLER.

A slim, well-spoken man, with a half-military appearance, as he had a well trimmed moustache, and was very cleanlily dressed, gave me the following account: "I have known the ginger-beer trade for eight years, and every branch of it. Indeed I think I've tried all sorts of street business. I've been a coster-monger, a lot-seller, a nut-seller, a secret-paper-seller (with straws, you know, sir), a cap-seller, a street-printer, a cakeman, a clown, an umbrella-maker, a toasting-fork maker, a sovereign seller, and a ginger-beer seller. I hardly know what I haven't been. I made my own when last I worked beer. Sunday was my best day, or rather Sunday mornings

when there's no public-houses open. Drinking Saturday nights make dry Sunday mornings. Many a time men have said to me: 'Let's have a bottle to quench a spark in my throat,' or 'My mouth's like an oven.' I've had to help people to lift the glass to their lips, their hands trembled so. They couldn't have written their names plain if there was a sovereign for it. But these was only chance customers; one or two in a morning, and five or six on a Sunday morning. I've been a teetotaller myself for fifteen years. No, sir, I didn't turn one—but I never was a drinker—not from any great respect for the ginger-beer trade, but because I thought it gave one a better chance of getting on. I once had saved money, but it went in a long sickness. I used to be off early on Sunday mornings sometimes to Hackney Marsh, and sell my beer there to gentlemen—oldish gentlemen some of them—going a fishing. Others were going there to swim. One week I took 35s. at 1d. a bottle, by going out early in a morning; perhaps 20s. of it was profit, but my earnings in the trade in a good season wasn't more than 12s. one week with another. All the trades in the streets are bad now, I think. Eight years back I could make half as much more in ginger-beer as could be made last summer. Working people and boys were my other customers. I stuck to ginger-beer in the season and then went into something else, for I can turn my hand to anything. I began a street life at eight years old by selling memorandum-books in the bull-ring at Birmingham. My parents were ill and hadn't a farthing in the house. I began with 1d. stock-money, and I bought three memorandum-books for it at Cheap Jack's thatched house. I've been in London seventeen or eighteen years. I'm a roulette-maker now; I mean the roulette boxes that gentlemen take with them to play with when travelling on a railway or such times. I make loaded dice, too, and supply gaming-houses. I think I know more gaming-houses than any man in London. I've sold them to gentlemen and to parsons, that is ministers of religion. I can prove that. I don't sell those sort of things in the streets. I could do very well in the trade, but it's so uncertain and so little's wanted compared to what would keep a man going, and I have a mother that's sixty to support. Altogether my present business is inferior to the ginger-beer; but the fountains will destroy all the fair ginger-beer trade."

OF THE STREET-SELLERS OF HOT ELDER
WINE.

THE sale of hot elder wine in the streets is one of the trades which have been long established, but it is only within these eight or ten years that it has been carried on in its present form. It continues for about four months in the winter.

Elder wine is made from the berries of the elder-tree. Elder syrup—also made from the berries — was formerly famous in the north of England as a curative for colds, and was frequently taken, with a small admixture of rum, at bedtime. Some of the street-sellers make the wine themselves; the majority, however, buy it of the British wine makers. The berries must be gathered when fully ripe, and on a dry day. They are picked, measured, and put into a copper, two gallons of water being added to every gallon of berries. They are then boiled till the berries are quite soft, when the liquor is strained and pressed from them through a strong hair sieve. The liquor thus expressed is again put into the copper, boiled an hour, skimmed, and placed in a tub along with a bread toast, on which yeast is spread thickly; it then stands two days, and is afterwards put into a cask, a few cloves and crusted ginger being hung in a muslin bag from the bung-hole, so as to flavour the liquor. Sometimes this spicing is added afterwards, when the liquor is warmed. The berries are sold in the markets, principally in Covent-garden,—the price varying, according to the season, from 1s. 6d. to 3s. a gallon. Of all elder-wine makers the Jews are the best as regards the street commodity. The costermongers say they "have a secret;" a thing said frequently enough when superior skill is shown, and especially when, as in the case of the Jews' elder wine, better pennyworths are given. The Jews, I am told, add a small quantity of raspberry vinegar to their "elder," so as to give it a "sharp pleasant twang." The heat and pungency of the elder wine sold in the streets is increased by some street-sellers by means of whole black pepper and capsicums.

The apparatus in which the wine is now kept for sale in the streets is of copper or brass, and is sometimes "handsome." It is generally an urn of an oblong form, erected on a sort of pedestal, with the lid or top ornamented with brass mouldings, &c. Three plated taps give vent to the beverage. Orifices are contrived and are generally hidden, or partially hidden, with some ornament, which act as safety-valves, or, as one man would have it, "chimneys." The interior of these urns holds three or four quarts of elder wine, which is surrounded with boiling water, and the water and wine are kept up to the boiling pitch by means of a charcoal fire at the foot of the vessel. Fruit of some kind is generally sold by the elder-wine men at their stand.

The elder wine urn is placed on a stand covered with an oil-cloth, six or eight glasses being ranged about it. It is sold at a half-penny and a penny a glass; but there is "little difference in some elder wines," I was told, "between the penn'orths and the ha'porths." A wine glass of the "regular" size is a half-quartern, or the eighth of a pint. Along with each glass of hot elder wine is given a small piece of toasted bread. Some buyers steep this bread in the wine, and so imbibe the flavour. "It ain't no good as I

know on," said an elder-wine seller, "but it's the fashion, and so people must have it." The purchasers of elder wine are the working classes—but not the better order of them—and the boys of the street. Some of these lads, I was told, were very choice and critical in their elder wines. Some will say: "It ain't such bad wine, but not the real spicy."—"The helder I thinks," said another, "is middlin', but somehow there's nothing but hotness for to taste."

Of these traders there are now perhaps fifty in London. One man counted up thirty of his brethren whom he knew personally, or knew to be then "working elder," and he thought that there might be as many more, but I am assured that fifty is about the mark. The sellers of elder wine have been for the most part mechanics who have adopted the calling for the reasons I have often given. None of them, in the course of my inquiry, depended entirely upon the sale of the wine, but sold fruit in addition to it. All complained of the bad state of trade. One man said, that four or five years back he had replenished the wine in a three quart urn twelve times a day, a jar of the wine being kept at the stall in readiness for that purpose. This amounted to 576 glasses sold in the course of the day, and a receipt—reckoning each glass at a penny—of 48s.; but probably not more than 40s. would be taken, as some would have halfpenny glasses. Now the same man rarely sells three quarts in a day, except perhaps on a Saturday, and on wet days he sells none at all. The elder wine can be bought at almost any pri e at the wine makers, from 4d. to 1s. 6d. the qu 1rt. The charge in the public-houses is twice as high as in the streets, but the inn wine, I was told by a person familiar with the trade, contains spirit, and is more highly spiced.

A decent-looking middle-aged man who had been in a gentleman's service, but was disabled by an accident which crushed his hand, and who thereupon resorted to street-selling and had since continued in it, in different branches, from fifteen to twenty years, gave me an account of his customers. He had not been acquainted with the elder-wine trade above four or five years when he bought an elder can for about 15s. among a cheap miscellaneous "lot" in Smithfield one Friday afternoon, and so he commenced:

"It's a poor trade, sir," he said. "I don't suppose any of us make 10s. a week at it alone, but it's a good help to other things, and I do middling. I should say less than a 1s. a day was above the average profits of the trade. Say 5s. a week, for on wet days we can't sell at all. No one will stop to drink elder wine in the wet. They'll rather have a pennor'th of gin, or half a pint of beer with the chill off, under shelter. I sell sometimes to people that say they're teetotallers and ask if there's any spirit in my wine. I assure them there's not, just the juice of the berry. I start when I think the weather's cold enough, and keep at it as long as there's any demand. My customers are boys and poor people, and I sell more ha'porths than pennor'ths. I've heard poor women that's bought of me say it was the only wine they ever tasted. The boys are hard to please, but I won't put up with their nonsense. It's not once in fifty times that a girl of the town buys my wine. It's not strong enough for her, I fancy. A sharp frosty dry day suits me best. I may then sell three or four quarts. I don't make it, but buy it. It's a poor trade, and I think it gets worse every year, though I believe there's far fewer of us."

One elder-wine stand in Tottenham-court-road cost, when new, 7l., but that was six or seven years ago. Calculating that 50 persons clear 5s. a week for 16 weeks, their profit being at least cent. per cent., the street outlay in this very British wine will be only 200l., and the street-consumption of it in the course of the year 1,500 gallons.

OF THE STREET SALE OF PEPPERMINT-WATER.

PERHAPS the only thing which can be called a cordial or a liqueur sold in the streets (if we except elder wine), is peppermint-water, and of this the sale is very limited. For the first 15 or 20 years of the present century, I was told by one who spoke from a personal knowledge, " a pepperminter" had two little taps to his keg, which had a division in the interior. From one tap was extracted "peppermint-water;" from the other, "strong peppermint-water." The one was at that time 1d. a glass, the other from 2d. to 4d., according to the size of the glass. With the "strong" beverage was mixed smuggled spirit, but so strongly impregnated with the odour of the mint, that a passer-by could not detect the presence of the illicit compound. There are six persons selling peppermint-water in the winter, and only half that number in the summer. The trade is irregular, as some pursue it only of a night, and generally in the street markets; others sell at Billingsgate, and places of great traffic, when the traffic is being carried on. They are stationary for awhile, but keep shifting their ground. The vendors generally " distilled their own mint," when the sale was greater, but within these six or eight years they have purchased it at a distilling chemist's, and have only prepared it for sale. Water is added to the distilled liquid bought of the chemist, to increase the quantity; but to enhance the heat of the draught—which is a draw to some buyers—black pepper (unground), or ginger, or, but rarely, capsicums, are steeped in the beverage. The peppermint-water is lauded by the vendors, when questioned concerning it, as an excellent stomachic; but nothing is said publicly of its virtues, the cry being merely, " Pep-permint water, a halfpenny a glass."

The sellers will generally say that they distil the peppermint-water themselves, but this is not now commonly the case. The process, however, is simple enough. The peppermint used

is gathered just as it is bursting into flower, and the leaves and buds are placed in a tub, with ust water enough to cover them. This steeping continues 24 hours, and then a still is filled three-parts full, and the water is "over" drawn rery slowly.

The price at the chemist's is 1s. a quart for the common mint-water; the street price is ½d. a glass, containing something short of the eighth of a pint. What costs 1s., the street-seller disposes of for 2s., so realising the usual cent. per cent.

To take 2s. is now accounted "a tidy day's work;" and calculating that four "pepperminters" take that amount the year round, Sundays excepted, we find that nearly 125l. is spent annually in peppermint-water and 900 gallons of it consumed every year in the streets of London.

The capital required is, keg, 3s. 6d., or jar, 2s. (for they are used indifferently); four glasses, 1s.; towel, 4d., and stock-money, 4s.; or, in all, about 8s. The "water"-keg, or jar, is carried by the vendor, but sometimes it is rested on a large stool carried for the purpose. A distilling apparatus, such as the street-sellers used, was worth about 10s. The vendors are of the same class of street-sellers as the ginger-beer people.

OF MILK SELLING IN ST. JAMES'S PARK.

THE principal sale of milk from the cow is in St. James's Park. The once fashionable drink known as syllabubs—the milk being drawn warm from the cow's udder, upon a portion of wine, sugar, spice, &c.—is now unknown. As the sellers of milk in the park are merely the servants of cow-keepers, and attend to the sale as a part of their business, no lengthened notice is required.

The milk-sellers obtain leave from the Home Secretary, to ply their trade in the park. There are eight stands in the summer, and as many cows, but in the winter there are only four cows. The milk-vendors sell upon an average, in the summer, from eighteen to twenty quarts per day; in the winter, not more than a third of that quantity. The interrupted milking of the cows, as practised in the Park, often causes them to give less milk, than they would in the ordinary way. The chief customers are infants, and adults, and others, of a delicate constitution, who have been recommended to take new milk. On a wet day scarcely any milk can be disposed of. Soldiers are occasional customers.

A somewhat sour-tempered old woman, speaking as if she had been crossed in love, but experienced in this trade, gave me the following account:

" It's not at all a lively sort of life, selling milk from the cows, though some thinks it's a gay time in the Park! I've often been dull enough, and could see nothing to interest one, sitting alongside a cow. People drink new milk for their health, and I've served a good many such. They're mostly young women, I think, that's delicate, and makes the most of it. There's twenty women, and more, to one man what drinks new milk. If they was set to some good hard work, t would do them more good than new milk, or ass's milk either, I think. Let them go on a milk-walk to cure them—that's what I say. Some children come pretty regularly with their nurses to drink new milk. Some bring their own china mugs to drink it out of; nothing less was good enough for them. I've seen the nurse-girls frightened to death about the mugs. I've heard one young child say to another: 'I shall tell mama that Caroline spoke to a mechanic, who came and shook hands with her.' The girl was as red as fire, and said it was her brother. Oh, yes, there's a deal of brothers comes to look for their sisters in the Park. The greatest fools I've sold milk to is servant-gals out for the day. Some must have a day, or half a day, in the month. Their mistresses ought to keep them at home, I say, and not let them out to spend their money, and get into nobody knows what company for a holiday; mistresses is too easy that way. It's such gals as makes fools of themselves in liking a soldier to run after them. I've seen one of them—yes, some would call her pretty, and the prettiest is the silliest and easiest tricked out of money, that's my opinion, anyhow—I've seen one of them, and more than one, walk with a soldier, and they've stopped a minute, and she's taken something out of her glove and given it to him. Then they've come up to me, and he's said to me, 'Mayn't I treat you with a little new milk, my dear?' and he's changed a shilling. Why, of course, the silly fool of a gal had given him that there shilling. I thought, when Annette Myers shot the soldier, it would be a warning, but nothing's a warning to some gals. *She* was one of those fools. It was a good deal talked about at the stand, but I think none of us know'd her. Indeed, we don't know our customers but by sight. Yes, there's now and then some oldish gentlemen—I suppose they're gentlemen, anyhow, they're idle men—lounging about the stand: but there's no nonsense there. They tell me, too, that there's not so much lounging about as there was; those that's known the trade longer than me thinks so. Them children's a great check on the nusses, and they can't be such fools as the servant-maids. I don't know how many of them I've served with milk along with soldiers: I never counted them. They're nothing to me. Very few elderly people drink new milk. It's mostly the young. I've been asked by strangers when the Duke of Wellington would pass to the Horse-Guards or to the House of Lords. He's pretty regular. I've had 6d. given me—but not above once or twice a year—to tell strangers where was the best place to see him from as he passed. I don't understand about this Great Exhibition, but, no doubt, more new milk will be sold when it's opened, and that's all I cares about."

OF THE STREET SALE OF MILK.

DURING the summer months milk is sold in Smithfield, Billingsgate, and the other markets, and on Sundays in Battersea-fields, Clapham-common, Camberwell - green, Hampstead-heath, and similar places. About twenty men are engaged in this sale. They usually wear a smock frock, and have the cans and yoke used by the regular milk-sellers; they are not itinerant. The skim milk—for they sell none else—is purchased at the dairies at 1½d. a quart, and even the skim milk is also further watered by the street-sellers. Their cry is "Half-penny half-pint! Milk!" The tin measure however in which the milk-and-water is served is generally a "slang," and contains but half of the quantity proclaimed. The purchasers are chiefly boys and children; rarely men, and never costermongers, I was told, "for they reckon milk sickly." These street-sellers —who have most of them been employed in the more regular milk-trade—clear about 1s. 6d. a day each, for three months; and as the profit is rather more than cent. per cent. it appears that about 4,000 gallons of milk are thus sold, and upwards of 260l. laid out upon these persons, yearly in its purchase.

A pair of cans with the yoke cost 15s., and 1l. is amply sufficient as capital to start in this trade, as the two measures used may be bought for 2s.; and 3s. can be devoted to the purchase of the liquid.

OF THE STREET-SALE OF CURDS AND WHEY.

THE preparations of milk which comprise the street-trade, are curds and whey and rice-milk, the oldest street-sellers stating that these were a portion of the trade in their childhood. The one is a summer, and the other a winter traffic, and both are exclusively in the hands of the same middle-aged and elderly women. The vendors prepare the curds and whey in all cases themselves. "Skim-milk," purchased at the dairies, is used by the street-purveyors, a gallon being the quantity usually prepared at a time. This milk gallon is double the usual quantity, or eight quarts. The milk is first "scalded," the pan containing it being closely watched, in order that the contents may not boil. The scalding occupies 10 or 15 minutes, and it is then "cooled" until it attains the lukewarmness of new milk. Half a pound of sugar is then dissolved in the milk, and a tea-spoonful of rennet is introduced, which is sufficient to "turn" a gallon. In an hour, or in some cases two, the milk is curded, and is ready for use. The street-sale is confined to stalls; the stall, which is the ordinary stand, being covered with a white cloth, or in some cases an oil-cloth, and on this the curds, in a bright tin kettle or pan, are deposited. There are six mugs on the board, and a spoon in each, but those who affect a more modern style have glasses. One of the neatest stalls, as regards the display of glass, and the bright cleanliness of the vessel containing the curds, is in Holborn; but the curd-seller there has only an average business. The mugs or glasses hold about the third of a pint, and " the full of one" is a penny-worth; for a halfpenny-worth the vessel is half filled. The season is during the height of summer, and continues three or four months, or, as one woman tersely and commercially expressed it, " from Easter to fruit." The number of street-saleswomen is about 100. Along with the curds they generally sell oranges, or such early fruit as cherries.

A woman who had sold " cruds " — as the street-people usually call it—for eighteen years, gave me the following account :—" Boys and girls is my best customers for cruds, sir. Perhaps I sell to them almost half of all I get rid of. Very little fellows will treat girls, often bigger than themselves, at my stall, and they have as much chaffing and nonsense about it's being ' stunning good for the teeth,' and such like, as if they was grown-up. Some don't much like it at first, but they gets to like it. One boy, whose young woman made faces at it—and it *was* a little sour to be sure that morning—got quite vexed and said, ' Wot a image you 're a-making on yourself!' I don't know what sort the boys are, only that they're the street-boys mostly. Quiet working people are my other customers, perhaps rather more women than men. Some has told me they was teetotallers. Then there 's the women of the town of the poorer sort, *they're* good customers,—as indeed I think they are for most cooling drinks at times, for they seem to me to be *always* thirsty. I never sell to dust-men or that sort of people. Saturday is my best day. If it's fine and warm, I sell a gallon then, which makes about 40 penn'orths; sometimes it brings me 3*s.*, sometimes 3*s.* 6*d.*; it's rather more than half profits. Take it altogether, I sell five gallons in fine dry weeks, and half that in wet; and perhaps there's what I call a set down wet week for every two dry. Nobody has a better right to pray against wet weather than poor women like me. Ten years ago I sold almost twice as much as I can now. There's so many more of us at present, I think, and let alone that there's more shops keeps it too."

Another old woman told me, that she used, " when days was longest," to be up all night, and sell her " cruds " near Drury-lane theatre, and often received in a few hours 5*s.* or 6*s.*, from " ladies and gentlemen out at night." But the men were so rackety, she said, and she'd had her stall so often kicked over by drunken people, and no help for it, that she gave up the night-trade, and she believed it was hardly ever followed now.

To start in the curds and whey line requires the following capital :—Saucepan, for the scalding and boiling, 2*s.*; stall, 5*s.*; 6 mugs, 6*d.*; or 6 glasses, 2*s.* 6*d.*; 6 spoons, 3*d.*; tin kettle on stall, 3*s.* 6*d.*; pail for water to rinse glasses, 1*s.* Then for stock-money : 1 gallon skimmed milk, 1*s.* 6*d.* or 1*s.* 8*d.*; and ¼ lb. sugar, 2*d.* In all,

14*s.* 1*d.*, reckoning the materials to be of the better sort.

Of the whole number of street curd-sellers, 50 dispose of as much as my informant, or 12½ gallons in 3 weeks; the other 50 sell only half as much. Taking the season at 3 months, we find the consumption of curds and whey in the street to be 2,812 double gallons (as regards the ingredient of milk), at a cost to the purchasers of 421*l.*, half of which is the profit accruing to the street-seller. The receipts of those having the better description of business being 9*s.* 4*d.* weekly; those of the smaller traders being 4*s.* 8*d.* There is a slight and occasional loss by the " cruds " being kept until unsaleable, in which case they are " fit for nothing but the hog-wash man."

OF THE STREET-SELLERS OF RICE-MILK.

To make rice-milk, the street-seller usually boils four quarts, of the regular measure, of " skim" with one pound of rice, which has been previously boiled in water. An hour suffices for the boiling of the milk; and the addition of the rice, swollen by the boiling water, increases the quantity to six quarts. No other process is observed, except that some sweeten their rice-milk before they offer it for sale; the majority, however, sweeten it to the customer's liking when he is " served," unless—to use the words of one informant—" he have a werry, werry sweet tooth indeed, sir ; and that can't be stood." For the sweetening of six quarts, half a pound of sugar is used ; for the " spicing," half an ounce of allspice, dashed over the milk freely enough from a pepper-castor. Rice-milk is always sold at stalls arranged for the purpose, and is kept in a tin pan fitted upon a charcoal brazier, so that the " drinkable" is always hot. This apparatus generally stands on the ground alongside the stall, and is elevated only by the feet of the brazier. The " rice-milk woman,"—for the street-sellers are generally females,—dips a large breakfast-cup, holding half a pint, into the pan, puts a tea-spoonful of sugar into it, browns the whole with allspice, and receives 1*d.* ; a halfpennyworth is, of course, half the quantity. The rice-milk women are also sellers of oranges, chestnuts, apples, or some other fruit, as well as the rice-milk ; but, sometimes, when the weather is *very* cold and frosty, they sell rice-milk alone. There are fifty street-sellers of rice-milk in London. Saturday night is the best time of sale, when it is not uncommon for a rice-milk woman to sell six quarts ; but, in a good trade, four quarts a day for six days of the week is an average. The purchasers are poor people ; and a fourth of the milk is sold to boys and girls, to whom it is often a meal. " Ah, sir," said one woman, " you should have seen how a poor man, last winter, swallowed a pen'n'orth. He'd been a-wandering all night, he said, and he looked it, and a gentleman gave him 2*d.*, for he took pity on his hungry look, and he spent 1*d.* with me, and I gave him another cup for charity. ' God bless the gentleman and you!' says he, 'it's saved my life; if I'd bought a penny loaf, I'd have choked on it.' He wasn't a beggar, for I never saw him before, and I've never seen him again from that day to this.'' The same informant told me, that she believed no rice-milk was bought by the women of the town: "it didn't suit the likes of them.'' Neither is it bought by those who are engaged in noisome trades. If there be any of the rice-milk left at night, and the saleswoman have doubts of its "keeping," it is re-boiled with fresh rice and milk. The profit is considerable; for the ingredients, which cost less than 1*s.* 6*d.*, are made into 96 pennyworths, and so to realize 8*s.* In some of the poorer localities, however, such as Rosemary-lane, only ½*d.* the half-pint can be obtained, and 4*s.* is then the amount received for six quarts, instead of 8*s.*

To start "in rice-milk" requires 13*s.* capital, which includes a pan for boiling the milk, 2*s.*; a kettle, with brazier, for stall, 4*s.*; stall or stand, 5*s.*; six cups, 9*d.*; for stock-money 15½*d.*, with which is bought 4 quarts of skim-milk, 9*d.*; 1 lb. of rice, 3*d.*; ½ lb. of sugar, 2*d.*; allspice, 1*d.*

The season continues for four months; and calculating—a calculation within the mark—that one half of the 50 sellers have as good a trade as my informant—24 quarts weekly—and that, of the remaining 25, one half sell 12 quarts each weekly, at 1*d.* the half-pint, and the other half vend 24 quarts at ½*d.* the half-pint, we find that 320*l.* is annually spent in rice-milk and about 3,000 gallons of it yearly consumed in the streets of London.

OF WATER-CARRIERS.

IT may surprise many to learn that there are still existing water-carriers in London, and some of them depending upon the trade for a livelihood; while others, the "odd men" of the neighbourhood, carry pails of spring water to the publicans or eating-house keepers, who may not have servants to send to the nearest pump for it, and who require it fresh and cool for those who drink it at their meals. Of these men there are, as near as I can ascertain, from 100 to 150; their charge is 1*d.* per pail. Their earnings per day 6*d.* to 1*s.* Perhaps none of them depend solely upon this labour for their support.

It is otherwise at Highgate and Hampstead, for in those places both men and women depend entirely for their daily bread on water carrying. At Hampstead the supply is derived from what may be called a double well, known as "the Conduit." The ground is flagged, and the water is seen at each corner of a wall built to the surface of the ground (about eight feet) and surmounted by an iron rail. The water is covered over, in one corner and not in the other, and the carrier descends a step or two, dips in his pails and walks away with them when filled. The water is carried by means of a "yoke,"

in the same way as we see the milk-pails carried in every street in London. The well and the field in which the Hampstead water is situated are the property of the Church, and the water is free to any one, in any quantity, either for sale or any other purpose, " without leave.'' In droughts or frosts the supply fails, and the carriers have sometimes to wait hours for their "turn," and then to bale the water into their pails with a basin. The nearest street to which the water is carried is half a mile distant. Some is carried three quarters of a mile, and some (occasionally) a mile. The two pails full, which contain seven gallons, are sold at 1½*d.* The weight is about 70 lbs. Seventeen years ago the price was 3*d.*; after which it fell to 2½*d.*, then to 2*d.*, and has been 1½*d.* these five or six years, while now there are three or four carriers who even "carry" at two pails a-penny to the nearer places. The supply of the well (apart from drought or frost) is fifty-six gallons an hour. The principal customers are the laundresses; but in wet weather their cisterns and water-tubs are filled, and the carriers, or the major part of them, are idle. The average earnings of the carriers are 5*s.* a week the year through. Two of them are men of seventy. There is a bench about midway to Hampstead, at which these labourers rest; and here on almost every fine day sits with them a palsied old soldier, a pensioner of about eighty, who regales them, almost daily, with long tales of Vinegar Hill, and Jemmy O'Brien (the informer), and all the terrors of the terrible times of the Irish rebellion of 1798; for the old man (himself an Irishman) had served through the whole of it. This appears to be a somewhat curious theme for constant expatiation to a band of London water-carriers.

There are now twenty individuals, fourteen men and six women, carrying at Hampstead, and twice that number at Highgate. Some leave the carrying when they get better work,—but three-fourths of the number live by it entirely. The women are the wives and widows of carriers. The men have been either mechanics or labourers, except six or eight youths (my informant was not certain which) who had been "brought up to the water, but would willingly get away from it if they could."

A well-spoken and intelligent-looking man, dressed in thick fustian, old and greasy, " but good enough for the carrying,'' gave me the following account.

" I was a copper-plate printer," he said, "and twenty years ago could earn my 25*s.* a week. But employment fell off. The lithographic injured it, and at last I could get very little work, and then none at all, so I have been carrying now between three and four years. My father-in-law was in the trade, and that made me think of it. My best day's work, and it's the same with all, is 2*s.*, which is sixteen turns. It's not possible to do more. If that could be done every day it would be very well, but in wet weather when the laundresses, who are my customers, don't want water, I can't make 1s. a week. Then in a drought or a frost one has to wait such a long time for his turn, that it's not 6d. a day; a dry spring's the worst. Last March I had many days to wait six turns, and it takes well on to an hour for a turn then. We sit by the well and talk when we're waiting. O, yes, sir, the Pope has had his turn of talk. There's water companies both at Hampstead and Highgate, but our well water (Hampstead) is asked for, for all that. It's so with Highgate. It is beautiful water, either for washing or drinking. Perhaps it's better with a little drop of spirit for drinking, but I seldom taste it that way. The fatigue's so great that we *must* take a little drop of spirit on a long day. No, sir, we don't mix it; that spoils two good things. I've been at the well first light in the morning, and in summer I've been at work at it all night. There's no rule among us, but it's understood that every one has his turn. There's a little chaff sometimes, and some get angry at having to wait, but I never knew a fight. I have a wife and three children. She works for a laundress, and has 2s. 6d. a day. She has two days regular every week, and sometimes odd turns as well. I think that the women earn more than the men in Hampstead. My rent is 1s. 6d. a week for an unfurnished room. There is no trade on Sundays, but on fine summer Sundays old —— attends at the well and sells glasses of cool water. He gets 2s. 6d. some days. He makes no charge; just what any one pleases to give. Any body might do it, but the old gentleman would grumble that they were taking his post."

Computing the number of water carriers at the two places at sixty, and their average earnings through the year at 5s. a week, it appears that these men receive 1,452l. yearly. The capital required to start in the business is 9s., the cost of a pair of pails and a yoke.

The old man who sells water on the summer Sunday mornings, generally leaving off his sale at church-time, told me that his best customers were ladies and gentlemen who loved an early walk, and bought of him "as it looked like a bit of country life," he supposed, more than from being thirsty. When such customers were not inhabitants of the neighbourhood, they came to him to ask their way, or to make inquiries concerning the localities. Sometimes he dispensed water to men who "looked as if they had been on the loose all night." One gentleman," he said, "looks sharp about him, and puts a dark-coloured stuff—very likely it's brandy—into the two or three glasses of water which he drinks every Sunday, or which he used to drink rather, for I missed him all last summer, I think. His hand trembled like an aspen; he mostly gave me 6d." The water-seller spoke with some indignation of boys, and sometimes men, going to the well on a Sunday morning and "drinking out of their own tins that they'd taken with 'em."

OF THE STREET-SELLERS OF PASTRY AND CONFECTIONARY.

THE cooked provisions sold in the streets, it has been before stated, consist of three kinds—solids, liquids, and pastry and confectionary. The two first have now been fully described, but the last still remains to be set forth.

The street pastry may be best characterised as of a *strong* flavour. This is, for the most part, attributable to the use of old or rancid butter,—possessing the all-important recommendation of cheapness,—or to the substitution of lard, dripping, or some congenial substance. The "strong" taste, however, appears to possess its value in the estimation of street pastry-buyers, especially among the boys. This may arise from the palates of the consumers having been unaccustomed to more delicate flavours, and having become habituated to the relish of that which is somewhat rank; just in the same way as the "*fumet*" of game or venison becomes dear to the palate of the more aristocratic *gourmand*. To some descriptions of street pastry the epithet strong-flavoured may seem inappropriate, but it is appropriate to the generality of these comestibles,—especially to the tarts, which constitute a luxury, if not to the meat pies or puddings that may supply a meal.

The articles of pastry sold in the London streets are meat and fruit pies, boiled meat and kidney puddings, plum "duff" or pudding, and an almost infinite variety of tarts, cakes, buns, and biscuits; while the confectionary consists of all the several preparations included under the wide denomination of "sweet-stuff," as well as the more "medicinal" kind known as "cough drops;" in addition to these there are the more "aristocratic" delicacies recently introduced into street traffic, viz., penny raspberry creams and ices.

OF STREET PIEMEN.

THE itinerant trade in pies is one of the most ancient of the street callings of London. The meat pies are made of beef or mutton; the fish pies of eels; the fruit of apples, currants, gooseberries, plums, damsons, cherries, raspberries, or rhubarb, according to the season—and occasionally of mince-meat. A few years ago the street pie-trade was very profitable, but it has been almost destroyed by the "pie-shops," and further, the few remaining street-dealers say "the people now haven't the pennies to spare." Summer fairs and races are the best places for the piemen. In London the best times are during any grand sight or holiday-making, such as a review in Hyde-park, the Lord Mayor's show, the opening of Parliament, Greenwich fair, &c. Nearly all the men of this class, whom I saw, were fond of speculating as to whether the Great Exposition would be "any good" to them, or not.

The London piemen, who may number about forty in winter, and twice that number in summer, are seldom stationary. They go along with

their pie-cans on their arms, crying, " Pies all
'ot! eel, beef, or mutton pies! Penny pies,
all 'ot — all 'ot!" The "can" has been
before described. The pies are kept hot by
means of a charcoal fire beneath, and there
is a partition in the body of the can to separate the hot and cold pies. The "can" has
two tin drawers, one at the bottom, where the hot
pies are kept, and above these are the cold pies.
As fast as the hot dainties are sold, their place
is supplied by the cold from the upper drawer.
A teetotal pieman in Billingsgate has a pony
and " shay cart." His business is the most extensive in London. It is believed that he sells
20s. worth or 240 pies a day, but his brother
tradesmen sell no such amount. " I was out
last night," said one man to me, " from four in
the afternoon till half-past twelve. I went
from Somers-town to the Horse Guards, and
looked in at all the public-houses on my way,
and I didn't take above 1s. 6d. I have been
out sometimes from the beginning of the evening till long past midnight, and haven't taken
more than 4d., and out of that I have to pay 1d.
for charcoal."

The pie-dealers usually make the pies themselves. The meat is bought in "pieces," of the
same part as the sausage-makers purchase—
the " stickings "—at about 3d. the pound.
" People, when I go into houses," said one
man, " often begin crying, ' Mee-yow,' or ' Bow-
wow-wow!' at me; but there's nothing of
that kind now. Meat, you see, is so cheap."
About five-dozen pies are generally made at a
time. These require a quartern of flour at 5d.
or 6d.; 2 lbs. of suet at 6d.; 1½ lb. meat at 3d.,
amounting in all to about 2s. To this must be
added 3d. for baking; 1d. for the cost of keeping hot, and 2d. for pepper, salt, and eggs with
which to season and wash them over. Hence the
cost of the five dozen would be about 2s. 6d., and
the profit the same. The usual quantity of meat
in each pie is about half an ounce. There are
not more than 20 *hot*-piemen now in London.
There are some who carry pies about on a tray
slung before them; these are mostly boys, and,
including them, the number amounts to about
sixty all the year round, as I have stated.

The penny pie-shops, the street men say, have
done their trade a great deal of harm. These shops
have now got mostly all the custom, as they make
the pies much larger for the money than those
sold in the streets. The pies in Tottenham-
court-road are very highly seasoned. " I
bought one there the other day, and it nearly
took the skin off my mouth; it was full of
pepper," said a street-pieman, with considerable bitterness, to me. The reason why so
large a quantity of pepper is put in is, because
persons can't exactly tell the flavour of the
meat with it. Piemen generally are not very
particular about the flavour of the meat they
buy, as they can season it up into anything.
In the summer, a street pieman thinks he is
doing a good business if he takes 5s. per day,
and in the winter if he gets half that. On a

Saturday night, however, he generally takes 5s.
in the winter, and about 8s. in the summer.
At Greenwich fair he will take about 14s. At
a review in Hyde-park, if it is a good one,
he will sell about 10s. worth. The generality
of the customers are the boys of London. The
women seldom, if ever, buy pies in the streets.
At the public-houses a few pies are sold, and
the pieman makes a practice of "looking in"
at all the taverns on his way. Here his customers are found principally in the tap-room.
" Here's all 'ot!" the pieman cries, as he
walks in; " toss or buy! up and win 'em!"
This is the only way that the pies can be got
rid of. " If it wasn't for tossing we shouldn't
sell one."

To "toss the pieman" is a favourite pastime
with costermongers' boys and all that class;
some of whom aspire to the repute of being
gourmands, and are critical on the quality of
the comestible. If the pieman win the toss,
he receives 1d. without giving a pie; if he lose,
he hands it over for nothing. The pieman
himself never " tosses," but always calls head
or tail to his customer. At the week's end it
comes to the same thing, they say, whether
they toss or not, or rather whether they win
or lose the toss : " I've taken as much as
2s. 6d. at tossing, which I shouldn't have had if
I had'nt done so. Very few people buy without
tossing, and the boys in particular. Gentlemen
' out on the spree' at the late public-houses will
frequently toss when they don't want the pies, and
when they win they will amuse themselves by
throwing the pies at one another, or at me.
Sometimes I have taken as much as half-a-
crown, and the people of whom I had the
money has never eaten a pie. The boys has
the greatest love of gambling, and they seldom,
if ever, buy without tossing." One of the
reasons why the street boys delight in tossing,
is, that they can often obtain a pie by such
means when they have only a halfpenny where-
with to gamble. If the lad wins he gets a
penny pie for his halfpenny.

For street mince-meat pies the pieman usually
makes 5lb. of mince-meat at a time, and for this
he will put in 2 doz. of apples, 1lb. of sugar,
1lb. of currants, 2lb. of "critlings" (critlings
being the refuse left after boiling down the
lard), a good bit of spice to give the critlings
a flavour, and plenty of treacle to make the
mince-meat look rich.

The "gravy" which used to be given with
the meat-pies was poured out of an oil-can,
and consisted of a little salt and water browned.
A hole was made with the little finger in the
top of the meat pie, and the "gravy" poured
in until the crust rose. With this gravy a person in the line assured me that he has known
pies four days old to go off very freely, and be
pronounced excellent. The street piemen are
mostly bakers, who are unable to obtain employment at their trade. " I myself," said one,
" was a bread and biscuit baker. I have been
at the pie business now about two years and a

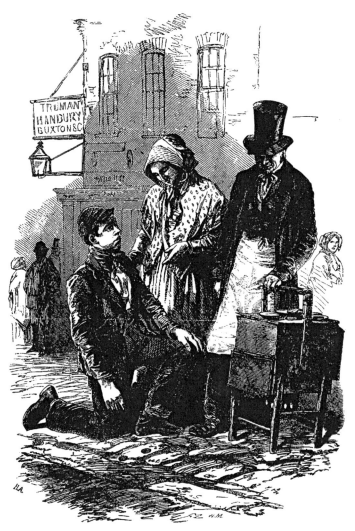

THE COSTER BOY AND GIRL TOSSING THE PIEMAN.

[*From a Daguerreotype by* BEARD.]

DOCTOR BOKANKY, THE STREET HERBALIST.

[*From a Daguerreotype by* BEARD.]

"Now then for the Kalibonca Root, that was brought from Madras in the East Indies. It'll cure the tooth-ache, head-ache, giddiness in the head, dimness of sight, rheumatics in the head, and is highly recommended for the ague; never known to fail; and I've sold it for this six and twenty year. From one penny to sixpence the packet. The best article in England."

half, and I can't get a living at it. Last week my earnings were not more than 7s. all the week through, and I was out till three in the morning to get that." The piemen seldom begin business till six o'clock, and some remain out all night. The best time for the sale of pies is generally from ten at night to one in the morning.

Calculating that there are only fifty street piemen plying their trade in London, the year through, and that their average earnings are 8s. a week, we find a street expenditure exceeding 3,000l., and a street consumption of pies amounting nearly to three quarters of a million yearly.

To start in the penny pie business of the streets requires 1l. for a "can," 2s. 6d. for a "turn-halfpenny" board to gamble with, 12s. for a gross of tin pie-dishes, 8d. for an apron, and about 6s. 6d. for stock money—allowing 1s. for flour, 1s. 3d. for meat, 2d. for apples, 4d. for eels, 2s. for pork flare or fat, 2d. for sugar, ½d. for cloves, 1d. for pepper and salt, 1d. for an egg to wash the pies over with, 6d. for baking, and 1d. for charcoal to keep the pies hot in the streets. Hence the capital required would be about 2l. in all.

OF THE STREET-SELLERS OF BOILED PUDDINGS.

THE sale of *boiled* puddings, meat and currant —which might perhaps be with greater correctness called dumplings—has not been known in London, I was informed by one in the trade, more than twelve or fourteen years. The ingredients for the meat puddings are not dissimilar to those I have described as required for the meat pies, but the puddings are boiled, in cotton bags, in coppers or large pans, and present the form of a round ball. The charge is a halfpenny each. Five or six years back a man embarked his means—said to be about 15l.—in the meat-pudding line, and prepared a superior article, which was kept warm in the street by means of steam, in a manner similar to that employed by the pieman. A mechanic out of work was engaged by this projector to aid him in the sale of his street luxuries, and the mechanic and his two boys made a living by this sale for two or three years. The original pudding-projector relinquished the street trade to go into business as a small shopkeeper, and the man who sold for him on a sort of commission, earning from 12s. to 18s. a week, made the puddings on his own account. His earnings, however, on his own account were not above from 1s. to 2s. 6d. a week beyond what he earned by commission, and a little while back he obtained work again at his own business,·but his two boys still sell puddings in the street.

The sale of boiled meat puddings is carried on only in the autumn and winter months, and only in the evenings, except on Saturdays, when the business commences in the afternoon. The sale, I was informed by one of the parties, has been as many as forty-five dozen puddings on a Saturday evening. The tins in which the puddings are carried about hold from four to six dozen, and are replenished from the pans— the makers always living contiguous to the street where the vend takes place—as fast as the demand requires such replenishment. An average sale on a fine dry winter Saturday evening is thirty dozen, but then, as in most street callings, "the weather"—a remark often made to me—"has considerable to do with it." A frost, I was told, helped off the puddings, and a rain kept them back. Next to Saturday the best business night is Monday; but the average sale on the Monday is barely half that on the Saturday, and on the other evenings of the week about a third. This gives a weekly sale by each street-seller of 85 dozen, or 1,020 puddings, and as I am informed there are now but six street-sellers (regularly) of this comestible, the weekly aggregate would be—allowing for bad weather—5,400, or 129,600 in a season of 24 weeks; an expenditure on the part of the street boys and girls (who are the principal purchasers), and of the poor persons who patronise the street-trade, of about 270l. per annum. The wandering street-musicians of the poorer class—such as "Old Sarey" and the Italian boys—often make their dinner off a meat pudding purchased on their rounds; for it is the rule with such people never to return home after starting in the morning till their day's work is done.

The boys who ply their callings in the street, or are much in the open air, are very fond of these puddings, and to witness the way in which they throw the pudding, when very hot, from hand to hand, eyeing it with an expression that shows an eagerness to eat with a fear of burning the mouth, is sometimes laughable and sometimes painful, because not unfrequently there is a look of keen hunger about the—probably outcast—lad. The currant puddings are, I believe, sold only at Billingsgate and Petticoat-lane.

OF THE STREET-SELLERS OF PLUM "DUFF" OR DOUGH.

PLUM dough is one of the street-eatables— though perhaps it is rather a violence to class it with the street-pastry — which is usually made by the vendors. It is simply a boiled plum, or currant, pudding, of the plainest description. It is sometimes made in the rounded form of the plum-pudding; but more frequently in the "roly-poly" style. Hot pudding used to be of much more extensive sale in the streets. One informant told me that twenty or thirty years ago, batter, or Yorkshire, pudding, "with plums in it," was a popular street business. The "plums," as in the orthodox plum-puddings, are raisins. The street-vendors of plum "duff" are now very few, only six as an average, and generally women, or if a man be the salesman he is the woman's husband. The sale is for the most part an evening sale, and some vend the plum dough only on a Saturday night. A woman in Leather-lane, whose trade is a Saturday night trade, is accounted "one of the best plum duffs" in London, as regards the quality of the comestible, but her trade is not considerable.

The vendors of plum dough are the street-sellers who live by vending other articles, and resort to plum dough, as well as to other things, "as a help." This dough is sold out of baskets in which it is kept hot by being covered with cloths, sometimes two and even three, thick; and the smoke issuing out of the basket, and the cry of the street-seller, "Hot plum duff, hot plum," invite custom. A quartern of flour, 5d.; ½ lb. Valentia raisins, 2d.; dripping and suet in equal proportions, 2½d.; treacle, ½d.; and allspice, ½d.—in all 10½d.; supply a roly-poly of twenty pennyworths. The treacle, however, is only introduced "to make the dough look rich and spicy," and must be used sparingly.

The plum dough is sold in slices at ½d. or 1d. each, and the purchasers are almost exclusively boys and girls—boys being at least three-fourths of the revellers in this street luxury. I have ascertained—as far as the information of the street-sellers enables me to ascertain—that take the year through, six "plum duffers" take 1s. a day each, for four winter months, including Sundays, when the trade is likewise prosecuted. Some will take from 4s. to 10s. (but rarely 10s.) on a Saturday night, and nothing on other nights, and some do a little in the summer. The vendors, who are all stationary, stand chiefly in the street-markets and reside near their stands, so that they can get relays of hot dough.

If we calculate then 42s. a week as the takings of six persons, for five months, so including the summer trade, we find that upwards of 200l. is expended in the street purchase of plum dough, nearly half of which is profit. The trade, however, is reckoned among those which will disappear altogether from the streets.

The capital required to start is: basket, 1s. 9d.; cloths, 6d.; pan for boiling, 2s.; knife, 2d.; stock-money, 2s.; in all about, 7s. 6d.

OF THE STREET-SELLERS OF CAKES, TARTS, &c.

THESE men and boys—for there are very few women or girls in the trade—constitute a somewhat numerous class. They are computed (including Jews) at 150 at the least, all regular hands, with an addition, perhaps, of 15 or 20, who seek to earn a few pence on a Sunday, but have some other, though poorly remunerative, employment on the week-days. The cake and tart-sellers in the streets have been, for the most part, mechanics or servants; a fifth of the body, however, have been brought up to this or to some other street-calling.

The cake-men carry their goods on a tray slung round their shoulders when they are offering their delicacies for sale, and on their heads when not engaged in the effort to do business. They are to be found in the vicinity of all public places. Their goods are generally arranged in pairs on the trays; in bad weather they are covered with a green cloth.

None of the street-vendors make the articles they sell; indeed, the diversity of those articles renders that impossible. Among the regular articles of this street-sale are "Coventrys," or three-cornered puffs with jam inside; raspberry biscuits; cinnamon biscuits; "chonkeys," or a kind of mince-meat baked in crust; Dutch butter-cakes; Jews' butter-cakes; "bowlas," or round tarts made of sugar, apple, and bread; "jumbles," or thin crisp cakes made of treacle, butter, and flour; and jams, or open tarts with a little preserve in the centre.

All these things are made for the street-sellers by about a dozen Jew pastry-cooks, the most of whom reside about Whitechapel. They confine themselves to the trade, and make every description. On a fine holiday morning their shops, or rather bake-houses, are filled with customers, as they supply the small shops as well as the street-sellers of London. Each article is made to be sold at a halfpenny, and the allowance by the wholesale pastry-cook is such as to enable his customers to realise a profit of 4d. in 1s.; thus he charges 4d. a dozen for the several articles. Within the last seven years there has been, I am assured, a great improvement in the composition of these cakes, &c. This is attributable to the Jews having introduced superior dainties, and, of course, rendered it necessary for the others to vie with them: the articles vended by these Jews (of whom there are from 20 to 40 in the streets) are still pronounced, by many connoisseurs in street-pastry, as the best. Some sell penny dainties also, but not to a twentieth part of the halfpenny trade. One of the wholesale pastry-cooks takes 40l. a week. These wholesale men, who sometimes credit the street-people, buy ten, fifteen, or twenty sacks of flour at a time whenever a cheap bargain offers. They purchase as largely in Irish butter, which they have bought at 3d. or 2½d. the pound. They buy also "scrapings," or what remains in the butter-firkins when emptied by the butter-sellers in the shops. "Good scrapings" are used for the best cakes; the jam they make themselves. To commence the wholesale business requires a capital of 600l. To commence the street-selling requires a capital of only 10s.; and this includes the cost of a tray, about 1s. 9d.; a cloth 1s.; and a leathern strap, with buckle, to go round the neck, 6d.; while the rest is for stock, with a shilling, or two as a reserve. All the street-sellers insist upon the impossibility of any general baker making cakes as cheap as those they vend. "It's impossible, sir," said one man to me; "it's a trade by itself; nobody else can touch it. They was miserable little things seven years ago."

An acute-looking man, decently dressed, gave me the following account. He resided with his wife—who went out charing—in a decent little back-room at the East-end, for which he paid 1s. a week. He had no children:—

"I'm a 'translator' (a species of cobbler) by

trade," he said, " but I've been a cake and a tart-seller in the streets for seven or eight years. I couldn't make 1s. 3d. a day of twelve hours' work, and sometimes nothing, by translating. Besides, my health was failing; and, as I used to go out on a Sunday with cakes to sell for a cousin of mine, I went into the trade myself, because I'd got up to it. I did middling the first three or four years, and I'd do middling still, if it wasn't for the bad weather and the police. I've been up three times for ' obstructing.' Why, sir, I never obstructed a quarter as much as the print-shops and newspaper-shops down there" (pointing to a narrow street in the City). " But the keepers of them shops can take a sight at the Lord Mayor from behind their tills. The first time I was up before the Lord Mayor—it's a few years back—I thought he talked like an old wife. ' You mustn't stand that way,' he says, ' and you mustn't do this, and you mustn't do that.' ' Well, my lord,' says I, ' then I mustn't live honestly. But if you'll give me 9s. a week, I'll promise not to stand here, and not to stand there; and neither to do this, nor that, nor anything at all, if that pleases you better.' They was shocked, they said, at my impudence—so young a ;fellow, too! I got off each time, but a deal of my things was spoiled. I work the City on week-days, and Victoria Park on Sundays. In the City, my best customers is not children, but young gents; real gents, some of them with gold watches. They buys twopenn'orth, mostly —that's four of any sort, or different sorts. They're clerks in banks and counting-houses, I suppose, that must look respectable like on a little, and so feeds cheap, poor chaps! for they dine or lunch off it, never doubt. Or they may be keeping their money for other things. To sell eleven dozen is a first-rate days' work; that's 1s. 9d. or 1s. 10d. profit. But then comes the wet days, and I can't trade at all in the rain; and so the things get stale, and I have to sell them in Petticoat-lane for two a halfpenny. Victoria Park—I'm not let inside with my tray —is good and bad as happens. It's chiefly a tossing trade there. Oh, I dare say I toss 100 times some Sundays. I don't like tossing the coster lads, they're the wide-awakes that way. The thieves are ' grays.' They're ha'-pennies, either both sides heads or both tails. Grays sell at from 2d. to 6d. I'm not often had that way, though. Working-people buy very few of me on Sundays; it's mostly boys; and next to the gents., why, perhaps, the boys is my best customers in the City. Only on Monday a lad, that had been lucky ' fiddling' " (holding horses, or picking up money anyhow) " spent a whole shilling on me. I clear, I think —and I'm among the cakes that's the top of the tree—about 10s. a week in summer, and hardly 7s. a week in winter. My old woman and me makes both ends meet, and that's all."

Reckoning 150 cake-sellers, each clearing 6s. a week, a sufficiently low average, the street outlay will be 2,340l., representing a street-consumption of 1,123,200 cakes, tarts, &c.

OF OTHER CAKE-SELLERS IN THE STREETS.

THE street cake-selling of London is not *altogether* confined to the class I have described; but the others engaged in it are not regular pursuers of the business, and do not exceed thirty in number. Some stock their trays with flare-cakes, which are round cakes, made of flour and " unrendered" (unmelted) lard, and stuck over freely with currants. They are sold at a farthing and a halfpenny each. Others, again, carry only sponge-cakes, made of flour and eggs, packed closely and regularly together, so as to present an uniform and inviting surface. Others carry only gingerbread, made of flour and treacle. These small trades are sometimes resorted to for a temporary purpose, rather than a street-seller's remaining in compulsory idleness. I learned also that cake-sellers in the regular line, when unable to command sufficient capital to carry on their trade in the way they have been accustomed to, sell " flayers," so called from being made with pig's or sheep's " flay," or any other cheap cakes, and so endeavour to retrieve themselves. The profits on these plainer sorts is 1d. in 1s. more than that on the others, but the sale rarely exceeds half as much. I heard, however, of one man who deposited in pence, in eight days, 1s. 10d. with a wholesale pastry-cook. He had saved this sum by almost starving himself, on the sale of the inferior cakes, and the dealer trusted him the 10d. to make up eight dozen in the regular cake business. To commence the street sale of cheap cakes requires a capital of less than 5s.; for tray, 1s. 6d.; cloth, 6d.; strap, 6d.; and stock-money, 1s. 6d.

Three or four men are occupied in selling plum-cakes. These are generally sold in half-penny and penny lots. The plum-cake is made by the same class of pastrycooks whom I have described as supplying the tarts, puffs, &c., and sold on the same terms. The profits are fifty per cent.—what cost 4s. bringing in 6s. One man who travels to all the fairs and races, and is more in the country than town in the summer and autumn, sells large quantities of plum-cake in Smithfield when in town, sometimes having 2l. worth and more on his stall. He sells cakes of a pound (ostensibly) at 4d., 6d., and 8d., according to quality. He sometimes supplies the street-sellers on the same terms as the pastrycooks, for he was once a baker.

From the best data at my command, it appears that the sale of these inferior cakes does not realise above a fifth of that taken by the other sellers, of whom I have treated, amounting to about 450l. in all.

OF THE STREET-SELLERS OF GINGERBREAD-NUTS, &c.

THE sale of gingerbread, as I have previously observed, was much more extensive in the streets than it is at present. Indeed, what was formerly known in the trade as "toy" gingerbread is now unseen in the streets, except occasionally, and that only when the whole has not been sold at the neighbouring fairs, at which it is still offered. But, even at these fairs, the principal, and sometimes the only, toy gingerbread that is vended is the "cock in breeches;" a formidable-looking bird, with his nether garments 'of gold. Twenty or thirty years ago, "king George on horseback" was popular in gingerbread. His Majesty, wearing a gilt crown, gilt spurs, and a gilt sword, bestrode the gilt saddle of his steed, and was eaten with great relish by his juvenile subjects. There were also sheep, and dogs, and other animals, all adorned in a similar manner, and looking as if they had been formed in close and faithful imitation of children's first attempts at cattle drawing. These edible toys were then sold in "white," as well as in "brown" gingerbread, the white being the same in all other respects as the brown, except that a portion of sugar was used in its composition instead of treacle.

There are now only two men in London who make their own gingerbread-nuts for sale in the streets. This preparation of gingerbread is called by the street-sellers, after a common elliptical fashion, merely "nuts." From the most experienced man in the street trade I had the following account : he was an intelligent, well-mannered, and well-spoken man, and when he laughed or smiled, had what may be best described as a pleasant look. After he had initiated me into the art and mystery of gingerbread making—which I shall detail separately —he said,

"I've been in the 'nut' trade 25 years, or thereabouts, and have made my own nuts for 20 years of that time. I bought of a gingerbread baker at first—there was plenty of them in them days — and the profit a living profit, too. Certainly it was, for what I bought for 5s. I could sell for 16s. I was brought up a baker, but the moment I was out of my time I started in the street nut trade for myself. I knew the profits of it, and thought it better than the slavery of a journeyman baker's life. You've mentioned, sir, in your work, a musical sort of a street-crier of gingerbread (see p. 160), and I think, and indeed I'm pretty certain, that it's the same man as was my partner 20 years back; aye, more than 20, but I can't tell about years." [The reader will have remarked how frequently this oblivion as to dates and periods characterises the statements of street-sellers. Perhaps no men take less note of time.] "At that time he was my partner in the pig trade. Dairy-fed, d'you say, sir? Not in the slightest. The outsides of the hanimals was paste, and the insides on 'em was all mince-meat. Their eyes was currants. We two was the original pigs, and, I believe, the only two pigs in the streets. We often made 15s. between us, in a day, in pigs alone. The musical man, as you call him—poor fellow, he dropped down dead in

the street one day as he was crying ; he was regular worn out—cried himself into his grave you *may* say—poor fellow, he used to sing out

'Here's a long-tailed pig, and a short-tailed pig,
    And a pig with a curly tail :
Here's a Yorkshire pig, and a Hampshire pig,
    And a pig without e'er a tail.'

"When I was first in the trade, I sold twice as many nuts as I do now, though my nuts was only 12 a penny then, and they're now 40. A little larger the 12 were, but not very much. I have taken 20s. and 24s. many and many a Saturday. I then made from 2l. to 2l. 10s. a week by sticking to it, and money might have been saved. I've taken between 7l. and 8l. at a Greenwich Fair in the three days, in them times, by myself. Indeed, last Easter, my wife and me—for she works as well as I do, and sells almost as much—took 5l. But gingerbread was money in the old times, and I sold 'lumps' as well as 'nuts;' but now lumps won't go off— not in a fair, no how. I've been in the trade ever since I started in it, but I've had turns at other things. I was in the service of a Customhouse agency firm ; but they got into bother about contrabands, and the revenue, and cut off to America—I believe they took money with them, a good bit of it—and I was indicted, or whatever they call it, in the Court of Exchequer—I never was in the Court in my life—and was called upon, one fine day, to pay to the Crown 1,580l., and some odd pounds and shillings besides ! I never understood the rights of it, but it was about smuggling. I was indicted by myself, I believe. When Mr. Candy, and other great houses in the City, were found out that way, *they* made it all right ; paid something, as I've heard, and sacked the profits. Well ; when *I* was called on, it wasn't, I assure you, sir—ha, ha, ha!—at all convenient for a servant—and I was only that—to pay the fifteen hundred and odd ; so I served 12 months and 2 days in prison for it. I'd saved a little money, and wasn't so uncomfortable in prison. I could get a dinner, and give a dinner. When I came out, I took to the nuts. It was lucky for me that I had a trade to turn to ; for, even if I could have shown I wasn't at all to blame about the Exchequer, I could never have got another situation—never. So the streets saved me : my nuts was my bread.

"At this present time, sir, if I make, the year through, 9s. a week, and my wife 1s. or 2s. less, that's the extent. When the Queen opened Parliament, the two on us took 10s. The Queen's good for that, anyhow, in person. If the opening was by proclamation" [so he called it, three or four times], "it wouldn't have been worth while going to—not at all. If there's not a crowd, the police interfere, and 'move on!' is the order. The Queen's popular with me, for her opening Parliament herself. I count it her duty. The police are a great trouble. I can't say they disturb me in the place (never mind mentioning it, sir) where you've seen me, but they do in

other places. They say there's no rest for the
wicked; but, in the streets, there's no rest for a
man trying to make an honest living, as I'm sure
I do. I could pitch anywhere, one time.
"My chief dependence is on working-men,
who buys my nuts to take home to their young
'uns. I never sell for parties, or desserts, that
I know of. I take very little from boys—very
little. The women of the town buy hardly any
of me. I used to sell a good many pigs to them,
in some of the streets about Brunswick-square;
kept misses, and such like—and very pleasant
customers they was, and good pay: but that's
all over now. They never 'bated me—never."
To make about 56 lbs. of the gingerbread-nuts
sold by my informant, takes 28 lbs. of treacle,
7s.; 48 lbs. of flour, 14s.; ½ lb. of ginger, 4d.;
and ¼ lb. of allspice, 4d. From 18 to 20
dozen of small nuts go to the pound. This
quantity, at 40 a penny, reckoning 18 dozen to
a pound, realises about 5d. per pound; or about
25s. for an outlay of 11s. 8d. The expense of
baking, however, and of "appurtenances," reduces the profit to little more than cent. per
cent.
The other nut-sellers in the streets vend the
"almond nuts." Of these vendors there are
not less than 150; of them, 100 buy their goods
of the bakers (what they sell for 1s. costing them
4d.), and the other 50 make their own. The
materials are the same as those of the gingerbread, with the addition of 4 lbs. of butter, 8d.
per lb.; 1 lb. of almonds, 1s. 4d.; and 2 lbs. of
volatile salts, 8d. Out of this material, 60 lbs.
of "almond nuts" may be made. A split
almond is placed in the centre of each of these
nuts; and, as they are three times as large as
the gingerbread nuts, 12 a penny is the price.
To sell 36 dozen a day—and so clearing 2s.—is
accounted a "very tidy day's work." With the
drawback of wet weather, the average weekly
earnings of the almond nut-sellers are, perhaps,
the same as the gingerbread nut man's—9s.
weekly. These almond nut-sellers are, for the
most part, itinerant, their localities of sale being
the same as in the "cake and tart" line. They
carry their goods, neatly done up in paper, on
trays slung from the shoulder. The gingerbread-
nuts are carried in a large basket, and are ready
packed in paper bags.
Some of the "almond" men call at the public-houses, but the sale in such places is very
small. Most of those who make their own nuts
have been brought up as bakers—a class of
workmen who seem to resort and adapt themselves to a street trade more readily than others.
The nuts are baked in the usual way, spread on
tin trays. To erect a proper oven for the purpose costs about 5l., but most of the men hire
the use of one.
I have already specified the materials required
to make 56 lb. of gingerbread nuts, the cost
being 11s. 8d. To that, the capital required to
start in the business must be added, and this
consists of basket, 6s.; baize cloth, 1s.; pan for
dough, 1s.; rolling-pin, 3d., and baking-tins, 1s.

In all about 21s. To begin in a small way in
the "almond" line, buying the nuts ready made,
requires as capital: tray, 2s.; leather strap, 6d.;
baize, 1s.; stock-money, 1s. 6d.—in all 5s. The
sale is prosecuted through the year, but hot
weather is unfavourable to it, as the nuts then
turn soft.
Calculating that 150 of these street-dealers
take 17s. each weekly (clearing 9s.), we find
6,630l. spent yearly in "spice" nuts in the
streets of London.

OF THE STREET-SELLERS OF HOT-CROSS
BUNS, AND OF CHELSEA BUNS.

PERHAPS no cry—though it is only for one
morning—is more familiar to the ears of a
Londoner, than that of "One-a-penny, two-a-
penny, hot-cross buns," on Good Friday. The
sale is unknown in the Irish capital; for among
Roman Catholics, Good Friday, I need hardly
say, is a strict fast, and the eggs in the buns
prevent their being used. One London gentleman, who spoke of fifty years ago, told me
that the street-bun-sellers used to have a not
unpleasing distich. On reflection, however,
my informant could not be certain whether he
had heard this distich cried, or had remembered hearing the elders of his family speak of
it as having been cried, or how it was impressed
upon his memory. It seems hardly in accordance with the usual style of street poetry :—

" One-a-penny, two-a-penny, hot-cross buns !
If your daughters will not eat them, give them to
    your sons.
But if you hav'n't any of those pretty little elves,
You cannot then do better than eat them all your-
    selves."

A tradesman who had resided more than
fifty years in the Borough had, in his boyhood,
heard, but not often, this ridiculous cry :—

" One-a-penny, poker; two-a-penny, tongs !
One-a-penny; two-a-penny, hot-cross buns."

The sellers of the Good Friday buns are
principally boys, and they are of mixed classes
—costers' boys, boys habitually and boys occasionally street-sellers, and boys street-sellers for
that occasion only. One great inducement to
embark in the trade is the hope of raising a
little money for the Greenwich Fair of the following Monday.
I am informed that 500 persons are employed
on Good Friday in the streets of London in the
sale of hot-cross buns, each itinerant selling
upon the day's average six dozen halfpenny,
and seven dozen penny buns, for which he will
take 12s. 6d. (his profits being 3d. in the shilling
or 3s. 1½d.). One person informed me that last
Good Friday he had sold during the day forty
dozen penny buns, for which he received 50s.
The bun-selling itinerants derive their supplies principally from the wholesale pastry-
cooks, and, in a less degree, from the small
bakers and pastrycooks, who work more for
"the trade" than themselves. The street hot-
cross bun trade is less than it was seven or eight

years ago, as the bakers have entered into it more freely, and send round for orders : so that the itinerants complain that they have lost many a good customer. One informant (a master pastry-cook, who had been in the business nearly fifty years) said to me : " Times are sadly altered to what they were when I was a boy. Why I have known my master to bake five sacks of flour in nothing but hot-cross buns, and that is sufficient for 20,000 buns " (one sack of flour being used for 4,000 buns, or 500 lbs. of raw material to the same quantity of buns). The itinerants carry their baskets slung on their arm, or borne upon the head. A flannel or green baize is placed at the bottom of the basket and brought over the buns, after which a white cloth is spread over the top of the baize, to give it a clean appearance.

A vendor of " hot-cross buns " has to provide himself with a basket, a flannel (to keep the buns warm), and a cloth, to give a clean appearance to his commodities. These articles, if bought for the purpose, cost—basket, 2s. 6d. ; flannel and cloth, 2s. ; stock-money, average, 5s. (largest amount 15s., smallest 2s. 6d.) ; or about 10s. in all.

There is expended in one day, in hot-cross buns purchased in the London streets, 300l., and nearly 100,000 buns thus bought.

The Chelsea buns are now altogether super-seded by the Bath and Alexander's buns. " People," the street-sellers say, " want so much for their money." There are now but two Chelsea bun-houses ; the one at Pimlico, and the other at Chelsea. The principal times Chelsea buns were sold in the streets was Good Friday, Easter, and Whitsuntide ; and, with the exception of Good Friday, the great sales were at Greenwich Fair, and then they were sold with other cakes and sweetmeats. I am informed that twenty years ago there was one man, with a rich musical voice, who sold these buns, about Westminster principally, all the year round ; his cry—which was one of the musical ones—was, " One a penny, two a penny, hot Chelsea buns ! Burning hot ! smoking hot ! r-r-r-reeking hot ! hot Chelsea buns ! "

Of Muffin and Crumpet-selling in the Streets.

THE street-sellers of muffins and crumpets rank among the old street-tradesmen. It is difficult to estimate their numbers, but they were computed for me at 500, during the winter months. They are for the most part boys, young men, or old men, and some of them infirm. There are a few girls in the trade, but very few women.

The ringing of the muffin-man's bell—attached to which the pleasant associations are not a few—was prohibited by a recent Act of Parliament, but the prohibition has been as inoperative as that which forbad the use of a drum to the costermonger, for the muffin bell still tinkles along the streets, and is rung vigorously in the suburbs. The sellers of muffins and crumpets are a mixed class, but I am told that more of them are the children of bakers, or worn-out bakers, than can be said of any other calling. The best sale is in the suburbs. " As far as I know, sir," said a muffin-seller, " it's the best Hackney way, and Stoke Newington, and Dalston, and Balls Pond, and Islington ; where the gents that's in banks—the steady coves of them—goes home to their teas, and the missuses has muffins to welcome them ; that's my opinion."

I did not hear of any street-seller who made the muffins or crumpets he vended. Indeed, he could not make the small quantity required, so as to be remunerative. The muffins are bought of the bakers, and at prices to leave a profit of 4d. in 1s. Some bakers give thirteen to the dozen to the street-sellers whom they know. The muffin-man carries his delicacies in a basket, wherein they are well swathed in flannel, to retain the heat : " People likes them warm, sir," an old man told me, " to satisfy them they're fresh, and they almost always *are* fresh ; but it can't matter so much about their being warm, as they have to be toasted again. I only wish good butter was a sight cheaper, and that would make the muffins go. Butter's half the battle." The basket and flannels cost the muffin-man 2s. 6d. or 3s. 6d. His bell stands him in from 4d. to 2s., " according as the metal is." The regular price of good-sized muffins from the street-sellers is a half-penny each ; the crumpets are four a penny. Some are sold cheaper, but these are generally smaller, or made of inferior flour. Most of the street-sellers give thirteen, and some even four-teen to the dozen, especially if the purchase be made early in the day, as the muffin-man can then, if he deem it prudent, obtain a further supply.

A sharp London lad of fourteen, whose father had been a journeyman baker, and whose mother (a widow) kept a small chandler's shop, gave me the following account :—

" I turns out with muffins and crumpets, sir, in October, and continues until it gets well into the spring, according to the weather. I carries a fust-rate article ; werry much so. If you was to taste 'em, sir, you'd say the same. If I sells three dozen muffins at ½d. each, and twice that in crumpets, it's a werry fair day, werry fair ; all beyond that is a *good* day. The profit on the three dozen and the others is 1s., but that's a great help, really a wonderful help, to mother, for I should be only mindin' the shop at home. Perhaps I clears 4s. a week, perhaps more, per-haps less ; but that's about it, sir. Some does far better than that, and some can't hold a candle to it. If I has a hextra day's sale, mother 'll give me 3d. to go to the play, and that hencourages a young man, you know, sir. If there's any unsold, a coffee-shop gets them cheap, and puts 'em off cheap again next morn-ing. My best customers is genteel houses, 'cause I sells a genteel thing. I likes wet days best, 'cause there's werry respectable ladies what don't keep a servant, and they buys to save themselves going out. We're a great conwenience to the ladies, sir—a great conwenience to them as likes a slap-up tea. I *have* made 1*s.* 8*d.* in a day; that was my best. I once took only 2½*d.*—I don't know why—that was my worst. The shops don't love me—I puts their noses out. Sunday is no better day than others, or werry little. I can read, but wish I could read easier."

Calculating 500 muffin-sellers, each clearing 4*s.* a week, we find 300*l.* a week expended on the metropolitan street sale of muffins; or, in the course of twenty weeks, 2,000*l.* Five shillings, with the price of a basket, &c., which is about 3*s.* 6*d.* more, is the capital required for a start.

OF THE STREET SALE OF SWEET-STUFF.

IN this sale there are now engaged, as one of the most intelligent of the class calculated, 200 individuals, exclusive of twenty or thirty Jew boys. The majority of the sellers are also the manufacturers of the articles they vend. They have all been brought up to the calling, their parents having been in it, or having been artizans (more especially bakers) who have adopted it for some of the general reasons I have before assigned. The non-makers buy of the cheap confectioners.

The articles now vended do not differ materially, I am informed by men who have known the street trade for forty years, from those which were in demand when they began selling in the streets.

A very intelligent man, who had succeeded his father and mother in the "sweet-stuff" business—his father's drunkenness having kept them in continual poverty—showed me his apparatus, and explained his mode of work. His room, which was on the second-floor of a house in a busy thoroughfare, had what I have frequently noticed in the abodes of the working classes—the decency of a turn-up bedstead. It was a large apartment, the rent being 3*s.* 6*d.* a week, unfurnished. The room was cheerful with birds, of which there were ten or twelve. A remarkably fine thrush was hopping in a large wicker cage, while linnets and bullfinches showed their quick bright eyes from smaller cages on all sides. These were not kept for sale but for amusement, their owner being seldom able to leave his room. The father and mother of this man cleared, twenty years ago, although at that time sugar was 6*d.* or 7*d.* the pound, from 2*l.* to 3*l.* a week by the sale of sweet-stuff; half by keeping a stall, and half by supplying small shops or other stall-keepers. My present informant, however, who has—not the best—but one of the best businesses in London, makes 24*s.* or 25*s.* a week from October to May, and sarcely 12*s.* a week during the summer months, "when people love to buy any cool fresh fruit instead of sweet-stuff." The average profits of the generality of the trade do not perhaps exceed 10*s.* 6*d.* or

12*s.* a week, take the year round. They reside in all parts.

Treacle and sugar are the ground-work of the manufacture of all kinds of sweet-stuff. "Hardbake," "almond toffy," "halfpenny lollipops," "black balls," the cheaper "bulls eyes," and "squibs" are all made of treacle. One informant sold more of treacle rock than of anything else, as it was dispensed in larger halfpennyworths, and no one else made it in the same way. Of peppermint rock and sticks he made a good quantity. Half-a-crown's worth, as retailed in the streets, requires 4 lbs. of rough raw sugar at 4¼*d.* per lb., 1½*d.* for scent (essence of peppermint), 1½*d.* for firing, and ½*d.* for paper—in all 1*s.* 8½*d.* calculating nothing for the labour and time expended in boiling and making it. The profit on the other things was proportionate, except on almond rock, which does not leave 2½*d.* in a shilling—almonds being dear. Brandy balls are made of sugar, water, peppermint, and a little cinnamon. Rose acid, which is a " transparent" sweet, is composed of loaf sugar at 6½*d.* per lb., coloured with cochineal. The articles sold in "sticks" are pulled into form along a hook until they present the whitish, or speckled colour desired. A quarter of a stone of materials will, for instance, be boiled for forty minutes, and then pulled a quarter of an hour, until it is sufficiently crisp and will "set" without waste. The flavouring—or "scent" as I heard it called in the trade—now most in demand is peppermint. Gibraltar rock and Wellington pillars used to be flavoured with ginger, but these "sweeties" are exploded.

Dr. Pereria, in his "Treatise on Diet," enumerates as many as ten different varieties and preparations of sugar used for dietetical purposes. These are (1) purified or refined sugar; (2) brown or raw sugar; (3) molasses or treacle —or fluid sugar; (4) aqueous solutions of sugar—or syrups; (5) boiled sugars, or the softer kinds of confectionary; (6) sugar-candy, or crystallized cane sugar; (7) burnt sugar, or caramel; (8) hard confectionary; (9) liquorice; (10) preserves. The fifth and eighth varieties alone concern us here.

Of the several preparations of *boiled sugar,* the Doctor thus speaks, "If a small quantity of water be added to sugar, the mixture heated until the sugar dissolves, and the solution boiled to drive off part of the water, the tendency of the sugar to crystallise is diminished, or, in some cases, totally destroyed. To promote this effect, confectioners sometimes add a small portion of cream of tartar to the solution while boiling. Sugar, thus altered by heat, and sometimes variously flavoured, constitutes several preparations sold by the confectioner. *Barley-sugar* and *acidulated drops* are prepared in this way from white sugar: powdered tartaric acid being added to the sugar while soft. *Hardbake* and *toffee* are made by a similar process from brown sugar. Toffee differs from hardbake from containing butter.

The ornamented sugar pieces, or *caramel*-tops, with which pastrycooks decorate their tarts, &c., are prepared in the same way. If the boiled and yet soft sugar be rapidly and repeatedly extended, and pulled over a hook, it becomes opaque and white, and then constitutes *pulled sugar*, or *penides*. Pulled sugar, variously flavoured and coloured, is sold in several forms by the preparers of hard confectionary.

"Concerning this *hard confectionary*," Dr. Pereira says, "sugar constitutes the base of an almost innumerable variety of hard confectionary, sold under the names of *lozenges, brilliants, pipe, rock, comfits, nonpareils,* &c. Besides sugar, these preparations contain some flavouring ingredient, as well as flour or gum, to give them cohesiveness, and frequently colouring matter. Carraway, fruits, almonds, and pine seeds, constitute the nuclei of some of these preparations."

One of the appliances of the street sweet-stuff trade which I saw in the room of the seller before mentioned was—Acts of Parliament. A pile of these, a foot or more deep, lay on a shelf. They are used to wrap up the rock, &c., sold. The sweet-stuff maker (I never heard them called confectioners) bought his "paper" of the stationers, or at the old book-shops. Sometimes, he said, he got works in this way in sheets which had never been cut (some he feared were stolen,) and which he retained to read at his short intervals of leisure, and then used to wrap his goods in. In this way he had read through two Histories of England! He maintained a wife, two young children, and a young sister, who could attend to the stall; his wife assisted him in his manufactures. He used 1 cwt. of sugar a week on the year's average, ½ cwt. of treacle, and 5 oz. of scents, each 8*d.* an oz.

The man who has the best trade in London streets, is one who, about two years ago, introduced—after much study, I was told—short sentences into his "sticks." He boasts of his secret. When snapped asunder, in any part, the stick presents a sort of coloured inscription. The four I saw were: "Do you love me?" The next of less touching character, "Do you love sprats?" The others were, "Lord Mayor's Day," and "Sir Robert Peel." This man's profits are twice those of my respectable informant's.

OF THE CUSTOMERS OF THE SWEET-STUFF STREET-SELLERS.

ANOTHER sweet-stuff man, originally a baker, but who, for a fortnight before I saw him, had been attending upon an old gentleman, disabled from an accident, gave me the following account of his customers. What I heard from the other street-sellers satisfies me of the correctness of the statement. It will be seen that he was possesed of some humour and observation:

"Boys and girls are my best customers, sir, and mostly the smallest of them; but then,

again, some of them's fifty, aye, turned fifty; Lor' love you. An old fellow, that hasn't a stump of a tooth in front, why, he '*ll* stop and buy a ha'porth of hard-bake, and he'll say, ' I've a deal of the boy left about me still.' He doesn't show it, anyhow, in his look. I'm sometimes a thinking I' ll introduce a softer sort of toffy—boiled treacle, such as they call Tom Trot in some parts, but it's out of fashion now, just for old people that's ' boys still.' It was rolled in a ha'penny stick, sir, and sold stunnin'. The old ones wants something to suck, and not to chew. Why, when I was a lad at school, there was Jews used to go about with boxes on their backs, offering rings and pencil-cases, and lots of things that's no real use to nobody, and they told everybody they asked to buy ' that they sold everything, and us boys used to say—' Then give 's a ha'porth of boiled treacle.' It was a regular joke. I wish I'd stuck more to my book then, but what can't be cured must be endured, you know. Now, those poor things that walks down there" (intimating, by a motion of the head, a thoroughfare frequented by girls of the town), "they're often customers, but not near so good as they was ten year ago; no, indeed, nor six or eight year. *They* like something that bites in the mouth, such as peppermint-rock, or ginger-drops. They used to buy a penn'orth or two and offer it to people, but they don't now, I think. I've trusted them ha'pennies and pennies, sometimes. They always paid me. Some that held their heads high like, might say : ' I really have no change ; I'll pay you to-morrow.' She hadn't no change, poor lass, sure enough, and she hadn't nothing to change either, I'll go bail. I've known women, that seemed working men's or little shopkeeper's wives, buy of me and ask which of my stuffs took greatest hold of the breath. I always knew what they was up to. They'd been having a drop, and didn't want it to be detected. Why, it was only last Saturday week two niceish-looking and niceish-dressed women, comes up to me, and one was going to buy peppermint-rock, and the other says to her: ' Don't, you fool, he'll only think you've been drinking gin-and-peppermint. Coffee takes it off best.' So I lost my customers. They hadn't had a *single* drain that night, I'll go bail, but still they didn't look like regular lushingtons at all. I make farthing's-worths of sweet-stuff, for children, but I don't like it ; it's an injury to trade. I *was* afraid that when half-farthings was coined, they'd come among children, and they'd want half a farthing of brandy-balls. Now, talking of brandy-balls, there's a gentleman that sometimes has a minute's chat with me, as he buys a penn'orth to take home to his children—(every reasonable man ought to marry and have children for the sake of the sweet-trade, but it ain't the women's fault that many's single still)—when one gentleman I knows buys brandy-balls, he says, quite grave, ' What kind o' brandy do you put in them?' ' Not a drop of British,' says I, ' I can assure you; not a single drop.' He's not finely dressed; indeed, he's a leetle seedy, but I know he's a gentleman, or what's the same thing, if he ain't rich; for a common fellow 'll never have his boots polished that way, every day of his life; *his* blacking bills must come heavy at Christmas. I can tell a gentleman, too, by his way of talk, 'cause he's never bumptious. It's the working people's children that's my great support, and they was a better support, by 2s. in every 10s., and more, when times was better; and next to them among my patrons is poor people. Perhaps, this last year, I've cleared 11s. a week, not more, all through. I make my own stuffs, except the drops, and they require machinery. I would get out of the streets if I could."

Another of these traders told me, that he took more in farthings, than in halfpennies or pennies.

Calculating 200 sweet-stuff sellers, each clearing 10s. weekly, the outlay in rocks, candies, hard-bakes, &c., in the streets is 5,200l. yearly, or nearly two and a half millions of halfpenny-worths.

To start in the sweet-stuff business requires a capital of 35s., including a saucepan in which to boil sugar, 2s.; weights and scales, 4s.; stock-money (average), 4s.; and barrow, 25s. If the seller be not his own manufacturer, then a tray, 1s. 9d.; and stock-money, 1s. 6d.; or 3s. 3d. in all will be sufficient.

OF THE STREET-SELLERS OF COUGH DROPS
AND OF MEDICAL CONFECTIONARY.

MR. STRUTT, in his "Sports and Pastimes of the People of England" (1800), says of the Mountebank: "It is uncertain at what period this vagrant dealer in physic made his appearance in England; it is clear, however, that he figured away with much success in this country during the last two centuries. . . . . . The mountebanks usually preface the vending of their medicines with pompous orations, in which they pay as little regard to truth as to propriety." I am informed by a gentleman observant of the matter, that within his knowledge, which extends to the commencement of the present century, no mountebank (proper) had appeared in the streets of London proclaiming the virtues of his medicines; neither with nor without his "fool." The last seen by my informant, perhaps the latest mountebank in England, was about twenty years ago, in the vicinity of Yarmouth. He was selling "cough drops" and infallible cures for asthma, and was dressed in a peruiwig and an embroidered coat, with ruffles at his wrist, a sword to his side, and was a representation, in shabby genteel, of the fine gentleman of the reign of Queen Anne. The mountebank's most legitimate successor in the street cajolery of London, as regards his "orations," is the "Patterer," as I shall show in my account of the street trade in stationery literature. His successor in the vending of curative confectionaries and (in a small degree)

of nostrums, salves, ointments, &c., are the sellers of "cough drops" and "horehound candy," and of the corn salves, and cures for bruises, sprains, burns, &c., &c., &c.

The street-traders in cough drops and their accompaniments, however, do not now exceed six, and of them only two—who are near relatives —manufacture their own stock-in-trade. I here treat of the street trade in "cough drops," as a branch of the itinerant sweet-stuff trade. The "mountebank" part of the business—that is to say, "the prefacing the vending of the medicines with *pompous orations*," I shall reserve till its proper place—viz. the "*pattering*" part of the street trade, of which an account will be given in the next Chapter.

The two principal vendors of cough drops wheel their stalls, which are fixed upon barrows, to different parts of town, but one principal stand is in Holborn. On their boards are displayed the cough cures, both in the form of "sticks" and "drops," and a model of a small distillery. The portion inclosing the still is painted to resemble brick-work, and a tin tube, or worm, appears to carry the distillation to a receiver. Horehound, colts-foot, and some other herbs lie in a dried state on the stall, but principally horehound, to which popular (street) opinion seems to attach the most and the greatest virtues. There are also on the stalls a few bottles, tied up in the way they are dispensed from a regular practitioner, while the cough drops are in the form of sticks ($\frac{1}{2}d$. each), also neatly wrapped in paper. The cry is both expressive and simply descriptive—" Long life candy! Candy from herbs!"

From the most experienced person in this curious trade, I had the following statement. He entertained a full assurance, as far as I could perceive, of the excellence of his remedies, and of the high art and mystery of his calling. In persons of his class, professing to heal, no matter in what capacity, or what may be the disease, this is an important element of success. My informant, whether answering my questions or speaking of his own accord, always took time to consider, and sometimes, as will be seen, declined replying to my inquiries. From him I received the following account:—

"The cough drop and herb trade is nothing now to what it was long ago. Thirty or forty years ago, it was as good as 3l. or 4l. a week to a person, and was carried on by respectable men. I know nothing of any 'humbugs' in the respectable part of the trade. What's done by those who are ignorant, and not respectable, is nothing to me. I don't know how many there were in the trade thirty or forty years ago; but I know that, ten or eleven years since, I supplied seven persons who sold cough drops, and such like, in the streets, and now I supply only myself and another. I sell only four or five months in the year—the cold months, in course; for, in the summer, people are not so subject to coughs and colds. I am the 'original' maker of my goods. I will cure any child of the hooping-cough, and very speedily. I defy any medical man to dispute it, and I'll do it—' no cure, no pay.' I never profess to cure asthma. Nobody but a gravedigger can put an end to that there; but I can relieve it. It's the same with consumption; it may be relieved, but the gravedigger is the only man as can put a stop to it. Many have tried to do it, but they've all failed. I sell to very respectable people, and to educated people, too; and, what's more, a good deal (of cough drops) to medical men. In course, they can analyse it, if they please. They can taste the bitter, and judge for themselves, just as they can taste wine in the Docks. Perhaps the wives of mechanics are among my best customers. They are the most numerous, but they buy only ha'porths and penn'orths. Very likely, they would think more of the remedy if they had to pay 13½d. for it, instead of the 1½d. The Government stamp makes many a stuff sell. Oh! I know nothing about quackery: you must inquire at the Stamp-office, if you want to know about them kind of medicines. They're the people that help to sell them. Respectable people will pay me 1s. or 2s. at a time; and those who buy once, buy again. I'm sent to from as far off as Woolwich. I'll undertake to cure, or afford relief, in coughs, colds, or wind in the chest, or forfeit 1s. I can dispel wind in two minutes. I sell bottles, too, for those cures (as well as the candy from herbs): I manufacture them myself. They're decoctions of herbs, and the way to prepare them is my secret. I sell them at from 2d. to 1s. Why, I use one article that costs 24s. a pound, foreign, and twice that English. I've sold hundred weights. The decoctions are my secret. I will instruct any person—and have instructed a good many—when I'm paid for it. In course, it would never do to publish it in your work, for thousands would then learn it for 2d. My secret was never given to any person—only with what you may call a fee—except one, and only to him when he got married, and started in the line. He's a connection of mine. All we sell is genuine.

"I sell herbs, too, but it's not a street sale: I supply them to orders from my connection. It's not a large trade. I sell horehound, for tea or decoctions; coltsfoot, for smoking as herb tobacco (I gather the coltsfoot myself, but buy the horehound as a shopkeeper, as it's cultivated); ground-ivy is sold only for the blood (but little of it); hyssop for wind; and Irish moss for consumption. I'm never asked for anything improper. They won't ask me for —— or ——. And I'm never asked for washes or cosmetics; but a few nettles are ordered of me for complexions.

"Well, sir, I'd rather not state the quantities I sell, or my profits, or prices. I make what keeps myself, my wife, and seven children, and that's all I need say about it. I'd rather say no more on that part of the business: and so, I'm sure you won't press me. I don't know what others in the trade make. They buy of confectioners, and are only imitators of me. They buy

coltsfoot-candy, and such like; how it's made so cheap, I don't know. In the summer, I give up cough-drop selling, and take to gold fish."

I am told that the cough-drop-makers, who are also street-sellers, prepare their sticks, &c., much in the same method as the manufacturers of the ordinary sweet-stuff (which I have described), using the decoction, generally of horehound or coltsfoot, as the "scents" are used. In the old times, it would appear that the preparation of a medicinal confection was a much more elaborate matter, if we may judge by the following extract from an obsolete medical work treating of the matter. The author styles such preparations "lohochs," which is an Arabic word, he says, and signifies "a thing to be licked." It would appear that the lohoch was not so hard as the present cough-drop. The following is one of the receipts, "used generally against diseases in the breast and lungs:"—

"*Lohoch de farfara,*" *the Lohoch of Coltsfoot.*

Take of coltsfoot roots cleansed 8 ozs.,marsh-mallow roots 4 ozs., boil them in a sufficient quantity of water, and press the pulp through a sieve, dissolve it again in the decoction, and let it boil once or twice; then take it from the fire, and add 2 lbs. of white sugar, honey of raisins 14 ozs., juice of liquorice 2½ drams, stir them well with a wooden pestle, sprinkling in of saffron and cloves in powder, of each 1 scruple, cinnamon and mace, of each 2 scruples; make them into a lohoch according to art. It is good for a cough and roughness of the windpipe.

Without wishing to infringe upon professional secrets, I may mention that the earnings of the principal man in the trade may be taken at 30s. a week for 20 weeks; that of another at 15s. for the same period; and those of the remaining four at 5s. each, weekly; but the latter sell acid drops, and other things bought of the chemists. Allowing the usual cent. per cent., we then find 130l. expended by street-buyers on cough-drops. The best cough-drop stall seen in the streets is a kind of barrow, which can be shut up like a piano: it cost 3l. 10s. complete with the distilling apparatus before described. Scales and weights cost 5s., and the stock-money for the supply of such a stall need not exceed 10s.; or, in all, about 4l. 10s. For an ordinary trade—ready-made articles forming the stock — the capital would be, stall and trestle, 7s.; scales and weights (which are not always used), 3s. 6d., and stock-money, 2s. 6d.; in all, 13s

OF THE STREET-SELLERS OF ICES AND OF ICE CREAMS.

I HAVE already treated of the street luxury of pine-apples, and have now to deal with the greater street rarity of ice-creams.

A quick-witted street-seller—but not in the "provision" line—conversing with me upon this subject, said: "Ices in the streets! Aye, and there'll be jellies next, and then mock turtle, and then the real ticket, sir. I don't know nothing of the difference between the real thing and the mock, but I once had some cheap mock in an eating-house, and it tasted like stewed tripe with a little glue. You'll keep your eyes open, sir, at the Great Exhibition; and you'll see a new move or two in the streets, take my word for it. Penny glasses of cham pagne, I shouldn't wonder."

Notwithstanding the sanguine anticipations of my street friend, the sale of ices in the streets has not been such as to offer any great encouragement to a perseverance in the traffic.

The sale of ice-creams was unknown in the streets until last summer, and was first introduced, as a matter of speculation, by a man who was acquainted with the confectionary business, and who purchased his ices of a confectioner in Holborn. He resold these luxuries daily to street-sellers, sometimes to twenty of them, but more frequently to twelve. The sale, however, was not remunerative, and had it not been generally united with other things, such as ginger-beer, could not have been carried on as a means of subsistence. The supplier of the street-traders sometimes went himself, and sometimes sent another to sell ice-cream in Greenwich Park on fine summer days, but the sale was sometimes insufficient to pay his railway expenses. After three or four weeks' trial, this man abandoned the trade, and soon afterwards emigrated to America.

Not many weeks subsequent to "the first start," I was informed, the trade was entered into by a street-seller in Petticoat-lane, who had become possessed, it was said, of Masters's Freezing Apparatus. He did not vend the ices himself for more than two or three weeks, and moreover confined his sale to Sunday mornings; after a while he employed himself for a short time in making ices for four or five street-sellers, some of whom looked upon the preparation as a wonderful discovery of his own, and he then discontinued the trade.

There were many difficulties attending the introduction of ices into street-traffic. The buyers had but a confused notion how the ice was to be swallowed. The trade, therefore, spread only very gradually, but some of the more enterprising sellers purchased stale ices from the confectioners. So little, however, were the street-people skilled in the trade, that a confectioner told me they sometimes offered ice to their customers in the streets, and could supply only water! Ices were sold by the street-vendors generally at 1*d.* each, and the trade left them a profit of 4*d.* in 1*s.*, when they served them " without waste," and some of the sellers contrived, by giving smaller modicums, to enhance the 4*d.* into 5*d.* ; the profit, however, was sometimes what is expressively called " nil." Cent. per cent.—the favourite and simple rate known in the streets as " half-profits " was rarely attained.

From a street-dealer I received the following account:—

" Yes, sir, I mind very well the first time as I ever sold ices. I don't think they'll ever take greatly in the streets, but there's no saying. Lord! how I've seen the people splutter when they've tasted them for the first time.

I did as much myself. They get among the teeth and make you feel as if you tooth-ached all over. I sold mostly strawberry ices. I haven't an idee how they're made, but it's a most wonderful thing in summer — freezing fruits in that way. One young Irish fellow—I think from his look and cap he was a printer's or stationer's boy—he bought an ice of me, and when he had scraped it all together with the spoon, he made a pull at it as if he was a drinking beer. In course it was all among his teeth in less than no time, and he stood like a stattey for a instant, and then he roared out,—'Jasus! I'm kilt. The could shivers is on to me!' But I said, 'O, you're all right, you are;' and he says, 'What d'you mane, you horrid horn,* by selling such stuff as that. An' you must have the money first, bad scran to the likes o' you!'

" The persons what enjoyed their ices most," the man went on, " was, I think, servant maids that gulped them on the sly. Pr'aps they'd been used, some on 'em, to get a taste of ices on the sly before, in their services. We sees a many dodges in the streets, sir—a many. I knew one smart servant maid, treated to an ice by her young man—they seemed as if they was keeping company—and he soon was stamping, with the ice among his teeth, but she knew how to take hern, put the spoon right into the middle of her mouth, and when she'd had a clean swallow she says: 'O, Joseph, why didn't you ask *me* to tell you how to eat your ice?' The conceit of sarvant gals is ridiculous. Don't you think so, sir? But it goes out of them when they gets married and has to think of how to get broth before how to eat ices. One hot day, about eleven, a thin tall gentleman, not very young, threw down 1*d.* to me, and says, says he, ' As much ice as you can make for that.' He knew how to take it. When he'd done, he says, says he, ' By G—, my good feller, you've saved my life. I've been keeping it up all night, and I was dying of a burnt-up throat, after a snooze, and had only 1*d.* So sick and hot was my stomach, I could have knelt down and taken a pull at the Thames'—we was near it at the time—' You've saved my life, and I'll see you again.' But I've never see'd him since. He was a gentleman, I think. He was in black, and wore a big black and gold ring—only one.

" The rest of my customers for ices, was people that bought out of curiosity, and there was gentlemen's servants among 'em, very little fellows some of 'em ; and doctors' boys; and mechanics as was young and seemed of a smartish sort ; and boys that seemed like schoolboys; and a few women of the town,— but mine's not much of a pitch for them."

From the information I obtained, I may state

* I inquired as to what was meant by the reproachful appellation, " horrid horn," and my informant declared that " to the best of his hearing," those were the words used ; but doubtless the word was " omad-haun," signifying in the Erse tongue, a half-witted fellow. My informant had often sold fruit to the same lad, and said he had little of the brogue, or of " old Irish words," unless " his temper was riz, and then it came out powerful. '

that, if the sale of street ices be calculated at twenty persons *taking*, not earning, 1s. 6d. daily for four weeks, it is as near the mark as possible. This gives an expenditure of 42l. in street ices, with a profit to the vendors of from 10 to 25 per cent. I am told that an unsuccessful start has characterised other street trades — rhubarb for instance, both in the streets and markets—which have been afterwards successful and remunerative.

For capital in the ice trade a small sum was

necessary, as the vendors had all stalls and sold other commodities, except the " original street ice man," who was not a regular street trader, but a speculator. A jar—in which the ices were neither sufficiently covered nor kept cooled, though it was often placed in a vessel or " cooler," containing cold water—cost 1s., three cups, 3d. (or three glasses, 1s.), and three spoons, 3d., with 2s. stock-money; the total is, presuming glasses were used, 4s., or, with a vessel for water, 5s.

OF THE CAPITAL AND INCOME OF THE STREET-SELLERS OF EATABLES AND DRINKABLES.

I now give a summary of the Capital and Income of the street-sellers of eatables and drinkables. But, first, I will endeavour to arrive at an estimate of the total number of people belonging to the class.

The street-sellers engaged in the sale of eatables and drinkables, are, summing the several items before given, altogether 6,347: of whom 300 sell pea-soup and hot eels; 150, pickled whelks; 300, fried fish; 300, sheeps trotters; 60, ham-sandwiches; 200, baked 'tatoes; 4, hot green peas; 150, meat; 25, bread; 1,000, cat and dogs' meat; 300, coffee and tea; 1,700, ginger-beer, lemonade, sherbet, &c.; 50, elder-wine; 4, peppermint-water; 28, milk; 100, curds and whey and rice-milk; 60, water; 50, pies; 6, boiled pudding; 6, plum "duff"; 150, cakes and tarts; 4, plum-cakes; 30, other cheaper cakes; 150, gingerbread-nuts; 500, cross-buns; 500, muffins and crumpets; 200, sweet stuff; 6, cough-drops; 20, ice-creams. But many of the above are only temporary trades. The street-sale of hot cross-buns, for instance, lasts only for a day; that of muffins and crumpets, baked potatoes, plum-"duff," cough-drops, elder-wine, and rice-milk, are all purely winter trades, while the sale of ginger-beer, lemonade, ice-creams, and curds and whey, is carried on solely in the summer. By this means the number of the street-sellers of eatables and drinkables, never at any one time reaches the amount before stated. In summer there are, in addition to the 10,000 costers before mentioned, about 3,000 people, and in winter between 4,000 and 5,000, engaged in the eatable and drinkable branch of the street-traffic.

As regards the Capital and Income, many minute accounts have been prepared.

To show the care, as well as the fulness with which these returns have been made, I give one of the Tables in its integrity, merely remarking, that similar tables relative to all the other articles have been made; but I condense the details, lest a repetition, however curious in its statistics, should prove wearisome:

CAPITAL, OR STOCK IN TRADE, OF THE STREET-SELLERS OF EATABLES AND DRINKABLES.

Street-sellers of Hot Eels.

	£	s.	d
200 stalls, at 6s.	60	0	0
100 baskets, at 1s.	5	0	0

	£	s.	d.
200 eel-kettles, at 3s. 6d.	35	0	0
100 jars for itinerants, at 6d.	2	10	0
300 stew-pans, at 2s.	30	0	0
300 strainers, at 1s.	15	0	0
300 ladles, at 4d.	5	0	0
2,400 cups, at 1d.	10	0	0
2,400 spoons, at 1d.	10	0	0
200 chafing-dishes, at 6d.	5	0	0
200 glasses for candles, at 3d.	2	10	0
240 vendors' stock-money, at 5s. each	60	0	0
60 ditto, at 25s. each	75	0	0
100 itinerants' ditto, at 2s. each	10	0	0
300 cloths, at 4d. each	5	0	0
300 pairs of sleeves, at 4d. per pair	5	0	0
300 aprons at 4d. each	5	0	0
	£339	10	0

Street-sellers of Pea Soup.

150 soup-kettles, 4s. each; 150 ladles, 6d. each; 150 pepper-boxes, 1d. each; 150 mint-boxes, 3d. each; 150 chafing-dishes, 6d. each; 1,800 basons, 1d. each; 1,800 spoons, 1d. each; stock-money, 3s. 6d. each * . 81 5 0

Street-sellers of Pickled Whelks.

100 stalls, 4s. each; 150 baskets, 2s. 6d. each; 150 tin boilers, 2s. 6d. each; 75 pans, 9d. each; 150 jars, 6d. each; 150 flour-dredgers, 4d. each; 1,800 saucers, ¼d. each; 150 table-spoons, 2d. each; 150 knives, 2d. each; 150 vinegar-bottles, 1d. each; 150 serge aprons, 2s. each; stock-money, for 150 vendors, 5s. each 125 18 9

Street-sellers of Fried Fish.

300 trays, 1s. 6d. each; 300 frying-pans, 1s. 6d. each; 300 salt-dredgers, 3d. each; 300 knives, 2d. each; 300 earthenware pans, 1s. each; 300 shallows, 1s. each; stock-money, for 150 vendors, 5s. each . 156 5 0

* The hot-eel trade being in conjunction with the pea-soup, the same stall, candles, towels, sleeves, and aprons do for both.

Street-sellers of Sheeps' Trotters.

300 baskets, 1s. 4d. each; 300
cotton cloths, 4d. each; 300 forks,
2d. each; 300 knives, 3d. each; 300
pepper-boxes, 1d. each; 300 salt-
cellars, 1d. each; stock-money, for
300 sellers, 1s. each 48 15 0

Street-sellers of Ham Sandwiches.

60 baskets, 2s. each; 60 tin boilers,
2s. each; 60 knives and forks, 6d.
per pair; 60 mustard-pots, 1d. each;
60 spoons, 1d. each; 60 cloths, 5d.
each; 60 aprons, 4d. each; 60 pairs
of sleeves, 4d. per pair; stock-money
for 60 vendors, 7s. 2d. weekly . . 38 15 0

Street-sellers of Baked 'Tatoes.

300 cans, 2l. each; 300 knives,
3d. each; 300 pepper-boxes, 1d.
each; stock-money for 300 vendors,
10s. each 755 0 0

Street-sellers of Hot Green Peas.

4 cans, 2s. 6d. each; 4 vinegar-
bottles, 1d. each: 4 pepper-boxes,
3d. each; 12 saucers, 1d. each; 12
spoons, 1d. each; 4 cloths, 4d. each;
stock-money for 4 vendors, 2s. each 1 2 8

Street-sellers of Meat ("Hawking Butchers.")

150 baskets, 4s. 6d. each; 150
saws, 2s. each; 150 cleavers, 1s. 6d.
each; 150 steels, 1s. 6d. each; 150
belts for baskets, 1s. each; 150 do.
for waist, 6d. each; 150 cloths, 6d.
each; 150 aprons, 6d. each; 150
pairs of sleeves, 4d. per pair; 150
vendors' stock-money, 6s each per
day 138 5 0

Street-sellers of Bread.

12 baskets, 4s. 6d. each; 12 barrows, 40s. each; 1 long bread-basket,
40s.; 1 barrow, 30s.; 13 sacks, 1s.
each; stock-money for 25 vendors,
at 1l. each 55 17 0

Street-sellers of Cats' and Dogs'-meat.

500 barrows, 18s. each; 1,000
baskets, 1s. 6d. each; 500 sets of
weights and scales, 4s. each; 1,000
knives, 8d. each; 1,000 steels, 1s.
each; stock-money of 1,500 vendors, 7s. 6d. per head 1,083 6 8

Street-sellers of Coffee and Tea.

150 tables, 2s. 6d. each; 75 stalls,
6s. each; 75 coffee-barrows, 1l. each;
400 coffee-cans (100 vendors having
two cans, and 200 only one), 8s. each;
1,200 half-pint cups and saucers, 3d.
each, and 900 pints, 6d. each; 2,100
spoons, 1d. each; 900 plates, 1½d.
each; 300 knives, 2d. each; 300
pans, 9d. each; 600 canisters, 5d.
each; 50 screens, 2s. 6d. each; stock-
money of 300 vendors, 5s. each . 435 12 0

Street-sellers of Ginger-beer.

300 barrows, 1l. each; 1,000 stalls,
5s. each; 175 fountains, 7l. each; 20
ditto, 20l. each; 3 ditto, 100l. each;
9,000 glasses, 5d. each; 1,500 tanks,
1s. each; 3,000 towels, 6d. each;
500 sets of brewing utensils, corks,
&c., 5s. each; 500 gross of bottles,
10s. per gross, and stock-money for
1,500 vendors, 5s. each 3,562 10 0

Street-sellers of Lemonade, Nectar, Sherbet, &c.

200 stalls, 6s. each; 500 stone
barrels, 5s. 6d. each; 1,200 glasses,
4½d. each; 400 towels, 6d. each; 200
jars, 2s. each; 2,400 glass bottles,
3d. each; stock-money for 200 vendors, 2s. 6d. each 305 0 0

Street-sellers of Elder-wine.

3 elder-wine carriages and apparatus, 7l. each; 47 ditto ditto, 3l. 10s.
each; 300 small wine-glasses, 2d.
each; stock-money, 3s. per head . 195 10 0

Street-sellers of Peppermint-water.

2 kegs, 3s. 6d. each; 2 jars, 2s.
each; 16 glasses, 3d. each; 4 cloths,
4d. each; stock-money, for four
vendors, 1s. each 1 0 4

Milk-sellers in the Park.

16 cows, 20l. each; 8 lockers, 3l.
each; 32 fixed seats, 3s. each; 48
forms, 3s. each; 48 glasses, 4½d.
each; 96 cups, 1d. each; 8 halters,
for cows, 6d. each; 8 pans, 1s. each;
16 towels, 6d. each 358 6 0

Milk-sellers in Markets, &c.

20 yokes and pairs of cans, 15s.
each; 20 sets of measures, 2s. per
set; stock-money for 20 vendors, 3s.
each 20 0 0

Street-sellers of Curds and Whey.

100 stalls, 5s. each; 100 saucepans, to scald the milk in, 2s. each;
300 cups, 1d. each; 300 glasses, 5d.
each; 600 spoons, ½d. each; 100
tin kettles, for stalls, at 3s. 6d. each;
100 small tubs, 1s each; 100 cloths,
3d. each; stock-money for 100 vendors, at 2s. each 77 10 0

Street-sellers of Rice-milk. †

50 kettles and braziers, for stall,
4s. the two; 300 spice or peppermint-
boxes, 1d. each; stock-money for
fifty vendors, 1s. 3d. each . . . 14 7 6

Water-carriers.

120 pails, 2s. each; 60 yokes, 5s.
each 27 0 0

* There are altogether 500 vendors of lemonade in
the streets, but 300 of these sell also ginger-beer, and
consequently do not have separate stalls, &c.
† The street-sellers of rice-milk are included in the
street-sellers of curds and whey; hence the stalls,
saucepans, cups, &c., of the two classes are the same.

Street Piemen.

	£	s.	d.
50 pie-cans, 1l. each ; 25 turn halfpenny boards, to gamble with, 2s. 6d. each ; 50 gross of tin pie-dishes, 12s. per gross ; 50 aprons, 8d. each ; 100 tins, 1s. each (for baking pies upon), stock-money, for 50 vendors, 6s. 6d. each	106	0	10

Street-sellers of Boiled Puddings.

6 stands, 6s. each ; 6 cans, 2s. 6d. each ; 6 pots (tin), 2s. each ; 6 chafing-dishes and stands, 5d. each ; 6 forks, 2d. each ; 6 cloths, 6d. each ; stock-money, for 6 vendors, 2s. 6d. each	4	4	6

Street-sellers of Plum-duff.

6 baskets, 1s. 9d. each ; 6 saucepans, 2s. each ; 6 cloths, 6d. each ; 6 knives, 2d. each ; stock-money, for 6 vendors, 2s. each	1	18	6

Street-sellers of Cakes, Tarts, &c.

150 trays, 1s. 9d. each ; 150 cloths, 1s. 3d. each ; 150 straps, 6d. each ; stock-money, 16s. 6d. each . . .	150	0	0

Other and inferior Cake-sellers.

30 trays, 1s. 9d. each ; 30 straps, 6d. each ; stock-money, 2s. 6d. each	7	2	6

Street-sellers of Plum-cake.

4 trays, 1s. 9d. each ; 4 baskets, 1s. 6d. each ; 4 cloths (oil-cloth covers for baskets), 1s. each ; 4 knives, 2d. each ; stock-money, for 4 sellers, 4s. each	1	18	8

Gingerbread-nut Makers and Sellers.

50 ovens, 5l. each ; 50 peels and rakes, 3s. the two ; 750 tins, 1s. each ; 50 lamps, for fairs, 6s. each ; 50 stalls, 6s. each ; 50 sets of scales and 100 sets of weights, half of them false, 7s. 6d. each ; 100 canisters, 2s. each ; 50 barrows, 30s. each ; 50 baskets, 6s. each ; 50 baizes, 1s. each ; 50 cloths to cover stall, 1s. each ; stock-money, for 50 makers and sellers, 14s. each	483	15	0

Gingerbread-nut Sellers (not Makers.)

150 trays, 1s. 9d. each ; 150 straps, 6d. each ; stock-money, for 150 sellers, 1s. 6d. each	28	5	6

Street-sellers of Hot cross Buns.

500 baskets, 2s. 6d. each ; 500 flannels and cloths, 2s. the two ; stock-money, for 500 sellers, 2s. 6d. each	175	0	0

Street-sellers of Muffins and Crumpets.

500 baskets, 2s. 6d. each ; 500 cloths, 1s. each ; stock-money, for 500 sellers, 5s. each	212	10	0

Street-sellers of Sweet-stuff.

	£	s.	d.
6 barrows, 1l. 10s. each ; 150 trays, 1s. 9d. each ; 50 saucepans, 2s. each ; 18 canisters (long tin), 2s. each ; 44 stalls, at 4s. each ; 50 sets of weights and scales, at 4s. each ; stock-money, for 150 vendors, 3s. each	70	4	6

Street-sellers of Cough Drops.

2 stills and barrows, 3l. 10s. each ; 4 stalls, 7s. each ; 6 weights and scales, 3s. 6d. each ; stock-money, for 6 sellers, 2s. 6d. each	10	4	0

Street-sellers of Ices.

20 jars, 1s. each ; 20 coolers, 2s. each ; 30 cups, 1d. each, and 30 glasses, 4d. each ; 60 spoons, 1d. each ; stock-money, for 20 vendors, 2s. per head	5	17	6

TOTAL CAPITAL INVESTED IN THE STREET SALE OF EATABLES AND DRINKABLES . . .	9,077	12	5

INCOME, OR "TAKINGS," OF STREET-SELLERS OF EATABLES AND DRINKABLES.

Street-sellers of Hot Eels.

There are upwards of 1,000,000 lbs. weight of hot eels sold yearly in the streets of London. 140 vendors each sell 6 lbs. of eels daily at their stands ; 60 sell 40 lbs. daily ; and 100 itinerant sell 5 lbs. nightly at the public-houses. The first mentioned take on an average 2s. daily ; the second 16s. ; and the third 1s. 8d. This gives a yearly street expenditure in the trade in hot eels amounting to £19,448

Street-sellers of Pea-soup.

The annual street consumption of pea-soup amounts to 1,680 gallons. 100 vendors sell each 4 gallons daily ; and 50 vendors, each sell upon an average 10 gallons daily. The first mentioned take 3s. a day ; and the last, 7s. 6d. This gives a street expenditure during the winter season of five months, of . . £4,050

Street-sellers of Pickled Whelks.

According to the Billingsgate returns, there are nearly 5,000,000 of whelks sold yearly in the streets of London. These are retailed in a boiled state, and flavoured with vinegar, at four a penny. 150 vendors take on an average 13s. weekly. This gives an annual street expenditure, of £5,000

Street-sellers of Fried Fish.

150 sellers make 10s. 6d. weekly, or yearly 27l. 6s. ; and 150 sellers make half that amount, 13l. 13s. per annum. Reckoning 20l. a year as a medium earning, and adding 90 per cent. for

profit, the annual consumption of fried fish supplied by London street-sellers amounts to 684,000 lbs., and the sum expended thereupon to £11,400

Street-sellers of Sheep's Trotters.

In the wholesale "trotter" establishment there are prepared, weekly, 20,000 sets, or 80,000 feet; giving a yearly average of 4,160,000 trotters, or the feet of 1,040,000 sheep. Of this quantity the street-folk buy seven-eighths, or 3,640,000 trotters yearly. The number of sheep trotter-sellers may be taken at 300; which gives an average of nearly 60 sets a week per individual. There is then expended yearly in London streets on trotters, calculating their sale, retail, at ½d. each, 6,500l.; but though the regular price is ½d., some trotters are sold at four for 1½d., very few higher than ½d., and some are kept until they are unsaleable, so that the amount thus expended may be estimated at £6,000

Street-sellers of Ham-sandwiches.

60 vendors, take 8s. a week, and sell annually 486,800 sandwiches, at a cost of £1,800

Street-sellers of Baked 'Tatoes.

300 vendors, sell upon an average ¾ cwt. of baked potatoes daily, or 1,755 tons in the season. The average takings of each vendor amount to 6s. a day; and the receipts of the whole number throughout the season (which lasts from the latter end of September till March inclusive), a period of 6 months, are . .£14,000

The Street-sellers of Hot Green Peas.

The chief man of business sells 3 gallons a day (which, at 1d. the quarter-pint, would be 8s., my informant said 7s.), the other three together sell the same quantity; hence there is an annual street consumption of 1,870 gallons, and a street expenditure on "hot green peas" of £250

Street-sellers of Meat.

The hawking butchers, taking their number at 150, sell 747,000 lbs. of meat, and take annually £12,450

Street-sellers of Bread.

25 men take 45s. a day for five months in the summer, and 12 regular traders take 1l. 12s. per day; this gives an annual street consumption of 700,000 quartern loaves of bread, and a street expenditure of £9,000

Street-sellers of Cats and Dogs' Meat.

There are 300,000 cats in the metropolis, and from 900 to 1,000 horses, averaging 2 cwt. of meat each, boiled down every week; the quantity of cats'

and dogs' meat used throughout London is about 200,000 lbs. per week, and this, sold at the rate of 2½d. per lb., gives 2,000l. a week for the money spent in cats' and dogs' meat, or per year, upwards of £100,000

Street-sellers of Coffee, Tea, &c.

Each coffee-stall keeper on an average clears 1l. a week, and his takings may be said to be at least double that sum; hence the quantity of coffee sold annually in the streets, is about 550,000 gallons, while the yearly street expenditure for tea, coffee, &c., amounts to . . .£31,200

Street-sellers of Ginger-beer.

The bottles of ginger-beer sold yearly in the streets number about 4,798,000, and the total street consumption of the same beverage may be said to be about 250,000 gallons per annum. 200 street-sellers of ginger-beer in the bottle trade of the penny class take 30s. a week each (thus allowing for inferior receipts in bad weather); 300 take 20s. each, selling their "beer" for the most part at ½d. the bottle, while the remaining 400 "in a small way" take 6s. each; hence there is expended in the bottled ginger-beer of the streets 11,480l. Adding the receipts from the fountains and the barrels, the barrel season continuing only ten weeks, the total sum expended annually in street ginger-beer amounts altogether to £14,660

Street-sellers of Lemonade, Sherbet, Nectar, &c.

There are 200 persons, chiefly men, selling solely lemonade, &c., and an additional 300 uniting the sale with that of ginger-beer. Their average receipts on fine days are 3s. 6d. a day, or, allowing for wet weather and diminished receipts, 10s. a week. The receipts, then, for this street luxury, show a street expenditure in such a summer as the last, of 2,800l., among those who do not unite ginger-beer with the trade. Calculating that those who do unite ginger-beer with it sell only one-half as much as the others, we find a total outlay of £4,900

Street-sellers of Elder-wine.

50 vendors clear 5s. a week for 16 weeks by the sale of elder-wine in the streets, their profit being at least cent. per cent.; hence the street consumption of this beverage in the course of the year is 1,500 gallons, and the outlay . . . £200

Street-sellers of Peppermint-water.

Calculating that 4 "pepperminters" take 2s. a day the year round, Sundays excepted, we find that 900 gallons of peppermint-water are consumed every year in the streets of London, while the sum expended in it amounts annually to £125

Street-sellers of Milk in the Markets, Parks, &c.

The vendors in the markets clear about 1s. 6d. a day each, for three months; and as the profit is rather more than cent. per cent., there are about 4,000 gallons of milk thus sold yearly. The quantity sold in the park averages 20 quarts a day for a period of nine months, or 1,170 gallons in the year. This is retailed at 4d. per quart; hence the annual expenditure is . . . £344

Street-sellers of Curds and Whey.

50 sellers dispose of 12½ gallons in 3 weeks; the other 50 sell only half as much. Taking the season at 3 months, the annual consumption of curds and whey in the streets is 2,812 double gallons (as regards the ingredients of milk), which is retailed at a cost to the purchasers of £412

Street-sellers of Rice-milk.

Calculating that 50 sellers dispose of 24 quarts weekly, while one-half of the remaining 25 sell 12 quarts each per week at 1d. the half-pint, and the other half vend 24 quarts at ½d. the half-pint, there are about 3,000 gallons of rice-milk yearly consumed in the streets of London, while the expenditure amounts to £320

Water-carriers.

The number of water-carriers are sixty, and their average earnings through the year 5s. a week; hence the sum annually expended in water thus obtained amounts to £780

Street Piemen.

There are fifty street piemen plying their trade in London, the year through, their average takings are one guinea a week; hence there is an annual street consumption of pies of nearly to three-quarters of a million, and a street expenditure amounting to £3,000

Street-sellers of Meat and Currant Puddings.

Each street-seller gets rid of, on an average, 85 dozen, or 1,020 puddings; there are now but six street-sellers (regularly) of these comestibles; hence the weekly aggregate would be—allowing for bad weather—5,400, and the total 129,600 meat and currant puddings sold in the streets, in a season of 24 weeks. This gives an annual expenditure on the part of the street boys and girls (who are the principal purchasers), and of the poor persons who patronise the street-trade, of about £270

Street-sellers of Plum "duff."

Calculating 42s. a week as the takings of six persons, for five months, we find there is yearly expended in the street purchase of plum dough upwards of . £250

Street-sellers of Cakes, Tarts, &c.

Reckoning 150 cake-sellers, each taking 6s. a week—a sufficiently low average — the street consumption of cakes, tarts, &c., will be 1,123,200 every year, and the street outlay about . . £2,350

Street-sellers of other and inferior Cakes.

The sale of the inferior street cakes realises about a fifth of that taken by the other cake-sellers; hence it may be estimated yearly at £450

Street-sellers of Gingerbread-nuts.

150 gingerbread-nut-sellers take 17s. each weekly (clearing 9s.); at this rate the sum spent yearly in "spice" nuts in the streets of London amounts to . £6,630

Street-sellers of Hot-cross Buns.

There are nearly 100,000 hot-cross buns sold every Good Friday in the streets of London; hence there is expended in one day, upon the buns thus bought about £300

Street-sellers of Muffins and Crumpets.

There are 500 muffin-sellers, each clearing 4s. and taking 12s. a week on an average; hence the metropolitan street sale of muffins and crumpets will be in 20 weeks about 120,000 dozen, and the sum expended thereon . . . £6,000

Street-sellers of Sweet-stuff.

The number of sweet-stuff sellers in London amounts to 200, each of whom, on an average, clears 10s., and takes 20s. weekly; the yearly consumption, therefore, of rocks, candies, hard-bakes, &c., purchased in the streets is nearly two and a half millions of halfpenny-worths, or (at the rate of ½d. an ounce) about 70 tons weight per annum, costing the consumers about £10,000

Street-sellers of Cough-drops.

The earnings of the principal man in the "cough-drop" street trade may be taken at 30s. a week for twenty weeks; that of another at 15s. for the same period; and those of the remaining four street-sellers of the same compound at 5s. each, weekly; allowing the usual cent. per cent., we find there is annually expended by street-buyers on cough-drops £130

Street-sellers of Ice Creams.

The sale of street ices may be calculated at twenty persons, taking 1s. 6d. daily for four weeks. This gives a street consumption of 10,000 penny ices, and an annual expenditure thereon of £42

TOTAL SUM EXPENDED YEARLY ON STREET EATABLES AND DRINKABLES £203,115

OF THE STREET-SELLERS OF STATIONERY, LITERATURE, AND THE FINE ARTS.

WE now come to a class of street-folk wholly distinct from any before treated of. As yet we have been dealing principally with the uneducated portion of the street-people—men whom, for the most part, are allowed to remain in nearly the same primitive and brutish state as the savage —creatures with nothing but their appetites, instincts, and passions to move them, and made up of the same crude combination of virtue and vice—the same generosity combined with the same predatory tendencies as the Bedouins of the desert—the same love of revenge and disregard of pain, and often the same gratitude and susceptibility to kindness as the Red Indian—and, furthermore, the same insensibility to female honour and abuse of female weakness, and the same utter ignorance of the Divine nature of the Godhead as marks either Bosjesman, Carib, or Thug.

The costers and many other of the street-sellers before described, however, are bad—not so much from their own perversity as from our selfishness. That they partake of the natural evil of human nature is not their fault but ours, —who would be like them if we had not been taught by others better than ourselves to controul the bad and cherish the good principles of our hearts.

The street-sellers of stationery, literature, and the fine arts, however, differ from all before treated of in the *general*, though far from universal, education of the sect. They constitute principally the class of street-orators, known in these days as "patterers," and formerly termed "mountebanks,"—people who, in the words of Strutt, strive to "help off their wares by pompous speeches, in which little regard is paid either to truth or propriety." To patter, is a slang term, meaning to speak. To indulge in this kind of oral puffery, of course, requires a certain exercise of the intellect, and it is the consciousness of their mental superiority which makes the patterers look down upon the costermongers as an inferior body, with whom they object either to be classed or to associate. The scorn of some of the "patterers" for the mere costers is as profound as the contempt of the pickpocket for the pure beggar. Those who have not witnessed this pride of class among even the most degraded, can form no adequate idea of the arrogance with which the skilled man, no matter how base the art, looks upon the unskilled. "We are the haristocracy of the streets," was said to me by one of the street-folks, who told penny fortunes with a bottle. "People don't pay us for what we gives 'em, but only to hear us talk. We live like yourself, sir, by the hexercise of our hintellects—we by talking, and you by writing."

But notwithstanding the self-esteem of the patterers, I am inclined to think that they are less impressionable and less susceptible of kindness than the costers whom they despise. Dr. Conolly has told us that, even among the insane, the educated classes are the most difficult to move and govern through their affections. They are invariably suspicious, attributing unworthy motives to every benefit conferred, and consequently incapable of being touched by any sympathy on the part of those who may be affected by their distress. So far as my experience goes it is the same with the street-patterers. Any attempt to befriend them is almost sure to be met with distrust. Nor does their mode of life serve in any way to lessen their misgivings. Conscious how much their own livelihood depends upon assumption and trickery, they naturally consider that others have some "dodge," as they call it, or some latent object in view when any good is sought to be done them. The impulsive costermonger, however, approximating more closely to the primitive man, moved solely by his feelings, is as easily humanized by any kindness as he is brutified by any injury.

The patterers, again, though certainly more intellectual, are scarcely less immoral than the costers. Their superior cleverness gives them the power of justifying and speciously glossing their evil practices, but serves in no way to restrain them; thus affording the social philosopher another melancholy instance of the evil of developing the intellect without the conscience—of teaching people to *know* what is morally beautiful and ugly, without teaching them at the same time to feel and delight in the one and abhor the other—or, in other words, of quickening the cunning and checking the emotions of the individual.

Among the patterers marriage is as little frequent as among the costermongers; with the exception of the older class, who "were perhaps married before they took to the streets." Hardly one of the patterers, however, has been bred to a street life: and this constitutes another line of demarcation between them and the costermongers.

The costers, we have seen, are mostly hereditary wanderers—having been as it were born to frequent the public thoroughfares; some few of the itinerant dealers in fish, fruit, and vegetables, have it is true been driven by want of employment to adopt street-selling as a means of living, but these are, so to speak, the aliens rather than the natives of the streets. The patterers, on the other hand, have for the most part neither been born and bred nor driven to a street life—but have rather *taken* to it from a natural love of what they call "roving." This propensity to lapse from a civilized into a nomad state—to pass from a settler into a wanderer—is a peculiar characteristic of the pattering tribe. The tendency however is by no means extraordinary; for ethnology teaches us, that whereas many abandon the habits of civilized life to adopt those of a nomadic state of existence, but few of the wandering tribes give up vagabondising and betake themselves to settled occupations. The innate "love of a roving life," which many of the street-people themselves speak of as the cause of their originally taking to the streets, appears to be accompanied by several peculiar characteristics ; among the most marked of these are an indomitable "self-will" or hatred of the least restraint or controul—an innate aversion to every species of law or government, whether political, moral, or domestic—a stubborn, contradictory nature—an incapability of continuous labour, or remaining long in the same place occupied with the same object, or attending to the same subject—an unusual predilection for amusements, and especially for what partakes of the ludicrous—together with a great relish of all that is ingenious, and so finding extreme delight in tricks and frauds of every kind. There are two patterers now in the streets (brothers)—well-educated and respectably connected — who candidly confess they prefer that kind of life to any other, and would not leave it if they could.

Nor are the patterers less remarkable than the costermongers for their utter absence of all religious feeling. There is, however, this distinction between the two classes—that whereas the creedlessness of the one is but the consequence of brutish ignorance, that of the other is the result of natural perversity and educated scepticism—as the street-patterers include many men of respectable connections, and even classical attainments. Among them, may be found the son of a military officer, a clergyman, a man brought up to the profession of medicine, two Grecians of the Blue-coat School, clerks, shopmen, and a class who have been educated to no especial calling—some of the latter being the natural sons of gentlemen and noblemen—and who, when deprived of the support of their parents or friends, have taken to the streets for bread. Many of the younger and smarter men, I am assured, reside with women of the town, though they may not be dependent for their livelihood on the wages got by the infamy of these women. Not a few of the patterers, too, in their dress and appearance, present but little difference to that of the "gent." Some wear a moustache, while others indulge in a Henri-Quatre beard. The patterers are, moreover, as a body, not distinguished by that good and friendly feeling one to another which is remarkable among costermongers. If an absence of heartiness and good fellowship be characteristic of an aristocracy—as some political philosophers contend—then the patterers may indeed be said to be the aristocrats of the streets.

The patterers or oratorical street-sellers include among their class many itinerant traders, other than the wandering "paper-workers"—

as those vending the several varieties of street-literature are generally denominated. The Cheap Jacks, or oratorical hucksters of hardware at fairs and other places, are among the most celebrated and humorous of this class. The commercial arts and jests of some of these people, display considerable cleverness. Many of their jokes, it is true, are traditional—and as purely a matter of parrotry as the witticisms of the "funny gentlemen" on the stage, but their ready adaptation of accidental circumstances to the purposes of their business, betrays a modicum of wit far beyond that which falls to the share of ordinary "low comedians." The street-vendors of cough drops—infallible cures for the toothache and other ailments—also belong to the pattering class. These are, as was before stated, the remains of the obsolete mountebanks of England and the *saltinbanque* of France—a class of *al fresco* orators who derived their names from the *bench*—the street pulpit, rostrum, or platform—that they ascended, in order the better to deliver their harangues. The street jugglers, actors, and showmen, as well as the street-sellers of grease-removing compositions, corn-salve, razor-paste, plating-balls, waterproof blacking, rat poisons, sovereigns sold for wagers, and a multiplicity of similar street-trickeries—such as oratorical begging — are other ingenious and wordy members of the same chattering, jabbering, or "pattering" fraternity. These will all be spoken of under the head of the different things they respectively sell or do. For the present we have only to deal with that portion of the "pattering" body who are engaged in the street sale of literature—or the "paper-workers" as they call themselves. The latter include the "running patterers," or "death-hunters;" being men (no women) engaged in vending last dying speeches and confessions—in hawking "se-cond edi-tions" of newspapers—or else in "working," that is to say, in getting rid of what are technically termed "cocks;" which, in polite language, means accounts of fabulous duels between ladies of fashion—of apochryphal elopements, or fictitious love-letters of sporting noblemen and certain young milliners not a hundred miles from the spot—"cooked" assassinations and sudden deaths of eminent individuals—pretended jealous affrays between Her Majesty and the Prince Consort (but these papers are now never worked) — or awful tragedies, including mendacious murders, impossible robberies, and delusive suicides.

The sellers of these choice articles, however, belong more particularly to that order or species of the pattering genus known as "running patterers," or "flying stationers," from the fact of their being continually on the move while describing the attractions of the "papers" they have to sell. Contradistinguished from them, however, are the "standing patterers," or those for whose less startling announcements a crowd is necessary, in order that the audience may have time to swallow the many marvels worked by their wares. The standing patterers require, therefore, what they term a "pitch," that is to say a fixed locality, where they can hold forth to a gaping multitude for, at least, some few minutes continuously. They are mainly such street-sellers as deal in nostrums and the different kinds of street "wonders." Occasionally, however, the running patterer (who is especially literary) transmigrates into a standing one, betaking himself to "board work," as it is termed in street technology, and stopping at the corners of thoroughfares with a large pictorial placard raised upon a pole, and glowing with a highly-coloured exaggeration of the interesting terrors of the pamphlet he has for sale. Thus is either "The Life of Calcraft, the Hangman," "The Diabolical Practices of Dr. —— on his Patients when in a state of Mesmerism," or "The Secret Doings at the White House, Soho," and other similar attractively-repulsive details. Akin to this "board work" is the practice of what is called "strawing," or selling straws in the street, and giving away with them something that is either really or fictionally forbidden to be sold,—as indecent papers, political songs, and the like. This practice, however, is now seldom resorted to, while the sale of "secret papers" is rarely carried on in public. It is true, there are three or four patterers who live chiefly by professing to dispose of "sealed packets" of obscene drawings and cards for gentlemen; but this is generally a trick adopted to extort money from old debauchees, young libertines, and people of degraded or diseased tastes; for the packets, on being opened, seldom contain anything but an odd number of some defunct periodical. There is, however, a large traffic in such secret papers carried on in what is called "the public-house trade," that is to say, by itinerant "paper-workers" (mostly women), who never make their appearance in the streets, but obtain a livelihood by "busking," as it is technically termed, or, in other words, by offering their goods for sale only at the bars and in the tap-rooms and parlours of taverns. The excessive indulgence of one appetite is often accompanied by the disease of a second; the drunkard, of course, is super-eminently a sensualist, and is therefore easily taken by anything that tends to stimulate his exhausted desires: so sure is it that one form of bestiality is a necessary concomitant of another. There is another species of patterer, who, though usually included among the standing patterers, belongs rather to an intermediate class, viz., those who neither stand nor "run," as they descant upon what they sell; but those walk at so slow a rate that, though never stationary, they can hardly be said to move. These are the reciters of dialogues, litanies, and the various street "squibs" upon passing events; they also include the public propounders of conundrums, and the "hundred and fifty popular song" enumerators—such as are represented in the engraving here given. Closely connected with them are the "chaunters," or those who do not cry, but (if one may so far

stretch the English language) *sing* the contents of the "papers" they vend.

These traffickers constitute the principal street-sellers of literature, or "paper-workers," of the "pattering" class. In addition to them there are many others vending "papers" in the public thoroughfares, who are mere traders resorting to no other acts for the disposal of their goods than a simple cry or exposition of them; and many of these are but poor, humble, struggling, and inoffensive dealers. They do not puff or represent what they have to sell as what it is not—(allowing them a fair commercial latitude). They are not of the "enterprising" class of street tradesmen. Among these are the street-sellers of stationery—such as note-paper, envelopes, pens, ink, pencils, sealing-wax, and wafers. Belonging to the same class, too, are the street-vendors of almanacs, pocket-books, memorandum and account-books. Then there are the sellers of odd numbers of periodicals and broadsheets, and those who vend either playing cards, conversation cards, stenographic cards, and (at Epsom, Ascot, &c.) racing cards. Besides these, again, there are the vendors of illustrated cards, such as those embellished with engravings of the Crystal Palace, Views of the Houses of Parliament, as well as the gelatine poetry cards—all of whom, with the exception of the racing-card sellers (who belong generally to the pattering tribe), partake of the usual characteristics of the street-selling class.

After these may be enumerated the vendors of old engravings out of inverted umbrellas, and the hawkers of coloured pictures in frames. Then there are the old book-stalls and barrows, and "the pinners-up," as they are termed, or sellers of old songs pinned against the wall, as well as the vendors of manuscript music. Moreover, appertaining to the same class, there are the vendors of playbills and "books of the performance" outside the theatre; and lastly, the pretended sellers of tracts—such as the Lascars and others, who use this kind of street traffic as a cloak for the more profitable trade of begging. The street-sellers of images, although strictly comprised within those who vend fine art productions in the public thoroughfares, will be treated of under the head of THE STREET ITALIANS, to which class they mostly belong.

OF THE FORMER AND PRESENT STREET-PATTERERS.

OF the street-patterers the running (or flying) trader announces the contents of the paper he is offering for sale, as he proceeds on his mission. It is usually the detail of some "barbarious and horrible murder," or of some extraordinary occurrence—such as the attack on Marshal Haynau—which has roused public attention; or the paper announced as descriptive of a murder, or of some exciting event, may in reality be some odd number of a defunct periodical. "It's astonishing," said one patterer to me, "how few people ever complain of having been took in. It hurts their feelings to lose a halfpenny, but it hurts their pride too much, when they're had, to grumble in public about it." On this head, then, I need give no further general explanation.

In times of excitement the running patterer (or "stationer," as he was and is sometimes called) has reaped the best harvest. When the Popish plot agitated England in the reign of Charles II. the "Narratives" of the design of a handful of men to assassinate a whole nation, were eagerly purchased in the streets and taverns. And this has been the case during the progress of any absorbing event subsequently. I was told by a very old gentleman, who had heard it from his grandfather, that in some of the quiet towns of the north of England, in Durham and Yorkshire, there was the greatest eagerness to purchase from the street-sellers any paper relative to the progress of the forces under Charles Edward Stuart, in 1745. This was especially the case when it became known that the "rebels" had gained possession of Carlisle, and it was uncertain what might be their route southward. About the period of the "affair of the '45," and in the autumn following the decisive battle of Culloden (in April, 1746), the "Northern Lights" were more than usually brilliant, or more than usually remarked, and a meteor or two had been seen. The street-sellers were then to be found in fairs and markets, vending wonderful accounts of these wonderful phenomena.

I have already alluded to the character of the old mountebank, and to his "pompous orations," having "as little regard to truth as to propriety." There certainly is little pompousness in the announcements of the patterers, though in their general disregard of truth they resemble those of the mountebank. The mountebank, however, addressed his audience from a stage, and made his address attractive by mixing up with it music, dancing, and tumbling; sometimes, also, equestrianism on the green of a village; and by having always the services of a merry-andrew, or clown. The nostrums of these quacks were all as unequalled for cheapness as for infallibility, and their impudence and coolness ensured success. Their practices are as well exposed in some of the *Spectators* of 1711-12 as the puppet-playing of Powel was good-humouredly ridiculed. One especial instance is cited, where a mountebank, announcing himself a native of Hammersmith, where he was holding forth, offered to make a present of 5s. to every brother native of Hammersmith among his audience. The mountebank then drew from a long bag a handful of little packets, each of which, he informed the spectators, was constantly sold for 5s. 6d., but that out of love to his native hamlet he would bate the odd 5s. to every inhabitant of the place. The whole assembly immediately closed with his generous offer."

There is a scene in Moncrieff's popular farce of "*Rochester*," where the hero personates a mountebank, which may be here cited as affording a good idea of the "pompous orations" indulged in by the street orators in days of yore:

"Silence there, and hear me, for my words are more precious than gold; I am the renowned and far-famed Doctor Paracelsus Bombastes Esculapus Galen dam Humbug von Quack, member of all the colleges under the Moon: M.D., L.M.D., F.R.S., L.L.D., *A.S.S.*—and all the rest of the letters in the alphabet: I am the seventh son of a seventh son—kill or cure is my motto —and I always do it; I cured the great Emperor of Nova Scotia, of a polypus, after he had been given over by all the faculty—he lay to all appearance dead : the first pill he took, he opened his eyes ; the second, he raised his head; and the third, he jumped up and danced a hornpipe. I don't want to sound my own praise—blow the trumpet, Balaam (*Balaam blows trumpet*); but I tapped the great Cham of Tartary at a sitting, of a terrible dropsy, so that I didn't leave a drop in him ! I cure the palsy, the dropsy, the lunacy, and all the sighs, without costing anybody a sigh; vertigo, pertigo, lumbago, and all the other go's are sure to go, whenever I come."

In his unscrupulousness and boldness in street announcements, and sometimes in his humour and satire, we find the patterer of the present day to be the mountebank of old descended from his platform into the streets—but without his music, his clown, or his dress.

There was formerly, also, another class, differing little from the habits of that variety of patterers of the present day who "busk" it, or "work the public-houses."

"The jestours," says Mr. Strutt, in his "Sports and Pastimes of the People of England," "or, as the word is often written in the old English dialect, 'gesters,' were the relaters of the gestes, that is, the actions of famous persons, whether fabulous or real; and these stories were of two kinds, the one to excite pity, and the other to move laughter, as we learn from Chaucer:

'And jestours that tellen tales,
Both of wepying and of game.'

The tales of 'game,' as the poet expresses himself were short jocular stories calculated to promote merriment, in which the reciters paid little respect to the claims of propriety or even of common decency. The tales of 'game,' however, were much more popular than those of weeping, and probably for the very reason that ought to have operated the most powerfully for their suppression. The gestours, whose powers were chiefly employed in the hours of conviviality, finding by experience that lessons of instruction were much less seasonable at such times, than idle tales productive of mirth and laughter, accommodated their narrations to the general taste of the times, regardless of the mischiefs they occasioned by vitiating the morals of their hearers. Hence it is that the author of the 'Vision of Pierce the Ploughman' calls them contemptibly 'Japers and Juglers, and Janglers of gests.' He describes them as haunters of taverns and common ale-houses, amusing the lower classes of the people with 'myrth of minstrelsy and losels' tales,' (loose vulgar tales,) and calls them tale-tellers and 'tutelers in ydell,' (tutors of idleness,) occasioning their auditory, 'for love of tales, in tavernes to drink,' where they learned from them to jangle and to jape, instead of attending to their more serious duties.

"The japers, I apprehend, were the same as the bourdours, or rybauders, an inferior class of minstrels, and properly called jesters in the modern acceptation of the word; whose wit, like that of the merry-andrews of the present day (1800) consisted in low obscenity accompanied with ludicrous gesticulation. They sometimes, however, found admission into the houses of the opulent. Knighton, indeed, mentions one of these japers who was a favourite in the English court, and could obtain any grant from the king 'a burdando,' that is, by jesting. They are well described by the poet:

'As japers and janglers, Judas' chyldren,
Fayneth them fantasies, and fooles them maketh."

"It was a very common and a very favourite amusement, so late as the 16th century, to hear the recital of verses and moral speeches, learned for that purpose by a set of men who obtained their livelihood thereby, and who, without ceremony, intruded themselves, not only into taverns and other places of public resort, but also into the houses of the nobility"

The resemblance of the modern patterer to the classes above mentioned will be seen when I describe the public-house actor and reciter of the present day, as well as the standing patterer, who does not differ so much from the running patterer in the quality of his announcements, as in his requiring more time to make an impression, and being indeed a sort of lecturer needing an audience; also of the present reciters " of verses and moral speeches." But of these curious classes I shall proceed to treat separately.

OF THE HABITS, OPINIONS, MORALS, AND RELIGION OF PATTERERS GENERALLY.

IN order that I might omit nothing which will give the student of that curious phase of London life in London streets—the condition of the patterers—a clear understanding of the subject, I procured the following account from an educated gentleman (who has been before alluded to in this work), and as he had been driven to live among the class he describes, and to support himself by street-selling, his remarks have of course all the weight due to personal experience, as well as to close observation:—

"If there is any truth in phrenology," writes the gentleman in question, "the patterers—to a man—are very large in the organ of 'self-esteem,' from which suggestion an enquiry arises, viz., whether they possess that of which they may justly pique themselves. To arrive at truth about the patterers is very difficult, and indeed the persons with whom they live are often quite in the dark about the history, or in some cases the pursuits of their lodgers.

" I think that the patterers may be divided into three classes. First,—those who were well born and brought up. Secondly, — those whose parents have been dissipated and gave them little education. Thirdly,—those who—whatever their early history—will not be or do anything but what is of an itinerant character. I shall take a glance at the *first* of these classes, presupposing that they were cradled in the lap of indulgence, and trained to science and virtue.

" If these people take to the streets, they become, with here and there an exception, the most reprobate and the least reclaimable. I was once the inmate of a lodging-house, in which there were at one time five University-men, three surgeons, and several sorts of broken-down clerks, or of other professional men. Their general habits were demoralised to the last degree—their oaths more horrid, extravagant, and farfetched than anything I ever heard: they were stupid in logic, but very original in obscenity. Most of them scoffed at the Bible, or perverted its passages to extenuate fraud, to justify violence, or construct for themselves excuses for incontinence and imposition. It will appear

strange that these educated persons, when they turn out upon the street, generally sell articles which have no connection with literature, and very little with art. The two brothers, who sell that wonder-working paste which removes grease from the outside of your collar by driving it further in, were both scholars of Christ's Hospital. They were second Grecians, and might have gone to college; but several visits to suburban fairs, and their accompanying scenes of debauch, gave them a *penchant* for a vagabond life, and they will probably never relinquish it. The very tall man—there are several others—who sells razors and paste on a red pagoda-looking stall, was apprenticed to a surgeon in Colchester, with a premium of 300 guineas; and the little dark-visaged man, who sells children's money-boxes and traps to catch vermin, is the son of a late upholsterer in Bath, who was also a magistrate of that city. The poor man alluded to was a law-student, and kept two terms in Trinity Hall, Cambridge. Many similar cases might be mentioned — cases founded on real observation and experience. Some light may be thrown upon this subject by pointing out the *modus operandi* by which a friend of mine got initiated into the ' art and mystery of patterism.' ' I had lived,' he said, ' more than a year among the tradesmen and tramps, who herd promiscuously together in low lodging-houses. One afternoon I was taking tea at the same table with a brace of patterers. They eyed me with suspicion; but, determined to know their proceedings, I launched out the only cant word I had then learned. They spoke of going to Chatham. Of course, I knew the place, and asked them, " Where do you stall to in the huey?" which, fairly translated, means, "Where do you lodge in the town?" Convinced that I was "fly," one of them said, "We drop the main toper (go off the main road) and slink into the crib (house) in the back drum (street)." After some altercation with the "mot" of the " ken" (mistress of the lodging-house) about the cleanliness of a knife or fork, my new acquaintance began to arrange " ground," &c., for the night's work. I got into their confidence by degrees; and I give below a vocabulary of their talk to each other:'

Word.	Meaning.
Crabshells	Shoes.
Kite	Paper.
Nests	Varieties.
Sticky	Wax.
Toff	Gentleman.
Burerk	Lady.
Camister	Minister.
Crocus	Doctor.
Bluff	An excuse.
Balmy	Insane.
Mill Tag	A shirt.
Smeesh	A shift.
Hay-bag	A woman.
Doxy	A wife.
Flam	A lie.
Teviss	A shilling

Bull . . . . A crown.
Flag . . . . An apron.

"The cant or slang of the patterer is not the cant of the costermonger, but a system of their own. As in the case of the costers, it is so interlarded with their general remarks, while their ordinary language is so smothered and subdued, that unless when they are profession-ally engaged and talking of their wares, they might almost pass for foreigners.

"There can be no doubt," continues my informant, "that the *second* class of street-patterers, to whom nature, or parents, or cir-cumstances have been unpropitious, are the most moral, and have a greater sense of right and wrong, with a quicksightedness about hu-mane and generous things, to which the 'aris-tocratic' patterer is a stranger. Of the dealers in useful or harmless wares—although, of course, they use allowable exaggeration as to the good-ness of the article—many are devout communi-cants at church, or members of dissenting bodies; while others are as careless about religion, and are still to be found once or twice a week in the lecture-rooms of the Mechanics' Institute nearest to their residence. Orchard-street, Westminster, is a great locality for this sort of patterers. Three well-known characters,—Bristol George, Corporal Casey, and Jemmy the Rake, with a very respectable and highly-informed man called 'Grocer,' from his having been apprenticed to that business,—have maintained a character for great integrity among the neighbours for many years.

"I come now to the *third* class of patterers,—those who, whatever their early pursuits and pleasures, have manifested a predilection for vagrancy, and neither can nor will settle to any ordinary calling. There is now on the streets a man scarcely thirty years old, conspicuous by the misfortune of a sabre-wound on the cheek. He is a native of the Isle of Man. His father was a captain in the Buffs, and himself a com-missioned officer at seventeen. He left the army, designing to marry and open a boarding-school. The young lady to whom he was be-trothed died, and *that* event *might* affect his mind; at any rate, he has had 38 situations in a dozen years, and will not keep one a week. He has a mortal antipathy to good clothes, and will not keep them one hour. He sells anything—chiefly needle-cases. He 'patters' very little in a *main drag* (public street); but in the little private streets he preaches an outline of his life, and makes no secret of his wandering propensity. His aged mother, who still lives, pays his lodgings in Old Pye-street.

"From the hasty glance I have taken at the patterers, any well-constructed mind may de-duce the following inference: because a great amount of intelligence sometimes consists with a great want of principle, that no education, or *mis*-education, leaves man, like a reed floating on the stream of time, to follow every direction which the current of affairs may give him.

"There is yet another and a larger class, who are wanderers from choice,—who would rather be street-orators, and quacks, and performers, than anything else in the world. In nine cases out of ten, the street-patterers are persons of intem-perate habits, no veracity, and destitute of any desire to improve their condition, even where they have the chance. One of this crew was lately engaged at a bazaar; he had 18*s.* a week, and his only work was to walk up and down and extol the articles exhibited. This was too monotonous a life; I happened to pass him by as he was taking his wages for the week, and heard him say, 'I shall cut this b—y work; I can earn more on the streets, and be my own master.'"

It would be a mistake to suppose that the patterers, although a vagrant, are a disorganized class. There is a telegraphic dispatch between them, through the length and breadth of the land. If two patterers (previously unac-quainted) meet in the provinces, the following, or something like it, will be their conversation: —"Can you 'voker romeny' (can you speak cant)? What is your 'monkeer' (name)?" —Perhaps it turns out that one is "White-headed Bob," and the other "Plymouth Ned." They have a "shant of gatter" (pot of beer) at the nearest "boozing ken" (ale-house), and swear eternal friendship to each other. The old saying, that "When the liquor is in, the wit is out," is remarkably fulfilled on these occa-sions, for they betray to the "flatties" (natives) all their profits and proceedings.

It is to be supposed that, in country districts, where there are no streets, the patterer is obliged to call at the houses. As they are mostly without the hawker's licence, and sometimes find wet linen before it is lost, the rural districts are not fond of their visits; and there are gene-rally two or three persons in a village reported to be "gammy," that is (unfavourable). If a patterer has been "crabbed," that is (offended) at any of the "cribbs" (houses), he mostly chalks a signal on or near the door. I give one or two instances:

◊ "Bone," meaning good.
▽ "Cooper'd," spoiled by the imprudence of some other patterer.
□ "Gammy," likely to have you taken up.
⊙ "Flummut," sure of a month in quod.

In most lodging-houses there is an old man who is the guide to every "walk" in the vicinity, and who can tell every house, or very round, that is "good for a cold 'tater." In many cases there is over the kitchen mantle-piece a map of the district, dotted here and there with memorandums of failure or success.

Patterers are fond of carving their names and avocations about the houses they visit. The old jail at Dartford has been some years a "padding-ken." In one of the rooms appears the following autographs:

"Jemmy, the Rake, bound to Bristol; bad beds, but no bugs. Thank God for all things."
"Razor George and his moll slept here the

day afore Christmas; just out of 'stir' (jail), for 'muzzling a peeler.'"

"Scotch Mary, with 'driz' (lace), bound to Dover and back, please God."

Sometimes these inscriptions are coarse and obscene; sometimes very well written and orderly. Nor do they want illustrations.

At the old factory, Lincoln, is a portrait of the town beadle, formerly a soldier; it is drawn with different-coloured chalks, and ends with the following couplet:

"You are a B for false swearing,
In hell they'll roast you like a herring."

Concubinage is very common among patterers, especially on their travels; they have their regular rounds, and call the peregrination "going on circuit." For the most part they are early risers; this gives them a facility for meeting poor girls who have had a night's shelter in the union workhouses. They offer such girls some refreshment,—swear they are single men,—and promise comforts certainly superior to the immediate position of their victims. Consent is generally obtained; perhaps a girl of 14 or 15, previously virtuous, is induced to believe in a promise of constant protection, but finds herself, the next morning, ruined and deserted; nor is it unlikely that, within a month or two, she will see her seducer in the company of a dozen incidental wives. A gray-headed miscreant called "Cutler Tom" boasts of 500 such exploits; and there is too great reason to believe that the picture of his own drawing is not greatly overcharged.

Some of the patterers are married men, but of this class very few are faithful to the solemn obligation. I have heard of a renowned patterer of this class who was married to four women, and had lived in criminal intercourse with his own sister, and his own daughter by one of the wives. This sad rule has, however, I am happy to state, some splendid exceptions. There is a man called "Andy"—well known as the companion of "Hopping Ned;" this "Andy" has a wife of great personal attractions, a splendid figure, and teeth without a parallel. She is a strictly-virtuous woman, a most devoted wife, and tender mother; very charitable to any one in want of a meal, and very constant (she is a Catholic) in her religious duties. Another man of the same school, whose name has escaped me, is, with his wife, an exception to the stigma on almost the whole class; the couple in question have no children. The wife, whose name is Maria, has been in every hospital for some complaint in her knees, probably white swelling: her beauty is the theme of applause, and whenever she opens her mouth silence pervades the "paddin' ken." Her common conversation is music and mathematics combined, her reading has been masculine and extensive, and the whisper of calumny has never yet attacked her own demeanour or her husband's.

Of patterers who have children, many are very exemplary; sending them to Day and Sunday-schools, causing them to say grace before and after meals, to attend public worship, and always to speak the truth: these, instances, however, stand in fearful contrast with the conduct of other parents.

"I have seen," proceeds my reverend informant, "fathers and mothers place their boys and girls in positions of incipient enormity, and command them to use language and gestures to each other, which would make an harlot blush, and almost a heathen tremble. I have hitherto viewed the patterer as a salesman,—having something in his hand, on whose merits, real or pretended, he talks people out of their money. By slow degrees prosperity rises, but rapid is the advance of evil. The patterer sometimes gets 'out of stock,' and is obliged, at no great sacrifice of conscience, to 'patter' in another strain. In every large town sham official documents, with crests, seals, and signatures, can be got for half-a-crown. Armed with these, the patterer becomes a 'lurker,'—that is, an impostor; his papers certify any and every 'ill that flesh is heir to.' Shipwreck is called a 'shake lurk;' loss by fire is a 'glim.' Sometimes the petitioner has had a horse, which has dropped dead with the mad staggers; or has a wife ill or dying, and six or seven children at once sickening of the small-pox. Children are borrowed to support the appearance; the case is certified by the minister and churchwardens of a parish which exists only in imagination; and as many people dislike the trouble of investigation, the patterer gets enough to raise a stock in trade, and divides the spoil between the swag-shop and the gin-palace. Sometimes they are detected, and get a 'drag' (three months in prison). They have many narrow escapes: one occurs to me, of a somewhat ludicrous character. A patterer and lurker (now dead) known by the name of 'Captain Moody,' unable to get a 'fakement' written or printed, was standing almost naked in the streets of a neighbouring town. A gentleman stood still and heard his piteous tale, but having been 'done' more than once, he resolved to examine the affair, and begged the petitioner to conduct him to his wife and children, who were in a garret on a bed of languishing, with neither clothes, food, nor fire, but, it appeared, with faith enough to expect a supply from 'Him who feedeth the ravens,' and in whose sacred name even a cold 'tater was implored. The patterer, or half-patterer and half-beggar, took the gentleman (who promised a sovereign if every thing was square) through innumerable and intricate windings, till he came to an outhouse or sort of stable. He saw the key outside the door, and begged the gentleman to enter and wait till he borrowed a light of a neighbour, to show him up-stairs. The illumination never arrived, and the poor charitable man found that the miscreant had locked him into the stable. The patterer went to the padding-ken,—told the story with great glee, and left that locality within an hour of the occurrence."

[Concerning the mendicancy and vagrancy of

patterers, I shall have more to say when I speak of vagrancy in general, and when I describe the general state and characteristics of the low lodging-houses in London, and those in the country, which are in intimate connection with the metropolitan abodes of the vagrant. My present theme is the London patterer, who is also a street-seller.]

OF THE PUBLISHERS AND AUTHORS OF STREET-LITERATURE.

THE best known, and the most successful printer and publisher of all who have directed their industry to supply the "paper" in demand for street sale, and in every department of street literature, was the late "Jemmy Catnach," who is said to have amassed upwards of 10,000*l.* in the business. He is reported to have made the greater part of this sum during the trial of Queen Caroline, by the sale of whole-sheet "papers," descriptive of the trial, and embellished with "splendid illustrations." The next to Catnach stood the late "Tommy Pitt," of the noted toy and marble-warehouse. These two parties were the Colburn and Bentley of the "paper" trade. Catnach retired from business some years ago, and resided in a country-house at Barnet, but he did not long survive his retirement. "He was an out and out sort," said one old paper-worker to me, "and if he knew you— and he could judge according to the school you belonged to, if he hadn't known you long—he was friendly for a bob or two, and sometimes for a glass. He knew the men that was stickers though, and there was no glass for them. Why, some of his customers, sir, would have stuck to him long enough, if there'd been a chance of another glass—supposing they'd managed to get *one*—and then would have asked him for a coach home! When I called on him, he used to say, in his north country way—he wasn't Scotch, but somewhere north of England—and he was pleasant with it, 'Well, d— you, how are you?' He got the cream of the pail, sir."

The present street literature printers and publishers are, Mrs. Ryle (Catnach's niece and successor), Mr. Birt, and Mr. Paul (formerly with Catnach), all of the Seven Dials; Mr. Powell (formerly of Lloyd's), Brick-lane, Whitechapel; and Mr. Good, Aylesbury-street, Clerkenwell. Mr. Phairs, of Westminster; Mr. Taylor, of the Waterloo-road; and Mr. Sharp, of Kent-street, Borough, have discontinued street printing. One man greatly regretted Mr. Taylor's discontinuing the business; "he was so handy for the New-cut, when it *was* the New-cut." Some classes of patterers, I may here observe, work in "schools" or "mobs" of two, three, or four, as I shall afterwards show.

The authors and poets who give its peculiar literature, alike in prose or rhyme, to the streets, are now six in number. They are all in some capacity or other connected with street-patter or song, and the way in which a narrative or a "copy of werses" is prepared for press is usually

this :—The leading members of the "schools," some of whom refer regularly to the evening papers, when they hear of any out-of-the-way occurrence, resort to the printer and desire its publication in a style proper for the streets. This is usually done very speedily, the school (or the majority of them) and the printer agreeing upon the author. Sometimes an author will voluntarily prepare a piece of street literature and submit it to a publisher, who, as in the case of other publishers, accepts or declines, as he believes the production will or will not prove remunerative. Sometimes the school carry the manuscript with them to the printer, and undertake to buy a certain quantity, to insure publication. The payment to the author is the same in all cases—a shilling.

Concerning the history and character of our street and public-house literature, I shall treat hereafter, when I can comprise the whole, and after the descriptions of the several classes engaged in the trade will have paved the way for the reader's better appreciation of the curious and important theme. I say, *important ;* because the street-ballad and the street-narrative, like all popular things, have their influence on masses of the people. Specimens will be found adduced, as I describe the several classes, or in the statements of the patterers.

It must be borne in mind that the street author is closely restricted in the quality of his effusion. It must be such as the patterers approve, as the chaunters can chaunt, the ballad-singers sing, and—above all—such as street-buyers will buy. One chaunter, who was a great admirer of the "Song of the Shirt," told me that if Hood himself had written the "Pitiful Case of Georgy Sloan and his Wife," it would not have sold so well as a ballad he handed to me, from which I extract a verse :

> " Jane Willbred we did starve and beat her very hard
> 　　I confess we used her very cruel,
> But now in a jail two long years we must bewail,
> 　　We don't fancy mustard in the gruel."

What I have said of the *necessity* which controls street authorship, may also be said of the art which is sometimes called in to illustrate it.

The paper now published for the streets is classed as quarter sheets, which cost (wholesale) 1*s.* a gross ; half sheets, which cost 2*s.* ; and whole or broad sheets (such as for executions), which cost 3*s.* 6*d.* a gross the first day, and 3*s.* the next day or two, and afterwards, but only if a ream be taken, 5*s.* 6*d.* ; a ream contains forty dozen. When "illustrated," the charge is from 3*d.* to 1*s.* per ream extra. The books, for such cases as the Sloanes, or the murder of Jael Denny, are given in books—which are best adapted for the suburban and country trade, when London is "worked" sufficiently—are the "whole sheet" printed so as to fold into eight pages, each side of the paper being then, of course, printed upon. A book is charged from 6*d.* to 1*s.* extra (to a whole sheet) per gross, and afterwards the same extra per ream.

OF LONG SONG-SELLERS.

I have this week given a daguerreotype of a well-known long-song seller, and have preferred to give it as the trade, especially as regards London, has all but disappeared, and it was curious enough. " Long songs" first appeared between nine and ten years ago.

The long-song sellers did not depend upon patter—though some of them pattered a little—to attract customers, but on the veritable cheapness and novel form in which they vended popular songs, printed on paper rather wider than this page, "three songs abreast," and the paper was about a yard long, which constituted the "three" yards of song. Sometimes three slips were pasted together. The vendors paraded the streets with their "three yards of new and popular songs" for a penny. The songs are, or were, generally fixed to the top of a long pole, and the vendor "cried" the different titles as he went along. This branch of "the profession" is confined solely to the summer; the hands in winter usually taking to the sale of song-books, it being impossible to exhibit "the three yards" in wet or foggy weather. The paper songs, as they fluttered from a pole, looked at a little distance like huge much-soiled white ribbons, used as streamers to celebrate some auspicious news. The cry of one man, in a sort of recitative, or, as I heard it called by street-patterers, "singsong," was, "Three yards a penny! Three yards a penny! Beautiful songs! Newest songs! Popular Songs! Three yards a penny! Song, song, songs!" Others, however, were generally content to announce merely "Three yards a penny!" One cried "Two under fifty a fardy!" As if two hundred and fifty songs were to be sold for a farthing. The whole number of songs was about 45. They were afterwards sold at a halfpenny, but were shorter and fewer. It is probable that at the best had the songs been subjected to the admeasurement of a jury, the result might have been as little satisfactory as to some tradesmen who, however, after having been detected in attempts to cheat the poor in weights and scales, and to cheat them hourly, are still "good men and true" enough to be jurymen and parliamentary electors. The songs, I am informed, were often about 2½ yards, (not as to paper but as to admeasurement of type); 3 yards, occasionally, at first, and not often less than 2 yards.

The crying of the titles was not done with any other design than that of expressing the great number of songs purchasable for "the small charge of one penny." Some of the patterers I conversed with would have made it sufficiently droll. One man told me that he had cried the following songs in his three yards, and he believed in something like the following order, but he had cried-penny song books, among other things, lately, and might confound his more ancient and recent cries:

"I sometimes began," he said, "with sing-ing, or trying to sing, for I'm no vocalist, the first few words of any song, and them quite loud. I'd begin

' The Pope he leads a happy life,
        He knows no care'——

' Buffalo gals, come out to-night;' 'Death of Nelson;' The gay cavalier;' 'Jim along Josey;' 'There's a good time coming;' 'Drink to me only;' 'Kate Kearney;' ' Chuckaroo - choo, choo - choo - choot - lah;' ' Chockala - roony - ninkaping - nang;' ' Paga - daway-dusty-kanty-key;' 'Hottypie-gunnypo-china-coo' (that's a Chinese song, sir); 'I dreamed that I dwelt in marble halls;' 'The standard bearer:' 'Just like love;' 'Whistle o'er the lave o't;' 'Widow Mackree;' 'I've been roaming;' 'Oh! that kiss;' 'The old English gentleman,' &c., &c. &c. I dares say they was all in the three yards, or was once, and if they wasn't there was others as good."

The chief purchasers of the "long songs" were boys and girls, but mostly boys, who expended 1d. or ½d. for the curiosity and novelty of the thing, as the songs were not in the most readable form. A few working people bought them for their children, and some women of the town, who often buy anything fantastic, were also customers.

When "the three yards was at their best," the number selling them was about 170; the wholesale charge is from 3d. to 5d. a dozen, according to size. The profit of the vendors in the first instance was about 8d. a dozen. When the trade had all the attractions of novelty, some men sold ten dozen on fine days, and for three or four of the summer months; so clearing between 6s. and 7s. a day. This, however, was not an average, but an average might be at first 21s. a week profit. I am assured that if twenty persons were selling long songs in the street last summer it was "the outside," as long songs are now "for fairs and races and country work." Calculating that each cleared 9s. in a week, and to clear that took 15s., the profit being smaller than it used to be, as many must be sold at ½d. each—we find 120l. expended in long songs in the streets. The character of the vendor is that of a patterer of inferior genius.

The stock-money required is 1s. to 2s.; which with 2d. for a pole, and ½d. for paste, is all the capital needed. Very few were sold in the public-houses, as the vendors scrupled to expose them there, "for drunken fellows would snatch them, and make belts of them for a lark."

OF RUNNING PATTERERS.

Few of the residents in London—but chiefly those in the quieter streets — have not been aroused, and most frequently in the evening, by a hurly-burly on each side of the street. An attentive listening will not lead any one to an accurate knowledge of what the clamour is about. It is from a "mob" or "school" of the running patterers (for both those words are

used), and consists of two, three, or four men.
All these men state that the greater the noise
they make, the better is the chance of sale, and
better still when the noise is on each side of a
street, for it appears as if the vendors were
proclaiming such interesting or important intelligence, that they were vieing with one another
who should supply the demand which must
ensue. It is not possible to ascertain with any
certitude *what* the patterers are so anxious to
sell, for only a few leading words are audible.
One of the cleverest of running patterers repeated to me, in a subdued tone, his announcements of murders. The words " Murder,"
" Horrible," " Barbarous," " Love," " Mysterious," " Former Crimes," and the like,
could only be caught by the ear, but there
was no announcement of anything like " particulars." If, however, the " paper " relate
to any well-known criminal, such as Rush,
the name is given distinctly enough, and so
is any new or pretended fact. The running
patterers describe, or profess to describe, the
contents of their papers as they go rapidly
along, and they seldom or ever stand still.
They usually deal in murders, seductions,
crim.-cons., explosions, alarming accidents,
" assassinations," deaths of public characters,
duels, and love-letters. But popular, or notorious, murders are the " great goes." The
running patterer cares less than other street-
sellers for bad weather, for if he " work " on
a wet and gloomy evening, and if the work be
" a cock," which is a fictitious statement or
even a pretended fictitious statement, there is
the less chance of any one detecting the *ruse.*
But of late years no new " cocks " have
been printed, excepting for temporary purposes, such as I have specified as under its
appropriate head in my account of " Death
and Fire-Hunters." Among the old stereotyped " cocks " are love-letters. One is well
known as " The Husband caught in a Trap,"
and being in an epistolary form subserves any
purpose : whether it be the patterer's aim to
sell the " Love Letters " of any well-known
person, such as Lola Montes, or to fit them
for a local (pretended) scandal, as the " Letters from a Lady in this neighbourhood to a
Gentleman not 100 miles off."
Of running patterers there are now in London from 80 to 100. They reside—some in their
own rooms, but the majority in lodging-houses
—in or near Westminster, St. Giles's, Whitechapel, Stratford, Deptford, Wandsworth, and
the Seven Dials. The " Dials," however, is
their chief locality, being the residence of the
longest-established printers, and is the " head
meet" of the fraternity.
It is not easy to specify with exactitude the
number of running or flying patterers at any
one time in London. Some of these men become,
occasionally, standing patterers, chaunters, or
ballad-singers—classes I shall subsequently describe—and all of them resort at intervals to
country rounds. I heard, also, many complaints

of boys having of late "taken to the running
patter" when anything attractive was before the
public, and of ignorant fellows—that wouldn't
have thought of it at one time—" trying their
hands at it." Waiving these exceptional aug-
mentations of the number, I will take the body
of running patterers, generally employed in their
peculiar craft in London, at 90. To ascertain
their earnings presents about the same difficulties as to ascertain their number ; for as all they
earn is spent—no patterer ever saving money—
they themselves are hardly able to tell their
incomes. If any new and exciting fact be before
the public, these men may each clear 20s. a
week ; when there is no suck fact, they may not
earn 5s. The profit is contingent, moreover, upon
their being able to obtain 1d., or only ½d., for
their paper. Some represented their average
weekly earnings at 12s. 6d. the year through ;
some at 10s. 6d. ; and others at less than half of
12s. 6d. Reckoning, however, that only 9s.
weekly is an average profit per individual, and
that 14s. be taken to realise that profit, we find
3,276l. expended yearly on running patterers in
London ; but in that sum the takings of the
chaunters must be included, as they are members of the same fraternity, and work with the
patterers.
The capital required to commence as a running
patterer is but the price of a few papers—from
2d. to 1s. The men have no distinctive dress :
" our togs," said one of them, " is in the latest
fashion of Petticoat-lane ;" unless on the very
rare occasions, when some character has to be
personated, and then coloured papers and glazed
calicoes are made available. But this is only a
venture of the old hands.

EXPERIENCE OF A RUNNING PATTERER.

FROM a running patterer, who has been
familiar with the trade for many years, I
received, upwards of a twelvemonth ago, the
following statement. He is well known for his
humour, and is a leading man in his fraternity.
After some conversation about "cocks," the
most popular of which, my informant said, was
the murder at Chigwell-row, he continued :
" That's a trump, to the present day. Why,
I'd go out now, sir, with a dozen of Chigwell-
rows, and earn my supper in half an hour off of
'em. The murder of Sarah Holmes at Lincoln
is good, too—that there has been worked for the
last five year successively every winter. Poor
Sarah Holmes ! Bless her ! she has saved me
from walking the streets all night many a time.
Some of the best of these have been in work
twenty years—the Scarborough murder has full
twenty years. It's called ' THE SCARBOROUGH
TRAGEDY.' I've worked it myself. It's about
a noble and rich young naval officer seducing a
poor clergyman's daughter. She is confined in
a ditch, and destroys the child. She is taken up
for it, tried, and executed. This has had a great
run. It sells all round the country places, and
would sell now if they had it out. Mostly all
our customers is females. They are the chief

dependence we have. The Scarborough Tragedy is very attractive. It draws tears to the women's eyes to think that a poor clergyman's daughter, who is remarkably beautiful, should murder her own child; it's very touching to every feeling heart. There's a copy of verses with it, too. Then there's the Liverpool Tragedy — that's very attractive. It's a mother murdering her own son, through gold. He had come from the East Indies, and married a rich planter's daughter. He came back to England to see his parents after an absence of thirty years. They kept a lodging-house in Liverpool for sailors; the son went there to lodge, and meant to tell his parents who he was in the morning. His mother saw the gold he had got in his boxes, and cut his throat—severed his head from his body; the old man, upwards of seventy years of age, holding the candle. They had put a washing-tub under the bed to catch his blood. The morning after the murder, the old man's daughter calls and inquires for a young man. The old man denies that they have had any such person in the house. She says he had a mole on his arm, in the shape of a strawberry. The old couple go up-stairs to examine the corpse, and find they have murdered their own son, and then they both put an end to their existence. This is a deeper tragedy than the Scarborough Murder. That suits young people better; they like to hear about the young woman being seduced by the naval officer; but the mothers take more to the Liverpool Tragedy— it suits them better. Some of the 'cocks' were in existence long before ever I was born or thought of. The 'Great and important battle between the two ye ladies of fortune,' is what we calls 'a ripper.' I should like to have that there put down correct," he added, "'cause I've taken a tidy lot of money out of it."

My informant, who had been upwards of 20 years in the running patter line, told me that he commenced his career with the "Last Dying Speech and Full Confession of William Corder." He was sixteen years of age, and had run away from his parents. "I worked that there," he said, "down in the very town (at Bury) where he was executed. I got a whole hatful of halfpence at that. Why, I wouldn't even give 'em seven for sixpence—no, that I wouldn't. A gentleman's servant come out and wanted half a dozen for his master and one for himself in, and I wouldn't let him have no such thing. We often sells more than that at once. Why, I sold six at one go to the railway clerks at Norwich about the Manning affair, only a fortnight back. But Steinburgh's little job—you know he murdered his wife and family, and committed suicide after —that sold as well as any 'die.' Pegsworth was an out-and-out lot. I did tremendous with him, because it happened in London, down Ratcliff-highway — that's a splendid quarter for working—there's plenty of feelings—but, bless you, some places you go to you can't move no how, they've hearts like paving-stones. They

wouldn't have 'the papers' if you'd give them to 'em — especially when they knows you. Greenacre didn't sell so well as might have been expected, for such a diabolical out-and-out crime as he committed; but you see he came close after Pegsworth, and that took the beauty off him. Two murderers together is never no good to nobody. Why there was Wilson Gleeson, as great a villain as ever lived—went and murdered a whole family at noon - day—but Rush coopered him—and likewise that girl at Bristol—made it no draw to any one. Daniel Good, though, was a first-rater; and would have been much better if it hadn't been for that there Madam Toosow. You see, she went down to Roehampton, and guv 2l. for the werry clogs as he used to wash his master's carriage in; so, in course, when the harristocracy could go and see the real things—the werry identical clogs—in the Chamber of 'Orrors, why the people wouldn't look at our authentic portraits of the fiend in human form. Hocker wasn't any particular great shakes. There was a deal expected from him, but he didn't turn out well. Courvoisier was much better; he sold werry well, but nothing to Blakesley. Why I worked him for six weeks. The wife of the murdered man kept the King's Head that he was landlord of open on the morning of the execution, and the place was like a fair. I even went and sold papers outside the door myself. I thought if she war'n't ashamed, why should I be? After that we had a fine 'fake'—that was the fire of the Tower of London—it sold rattling. Why we had about forty apprehended for that—first we said two soldiers was taken up that couldn't obtain their discharge, and then we declared it was a well-known sporting nobleman who did it for a spree. The boy Jones in the Palace wasn't much of an affair for the running patterers; the ballad singers—or street screamers, as we calls 'em—had the pull out of that. The patter wouldn't take; they had read it all in the newspapers before. Oxford, and Francis, and Bean were a little better, but nothing to crack about. The people doesn't care about such things as them. There's nothing beats a stunning good murder, after all. Why there was Rush—I lived on him for a month or more. When I commenced with Rush, I was 14s. in debt for rent, and in less than fourteen days I astonished the wise men in the east by paying my landlord all I owed him. Since Dan'el Good there had been little or nothing doing in the murder line —no one could cap him—till Rush turned up a regular trump for us. Why I went down to Norwich expressly to work the execution. I worked my way down there with '*a sorrowful lamentation*' of his own composing, which I'd got written by the blind man expressly for the occasion. On the morning of the execution we beat all the regular newspapers out of the field; for we had the full, true, and particular account down, you see, by our own express, and that can beat anything that ever they can publish; for we gets it printed several days afore it comes off, and goes and stands with it right under the drop; and many's the penny I've turned away when I've been asked for an account of the whole business *before* it happened. So you see, for herly and correct hinformation, we can beat the *Sun*—aye, or the moon either, for the matter of that. Irish Jem, the Ambassador, never goes to bed but he blesses Rush the farmer; and many's the time he's told me we should never have such another windfall as that. But I told him not to despair; there's a good time coming, boys, says I, and, sure enough, up comes the Bermondsey tragedy. We might have done very well, indeed, out of the Mannings, but there was too many examinations for it to be any great account to us. I've been away with the Mannings in the country ever since. I've been through Hertfordshire, Cambridgeshire, and Suffolk, along with George Frederick Manning and his wife—travelled from 800 to 1,000 miles with 'em, but I could have done much better if I had stopped in London. Every day I was anxiously looking for a confession from Mrs. Manning. All I wanted was for her to clear her conscience afore she left this here whale of tears (that's what I always calls it in the patter), and when I read in the papers (mind they was none of my own) that her last words on the brink of heternity was, ' I've nothing to say to you, Mr. Rowe, but to thank you for your kindness,' I guv her up entirely—had completely done with her. In course the public looks to us for the last words of all monsters in human form, and as for Mrs. Manning's, they were not worth the printing."

Of the Recent Experience of a Running Patterer.

From the same man I had the following account of his vocation up to the present time:

"Well, sir," he said, "I think, take them altogether, things hasn't been so good this last year as the year before. But the Pope, God bless him! he's been the best friend I've had since Rush, but Rush licked his Holiness. You see, the Pope and Cardinal Wiseman is a one-sided affair; of course the Catholics won't buy anything against the Pope, but *all* religions could go for Rush. Our mob once thought of starting a cardinal's dress, and I thought of wearing a red hat myself. I did wear a shovel hat when the Bishop of London was our racket; but I thought the hat began to feel too hot, so I shovelled it off. There was plenty of paper that would have suited to work with a cardinal's hat. There was one,—'Cardinal Wiseman's Lament,'—and it was giving his own words like, and a red hat would have capped it. It used to make the people roar when it came to snivelling, and grumbling at little Jack Russell —by Wiseman, in course; and when it comes to this part—which alludes to that 'ere thundering letter to the Bishop of Durham—the people was stunned:

' He called me a buffalo, bull, and a monkey,
And then with a soldier called Old Arthur conkey
Declared they would buy me a ninepenny donkey,
And send me to Rome to the Pope.'

"They shod me, sir. *Who's* they? Why, the Pope and Cardinal Wiseman. I call my clothes after them I earn money by to buy them with. My shoes I call Pope Pius; my trowsers and braces, Calcraft; my waistcoat and shirt, Jael Denny; and my coat, Love Letters. A man must show a sense of gratitude in the best way he can. But I didn't start the cardinal's hat; I thought it might prove disagreeable to Sir Robert Peel's dress lodgers." [What my informant said further of the Pope, I give under the head of the Chaunter.] "There was very little doing," he continued, "for some time after I gave you an account before; hardly a slum worth a crust and a pipe of tobacco to us. A slum's a paper fake,—make a foot-note of that, sir. I think Adelaide was the first thing I worked after I told you of my tomfooleries. Yes it was,—her helegy. She weren't of no account whatsomever, and Cambridge was no better nor Adelaide. But there was poor Sir Robert Peel,— he *was* some good; indeed, I think he was as good as 5s. a day to me for the four or five days when he was freshest. Browns were thrown out of the windows to us, and one copper cartridge was sent flying at us with 13½d. in it, all copper, as if it had been collected. I worked Sir Robert at the West End, and in the quiet streets and squares. Certainly we had a most beautiful helegy. Well, poor gentleman, what we earned on him was some set-off to us for his starting his new regiment of the Blues—the Cook's Own. Not that they've troubled us much. I was once before Alderman Kelly, when he was Lord Mayor, charged with obstructing, or some humbug of that sort. ' What are you, my man?' says he quietly, and like a gentleman. ' In the same line as yourself, my lord,' says I. ' How's that?' says he. ' I'm a paper-worker for my living, my lord,' says I. I was soon discharged; and there was such fun and laughing, that if I'd had a few slums in my pocket, I believe I could have sold them all in the justice-room.

"Haynau was a stunner, and the drayman came their caper just in the critical time for us, as things was growing very taper. But I did best with him in chaunting; and so, as you want to hear about chaunting, I'll tell you after. We're forced to change our patter—first running, then chaunting, and then standing—oftener than we used to.

"Then Calcraft was pretty tidy browns. He was up for starving his mother,—and what better can you expect of a hangman? Me and my mate worked him down at Hatfield, in Essex, where his mother lives. It's his native, I believe. We sold her one. She's a limping old body. I saw the people look at her, and they told me arterards who she was. ' How much?' says she. ' A penny, marm,' say I. ' Sarve him right,' says she. We worked it, too, in the street in Hoxton where he lives, and he sent out for two, which shows he's a sensible sort of character in some points, after all. Then we had a ' Woice from the Gaol ! or the Horrors

Horrible and Bar-bari-ous Murder of Poor
JAEL DENNY,
THE ILL-FATED VICTIM OF THOMAS DRORY.

of the Condemned Cell! Being the Life of William Calcraft, the present Hangman.' It's written in the high style, and parts of it will have astonished the hangman's nerves before this. Here's a bit of the patter, now:

" Let us look at William Calcraft," says the eminent author, " in his earliest days. He was born about the year 1801, of humble but industrious parents, at a little village in Essex. His infant ears often listened to the children belonging to the Sunday schools of his native place, singing the well-known words of Watt's beautiful hymn,

' When e'er I take my walks abroad,
How many poor I see, &c.'

But alas for the poor farmer's boy, he never had the opportunity of going to that school to be taught how to shun ' the broad way leading to destruction.' To seek a chance fortune he travelled up to London where his ignorance and forlorn condition shortly enabled that fell demon which ever haunts the footsteps of the wretched, to mark him for her own."

" Isn't that stunning, sir? Here it is in print for you. ' Mark him for her own!' Then, poor dear, he's so sorry to hang anybody. Here's another bit:

' But in vain he repents, he has no real friend in the world but his wife, to whom he can communicate his private thoughts, and in return receive consolation, can any lot be harder than this? Hence his nervous system is fast breaking down, every day rendering him less able to endure the excruciating and agonizing torments he is hourly suffering, he is haunted by remorse heaped upon remorse, every fresh victim he is required to strangle being so much additional fuel thrown upon that mental flame which is scorching him.'

" You may believe me, sir, and I can prove the fact—the author of that beautiful writing ain't in parliament! Think of the mental flame, sir! O, dear.'

" Sirrell was no good either. Not salt to a herring. Though we worked him in his own neighbourhood, and pattered about gold and silver all in a row. ' Ah!' says one old woman, ' he was a 'spectable man.' ' Werry, marm,' says I.

" Hollest weren't no good either, 'cause the wictim was a parson. If it had happened a little later, we'd have had it to rights; the newspapers didn't make much of it. We'd have shown it was the ' Commencement of a Most Horrid and Barbarious Plot got up by the Pope and Cardinal Wiseman *for-r* the Mas-ser-cree-ing of all good Protestant Ministers.' That would have been the dodge, sir! A beautiful idear, now, isn't it? But the murder came off badly, and you can't expect fellows like them murderers to have any regard for the interest of art and literature. Then there's so long to wait between the murder and the trial, that unless the fiend in human form keeps writing beautiful love-letters, the excitement can't be kept up. *We* can write the love-letters for the fiend in human? That's quite true, and we once had a great pull that way over the newspapers. But Lord love you, there's plenty of 'em gets more and more into our line. They treads in our footsteps, sir; they follows our bright example. O! isn't there a nice rubbing and polishing up. This

here copy won't do. This must be left out, and that put in; 'cause it suits the walk of the paper. Why, you must know, sir. *I* know. Don't tell me. You can't have been on the *Morning Chronicle* for nothing.

" Then there was the ' Horrid and Inhuman Murder, Committed by T. Drory, on the Body of Jael Denny, at Donninghurst, a Village in Essex.' We worked it in every way. Drory had every chance given to him. We had half-sheets, and copies of werses, and books. A very tidy book it was, setting off with showing how ' The secluded village of Donninghurst has been the scene of a most determined and diabolical murder, the discovery of which early on Sunday, the 12th, in the morning has thrown the whole of this part of the country into a painful state of excitement.' Well, sir, well—very well; that bit was taken from a newspaper. Oh, we're not above acknowledging when we condescends to borrow from any of 'em. If you remember, when I saw you about the time, I told you I thought Jael Denny would turn out as good as Maria Martin. And without any joke or nonsense, sir, it really is a most shocking thing. But she didn't. The weather coopered her, poor lass! There was money in sight, and we couldn't touch it; it seemed washed away from us, for you may remember how wet it was. I made a little by her, though. For all that, I haven't done with Master Drory yet. If God spares my life, he shall make it up to me. Why, now, sir, is it reasonable, that a poor man like me should take so much pains to make Drory's name known all over the country, and walk miles and miles in the rain to do it, and get only a few bob for my labour? It can't be thought on. When the Wile and Inhuman Seducer takes his trial, he must pay up my just claims. I'm not going to take all that trouble on his account, and let him off so easy."

My informant then gave me an account of his sale of papers relating to the Pope and Cardinal Wiseman, but as he was then a chaunter, rather than a patterer (the distinction is shown under another head), I give his characteristic account, as the statement of a chaunter. He proceeded after having finished his recital of the street business relating to the Pope, &c.:

" My last paying caper was the Sloanes. They beat Haynau. I declare to you, sir, the knowingest among us couldn't have invented a cock to equal the conduct of them Sloanes. Why, it's disgusting to come near the plain truth about them. I think, take it altogether, Sloane was as good as the Pope, but he had a stopper like Pius the Ninth, for that was a one-sided affair, and the Catholics wouldn't buy; and Sloane was too disgusting for the gentry, or better sort, to buy him. But I've been in little streets where some of the windows was without sashes, and some that had sashes had stockings thrust between the frames, and I've taken half a bob in ha'pennies. Oh! you should have heard what poor women said about him, for it was women that bought him most. They was more savage against him than against her. Why, they had fifty deaths for him. Rolling in a barrel, with lots of sharp nails inside, down Primrose-hill, and turned out to the women on Kennington-common, and boiled alive in oil or stuff that can't be mentioned, or hung over a slow fire. ' O, the poor dear girl,' says they, ' what she's suffered.' We had accounts of Mistress Sloane's apprehension before the papers. We had it at Jersey, and they had it at Boulogne, but we were first. Then we discovered, because we *must* be in advance of the papers, that Miss Devaux was Sloane's daughter by a former wife, and Jane Wilbred was Mrs. Sloane's daughter by a former husband, and was entitled to 1,000*l.* by rights. Haynau was a fool to Sloane. "I don't know of anything fresh that's in hand, sir. One of our authors is coming out with something spicy, against Lord John, for doing nothing about Wiseman ; 'cause he says as no one thing that he's written for Lord John ever sold well, something against him may."

Of the Chaunters.

"As the minstrel's art," writes Mr. Strutt, in his " Sports and Pastimes," " consisted of several branches, the professors were distinguished by different denominations, as ' rimours, *chanterres*, conteours, jougleours or jongleurs, jestours, lecours, and troubadours or trouvers :' in modern language, rhymers, singers, story-tellers, jugglers, relaters of heroic actions, buffoons, and poets ; but all of them were included under the general name of minstrel. An eminent French antiquary says of the minstrels, that some of them themselves composed the subjects they sang or related, as the trouvers and the conteurs ; and some of them used the compositions of others, as the jougleours and the chanteurs. He further remarks, that the trouvers may be said to have embellished their productions with rhyme, while the conteurs related their histories in prose ; the jougleours, who in the middle ages were famous for playing upon the vielle" [a kind of hurdy-gurdy], " accompanied the songs of the trouvers. These jougleours were also assisted by the chanteurs ; and this union of talents rendered the compositions more harmonious and more pleasing to the auditory, and increased their rewards, so that they readily joined each other, and travelled together in large parties. It is, however, very certain that the poet, the songster, and the musician were frequently united in the same person." My account of the authors, &c., of street literature shows that the analogy still holds.

The French antiquary quoted was Fauchet, in his " Origine de la Langue et Poësie Francoise" (1581) ; and though he wrote concerning his own country, his descriptions apply equally to the English minstrels, who were principally Normans, for many reigns after the Conquest, and were of the same race, and habits, and manners as on the French side of the Channel.

Of the minstrels, I shall have more to say when I treat of the ballad-singers and the bands of street and public-house musicians of to-day, between whom and the minstrels of old there is, in many respects, a somewhat close resemblance. Minstrelsy fell gradually from its high estate, and fell so low that, in the 39th year of Elizabeth's reign—a period when the noblest poetry of any language was beginning to command the ear of the educated in England—the minstrels were classed in a penal statute with rogues, vagabonds, and sturdy beggars! Putenham, in his " Arte of English Poesie" (1589), speaks of " taverne minstrels that give a fit of mirth for a groat." One of the statutes enacted in Cromwell's Protectorate was directed against all persons " commonly called fidlers or minstrells."

In the old times, then, the jougeleurs and jestours were assisted by the chanteurs. In the present day the running patterer—who, as I have shown, is the sufficiently legitimate descendant of the jestour, and in some respects descendant of the mountebank—is accompanied generally by a chaunter, so presenting a further point of resemblance between ancient and modern streetfolk. The chaunter now not only sings, but fiddles, for within these few years the running patterers, to render their performances more attractive, are sometimes accompanied by musicians. The running performer then, instead of hurrying along with the members of his mob, making sufficient noise to arouse a whole street, takes his stand with the chaunter in any promising place, and as the songs which are the most popular are—as is the case at many of the concert-rooms—sometimes " spoken" as well as sung, the performers are in their proper capacity, for the patterer not only " speaks," but speaks more than is set down for him, while the chaunter fiddles and sings. Sometimes the one patters while the other sings, and their themes are the same.

I am told, however, that there are only fifty running patterers who are regularly their own chaunters, fiddling to their songs, while the mob work as usual, or one man sings, or speaks and sings, with the chaunter. Two of these men are known as Brummagem Jack, and the Country Paganini. From twenty to thirty patterers, however, are chaunters also, when they think the occasion requires it.

Further to elucidate chaunting, and to show the quality of the canticles, and the way of proceeding, I cite a statement of his experience as a chaunter, from the running patterer, whose details of his more especial business I have already given, but who also occasionally chaunts :—

Of the Experience of a Chaunter.

"The Pope, sir," he began, " was one-sided to chaunt as to patter, in course. We had the Greeks (the lately-arrived Irish) down upon us more than once. In Liverpool-street, on the night of the meeting at Guildhall about the Papal Aggression, we had a regular skrimmage. One gentleman said : ' Really, you shouldn't sing such improper songs, my men.' Then up comes another, and he was a little crusted with port wine, and he says : ' What, against that cove the Pope ! Here, give me half a dozen of the papers.' The city was tidy for the patter, sir, or the chaunt ; there was sixpences ; but there was shillings at the West End. And for the first time in their innocent lives, the parsons came out as stunning patrons of the patter. One of 'em as we was at work in the street give a bit of a signal and was attended to without any parade to the next street, and was good for half-a-crown ! Other two stopped, that wery same day, and sent a boy to us with a Joey. Then me and my mate went to the Rev. W.'s, him as came it so strong for the fire-works on the Fifth of November. And we pattered and we pattered, and we chaunted and we chaunted, but no go for a goodish bit. His servant said he weren't at home. In course *that* wouldn't do for us, so down he came his-self at last, and says, werry soft : ' Come to-morrow morning, my men, and there'll be two gentlemen to hear you.' We stuck to him for something in hand, but he said the business had cost him so much already, he really couldn't. Well, we bounced a bob out of him, and didn't go near him again. After all we did for his party, a shilling was black ingratitude. Of course *we* has no feeling either for it or agin the Pope. *We* goes to it as at an election ; and let me tell you, sir, we got very poorly paid, it couldn't be called paid, for working for Lord John at the City Election ; and I was the original of the live rats, which took well. But there's a good time coming to pay Lord Johnny off.

" Some of the tunes—there's no act of parliament about tunes, you know, sir—was stunners on the fiddle ; as if a thousand bricks was falling out of a cart at once. I think ' The Pope and Cardinal Wiseman,' one of the first of the songs, did as well as any. This werse was greatly admired :—

' Now Lord John Russell did so bright,
    to the Bishop of Durham a letter write
Saying while I've a hand I'll fight,
    The pope and cardinal wiseman,
Lord John's ancestor as I tell,
    Lord William Russell then known well
His true religion would not sell,
    A martyr he in glory fell,
And now Lord John so bold and free,
    Has got a rope as we may see,
To hang up on each side of a tree,
    The pope and cardinal wiseman.'

" This finishing werse, too, was effective, and out came a few browns :—

' Now we don't care a fig for Rome,
    why can't they let the girls alone,
And mind their business at home,
    the pope and cardinal wiseman.
With their monsical red cardinals hat,
    And lots of wafers in a sack,
If they come here with all their clack,
    we'll wound them fil fal la ra whack,
In England they shall not be loose,
    Their hum bugging is all no use,

If they come here we'll cook their goose,
    The pope and Cardinal Wiseman.
    CHORUS
Monks and Nuns and fools afloat,
    We'll have no bulls shoved down our throat,
Cheer up and shout down with the Pope,
    And his bishop cardinal Wiseman.'

" Then there was another, sir. ' The Pope he is coming ; oh, crikey, oh dear ! ' to the tune of the ' Camels are coming.' There was one bit that used to tickle them. I mayn't exactly remember it, for I didn't do anything beyond a spurt in it, and haven't a copy for you, but it tickled 'em with others. This was the bit :—

' I've heard my old grandmother's grandmother say,
They burnt us in Smithfield full ten every day.
O, what shall I do, for I feel very queer,
The Pope he's a-coming, oh ! crikey, oh, dear !'

" Bless you, sir, if I see a smart dressed servant girl looking shyly out of the street-door at us, or through the area railings, and I can get a respectful word in and say, ' My good young lady, do buy of a poor fellow, we haven't said a word to your servants, we hasn't seen any on 'em,' then she's had, sir, for 1*d*. at least, and twice out of thrice ; that ' good young lady ' chloroforms her.

" Then this one, now, is stunning. It's part of what the Queen was a going to sing at the opening of the parliament, but she changed her mind, and more's the pity, for it would have had a grand effect. It's called ' The Queen, the Pope, and the Parliament,' and these is the best of the stanzas ; I calls them werses in common, but stanzas for Wick :

' My lords and my gentlemen all,
    The bishops and great house of commons
On you for protection I call,
    For you know I am only a woman,
I am really quite happy indeed—
    To meet you like birds of a feather,
So I hope you will all struggle with me,
    And pull away boys altogether,
My name is Victoria the Queen.

' Our bishops and deans did relent,
    And say they for ever was undone,
Bishop Philpott a long challenge sent
    To his lordship the bishop of London,
To fight him on Hounslow Heath—
    But the bishop of London was coosey,
He gave him one slap in the mouth,
    And then sent a letter to pusey,
No humbuggery stories for vick—

' I heard my old grandfather say
    His great grandmother easily loved reckon
When they made a fool run away,
    Whose name was king Jemmy the second.
Billy gave him a ticket for soup,
    Though Bill married old Jemmy's daughter
He knocked him from old Palace yard,
    To Ireland, across the Boyne water,
Long life to Victoria the Queen.

' Come here my old friend Joey Hume,
    I know you in silence wont mope now,
Go up and get inside the moon
    And make fast a great torry rope now,
And then give a spring and a jump
    And you to a peerage shall rise then,
For we'll swing up old Pius the Pope
    And his eminence cardinal Wiseman,
Old England and down with the Pope.'

"Then there wasn't no risk with Haynau—I told you of the Pope first, 'cause he was most chaunted—no fear of a *ferricadouzer* for the butcher. How is it spelled, sir? Well, if you can't find it in the dictionary, you must use your own judgment. What does it mean? It means a dewskitch (a good thrashing). I've been threatened with dark nights about the Pope, after the Greeks has said: 'Fat have you to say agin the holy gintleman? To the divil wid all the likes o' ye.' Haynau was a fair stage and no favour. This werse was best liked:—

'The other day as you must know,
In Barclay's brewhouse he did go
And signed his bloody name " Haynau.
The fellow that flogged the women.
Baron Rothchild did him shend,
And in the letter which he penn'd
He shaid the sheneral wash his friend,
And so good a man he could not mend.

CHORUS
Rumpsey bumsey—bang him well—
Make his back and sides to swell
Till he roars aloud with dreadful yell,
The fellow that flogged the women.'

"The women bought very free; poor women, mostly; we only worked him to any extent in the back drags. One old body at Stepney was so pleased that she said, ' O, the bloody-minded willain! Whenever you come this way again, sir, there's always 1d. for you.' She didn't pay in advance though.

"Then it ended, sir, with a beautiful moral as appeals to every female bosom :—

'That man who would a female harm,
Is never fit to live.'

"We always likes something for the ladies, bless 'em. They're our best customers.

"Then there was poor Jael Denny, but she was humped, sir, and I've told you the reason. Her copy of werses began :—

'Since Corder died on Buystree,
No mortal man did read or see,
Of such a dreadful tragedy,
As I will now unfold.
A maid in bloom—to her silent tomb,
Is hurried in the prime of life,
How could a villain cause such strife
She worthy was a famous wife.
The like was seldom told.

CHORUS.
She was young and gay,
Like the flowers of may,
In youth and vigour health and bloom,
She is hurried to the silent tomb.
Through Essex, such a dreadfull gloom,
Jael Denny's murder caused.'

"My last chaunt was Jane Wilbred; and her werses—and they did tidy well—began :—

'A Case like this you seldom read,
Or one so sad and true,
And we sincerely hope the perper-
trators both will rue
To serve a friendless servant girl,
Two years they did engage,
Her name it is Jane Willbred,
And eighteen years of age.'

"What do you think of the Great Exhibition, sir? I shall be there. Me and my mates. We are going to send in a copy of werses in letters of gold for a prize. *We'll* let the foreigners know what the real native melodies of England is, and no mistake."

OF THE DEATH AND FIRE HUNTERS.

I have described the particular business of the running patterer, who is known by another and a very expressive cognomen — as a "Death Hunter." This title refers not only to his vending accounts of all the murders that become topics of public conversation, but to his being a "murderer" on his own account, as in the sale of "cocks" mentioned incidentally in this narrative. If the truth be saleable, a running patterer prefers selling the truth, for then—as one man told me—he can " go the same round comfortably another day." If there be no truths for sale—no stories of criminals' lives and loves to be condensed from the diffusive biographies in the newspapers—no "helegy" for a great man gone—no prophecy and no crim. con.—the death hunter invents, or rather announces, them. He puts some one to death for the occasion, which is called "a cock." The paper he sells may give the dreadful details, or it may be a religious tract, "brought out in mistake," should the vendor be questioned on the subject; or else the poor fellow puts on a bewildered look and murmurs, "O, it's shocking to be done this way—but I can't read." The patterers pass along so rapidly that this detection rarely happens.

One man told me that in the last eight or ten years, he, either singly or with his "mob," had twice put the Duke of Wellington to death, once by a fall from his horse, and the other time by a "sudden and myst-erious" death, without any condescension to particulars. He had twice performed the same mortal office for Louis Phillipe, before that potentate's departure from France; each death was by the hands of an assassin; "one was stabbing, and the other a shot from a distance." He once thought of poisoning the Pope, but was afraid of the street Irish. He broke Prince Albert's leg, or arm, (he was not sure which), when his royal highness was out with his harriers. He never had much to say about the Queen; "it wouldn't go down," he thought, and perhaps nothing had lately been said. "Stop, there, sir," said another patterer, of whom I inquired as to the correctness of those statements, (after my constant custom in sifting each subject thoroughly,) "stop, stop, sir. I *have* had to say about the Queen lately. In coorse, nothing can be said against her, and nothing ought to; that's true enough, but the last time she was confined, I cried her *accouchement* (the word was pronounced as spelt to a merely English reader, or rather more broadly) of *three!* Lord love you, sir, it would have been no use crying *one;* people's so used to that; but a Bobby came up and stops me, and said it was some impudence about the Queen's *coachman!* Why look at it, says I, fat-head—I knew I was safe—and see if there's anything in it about the Queen or her coach-man! And he looked, and in coorse there was nothing. I forget just now what the paper *was* about." My first-mentioned informant had ap-prehended Feargus O'Connor on a charge of high treason. He assassinated Louis Napoleon, "from a *fourth* edition of the *Times*," which "did well." He caused Marshal Haynau to die of the assault by the draymen. He made Rush hang himself in prison. He killed Jane Wilbred, and put Mrs. Sloane to death; and he announced the discovery that Jane Wilbred was Mrs. Sloane's daughter.

This informant did not represent that he had originated these little pieces of intelligence, only that he had been a party to their sale, and a party to originating one or two. Another patterer and of a higher order of genius—told me that all which was stated was undoubtedly correct, "but me and my mates, sir," he said, "did Haynau in another style. A splendid slum, sir! Capital! We assassinated him—*mys*-te-rious. Then about Rush. His hanging hisself in prison was a fake, I know; but we've had him lately. His ghost appeared—as is shown in the Australian papers—to Emily Sandford, and threatened her; and took her by the neck, and there's the red marks of his fingers to be seen on her neck to this day!" The same informant was so loud in his praise of the "Ass-sass-sina-tion" of Haynau that I give the account. I have little doubt it was his own writing. It is confused in passages, and has a blending of the "I" and the "we:"—

"We have just received upon undisputed authority, that, that savage and unmanly tyrant, that enemy to civil and religious liberty, the inhuman Haynau has at last finished his career of guilt by the hand of an assassin, the term assassin I have no doubt will greet harshly upon the ears of some of our readers, yet never the less I am compelled to use it although I would gladly say the *average* of outraged innocence, which would be a name more suitable to one who has been the means of ridden the world of such a despicable monster."

[My informant complained bitterly, and not without reason, of the printer. "Average," for instance (which I have *italicised*), should be "avenger." The "average of outraged inno-cence!"]

"It appears by the Columns of the Corour le Con-stituonal of Brussels," runs the paper, "that the even-ing before last, three men one of which is supposed to be the miscreant, Haynau entered a Cafe in the Neigh-bourhood of Brussels kept by a man in the name of Priduex, and after partaking of some refreshments which were ordered by his two companions they de-sired to be shown to their chambers, during their stay in the public or Travellers Room, they spoke but little and seemed to be very cautious as to joining in the conversations which was passing briskly round the festive board, which to use the landlord's own words was rather strange, as his Cafe was mostly frequented by a set of jovial fellows, M. Priduex goes on to state that after the three strangers had retired to rest some time a tall and rather noble looking man enveloped in a large cloak entered and asked for a bed, and after calling for some wine he took up a paper and appeared to be reading it very attentively, in due time he was shown to bed and all passed on without any appear-ance of anything wrong until about 6 o'clock in the morning, when the landlord and his family, were roused by a noise over head and cries of murder, and

upon going up stairs to ascertain the cause, he disco-vered the person who was [known] to be Marshal Haynau, lying on his bed with his throat cut in a frightful manner, and his two companions standing by his bed side bewailing his loss. On the table was dis-covered a card, on which was written these words 'Monster, I am avenged at last. Suspicion went upon the tall stranger, who was not anywhere to be found, the Garde arms instantly were on the alert, and are now in active persuit of him but up to the time of our going to press nothing further has transpired."

It is very easy to stigmatise the death-hunter when he sets off all the attractions of a real or pretended murder,—when he displays on a board, as does the standing patterer, "illustrations" of "the 'dentical pick-axe" of Manning, or the stable of Good,—or when he invents or embel-lishes atrocities which excite the public mind. He does, however, but follow in the path of those who are looked up to as "the press,"—as the "fourth estate." The conductors of the *Lady's Newspaper* sent an artist to Paris to give drawings of the scene of the murder by the Duc de Praslin,—to "illustrate" the blood-stains in the duchess's bed-chamber. The *Illustrated London News* is prompt in depicting the locality of any atrocity over which the curious in crime may gloat. The *Observer*, in costly advertisements, boasts of its 20 columns (sometimes with a supplement) of details of some vulgar and mercenary bloodshed,—the details being written in a most honest depre-cation of the morbid and savage tastes to which the writer is pandering. Other weekly papers have engravings—and only concerning murder —of any wretch whom vice has made notorious. Many weekly papers had expensive telegraphic despatches of Rush's having been hung at Norwich, which event, happily for the interest of Sunday newspapers, took place in Norwich at noon on a Saturday. [I may here remark, that the patterers laugh at telegraphs and ex-press trains for rapidity of communication, boasting that the press strives in vain to rival them,—as at a "hanging match," for instance, the patterer has the full particulars, dying speech, and confession included—if a confes-sion be feasible—ready for his customers the moment the drop falls, and while the criminal may still be struggling, at the very scene of the hanging. "If the *Times* was cross-examined about it," observed one patterer, "he must con-fess he's outdone, though he's a rich *Times*, and we is poor fellows." But to resume—]

A penny-a-liner is reported, and without con-tradiction, to have made a large sum by having hurried to Jersey in Manning's business, and by being allowed to accompany the officers when they conducted that paltry tool of a vindictive woman from Jersey to Southampton by steamer, and from Southampton to London by "special engine," as beseemed the popularity of so dis-tinguished a rascal and homicide; and next morning the daily papers, in all the typo-graphical honour of "leads" and "a good place," gave details of this fellow's—this Man-ning's—conversation, looks, and demeanour.

Until the "respectable" press become a more healthful public instructor, we have no right to blame the death-hunter, who is but an imitator —a follower—and that for a meal. So strong has this morbid feeling about criminals become, that an earl's daughter, who had " an order" to see Bedlam, would not leave the place until she had obtained Oxford's autograph for her album! The rich vulgar are but the poor vulgar—without an excuse for their vulgarity.

"Next to murders, fires are tidy browns," I was told by a patterer experienced both in "murders" and "fires." The burning of the old Houses of Parliament was very popular among street-sellers, and for the reason which ensures popularity to a commercial people; it was a source of profit, and was certainly made the most of. It was the work of incendiaries,— of ministers, to get rid of perplexing papers,— of government officers with troublesome accounts to balance,—of a sporting lord, for a heavy wager,—of a conspiracy of builders,—and of " a unsuspected party." The older "hands" with whom I conversed on the subject, all agreed in stating that they "did well" on the fire. One man said, "No, sir, it wasn't only the working people that bought of me, but merchants and their clerks. I s'pose they took the papers home with 'em for their wives and families, which is a cheap way of doing, as a newspaper costs 3d. at least. But stop, sir,—stop ; there wasn't no threepennies then,—nothing under 6d., if they wasn't more ; I can't just say, but it was better for us when newspapers was high. I never heard no sorrow expressed,—not *in* the least. Some said it was a good job, and they wished the ministers was in it." The burning of the Royal Exchange was not quite so beneficial to the street-sellers, but "was uncommon tidy." The fire at the Tower, however, was almost as great a source of profit as that of the Houses of Parliament, and the following statement shows the profit reaped.

My informant had been a gentleman's servant, his last place being with a gentleman in Russell-square, who went to the East Indies, and his servant was out of a situation so long that he "parted with everything." When he was at the height of his distress, he went to see the fire at the Tower, as he "had nothing better to do." He remained out some hours, and before he reached his lodging, men passed him, crying the full and true particulars of the fire. "I bought one," said the man, "and changed my last shilling. It was a sudden impulse, for I saw people buy keenly. I never read it, but only looked at the printer's name. I went to him at the Dials, and bought some, and so I went into the paper trade. I made 6s. or 7s. some days, while the Tower lasted ; and 3s. and 4s. other days, when the first polish was off. I sold them mostly at 1d. a piece at first. It was good money then. The Tower was good, or middling good, for from 14 to 20 days. There was at least 100 men working nothing but the

Tower. There's no great chance of any more great buildings being burnt; worse luck. People don't care much about private fires. A man in this street don't heed so much who's burnt to death in the next. But the foundation-stone of the new Royal Exchange—fire led to that—was pretty fair, and portraits of Halbert went off, so that it was for two or three days as good as the Tower. Fires is our best friends next to murders, if they're *good* fires. The hopening of the Coal Exchange was rather tidy. I've been in the streets ever since, and don't see how I could possibly get out of them. At first I felt a great degradation at being driven to the life. I shunned grooms and coachmen, as I might be known to them. I didn't care for others. That sort of feeling wears out though. I'm a widower now, and my family feels, as I did at first, that what I'm doing is 'low.' They won't assist— though they may give me 1s. now and then—but they won't assist me to leave the streets. They'll rather blame me for going into them, though there was only that, or robbing, or starving. The fire at Ben. Caunt's, where the poor children was burnt to hashes, was the best of the private house fires that I've worked, I think. I made 4s. on it one day. He was the champion once, and was away at a fight at the time, and it was a shocking thing, and so people bought."

After the burning of York Minster by Jonathan Martin, I was told by an old hand, the (street) destruction of the best known public buildings in the country was tried ; such as Canterbury Cathedral, Dover Castle, the Brighton Pavilion, Edinburgh Castle, or Holyrood House—all known to "travelling" patterers— but the success was not sufficiently encouraging. It was no use, I was told, firing such places as Hampton Court or Windsor Castle, for unless people *saw* the reflection of a great fire, they wouldn't buy.

OF THE SELLERS OF SECOND EDITIONS.

THESE "second editions" are, and almost universally, second or later editions of the newspapers, morning and evening, but three-fourths of the sale may be of the evening papers, and more especially of the *Globe* and *Standard.*

I believe that there is not now in existence— unless it be in a workhouse and unknown to his fellows, or engaged in some other avocation and lost sight of by them—any one who sold "second editions" (the *Courier* evening paper being then in the greatest demand) at the time of the Duke of York's Walcheren expedition, at the period of the battle of the Nile, during the continuance of the Peninsular war, or even at the battle of Waterloo. There were a few old men—some of whom had been soldiers or sailors, and others who have simulated it—surviving within these 5 or 6 years, and some later, who "worked Waterloo," but they were swept off, I was told, by the cholera.

"I was assured by a gentlemen who had a perfect remembrance of the "second editions" (as they were generally called) sold in the streets, and who had often bought them upwards of forty years ago, that a sketch in the "Monthly Review," in a notice of Scott's "Lord of the Isles" (published in 1815), gave the best notion he had met with of what the second edition sale really was. At the commencement of the sixth canto of his poem, Sir Walter, somewhat too grandiloquently, in the judgment of his reviewer, asks—

"O who, that shared them, ever shall forget
The emotions of the spirit-rousing time,
When breathless in the mart the couriers met,
Early and late, at evening and at prime?"

"Who," in his turn asks the reviewer, "can avoid conjuring up the idea of men with broad sheets of foolscap, scored with 'victories' rolled round their hats, and horns blowing loud defiance in each other's mouth, from the top to the bottom of Pall-mall or the Haymarket, when he reads such a passage? We actually hear the Park and Tower guns, and the clattering of ten thousand bells, as we read, and stop our ears from the close and sudden intrusion of some hot and *horn-fisted* patriot, blowing ourselves, as well as Bonaparte to the devil!"

The horn carried by these "*horn*-fisted" men was a common tin tube, from two to three feet long, and hardly capable of being made to produce any sound beyond a sudden and discordant "trump, trump." The men worked with papers round their hats, in a way not very dissimilar to that of the running patterers of to-day.

The "editions" cried by these men during the war-time often contained spurious intelligence, but for that the editors of the journals were responsible—or the stock-jobbers who had imposed upon them. Any one who has consulted a file of newspapers of the period to which I have referred, will remember how frequent, and how false, were the announcements, or the rumours, of the deaths of Bonaparte, his brothers, or his marshals, in battle or by assassination.

As there was no man who was personally conversant with this traffic in what is emphatically enough called the "war-time," I sought out an old street-patterer who had been acquainted with the older hands in the trade, whose experience stretched to the commencement of the present century, and from him I received the following account:—

"Oh, yes," he began, "I've worked 'seconds.' We used to call the editions generally seconds, and cry them sometimes, as the *latest* editions, whatever it was. There was Jack Griffiths, sir,—now wasn't he a hand at a second edition? I believe you. I do any kind of patter now myself, but I've done tidy on second editions, when seconds was to be had. Why, Jack Griffiths, sir—he'd been a sailor and was fond of talking about the sea—Jack Griffiths—you would have liked to have heard him—Jack told me that he once took 10s. 6d.—it was Hyde Park way—for a second edition of a paper when Queen Caroline's trial was over. Besides

Jack, there was Tom Cole, called the Wooden Leg (he'd been a soldier I believe), and Whitechapel, and Old Brummagem, and Hell-fire Jack. Hell-fire Jack was said to be something to a man that was a trainer, and a great favourite of the old Duke of Queensberry, and was called Hell-fire Dick ; but I can't say how it was. I began to work second editions, for the first time when George IV. died. They went off pretty well at 1s. a piece, and for three or four I got 2s. 6d. If it's anything good I get 1s. still, but very seldom any more. I always show anybody that asks that the paper *is* just what I've cried it. There's no regular cry ; we cries what's up : '*Here's* the second edition of the *Globe* with the full perticlers of the death of his Majesty King George IV.' We work much in the same way as the running patter. Three of us shouts in the same spot. I was one of three who one night sold five quires, mostly *Globe* and *Standard*. It was at the Reform Bill time, and something about the Reform Bill. I never much heeded what the paper was about. I only wanted the patter, and soon got it. A mate, or any of us, looks out for anything good in the evening papers, to be ready. Why that night I speak of I was kept running backards and for'ards to the newspaper offices—and how they does keep you waiting at times!—mostly the *Globe* and *Standard ;* we worked them all at the West End. There's twenty-seven papers to a quire, and we gave 4d. a piece for 'em and sold none, as well as I mind, for under 1s. I carried them mostly under my arm or in my hat, taking care they wasn't spoiled. Belgrave-square way, and St. George's, Hanover-square way, and Hyde Park way, are the best. The City's no good. There's only sixpences there. The coffee-shops has spoiled the City, as I'm afeard they will other parts. Murders in second editions don't sell now, and aren't tried much, beyond a few, if there's a late verdict. Curviseer (Courvoisier) was tidy. The trial weren't over 'til evening, and I sold six papers, and got 7s. for them, to gentlemen going away by the mail. I've heard that Greenacre was good in the same way, but I wasn't in town at the time. The French Revolution—the last one—was certainly a fairish go. Lewis Fillup was good many ways. When he used to be shot at—if the news weren't too early in the day—and when he got to England, and when he was said to have got back, or to have been taken. Why, of course he wern't to compare with Rush in the regular patter, but he was very fair. I have nothing to say against him, and wish he was alive, and could do it all over again. Lord Brougham's death wern't worth much to us. You remember the time, I dare say, sir, when they said he killed hisself in the papers, to see what folks would say on him. The resignation of a prime minister is mostly pretty good. Lord Melbourne was, and so was Sir Robert Peel. There's always somebody to say,

'Hurra! that's right!' and to buy a paper because he's pleased. I had a red paper in my hat when I worked the French Revolution. French news is generally liked in a fashionable drag. Irish news is no good, for people don't seem to believe it. Smith O'Brien's battle, though, did sell a little. It's not possible to tell you exactly what I've made on seconds. How can I? One week I may have cleared 1*l.* in them, and for six months before not a blessed brown. Perhaps—as near as I can recollect and calculate—I've cleared 3*l.* (if that) each year, one with another, in second editions in my time, and perhaps twenty others has done the same."

Another man who also knew the old hands said to me: "Lord bless us, how times is changed! you should have heard Jack Griffiths tell how he cried his gazettes: '*He-ere's* the *London Gazette* Ex-terorary, containing the hof-ficial account of the bloody and decisive wictory of Sally-manker.' Something that way. Patter wern't required then; the things sold theirselves. Why, the other day I was talking to a young chap that conceits hisself to be a hout-and-houter in patter, and I mentions Jack's crying *Gazettes* and getting 5*s.* apiece for many a one on 'em, and this young chap says, says he: '*Gazettes!* What did they cry *Gazettes?*—bankrupts, and all that?' 'Bankrupts be blowed!' said I, 'wictories!' I heerd Waterloo cried when I was a little 'un. The speeches on the opening of parliament, which the newspapers has ready, has no sale in the crowd to what they had. I only sold two papers at 6*d.* each this last go. I ventured on no more, or should have been a loser. If the Queen isn't there, none's sold. But we always has a speech ready, as close as can be got from what the morning papers says. One gent. said to me: 'But that ain't the real speech!' 'It's a far better,' says I, and so it is. Why now, sir, there's some reading and spirit in this bit. The Queen says:

'It is my determination by the assistance of divine providence to uphold and protect the Protestant Church of the British Empire, which has been enjoyed three hundred years without interuption, the Religion which our ancestors struggled to obtain. And as long as it shall please God to spare me, I will endeavour to maintain the rights and perogatives of our holy Protestant Church. And now my Lords, I leave you to your duties, to the helm of the state, to the harbour of peace, and happiness.'"

This man showed me the street speech, which was on a broad sheet set off with the royal arms. The topics and arrangement were the same as those in the speech delivered by her Majesty.

On Monday morning last (Feb. 24), I asked the man who told me that prime ministers' resignations were "pretty good" for the street traffic, if he had been well remunerated by the sale of the evening papers of Saturday, with the account of Lord John Russell's resignation. "It wern't tried, sir," he answered; "there was nothing new in the evenings, and we thought nobody seemed to care about it. The newspaper offices and their boarders (as he called the men going about with announcements on boards) didn't make very much of it, so we got up a song instead; but it was no good,—not salt to a fresh herring—for there was some fresh herrings in. It was put strong, though. This was the last verse:

'From the House to the Palace it has caused a bother,
Old women are tumbling one over another,
The Queen says it is with her, one thing or 'tother,
    They must not discharge Little John;
Her Majesty vows that she is not contented,
And many ere long will have cause to repent it,
Had she been in the house she would nobly resent it,
    And fought like a brick for Lord John.'"

Adopting the calculation of my first informant, and giving a profit of 150 per cent., we find 150*l.* yearly expended in the streets, in second editions, or probably it might be more correct to say 200*l.* in a year of great events, and 50*l.* in a year when such events are few.

OF THE STANDING PATTERERS.

THE standing patterer I have already described in his resemblance to the mountebank of old, and how, like his predecessor, he required a "pitch" and an audience. I need but iterate that these standing patterers are men who remain in one place, until they think they have exhausted the custom likely to accrue there, or until they are removed by the police; and who endeavour to attract attention to their papers, or more commonly pamphlets, either by means of a board with coloured pictures upon it, illustrative of the contents of what they sell, or else by gathering a crowd round about them, in giving a lively or horrible description of the papers or books they are "working." The former is what is usually denominated in street technology, "board work." A few of the standing patterers give street recitations or dialogues.

Some of the "illustrations" most "in vogue" of late for the boards of the standing patterers were,—the flogging of the nuns of Minsk, the blood streaming from their naked shoulders, (anything against the Emperor of Russia, I was told, was a good street subject for a painting); the young girl, Sarah Thomas, who murdered her mistress in Bristol, dragged to the gallows by the turnkeys and Calcraft, the hangman; Calcraft himself, when charged with "starving his mother;" Haynau, in the hands of the draymen; the Mannings, and afterwards the Sloanes. The two last-mentioned were among the most elaborate, each having a series of "compartments," representing the different stages of the events in which those heroes and heroines flourished. I shall speak afterwards of street-artists who are the painters of these boards, and then describe the pictures more fully. There are also, as before alluded to, what may be called "cocks" in street paintings, as well as street literature.

Two of the most favourite themes of the standing patterers were, however, the "Annals of the White House in Soho-square," and the

"Mysteries of Mesmerism." Both supplied subjects to the boards.

The White House was a notorious place of ill fame. Some of the apartments, it is said, were furnished in a style of costly luxury; while others were fitted up with springs, traps, and other contrivances, so as to present no appearance other than that of an ordinary room, until the machinery was set in motion. In one room, into which some wretched girl might be introduced, on her drawing a curtain as she would be desired, a skeleton, grinning horribly, was precipitated forward, and caught the terrified creature in his, to all appearance, bony arms. In another chamber the lights grew dim, and then seemed gradually to go out. In a little time some candles, apparently self-ignited, revealed to a horror stricken woman, a black coffin, on the lid of which might be seen, in brass letters, ANNE, or whatever name it had been ascertained the poor wretch was known by. A sofa, in another part of the mansion, was made to descend into some place of utter darkness; or, it was alleged, into a room in which was a store of soot or ashes.

Into the truth or exaggeration of these and similar statements, it is not my business to inquire; but the standing patterer made the most of them. Although the house in question has been either rebuilt or altered—I was told that each was the case—and its abominable character has ceased to apply to it for some years, the patterer did not scruple to represent it as still in existence (though he might change the venue as to the square at discretion) and that all the atrocities perpetrated—to which I have not ventured even to allude—were still the ordinary procedures of "high life." Neither did the standing patterer scruple, as one man assured me, to "name names;" to attribute vile deeds to any nobleman or gentleman whose name was before the public; and to embellish his story by an allusion to a recent event. He not unfrequently ended with a moral exhortation to all ladies present to avoid this "abode of iniquity for the rich." The board was illustrated with skeletons, coffins, and other horrors; but neither on it, nor in a hardly intelligible narrative which the patterer sold, was there anything indecent.

The "Mysteries of Mesmerism" was an account of the marvels of that "newly-discovered and most wonderful power in natur and art." With it Dr. Elliotson's, or some well-known name, was usually associated, and any marvel was "pattered," according to the patterer's taste and judgment. The illustrations were of persons, generally women, in a state of coma, but in this also there was no indecency; nor was there in the narrative sold.

Of these two popular exhibitions there are, I am informed, none now in town, and both, I was told, was more the speculations of a printer, who sent out men, than in the hands of the regular patterers.

It may tend somewhat to elucidate the cha-

racter of the patterers, if I here state, that in my conversation with the whole of them, I heard from their lips strong expressions of disgust at Sloane,—far stronger than were uttered in abhorrence of any murderer. Rush, indeed, was, and is, a popular man among them. One of them told me, that not long before Madame Tussaud's death, he thought of calling upon that "wenerable lady," and asking her, he said, "to treat me to something to drink the immortal memory of Mr. Rush, my friend and her'n."

It is admitted by all concerned in the exercise of street elocution, that "the stander" must have "the best of patter." He usually works alone,—there are very rarely two at standing patter,—and beyond his board he has no adventitious aids, as in the running patter, so that he must be all the more effective; but the board is pronounced "as good as a man." When the standing patterer visits the country, he is accompanied by a mate, and the "copy of werses" is then announced as being written by an "underpaid curate" within a day's walk. "It tells mostly, sir," said one man; "for it's a blessing to us that there always is a journeyman parson what the people knows, and what the patter fits." Sometimes the poetry is attributed to a sister of mercy, or to a popular poetess; very frequently, by the patterers who best understand the labouring classes, to Miss Eliza Cook. Sometimes the verses are written by "a sympathising gent. in that parish," but his name wasn't to be mentioned. Another intelligent patterer whom I questioned on the subject, told me that my information was correct. "It's just the same in the newspapers," he continued; "why the 'sympathising gent.' is the same with us as what in the newspapers is called "other intelligence (about any crime), to publish which might defeat the ends of justice." That means, they know nothing at all about it, and can't so much as venture on a guess. I've known a little about it for the papers, sir,—it doesn't matter in what line."

Some standing patterers are brought up to the business from childhood. Some take to it through loss of character, or through their inability to obtain a situation from intemperate habits, and some because "a free life suits me best." In a former inquiry into a portion of this subject, I sought a standing patterer, whom I found in a threepenny lodging-house in Mint-street, Southwark. On my inquiring what induced him to adopt, or pursue, that line of life, he said:—

"It was distress that first drove me to it. I had learnt to make willow bonnets, but that branch of trade went entirely out. So, having a wife and children, I was drove to write out a paper that I called 'The People's Address to the King on the Present State of the Nation.' I got it printed, and took it into the streets and sold it. I did very well with it, and made 5s. a day while it lasted. I never was brought up to any mechanical trade. My father was a clergyman" [here he cried bitterly]. "It breaks my heart when I think of it. I have as good a wife as ever lived, and I would give the world to get out of my present life. It would be heaven to get away from the place where I am. I am obliged to cheer up my spirits. If I was to give way to it, I shouldn't live long. It's like a little hell to be in the place where we live" [crying], "associated with the ruffians that we are. My distress of mind is awful, but it won't do to show it at my lodgings—they'd only laugh to see me down-hearted; so I keep my trouble all to myself. Oh, I am heartily sick of this street work—the insults I have to 'put up with—the drunken men swearing at me. Yes, indeed, I am heartily sick of it."

This poor man had some assistance forwarded to him by benevolent persons, after his case had appeared in my letter in the *Morning Chronicle*. This was the means of his leaving the streets, and starting in the "cloth-cap trade." He seemed a deserving man.

EXPERIENCE OF A STANDING PATTERER.

FROM one of this body I received, at the period just alluded to, the following information:—

" I have taken my 5s. a day (said my informant); but 'paper' selling now isn't half so good as it used to be. People haven't got the money to lay out; for it all depends with the working man. The least we take in a day is, upon an average, sixpence; but taking the good and bad together, I should say we take about 10s. a week. I know there's some get more than that, but then there's many take less. Lately, I know, I haven't taken 9s. a week myself, and people reckon me one of the best patterers in the trade. I'm reckoned to have the gift—that is, the gift of the gab. I never works a last dying speech on any other than the day of execution—all the edge is taken off of it after that. The last dying speeches and executions are all printed the day before. They're always done on the Sunday, if the murderers are to be hung on the Monday. I've been and got them myself on the Sunday night, over and over again. The flying stationers goes with the papers in their pockets, and stand under the drop, and as soon as ever it falls, and long before the breath is out of the body, they begin bawling out." [Here my informant gave a further account of the flying stationers under the gallows, similar to what I have given. He averred that they "invented every lie likely to go down."] "'Here you have also an exact likeness,' they say, 'of the murderer, taken at the bar of the Old Bailey!' when all the time it is an old wood-cut that's been used for every criminal for the last forty years. I know the likeness that was given of Hocker was the one that was given for Fauntleroy; and the wood-cut of Tawell was one that was given for the Quaker that had been hanged for forgery twenty years before. Thurtell's likeness was done expressly for the 'papers;' and so was the Mannings' and Rush's likenesses too. The murders are bought by men,

women, and children. Many of the tradespeople bought a great many of the affair of the Mannings. I went down to Deptford with mine, and did uncommonly well. I sold all off. Gentlefolks won't have anything to do with murders sold in the street; they've got other ways of seeing all about it. We lay on the horrors, and picture them in the highest colours we can. We don't care what's in the 'papers' in our hands. All we want to do is to sell 'em; and the more horrible we makes the affairs, the more sale we have. We do very well with 'love-letters.' They are 'cocks;' that is, they are all fictitious. We give it out that they are from a tradesman in the neighbourhood, not a hundred yards from where we are a-standing. Sometimes we say it's a well-known sporting butcher; sometimes it's a highly respectable publican— just as it will suit the tastes of the neighbourhood. I got my living round Cornwall for one twelvemonth with nothing else than a love-letter. It was headed, 'A curious and laughable love-letter and puzzle, sent by a sporting gentleman to Miss H—s—m, in *this* neighbourhood;' that suits any place that I may chance to be in; but I always patter the name of the street or village where I may be. This letter, I say, is so worded, that had it fallen into the hands of her mamma or papa, they could not have told what it meant; but the young lady, having so much wit, found out its true meaning, and sent him an answer in the same manner. You have here, we say, the number of the house, the name of the place where she lives (there is nothing of the kind, of course), and the initials of all the parties concerned. We dare not give the real names in full, we tell them; indeed, we do all we can to get up the people's curiosity. I did very well with the 'Burning of the House of Commons.' I happened by accident to put my pipe into my pocket amongst some of my papers, and burnt them. Then, not knowing how to get rid of them, I got a few straws. I told the people that my burnt papers were parliamentary documents that had been rescued from the flames, and that, as I dare not sell them, I would let them have a straw for a penny, and give them one of the papers. By this trick I got rid of my stock twice as fast, and got double the price that I should have done. The papers had nothing at all to do with the House of Commons. Some was 'Death and the Lady,' and 'Death and the Gentleman,' and others were the 'Political Catechism,' and 365 lies, Scotch, English, and Irish, and each lie as big round as St. Paul's. I remember a party named Jack Straw, who laid a wager, half-a-gallon of beer, that he'd bring home the money for two dozen blank papers in one hour's time. He went out into the Old-street-road, and began a patter about the political affairs of the nation, and Sir Robert Peel, and the Duke of Wellington, telling the public that he dared not sell his papers, they were treasonable; so he gave them with a straw—that he sold for one penny. In less than the hour he was sold clean out, and returned and drank the beer. The chief things that I work are quarter-sheets of recitations and dialogues. One is ' Good Advice to Young Men on Choosing their Wives.' I have done exceedingly well with that—it's a good moral thing. Another is the ' Drunkard's Catechism ;' another is ' The Rent Day ; or, the Landlord gathering his Rents.' This is a dialogue between the landlord and his tenant, beginning with ' Good morning, Mrs. Longface ; have you got my rent ready, ma'am?' The next one is ' The Adventures of Larry O'Flinn.' It's a comic story, and a very good got-up thing. Another is ' A Hint to Husbands and Wives ;' and ' A Pack of Cards turned into a Bible, a Prayer-book, and an Almanack.' These cards belonged to Richard Middleton, of the 60th regiment of foot, who was taken a prisoner for playing at cards in church during divine service. But the best I do is ' The Remarkable Dream of a Young Man of loose character, who had made an agreement to break into a gentleman's house at twelve at night on Whitsun Monday, but, owing to a little drink that he took, he had a remarkable dream, and dreamed he was in hell. The dream had such influence on his mind that he refused to meet his comrade. His comrade was taken up for the burglary, found guilty, and executed for it. This made such an impression on the young man's mind that he became a reformed character.' There is a very beautiful description of hell in this paper," said my informant, " that makes it sell very well among the old women and the apprentice lads, for the young man was an apprentice himself. It's all in very pretty poetry, and a regular ' cock.' The papers that I work chiefly are what are called ' the standing patters ;' they're all of 'em stereotype, and some of them a hundred years old. We consider the ' death hunters' are the lowest grade in the trade. We can make most money of the murders while they last, but they don't last, and they merely want a good pair of lungs to get them off. But it's not every one, sir, that can work the standing patters. Many persons I've seen try at it and fail. One old man I knew tried the ' Drunkard's Catechism' and the ' Soldier's Prayer-book and Bible.' He could manage to patter these because they'll almost work themselves ; but ' Old Mother Clifton' he broke down in. I heard him do it in Sun-street and in the Blackfriars-road ; but it was such a dreadful failure—he couldn't humour it a bit—that, thinks I to myself, you'll soon have to give up, and sure enough he's never been to the printer's since. He'd a very poor audience, chiefly boys and girls, and they were laughing at him because he made so many blunders in it. A man that's never been to school an hour can go and patter a dying speech or ' A Battle between Two Ladies of Fortune.' They require no scholarship. All you want is to stick a picture on your hat, to attract attention, and to make all the noise you can. It's all the same when they does an ' Assassination of Louis Philippe,' or a ' Diabolical Attempt on the Life

of the Queen'—a good stout pair of lungs and plenty of impudence is all that is required. But to patter ' Bounce, the Workhouse Beadle, and the Examination of the Paupers before the Poor-law Commissioners,' takes a good head-piece and great gift of the gab, let me tell you. It's just the same as a play-actor. I can assure you I often feel very nervous. I begin it, and walk miles before I can get confidence in myself to make the attempt. I got rid of two quire last night. I was up among the gentlemen's servants in Crawford-street, Baker-street, and I had a very good haul out of the grown-up people. I cleared 1s. 8d. altogether. I did that from seven till nine in the evening. It's all chance-work. If it's fine, and I can get a crowd of grown-up people round me, I can do very well, but I can't do anything amongst the boys. There's very little to be done in the day-time. I begin at ten in the day, and stop out till one. After that I starts off again at five, and leaves off about ten at night. Marylebone, Paddington, and Westminster I find the best places. The West-end is very good the early part of the week, for any thing that's genteel, such as the ' Rich Man and his Wife quarrelling because they have no Family.' Our customers there are principally the footmen, the grooms, and the maid-servants. The east end of the town is the best on Friday and Saturday evenings. I very often go to Limehouse on Friday evening. Most part of the dock-men are paid then, and anything comic goes off well among them. On Saturdays I go to the New-cut, Ratcliff-highway, the Brill, and such places. I make mostly 2s. clear on a Saturday night. After nineteen years' experience of the patter and paper line in the streets, I find that a foolish nonsensical thing will sell twice as fast as a good moral sentimental one ; and, while it lasts, a good murder will cut out the whole of them. It's the best selling thing of any. I used at one time to patter religious tracts in the street, but I found no encouragement. I did the ' Infidel Blacksmith'—that would not sell. ' What is Happiness? a Dialogue between Ellen and Mary'—that was no go. No more was the ' Sorrows of Seduction.' So I was driven into the comic standing patters."

The more recent " experiences " of standing patterers, as they were detailed to me, differ so little in subject, or anything else, from what I have given concerning running patterers, that to cite them would be a repetition.

From the best information to be obtained, I have no doubt that there are always at least 20 standing patterers—sometimes they are called " boardmen"—at work in London. Some of them " run " occasionally, but an equal number or more, of the regular " runners " resort now and then to the standing patter, so the sum is generally kept up.

Notwithstanding the drawbacks of bad weather, which affects the standing, and does not affect the running, patterer ; and notwithstanding the more frequent interruptions of the police, I am of opinion that the standing patterer earns

on an average 1s. a week more than his running
brother. His earnings too are often all his
own; whereas the runners are a 'school,' and,
their gains divided. More running patterers
become, on favourable occasions, stationary,
with boards, perhaps in the proportion of five to
four, than the stationary become itinerant. One
standing patterer told me, that, during the excitement about the Sloanes, he cleared full 3s. a
day for more than a week; but at other times
he had cleared only 1s. 6d. in a whole week,
and he had taken nothing when the weather
was too wet for the standing work, and there
was nothing up to "run" with.

If, then, 20 standing patterers clear 10s.
weekly, each, the year through—"taking" 15s.
weekly—we find that 780l. is yearly expended
in the standing patter of London streets.

The capital required for the start of the
standing is greater than that needed by the
running patterer. The painting for a board
costs 3s. 6d.; the board and pole, with feet, to
which it is attached, 5s. 6d.; and stock-money,
2s.; in all, 11s.

OF POLITICAL LITANIES, DIALOGUES, ETC.

To "work a litany" in the streets is considered
one of the higher exercises of professional skill
on the part of the patterer. In working this, a
clever patterer—who will not scruple to introduce anything out of his head which may strike
him as suitable to his audience—is very particular in his choice of a mate, frequently changing
his ordinary partner, who may be good "at a
noise" or a ballad, but not have sufficient acuteness or intelligence to patter politics as if he
understood what he was speaking about. I am
told that there are not twelve patterers in London whom a critical professor of street elocution
will admit to be capable of 'working a catechism' or a litany. "Why, sir," said one patterer, "I've gone out with a mate to work a
litany, and he's humped it in no time." To
'hump,' in street parlance, is equivalent to
'botch,' in more genteel colloquialism. "And
when a thing's humped," my informant continued, "you can only 'call a go.'" To 'call a
go,' signifies to remove to another spot, or adopt
some other patter, or, in short, to resort to some
change or other in consequence of a failure.

An elderly man, not now in the street trade,
but who had "pattered off a few papers" some
years ago, told me that he had heard three or
four old hands—"now all dead, for they're a
short-lived people"—talk of the profits gained
and the risk ran by giving Hone's parodies on
the Catechism, Litany, St. Athanasius' Creed, &c.
in the streets, after the three consecutive trials
and the three acquittals of Hone had made the
parodies famous and Hone popular. To work
them in the streets was difficult, "for though,"
said my informant, "there was no new police in
them days, there was plenty of officers and constables ready to pull the fellows up, and though
Hone was acquitted, a beak that wanted to please
the high dons, would find some way of stopping

them that sold Hone's things in the street, and
so next to nothing could be done that way, but
a little was done." The greatest source of profit,
I learned from the reminiscences of the same
man, was in the parlours and tap-rooms of public-houses, where the patterers or reciters were
well paid "for going through their catechisms,"
and sometimes, that there might be no interruption, the door was locked, and even the landlord
and his servants excluded. The charge was
usually 2d. a copy, but 1d. was not refused.

During Queen Caroline's trial there were the
like interruptions and hindrances to similar performances; and the interruptions continued during the passing of the Catholic Emancipation
Bill until about the era of the Reform Bill, and
then the hindrance was but occasional. "And
perhaps it was our own fault, sir," said one patterer, "that we was then molested at all in the
dialogues and catechisms and things; but we
was uncommon bold, and what plenty called
sarcy, at that time: we was so."

Thus this branch of a street profession continued to be followed, half surreptitiously, until
after the subsidence of the political ferment
consequent on the establishment of a new fran-
chise and the partial abolition of an old one.
The calling, however, has never been popular
among street purchasers, and I believe that it
is sometimes followed by a street-patterer as
much from the promptings of the pride of art
as from the hope of gain.

The street-papers in the dialogue form have
not been copied nor derived from popular productions—but even in the case of Political
Litanies and Anti-Corn-law Catechisms and
Dialogues are the work of street authors.

One intelligent man told me, that properly to
work a political litany, which referred to ecclesiastical matters, he "made himself up," as
well as limited means would permit, as a
bishop! and "did stunning, until he was afraid
of being stunned on skilly." Of the late papers
on the subject of the Pope, I cite the one which
was certainly the best of all that appeared, and
concerning which indignant remonstrances were
addressed to some of the newspapers. The
"good child" in the patter, was a tall bulky
man; the examiner (also the author), was
rather diminutive:—

"*The old English Bull John v. the Pope's Bull of*
of Rome.

"My good Child as it is necessary at this very
important crisis; when, that good pious and very reasonable old gentleman Pope Pi-ass the nineth has
promised to favor us with his presence, and the pleasures of Popery—and trampled on the rights and pri-
vilages which, we, as Englishmen, and Protestants,
have engaged for these last three hundred years—
Since Bluff, king Hal, began to take a dislike to the
broad brimmed hat of the venerable Cardinal Wolsey,
and proclaimed himself an heretic; It is necessary I
say, for you, and all of you, to be perfect in your Lessons so as you may be able to verbly chastize this
saucy prelate, his newly made Cardinal Foolishman,
and the whole host of Puseites and protect our beloved
Queen, our Church, and our Constitution.

"Q. Now my boy can you tell me what is your
Name?

"A. B—— Protestant.

"*Q.* How came you by that name?

"*A.* At the time of Harry the stout, when Popery was in a galloping consumption the people protested against the surpremacy and instalence of the Pope; and his Colleges had struck deep at the hallow tree of superstition I gained the name of Protestant, and proud anf'I, and ever shall be to stick to it till the day of my death.

"*Let us say.*

"From all Cardinals whether wise or foolish. Oh! Queen Spare us.

"*Spare us, Oh Queen.*

"From the pleasure of the Rack, and the friendship of the kind hearted officers of the Inquisition. Oh! Johnny hear us.

"*Oh! Russell hear us.*

"From the comforts of being frisled like a devil'd kindney. Oh! Nosey save us.

"*Hear us Oh Arthur.*

"From such saucy Prelates, as Pope Pi-ass. Oh! Cumming's save us.

"*Save us good Cumming.*

"And let us have no more Burnings in smithfield, no more warm drinks in the shape of boiled oil, or, molten lead, and send the whole host of Pusyites along with the Pope, Cardinals to the top of mount Vesuvius there to dine off of hot lava, so that we may live in peace & shout long live our Queed, and No Popery!"

For some pitches the foregoing was sufficient, for a street auditory "hates too long a patter;" but where a favourable opportunity offered, easily tested by the pecuniary beginnings, the "Lesson of the Day" was given in addition, and was inserted after the second "Answer" in the foregoing parody, so preceding the "Let us say:"

"*The Lesson of the Day.*

"You seem an intelligent lad, so I think you are quite capable of Reading with me the Lessons for this day's service.

"Now the Lesson for the day is taken from all parts of the Book of Martyr's, beginning at just where you like.

"It was about the year 1835, that a certain renegade of the name of Pussy—I beg his pardon, I mean Pusey, like a snake who stung his master commenced crawling step by step, from the master; he was bound to serve to worship a puppet, arrayed in a spangle and tincel of a romish showman.

"And the pestelance that he shed around spread rapidly through the minds of many unworthy members of our established Church; even up to the present year, 1850, inasmuch that St Barnabus, of Pimlico, unable to see the truth by the aid of his occulars, mounted four pounds of long sixes in the mid-day, that he might see through the fog of his own folly, by which he was surrounded.

"And Pope Pi-ass the nineth taking advantage of the hubub, did create unto himself a Cardinal in the person of one Wiseman of Westminster.

"And Cardinal broadbrim claimed four counties in England as his dioces, and his master the Pope claimed as many more as his sees, but the people of England could not see that, so they declared aloud they would see them blowed first.

"So when Jack Russell heard of his most impudent intentions, he sent him a Letter saying it was the intention of the people of England never again to submit to their infamous mumerys for the burnings in Smithfield was still fresh in their memory.

"And behold great meetings were held in different parts of England where the Pope was burnt in effigy, like unto a Yarmouth Bloater, as a token of respect for him and his followers.

"And the citizens of London were stanch to a man, and assembled together in the Guildhall of our mighty City and shouted with stentarian lungs, long live the Queen and down with the Pope, the sound of which might have been heard even unto the vatican of Rome.

"And when his holyness the Pope heard that his power was set at naught, his nose became blue even as a bilberry with rage and declared Russell and Cummings or any who joined in the No Popery cry, should ever name the felisity of kissing his pious great toe.

"*Thus Endeth the Lesson.*"

In the course of my inquiries touching this subject I had more than once occasion to observe that an acute patterer had always a reason, or an excuse for anything. One quick-witted Irishman, whom I knew to be a Roman Catholic, was "working" a "patter against the Pope," (not the one I have given), and on my speaking to him on the subject, and saying that I supposed he did it for a living, he replied: "That's it then, sir. You're right, sir, yes. I work it just as a Catholic lawyer would plead against a Catholic paper for a libel on Protestants— though in his heart he knew the paper was right —and a Protestant lawyer would defend the libel hammer and tongs. Bless you, sir, you'll not find much more honour that way among us (laughing) than among them lawyers; not much." The readiness with which the sharpest of those men plead the doings not only of tradesmen, but of the learned and sacred professions, to justify themselves, is remarkable.

Sometimes a dialogue is of a satirical nature. One man told me that the "Conversation between Achilles and the Wellington Statue," of which I give the concluding moiety, was "among the best," (he meant for profit), "but no great thing." My informant was Achilles—or, as he pronounced it, Atchilees—and his mate was the statue, or "man on the horse." The two lines, in the couplet form, which precede every two paragraphs of dialogue, seem as if they represent the speakers wrongfully. The answer should be attributed, in each case, to Achilles.

"The hoarse voice it came from the statue of Achilles
And 'twas answer'd thus by the man on the horse.

"Little man of little mind havn't I now got iron blinds, and bomb-proof rails when danger assails, a cunning devised job, to keep out an unruly mob, with high and ambitious views and remarkable queer shoes; I say, Old Nakedness, I say, come and see my frontage over the way, but I believe you can't get out after ten!

"No, you're as near where you are as at Quatre Bras, I hear a great deal what the public think and feel, plain as the nose on your face, we're deemed a national disgrace; they grumble at your high-ness, and at my want of shyness, and say many unpleasant things of Ligny and Marchienne!

"The hoarse voice it came from the statue of Achilles
And 'twas answer'd thus by the man on the horse.

"Ah! its a few days since the Nive, where Soult found me all alive, and the grand toralloo I made at Bordeaux; wasn't I in a nice mess, when Boney left Elba and left no address, besides 150 other jobs with the chill off I could bring to view.

"But then people will say, poor unfortunate Ney, and that you were dancing at a ball, and not near Hogumont at all, and that the job of St. Helena might have been done rather cleaner, and it was a shameful go to send Sir Hudson Lowe, and that you took particular care of No. 1, at Waterloo.

"The hoarse voice it came from the statue of Achilles
And 'twas answer'd thus by the man on the horse.

"Why flog 'em and 'od 'rot em, who said ' Up Guards and at 'em !' and you know that nice treat I received in Downing Street, when hooted by a thousand or near, defended by an old grenadier, so no whopping I got, good luck to his old tin pot, oh! there's a deal of brass in me I'll allow.

" Its prophecied you'll break down, they're crying it about town, and many jokes are past, that you're brought to the scaffold at last, and they say I look black, because I've no shirt to my back, and its getting broad daylight, I vow!

" The hoarse voice it came from the statue of Achilles But 'twas answer'd thus by the man on the horse.
" II. V. HOOKER."

Of parodies other than the sort of compound of the Litany and other portions of the Church Service, which I have given, there are none in the streets—neither are there political duets. Such productions as parodies on popular songs, " Cab! cab! cab!" or " Trip! trip! trip!" are now almost always derived, for street-service, from the concert-rooms. But they relate more immediately to ballads, or street song; and not to patter.

OF " COCKS," ETC.

THESE " literary forgeries," if so they may be called, have already been alluded to under the head of the " Death and Fire Hunters," but it is necessary to give a short account of a few of the best and longest know nof those stereotyped; no new cocks, except for an occasion, have been printed for some years.

One of the stereotyped cocks is, the "Married Man Caught in a Trap." One man had known it sold " for years and years," and it served, he said, when there was any police report in the papers about sweethearts in coal-cellars, &c. The illustration embraces two compartments. In one a severe-looking female is assaulting a man, whose hat has been knocked off by the contents of a water-jug, which a very stout woman is pouring on his head from a window. In the other compartment, as if from an adjoining room, two women look on encouragingly. The subject matter, however, is in no accordance with the title or the embellishment. It is a love-letter from John S—n to his most "adorable Mary." He expresses the ardour of his passion, and then twits his adored with something beyond a flirtation with Robert E—, a " decoyer of female innocence." Placably overlooking this, however, John S—n continues : —

" My dearest angel consent to my request, and keep me no longer in suspense—nothing, on my part, shall ever be wanting to make you happy and comfortable. My apprenticeship will expire in four months from hence, when I intend to open a shop in the small ware line, and your abilities in dress-making and self-adjusting stay-maker, and the assistance of a few female mechanics, we shall be able to realize an independency."

" Many a turn in seductions talked about in the papers and not talked about nowhere," said one man, " has that slum served for, besides other things, such as love-letters, and confessions of a certain lady in this neighbourhood."

Another old cock is headed, " Extraordinary and Funny Doings in this Neighbourhood." The illustration is a young lady, in an evening dress, sitting with an open letter in her hand, on a sort of garden-seat, in what appears to be a churchyard. After a smart song, enforcing the

ever-neglected advice that people should " look at home and mind their own business," are two letters, the first from R. G.; the answer from S. H. M. The gentleman's epistle commences :—

" Madam,
" The love and tenderness I have hitherto expressed for you is false, and I now feel that my indifference towards you increases every day, and the more I see you the more you appear ridiculous in my eyes and contemptible— I feel inclined & in every respect disposed & determined to hate you. Believe me, I never had any inclination to offer you my hand."

The lady responds in a similar strain, and the twain appear very angry, until a foot-note offers an explanation : " By reading every other line of the above letters the true meaning will be found."

Of this class of cocks I need cite no other specimens, but pass on to one of another species — the " Cruel and Inhuman Murder Committed on the Body of Capt. Lawson." The illustration is a lady, wearing a coronet, stabbing a gentleman, in full dress, through the top button of his waistcoat. The narrative commences :—

" WITH surprise we have learned that this neighbourhood for a length of time was amazingly alarmed this day by a crowd of people carrying the body of Mr. James Lawless, to a doctor while streams of blood besmeared the way in such a manner that the cries of Murder re-echoed the sound of numerous voices. It appears that the cause of alarm, originated through a court-ship attended with a solemn promise of mar riage between him and miss Lucy Guard, a handsome young Lady of refined feelings with the intercourse of a superior enlightened mind she lived with her aunt who spared neither pain nor cost to improve the talents of miss G. those seven years past, since the death of her mother in Ludgate Hill, London, and bore a most excellent character until she got entangled by the delumps alcurement of Mr. L."

The writer then deplores Miss Guard's fall from virtue, and her desertion by her betrayer. " on account of her fortune being small." Capt. Lawson, or Mr. James Lawless, next woos a wealthy City maiden, and the banns are published. What follows seems to me to be a rather intricate detail :—

" We find that the intended bride learned that miss Guard, held certain promissory letters of his, and that she was determined to enter an action against him for a breach of promise, which moved clouded Eclipse over the extacy of the variable miss Lawless who knew that Miss G had Letters of his sufficient to substan- tiate her claims in a court."

Lawson visits Miss Guard to wheedle her out of his letters, but " she drew a large carving-knife and stabbed him under the left breast." At the latest account the man was left without hope of recovery, while " the valiant victress" was " ordered to submit to judicial decorum in the nineteenth year of her age." The murders and other atrocities for which this " cock" has been spoken, are — I was informed emphatically—a thundering lot!

I conclude with another cock, which may be called a narrative " on a subject," as we have " ballads on a subject " (afterwards to be de- scribed), but with this difference, that the narra- tive is fictitious, and the ballad must be founded

Murder of Captain Lawson.
(A "COCK.")

HINDOO TRACT SELLER.

[From a Daguerreotype by BEARD.]

on a real event, however embellished. The highest newspaper style, I was told, was aimed at. Part of the production reads as if it had done service during the Revolution of February, 1848.

"Express from Paris. Supposed Death of LOUIS NAPOLEON. We stop the press to announce, that Luis Napoleon has been assasinated, by some it is said he is shot dead, by others that he is only wounded in the right arm.

"We have most important intelligence from Paris. That capital is in a state of insurrection. The vivacious people, who have herefore defeated the goverment by paving-stones, have again taken up those missiles. On Tuesday the Ministers forbade the reform banquet, and the prefect of police published a proclamation warning the people to respect the laws, which he declared were violated, and he meant to enforce them. But the people dispised the proclamation and rejected his authority. They assembled in great multitudes round the Chambers of Deputies, and forced their way over the walls. They were attacked by the troops and dispersed, but, re-assembled in various quarters. They showed their hatred of M. Guizot by demolishing his windows and attempting to force an entrance into his hotel, but were again repulced by the troops. All the military in Paris, and all the National Guard, have been summoned to arms, and every preparation made on the part of the government to put down the people.

"The latter have raised barricades in various places, and have unpaved the streets, overturned omnibusses, and made preparations for a vigorous assault, or a protracted resistance.

"Five o'Closk—At this momont the Rue St. Honore is blockaded by a detachment dragoons, who fill the market-place near the Rue des Petits Champs, and are charging the people sword in hand, carriages full of deople are being taken to the hospitals.

"In fact the maddest excitement reigns throughout the capital.

"Half past Six.—During the above we have instituted enquiries at the Foreign office, they have not received any inteligence of the above report, if it has come, it must have been by pigeon express. We have not given the above in our columns with a view of its authenticity, any further information as soon as obtained shall be immediately announced to the public."

Of "Strawing."

I have already alluded to "strawing," which can hardly be described as quackery. It is rather a piece of mountebankery. Many a quack—confining the term to its most common signification, that of a "quack doctor"—has faith in the excellence of his own nostrums, and so proffers that which he believes to be curative: the strawer, however, sells what he *knows* is not what he represents it.

The strawer offers to *sell* any passer by in the streets a straw and to *give* the purchaser a paper which he *dares not* sell. Accordingly as he judges of the character of his audience, so he intimates that the paper is political, libellous, irreligious, or indecent.

I am told that as far back as twenty-five or twenty-six years, straws were sold, but only in the country, with leaves from the *Republican*, a periodical published by Carlile, then of Fleet-street, which had been prosecuted by the government; but it seems that the trade died away, and was little or hardly known again until the time of the trial of Queen Caroline, and then but sparingly. The straw sale reached its highest commercial pitch at the era of the Reform Bill. The most successful trader in the article is remembered among the patterers as "Jack Straw," who was oft enough represented to me as the original strawer. If I inquired further, the answer was: "He was the first in my time." This Jack Straw was, I am told, a fine-looking man, a natural son of Henry Hunt, the blacking manufacturer. He was described to me as an inveterate drunkard and a very reckless fellow. One old hand was certain that this man was Hunt's son, as he himself had "worked" with him, and was sometimes sent by him when he was "in trou-ble," or in any strait, to 32, Broadwall, Blackfriars, for assistance, which was usually rendered. (This was the place where Hunt's "Matchless Blacking" and "Roasted Corn" were vended.) Jack Straw's principal "pitch" was at Hyde Park Corner, "where," said the man whom I have mentioned as working with him, "he used to come it very strong against Old Nosey, the Hyde Park bully as he called him. To my knowledge he's made 10s., and he's made 15s. on a night. O, it didn't matter to him what he sold with his straws, religion or anything. There was no three-pennies (threepenny newspapers) then, and he had had a gentleman's education, and knew what to say, and so the straws went off like smoke." The articles which this man "durst not sell" were done up in paper, so that no one could very well peruse them on the spot, as a sort of stealth was implied. On my asking Jack Straw's co-worker if he had ever drank with him, "Drank with him!" he answered, "Yes, many a time. I've gone out and pattered, or chaunted, or anything, to get money to buy him two glasses of brandy—and good brandy was very dear then—before he could start, for he was all of a tremble until he had his medicine. If I couldn't get brandy, it was the best rum, 'cause he had all the tastes of a gentleman. Ah! he's been dead some years, sir, but where he died I don't know. I only heard of his death. He was a nice kindly fellow."

The *ruse* in respect of strawing is not remarkable for its originality. It was an old smuggler's trick to *sell* a sack and *give* the keg of contraband spirit placed within it and padded out with straw so as to resemble a sack of corn. The hawkers, prior to 1826, when Mr. Huskisson introduced changes into the Silk Laws, *gave* "real Ingy handkerchiefs" (sham) to a customer, and *sold* him a knot of tape or thread at 4s. The price of a true Bandana, then prohibited, and sold openly in the draper's shops, was about 8s. The East India Company imported about a million of Bandanas yearly; they were sold by auction for exportation to Hamburgh, &c., at about 4s. each, and were nearly all smuggled back again to England, and disposed of as I have stated.

It is not possible to give anything like statistics as to the money realised by strawing. A well-informed man calculated that when the trade was at its best, or from 1832 to 1836, there might be generally fifty working it in the country and twenty in London; they did not confine themselves, however, to strawing, but resorted to it only on favourable opportunities. Now there are none in London—their numbers diminished gradually—and very rarely any in the country.

OF THE SHAM INDECENT STREET-TRADE.

THIS is one of those callings which are at once repulsive and ludicrous; repulsive, when it is considered under what pretences the papers are sold, and ludicrous, when the disappointment of the gulled purchaser is contemplated.

I have mentioned that one of the allurements held out by the strawer was that his paper—the words used by Jack Straw—could "not be admitted into families." Those following the "sham indecent trade" for a time followed his example, and professed to sell straws and give away papers; but the London police became very observant of the sale of straws—more especially under the pretences alluded to—and it has, for the last ten years, been rarely pursued in the streets.

The plan now adopted is to sell the sealed packet itself, which the "patter" of the street-seller leads his auditors to believe to be some improper or scandalous publication. The packet is some coloured paper, in which is placed a portion of an old newspaper, a Christmas carol, a religious tract, or a slop-tailor's puff (given away in the streets for the behoof of another class of gulls). The enclosed paper is, however, never indecent.

From a man who had, not long ago, been in this trade, I had the following account. He was very anxious that nothing should be said which would lead to a knowledge that he was my informant. After having expressed his sorrow that he had ever been driven to this trade from distress, he proceeded to justify himself. He argued—and he was not an ignorant man—that there was neither common sense nor common justice in interfering with a man like him, who, "to earn a crust, pretended to sell what *shopkeepers*, that must pay church and all sorts of rates, sold without being molested." The word "shopkeepers" was uttered with a bitter emphasis. There are, or were, he continued, shops —for he seemed to know them all—and some of them had been carried on for years, in which shameless publications were not only sold, but exposed in the windows; and why should he be considered a greater offender than a shopkeeper, and be knocked about by the police? There are, or lately were, he said, such shops in the Strand, Fleet-street, a court off Ludgate-hill, Holborn, Drury-lane, Wych-street, the courts near Drury-lane Theatre, Haymarket, High-street, Bloomsbury, St. Martin's-court, May's buildings, and elsewhere, to say nothing of Holywell-street! Yet *he* must be interfered with!

[I may here remark, that I met with no street-sellers who did not disbelieve, or affect to disbelieve, that they were really meddled with by the police for obstructing the thoroughfare. They either hint, or plainly state, that they are removed solely to please the shop-keepers. Such was the reiterated opinion, real or pretended, of my present informant.]

I took a statement from this man, but do not care to dwell upon the subject. The trade, in the form I have described, had been carried on, he thought, for the last six years. At one time, 20 men followed it; at present, he believed there were only 6, and they worked only at intervals, and as opportunities offered: some going out, for instance, to sell almanacs or memorandum books, and, when they met with a favourable chance, offering their sealed packets. My informant's customers were principally boys, young men, and old gentlemen; but old gentlemen chiefly when the trade was new. This street-seller's "great gun," as he called it, was to make up packets, as closely resembling as he could accomplish it, those which were displayed in the windows of any of the shops I have alluded to. He would then station himself at some little distance from one of those shops, and, if possible, so as to encounter those who had stopped to study the contents of the window, and would represent—broadly enough, he admitted, when he dared—that he could sell for 6d. what was charged 5s., or 2s. 6d., or whatever price he had seen announced, "in that very neighbourhood." He sometimes ventured, also, to mutter something, unintelligibly, about the public being imposed upon! On one occasion, he took 6s. in the street in about two hours. On another evening he took 4s. 8d. in the street and was called aside by two old gentlemen, each of whom told him to come to an address given (at the West-end), and ask for such and such initials. To one he sold two packets for 2s.; to the other, five packets, each 1s.—or 11s. 8d. in one evening. The packets were in different coloured papers, and had the impressions of a large seal on red wax at the back; and he assured the old gents., as he called them, one of whom, he thought, was "silly," that they were all different. "And very likely," he said, chucklingly, "they were different; for they were made out of a lot of missionary tracts and old newspapers that I got dirt cheap at a 'waste' shop. I should like to have seen the old gent.'s face, as he opened his 5s. worth, one after another!" This trade, however, among old gentlemen, was prosperous for barely a month: "It got blown then, sir, and they wouldn't buy any more, except a very odd one."

This man—and he believed it was the same with all the others in the trade—never visited the public-houses, for a packet would soon have been opened and torn there, which, he said, people was ashamed to do in the public streets. As well as he could recollect, he had never sold a single packet to a girl or a woman. Drunken women of the town had occasionally made loud comments on his calling, and offered to purchase; but on such occasions, fearful of a disturbance, he always hurried away.

I have said that the straw trade is now confined to the country, and I give a specimen of the article vended there, by the patterer in the sham indecent trade. It was purchased of a man, who sold it folded in the form of a letter, and is addressed, "On Royal Service. By Express. Private. To Her Royal Highness, Victoria, Princess Royal. Kensington Palace, London. Entered at Stationer's Hall." The man who sold it had a wisp of straw round his neck, and introduced his wares with the following patter:

"I am well aware that many persons here present will say what an absurd idea—the idea of selling straws for a halfpenny each, when there are so many lying about the street; but the reason is simply this: I am not allowed by the authorities to sell these papers, so I give them away and sell my straws. There are a variety of figures in these papers for gentlemen; some in the bed, some on the bed, some under the bed." The following is a copy of the document thus sold:—

"Bachelors or Maidens, Husbands and Wives,
Will love each other and lead happy lives;
If both these Letters to read are inclined,
Secrets worth knowing therein they will find.

"Dated from the Duchy of Coburg.

"My Dearest Victoria,
Hiƨhuessəs' ɐnsʍeɹ,]bəƨ ləʌe ʇosnbscɹiqe ɯyseʃf
plepgəsof aʃʃeɔʇiou—ɐuxiouslyɐwɐiʇiug ʎonr royal-
ɹoʎaʅqɹipe aud fnʇnrəsovərəign, ʌeɹy mɐuʎaud ʅiʌiug
snrəd ou mʎpɹinɔeʅy qouour, ʇʮaʇI ʍiʅl aʍaɹdʇo ɯy
ɯeɟo ʇhɐt euvɪepstɐtion oʃqeiuƨʇqy husqaud, rəsʇas-
ɪnɔhɹisʇeudom; aud ʍhənʇhon ʮast doiƨnədʇo əxʮalt
bəudep kueəs, ʇo ɟaʌonr ɯʎsnit, aqoʌe ɐnyoʇʮer drɪnce
oɟ aʅl ʮeirsʇo ɐbɹiʇisʮdɪadəm—I iɯpʅoɹeʇhəe ou uʎ
amɪɐbʅe oɟ Eugʅaup'sdɹiuɔessəs—ɐnd tqə ɯosʇ ʌiɹʇuons
quiyʮiuisəʅʇ ʍiʇhiu tʮy oʍndoʍuʎ dlnmɐƨe! Mosʇ
əherɯiug uoʇes, audʍiʇh ɟlnʇʇeɹiug ʍiugswisʮes ʇo
ʍʮo ʅiʞe ɐbɪrpoɟ perɐdɪse, ɪsɔalʅiuƨtʮeəto ʅisʇeu ʇo his
ɔome ʇo ɯyʅougiuƨ aɹaɯs—ɪt ɪs oulʎʇʮʎ peɐr Aʅqərt,
ɐmɪaqlə Vɪcʇoɹɪɐ, theɯosʇ duɹe ɐnp sdoʇləss oɟ virƨius,
fnʇnrɪʇʎ,audɔoutɪnne ʇo prəaɯoɟ loʌə ɐnptʮeə! Ɯy
sʮaʅqe ənɔʮanʇep wɪʇʮʇʮe mosʇ bəantɪfnl visiousoɟ
ɯənt oɟ ʇhɐt qalmʎsʅeəd I hɐvəbəen ʅouƨ ʍɐntiuƨ, I
nom sʅeəpʅess ɔonch,aud resiniuƨ ɯysouʅ ʇo tʮeenjoʎ-
wonnps—⅃ʮenʍiʅl I dlɐasɐuʇʅʎ rədose ɯysəʅɟ ou ɯʎ
bɪtcoɯe ɐnp ponr tʮy ʮeɐʅiuƨ bɐlsɐmiuʇo ɯʎ suɐɹtiug
ʌəuʅysɐmɐriten, pass uoʇaʍaʎ ɟrom ʇʮyɐdoɹiug ɐlqeɹʇ;
iugʅovə! Ⅎhənʮasʇeu ɯy ƨloɹiousəhərnb—ʇhou həa-
wʮoʅeqopy ɪs qeiuƨcousnmepin tʮeɟurnɐsə oɟ eʌeɹlɐsʇ-
tɐʅisəd ʍiʇhʌɐriəd aud ɔoufʅiɔtiuƨ eɯoʇious, aud mʎ
ɟusəto po ʇhəiɹoʃʃicə; əvəɹʎ oueoɟ ɯy ɯeɯbərsɐrə ʇɐn-
fɪrə, ɯyɟeəʇ sʇuɯbʅes—ʎeɐ, mʎ ɐrɯs audɯy ləgs ɹe-
ɯy sənsəsʍaudər, ɯy ʮairsʇauds ou eup, mʎ ʮeɐd isou
əlɐsdtʮeəiu ɯyaɹms—Mʎ qosomʮeɐvəs, ɯy ʮeaɹʇpɐnʇs,
tʮylovəlʎ forɯ, audʅoug for ʇhəhɐpdy ʮonr wʮeuʅ sʮall
royɐlqiƨhuess—ɯy sʍeeʇestauƨeʅ, oʮ! ʮow I po apore
doʍuʇo tʮe pəʅiƨhʇfuʅtɐsk oɟ ʍriʇiuƨa loʌe ʅəʇʇeɹto ʇhʎ
— — nəvərpip I eujoʎgɹɐɐtər qʅiss, ʇhauwʮeuI sɐʇ

"Your adored Lover,
"ALBERT,
"Prince of Coburg."

On the back of this page is the following cool initiation of the purchaser into the mysteries of the epistle:

"Directions for the purchasers to understand the *Royal Love Letters*, and showing them how to practise the art of Secret Letter Writing:—

"Proceed to lay open 'Albert's Letter' by the side of 'Victoria's,' and having done so, then look carefully down them until you have come to a word at the left hand corner, near the end of each Letter, having two marks thus — —, when you must commence with that word, and read from left to right after you have turned them bottom upwards before a looking glass so that you may peruse the copy reflected therein. But you must notice, throughout all the words every other letter is upside down, also every other word single; but the next two words being purposely joined together, therefore they are double; and in addition to those letters placed upside down, makes it more mysterious in the reading. The reader is recommended to copy each word in writing, when he will be able to read the letters forward, and after a little practice he can soon learn to form all his words in the same curious manner, when he wants to write a 'secret letter.'

"Be sure when holding it up side down before a looking-glass, that the light of a candle, is placed between then by the reflection it will show much plainer, and be sooner discovered.

"If you intend to practise a *Joke* and make it answer the purpose of a Valentine, write what you think necessary on the adjoining *blank page*; then post it, with the superscription filled up in this manner:—After the word To, *write the name and address of the party* also place the word FROM *before* 'VICTORIA'S' name: then the address on the outside of this letter will read somewhat after the following fashion:—To Mr. or Mrs. so and so, (with the number if any,) in such and such a street: at the same time your letter will appear as if it came from Royalty.

"N.B. You must first buy both the letters, as the other letter is an answer to this one; and because, without the reader has got both letters, he will not have the secrets perfect."

Notwithstanding the injunction to buy *both* letters, and the seeming necessity of having both to understand the "directions," the patterer was selling only the one I have given.

That the trade in sham indecent publications was, at one time, very considerable, and was not unobserved by those who watch, as it is called, "the signs of the times," is shown by the circumstance that the Anti-Corn-Law League paper, called the *Bread Basket*, could only be got off by being done up in a sealed packet, and sold by patterers as a pretended improper work.

The really indecent trade will be described hereafter.

For a month my informant thought he had cleared *35s.* a week; for another month, *20s.*; and as an average, since that time, from *5s.* to *7s. 6d.* weekly, until he discontinued the trade. It is very seldom practised, unless in the evening, and perhaps only one street-seller depends entirely upon it.

Supposing that 6 men last year each cleared *6s.* weekly, we find upwards of *93l.* expended yearly in the streets on this rubbish.

The capital required to start in the business is *6d.* or *1s.*, to be expended in paper, paste, and sometimes sealing-wax.

Of Religious Tract Sellers.

The sellers of religious tracts are now, I am informed, at the least, about 50, but they were at one time, far more numerous. When penny books were few and very small, religious tracts were by far the cheapest things in print. It is common, moreover, for a religious society, or an individual, to give a poor person, children especially, tracts for sale. A great many tract sellers, from 25 to 35 years ago, were, or pretended to be, maimed old soldiers or sailors. The traffic is now in the hands of what may be called an anomalous body of men. More than one half of the tract sellers are foreigners, such as Malays, Hindoos, and Negros. Of them, some cannot speak English, and some—who earn a spare subsistence by selling Christian tracts — are Mahometans, or worshippers of Bramah! The man whose portrait supplies the daguerreotyped illustration of this number is unable to speak a word of English, and the absence of an interpreter, through some accident, prevented his statement being taken at the time appointed. I shall give it, however, with the necessary details on the subject, under another head.

With some men and boys, I am informed, tract-selling is but a pretext for begging.

Of a Benefit Society of Patterers.

In the course of my inquiries, I received an account of an effort made by a body of these people to provide against sickness,—a step so clearly in the right direction, and perhaps so little to be expected from the habits of the class, that I feel bound to notice it. It was called the " Street-sellers' Society;" but as nearly all the *bonâ-fide* members (or those who sought benefit from its funds) were patterers in paper, or ballad-singers, I can most appropriately notice their proceedings here.

The society " sprung up accidental," as it was expressed to me. A few paper-workers were conversing of the desirableness of such an institution, and one of the body suggested a benefit club, which it was at once determined to establish. It was accordingly established between six and seven years ago, and was carried on for about four years. The members varied in number from 40 to 50; but of a proportion of 40, as many as 18 might be tradesmen who were interested in the street-trade, either in supplying the articles in demand for it, or from keeping public-houses resorted to by the fraternity, or any such motive, or who were merely curious to mix in such society. Mr. C—— was conductor; Mr. J. H—— (a poet, and the writer of " Black Bess," " the Demon of the Sea," and other things which " took" in the streets), secretary; and a well-known patterer was under-conductor, with which office was mixed up the rather onerous duties of a kind of master of the ceremonies on meeting-nights. None of the officers were paid.

The subscription was 2*d.* a week, and meetings of the members were held once a week. Each member, not an officer, paid ½*d.* for admission to the fund, and could introduce a visitor, who also paid ½*d.* No charge was made for the use of the club-room (in a public-house), which was entirely in the control of the members. Every one using bad language, or behaving improperly, was fined ½*d.*, and on a second offence was ejected, and sometimes, if the misbehaviour was gross, on the first. Any one called upon to sing, and refusing, or being

unable, was fined ½*d.*, and was liable to be called upon again, and pay another fine. A visitor sometimes, instead of ½*d.*, offered 6*d.* when fined; but this was not accepted,—only ½*d.* could be received. The members' wives could and did often accompany their husbands to the meetings; but women of the town, whether introduced by members or not, were not permitted to remain. " They found their way in a few times," said the man who was under-conductor to me, " but I managed to work them out without any bother, and without insulting them—God forbid ! "

The assistance given was 5*s.* weekly to sick members, who were not in arrear in their subscriptions. If the man had a family to support, a gathering was made for him, in addition to his weekly allowance,—for the members were averse to " distress the box" (fund). There was no allowance for the burial of a member, but a gathering took place, and perhaps a raffle, to raise funds for a wake (sometimes) and an interment ; and during the existence of the society, three members, I was told, were buried that way " comfortably." The subscriptions were paid up regularly enough ; " indeed," said a member to me, " if a man earned anything, his mates knew of it : we all know how the cat jumps that way, so he must either pay or be scratched." The members not unfrequently lent each other money to pay up their subscriptions. Fashionable young " swells," I was told, often visited the house, and stayed till 3 or 4 in the morning, but were very seldom in the club-room, which was closed regularly at 12. After that hour, the " swells" who were bent upon seeing life —(and they are a class whom the patterers, on all such occasions, not so very unreasonably consider " fair game " for bamboozling)—could enjoy the society congenial to their tastes or gratifying to their curiosity. On one occasion two policemen were among the visitors, and were on friendly terms enough with the members, some of whom they had seen before.

From the beginning there seems to have been a distrust of one another among the members, but a distrust not invincible or the club would never have been formed. Instead of the " box," or fund (the money being deposited in a box), being allowed to accumulate, so that an investment might be realised, available for any emergency, the fund was divided among the members quarterly, and then the subscription went on anew. The payments, however, fell off. The calling of the members was precarious, their absence in the country was frequent, and so the society ceased to exist, but the members were satisfied that every thing was done honourably.

The purpose to which the funds, on a quarterly division, were devoted, was one not confined to such men as the patterers—to a supper. " None of your light suppers, sir," said a member ; " not by no means. And we were too fly to send anybody to market but ourselves. We used to go to Leadenhall, and buy a cut off a sirloin, which was roasted prime, and smelt like a angel. But not so often, for its a dear jint, the bones is heavy. One of the favouritest jints was a boiled leg of mutton with caper trimmings. That *is* a good supper,—I believe you, my hero."

OF THE ABODES, TRICKS, MARRIAGE, CHA-
RACTER, AND CHARACTERISTICS OF THE
DIFFERENT GRADES OF PATTERERS.

HAVING now giving an account of those who may be called the literary patterers (proper), or at any rate of those who do not deem it vain so to account themselves, because they "work paper," I proceed to adduce an account of the different grades of patterers generally, for patter has almost as many divisions as literature. There is patter pathetic, as from beggars; bouncing, to puff off anything of little or no value; comic, as by the clowns; descriptive, as in the cases where the vendor describes, however ornately, what he really sells; religious, as occasionally by the vendors of tracts; *real patter* (as it is understood by the profession) to make a thing believed to be what it is not; classical, as in the case of the sale of stenographic cards, &c.; and sporting, as in race cards.

The pattering tribe is by no means confined to the traffic in paper, though it may be the principal calling as regards the acuteness of its professors. Among these street-folk are the running and standing patterers (or stationers as they are sometimes, but rarely, styled)—and in these are included, the Death and Fire Hunters of whom I have spoken; Chaunters; Second Edition-sellers; Reciters; Conundrum-sellers; Board-workers; Strawers; Sellers of (Sham) Indecent Publications; Street Auctioneers; Cheap Jacks; Mountebanks (quacks); Clowns; the various classes of Showmen; Jugglers; Conjurors; Ring-sellers for wagers; Sovereign-sellers; Corn-curers; Grease-removers; French-polishers; Blacking-sellers; Nostrum-vendors; Fortune-tellers; Oratorical-beggars; Turnpike-sailors; the classes of Lurkers; Stenographic Card-sellers, and the Vendors of Race-cards or lists.

The following accounts have been written for me by the same gentleman who has already described the Religion, Morals, &c., of patterers. He has for some years resided among the class, and has pursued a street calling for his existence. What I have already said of his opportunities of personal observation and of dispassionate judgment I need not iterate.

"I wish," says the writer in question, "in the disclosures I am now about to make concerning the patterers generally, to *do more* than merely put the public on their guard. I take no cruel delight in dragging forth the follies of my fellow-men. Before I have done with my subject, I hope to draw forth and exhibit some of the latent virtues of the class under notice, many of whom I know to sigh in secret over that *one* imprudent step (whatever its descrip-

tion), which has furnished the censorious with a weapon they have been but too ready to wield. The first thing for me to do is to give a glance at the *habitations* of these outcasts, and to set forth their usual conduct, opinions, conversation and amusements. As London (including the ten mile circle), is the head quarters of lodging-house life, and least known, because most crowded, I shall lift the veil which shrouds the vagrant hovel where the patterer usually resides.

"As there are many individuals in lodging-houses who are not regular patterers or professional vagrants, being rather, as they term themselves, 'travellers' (or tramps), so there are multitudes who do *not* inhabit such houses who really belong to the fraternity, pattering, or vagrant. Of these some take up their abode in what they call 'flatty-kens,' that is, houses the landlord of which is not 'awake' or 'fly' to the 'moves' and dodges of the trade; others resort to the regular 'padding-kens,' or houses of call for vagabonds; while others—and especially those who have families—live constantly in furnished rooms, and have little intercourse with the 'regular' travellers, tramps, or wanderers.

"The medium houses the London vagrant haunts, (for I have no wish to go to extremes either way,) are probably in Westminster, and perhaps the fairest 'model' of the '*monkry*' is the house in Orchard-street—once the residence of royalty—which has been kept and conducted for half a century by the veteran who some fifty years ago was the *only* man who amused the population with that well-known ditty,

'If I'd as much money as I could tell,
I would not cry young lambs to sell.'

Mister (for that is the old man's title) still manufactures lambs, but seldom goes out himself; his sons (obedient and exemplary young men) take the toys into the country, and dispose of them at fairs and markets. The wife of this man is a woman of some beauty and good sound sense, but far too credulous for the position of which she is the mistress.

"So much for the establishment. I have now to deal with the inmates.

"No one could be long an inmate of Mr. ——'s without discerning in the motley group persons who had seen better days, and, seated on the same bench, persons who are 'seeing' the best days they *ever* saw. When I took up my abode in the house under consideration, I was struck by the appearance of a middle-aged lady-like woman, a native of Worcester, bred to the glove trade, and brought up in the lap of plenty, and under the high sanction of religious principle. She had evidently some source of mental anguish. I believe it was the conduct of her husband, by whom she had been deserted, and who was living with a woman to whom, it is said, the wife had shown much kindness. By her sat a giant in size, and candour demands that I should say a 'giant in sin.' When Navy Jem, as he is called, used to *work* for his living (it was a long while ago) he drove a barrow at the formation of the Great Western Railway. At present the man lies in bed till mid-day, and when he makes his appearance in the kitchen,

'The very kittens on the hearth
They dare not even play.'

His breakfast embraces all the good things of the season. He divides his delicacies with a silver fork—where did he get it? The mode in which this man obtains a livelihood is at once a mixture and a mystery. His prevailing plan is to waylay gentlemen in the decline of life, and to extort money by threats of accusation and exposure, to which I can do no more than allude. His wife, a notorious shoplifter, is now for the third time 'expiating her offences' in Coldbath-fields.

"Next to Navy Jem may be perceived a little stunted woman, of pretended Scotch, but really Irish extraction, whose husband has died in the hospital for consumption at least as many times as the hero of Waterloo has seen engagements. At last the man *did* die, and his widow has been collecting money to bury him for eight years past, but has not yet secured the required sum. This woman, whose name I never knew, has a boy and a girl; to the former she is very kind, the latter she beats without mercy, always before breakfast, and with such (almost) unvaried punctuality that her brother will sometimes whisper (after saying grace), 'Mother, has our Poll had her licks yet?'

"Among the records of mortality lately before the public, is the account of a notorious woman, who was found suffocated in a stagnant pool, whether from suicide or accident it was impossible to determine. She had been in every hospital in town and country, suffering from a disease, entirely self-procured. She applied strong acids to wounds previously punctured with a pin, and so caused her body to present one mass of sores. She was deemed incurable by the hospital doctors, and liberal collections were made for her among the benevolent in various places. The trick, however, was ultimately discovered, and the failure of her plan (added to the bad state of health to which her bodily injuries had gradually led) preyed upon her mind and hastened her death.

"This woman had been the paramour of 'Peter the crossing-sweeper,' a man who for years went about showing similar wounds, which he pretended had been inflicted while fighting in the Spanish Legion—though, truth to say, he had never been nearer Spain than Liverpool is to New York. He had followed the 'monkry' from a child, and chiefly, since manhood, as a 'broken-down weaver from Leicester,' and after singing through every one of the provinces 'We've got no work to do,' he scraped acquaintance with a 'school of shallow coves;' that is, men who go about half-naked, telling frightful tales about ship-

wrecks, hair-breadth escapes from houses on fire, and such like aqueous and igneous calamities. By these Peter was initiated into the 'scaldrum dodge,' or the art of burning the body with a mixture of acids and gunpowder, so as to suit the hues and complexions of the accident to be deplored. Such persons hold every morning a 'committee of ways and means,' according to whose decision the movements of the day are carried out. Sometimes when on their country rounds, they go singly up to the houses of the gentry and wealthy farmers, begging shirts, which they hide in hedges while they go to another house and beg a similar article. Sometimes they go in crowds, to the number of from twelve to twenty; they are most successful when the 'swell' is not at home; if they can meet with the 'Burerk' (Mistress), or the young ladies, they 'put it on them for dunnage' (beg a stock of general clothing), flattering their victims first and frightening them afterwards. A friend of mine was present in a lodging-house in Plymouth, when a school of the shallow coves returned from their day's work with *six suits of clothes, and twenty-seven shirts, besides children's apparel and shoes,* (all of which were sold to a broker in the same street), and, besides these, the donations in money received amounted to 4s. 4d. a man.

"At this enterprise 'Peter' continued several years, but—to use his own words—'everything has but a time,' the country got 'dead' to him, and people got 'fly' to the 'shallow brigade;' so Peter came up to London to 'try his hand at something else.' Housed in the domicile of 'Sayer the barber,' who has enriched himself by beer-shops and lodging-house-keeping, to the tune it is said of 20,000l., Peter amused the 'travellers' of Wentworth-street, Whitechapel, with recitals of what he had seen and done. Here a profligate, but rather intelligent man, who had really been in the service of the Queen of Spain, gave him an old red jacket, and with it such instructions as equipped him for the imposition. One sleeve of this jacket usually hung loosely by his side, while the arm it should have covered was exposed naked, and to all appearance withered. His rule was to keep silence till a crowd assembled around him, when he began to '*patter*' to them to the following effect: 'Ladies and gentlemen, it is with feelings of no common reluctance that I stand before you at this time; but although I am not without *feelings*, I am totally without friends, and frequently without food. This wound (showing his disfigured arm) I received in the service of the Queen of Spain, and I have many more on different parts of my person. I received a little praise for my brave conduct, but not a penny of pension, and here I am (there's no deception you see) ill in health—poor in pocket, and exposed without proper nourishment to wind and weather—the cold is blowing through me till I am almost perished.' His '*Doxy*' stood by and received the 'voluntary contributions' of the audience in a soldier's cap, which our hero emptied into his pocket, and after snivelling out his thanks, departed to renew the exhibition in the nearest available thoroughfare. Peter boasted that he could make on an average fifteen of these pitches a day, and as the proceeds were estimated at something considerable in each pitch (he has been known to take as much as half-a-crown in pence at one standing), he was able to sport his figure at Astley's in the evening—to eat 'spring lamb,' and when reeling home under the influence of whiskey, to entertain the peaceful inhabitants with the music of—'We won't go home till morning————'

"Whether the *game* got *stale*, or Peter became honest, is beyond the purport of my communication to settle. If any reader, however, should make his purchases at the puffing fish-monger's in Lombard-street, they may find Peter now pursuing the more honest occupation of sweeping the crossing, by the church of St. Gabriel, Fenchurch-street.

"Among the most famous of the 'lurking patterers' was 'Captain Moody,' the son of poor but honest parents in the county of Cornwall, who died during his boyhood, leaving him to the custody of a maiden aunt. This lady soon, and not without reason, got tired of her incorrigible charge. Young Moody was apprenticed successively to three trades, and wanted not ability to become expert in any of them, but having occasional interviews with some of the gipsey tribe, and hearing from themselves of their wonderful achievements, he left the sober walks of life and joined this vagrant fraternity.

"His new position, however, was attractive only while it was novel. Moody, who had received a fair education, soon became disgusted with the coarseness and vulgarity of his associates. At the solicitation of a neighbouring clergyman, he was restored to the friendship of his aunt, who had soon sad reason to regret that her compassion had got the better of her prudence; for one Sunday afternoon, while she was absent at church, young Moody who had pleaded indisposition and so obtained permission to stay at home, decamped (after dispatching the servant to the town, a mile distant, to fetch the doctor) in the meantime, emptying his aunt's 'safety cupboard' of a couple of gold watches and £72 in cash and country notes.

"His roving disposition then induced him to try the sea, and the knowledge he obtained during several voyages fitted him for those maritime frauds which got him the name of 'Captain Moody, the lurker.' The frauds of this person are well known, and often recounted with great admiration among the pattering fraternity. On one occasion, the principal butcher in Gosport was summoned to meet a gentleman at an hotel. The *Louisa*, a brig, had just arrived at Portsmouth, the captain's name was Young, and this gentleman Moody personated for the time being. 'I have occasion,' said he

to the butcher, 'for an additional supply of beef for the *Louisa;* I have heard you spoken of by Captain Harrison' (whom Moody knew to be an old friend of the butcher's), 'and I have thus given you the preference. I want a bullock, cut up in 12 lb. pieces; it must be on board by three to-morrow.' The price was agreed upon, and the captain threw down a few sovereigns in payment, but, of course, discovered that he had not gold enough to cover the whole amount, so he proposed to give him a cheque he had just received from Captain Harrison for £100, and the butcher could give him the difference. The tradesman was nothing loth, for a cheque upon 'Vallance, Mills, and West,' with Captain Harrison's signature, was reckoned equal to money any day, and so the butcher considered the one he had received, until the next morning, when the draft and the order proved to be forgeries. The culprit was, of course, nowhere to be found, nor, indeed, heard of till two years after, when he had removed the scene of his depredations to Liverpool.

"In that port he had a colleague, a man whose manners and appearance were equally prepossessing. Moody sent his 'pal' into a jeweller's shop, near the corner of Lord-street, who there purchased a small gold seal, paid for it, and took his leave. Immediately afterwards, Moody entered the shop under evident excitement, declaring that he had seen the person, who had just left the shop secrete two, if not three, seals up his coat-sleeve; adding, that the fellow had just gone through the Exchange, and that if the jeweller were quick he would be sure to catch him. The jeweller ran out without his hat, leaving his kind friend in charge of the shop, and soon returned with the supposed criminal in his custody. The 'captain,' however, in the mean time, had decamped, taking with him a tray from the window, containing precious materials to the value of 300*l.*

"At another time, the 'captain' prepared a document, setting forth 'losses in the Baltic trade,' and a dismal variety of disasters; and concluding with a melancholy shipwreck, which had really taken place just about that time in the German Ocean. With this he travelled over great part of Scotland, and with almost unprecedented success. Journeying near the Frith of Forth, he paid a visit to Lord Dalmeny—a nobleman of great benevolence—who had read the account of the shipwreck in the local journals, and wondered that the petition was not signed by influential persons *on the spot;* and, somewhat suspicious of the reality of the 'captain's' identity, placed a terrestrial globe before him, and begged to be shown 'in what latitude he was cast away.' The awkwardness with which Moody handled the globe showed that he was 'out of *his* latitude' altogether. His lordship thereupon committed the document to the flames, but generously gave the 'captain' a sovereign and some good advice; the former he appropriated at the nearest public-house, of the latter he never made the least use.

"Old, and worn out by excesses and imprisonment, he subsists now by 'sitting pad' about the suburban pavements; and when, on a recent evening, he was recognised in a low public-house in Deptford, he was heard to say, with a sigh: 'Ah! once I could "screeve a fakement" (write a petition) or "cooper a monekur" (forge a signature) with any man alive, and my heart's game now; but I'm old and asthmatic, and got the rheumatis, so that I ain't worth a d—n.'

"'The Lady Lurker.'—Of this person very little is known, and *that* little, it is said, makes her an object of pity. Her father was a dissenting minister in Bedfordshire. She has been twice married; her first husband was a schoolmaster at Hackney, and nephew of a famous divine who wrote a Commentary on the Bible, and was chaplain to George III. She afterwards married a physician in Cambridgeshire (a Dr. S——), who is alleged to have treated her ill, and even to have attempted to poison her. She has no children; and, since the death of her husband, has passed through various grades, till she is now a cadger. She dresses becomingly in black, and sends in her card (Mrs. Dr. S——) to the houses whose occupants are known, or supposed, to be charitable. She talks with them for a certain time, and then draws forth a few boxes of lucifers, which, she says, she is compelled to sell for her living. These lucifers are merely excuses, of course, for begging; still, nothing is known to have ever transpired in her behaviour wholly unworthy of a distressed gentlewoman. She lives in private lodgings."

I continue the account of these habitations, and of their wretched occupants, from the pen of the same gentleman whose vicissitudes (partly self-procured) led him to several years' acquaintance with the subject.

"Padding-kens" (lodging-houses) in the country are certainly preferable abodes to those of St. Giles's, Westminster, or Whitechapel; but in country as in town, their condition is extremely filthy and disgusting; many of them are scarcely ever washed, and as to sweeping, once a week is miraculous. In most cases they swarm with vermin, and, except where their position is very airy, the ventilation is imperfect, and frequent sickness the necessary result. It is a matter of surprise that the nobility, clergy, and gentry of the realm should permit the existence of such horrid dwellings.

"I think," continues my informant, "that the majority of these poor wretches are without even the idea of respectability or 'home comforts,'—many of them must be ranked among the worst of our population. Some, who could live elsewhere, prefer these wretched abodes, because they answer various evil purposes. With beggars, patterers, hawkers, tramps, and vendors of their own manufacture, are mingled thieves, women of easy virtue, and men of no virtue at all; a few, and by far the smallest portion, are persons who once filled posts of credit and affluence, but whom bankruptcy, want of em-ployment, or sickness has driven to these dismal retreats. The vast majority of London vagrants take their summer vacation in the country, and the 'dodges' of both are interchanged, and every new 'move' circulates in almost no time.

"I will endeavour to sketch a few of the most renowned 'performers' on this theatre of action. By far the most illustrious is 'Nicholas A——,' an ame known to the whole cadging fraternity as a *real* descendant from Bamfylde Moore Carew, and the 'prince of lurkers' and patterers for thirty years past. This man owes much of his success to his confessedly imposing appearance, and many of his escapes to the known respectability of his connections. His father—yet alive—is a retired captain in the Royal Navy, a gentleman of good private property, and one of her Majesty's justices of peace for the county of Devon—the southern extremity of which was the birth-place of Nicholas. But little is known of his early days. He went to school at Tavistock, where he received a good education, and began life by cheating his schoolfellows.

"The foolish fondness of an indulgent mother, and some want of firmness in paternal discipline, accelerated the growth of every weed of infamy in Nicholas, and baffled every experiment, by sea and land, to 'set' him up in life.

"Scarcely was he out of his teens, when he honoured the sister country with his visits and his depredations. About the centre of Sackville-street, Dublin, there lived a wealthy silversmith of the name of Wise. Into his shop (accompanied by one of his *pals* in livery) went Nicholas, whose gentlemanly exterior, as I have already hinted, would disarm suspicion in a stranger.

"'Good morning sir, is your name Wise?—Yes, sir.—Well, that is *my* name.—Indeed, of the English family, I suppose?—Yes, sir, East Kent.—Oh, indeed! related to 'the ladies of Leeds Castle, I presume?—I have the honour to be their brother.—James, is your name James or John?—Neither, sir, it is Jacob.—Oh, indeed! a very ancient name.—Well, I have occasion to give a party at the Corn Exchange Tavern, and I want a little plate on hire, can you supply me?'—A very polite affirmative settled this part of the business. Plate to the amount of 150*l.* was selected and arranged, when Nicholas discovered that his pocket-book was at home (to complete the deception, his right arm was in a sling). 'Will you, Mr. Wise (you see my infirmity), write me a few lines?—With the greatest pleasure,' was the silversmith's reply.—'Well, let me see. *My dear, do not be surprised at this; I want 150l., or all the money you can send, per bearer; I will explain at dinner-time. J. Wise.*'

"'Now, John, take this to your mistress, and be quick.' As John was not very hasty in his return, Nicholas went to look for him, leaving a strict injunction that the plate should be sent to the Corn Exchange Tavern, as soon as the deposit was received. This happened at eleven in the forenoon—the clock struck five and no return of either the master or the man.

"The jeweller left a message with his apprentice, and went home to his dinner. He was met at the door of his suburban villa by his 'better half,' who wondered what made him so late, and wished to know the nature of the exigency which had caused him to send home for so much money? The good man's perplexity was at an end when he saw his own handwriting on the note; and every means within the range of constabulary vigilance was taken to capture the offender, but Nicholas and his servant got clear off.

"This man's ingenuity was then taxed as to the next move, so he thought it expedient to tax somebody else. He went with his 'pal' to a miscellaneous repository, where they bought a couple of old ledgers—useful only as waste paper, a bag to hold money, two ink-bottles, &c. Thus equipped, they waited on the farmers of the district, and exhibited a 'fakement,' setting forth parliamentary authority for imposing a tax upon the geese! They succeeded to admiration, and weeks elapsed before the hoax was discovered. The coolness of thus assuming legislatorial functions, and being, at the same time, the executive power, has rarely been equalled.

"There is an old proverb, that 'It is an ill wind that blows nobody good.' The gallant 'captain' was domiciled at a lodging-house in Gainsborough, Lincolnshire, where he found all the lodgers complaining of the badness of the times—most of them were makers of nets. He sallied forth to all the general shops, and left his (fictitious) 'captain' card at each, with an order for an unusual number of nets. This 'dodge' gave a week's work to at least twenty poor people; but whether the shopkeepers were 'caught in a net,' or the articles were paid for and removed by the 'captain,' or whether it was a piece of pastime on his part, I did not stay long enough to ascertain.

"Nicholas A—— is now in his sixty-second year, a perfect hypochondriac. On his own authority—and it is, no doubt, too true—he has been 'lurking' on every conceivable system, from forging a bill of exchange down to 'maundering on the fly,' for the greater part of his life; and, excepting the 'hundred and thirteen times' he has been in provincial jails, society has endured the scourge of his deceptions for a quarter of a century at least. He now lives with a young prostitute in Portsmouth, and contributes to her wretched earnings an allowance of 5s. a week, paid to him by the attorney of a distant and disgusted relative."

The writer of this account was himself two whole years on the "monkry," before he saw a lodging-house for tramps; and the first he ever saw was one well-known to every patterer in Christendom, and whose fame he says is "gone out into all lands," for its wayfaring inmates are very proud of its popularity.

"It may be as well," writes the informant in question, "before submitting the following account, to state that there are other, and more elaborate marks—the hieroglyphics of tramping—than those already given. I will accordingly explain them.

"Two hawkers (pals) go together, but separate when they enter a village, one taking each side of the road, and selling different things; and, so as to inform each other as to the character of the people at whose houses they call, they chalk certain marks on their door-posts:

"⌒ means 'Go on. I have called here; don't you call—it's no go.'

"⌒+ means 'Stop—you may call here; they want' (for instance) 'what you sell, though not what I sell;' or else, 'They had no change when I was there, but may have it now;' or, 'If they don't buy, at least they'll treat you civilly.'

"⋗ on a corner-house, or a sign-post, means, 'I went this way;' or 'Go on in this direction.'

"⋗+ on a corner-house, or sign-post, means 'Stop—don't go any further in this direction.'

"⊙ as before explained, means 'danger.'

"Like many other young men, I had lived above my income, and, too proud to crave parental forgiveness, had thrown off the bonds of authority for a life of adventure. I was now homeless upon the world. With a body capable of either exertion or fatigue, and a heart not easily terrified by danger, I endured rather than enjoyed my itinerant position. I sold small articles of Tunbridge ware, perfumery, &c.. &c., and by 'munging' (begging) over them—sometimes in Latin—got a better living than I expected, or probably deserved. I was always of temperate and rather abstemious habits, but ignorant of the haunts of other wanderers, (whom I saw in dozens every day upon every road, and every conceivable pursuit) I took up my nightly quarters at a sort of third-rate public-houses, and supposed that my contemporaries did the same. How long my ignorance might have continued (if left to myself) I can hardly determine; an adventure at a road-side inn, however, removed the veil from my eyes, and I became gradually and speedily 'awake' to 'every move on the board.' It was a lovely evening in July, the air was serene and the scenery romantic; my own feelings were in unison with both, and enhanced perhaps by the fact that I had beguiled the last two miles of my deliberate walk with a page out of my pocket-companion, 'Burke on the Sublime and Beautiful.' I was now smoking my pipe and quaffing a pint of real 'Yorkshire stingo' in the 'keeping room' (a term which combines parlour and kitchen in one word) of a real 'Yorkshire village,' Dranfield, near Sheffield. A young person of the other sex was my only and accidental companion; she had been driven into the house by the over-officiousness of a vigilant village constable, who finding that she sold lace without a license, and—infinitely worse—refused to listen to his advances, had warned her to 'make herself scarce' at her 'earliest possible convenience.'

"Having elicited what I did for a living, she popped the startling question to me, 'Where do you "hang out" in Sheffield?' I told her that I had never been in Sheffield, and did not 'hang out' my little wares, but used my persuasive art to induce the purchase of them. The lady said, 'Well, you are "green." I mean, where do you *dos?*' This was no better, it seemed something like Greek,—'*delta, omicron, sigma,*' (I retain the "patterer's" own words to show the education of the class)—but the etymology was no relief to the perplexity. 'Where do you mean to sleep?' she inquired. I referred to my usual practice of adjourning to an humble public-house. My companion at once threw off all manner of disguise, and said, 'Well, sir, you are a young man that I have taken a liking to, and if you think you should like my company, I will take you to a lodging where there is plenty of travellers, and you will see "all sorts of life."' I liked the girl's company, and our mutual acquiescence made us companions on the road. We had not got far before we met the aforesaid constable in company with an unmistakeable member of the Rural Police. They made some inquiries of me, which I thought exceeded their commission. I replied to them with a mutilated Ode of Horace, when they both determined that I was a Frenchman, and allowed us to 'go on our way rejoicing.'

"The smoky, though well-built, town of Sheffield was now near at hand. The daylight was past,' and the 'shades of the evening were stretching out;' we were therefore enabled to journey through the thoroughfares without impertinent remarks, or perhaps any observation, except from a toothless old woman, of John Wesley's school, who was 'sorry to see two such nice young people going about the country,' and wondered if we 'ever thought of eternity!'

"After a somewhat tedious ramble, we arrived at Water-lane;—at the 'Bug-trap,' which from time immemorial has been the name of the most renowned lodging-house in that or perhaps any locality. Water-lane is a dark narrow street, crowded with human beings of the most degraded sort—the chosen atmosphere of cholera, and the stronghold of theft and prostitution. In less than half an hour, my fair companion and myself were sipping our tea, and eating Yorkshire cake in this same lodging-house.

"'God bless every happy couple!' was echoed from a rude stentorian voice, while a still ruder hand bumped down upon our tea-table a red earthen dish of no small dimensions, into which was poured, from the mouth of a capacious bag, fragments of fish, flesh, and fowl, viands and vegetables of every sort, intermingled with bits of cheese and dollops of Yorkshire pudding. The man to whom this heterogeneous mass belonged, appeared anything but satisfied with his lot. 'Well,' said he, 'I don't know what this 'ere monkry *will* come to, after a bit. Three bob and a tanner, and that there dish o' scra n (enough to feed two families for a fortnight) 'is

all I got this blessed day since seven o'clock in the morning, and now it's nine at night.' I ventured to say something, but a remark, too base for repetition, 'put the stunners on me,' and I held my peace.

"I was here surprised, on conversing with my young female companion, to find that she went to church, said her prayers night and morning, and knew many of the collects, some of which she repeated, besides a pleasing variety of Dr. Watts's hymns. At the death of her mother, her father had given up housekeeping; and, being too fond of a wandering life, had led his only child into habits like his own.

"As the night advanced, the party at the 'Bug-trap' more than doubled. High-flyers, shallow-coves, turnpike-sailors, and swells out of luck, made up an assembly of fourscore human beings, more than half of whom were doomed to sleep on a 'make-shift'—in other words, on a platform, raised just ten inches above the floor of the garret, which it nearly equalled in dimensions. Here were to be huddled together, with very little covering, old men and women, young men and children, with no regard to age, sex, or propensities.

"The 'mot' of the 'ken' (nickname for 'matron of the *establishment*') had discovered that I was a 'more bettermost' sort of person, and hinted that, if I would 'come down' with twopence more (threepence was the regular nightly charge), I, 'and the young gal as I was with,' might have a little 'crib' to ourselves in a little room, along with another woman wot was married and had a 'kid,' and whose husband had got a month for 'griddling in the main drag' (singing in the high street), and being 'cheekish' (saucy) to the beadle.

"Next morning I bade adieu to the 'Bug-trap,' and I hope for ever."

The same informant further stated that he was some time upon "tramp" before he even knew of the existence of a common lodging-house : "After I had 'matriculated' at Sheffield," he says, "I continued some time going to public-houses to sleep, until my apparel having got shabby and my acquintance with misfortune more general, I submitted to be the associate of persons whom I never spoke to out of doors, and whose even slight acquaintance I have long renounced. My first introduction to a London paddin' ken was in Whitechapel, the place was then called Cat and Wheel-alley (now Commercial-street). On the spot where St. Jude's church now stands was a double lodging-house, kept by a man named Shirley—one side of it was for single men and women, the other married couples ; as these 'couples' made frequent exchanges, it is scarcely probable that Mr. Shirley ever 'asked to see their marriage lines.' These changes were, indeed, as common as they were disgusting. I knew two brothers (Birmingham nailers) who each brought a young woman out of service from the country. After a while each became dissatisfied with his partner. The mistress of the house (an old procuress from Portsmouth) proposed that they should change their wives. They did so, to the amusement of nine other couples sleeping on the same floor, and some of whom followed the example, and more than once during the night.

"When Cat and Wheel-alley was pulled down, the crew removed to George-yard; the proprietor died, and his wife sold the concern to a wooden-legged Welshman named Hughes (commonly called 'Taff'). I was there some time. 'Taff' was a notorious receiver of stolen goods. I knew two little boys, who brought home six pairs of new Wellington boots, which this miscreant bought at 1s. per pair; and, when they had no luck, he would take the strap off his wooden-leg, and beat them through the nakedness of their rags. He boarded and lodged about a dozen Chelsea and Greenwich pensioners. These he used to follow and watch closely till they got paid; then (after they had settled with him) he would make them drunk, and rob them of the few shillings they had left.

"One of these dens of infamy may be taken as a specimen of the whole class. They have generally a spacious, though often ill-ventilated, kitchen, the dirty dilapidated walls of which are hung with prints, while a shelf or two are generally, though barely, furnished with crockery and kitchen utensils. In some places knives and forks are not provided, unless a penny is left with the 'deputy,' or manager, till they are returned. A brush of any kind is a stranger, and a looking-glass would be a miracle. The average number of nightly lodgers is in winter 70, and in summer (when many visit the provinces) from 40 to 45. The general charge is, if two sleep together, 3d. per night, or 4d. for a single bed. In either case, it is by no means unusual to find 18 or 20 in one small room, the heat and horrid smell from which are insufferable; and, where there are young children, the staircases are the lodgment of every kind of filth and abomination. In some houses there are rooms for families, where, on a rickety machine, which they dignify by the name of a bedstead, may be found the man, his wife, and a son or daughter, perhaps 18 years of age; while the younger children, aged from 7 to 14, sleep on the floor. If they have linen, they take it off to escape vermin, and rise naked, one by one, or sometimes brother and sister together. This is no ideal picture; the subject is too capable of being authenticated to need that meaningless or dishonest assistance called 'allowable exaggeration.' The amiable and deservedly popular minister of a district church, built among lodging-houses, has stated that he has found 29 human beings in one apartment; and that having with difficulty knelt down between two beds to pray with a dying woman, his legs became so jammed that he could hardly get up again.

"Out of some fourscore such habitations," continues my informant, "I have only found

two which had any sort of garden; and, I am happy to add, that in neither of these two was there a single case of cholera. In the others, however, the pestilence raged with terrible fury.

"Of all the houses of this sort, the best I know is the one (previously referred to) in Orchard-street, Westminister, and another in Seven Dials, kept by a Mr. Mann (formerly a wealthy butcher). Cleanliness is inscribed on every wall of the house; utensils of every kind are in abundance, with a plentiful supply of water and gas. The beds do not exceed five in a room, and they are changed every week. There is not one disorderly lodger; and although the master has sustained heavy losses, ill health, and much domestic affliction, himself and his house may be regarded as patterns of what is wanted for the London poor.

"As there is a sad similarity between these abodes, so there is a sort of *caste* belonging in general to the inmates. Of them it may be averred that whatever their pursuits, they are more or less alike in their views of men and manners. They hate the aristocracy. Whenever there is a rumour or an announcement of an addition to the Royal Family, and the news reaches the padding-ken, the kitchen, for half-an-hour, becomes the scene of uproar—'another expense coming on the b—y country!' The 'patterers' are very fond of the Earl of Carlisle, whom, in their attachment, they still call Lord Morpeth; they have read many of his lordship's speeches at *soirées*, &c., and they think he wishes well to a poor man. Sir James Graham had better not show face among them; they have an idea (whence derived we know not) that this nobleman invented fourpenny-pieces, and, now, they say, the swells give a 'joey' where they used to give a 'tanner.' The hero of Waterloo is not much amiss 'if he lets politics alone.' The name of a bishop is but another name for a Beelzebub; but they are very fond of the inferior clergy. Lay-agents and tract-distributors they cannot bear; they think they are spies come to see how much 'scran' (food) they have got, and then go and 'pyson' the minds of the public against poor people.

"I was once (says our informant) in a house of this kind, in George-street, St. Giles's,—the missionary who visited them on that occasion (Sunday afternoon) had the misfortune to be suspected as the author of some recent exposure in the newspapers.—They accused him, and he rebutted the accusation; they replied, and he rejoined; at last one of the men said, 'What do you want poking your nose in here for?' 'The City Mission,' was the answer, 'had authorised ——.' 'Authorised be d—d! are you ordained?' 'No, not yet, friend.' The women then tore the poor gentleman's nether garments in a way I must not describe. The men carried him into the yard, filled his mouth with flour of mustard and then put him in a water-butt.

"It is, I am satisfied, quite a mistake to

suppose that there is much real infidelity among these outcast beings. They almost all believe in a hereafter; most of them think that the wicked will be punished for a few years, and then the whole universe of people be embraced in the arms of one Great Forgiving Father. Some of them think that the wicked will not rise at all; the punishment of 'losing Heaven' being as they say 'Hell enough for anybody.' Points of doctrine they seldom meddle with.

" There are comparatively few Dissenters to be found in padding-kens, though many whose parents were Dissenters. My own opinion (writes my informant) is, that dissent seldom lasts long in one family. In eight years' experience I have found two hundred apparently pious men and women, and at least two thousand who call themselves Protestants, but never go to any church or chapel.

" The politics of these classes are, perhaps, for the most part, ' liberal Tory.' In most lodging-houses they take one or two papers: the *Weekly Dispatch*, and *Bell's Weekly Messenger*, are the two usually taken. I know of no exception to this rule. The beggars hate a Whig Ministry, and I know that many a tear was shed in the hovels and cellars of London when Sir Robert Peel died. I know a publican, in Westminster, whose daily receipts are enormous, and whose only customers are soldiers, thieves, and prostitutes, who closed his house the day of the funeral, and put himself, his family, and even his beer-machines and gas-pipes, into mourning for the departed statesman.

" The pattering fraternity, that I write of, are generally much given to intemperance. Their amusements are the theatre, the free-and-easy, the skittle-ground, and sometimes cards and dominoes. They read some light works, and some of them subscribe to libraries, and a few, very few, attend lectures. Eliza Cook is a favourite writer with them, and Capt. Marryatt, the ' top-sawyer,' as a novelist. Ainsworth is the idol of another class, when they can read. Mr. Dickens *was* a favourite, but he has gone down sadly in the scale since his *Household Words* 'came it so strong' against the begging letter department. These poor creatures seldom rise in society. They make no effort to extricate themselves, while by others they are unpitied because unknown. To this rule, however, there are some happy and honourable exceptions.

" Taken as a body, patterers, lurkers, &c. are by no means quick-sighted as to the sanctions of moral obligation. They would join the hue and cry against the persecutors of Jane Wilbred, but a promiscuous robbery, even accompanied by murder—if it was ' got up clever' and ' done clean,' so long as the parties escaped detection—might call forth a remark that ' there was no great harm done,' and perhaps some would applaud the perpetrators."

Before quitting this part of my subject (viz. the character, habits, and opinions of *all* classes of patterers), I will give an account of the pre-tended missionary proceedings of a man, well-known to the vagrant fraternity as " Chelsea George." I received the following narrative from the gentleman whose statements I have given previously. The scheme was concocted in a low lodging-house:

" After a career of incessant ' lurking' and deceit, Chelsea George left England, and remained abroad," writes my informant, " four or five years. Exposure to the sun, and allowing his beard to grow a prodigious length, gave him the appearance of a foreigner. He had picked up enough French and Italian, with a little Dutch and German, and a smattering of Spanish, to enable him to ' hail for any part of the globe,' and from the designed inarticulateness with which he spoke (sometimes four languages in one sentence) added to his sun-burnt and grotesque appearance, it was difficult to *pall* him upon any *racket* (detect him in any pretence), so that the most incredulous,—though often previously imposed upon—gave credence to his story, relief to his supposed necessities, and sometimes letters of introduction to their friends and neighbours.

" Some time after his return to England, and while pursuing the course of a ' high-flyer' (genteel beggar), he met with an interruption to his pursuits which induced him to alter his plan without altering his behaviour. The newspapers of the district, where he was then located, had raised before the eye and mind of the public, what the ' patterers' of his class proverbially call a ' stink,'—that is, had opened the eyes of the unwary to the movements of ' Chelsea George;' and although he ceased to renew his appeals from the moment he heard of the notice of him, his appearance was so accurately described that he was captured and committed to Winchester jail as a rogue and vagabond. The term of his imprisonment has escaped my recollection. As there was no definite charge against him, probably he was treated as an ordinary vagrant and suffered a calendar month in durance. The silent system was not then in vogue, consequently there existed no barrier to mutual intercourse between prisoners, with all its train of conscience-hardening tendencies. I do not say this to intimate unqualified approval of the solitary system, I merely state a fact which has an influence on my subject.

" George had by this time scraped acquaintance with two fellow-prisoners—Jew Jem and Russia Bob. The former in ' quod' for ' pattering' as a ' converted Jew,' the latter for obtaining money under equally false, though less theological, pretences.

" Liberated about one time, this trio laid their heads together,—and the result was a plan to evangelize, or rather victimize, the inhabitants of the collier villages in Staffordshire and the adjoining counties. To accomplish this purpose, some novel and imposing representation must be made, both to lull suspicion and give the air of piety to the plan, and disinterestedness to the agents by whom it was carried out.

"THE KITCHEN," FOX COURT, GRAY'S-INN-LANE.

" George and his two fellow-labourers were 'square-rigged'—that is, well dressed. Something, however, must be done to colour up the scene, and make the appeal for money touching, unsuspected, and successful. Just before the time to which I allude, a missionary from Sierra Leone had visited the larger towns of the district in question, while the inhabitants of the surrounding hamlets had been left in ignorance of the 'progress of missions in Africa and the East.' George and his comrades thought it would be no great harm at once to enlighten and fleece this scattered and anxious population. The plan was laid in a town of some size and facility. They 'raised the wind' to an extent adequate to some alteration of their appearances, and got bills printed to set forth the merits of the cause. The principal actor was Jew Jim, a converted Israelite, with 'reverend' before his name, and half the letters of the alphabet behind it. He had been in all the islands of the South Sea, on the coast of Africa, all over Hindostan, and half over the universe; and after assuring the villagers of Torryburn that he had carried the Gospel to various dark and *uninhabited* parts of the earth, he introduced Russia Bob (an Irishman who had, however, been in Russia) as his worthy and self-denying colleague, and Chelsea George as the first-fruits of their ministry—as one who had left houses and land, wife and children, and taken a long and hazardous voyage to show Christians in England that their sable brethren, children of one common Parent, were beginning to cast their idols to the moles and to the bats. Earnest was the gaze and breathless the expectation with which the poor deluded colliers of Torry-burn listened to this harangue; and as argument always gains by illustration, the orator pulled out a tremendous black doll, bought for a 'flag' (fourpence) of a retired ragmerchant, and dressed up in Oriental style. This, Jew Jim assured the audience, was an idol brought from Murat in Hindostan. He presented it to Chelsea George for his worship and embraces. The convert indignantly repelled the insinuation, pushed the idol from him, spat in its face, and cut as many capers as a dancing-bear. The trio at this stage of the performances began 'puckering' (talking privately) to each other in murdered French, dashed with a little Irish; after which, the missionaries said that their convert (who had only a few words of English) would now profess his faith. All was attention as Chelsea George came forward. He stroked his beard, put his hand in his breast to keep down his dickey, and turning his eyes upwards, said : ' I believe in Desus Tist—dlory to 'is 'oly Name !'

" This elicited some loud 'amens' from an assemblage of nearly 1,000 persons, and catching the favourable opportunity, a 'school of pals,' appointed for the purpose, went round and made the collection. Out of the abundance of their credulity and piety the populace contributed sixteen pounds ! The whole scene was enacted out of doors, and presented to a stranger very pleasing impressions. I was present on the occasion, but was not then aware of the dodge. One verse of a hymn, and the blessing pronounced, was the signal for separation. A little shaking of hands concluded the exhibition, and 'every man went into his own house.'

" The missionary party and their 'pals' took the train to Manchester, and as none of them were teetotallers, the proceeds of their imposition did not last long. They were just putting on their considering caps, for the contrivance of another dodge, when a gentleman in blue clothes came into the tap-room, and informed Jew Jem that he was 'wanted.' It appears that 'Jem' had come out of prison a day or two before his comrades, and being 'hard up,' had ill-used a lady, taken her purse, and appropriated its contents. Inquiries, at first useless, had now proved successful—the 'missionary' stood his trial, and got an 'appointment' on Norfolk Island. Russia Bob took the cholera and died, and 'George the convert' was once more left alone to try his hand at something else."

OF THE LOW LODGING-HOUSES OF LONDON.

THE patterers, as a class, usually frequent the low lodging-houses. I shall therefore now proceed to give some further information touching the abodes of these people—reminding the reader that I am treating of patterers in general, and not of any particular order, as the " paper workers."

In applying the epithet " low " to these places, I do but adopt the word commonly applied, either in consequence of the small charge for lodging, or from the character of their frequenters. To some of these domiciles, however, as will be shown, the epithet, in an opprobrious sense, is unsuited.

An intelligent man, familiar for some years with some low lodging-house life, specified the quarters where those abodes are to be found, and divided them into the following districts, the correctness of which I caused to be ascertained.

Drury-lane District. Here the low lodging-houses are to be found principally in the Coal-yard, Charles-street, King-street, Parker-street, Short's-gardens, Great and Little Wyld-streets, Wyld-court, Lincoln-court, Newton-street, Star-court.

Gray's - inn Lane. Fox - court, Charlotte-buildings, Spread Eagle-court, Portpool-lane, Bell-court, Baldwin's-gardens, Pheasant-court, Union-buildings, Laystall-street, Cromer-street, Fulwood's-rents (High Holborn).

Chancery-lane. Church-passage, and the Liberty of the Rolls.

Bloomsbury. George - street, Church - lane, Queen-street, Seven - dials, Puckeridge - street (commonly called the Holy Land).

Saffron-hill and Clerkenwell. Peter-street, Cow-cross, Turnmill-street, Upper and Lower White-cross-street, St. Helen's-place, Playhouse-yard, Chequer-alley, Field-lane, Great Saffron-hill.

Westminster. Old and New Pye-streets, Ann-

street, Orchard-street, Perkins's-rents, Roches-
ter-row.

Lambeth.   Lambeth-walk, New-cut.
Marylebone.   York-court, East-street.
St. Pancras.   Brooke-street.
Paddington.   Chapel-street, Union-court.
Shoreditch.   Baker's-rents, Cooper's-gardens.
Islington.   Angel-yard.
Whitechapel, Spitalfields, &c.   George-yard,
Thrawl-street, Flower and Dean-street, Went-
worth - street, Keate - street, Rosemary - lane,
Glasshouse-yard, St. George's-street, Lambeth-
street, Whitechapel, High-street.
Borough.   Mint-street, Old Kent-street, Long-
lane, Bermondsey.
Stratford.   High-street.
Limehouse.   Hold (commonly called Hole).
Deptford.   Mill-lane, Church-street, Gifford-
street.

There are other localities, (as in Mile-end,
Ratcliffe-highway, Shadwell, Wapping, and
Lisson-grove,) where low lodging-houses are to
be found; but the places I have specified may
be considered the *districts* of these hotels for
the poor. The worst places, both as regards
filth and immorality, are in St. Giles's and
Wentworth-street, Whitechapel. The best are in
Orchard-street, Westminster (the thieves having
left it in consequence of the recent alterations
and gone to New Pye-street), and in the Mint,
Borough. In the last-mentioned district, indeed, some of the proprietors of the lodging-
houses have provided considerable libraries for
the use of the inmates. In the White Horse,
Mint-street, for instance, there is a collection of
500 volumes, on all subjects, bought recently,
and having been the contents of a circulating
library, advertised for sale in the *Weekly Dispatch.*

Of lodging-houses for "travellers" the
largest is known as the Farm House, in the
Mint: it stands away from any thoroughfare,
and lying low is not seen until the visitor stands
in the yard. Tradition rumour states that the
house was at one time Queen Anne's, and was
previously Cardinal Wolsey's. It was probably some official residence. In this lodging-
house are forty rooms, 200 beds (single and
double), and accommodation for 200 persons.
It contains three kitchens,—of which the largest,
at once kitchen and sitting-room, holds 400
people, for whose uses in cooking there are two
large fire-places. The other two kitchens are
used only on Sundays; when one is a preach-
ing-room, in which missionaries from Surrey
Chapel (the Rev. James Sherman's), or some
minister or gentleman of the neighbourhood,
officiates. The other is a reading-room, supplied with a few newspapers and other periodicals; and thus, I was told, the religious and
irreligious need not clash. For the supply of
these papers each person pays 1d. every Sunday morning; and as the sum so collected is
more than is required for the expenses of the
reading-room, the surplus is devoted to the
help of the members in sickness, under the

management of the proprietor of the lodging-
house, who appears to possess the full confidence of his inmates. The larger kitchen is
detached from the sleeping apartments, so that
the lodgers are not annoyed with the odour of
the cooking of fish and other food consumed by
the poor; for in lodging-houses every sojourner
is his own cook. The meal in most demand is
tea, usually with a herring, or a piece of bacon.

The yard attached to the Farm House, in
Mint-street, covers an acre and a half; in it
is a washing - house, built recently, the yard
itself being devoted to the drying of the clothes
—washed by the customers of the establishment.
At the entrance to this yard is a kind of porter's
lodge, in which reside the porter and his wife
who act as the "deputies" of the lodging-
house. This place has been commended in
sanitary reports, for its cleanliness, good order,
and care for decency, and for a proper division
of the sexes. On Sundays there is no charge
for lodging to known customers; but this is a
general practice among the low lodging-houses
of London.

In contrast to this house I could cite many
instances, but I need do no more in this place
than refer to the statements, which I shall proceed
to give; some of these were collected in the course
of a former inquiry, and are here given because
the same state of things prevails now. I was
told by a trustworthy man that not long ago
he was compelled to sleep in one of the lowest
(as regards cheapness) of the lodging-houses.
All was dilapidation, filth, and noisomeness.
In the morning he drew, for purposes of ablu-
tion, a basinfull of water from a pailfull kept
in the room. In the water were floating
alive, or apparently alive, bugs and lice,
which my informant was convinced had fallen
from the ceiling, shaken off by the tread
of some one walking in the rickety apartments
above!

"Ah, sir," said another man with whom I
conversed on the subject, "if you had lived in
the lodging-houses, you would say what a vast
difference a penny made,—it's often all in all.
It's 4d. in the Mint House you've been asking
me about; you've sleep and comfort there, and
I've seen people kneel down and say their
prayers afore they went to bed. Not so many,
though. Two or three in a week at nights,
perhaps. And it's wholesome and sweet enough
there, and large separate beds; but in other
places there's nothing to smell or feel but bugs.
When daylight comes in the summer—and it's
often either as hot as hell or as cold as icicles
in those places; but in summer, as soon as its
light, if you turn down the coverlet, you'll
see them a-going it like Cheapside when it's
throngest." The poor man seemed to shudder
at the recollection.

One informant counted for me 180 of these
low lodging-houses; and it is reasonable to say
that there are, in London, at least 200 of them.
The average number of beds in each was computed for me, by persons cognizant of such

matters, from long and often woful experience, at 52 single or 24 double beds, where the house might be confined to single men or single women lodgers, or to married or pretendedly married couples, or to both classes. In either case, we may calculate the number that can be, and generally are, accommodated at 50 per house; for children usually sleep with their parents, and 50 may be the lowest computation. We have thus no fewer than 10,000 persons domiciled, more or less permanently, in the low lodging-houses of London—a number more than doubling the population of many a parliamentary borough.

The proprietors of these lodging-houses mostly have been, I am assured, vagrants, or, to use the civiller and commoner word, "travellers" themselves, and therefore sojourners, on all necessary occasions, in such places. In four cases out of five I believe this to be the case. The proprietors have raised capital sufficient to start with, sometimes by gambling at races, sometimes by what I have often, and very vaguely, heard described as a "run of luck;" and sometimes, I am assured, by the proceeds of direct robbery. A few of the proprietors may be classed as capitalists. One of them, who has a country house in Hampstead, has six lodging-houses in or about Thrawl-street, Whitechapel. He looks in at each house every Saturday, and calls his deputies—for he has a deputy in each house —to account; he often institutes a stringent check. He gives a poor fellow money to go and lodge in one of his houses, and report the number present. Sometimes the person so sent meets with the laconic repulse—"Full;" and woe to the deputy if his return do not evince this fulness. Perhaps one in every fifteen of the low lodging-houses in town is also a beer-shop. Very commonly so in the country.

To "start" a low lodging-house is not a very costly matter. Furniture which will not be saleable in the ordinary course of auction, or of any traffic, is bought by a lodging-house "starter." A man possessed of some money, who took an interest in a bricklayer, purchased for 20*l.*, when the Small Pox Hospital, by King's-cross, was pulled down, a sufficiency of furniture for *four* lodging-houses, in which he "started" the man in question. None others would buy this furniture, from a dread of infection.

It was the same at Marlborough-house, Peckham, after the cholera had broken out there. The furniture was sold to a lodging-house keeper, at 9*d.* each article. "Big and little, sir," I was told; "a penny pot and a bedstead —all the same; each 9*d.* Nobody else would buy."

To about three-fourths of the low lodging-houses of London, are "deputies." These are the conductors or managers of the establishment, and are men or women (and not unfrequently a married, or proclaimed a married couple), and about in equal proportion. These deputies are paid from 7*s.* to 15*s.* a week each,

according to the extent of their supervision; their lodging always, and sometimes their board, being at the cost of "the master." According to the character of the lodging-house, the deputies are civil and decent, or roguish and insolent. Their duty is not only that of general superintendence, but in some of the houses of a nocturnal inspection of the sleeping-rooms; the deputy's business generally keeping him up all night. At the better-conducted houses strangers are not admitted after twelve at night; in others, there is no limitation as to hours.

The rent of the low lodging-houses varies, I am informed, from 8*s.* to 20*s.* a week, the payment being for the most part weekly; the taxes and rates being of course additional. It is rarely that the landlord, or his agent, can be induced to expend any money in repairs,—the wear and tear of the floors, &c., from the congregating together of so many human beings being excessive: this expenditure in consequence falls upon the tenant.

Some of the lodging-houses present no appearance differing from that of ordinary houses; except, perhaps, that their exterior is dirtier. Some of the older houses have long flat windows on the ground-floor, in which there is rather more paper, or other substitutes, than glass. "The windows there, sir," remarked one man, "are not to let the light in, but to keep the cold out."

In the abodes in question there seems to have become tacitly established an arrangement as to what character of lodgers shall resort thither; the thieves, the prostitutes, and the better class of street-sellers or traders, usually resorting to the houses where they will meet the same class of persons. The patterers reside chiefly in Westminster and Whitechapel.

Some of the lodging-houses are of the worst class of low brothels, and some may even be described as brothels for children.

On many of the houses is a rude sign, " Lodgings for Travellers, 3*d.* a night. Boiling water always ready," or the same intimation may be painted on a window-shutter, where a shutter is in existence. A few of the better order of these housekeepers post up small bills, inviting the attention of "travellers," by laudations of the cleanliness, good beds, abundant water, and "gas all night," to be met with. The same parties also give address-cards to travellers, who can recommend one another.

The beds are of flock, and as regards the mere washing of the rug, sheet, and blanket, which constitute the bed-furniture, are in better order than they were a few years back; for the visitations of the cholera alarmed even the reckless class of vagrants, and those whose avocations relate to vagrants. In perhaps a tenth of the low lodging-houses of London, a family may have a room to themselves, with the use of the kitchen, at so much a week—generally 2*s.* 6*d.* for a couple without family, and 3*s.* 6*d.* where there are children. To let out "beds" by the night is however the general rule.

The illustration presented this week is of a place in Fox-court, Gray's-inn-lane, long notorious as a " thieves' house," but now far less frequented. On the visit, a few months back, of an informant (who declined staying there), a number of boys were lying on the floor gambling with marbles and halfpennies, and indulging in savage or unmeaning blasphemy. One of the lads jumped up, and murmuring something that it wouldn't do to be idle any longer, induced a woman to let him have a halfpenny for "a stall;" that is, as a pretext with which to enter a shop for the purpose of stealing, the display of the coin forming an excuse for his entrance. On the same occasion a man walked into " the kitchen," and coolly pulled from underneath the back of his smock-frock a large flat piece of bacon, for which he wanted a customer. It would be sold at a fourth of its value.

I am assured that the average takings of lodging-house keepers may be estimated at 17s. 6d. a night, not to say 20s.; but I adopt the lower calculation. This gives a weekly payment by the struggling poor, the knavish, and the outcast, of 1,000 guineas weekly, or 52,000 guineas in the year. Besides the rent and taxes, the principal expenditure of the lodging-house proprietors is for coals and gas. In some of the better houses, blacking, brushes, and razors are supplied, without charge, to the lodgers: also pen and ink, soap, and, almost always, a newspaper. For the meals of the frequenters salt is supplied gratuitously, and sometimes, but far less frequently, pepper also; never vinegar or mustard. Sometimes a halfpenny is charged for the use of a razor and the necessary shaving apparatus. In one house in Kent-street, the following distich adorns the mantel-piece:

> "To save a journey up the town,
> A razor lent here for a *brown:*
> But if you think the price too high,
> I beg you won't the razor try."

In some places a charge of a halfpenny is made for hot water, but that is very rarely the case. Strong drink is admitted at almost any hour in the majority of the houses, and the deputy is generally ready to bring it; but little is consumed in the houses, those addicted to the use or abuse of intoxicating liquors preferring the tap-room or the beer-shop.

OF THE FILTH, DISHONESTY, AND IMMORALITY OF LOW LODGING-HOUSES.

IN my former and my present inquiries, I received many statements on this subject. Some details, given by coarse men and boys in the grossest language, are too gross to be more than alluded to, but the full truth must be manifested, if not detailed. It was remarked when my prior account appeared, that the records of gross profligacy on the part of some of the most licentious of the rich (such as the late Marquis of Hertford and other worthies of the same depraved habits) were equalled, or nearly equalled, by the account of the orgies of the lowest lodging-

houses. Sin, in any rank of life, shows the same features.

And first, as to the want of cleanliness, comfort, and decency : " Why, sir," said one man, who had filled a commercial situation of no little importance, but had, through intemperance, been reduced to utter want, " I myself have slept in the top room of a house not far from Drury-lane, and you could study the stars, if you were so minded, through the holes left by the slates having been blown off the roof. It was a fine summer's night, and the openings in the roof were then rather an advantage, for they admitted air, and the room wasn't so foul as it might have been without them. I never went there again, but you may judge what thoughts went through a man's mind—a man who had seen prosperous days—as he lay in a place like that, without being able to sleep, watching the sky."

The same man told me (and I received abundant corroboration of his statement, besides that incidental mention of the subject occurs elsewhere), that he had scraped together a handful of bugs from the bed-clothes, and crushed them under a candlestick, and had done that many a time, when he could only resort to the lowest places. He had slept in rooms so crammed with sleepers—he believed there were 30 where 12 would have been a proper number—that their breaths in the dead of night and in the unventilated chamber, rose (I use his own words) " in one foul, choking steam of stench." This was the case most frequently a day or two prior to Greenwich Fair or Epsom Races, when the congregation of the wandering classes, who are the supporters of the low lodging-houses, was the thickest. It was not only that two or even three persons jammed themselves into a bed not too large for one full-sized man; but between the beds—and their partition one from another admitted little more than the passage of a lodger—were placed shakes-down, or temporary accommodation for nightly slumber. In the better lodging-houses the shake-downs are small palliasses or mattresses; in the worst, they are bundles of rags of any kind; but loose straw is used only in the country for shake-downs. One informant saw a traveller, who had arrived late, eye his shake-down in one of the worst houses with anything but a pleased expression of countenance; and a surly deputy, observing this, told the customer he had his choice, " which," the deputy added, " it's not all men as has, or I shouldn't have been waiting here on you. But you has your choice, I tell you;—sleep there on that shake-down, or turn out and be d——; that's fair." At some of the busiest periods, numbers sleep on the kitchen floor, all huddled together, men and women (when indecencies are common enough), and without bedding or anything but their scanty clothes to soften the hardness of the stone or brick floor. A penny is saved to the lodger by this means. More than 200 have been accommodated in this way in a large house. The Irish, at harvest-time, very often resort to this mode of passing the night.

I heard from several parties, of the surprise, and even fear or horror, with which a decent mechanic—more especially if he were accompanied by his wife—regarded one of these foul dens, when destitution had driven him there for the first time in his life. Sometimes such a man was seen to leave the place abruptly, though perhaps he had pre-paid his last half-penny for the refreshment of a night's repose. Sometimes he was seized with sickness. I heard also from some educated persons who had "seen better days," of the disgust with themselves and with the world, which they felt on first entering such places. "And I have some reason to believe," said one man, "that a person, once well off, who has sunk into the very depths of poverty, often makes his first appearance in one of the worst of those places. Perhaps it is because he keeps away from them as long as he can, and then, in a sort of desperation fit, goes into the cheapest he meets with; or if he knows it's a vile place, he very likely says to himself—I did—' I may as well know the worst at once.' "

Another man who had moved in good society, said, when asked about his resorting to a low lodging-house: "When a man's lost caste in society, he may as well go the whole hog, bristles and all, and a low lodging-house is the entire pig."

Notwithstanding many abominations, I am assured that the lodgers, in even the worst of these habitations, for the most part sleep soundly. But they have, in all probability, been out in the open air the whole of the day, and all of them may go to their couches, after having walked, perhaps, many miles, exceedingly fatigued, and some of them half-drunk. "Why, in course, sir," said a "traveller," whom I spoke to on this subject, "if you is in a country town or village, where there's only one lodging-house, perhaps, and that a bad one—an old hand can always suit his-self in London—you *must* get half-drunk, or your money for your bed is wasted. There's so much rest owing to you, after a hard day; and bugs and bad air'll prevent its being paid, if you don't lay in some stock of beer, or liquor of some sort, to sleep on. It's a duty you owes yourself; but, if you haven't the browns, why, then, in course, you can't pay it." I have before remarked, and, indeed, have given instances, of the odd and sometimes original manner in which an intelligent patterer, for example, will express himself.

The information I obtained in the course of this inquiry into the condition of low lodging-houses, afforded a most ample corroboration of the truth of a remark I have more than once found it necessary to make before—that persons of the vagrant class will sacrifice almost anything for warmth, not to say heat. Otherwise, to sleep, or even sit, in some of the apartments of these establishments would be intolerable.

From the frequent state of weariness to which I have alluded, there is generally less conversation among the frequenters of the low lodging-houses than might be expected. Some are busy cooking, some (in the better houses) are reading, many are drowsy and nodding, and many are smoking. In perhaps a dozen places of the worst and filthiest class, indeed, smoking is permitted even in the sleeping-rooms; but it is far less common than it was even half-a-dozen years back, and becomes still less common yearly. Notwithstanding so dangerous a practice, fires are and have been very unfrequent in these places. There is always some one awake, which is one reason. The lack of conversation, I ought to add, and the weariness and drowsiness, are less observable in the lodging-houses patronised by thieves and women of abandoned character, whose lives are comparatively idle, and whose labour a mere nothing. In their houses, if the conversation be at all general, it is often of the most unclean character. At other times it is carried on in groups, with abundance of whispers, shrugs, and slang, by the members of the respective schools of thieves or lurkers.

I have now to speak of the habitual violation of all the injunctions of law, of all the obligations of morality, and of all the restraints of decency, seen continually in the vilest of the lodging-houses. I need but cite a few facts, for to detail minutely might be too disgust. In some of these lodging-houses, the proprietor—or, I am told, it might be more correct to say, the proprietress, as there are more women than men engaged in the nefarious traffic carried on in these houses—are "fences," or receivers of stolen goods in a small way. *Their* "fencing," unless as the very exception, does not extend to any plate, or jewellery, or articles of value, but is chiefly confined to provisions, and most of all to those which are of ready sale to the lodgers.

Of very ready sale are "fish got from the gate" (stolen from Billingsgate); "sawney" (thieved bacon), and "flesh found in Leadenhall" (butcher's-meat stolen from that market). I was told by one of the most respectable tradesmen in Leadenhall-market, that it was infested—but not now to so great an extent as it was—with lads and young men, known there as "finders." They carry bags round their necks, and pick up bones, or offal, or pieces of string, or bits of papers, or "anything, sir, please, that a poor lad, that has neither father nor mother, and is werry hungry, can make a ha'penny by to get him a bit of bread, please, sir." This is often but a cover for stealing pieces of meat, and the finders, with their proximate market for disposal of their meat in the lowest lodging-houses in Whitechapel, go boldly about their work, for the butchers, if the "finder" be detected, "won't," I was told by a sharp youth who then was at a low lodging-house in Keate-street, "go bothering theirselves to a beak, but gives you a scruff of the neck and a kick and lets you go. But some of them kicks werry hard." The tone and manner of this boy — and it is a common case enough with the "prigs"—showed that he regarded hard kicking merely as one of the inconveniences to which his business-pursuits were unavoidably subjected; just as a struggling housekeeper might complain of the unwelcome calls of the tax-gatherers. These depredations are more frequent in Leadenhall-market than in any of the others, on account of its vicinity to Whitechapel. Even the Whitechapel meat-market is less the scene of prey, for it is a series of shops, while Leadenhall presents many stalls, and the finders seem loath to enter shops without some plausible pretext.

Groceries, tea especially, stolen from the docks, warehouses, or shops, are things in excellent demand among the customers of a lodging-house fence. Tea, known or believed to have been stolen " genuine " from any dock, is bought and sold very readily; 1s. 6d., however, is a not unfrequent price for what is known as 5s. tea. Sugar, spices, and other descriptions of stolen grocery, are in much smaller request.

Wearing-apparel is rarely bought by the fences I am treating of; but the stealers of it can and do offer their wares to the lodgers, who will often, before buying, depreciate the garment, and say " It's never been nothing better nor a Moses."

" Hens and chickens " are a favourite theft, and " go at once to the pot," but in no culinary sense. The hens and chickens of the roguish low lodging-houses are the publicans' pewter measures; the bigger vessels are " hens;" the smaller are " chickens." Facilities are provided for the melting of these stolen vessels, and the metal is sold by the thief—very rarely if ever, by the lodging-house keeper, who prefers dealing with the known customers of the establishment—to marine-store buyers.

A man who at one time was a frequenter of a thieves' lodging-house, related to me a conversation which he chanced to overhear—he himself being then in what his class would consider a much superior line of business—between a sharp lad, apparently of twelve or thirteen years of age, and a lodging-house (female) fence. But it occurred some three or four years back. The lad had " found " a piece of Christmas beef, which he offered for sale to his landlady, averring that it weighed 6 lbs. The fence said and swore that it wouldn't weigh 3 lbs., but she would give him 5d. for it. It probably weighed above 4 lbs. " Fip-pence!" exclaimed the lad, indignantly; " you haven't no fairness. Vy, its sixpun' and Christmas time. Fip-pence! A tanner and a flag (a sixpence and a four-penny piece) is the werry lowest terms." There was then a rapid and interrupted colloquy, in which the most frequent words were: " Go to blazes!" with retorts of " You go to blazes!" and after strong and oathful imputations of dishonest endeavours on the part of each contracting party, to over-reach the other, the meat was sold to the woman for 6d.

Some of the " fences " board, lodge, and clothe, two or three boys or girls, and send them out regularly to thieve, the fence usually taking all the proceeds, and if it be the young thief has been successful, he is rewarded with a trifle of pocket-money, and is allowed plenty of beer and tobacco.

One man, who keeps three low lodging-houses (one of which is a beer-shop), not long ago received from a lodger a valuable greatcoat, which the man said he had taken from a gig. The fence (who was in a larger way of business than others of his class, and is reputed rich,) gave 10s. for the garment, asking at the same time, " Who was minding the gig?" " A charity kid," was the answer. " Give him a deuce" (2d.), " and stall him off" (send him an errand), said the fence, " and bring the horse and gig, and I'll buy it." It was done, and the property was traced in two hours, but only as regarded the gig, which had already had a new pair of wheels attached to it, and was so metamorphosed, that the owner, a medical gentleman, though he had no moral doubt on the subject, could not swear to his own vehicle. The thief received only 4l. for gig and horse; the horse was never traced.

The licentiousness of the frequenters, and more especially of the juvenile frequenters, of the low lodging-houses, must be even more briefly alluded to. In some of these establishments, men and women, boys and girls,—but perhaps in no case, or in very rare cases, unless they are themselves consenting parties, herd together promiscuously. The information which I have given from a reverend informant indicates the nature of the proceedings, when the sexes are herded indiscriminately, and it is impossible to present to the reader, in full particularity, the records of the vice practised.

Boys have boastfully carried on loud conversations, and from distant parts of the room, of their triumphs over the virtue of girls, and girls have laughed at and encouraged the recital. Three, four, five, six, and even more boys and girls have been packed, head and feet, into one small bed; some of them perhaps never met before. On such occasions any clothing seems often enough to be regarded as merely an incumbrance. Sometimes there are loud quarrels and revilings from the jealousy of boys and girls, and more especially of girls whose "chaps" have deserted or been inveigled from them. At others, there is an amicable interchange of partners, and next day a resumption of their former companionship. One girl, then fifteen or sixteen, who had been leading this vicious kind of life for nearly three years, and had been repeatedly in prison, and twice in hospitals—and who expressed a strong desire to "get out of the life" by emigration—said: "Whatever that's bad and wicked, that any one can fancy could be done in such places among boys and girls that's never been taught, or won't be taught, better, *is* done, and night after night." In these haunts of low iniquity, or rather in the room into which the children are put, there are seldom persons above twenty. The younger lodgers in such places live by thieving and pocket-picking, or by prostitution. The charge for a night's lodging is generally 2*d.*, but smaller children have often been admitted for 1*d.* If a boy or girl resort to one of these dens at night without the means of defraying the charge for accommodation, the "mot of the ken" (mistress of the house) will pack them off, telling them plainly that it will be no use their returning until they have stolen something worth 2*d.* If a boy or girl do not return in the evening, and have not been heard to express their intention of going elsewhere, the first conclusion arrived at by their mates is that they have "got into trouble" (prison).

The indiscriminate admixture of the sexes among adults, in many of these places, is another evil. Even in some houses considered of the better sort, men and women, husbands and wives, old and young, strangers and acquaintances, sleep in the same apartment, and if they choose, in the same bed. Any remonstrance at some act of gross depravity, or impropriety on the part of a woman not so utterly hardened as the others, is met with abuse and derision. One man who described these scenes to me, and had long witnessed them, said that almost the only women who ever hid their faces or manifested dislike of the proceedings they could not but notice (as far as he saw), were poor Irishwomen, generally those who live by begging: "But for all that," the man added, "an Irishman or Irishwoman of that sort will sleep anywhere, in any mess, to save a halfpenny, though they may have often a few shillings, or a good many, hidden about them."

There is no provision for purposes of decency in some of the places I have been describing, into which the sexes are herded indiscriminately; but to this matter I can only allude. A policeman, whose duty sometimes called him to enter one of those houses at night, told me that he never entered it without feeling sick.

There are now fewer of such filthy receptacles than there were. Some have been pulled down —especially for the building of Commercial-street, in Whitechapel, and of New Oxford-street—and some have fallen into fresh and improved management. Of those of the worst class, however, there may now be at least thirty in London ; while the low lodgings of all descriptions, good or bad, are more frequented than they were a few years back. A few new lodging-houses, perhaps half a dozen, have been recently opened, in expectation of a great influx of "travellers" and vagrants at the opening of the Great Exhibition.

OF THE CHILDREN IN LOW LODGING-HOUSES.

THE informant whose account of patterers and of vagrant life in its other manifestations I have already given, has written from personal knowledge and observation the following account of the children in low lodging-houses:

"Of the mass of the indigent and outcast," he says, "of whom the busy world know nothing, except from an occasional paragraph in the newspaper, the rising generation, though most important, is perhaps least considered. Every Londoner must have seen numbers of ragged, sickly, and ill-fed children, squatting at the entrances of miserable courts, streets, and alleys, engaged in no occupation that is either creditable to themselves or useful to the community. These are, in many cases, those whose sole homes are in the low lodging-houses ; and I will now exhibit a few features of the ' juvenile performers ' among the ' London Poor.'

" In many cases these poor children have lost *one* of their parents ; in some, they are without either father or mother ; but even when both parents are alive, the case is little mended, for if the parents be of the vagrant or dishonest class, their children are often neglected, and left to provide for the cost of their food and lodging as they best may. The following extract from the chaplain's report of one of our provincial jails, gives a melancholy insight into the training of many of the families. It is not, I know, without exception ; but, much as we could wish it to be otherwise, it is so general an occurrence, varied into its different forms, that it may be safely accounted as the rule of action.

" ' J. G. was born of poor parents. At five years old his father succeeded to a legacy of 500*l.* He was quiet, indolent, fond of drink, a good scholar, and had twelve children. He never sent any of them to school! "Telling lies," said the child, "I learned from my mother ; she did things unknown to father, and gave me a penny not to tell him ! " The father (on leaving home) left, by request of the mother, some money to pay a man ; she slipped up stairs, and told the children to say she was out.

" ' From ten to twelve years of age I used to go to the ale-house. I stole the money from my father, and got very drunk. My father never punished me for all this, as he ought to have done. In course of time I was apprenticed to a tanner ; he ordered me to chapel, instead of which I used to play in the fields. When out of my time I got married, and still carried on the same way, starving my wife and children. I used to take my little boy, when only five years old, to the public-house, and make him drunk with whatever I drank myself. A younger one could act well a drunken man on the floor. My wife was a sober steady women ; but, through coming to fetch me home she learned to drink too. One of our children used to say, "Mam, you are drunk, like daddy."'

"It may be argued that this awful 'family portrait' is not the average character, but I have witnessed too many similar scenes to doubt the *general* application of the sad rule.

"Of those children of the poor, as has been before observed, the most have either no parents, or have been deserted by them, and have no regular means of living, nor moral superintendance on the part of relatives or neighbours; consequently, they grow up in habits of idleness, ignorance, vagrancy, or crime. In some cases they are countenanced and employed. Here and there may be seen a little urchin holding a few onions in a saucer, or a diminutive sickly girl standing with a few laces or a box or two of lucifers. But even *these* go with the persons who have 'set them up' daily to the public-house (and to the lodging-house at night); and after they have satisfied the cravings of hunger, frequently expend their remaining halfpence (if any) in gingerbread, and as frequently in gin. I have overheard a proposal for 'half-a-quartern and a two-out' (glass) between a couple of shoeless boys under nine years old. One little fellow of eleven, on being remonstrated with, said that it was the only pleasure in life that he had, and he weren't a-going to give that up. Both sexes of this juvenile class frequent, when they can raise the means, the very cheap and 'flash' places of amusement, where the precocious delinquent acquires the most abandoned tastes, and are often allured by elder accomplices to commit petty frauds and thefts.

"Efforts have been made to redeem these young recruits in crime from their sad career, with its inevitable results. In some cases, I rejoice to believe that success has crowned the endeavour. There is that, however, in the cunning hardihood of the majority of these immature delinquents, which presents almost insuperable barriers to benevolence, and of this I will adduce an instance.

"A gentleman, living at Islington, who attends one of the city churches, is in the habit of crossing the piece of waste ground close to Saffron-hill. Here he often saw (close to the ragged school) a herd of boys, and as nearly as he could judge always the *same* boys. One of them always bowed to him as he passed. He thought—and thought right—that they were gambling, and after, on one occasion, talking to them very seriously, he gave each of them twopence and pursued his way. However, he found himself followed by the boy before alluded to, accompanied by a younger lad, who turned out to be his brother. Both in one breath begged to know if 'his honour' could please to give them any sort of a job. The gentleman gave them his card, inquired their place of residence (a low lodging-house) and the next morning, at nine o'clock, both youths were at his door. He gave them a substantial breakfast, and then took them into an out-house where was a truss of straw, and having

himself taken off the band, he desired them to convey the whole, *one straw at a time*, across the garden and deposit it in another out-house. The work was easy and the terms liberal, as each boy was to get dinner and tea, and one shilling per day as long as his services should be required. Their employer had to go to town, and left orders with one of his domestics to see that the youths wanted nothing, and to watch their proceedings; their occupation was certainly not laborious, but then it was *work*, and although that was the first of their requests, it was also the last of their wishes.

"Taking advantage of an adjoining closet, the servant perceived that the weight even of a straw had been too much for these hopeful boys. They were both seated on the truss, and glibly recounting some exploits of their own, and how they had been imposed upon by others. The eldest—about fourteen—was vowing vengeance upon 'Taylor Tom' for attempting to 'walk the barber' (seduce his 'gal'); while the younger—who had scarcely seen eleven summers—averred that it was 'very good of the swell to give them summut to eat,' but 'precious bad to be shut up in that crib all day without a bit o' backer'). Before the return of their patron they had transported all the straw to its appointed designation; as it was very discernible, however, that this had been effected by a wholesale process, the boys were admonished, paid, and dismissed. They are now performing more ponderous work in one of the penal settlements. Whether the test adopted by the gentleman in question was the best that might have been resorted to, I need not now inquire.

"It would be grateful to my feelings if in these disclosures I could omit the misdemeanors of the other sex of juveniles; but I am obliged to own, on the evidence of personal observation, that there are girls of ages varying from eleven to fifteen who pass the day with a 'fakement' before them ('Pity a poor orphan'), and as soon as evening sets in, loiter at shop-windows and ogle gentlemen in public walks, making requests which might be expected only from long-hardened prostitution. Their nights are generally passed in a low lodging-house. They frequently introduce themselves with 'Please, sir, can you tell me what time it is?' If they get a kindly answer, some other casual observations prepare the way for hints which are as unmistakeable as they are unprincipled.

OF THE LOW LODGING-HOUSES THROUGH-OUT THE COUNTRY.

FURTHER to elucidate this subject, full of importance, as I have shown, I give an account of low lodging-houses (or "padding-kens") at the "stages" (so to speak) observed by a patterer "travelling" from London to Birmingham.

I give the several towns which are the usual sleeping places of the travellers, with the character and extent of the accommodation provided for them, and with a mention of such incidental matters as seemed to me, in the account I received, to be curious or characteristic. Circuitous as is the route, it is the one generally followed. Time is not an object with a travelling patterer. "If I could do better in the way of tin," said one of the fraternity to me, "in a country village than in London, why I'd stick to the village—if the better tin lasted—for six months; aye, sir, for six years. What's places to a man like me, between grub and no grub?" It is probable that on a trial, such a man would soon be weary of the monotony of a village life; but into that question I need not now enter.

I give each stage without the repetition of stating that from "here to there" is so many miles; and the charge for a lodging is at such and such a rate. The distance most frequently "travelled" in a day varies from ten to twenty miles, according to the proximity of the towns, and the character and capabilities (for the patterer's purposes) of the locality. The average charge for a lodging, in the better sort of country lodging-houses, is 4*d.* a night,—at others, 3*d.* In a slack time, a traveller, for 4*d.*, has a bed to himself. In a busy time—as at fairs or races—he will account himself fortunate if he obtain *any* share of a bed for 4*d.* At some of the places characterised by my informant as "rackety," "queer," or "Life in London," the charge is as often 3*d.* as 4*d.*

The first stage, then, most commonly attained on tramp, is—

Romford.—"It's a good circuit, sir," said my principal informant, "and if you want to see life between from London to Birmingham, why you can stretch it and see it for 200 miles." The Romford "house of call" most frequented by the class of whom I treat, is the King's Arms (a public-house.) There is a back-kitchen for the use of travellers, who pay something extra if they choose to resort, and are decent enough to be admitted, into the tap-room. "Very respectable, sir," said an informant, "and a proper division of married and single, of men and women. Of course they don't ask any couple to show their marriage lines; no more than they do any lord and lady, or one that ain't a lady, if she's with a lord, at any fash'nable hotel at Brighton. I've done tidy well on slums about 'ladies in a Brighton hotel,' just by the Steyne; werry tidy." In this house they make up forty beds; some of them with curtains.

Chelmsford.—The Three Queens (a beer-shop.) "A rackety place, sir," said the man, "one of the showfuls; a dicky one; a free-and-easy. You can get a pint of beer and a punch of the head, all for 2*d.* As for sleeping on a Saturday night there, 'O, no, we never mention it.' It mayn't be so bad, indeed it ain't, as some London lodging-houses, because there ain't the chance, and there's more known about it." Fourteen beds.

Braintree.—The Castle (a beer-shop.) "Takes in all sorts and all sizes; all colours and all nations; similar to what's expected of the Crys-

tal Palace. I was a *muck-snipe* when I was there—why, a muck-snipe, sir, is a man regularly done up, coopered, and humped altogether—and it was a busyish time, and when the deputy paired off the single men, I didn't much like my bed-mate. He was a shabby-genteel, buttoned up to the chin, and in the tract line. I thought of Old Scratch when I looked at him, though he weren't a Scotchman, I think. I tipped the wink to an acquaintance there, and told him I thought my old complaint was coming on. That was, to kick and bite like a horse, in my sleep, a'cause my mother was terrified by a wicious horse not werry long afore I was born. So I dozed on the bed-side, and began to whinny; and my bed-mate jumped up frightened, and slept on the floor." Twenty-two beds.

Thaxton.—"A poor place, but I stay two days, it's so comfortable and so country, at the Rose and Crown. It's a sort of rest. It's decent and comfortable too, and it's about 6*d.* a night to me for singing and patter in the tap-room. That's my cokum (advantage)." Ten beds.

Saffron Walden.—The Castle. "Better now—was very queer. Slovenly as could be, and you had to pay for fire, though it was a house of call for curriers and other tradesmen, but they never mix with us. The landlord don't care much whose admitted, or how they go on." Twenty-four beds.

Cambridge.—"The grand town of all. London in miniature. It would be better but for the police. I don't mean the college bull-dogs. They don't interfere with us, only with women. The last time I was at Cambridge, sir, I hung the Mannings. It was the day, or two days, I'm not sure which, after their trial. We pattered at night, too late for the collegians to come out. We 'worked' about where we knew they lodged—I had a mate with me—and some of the windows of their rooms, in the colleges themselves, looks into the street. We pattered about later news of Mr. and Mrs. Manning. Up went the windows, and cords was let down to tie the papers to. But we always had the money first. We weren't a-going to trust such out-and-out going young coves as them. One young gent. said: 'I'm a sucking parson; won't you trust *me*?' 'No,' says I, 'we'll not trust Father Peter.' So he threw down 6*d.* and let down his cord, and he says, 'Send six up.' We saw it was Victoria's head all right, so we sends up three. 'Where's the others?' says he. 'O,' says I, 'they're 1*d.* a piece, and 1*d.* a piece extra for hanging Mr. and Mrs. Manning, as we have, to a cord; so it's all right.' Some laughed, and some said, 'D—n you, wait till I see you in the town.' But they hadn't that pleasure. Yorkshire Betty's is the head quarters at Cambridge,—or in Barnwell, of course, there's no such places in Cambridge. It's known as 'W— and Muck Fort.' It's the real college touch—the seat of learning, if you're seeing life. The college lads used to look in there oftener than they do now. They're getting shyer." Men won't put up with black eyes for nothing. Old Yorkshire Betty's a motherly body, but she's no ways particular in her management. Higgledy-piggledy; men and women; altogether." Thirty beds.

Newmarket.—" The Woolpack. A lively place; middling other ways. There's generally money to be had at Newmarket. I don't stay there so long as some, for I don't care about racing; and the poorest snob there's a sporting character." Six beds.

Bury St. Edmund's.—" Old Jack Something's. He was a publican for forty years. But he broke, and I've heard him say that if he hadn't been a player on the fiddle, he should have destroyed his-self. But his fiddle diverted him in his troubles. He has a real Cremona, and can't he play it? He's played at dances at the Duke of Norfolk's. I've heard him give the tune he played on his wedding night, years and years back, before I was born. He's a noble-looking fellow; the fac-simile of Louis Philippe. It's a clean and comfortable, hard and honest place." Twelve beds.

Mildenhall.—" A private house; I forget the landlord's name. The magistrates is queer there, and so very little work can be done in my way. I've been there when I was the only lodger." Seven beds.

Ely.—" The Tom and Jerry. Very queer. No back kitchen or convenience. A regular rough place. Often quarrelling there all night long. Any caper allowed among men and women. The landlord's easy frightened." Five beds.

St. Ives.—" Plume of Feathers. Passable." Eleven beds.

St. Neot's.—" Bell and Dicky, and very dicky too. Queer doings in the dos (sleeping) and everything. It's an out-of-the-way place, or the town's people might see to it, but they won't take any notice unless some traveller complains, and they won't complain. They're a body of men, sir, that don't like to run gaping to a beak. The landlord seems to care for nothing but money. He takes in all that offer. Three in a bed often; men, women, and children mixed together. It's anything but a tidy place." Thirteen beds.

Bedford.—The Cock. " Life in London, sir; I can't describe it better. Life in Keate-street, Whitechapel." Fifteen beds.

Irchester.—" I don't mind the name. A most particular place. You must go to bed by nine, or be locked out. It's hard and honest; clean and rough." Six beds.

Wellingborough.—" A private house. Smith or Jones, I know, or some common name. Ducker, the soldier that was shot in the Park by Annette Meyers, lived there. I worked him there myself, and everybody bought. I did the gun-trick, sir, (had great success.) It's an inferior lodging place. They're in no ways particular, not they, who they admit or how they dos. At a fair-time, the goings on is anything but fair." Ten beds.

Northampton.—" Mrs. Bull's. Comfortable and decent. She takes in the *Dispatch*, to oblige her travellers. It's a nice, quiet, Sunday house." Twelve beds.

Market Harborough.—" There's a good lady there gives away tracts and half-a-crown. A private house is the traveller's house, and some new name. Middling accommodation." Nine beds.

Lutterworth.—" A private house, and I'll go there no more. Very queer. Not the least comfort or decency. They're above their business, I think, and take in too many, and care nothing what the travellers do. Higgledy-piggledy together." Ten beds.

Leicester.—" The Rookery. Rosemary-lane over again, sir, especially at Black Jack's. He shakes up the beds with a pitchfork, and brings in straw if there's more than can possibly be crammed into the beds. He's a fighting man, and if you say a word, he wants to fight you." Twelve beds.

Hinckley.—" The Tea-board. Comfortable." Eight beds.

Nuneaton.—" The same style as Hinckley. A private house." Eight beds.

Coventry.—" Deserves to be sent further. Bill Cooper's. A dilapidated place, and no sleep, for there's armies of bugs,—great black fellows. I call it the Sikh war there, and they're called Sikhs there, or Sicks there, is the vermin; but I'm sick of all such places. They're not particular there,—certainly not." Twenty beds.

Birmingham.—" Mrs. Leach's. Comfortable and decent, and a good creature. I know there's plenty of houses in Birmingham bad enough,—London reduced, sir; but I can't tell you about them from my own observation, 'cause I always go to Mrs. Leach's." Thirty beds.

Here, then, in the route most frequented by the pedestrian "travellers," we find, taking merely the accommodation of one house in each place (and in some of the smaller towns there is but one), a supply of beds which may nightly accommodate, on an average, 489 inmates, reckoning at the rate of 12 sleepers to every 8 beds. At busy times, double the number will be admitted. And to these places resort the beggar, the robber, and the pick-pocket; the street-patterer and the street-trader; the musician, the ballad-singer, and the street-performer; the diseased, the blind, the lame, and the half-idiot; the outcast girl and the hardened prostitute; young and old, and of all complexions and all countries.

Nor does the enumeration end here. To these places must often resort the wearied mechanic, travelling in search of employment, and even the broken-down gentleman, or scholar, whose means do not exceed 4d.

A curious history might be written of the frequenters of low lodging-houses. Dr. Johnson relates, that when Dean Swift was a young man, he paid a yearly visit from Sir William Temple's seat, Moor Park, to his mother at Leicester.

"He travelled on foot, unless some violence of weather drove him into a waggon; and at night he would go to a penny lodging, where he purchased clean sheets for sixpence. This practice Lord Orrery imputes to his (Swift's) innate love of grossness and vulgarity; some may ascribe it to his desire of surveying human life through all its varieties." Perhaps it might not be very difficult to trace, in Swift's works, the influence upon his mind of his lodging-house experience.

The same author shows that his friend, Richard Savage, in the bitterness of his poverty, was also a lodger in these squalid dens: "He passed the night sometimes in mean houses, which are set open at night to any casual wanderer; sometimes in cellars, among the riot and filth of the meanest and most profligate of the rabble." A Richard Savage of to-day might, under similar circumstances, have the same thing said of him, except that "cellars" might now be described as "ground-floors."

The great, and sometimes the only, luxury of the frequenters of these country lodging-houses is tobacco. A man or women who cannot smoke, I was told, or was not "hardened" to tobacco smoke, in a low lodging-house was half-killed with coughing. Sometimes a couple of men, may be seen through the thick vapour of the tobacco-smoke, peering eagerly over soiled cards, as they play at all-fours. Sometimes there is an utter dulness and drowsiness in the common sitting-room, and hardly a word exchanged for many minutes. I was told by one man of experience in these domiciles, that he had not very unfrequently heard two men who were conversing together in a low tone, and probably agreeing upon some nefarious course, stop suddenly, when there was a pause in the general conversation, and look uneasily about them, as if apprehensive and jealous that they had been listened to. A "stranger" in the lodging-house is regarded with a minute and often a rude scrutiny, and often enough would not be admitted, were not the lodging-house keeper the party concerned, and he of course admits "all what pays."

One patterer told me of two "inscriptions," as he called them, which he had noticed in country lodgings he had lately visited; the first was:—

"He who smokes, thinks like a philosopher, and feels like a philanthropist."—*Bulwer's Night and Morning.*

The second was an intimation from the proprietor of the house, which, in spite of its halting explanation, is easily understood:—

"No sickness allowed, unles by order of the Mare."

OF THE STREET STATIONERS, AND THE STREET CARD-SELLERS.

I have before mentioned that the street-stationers—the sellers of writing-paper, envelopes, pens, and of the other articles which constitute the stationery in the most general demand—were not to be confounded with the pattering

"paper-workers." They are, indeed, a different class altogether. The majority of them have been mechanics, or in the employ of tradesmen whose callings were not mechanical (as regards handicraft labour), but what is best described perhaps as commercial; or as selling but not producing; as in the instances of the large body of "warehousemen" in the different departments of trade. One street-stationer thought that of his entire body, not more than six had been gentlemen's servants. He himself knew four who had been in such employment, and one only as a boy—but there might be six.

The card-sellers are, in the instances I shall show, more akin to the class of patterers, and I shall, therefore, give them first. The more especially as I can so preserve the consecutiveness of the accounts, in the present number, by presenting the reader with a sketch of the life of an informant, in whose revelations I find that many have taken a strong interest.

OF THE SELLER OF THE PENNY SHORT-HAND CARDS.

ALL ladies and gentlemen who "take their walks abroad," must have seen, and of course heard, a little man in humble attire engaged in selling at one penny each a small card, containing a few sentences of letter-press, and fifteen stenographic characters, with an example, by which, it is asserted, anybody and everybody may "learn to write short-hand in a few hours." With the merits of the production, self-considered, this is not the place to meddle; suffice it that it is one of the many ways of getting a crust common to the great metropolis, and perhaps the most innocent of all the street performances. A kind of a street lecture is given by the vendor, in which the article is sufficiently puffed off. Of course this lecture is, so to speak, stereotyped, embracing the same ideas in nearly the same words over and over and over again. The exhibitor, however, pleads that the constant exchange and interchange of passengers, and his desire to give each and all a fair amount of information, makes the repetition admissible, and even necessary. It is here given as a specimen of the style of the educated "patterer."

The Lecture.

"Here is an opportunity which has seldom if ever been offered to the public before, whereby any person of common intellect may learn to write short-hand in a few hours, without any aid from a teacher. The system is entirely my own. It contains no vowels, no arbitrary characters, no double consonants, and no terminations; it may therefore properly be called 'stenography,' an expression which conveys its own meaning; it is derived from two Greek words; *stenos*, short, and *grapho*, I write, or *graphi*, the verb *to* write, and embraces all tha. is necessary in fifteen characters. I know that a prejudice obtains to a great extent against anything and everything said or done in the street, but I have nothing to do with either the majority or minority of street pretenders. I am an educated man, and not a mere pretender, and if the justice or genuineness of a man's pretensions would always lead him to success I had not been here to-day. But against the tide of human disappointment, the worthy and the undeserving are so equally compelled to struggle, and so equally liable to be overturned by competition, that till you can prove that wealth is the guage of character, it may be difficult to determine the ability or morality of a man from his position. I was lately reading an account of the closing life of that leviathan in literature, Dr. Johnson, and an anecdote occurred, which I relate, conceiving that it applies to one of the points at issue—I mean the ridicule with which my little publication has sometimes been treated by passers-by, who have found it easier to speculate on the texture of my coat, than on the character of my language. The Doctor had a niece who had embraced the peculiarities of Quakerism; after he had scolded her some time, and in rather unmeasured terms, her mother interfered and said, 'Doctor, don't scold the girl—you'll meet her in heaven, I hope.'— 'I hope not,' said the Doctor, 'for I hate to meet *fools* anywhere.' I apply the same observation to persons who bandy about the expressions 'gift of the gab,' 'catch-penny,' &c., &c., which in my case it is somewhat easier to circulate than to support. At any rate they ought to be addressed to *me* and not to the atmosphere. The man who meets a foe to the face, gives him an equal chance of defence, and the sword openly suspended from the belt is a less dangerous, because a less cowardly weapon than the one which, like that of Harmodius, is concealed under the wreaths of a myrtle.

"If you imagine that professional disappointment is confined to people out of doors, you are very much mistaken. Look into some of the middle-class streets around where we are standing: you will find here and there, painted or engraved on a door, the words 'Mr. So-and-so, surgeon.' The man I am pre-supposing shall be qualified, — qualified in the technical sense of the expression, a Member of the College of Surgeons, a Licentiate of Apothecaries' Hall, and a Graduate of some University. He may possess the talent of Galen or Hippocrates; or, to come to more recent date, of Sir Astley Cooper himself, but he never becomes popular, and dies unrewarded because unknown: before he dies, he may crawl out of his concealed starvation into such a thoroughfare as this, and see Professor Morrison, or Professor Holloway, or the Proprietor of Parr's Life Pills, or some other quack, ride by in their carriage; wealth being brought them by the same waves that have wafted misfortune to himself; though that wealth has been procured by one undeviating system of Hypocrisy and Humbug, of Jesuitism and Pantomime, such as affords no parallel since the disgusting period of Oliverian ascendancy.

Believe me, my friends, a man may form his plans for success with profound sagacity, and guard with caution against every approach to extravagance, but neither the boldness of enterprise nor the dexterity of stratagem will always secure the distinction they deserve. Else that policeman would have been an inspector!

"I have sometimes been told, that if I possessed the facilities I professedly exhibit, I might turn them to greater personal advantage: in coarse, unfettered, Saxon English, 'That's a LIE;' for on the authority of a distinguished writer, there are 2,000 educated men in London and its suburbs, who rise every morning totally ignorant where to find a breakfast. Now I am not *quite* so bad as that, so that it appears I am an exception to the rule, and not the rule open to exception. However, it is beyond all controversy, that the best way to keep the fleas from biting you in bed is to 'get out of bed;' and by a parity of reasoning, the best way for you to sympathize with me for being on the street is to take me off, as an evidence of your sympathy. I remember that, some twenty years ago, a poor man of foreign name, but a native of this metropolis, made his appearance in Edinburgh, and advertised that he would lecture on mnemonics, or the art of memory. As he was poor, he had recourse to an humble lecture-room, situated up a dirty court. Its eligibility may be determined by the fact that sweeps' concerts were held in it, at $\frac{1}{2}d$. per head, and the handbill mostly ended with the memorable words: 'N. B.—No gentleman admitted without shoes and stockings.' At the close of his first lecture (the admission to which was 2d.), he was addressed by a scientific man, who gave him 5s.—(it will relieve the monotony of the present address if some of you follow his example)—and advised him to print and issue some cards about his design, which he did. I saw one of them—the ink on it scarcely dry— as he had got it back at the house of a physician, and on it was inscribed: 'Old birds are not caught with chaff. From Dr. M——, an old bird.' The suspicious doctor, however, was advised to hear the poor man's twopenny lecture, and was able, at the end of it, to display a great feat of memory himself. What was the result? The poor man no longer lectured for 2d. But it is tedious to follow him through a series of years. He was gradually patronised throughout the kingdom, and a few months ago he was lecturing in the Hanover-square Rooms, with the Earl of Harrowby in the chair. Was he not as clever a man when he lectured in the sweeps' concert-room? Yes; but he had not been brought *under the shadow of a great name.* Sometimes that 'great name' comes too late. You are familiar with the case of Chatterton. He had existed, rather than lived, three days on a penny loaf; then he committed suicide, and was charitably buried by strangers. Fifty years or more had elapsed, when people found out how clever he had been, and collected money for the erection of that monument which now stands to his memory by St. Mary Redcliff Church, in Bristol. Now, if you have any idea of doing that for me, please to collect some of it while I am *alive !*"

On occasions when the audience is not very liberal, the lecturer treats them to the following hint:

"When in my golden days—or at the least they were silver ones compared to these—I was in the habit of lecturing on scientific subjects, I always gave the introductory lecture *free*. I suppose this is an 'introductory lecture,' for it yields very little money at present. I have often thought, that if everybody a little richer than myself was half as conscientious, I should either make a rapid fortune, or have nobody to listen to me at all; for I never sanction long with my company anything I don't believe. Now, if what I say is untrue or grossly improbable, it does not deserve the sanction of an audience; if otherwise, it must be meritorious, and deserve more efficient sanction. As to any insults I receive, Christianity has taught me to forgive, and philosophy to despise them."

These very curious, and perhaps unique, specimens of street elocution are of course interrupted by the occasional sale of a card, and perhaps some conversation with the purchaser. The stenographic card-seller states that he has sometimes been advised to use more commonplace language. His reply is germane to the matter. He says that a street audience, like some other audiences, is best pleased with what they least understand, and that the way to appear sublime is to be incomprehensible. He can occasionally be a little sarcastic. A gentleman informed me that he passed him at Bagnigge-wells on one occasion, when he was interrupted by a "gent." fearfully disfigured by the small-pox, who exclaimed: "It's a complete humbug." "No, sir," retorted Mr. Shorthand, "but if any of the ladies present were to call you handsome, *that* would be a humbug." On another occasion a man (half-drunk) had been annoying him some time, and getting tired of the joke, said: "Well—I see you are a learned man, you must pity my ignorance." "No," was the reply, "but I pity your father." "Pity my father!—why?" was the response. "Because Solomon says, 'He that begetteth a fool shall have sorrow of him.'" This little *jeu-d'ésprit*, I was told, brought forth loud acclamations from the crowd, and a crown-piece from a lady who had been some minutes a listener. These statements are among the most curious revelations of the history of the streets.

The short-hand card-seller, as has partly appeared in a report I gave of a meeting of street-folk, makes no secret of having been fined for obstructing a thoroughfare,—having been bound down to keep the peace, and several times imprisoned as a defaulter. He tells me that he once "got a month" in one of the metropolitan jails. It was the custom of the chaplain of the prison in which he was confined, to question the prisoners every Wednesday,

from box to box (as they were arranged before him) on some portion of Holy Writ, and they were expected, if able, to answer. On one occasion, the subject being the Excellence of Prayer, the chaplain, remarked that, "even among the heathen, every author, without exception, had commended prayer to a real or supposed Deity." The card-seller, I am told, cried out "Question!" "Who is that?" said the chaplain. The turnkey pointed out the questioner. "Yes," said the card-seller, "you know what Seneca says:—'Quid opus votis? Fac teipsum felicem, vel bonum.' 'What need of prayer? Make thou thyself happy and virtuous.' Does *that* recommend prayer?" The prisoners laughed, and to prevent a mutiny, the classical querist was locked up, and the chaplain closed the proceedings. It is but justice, however, to the worthy minister to state, his querist came out of durance vile better clothed than he went in.

The stenographic trade, of which the informant in question is the sole pursuer, was commenced eleven years ago. At that time 300 cards were sold in a day; but the average is now 24, and about 50 on a Saturday night. The card-seller tells me that he is more frequently than ever interrupted by the police, and his health being delicate, wet days are "nuisances" to him. He makes an annual visit to the country, to see his children, who have been provided for by some kind friends. About two years ago he was returning to London and passed through Oxford. He was "hard up," he says, having left his coat for his previous night's lodging. He attended prayers (without a coat) at St. Mary's church, and when he came out, seated himself on the pavement beside the church, and wrote with chalk inside an oval border.

"Δε λίμῳ ἀπολλυμαί."—Lucam xv. 17.
" I perish with hunger."

He was not long unnoticed, he tells me, by the scholars; some of whom "rigged him out," and he left Oxford with 6*l*. 10*s*. in his pocket.

" Let us indulge the hope," writes one who knows this man well, " that whatever indiscretions may have brought a scholar, whom few behold without pity, or converse with without respect for his acquirements, to be a streetseller, nevertheless his last days will be his best days, and that, as his talents are beyond dispute and his habits strictly temperate, he may yet arise out of his degradation."

Of this gentleman's history I give an account derived from the only authentic source. It is, indeed, given in the words of the writer from whom it was received.—

"The *Reverend* Mr. Shorthand" [his real name is of no consequence—indeed, it would be contrary to the rule of this work to print it] "was born at Hackney, in the county of Middlesex, on Good Friday, the 15th of April, 1808; he is, therefore, now in his 43rd year. Of his parents very little is known; he was brought up by guardians, who were 'well to do,' and who gave him every indulgence and every good instruction and example. From the earliest dawn of reason he manifested a strong predilection for the church; and, before he was seven years old, he had preached to an infant audience, read prayers over a dead animal, and performed certain mimic ceremonies of the church among his schoolfellows.

"The directors of his youthful mind were strong Dissenters, of Antinomian sentiments. With half-a-dozen of the same denomination he went, before he was thirteen, to the anniversary meeting of the Countess of Huntingdon's College, at Cheshunt. Here, with a congregation of about forty persons, composed of the students and a few strangers, he adjourned, while the parsons were dining at the 'Green Dragon,' to the College Chapel, where, with closed doors, the future proprietor of the 'penny short-hand' delivered his first public sermon.

"Before he was quite fourteen, the stenographic card-seller was apprenticed to a draper in or near Smithfield. In this position he remained only a few months, when the indentures were cancelled by mutual consent, and he resumed his studies, first at his native place, and afterwards as a day-scholar at the Charterhouse. He was now sixteen, and it was deemed high time for him to settle to some useful calling. He became a junior clerk in the office of a stockbroker, and afterwards amanuensis to an 'M.D.,' who encouraged his thirst for learning, and gave him much leisure and many opportunities for improvement. While in this position he obtained two small prizes in the state lottery, gave up his situation, and went to Cambridge with a private tutor. As economy was never any part of his character, he there 'overrun the constable,' and to prevent," he says, "any constable running after him. He decamped in the middle of the night, and came to London by a waggon—all his property consisting of a Greek Prayer-book, Dodd's Beauties of Shakspere, two shirts, and two half-crowns.

"At this crisis a famous and worthy clergyman, forty years resident in Hackney (the Rev. H. H. N——, lately deceased), had issued from the press certain strictures against the Society for promoting Christianity among the Jews. The short-hand seller wrote an appendix to this work, under the title of the 'Church in Danger.' He took it to Mr. N——, who praised the performance and submitted it to the publication. The impression cast off was limited, and the result unprofitable. It had, however, one favourable issue; it led to the engagement of its author as private and travelling tutor to the children of the celebrated Lady S——, who, though (for adultery) separated from her husband, retained the exclusive custody of her offspring. While in this employment, my informant resided chiefly at Clifton, sometimes in Bath, and sometimes on her ladyship's family property in Derbyshire. While here, he took deacon's orders, and became a popular preacher. In whatever virtues he might

be deficient, his charities, at least, were unbounded. This profusion ill suited a limited income, and *a forgery* was the first step to suspension, disgrace, and poverty. In 1832 he married; the union was not felicitous.

"About this date my informant relates, that under disguise and change of name he supplied the pulpits of several episcopal chapels in Scotland with that which was most acceptable to them. Unable to maintain a *locus standi* in connexion with the Protestant church, he made a virtue of necessity, and avowed himself a seceder. In this new disguise he travelled and lectured, proving to a demonstration (always pecuniary) that 'the Church of England was the hospital of Incurables.'

"Always in delicate health, he found continued journeys inconvenient. The oversight of a home missionary station, comprising five or six villages, was advertised; the card-seller was the successful candidate, and for several years performed Divine service four times every Sunday, and opened and taught *gratuitously* a school for the children of the poor. Here report says he was much beloved, and here he ought to have remained; but with that restlessness of spirit which is so marked a characteristic of the class to which he now belongs, he thought otherwise, and removed to a similar sphere of labour near Edinburgh. The town, containing a population of 14,000, was visited to a dreadful extent with the pestilence of cholera. The future street-seller (to his honour be it spoken) was the only one among eight or ten ministers who was not afraid of the contagion. He visited many hundreds of cases, and, it is credibly asserted, added medicine, food, and nursing to his spiritual consolations. The people of his charge here embraced the Irving heresy; and unable, as he says, to determine the sense of 'the unknown tongues,' he resigned his charge, and returned to London in 1837. After living some time upon his money, books, and clothes, till all was expended, he tried his hand at the 'begging-letter trade.' About this time, the card-seller declares that a man, also from Scotland, and of similar history and personal appearance, lodged with him at a house in the Mint, and stole his coat, and with it his official and other papers. This person had been either a city missionary or scripture-reader, having been dismissed for intemperance. The street card-seller states that he has 'suffered much persecution from the officers of the Mendicity Society, and in the opinion of the public, by the blending of his own history with that of the man who robbed him.'' Be the truth as it may, or let his past faults have been ever so glaring, still it furnishes no present reason why he should be maltreated in the streets, where he is *now* striving for an honest living. Since the card-seller's return to London, he has been *five* times elected and re-elected to a temporary engagement in the Hebrew School, Goodman's-fields; so that, at the worst, his habits of life cannot be *very* outrageous."

The " pomps and vanities of this wicked world," have, according to his own account, had very little share in the experience of the short-hand parson. He states, and there is no reason for doubting him, that he *never witnessed any sort of public amusement in his life;* that he was a hard student when he was young, and now keeps no company, living much in retirement. He " attends the ministry," he says, " of the Rev. Robert Montgomery,—reads the daily lessons at home, and receives the communion twice every month at the early service in Westminster Abbey."

Of course these are matters that appear utterly inconsistent with his present mode of life. One well-known peculiarity of this extraordinary character is his almost idolatrous love of children, to whom, if he " makes a good Saturday night," he is very liberal on his way home. This is, perhaps, his " ruling passion " (an acquaintance of his, without knowing why I inquired, fully confirmed this account); and it displays itself sometimes in strong emotion, of which the following anecdote may be cited as an instance :—One of his favourite spots for stenographic demonstration is the corner of Playhouse-yard, close to the *Times* office. Directly opposite lives a tobacconist, who has a young family. One of his little girls used to stand and listen to him; to her he was so strongly attached, .'at when he heard of her death (he had missed her several weeks), he went home much affected, and did not return to the spot for many months. At the death of the notorious Dr. Dillon, the card-seller offered himself to the congregation as a successor ; they, however, declined the overture.

OF THE SELLERS OF RACE CARDS AND LISTS.

THIS trade is not carried on in town ; but at the neighbouring races of Epsom and Ascot Heath, and, though less numerously, at Goodwood, it is pursued by persons concerned in the street paper-trade of London.

At Epsom I may state that the race-card sale is in the hands of two classes (the paper or sheet-lists sale being carried on by the same parties) — viz. those who confine themselves to " working " the races, and those who only resort to such work occasionally. The first-mentioned sellers usually live in the country, and the second in town,

Between these two classes, there is rather a strong distinction. The country race-card sellers are not unfrequently " sporting characters." The town professor of the same calling feels little interest in the intrigues or great " events " of the turf. Of the country traders in this line some act also as touters, or touts ; they are for the most part men, who having been in some capacity or other, connected with racing or with race-horses, and having fallen from their position or lost their employment, resort to the selling of race-cards as one means of a livelihood, and to touting,

or watching race-horses, and reporting anything concerning them to those interested, as another means. These men, I am assured, usually " make a book " (a record and calculation of their bets) with grooms, or such gentlemen's servants, as will bet with them, and sometimes one with another.

The most notorious of the race-card selling fraternity is known as Captain Carrot. He is the successor, I am told, of Gentleman Jerry, who was killed some time back at Goodwood races—having been run over. Gentleman Jerry's attire, twenty-five to thirty-five years ago, was an exaggeration of what was then accounted a gentleman's style. He wore a light snuff-coloured coat, a " washing " waistcoat of any colour, cloth trowsers, usually the same colour as his coat, and a white, or yellow white, and ample cravat of many folds. His successor wears a military uniform, always with a scarlet coat, Hessian boots, an old umbrella, and a tin eye-glass. Upon the card-sellers, however, who confine their traffic to races, I need not dwell, but proceed to the metropolitan dealers, who are often patterers when in town.

It is common, for the smarter traders in these cards to be liberal of titles, especially to those whom they address on the race-ground. " This is the sort of style, sir," said one race-card-seller to me, " and it tells best with cockneys from their shops. ' Ah, my lord. I hope your lordship's well. I've backed your horse, my lord. He'll win, he'll win. Card, my lord, correct card, only 6*d.* I'll drink your lordship's health after the race.' Perhaps this here ' my lord,' may be a barber, you see, sir, and never had so much as a donkey in his life, and he forks out a bob; but before he can get his change, there always *is* somebody or other to call for a man like me from a little distance, so I'm forced to run off and cry, ' Coming, sir, coming. Coming, your honour, coming.' "

The mass of these sellers, however, content themselves with the customary cry : " Here's Dorling's Correct Card of the Races.—Names, weights, and colours of the Riders.—Length of Bridle, and Weight of Saddle."

One intelligent man computed that there were 500 men, women, and children, of all descriptions of street-callings, who on a " Derby day " left London for Epsom. Another considered that there could not be fewer than 600, at the very lowest calculation. Of these, I am informed, the female sellers may number something short of a twentieth part from London, while a twelfth of the whole number of regular street-sellers attending the races vend at the races cards. But card-selling is often a cloak, for the females—and especially those connected with men who depend solely on the races—vend improper publications (usually at 6*d.*), making the sale of cards or lists a pretext for the more profitable traffic.

If a man sell from ten to twelve dozen cards on the " Derby day," it is accounted " a good day ;" and so is the sale of three-fourths of that quantity on the Oaks day. On the other, or "off" days, 2s. is an average earnig.

The cards are all bought of Mr. Dorling, the printer, at 2s. 6d. a dozen. The price asked is always 6d. each. "But those fourpenny bits," said one card-seller, "is the ruination of every thing. And now that they say that the three-penny bits is coming in more, things will be wuss and wuss." The lists vary from 1s. 6d. to 2s. 6d. the dozen, according to size. To clear 10s. and 8s. on the two great days is accounted "tidy doings," but that is earned only by those who devote themselves to the sale of the race-cards, which all the sellers do not. Some, for instance, are ballad-singers, who sell cards immediately before a race comes off, as at that time they could obtain no auditory for their melodies. Ascot-heath races, I am told, are rather better for the card seller than Epsom, as "there's more of the nobs there," and fewer of the London vendors of cards. The sale of the "lists" is less than one-eighth that of the sale of cards. They are chiefly "return lists," (lists with a specification of the winning horses, &c., "returned" as they acquitted themselves in each race), and are sold in the evening, or immediately after the conclusion of the "sport," for the purpose of being posted or kept.

OF THE STREET-SELLERS OF GELATINE, OF ENGRAVED, AND OF PLAYING CARDS, &c.

THERE are yet other cards, the sale of which is carried on in the streets; of these, the principal traffic has lately been in "gelatines" (gelatine cards). Those in the greatest demand contain representations of the Crystal Palace, the out-lines of the structure being given in gold deli-neation on the deep purple, or mulberry, of the smooth and shining gelatine. These cards are sold in blank envelopes, for the convenience of posting them as a present to a country friend; or of keeping them unsoiled, if they are retained as a memento of a visit to so memorable a build-ing. The principal sale was on Sunday morn-ings, in Hyde Park, and to the visitors who employed that day to enjoy the sight of the "palace." But on the second Sunday in Fe-bruary—as well as my informant could recollect, for almost all street-traders will tell you, if not in the same words as one patterer used, that their recollections are "not worth an old button without a neck"—the police "put down" the sale of these Exhibition cards in the Park, as well as that of cakes, tarts, gingerbread, and such like dainties. This was a bitter disap-pointment to a host of street-sellers, who looked forward very sanguinely to the profits they might realise when the Great Exhibition was in full operation, and augured ill to their prospects from this interference. I am inclined to think, that, on this occasion, the feelings of animosity enter-tained by the card-sellers towards the police and the authorities were even bitterer than I have described as affecting the costermongers. "Why," said one man, "when I couldn't be

let sell my cards, I thrust my hands into my empty pockets, and went among the crowd near the Great Exhibition place to look about me. There was plenty of ladies and gentlemen—say about 12 o'clock at Sunday noon, and as many as could be. Plenty of 'em had nice paper bags of biscuits, or cakes, that, of course, they'd bought that morning at a pastrycook's, and they handed 'em to their party. Some had news-papers they was reading—about the Exhibition, I dare say—papers which was bought, and, per-haps, was printed that very blessed morning; but for us to offer to earn a crust then—oh, it's agen the law. In course it is."

Some of the gelatine cards contain pieces of poetry, in letters of gold, always—at least, I could hear of no exceptions—of a religious or sentimental character. "A Hymn," "The Child's Prayer," "The Christian's Hope," "To Eliza," "To a Daisy," "Forget-me-not," and "Affection's Tribute," were among the titles. Some contained love-verses, and might be used for valentines, and some a sentimental song.

In the open-air sale, nearly all the traffic was in "Exhibition gelatines," and the great bulk were sold in and near Hyde Park. For two or three months, from as soon as the glass palace had been sufficiently elevated to command public attention, there were daily, I am told, 20 persons selling those cards in the Park and its vicinity, and more than twice that number on Sundays. One man told me, that, on one fine bright Sunday, the sale being principally in the morning, he had sold 10 dozen, with a profit of about 5s. On week-days three dozen was a good sale; but on wet, cold, or foggy days, none at all could be disposed of. If, therefore, we take as an average the sale of two dozen daily per each individual, and three dozen on a Sun-day, we find that 180l. was expended on street-sold "gelatines." The price to the retailer is 5d. a dozen, with 1d. or 1¼d. for a dozen of the larger-sized envelopes, so leaving the usual profit—cent. per cent. The sellers were not a distinct class, but in the hands of the less enter-prising of the paper-workers or patterers. The "poetry gelatines" were hardly offered at all in the streets, except by a few women and children, with whom it was a pretext for begging.

Of "engraved" Exhibition-cards, sold under similar circumstances, there might be one third as many sold as of the gelatines, or an expen-diture of 60l.

The sale of playing-cards is only for a brief interval. It is most brisk for a couple of weeks before Christmas, and is hardly ever attempted in any season but the winter. The price varies from 1d. to 6d., but very rarely 6d.; and seldom more than 3d. the pack. The sellers for the most part announce their wares as "New cards. New playing-cards. Two-pence a pack." This subjects the sellers (the cards being unstamped) to a penalty of 10l., a matter of which the street-traders know and care nothing; but there is no penalty on the sale of second-hand cards. The best of the cards are generally sold by the street-sellers to the landlords of the public-houses and beer-shops where the customers are fond of a "hand at cribbage," a "cut-in at whist," or a "game at all fours," or "all fives." A man whose business led him to public-houses told me that for some years he had not observed any other games to be played there, but he had heard an old tailor say that in his youth, fifty years ago, "put" was a common public-house game. The cheaper cards are frequently imperfect packs. If there be the full number of fifty-two, some perhaps are duplicates, and others are consequently wanting. If there be an ace of spades, it is unaccompanied by those flourishes which in the duly stamped cards set off the announcement, "Duty, One Shilling;" and sometimes a blank card supplies its place. The smaller shop-keepers usually prefer to sell playing-cards with a piece cut off each corner, so as to give them the character of being second-hand; but the street-sellers prefer vending them without this precaution. The cards—which are made up from the waste and spoiled cards of the makers—are bought chiefly, by the retailers, at the "swag shops."

Playing cards are more frequently sold with other articles—such as almanacks—than otherwise. From the information I obtained, it appears that if twenty dozen packs of cards are sold daily for fourteen days, it is about the quantity, but rather within it. The calculation was formed on the supposition that there might be twenty street playing-card sellers, each disposing (allowing for the hinderances of bad weather, &c.), of one dozen packs daily. Taking the average price at 3d. a pack, we find an outlay of 42l. The sale used to be far more considerable and at higher prices, and was "often a good spec. on a country round."

There is still another description of cards sold in the streets of London; viz., conversation-cards; but the quantity disposed of is so trifling as to require no special comment.

OF THE STREET-SELLERS OF STATIONERY.

OF this body of street-traders there are two descriptions, the itinerant and the "pitching." There are some also who unite the two qualities, so far as that they move a short distance, perhaps 200 yards, along a thoroughfare, but preserve the same locality.

Of the itinerant again, there are some who, on an evening, and more especially a Saturday evening, take a stand in a street-market, and pursue their regular "rounds" the other portions of the day.

The itinerant trader carries a tray, and in no few cases, as respects the "display" of his wares, emulates the tradesman's zeal in "dressing" a window temptingly. The tray most in use is painted, or mahogany, with "ledges," front and sides; or, as one man described it, "an upright four-inch bordering, to keep things in their places." The back of the tray, which rests against the bearer's breast, is about twelve inches high. Narrow pink tapes are generally attached to the "ledges" and back, within which are "slipped" the articles for sale. At the bottom of the tray are often divisions, in which are deposited steel pens, wafers, wax, pencils, pen-holders, and, as one stationer expressed it, "packable things that you can't get much show out of." One man—who rather plumed himself on being a thorough master of his trade—said to me: "It's a grand point to display, sir. Now, just take it in this way. Suppose you yourself, sir, lived in my round. Werry good. You hear me cry as I'm a approaching your door, and suppose you was a customer, you says to yourself: 'Here's Penny-a-quire,' as I'm called oft enough. And I'll soon be with you, and I gives a extra emphasis at a customer's door. Werry good, you buys the note. As you buys the note, you gives a look over my tray, and then you says, 'O, I want some steel pens, and is your ink good?' and you buys some. But for the 'display,' you'd have sent to the shopkeeper's, and I should have lost custom, 'cause it wouldn't have struck you."*

The articles more regularly sold by the street-sellers of stationery are note-paper, letter-paper, envelopes, steel pens, pen-holders, sealing-wax, wafers, black-lead pencils, ink in stonebottles, memorandum-books, almanacks, and valentines. Occasionally, they sell India-rubber, slate-pencil, slates, copy-books, story-books, and arithmetical tables.

The stationery is purchased, for the most part, in Budge-row and Drury-lane. The half-quires (sold at 1d.) contain, generally, 10 sheets; if the paper, however, be of superior quality, only 8 sheets. In the paper-warehouses it is known as "outsides," with no more than 10 sheets to the half-quire, the price varying from 4s. to 6s. the ream (20 quires); or, if bought by weight, from 7d. to 9d. the pound. The envelopes are sold (wholesale) at from 6d. to 15d. the dozen; the higher-priced being adhesive, and with impressions—now, generally, the Crystal Palace—on the place of the seal. The commoner are retailed in the streets at 12, and the better at 6, a penny. Sometimes "a job-lot," soiled, is picked up by the street-stationer at 4d. a pound. The sealing, a pound, retailed at ½d. each; the "flat" wax, however, is 1s. 4d. per lb., containing from 30 to 36 sticks, retailed at 1d. each. Wafers (at the same swag shops) are 3d. or 4d. the lb.—in small boxes, 9d. the gross; ink, 4½d. or 5d. the dozen bottles; pencils, 7d. to 8s. a gross; and steel pens from 4d. (waste) to 3s. a gross; but the street-stationers do not go beyond 2s. the gross, which is for magnum bonums,

OF THE EXPERIENCE OF A STREET-STATIONER.

A middle-aged man gave me the following

* I may here observe that I have rarely heard tradesmen dealing in the same wares as street-sellers, described by those street-sellers by any other term than that of "shopkeepers."

account. He had pursued the trade for upwards of twelve years. He was a stout, cosey-looking man, wearing a loose great coat. The back of his tray rested against his double-breasted waistcoat; the pattern of which had become rather indistinct, but which was buttoned tightly up to his chin, as if to atone for the looseness of his coat. The corner of his mouth, toward his left ear, was slightly drawn down, for he seemed in "crying" to pitch his voice (so that it could be heard a street off) out of the corner of his only partially-opened mouth.

"Middlin', sir," he said, "times is middlin' with me; they might be better, but then they might be worse. I can manage to live. The times is changed since I was first in the business. Theie wasn't no 'velops (envelopes) then, and no note-paper—least I had none; but I made as good or a better living than I do now; a better indeed. When the penny-postage came in—I don't mind the year, but I hadn't been long in the trade [it was in 1840]—I cried some of the postage 'velops. They was big, figured things at first, with elephants and such like on them, and I called them at prime cost, if anything was bought with 'em. The very first time, a p'liceman says, 'You mustn't sell them covers. What authority have you to do it?' 'Why, the authority to earn a dinner,' says I; but it was no go. Another peeler came up and said I wasn't to cry them again, or he'd have me up; and so that spec. came to nothing. I sell to ladies and gentlemen, and to servant-maids, and mechanics, and their wives; and indeed all sorts of people. Some fine ladies, that call me to the door on the sly, do behave very shabby. Why, there was one who wanted five half-quire of note for 4d., and I told her I couldn't afford it, and so she said ' that she knew the world, and never gave nobody the price they first asked.' ' If that's it, ma'am,' says I, ' people that knows your plan can 'commodate you.' That knowing card of a lady, sir, as she reckons herself, had as much velvet to her body—such a gown!— as would pay my tailor's bills for twenty year. But I don't employ a fashionable tailor, and can patch a bit myself, as I was two years with a saddler, and was set to work to make girths and horse-clothes. My master died, and all went wrong, and I had to turn out, without nobody to help me,—for I had no parents living; but I was a strong young fellow of sixteen. I first tried to sell a few pairs of girths, and a roller or two, to livery-stable keepers, and horse-dealers, and job-masters. But I was next to starving. They wouldn't look at anything but what was good, and the stuff was too high, and the profit too little—for I couldn't get regular prices, in course—and so I dropped it. There's no men in the world so particular about good things as them as is about vallyable horses. I've often thought if rich people cared half as much about poor men's togs, that was working or them for next to nothing, as they cared for their horse-clothes, it would be a better world. I was dead beat at last; but I went

down to Epsom and sold a few race-cards. I'd borrowed 1s. of a groom to start with, and he wouldn't take it back when I offered it; and that wax is bought at general warehouses, known as "swag shops" (of which I may speak hereafter), at 8d. the pound, there being 48 round sticks in, was my beginning in the paper trade. I felt queer at first, and queerer when I wasn't among horses, as at the races like—but one get's reconciled to anything, 'cept, to a man like me, a low lodging-house. A stable's a palace to it. I got into stationery at last, and it's respectable.

" I've heard people say how well they could read and write, and it was no good to them. It has been, and is still, a few pence to me; though I can only read and write middlin'. I write notes and letters for some as buys paper of me. Never anything in the beggin' way— never. It wouldn't do to have my name mixed up that way. I've often got extra pennies for directing and doing up valentines in nice 'velops. Why, I spoke to a servant girl the other day; she was at the door, and says I, ' Any nice paper to-day, to answer your young man's last love-letter, or to write home and ask your mother's consent to your being wed next Monday week?' That's the way to get them to listen, sir. Well, I finds that she can't write, and so I offers to do it for a pint of beer, and she to pay for paper of course. And then there was so many orders what to say. Her love to no end of aunts, and all sorts of messages and inquiries about all sorts of things; and when I'd heard enough to fill a long ' letter' sheet, she calls me back and says, ' I'm afraid I've forgot uncle Thomas.' I makes it all short enough in the letter, sir. ' My kind love to all inquiring friends,' takes in all uncle Thomases. I writes them when I gets a bite of dinner. Sometimes I posts them, if I'm paid beforehand; at other times I leaves them next time I pass the door. There's no mystery made about it. If a missus says, ' What's that?' I've heard a girl answer, ' It's a letter I've got written home, ma'am. I haven't time myself,' or ' I'm no scholar, ma'am.' But that's only where I'm known. I don't write one a week the year round—perhaps forty in a year. I charge 1d. or 2d., or if it's a very poor body, and no gammon about it, nothing. Well, then, I think I never wrote a love-letter. Women does that one for another, I think, when the young housemaid can't write as well as she can talk. I jokes some as I knows, and says I writes all sorts of letters but love-letters, and for them, you see, says I, there's wanted the best gilt edge, and a fancy 'velop, and a Dictionary. I take more for note and 'velops than anything else, but far the most for note. Some has a sheet folded and fitted into a 'velop when they buys, as they can't fit it so well theirselves, they say. Perhaps I make 2s. a day, take it all round. Some days I may make as much as 3s. 6d.; at others, 'specially wet days, not 1s. But I call mine a tidy round, and better than an average. I've only myself, and pays 1s. 9d. a week for a tidy room, with a few of my own sticks in it. I buy sometimes in Budge-row, and sometimes in Drury-lane. Very seldom at a swag-shop (Birmingham house), for I don't like them.

"Well, now, I've heard, sir, that poor men like me ain't to be allowed to sell anything in the Park at the Great Exhibition. How's that, sir?" I told him I could give no information on the subject.

"It's likely enough to be true," he resumed; "the nobs 'll want to keep it all to theirselves. I read *Lloyd's Weekly Newspaper* on a Sunday, and what murders and robberies there is now! What will there be when the Great Exhibition opens! for rogues is worst in a crowd, and they say they'll be plenty come to London from all arts and parts? Never mind; if I can see anything better to do in a fair way at the Exhibition, I'll cut the streets.

"Perhaps my earnings is half from working people and half from private houses; that's about it. But working people's easiest satisfied."

I have given this man's statement more fully than I should have thought necessary, that I might include his account of letter-writing. The letter-writer was at one period a regular street-labourer in London, as he is now in some continental cities—Naples, for instance. The vocation in London seems in some respects to have fallen into the hands of the street-stationer, but the majority of letters written for the uneducated—and their letter-receiving or answering is seldom arduous—is done, I believe, by those who are rather vaguely but emphatically described as—"friends."

I am told that there are 120 street-stationers in London, a small majority of whom may be itinerant, but chiefly on regular rounds. On a Sunday morning, in such places as the Brill, are two or three men, but not regularly, who sell stationery only on Sunday mornings. Taking the number, however, at 120, I am assured that their average profits may be taken at 8s. weekly, each stationer. On note-paper of the best sort the profit is sometimes only 50 per cent.; but, take the trade altogether, we may calculate it at cent. per cent. (on some things it is higher); and we find 4,992l. yearly expended in street-stationery.

OF A "REDUCED" GENTLEWOMAN, AND A "REDUCED" TRADESMAN, AS STREET-SELLERS OF STATIONERY.

I now give two statements, which show the correctness of my conclusion, that among the street-stationers were persons of education who had known prosperity, and that, as a body, those engaged in this traffic were a better class than the mass of the "paper-workers." They are also here cited as illustrations of the causes which lead, or rather force, many to a street-life.

The first statement is that of a lady:—

"My father," she said, "was an officer in the army, and related to the Pitt family. After his death, I supported myself by teaching music. I was considered very talented by my profession, both as teacher and composer." (I may here interrupt the course of the narrative by saying, that I myself have had printed proofs of the lady's talents in this branch of art.) "A few years ago, a painful and protracted illness totally incapacitated me from following my profession; consequently, I became reduced to a state of great destitution. For many weeks I remained ill in my own room. I often, during that time, went without nourishment the day through. I might have gone into an hospital; but I seemed to dread it so much, that it was not until I was obliged to give up my room that I could make up my mind to enter one. From that time, until within a few weeks ago, I have been an inmate of several hospitals: the last I was in was the Convalescent Establishment at Carshalton. On my coming to London, I found I had to begin the world again, as it were, in a very different manner from what I have been accustomed to. I had no head to teach—I felt that; and what to do I hardly knew. I had no home to go to, and not a halfpenny in the world. I had heard of the House of Charity, in Soho-square, and, as a last resource, I went there; but before I could have courage to ask admittance, I got a woman to go in and see what kind of a place it was —I seemed to fear it so much. I met with great kindness there, however; and, by the time I left, the care they had bestowed upon me had restored my health in a measure, but not my head. The doctors advised me to get some outdoor occupation (I am always better in the open air); but what to do I could not tell. At last I thought of a man I had known, who made fancy envelopes. I went to him, and asked him to allow me to go round to a few houses with some of them for a small per centage. This he did, and I am thereby enabled, by going along the streets and calling to offer my envelopes at any likely house, just to live. None but those who have suffered misfortunes (as I have done) can tell what my feelings were on first going to a house. I *could* not go where I was known; I had not the courage, nor would my pride allow me. My pupils had been very kind to me during my illnesses, but I could not bear the idea of going to them and offering articles for sale. "My fear of strangers is so great, that I tremble when I knock at a door—lest I should meet with an angry word. How few have any idea of the privations and suffering that have been endured before a woman (brought up as I have been) can make up her mind to do as I am obliged to do! I am now endeavouring to raise a little money to take a room, and carry on the envelope business myself. I might do pretty well, I think; and, should my head get better, in time I might get pupils again. At present I could not teach, the distressed state of my mind would not allow me."

The tradesman's statement he forwarded to me in writing, supplying me with every facility to test the full accuracy of his assertions, which it is right I should add I have done, and found all as he has stated. I give the narrative in the writer's words (and his narrative will be found at once diffuse and minute), as a faithful representation of a " reduced" tradesman's struggles, thoughts, and endurances, before being forced into the streets.

" I was brought up," he writes, " as a linendraper. After filling every situation as an assistant, both in the wholesale and retail trade, I was for a considerable time in business. Endeavouring to save another from ruin, I advanced what little money I had at my banker's, and became security for more, as I thought I saw my way clear. But a bond of judgment was hanging over the concern (kept back from me of course) and the result was, I lost my money to the amount of some hundreds, of which I have not recovered one pound. Since that time I have endeavoured to gain a livelihood as a town traveller. In 1845 I became very much afflicted, and the affliction continued the greater part of the following year. At one time I had fifteen wounds on my body, and lost the use of one side. I was reduced by bodily disease, as well as in circumstances. My wife went to reside among her friends, and I, after my being an out-patient of Bartholomew's Hospital went, through necessity, to Clerkenwell Workhouse. When recovered, I made another effort to do something among my own trade, and thought, after about two years struggle, I should recover in a measure my position. In August, 1849, I sent for a few shillings-worth of light articles from London (being then at Dunstable). I received them, and sold one small part ; I went the following day to the next village nearer London. There I had a violent attack of cholera ; which once more defeated my plans, leaving me in a weak condition. I was obliged to seek the refuge of my parish, and consider that very harshly was I treated there. They refused me admittance, and suffered me to walk the street two days and two nights. I had no use of my arm, was ill and disabled. About half-past seven on the third night, a gentleman, hearing of my sufferings, knocked at the door of the Union, took me inside, and dared them to turn me thence. This was in October, 1849. I lay on my bed there for seven weeks nearly, and a few days before Christmas-day the parish authorities brought me before the Board, and turned me out, with one shilling and a loaf; one of the overseers telling me to go to h—ll and lodge anywhere. I came to lodge at the Model Lodging-house, King-street, Drury-lane ; but being winter-time they were full. Although I remained there in the day-time, I was obliged to sleep at another house. At this domicile I saw how many ways there were of getting what the very poor call a living, and various suggestions were offered. I was promised a gift of 2s. 6d. by an individual, on a certain day,—but I had to live till that day, and many were the feelings of my mind, how to dispose of what might remain when I received the 2s. 6d., as I was getting a little into debt. My debt, when paid, left me but 9½d. out of the

2s. 6d. to trade with. I had never hawked an article before that time ; to stand the streets was terrible to my mind, and how to invest this small sum sadly perplexed me. My mind was racked by painful anxiety ; one moment almost desponding, the next finding so much sterling value in a shilling, that I saw in it the means of rescuing me from my degradation. Wanting many of the necessaries of life, but without suitable attire for my own business, and still weak from illness, I made up my mind. On the afternoon of 2nd Jan., 1850, I purchased 1½ doz. memorandum-books, of a stationer in Clerkenwell, telling him my capital. I obtained the name of ' Ninepence-halfpenny Man ' (the amount of my funds) at that shop. The next step was how to dispose of my books. I thought I would go round to some coffee and public-houses, as I could not endure the streets. I went into one, where I was formerly known, and sold 6d.-worth, and meeting a person who was once in my own line, at another house, I sold 4d.-worth more. The first night, therefore, I got over well. The next day I did a little, but not so well, and I found out that what I had bought was not the most ready sale. My returns that week were only 6s. 2d. I found I must have something different,—one thing would not do alone ; so I bought a few childrens' books and almanacks— sometimes going to market with as little as seven farthings. I could not rise to anything better in the way of provisions during this time than dry toast and coffee, as the rent must be looked to. I struggled on, hoping against hope. At one period I had a cold and lost my voice. Two or three wet days in a week made me a bankrupt. If I denied myself food, to increase my stock, and went out for a day or two to some near town, I found that with small stock and small returns I could not stem the tide.

" I always avoided associating with any but those a step higher in the grades of society—a circumstance that caused me not to know as much of the market for my cheap articles as I might have done. I am perhaps looked on as rather an ' aristocrat,' as I am not often seen by the street-sellers at a stand. My difficulties have been of no ordinary kind ; with a desire for more domestic comfort on one hand, and painful reflections from want of means on the other, I have had to call to my aid all the philosophy I possess, to keep up a proper equilibrium, lest I should be tempted to anything derogatory or dishonest. I am desirous of a rescue at the only time likely for it to take place with advantage, as I am persuaded when persons continue long in a course that endangers their principles and self-respect, a rescue becomes hopeless. Should I have one small start with health, the privations I have undergone show not what comforts I have had, or may hope ever to have, but what I can absolutely do without.

" I found the first six months not quite so good as the latter ; March and May being the worst. The entire amount taken from January 2nd to December 31st, 1850 ; was 28l. 10s. 6d.,—

an average of about 11s. 4d. a week; say for cost of goods, 6s. per week; and rent, 1s. 9d.; leaving me but 3s. 7d. clear for living. This statement, sir, is strictly correct, as I do not get cent. per cent. on all the articles; and yet with so small a return I am not behind one single crown at the present time.

"On New Year's-day last, I had but the cost price of stock, 5d. Up to the evening of February 10th, I have taken 2l. 19s. 8d.;—having paid for goods, 1l. 10s. 5d.; and for rent, 8s. 10d.: leaving me 1l. 5d. to exist on during nearly six weeks. These facts and figures show that without a little assistance it is impossible to rise; and remember this circumstance—I have had to walk on some occasions as much as twenty or twenty-two miles in a day. If those whom Providence has blessed with a little more than their daily wants would only enter into the conflicts of the really reduced person, they would not be half so niggardly in spending a few coppers for useful articles, at least, nor overbearing in their requirements as to bulk, when purchasing of the itinerant vendor. Did they but reflect that they themselves might be in the same condition, or some of their families, I am sure they would not act as they do; for I would venture to say that the common street beggar does not get more rebuffs or insults than the educated and unfortunate reduced tradesmen in the streets. The past year has been one of the most trying and painful, yet I hope instructive, periods of my existence, and one of which I trust I never shall see the like again."

I subjoin one of the testimonies that have been furnished me, as to this man's character, and which I thought it right to procure before giving publicity to the above statement. It is from a minister of the gospel—the street-seller's father-in-law.

"Dear Sir,—I received a letter, last Tuesday, from Mr. Knight, intimating that he was requested by you to inquire into the character of Mr. J—— N——.

"It is quite correct, as he states, that his wife is my daughter. They lived together several years in London; but eventually, notwithstanding her efforts in the millinery and straw-work, they became so reduced that their circumstances obliged my daughter to take her two little girls with herself to us.

"This was in the summer, 1845. His wife and children have been of no expense to Mr. N. since that time. The sole cause of their separation was poverty.

"I consider him to have acted imprudently in giving up his situation to depend on an income arising from a small capital; whereas, if he had kept in a place, whilst she attended to her own business, they might have gone on comfortably; and should they, through the interposition of a kind Providence, gain that position again, it is to be hoped that they will improve the circumstance to the honour and glory of the Author of all our mercies, and with gratitude to the Instrument who may be raised up for their good.

"I am, dear Sir, respectfully yours,
"J. D."

Other vouchers have been received, and all equally satisfactory.

Of the Street-sale of Memorandum-books and Almanacks.

The memorandum-books in demand in street-sale are used for weekly "rent-books." The payment of the rent is entered by the landlord, and the production of one of these books, showing a punctuality of payment, perhaps for years, is one of the best "references" that can be given by any one in search of a new lodging. They are bought also for the entrance of orders, and then of prices, in the trade at chandler's shops, &c., where weekly or monthly accounts are run. All, or nearly all, the street-stationers sell memorandum-books, and in addition to them, there may be, I am told, sometimes as many as fifty poor persons, including women and children, who sell memorandum-books with other trifling articles, not necessarily stationery, but such things as stay-laces or tapes. If a man sell memorandum-books alone it is because his means limit him to that stock, he being at the time, what I heard a patterer describe as, a "dry-bread cove." The price is 6d. the dozen, or 9d. (with almanacks pasted inside the cover), and thirteen to the dozen. No more than 1d. is obtained in the streets for any kind of memorandum-books.

The almanack street trade, I heard on all hands, had become a mere nothing. "What else can you expect, sir," said one street-seller, "when so many publicans sends almanacks round, or gives them away to their customers; and when the slop tailors' shilling-a-day men thrust one into people's hands at every corner? It was a capital trade once, before the duty was taken off—capital! The duty wasn't in our way so much as in the shop-keepers', though they did a good deal on the sly in unstamped almanacks. Why of a night in October I've many a time cleared 5s. and more by selling in the public-houses almanacks at 2d. and 3d. a-piece (they cost me 1s. and 1s. 2d. a dozen at that time). Anything that way, when Government's done, has a ready sale; people enjoys it; and I suppose no man, as ever was, thinks it much harm to do a tax-gatherer! I don't pay the income-tax myself (laughing). One evening I sold, just by Blackfriars-bridge, fourteen dozen of diamond almanacks to fit into hat-crowns. I was liable, in course, and ran a risk. I sold them mostly at 1d. a piece, but sometimes got 6d. for three. I cleared between 6s. and 7s. The 'diamonds' cost me 8d. a dozen."

The street almanack trade is now carried on by the same parties as I have specified in my account of memorandum-books. Those sold are of any cheap kind, costing wholesale 6d. a dozen, but they are almost always announced as "Moore's."

Of the Street-sale of Pocket-books and Diaries.

The sale of pocket-books, in the streets, is not, I was told by several persons, "a living for a man now-a-days." Ten years ago it was common to find men in the streets offering "half-crown pocket-books" for 1s., and holding them open so as to display the engravings, if there were any. The street-sale usually takes place in March, when the demand for the regular trade has ceased, and the publishers dispose of their unsold stock. The trade is now, I am assured, only about a tenth of its former extent. The reason assigned for the decline is that almanacks, diaries, &c., are so cheap that people look upon 1s. as an enormous price, even for a "beautiful morocco-bound pocket-book," as the street-seller proclaims it. The binding is roan (a dressed sheep-skin, morocco being a goat-skin), an imitation of morocco, but the pocket-books are really those which in the October preceding have been published in the regular way of trade. Some few of them may, however, have been damaged, and these are bought by the street-people as a "job lot," and at a lower price than that paid in the regular way; which is 4s. 6d. to 5s. 6d. the dozen, thirteen to the dozen. The "job lot" is sometimes bought for 2s. 6d. a dozen, and sold at 6d. each, or as low as 4d.,—for street-sellers generally bewail their having often to come down to "fourpenny-bits, as they're going so much now." One man told me that he was four days last March in selling a dozen pocket-books, and that the weather was not unfavourable, and that his profit was 5s. Engravings of the "fashions," the same man told me, were "no go now." Even poorly-dressed women (but they might, he thought, be dress-makers) had said to him the last time he displayed a pocket-book with fashions—"They're out now." The principal supplier of pocket-books, &c., to the street-trade is in Bride-lane, Fleet-street. Commercial diaries are bought and sold at the same rate as pocket-books; but the sale becomes smaller and smaller.

I am informed that "last season" there were twenty men, all street-traders in "paper," or "anything that was up," at other times, selling pocket-books and diaries. For this trade Lei-cester-square is a favourite place. Calculating, from the best data I can command, that each of those men took 15s. weekly for a month (half of it their profit), we find 60l. expended in the streets in this purchase. Ledgers are some-times sold in the streets; but as the sale is more a hawker's than a regular street-seller's, an ac-count of the traffic is not required by my present subject.

OF THE STREET-SELLERS OF SONGS.

THESE street-traffickers, with the exception, in a great degree, of the "pinners-up," are of the same class, but their callings are diversified. There are long song-sellers, ballad-sellers (who are generally singers of the ballads they vend, unless they are old and infirm, and offer ballads instead of begging), chaunters, pinners-up, and song-book-sellers. The three first-mentioned classes I have already described in their con-nection with the patterers; and I now proceed to deal with the two last-mentioned.

The "pinners-up" (whom I have mentioned as an exceptional body), are the men and women —the women being nearly a third of the num-

ber of the men—who sell songs which they have "pinned" to a sort of screen or large board, or have attached them, in any convenient way, to a blank wall; and they differ from the other song-sellers, inasmuch as that they are not at all connected with patter, and have generally been mechanics, porters, or servants, and re-duced to struggle for a living as "pinners-up."

OF THE STREET "PINNERS-UP," OR WALL SONG-SELLERS.

THESE street-traders, when I gave an account of them in the winter of 1849, were not 50 in number; they are now, I learn, about 30. One informant counted 28, and thought "that was nearly all."

I have, in my account of street song-sellers, described the character of the class of pinners-up. Among the best-accustomed stands are those in Tottenham-court Road, the New-road, the City-road, near the Vinegar-works, the Westminster-road, and in Shoreditch, near the Eastern Counties Station. One of the best-known of the pinners-up was a stout old man, wearing a great-coat in all weathers, who "pinned-up" in an alley leading from White-friars-street to the Temple, but now thrown into an open street. He had old books for sale on a stall, in addition to his ballads, and every morn-ing was seen reading the newspaper, borrowed from a neighbouring public-house which he "used," for he was a keen politician. "He would quarrel with any one," said a person who then resided in the neighbourhood—an account confirmed to me at the public-house in question —"mostly about politics, or about the books and songs he sold. Why, sir, I've talked to him many a time, and have stood looking through his books; and if a person came up and said, 'Oh, Burn's Works, 1s.; I can't understand him,'—then the old boy would abuse him for a fool! Suppose another came and said—for I've noticed it myself—'Ah! Burns—he was a poet!' that didn't pass; for the jolly old pinner-up would say, 'Well, now, I don't know about that.' In my opinion, he cared nothing about this side or that—this notion or the opposite—but he liked to *shine*." The old man was carried off in the prevalence of the cholera in 1849.

At the period I have specified, I received the following statement from a man who at that time pinned-up by Harewood-place, Oxford-street:

"I'm forty-nine," he said. "I've no chil-dren, thank God, but a daughter, who is eighteen, and no incumbrance to me, as she is in a 'house of business;' and as she has been there nine years, her character can't be so very bad. (This was said proudly.) I worked twenty-two years with a great sculptor as a marble polisher, and besides that, I used to run errands for him, and was a sort of porter, like, to him. I couldn't get any work, because he hadn't no more marble-work to do; so nine or ten years back I went into this line. I knew a man what done well in it—but times

LONG-SONG SELLER.

"Two under fifty for a fardy'!"

[From a Daguerreotype by BEARD.*]*

was better then—and that put it into my head. It cost me 2*l.* 10*s.* to stock my stall, and get all together comfortable; for I started with old books as well as songs. I got leave to stand here from the landlord. I sell ballads and manuscript music (beautifully done these music sheets were), which is 'transposed' (so he worded it) from the nigger songs. There's two does them for me. They're transposed for the violin. One that does them is a musicianer, who plays outside public-houses, but I think his daughter does most of it. I sell my songs at a halfpenny,—and, when I can get it, a penny a piece. Do I yarn a pound a week? Lor' bless you, no. Nor 15*s.*, nor 12*s.* I don't yarn, one week with another, not 10*s.*, sometimes not 5*s.* My wife don't yarn nothing. She used to go out charing, but she can't now. I am at my stall at nine in the morning, and sometimes I have walked five or six miles to buy my 'pubs' before that. I stop till ten at night oft enough. The wet days is the ruin of us; and I think wet days increases. [This was said on a rainy day.] Such a day as yesterday now I didn't take, not make,—but I didn't *take* what would pay for a pint of beer and a bit of bread and cheese. My rent's 2*s.* 3*d.* a week for one room, and I've got my own bits of sticks there. I've always kept *them*, thank God!''

Generally, these dealers know little of the songs they sell,—taking the printer's word, when they purchase, as to ''what was going.'' The most popular comic songs (among this class I heard the word *song* used far more frequently than *ballad*) are not sold so abundantly as others,—because, I was told, boys soon picked *them* up by heart, hearing them so often, and so did not buy them. Neither was there a great demand for nigger songs, nor for ''flash ditties,'' but for such productions as ''A Life on the Ocean Wave,'' '' I'm Afloat,'' ''There's a Good Time coming,'' ''Farewell to the Mountain,'' &c., &c. Three-fourths of the customers of these traders, one man assured me, were boys.

Indecent songs are not sold by the pinners-up. One man of whom I made inquiries was quite indignant that I should even think it necessary to ask such questions. The ''songs'' cost the pinners-up, generally, 2*d.* a dozen, sometimes 2½*d.*, and sometimes less than 2*d.*, according to the quality of the paper and the demand.

On fine summer days the wall song-sellers take 2*s.* on an average. On short wintry days they may not take half so much, and on very foggy or rainy days they take nothing at all. Their ballads are of the same sort as those I proceed to describe under especial heads, and I have shown what are of readiest sale. Reckoning that each pinner-up, thirty in number, now takes 10*s.* 6*d.* weekly (7*s.* being the profit), we find that 780 guineas are yearly expended in London streets, in the ballads of the pinners-up.

OF ANCIENT AND MODERN STREET BALLAD MINSTRELSY.

MR. STRUTT, in his ''Sports and Pastimes of the People of England,'' shows, as do other authorities, that in the reigns subsequent to the Norman Conquest the minstrels ''were permitted to perform in the rich monasteries, and in the mansions of the nobility, which they frequently visited in large parties, and especially upon occasions of festivity. They entered the castles without the least ceremony, rarely waiting for any previous invitation, and there exhibited their performances for the entertainment of the lord of the mansion and his guests. They were, it seems, admitted without any difficulty, and handsomely rewarded for the exertion of their talents.''

Of the truth of this statement all contemporary history is a corroboration. The minstrels then, indeed, constituted the theatre, the opera, and the concert of the powerful and wealthy. They were decried by some of the clergy of that day,—as are popular performers and opera singers (occasionally) by some zealous divine in our own era. John of Salisbury stigmatizes minstrels as ''ministers of the devil.''

''The large gratuities collected by these artists,'' the same antiquarian writer further says, ''not only occasioned great numbers to join their fraternity, but also induced many idle and dissipated persons to assume the characters of minstrels, to the disgrace of the profession. These evils became at last so notorious, that in the reign of King Edward II. it was thought necessary to restrain them by a public edict, which sufficiently explains the nature of the grievance. It states, that many indolent persons, under the colour of minstrelsy, intruded themselves into the residences of the wealthy, where they had both meat and drink, but were not contented without the addition of large gifts from the householder. To restrain this abuse, the mandate ordains, that no person should resort to the houses of prelates, earls, or barons, to eat, or to drink, who was not a professed minstrel; nor more than three or four minstrels of honour at most in one day (meaning, I presume, the king's minstrels of honour and those retained by the nobility), except they came by invitation from the lord of the house.''

The themes of the minstrels were the triumphs, victories, pageants, and great events of the day; commingled with the praise, or the satire of individuals, as the humour of the patron or of the audience might be gratified. It is stated that Longchamp, the favourite and justiciary of Richard Cœur-de-lion, not only engaged poets to make songs and poems in his, Bishop Longchamp's, praise, but the best singers and minstrels to sing them in the public streets! In the ninth year of the reign of Edward IV. another royal edict was issued, as little favourable to the minstrels as the one I have given an account of; and those functionaries seem to have gradually fallen in the estimation of the public, and to have been contemned by the law, down to the statute of Elizabeth, already alluded to, subjecting them to the same treatment as rogues, vagabonds, and sturdy beggars. A writer of the period (1589) represents the (still-styled) minstrels, singing " ballads and small popular musickes" for the amusement of boys and others "that passe by them in the streete." It is related also that their "matters were for the most part stories of old time; as the tale of Sir Topas, Bevis of Southampton, Guy of Warwick, Adam Bell, and Clymme of the Clough, and such other old romances or historical rhymes, made purposely for the recreation of the common people at Christmas dinners and bride ales, and in tavernes and alehouses, and such other places of base resort."

These "stories of old time" are now valuable as affording illustrations of ancient manners, and have been not unfertile as subjects of antiquarian annotation.

Under the head of the " Norman Minstrels," Mr. Strutt says: " It is very certain that the poet, the songster, and the musician were frequently united in the same person."

From this historical sketch it appears evident that the ballad-singer and seller of to-day is the sole descendant, or remains, of the minstrel of old, as regards the business of the streets; he is, indeed, the minstrel having lost caste, and being driven to play cheap.

The themes of the minstrels were wars, and victories, and revolutions; so of the modern man of street ballads. If the minstrel celebrated with harp and voice the unhorsings, the broken bones, the deaths, the dust, the blood, and all the glory and circumstance of a tournament,—so does the ballad-seller, with voice and fiddle, glorify the feelings, the broken bones, the blood, the deaths, and all the glory and circumstance of a prize-fight. The minstrel did not scoff at the madness which prevailed in the lists, nor does the ballad-singer at the brutality which rules in the ring. The minstrels had their dirges for departed greatness; the ballad-singer, like old Allan Bane, also "pours his wailing o'er the dead"—for are there not the street " helegies " on all departed greatness? In the bestowal of flattery or even of praise the modern minstrel is far less liberal than was his prototype; but the laudation was, in the good old times, very often " paid for " by the person whom it was sung to honour. Were the same measure applied to the ballad-singer and writer of to-day, there can be no reason to doubt that it would be attended with the same result. In his satire the modern has somewhat of an advantage over his predecessor. The minstrel not rarely received a "largesse" to satirize some one obnoxious to a rival, or to a disappointed man. The ballad-singer (or chaunter, for these remarks apply with equal force to both of these street-professionals), is seldom hired to abuse. I was told, indeed, by a clever chaunter, that he had been sent lately by a strange gentleman to

sing a song—which he and his mate (a patterer) happened at the time to be working—in front of a neighbouring house. The song was on the rogueries of the turf; and the " move" had a doubly advantageous effect. " One gentleman, you see, sir, gave us 1s. to go and sing; and afore we'd well finished the chorus, somebody sent us from the house another 1s. to go away agin." I believe this to be the only way in which the satire of a ballad-singer is rewarded, otherwise than by sale to his usual class of customers in the streets or the public-houses. The ancient professors of street minstrelsy unquestionably played and sung satirical lays, depending for their remuneration on the liberality of their out-of-door audience; so is it precisely with the modern. The minstrel played both singly and with his fellows; the ballad-singer " works " both alone (but not frequently) and with his " mates " or his "school."

In the persons of some of these modern street professionals, as I have shown and shall further show, are united the functions of "the poet, the songster, and the musician." So in the days of yore. There are now female ballad-singers; there were female minstrels, or glee-women. The lays which were poured forth in our streets and taverns some centuries back, either for the regalement of a miscellaneous assemblage, or of a select few, were sometimes of an immoral tendency. Such, it cannot be denied, is the case in our more enlightened days at our Cyder-cellars, Coal-holes, Penny Gaffs, and such like places. Rarely, however, are such things sung in the streets of London; but sometimes at country fairs and races.

In one respect the analogy between the two ages of these promoters of street enjoyment does not hold. The minstrel's garb was distinctive. It was not always the short laced tunic, tight trousers, and russet boots, with a well plumed cap,—which seems to be the modern notion of this tuneful itinerant. The king's and queen's minstrels wore the royal livery, but so altered as to have removed from its appearance what might seem menial. The minstrels of the great barons also assumed their patron's liveries, with the like qualification. A minstrel of the highest class might wear " a fayre gowne of cloth of gold," or a military dress, or a "tawnie coat," or a foreign costume, or even an ecclesiastical garb,—and some of them went so far as to shave their crowns, the better to resemble monks. Of course they were imitated by their inferiors. The minstrel, then, wore a particular dress; the ballad-singer of the present day wears no particular dress. During the terrors of the reign of Henry VIII., and after the Reformation, a large body of the minstrels fell into meanness of attire; and in that respect the modern ballad-singer *is* analogous.

It must be borne in mind that I have all along spoken—except when the description is necessarily general—of the *street*, or itinerant, minstrel of old. The highest professors of the art were poets and composers, men often of genius, learning, and gravity, and were no more to be ranked with the mass of those I have been describing than is Alfred Tennyson with any Smithfield scribbler and bawler of some Newgate " Copy of Verses."

How long " Sir Topas " and the other " old stories " continued to be sung in the streets there are no means of ascertaining. But there are old songs, as I ascertained from an intelligent and experienced street-singer, still occasionally heard in the open air, but more in the country than in the metropolis. Among those still heard, however rarely, are the Earl of Dorset's song, written on the night before a naval engagement with the Dutch, in 1665 :

" To all you ladies now on land,
We men at sea indite."

I give the titles of the others, not chronologically, but as they occurred to my informant's recollection—" A Cobbler there was, and he liv'd in a Stall "—Parnell's song of " My Days have been so wond'rous Free," now sung in the streets to the tune of Gramachree." A song (of which I could not procure a copy, but my informant had lately heard it in the street) about the Cock-lane Ghost—

" Now ponder well, you parents dear
The words which I shall write ;
A doleful story you shall hear,
In time brought forth to light."

the " Children in the Wood " and " Chevy-chase." Concerning this old ditty one man said to me : " Yes, sir, I've sung it at odd times and not long ago in the north of England, and I've been asked whereabouts Chevy-chase lay, but I never learned."

" In Scarlet towne, where I was borne,
There was a faire maid dwellin',
Made every youth crye, Well-awaye !
Her name was Barbara Allen."

" Barbara Allen's selling yet," I was told. " Gilderoy was a Bonnie Boy," is another song yet sung occasionally in the streets.

" The ballad," says a writer on the subject, " may be considered as the native species of poetry of this country. It very exactly answers the idea formerly given of original poetry, being the rude uncultivated verse in which the popular tale of the time was recorded. As our ancestors partook of the fierce warlike character of the northern nations, the subjects of their poetry would chiefly consist of the martial exploits of their heroes, and the military events of national history, deeply tinctured with that passion for the marvellous, and that superstitious credulity, which always attend a state of ignorance and barbarism. Many of the ancient ballads have been transmitted to the present times, and in them the character of the nation displays itself in striking colours."

The " Ballads on a Subject," of which I shall proceed to treat, are certainly " the rude uncultivated verse in which the popular tale of the times is recorded," and what may be the cha-racter of the nation as displayed in them I leave to the reader's judgment.

OF STREET " BALLADS ON A SUBJECT."

THERE is a class of ballads which may with perfect propriety be called *street* ballads, as they are written by street authors for street singing (or chaunting) and street sale. These effusions, however, are known in the trade by a title appropriate enough — " Ballads on a Subject." The most successful workers in this branch of the profession, are the men I have already described among the patterers and chaunters.

The " Ballads on a Subject " are always on a political, criminal, or exciting public event, or one that has interested the public, and the celerity with which one of them is written, and then sung in the streets, is in the spirit of " these railroad times." After any great event, " a ballad on the subject " is often enough written, printed, and sung in the street, in little more than an hour. Such was the case with a song " in honour," it was announced, " of Lord John Russell's resignation." Of course there is no time for either the correction of the rhymes or of the press ; but this is regarded as of little consequence—while an early " start " with a new topic is of great consequence, I am assured ; " yes, indeed, both for the sake of meals and rents." If, however, the songs were ever so carefully revised, their sale would not be greater.

I need not treat this branch of our street literature at any great length, as specimens of the " Ballad on a Subject " will be found in many of the preceding statements of paper-workers.

It will have struck the reader that all the street lays quoted as popular have a sort of burthen or jingle at the end of each verse. I was corrected, however, by a street chaunter for speaking of this burthen as a jingle. " It's a chorus, sir," he said. " In a proper ballad on a subject, there's often twelve verses, none of them under eight lines,—and there 's a four-line chorus to every verse ; and, if it 's the right sort, it 'll sell the ballad." I was told, on all hands, that it was not the words that ever " made a ballad, but the subject ; and, more than the subject,—the chorus ; and, far more than either,—*the tune !*" Indeed, many of the street-singers of ballads on a subject have as supreme a contempt for words as can be felt by any modern composer. To select a tune for a ballad, however, is a matter of deep deliberation. To adapt the ballad to a tune too common or popular is injudicious ; for then, I was told, any one can sing it—boys and all. To select a more elaborate and less-known air, however appropriate, may not be pleasing to some of the members of " the school " of ballad-singers, who may feel it to be beyond their vocal powers ; neither may it be relished by the critical in street song, whose approving criticism induces them to purchase as well as to admire.

The license enjoyed by the court jesters, and, in some respects, by the minstrels of old, is certainly enjoyed, undiminished, by the street-writers and singers of ballads on a subject. They are unsparing satirists, who, with a rare impartiality, lash all classes and all creeds, as well as any individual. One man, upon whose information I can rely, told me that, eleven years ago, he himself had "worked," in town and country, 23 different songs at the same period and on the same subject—the marriage of the Queen. They all "sold,"—but the most profitable was one "as sung by Prince Albert in character." It was to the air of the "Dusty Miller;" and "it was good," said the balladman, "because we could easily dress up to the character given to Albert." I quote a verse:

"Here I am in rags
From the land of All-dirt,
To marry England's Queen,
And my name it is Prince Albert."

"And what's more, sir," continued my informant, "not very long after the honeymoon, the Duchess of L—— drove up in her carriage to the printer's, and bought all the songs in honour of Victoria's wedding, and gave a sovereign for them and wouldn't take the change. It was a duchess. Why I'm sure about it—though I can't say whether it were the Duchess of L—— or S——; for didn't the printer, like an honest man, when he'd stopped the price of the papers, hand over to us chaps the balance to drink, and *didn't* we drink it! There can't be a mistake about *that.*"

Of street ballads on political subjects, or upon themes which have interested the whole general public, I need not cite additional instances. There are, however, other subjects, which, though not regarded as of great interest by the whole body of the people are still eventful among certain classes, and for them the street author and ballad-singer cater.

I first give a specimen of a ballad on a Theatrical Subject. The best I find, in a large collection of these street effusions, is entitled "Jenny Lind and Poet B." After describing how Mr. Bunn "flew to Sweden" and engaged Miss Lind, the poet proceeds,—the tune being "Lucy Long":

"After Jenny sign'd the paper,
She repeated what she'd done,
And said she must have been a cake,
To be tempted by A. Bunn.
The English tongue she must decline,
It was such awkward stuff,
And we find 'mongst our darling dames,
That one tongue's quite enough.

CHORUS.

So take your time Miss Jenny,
Oh, take your time Miss Lind,
You're only to raise your voice,
John Bull, will raise the wind.

Says Alfred in the public eye,
My name you shan't degrade,
So birds that can and won't sing
Why in course they must be made
This put Miss Jenny's pipe out,
Says Bunn your tricks I see,

Altho' you are a Nightingale,
You shan't play larks with me.

The Poet said he'd seek the law,
No chance away he'd throw;
Says Jenny if you think I'll come,
You'll find it is no go!
When a bird-catcher named 'Lummy
With independence big,
Pounced down upon the Nightingale,
And with her hopp'd the twig!"

I am inclined to think—though I know it to be an unusual case—that in this theatrical ballad the street poet was what is tenderly called a "plagiarist." I was assured by a chaunter that it was written by a street author,—but probably the chaunter was himself in error or forgetfulness.

Next, there is the Ballad on a Civic Subject. In the old times the Lord Mayor had his laureate. This writer, known as "poet to the City of London," eulogised all lord mayors, and glorified all civic pageants. That of the 9th November, especially, "lived in Settle's numbers, one day more,"—but Elkanah Settle was the last of such scribes. After his death, the city eschewed a poet. The office has now descended to the street bard, who annually celebrates the great ceremony. I cite two stanzas and the chorus from the latest of these civic Odes:

"Now Farncombe's out and Musgrove's in,
And grand is his position,
Because he will be made a king,
At the Hyde Park Exhibition;
A feast he'll order at Guildhall,
For hypocrites and sinners,
And he has sent Jack Forester to Rome,
To invite the Pope to dinner!

A day like this we never saw,
The truth I am confessing,
Batty's astonishing menagerie,
Is in the great procession;
There's lions, tigers, bears and wolves,
To please each smiling feature,
And elephants in harness drawing
Drury Lane Theatre!

CHORUS.

"It is not as it used to be,
Cut on so gay and thrifty,
The funny Lord Mayor's Show to see,
In eighteen hundred and fifty."

There is, beside the descriptions of ballads above cited, the Ballad Local. One of these is headed the "Queer Doings in Leather-lane," and is on a subject concerning which streetsellers generally express themselves strongly—Sunday trading. The endeavour to stop street trading (generally) in Leather-lane, with its injurious results to the shopkeepers, has been already mentioned. The ballad on this local subject presents a personality now, happily, almost confined to the street writers:

"A rummy saintly lot is there,
A domineering crew,
A Butcher, and a Baker,
And an Undertaker too,
Besides a cove who deals in wood,
And makes his bundles small,
And looks as black on Sunday
As the Undertaker's pall.

CHORUS.
You must not buy, you must not sell,
Oh! is it not a shame?
It is a shocking place to dwell,
About sweet Leather Lane.

The Butcher does not like to hear
His neighbours holla, buy!
Although he on the Sunday
Sells a little on the sly;
And the Coffin Maker struts along
Just like the great Lord Mayor,
To bury folks on Sundays,
Instead of going to prayers."

There are yet three themes of these street
songs, of which, though they have been alluded
to, no specimens have been given. I now supply
them. The first is the election ballad. I quote
two stanzas from " Middlesex and Victory! or,
Grosvenor and Osborne for ever!"

" Now Osborne is the man
To struggle for your rights,
He will vote against the Bishops,
You know, both day and night,
He will strive to crush the Poor Law Bill,
And that with all his might,
And he will never give his vote
To part a man from his wife.

CHORUS.
Then cheer Osborne and Lord Grosvenor,
Cheer them with three times three,
For they beat the soldier, Tommy Wood,
And gained the victory.

I have not forgot Lord Grosvenor,
Who nobly stood the test,
For the electors of great Middlesex
I know he'll do his best;
He will pull old Nosey o'er the coals,
And lay him on his back,
And he swears that little Bob's head
He will shove into a rat trap."

Then come the " elegies." Of three of these
I cite the opening stanza. That on the " Death
of Queen Adelaide" has for an illustration a
figure of Britannia leaning on her shield, with
the " Muse of History," (as I presume from her
attributes,) at Britannia's feet. In the distance
is the setting sun:

" Old England may weep, her bright hopes are fled,
The friend of the poor is no more;
For Adelaide now is numbered with the dead,
And her loss we shall sadly deplore.
For though noble her birth, and high was her station
The poor of this nation will miss her,
For their wants she relieved without ostentation,
But now she is gone, God bless her!
God bless her! God bless her!
But now she is gone, God bless her!"

The elegy on the " Death of the Right Honourable Sir Robert Peel, Bart. M.P.," is set
off with a very fair portrait of that statesman.

" Britannia! Britannia! what makes thee complain,
O why so in sorrow relenting,
Old England is lost, we are born down in pain,
And the nation in grief is lamenting,
That excellent man—the pride of the land,
Whom every virtue possessed him,
Is gone to that Home, from whence no one returns,
Our dear friend, Sir Robert, God rest him.

The verses which bewail the " Death of
H. R. H. the Duke of Cambridge," and which
are adorned with the same illustration as those
upon Queen Adelaide, begin

" Oh! death, thou art severe, and never seems contented,
Prince Adolphus Frederick is summoned away,

The death of Royal Cambridge in sorrow lamented,
Like the good Sir Robert Peel, he no longer could
stay;
His virtues were good, and noble was his actions,
His presence at all places caused much attraction,
Britannia for her loss is driven to distraction,
Royal Cambridge, we'll behold thee no more!"

The third class of street-ballads relates to
" fires." The one I quote, " On the Awful Fire
at B. Caunt's, in St. Martin's-lane," is preceded
by an engraving of a lady and a cavalier, the
lady pointing to a column surmounted by an
urn. I again give the first stanza:

" I will unfold a tale of sorrow,
List, you tender parents dear,
It will thrill each breast with horror,
When the dreadful tale you hear.
Early on last Wednesday morning,
A raging fire as we may see,
Did occur, most sad and awful,
Between the hours of two and three."

In a subsequent stanza are four lines, not without some rough pathos, and adapted to move
the feelings of a street audience. The writer is
alluding to the grief of the parents who had lost
two children by a terrible death:

" No more their smiles they'll be beholding,
No more their pretty faces see,
No more to their bosoms will they fold them,
Oh! what must their feelings be."

I find no difference in style between the ballads on a subject of to-day, and the oldest which
I could obtain a sight of, which were sung in
the present generation—except that these poems
now begin far less frequently with what at one
time was as common as an invocation to the
Muse—the invitation to good Christians to attend
to the singer. One on the Sloanes, however,
opens in the old fashion:

" Come all good Christians and give attention,
Unto these lines I will unfold,
With heartfelt feelings to you I'll mention,
I'm sure 'twill make your blood run cold."

I now conclude this account of street-ballads
on a subject with two verses from one on
the subject of " The Glorious Fight for the
Championship of England." The celebration
of these once-popular encounters is, as I have
already stated, one of the points in which the
modern ballad-man emulates his ancient brother
minstrel:

" On the ninth day of September,
Eighteen hundred and forty five,
From London down to Nottingham
The roads were all alive;
Oh! such a sight was never seen,
Believe me it is so,
Tens of thousands went to see the fight,
With Caunt and Bendigo.

And near to Newport Pagnell;
Those men did strip so fine,
Ben Caunt stood six feet two and a half,
And Bendigo five foot nine;
Ben Caunt, a giant did appear,
And made the claret flow,
And he seemed fully determined
Soon to conquer Bendigo.

CHORUS.
With their hit away and slash away,
So manfully you see,
Ben Caunt has lost and Bendigo
Has gained the victory."

Of the Street Poets and Authors.

Authorship, for street sale, is chiefly confined to the production of verse, which, whatever be its nature, is known through the trade as "ballads." Two distinctions, indeed, are recognised—"Ballads" and "Ballads on a Subject." The last-mentioned is, as I have said and shown, the publication which relates to any specific event; national or local, criminal or merely extraordinary, true or false. Under the head "Ballads," the street-sellers class all that does not come under the description of "Ballads on a Subject."

The same street authors—now six in number—compose indiscriminately any description of ballad, including the copy of verses I have shown to be required as a necessary part of all histories or trials of criminals. When the printer has determined upon a "Sorrowful Lamentation," he sends to a poet for a copy of verses, which is promptly supplied. The payment I have already mentioned—1s.; but sometimes, if the printer (and publisher) like the verses, he "throws a penny or two over;" and sometimes also, in case of a great sale, there is the same over-sum.

Fewer ballads, I was assured, than was the case ten or twelve years ago, are now written expressly for street sale or street minstrelsy. "They come to the printer, for nothing, from the concert-room. He has only to buy a 'Ross' or a 'Sharp'" [song-books] "for 1d., and there's a lot of 'em; so, in course, a publisher ain't a-going to give a bob, if he can be served for a farthing, just by buying a song-book."

Another man, himself not a "regular poet," but a little concerned in street productions, said to me, with great earnestness: "Now look at this, sir, and I hope you'll just say, sir, as I tell you. You've given the public a deal of information about men like me, and some of our chaps abuses you for it like mad; but I say it's all right, for it's all true. Now you'll have learned, sir, or, any way, you will learn, that there's songs sung in the streets, and sometimes in some tap-rooms, that isn't decent, and relates to nothing but wickedness. There wasn't a few of those songs once written for the streets, straight away, and a great sale they had, I know—but far better at country fairs and races than in town. Since the singing-houses—I don't mean where you pay to go to a concert, no! but such as your Cyder-cellars, and your night-houses, where there's lords, and gentlemen, and city swells, and young men up from the colleges—since these places has been up so flourishing, there hasn't, I do believe, been *one* such song written by one of our poets. They all come from the places where the lords, and genelmen, and collegians is capital customers; and they never was a worse sort of ballads than now. In course those houses is licensed, and perticler respectable, or it wouldn't be allowed; and if I was to go to the foot of the bridge, sir (Westminster-bridge), and chaunt any such songs, and my mate should sell them, why we should very soon be taking reg'lar exercise on Colonel Chesterton's everlasting staircase. We has a great respect for the law—O, certainly!"

Parodies on any very popular song, which used to be prepared expressly for street trade, are now, in like manner, derived from the nighthouse or the concert-room; but not entirely so. The parody "Cab, cab, cab!" which was heard in almost every street, was originated in a concert-room.

The ballads which have lately been written, and published expressly for the street sale, and have proved the most successful, are parodies or imitations of "The Gay Cavalier." One street ballad, commencing in the following words, was, I am told, greatly admired, both in the streets and the public-houses:

> "'Twas a dark foggy night,
> And the moon gave no light,
> And the stars were all put in the shade:
> When leary Joe Scott,
> Dealt in 'Donovan's hot'
> Said he'd go to court his fair maid."

I now give three stanzas of "The Way to Live Happy Together,"—a ballad said to have been written expressly for street sale. Its popularity is anything but discreditable to the street-buyers:

> "From the time of this world's first formation
> You will find it has been the plan,
> In every country and nation,
> That woman was formed to please man;
> And man for to love and protect them,
> And shield them from the frowns of the world,
> Through the smooth paths of life to direct them,
> And he who would do less is a churl.
> Then listen to me!
> If you would live happy together,
> As you steer through the troubles of life,
> Depend that this world's greatest treasure,
> Is a kind and a good-tempered wife.
>
> Some men will ill-use a good woman,
> And say all they do turns out wrong,
> But as I mean to offend no one,
> You'll find faults to both sides belong;
> But if both were to look at the bright side,
> And each other's minds cease to pain,
> They would find they have looked at the right side,
> For all would be summer again.
> Then listen to me!
> If you would live happy together, &c.
>
> Married women, don't gossip or tattle,
> Remember it oft stirs up strife,
> But attend to your soft children's soft prattle,
> And the duties of mother and wife.
> And men, if you need recreation,
> With selfish companions don't roam,
> Who might lead you to sad degradation,
> But think of your comforts at home.
> Then listen to me!
> If you would live happy together, &c."

"It's all as one, sir," was the answer of a man whom I questioned on the subject; "it's the same poet; and the same tip for any ballad. No more nor a bob for nothing."

A large number of ballads which I procured, and all sold and sung in the street, though not written expressly for the purpose, presented a curious study enough. They were of every class. I specify a few, to show the nature of

Mr. PATRICK CONNOR.*

ILLUSTRATIONS TO STREET-BALLADS.

THE
AMOROUS WATERMAN.
Of St. JOhn's Wood.

* This is evidently a rude copy of Lawrence's picture of George the Fourth.

THE QUEEN'S GLORIOUS SPEECH.

GENERAL HAYNAU.*

THE POACHERS.

The Heart that can feel for Another.

The Miller's Ditty.

ROSIN THE BEAU.

Broken Hearted Gardener.

This originally was an illustration to "Thump em the Drummer," in one of Fairburn's Song-books.

the collection (not including ballads on a subject): " Ye Banks and Braes o' Bonnie Doun," with (on the same sheet) " The Merry Fiddler," (an indecent song)—" There's a good Time coming, Boys," " Nix, my Dolly," " The Girls of —— shire," (which of course is available for any county) — " Widow Mahoney," " Remember the Glories of Brian the Brave," " Clementina Clemmins," " Lucy Long," " Erin Go Bragh," " Christmas in 1850," " The Death of Nelson," " The Life and Adventures of Jemmy Sweet," " The Young May Moon," " Hail to the Tyrol," " He was sich a Lushy Cove," &c. &c.

I may here mention—but a fuller notice may be necessary when I treat of street art—that some of these ballads have an " illustration " always at the top of the column. " The Heart that can Feel for Another " is illustrated by a gaunt and savage-looking lion. " The Amorous Waterman of St. John's Wood," presents a very short, obese, and bow-legged grocer, in top-boots, standing at his door, while a lady in a huge bonnet is " taking a sight at him," to the evident satisfaction of a " baked 'tater" man. " Rosin the Beau " is heralded by the rising sun. " The Poachers " has a cut of the Royal Exchange above the title. " The Miller's Ditty " is illustrated by a perfect dandy, of the slimmest and straightest fashion; and " When I was first Breeched," by an engraving of a Highlander. Many of the ballads, however, have engravings appropriate enough.

Of the Experience of a Street Author, or Poet.

I have already mentioned the present number of street authors, as I most frequently heard them styled, though they write only verses. I called upon one on the recommendation of a neighbouring tradesman, of whom I made some inquiries. He could not tell me the number of the house in the court where the man lived, but said I had only to inquire for the Tinker, or the Poet, and any one would tell me.

I found the poor poet, who bears a good character, on a sick bed; he was suffering, and had long been suffering, from abscesses. He was apparently about forty-five, with the sunken eyes, hollow cheeks, and, not pale but thick and rather sallow complexion, which indicate ill-health and scant food. He spoke quietly, and expressed resignation. His room was not very small, and was furnished in the way usual among the very poor, but there were a few old pictures over the mantel-piece. His eldest boy, a lad of thirteen or fourteen, was making dog-chains; at which he earned a shilling or two, sometimes 2s. 6d., by sale in the streets.

" I was born at Newcastle-under-Lyne," the man said, " but was brought to London when, I believe, I was only three months old. I was very fond of reading poems, in my youth, as soon as I could read and understand almost. Yes, very likely, sir; perhaps it was that put it into my head to write them afterwards. I was

taught wire-working, and jobbing, and was brought up to hawking wire-work in the streets, and all over England and Wales. It was never a very good trade—just a living. Many and many a weary mile we've travelled together,—I mean, my wife and I have : and we've sometimes been benighted, and had to wander or rest about until morning. It wasn't that we hadn't money to pay for a lodging, but we couldn't get one. We lost count of the days sometimes in wild parts; but if we did lose count, we had, I could always tell when it was Sunday morning by the look of nature; there was a mystery and a beauty about it to me. I was very fond of Goldsmith's poetry always. I can repeat ' Edwin and Emma' now. No, sir; I never read the ' Vicar of Wakefield.' I found ' Edwin and Emma' in a book called the ' Speaker.' I often thought of it in travelling through some parts of the country.

" Above fourteen years ago I tried to make a shilling or two by selling my verses. I'd written plenty before, but made nothing by them. Indeed I never tried. The first song I ever sold was to a concert-room manager. The next I sold had great success. It was called the ' Demon of the Sea,' and was to the tune of ' The Brave Old Oak.' Do I remember how it began ? Yes, sir, I remember every word of it. It began :

Unfurl the sails,
We've easy gales;
And helmsman steer aright,
Hoist the grim death's head—
The Pirate's head—
For a vessel heaves in sight !

That song was written for a concert-room, but it was soon in the streets, and ran a whole winter. I got only 1s. for it. Then I wrote the ' Pirate of the Isles,' and other ballads of that sort. The concert-rooms pay no better than the printers for the streets.

" Perhaps the best thing I ever wrote was the ' Husband's Dream.' I'm very sorry indeed that I can't offer you copies of some of my ballads, but I haven't a single copy myself of any of them, not one, and I dare say I've written a thousand in my time, and most of them were printed. I believe 10,000 were sold of the ' Husband's Dream.' It begins :

O Dermot, you look healthy now,
Your dress is neat and clean ;
I never see you drunk about,
Then tell me where you've been.

Your wife and family—are they well ?
You once did use them strange :
O, are you kinder to them grown,
How came this happy change ?

" Then Dermot tells how he dreamed of his wife's sudden death, and his childrens' misery as they cried about her dead body, while he was drunk in bed, and as he calls out in his misery, he wakes, and finds his wife by his side. The ballad ends :

' I pressed her to my throbbing heart,
Whilst joyous tears did stream ;
And ever since, I've heaven blest,
For sending me that dream.'

" Dermot turned teetotaller. The teetotallers were very much pleased with that song. The printer once sent me 5s. on account of it.

" I have written all sorts of things—ballads on a subject, and copies of verses, and anything ordered of me, or on anything I thought would be accepted, but now I can't get about. I've been asked to write indecent songs, but I refused. One man offered me 5s. for six such songs.—'Why, that's less than the common price,' said I, 'instead of something over to pay for the wickedness.'—All those sort of songs come now to the streets, I believe all do, from the concert-rooms. I can imitate any poetry. I don't recollect any poet I've imitated. No, sir, not Scott or Moore, that I know of, but if they've written popular songs, then I dare say I have imitated them. Writing poetry is no comfort to me in my sickness. It might if I could write just what I please. The printers like hanging subjects best, and I don't. But when any of them sends to order a copy of verses for a ' Sorrowful Lamentation' of course I must supply them. I don't think much of what I've done that way. If I'd my own fancy, I'd keep writing acrostics, such as one I wrote on our rector." " God bless him," interrupted the wife, " he's a good man." " That he is," said the poet, " but he's never seen what I wrote about him, and perhaps never will." He then desired his wife to reach him his big Bible, and out of it he handed me a piece of paper, with the following lines written on it, in a small neat hand enough :

" C elestial blessings hover round his head,
H undreds of poor, by his kindness were fed,
A nd precepts taught which he himself obeyed.
M an. erring man, brought to the fold of God,
P reaching pardon through a Saviour's blood.
N o lukewarm priest, but firm to Heaven's cause;
E xamples showed how much he loved its laws.
Y outh and age, he to their wants attends,
S teward of Christ—the poor man's sterling friend."

" There would be some comfort, sir," he continued, " if one could go on writing at will like that. As it is, I sometimes write verses all over a slate, and rub them out again. Live hard! yes, indeed, we do live hard. I hardly know the taste of meat. We live on bread and butter, and tea; no, not any fish. As you see, sir, I work at tinning. I put new bottoms into old tin tea-pots, and such like. Here's my sort of bench, by my poor bit of a bed. In the best weeks I earn 4s. by tinning, never higher. In bad weeks I earn only 1s. by it, and sometimes not that,—and there are more shilling than four shilling weeks by three to one. As to my poetry, a good week is 3s., and a poor week is 1s.—and sometimes I make nothing at all that way. So I leave you to judge, sir, whether we live hard; for the comings in, and what we have from the parish, must keep six of us—myself, my wife, and four children. It's a long, hard struggle." " Yes, indeed," said the wife, " it's just as you've heard my husband tell, sir. We've 2s. a week and four loaves of bread from the parish, and the rent 's 2s. 6d., and the land-lord every week has 2s.,—and 6d. he has done for him in tinning work. Oh, we do live hard, indeed."

As I was taking my leave, the poor man expressed a desire that I would take a copy of an epitaph which he had written for himself. " If ever," he said, " I am rich enough to provide for a tomb-stone, or my family is rich enough to give me one, this shall be my epitaph" [I copied it from a blank page in his Bible :]

" Stranger, pause, a moment stay,
   Tread lightly o'er this mound of clay.
Here lies J—— H——, in hopes to rise,
   And meet his Saviour in the skies.
Christ his refuge, Heaven his home,
   Where pain and sorrow never come.
His journey's done, his trouble's past,
   With God he sleeps in peace at last."

OF THE STREET-SELLERS OF BROAD-SHEETS.

THE broad-sheet known in street-sale is an unfolded sheet, varying in size, and printed on one side. The word is frequently used to signify an account of a murder or execution, but it may contain an account of a fire, an " awful accident and great loss of life," a series of conundrums, as in those called " Nuts to Crack," a comic or intended comic engraving, with a speech or some verses, as recently in satire of the Pope and Cardinal Wiseman (these are sometimes called " comic exhibitions"), or a " bill of the play." The " cocks" are more frequently a smaller size than the broad-sheet.

The sellers of these articles (play-bills excepted), are of the class I have described as patterers. The play-bill sellers are very rarely patterers on other " paper work." Some of them are on the look-out during the day for a job in porterage or such like, but they are not mixed up with any pattering,—and a regular patterer looks down upon a play-bill seller as a poor creature, " fit for nothing but play-bills." I now proceed to describe such of these classes as have not been previously given.

OF THE "GALLOWS" LITERATURE OF THE STREETS.

UNDER this head I class all the street-sold publications which relate to the hanging of malefactors. That the question is not of any minor importance must be at once admitted, when it is seen how very extensive a portion of the reading of the poor is supplied by the " Sorrowful Lamentations" and " Last Dying Speech, Confession, and Execution" of criminals. One paper-worker told me, that in some small and obscure villages in Norfolk, which, he believed, were visited only by himself in his line, it was not very uncommon for two poor families to *club* for 1d. to purchase an execution broad-sheet! Not long after Rush was hung, he saw, one evening after dark, through the uncurtained cottage window, eleven persons, young and old, gathered round a scanty fire, which was made to blaze by being fed with a few sticks. An old man was reading, to an attentive audience, a broad-sheet of Rush's execution, which my informant had sold to him; he read by the fire-light; for the very poor in those villages, I was told, rarely lighted a candle on a spring evening, saying that "a bit o' fire was good enough to talk by." The scene must have been impressive, for it had evidently somewhat impressed the perhaps not very susceptible mind of my informant.

The procedure on the occasion of a "good" murder, or of a murder expected to "turn out well," is systematic. First appears a quarter-sheet (a hand-bill, 9½ in. by 7½ in.) containing the earliest report of the matter. Next come half-sheets (twice the size) of later particulars, or discoveries, or—if the supposed murderer be in custody—of further examinations. The sale of these bills is confined almost entirely to London, and in their production the newspapers are for the most part followed closely enough. Then are produced the whole, or broad-sheets (twice the size of the half-sheets), and, lastly, but only on great occasions, the *double* broad-sheet. [I have used the least technical terms that I might not puzzle the reader with accounts of "crowns," "double-crowns," &c.]

The most important of all the broad-sheets of executions, according to concurrent, and indeed unanimous, testimony is the case of Rush. I speak of the testimony of the street-folk conerned, who all represent the sale of the papers relative to Rush, both in town and country, as the best in their experience of late years.

The sheet bears the title of "The Sorrowful Lamentation and Last Farewell of J. B. Rush, who is ordered for Execution on Saturday next, at Norwich Castle." There are three illustrations. The largest represents Rush, cloaked and masked, "shooting Mr. Jermy, Sen." Another is of "Rush shooting Mrs. Jermy." A prostrate body is at her feet, and the lady herself is depicted as having a very small waist and great amplitude of gown-skirts. The third is a portrait of Rush,—a correct copy, I was assured, and have no reason to question the assurance,—from one in the *Norwich Mercury.* The account of the trial and biography of Rush, his conduct in prison, &c., is a concise and clear enough condensation from the newspapers. Indeed, Rush's Sorrowful Lamentation is the best, in all respects, of any execution broad-sheet I have seen; even the "copy of verses" which, according to the established custom, the criminal composes in the condemned cell—his being unable, in some instances, to read or write being no obstacle to the composition—seems, in a literary point of view, of a superior strain to the run of such things. The matters of fact, however, are introduced in the same peculiar manner. The worst part is the morbid sympathy and intended apology for the criminal. I give the verses entire:

"This vain world I soon shall leave,
Dear friends in sorrow do not grieve;
Mourn not my end, though 'tis severe,
For death awaits the murderer.

Now in a dismal cell I lie,
For murder I'm condemn'd to die;
Some may pity when they read,
Oppression drove me to the deed.

My friends and home to me were dear,
The trees and flowers that blossom'd near;
The sweet loved spot where youth began
Is dear to every Englishman.

I once was happy—that is past,
Distress and crosses came at last;
False friendship smiled on wealth and me,
But shunned me in adversity.

The scaffold is awaiting me,
For Jermy I have murdered thee;
Thy hope and joys—thy son I slew,
Thy wife and servant wounded too.

I think I hear the world to say—
'Oh, Rush, why didst thou Jermy slay?
His dear loved son why didst thou kill,
For he had done to thee no ill.'

If Jermy had but kindness shown,
And not have trod misfortune down,
I ne'er had fired the fatal ball
That caus'd his son and him to fall.

My cause I did defend alone,
For learned counsel I had none;
I pleaded hard and questions gave,
In hopes my wretched life to save.

The witness to confound did try,
But God ordained that I should die;
Eliza Chestney she was there,—
I'm sorry I have injured her.

Oh, Emily Sandford, was it due
That I should meet my death through you?
If you had wish'd me well indeed,
How could you thus against me plead?

I've used thee kind, though not my wife:
Your evidence has cost my life;
A child by me you have had born,
Though hard against me you have sworn.

The scaffold is, alas! my doom,—
I soon shall wither in the tomb:
God pardon me—no mercy's here
For Rush—the wretched murderer!"

Although the execution broad-sheet I have cited may be the best, taken altogether, which has fallen under my observation, nearly all I have seen have one characteristic—the facts can be plainly understood. The narrative, embracing trial, biography, &c., is usually prepared by the printer, being a condensation from the accounts in the newspapers, and is perhaps intelligible, simply because it *is* a condensation. It is so, moreover, in spite of bad grammar, and sometimes perhaps from an unskilful connection of the different eras of the trial.

When the circumstances of the case permit, or can be at all constrained to do so, the Last Sorrowful Lamentation contains a "Love Letter," written—as one patterer told me he had occasionally expressed it, when he thought his audience suitable—"from the depths of the condemned cell, with the condemned pen, ink, and paper." The style is stereotyped, and usually after this fashion:

"Dear ——,—Shrink not from receiving a letter from one who is condemned to die as a murderer. Here, in my miserable cell, I write to one whom I have from my first acquaintanceship, held in the highest esteem, and whom, I believe, has also had the same kindly feeling towards myself. Believe me, I forgive all my enemies and bear no malice. O, my dear ——, guard against giving way to evil passions, and a fondness for drink. Be warned by my sad and pitiful fate."

If it be not feasible to have a love-letter—which can be addressed to either wife or sweetheart—in the foregoing style, a "last letter" is given, and this can be written to father, mother, son, daughter, or friend; and is usually to the following purport:

"Condemned Cell, ——

"My Dear ——,—By the time you receive this my hours, in this world, will indeed be short. It is an old and true saying, that murderers will one day meet their proper reward. No one can imagine the dreadful nights of anguish passed by me since the commital of the crime on poor ——. All my previous victims have appeared before me in a thousand different shapes and forms. My sufferings have been more than I can possibly describe. Let me entreat you to turn from your evil ways and lead a honest and sober life. I am suffering so much at the present moment both from mind and body that I can write no longer. Farewell! farewell!

"Your affectionate ——."

I have hitherto spoken of the Last Sorrowful Lamentation sheets. The next broad-sheet is the "Life, Trial, Confession, and Execution." This presents the same matter as the "Lamentation," except that a part—perhaps the judge's charge at the trial, or perhaps the biography—is removed to make room for the "Execution," and occasionally for a portion of the "Condemned Sermon." To judge by the productions I treat of, both subjects are marvellously similar on all occasions. I cite a specimen of the Condemned Sermon, as preached, according to the broad-sheet, for Hewson, condemned for the murder of a turnkey It will be seen that it is of a character to fit *any* condemned sermon whatever:

"The rev. gent. then turned his discourse particularly to the unhappy prisoner doomed to die on the morrow, and told him to call on Him who alone had the power of forgiveness; who had said, 'though his sins were red as scarlet,' he would 'make them white as snow,' though he had been guilty of many heinous crimes, there was yet an opportunity of forgiveness.— During the delivery of this address, the prisoner was in a very desponding state, and at its conclusion was helped out of the chapel by the turnkeys."

The "Execution" is detailed generally in this manner. I cite the "Life, Trial, Confession, and Execution of Mary May, for the Murder of W. Constable, her Half-brother, by Poison, at Wix, near Manningtree:"

"At an early hour this morning the space before the prison was very much crowded by persons anxious to witness the execution of Mary May, for the murder of William Constable, her half-brother, by poison, at Wix, Manningtree, which gradually increased to such a degree, that a great number of persons suffered extremely from the pressure, and gladly gave up their places on the first opportunity to escape from the crowd. The sheriffs and their attendants arrived at the prison early this morning and proceeded to the condemn cell, were they found the reverend ordinary engaged in prayer with the miserable woman. After the usual formalities had been observed of demanding the body of the prisoner into their custody she was then conducted to the press-room. The executioner with his assistants then commenced pinioning her arms, which opporation they

skillfully and quickly dispatched. During these awful preparations the unhappy woman appeared mently to suffer severely, but uttered not a word when the hour arrived and all the arrangements having been completed, the bell commenced tolling, and then a change was observed, to come over the face of the prisoner, who trembling violently, walked with the melancholy procession, proceeded by the reverend ordinary, who read aloud the funeral service for the dead. When the bell commenced tolling a moment was heard from without, and the words "Hats off," and "Silence," were distinctly heard, from which time nothing but a continual sobbing was heard. On arriving at the foot of the steps leading to the scaffold she thanked the sheriff's and the worthy governor of the prison, for their kind attentions to her during her confinement; & then the unfortunate woman was seen on the scaffold, there was a death like silence prevailed among the vast multitude of people assembled. In a few seconds the bolt was drawn, and, after a few convulsive struggles, the unhappy woman ceased to exist."

I cannot refrain from calling the reader's attention to the "copy of verses" touching Mary May. I give them entire, for they seem to me to contain all the elements which made the old ballads popular—the rushing at once into the subject—and the homely reflections, though crude to all educated persons, are, nevertheless, well adapted to enlist the sympathy and appreciation of the class of hearers to whom they are addressed:

COPY OF VERSES.

"The solemn bell for me doth toll,
　And I am doom'd to die
(For murdering by brother dear,)
　Upon a tree so high.
For gain I did premeditate
　My brother for to slay,—
Oh, think upon the dreadful fate
　Of wretched Mary May.

CHORUS.

Behold the fate of Mary May,
Who did for gain her brother slay.

In Essex boundry I did dwell,
　My brother lived with me,
In a little village called Wix,
　Not far from Manningtree.
In a burial club I entered him,
　On purpose him to slay;
And to obtain the burial fees
　I took his life away.

One eve he to his home return'd,
　Not thinking he was doom'd,
To be sent by a sister's hand
　Unto the silent tomb.
His tea for him I did prepare,
　And in it poison placed,
To which I did administer,—
　How dreadful was his case.

Before he long the poison took
　In agony he cried;
Upon him I in scorn did look,—
　At length my brother died.
Then to the grave I hurried him,
　And got him out of sight,
But God ordain'd this cruel deed
　Should soon be brought to light.

I strove the money to obtain,
　For which I did him slay,
By which, also, suspicion fell
　On guilty Mary May.
The poison was discovered,
　Which caused me to bewail,
And I my trial to await
　Was sent to Chelmsford jail.

And for this most atrocious deed
  I at the bar was placed,
The Jury found me guilty,—
  How dreadful was my case.
The Judge the dreadful sentence pass'd,
  And solemn said to me,
'You must return from whence you came,
  And thence unto the tree.'

On earth I can no longer dwell,
  There's nothing can me save;
Hark! I hear the mournful knell
  Which calls me to the grave.
Death appears in ghostly forms,
  To summon me below;
See, the fatal bolt is drawn,
  And Mary May must go.

Good people all, of each degree,
  Before it is too late,
See me on the fatal tree,
  And pity my sad fate.
My guilty heart stung with grief,
  With agony and pain,—
My tender brother I did slay
  That fatal day for gain."

This mode of procedure in "gallows" literature, and this style of composition, have prevailed for from twenty to thirty years. I find my usual impossibility to *fix* a date among these street-folk; but the Sorrowful Lamentation sheet was unknown until the law for prolonging the term of existence between the trial and death of the capitally-convicted, was passed. "Before that, sir," I was told, "there wasn't no time for a Lamentation; sentence o' Friday, and scragging o' Monday. So we had only the Life, Trial, and Execution." Before the year 1820, the Execution broad-sheets, &c., were "got up" in about the same, though certainly in an inferior and more slovenly manner than at present; and *one* copy of verses often did service for the canticles of all criminals condemned to be hung. These verses were to sacred or psalm tunes, such as Job, or the Old Hundredth. I was told by an aged gentleman that he remembered, about the year 1812, hearing a song, or, as he called it, "stave," of this description, not only given in the street with fiddle and nasal twang, to the tune of the Old Hundredth, but commencing in the very words of Sternhold and Hopkins—

"All people that on earth do dwell."

These "death-verses," as they were sometimes called, were very frequently sung by blind people, and in some parts of the country blind men and women still sing—generally to the accompaniment of a fiddle—the "copy of verses." A London chaunter told me, that, a few years back, he heard a blind man at York announce the "verses" as from the "solitudes" of the condemned cell. At present the broad-sheet sellers usually sing, or chaunt, the copy of verses.

An intelligent man, now himself a street-trader, told me that one of the latest "execution songs" (as he called them) which he remembered to have heard in the old style—but "no doubt there were plenty after that, as like one another as peas in a boiling"—was on the murder of Weare, at Elstree, in Hertfordshire.

He took great interest in such things when a boy, and had the song in question by heart, but could only depend upon his memory for the first and second verses:

"Come, all good Christians, praise the Lord,
  And trust to him in hope.
God in his mercy Jack Thurtell sent
  To hang from Hertford gallows rope.

Poor Weare's murder the Lord disclosed—
  Be glory to his name:
And Thurtell, Hunt, and Probert too,
  Were brought to grief and shame."

Another street paper-worker whom I spoke to on the subject, and to whom I read these two verses, said: "That's just the old thing, sir; and it's quite in old Jemmy Catnach's style, for he used to write werses—anyhow, he said he did, for I've heard him say so, and I've no doubt he did in reality—it was just his favourite style, I know, but the march of intellect put it out. It did so."

In the most "popular" murders, the street "papers" are a mere recital from the news-papers, but somewhat more brief, when the suspected murderer is in custody; but when the murderer has not been apprehended, or is unknown, "then," said one Death-hunter, "we has our fling, and I've hit the mark a few chances that way. We had, at the werry least, half-a-dozen coves pulled up in the slums that we printed for the murder of 'The Beautiful Eliza Grimwood, in the Waterloo-road.' I did best on Thomas Hopkins, being the guilty man —I think he was Thomas Hopkins—'cause a strong case was made out again him."

I received similar accounts of the street-doings in the case of "mysterious murders," as those perpetrations are called by the paper workers, when the criminal has escaped, or was unknown. Among those leaving considerable scope to the patterer's powers of invention were the murders of Mr. Westwood, a watchmaker in Prince's-street, Leicester-square; of Eliza Davis, a bar-maid, in Frederick-street, Hampstead-road; and of the policeman in Dagenham, Essex. One of the most successful "cocks," relating to murders which actually occurred, was the "Confession to the Rev. Mr. Cox, Chaplain of Aylesbury Gaol, of John Tawell the Quaker." I had some conversation with one of the authors of this "Confession," —for it was got up by three patterers; and he assured me that "it did well, and the facts was soon in some of the newspapers—as what we 'riginates often is." This sham confession was as follows:

"The Rev. Mr. Cox, the chaplain of Aylesbury Gaol, having been taken ill, and finding his end approaching, sent for his son, and said, 'Take this confession; now I am as good as my word; I promised that unhappy man, John Tawell, that while I lived his confession should not be made public, owing to the excited state of the public mind. Tawell confessed to me, that besides the murder of Sarah Hart, at Salt-hill, for while he suffered the last penalty of the law at Aylesbury, he was guilty of two other barbarous murders which abroad as a transport in Van Dieman's Land. One of these barbarous and horrid murders was on the body of one of the keepers. He knocked him down with the keys, which he wrenched from him, and then cut his throat with his own knife, leaving the body locked up in his cell; and before that, to have the better opportunity of having the turnkey single-handed, John Tawell feigned illness. He then locked the keeper, in the cell, and went to a young woman in the town, a beautiful innkeeper's daughter, whom he had seduced as he worked for her father, as he had the privilege of doing in the day-times. He went to her, and she, seeing him in a flurried state, with blood upon his hand, questioned him. He told the unhappy young woman how he had killed the keeper for the love of her, and the best thing to be done was for her to get possession of all the money she could, and escape with him to this country, where he would marry her, and support her like a lady. The unhappy young woman felt so terrified, that at the moment she was unable to say yes or no. He became alarmed for his safety, and with the identical knife that he killed the keeper with, he left his unhappy victim a welter-ing in her gore. He then fled from the house unob-served, and went into the bush, where he met three men, who had escaped through his killing the keeper. He advised them to go down with him to an English vessel lying off the coast. When they reached the shore, they met a crew in search of fresh water; to them they made out a pitiful story, and were taken on board the ship. All being young men, and the captain being short of hands, and one of them having been really a seaman transported for mutiny, the captain, after putting questions which the seaman answered, engaged them to work their passage home. Tawell was the captain of the gang, and was most looked up to. They worked their passage home, behaving well during the voyage, so that the captain said he would make each of them a present, and never divulge. When they reached Liverpool, Tawell robbed the cap-tain's cabin of all the money contained in it, which was a very considerable sum. After that he left Liver-pool, and adopted the garb of a Quaker, in which he could not easily be recognized, and then pursued the course of wickedness and crime which led him to a shameful death."

The " confession" of Rush to the chaplain of Norwich Castle, was another production which was remunerative to the patterers. " There was soon a bit of it in the newspapers," said one man, " for us and them treads close on one another's heels. The newspapers ' screeved ' about Rush, and his mother, and his wife ; but we, in our patter, made him confess to having murdered his old grandmother fourteen years back, and how he buried her under the apple-tree in the garden, and how he murdered his wife as well."

These ulterior Confessions are very rarely in-troduced, in lieu of some matter displaced, into the broad-sheet, but form separate bills. It was necessary to mention them here, however, and so preserve the sequence of the whole of the traffic consequent upon a conviction for murder, in this curious trade.

Sometimes the trial, &c., form also separate bills, as well as being embodied afterwards in the Sorrowful Lamentation. This is only, how-ever, in cases which are deemed important. One of the papers I obtained, for instance, is the " Trial of Mr. and Mrs. Manning for the Murder of Mr. Patrick O'Connor." The trial alone occupies a broad-sheet; it is fairly " got up." A portrait of Mr. Patrick O'Connor heads the middle column. From the presence of a fur collar to the coat or cloak, and of what is evidently an order with its insignia, round the neck, I have little doubt that the portrait of Mr. O'Connor was originally that of the sovereign in whose service O'Connor was once an excise-officer—King William IV.

The last publication to which the trade has recourse is " the book." This is usually eight pages, but sometimes only four of a larger size. In authorship, matter, or compilation, it differs little from the narratives I have described. The majority of these books are prepared by one man. They are in a better form for being pre-served as a record than is a broad-sheet, and are frequently sold, and almost always offered by the patterers when they cry a new case on a sheet, as " people that loves such reading likes to keep a good account of the best by them ; and so, when I've sold Manning's bills, I've often shoved off Rush's books." The books, like the bills, have generally the letters and the copy of verses.

Some of these books have the title-page set forth in full display,— for example : " *Horrible Murder and Mutilation of Lucy Game, aged* 15, *by her Cruel Brother, William Game, aged* 9, *at Westmill, Hertfordshire. His Committal and Confession. With a Copy of Letter. Also, Full Particulars of the Poisonings in Essex.*" Here, as there was no execution, the matter was extended, to include the poisonings in Essex. The title I have quoted is expanded into thir-teen lines. Sometimes the title-page is adorned with a portrait. One, I was told, which was last employed as a portrait of Calcraft, had done severe service since Courvoisier's time,—for my informant thought that Courvoisier was the original. It is the bust of an ill-looking man, with coat and waistcoat fitting with that un-wrinkled closeness which characterises the figures in tailors' " fashions."

The above style of work is known in the trade as " the book ;" but other publications, in the book or pamphlet form, are common enough. In some I have seen, the title-page is a history in little. I cite one of these :—" *Founded on Facts. The Whitby Tragedy ; or, the Gambler's Fate. Containing the Lives of Joseph Carr, aged* 21, *and his sweetheart, Maria Leslie, aged* 19, *who were found Dead, lying by each other, on the morning of the* 23rd *of May. Maria was on her road to Town to buy some Ribbon, &c., for her Wedding Day, when her lover in a state of intoxication fired at her, and then run to rob his prey, but finding it to be his Sweetheart, reloaded his Gun, placed the Muzzle to his Mouth, and blew out his Brains, all through cursed Cards, Drink, &c. Also, an affec-tionate Copy of Verses.*"

To show the extent of the trade in execution broad-sheets, I obtained returns of the number of copies relating to the principal executions of late, that had been sold :

Of Rush	2,500,000	copies.
„ the Mannings .	2,500,000	„
„ Courvoisier . .	1,666,000	„
„ Good	1,650,000	„
„ Corder . . .	1,650,000	„
„ Greenacre . .	1,666,000	„

Of Thurtell I could obtain no accounts—" it was so long ago ;" but the sale, I was told, was enormous. Reckoning that each copy was sold for 1*d.* (the regular price in the country, where the great sale is,) the money expended for such things amounts to upwards of 48,500*l.* in the case of the six murderers above given. All this number was printed and got up in London; a few "broad-sheets" concerning Rush were printed also in Norwich.

Touching the issue of " cocks," a person connected with the trade calculated for me, from data at his command, that 3,456 copies were struck off weekly, and sold in the streets, in the metropolis ; and reckoning them at only a ½*d.* each, we have the sum of 7*l.* 4*s.* spent every week in this manner. At this rate, there must be 179,712 copies of " cocks " printed in a year, on which the public expend no less than 374*l.* 8*s.*

Of the style of illustrations usually accompanying this class of street literature the two large engravings here given are *fac similes*—while the smaller ones are faithful copies of the average embellishments to the halfpenny ballads. On another occasion I shall speak at length on " Street-Art."

OF THE STREET-SELLERS OF CONUNDRUMS.

AMONG the more modern street sales are " conundrums," generally vended, both in the shops and the streets, as " Nuts to Crack," when not in the form of books. This is another of the " broad-sheets," and is sufficiently clever and curious in its way.

In the centre, at the top, is the " Wonderful Picture," with the following description : " This Picture when looked at from a particular point of view, will not only appear perfect in all respects and free from distortion, but the figures will actually appear to stand out in relief from the paper." The wonderful picture, which is a rude imitation of a similar toy picture sold in a box, " with eye-piece complete," at the shops, presents a distorted view of a church-spire, a light-house, a donjon-keep, castellated buildings backed by mountains, a moat on which are two vessels, an arch surmounted by a Britannia, a palm-tree (I presume), and a rampart, or pier, or something that way, on which are depicted two figures, with the gestures of elocutionists. The buildings are elongated, like shadows at sunset or sunrise. What may be the " particular point of view" announced in the description of the Wonderful Picture, is not described in the " Nuts," but the following explanation is given in a little book, published simultaneously, and entitled, " The Nutcrackers, a Key to Nuts to Crack, or Enigmatical Repository:"

"THE WONDERFUL PICTURE.—Cut out a piece of cardboard 2½ inches long, make a round hole about the size of a pea in the top of it ; place this level with the right-hand side of the Engraving and just 1½ inches distant from it, then apply your eye to the little hole and look at the picture, and you will find that a beautiful symmetry pervades the landscape, there is not the slightest appearance of distortion, and the different

parts appear actually to stand up in relief on the paper."

Below the " Wonderful Picture " are other illustrations ; and the border of the broadsheet presents a series of what may be called pictorial engravings. The first is,

```
          D I O
          C  C
1.—Lately presented to a " Wise
    man " by a usurper.
```

The answer being evidently " Diocese." No. 26 is

```
          A 4
26.—The Child's " Tidy."
```

" Pinafore " is the solution. Of the next " hieroglyphic"—for a second title to the " Nuts " tells of " 200 Hieroglyphics, Enigmas, Conundrums, Curious Puzzles, and other Ingenious Devices," — I cannot speak very highly. It consists of " AIMER," (a figure of a hare at full speed,) and " EKA." Answer.—" America." In the body of the broad-sheet are the Enigmas, &c., announced ; of each of which I give a specimen, to show the nature of this street performance or entertainment. Enigma 107 is—

" I've got no wings, yet in the air
    I often rise and fall ;
I've got no feet, yet clogs I wear,
    And shoes, and boots, and all."

As the answer is foot-ball, the two last lines should manifestly have been placed first.

The " Conundrums" are next in the arrangement, and I cite one of them :

" Why are there, strictly speaking, only 325 days in the year ?"

" Because," is the reply, " forty of them are lent and never returned." The " Riddles " follow in this portion of the " Nuts to Crack." Of these, one is not very difficult to be solved, though it is distinguished for the usual grammatical confusion of tenses :

" A man has three daughters, and each of these have a brother. How many children had he ?"

The " Charades" complete the series. Of these I select one of the best :

" I am a word of letters seven,
    I'm sinful in the sight of heaven,
    To every virtue I'm opposed,
Man's weary life I've often closed.
If to me you prefix two letters more,
    I mean exactly what I meant before."

The other parts of the letter-press consist of " Anagrams," " Transpositions," &c.

When a clever patterer " works conundrums " —for the trade is in the hands of the pattering class—he selects what he may consider the best, and reads or repeats them in the street, sometimes with and sometimes without the answer. But he does not cripple the probable quickness of his sale by a slavish adherence to what is in type. He puts the matter, as it were, personally. "What gentleman is it," one man told me he would ask, "in this street, that has—

'Eyes like saucers, a back like a box,
A nose like a pen-knife, and a voice like a fox?'

You can learn for a penny. Or sometimes I'll go on with the patter, thus," he continued, "What lady is it that we have all seen, and who can say truly—

'I am brighter than day, I am swifter than light,
And stronger than all the momentum of might?'

More than once people have sung out 'the Queen,' for they seem to think that the momentum of might couldn't fit any one else. It's 'thought' as is the answer, but it wouldn't do to let people think it's anything of the sort. It must seem to fit *somebody*. If I see a tailor's name on a door, as soon as I've passed the corner of the street, and sometimes in the same street, I've asked—

'Why is Mr. So-and-so, the busy tailor of this (or the next street) never at home?'

'Because he's always cutting out.' I have the same questions for other tradesmen, and for gentlemen and ladies in this neighbourhood, and no gammon. All for a penny. Nuts to Crack, a penny. A pair of Nutcrackers to crack 'em, only one penny."

Sometimes this man, who perhaps is the smartest in the trade, will take a bolder flight still, and when he knows the residence of any professional or public man, he will, if the allusion be complimentary, announce his name, or —if there be any satire—indicate by a motion of the head, or a gesture of the hand, the direction of his residence. My ingenuous, and certainly ingenious, informant obliged me with a few instances:—"In Whitechapel parish I've said—it ain't in the print, it was only in the patter—'Why won't the Reverend Mr. Champneys lay up treasures on earth?'—'Because he'd rather lay up treasures in heaven.' That's the reverend gentleman not far from this spot; but in this sheet—with nearly 100 engravings by the first artists, only a penny—I have other questions for other parsons, not so easy answered; nuts as is hard to crack. 'Why is the Reverend Mr. Popjoy,' or the Honourable Lawyer Bully, or Judge Wiggem,—and then I just jerks my thumb, sir, if it's where I know or think such people live —'Why is the Reverend Mr. Popjoy (or the others) like *two* balloons, one in the air to the east, and the 'tother in the air to the west, in this parish of St. George's, Hanover-square?' There's no such question, and as it's a sort of a 'cock,' of course there's no answer. I don't know one. But a gentleman's servant once sung out: ''Cause he's uppish.' And a man in a leather apron once said: 'He's a raising the wind,' which was nonsense. But I like that sort of interruption, and have said—'You'll not find *that* answer in the Nutcrackers,' only a penny—and, Lord knows, I told the truth when

I said so, and it helps the sale. No fear of any one's finding out all what's in the sheet before I'm out of the 'drag.' Not a bit. And you must admit that any way it's a cheap pennorth." That it is a cheap harmless pennyworth is undeniable.

The street-sale of conundrums is carried on most extensively during a week or two before Christmas; and on summer evenings, when the day's work is, or ought to be, over even among the operatives of the slop employers. As the conundrum patterer requires an audience, he works the quieter streets, preferring such as have no horse-thoroughfare—as in some of the approaches from the direction of Golden-square to Regent-street. The trade is irregularly pursued, none following it all the year; and from the best information I could acquire, it appears that fifteen men may be computed as working conundrums for two months throughout the twelve, and clearing 10s. weekly, per individual. The cost of the "Nuts to Crack" (when new) is 5d. a doz. to the seller; but old "Nuts" often answer the purpose of the street-seller, and may be had for about half the price; the cost of the "Nut-crackers" 2s. to 2s. 6d. It may be calculated, then, that to realize the 10s. 6d., 15s. must be taken. This shows the street expenditure in "Nuts to Crack" and "Nut-crackers" to be 90l. yearly.

OF THE STREET-SELLERS OF COMIC EXHIBITIONS, MAGICAL DELUSIONS, &c.

THE street sale of "Comic Exhibitions" (properly so called) is, of course, as modern as the last autumn and winter; and it is somewhat curious that the sale of any humorous, or meant to be humorous sheet of engravings, is now becoming very generally known in the street sale as a "Comic Exhibition." Among these—as I have before intimated—are many caricatures of the Pope, the Church of Rome, Cardinal Wiseman, the Church of England, the Bishop of London (or any bishop or dignitary), or of any characteristic of the conflicting creeds. In many of these, John Bull figures personally, and so does the devil.

The Comic Exhibition (proper) is certainly a very cheap pennyworth. No. 1 is entitled, "The Ceremonial of the Opening of the Great Exhibition, in 1851, with Illustrations of the Contributions of All Nations." The "contributions," however, are reserved for Nos. 2 and 3. Two larger "cuts," at the head of the broad-sheet, may be considered geographical, as regards the first, and allegorical as regards the second. "Table Bay" presents a huge feeder (evidently), and the "Cape of Good Hope" is a spare man obsequiously bowing to the table and its guest in good hope of a dinner. Of the Sandwich Islands and Hung(a)ry, the "exhibition" is of the same description. The second larger cut shows the Crystal Palace ascending by the agency of a balloon, a host of people of all countries looking on. Then comes the

'Procession from Palace-yard to Hyde Park."
The first figure in this procession is described
as "Beefeaters piping hot and well puffed out,"
though there is but one beefeater, with head
larger than his body and legs ridiculously, small
(as have nearly all the sequent figures), smoking a pipe as if it were a trombone, duly
followed by "Her Majesty's Spiritual Body-
guard" (five beefeaters, drunk), and by "Prince
Albert blowing his own trumpet" (from the
back of a very sorry steed), with "Mops and
brooms," and a "Cook-oo" (a housemaid and
cook) as his supporters. Then follow figures,
grotesque enough, of which the titles convey
the character: "A famous Well-in-Town;"
"Nae Peer-ye;" "Humorous Estimates"
(Mr. Hume); "A Jew-d' esprit" (Mr. D'Is-
raeli); "An exemplification of Cupidity in
Pummicestone" (Lord Palmerston); "Old
Geese" and "Young Ducks" (old and angry-
looking and young and pretty women); "Some
gentlemen who patronise Moses in the Minories" (certainly no credit to the skill of a tailor);
"A Jew Lion" (M. Jullien); "Fine high
screams" (ice-creams) and "Capers" (chorister
boys and ballet-girls); "Hey-day, you don't
take advantage here" (Joseph Ady); and
"Something to give the milk a head" (a man
with a horse's head on a tray). These, however,
are but a portion of the figures. The Comic
Exhibition-sheet contains ninety such figures,
independent of those in the two cuts mentioned
as headings.

"Galleries of Comicalities," or series of figures
sometimes satirically, sometimes grotesquely
given without any aim at satire, are also sold by
the same parties, and are often announced as a
"Threepenny gallery for a penny!—and dirt
cheap at threepence. As big as a newspaper."

Another broad-sheet sold this winter in the
streets is entitled, "Optical and Magical Delusions," and was announced as "Dedicated to
and Prepared for his Royal Highness the Prince
of Wales—the only original copy." The engravings are six in number, and are in three
rows, each accompanying engraving being re-
versed from its fellow: where the head is erect on
one side, it is downward on the other. The first
figure is a short length of a very plain woman,
while on the opposite side is that of a very plain
man, both pleased and smirking in accordance
with a line below: "O what joy when our lips
shall meet!" "Cat-a-gorical" is a spectacled
and hooded cat. "Dog-matical" is a dog with
the hat, wig, and cane once held proper to a
physician. "Cross purposes" is an austere
lady in a monster cap, while her opposite husband is pointing bitterly to a long bill. The
purport of these figures is shown in the following

"DIRECTIONS—Paste all over the Back of the
sheet, and put a piece of thick paper between, to stiffen
it, then fold it down the centre, so that the marginal
lines fall exactly at the back of each other, (which may
be ascertained by holding it to the light)—press it quite
flat—when cut separate they will make three cards—
shave them close to the margin—then take a needle-

full of double thread and pass it through the dot at
each end of the card; cut the thread off about three
inches long. By twisting the threads between your
fore fingers and thumbs, so as to spin the card round
backwards and forwards with a rapid motion, the
figures will appear to connect and form a pleasing
delusion."

Then there are the "Magical Figures," or
rude street imitations of Dr. Paris' ingenious
toy, called the "Thaumascope." Beside these
are what at the first glance appear mere black,
and very black, marks, defining no object; but
a closer examination shows the outlines of a
face, or of a face and figure. Of such there are
sometimes four on a broad-sheet, but they are
also sold separately, both in the streets and the
small stationers' shops. When the white or
black portion of the paper is cut away (for both
colours are so prepared), what remains, by a
disposition of the light, throws a huge shadow
of a grotesque figure on the wall, which may
be increased or diminished according to the
motions of the exhibitor. The shadow-figures
sold this winter by one of my informants were
of Mr. and Mrs. Manning, the Queen, Prince
Albert, the Princess Royal, and the Prince of
Wales; "but you see, sir," observed the man,
"the Queen and the Prince does for any father
and mother—for she hasn't her crown on—and
the Queen's kids for anybody's kids."

I mention these matters more particularly, as
it certainly shows something of a change in the
winter-evenings' amusements of the children of
the working-classes. The principal street customers for these penny papers were mechanics,
who bought them on their way home for the
amusement of their families. Boys, however,
bought almost as many.

The sale of these papers is carried on by the
same men as I have described working conundrums. A superior patterer, of course, shows
that his magical delusions and magical figures
combine all the wonders of the magic lantern
and the dissolving views, "and all for one
penny." The trade is carried on only for a
short time in the winter as regards the magical
portion; and I am informed that, including the
"Comic Exhibitions," it extends to about half of
the sum taken for conundrums, or to about 45l.

OF THE STREET SELLERS OF PLAY-BILLS.

THE sellers of play-bills carry on a trade which
is exceedingly uncertain, and is little remunerative. There are now rather more than 200
people selling play-bills in London, but the
number has sometimes been as high as 400.
"Yes, indeed," a theatrical gentleman said to
me, "and if a dozen more theatres were opened
to-morrow, why each would have more than its
twenty bill-sellers the very first night. Where
they come from, or what they are, I haven't a
notion."

The majority of the play-bill sellers are either
old or young, the sexes being about equally
engaged in this traffic. Some of them have
followed the business from their childhood. I
met with very few indeed who knew anything of

theatres beyond the names of the managers and of the principal performers, while some do not even enjoy that small modicum of knowledge, and some can neither read nor write. The boys often run recklessly alongside the cabs which are conveying persons to the theatre, and so offer their bills for sale. One of these youths said to me, when I spoke of the danger incurred, "The cabman knows how to do it, sir, when I runs and patters ; and so does his hoss." An intelligent cabman, however, who was in the habit of driving parties to the Lyceum, told me that these lads clung to his cab as he drove down to Wellington-street in such a way, for they seemed never to look before them, that he was in constant fear lest they should be run over. Ladies are often startled by a face appearing suddenly at the cab window, " and thro' my glass," said my informant, " a face would look dirtier than it really is." And certainly a face gliding along with the cab, as it were, no accompanying body being visible, on a winter's night, while the sound of the runner's footsteps is lost in the noise of the cab, has much the effect of an apparition.

I did not hear of one person who had been in any way connected with the stage, even as a supernumerary, resorting to play-bill selling when he could not earn a shilling within the walls of a theatre. These bill-sellers, for the most part, confine themselves, as far as I could ascertain, to that particular trade. The youths say that they sometimes get a job in errand-going in the daytime, but the old men and women generally aver they can do nothing else. An officer, who, some years back, had been on duty at a large theatre, told me that at that time the women bill-sellers earned a trifle in running errands for the women of the town who attended the theatres ; but, as they were not permitted to send any communication into the interior of the house, their earnings that way were insignificant, for they could only send in messages by any other " dress woman " entering the theatre subsequently.

In the course of my inquiries last year, I met with a lame woman of sixty-eight, who had been selling play-bills for the last twelve years. She had been, for six or eight months before she adopted that trade, the widow of a poor mechanic, a carpenter. She had first thought of resorting to that means of a livelihood owing to a neighbouring old woman having been obliged to relinquish her post from sickness, when my informant " succeeded her." In this way, she said, many persons " succeeded " to the business, as the recognised old hands were jealous of and uncivil to any additional new comers, but did not object to a " successor." These parties generally know each other ; they murmur if the Haymarket hands, for instance, resort to the Lyceum for any cause, or *vice versâ*, thus overstocking the business, but they offer no other opposition. The old woman further informed me that she commenced selling play-bills at Astley's, and then realized a profit of 4s. per week. When the old Amphitheatre was burnt down,

she went to the Victoria ; but " business was not what it was," and her earnings were from 6d. to 1s. a week less ; and this, she said, although the Victoria was considered one of the most profitable stations for the play-bill seller, the box-keeper there seldom selling any bill in the theatre. "The boxes," too, at this house, more frequently buy them outside. Another reason why " business" was better at the Victoria than elsewhere was represented to me, by a person familar with the theatres, to be this : many go to the Victoria who cannot read, or who can read but imperfectly, and they love to " make-believe" they are " good scholards" by parading the consulting of a play-bill !

On my visit the bill-sellers at the Victoria were two old women (each a widow for many years), two young men, besides two or three, though there are sometimes as many as six or seven children. The old women " fell into the business" as successors by virtue of their predecessors' leaving it on account of sickness. The children were generally connected with the older dealers. The young men had been in this business from boyhood ; some sticking to the practice of their childhood unto manhood, or towards old age. The number at the Victoria is now, I am informed, two or three more, as the theatre is often crowded. The old woman told me that she had known two and even four visitors to the theatre club for the purchase of a bill, and then she had sometimes to get farthings for them.

A young fellow—who said he believed he was only eighteen, but certainly looked older—told me that he was in the habit of selling play-bills, but not regularly, as he sometimes had a job in carrying a board, or delivering bills at a corner, " or the likes o' that ;"—he favoured me with his opinion of the merits of the theatres he was practically acquainted with as regarded their construction for the purposes of the bill-seller. His mother, who had been dead a few years, had sold bills, and had put him into the business. His ambition seemed to be to become a general bill-sticker. He could not write but could read very imperfectly.

" Vy, you see, sir," he said, " there's sets off. At the Market (Haymarket), now, there's this : there's only one front, so you may look sharp about for there goes, boxes, pit, and gallery. The 'Delphis as good that way, and so is the Surrey, but them one's crowded too much. The Lyceum's built shocking orkered. Vy, the boxes is in one street, and the pit in another, and the gallery in another ! It's true, sir. The pit's the best customer in most theatres, I think. Ashley's and the Wick is both spoiled that way—Ashley's perticler—as the gallery's a good step from the pit and boxes ; at the Wick it's round the corner. But the shilling gallery aint so bad at Ashley's. Sadler's Wells I never tried, it's out of the way, and I can't tell you much about the 'Lympic or the Strand. The Lane is middling. I don't know that either plays or actors makes much difference to me. Perhaps it's rather vorser ven it's anything werry prime, as everybody seems to know every think about it aforehand. No, sir, I can't say, sir, that Mr. Macready did me much good. I sometimes runs along by a cab because I've got a sixpence from a swell for doing it stunnin', but werry seldom, and I don't much like it; though ven you're at it you don't think of no fear. I makes 3s. or rather more a week at bill-selling, and as much other vays. I never saw a play but once at the Wick. I'd rather be at a Free and Heasy. I don't know as I knows any of the actors or actresses, either hes or shes."

The sellers of play-bills purchase their stock of the printer, at 3s. 4d. the hundred, or in that proportion for half or quarter-hundreds. If a smaller quantity be purchased, the charge is usually thirteen for 6d.; though they used to be only twelve for 6d. These sellers are among the poorest of the poor; after they have had one meal, they do not know how to get another. They reside in the lowest localities, and some few are abandoned and profligate in character. They reckon it a good night to earn 1s. clear, but upon an average they clear but 3s. per week. They lose sometimes by not selling out their nightly stock. What they have left, they are obliged to sell for waste-paper at 2d. per lb. Christmas, Easter, and Whitsuntide are generally their best times—they will then make 9d. per night clear. The printer of the play-bills prints but a certain number, the demand being nearly ascertained week by week. These are all sold (by the printer or some person appointed) to the regular customers, in preference to others, but the "irregulars" can get supplied, though often not without trouble. The profit on all sold is rather more than cent. per cent. As I have intimated, when some theatres are closed, the bill-sellers are driven to others; and as the demand is necessarily limited, a superflux of sellers affects the profits, and then 2s. 6d. is considered a good week's work. During the opera season, I am told, a few mechanics, out of work, will sell bills there and books of the opera, making about 6s. a week, and doing better than the regular hands, as they have a better address and are better clad.

Taking the profits at 3s. a week at cent. per cent. on the outlay, and reckoning 200 sellers, including those at the saloons, concert-rooms, &c., we find that 60l. is now expended weekly on play-bills purchased in the streets of London.

Of the Street-sellers of Periodicals, Pamphlets, Tracts, Books, etc.

These street-sellers are a numerous body, and the majority of them show a greater degree of industry and energy than is common to many classes of street-folk. They have been for the most part connected with the paper, newspaper, or publishing trade, and some of them have "known better days." One intelligent man I met with, a dealer in "waste" (paper), had been brought up as a compositor, but late hours and glaring gas-lights in the printing-office

affected his eyes, he told me; and as a half-blind compositor was about of as little value, he thought, as a "horse with a wooden leg," he abandoned his calling for out-of-door labour. Another had been a gun-smith, and when out of his apprenticeship was considered a "don hand at hair triggers, for hair triggers were more wanted then," but an injury to his right hand and arm had disabled him as a mechanic, and he had recourse to the streets. A third had been an ink-maker's "young man," and had got to like the streets by calling for orders, and delivering bottles of ink, at the shops of the small stationers and chandlers, and so he had taken to them for a living. Of the book-stall-keepers I heard of one man who had died a short time before, and who "once had been in the habit of buying better books for his own pleasure than he had afterwards to sell for his bread." Of the book-stall proprietors, I have afterwards spoken more fully.

All the street-sellers in question are what street estimation pronounces to be educated men; they can all, as far as I could ascertain, read and write, and some of them were "keenish politicians, both free-traders, and against free-trade when they was a-talking of the better days when they was young." Nearly all are married men with families.

The divisions into which these street traffickers may be formed are — Odd Number-sellers — Steamboat Newsvendors — Railway Newsvendors, (though the latter is now hardly a street traffic),—the Sellers of Second Editions (which I have already given as a portion of the patterers)—Board-workers (also previously described, and for the same reason)—Tract-sellers (of whom I have given the number, character, &c., and who are regarded by the other street-sellers as the idlers, beggars, and pretenders of the trade,—the Sellers of Childrens' Books and Song Books—Book-auctioneers, and Book-stall-keepers.

Of the Street-sale of Back Numbers.

This trade is carried on by the same class of patterers as work race-cards, second editions, &c. The collectors of waste-paper frequently find back numbers of periodicals in "a lot" they may have purchased at a coffee-shop. These they sell to warehousemen who serve the street-sellers. The largest lot ever sold at one time was some six or seven years ago, of the *Pictorial Times*, at least a ton weight. A dealer states—

"I lost the use of this arm ever since I was three months old. My mother died when I was ten years of age, and after that my father took up with an Irishwoman, and turned me and my youngest sister (she was two years younger than me) out into the streets. My youngest sister got employment at my father's trade, but I couldn't get no work because of my crippled arm. I walked about, till I fell down in the streets for want. At last, a man, who had a sweetmeat-shop, took pity on me. His wife made the sweetmeats, and minded the shop while he went out a juggling in the streets, in the Ramo Samee line. He told me as how, if I would go round the country with him and sell a few prints while he was a juggling in the public-houses, he'd find me in wittles, and pay my lodging. I joined him, and stopped with him two or three year. After that I went to work for a werry large waste-paper dealer. He used to buy up all the old back numbers of the cheap periodicals and penny publications, and send me out with them to sell at a farden' a piece. He used to give me 4d. out of every shilling, and I done very well with that, till the periodicals came so low, and so many on 'em, that they wouldn't sell at all. Sometimes I could make 15s. on a Saturday night and a Sunday morning, a-selling the odd numbers of periodicals,—such as tales ; 'Tales of the Wars,' 'Lives of the Pirates,' 'Lives of the Highwaymen,' &c. I've often sold as many as 2,000 numbers on a Saturday night in the New-cut, and the most of them was works about thieves, and highwaymen, and pirates. Besides me, there was three others at the same business. Altogether, I dare say my master alone used to get rid of 10,000 copies of such works on a Saturday night and a Sunday morning. Our principal customers was young men. My master made a good bit of money at it. He had been about eighteen years in the business, and had begun with 2s. 6d. I was with him fifteen year, on and off, and at the best time. I used to earn my 30s. a week full at that time. But then I was foolish, and didn't take care of my money. When I was at the 'odd number business,' I bought a peepshow, and left the trade to go into that line."

Of the Sale of Waste Newspapers at Billingsgate.

This trade is so far peculiar that it is confined to Billingsgate, as in that market alone the demand supplies a livelihood to the man who carries it on. His principal sale is of newspapers to the street-fishmongers, as a large surface of paper is required for the purposes of a fish-stall. The "waste" trade—for "waste" and not "waste-paper" is the word always applied—is not carried on with such facility as might be expected, for I was assured that "waste" is so scarce that only a very insufficient supply of paper can at present be obtained. "I hope things will change soon, sir," said one collector, gravely to me, "or I shall hardly be able to keep myself and my family on my waste."

This difficulty, however, does not affect such a street-seller as the man at Billingsgate, who buys of the collectors—"collecting," however, a portion himself at the neighbouring coffeeshops, public-houses, &c.; for the wants of a regular customer must, by some means or other, be supplied.

The Billingsgate paper-seller carries his paper round, offering it to his customers, or to those he wishes to make purchasers ; some fishmongers,

however, obtain their "waste" first-hand from the collectors, or buy it at a news-agent's.

The retail price varies from 2d. to 3½d. the pound, but 3½d. is only given for "very clean and prime, and perhaps uncut," newspapers ; for when a newsvendor has, as it is called, "over-stocked" himself, he sells the uncut papers at last to the collector, or the "waste" consumer. This happens, I was told, twenty times as often with the "weeklys" as the "dailys ;" for, said my informant, "suppose it's a wet Sunday morning—and all newsvendors as does pray, prays for wet Sundays, because then people stays at home and buys a paper, or some number, to read and pass away the time. Well, sir, suppose it's a soaker in the morning, the newsman buys a good lot, an extra nine, or two extra nines, or the like of that, and then may be, after all, it comes out a fine day, and so he's over-stocked ; in which case there's some for the waste."

When they consider it a favourable opportunity, the workers carry waste to offer to the Billingsgate salesmen ; but the chief trade is in the hands of the regular frequenter of the market.

From the best information I could obtain, it appears that from 70 to 100 pounds weight of "waste"—about three-fourths being newspapers, of which some are foreign—is supplied to Billingsgate market and its visitants. Two numbers of the *Times*, with their supplements, one paper-buyer told me, "when cleverly damped, and they're never particularly dry," will weigh about a pound. The average price is not less than 2½d. a pound, or from that to 3d. A single paper is 1d. At 2½d. per pound, and 85 pounds a day, upwards of 275l. is spent yearly in waste paper at Billingsgate, in the street or open-air purchase alone.

Of the Sale of Periodicals on the Steam-boats and Steam-boat Piers.

In this traffic are engaged about 20 men, "when the days are light until eight o'clock ;" from 10 to 15, if the winter be a hard winter ; and if the river steamers are unable to run—none at all. This winter, however, there has been no cessation in the running of the "boats," except on a few foggy days. The steam-boat paper-sellers are generally traders on their own account (all, I believe, have been connected with the newsvendors' trade); some few are the servants of newsvendors, sent out to deal at the wharfs and on board the boats.

The trade is not so remunerative that any payment is made to the proprietors of the boats or wharfs for the privilege of selling papers there (as in the case of the railways), but it is necessary to "obtain leave," from those who have authority to give it.

The steam-boat paper-seller steps on board a few minutes before the boat starts, when there are a sufficient number of voyagers assembled. He traverses the deck and dives into the cabins, offering his "papers," the titles of which he announces: " Punch, penny Punch, *real* Punch, last number for 3*d.*—comic sheets, a penny— all the London periodicals — Guide to the Thames."

From one of these frequenters of steam-boats for the purposes of his business, I had the following account:

" I was a news-agent's boy, sir, near a pier, for three or four year, then I got a start for myself, and now I serve a pier. It's not such a trade as you might think, still it's bread and cheese and a drop of beer. I go on board to sell my papers. It's seldom I sell a news-paper; there's no call for it on the river, ex-cept at the foreign-going ships—a few as is sold to them—but I don't serve none on 'em. People reads the news for nothing at the cof-fee-shops when they breakfasts, I s'pose, and goes on as if they took in the *Times, Chron,* and '*Tiser*—pubs. we calls the '*Tiser*—all to their own cheek. It's penny works I sell the most of; indeed, it's very seldom I offer anything else, 'cause it's little use. Penny Punches is fair sale, and I calls it ' Punch '—just Punch. It's dead now, I believe, but there's old num-bers; still they'll be done in time. The real Punch—I sell from six to twelve a week—I call that there as the reel Punch. Galleries of Comicalities is a middling sale ; people take them home with them, I think. Guides to the Thames is good in summer. They're illus-trated ; but people sometimes grumbles and calls them catchpennies. It ain't my fault if they're not all that's expected, but people ex-pects everything for 1*d.* Joe Millers and 'Sto-phelees" (Mephistopheles) " I've sold, and said they was oppositions to Punch ; that's a year or more back, but they was old, and to be had cheap. I sell Lloyd's and Reynolds's pennies —fairish, both of them ; so's the Family He-rald and the London Journal—very fair. I don't venture on any three-halfpenny books on anything like a spec., acause people says at once : ' A penny—I'll give you a penny.' I sell seven out of eight of what I do sell to gents. ; more than that, perhaps ; for you'll not often see a woman buy nothing wots in-tended to improve her mind. A young woman, like a maid of all work, buys sometimes and looks hard at the paper ; but I some-times thinks it's to show she can read. A summer Sunday's my best time, out and out. There's new faces then, and one goes on bolder. I've known young gents. buy, just to offer to young women, I'm pretty well satisfied. It's a introduction. *I have* met with real gentlemen. They've looked over all I offered for sale and then said : ' Nothing I want, my good fellow, but here's a penny for your trouble.' I wish there was more of them. I do sincerely. Sometimes I've gone on board and not sold one paper. I buy in the regular way, 9*d.* for a dozen (sometimes thirteen to the dozen) of penny pubs. I don't know what I make, for I keep no count ; perhaps a sov. in a good week and a half in another."

I am informed that the average earnings of these traders, altogether, may be taken at 15*s.* weekly ; calculating that twelve carry on the trade the year through, we find that (assuming each man to sell at thirty-three per cent. pro-fit—though in the case of old works it will be cent. per cent.) upwards of 1,500*l.* are ex-pended annually in steam-boat papers.

OF THE SALE OF NEWSPAPERS, BOOKS, &c., AT THE RAILWAY STATIONS.

ALTHOUGH the sale of newspapers at the rail-way termini, &c., cannot strictly be classed as a street-sale, it is so far an open-air traffic as to require some brief notice, and it has now become a trade of no small importance.

The privilege of selling to railway-passengers, within the precincts of the terminus, is disposed of by tender. At present the newsvendor on the North-Western Line, I am informed, pays to the company, for the right of sale at the Euston-square terminus, and the provincial stations, as large a sum as 1,700*l.* per annum. The amount usually given is of course in proportion to the number of stations, and the traffic of the rail-way.

The purchaser of this exclusive privilege sends his own servants to sell the newspapers and books, which he supplies to them in the quantity required. The men thus engaged are paid from 20*s.* to 30*s.* a week, and the boys receive from 6*s.* to 10*s.* 6*d.* weekly, but rarely 10*s.* 6*d.*

All the morning and evening papers are sold at the Station, but of the weekly press, those are sent for sale which in the manager's judgment are likely to sell, or which his agent informs him are " asked for." It is the same with the weekly unstamped publications. The reason seems obvious ; if there be more than can be sold, a dead loss is incurred, for the surplusage, as regards newspapers, is only saleable as waste paper.

The books sold at railways are nearly all of the class best known as " light reading," or what some account light reading. The price does not often exceed 1*s.* ; and among the books offered for sale in these places are novels in one volume, published at 1*s.*—sometimes in two volumes, at 1*s.* each ; " monthly parts " of works issued in weekly numbers ; shilling books of poetry ; but rarely political or controversial pamphlets. One man, who understood this trade, told me that " a few of the pamphlets about the Pope and Cardinal Wiseman sold at first ; but in a month or six weeks, people began to say, ' A shilling for that! I'm sick of the thing.' "

The large sum given for the privilege of an exclusive sale, shows that the number of books and papers sold at railway stations must be very considerable. But it must be borne in mind, that the price, and consequently the profit on the daily newspapers, sold at the railways, is greater than elsewhere. None are charged less than 6*d.*, the regular price at a news-agent's shop being 5*d.*, so that as the cost price is 4*d.*

the profit is double. Nor is it unusual for a passenger by an early train, who grows impatient for his paper, to cry out, "A shilling for the *Times !* " This, however, is only the case, I am told, with those who start very early in the morning ; for the daily papers are obtained for the railway stations from among the earliest impressions, and can be had at the accustomed price as early as six o'clock, although, if there be exciting news and a great demand, a larger amount may be given.

OF THE STREET BOOKSELLERS.

THE course of my inquiry now leads me to consider one of the oldest, and certainly not least important of the street traffics—that of the book-stalls. Of these there are now about twenty in the London streets, but in this number I include only those which are *properly* street-stalls. Many book-stalls, as in such a locality as the London-road, are appendages to shops, being merely a display of wares outside the bookseller's premises ; and with these I do not now intend to deal.

The men in this trade I found generally to be intelligent. They have been, for the most part, engaged in some minor department of the bookselling or newspaper trade, in the regular way, and are unconnected with the street-sellers in other lines, of whose pursuits, habits, and characters, they seem to know nothing.

The street book-stalls are most frequent in the thoroughfares which are well-frequented, but which, as one man in the trade expressed himself, are not so "shoppy" as others—such as the City-road, the New-road, and the Old Kent-road. "If there's what you might call a recess," observed another street book-stall-keeper, "*that's* the place for us; and you'll often see us along with flower-stands and pinners-up." The stalls themselves do not present any very smart appearance ; they are usually of plain deal. If the stock of books be sufficiently ample, they are disposed on the surface of the stall, "fronts up," as I heard it described, with the titles, when lettered on the back, like as they are presented in a library. If the "front" be unlettered, as is often the case with the older books, a piece of paper is attached, and on it is inscribed the title and the price. Sometimes the description is exceeding curt, as, " Poetry," " French," " Religious," " Latin " (I saw an odd volume, in Spanish, of Don Quixote, marked " Latin," but it was at a shop-seller's stall,) " Pamphlets," and such like ; or where it seems to have been thought necessary to give a somewhat fuller appellation, such titles are written out as " Locke's Understanding," " Watts's Mind," or " Pope's Rape." If the stock be very scant, the side of the book is then shown, and is either covered with white paper, on which the title and price are written, or " brushed," or else a piece of paper is attached, with the necessary announcement.

Sometimes these announcements are striking

enough, as where a number of works of the same size have been bound together (which used to be the case, I am told, more frequently than it is now) ; or where there has been a series of stories in one volume. One such announcement was, " Smollett's Peregrine Pickle Captain Kyd Pirate Prairie Rob of the Bowl Bamfyeld Moore Carew 2s." Alongside this miscellaneous volume was, " Wilberforce's Practical View of Christianity, 1s. ;" " Fenelon's Aventures de Télémaque, plates, 9d. ;" " Arres, de Predestinatione, 1s." (the last-mentioned work, which, at the first glance, seems as if it were an odd mixture of French and Latin, was a Latin quarto); " Coronis ad. Collationem Hagiensem, &c. &c., Gulielmo Amesio." Another work, on another stall, had the following description : " Lord Mount Edgecumbe's Opera What is Currency Watts's Scripture History Thoughts on Taxation only 1s. 3d." Another was, " Knickerbocker Bacon 1s." As a rule, however, the correctness with which the work is described is rather remarkable.

At some few of the street-stalls, and at many of the shop-stalls, are boxes, containing works marked, " All 1d.," or 2d., 3d., or 4d. Among these are old Court- Guides, Parliamentary Companions, Railway Plans, and a variety of sermons, and theological, as well as educational and political pamphlets. To show the character of the publications thus offered—not, perhaps, as a rule, but generally enough, for sale— I copied down the titles of some at 1d. and 2d.

" *All these at* 1d.—' Letters to the Right Honourable Lord John Russell, on State Education, by Edward Baines, jun. ;' ' A Pastoral Letter to the Clergy and Members of the Protestant Episcopal Church in the United States of America ;' ' A Letter to the Protestant Dissenters of England and Wales, by the Rev. Robert Ainslie ;' ' Friendly Advice to Conservatives ;' ' Elementary Thoughts on the Principles of Currency and Wealth, and on the Means of Diminishing the Burthens of the People, by J. D. Basset, Esq., price 2s. 6d.' " The others were each published at 1s.

" *All these at* 2d.—' Poems, by Eleanor Tatlock, 1811, 2 vols., 9s. ;' ' Two Sermons, on the Fall and Final Restoration of the Jews, by the Rev. John Stuart ;' ' Thoughts and Feelings, by Arthur Brooke, 1820 ;' ' The Amours of Philander and Sylvia, being the third and last part of Love-letters between a Nobleman and his Sister. Volume the Second. The Seventh Edition. London.' "

From a cursory examination of the last-mentioned twopenny volume, I could see nothing of the nobleman or his sister. It is one of an inane class of books, originated, I believe, in the latter part of the reign of Charles II. Such publications professed to be (and some few were) records of the court and city scandal of the day, but in general they were works founded on the reputation of the current scandal. In short, to adopt the language of patterers, they were " cocks" issued by the publishers of that period ; and they continued to be published until the middle of the eighteenth century, or a little later. I notice this description of literature the more, particularly as it is still frequently to be met with in street-sale. "There's oft enough," one street-bookseller said to me, "works of that sort making up a 'lot' at a sale, and in very respectable rooms. As if they were make-weights, or to make up a sufficient number of books, and so they keep their hold in the streets."

As many of my readers may have little, if any, knowledge of this class of street-sold works, I cite a portion of the "epistle dedicatory," and a specimen of the style, of "Philander and Sylvia," to show the change in street, as well as in general literature, as no such works are now published:

"To the Lord Spencer, My Lord, when a new book comes into the world, the first thing we consider is the dedication; and according to the quality and humour of the patron, we are apt to make a judgment of the following subject. If to a statesman we believe it grave and politic; if to a gownman, law or divinity; if to the young and gay, love and gallantry. By this rule, I believe the gentle reader, who finds your lordship's name prefixed before this, will make as many various opinions of it, as they do characters of your lordship, whose youthful sallies have been the business of so much discourse; and which, according to the relator's sense or good nature, is either aggravated or excused; though the woman's quarrel to your lordship has some more reasonable foundation, than that of your own sex; for your lordship being formed with all the beauties and graces of mankind, all the charms of wit, youth, and sweetness of disposition (derived to you from an illustrious race of heroes) adapting you to the noblest love and softness, they cannot but complain on that mistaken conduct of yours, that so lavishly deals out those agreeable attractions, squandering away that youth and time on many, which might be more advantageously dedicated to some one of the fair; and by a liberty (which they call not being discreet enough) rob them of all the hopes of conquest over that heart which they believe can fix no where; they cannot caress you into tameness; or if you sometimes appear so, they are still upon their guard with you; for like a young lion you are ever apt to leap into your natural wildness; the greatness of your soul disdaining to be confined to lazy repose; though the delicacy of your person and constitution so absolutely require it; your lordship not being made for diversions so rough and fatiguing, as those your active mind would impose upon it."

The last sentence is very long, so that a shorter extract may serve as a specimen of the staple of this book-making:

"To Philander,—False and perjured as you are, I languish for a sight of you, and conjure you to give it me as soon as this comes to your hands. Imagine not that I have prepared those instruments of revenge that are so justly due to your perfidy; but rather, that I have yet too tender sentiments for you, in spite of the outrage you have done my heart; and that for all the ruin you have made, I still adore you: and though I know you are now another's slave, yet I beg you would vouchsafe to behold the spoils you have made, and allow me this recompense for all, to say—Here was the beauty I once esteemed, though now she is no more Philander's Sylvia."

Having thus described what may be considered the divisional parts of this stall trade, I proceed to the more general character of the class of books sold.

OF THE CHARACTER OF BOOKS OF THE STREET-SALE.

THERE has been a change, and in some respects a considerable change, in the character or class of books sold at the street-stalls, within the last 40 or 50 years, as I have ascertained from the most experienced men in the trade. Now sermons, or rather the works of the old divines, are rarely seen at these stalls, or if seen, are rarely purchased. Black-letter editions are very unfrequent at street book-stalls, and it is twenty times more difficult, I am assured, for street-sellers to pick up anything really rare and curious, than it was in the early part of the century.

One reason assigned for this change by an intelligent street-seller was, that black-letter or any ancient works, were almost all purchased by the second-hand booksellers, who have shops and issue catalogues, as they had a prompt sale for them whenever they could pick them up at book-auctions or elsewhere. "Ay, indeed," said another book-stall keeper, "anything scarce or curious, when it's an old book, is kept out of the streets; if it's not particular decent, sir," (with a grin), "why it's reckoned all the more curious,—that's the word, sir, I know,—'curious.' I can tell how many beans make five as well as you or anybody. Why, now, there's a second-hand bookseller not a hundred miles from Holborn—and a pleasant, nice man he is, and does a respectable business—and he puts to the end of his catalogue—they all have catalogues that's in a good way—two pages that he calls 'Facetiæ.' They're titles and prices of queer old books in all languages—indecent books, indeed. He sends his catalogues to a many clergymen and learned people; and to any that he thinks wouldn't much admire seeing his 'Facetiæ,' he pulls the last leaf out, and sends his catalogue, looking finished without it. Those last two pages aren't at all the worst part of his trade among buyers that's worth money."

In one respect a characteristic of this trade is unaltered; I allude to the prevalence of "odd volumes" at the cheaper stalls,—not the odd volumes of a novel, but more frequently of one of the essayists—the "Spectator" especially. One stall-keeper told me, that if he purchased an old edition of the "Spectator," in eight vols., he could more readily sell it in single volumes, at 4d. each, than sell the eight vols. altogether for 2s., or even 1s. 4d., though this was but 2d. a volume.

"There's nothing in my trade," said one street-bookseller with whom I conversed on the subject, "that sells better, or indeed so well, as English classics. I can't offer to draw fine distinctions, and I'm just speaking of my own plain way of trade; but *I* call English classics such works as the 'Spectator,' 'Tatler,' 'Guardian,' 'Adventurer,' 'Rambler,' 'Rasellas,' 'The Vicar of Wakefield,' 'Peregrine Pickle,' 'Tom Jones, 'Goldsmith's Histories of Greece, Rome, and England' (they all sell quick), 'Enfield's Speaker,' 'mixed plays,' the 'Sentimental Journey,' no, sir, 'Tristram Shandy,' rather hangs on hand, the 'Pilgrim's Progress' (but it must be sold *very* low), 'Robinson Crusoe,' 'Philip Quarles,' 'Telemachus,' 'Gil Blas,' and 'Junius's Letters.' I don't remember more at this moment, such as are of good sale. I haven't included poetry, because I'm speaking of English classics, and of course they must be oldish works to be classics."

Concerning the street sale of poetical works I learned from street book-sellers, that their *readiest* sale was of volumes of Shakespeare, Pope, Thomson, Goldsmith, Cowper, Burns, Byron, and Scott. "You must recollect, sir," said one dealer, "that in nearly all those poets there's a double chance for sale at book-stalls. For what with old editions, and new and cheap editions, there's always plenty in the market, and very low. No, I can't say I could sell Milton as quickly as any of those mentioned, nor 'Hudibras,' nor 'Young's Night Thoughts,' nor Prior, nor Dryden, nor 'Gay's Fables.' It's seldom that we have any works of Hood, or Shelley, or Coleridge, or Wordsworth, or Moore at street stalls—you don't often see them, I think, at booksellers' stalls—for they're soon picked up. Poetry sells very fair, take it altogether."

Another dealer told me that from twenty to thirty years ago there were at the street-stalls a class of works rarely seen now. He had known them in all parts and had disposed of them in his own way of business. He specified the "Messiah" (Klopstock's) as of this class, the "Death of Abel," the "Castle of Otranto" ("but that's seen occasionally still," he observed), the "Old English Baron" ("and that's seen still too, but nothing to what it were once"), the "Young Man's Best Companion" "Zimmerman on Solitude," and "Burke on the Sublime and Beautiful" ("but I have that yet sometimes.") These works were of heavy sale in the streets, and my informant thought they had been thrown into the street-trade because the publishers had not found them saleable in the regular way. "I was dead sick of the 'Death of Abel,'" observed the man, "before I could get out of him." Occasionally are to be seen at most of the stalls, works of which the majority of readers have heard, but may not have met with. Among such I saw "Laura," by Capel Lloftt, 4 vols. 1s. 6d. "Darwin's Botanic Garden," 2s. "Alfred, an Epic Poem," by H. J. Pye, Poet Laureate, 10d. "Cœlebs in search of a Wife," 2 vols. in one, 1s.

The same informant told me that he had lived near an old man who died twenty-five years ago, or it might be more, with whom he was somewhat intimate. This old man had been all his life familiar with the street trade in books, which he had often hawked—a trade now almost unknown; his neighbour had heard him say that fifty to seventy years ago, he

made his two guineas a week "without distressing hisself," meaning, I was told, that he was drinking every Monday at least. This old man used to tell that in his day, the "Whole Duty of Man," and the "Tale of a Tub," and "Pomfret's Poems," and "Pamela," and "Sir Charles Grandison" went off *well*, but "Pamela" the best. "And I've heard the old man say, sir," I was further told, "how he had to tread his shoes straight about what books he showed publicly. He sold 'Tom Paine' on the sly. If anybody bought a book and would pay a good price for it, three times as much as was marked, he'd *give* the 'Age of Reason' in. I never see it now, but I don't suppose anybody would interfere if it was offered. A sly trade's always the best for paying, and for selling too. The old fellow used to laugh and say his stall was quite a godly stall, and he wasn't often without a copy or two of the 'Anti-Jacobin Review,' which was all for Church and State and all that, though he had 'Tom Paine' in a drawer."

The books sold at the street-stalls are purchased by the retailers either at the auctions of the regular trade, or at "chance," or general auctions, or of the Jews or others who may have bought books cheap under such circumstances. Often, however, the stall-keeper has a market peculiarly his own. It is not uncommon for working men or tradesmen, if they become "beaten-down and poor" to carry a basket-full of books to a stall-keeper, and say, "Here, give me half-a-crown for these." One man had forty parts, each issued at 1s., of a Bible, offered to him at 1d. a part, by a mechanic who could not any longer afford to "take them in," and was at last obliged to sell off what he had. Of course such things are nearly valueless when imperfect. Very few works are bought for street-stall sale of the regular booksellers.

OF THE EXPERIENCE OF A STREET BOOK-SELLER.

I now give a statement, furnished to me by an experienced man, as to the nature of his trade, and the class of his customers. Most readers will remember having seen an account in the life of some poor scholar, having read—and occasionally, in spite of the remonstrances of the stall-keeper—some work which he was too needy to purchase, and even of his having read it through at intervals. That something of this kind is still to be met with will be found from the following account:

"My customers, sir, are of all sorts," my informant said. "They're gentlemen on their way from the City, that have to pass along here by the City-road. Bankers' clerks, very likely, or insurance-office clerks, or such like. They're faiiish customers, but they often screw me. Why only last month a gentleman I know very well by sight, and I see him pass in his brougham in bad weather, took up an old Latin book—if I remember right it was an odd volume of a French edition of Horace—and though it was marked only 8*d.*, it was long before he would consent to give more than 6*d.* And I should never have got my price if I hadn't heard him say quite hastily, when he took up the book, 'The very thing I've long been looking for!' Mechanics are capital customers for scientific or trade books, such as suit their business; and so they often are for geography and history, and some for poetry; but *they're* not so screwy. I know a many such who are rare ones for searching into knowledge. Women buy very little of me in comparison to men; sometimes an odd novel, in one volume, when its cheap, such as 'The Pilot,' or 'The Spy,' or 'The Farmer of Inglewood Forest,' or 'The Monk.' No doubt some buy 'The Monk,' not knowing exactly what sort of a book it is, but just because it's a romance; but some young men buy it, I know, because they have learned what sort it's like. Old three vol. novels won't sell at all, if they're ever so cheap. Boys very seldom buy of me, unless it's a work about pigeons, or something that way.

" I can't say that odd vols. of Annual Registers are anything but a bad sale, but odd vols. of old Mags. (magazines), a year or half-year bound together, are capital. Old London Mags., or Ladies', or Oxford and Cambridges, or Town and Countrys, or Universals, or Monthly Reviews, or Humourists, or Ramblers, or Europeans, or any of any sort, that's from 40 to 100 years old, no matter what they are, go off rapidly at from 1*s.* 6*d.* to 3*s.* 6*d.* each, according to size, and binding, and condition. Odd numbers of Mags. are good for little at a stall. The old Mags. in vols. are a sort of reading a great many are very fond of. Lives of the Princess Charlotte are a ready penny enough. So are Queen Carolines, but not so good. Dictionaries of all kinds are nearly as selling as the old Mags., and so are good Latin books. French are only middling; not so well as you might think."

My informant then gave me a similar account to what I had previously received concerning English classics, and proceeded: " Old religious books, they're a fair trade enough, but they're not so plentiful on the stalls now, and if they're black-letter they don't find their way from the auctions or anywhere to any places but the shops or to private purchasers. Mrs. Rowe's 'Knowledge of the Heart' goes off, if old. Bibles, and Prayer-books, and Hymn-books, are very bad." [This may be accounted for by the cheapness of these publications, when new, and by the facilities afforded to obtain them gratuitously.] " Annuals are dull in going off; very much so, though one might expect different. I can hardly sell 'Keepsakes' at all. Children's books, such as are out one year at 2*s.* 6*d.* apiece, very nicely got up, sell finely next year at the stalls for from 6*d.* to 10*d.* Genteel people buy them of us for presents at holiday times. They'll give an extra penny quite cheerfully if there's 'Price 2*s.* 6*d.*' or 'Price 3*s.* 6*d.*' lettered on the back or part of the title-page. School-books in good

condition don't stay long on hand, especially Pinnock's. There's not a few people who stand and read and read for half an hour or an hour at a time. It's very trying to the temper when they take up room that way, and prevent others seeing the works, and never lay out a penny theirselves. But they seem quite lost in a book. Well, I'm sure I don't know what they are. Some seem very poor, judging by their dress, and some seem shabby genteels. I can't help telling them, when I see them going, that I'm much obliged, and I hope that perhaps next time they'll manage to say ' thank ye,' for they don't open their lips once in twenty times. I know a man in the trade that goes dancing mad when he has customers of this sort, who aren't customers. I dare say, one day with another, I earn 3*s.* the year through; wet days are greatly against us, for if we have a cover people won't stop to look at a stall. Perhaps the rest of my trade earn the same?" This man told me that he was not unfrequently asked, and by respectable people, for indecent works, but he recommended them to go to Holywell-street themselves. He believed that some of his fellow-traders *did* supply such works, but to no great extent.

An elderly man, who had known the street book-trade for many years, but was not concerned in it when I saw him, told me that he was satisfied he had sold old books, old plays often, to Charles Lamb, whom he described as a stuttering man, who, when a book suited him, sometimes laid down the price, and smiled and nodded, and then walked away with it in his pocket or under his arm, without a word having been exchanged. When we came to speak of dates, I found that my informant—who had only conjectured that this was Lamb—was unquestionably mistaken. One of the best customers he ever had for anything old or curious, and in Italian, if he remembered rightly, as well as in English, was the late Rev. Mr. Scott, who was chaplain on board the Victory, at the time of Nelson's death at Trafalgar. "He had a living in Yorkshire, I believe it was," said the man, "and used to come up every now and then to town. I was always glad to see his white head and rosy face, and to have a little talk with him about books and trade, though it wasn't always easy to catch what he said, for he spoke quick, and not very distinct. But he was a pleasant old gentleman, and talked to a poor man as politely as he might to an admiral. He was very well known in my trade, as I was then employed."

The same man once sold to a gentleman, he told me, and he believed it was somewhere about twenty-five years ago, if not more, a Spanish or Portuguese work, but what it was he did not know. It was marked 1*s.* 9*d.*, being a good-sized book, but the stall-keeper was tired of having had it a long time, so that he gladly would have taken 9*d.* for it. The gentleman in question handed him half-a-crown, and, as he had not the change, the purchaser said: "O, don't mind; it's worth far more than half-a-crown to me." When this liberal customer had walked away, a gentleman who had been standing at the stall all the time, and who was an occasional buyer, said, "Do you know him?" and, on receiving an answer in the negative, he rejoined, "That's Southey."

Another stall-keeper told me that his customers—some of whom he supplied with any periodical in the same way as a newsvendor—had now and then asked him, especially "the ladies of the family," who glanced, when they passed, at the contents of his stall, why he had not newer works? "I tell them," said the stall-keeper, "that they haven't become cheap enough yet for the streets, but that they would come to it in time." After some conversation about his trade, which only confirmed the statements I have given, he said laughingly, "Yes, indeed, you all come to such as me at last. Why, last night I heard a song about all the stateliest buildings coming to the ivy, and I thought, as I listened, it was the same with authors. The best that the best can do is the book-stall's food at last. And no harm, for he's in the best of company, with Shakespeare, and all the great people."

Calculating 15s. weekly as the average earnings of the street book-stall keepers—for further information induces me to think that the street bookseller who earned 18s. a week regularly, cleared it by having a "tidy pitch"—and reckoning that, to clear such an amount, the bookseller takes, at least, 1l. 11s. 6d. weekly, we find 5,460 guineas yearly expended in the purchase of books at the purely street-stalls, independently of what is laid out at the open-air stalls connected with book-shops.

Of Street Book-auctioneers.

The sale of books by auction, in the streets, is now inconsiderable and irregular. The "auctioning" of books—I mean of new books—some of which were published principally with a view to their sale by auction, was, thirty to forty years ago, systematic and extensive. It was not strictly a street-sale. The auctioneer offered his books to the public, nine cases out of ten, in town, in an apartment (now commonly known as a "mock-auction room"), which was so far a portion of the street that access was rendered easier by the removal of the door and window of any room on a ground-floor, and some of the bidders could and did stand in the street and take part in the proceedings. In the suburbs—which at that period were not so integral a portion of the metropolis as at present—the book-auction sales were carried on strictly in the open air, generally in front of a public-house, and either on a platform erected for the purpose, or from a covered cart; the books then being deposited in the vehicle, and the auctioneer standing on a sort of stage placed on the propped-up shafts. In the country, however, the auction was often carried on in an inn.

The works thus sold were generally standard works. The poems were those of Pope, Young, Thomson, Goldsmith, Falconer, Cowper, &c. The prose writings were such works as "The Pilgrim's Progress," "The Travels of Mr. Lemuel Gulliver," "Johnson's Lives of the Poets," "The Vicar of Wakefield," the most popular of the works of Defoe, Fielding, and Smollett, and "Hervey's Meditations among the Tombs" (at one time highly popular). These books were not correctly printed, they were printed, too, on inferior paper, and the frontispiece—when there was a frontispiece—was often ridiculous. But they certainly gave to the public what is called an "impetus" for reading. Some were published in London (chiefly by the late Mr. Tegg, who at one time, I am told, himself "offered to public competition," by auction, the works he published); others were printed in Edinburgh, Aberdeen, Newcastle-upon-Tyne, Ipswich, Bungay, &c.

One of my informants remembered being present at a street-sale, about twenty or thirty years ago; he perfectly remembered, however, the oratory of the auctioneer, of whom he purchased some books. The sale was in one of the streets in Stoke Newington, a door or two from a thoroughfare. My informant was there—as he called it—"accidentally," and knew little of the neighbourhood. The auctioneer stood at the door of what appeared to have been a coach-house, and sold his books, which were arranged within, very rapidly: "Byron," he exclaimed; "Lord Byron's latest and best po'ms. Sixpence! Sixpence! Eightpence! I take penny bids under a shilling. Eightpence for the poems written by a lord—Gone! Yours, sir" (to my informant). The auctioneer, I was told, "spoke very rapidly, and clipped many of his words." The work thus sold consisted of some of Byron's minor poems. It was in the pamphlet form, and published, I have no doubt, surreptitiously; for there was, in those days, a bold and frequent piracy of any work which was thought distasteful to the Government, or to which the Court of Chancery might be likely to refuse the protection of the law of copyright.

The auctioneer went on: "Coop'r—Coop'r! Published at 3s. 6d., as printed on the back. Superior to Byron — Coop'r's 'Task.' No bidders? Thank you, sir. One - and - six, your's, sir. Young—'Young's Night Thoughts. Life, Death, and Immortality,'—great subjects. London edition, marked 3s. 6d. Going!—last bidder—two shillings—gone!" The purchaser then complained that the frontispiece—a man seated on a tombstone—was exactly the same as to a copy he had of "Hervey's Meditations," but the auctioneer said it was impossible.

I have thus shown what was the style and nature of the address of the street book-auctioneer, formerly, to the public. If it were not strictly "patter," or "pompous oration," it certainly partook of some of the characteristics of patter. At present, however, the street book-auctioneer may be described as a true patterer.

It will be seen from the account I have

THE STREET-STATIONER.

[*From a Daguerreotype by* BEARD.]

given, that the books were then really "sold by auction"—knocked down to the highest bidder. This however was, and is not always the case. Legally to sell by auction, necessitates the obtaining of a licence, at an annual cost of 5*l.*; and if the bookseller conveys his stock of books from place to place, a hawker's licence is required as well,—which entails an additional expenditure of 4*l.* The itinerant bookseller evades, or endeavours to evade, the payment for an auctioneer's licence, by "putting-up" his books at a high price, and *himself* decreasing the terms, instead of offering them at a low price, and allowing *the public* to make a series of "advances." Thus, a book may be offered by a street-auctioneer at half-a-crown—two shillings—eighteenpence—a shilling—tenpence, and the moment any one assents to a specified sum, the volume handed to him; so that there is no competition—no bidding by the public one in advance of another. Auction, however, is resorted to as often as the bookseller dares.

One experienced man in the book-stall trade calculated that twenty years ago there might be twelve book-auctioneers in the streets of London, or rather, of its suburbs. One of these was a frequenter of the Old Kent-road; another, "Newington way;" and a third resorted to "any likely pitch in Pimlico"—all selling from a sort of van. Of these twelve, however, my informant thought that there were never more than six in London at one time, as they were all itinerant; and they have gradually dwindled down to two, who are now not half their time in town. These two traders are brothers, and sell their books from a sort of platform erected on a piece of waste-ground, or from a barrow. The works they sell are generally announced as new, and are often uncut. They are all recommended as explanatory of every topic of the day, and are often set forth as "spicy." Three or four years ago, a gentleman told me how greatly he was amused with the patter of one of these men, who was selling books at the entrance of a yard full of caravans, not far from the School for the Blind, Lambeth. One work the street-auctioneer announced at the top of his voice, in the following terms, as far as a good memory could retain them : "' The Rambler!' Now you rambling boys—now you young devils, that's been staring those pretty girls out of countenance—here's the very book for you, and more shame for you, and perhaps for me too; but I must sell—I must do business. If any lady or gen'lman 'll stand treat to a glass of brandy and water, ' warm with,' I'll tell more about this ' Rambler'—I'm too bashful, as it is. Who bids? Fifteen-pence—thank'ee, sir. Sold again!" The "Rambler" was Dr. Johnson's !

The last time one of my informants heard the " patter " of the smartest of the two brothers, it was to the following effect: " Here is the ' History of the Real Flying Dutchman,' and *no* mistake; no fiction, I assure you, upon

my honour. Published at 10*s.*—who bids half-a-crown? Sixpence; thank you, sir. Ninepence ; going—going! Any more?—gone! "

A book-stall-keeper, who had sold goods to a book-auctioneer, and attended the sales, told me he was astonished to hear how his own books—" old new books," he called them, were set off by the auctioneer : " Why, there was a vol. lettered ' Pamphlets,' and I think there *was* something about Jack Sheppard in it, but it was all odds and ends of other things, I know. ' Here's the *real* Jack Sheppard,' sings out the man, ' and no gammon!' The real edition—no spooniness here, but set off with other interesting histories, valuable for the rising generation and all generations. This is the real Jack. This will

. '—— put you up to the time o' day,
    Nix, my dolly pals, bid away.'

" Then he went on : ' Goldsmith's History of England. Continued by the first writers of the day—to the very last rumpus in the palace, and no mistake. Here it is ; genuine.' Well, sir," the stall-keeper continued, " the man didn't do well ; perhaps he cleared 1*s.* 6*d.* or a little more that evening on books. People laughed more than they bought. But it's no wonder the trade's going to the dogs — they're not allowed to have a pitch now; I shouldn't be surprised if they was not *all* driven out of London next year. It's contrary to Act of Parliament to get an honest living in the streets now-a-days."

A man connected with the street book-trade considered that if one of these auctioneers earned a guinea in London streets in the six days it was a "good week." Half-a-guinea was nearer the average, he thought, " looking at the weather and everything." What amount is expended to enable this street-dealer to earn his guinea or half-guinea, is so uncertain, from the very nature of an auction, that I can obtain no data to rely upon.

The itinerant book-auctioneer is now confined chiefly to the provincial towns, and especially the country markets. The reason for this is correctly given in the statement above cited. The street-auction requires the gathering of so large a crowd that the metropolitan police consider the obstruction to the public thoroughfares warrants their interference. The two remaining book-auctioneers in London generally restrict their operations to the outskirts — the small space which fronts "the George Inn " in the Commercial-road, and which lays a few yards behind the main thoroughfare, and similar suburban "retreats " being favourite "pitches." The trade is, as regards profits, far from bad—the books sold consisting chiefly of those picked up in cheap "lots " at the regular auctions; so that what fetches 6*d.* in the streets has generally been purchased for less than a penny. The average rate of profit may be taken at 250*l.* per cent. at the least. Exorbitant however as this re-turn may appear, still it should be remembered that the avocation is one that can be pursued only occasionally, and that solely in fine weather. Books are now more frequently sold in the London streets from barrows. This change of traffic has been forced upon the street-sellers by the commands of the police—that the men should "keep moving." Hence the well-known light form of street conveyance is now fast superseding not only the book-auctioneer, but the book-stall in the London streets. Of these book-barrowmen there is now about fifty trading regularly in the metropolis, and taking on an average from 3s. to 5s. 6d. a day.

OF THE STREET-SALE OF SONG-BOOKS, AND OF CHILDREN'S BOOKS.

THE sale of song-books in the streets, at 1d. and at ½d. each, is smaller than it was two years ago. One reason that I heard assigned was that the penny song-books—styled "The Universal Song-book," "The National," "The Bijou," &c.— were reputed to be so much alike (the same songs under a different title), that people who had bought one book were averse to buy another. "There's the ' Ross' and the ' Sam Hall' song-books," said one man, "the 'eighteenth series,' and I don't know what; but I don't like to venture on working them, though they're only a penny. There's lots to be seen in the shop-windows; but they might be stopped in the street, for they an't decent—'specially the flash ones."

One of the books which a poor man had found the most saleable is entitled, "The Great Exhibition Song-book; a Collection of the Newest and Most Admired Songs. Embellished with upwards of one Hundred Toasts and Sentiments." The toasts and sentiments are given in small type, as a sort of border to the thirty-two pages of which the book consists. The toast on the title-page is as follows:

"I'll toast England's daughters, let all fill their glasses, Whose beauty and virtue the whole world surpasses."

To show the nature of the songs in street demand, I cite those in the book: "The Gathering of the Nations," "Bloom is on the Rye," "Wilt thou Meet me there, Love?" "Minna's Tomb," "I'll Love thee ever Dearly" (Arnold), "When Phœbus wakes the Rosy Hours," "Money is your Friend," "Julia and Caspar" (G. M. Lewis), "That pretty word, Yes" (E. Mackey), "Farewell, Forget me Not," "The Queen and the Navy" (music published by H. White, Great Marlborough-street), "I resign Thee every Token" (music published by Duff and Co.), "Sleep, gentle Lady;" a serenade (H. J. Payne), "The Warbling Waggoner," "The Keepsake," "A Sequel to the Cavalier," "There's room enough for All" (music at Mr. Davidson's), "Will you Come to the Dale?" "Larry O'Brian," "Woman's Love," "Afloat on the Ocean" (sung by Mr. Weiss, in the Opera of the "Heart of Mid Lothian," music published by Jefferys, Soho-square), "Together, Dearest, let us Fly" (sung by Mr. Braham, in the Opera of the "Heart of Mid Lothian," music published

by Jefferys, Soho-square), "The Peremptory Lover" (Tune—"John Anderson, my Joe"). There are forty-seven songs in addition to those whose titles I have quoted, but they are all of the same character.

The penny song-books (which are partly indecent), and entitled the "Sam Hall" and "Ross" Songsters, are seldom or never sold in the streets. Many of those vended in the shops outrage all decency. Some of these are styled the "Coal-Hole Companion," "Cider-Cellar Songs," "Captain Morris's Songs," &c. (the filthiest of all.) These are generally marked 1s. and sold at 6d.; and have a coloured folded frontispiece. They are published chiefly by H. Smith, Holywell-street. The titles of some of the songs in these works are sufficient to indicate their character. "The Muff," "The Two Miss Thys," "George Robins's Auction," "The Woman that studied the Stars," "A Rummy Chaunt" (frequently with no other title), "The Amiable Family," "Joe Buggins' Wedding," "Stop the Cart," "The Mot that can feel for another," "The Irish Giant," "Taylor Tim," "The Squire and Patty."

Some titles are unprintable.

The children's books in best demand in the street-trade, are those which have long been popular: "Cinderella," "Jack the Giant-killer," "Baron Munchausen," "Puss and the Seven-leagued Boots," "The Sleeping Beauty," "The Seven Champions of Christendom," &c. &c. "There's plenty of ' Henry and Emmas,'" said a penny bookseller, "and ' A Present for Christmas,' and ' Pictorial Alphabets,' and ' Good Books for Good Boys and Girls;' but when people buys really for their children, they buys the old stories—at least they does of me. I've sold ' Penny Hymns' (hymn-books) sometimes; but when they're bought, or ' Good Books' is bought, it's from charity to a poor fellow like me, more than anything else."

The trade, both in songs and in children's books, is carried on in much the same way as I have described of the almanacks and memorandum-books, but occasionally the singers of ballads sell books. Sometimes poor men, old or infirm, offer them in a tone which seems a whine for charity rather than an offer for sale, "Buy a penny book of a poor old man—very hungry, very hungry." Children do the same, and all far more frequently in the suburbs than in the busy parts of the metropolis. Those who purchase really for the sake of the books, say, one street-seller told me, "Give me something that'll interest a child, and set him a-thinking. They can't understand—poor little things!—your fine writing; do you understand that?" Another man had said, "Fairy tales! bring me nothing but fairies; they set children a-reading." The price asked is most frequently a penny, but some are offered at a halfpenny, which is often given (without a purchase) out of compassion, or to be rid of importunity. The profit is at least cent. per cent.

Of the Street-sellers of Account-books.

THE sale of account-books is in the hands of about the same class of street-sellers as the stationery, but one man in the trade thought the regular hands were more trusted, if anything, than street-stationers. "People, you see," he said, "won't buy their ' accounts ' of raff ; they won't have them of any but respectable people." The books sold are bought at 4s. the dozen, or 4½d. a piece, up to 70s. the dozen, or 5s. 9d., or 6s. a piece. It is rarely, however, that the street account-bookseller gives 4s. 9d., and very rarely that he gives as much as 5s. 9d. for his account-books. His principal sale is of the smaller "waste," or "day-books," kept by the petty traders; the average price of these being 1s. 9d. The principal purchasers are the chandlers, butchers, &c., in the quieter streets, and more especially "a little way out of town, where there ain't so many cheap shops." A man, now a street-stationer, with a "fixed pitch," had carried on the account-book trade until an asthmatic affliction compelled him to relinquish it, as the walking became impossible to him, and he told me that the street-trade was nothing to what it once was. "People," he said, " aren't so well off, I think, sir; and they'll buy half a quire of outside foolscap, or outside post, for from 5d. to 8d., and stitch it together, and rule it, and make a book of it. Rich tradesmen do that, sir. I bought of a stationer some years back, and he told me that he was a relation of a rich grocer, and had befriended him in his (the grocer's) youth, but he wouldn't buy account-books, for he said, the make-shift books that his shopman stitched together for him opened so much easier. People never want a good excuse for acting shabby."

There are now, I am informed, twelve men selling account-books daily, which they carry in a covered basket, or in a waterproof bag, or, in fine weather, under the arm. Some of these street-sellers are not itinerant when there is a congregation of people for business, or indeed for any purpose; at other times they "keep moving." The fixed localities are, on market days, at Smithfield and Mark-lane : and to Hungerford-market, an old man, unable to "travel," resorts daily. The chief trade, however, is in carrying, or hawking these account-books from door to door. A man, "having a connection," does best "on a round;" if he be known, he is not distrusted, and sells as cheap, or rather cheaper, than the shop-keepers.

The twelve account-book sellers (with connections) may clear 2s. 6d. a day each, taking, for the realisation of such profit, 7s. per diem. Thus 1,310l. will be taken by these street-sellers in the course of a year. The capital required to start is, stock-money, 15s.; basket, 3s. 6d ; waterproof bag, 2s. 6d ; 21s. in all.

Of the Street-sellers of Guide-books, &c.

THIS trade, as regards a street-sale, has only been known for nine or ten years, and had its origination in the exertions of Mr. Hume, M.P., to secure to persons visiting the national exhibitions the advantage of a cheap catalogue. The guide-books were only sold, prior to this time, within any public exhibition; and the profits—as is the case at present—were the perquisite of some official. When the sale was a monopoly, the profit must have been considerable, as the price was seldom less than 6d., and frequently 1s. The guide-books, or, as they are more frequently called, catalogues, are now sold by men who stand at the entrance, the approaches, at a little distance on the line, or at the corners of the adjacent streets, at the following places : — the National Gallery, the Vernon Gallery, the British Museum, Westminster Abbey, the House of Lords, the Society of Arts (occasionally), the Art-Union (when open " free "), Greenwich Hospital, the Dulwich Gallery, Hampton Court, Windsor Castle, and Kew Gardens.

At any temporary exhibition, also, the same trade is carried on—as it was largely when the "designs," &c., for the decoration of the New Houses of Parliament were exhibited in Westminster Hall. There are, of course, very many other catalogues, or explanatory guides, sold to the visitors of other exhibitions, but I speak only of the street-sale.

There are now, at the National Gallery, three guidebook-sellers plying their trade in the streets; eight at the British Museum; two at Westminster Abbey; one at the House of Lords, but only on Saturdays, when the House is shown, by orders obtained gratuitously at the Lord Chamberlain's office, or "when appeals are on;" one at the Vernon Gallery; two at Dulwich (but not regularly, as there are none at present), two at Hampton Court, "one near each gate ;" and one, and sometimes three, at Windsor (generally sent out by a shopkeeper there). There used to be one at the Thames Tunnel, but "it grew so bad at last," I was told, "that a rat couldn't have picked up his grub at it—let alone a man."

Among all these sellers I heard statements of earning a most wretched pittance, and all attributed it to the same cause. By the National Gallery is a board, on which is an announcement that the only authorized catalogue of the works of art can be obtained in the hall. There are similar announcements at other public places. One man who had been in this street trade, but had abandoned it, spoke of these "boards," as he called them, with intense bitterness. "They're the ruin of any trade in the streets," he said. "You needn't think because I'm out of it now, that I have a pleasure in abusing the regulations ; no, sir, I look at it this way. Mr. Hume had trouble enough, I know, to get the public a cheap catalogue, and poor men were allowed to earn honest bread by selling them in the streets, and honest bread they would earn still, if it weren't for the board. I declare solemnly a man can't get a living at the trade. The publishers can't prepare their catalogues without leave, and when they've got leave, and do prepare and print them, why isn't a man allowed to sell them in the streets, as I've sold second editions of the *Globe* without ever the office putting out a notice that the only authorized copy was to be had within? God bless your soul, sir, it's shocking, shocking, poor men being hindered every way. Anybody that looks on the board looks on us as cheats and humbugs, and thinks that our catalogues are all takes-in. But I've heard gentlemen, that I'm sure knew what they were talking about, say, in case they'd bought in the street first, and then seen the board and bought within after, so as to be sure of the real thing—I've heard gentlemen, say, sir,—' Why what we got in the street is the best after all.' Free trade! There's plenty said about free trade, but that board, sir, or call it what you please, gives a monopoly against us. What I have said, when I was starving on catalogues, is this: Kick us out of the streets, commit us for selling catalogues, as rogues and vagabonds; or give us a fair chance. If we *may* sell, why is the only authorised catalogue sold only within? I wish Mr. Hume, or Mr. Cobden, either, only understood the rights of the matter —it's of no account to me myself now—and I think they'd soon set it to rights. Free trade! Over the left, and with more hooks than one."

I have no doubt that this representation and this opinion would have been echoed by the street catalogue-sellers, but they were evidently unwilling to converse freely on this branch of the subject, knowing the object for which I questioned them, and that publicity would follow. I attribute this reluctance chiefly to the fact that, all these poor men look forward to the opening of the Great Exhibition with earnest hope and anxiety that the influx of visiters will add greatly to their sale and profits; and they are unwilling to jeopardise their privilege of sale.

One man told me that he believed, from his own knowledge, for he had not always "sold outside," that the largest buyers of these publications were country people, sight-seeing in London, for they bought the book not only as an explanatory guide, but to preserve as a memento of their visit. Such customers, however, I heard from several quarters, the moment they saw a "notice" as to the only authorised copy, looked upon the street-sellers as a systematised portion of the London sharpers, seeking whom they might devour, and so bought their catalogues "within."

The best customers in the streets for the catalogues are, I am assured, the working-classes, who visit the national exhibitions on a holiday. " I've oft enough heard them say," one man stated, " ' I'd rather pay a poor man 2d. any day, when I can spare it, than rich people 1d. I know what it is to fight for a crust.' "

At the National Gallery, the street-sold catalogues are 1d., 3d., and 6d.; in the hall, the authorised copy is sold at 4d. and 1s. At the British Museum, the street-charges are 3d. and 6d.; there were 1d. catalogues of this institution, but they have been discontinued for the last half-year, being found too meagre. At the Vernon Gallery, the charge is 1d.; but the 6d. guide-book to the National Gallery contains also an account of the pictures in the Vernon Gallery. At Westminster Abbey the price is 6d., and the same at the House of Lords. At Hampton-court it is 2d., 4d., and 6d., and at the same rate as regards the other places mentioned. At Hampton-court, I was told, the street-sellers were not allowed to approach the palace nearer than a certain space. One man told me that he was threatened with being " had in for trespassing, and Mr. G—— would make him wheel a roller. Of course," the man continued, " there's an authorised catalogue there."

The best sale of catalogues in the streets was at the exhibition of the works of art for the Houses of Parliament. The sellers, then— about 20 in number, among whom were four women—cleared 2s. and 2s. 6d. each daily. At present, I am assured, that a good week is considered one in which 5s. is made, but that 3s. is more frequently the weekly earning. It must be borne in mind, that at the two places most resorted to—the National Gallery and the British Museum—the street sale is only for four days in the week at the first mentioned, and three days at the second. "You may think that more is made," said one man, " but it isn't. Sweeping a good crossing is far better, far. Bless your soul, only stand a few minutes looking on, any day, and see what numbers and numbers of people pass in and out of a free admission place without ever laying out 1d. Why, only last Monday and Wednesday (March 17 and 19, both very rainy days) I took only 5d. I didn't *take* more than 5d., and I leave you to judge the living I shall *clear* out of that; and I know that the man with the catalogue at another place, didn't take 1d. It's sad work, sir, as you stand in the wet and cold, with no dinner for yourself, and no great hope of taking one home to your family."

These street-sellers contrive, whenever they can, to mix up other avocations with catalogue selling, as the public institutions close early. One, on every occasion, sells second editions of the newspapers; another has "odd turns at portering;" a third sells old umbrellas in the streets; some sold exhibition cards in the Park, on Sundays, until the sale was stopped; another sells a little stationery; and nearly the whole of them resort, on favourable opportunities, to the sale of "books of the play," or of "the opera."

Reckoning that there are regularly sixteen street-sellers of guide-books—they do not interfere with each other's stations—and that each clears 4s. weekly, we find £832 expended in this street traffic. I have calculated only on the usual bookseller's allowance of 25 per cent., though, in some instances, these sellers are supplied on lower terms — besides having, in some of the catalogues, thirteen to the dozen ; but the amount specified does not exceed the mark.

The greatest number of these guide-books which I heard of as having been sold, in any one day, was four dozen, disposed of on a fine Whit-Monday, and for these the street-seller only took 6s. 8d. There are, I was informed, half as many more "threepennies" as "sixpennies" sold, and three times as many "pennies" as the other two together.

The capital required to start is what may suffice to "lay in" a stock of books—5s. generally.

Of the Street-sellers of Fine Arts.

These traders may be described as partaking more of the characteristics of the street stationers than of the "paper-workers," as they are not patterers. The trade is less exclusively than the "paper-trade" in the hands of men. Those carrying on this branch of the street-traffic may be divided into the sellers of pictures in frames, and of engravings (of all kinds), in umbrellas. Under this head may also be ranked the street-artists (though this is a trade associated with street-life rather than forming an integrant part of it), I allude more particularly to the illustrated "boards" which are prepared for the purposes of the street-patterers, and are adapted for no other use. The same artist that executes the greater portion of the street-art, also prepares the paintings which decorate the exterior of shows. There are also the writers of manuscript music, and the makers and sellers of "images" of all descriptions, but this branch of the subject I shall treat under the head of the street-Italians. Under the same curious head I shall also speak of the artists whose skill produces the street-sold medallions, in wax or plaster, they being of the same class as the "image" men. In both "images" and "casts" and "moulded" productions of all kinds the change and improvement that have taken place, from the pristine rudeness of "green parrots" is most remarkable and creditable to the taste of working people, who are the chief purchasers of the smaller articles.

Of Street Art.

The artists who work for the street-sellers are less numerous than the poets for the same trade. Indeed, there is now but one man who can be said to be *solely* a street-artist. The inopportune illustration of ballads of which specimens have already been given—or of any of the street papers—are the work of cheap wood-engravers, who give the execution of these orders to their boys. But it is not often that illustrations are prepared expressly for anything but what I have described as "Gallows literature." Of these, samples have also been furnished. The one of a real murder, and the other of a fabulous

one, or "cock," together with a sample (in the case of Mr. Patrick Connor) of the portraits given in such productions. The cuts for the heading of ballads are very often such as have been used for the illustration of other works, and are "picked up cheap."

The artist who works especially for the street trade—as in the case of the man who paints the patterers' boards—must address his art plainly to the eye of the spectator. He must use the most striking colours, be profuse in the application of scarlet, light blue, orange—not yellow I was told, it ain't a good candlelight colour—and must leave nothing to the imagination. Perspective and back-grounds are things of but minor consideration. Everything must be sacrificed for effect.

These paintings are in water colours, and are rubbed over with a solution of some gum-resin to protect them from the influence of rainy weather. Two of the subjects most in demand of late for the patterers' boards were "the Sloanes" and "the Mannings." The treatment of Jane Wilbred was "worked" by twenty boardmen, each with his "illustration" of the subject. The illustrations were in six "compartments." In the first Mr. and Mrs. Sloane are "picking out" the girl from a line of workhouse children. She is represented as plump and healthy, but with a stupid expression of countenance. In another compartment, Sloane is beating the girl, then attenuated and wretched-looking, with a shoe, while his wife and Miss Devaux (a name I generally heard pronounced among the street-people as it is spelt to an English reader) look approvingly on. The next picture was Sloane compelling the girl to swallow filth. The fourth represented her as in the hospital, with her ribs protruding from her wasted body —"just as I've worked Sarah Simpole," said a patterer, "who was confined in a cellar and fed on 'tato peels. Sarah was a cock, sir, and a ripper." Then came the attack of the people on Sloane, one old woman dressed after the fashion of Mrs. Gamp, "prodding" him with a huge and very green umbrella. The sixth and last was, as usual, the trial.

I have described the "Sloanes' board" first, as it may be more fresh in the remembrance of any reader observant of such things. In the "Mannings' board" there were the same number of compartments as in the Sloanes'; showing the circumstances of the murder, the discovery of the body of Connor, the trial, &c. One standing patterer, who worked a Mannings' board, told me that the picture of Mrs. Manning, beautifully "dressed for dinner" in black satin, with "a low front," firing a pistol at Connor, who was "washing himself," while Manning, in his shirt sleeves, looked on in evident alarm, was greatly admired, especially out of town. "The people said," observed the patterer, "'O, look at him a-washing hisself; he's a doing it so nattral, and ain't a-thinking he's a-going to be murdered. But was he really so ugly as that? Lor! such a beautiful woman to have to do with him.' You see, sir, Connor weren't flattered, and perhaps Mrs. Manning was. I have heard the same sort of remarks both in town and country. I patters hard on the women such times, as I points them out on my board in murders or any crimes. I says: ' When there 's mischief a woman 's always the first. Look at Mrs. Manning there on that werry board—the work of one of the first artists in London—it 's a faithful likeness, taken from life at one of her examinations, look at *her.* She fires the pistol, as you can see, and her husband was her tool.' I said, too, that Sloane was Mrs. Sloane's tool. It answers best, sir, in my opinion, going on that patter. The men likes it, and the women doesn't object, for they 'll say: ' Well, when a woman is bad, she *is* bad, and is a disgrace to her sex.' There's the board before them when I runs on that line of patter, and when I appeals to the 'lustration, it seems to cooper the thing. They *must* believe their eyes."

When there is "a run" on any particular subject, there are occasionally jarrings—I was informed by a "boardman"—between the artist and his street-customers. The standing patterers want " something more original" than their fellows, especially if they are likely to work in the same locality, while the artist prefers a faithful copy of what he has already executed. The artist, moreover, and with all reasonableness, will say: " Why, you must have the facts. Do you want me to make Eliza Chestney killing Rush ? " The matter is often compromised by some change being introduced, and by the characters being differently dressed. One man told me, that in town and country he had seen Mrs. Jermy shot in the following costumes, "in light green welwet, sky-blue satin, crimson silk, and vite muslin." It was the same with Mrs. Manning.

For the last six or eight years, I am told, the artist in question has prepared all the boards in demand. Previously, the standing patterers prepared their own boards, when they fancied themselves capable of such a "reach of art," or had them done by some unemployed painter, whom they might fall in with at a lodging-house, or elsewhere. This is rarely done now, I am told ; not perhaps more than six times in a twelve-month, and when done it is most frequently practised of " cock-boards ;" for, as was said to me, " if a man thinks he 's getting up a fake-ment likely to take, and wants a board to help him on with it, he'll try and keep it to hisself, and come out with it quite fresh."

The charge of the popular street-artist for the painting of a board is 3s. or 3s. 6d., according to the simplicity or elaborateness of the details ; the board itself is provided by the artist's employer. The demand for this peculiar branch of street art is very irregular, depending entirely upon whether anything be "up" or not; that is, whether there has or has not been perpetrated any act of atrocity, which has riveted, as it is called, the public attention. And so great is the uncertainty felt by the street-folk, whether " the most beautiful murder will take or not," that it is rarely the patterer will order, or the artist will speculate, in anticipation of a demand, upon preparing the painting of any event, until satisfied that it has become "popular." A deed of more than usual daring, deceit, or mystery, may be at once hailed by those connected with murder-patter, as " one that will do," and some speculation may be ventured upon; as it was, I am informed, in the cases of Tawell, Rush, and the Mannings; but these are merely exceptional. Thus, if the artist have a dozen boards ordered " for this ten days, he may have two, or one, or none for the next ten ;" so uncertain, it appears, is all that depends, without intrinsic merit, on mere popular applause.

I am unable to give—owing to the want of account-books, &c., which I have so often had to refer to as characteristic of street-people—a precise account of the average number of boards thus prepared in a year. Perhaps it may be as close to the fact as possible to conclude that the artist in question who, unlike the majority of the street-poets, is not a street-seller, but works, as a professional man, *for* but not *in* the streets, realises on his boards a profit of 7s. 6d. weekly. The pictorial productions for street-shows will be more appropriately described in the account of street-performers and showmen.

This artist, as I have shown concerning some of the street-professors of the sister art of poesy, has the quality of knowing how to adapt his works exactly to the taste of his patrons the sellers, and of their patrons, the buyers in the streets.

Of the Street-sellers of Engravings, etc., in Umbrellas, etc.

The sale of "prints," "pictures," and "engravings"—I heard them designated by each term—in umbrellas in the streets, has been known, as far as I could learn from the street-folk for some fifteen years, and has been general from ten to twelve years. In this traffic the umbrella is inverted and the "stock" is disposed within its expanse. Sometimes narrow tapes are attached from rib to rib of the umbrella, and within these tapes are placed the pictures, one resting upon another. Sometimes a few pins are used to attach the larger prints to the cotton of the umbrella, the smaller ones being " fitted in at the side " of the bigger. " Pins is best, sir, in my opinion," said a little old man, who used to have a " print umbrella " in the New Cut; "for the public has a more unbrokener display. I used werry fine pins, though they's dearer, for people as has a penny to spare likes to see things nice, and big pins makes big holes in the pictures."

This trade is most pursued on still summer evenings, and the use of an inverted umbrella seems so far appropriate that it can only be so used, in the street, in *dry* weather. " I used to keep a sharp look-out, sir," said the same informant, " for wind or rain, and many's the time them devils o' boys—God forgive me, they's on'y poor children—but they *is* devils—has come up to me and has said—one in particler, standin' afore the rest: 'It'll thunder in five minutes, old bloke, so hup with yer humbereller, and go 'ome; hup with it jist as it is; it'll show stunnin; and sell as yer goes.' O, they're a shocking torment, sir; nobody can feel it like people in the streets,—shocking."

The engravings thus sold are of all descriptions. Some have evidently been the frontispieces of sixpenny or lower-priced works. These works sometimes fall into hands of the "waste collectors," and any "illustrations" are extracted from the letter-press and are disposed of by the collectors, by the gross or dozen, to those warehousemen who supply the small shop-keepers and the street-sellers. Sometimes, I was informed, a number of engravings, which had for a while appeared as "frontispieces" were issued for sale separately. Many of these were and are found in the "street umbrellas;" more especially the portraits of popular actors and actresses. "Mr. J. P. Kemble, as Hamlet"—"Mr. Fawcett, as Captain Copp"—"Mr. Young, as Iago"—"Mr. Liston, as Paul Pry"—"Mrs. Siddons, as Lady Macbeth"—"Miss O'Neil, as Belvidera," &c., &c. In the course of an inquiry into the subject nearly a year and a half ago, I learned from one "umbrella man" that, six or seven years previously, he used to sell more portraits of "Mr. Edmund Kean, as Richard III.," than of anything else. Engravings, too, which had first been admired in the "Annuals"—when half-a-guinea was the price of the "Literary Souvenir," the "Forget-me-not," "Friendship's Offering," the "Bijou," &c., &c.—are frequently found in these umbrellas; and amongst them are not unfrequently seen portraits of the aristocratic beauties of the day, from "waste" "Flowers of Loveliness" and old "Court Magazines," which "go off very fair." The majority of these street-sold "engravings" are "coloured," in which state the street-sellers prefer them, thinking them much more saleable, though the information I received hardly bears out their opinion.

The following statement, from a middle-aged woman, further shows the nature of the trade, and the class of customers:

"I've sat with an umbrella," she said, "these seven or eight years, I suppose it is. My husband's a penny lot-seller, with just a middling pitch" [the vendor of a number of articles, sold at a penny "a lot"] "and in the summer I do a little in engravings, when I'm not minding my husband's 'lots,' for he has sometimes a day, and oftener a night, with portering and packing for a tradesman, that's known him long. Well, sir, I think I sell most 'coloured.' 'Master Toms' wasn't bad last summer. 'Master Toms' was pictures of cats, sir—you must have seen them—and I had them different colours. If a child looks on with its father, very likely, it'll want 'pussy,' and if the child cries for it, it's almost a sure sale, and

more, I think, indeed I'm sure, with men than with women. Women knows the value of money better than men, for men never understand what housekeeping is. I have no children, thank God, or they might be pinched, poor things. 'Miss Kitties' was the same sale. Toms is hes, and Kitties is she cats. I've sometimes sold to poor women who was tiresome; they must have just what would fit over their mantel-pieces, that was papered with pictures." [My readers may remember that some of the descriptions I have given, long previous to the present inquiry, of the rooms of the poor, fully bear out this statement.] "I seldom venture on anything above 1*d*., I mean to sell at 1*d*. I've had Toms and Kitties at 2*d*. though. 'Fashions' isn't worth umbrella room; the poorest needlewoman won't be satisfied with them from an umbrella. 'Queens' and 'Alberts' and 'Wales's' and the other children isn't near so good as they was. There's so many 'fine portraits of Her Majesty,' or the others, given away with the first number of this or of that, that people's overstocked. If a working-man can buy a newspaper or a number, why of course he may as well have a picture with it. They gave away glasses of gin at the opening of that baker's shop there, and it's the same doctrine" [The word she used]. "I never offer penny theatres, or comic exhibitions, or anything big; they spoils the look of the umbrella, and makes better things look mean. I sell only to working people, I think; seldom to boys, and seldomer to girls; seldom to servant-maids and hardly ever to women of the town. I *have* taken 6*d*. from one of them though. I think boys buy pictures for picture books. I never had what I suppose was old pictures. To a few old people, I've known, 'Children' sell fairly, when they're made plump, and red cheeked, and curly haired. They sees a resemblance of their grandchildren, perhaps, and buys. Young married people does so too, but not so oft, I think. I don't remember that ever I have made more than 1*s*. 10*d*. on an evening; I don't sell, or very seldom indeed, at other times, and only in summer, and when its fine. If I clear 5*s*. I counts that a good week. It's a great help to the lot-selling. I seldom clear so much. Oftener 4*s*."

The principal sale of these "pictures," in the streets, is from umbrellas. Occasionally, a street-stationer, or even a miscellaneous lot-seller, when he has met with a cheap lot, especially of portraits of ladies, will display a collection of prints, pyramidally arranged on his stall,—but these are exceptions. Sometimes, too, an "umbrella print-seller" will have a few "pictures in frames," on a sort of stand alongside the umbrella.

The pictures for the umbrellas are bought at the warehouse, or the swag-shops, of which I have before spoken. At these establishments "prints" are commonly supplied from 3*d*. to 5*s*. the dozen. The street-sellers buy at 5*d*. and 6*d*. the dozen, to sell at a 1*d*. a piece; and at 3d. to sell at ½d. *None* of the pictures thus sold are prepared expressly for the streets.

In so desultory and—as one intelligent street-seller with whom I conversed on the subject described it—so *weathery* a trade, it is difficult to arrive at exact statistics. From the best data at my command, it may be computed, that for twelve weeks of the year, there are thirty umbrella print-sellers (all exceptional traders therein included) each clearing 6s. weekly, and taking 12s. Thus it appears that 216l. is yearly expended in the streets in this purchase. Many of the sellers are old or infirm; one who was among the most prosperous before the changes in the streets of Lambeth, was dwarfish, and was delighted to be thought " a character."

OF THE STREET-SELLERS OF PICTURES IN FRAMES.

FROM about 1810, or somewhat earlier, down to 1830, or somewhat later, the street-sale of pictures in frames was almost entirely in the hands of the Jews. The subjects were then nearly all scriptural: " The Offering up of Isaac;" " Jacob's Dream;" " The Crossing of the Red Sea;" " The Death of Sisera;" and " The Killing of Goliath from the Sling of the youthful David." But the Jew traders did not at all account it necessary to confine the subjects of their pictures to the records of the Old—their best trade was in the illustrations of the New Testament. Perhaps the " Stoning of St. Stephen" was their most saleable " picture in a frame." There were also " The Nativity;" " The Slaying of the Children, by order of Herod" (with the quotation of St. Matthew, chap. ii. verse 17, " Then was fulfilled that which was spoken by Jeremy the prophet"); " The Sermon on the Mount;" " The Beheading of John the Baptist;" " The Entry of Christ into Jerusalem;" " The Raising of Lazarus;" " The Betrayal on the part of Judas;" " The Crucifixion;" and " The Conversion of St. Paul." There were others, but these were the principal subjects. All these pictures were coloured, and very deeply coloured. St. Stephen was stoned in the lightest of sky-blue short mantles. The pictures were sold in the streets of London, mostly in the way of hawking; but ten times as extensively, I am told, in the country, as in town. Indeed, at the present time, many a secluded village ale-house has its parlour walls decorated with these scriptural illustrations, which seem to have superseded

" The pictures placed for ornament and use;
The twelve good rules; the royal game of goose,"

mentioned by Goldsmith as characteristic of a village inn. These " Jew pictures" are now yielding to others.

Most of these articles were varnished, and 2s. or 2s. 6d. each was frequently the price asked, 1s. 6d. being taken " if no better could be done," and sometimes 1s. A smaller amount per single picture was always taken, if a set

were purchased. These productions were prepared principally for street-sale and for hawkers. The frames were narrower and meaner-looking than in the present street-pictures of the kind; they were stained like the present frames, in imitation of maple, but far less skilfully. Sometimes they were a black japan; sometimes a sorry imitation of mahogany.

In the excitement of the Reform Bill era, the street-pictures in frames most in demand were Earl Grey, Earl Spencer's (or Lord Althorp), Lord Brougham's, and Lord John Russell's. O'Connell's also " sold well," as did William IV. " Queen Adelaide," I was told, " went off middling, not much more than half as good as William." Towards the close of King William's life, the portraits of the Princess Victoria and her Royal Highness was certainly represented as a young lady of undue plumpness, and had hardly justice done to her portraiture. The Duchess of Kent, also, I was informed, " sold fairish in the streets." In a little time, the picture in a frame of the Princess Victoria of Kent, with merely an alteration in the title, became available as Queen Victoria I., of Great Britain and Ireland. Since that period, there have been the princes and princesses, her Majesty's offspring, who present a strong family resemblance.

The street pictures, so to speak, are not unfrequently of a religious character. Pictures of the Virgin and Child, of the Saviour seated at the Last Supper, of the Crucifixion, or of the different saints, generally coloured. The principal purchasers of these " religious pictures" are the poorer Irish. I remember seeing, in the course of an inquiry among street-performers last summer, the entire wall of a poor street-dancer's one room, except merely the space occupied by the fireplace, covered with small coloured pictures in frames, the whole of which, the proprietor told me, with some pride, he had picked up in the streets, according as he could spare a few pence. Among them were a crucifix (of bone), and a few medallions, of a religious character, in plaster or wax. This man was of Italian extraction; but I have seen the same thing in the rooms of the Roman Catholic Irish, though never to the same extent.

The general subjects now most in demand for street-sale are, " Lola Montes," " Louis Philippe and his Queen," " The Sailor's Return," " The Soldier's Return," and the " Parting" of the same individuals, Smugglers, in different situations, Poachers also; " Turpin's Ride to York," the divers feats attributed to Jack Sheppard (but less popular than " Turpin's Ride,") " Courtship," " Marriage" (the one a couple caressing, and the other bickering, and the other in very black large boots), " Napoleon Bonaparte crossing the Alps," and his " Farewell to his Troops at Fontainebleau," " Scenes of Piracy." None of these subjects are modern; " Lola Montes" (a bold-faced woman, in a riding-habit), being the newest. "Why," said one man familiar with the trade, "there hasn't been no Louis Napoleon in a frame-picture for the streets, nor Cobdens, nor Feargus O'Connors, nor Sir John Franklins ; what is wanted for us is something exciting."

The prices of frame-pictures (as I sometimes heard them called) made expressly for street-sale, vary from 1*d.* to 1*s.* a pair. The 1*d.* a pair are about six inches by four, very rude, and on thin paper, and with frames made of lath-wood (stained), but put together very compactly. The cheaper sorts are of prints bought at the swag-shops, or of waste-dealers, sometimes roughly coloured, and sometimes plain. The greatest sale is of those charged from 2*d.* to 4*d.* the pair.

Some of the higher-priced pictures are painted purposely for the streets, but are always copies of some popular engraving, and their sale is not a twentieth of the others. These frame-pictures were, and are, generally got up by a family, the girls taking the management of the paper-work, the boys of the wood. The parents have, many of them, been paper-stainers. This division of labour is one reason of the exceeding cheapness of this street branch of the fine arts. These working artists — or whatever they are to be called—also prepare and frame for street-sale the plates given away in the first instance with a number of a newspaper or a periodical, and afterwards "to be had for next to nothing." The prevalence of such engravings has tended greatly to diminish the sale of the pictures prepared expressly for the streets.

Ten years ago this trade was ten times greater than it is now. The principal sale still is, and always was, at the street-markets on Saturday evenings. They are sold piled on a small stall, or carried under the arm. To sell 10*s.* worth on a Saturday night is an extraordinary sale, and 2*s.* 6*d.* is a bad one, and the frame-picturer must have "middling patter to set them off at all. 'Twopence a pair !' he'll say ; 'only twopence a pair ! Who'd be without an ornament to his dwelling ? ' "

There are now about fifty persons engaged in this sale on a Saturday night, of whom the majority are the artists or preparers of the pictures. On a Monday evening there are about twenty sellers; and not half that number on other evenings—but some "take a round in the suburbs."

If these people take 10*s.* weekly for frame-pictures the year through, 1,040*l.* is yearly expended in this way. I estimate the average number at twenty daily. Their profits are about cent. per cent. ; boys and working people buy the most. The trade is often promoted by a raffle at a public-house. Many mechanics, I was told, now frame their own pictures.

OF THE STREET-SELLERS OF MANUSCRIPT
AND OTHER MUSIC.

THIS trade used to be more extensively carried on in the streets than it is at present. The reasons I heard assigned for the decadence were the greater cheapness of musical productions generally, and the present fondness for lithographic embellishments to every polka, waltz, quadrille, ballad, &c., &c. "People now hates, I do believe, a *bare* music-sheet," one street-seller remarked.

The street manuscript-music trade was, certainly, and principally, piratical. An air became popular perhaps on a sudden, as it was pointed out to me, in the case, of "Jump, Jim Crow." At a musical publisher's, such an affair in the first bloom of its popularity, would have been charged from 2*s.* to 3*s.* 6*d.*, twenty-five years ago, and the street-seller at that time, often also a book-stall keeper, would employ, or buy of those who offered them for sale, and who copied them for the purpose, a manuscript of the demanded music, which he could sell cheap in comparison.

A man who, until the charges of which I have before spoken, kept a second-hand book-stall, in a sort of arched passage in the New Cut, Lambeth, sold manuscript-music, and was often " sadly bothered," he said, at one time by the musical propensities of a man who looked like a journeyman tailor. This man, whenever he had laid out a trifle at the book-stall, looked over the music, and often pulled a small flute from his pocket, and began to play a few bars from one of the manuscripts, and this he continued doing, to the displeasure of the stall-keeper, until a crowd began to assemble, thinking, perhaps, that the flute-player was a street-musician ; he was then obliged to desist. Of the kind of music he sold, or of its mode of production, this street-bookseller knew nothing. He purchased it of a man who carried it to his stall, and as he found it sell tolerably well, he gave himself no further trouble concerning it. The supplier of the manuscript pencilled on each sheet the price it was to be offered at, allowing the stall-keeper from 50 to 150 per cent. profit, if the price marked was obtained. "I haven't seen anything of him, sir," said the street-bookseller, "for a long while. I dare say he was some poor musicianer, or singer, or a reduced gentleman, perhaps, for he always came after dusk, or else on bad dark days."

Although but partially connected with street-art, I may mention as a sample of the music sometimes offered in street-sale, that a book-stall keeper, three weeks ago showed me a pile of music which he had purchased from a "waste collector," about eight months before, at 2½*d.* the pound. Among this was some MS. music, which I specify below, and which the book-stall keeper was confident, on very insufficient grounds, I think, had been done for street-sale.

The music had, as regards three-fourths of it, evidently been bound, and had been torn from the boards of the book, as only the paper portion is purchased for "waste." Some, however, were loose sheets, which had evidently never been subjected to the process of stitching. I now cite some of the titles of this street-sale: "Le Petit Tambour. Sujet d'un Grand Rondeau pour le Piano Forte. Composé par L. Zerbini," (MS.) "Di Tanti Palpiti. The Celebrated Cavatina, by Rossini, &c." "Twenty Short Lessons, or Preludes in the most Convenient Keys for the Harp. Composed and Respectfully Dedicated to Lady Ann Collins. By John Baptist Meyer. Price 5s." "An Cota Caol (given in the ancient Irish character.) The Slender Coat," (MS.) "Cailin beog chruite na mbo (also in Irish). The Pretty Girl Milking the Cow," (MS.)

There are now no persons regularly employed in preparing MS. music for the streets. But occasionally a person skilled in music writing will, when he or she, I was told, had nothing better in hand, do a little for the street sale, disposing of the MSS. to any street-stationer or bookseller. If four persons are this way employed, receiving 4s. a week each, the year through—which I am assured is the extent—we find upwards of 40l. thus earned, and about twice that sum taken by the street retailers.

OF THE CAPITAL AND INCOME OF THE STREET-SELLERS OF STATIONERY, LITERATURE, AND THE FINE ARTS.

I now proceed to give a summary of the capital, and income of the above classes. I will first however, endeavour to give a summary of the number of individuals belonging to the class. This appears to be made up (so far as I am able to ascertain) of the following items:—120 sellers of stationery; 20 sellers of pocket-books and diaries; 50 sellers of almanacks and memorandum-books; 12 sellers of account-books; 31 card-sellers; 6 secret papers-sellers; 250 sellers of songs and ballads; 90 running patterers; 20 standing patterers; 8 sellers of "cocks" (principally elopements); 15 selling conundrums, "comic exhibitions," &c.; 200 selling play-bills and books for the play; 40 back-number-sellers; 4 waste paper-sellers at Billingsgate; 40 sellers of tracts and pamphlets; 12 newsvenders, &c., at steam-boat piers; 2 book auctioneers; 70 book-stall keepers and book barrow-men; 16 sellers of guide-books; 30 sellers of song-books and children's books; 40 dealers in pictures in frames; 30 vendors of engravings in umbrellas, and 4 sellers of manuscript music—making altogether a total of 1,110. Many of the above street-trades are, however, only temporary. As, for instance, the street-sale of playing-cards, continues only fourteen days in the year; pocket-books and diaries, four weeks; others, again, are not regularly pursued from day to day, as the sale of prints and engravings in umbrellas, which affords employment for but twelve weeks out of the fifty-two, and conundrums for two months. One trade, however, (namely, that of "Comic Exhibition Papers," gelatine and engraved cards of the Exhibition) is entirely now in the streets. In the broad-sheet trade, again, the "running patterers" work what are called "cocks," when there are no incidents happening to incite the public mind. Hence, making due allowances for such variations, we may fairly assume that the street-sellers belonging to this class number at least 1,000. The following statistics will show the whole amount of capital, and the gross income of this branch of street traffic :

CAPITAL OR VALUE OF THE STOCK-IN-TRADE OF THE STREET-SELLERS OF STATIONERY, LITERATURE AND THE FINE ARTS.

Street-sellers of Stationery.

40 stalls, 4s. each; 80 boxes,

	£	s.	d.
3s. 6d. each; and stock-money for 120 sellers, 10s. each	82	0	0

Street-sellers of Pocket-books and Diaries.

| Stock-money for 20 vendors, 10s. each . . . . | 10 | 0 | 0 |

Street-sellers of Almanacks and Memorandum-books.

| Stock-money for 50 vendors, 1s. per head . . . . | 2 | 10 | 0 |

Street-sellers of Account-books.

| 12 baskets, 3s. each; 12 waterproof bags, 2s. 6d. each; stock-money for 12 sellers, 15s. each . . . . | 12 | 6 | 0 |

Street-sellers of Cards.

| Stock-money for 20 sellers, 1s. 6d. each . . . . | 2 | 5 | 0 |

Street-seller of Stenographic-cards.

| Stock-money for 1 seller . . . | 0 | 1 | 6 |

Street-sellers of Long-songs.

| 20 poles to which songs are attached, 2d. each; stock-money for 20 sellers, 1s. each . . . . . | 1 | 3 | 4 |

Street-sellers of Wall-songs ("Pinners-up.")

| 30 canvass frames, to which songs are hung, 2s. each; stock-money for 30 sellers, 1s. each . . . . . | 4 | 10 | 0 |

Street-sellers of Ballads ("Chaunters.")

| 2 fiddles, 7s. each; stock-money for 200 chaunters, 1s. each . . . | 10 | 14 | 0 |

Street-sellers of "Dialogues," "Litanies," &c. ("Standing Patterers.")

| 20 boards with appendages "for pictures," 5s. each; 20 paintings for boards, 3s. 6d. each; stock-money for 20 vendors, 1s. each . . | 10 | 0 | 0 |

Street-sellers of Executions, &c. ("Running Patterers.")

| Stock-money for 90 sellers, 1s. each . . . . | 4 | 10 | 0 |

Street-sellers of "Cocks."

| Stock-money for 8 sellers, 1s. each | 0 | 8 | 0 |

Street-sellers of Conundrums and Nuts to Crack.

| Stock-money for 15 sellers, 1s. each . . . . | 0 | 15 | 0 |

Street-sellers of Exhibition Papers, Magical Delusions, &c.
Stock-money for 15 sellers, 1s.
each 0 15 0

Street-sellers of Secret Papers.
Stock-money for 6 vendors, 1s.
each 0 6 0

Street-sellers of Play-bills and Books of the Play.
Stock-money for 200 vendors, 2s.
each 20 0 0

Street-sellers of Back Numbers.
Stock-money for 40 sellers, 5s.
each . . . . , . . 10 0 0

Street-sellers of Waste-paper at Billingsgate.
Stock-money for 4 sellers, 5s. each 1 0 0

Street-sellers of Tracts and Pamphlets.
Stock-money for 40 sellers, 6d.
each 1 0 0

Street-sellers of Newspapers (Second Edition).
Stock-money for 20 sellers, 2s. 6d.
each 2 10 0

Street-sellers of Newspapers, &c., on board Steam-boats.
Stock-money for 12 sellers, 5s.
each 3 0 0

Street-sellers of Books by Auction.
Stock-money for 2 sellers, 2l.
each; 2 barrows, 1l. each; 2 boards,
for barrows, 3s. each 6 6 0

Street-sellers of Books on Stalls and Barrows.
20 stalls, 4s. each; 50 barrows,
1l. each; 50 boards, for barrows, 3s.
each; stock-money, for 70 sellers,
2l. each 201 10 0

Street-sellers of Guide-books.
Stock-money, for 16 sellers, 5s.
each 4 0 0

Street-sellers of Song Books and Children's Books.
Stock-money, for 30 vendors, 1s.
each 1 10 0

Street-sellers of Pictures in Frames.
40 stalls, 2s. 6d. each; stock-
money, for 40 sellers, 5s. each . . 15 0 0

Street-sellers of Engravings in Umbrellas.
Umbrellas, 2s. 6d. each; stock-
money, for 30 sellers, 2s. each . . 3 0 0

Street-sellers of Manuscript-music.
Stock-money, for 4 sellers, 1s. 6d.
each 0 6 0

TOTAL CAPITAL INVESTED IN
THE STREET-SALE OF STATIONERY,
LITERATURE, AND THE FINE
ARTS 411 5 10

INCOME, OR AVERAGE ANNUAL " TAKINGS,"
OF THE STREET-SELLERS OF STATIONERY,
LITERATURE, AND THE FINE ARTS.

Street-sellers of Stationery.

There are 120 vendors of stationery,
who sell altogether during the year,

224,640 quires of writing paper at 3d.
per quire; 149,760 doz. envelopes, at
1½d. per doz.; 37,440 doz. pens, at 3d.
per doz.; 24,960 bottles of ink, at 1d.
each; 112,320 black lead pencils, at
1d. each; 24,960 pennyworths of
wafers, and 49,920 sticks of sealing-
wax, at ½d. per stick; amounting altogether to £4,992

Street-sellers of Pocket-books and Diaries.
During the year 1,440 pocket-books,
at 6d. each, and 960 diaries, at 6d.
each, are sold in the streets by 20
vendors; amounting to £60

Street-sellers of Almanacks and Memorandum-books.
There are sold during the year, in
the streets of London, 280,800 memorandum-books, at 1d. each, and 4,800
almanacks at 1d. each, among 50 vendors, altogether amounting to . . . £1,190

Street-sellers of Account-books.
There are now 12 itinerants vending
account-books in various parts of the
metropolis, each of whom sells daily,
upon an average, 4 account-books, at
1s. 9d. each; the number sold during
the year is therefore 14,976, and the
sum expended thereon amounts to . . £1,310

Street-sellers of " Gelatine," " Engraved," and " Playing-cards."
There are 20 street-sellers vending
gelatine and engraved cards during the
day, and 30 selling playing-cards (for
14 days) at night. These vendors get
rid of, among them, in the course of the
year, 43,200 gelatine, and 14,400 engraved cards, at 1d. each, and 3,360
packs of playing-cards, at 3d. per
pack; so that the money spent in the
streets on the sale of engraved, gelatine, and playing-cards, during the
year, amounts to £282

Street-seller of Stenographic Cards.
There is only 1 individual "working " stenographic cards in the streets
of London, and the number he sells in
the course of the year is 7,448 cards,
at 1d. each, amounting to £31 4

Street-sellers of Long Songs.
I am assured, that if 20 persons were
selling long songs in the street last
summer (during a period of 12 weeks),
it was " the outside;" as long songs
are now " for fairs and races, and
country work." Calculating that each
cleared 9s. in a week, and to clear that
took 15s., we find there is expended in
long songs in the streets annually . . £180

Street-sellers of Wall Songs (" Pinners-up.")
On fine summer days, the wall song-
sellers (of whom there are 30) take 2s.
on an average. On short wintry days

they may not take half so much, and on very foggy or rainy days they take nothing at all. Reckoning that each wall song-man now takes 10s. 6d. weekly (7s. being the profit), we find there is expended yearly in London streets, in the ballads of the pinners-up   £810

Street-sellers of Ballads (" Chaunters.")

There are now 200 chaunters, who also sell the ballads they sing; the average takings of each are 3s. per day; altogether amounting to . . . £4,680

Street-sellers of Executions, &c. (" Running Patterers.")

Some represent their average weekly earnings at 12s. 6d. the year through; some at 10s. 6d.; and others at less than half of 12s. 6d. Reckoning, however, that only 9s. weekly is an average profit per individual, and that 14s. be taken to realise that profit, we find there is expended yearly, on executions, fires, deaths, &c., in London   . . . £3,276

Street-sellers of Dialogues, Litanies, &c. (Standing Patterers.)

If 20 standing patterers clear 10s. weekly, each, the year through, and take 15s. weekly, we find there is yearly expended in the standing patter of London streets £780

Street-sellers of "Cocks" (Elopements, Love Letters, &c.

There are now 8 men who sell nothing but " Cocks," each of whom dispose daily of 6 dozen copies at ½d. per copy, or altogether, during the year, 179,712 copies, amounting to £374 8s.

Street-sellers of Conundrums—" Nuts to Crack," &c.

From the best information I could acquire, it appears that fifteen men may be computed as working conundrums for two months throughout the twelve, and clearing 10s. 6d. per individual. The cost of the "Nuts to Crack" (when new) is 5d. a dozen to the seller; but old "Nuts" often answer the purpose of the street-seller, and may be had for about half the price; the cost of the "Nut-crackers" is 2s. to 2s. 6d. It may be calculated, then, that to realize the 10s. 6d. above-mentioned 15s. must be taken. This shows the street expenditure in "Nuts to Crack" and "Nut-crackers" to be yearly . . £90

Street-sellers of Exhibition Papers, Magical Delusions, &c.

This trade is carried on only for a short time in the winter, as regards the magical portion; and I am informed that, including the "Comic Exhibitions," it extends to about half of

the sum taken for conundrums; or to about £45

Street-sellers of Secret Papers.

Supposing that 6 men last year each cleared 6s. weekly, we find expended yearly in the streets on this rubbish £93

Street-sellers of Play-bills and Books.

Taking the profits at 3s. a week, at cent. per cent. on the outlay, and reckoning 200 sellers, including those at the saloons, concert-rooms, &c., there is expended yearly on the sale of play-bills purchased in the streets of London £3,120

Street-sellers of Back Numbers.

There are now 40 vendors in the streets of London, each selling upon an average 3 dozen copies daily, at ⅓d. each, or during the year 336,960 odd numbers. Hence, the sum expended annually in the streets for back numbers of periodicals amounts to upwards of £700

Street-sellers of Waste-paper at Billingsgate.

There are 4 individuals selling waste-paper at Billingsgate, one of whom informed me that from 70 to 100 pounds weight of " waste "— about three-fourths being newspapers—is supplied to Billingsgate market and its visitants. The average price is not less than 2½d. a pound, or from that to 3d. A single paper is 1d. Reckoning that 85 pounds of waste-paper are sold a day, at 2½d. per pound, we find that the annual expenditure in waste-paper at Billingsgate is upwards of £275

Street-sellers of Tracts and Pamphlets.

From the information I obtained from one of this class of street-sellers, I find there are 40 individuals gaining a livelihood in selling tracts and pamphlets in the streets, full one half are men of colour, the other half consists of old and infirm men, and young boys, the average takings of each is about 1s. a day, the year through; the annual street expenditure in the sale of tracts and pamphlets is thus upwards of £620

Street-sellers of Newspapers (Second Edition.)

There are 20 who are engaged in the street sale of newspapers, second edition, each of whom take weekly (for a period of 6 weeks in the year) 1l. 5s.; so that, adopting the calculation of my informant, and giving an profit of 150 per cent., the yearly expenditure in the streets, in second editions, amounts to £150

Street-sellers of Newspapers, &c., at Steam-Boat Piers.

I am informed that the average earnings of these traders, altogether, may be taken at 15s. weekly; calculating that twelve carry on the trade the year through, we find that that (assuming each man to sell at thirty-three per cent. profit—though in the case of old works it will be often cent. per cent.), the sum expended annually in steam-boat papers is upwards of .£1,500

Street-sellers of Books (by Auction).

There are at present only 2 street-sellers of books by auction in London, whose clear weekly earnings are 10s. 6d. each. Calculating their profits at 250l. per cent., their weekly receipts will amount to 35s. each per week; giving a yearly expenditure of £91

Street-sellers of Books on Stalls and Barrows.

The number of book-stalls and barrows in the streets of the metropolis is 70. The proprietors of these sell weekly upon an average 42 volumes each. The number of volumes annually sold in the streets is thus 1,375,920, and reckoning each volume sold to average 9d., we find that the yearly expenditure in the sale of books in the street amounts to £5,733

Street-sellers of Guide-books.

The street-sellers of guide-books to public places of amusement, are 16 in number, the profit of each is 4s. weekly, at 25 per cent., hence the takings must be 20s.; thus making the annual expenditure in the street-sale of such books amount to £832

Street-sale of Song-books and Chidren's books.

There are 30 street-sellers who vend children's books and song-books, and dispose of, among them, 2 dozen each daily, or during the year 224,640 books, at 1d. each; hence the sum yearly expended in the street-sale of children's books and song-books is £936

Street-sellers of Pictures in Frames.

If we calculate 40 persons selling pictures in frames, and each taking 10s. weekly; we find the annual amount spent in the streets in the sale of these articles is £1,040

Street-sellers of Prints and Engravings in Umbrellas.

The street-sale of prints and engravings in umbrellas lasts only 12 weeks. There are 30 individuals who gain a livelihood in the sale of these articles during that period. The average takings of each seller is 12s. weekly; so that the annual street-expenditure upon prints and engravings is £216

Street-sellers of Manuscript Music.

There are only 4 sellers of manuscript music in the streets, who take on an average 4s. each weekly; hence we find the annual expenditure in this article amounts in round numbers to . . . £40

TOTAL SUM EXPENDED YEARLY IN THE STREETS ON STATIONERY, LITERATURE, AND THE FINE ARTS . . . . £33,446 12s.

AN EPITOME OF THE PATTERING CLASS.

I wish, before passing to the next subject—the street-sellers of manufactured articles (of one of whom the engraving here given furnishes a well-known specimen)—I wish, I say, as I find some mistakes have occurred on the subject, to give the public a general view of the patterers, as well as to offer some few observations concerning the means of improving the habits of street-people in general.

The patterers consist of three distinct classes; viz., those who sell something, and patter to help off their goods; those who exhibit something, and patter to help off the show; and those who do nothing but patter, with a view to elicit alms. Under the head of "Patterers who sell" may be classed

Paper Workers,	Dealers in Razor Paste,
Quack Doctors,	„ French Polish,
Cheap Jacks,	„ Plating Balls,
Grease Removers,	„ CandleShades,
Wager Patterers,	„ Rat Poisons, &
Ring Sellers,	„ Blacking,
Dealers in Corn Salve,	Book Auctioneers.

The second class of patterers includes jugglers, showmen, clowns, and fortune-tellers; beside several exhibitors who invite public notice to the wonders of the telescope or microscope.

The third and last class of patterers are those who neither sell nor amuse, but only victimise those who get into their clutches. These (to use their own words) "do it on the bounce." Their general resort is an inferior public-house, sometimes a brothel, or a coffee-shop. One of the tricks of these worthies is to group together at a window, and if a well-dressed person pass by, to salute him with the contents of a flour-bag. One of their pals—better dressed than the rest—immediately walks out, declares it was purely accidental, and invites the gentleman in "to be brushed." Probably he consents, and still more probably, if he be "good-natured," he is plied with liquor, drugged with snuff for the occasion, and left in some obscure court, utterly stupified. When he awakes, he finds that his watch, purse, &c., are gone.

"A casual observer, or even a stranger, may be induced to contract a wayside acquaintance with the parties to whom I allude," says one of the pattering class, from whom I have received much valuable information; "and if he be a visitor of fairs and races, that acquaintance, though slight, may sometimes prove expensive.

But casual observers cannot, from the complexity and varied circumstances of the characters now under notice, form anything like a correct view of them. I am convinced that no one can, but those who have visited their haunts and indeed lived among them for months together. They are not to be known, any more than the great city was to be built, in a day. This advantage—if so it may be called—has fallen to my lot."

The three classes of patterers above enumerated must not be confounded. The two first are essentially distinct from the last—at least they do *something* for their living; and though the pattering street-tradesmen may generally overstep the bounds of truth in their glowing descriptions of the virtues of the goods they sell, still it should be remembered they are no more dishonest in their dealings than the "enterprising" class of shopkeepers, who resort to the *printed* mode of puffing off their wares,—indeed the street-sellers are far less reprehensible than their more wealthy brother puffers of the shops, who cannot plead want as an excuse for their dishonesty. The recent revelations made by the *Lancet*, as to the adulteration of the articles of diet sold by the London grocers, show that the patterers who sell, practise far less imposition than some of our "merchant princes."

"A tradesman in Tottenham-court Road, whose address the *Lancet* advertises gratis, thus proclaims the superior qualities of his ' *Finest* WHITE PEPPER. One package of this article, which is the interior part of the kernel of the finest pepper, being equal in strength to nearly three times the quantity of black pepper (which is the inferior, small, shrivelled berries, and often little more than husks), it will be not only the best but the cheapest for every purpose.' This super-excellent pepper, 'sold in packages, price 1*d*.' was found on analysis to consist of finely-ground *black pepper, and a very large quantity of wheat-flour.*"

Indeed the *Lancet* has demonstrated that as regards tea, coffee, arrow-root, sugar, and pepper sold by "pattering" shopkeepers, the rule invariably is that those are articles which are the most puffed, and "warranted free from adulteration," and "to which the attention of families and *invalids* is particularly directed as being of the finest quality ever imported into this country," are uniformly the most scandalously adulterated of all.

We should, therefore, remember while venting our indignation against pattering street-sellers, that they are not the only puffers in the world, and that they, at least, can plead poverty in extenuation of their offence; whereas, it must be confessed, that shopkeepers can have no other cause for their acts but their own brutalizing greed of gain.

The class of patterers with whom we have here to deal are those who patter to help off their goods—but while describing them it has been deemed advisable to say a few words, also, on the class who *do nothing but patter*, as a means of exciting commiseration to their assumed calamities. These parties, it should be distinctly understood, are in no way connected with the puffing street-sellers, but in the exaggerated character of the orations they deliver, they are mostly professional beggars—or bouncers (that is to say cheats of the lowest *kind*), and *will* not work or do anything for their living. This, at least, cannot be urged against the pattering street-sellers who, as was before stated, do *something* for the bread they eat.

Further to show the extent, and system, of the lodging and routes throughout the country of the class of "lurkers," &c., here described—as all resorting to those places—I got a patterer to write me out a list, from his own knowledge, of divers routes, and the extent of accommodation in the lodging-houses. I give it according to the patterer's own classification.

"*Brighton* is a town where there is a great many furnished cribs, let to needys (nightly lodgers) that are molled up," [that is to say, associated with women in the sleeping-rooms.]

SURREY AND SUSSEX.

	Dossing Cribs, or Lodging-houses	Beds.	Needys, or Nightly Lodgers.
Wandsworth	6	9	108
Croydon	9	8	144
Reigate	5	6	60
Cuckfield.	2	8	32
Horsham	3	7	52
Lewis	7	6	84
Kingston	12	8	192
Brighton	16	9	228

"*Bristol*.—A few years back an old woman kept a padding-ken here. She was a strong Methodist, but had a queer method. There was thirty standing beds, besides make-shifts and furnished rooms, which were called 'cottages.' It's not so bad now. The place was well-known to the monkry, and you was reckoned flat if you hadn't been there. The old woman, when any female, old or young, who had no tin, came into the kitchen, made up a match for her with some men. Fellows half-drunk had the old women. There was always a broomstick at hand, and they was both made to jump over it, and that was called a broomstick wedding. Without that ceremony a couple weren't looked on as man and wife. In course the man paid, in such case, for the dos (bed.)

Kensington	6	7	84
Brentford	12	8	192
Hounslow	6	5	60
Colebrook	2	7	20
Windsor	7	10	140
Maidenhead	4	5	40
Reading	12	9	216
Oxford	14	7	196
Banbury	10	12	240
Marlboro'	8	7	112
Bath	10	8	160
Bristol	20	11	440

"*Counties of Kent and Essex.*—Here is the best places in England for 'skipper-birds;' (parties that never go to lodging-houses, but to barns or outhouses, sometimes without a blanket.) The Kent farmers permit it to their own travellers, or the travellers they know. In Essex it's different. There a farmer will give 1*s*. rather than let a traveller sleep on his premises, for fear of robbery. 'Keyhole whistlers,' the skipper-birds are sometimes called, but they're regular travellers. Kent's the first county in England for them. They start early to good houses for victuals, when gentlefolk are not up. I've seen them doze and sleep against the door. They like to be there before any one cuts their cart (exposes their tricks). Travellers are all early risers. It's good morning in the country when it's good night in town.

KENT.

	Dossing Cribs, or Lodging-houses	Beds.	Needys, or Nightly Lodgers.
Deptford	18	9	324
Greenwich	6	8	26
Woolwich	9	8	144
Gravesend	6	7	84
Chatham	20	10	400
Maidstone	5	7	70
Sittingbourne	3	6	36
Sheerness	4	5	40
Faversham	3	5	30
Canterbury	11	8	176
Dover	12	9	216
Ramsgate	4	5	40
Margate	6	6	72

ESSEX.

Stratford	10	9	180
Ilford	3	7	52
Barking	4	6	48
Billericay	5	7	70
Orsett	2	8	32
Rayleigh	3	9	54
Rochford	3	8	48
Leigh	4	8	64
Prettywell	2	7	28
Southend	3	8	48
Maldon	5	9	90
Witham	4	8	64
Colchester	15	10	300

"*Windsor.*—At Ascot race-time I've paid many 1s. just to sit up all night.

"*Colchester.*—Life in London at the Bugle; called 'Hell upon earth' sometimes.

Barnet	5	1	80
Watford	6	8	90
Hemel-Hempstead	3	5	30
Uxbridge	6	7	84
Tring	2	6	24
Dunstable	6	5	60
Stony-Stratford	3	6	36
Northampton	13	9	234
Towcester	4	7	56
Daventry	5	9	90
Coventry	16	9	288
Birmingham	50	11	1100

HERTS AND BEDFORDSHIRE.

Edmonton	14	7	196
Waltham-Abbey	3	6	36
Cheshunt-Street	2	7	28
Hoddesden	3	8	48
Hertford	9	9	162
Ware	7	10	140
Puckeridge	2	5	20
Buntingford	3	8	48
Royston	4	10	40
Hitchin	7	9	126
Luton	6	8	96
Bedford	9	7	126
St. Alban's	8	6	96

SUFFOLK AND NORFOLK.

Ipswich	24	8	384
Hadleigh	8	7	112
Halsted	5	6	60
Stowmarket	4	7	56
Woodbridge	6	5	60
Sudbury	4	7	56

	Dossing Cribs, or Lodging-houses	Beds.	Needys, or Nightly Lodgers.
Bury St. Edmund's	8	8	128
Thetford	3	6	36
Attleboro'	2	5	20
Wymondham	1	11	22
Norwich	40	9	720
Yarmouth	16	8	256

OF THE "SCREEVERS," OR WRITERS OF BEGGING-LETTERS AND PETITIONS.

"SCREEVING"—that is to say, *writing* false or exaggerated accounts of afflictions and privations, is a necessary corollary to "Pattering," or making pompous *orations* in public—and I here sub-join a brief description of the " business "—for although the " screevers," " economically " con-sidered, belong properly to the class who will *not work*, yet as they are intimately connected with the street-trade of begging I have thought it best to say a few words on the subject here, reserving a more comprehensive and scientific view of the subject till such time as I come to treat of the *professional* beggar, under the head of those who are *able* but *unwilling* to labour for their livelihood, in contradistinction to the involuntary beggars, who belong more properly to those who are *willing* but *unable* to work. The subjoined information has been obtained from one who has had many oppor-tunities of making himself acquainted with the habits and tricks of the class here treated of,—indeed, at one part of his life he himself belonged to the "profession."

"In England and Wales the number of vagrants committed to prison annually amounts to 19,621; and as many are not imprisoned more than a dozen times during their lives, and a few never at all, the number of tramps and beggars may be estimated, at the very lowest, at 22,000 throughout England and Wales. The returns from Scotland are indeterminate. Of this wretched class many are aged and infirm; others are destitute orphans; while not a few are persons whose distress is real, and who suffer from temporary causes.

"With this excusable class, however, I have not now to do. Of professional beggars there are two kinds—those who 'do it on the blob' (by word of mouth), and those who do it by 'screeving,' that is, by petitions and letters, setting forth imaginary cases of distress.

"Of these documents there are two sorts, 'slums' (letters) and 'fakements' (petitions). These are seldom written by the persons who present or send them, but are the production of a class of whom the public little imagine either the number or turpitude. I mean the 'professional begging-letter writers.'

"Persons who write begging-letters for others sometimes, though seldom, beg themselves. They are in many cases well supported by the fraternity for whom they write. A professional of this kind is called by the 'eadgers,' 'their man of business.' Their histories vary as much as their abilities; generally speaking they have been clerks, teachers, shopmen, reduced gentlemen, or the illegitimate sons of members of the aristocracy ; while others, after having received a liberal education, have broken away from parental control, and commenced the 'profession' in early life, and will probably pursue it to their graves.

" I shall take a cursory view of the various pretences set forth in these begging documents," says my informant, " and describe some of the scenes connected with their preparation. The documents themselves are mournful catalogues of all the ills that flesh is heir to.

" I address myself first to that class of petitions which represent losses by sea, or perhaps shipwreck itself. These documents are very seldom carried by one person, unless indeed he is really an old sailor; and, to the credit of the navy be it spoken, this is very seldom the case. When the imposition under notice has to be carried out, it is, for the most part, conducted by half-a-dozen worthless men, dressed in the garb of seamen (and known as turnpike sailors), one of their number having really been at sea and therefore able to reply to any nautical inquiries which suspicion may throw out. This person mostly carries the document; and is, of course, the spokesman of the company. Generally speaking, the gang have a subscription-book, sometimes only a fly-leaf or two to the document, to receive the names of contributors.

" It may not be out of place here, to give a specimen—drawn from memory—of one of those specious but deceitful ' fakements' upon which the ' swells,' (especially those who have ' been in the service,') ' come down with a *couter*' (sovereign) if they ' granny the mauley' (perceive the signature) of a brother officer or friend. The document is generally as follows—

" ' 𝕿𝖍𝖊𝖘𝖊 𝖆𝖗𝖊 𝖙𝖔 𝕮𝖊𝖗𝖙𝖎𝖋𝖞, to all whom it may concern, that the THUNDERER, Captain Johnson, was returning on her homeward-bound passage from China, laden with tea, fruit, &c., and having beside, twenty passengers, chiefly ladies, and a crew of thirty hands, exclusive of the captain and other officers. That the said vessel encountered a tremendous gale off the banks of Newfoundland, and was dismasted, and finally wrecked at midnight on' (such a day, including the hour, latitude, and other particulars). ' That the above-named vessel speedily foundered, and only the second mate and four of the crew (the bearers of this certificate) escaped a watery grave. These, after floating several days on broken pieces of the ship, were providentially discovered, and humanely picked up by the brig INVINCIBLE, Captain Smith, and landed in this town and harbour of Portsmouth, in the county of Hants. That we, the Master of Customs, and two of her Majesty's Justices of the Peace for the said harbour and county, do hereby grant and afford to the said' (here follows the names of the unfortunate mariners) 'this our vouchment of the truth of the said wreck, and their connection there-

with, and do empower them to present and use this certificate for twenty-eight days from the date hereof, to enable them to get such temporal aid as may be adequate to reaching their respective homes, or any sea-port where they may be re-engaged. And this certificate further showeth, that they are not to be interrupted in the said journey by any constabulary or other official authority; provided, that is to say, that no breach of the peace or other cognizable offence be committed by the said Petitioners,

' As witness our hands,

John Harris, M.C. . . .	£1 0 0
James Flood, J.P.	1 0 0
Capt. W. Hope, R.N., J.P. .	1 10 0

' Given at Portsmouth, this 10th day of October, 1850.

' GOD SAVE THE QUEEN.'

Rev. W. Wilkins	£1 0 0
An Officer's Widow . . .	0 10 0
An Old Sailor	0 5 0
A Friend	0 2 6 '

" I have already hinted at the character and description of the persons by whom these forgeries are framed. It would seem, from the example given, that such documents are available in every sea-port or other considerable town; but this is not the case. It is true that certain kinds of documents, especially sham hawkers' licenses, may be had in the provinces, at prices suited to the importance of their contents, or to the probable gains of their circulation; but all the ' regular bang-up fakes' are manufactured in the ' Start' (metropolis), and sent into the country to order, carefully packed up, and free from observation. The following note, sent to ' Carotty Poll, at Mrs. Finder's Login-ouse facin the orse and trumpet bere shop han street Westminster London with spede,' may tend to illuminate the uninitiated as to how such ' fakements' are obtained :

' Dere pol—I ope this will find yu an george in good helth and spirits—things is very bad ere, yure sister Lizer has been konfined an got a fine strappin boye, they was very bad off wen it happend. they say in mi industry it never ranes but it pores and so it was pol, for mi William as got a month along with Cockny Harry for a glim lurk and they kum out nex Mundie and i av porned my new shift and every indivigual thing to get them a brekfust and a drop a rum the mornin they kums out. They wont hav no paper to work and I dont know what they will do. Tayler Tom lent me a shillin wish I send inklosed and yu must porn sumthing for anuther shilling and get Joe the Loryer to rite a fake for William not a glim' (loss by fire) ' but a brake say as e ad a hors fell downe with the mad staggurs an broke all is plates and dishes an we are starvin you can sa that the children is got the mesuls—they av ben ill thats *no* lie—an we want to rase a little munney to git anuther hanimul to dror the kart put a fu monekurs' (names) · tu it and make it durty and date it sum time bak do not neglect and dont fale to pay the post no more at preasant from yure luvin sister Jane N—— at Mister John H—— the Sweep—nex dore to the five Bels grinsted Colchester Essex. good by.'

" The person from whom the above letter was obtained, was in the lodging-house when it arrived, and had it given him to read and retain for reference. Lawyer Joe was soon sent for; and the following is an outline of the scene that occurred, given in my informant's own words:

" I had called at the house whither the above letter had been addressed, to inquire for a man whom I had known in his and my own better days. The kitchen-door, or rather cellar-door, was thrust open, and in came Carrotty Poll herself.

" ' Well, Poll,' asked the deputy, ' how does the world use you ? '

" ' B— bad,' was the reply, ' where's Lawyer Joe ? '

" ' Oh, he's just gone to Mother Linstead's for some tea and sugar; here he comes.'

" ' Joe, I've a job for you. How much do you charge for screeving a " brake ? " ' '

" ' Oh, half a bull (half-a-crown).'

" ' No, I'll give you a deuce o' deeners (two shillings), co's don't ye see the poor b— is in " stir " (prison).'

" ' Well, well, I shan't stand for a tanner. Have you got paper ? '

" ' Yes, and a Queen's head, and all.'

" The pen and ink were found, a corner of the table cleared, and operations commenced.

" ' He writes a good hand,' exclaimed one, as the screever wrote the petition.

" ' I wish I could do it,' said another.

" ' If you could, you'd soon be transported,' said a third ; while the whole kitchen in one chorus, immediately on its completion, proclaimed, that it was d—d well done, adding to that, not one ' swell ' in a score would view it in any other light than a ' ream' (genuine) concern.

" Lawyer Joe was up to his trade—he folded the paper in official style—creased it as if it was long written and often examined, attached the signatures of the minister and churchwardens, and dipping his fingers under the fireplace, smeared it with ashes, and made the whole the best representation of a true account of ' a horse in the mad staggers ' and ' a child in the measles ' that could be desired by the oldest and best cadger on the monkry.

" These professional writers are in possession of many autographs of charitable persons, and as they keep a dozen or more bottles of different shades of ink, and seldom write two documents on exactly the same sort of paper, it is difficult to detect the imposition. A famous lurker who has been previously alluded to in this work, was once taken before a magistrate at York whose *own* signature was attached to his fakement. The imitation was excellent, and the ' lurker' swore hard and fast to the worthy justice that he (the justice) *did* write it in his own saddle-room, as he was preparing to ride, and gave him five shillings, too. The effrontery and firmness of the prisoner's statement gained him his discharge!

" It is not uncommon in extensive districts— say, for instance, a section of a county taking in ten or a dozen townships—for a school of lurkers to keep a secretary and remit his work and his pay at the same time. In London this functionary is generally paid by commission, and sometimes partly in food, beer, and tobacco. The following is a fair estimate of the scale of charges :

	s.	d.
Friendly letter	0	6
Long ditto	0	9
Petition	1	0
Ditto, with ream monekurs (genuine signatures) . . .	1	6
Ditto, with gammy monekurs (forged names)	2	6
Very " heavy " (dangerous) .	3	0
Manuscript for a broken down author	10	0
Part of a play for ditto . . .	7	6

" To this I may add the prices of other articles in the begging line.

	s.	d.
Loan of one child, without grub	0	9
Two ditto	1	0
Ditto, with grub and Godfrey's Cordial	0	9
If out after twelve at night, for each child, extra	0	2
For a school of children, say half-a-dozen	2	6
Loan of any garment, per day	0	2
Going as a pal to vindicate any statement	1	0

" Such is an outline, open to circumstantial variation, of the pay received for the sort of accommodation required.

" There is a very important species of ' lurking' or ' screeving,' which has not yet been alluded to.

" It is well-known that in the colliery districts an explosion of fire-damp frequently takes place, when many lives are lost, and the men who escape are often so wounded as to render amputation of a leg or arm the only probable means of saving them from the grave. Of course the accident, with every particular as to date and locality, goes the round of the newspapers. Such an event is a sort of God-send to the begging-letter writer. If he is anything of a draughtsman, so much the better. He then procures a sheet of vellum, and heads it with a picture of an explosion, and exhibiting men, boys, and horses up in the air, and a few nearer the ground, minus a head, a leg, or an arm ; with a background of women tearing their hair, and a few little girls crying. Such a ' fakement,' professionally filled up and put into the hands of an experienced lurker, will bring the ' amanuensis,' or ' screever,' two guineas at least, and the proceeds of such an expedition have in many cases averaged 60*l.* per week. The lurker presenting this would have to take with him three or four countrymen, dressed in the garb of colliers, one at least knowing something of underground work. These he would engage at ' a bob a nob ' (one shilling each), and if he made a good day, give them a 'toothful o' rum' beside. As such men are always le; ' outside the jigger (door) of the houses, they are of course ignorant of the state of the subscription-list.

" A famous lurker, to whom we have previously referred, Nicholas A——, kept ' a man of business' to himself, and gave him from 5s. to 10s. 6d. per day. Nicholas, who was tolerably educated, could write very well, but as his ' secretary' could imitate twelve different hands, he was of course no trifling acquisition.

" It would not be easy to trace the history of all, or even many of the men, who pursue the begging-letter trade as professional writers. Many of the vagrant tribe write their own letters, but the vast majority are obliged to have assistance. Of course, they are sometimes detected by the fact that their conversation does not tally with the rhetorical statement of the petition. The few really deserving persons, well-born and highly educated, who subsist by begging, are very retired and cautious in their appeals. They write concisely, and their statements are generally true to a certain extent, or perhaps rigidly so in relation to an earlier part of their history. These seldom live in the very common lodging-houses.

"The most renowned of the tribe who write for others, and whose general trade lies in forged certificates of bankruptcy, seizure of goods for rent, and medical testimonies to infirmity, is an Irishman, brought up in London, and who may be seen almost every night at the bar of a certain public-house in Drury-lane. He lives, or did live, at one of the model lodging-houses. Very few persons know his occupation. They suppose that he is ' connected with the press.' Several years ago this person, says one who knew this trade well, was ' regularly hard up,' and made a tender of his services to a distinguished M.P., who took a lively interest in the emancipation of the Jews. He offered to visit the provinces, hold meetings, and get up petitions. The hon. member tested his abilities, and gave him clothes and a ten-pound note to commence operations. ' I saw him' (says my informant) ' the same night, and he mooted the subject to me over a glass of whiskey-punch. ' Not that *I* care (said he) if all the b—y Jews were in h—ll, but I must do something.'

"' But how,' asked my informant, ' will you get up the meetings?—and then the signatures, you know !'

"' ' Meetings!' was the reply, ' don't mention it ; I can get *millions of signatures !*'

" The pretended Jewish Advocate never left London. He got (from Ireland) a box of old documents relative to bygone petitions for repeal, &c., and on these he put a frontispiece suited to his purpose — got them sent to Bath and Bristol, and thence transmitted to his employer—who praised his perseverance, and sent more money to the post-office of one of the above-named towns ; this was countermanded to London, and jovially spent at ' Tom Spring's' in Holborn.

" Hitherto the movements of the begging-letter writer—self-considered—have been chiefly dwelt upon. There is another class of the fraternity, however, of whom some notice must here be taken ; viz., those, who to meet cases of great pretension, and consequent misgivings on the part of the noblemen or gentry to whom fakements are presented, become referees to professional beggars. These referees are kept by local ' schools' of beggars in well-furnished apartments at respectable houses, and well dressed ; their allowance varies from 1l. to 3l. per week.

" But the most expert and least suspected dodge is referring to some dignified person in the country ; a person however who exists nowhere but in imagination. Suppose (says my informant) I am a beggar, I apply to you for relief. Perhaps I state that I am in prospect of lucrative employment, if I could get enough money to clothe myself. You plead the number of impositions; I consent to that fact, but offer you references as to the truth of my statement. I refer you to the Hon. and Rev. Mr. Erskine, at Cheltenham (any name or place will do). You promise to write, and tell me to call in a few days; meanwhile, I assume the name of the gentleman to whom I have referred you, and write forthwith to the post-master of the town in question, requesting that any letter coming there directed to the Hon. and Rev. Mr. Erskine, may be forwarded to my present address. I thus discover what you have written, frame a flattering reply, and address it to you. I send it (under cover) to a pal of mine at Cheltenham, or elsewhere, who posts it ; I call half an hour after you receive it, and, being satisfied, you give me a donation, and perhaps introduce me to some of your friends. Thus I raise a handsome sum, and the fraud is probably never found out.

" One of the London lurkers, who has good means of forming a calculation on the subject, assures me that the average earnings of ' lurkers' in London alone (including those who write for them), cannot be less than 6,000l. per annum.

" Two of the class were lately apprehended, at the instance of the Duke of Wellington ; on their persons was found fifteen sovereigns, one five-pound note, a silver watch with gold guard, and two gold watches with a ribbon attached to each ; their subscription - book showed that they had collected 620l. during the current year.

" A man named M'Kensie—who was transported at the last Bristol Assizes — had just received a cheque for 100l. from a nobleman lately deceased.

" Most of the ' professionals' of this class include a copy of the ' Court Guide ' among their stock in trade. In this all the persons known to be charitable, have the mark ⊕ set against their names. I have been furnished with a list of such persons, accompanied with comments, from the note-book of ' an old stager' ' thirty years on the monkery,' and, as he adds, ' never quodded but twice.'

" The late Queen Dowager.
Hon. Wm. Ashley.
The Bishop of Norwich.
Serjeant Talfourd.
Charles Dickins.
Samuel Rogers, the Poet.
Samuel Warren (Author of ' Extracts from the Diary of a Physician).
Hon. G. C. Norton, the ' beak' (magistrate), but good for all that.
Rev. E. Holland, Hyde-park-gardens.
The late Sir Robert Peel.
Countess of Essex (only good to sickness, or distressed authorship).
Marquess of Bredalbane (good on anything religious).
The Editor of the ' Sun.'
Madame Celeste.
Marquess of Blandford.
Duke of Portland.
Duke of Devonshire.
Lord George Bentinck (deceased ; God A'mighty wouldn't let him live ; he was too good for this world.)
Lord Skelmersdale.
Lord John Manners.
Lord Lyttleton.
Mrs. Elder, Exeter.
Lady Emily Ponsonby (a devilish pretty wench).
Miss Burdett Coutts.
F. Stewart, Esq., Bath.
Mrs. Groves, Salisbury.
Mrs. Mitchell, Dorchester.
Mrs. Taggart, Bayswater (her husband is a Unitarian minister, not so good as she, but he'll stand a ' bob' if you look straight at him and keep to one story.)
Archdeacon Sinclair, at Kensington (but not so good as Archdeacon Pott, as was there afore him ; he was a good man ; he couldn't refuse a dog, much more a Christian ; but he had a butler, a regular ' knark,' who was a b— and a half, good weight,)
Lady Cottenham used to be good, but she is ' coopered' (spoilt) now, without you has a ' slum,' any one as she knows, and then she won't stand above a ' bull' (five shillings)."

OF THE PROBABLE MEANS OF REFORMATION.

I shall now conclude this account of the patterers, lurkers, and screevers, with some observations from the pen of one who has had ample means of judging as to the effect of the several plans now in operation for the reformation or improvement of the class.

" In looking over the number of institutions," writes the person alluded to, " designed to reform and improve the classes under review, we are, as it were, overwhelmed with their numerous branches ; and though it is highly gratifying to see so much good being done, it is necessary to confine this notice to the examination of only the

most prominent, with their general characteristics.

" The churches, on many considerations— personal feelings being the smallest, but not unknown—demand attention first. I must treat this subject (for your work is not a theological magazine) without respect to doctrine, principle, or legislation.

" The object of erecting churches in poor neighbourhoods is to benefit the poor ; why is it, then, that the instruction communicated should exercise so little influence upon the vicious, the destitute, and the outcast ? Is it that Christian ordinances are less adapted to them than to others ? Or, rather, is it not that the public institutions of the clergy are not made interesting to the wretched community in question? The great hindrance (in my opinion) to the progress of religion among the unsettled classes is, that having been occasionally to church or chapel, and heard nothing but doctrinal lectures or feverish mental effusions, they cannot see the application of these to every-day trade and practice ; and so they arrive at the conclusion, that they can get as much or more good at home.

" Our preachers seem to be afraid of ascertaining the sentiments, feelings, and habits of the more wretched part of the population ; and, without this, their words will die away upon the wind, and no practical echo answer their addresses.

" It will, perhaps, relieve the monotony of this statement if I give an illustration communicated to me by a person well qualified to determine the merits of the question.

" Your readers will probably recollect the opposition experienced by Dr. Hampden on his promotion to the bishopric of Hereford. Shortly after the affair was settled, his lordship accepted an invitation to preach on behalf of the schools connected with the ' ten new churches' of Bethnal-green. The church selected for the purpose was the one on Friar's-mount. It was one July Sunday in 1849, and, as I well remember, the morning was very wet ; but, supposing the curiosity, or better motives, of the public would induce a large congregation, I went to the church at half-past ten. The free-seats occupying the middle aisle were all filled, and chiefly with persons of the lowest and worst classes, many of whom I personally knew, and was agreeably surprised to find them in such a place.

" I sat in the midst of the group, and at the elbow of a tall attenuated beggar, known by the name of ' Lath and Plaster,' of whom it is but justice to say that he repeated the responsive parts of the service very correctly. It is true he could not read ; but having ' larned a few prayers' in the ' Downs' (Tothill-fields prison), ' he always sed 'em, night and morning, if he wasn't drunk, and then he sed 'em twice next day, 'cos,' reasoned he, ' I likes to rub off as I goes on.'

" In course of time, the bishop made his appearance in the pulpit. His subject was neglected education, and he illustrated it from the history of Eli.

"I thought proper to hang back, and observe the group as they passed out of church. There was Tailor Tom, and Brummagem Dick, and Keate-street Nancy, and Davy the Duke, and Stationer George, and at least two dozen more, most of whom were miserably clad, and several apparently without a shirt. They were not, however, without halfpence; and as I was well known to several of the party, and flattered as being 'a very knowledgeable man,' I was invited to the Cat and Bagpipes afterwards, to 'have share of what was going.'

"I was anxious," continues my informant, "to learn from my companions their opinion of the right reverend prelate. They thought, to use their own words, 'he was a jolly old brick.' But did they think he was sound in opinion about the Trinity, or was he (as alleged) a Unitarian? They did not even understand the meaning of these words. All they *did* understand was, that 'a top-sawyer parson at Oxford, called Dr. Pussy,' had 'made himself disagreeable,' and that some of the bishops and nobility had 'jined him;' that these had persecuted Dr. Hampden, because he was 'more cleverer' than themselves; and that Lord John Russell, who, generally speaking, was 'a regular muff,' had 'acted like a man' in this instance, and 'he ought to be commended for it; and,' added the man who pronounced the above sentiment, '*it's just a picture of ourselves.*' To other ears than mine, the closing remark would have appeared impertinent, but I 'tumbled to' it immediately. It was a case of oppression; and whether the oppressors belonged to Oxford University or to Scotland-yard militated nothing against the aphorism: 'it's just a picture of ourselves !'

"It seems to me that these poor creatures understood the *circumstances* better than they did the sermon; and my inference is, that whether from the parochial pulpit, or the missionary exhortation, or in the printed form of a tract, those who wish to produce a practical effect must themselves be practical men. I, who have been in the Christian ministry, and am familiar, unhappily, with the sufferings of men of every grade among the outcast, would say: 'If you wish to do these poor outcasts real good, you must mould your language to their ideas, get hold of their common phrases—those which tell so powerfully when they are speaking to each other — let them have their own *fashion* of things, and, where it does not interfere with order and decency, use yourselves language which their unpolished minds will appreciate; and then, having gained their entire confidence, and, perhaps, their esteem, you may safely strike home, though it be as with a sledge-hammer, and they will even 'love you for the smart.'

"The temperance movement next claims attention, and I doubt not that much crime and degradation has been prevented by total absti-

nence from all intoxicating drinks; but I would rather raise the tone of moral feeling by intelligent and ennobling means than by those spasmodic efforts, which are without deliberation, and often without permanency. The object sought to be obtained, however, is good,—so is the motive,—and I leave to others to judge what means are most likely to secure it.

"I may also allude, as another means of reformation, to the Ragged-schools which are now studding the localities of the poorest neighbourhoods. The object of these schools is, one would hope, to take care of the uncared for, and to give instruction to those who would be otherwise running wild and growing up as a pest to society. A few instances of real reform stand, however, in juxtaposition with many of increased hardihood. I, as a man, seeing those who resort to ragged-schools, cannot understand the propriety of insulting an honest though ragged boy by classing him with a young thief; or the hope of improving the juvenile female character where the sexes are brought in promiscuous contact, and left unrestrained on their way home to say and do everything subversive of the good instruction they have received." [It is right I should here state, that these are my informant's own unbiassed sentiments, delivered without communication with myself on the subject. I say thus much, because, my own opinions being known, it might perhaps appear as if I had exerted some influence over the judgment of my correspondent.]

"The most efficient means of moral reform among the street-folk, appear to have been consulted by those who, in Westminster and other places, have opened institutions cheaper, but equally efficient, as the mechanics' institutes of the metropolis. In these, for one farthing per night, three-halfpence a week, or sixpence a month, lectures, exhibitions, newspapers, &c., are available to the *very* poor. These, and such as these, I humbly but earnestly would commend to public sympathy and support, believing that, under the auspices of heaven, they may 'deliver the outcast and poor' from their own mistaken views and practices, and make them ornamental to that society to which they have long been expensive and dangerous."

Another laudable attempt to improve the condition of the poorer class is by the erection of model lodging-houses. The plan which induced this measure was good, and the success has been tolerable; but I am inclined to think the management of these houses, as well as their internal regulation, is scarcely what their well-meaning founders designed. The principal of these buildings is in George-street, St. Giles's; the building is spacious and well ventilated, there is a good library, and the class of lodgers very superior to what might be expected This latter circumstance makes the house in question scarcely admissible to the catalogue of reformed lodging-houses for the *very* poor.

" The next 'model lodging-house' in importance is the one in Charles-street, Drury-lane. This, from personal observation (having lodged in it more than four months)," says my informant, " I can safely say (so far as social reform is concerned), is a miserable failure. The bed-rooms are clean, but the sitting-room, though large, is the scene of dirt and disorder. Noise, confusion, and intemperance abound from morning till night.

" There is a model lodging-house in Westminster, the private property of Lord Kinnaird. It is generally well conducted. His lordship's agent visits the place once a week. There is an almost profuse supply of cooking utensils and other similar comforts. There are, moreover, two spacious reading-rooms, abundance of books and periodicals, and every lodger, on payment of 6d., is provided with two lockers—one in his bed-room, and the other below-stairs. The money is returned when the person leaves the house. There is divine service every day, conducted by different missionaries, and twice on Sundays. Attendance on these services is optional; and as there are two ways of ingress and egress, the devout and undevout need not come in contact with each other. The kitchen is very large and detached from the house. The master of this establishment is a man well fitted for his situation. He is a native of Saffron Walden in Essex, where his father farmed his own estate. He received a superior education, and has twice had a fortune at his own disposal. He *did* dispose of it, however; and ' after many roving years,' as a ' traveller,' ' lurker,' and ' patterer,' he has settled down in his present situation, and maintained it with great credit for a considerable period. The beds in this house are only 3d. per night, and no small praise is due to Lord Kinnaird for the superiority of this ' model ' over others of the same denomination.

" Such are a few of the principal of these establishments. Giving every credit to their founders, however, for purity and even excellence of motive, I doubt if ' model lodging-houses,' as at present conducted, are likely to accomplish much real good for those who get their living in the streets. Ever and anon they are visited by dukes and bishops, lords and ladies, who march in procession past every table, scrutinise every countenance, make their remarks upon the quantity and quality of food, and then go into the lobby, sign their names, jump into their carriages, and drive away, declaring that ' after all ' there is not so much poverty in London as they supposed.

" The poor inmates of these houses, moreover," adds my informant, " are kept in bondage, and made to *feel* that bondage, to the almost annihilation of old English independence. It is thought by the managers of these establishments, and with some share of propriety, that persons who get their living by any honest means may get home and go to bed, according to strict rule, at a certain prescribed hour—in one house it is ten o'clock, in the others eleven. But many

of the best-conducted of these poor people, if they be street-folk, are at those very hours in the height of their business, and have therefore to pack up their goods, and carry homeward their cumbersome and perhaps heavy load a distance usually varying from two or three to six or seven miles. *If they are a minute beyond time, they are shut out, and have to seek lodgings in a strange place. On their return next morning, they are charged for the bed they were prevented from occupying, and if they demur they are at once expelled!* Thus the ' model ' lodgers are kept, as it were, in leading-strings, and triumphed over by lords and ladies, masters and matrons, who, while they pique themselves on the efforts they are making to ' better the condition of the poor,' are making them their slaves, and driving them into unreasonable thraldom ; while the rich and noble managers, reckless of their own professed benevolence, are making the poor poorer, by adding insult to wretchedness. If my remarks upon these establishments appear," adds the writer of the above remarks, " to be invidious, it is only in ' appearance ' that they are so. I give their promoters credit for the best intentions, and, as far as sanitary and moral measures are concerned, I rejoice in the benefit while suggesting the improvement.

" Everything even moderately valuable has its counterfeit. We have counterfeit money, counterfeit virtue, counterfeit modesty, counterfeit religion, and last, but not least, ' counterfeit model lodging-houses.' Many private adventurers have thus dignified their domiciles, and some of them highly merit the distinction, while with others it is only a cloak for greater uncleanliness and grosser immorality.

" There has come to my knowledge the case of one man, who owns nearly a dozen of these dens of infamy, in one of which a poor girl under fifteen was lately ruined by a gray-headed monster, who, according to the pseudo-' model ' regulations, slept in an adjoining bed. The sham model-houses to which I more particularly allude," says my correspondent, " are in Short's-gardens, Drury-lane; Mill-yard, Cable-street; Keate-street, Flower and Dean-street, Thrawl-street, Spitalfields; Plough-court, Whitechapel; and Union-court, Holborn. All of these are, *without exception,* twopenny brothels, head-quarters of low-lived procuresses, and resorts of young thieves and prostitutes. Each of the houses is managed by a ' deputy,' who receives an income of 8s. 2d. per week, out of which he has to provide coke, candles, soap, &c. Of course it is impossible to do this from such small resources, and the men consequently increase their salaries by ' taking in couples for a little while,' purchasing stolen goods, and other nefarious practices. *Worse than all, the person owning these houses is a member of a strict Baptist church, and the son of a deceased minister. He lives in great splendour in one of the fashionable streets in Pimlico.*

" It still remains for me," my correspondent continues, " to contemplate the best agency for promoting the reformation of the poor. The 'City Mission,' if properly conducted, as it brings many good men in close contact with the 'outcast and poor,' might be made productive of real and extensive good. Whether it has done so, or done so to any extent, is perhaps an open question. Our town missionary societies sprang up when our different Christian denominations were not fully alive to the apprehension of their own duties to their poorer brethren, who were lost to principle, conscience, and society. That the object of the London City Mission is most noble, needs no discussion, and admits of no dispute. The method of carrying out this great object is by employing agents, who are required to give their whole time to the work, without engaging in any secular concerns of life ; and regarding the operation of the work so done, I must say that great good has resulted from the enterprise. At the commencement of the labours of the Mission in any particular locality great opposition was manifested, and a great amount of prejudice, with habits of the most immoral kind —openly carried on without any public censure—had to be overcome. The statements of the missionaries have from time to time been published, and lie recorded against us as a nation, of the glaring evils and ignorance of a vast portion of our people. It is principally owing to the city missionaries that the other portions of society have known what they now do of the practices and habits of the poor ; it is principally due to their exertions that schools have been established in connection with their labours ; and the Ragged-schools—one of the principal movements of the last few years—are mainly to be attributed to their efforts.

" A man," says my informant in conclusion, " can receive little benefit from a thing he does not understand ; the talk which will do for the senate will not do for the cottage, and the argument which will do for the study will not do for the man who spends all his spare time in a public-house. These remarks will apply to the distribution of tracts, which should be couched in the very language that is used by the people to whom they are addressed ; then the ideas will penetrate their understanding. Some years back I met with an old sailor in a lodging-house in Westminster, who professed a belief that there had *once* been a God, but that he was either dead, or grown old and diseased. He did not dispute the inspiration of the Bible. He believed that there had been revelations made to our forefathers when God was alive and active, but that now the Almighty did not 'fash' (trouble) himself about his creatures at all !

" I endeavoured to instruct the man in his own rude language and ideas ; and after he had thus been made to comprehend the doctrine of the Atonement, he said, ' I see it all plain enough—though I've liked a drop o' drink, and been a devil among the gals, and all that, in my time, if I'll humble myself I can have it all wiped off; and, as the song says, "We may be

happy yet," because, as the saying is, it's all square with God A'mighty.' Whether the sailor permanently reformed, I am unable to say, for I lost sight of him shortly after ; at any rate he *understood* the subject, and was thus qualified to profit by it. And what can the teachers of Christianity among the British heathen—herded together in courts and alleys —tell their poor ignorant hearers better than the old sailor's aphorism, 'You have, indeed, gone astray from your greatest and best Friend, but, if you so desire, "You may be happy yet," because it's all square with God A'mighty?'

" Before quitting this subject, I would add, if you really wish to do these poor creatures good, you must remember that your instructions are not intended for so-called fashionable society, but for those who have a fashion of their own. If you lose sight of this fact, your words will die away upon the wind, and no echo in the hearts of these poor people will answer your addresses."

The above observations are from the pen of one who has not only had the means, but is likewise possessed of the power, of judging as to the effect of the several plans (now in course of operation) for the reformation and improvement of the London poor. I have given the comments in the writer's own language, because I was anxious that the public should know the opinions of the best informed of the street-people themselves on this subject; and I trust I need not say that I have sought in no way to influence my correspondent's judgment.

I now subjoin a communication from a clergyman in the country, touching the character of the tramps and lurkers frequenting his neighbourhood, together with some suggestions concerning the means of improving the condition of the London poor. These I append, because it is advisable that in so difficult a matter the sentiments of every one having sufficient experience, judgment, and heart to fit him to speak on the subject should be calmly attended to, so that amid much counsel there may be at least some little wisdom.

" The subject of the welfare of our poorer brethren was one which engaged much of my attention twenty years ago, when studying for the bar at Lincoln's Inn, before I entered into orders; and the inquiries, &c., then made by me in reference to London, are recalled by many of your pages. I have pursued the same course, according to my limited means and opportunities (for my *benefice*, like thousands of others, is but 100*l.* a-year) in this neighbourhood, and there are very many of my clerical brethren, also, deeply anxious and exerting their means for the country poor. The details given in your numbers as to the country tramps and patterers, I can fully corroborate from personal experience and knowledge, so far as the country part of it. We *never* give money to beggars here, on any pretence whatever. We never give clothes. We never give relief to a *naked* or *half-naked* man if we can avoid it (the imposture is too barefaced).

Medicine I *do* give occasionally to the sick, or pretended sick, and *see* them take it. Every beggar may have *dry bread*, or three or four tracts to sell, but never both. I know we are even thus *often* imposed on ; but it is better to run this risk than to turn away, by chance, a starving man; and I do see the mendicants often sit down on a field near, and eat the dry bread with ravenous look. The tramps sometimes come to church on Sunday, and *then* beg : but we never give even bread on Sunday, because on that day they can get help at the Union workhouse, and it only tempts idlers. Sometimes we are days without a beggar, and then there will be ten to twenty per day, and then all at once the stream stops. There are no tramp lodginghouses in my parish (which is a village of 600 or 700 people). Most of the burglaries hereabouts seem connected with some inroad of tramps into the neighbourhood. The lodginghouses are very bad in some of the small towns near, but somehow the magistrates cannot get them put down. The gentry are alive here to the evil of crowded cottages, &c., and are using efforts to build better and more decent ones. But the evil results from the little landowners, who have an acre or two, or less, and build rows of cottages on them of the scantiest dimensions, at high rents,—ten per cent. on the cost of building. The rents of the gentry and nobility are very moderate to the poor, viz., scarcely two per cent. (beyond the yearly repairs) on the market value of the cottage.

" In 1832 I succeeded in getting land allotments for the poor here, and most of the parishes round have followed our example since. The success *to the poor* has always depended on the rent being a *real* rent, such as is paid by the land round about, and on the rules of good management and of payment of rent being rigidly enforced.

" The character of the poor of England *must* be raised, as well as their independence. They must not be left to lean on charity. I am sure that the sterling worth of the English character can only be raised by that means *to the surface* of society among the poor. The " English " is a fine material, but the poor neither value, nor are benefited, by mawkish nonsense or excessive feeling.

" I believe this parish was one of the most fearfully demoralized twenty years ago. It was said there was not *one* young female cottager of virtuous character. There was not one man who was not, or had not been, a drunkard ; and theft, fighting, &c., &c., were universal. It is greatly better now — totally different— and I attribute the change to the land allotments, the provident society, the village horticultural society, the lending library, the clothing club, the coal club, the cultivating a taste for music, &c., &c., as subsidiary to the more directly pastoral work of a clergyman, and the schools, &c.

" I am probably visionary in my ideas, but the perusal of your pages has led me to think that, were I clergyman of a parish where the street-folks *lived*, I should aim at some schemes of this style, in addition to the benefit society and loan society (the last *most* important) as proposed by yourself.

"(1) To get music taught at $\frac{1}{2}d.$ a week, or something of the kind—*a ragged-school musicroom*, if the people would learn gratis, would be still better—as a *step* to a " superior " music class at 1*d.* per week.

"(2) To get the poor to adorn their rooms *plentifully* with a better class of pictures—of places, of people, of natural history, and of historical and religious subjects — just as they might like, and a circulating library for pictures if they preferred change. This I find takes with the village poor. Provide these things excessively cheap for them—at *nominal prices*, just high enough to prevent them being *sold* at a profit by the poor.

"(3) To establish a monthly or fortnightly sheet—or little book for the poor—at $\frac{1}{2}d.$, or some trifle, *full of pictures* such as they would like, but free from impropriety. It might be called ' The Coster's Barrow,' or some name which would take their fancy, and contain pictures for those who cannot read, and reading for those who can. Its contents should be instructive, and yet lively ; as for instance, the ' History of London Bridge,' ' History of a Codfish,' ' Travels of Whelks,' ' Dreams of St. Paul's,' (old History of England), ' Voice from the Bottom of the Coal Exchange' (Roman tales), ' True Tale of Trafalgar,' &c., &c. All *very short articles*, at which perhaps they might be angry, or praise, or abuse, or *do anything*, but still would read, or hear, and talk about. If possible, the little work might have a corner called, ' The Next World's Page,' or any name of the kind, with *nothing* in it but the Lord's Prayer, or the Creed, or the Ten Commandments, or a Parable, or Miracle, or discourse of Christ's—in the exact words of Scripture—without *any* commentary.; which could neither annoy the Roman Catholics nor others. Those parts in which the Douay version differs from ours might be avoided, and the Romanists be given to understand that they would *always* be avoided.

" The more difficult question of cheap amusements instead of the demoralizing ones now popular, is one which as yet I cannot see my way through—but it is one which *must* be grappled with if any good is to be done.

" I write thus," adds my correspondent, "because I feel you are a fellow-worker—so far as your labours show it, for the cause of God's poor—and therefore will sympathize in anything another worker can say from experience on the same subject."

Such are the opinions of two of my correspondents—each looking at the subject from different points of view—the one living among the people of whom he treats, and daily witnessing the effects of the several plans now in operation for the moral and physical improvement of the poor, and the other in frequent intercourse with the tramps and lurkers, on their vagrant excursions through the country, as well as with the resident poor of his own parish—the former living in friendly communion with those of whom he writes, and the latter visiting them as their spiritual adviser and material benefactor.

I would, however, before passing to the consideration of the next subject, here pause to draw special attention to the distinctive features of the several classes of people obtaining their livelihood in the streets. These viewed in regard to the *causes* which have induced them to adopt this mode of life, may be arranged in three different groups, viz. :

(1.) Those who are *bred* to the streets.
(2.) Those who *take* to the streets.
(3.) Those who are *driven* to the streets.

The class bred to the streets are those whose fathers having been street-sellers before them, have sent them out into the thoroughfares at an early age to sell either watercresses, lavender, oranges, nuts, flowers, apples, onions, &c., as a means of eking out the family income. Of such street-apprenticeship several notable instances have already been given; and one or two classes of juvenile street-sellers, as the lucifer match, and the blacking-sellers, still remain to be described. Another class of street-apprentice is to be found in the boys engaged to wheel the barrows of the costers, and who are thus at an early age tutored in all the art and mystery of street traffic, and who rarely abandon it at maturity. These two classes may be said to constitute the *natives* of the streets—the tribe *indigenous* to the paving-stones—imbibing the habits and morals of the gutters almost with their mothers' milk. To expect that children thus nursed in the lap of the kennel, should when men not bear the impress of the circumstances amid which they have been reared, is to expect to find costermongers heroes instead of ordinary human beings. We might as well blame the various races on the face of the earth for those several geographical peculiarities of taste, which constitute their national characteristics. Surely there is a moral acclimatisation as well as a physical one, and the heart may become inured to a particular atmosphere in the same manner as the body; and even as the seed of the apple returns, unless grafted, to its original crab, so does the child, without training, go back to its parent stock—the vagabond savage. For the bred and born street-seller, who inherits a barrow as some do coronets, to be other than he is—it has here been repeatedly enunciated—is no fault of his but of ours, who could and yet *will* not move to make him otherwise. Might not " the finest gentleman in Europe" have been the greatest blackguard in Billingsgate, had he been born to carry a fish-basket on his head instead of a crown? and by a parity of reasoning let the roughest " rough" outside the London fish-market have had his lot in life cast, "by the Grace of God, King, Defender of the Faith,"

and surely his shoulders would have glittered with diamond epaulettes instead of fish scales.

I say thus much, to impress upon the reader a deep and devout sense, that we who have been appointed to another state, are, by the grace of God, what we are, and from no special merit of our own, to which, in the arrogance of our self-conceit, we are too prone to attribute the social and moral differences of our nature. Go to a lady of fashion and tell her she could have even become a fishfag, and she will think you some mad ethnologist (if indeed she had ever heard of the science). Let me not, however, while thus seeking to impress the reader's mind with a sense of the "antecedents" of the human character, be thought to espouse the doctrine that men are *merely* the creatures of events. All I wish to enforce is, that the three common causes of the social and moral differences of individuals are to be found in *race*, *organization*, and *circumstances*—that none of us are entirely proof against the influence of these three conditions—the *ethnological*, the *physiological*, and the *associative* elements of our idiosincracy. But, while I admit the full force of external nature upon us all, while I allow that we are, in many respects, merely patients, still I cannot but perceive that, in other respects we are self-agents, moving rather than being moved, by events—often stemming the current of circumstances, and at other times giving to it a special direction rather than being swept along with it. I am conscious that it is this directive and controlling power, not only over external events, but over the events of my own nature, that distinguishes me as well from the brute of the fields as it does my waking from my sleeping moments. I know, moreover, that in proportion as a man is active or passive in his operations, so is his humanity or brutality developed; that true greatness lies in the superiority of the internal forces over the external ones; and that as heroes, or extraordinary men are heroes, because they overcome the sway of one or other, or all, of the three material influences above-named, so ordinary people are ordinary, simply because they lack energy—principle—will (call it what you please) to overcome the material elements of their nature with the spiritual. And it is precisely because I know this, that I *do* know that those who are bred to the streets must bear about them the moral impress of the kennel and the gutter—unless *we* seek to develope the inward and controlling part of their constitution. If we allow them to remain the creatures of circumstances, to wander through life principleless, purposeless, conscienceless—if it be their lot to be flung on the wide waste of waters without a "guiding star" above, or a rudder or compass within, how can *we* (the well-fed) *dare* to blame them because, wanting bread, they prey and live upon their fellow-creatures?

I say thus much, because I feel satisfied that a large portion of the street-folk—and especially those who have been *bred* to the business—

are of improvable natures; that they crave knowledge, as starving men for "the staff of life;" that they are most grateful for instruction; that they are as deeply moved by any kindness and sympathy (when once their suspicion has been overcome) as they are excited by any wrong or oppression—and I say it moreover, because I feel thoroughly convinced of the ineffectiveness of the present educational resources for the poor. We think, if we teach them reading and writing, and to chatter a creed, that we have armed them against the temptations, the trials, and the exasperations of life, believing, because we have put the knife and fork in their hands that we have really filled with food the empty bellies of their brains. We exercise their memories, make them human parrots, and then wonder that they do not act as human beings. The intellect, the conscience, the taste, indeed all that refines, enlightens, and ennobles our nature, we leave untouched, to shrivel and wither like unused limbs. The beautiful, the admirable, the true, the right, are as hidden to them as at their first day's schooling. We impress them with no purpose, animate them with no principle; they are still the same brute creatures of circumstances—the same passive instruments—human waifs and strays—left to be blown about as the storms of life may whirl them.

Of the second group, or those who *take* to the streets, I entertain very different opinions. This class is distinguished from that above mentioned, in being wanderers by choice, rather than wanderers by necessity. In the early chapters of this work, I strove to point out to my readers that the human race universally consisted of two distinct classes: the wanderers and the settlers—the civilized and the savage—those who *produced* their food, and those who merely *collected* it. I sought further to show, that these two classes were not necessarily isolated, but that, on the contrary, almost every civilized tribe had its nomadic race, like parasites, living upon it. These nomadic races I proved, moreover, to have several characteristics common to the class, one of the most remarkable of which was, their adoption of a *secret* language, with the intent of concealing their designs and exploits. "Strange to say," I then observed, "that despite its privations, dangers, and hardships, those who have once taken to a wandering life rarely abandon it. There are countless instances," I added, "of white men adopting all the usages of an Indian hunter; but there is not one example of the Indian hunter or trapper, adopting the steady and regular habits of civilized society." That this passion for "a roving life" (to use the common expression by which many of the street-people themselves designate it), is a marked feature of some natures, there cannot be a doubt in the mind of any one who has contemplated even the surface differences of human beings; and nevertheless it is a point to which no social philosopher has yet drawn attention. To my mind, it is essentially the *physical* cause of crime. Too

restive and volatile *to* pursue the slow process of production, the wanderers, and consequently the *collectors*, of subsistence must (in a land where all things are appropriated) live upon the stock of the *producers*. The nomadic or vagrant class have all an universal type, whether they be the Bushmen of Africa or the "tramps" of our own country; and Mr. Knapp, the intelligent master of the Wandsworth and Clapham Union, to whom I was referred at the time of my investigations touching the subject of vagrancy, as having the greatest experience upon the matter, gave me the following graphic account, which, as I said at the time of its first publication, had perhaps never been surpassed as an analysis of the habits and propensities of the vagabond class:

"Ignorance," to use the gentleman's own words, "is certainly not their prevailing characteristic: indeed, with a few exceptions, it is the reverse. The vagrants are mostly distinguished by their aversion to continuous labour of any kind. He never knew them to work. Their great inclination is to be on the move, and wandering from place to place, and they appear to receive a great deal of pleasure from the assembly and conversation of the casual ward. They are physically stout and healthy, and certainly not emaciated or sickly. They belong especially to the able-bodied class, being, as he says, full of health and mischief. They are very stubborn and self-willed. They are a most difficult class to govern, and are especially restive under the least restraint; they can ill brook control, and they find great delight in thwarting the authorities. They are particularly fond of amusements of all kinds. He never knew them love reading. They mostly pass under fictitious names. They are particularly distinguished by their libidinous propensities. They are not remarkable for a love of drink. He considers them to be generally a class possessing the keenest intellect, and of a highly enterprising character. They seem to have no sense of danger, and to be especially delighted with such acts as involve any peril. They are likewise characterised by their exceeding love of mischief. They generally are of a most restless and volatile disposition. They have great quickness of perception, but little power of continuous attention or perseverance. They have a keen sense of the ridiculous, and are not devoid of deep feeling. In the summer they make regular tours through the country, visiting all places that they have not seen. They are perfectly organized, so that any regulation affecting their comforts or interests becomes known among the whole body in a remarkably short space of time."

Every day my inquiries add some fresh proof to the justice of the above enumeration of the several phenomena distinguishing this class. To the more sedate portion of the human family, the attractions of "a roving life" are inexplicable. Nevertheless, there can be no doubt that, to the more volatile, the mere muscular exercise and the continual change of scene, together with the wild delight which attends the overcoming of any danger, are sources of pleasure sufficient to compensate for all the privations and hardships attending such a state of existence.

Mr. Ruxton, one of the many who have passed from settlers to wanderers, has given us the following description of the enjoyments of a life in the wilderness:

"Although liable to an accusation of barbarism, I must confess that the very happiest moments of my life have been spent in the wilderness of the Far West; and I never recall, but with pleasure, the remembrance of my solitary camp in the Bayou Solade, with no friend near me more faithful than my rifle, and no companions more sociable than my good horse and mules, or the attendant cayute which nightly serenaded us. Seldom did I ever wish to change such hours of freedom for all the luxuries of civilized life; and unnatural and extraordinary as it may appear, yet such is the fascination of the life of the mountain hunter, that I believe not one instance could be adduced of even the most polished and civilized of men, who had once tasted the sweets of its attendant liberty and freedom from every worldly care, not regretting the moment when he exchanged it for the monotonous life of the settlements, nor sighing and sighing again once more to partake of its pleasures and allurements."

To this class of voluntary wanderers belong those who *take* to the streets, glad to exchange the wearisomeness and restraint of a settled occupation for tne greater treedom ana iicense of a nomad mode of life. As a class, they are essentially the non-working, preferring, as I said before, to *collect*, rather than *produce*, what they eat. If they sell, they do so because for sundry reasons they fear to infringe the law, and as traders their transactions certainly are not marked by an excess of honesty. I am not aware that any of them are professional thieves (for these are the more daring portion of the same vagrant fraternity), though the majority assuredly are habitual cheats—delighting in proving their cleverness by imposing upon simple-minded citizens—viewing all society as composed of the same dishonest elements as their own tribes, and looking upon all sympathy and sacrifice, even when made for their own benefit, as some "artful dodge" or trick, by which to snare them.

It should be remembered, however, that there are many grades of vagrants among us, and that though they are all essentially non-producing and, consequently, predatory, still many are in no way distinguished from a large portion of even our wealthy tradesmen—our puffing grocers and slopsellers. To attempt to improve the condition of the voluntary street-sellers by teaching of any kind, would be to talk to the wind. We might as well preach to Messrs. Moses, Nicol, and Co., in the hope of Christianising them. Those who *take* to the streets are *not*, like those who are *bred* to it, an uneducated class. They are intelligent and "knowing" enough, and it is this development of their intellect at the expense of their conscience which gives rise to that excessive admiration of mere cleverness, which makes skill the sole standard of excellence with them. They approve, admire, venerate nothing but what is ingenious. Wrong with them is mere folly—right, cunning; and those who think the simple cultivation of the intellect the great social panacea of the time, have merely to study the characteristics of this class to see how a certain style of education can breed the very vice it seeks to destroy. Years ago, I wrote and printed the following passage, and every year since my studies have convinced me more and more of its truth:

"Man, if deprived of his intellect, would be the most miserable and destitute,—if of his sympathy, the most savage and cunning, of all the brute creation: consequently, we may infer that, according as solely the one or the other of these powers is expanded in us, so shall we approximate in our nature either to the instinct of the brute or to the artifice of the demon, and that only when they are developed in an equal degree, can Man be said to be educated as Man. We should remember that the intellect simply executes; it is either the selfish or moral propensity that designs. The intellectual principle enables us to perceive the means of attaining any particular object; it is the selfish or else the moral principle in us, that causes us originally to desire that object. The two latter principles are the springs, the former is merely the instrument of all human action. They are masters, whereas the intellect is but the servant of the will; and hence it is evident that in proportion as the one or the other of these two predominant principles—as either the selfish or the moral disposition is educed in man, and thus made the chief director and stimulus of the intellectual power within him, so will the cultivation of that power be the source of happiness or misery to himself and others."

The third and last class, namely, those who are *driven* to the streets, is almost as large as any. Luckily, those who *take* to that mode of life, are by far the least numerous portion of the street-folk; and if those who are bred to the business are worthy of our pity, assuredly those who are driven to it are equally, if not more, so. With some who are deprived of the means of obtaining a maintenance for themselves, the sale of small articles in the streets may, perhaps, be an excuse for begging; but in most cases, I am convinced it is adopted from a horror of the workhouse, and a disposition to do, at least, *something* for the food they eat. Often is it the last struggle for independence—the desire to give something like an equivalent for what they receive. Over and over again have I noticed this honourable pride, even in individuals who, from some privations or affliction that rendered them utterly incompetent to labour for their living, had a just claim on our sympathies and assistance. The blind—the cripple—the maimed—

the very old—the very young—all have generally adopted a street-life, because they could do nothing else. With many it is the last resort of all. The smallness of the stock-money required—for a shilling, it has been shown, is sufficient to commence several street-trades—is one of the principal causes of so many of those who are helpless taking to the street-traffic. Moreover, the severity of the Poor-laws and the degradation of pauperism, and the aversion to be thought a common beggar by all, except the very lowest, are, I have no doubt, strong incentives to this course. There are many callings which are peculiar, as being followed principally by the disabled. The majority of the blind are musicians, or boot-lace or tape-sellers. The very old are sellers of water-cresses, lucifers, pincushions, ballads, and pins and needles, stay-laces, and such small articles as are light to carry, and require but a few pence for the outlay. The very young are sellers of flowers, oranges, nuts, onions, blacking, lucifers, and the like. Many of those who have lost an arm, or a leg, or a hand, turn showmen, or become sellers of small metal articles, as knives or nutmeg-graters; and many who have been born cripples may be seen in the streets struggling for self-support. But all who are *driven* to the streets have not been physically *disabled* for labour. Some have been *reduced* from their position as tradesmen or shopmen; others, again, have been gentlemen's servants and clerks; all, dragged down by a series of misfortunes, sometimes beyond their control, and sometimes brought about by their own imprudence or sluggishness. As we have seen, many are reduced to a state of poverty by long illness, and on their recovery are unable, from want of clothes or friends, to follow any other occupation.

But a still larger class than all, are the beaten-out mechanics and artizans, who, from want of employment in their own trade, take to make up small things (as clothes-horses, tin-ware, cutlery, brushes, pails, caps, and bonnets)

on their own account. The number of artizans in the London streets speaks volumes for the independence of the working-men of this country; as well as for the difficulty of their obtaining employment at their own trades. Those who are unacquainted with the sterling pride of the destitute English mechanic, know not what he will suffer before becoming an inmate of a workhouse, or sinking to the debasement of a beggar. That handicraftsmen do occasionally pass into "lurkers" I know well; but these, I am convinced, have gradually been warped to the life by a long course of tramping, aided by the funds of their societies, and thus becoming disused to labour, have, after forfeiting all claims upon the funds of their trade, adopted beggary as a means of subsistence. But, that this is the exception rather than the rule, the following is sufficient to show:

"The destitute mechanics," said the Master of the Wandsworth and Clapham Union to me, "are entirely a different class from the regular vagrants; they have different habits, and indeed different features. During the whole of my experience I never knew a distressed artizan who applied for a night's shelter, commit an act of theft; and I have seen them," he added, "in the last stage of destitution. Occasionally they have sold the shirt and waistcoat off their backs before they applied for admittance into the workhouse, while some of them have been so weak from long starvation that they could scarcely reach the gate, and indeed had to be kept for several days in the Infirmary before their strength was recruited sufficiently to continue their journey." "The poor mechanic," said another of my informants, "will sit in the casual ward like a lost man, scared. Its shocking to think a decent mechanic's houseless. When he's beat out he's like a bird out of a cage; he doesn't know where to go, or how to get a bit."

I shall avail myself of another occasion to discuss the means of improving the condition of the street-people.

OF THE STREET-SELLERS OF MANUFACTURED ARTICLES.

THESE traders consist of: (1) The vendors of metal articles; (2) Of chemical articles; (3) Of China, glass, and stone articles; (4) Of linen, cotton, and other textile fabrics; and (5) Of miscellaneous articles. In this classification I do not include second-hand articles, nor yet the traffic of those who make the articles they sell, and who are indeed street-artizans rather than street-sellers.

Under the first head are included, the vendors of razors, table and penknives, tea-trays, dog-collars, key-rings, articles of hardware, small coins and medals, pins and needles, jewellery, snuffers, candlesticks, articles of tin-ware, tools, card-counters, herring-toasters, trivets, gridirons,

pans, tray-stands (as in the roasting of meat), and Dutch ovens.

Of the second description are the vendors of blacking, black-lead, lucifer matches, corn-salves, grease-removing compositions, china and glass cements, plating-balls, rat and beetle poisons, crackers, detonating-balls, and cigar-lights.

Under the third head come all street-sold articles of China, glass, or stone manufacture, including not only "crockery," but vases, chimney-ornaments, and stone fruit.

The fourth head presents the street-vending of cotton, silken, and linen-manufactures; such as sheetings, shirtings, a variety of laces, sewing cotton, threads and tapes, articles of haberdashery and of millinery, artificial flowers, handkerchiefs, and pretended smuggled goods.

Among the fifth class, or the "miscellaneous" street-sellers, are those who vend cigars, pipes, tobacco and snuff-boxes and cigar-cases, accordions, spectacles, hats, sponge, combs and hair-brushes, shirt-buttons and coat-studs, "lots," rhubarb, wash-leather, paper-hangings, dolls, Bristol and other toys, saw-dust, fire-wood, and pin-cushions.

There are many other manufactured articles sold in the streets, but their description will be more proper under the head of Street Artisans.

The street-sellers of manufactured articles present, as a body, so many and often such varying characteristics, that I cannot offer to give a description of them as a whole, as I have been able to do with other and less diversified classes.

Among them are several distinct and peculiar street-characters, such as the pack-men, who carry their cotton or linen goods in packs on their backs, and are all itinerants. Then there are duffers, who vend pretended smuggled goods, handkerchiefs, silks, tobacco or cigars; also, the sellers of sham sovereigns and sham gold rings for wagers. The crockery-ware and glass-sellers (known in the street-trade as "crocks"), are peculiar from their principle of *bartering.* They will sell to any one, but they *sell* very rarely, and always clamour in preference for an exchange of their wares for wearing-apparel of any kind. They state, if questioned, that their reason for doing this is—at least I heard the statement from some of the most intelligent among them—that they do so because, if they "sold outright," they required a hawker's license, and could not sell or "swop" so cheap.

Some of the street-sellers of manufactured articles are also patterers. Among these are the "cheap Jacks," or "cheap Johns;" the grease and stain removers; the corn-salve and plate-ball vendors; the sellers of sovereigns and rings for wagers; a portion of the lot-sellers; and the men who vend poison for vermin and go about the streets with live rats clinging to, or running about, their persons.

This class of street-sellers also includes many of the very old and the very young; the diseased, crippled, maimed, and blind. These poor creatures sell, and sometimes obtain a charitable penny, by offering to sell such things as boxes of lucifer-matches; cakes of blacking; boot, stay, and other laces; pins, and sewing and knitting-needles; tapes; cotton-bobbins; garters; pincushions; combs; nutmeg-graters; metal skewers and meat-hooks; hooks and eyes; and shirt-buttons.

The rest of the class may be described as merely street-sellers; toiling, struggling, plodding, itinerant tradesmen.

OF THE STREET-SELLERS OF MANUFACTURED ARTICLES IN METAL.

THESE street-sellers are less numerous than might be imagined, when—according to my present division—the class is confined to the sellers of articles which they do not manufacture. The metal wares thus sold I have already enumerated, and I have now to describe the characteristics of the sellers.

The result of my inquiries leads me to the conclusion, that the street-vendors of any article which is the product of the skill of the handicraftsman, have been, almost always, in their first outset in a street life, connected in some capacity or other with the trade, the manufactures of which they vend.

One elderly man, long familiar with this branch of the street-trade, expressed to me his conviction that when a mechanic sought his livelihood in the streets, he naturally "gave his mind to sell what he understood. Now, in my own case," continued my informant, "I was born and bred a tinman, and when I was driven to a street-life, I never thought of selling anything but tins. How could I, if I wished to do the thing square and proper?—it would be like trying to speak another language. If I'd started on slippers—and I knew a poor man who was set up in the streets by a charitable lady on a stock of gentlemen's slippers—what could I have done? Why, no better than he told me he did. He was a potter down at Deptford, and knew of nothing but flower-pots, and honey-jars for grocers, and them red sorts of pottery. Poor fellow, he might have died of hunger, only the cholera came quickest. But when I'm questioned about my tins, I'm my own man; and it's a great thing, I'm satisfied, in a street-trade, when there's so many cheap shops, and the police and all again you, to understand the goods you're talking about."

This statement, I may repeat, is undoubtedly correct, so far as that a "beaten-out" mechanic, when driven to the streets, in the first instance offers to the public wares of which he understands the value and quality. Afterwards, in the experience or vagaries of a street-life, other commodities may be, or may appear to be, more remunerative, and for such the mechanic may relinquish his first articles of street-traffic. "Why, sir," I was told, "there was one man who left razors for cabbages; 'cause one day a costermonger wot lived in the same house with him and was taken ill, asked him to go out with a barrow of summer cabbages—the costermonger's boy went with him—and they went off so well that Joe [the former razor-seller] managed to start in the costering line, he was so encouraged."

The street-trade in metal manufactured articles is principally itinerant. Perhaps during the week upwards of three-fourths of those carrying it on are itinerant, while on a Saturday night, perhaps, all are stationary, and almost always in the street-markets. The itinerant trade is carried on, and chiefly in the suburbs, by men, women, and children; but the children are always, or almost always, the offspring of the adult street-sellers.

The metal sold in the street may be divided into street-hardware, street-tinware, and street-jewellery. I shall begin with the former.

The street-sellers of hardware are, I am assured, in number about 100, including single men and families; for women "take their share" in the business, and children sell smaller things, such as snuffers or bread-baskets. The people pursuing the trade are of the class I have above described, with the exception of some ten or twelve who formerly made a living as servants to the gaming-booths at Epsom, Ascot, &c., &c., and "managed to live out of the races, somehow, most of the year;" since the gaming-booths have been disallowed, they have "taken to the street hardware."

All these street-sellers obtain their supplies at "the swag-shops;" of which I shall speak hereafter. The main articles of their trade are tea-boards, waiters, snuffers, candlesticks, bread-baskets, cheese-trays, Britannia metal tea-pots and spoons, iron kettles, pans, and coffee-pots. The most saleable things, I am told by a man who has been fifteen years in this and similar street trades, are at present 18-in. tea-boards, bought at "the swags" at from 10s. 6d. a doz., to 4s. each; 24-in. boards, from 20s. the doz. to 5s. each; bread-baskets, 4s. 6d. the doz.; and Britannia metal tea-pots, 10s. the doz. These tea-pots have generally what is called "loaded bottoms;" the lower part of the vessel is "filled with composition, so as to look as if there was great weight of metal, and as if the pot would melt for almost the 18d. which is asked for it, and very often got."

I learned from the same man, however, and from others in the trade, that it is far more difficult now than it was a few years ago, to sell "rubbish." There used to be also, but not within these six or eight years, a tolerable profit realised by the street-sellers of hardware in the way of "swop." It was common to take an old metal article, as part payment for a new one; and if the old article were of good quality, it was polished and tinkered up for sale in the Saturday evening street-markets, and often "went off well." This traffic, however, has almost ceased to exist, as regards the street-sellers of hardware, and has been all but monopolised by the men who barter "crocks" for wearing-apparel, or any old metal. Some hardware-men who have become well known on their "rounds"—for the principal trade is in the suburbs—sell very good wares, and at moderate profits.

"It's a poor trade, sir, is the hardware," said one man carrying it on, "and street trades are mostly poor trades, for I've tried many a one of them. I was brought up a clown, I may say; my father died when I was a child, and I might have been a clown still but for an accident (a rupture). That's long ago,—I can't say how long; but I know that before I was fifteen, I

many a time wished I was dead, and I have many a time since. Why the day before yesterday, from 9 in the morning to 11 at night, I didn't take a farthing. Some days I don't earn 1s., and I have a mother depending upon me who can do little or nothing. I'm a tee-totaller; if I wasn't we shouldn't have a meal a day. I never was fond of drink, and if I'm ever so weary and out of sorts, and worried for a meal's meat, I can't say I ever long for a drop to cheer me up. Sometimes I can't get coffee, let alone anything else. O, I suffer terribly. Day after day I get wet through, and have nothing to take home to my mother at last. Our principal food is bread and butter, and tea. Not fish half so often as many poor people. I suppose, because we don't care for it. I know that our living, the two of us, stands to less than 1s. a day,—not 6d. a piece. Then I have two rents to pay. No, sir, not for two places; but I pay 2s. a week for a room, a tidy bit of a chamber, furnished, and 1s. a week rent, —I call it rent, for a loan of 5s. I've paid 1s. a week for four weeks on it, and must keep paying until I can hand over the 5s., with 1s. for rent added to it, all in one sum. If I could tip up the 5s. the day after I'd paid the last week's 1s., I must pay another shilling. The man who lends does nothing else; he lives by lending, and by letting out a few barrows to costermongers, and other street-people. I wish I could take a farewell sight of them."

The principal traffic carried on by these street-sellers is in the suburbs. Women constitute their sole customers, or nearly so. Their profits fluctuate from 20 per cent. to 100 per cent. The bread-baskets, which they buy at 4s. 6d. the doz., they retail at 6d. each; for it is very difficult, I have frequently been told, to get a price between 6d. and 1s. This, however, relates only to those things which are not articles of actual necessity. Half of these street-sellers, I am assured, take on an average from 20s. to 25s. weekly the year through; a quarter take 15s., and the remaining quarter from 7s. 6d. to 10s. Calculating an average taking of 15s. each per week, throughout the entire class, men, women, and children, we find 780l. expended in street-sold hardwares. Ten years ago, I am told, the takings were not less than 2,000l.

The following is an extract from accounts kept, not long ago, by a street-seller of hardware. His principal sale was snuffers, knives and forks, iron candlesticks, padlocks, and bed-screws. His stock cost him 35s. on the Monday morning, and his first week was his *best*, which I here subjoin:

	Receipts.	Profits.
Monday	8s.	3s. 0d.
Tuesday	5	2 3
Wednesday	4	1 6
Thursday (always a slack day)	3	
Friday (a better day about the docks, when people are paid)	7	3 0
Saturday Morning and Even.	23	6 1
	50	15 10

The following is the *worst* week in the account-books. The street-seller after this (about half a year ago) sold his stock to a small shopkeeper, and went into another business.

	Receipts.		Profits.	
	s.	d.	s.	d.
Monday (very cold) a common bed-screw	0	4	0	1¼
Tuesday	—	—	—	—
Wednesday	1	0	0	5
Thursday (sold cheap) . .	1	1	0	3
Friday	—	—	—	—
Saturday	1	7	0	8
	4	0	1	5¼

Of the Cheap Johns, or Street Han-sellers.

This class of street-salesmen, who are perhaps the largest dealers of all in hardware, are not so numerous as they were some few years ago—the Excise Laws, as I have before remarked, having interfered with their business. The principal portion of those I have met are Irishmen, who, notwithstanding, generally "hail" from Sheffield, and all their sales are effected in an attempt at the Yorkshire dialect, interspersed, however, with an unmistakeable brogue. The brogue is the more apparent when cheap John gets a little out of temper—if his sales are flat, for instance, he'll say, "By J—s, I don't belaive you've any money with you, or that you've lift any at home, at all, at all. Bad cess to you!"

There are, however, many English cheap Johns, but few of them are natives of Sheffield or Birmingham, from which towns they invariably "hail." Their system of selling is to attract a crowd of persons by an harangue after the following fashion: "Here I am, the original cheap John from Sheffield. I've not come here to get money; not I; I've come here merely for the good of the public, and to let you see how you've been imposed upon by a parcel of pompous shopkeepers, who are not content with less than 100 per cent. for rubbish. They got up a petition—which I haven't time to read to you just now—offering me a large sum of money to keep away from here. But no, I had too much friendship for you to consent, and here I am, cheap John, born without a shirt, one day while my mother was out, in a haystack; consequently I've no parish, for the cows eat up mine, and therefore I've never no fear of going to the workhouse. I've more money than the parson of the parish—I've in this cart a cargo of useful and cheap goods; can supply you with anything, from a needle to an anchor. Nobody *can* sell as cheap as me, seeing that I gets all my goods upon credit, and never means to pay for them. Now then, what shall we begin with? Here's a beautiful guard-chain; if it isn't silver, it's the same colour—I don't say it isn't silver, nor I don't say it is—in that affair use your own judgment. Now, in the reg'lar way of trade, you shall go into any shop in town, and they will ask you 1*l.* 18*s.* 6*d.* for an article

not half so good, so what will you say for this splendid chain? Eighteen and sixpence without the pound? What, that's too much! Well, then say 17, 16, 15, 14, 13, 12, 11, 10 shillings; what, none of you give ten shillings for this beautiful article? See how it improves a man's appearance" (hanging the chain round his neck). "Any young man here present wearing this chain will always be shown into the parlour instead of the tap-room; into the best pew in church, when he and—but the advantages the purchaser of this chain will possess I haven't time to tell. What! no buyers? Why, what's the matter with ye? Have you no money, or no brains? But I'll ruin myself for your sakes. Say 9*s.* for this splendid piece of jewellery—8, 7, 6, 5, 4, 3, 2, 1—a shilling, will anybody give a shilling? Well, here 11*d.*, 10*d.*, 9*d.*, 8*d.*, 7*d.*, 6½*d.*, 6*d.*! Is there ever a buyer at sixpence? Now I'll ask no more and I'll take no less; sell it or never sell it." The concluding words are spoken with peculiar emphasis, and after saying them the cheap John never takes any lower sum. A customer perhaps is soon obtained for the guard-chain, and then the vendor elevates his voice: "Sold to a very respectable gentleman, with his mouth between his nose and chin, a most remarkable circumstance. I believe I've just one more—this is better than the last; I must have a shilling for this. Sixpence? To you, sir. Sold again, to a gentleman worth 30,000*l.* a year; only the right owner keeps him out of it. I believe I've just one more; yes, here it is; it's brighterer, longerer, strongerer, and betterer than the last. I must have at least tenpence for this. Well then, 9, 8, 7, 6; take this one for a sixpence. Sold again, to a gentleman, his father's pet and his mother's joy. Pray, sir, does your mother know you're out? Well, I don't think I've any more, but I'll look; yes, here is *one* more. Now this is better than all the rest. Sold again, to a most respectable gentleman, whose mother keeps a chandler's shop, and whose father turns the mangle." In this manner the cheap John continues to sell his guard-chain, until he has drained his last customer for that particular commodity. He has always his remark to make relative to the purchaser. The cheap John always takes care to receive payment before he hazards his jokes, which I need scarcely remark are ready made, and most of them ancient and worn threadbare, the joint property of the whole fraternity of cheap Johns. After supplying his audience with one particular article, he introduces another: "Here is a carving-knife and fork, none of your wasters, capital buck-horn handle, manufactured of the best steel, in a regular workmanlike manner; fit for carving in the best style, from a sparrow to a bullock. I don't ask 7*s.* 6*d.* for this—although go over to Mr. —, the ironmonger, and he will have the impudence to ask you 15*s.* for a worse article." (The cheap Johns always make comparisons as to their own prices and the shopkeepers, and sometimes mention their names.) "I say 5*s.*

for the carving-knife and fork. Why, it's an article that'll almost fill your children's bellies by looking at it, and will always make 1 lb. of beef go as far as 6 lb. carved by any other knife and fork. Well, 4*s.*, 3*s.*, 2*s.*, 1*s.* 11*d.*, 1*s.* 10*d.*, 1*s.* 9*d.*, 1*s.* 8*d.*, 1*s.* 7*d.*, 18*d.* I ask no more, nor I'll take no less." The salesman throughout his variety of articles indulges in the same jokes, and holds out the same inducements. I give a few.

" *This* is the original teapot " (producing one), " formerly invented by the Chinese; the first that ever was imported by those celebrated people—only two of them came over in three ships. If I do not sell this to-day, I intend presenting it to the British Museum or the Great Exhibition. It is mostly used for making tea,—sometimes by ladies, for keeping a little drop on the sly; it is an article constructed upon scientific principles, considered to require a lesser quantity of tea to manufacture the largest quantity of tea-water, than any other teapot now in use—largely patronised by the tea-totallers. Now, here's a fine pair of bellows! Any of you want to raise the wind? This is a capital opportunity, if you'll try. I'll tell you how; buy these of me for 3*s.* 6*d.*, and go and pawn them for 7*s.* Will you buy 'em, sir? No! well, then, you be blowed! Let's see—I said 3*s.* 6*d.*; it's too little, but as I have said it, they must go; well—3*s.*," &c. &c. " Capital article to chastise the children or a drunken husband. Well, take 'em for 1*s.*—I ask no more, and I'll take no less."

These men have several articles which they sell singly, such as tea-trays, copper kettles, fire-irons, guns, whips, to all of which they have some preamble; but their most attractive lot is a heap of miscellaneous articles :—" I have here a pair of scissors; I only want half-a-crown for them. What! you won't give 1*s.*? well, I'll add something else. Here's a most useful article—a knife with eight blades, and there's not a blade among you all that's more highly polished. This knife's a case of instruments in addition to the blades ; here's a cork-screw, a button-hook, a file, and a picker. For this capital knife and first-rate pair of scissors I ask 1*s.* Well, well, you've no more con-science than a lawyer; here's something else —a pocket-book. This book no gentleman should be without; it contains a diary for every day in the week, an almanack, a ready-reckoner, a tablet for your own memorandums, pockets to keep your papers, and a splendid pencil with a silver top. No buyers! I'm astonished; but I'll add another article. Here's a pocket-comb. No young man with any sense of decency should be without a pocket-comb. What looks worse than to see a man's head in an uproar? Some of you look as if your hair hadn't seen a comb for years. Surely I shall get a customer now. What! no buyers—well I never! Here, I'll add half-a-dozen of the very best Britannia metal tea-spoons, and if you don't buy, you must be spoons yourselves. Why, you perfectly

astonish me! I really believe if I was to offer all in the shop, myself included, I should not draw 1*s.* out of you. Well, I'll try again. Here, I'll add a dozen of black-lead pencils. Now, then, look at these articles "—(he spreads them out, holding them between his fingers to the best advantage)—" here's a pair of first-rate scissors, that will almost cut of themselves, —this valuable knife, which comprises within itself almost a chest of tools,—a splendid pocket-book, which must add to the respectability and consequence of any man who wears it,—a pocket-comb which possesses the peculiar property of making the hair curl, and dyeing it any colour you wish,—a half-dozen spoons, nothing inferior to silver, and that do not require half the usual quantity of sugar to sweeten your tea,—and a dozen beautiful pencils, at least worth the money I ask for the whole lot. Now, a reasonable price for these articles would be at least 10*s.* 6*d.* ; I'll sell them for 1*s.* I ask no more, I'll take no less. Sold again! "

The opposition these men display to each other, while pursuing their business, is mostly assumed, for the purpose of attracting a crowd. Sometimes, when in earnest, their language is disgusting; and I have seen them, (says an informant), after selling, try and settle their differences with a game at fisticuffs ; but this occurred but seldom. One of these men had a wife who used to sell for him,—she was considered to be the best " chaffer " on the road ; not one of them could stand against her tongue : but her language abounded with obscenity. All the "cheap Johns" were afraid of her.

They never under-sell each other (unless they get in a real passion); this but seldom happens, but when it does they are exceedingly bitter against each other. I cannot state the language they use, further than that it reaches the very summit of blackguardism. They have, however, assumed quarrels, for the purpose of holding a crowd together, and chaff goes round, intended to amuse their expected customers.

" He's coming your way to-morrow," they'll say one of the other, " mind and don't hang your husbands' shirts to dry, ladies, he's very lucky at finding things before they're lost; he sells very cheap, no doubt—but mind, if you handle any of his wares, he don't make you a present of a Scotch fiddle for nothing. His hair looks as if it had been cut with a knife and fork."

The Irishmen, in these displays, generally have the best of it ; indeed, most of their jokes have originated with the Irishmen, who complain of the piracies of other " cheap Johns," for as soon as the joke is uttered it is the property of the commonwealth, and not unfrequently used against the inventor half an hour after its first appearance.

A few of them are not over particular as to the respectability of their transactions. I recollect one purchasing a brick at Sheffield ; the brick was packed up in paper, with a knife tied on the outside, it appeared like a package of knives, containing several dozens. The "cheap John " made out that he bought them as stolen property ; the biter was deservedly bitten. A few of the fraternity are well-known " Fences," and some of them pursue the double calling of " cheap John " and gambler—keeping gambling tables at races. However the majority are hard-working men, who unite untiring industry with the most indomitable perseverance, for the laudable purpose of bettering their condition.

I believe the most successful in the line have worked their way up from nothing, gaining experience as they proceeded. I have known two or three start the trade with plenty of stock, but, wanting the tact, they have soon been knocked off the road. There is a great deal of judgment required in knowing the best fairs, and even when there, as to getting a good stand ; and these matters are to be acquired only by practice.

In the provinces, and in Scotland, there may be 100 " cheap Johns," or, as they term themselves, "Han-sellers." They are generally a most persevering body of men, and have frequently risen from small hawkers of belts, braces, &c. Their receipts are from 5l. to 30l. per day, their profits from 20 to 25 per cent.; 20l. is considered a good day's work ; and they can take about three fairs a week during the summer months. "I have known many of these men," a man well acquainted with them informs me, "who would walk 20 miles to a fair during the night, hawk the public-houses the whole of the day, and start again all night for a fair to be held 20 miles off upon the following day. I knew two Irish lads, named ——, and I watched their progress with some interest. Each had a stock of goods worth a few shillings ; and now each has a wholesale warehouse,—one at Sheffield, in the cutlery line, and the other at Birmingham, in general wares."

The goods the han-seller disposes of are mostly purchased at Sheffield and Birmingham. They purchase the cheapest goods they can obtain. Many of the han-sellers have settled in various parts of England as "swag-shop keepers." There are two or three in London, I am told, who have done so ; one in the Kent-road, a large concern, —the others I am not aware of their locality. Their mode of living while travelling is rather peculiar. Those who have their caravans, sleep in them, some with their wives and families ; they have a man, or more generally a boy, to look after the horse, and other drudgery, and sometimes at a fair, to hawk, or act as a button (a decoy), to purchase the first lot of goods put up. This boy is accommodated with a bed made between the wheels of the cart or wagon, with some old canvas hung round to keep the weather out—not the most comfortable quarters, perhaps, —but, as they say, " it's nothing when you're used to it." The packing up occurs when there's no more chance of effecting sales ; the horse is put to, and the caravan proceeds on the road towards the next town intended to visit. After a sufficient days' travel, the " cheap

John " looks out for a spot to encamp for the night. A clear stream of water, and provender for the horse, are indispensable; or perhaps the han-seller has visited that part before, and is aware of the halting-place. After having released the horse, and secured his fore-feet, so that he cannot stray, the next process is to look for some crack (some dry wood to light a fire); this is the boy's work. He is told not to despoil hedges, or damage fences : "cheap John" doesn't wish to offend the farmers ; and during his temporary sojourn in the green lanes, he frequently has some friendly chat with the yeomen and their servants, sometimes disposes of goods, and often barters for a piece of fat bacon or potatoes. —a stick placed across, upon which is suspended the cookery utensil. When the meal is concluded, the parties retire to bed,—the master within the caravan, and the boy to his chamber between the wheels. Sometimes they breakfast before they proceed on their journey; at other times they travel a few miles first.

Those who have children bring them up in such a manner as may be imagined considering their itinerant life: but there are very few who have families travelling with them; though in most cases a wife; generally the children of the " cheap John " are stationary, either out at nurse or with relatives.

Some of the " cheap Johns " have wagons upon four wheels, others have carts ; but both are fitted up with a wooden roof. The proprietor invariably sleeps within his portable house, both for the protection of his property and also upon the score of economy. The vans with four wheels answer all the purposes of a habitation. The furniture consists of a bed placed upon boxes, containing the stock in trade. The bed extends the whole width of the vehicle, about 6 ft. 6 in., and many generally extend about 5 ft. into the body of the van, and occupies the farthest end of the machine from the door,— which door opens out upon the horse. The four-wheeled vans are 12 ft. long, and the two-wheeled carts 9 ft. During business hours the whole of the articles most likely to be wanted are spread out upon the bed, and the assistant (either the wife or a boy) hands them out as the salesman may require them. The furniture, in addition to the bed, is very scarce ; indeed they are very much averse to carry more than is really necessary. The pail, the horse takes his corn and beans from (I don't know why, but they never use nose-bags,) serves the purpose of a wash-hand basin or a washing-tub. It is generally painted the same colour as the van, with the initials of the proprietor painted upon it, and, when travelling, hangs upon a hook under the machine. They mostly begin with a two-wheeled machine, and if successful a four-wheeler follows. The tables and chairs are the boxes in which the goods are packed. A tea-kettle and saucepan, and as few delf articles as possible, and corner-cupboard, and these comprise the whole of the furniture of the van.

LONDON LABOUR AND THE LONDON POOR.

In the four-wheeled wagons there is always a fire-place similar to those the captains of ships have in their cabins, but in the two-wheeled carts fire-places are dispensed with. These are mostly brass ones, and are kept very bright; for the " cheap Johns" are proud of their van and its contents. They are always gaudily painted, sometimes expensively; indeed they are most expensive articles, and cost from 80*l*. to 120*l*. The principal person for making these machines is a Mr. Davidson of Leeds. The showman's caravans are still more expensive; the last purchased by the late Mr. Wombwell cost more than 300*l*., and is really a curiosity. He termed it, as all showmen do —the living wagon; viz. to live in—it has parlour and kitchen, and is fitted up most handsomely; its exterior presents the appearance of a first-class railway-carriage. The front exterior of the van during the trading operations of the "cheap Johns," is hung round with guns, saws, tea-trays, bridles, whips, centre-bits, and other articles, displayed to the best advantage. The name of the proprietor is always prominently displayed along the whole side of the vehicle, added to which is a signification that he is a wholesale hardwareman, from Sheffield, Yorkshire, or Birmingham, Warwickshire, and sometimes an extra announcement.

"*The original cheap John.*"

I do not know any class of men who are more fond of the good things of this life than " cheap John;" his dinner, during a fair, is generally eaten upon the platform outside his van, where he disposes of his wares, and invariably consists of a joint of baked meat and potatoes—that is where they can get a dinner baked. As little time as possible is occupied in eating, especially if trade is good. At a hill fair (that is where the fair is held upon a hill away from a town), a fire is made behind the cart, the pot is suspended upon three sticks, and dinner prepared in the usual camp fashion. The wife or boy superintends this. Tea and coffee also generally find their way to their table; and if there's no cold meat a plentiful supply of bacon, beef-steaks, eggs, or something in the shape of a relish, seem to be with " cheap John" indispensable. His man or boy (if John is unmarried) appears to be upon an equality with the master in the eating department; he is not allowanced, neither has he to wait until his superior has finished. Get it over as quick as you can seems to be the chief object. Perhaps from the circumstance of their selling guns, and consequently always having such implements in their possession, these men, when they have time on their hands, are fond of the sports of the field, and many a hare finds its way into the camp-kettle of " cheap John." I need not say that they practise this sport with but little respectful feeling towards the Game-laws; but they are careful when indulging in such amusement, and I never heard of one getting into a hobble.

During the winter (since the " cheap John " has been obliged to become a licensed auctioneer), some of them take shops and sell their goods by auction, or get up mock-auctions. I have been told by them that sometimes its a better game than " han-selling."

The commencement of the " cheap John's " season is at Lynn in Norfolk; there is a mart there commencing 14th February, it continues fourteen days. After this, there is Wisbeach, Spalding, Grantham, and other marts in Norfolk and Lincolnshire; which bring them up to Easter. At Easter there are many fairs—Manchester, Knott Mill, Blackburn, Darlington, Newcastle, &c., &c. The " cheap Johns " then disperse themselves through different parts of the country. Hill-fairs are considered the best; that is cattle-fairs, where there are plenty of farmers and country people. Hirings for servants are next to them. It may appear curious, but Sheffield and Birmingham fairs are two of the best for the " cheap John's " business in England. There are two fairs at each place during the year. Sheffield, at Whitsuntide and November; Birmingham, Whitsuntide and September. Nottingham, Derby, Leeds, Newcastle, Bristol, Glasgow—in fact, where the greatest population is, the chances for business are considered the best, and if I may judge from the number of traders in this line, who attend the largest towns, I should say they succeed better than in smaller towns.

If we calculate that there are 100 "cheap Johns" in London and in the country, and they are more or less itinerant, and that they each take 4*l*. per day for nine months in the year, or 24*l*. per week; this amounts to 2,400*l*. per week, or about 90,000*l*. in nine months. Supposing their profits to be 20 per cent., it would leave 18,000*l*. clear income. Say that during the winter there are seventy-five following the business, and that their receipts amount to 15*l*. each per week, this amounts to 3,500*l*. additional; and, at the rate of 20 per cent. profit, comes to 700*l*.,—making throughout the year the profits of the 100 "cheap Johns" 25,000*l*., or 250*l*. a man.

The "cheap Johns" seldom frequent the crowded thoroughfares of London. Their usual pitches in the metropolis are, King's-cross, St. George's-in-the-East, Stepney, round about the London Docks, Paddington, Kennington, and such like places.

THE CRIPPLED STREET-SELLER OF NUT-MEG-GRATERS.

I now give an example of one of the classes *driven* to the streets by utter inability to labour. I have already spoken of the sterling independence of some of these men possessing the strongest claims to our sympathy and charity, and yet preferring to *sell* rather than *beg*. As I said before, many ingrained beggars certainly use the street *trade* as a cloak for alms-seeking, but as certainly many more, with every title to our assistance, use it as a means of redemption from beggary. That the nutmeg-grater seller is a noble example of the latter class, I have not the least doubt. I have made all due inquiries to satisfy myself as to his worthiness, and I feel convinced that when the reader looks at the portrait here given, and observes how utterly helpless the poor fellow is, and then reads the following plain unvarnished tale, he will marvel like me, not only at the fortitude which could sustain him under all his heavy afflictions, but at the resignation (not to say philosophy) with which he bears them every one. His struggles to earn his own living (notwithstanding his physical incapacity even to put the victuals to his mouth after he has earned them), are instances of a nobility of pride that are I believe without a parallel. The poor creature's legs and arms are completely withered; indeed he is scarcely more than head and trunk. His thigh is hardly thicker than a child's wrist. His hands are bent inward from contraction of the sinews, the fingers being curled up and almost as thin as the claws of a bird's foot. He is unable even to stand, and cannot move from place to place but on his knees, which are shod with leather caps, like the heels of a clog, strapped round the joint; the soles of his boots are on the *upper* leathers, that being the part always turned towards the ground while he is crawling along. His countenance is rather handsome than otherwise; the intelligence indicated by his ample forehead is fully borne out by the testimony as to his sagacity in his business, and the mild expression of his eye by the statements as to his feeling for all others in affliction.

"I sell nutmeg-graters and funnels," said the cripple to me; "I sell them at 1d. and 1½d. a piece. I get mine of the man in whose house I live. He is a tinman, and makes for the street-trade and shops and all. I pay 7d. a dozen for them, and I get 12d. or 18d. a dozen, if I can when I sell them, but I mostly get only a penny a piece—it's quite a chance if I have a customer at 1½d. Some days I sell only three—some days not one—though I'm out from ten o'clock till six. The most I ever took was 3s. 6d. in a day. Some weeks I hardly clear my expenses—and they're between 7s. and 8s. a week; for not being able to dress and ondress myself, I'm obligated to pay some one to do it for me—I think I don't clear more than 7s. a week take one week with another. When I don't make that much, I go without—sometimes friends who are kind to me give me a trifle, or else I should starve. As near as I can judge, I *take* about 15s. a week, and out of that I clear about 6s. or 7s. I pay for my meals as I have them—3d. or 4d. a meal. I pay every night for my lodging as I go in, if I can; but if not my landlady lets it run a night or two. I give her 1s. a week for my washing and looking after me, and 1s. 6d. for my lodging. When I do very well I have three meals a day, but it's oftener only two—breakfast and supper—unless of Sunday. On a wet day when I can't get out, I often go without food. I may have a bit of bread and butter give me, but that's all—then I lie a-bed.

I feel miserable enough when I see the rain come down of a week day, I can tell you. Ah, it *is* very miserable indeed lying in bed all day, and in a lonely room, without perhaps a person to come near one—helpless as I am—and hear the rain beat against the windows, and all that without nothing to put in your lips. I've done *that* over and over again where I lived before; but where I am now I'm more comfortable like. My breakfast is mostly bread and butter and tea; and my supper, bread and butter and tea with a bit of fish, or a small bit of meat. What my landlord and landlady has I share with them. I never break my fast from the time I go out in the morning till I come home—unless it is a halfpenny orange I buy in the street; I do that when I feel faint. I have only been selling in the streets since this last winter. I was in the workhouse with a fever all the summer. I was destitute afterwards, and obliged to begin selling in the streets. The Guardians gave me 5s. to get stock. I had always dealt in tin ware, so I knew where to go to buy my things. It's very hard work indeed is street-selling for such as me. I can't walk no distance. I suffer a great deal of pains in my back and knees. Sometimes I go in a barrow, when I'm travelling any great way. When I go only a short way I crawl along on my knees and toes. The most I've ever crawled is two miles. When I get home afterwards, I'm in great pain. My knees swell dreadfully, and they're all covered with blisters, and my toes ache awful. I've corns all on top of them.

"Often after I've been walking, my limbs and back ache so badly that I can get no sleep. Across my lines it feels as if I'd got some great weight, and my knees are in a heat, and throb, and feel as if a knife was running into them. When I go up-stairs I have to crawl upon the back of my hands and my knees. I can't lift nothing to my mouth. The sinews of my hands is all contracted. I am obliged to have things held to my lips for me to drink, like a child. I *can* use a knife and fork by leaning my arm on the table and then stooping my head to it. I can't wash nor ondress myself. Sometimes I think of my helplessness a great deal. The thoughts of it used to throw me into fits at one time—very bad. It's the Almighty's will that I am so, and I must abide by it. People says, as they passes me in the streets, 'Poor fellow, it's a shocking thing;' but very seldom they does any more than pity me; some lays out a halfpenny or a penny with me, but the most of 'em goes on about their business. Persons looks at me a good bit when I go into a strange place. I *do* feel it very much, that I haven't the power to get my living or to do a thing for myself, but I never begged for nothing. I'd sooner starve than I'd do that. I never thought that people whom God had given the power to help theirselves ought to help me. I *have* thought that I'm as I am—obliged to go on my hands and knees, from no fault of my own. Often I've done that, and I've over and over again laid in

THE STREET-SELLER OF NUTMEG-GRATERS.

[*From a Daguerreotype by* BEARD.]

bed and wondered why the Almighty should send me into the world in such a state; often I've done that on a wet day, with nothing to eat, and no friend to come a-nigh me. When I've gone along the streets, too, and been in pain, I've thought, as I've seen the people pass straight up, with all the use of their limbs, and some of them the biggest blackguards, cussing and swearing, I've thought, Why should I be deprived of the use of mine? and I've felt angry like, and perhaps at that moment I couldn't bring my mind to believe the Almighty was so good and merciful as I'd heard say; but then in a minute or two afterwards I've prayed to Him to make me better and happier in the next world. I've always been led to think He's afflicted me as He has for some wise purpose or another that I can't see. I think as mine is so hard a life in this world, I shall be better off in the next. Often when I couldn't afford to pay a boy, I've not had my boots off for four or five nights and days, nor my clothes neither. Give me the world I couldn't take them off myself, and then my feet has swollen to that degree that I've been nearly mad with pain, and I've been shivering and faint, but still I was obliged to go out with my things; if I hadn't I should have starved. Such as I am can't afford to be ill—it's only rich folks as can lay up, not we; for us to take to our beds is to go without food altogether. When I was without never a boy, I used to tie the wet towel round the back of one of the chairs, and wash myself by rubbing my face up against it. I've been two days without a bit of anything passing between my lips. I couldn't go and beg for victuals—I'd rather go without. Then I used to feel faint, and my head used to ache dreadful. I used then to drink a plenty of water. The women sex is mostly more kinder to me than the men. Some of the men fancies, as I goes along, that I can walk. They often says to me, 'Why, the sole of your boot is as muddy as mine;' and one on 'em is, because I always rests myself on that foot—the other sole, you see, is as clean as when it was first made. The women never seem frightened on me. My trade is to sell brooms and brushes, and all kinds of cutlery and tin-ware. I learnt it myself. I never was brought up to nothing, because I couldn't use my hands. Mother was a cook in a nobleman's family when I were born. They say as I was a love-child. I was not brought up by mother, but by one of her fellow-servants. Mother's intellects was so weak, that she couldn't have me with her. She used to fret a great deal about me, so her fellow-servant took me when she got married. After I were born, mother married a farmer in middling circumstances. They tell me as my mother was frightened afore I was born. I never knew my father. He went over to Buonos Ayres, and kept an hotel there—I've heard mother say as much. No mother couldn't love a child more than mine did me, but her feelings was such she couldn't bear to see me. I never

went to mother's to live, but was brought up by the fellow-servant as I've told you of. Mother allowed her 30l. a-year. I was with her till two years back. She was always very kind to me—treated me like one of her own. Mother used to come and see me about once a-year—sometimes not so often: she was very kind to me then. Oh, yes; I used to like to see her very much. Whatever I wished for she'd let me have; if I wrote to her, she always sent me what I wanted. I was very comfortably then. Mother died four years ago; and when I lost her I fell into a fit—I was told of it all of a sudden. She and the party as I was brought up with was the only friends as I had in the world—the only persons as cared anything about a creature like me. I was in a fit for hours, and when I came to, I thought what would become of me: I knew I could do nothing for myself, and the only friend as I had as could keep me was gone. The person as brought me up was very good, and said, while she'd got a home I should never want; but, two years after mother's death, she was seized with the cholera, and then I hadn't a friend left in the world. When she died I felt ready to kill myself; I was all alone then, and what could I do — cripple as I was? She thought her sons and daughters as I'd been brought up with—like brothers and sisters—would look after me; but it was not in their power — they was only hard-working people. My mother used to allow so much a year for my schooling, and I can read and write pretty well." (He wrote his name in my presence kneeling at the table; holding the pen almost as one might fancy a bird would, and placing the paper sideways instead of straight before him.) "While mother was alive, I was always foraging about to learn something unbeknown to her. I wanted to do so, in case mother should leave me without the means of getting a living. I used to buy old bedsteads, and take them to a man, and get him to repair them, and then I'd put the sacking on myself; I can hold a hammer somehow in my right hand. I used to polish them on my knees. I made a bench to my height out of two old chairs. I used to know what I should get for the bedsteads, and so could tell what I could afford to give the man to do up the parts as I couldn't manage. It was so I got to learn something like a business for myself. When the person died as had brought me up, I could do a little; I had then got the means. Before her death I had opened a kind of shop for things in the general line; I sold tin-ware, and brass-work, and candlesticks, and fire-irons, and all old furniture, and gown-prints as well. I went into the tally business, and that ruined me altogether. I couldn't get my money in; there's a good deal owing to me now. Me and a boy used to manage the whole. I used to make all my account-books and everything. My lodgers didn't pay me my rent, so I had to move from the house, and live on what stock I had. In my new lodging

I went on as well as I could for a little while; but about eighteen months ago I could hold on no longer. Then I borrowed a little, and went hawking tin-ware and brushes in the country. I sold baking-dishes, Dutch ovens, roasting-jacks, skewers and gridirons, teapots, and sauce-pans, and combs. I used to exchange some-times for old clothes. I had a barrow and a boy with me; I used to keep him, and give him 1s. a week. I managed to get just a living that way. When the winter came on I gave it up; it was too cold. After that I was took bad with a fever; my stock had been all gone a little while before, and the boy had left because I couldn't keep him, and I had to do all for myself. All my friends was dead, and I had no one to help me, so I was obligated to lay about all night in my things, for I couldn't get them off alone; and that and want of food brought on a fever. Then I was took into the workhouse, and there I stopped all the summer, as I told you. I can't say they treated me bad, but they certainly didn't use me well. If I could have worked after I got better, I could have had tea; but 'cause I couldn't do nothing, they gave me that beastly gruel morning and night. I had meat three times a week. They would have kept me there till now, but I would die in the streets rather than be a pauper. So I told them, if they would give me the means of getting a stock, I would try and get a living for myself. After refusing many times to let me have 10s., they agreed to give me 5s. Then I came out, but I had no home, and so I crawled about till I met with the people where I am now, and they let me sit up there till I got a room of my own. Then some of my friends collected for me about 15s. altogether, and I did pretty well for a little while. I went to live close by the Blackfriars-road, but the people where I lodged treated me very bad. There was a number of girls of the town in the same street, but they was too fond of their selves and their drink to give nothing. They used to buy things of me and never pay me. They never made game of me, nor played me any tricks, and if they saw the boys doing it they would protect me. They never offered to give me no victuals; indeed, I shouldn't have liked to have eaten the food they got. After that I couldn't pay my lodgings, and the parties where I lodged turned me out, and I had to crawl about the streets for four days and nights. This was only a month back. I was fit to die with pain all that time. If I could get a penny I used to go into a coffee-shop for half-a-pint of coffee, and sit there till they drove me out, and then I'd crawl about till it was time for me to go out selling. Oh! dreadful, dreadful, it was to be all them hours—day and night—on my knees. I couldn't get along at all, I was forced to sit down every minute, and then I used to fall asleep with my things in my hand, and be woke up by the police to be pushed about and druv on by them. It seemed like as if I was walking on the bare bones of my knees. The pain in them was like the cramp,

only much worse. At last I could bear it no longer, so I went afore Mr. Secker, the magis-trate, at Union Hall, and told him I was destitute, and that the parties where I had been living kept my bed and the few things I had, for 2s. 6d. rent, that I owed them. He said he couldn't believe that anybody would force me to crawl about the streets, for four days and nights, cripple as I was, for such a sum. One of the officers told him I was a honest and striving man, and the magistrate sent the officer, with the money, to get my things, but the landlady wouldn't give them till the officer compelled her, and then she chucked my bed out into the middle of the street. A neighbour took it in for me and took care of it till I found out the tinman who had before let me sit up in his house. I should have gone to him at first, but he lived farther than I could walk. I am stopping with him now, and he is very kind to me. I have still some rela-tions living, and they are well to do, but, being a cripple, they despise me. My aunt, my mother's sister, is married to a builder, in Petersham, near Richmond, and they are rich people—having some houses of their own besides a good business. I have got a boy to wheel me down on a barrow to them, and asked assistance of them, but they will have nothing to do with me. They won't look at me for my affliction. Six months ago they gave me half-a-crown. I had no lodgings nor victuals then; and that I shouldn't have had from them had I not said I was starving and must go to the parish. This winter I went to them, and they shut the door in my face. After leaving my aunt's, I went down to Ham Common, where my father-in-law lives, and there his daughter's husband sent for a policeman to drive me away from the place. I told the husband I had no money nor food; but he advised me to go to begging, and said I shouldn't have a penny of them. My father-in-law was ill up-stairs at the time, but I don't think he would have treated me a bit better—and all this they do because the Almighty has made me a cripple. I can, indeed, solemnly say, that there is nothing else against me, and that I strive hard and crawl about till my limbs ache enough to drive me mad, to get an honest livelihood. With a couple of pounds I could, I think, manage to shift very well for myself. I'd get a stock, and go into the country with a barrow, and buy old metal, and exchange tin ware for old clothes, and, with that, I'm almost sure I could get a decent living. I'm accounted a very good dealer."

In answer to my inquiries concerning the character of this man, I received the following written communication:

"I have known C—— A—— twelve years; the last six years he has dealt with me for tinware. I have found him honest in all his dealings with me, sober and industrious.

"C—— H——, Tinman."

From the writer of the above testimonial I

received the following account of the poor cripple:—

"He is a man of generous a disposition, and very sensitive for the afflictions of others. One day while passing down the Borough he saw a man afflicted with St. Vitus's dance shaking from head to foot, and leaning on the arm of a woman who appeared to be his wife." The cripple told my informant that he should never forget what he felt when he beheld that poor man. "I thought," he said, "what a blessing it is I am not like him." Nor is the cripple, I am told, less independent than he is generous. In all his sufferings and privations he never pleads poverty to others; but bears up under the trials of life with the greatest patience and fortitude. When in better circumstances he was more independent than at present, having since, through illness and poverty, been much humbled.

"His privations have been great," adds my informant. "Only two months back, being in a state of utter destitution and quite worn out with fatigue, he called at the house of a person (where my informant occupied a room) about ten o'clock at night, and begged them to let him rest himself for a short while, but the inhuman landlady and her son laid hold of the wretched man, the one taking him by the arms and the other by the legs, and literally hurled him into the street. The next morning," my informant continued, "I saw the poor creature leaning against a lamp-post, shivering with the cold, and my heart bled for him; and since that he has been living with me."

OF THE SWAG-SHOPS OF THE METROPOLIS.

By those who are not connected with the street trade, the proprietors of the swag-shops are often called "warehousemen" or "general dealers," and even "slaughterers." These descriptions apply but partially. "Warehousemen" or "general dealers" are vague terms, which I need not further notice. The wretchedly underpaid and over-worked shoe-makers, cabinet-makers and others call these places "slaughter-houses," when the establishment is in the hands of tradesmen who buy their goods of poor workmen without having given orders for them. On Saturday afternoons pale-looking men may be seen carrying a few chairs, or bending under the weight of a cheffonier or a chest of drawers, in Tottenham-court Road, and thoroughfares of a similar character in all parts. These are "small masters," who make or (as one man said to me, "No, sir, I don't make these drawers, I put them together, it can't be called making; it's not workmanship") who "put together" in the hastiest manner, and in any way not positively offensive to the eye, articles of household furniture. The "slaughterers" who supply all the goods required for the furniture of a house, buy at "starvation prices" (the common term), the artificer being often kept waiting for hours, and treated with every indignity. One East-end "slaughterer" (as I ascertained in a former inquiry) used habitually to tell that he prayed for wet Saturday afternoons, because it put 20l. extra into his pocket! This was owing to the damage sustained in the appearance of any painted, varnished, or polished article, by exposure to the weather; or if it had been protected from the weather, by the unwillingness of the small master to carry it to another slaughter-house in the rain. Under such circumstances—and under most of the circumstances of this unhappy trade—the poor workman is at the mercy of the slaughterer.

I describe this matter more fully than I might have deemed necessary, had I not found that both the "small masters" spoken of—for I called upon these again—and the street-sellers, very frequently confounded the "swag-shop" and the "slaughter-house." The distinction I hold to be this:—The slaughterer buys as a rule, with hardly an exception, the furniture, or whatever it may be, made for the express purpose of being offered to him on speculation of sale. The swag shop-keeper *orders* his goods as a rule, and buys, as an exception, in the manner in which the slaughterer buys ordinarily. The slaughterer sells by retail; the swag-shop keeper only by wholesale.

Most of the articles, of the class of which I now treat, are "Brummagem made." An experienced tradesman said to me: "All these low-priced metal things, fancy goods and all, which you see about, are made in Birmingham; in nineteen cases out of twenty at the least. They may be marked London, or Sheffield, or Paris, or any place—you can have them marked North Pole if you will—but they're genuine Birmingham. The carriage is lower from Birmingham than from Sheffield—that's one thing."

The majority of the swag-shop proprietors are Jews. The wares which they supply to the cheap shops, the cheap John's, and the street-sellers, in town and country, consist of every variety of article, apart from what is eatable, drinkable, or wearable, in which the trade class I have specified can deal. As regards what is wearable, indeed, such things as braces, garters, &c., form a portion of the stock of the swag-shop.

In one street (a thoroughfare at the east-end of London) are twenty-three of these establishments. In the windows there is little attempt at display; the design aimed at seems to be rather to *crowd* the window—as if to show the amplitude of the stores within, "the wonderful resources of this most extensive and universal establishment"—than to tempt purchasers by exhibiting tastefully what may have been tastefully executed by the artificer, or what it is desired should be held to be so executed. In one of these windows the daylight is almost precluded from the interior by what may be called a perfect wall of "pots." A street-seller who accompanied me called them merely "pots" (the trade term), but they were all pot ornaments. Among them were great store of shepherdesses, of greyhounds of a gamboge colour. of what I heard called "figures" (allegorical nymphs with and without birds or wreaths in their hands), very tall-looking Shaksperes (I did not see one of these windows without its Shakspere, a sitting figure), and some "pots" which seem to be either shepherds or musicians; from what I could learn, at the pleasure of the seller, the buyer, or the inquirer. The shepherd, or musician is usually seated under a tree; he wears a light blue coat, and yellow breeches, and his limbs, more than his body, are remarkable for their bulk; to call them merely fat does not sufficiently express their character, and in some "pots," they are as short and stumpy as they are bulky. On my asking if the dogs were intended for Italian greyhounds, I was told, "No, they are German." I alluded however to the species of the animal represented; my informant to the place of manufacture, for the pots were chiefly German. A number of mugs however, with the Crystal Palace very well depicted upon them, were unmistakably English. In another window of the same establishment was a conglomeration of pincushions, shaving-brushes, letter-stamps (all in bone), cribbage-boards and boxes (including a pack of cards), necklaces, and strings of beads.

The window of a neighbouring swag-shop presented, in the like crowding, and in greater confusion, an array of brooches (some in coloured glass to imitate rubies, topazes, &c., some containing portraits, deeply coloured, in purple attire, and red cheeks, and some being very large cameos), time-pieces (with and without glasses), French toys with moveable figures, telescopes, American clocks, musical boxes, shirt-studs, backgammon-boards, tea-trays (one with a nondescript bird of most gorgeous green plumage forming a sort of centrepiece), razor-strops, writing-desks, sailors' knives, hair-brushes, and tobacco-boxes.

Another window presented even a more "miscellaneous assortment;" dirks (apparently not very formidable weapons), a mess of steel pens, in brown-paper packages and cases, and of black-lead pencils, pipe-heads, cigar-cases, snuff-boxes, razors, shaving-brushes, letter-stamps, metal tea-pots, metal tea-spoons, glass globes with artificial flowers and leaves within the glass (an improvement one man thought on the old ornament of a reel in a bottle), Peel medals, Exhibition medals, roulette-boxes, scent bottles, quill pens with artificial flowers in the feathery part, fans, side-combs, glass pen-holders, and pot figures (caricatures) of Louis Philippe, carrying a very red umbrella, Marshal Haynau, with some instrument of torture in his hand, while over all boomed a huge English seaman, in yellow waistcoat and with a brick-coloured face.

Sometimes the furniture of a swag-shop window is less plentiful, but quite as heterogenous. In one were only American clocks, French toys (large), opera-glasses, knives and forks, and powder-flasks.

In some windows the predominant character is jewellery. Ear-drops (generally gilt), rings of all kinds, brooches of every size and shade of coloured glass, shawl-pins, shirt-studs, necklaces, bead purses, small paintings of the Crystal-palace, in "burnished 'gold' frames," watch-guards, watch-seals (each with three impressions or mottoes), watch-chains and keys, "silver" tooth-picks, medals, and snuff-boxes. It might be expected that the jewellery shops would present the most imposing display of any; they are, on the contrary, among the dingiest, as if it were not worth the trouble to put clean things in the window, but merely what sufficed to characterise the nature of the trade carried on.

Of the twenty-three swag-shops in question, five were confined to the trade in all the branches of stationery. Of these I saw one, the large window of which was perfectly packed from bottom to top with note-paper, account and copy-books, steel-pens, pencils, sealing-wax, enamelled wafers (in boxes), ink-stands, &c.

Of the other shops, two had cases of watches, with no attempt at display, or even arrangement. "Poor things," I was told by a person familiar with the trade in them, "fit only to offer to countrymen when they've been drinking at a fair, and think themselves clever."

I have so far described the exterior of these street-dealers' bazaars, the swag-shops, in what may be called their head-quarters. Upon entering some of these places of business, spacious rooms are seen to extend behind the shop or warehouse which opens to the street. Some are almost blocked up with what appears a litter of packing-cases, packages, and bales—but which are no doubt ordered systematically enough—while the shelves are crammed with goods in brown paper, or in cases or boxes. This uniformity of package, so to speak, has the effect of destroying the true character of these swag store-rooms; for they present the appearance of only three or four different kinds of merchandise being deposited on a range of shelves, when, perhaps, there are a hundred. In some of these swag-shops it appears certain, both from what fell under my own observation, and from what I learned through my inquiries of persons long familiar with such places, that the "litter" I have spoken of is disposed so as to present the appearance of an affluence of goods without the reality of possession.

In no warehouses (properly "swag," or wholesale traders) is there any arranged display of the wares vended. "Ve don't vant people here," one street-seller had often heard a swag-shopkeeper say, "as looks about them, and says, ''Ow purty!—Vot nice things!' Ve vants to sell, and not to show. Ve is all for bisness, and be d——d." All of these places which I saw were dark, more or less so, in the interior, as if a customer's inspection were uncared for.

Some of the swag-shop people present cards, or "circulars with prices," to their street and other customers, calling attention to the variety of their wares. These circulars are not given without inquiry, as if it were felt that one must not be wasted. On one I find the following enumeration:—

Shopkeepers and Dealers supplied with the following Articles:—

CLOCKS—American, French, German, and English eight-day dials.
WATCHES—Gold and Silver.
MUSICAL BOXES—Two, Four, Six, and Eight Airs.
WATCH-GLASSES—Common Flint, Geneva, and Lunettes.
MAIN-SPRINGS—Blue and Straw-colour, English and Geneva.
WATCH MATERIALS—Of every description.
JEWELLERY—A general assortment.
SPECTACLES—Gold, Silver, Steel, Horn, and Metal Frames, Concave, Convex, Coloured, and Smoked Eyes.
TELESCOPES—One, two, and three draws.
MATHEMATICAL INSTRUMENTS.
COMBS—Side, Dressing, Curl, Pocket, Ivory, Small-Tooth, &c.
MUSICAL INSTRUMENTS—Violins, Violincellos, Bows, &c., Flutes, Clarionets, Trombones, Ophioclides, Cornopeans, French-Horns, Post-Horns, Trumpets, and Passes, Violin Tailboards, Pegs, and Bridges.
ACCORDIONS—French and German of every size and style.

It must not be thought that swag-shops are mainly repositories of "fancy" articles, for such is not the case. I have described only the "windows" and outward appearances of these places—the interior being little demonstrative of the business; but the bulkier and more useful articles of swag traffic cannot be exposed in a window. In the miscellaneous (or Birmingham and Sheffield) shops, however, the useful and the "fancy" are mixed together; as is shown by the following extracts from the Circular of one of the principal swag-houses. I give each head, with an occasional statement of prices. The firm describe themselves as "Wholesale, Retail, and Export Furnishing Ironmongers, General Hardwaremen, Manufacturers of Clocks, Watches, and Steel Pens, and Importers of Toys, Beads, and other Foreign Manufactures."

Table Cutlery.

	s.	d.
Common knives and forks, per doz.	2	0
Ivory-handle table knives and fork, per set of fifty-pieces	30	0
Tables, per doz.	15	0
Desserts, per doz.	11	3
Carvers, per pair	4	0

Fire-Irons.

	s.	d.
Strong wrought-iron for kitchens, per set 2s. to	6	0
Ditto for parlours or libraries, bright pans, 4s. 6d. to	7	0

Fenders.

	s.	d.
Kitchen fenders, 3 ft. long, with sliding bar	3	0
Green ditto, brass tops, for bed rooms	1	8

"Britannia Metal Goods" (tea-pots, &c.), "German Silver Goods" (tea-spoons, 1s. to 2s. per dozen, &c.).

Bellows.

	s.	d.
Kitchen, each	10d. to 2	0
Parlour ditto, brass pipes and nails 2s 3d. to	3	0

Japanned goods, brass goods, iron saucepans, oval iron pots, iron tea-kettles, &c., iron stew-pans, &c. The prices here run very systematically:—

	s.	d.
One quart	1	2
Three pints	1	8
Two quarts	2	0
Three quarts	3	0
Four quarts	3	9
Five quarts	4	0

Patent enamelled saucepans, oval tin boilers, tin saucepans, tea-kettles, coffee-pots. In all these useful articles the prices range in the same way as in the iron stew-pans. Copper goods (kettles, coal-scoops, &c.), tin fish-kettles, dish-covers, rosewood workboxes, glass, brushes (tooth, hair, clothes, scrubbing, stove, shoe, japanned hearth, banister, plate, carpet, and dandy), tools, plated goods (warranted silver edges), snuffers, beads, musical instruments (accordions from 1s. to 5s., &c.). Then come dials and clocks, combs, optics, spectacles, eye-glasses, telescopes, opera glasses, each 10d. to 10s., China ornaments, lamps, sundries (these I give verbatim, to show the nature of the trade), crimping and goffering-machines, from 14s., looking-glasses, pictures, &c., beads of every kind, watch-guards, shaving-boxes, guns, pistols, powder-flasks, belts, percussion caps, &c., corkscrews, 6d. to 2s., nut-cracks, 6d. to 1s. 6d., folding measures, each 2s. to 4s., silver spoons, haberdashery, skates per pair 2s. to 10s., carpet bags, each 3s. to 10s., egg-boilers, tapers, flat and box irons, Italian irons and heaters, earthenware jugs, metal covers, tea-pots, plaited straw baskets, sieves, wood pails, camera-obscuras, medals, amulets, perfumery and fancy soaps of all kinds, mathematical instruments, steel pens, silver and German silver patent pencil-cases and leads, snuff-boxes "in great variety," strops, ink, slates, metal eyelet-holes and machines, padlocks, braces, belts, Congreves, lucifers, fuzees, pocket-books, bill-cases, bed-keys, and a great variety of articles too numerous to mention.

Notwithstanding the specific character and arrangement of the "Circulars with prices," it is common enough for the swag-shop proprietors to intimate to any one likely to purchase that those prices are not altogether to be a guidance, as thirty-five per cent. discount is allowed on the amount of a ready-money purchase. One of the largest "swags" made such an allowance to a street-seller last week.

The swag-shops (of which I state the numbers in a parenthesis) are in Houndsditch (their principal locality (23), Minories (4), Whitechapel (2), Ratcliffe-highway (20), Shoreditch (1), Long-lane, Smithfield (4), Fleet-lane (2), Holywell-street, Strand (1), Tothill-street (4), Compton-street, Soho (1), Hatton-garden (2), Clerkenwell (10), Kent-street, Borough (8), New-cut (6), Blackman-street (2), Tooley-street (3), London-road (3), Borough-road (1), Waterloo-road (4)—in all 101; but a person who had been upwards of twenty years a frequenter of these places counted up fifty others, many of them in obscure courts and alleys near Houndsditch, Ratcliffe Highway, &c., &c. These "outsiders" are generally of a smaller class than those I have described; "and I can tell you, sir," the same man said, "some of them—ay, and some of the big ones, too—are real *swag*-shops still,—partly so, that is; you understand me, sir." The word "swag," I should inform my polite readers, means in slang language, "plunder."

It may be safely calculated, then, that there are 150 swag-shops to which the different classes of street-sellers resort for the purchase of stock. Among these establishments are pot swag, stationery swag, haberdashery swag, jewellery swag, and miscellaneous swag—the latter comprise far more than half of the entire number, and constitute the warehouses which are described by their owners as "Birmingham and Sheffield," or "English and Foreign," or "English and German." It is in these last-mentioned "swags" that the class I now treat of—the street-sellers of metal manufactures—find the commodities of their trade. To this, however, there is one exception. Tins for household use are not sold at the general swag-shops; but "fancy tins," such as japanned and embellished trays, are vended there extensively. The street-sellers of this order are supplied at the "tin-shops,"—the number of the wholesale tin-men supplying the street-sellers is about fifty. The principle on which the business is conducted is precisely that of the more general swag-shop; but I shall speak of them when I treat of the street-sellers of tins.

An intelligent man, who had been employed in different capacities in some of the principal swag-shops, told me of one which had been carried on by the same family, from father to son, for more than seventy years. In the largest of the "swags" about 200 "hands" are employed, in the various capacities of salesmen, buyers, clerks, travellers, unpackers, packers, porters, &c., &c. On some mornings twenty-five large packages—some of small articles entirely—are received from the carriers. In one week, when my informant assisted in "making up the books," the receipts were upwards of 3000l. "In my opinion, sir," he said, "and it 's from an insight into the business, Mr. ——'s profit on that 3000l. was not less than thirty-five per cent. ; for he's a great capitalist, and pays for everything down upon the nail ; that 's more than 1000l. profit in a week. Certainly it was an extra week, and there's the 200 hands to pay,—but that wouldn't range higher than 300l., indeed, not so high ; and there 's heavy rent and taxes, and rates, no doubt, and he (the proprietor is a Jew) is a fair man to the trade, and not an uncharitable man—but he will drive a good bargain where it 's possible ; so considering everything, sir, the profits must be very great, and they are mostly made out of poor buyers, who sell it to poor people in the streets, or in small shops. It's a wonderful trade."

From the best information I could obtain I come to the conclusion that, including small and large shops, 3000l. yearly is the average receipt of each—or, as it is most frequently expressed, that sum is "turned over" by the swag-shop keepers yearly. There is great competition in the trade, and much of what is called "cutting," or one tradesman underselling another. The profit consequently varies from twenty to thirty-five and

(rarely) fifty per cent. Sometimes a swag-shop proprietor is "hung-up" with a stock the demand for which has ceased, and he must dispose of it as "a job lot," to make room for other goods, and thus is necessarily "out of pocket." The smaller swag-shops do not "turn over" 500l. a year. The calculation I have given shows an outlay, yearly, of 450,000l. at the swag-shops of London ; "but," said a partner in one of these establishments, "what proportion of the goods find their way into the streets, what to the shops, what to the country, and what for shipping, I cannot form even a guess, for we never ask a customer for what purpose he wants the goods, though sometimes he will say, ' I must have what is best for such or such a trade.' Say half a million turned over in a year, sir, by the warehousemen who sell to the street-people, among others, and you 're within the mark."

I found the street-sellers characterize the "swags" as hard and grinding men, taking every advantage "in the way of trade." There is, too, I was told by a man lately employed in a swag-shop, a constant collision of clamour and bargaining, not to say of wits, between the smarter street-sellers—the pattering class especially—and the swag-men with whom they are familiar.

The points in which the "swag-shops" resemble the "slaughter-houses," are in the traffic in work-boxes, desks, and dressing-cases.

OF THE LIFE OF A CHEAP-JOHN.

THE following narrative, relative to this curious class, who, in many respects, partake of the characteristics which I have pointed out as proper to the mountebank of old, was taken from one of the fraternity. It may be cited as an example of those who are bred to the streets:—"My father and mother," said he, "both followed a travelling occupation, and were engaged in vending different things, from the old brimstone matches up to clothes lines, clothes props, and clothes pegs. They never got beyond these,—the other articles were thread, tapes, nutmeg graters, shoe-ties, stay-laces, and needles. My father, my mother used to tell me, was a great scholard, and had not always been a travelling vagrant. My mother had never known any other life. I, however, did not reap any benefit from my father's scholarship. At a very early age, five or six perhaps, I recollect myself a poor little neglected wretch, sent out each day with a roll of matches, with strict injunctions not to come home without selling them, and to bring home a certain sum of money, upon pain of receiving a sound thrashing, which threat was mostly put into execution whenever I failed to perform the task imposed upon me. My father seldom worked, that is, seldom hawked, but my mother, poor thing, had to travel and work very hard to support four of us—my father, myself, and a sister, who is since dead. I was but little assistance, and sometimes when I did not bring home the sum required, she would make it up, and tell my father I had been a good boy. My father was an inveterate drinker, and a very violent temper. My mother, I am sorry to say, used to drink too, but I believe that ill-usage drove her to it. They led a dreadful life; I scarcely felt any attachment for them; home we had none, one place was as good another to us. I left my parents when scarcely eight years old. I had received a thrashing the day before for being a defaulter in my sale, and I determined the following morning to decamp; and accordingly, with my nine-pennyworth of matches (the quantity generally allotted me), I set out to begin the world upon my own account. Although this occurred 25 years ago, I have never met my parents since. My father, I heard, died a few years after my leaving, but my mother I know not whether she be living or dead. I left my parents at Dover, and journeyed on to London. I knew there were lodging-houses for travellers in every town, some of them I had stopped at with my father and mother. I told the people of these houses that my parents would arrive the following day, and paid my 2d. for the share of a third, fourth, fifth, or even sixth part of a bed, according to the number of children who inhabited the lodging-house upon that particular night. My matches I could always sell if I tried, but I used to play my time away, and many times night has arrived before I thought of effecting sales sufficient to pay my expenses at the beggar's hotel. Broken victuals I got in abundance, indeed more than sufficient for my own consumption. The money I received for the matches, after paying my lodging, and purchasing a pennyworth of brimstone to make more (the wood I begged at the carpenters, I gambled away at cards. Yes, young as I was, I understood Blind Hookey. I invariably lost; of course I was cheated.

"I remained in a lodging house in Mill-lane, Deptford, for two years, discontinued the match-selling, and, having a tidy voice, took to hawking songs through the public-houses. The sailors used to ask me to sing, and there were few days that I did not accumulate 2s. 6d., and from that to 4s., especially when I chose to be industrious; but my love of pitch and toss and blind hookey always kept me poor. I often got into debt with my landlady, and had no difficulty in doing so, for I always felt a pride in paying. From selling the printed songs, I imbibed a wish to learn to read, and, with the assistance of an old soldier, I soon acquired sufficient knowledge to make out the names of each song, and shortly afterwards I could study a song and learn the words without any one helping me. I stopped in Deptford until I was something more than twelve years old. I had then laid the songs aside, and taken to hawking small wares, tapes, thread, &c.; and in the winter season I was a buyer of rabbit and hare skins. I kept at this for about three years, sometimes entirely without a stock. I had run it out, perhaps gambled it away; and at such times I suffered great privations. I never could beg. I have often tried, but never could. I have approached a house with a begging intention, knocked at the door, and when it has been opened I have requested a drink of water. When I was about 16 I joined in partnership with

a man who used to make phosphorus boxes. I sold them for him. A piece of phosphorus was stuck in a tin tube, the match was dipped into the phosphorus, and it would ignite by friction. I was hawking these boxes in Norwich, when the constable considered they were dreadful affairs, and calculated to encourage and assist thieves and burglars. He took me before the magistrate, at the beak's own private house, and he being equally horrified, I was sent to prison for a month. I have often thought since that the proceeding was illegal. What would be said now if a man was to be sent to jail for selling lucifer matches? In Norwich prison I associated with the rest, and if I had been inclined to turn thief I had plenty of opportunities and offers of gratuitous instruction. The separate or silent system was not in vogue then. I worked on the treadmill. Dinner was allowed to be sent in on the Sunday by the prisoner's friends. My dinner was sent in on the first Sunday by the man I sold the boxes for, as it was on the second, third, and fourth; but I had lost it before I received it. I had always gambled it away, for there were plenty of opportunities of doing so in the prisons then. On leaving the jail I received 1s.; with this I purchased some songs and travelled to Yarmouth. I could do best among sailors. After a few weeks I had accumulated about 8s., and with that sum I purchased some hardware at the swag-shop, commenced hawking, and cut the vocal department altogether; still I gambled and kept myself in poverty. In the course of time, however, I had amassed a basket of goods, worth, perhaps, 3l. I gambled and lost them all in one night. I was so downcast and unhappy from this circumstance, that it caused me to reflect seriously, and I made an oath that I never would gamble again. I have kept it, and have reason to bless the day that I made so good a resolution. After losing my basket of goods, the winner gave me articles amounting to a few shillings, and I began the world once more. Shortly afterwards I commenced rag gatherer, and changed my goods for old rags, of course not refusing cash in payment. My next step was to have some bills printed, whereon I requested all thrifty wives to look out their old rags or old metal, or old bones, &c.; stating at the bottom that the bill would be called for, and that a good price in ready money would be given for all useless lumber, &c. Some months at this business realized me a pretty sum of money. I was in possession of nearly 5l. Then I discontinued the rag-gathering; not that the trade was declining, but I did not like it—I was ambitious. I purchased a neat box, and started to sell a little Birmingham jewellery. I was now respectably dressed, was getting a living, and had entirely left off stopping at common lodging-houses; but I confined my visits to small villages—I was afraid of the law; and as I was pursuing my calling near Wakefield, a constable inquired for my hawker's licence. I had none to produce. He took me into custody, and introduced me to a magistrate, who committed me to prison for a month, and took away my box of goods. I endured the month's imprisonment upon the silent system; they cut my hair short; and at the expiration of the term I was thrust out upon the world heart-broken, without a shilling, to beg, to steal, or to starve.

"I proceeded to Leeds, the fair was on at this time. I got engaged to assist a person, from whom I had been accustomed occasionally to purchase goods. He was a 'Cheap-John.' In the course of the day he suggested that I should have a try at the hand-selling. I mounted the platform, and succeeded beyond my own expectations or that of my master. He offered me a regular engagement, which I accepted. At times I would help him sell, and at other times I hawked with his licence. I had regular wages, besides all I could get above a certain price that he placed upon each of the goods. I remained with this person some fifteen months, at the end of which period I commenced for myself, having saved nearly 25l. I began at once the hand-selling, and purchased a hawker's licence, which enabled me to sell without danger. Then I always called at the constable's house, and gave a louder knock at his door than any other person's, proud of my authority, and assured of my safety. At first I borrowed an empty cart, in which I stood and sold my wares. I could chaff as well as the best, and was as good a salesman as most of them. After that I purchased a second-hand cart from a person who had lately started a waggon. I progressed and improved in circumstances, and at last bought a very handsome waggon for myself. I have now a nice caravan, and good stock of goods, worth at least 500l. Money I have but little. I always invest in goods. I am married, and have got a family. I always travel in the summer, but remain at home during the winter. My wife never travels. She remains behind, and manages a little swag-shop, which always turns in at least the family expenses."

THE STREET-SELLERS OF CUTLERY.

THE cutlery sold in the streets of London consists of razors, pen-knives, pocket-knives, table and carving-knives and forks, scissors, shears, nail-filers, and occasionally (if ordered) lancets. The knives are of various kinds—such as sailors' knives (with a hole through the handle), butchers' knives, together with choppers and steels (sold principally at Newgate and Billingsgate Markets, and round about the docks), oyster and fish-knives (sold principally at Billingsgate and Hungerford Markets), bread-knives (hawked at the bakers' shops), ham and beef knives (hawked at the ham and beef shops), cheese-knives with tasters, and ham-triers, shoemakers' knives, and a variety of others. These articles are usually purchased at the "swag-shops," and the prices of them vary from 2½d. to 1s. 1½d. each. They are bought either by the dozen, half-dozen, or singly, according to the extent of the street-seller's stock-money. Hence it would appear that the street-seller of cutlery can begin business with only a few pence; but it is only when the swag-shop keeper

has known the street-seller that he will consent to sell one knife alone "to sell again;" to street-sellers with whom he is unacquainted, he will not vend less than half-a-dozen. Even where the street-seller is known, he has, if "cracked-up," to beg hard, I am told, before he can induce the warehouseman to let him have only one article. "The swag-shops won't be bothered with it," say the men—"what are our troubles to them? if the rain starves us out and makes us eat up all our stock-money, what is it to such folks? They wouldn't let us have even a row of pins without the money for 'em—no, not if we was to drop down dead for want of bread in their shops. They have been deceived by such a many that now they won't listen to none." I subjoin a list of the prices paid and received by the street-sellers of cutlery for the principal articles in which they deal:

	Lowest price paid per half-dozen.	Sold at in streets.	Highest price paid per half-dozen.	Sold at in streets.
	s. d.	s. d.	s. d.	s. d.
Table-knives and forks..	1 3	2 0	5 0	7 6
Ditto, without forks	0 9	1 3	4 0	6 0
Pocket-knives	1 0	1 6	4 0	6 0
Pen-knives	1 9	2 6	2 6	3 9
Razors	1 9	2 6	5 0	7 6
Scissors	0 3½	0 6	1 9	2 6

Their usual rate of profit is 50 per cent., but rather than refuse a ready sale the street cutlery-seller will often take much less. Many of the sellers only pursue the trade for a few weeks in the year. A number of the Irish labourers take to it in the winter-time when they can get no work. Some few of the sellers are countrymen, but these mostly follow the business continuously. "I don't see as there is hardly one upon the list as has ever been a cutler by trade," said one street-seller to me, "and certainly none of the cutlery-sellers have ever belonged to Sheffield—they may say so, but its only a dodge." The cutlery street-sellers are not one-quarter so numerous as they were two years back. "The reason is," I am told, "that things are got so bad a man can't live by the trade—mayhap he has to walk three miles now before he can sell for 1s. a knife that has cost him 8½d., and then mayhap he is faint, and what's 3½d., sir, to keep body and soul together, when a man most likely has had no victuals all the day before." If they had a good bit of stock they might perhaps get a crust, they say. "Things within the last two or three years," to quote the words of one of my informants, "have been getting much worse in the streets; 'specially in the cutlery line. I can't give no account for it, I'm sure, sir; the sellers have not been half as many as they were. What's become of them that's gone, I can't tell; they're in the workhouse, I dare say." But, notwithstanding this decrease in the number of sellers, there is a greater difficulty to vend their goods now than formerly. "It's all owing to the times, that's all I can say. People, shopkeepers, and all says to me, I can't tell why things is so bad, and has been so bad in trade; but so they is. We has to walk farther to sell our goods, and people beat us down so terrible hard, that we can't get a penny out of them when we do sell. Sometimes they offers me 9*d*., yes, and often 6*d*. for an 8½*d*. knife; and often enough 4*d*. for one that stands you in 3¾*d*. —a ¼*d*. profit, think of that, sir. Then they say, 'Well, my man, will you take my money?' and so as to make you do so, they'll flash it before your eyes, as if they knew you was a starving, and would be sure to be took in by the sight of it. Yes, sir, it is a very hard life, and we has to put up with a good deal—a good deal—starvation and hard-dealing, and insults and knockings about, and all. And then you see the swag-shops is almost as hard on us as the buyers. The swag-men will say, if you merely makes a remark, that a knife they've sold you is cracked in the handle, 'Oh, is it; let me see whereabouts;' and when you hands it to 'em to show it 'em, they'll put it back where they took it from, and tell you, 'You're too particular by half, my man. You'd better go and get your goods somewhere else; here take your money, and go on about your business, for we won't sarve you at all.' They'll do just the same with the scissors too, if you complains about their being a bit rusty. 'Go somewhere else,' they'll say, 'We won't sarve you.' Ah, sir, that's what it is to be a poor man; to have your poverty flung in your teeth every minute. People says, 'to be poor and seem poor is the devil;' but to be poor, and be treated like a dog merely because you *are* poor, surely is ten thousand times worse. A sreet-seller now-a-days is looked upon as a 'cadger,' and treated as one. To try to get a living for one's self is to do something shameful in these times."

The man then gave me the following history of himself. He was a kindly-looking and hearty old man. He had on a ragged fustian jacket, over which he wore a black greasy-looking and tattered oilskin coat—the collar of this was torn away, and the green baize lining alone visible. His waistcoat was patched in every direction, while his trousers appeared to be of corduroy; but the grease and mud was so thick upon them, that it was difficult to tell of what material they were made. His shoes—or rather what remained of them—were tied on his feet with pieces of string. His appearance altogether denoted great poverty.

"My father was a farmer, sir. He had two farms, about 800 acres in all. I was one of eleven (ten sons and one daughter). Seven years before my father's death he left his farm, and went to live on his money. He had made a good bit at farming; but when he died it was all gone, and we was left to shift as we could. I had little or no education. My brothers could read and write, but I didn't take to it; I went a bird's-nesting, boy-like, instead, so that what little I did larn I have forgot. I am very sorry for that now. I used to drive the plough, and go a harrowing for father. I was brought up to nothing else. When father died, I thought as I should like to see London. I was a mere lad—about 20—and so I strolled up to town. I had 10*s*.

with me, and that, with a bundle, was all that I possessed in the world. When I got to London I went to lodge at a public-house—the Red Lion—in Great Wild-street; and while I was there I sought about for work, but could not get any; when all was gone, I was turned out into the streets, and walked about for two days and two nights, without a bed, or a bit to eat, unless what I picked out of the gutter, and eat like a dog—orange-peel and old cabbage-stumps, indeed *anything* I could find. When I was very hard put to it, I was coming down Drury-lane, and I looked in, quite casual like, to ask for a job of work at the shop of Mr. Bolton, the needle-maker from Redditch. I told him as how I was nigh starving, and would do anything to get a crust; I didn't mind what I put my hand to. He said he would try me, and gave me two packets of needles to sell—they was the goolden-eyed ones of that time of day—and he said when I had got rid of them I was to come back to him, and I should have two packets more. He told me the price to ask—sixpence a paper—and away I went like a sand-boy, and got rid of the two in an hour and a half. Then I went back, and when I told him what I'd done, he shook hands with me, and said, as he burst out laughing, "Now, you see I've made a man of you." Oh, he was an uncommon nice gentleman! Then he told me to keep the shilling I had taken, and said he would trust me with two more packets. I sold them, and two others besides, that day. Then, he says, 'I shall give you something else,' and he let me have two packets of tailors' needles and half a dozen of tailors' thimbles. He told me how to sell them, and where to go, and on them I did better. I went round to the tailors' shops and sold a good lot, but at last they stopped me, because I was taking the bread out of the mouths of the poor blind needle-sellers what supplies the journeymen tailors at the West-end. Then Mr. Bolton sent me down to one of his relations, a Mr. Crooks, in Fetter Lane, who was a Sheffield man, and sold cutlery to the hawkers; and Mr. Crooks and Mr. Bolton sot me up between them, and so I've followed the line ever since. I dare say I shall continue in it to my dying day. After I got fairly set agoing, I used to make—take good and bad, wet and dry days together—18*s*. a week; three shillings a day was what I calculated on at the least, and to do that I was obligated to take between 2*l*. and 3*l*. a week, or about eight or nine shillings each day. I went on doing this for upwards of thirty year. I have been nearly forty years, altogether, in the streets, selling cutlery. I did very tidy till about 4 years back—I generally made from 18*s*. to 1*l*. a week up to that time. I used to go round the country—to Margate, Brighton, Portsmouth—I mostly travelled by the coast, calling at all the sea-port towns, for I always did best among the sailors. I went away every Spring time, and came to London again at the fall of the year. Sixteen year ago, I married the widow of a printer—a pressman—she had no money, but you see I had no home, and I thought I should be more comfortable, and so

I have been—a great deal more comfortable—and so I should be now, if things hadn't got so bad. Four year ago, as I was a telling you, it was just after the railways had knocked off work, things began to get uncommon bad—before then, I had as good as 30s. or 40s. stock, and when things got slack, it went away, little by little. I couldn't make profit enough to support me and my old woman—she has got the rheumatics and can't earn me a halfpenny or a farden in the world; she hasn't done so for years. When I didn't make enough to live upon, of course I was obligated to break into my stock; so there it kept going shilling by shilling, and sixpence by sixpence, until I had got nothing left to work upon —not a halfpenny. You see, four or five months ago, I was took very bad with the rheumatic fever and gout. I got wet through in the streets, and my clothes dried on me, and the next day I was taken bad with pains in my limbs, and then everything that would fetch me a penny went to the pawn-shop; all my own and my old woman's clothes went to get us food—blankets, sheets and all. I never would go nigh the parish; I couldn't bring myself to have the talk about it. When I got well and out into the streets again, I borrowed 2s. or 3s. of my landlady—I have lived with her these three years—to get my stock again, but you see that got me so few things, that I couldn't fetch myself up. I lost the greater portion of my time in going backards and forrards to the shop to get fresh goods as fast as I sold them, and so what I took wasn't enough to earn the commonest living for me and my missus. Since December we have been nearly starving, and that's as true as you have got the pen in your very hand. Sunday after Sunday we have been without a bit of dinner, and I have laid a-bed all day because we have had no coal, and then been obligated to go out on Monday morning without a bit of victuals between my lips. I've been so faint I couldn't hardly walk. I've picked the crusts off the tables of the tap-rooms where I have been to hawk my goods, and put them in my pocket to eat them on the sly. Wet and dry I'm obligated to be out; let it come down ever so hard I must be in it, with scarcely a bit of shoe, and turned 60 years old, as I am. Look here, sir," he said, holding up his foot; "look at these shoes, the soles is all loose, you see, and let water. On wet days I hawk my goods to respectable shops; tap-rooms is no good, decent people merely get insulted there. But in most of the shops as I goes to people tells me, 'My good man it is as much as we can do to keep ourselves and our family in these cutting times.' Now, just to show you what I done last week. Sunday, I laid a-bed all day and had no dinner. Monday, I went out in the morning without a morsel between my lips, and with only 8½d. for stock-money; with that I bought a knife and sold it for a shilling, and then I got another and another after that, and that was my day's work—three times 3½d. or 10½d. in all, to keep the two of us. Tuesday, I sold a pair of small scissors and two little pearl-handled knives,

at 6d. each article, and cleared 10½d. on the whole, and that is all I did. Wednesday, I sold a razor-strop for 6d., a four-bladed knife for a shilling, and a small hone for 6d.; by these I cleared 10d. altogether. Thursday, I sold a pair of razors for a shilling, clearing by the whole 11½d. Friday, I got rid of a pair of razors for 1s. 9d., and got 9d. clear." I added up the week's profits and found they amounted to 4s. 3½d. "That's about right," said the man, "out of that I shall have to pay 1s. for my week's rent; we've got a kitchen, so that I leave you to judge how we two can live out of what's remaining." I told him it would'nt average quite 6d. a day. "That's about it," he replied, "we have half a loaf of bread a day, and that thank God is only five farthings now. This lasts us the day, with two-penny-worth of bits of meat that my old woman buys at a ham-shop, where they pare the hams and puts the parings by on plates to sell to poor people; and when she can't get that, she buys half a sheep's head, one that's three or four days old, for then they sells 'em to the poor for 1¼d. the half; and these with ¾d. worth of tea, and ½d. worth of sugar, ¼d. for a candle, 1d. of coal—that's seven pounds—and ¾d. worth of coke—that's half a peck—makes up all we gets." These items amount to 6½d. in all. "That's how we do when we can't get it, and when we can't, why we lays in bed and goes without altogether."

OF THE BLIND STREET-SELLERS OF TAILORS' NEEDLES, ETC.

IT is customary with many trades, for the journeymen to buy such articles as they require in their business of those members of their craft who have become incapacitated for work, either by old age, or by some affliction. The tailors—the shoemakers—the carpenters—and many others do this. These sellers are, perhaps, the most exemplary instances of men *driven* to the streets, or to hawking for a means of living; and they, one and all, are distinguished by that horror of the workhouse which I have before spoken of as constituting a peculiar feature in the operative's character. At present I purpose treating of the street-sellers of needles and "trimmings" to the tailors.

There are, I am informed, two dozen "brokendown" journeymen tailors pursuing this avocation in and around London. "There may be more," said one who had lost his sight stitching, "but I get my information from the needle warehouse, where we all buy our goods; and the lady there told me she knew as many as twenty-four hawkers who were once tailors. These are all either decayed journeymen, or their widows. Some are vicapicated by age, being between sixty and seventy years old; the greater part of the aged journeymen, however, are inmates of the tailors' almshouses. I am not aware," said my informant, "of there being more than one very old man hawking needles to the tailors, though there may be many that I know nothing about. The one I am acquainted with is close upon eighty, and he is a very respectable man, much esteemed in St.

James's and St. George's; he sells needles, and
'London Labour and the London Poor' to the journeymen: he is very feeble indeed, and can scarcely
get along." Of the two dozen needle-sellers above
mentioned, there are only six who confine their
"rounds" solely to the metropolis. Out of these
six my informant knew two who were blind
beside himself (one of these sells to the journeymen in the city). There are other blind tailors
who were formerly hawkers of needles, but being
unable to realize a subsistence thereby, have been
obliged to become inmates of the workhouses; others
have recently gained admission into the almshouses.
Last February, I am assured, there were two blind
needle-sellers, and two decrepit, in St. James's
workhouse. There are, moreover, two widows selling tailors' needles in London. One of these, I am
told, is wretchedly poor, being "eat up with the
rheumatics, and scarcely able to move"—she is
the relict of a blind journeyman, and well known
in St. James's. The other widow is now in St.
Pancras Workhouse, having been unable, to use
the words of my informant, "to get anything to
keep life and soul together at the needle trade;"
she, too, I am told, is well known to the journeymen. The tailors' needle-sellers confining themselves more particularly to London consist of, at
present, one old man, three blind, one paralyzed,
and one widow; besides these, there are now in
the alms-houses, two decrepit and one paralyzed;
and one widow in the workhouse, all of whom,
till recently, were needle-sellers, and originally
connected with the trade.

"That is all that I believe are now in London," said one to me, "I should, I think, know
if there were more; for it is not from one place
we get our articles, but many; and there I hear
that six is about the number of tailors' hawkers in
town; the rest of the two dozen hawkers that I
spoke of go a little way out into the suburbs.
The six, however, stick to London altogether."
The needle-sellers who go into the country, I am
told, travel as far as Reading, westward, and to
Gravesend, in the opposite direction, or Brentwood, in Essex, and they will keep going
back'ards and for'ards to the metropolis immediately their stock is exhausted. These persons
sell not only tailors' needles, but women's needles
as well, and staylaces and cottons, and small ware
in general, which they get from Shepherd's, in
Compton Street; they have all been tailors, and
are incapacitated from labour, either by old age or
some affliction. There was one widow of a tailor
among the number, but it is believed she is now
either too old to continue her journeys, or else
that she is deceased. The town-sellers confine their peregrinations mostly to the parishes
of St. James's and St. George's (my informant
was not aware that any went even into Marylebone). One travels the City, while the other
five keep to the West End; they all sell
thimbles, needles, inch-measures, bodkins, inch
sticks, scissars ("when they can get them," I was
told, "and that 's very seldom"), and bees'-wax,
basting cotton, and, many of them, publications.
The publications vended by these men are princi-

pally the cheap periodicals of the day, and two of
these street-sellers, I am informed, do much better
with the sale of publications than by the "trimmings." "*They* get money, sir," said one man to
me, "while *we* are starving. They have their set
customers and have only to go round and leave
the paper, and then to get their money on the
Monday morning."

The tailors' hawkers buy their trimmings mostly
at the retail shops. They have not stock-money
sufficient, I am assured, to purchase at the wholesale houses, for "such a thing as a paper of
needles large tradesmen don't care about of
selling us poor men." They tell me that if they
could buy wholesale they could get their goods one-
fourth cheaper, and to be "obligated" to purchase
retail is a great drawback on their profits. They
call at the principal tailors' workshops, and solicit
custom of the journeymen; they are almost all
known to the trade, both masters and men, and,
having no other means of living, they are allowed
to enter the masters' shops, though some of the
masters, such as Allen, in Bond-street; Curlewis,
Jarvis, and Jones, in Conduit-street, and others,
refuse the poor fellows even this small privilege.
The journeymen treat them very kindly, the
needle-sellers tell me, and generally give them
part of the provisions they have brought with
them to the shop. If it was not for this the
needle-sellers, I am assured, could hardly live at
all. "There's that boy there," said a blind
tailor, speaking of the youth who had led him
to my house, and who sat on the stool fast asleep
by the fire,—"I 'm sure he must have starved
this winter if it hadn't been for the goodness of
the men to us, for it 's little that me and his
mother has to give him; she 's gone almost as
blind as myself working at the 'sank work'
(making up soldiers' clothing). Oh, ours is a
miserable life, sir!—worn out—blind with over
work, and scarcely a hole to put one's head in, or a
bit to put in one's mouth. God Almighty knows
that's the bare truth, sir." Sometimes the hawkers
go on their rounds and take only 2*d.*, but that is
not often; sometimes they take 5*s.* in a day, and
"that is the greatest sum," said my informant,
"I ever took; what others might do I can't say,
but that I 'm confident is about the highest
takings." In the summer three months the average
takings rise to 4*s.* per day; but in the winter
they fall to 1*s.*, or at the outside 1*s.* 6*d.* The
business lasts only for three hours and a half each
day, that is from eight till half-past eleven in
the morning; after that no good is to be
done. Then the needle-sellers, I am told, go
home, and the reason of this is, I am told, if
they appear in the public streets selling or so-
liciting alms, the blind are exempted from becoming recipients of the benefits of many of the
charitable institutions. The blind man whom I saw,
told me that after he had done work and returned
home, he occupied himself with pressing the
seams of the soldiers' clothes when his "missus"
had sewed them. The tailors' needle-sellers are
all married, and one of the wives has a mangle;
and "perhaps," said my informant, "the blind

husband turns the mangle when he goes home, but I can't say." Another wife is a bookfolder, but she has no work. The needles they usually sell five a penny to the journeymen, but the most of the journeymen will take but four; they say "we can't get a living at all if we sell the needles cheaper. The journeymen are mostly very considerate—very indeed; much more than the masters; for the masters won't hardly look at us. I don't know that a master ever gave me a farden—and yet there's some of them very soothing and kind in speaking." The profit in the needles, I am told, is rather more than 100 per cent.; "but," say the sellers, "only think, sir, we must get rid of 150 needles even to take 3s. The most we ever sell in one shop is 6d. worth—and the usual amount is 2d. worth. You can easy tell how many shops we must travel round to, in order to get rid of 3s. worth." Take one shop with another, the good with the bad, they tell me they make about 1d. profit from each they visit. The profit on the rest of the articles they vend is about 20 per cent., and they calculate that all the year round, summer and winter, they may be said to take 2s. a day, or 12s. a week; out of which they clear from 5s. to 5s. 6d. They sell far more needles than anything else. Some of the blind needle-sellers make their own bees'-wax into "shapes," (pennyworths) themselves, melting into and pouring into small moulds.

The blind needle-seller whom I saw was a respectable-looking man, with the same delicacy of hand as is peculiar to tailors, and which forms so marked a contrast to the horny palms of other workmen. He was tall and thin, and had that upward look remarkable in all blind men. His eyes gave no signs of blindness (the pupils being full and black), except that they appeared to be directed to no one object, and though fixed, were so without the least expression of observation. His long black surtout, though faded in colour, was far from ragged, having been patched and stitched in many places, while his cloth waistcoat and trowsers were clean and neat—very different from the garments of street-sellers in general. In his hand he carried his stick, which, as he sat, he seemed afraid to part with, for he held it fast between his knees. He came to me accompanied by his son, a good-looking rough-headed lad, habited in a washed-out-blue French kind of pinafore, and whose duty it was to lead his blind father about on his rounds. Though the boy was decently clad, still his clothes, like those of his father, bore many traces of that respectable kind of poverty which seeks by continuous mending to hide its rags from the world. The face of the father, too, was pinched, while there was a plaintiveness about his voice that told of a wretched spirit-broken and afflicted man. Altogether he was one of the better kind of handicraftsmen—one of those fine specimens of the operatives of this country—independent even in their helplessness, scorning to beg, and proud to be able to give some little equivalent for the money bestowed on them. I have already given accounts of the "beaten-out" mechanic from those

who certainly cannot be accused of an excess of sympathy for the poor—namely the Poor Law Commissioners and masters of workhouses; and I can only add, that all my experience goes fully to bear out the justice of these statements. As I said before, the class who are *driven* to the streets to which the beaten-out or incapacitated operative belongs, is, of all others, the most deserving of our sympathy; and the following biography of one of this order is given to teach us to look with a kindly eye upon the many who are forced to become street-sellers as the sole means of saving themselves from the degradation of pauperism or beggary.

"I am 45 years of age next June," said the blind tailor. "It is upwards of 30 years since I first went to work at the tailoring trade in London. I learnt my business under one of the old hands at Mr. Cook's, in Poland-street, and after that went to work at Guthrie's, in Bond-street. I belonged to the Society held at the Old White Hart. I continued working for the honourable trade and belonging to Society for about 15 years. My weekly earnings then averaged 1l. 16s. a week while I was at work, and for several years I was seldom out of work, for when I got into a shop it was a long time before I got out again. I was not married then. I lived in a first floor back room, well-furnished, and could do very comfortably indeed. I saved often my 15s. or 16s. in a week, and was worth a good bit of money up to the time of my first illness. At one period I had nearly 50l. by me, and had it not been for "vacations" and "slack seasons" I should have put by more; but you see to be out of work even a few weeks makes a large hole in a journeyman's savings. All this time I subscribed regularly to Society, and knew that if I got superannuated I should be comfortably maintained by the trade. I felt quite happy with the consciousness of being provided for in my old age or affliction then, and if it had not been for that perhaps I might have saved more even than I did. I went on in this way, as I said before, for 15 years, and no one could have been happier than I was—not a working man in all England couldn't. I had my silver watch and chain. I could lay out my trifle every week in a few books, and used to have a trip now and then up and down the river, just to blow the London smoke off, you know. About 15 years ago my eyes began to fail me without any pain at all; they got to have as it were a thick mist, like smoke, before them. I couldn't see anything clear. Working by gas-light at first weakened and at last destroyed the nerve altogether. I'm now in total darkness. I can only tell when the gas is lighted by the heat of it.

"It is not the black clothes that is trying to the sight—black is the steadiest of all colours to work at; white and all bright colours makes the eyes water after looking at 'em for any long time; but of all colours scarlet, such as is used for regimentals, is the most blinding, it seems to burn the eye-balls, and makes them ache dreadful. After working at red there's always flying colours before the eyes; there's no steady colour to be seen in anything for some time. Everything seems all of a twitter, and to keep changing its tint. There's more military tailors blind than any others. A great number of tailors go blind, but a great many more has lost their sight since gas-light has come up. Candle-light was not half so pernicious to the sight. Gas-light is so very heating, and there's such a glare with it that it makes the eyes throb, and shoot too, if you work long by it. I've often continued working past midnight with no other light than that, and then my eyes used to feel like two bits of burning coals in my head. And you see, sir, the worst of it was, as I found my sight going bad I was obliged to try it more, so as to keep up with my mates in the shop. At last my eyes got so weak that I was compelled to give up work, and go into the country, and there I stopped, living on my savings, and unable to do any work for fear of losing my sight altogether. I was away about three years, and then all my money was gone, and I was obligated, in spite of my eyes, to go back to work again. But then, with my sight defective as it was, I could get no employ-ment at the honourable trade, and so I had to take a seat in a shop at one of the cheap houses in the city, and that was the ruin of me entirely ; for working there, of course I got " scratched " from the trade Society, and so lost all hope of being provided for by them in my helplessness. The workshop at this cheap house was both small and badly ventilated. It was about seven foot square, and so low, that as you sot on the floor you could touch the ceiling with the tip of your finger. In this place seven of us worked—three on each side and one in the middle. Two of my shopmates were boys, or else I am sure it would not have held us all. There was no chimney, nor no window that could be opened to let the air in. It was lighted by a skylight, and this would neither open nor shut. The only means for letting out the foul air was one of them working ventilators—like cockades, you know, sir—fixed in one of the panes of glass ; but this wouldn't work, so there we were, often from 5 in the morning till 10 at night, working in this dreadful place. There was no fire in the winter, though we never needed one, for the workshop was over-hot from the suffocation, and in the summer it was like an oven. This is what it was in the daytime, but mortal tongue can't tell what it was at night, with the two gas-lights burning away, and almost stifling us. Many a time some of the men has been carried out by the others fainting for air. They all fell ill, every one of them, and I lost my eyes and my living entirely by it. We spoke to the master repeatedly, telling him he was killing us, and though when he came up to the workshop hisself, he was nearly blown back by the stench and heat, he would not let us have any other room to work in—and yet he'd plenty of convenience up stairs. He paid little more than half the regular wages, and employed such men as myself—only those who couldn't get anything better to do. What with ill-ness and all, I don't think my wages there averaged

above 12*s.* a week : sometimes I could make 1*l.* in the week, but then, the next week, maybe I'd be ill, and would get but a few shillings. It was impossible to save anything then—even to pay one's way was a difficulty, and, at last, I was seized with rheumatics on the brain, and obliged to go into St. Thomas's Hospital. I was there eleven months, and *came out stone blind.* I am convinced I lost my eyesight by working in that cheap shop ; nothing on earth will ever persuade me to the contrary, and what's more, my master robbed me of a third of my wages and my sight too, and left me helpless in the world, as, God knows, I am now. It is by the ruin of such men as me that these masters are enabled to undersell the better shops ; they get hold of the men whose eyes are just beginning to fail them, like mine did, because they know they can get them to cheapwork, and then, just at the time when a journeyman re-quires to be in the best of shops, have the best of air, and to work as little by gas-light as possible, they puts him into a hole of a place that would stifle a rat, and keeps him working there half the night through. That's the way, sir, the cheap clothes is produced, by making blind beggars of the workmen, like myself, and throwing us on the parish in our old age. You are right, sir, they not only robs the men but the ratepayers too.

" Well, sir, as I said, I come out of the hospi-tal stone blind, and have been in darkness ever since, and that's near upon ten years ago. I often dream of colours, and see the most delightful pic-tures in the world ; nothing that I ever beheld with my eyes can equal them—they're so brilliant, and clear and beautiful. I see then the features and figures of all my old friends, and I can't tell you how pleasureable it is to me. When I have such dreams they so excite me that I am ill all the next day. I often see, too, the fields, with the cows grazing on a beautiful green pasture, and the flowers, just at twilight like, closing up their blossoms as they do. I never dream of rivers ; nor do I ever remember seeing a field of corn in my visions ; it's strange I never dreamt in any shape of the corn or the rivers, but maybe I didn't take so much notice of them as of the others. Sometimes I see the sky, and very often indeed there's a rainbow in it, with all kinds of beautiful colours. The sun is a thing I often dream about seeing, going down like a ball of fire at the close of the day. I never dreamt of the stars, nor the moon—it's mostly bright colours that I see.

" I have been under all the oculists I could hear of—Mr. Turnbull, in Russell-square, but he did me no good ; then I went to Charing-cross, under Mr. Guthrie, and he gave me a blind certificate, and made me a present of half-a-sovereign ; he told me not to have my eyes tampered with again, as the optic nerve was totally decayed. Oh, yes ; if I had all the riches in the world I'd give them every one to get my sight back, for it's the greatest pressure to me to be in darkness. God help me ! I know I am a sinner, and believe I'm so afflicted on account of my sins. No, sir, it's nothing like when you shut your eyes ; when I had my sight, and closed mine, I remember I could still see the light through the lids, the very same as when you hold your hand up before the candle; but mine's far darker than that—pitch black. I see a dark mass like before me, and never any change—everlasting darkness, and no chance of a light or shade in this world. But I feel consolated some how, now it is settled; although it's a very poor comfort after all. I go along the streets in great fear. If a baby have hold of me, I am firm, but by myself, I reel about like a drunken man. I feel very timid unless I have hold of something—not to support me, but to assure me I shall not fall. If I was going down your staircase, sir, I should be all right so long as I touched the bannister, but if I missed that, I'm sure I should grow so giddy and nervous I should fall from the top to the bottom. After losing my sight, I found a great difficulty in putting my food into my mouth, for a long time—six months or better—and I was obliged to have some one to guide my hand, for I used often to put the fork up to my forehead instead of my mouth. Shortly after my becoming quite blind, I found all my other senses much quickened—my hearing—feeling—and reckoning. I got to like music very much indeed; it seemed to elevate me —to animate and cheer me much more than it did before, and so much so now, that when it ceases, I feel duller than ever. It sounds as if it was in a wilderness to me—I can't tell why, but that's all I can compare it to; as if I was quite alone with it. My smell and taste is very acute" (he was given some violets to smell)—"Oh, that's beautiful," he cried, "very reviving indeed. Often of an evening, I can see things in my imagination, and that's why I like to sit alone then; for of all the beautiful thoughts that ever a man possessed, there's none to equal a blind man's, when he's by hisself.

"I don't see my early home, but occurrences that has recently took place. I see them all plain before me, in colours as vivid as if I had my sight again, and the people all dressed in the fashion of my time; the clothes seem to make a great impression on me, and I often sit and see in my mind master tailors trying a coat on a gentleman, and pulling it here and there. The figures keep passing before me like soldiers, and often I'm so took by them that I forget I'm blind, and turn my head round to look after them as they pass by me. But that sort of thinking would throw me into a melancholly—it's too exciting while it lasts, and then leaves me dreadful dull afterwards. I have got much more melancholy since my blindness; before then, I was not seriously given, but now I find great consolation in religion. I think my blindness is sent to try my patience and resignation, and I pray to the Almighty to give me strength to bear with my affliction. I was quick and hot-tempered before I was blind, but since then, I have got less hasty like; all other troubles appears nothing to me. Sometimes I revile against my affliction—too frequently—but that is at my thoughtless moments, for when I'm calm and serious, I feel thankful that the Almighty has touched me with his cor-

recting rod, and then I'm happy and at peace with all the world. If I had run my race, and not been stopped, I might never have believed there was a God. My wife works at the 'sank work.' She makes soldiers' coats; she gets 1s. 1d. for making one, and that's nearly a day and a half's work; then she has to find her own trimmings, and they're 1d. It takes her 16 hours to finish one garment, and the over-work at that is beginning to make her like as I was myself. If she takes up a book to read to me now, it's all like a dirty mass before her, and that's just as my sight was before I lost it altogether. She slaves hard to help me; she's anxious and willing—indeed too much so. If she could get constant work, she might perhaps make about 7s. a week; but as it is, her earnings are, take one week with another, not more than 3s. Last week she earned 5s.; but that was the first job of work she'd had to do for two months. I think the two of us make on an average about 8s.; and out of that there is three people to keep—our two selves and our boy. Our rent is 2s. 6d., so that after paying that, we has about 5s. 6d. left for food, firing, and clothing for the whole of us. How we do it I can't tell; but I know we live very, very hard: mostly on pieces of bread that the men gives to me and my boy, as we go round to the workshops. If we was any of us to fall ill, we must all go to the parish; if my boy was to go sick, I should be left without any one to lead me about, and that would be as bad as if I was laid-up myself; and if anything was to happen to my wife, I'd be done clean altogether. But yet the Lord is very good, and we'd get out of that, I dare say. If anything was to drive me to the parish, I should lose all hopes of getting some help from the blind institutions; and so I dread the workhouse worse than all. I'd sooner die on the step of a door, any time, than go there and be what they call well kept. I don't know why I should have a dislike to going there, but yet I do possess it. I do believe, that any one that is willing to work for their bread, hates a workhouse; for the workhouse coat is a slothful, degrading badge. After a man has had one on his back, he's never the same. I would'nt go for an order for relief so long as I could get a half-penny loaf in twenty-four hours. If I could only get some friend to give me a letter of recommendation to Mr. Day's Charity for the Blind, I should be happy for the rest of my days. I could give the best of references to any one who would take pity on me in my affliction."

THE PUBLIC-HOUSE HAWKERS OF METAL SPOONS, ETC.

THE public-house hawkers are never so prosperous as those who confine their calling to private houses; they are often invited to partake of drink; are not the most industrious class of hawkers, and, to use their own language, are more frequently *hard up* than those who keep away from tap-room selling. The profits of the small hawkers in public-houses vary considerably. Some of them, when they have earned a shilling or two, are content to spend it before they leave the tap-room, and so they lose both their stock and profit. I do not mean to infer that this is the case with the whole of the public-house hawkers, for some among them strive hard to better their condition, and occasionally succeed ; but there are too many who are content to drawl out their existence by always suffering to-morrow to provide for itself. The man who gave me the routine of small hawkers' business I found in a tap-room in Ratcliffe Highway. He was hawking tea-spoons, and all the stock he possessed was half-a-dozen. These he importuned me to purchase with great earnestness. He prayed of me to lay out a trifle with him. He had not taken a penny the whole day he said, and had nothing to eat. "What's much worse for such as me," he added, "I'm dying for a glass of rum." I might have his tea-spoons, he told me, at any price. If I would but pay for a glass of rum for him they should be mine. I assured him some bread and cheese would do him more good, as he had not eaten anything that day ; but still he *would* have the rum. With a trembling hand he threw the liquor down his throat, smacked his lips, and said "that there dram has saved my life." A few minutes afterwards he sold his spoons to a customer for sixpence ; and he had another glass of rum. "*Now*," said he, "I'm all right for business ; if I'd twopence more I could buy a dozen tea-spoons, and I should earn a 'bob' or two yet before I went to bed." After this he grew communicative, and told me he was as good a hawker as there was in London, and he thought he could do more than any other man with a small stock. He had two or three times resolved to better himself, and had '*put in the pin*,' meaning he had made a vow to refrain from drinking ; but he had broken out again and gone on in his old course until he had melted the whole of his stock, though twice it had, during his sobriety, amounted to 5*l.*, and was often worth between 2*l.* and 3*l.* It was almost maddening when he came to his senses, he said, to find he had acted so foolishly ; indeed, it was so disheartening to discover all the result of his good resolutions dissipated in a moment, that he declared he never intended to try again. After having drunk out his stock, he would if possible commence with half-a-dozen Britannia metal tea-spoons ; these cost him 6*d.*, and would sell for 9*d.* or 1*s.* When one half-dozen were disposed of he would procure another, adding a knife, or a comb or two. If entirely destitute, he would stick a needle in a cork, and request to know of "the parties" assembled in some tap-room, if they wanted anything in the ironmongery line, though the needle was all the stock he had. This was done for the purpose of "raising the wind ;" and by it he would be sure to obtain a glass or two of ale if he introduced himself with his "ironmongery establishment" among the sailors. Sometimes he would manage to beg a few pence, and then he would purchase a knife, pair of braces, or half-a-dozen tea-spoons, and begin to practise his trade in a legitimate manner. In answer to my inquiry he said he had not always been a hawker. His father had been a soldier,

and he had worked in the armoury. His father had been discharged upon a pension, and he (the hawker) left the army with his parents. He had never enlisted while his father was a soldier, but he had since. His mother adopted the business of a hawker upon the receipt of his father's first quarter's pension ; and then he used to accompany her on her rounds. With the pension and the mother's exertions they managed to subsist tolerably well. "Being the only child, I was foolishly spoilt by my parents," he said ; "and when I was a very young man—15 or 16—I became a great trouble to them. At 18 I enlisted in the 7th Fusileers, remained in the regiment three months, and then, at my own request, was bought off. My mother sold off most of her stock of goods to raise the money (twenty pounds). When I returned home I could not think of trudging by my mother's side, as I had been used to do when carrying the goods ; nor did I feel inclined to exert myself in any way for my own support. I considered my mother had a right to keep me without my working, and she, poor thing, thought so too. I was not only supported in idleness, but my mother would give me many a shilling, though she could ill afford it, for me to spend with my companions. I passed most of my time in a skittle ground. I was not what you might term a skittle sharp, for I never entered into a plot to victimise any person, although I confess I have often bet upon the 'greenness' of those who were silly enough to make wagers that they could not possibly win. Sometimes, after I had lost the trifle supplied me by my mother, I would return, and be blackguard enough to assume the bully unless my demands on her for a further supply were attended to. Poor thing, she was very meek, and with tears in her eyes she would grant my request. I often weep when I think how I treated her" (here the tears trickled down the man's cheek), "and yet, badly as I used her, in my heart I loved her very much. I got tired of the skittle grounds in consequence of getting into a hobble relative to a skittle swindle : some sharpers had obtained a flat ; I was speculating in a small way, betting pennies and twopences in such a manner as always to win ; I was practising upon the flat upon my own account, without having any connection with the others ; they fleeced their dupe out of several pounds, and he made a row about it. The police interfered, and I was singled out as one of the gang ; the principals were also apprehended ; they got six months each, and I was accommodated with a month's board and lodging at the expense of the nation. I thought this at the time unjust, but I was as culpable as any of them, for at the time I only regretted I had not more money to stake larger wagers, and envied the other parties who were making a better thing of the business than I was. When I came out of jail, my poor mother treated me as a martyr. She thought I was as innocent as a child. Shortly after my release from prison my father died, and with him went the pension of course. I was then obligated to do something for myself. A few shillings' worth of goods only were procured—for my father's funeral and my extravagances had sadly crippled my mother's means. I behaved very well for a short time. My mother then was often ill, and she never recovered the death of my father. In about a year after my father died I lost my mother ; our stock of goods had dwindled down to a very poor lot, and I was obligated to ask relief of the parish towards her funeral expenses. When all was over, the value of my goods and cash did not amount to 20s. Ten years have elapsed since my mother's death, and I don't think I have ever been, during the whole period, sober for a month together."

While I sat in this tap-room, I counted in the course of an hour and a quarter,—4 hawkers of sheep's trotters, who visited the place ; 3 sellers of shrimps, pickled whelks, and periwinkles ; 2 baked potato-sellers ; 8 song-hawkers ; the same number with lucifer matches ; and 3 with braces, &c. Not one of these effected a sale.

Of the Street-Sellers of Jewellery.

The jewellery now sold in the streets far exceeds, both in cheapness and quality, what was known even ten years ago. Fifty years ago the jewellery itinerant trade was almost entirely, if not entirely, in the hands of Jews, who at any rate professed to sell really gold articles, and who asked large prices ; but these traders have lost their command over this, as I have shown that they have over other street callings, as not a twelfth of the street-jewellers are now Jews. A common trade among such street and country itinerant jewellers was in large watch seals, the bodies of which were of lead, more or less thickly plated with gold, and which were unsaleable even as old metal until broken to pieces,—but not always saleable then. The street or itinerant trade was for a long time afterwards carried on only by those who were regularly licensed as hawkers, and who preferred " barter" or " swopping" to actual sale, the barter being usually for other and more solid articles of the goldsmith's trade.

The introduction of " mosaic" and other cheap modes of manufacturing *quasi* gold ornaments, brought about considerable changes in the trade, pertaining, however, more to the general manufacture, than to that prepared for the streets.

The itinerants usually carry their wares in boxes or cases, which shut up close, and can be slung on the shoulder for conveyance, or hung round the neck for the purposes of sale. These cases are nearly all glazed ; within them the jewellery is disposed in such manner as, in the street-seller's judgment, is the most attractive. A card of the larger brooches, or of cameos, often forms the centre, and the other space is occupied with the shawl-pins, with their globular tops of scarlet or other coloured glass : rings, armlets, necklaces, a few earrings and ear-drops, and sometimes a few side-combs, small medals for keepsakes, clasps, beads, and bead-purses, ornamental buttons for dresses, gilt buckles for waist-belts, thimbles, &c., constitute the street jeweller's stock-in-trade. The usual prices are from 2d. to

1s. 6d. ; the price most frequently obtained for any article being 3d. It will be seen from the enumeration of the articles, that the stock is such as is required " for women's wear," and women are now almost the sole customers of the street-jewellers. " In my time, sir," said one elderly street-trader, " or rather, when I was a boy, and in my uncle's time—for he was in jewellery, and I helped him at times—quite different sorts of jewellery was sold, and quite different prices was had ; what's a high figure now was a low figure then. I've known children's coral and bells in my uncle's stock—well, I don't know whether it was real coral or not—and big watch keys with coloured stones in the centre on 'em, such as I've seen old gents keep spinning round when they was talking, and big seals and watch-chains ; there weren't no guards then, as I remember. And there was plated fruit-knives—silver, as near as a toucher—and silver pencils (pencil-cases), and gilt lockets, to give your sweetheart your hair in for keepsakes. Lor' bless you ! times is turned upside down."

The disposition of the street-stalls is somewhat after the same fashion as that in the itinerant's box, with the advantage of a greater command of space. Some of the stalls—one in Tottenham-court Road, I may instance, and another in Whitechapel—make a great show.

I did not hear of any in this branch of the jewellery trade who had been connected with it as working jewellers. I heard of two journeymen watchmakers and four clockmakers now selling jewellery (but often with other things, such as eye-glasses) in the street, but that is all. The street mass selling jewellery in town and country are, I believe, composed of the various classes who constitute the street-traders generally.

Of the nature of his present trade, and of the class of his customers, I had the following account from a man of twelve years' experience in the vending of street jewellery :—

" It's not very easy to tell, sir," he said, " what sells best, for people begins to suspect everything, and seems to think they 're done if they give 3d. for an agate brooch, and finds out it ain't set in gold. I think agate is about the best part of the trade now. It seems a stone as is easy imitated. Cornelians, too, ain't so bad in brooches—people likes the colour ; but not what they was, and not up to agates. But nothing is up to what it once was ; not in the least. Sell twice as much—when you can, which often stands over till to-morrow come-never—and get half the profit. I don't expect very much from the Great Exhibition. They sends goods so cheap from Germany, they 'll think anything dear in London, if it 's only at German prices. I think it 's a mistake to fancy that the cheaper a jewellery article is the more you 'll sell of it. You won't. People 's of opinion—at least that 's my notion of it—that it 's so common everybody 'll have it, and so they won't touch it. It 's Thames water, sir, against beer, is poor low-priced jewellery, against tidy and fair-priced ; but then the low-priced has now ruined the other sorts, for they 're all thought to go under the same umbrella,—all of a sort; 1s. or 1d. Why, as to who's the best customers, that depends on where you pitches your pitch, or works your round, and whether you are known, or are merely a upstart. But I can tell you, sir, who's been my best customers—and is yet, but not so good as they was —and that's women of the town; and mostly (for I've tried most places) about Ratcliff Highway, Whitechapel, Mile-end-road, Bethnal-green, and Oxford-street. The sailors' gals is the best of all; but a'most all of them is very particular, and some is rather tiresome. 'I'm afeard,' they says, 'this colour don't suit my complexion; it's too light, or it's too dark. How does that ring show on my finger?' I've known some of the fat and fair ones—what had been younger, but would be older—say, 'Let me have a necklace of bright black beads;' them things shows best with the fat 'uns—but in gen'ral them poor creatures is bad judges of what becomes them. The things they're the most particular of all in is necklaces. Amber and pearl sells most. I have them from 6d. to 1s. 6d. I never get more than 1s. 6d. Cornelian necklaces is most liked by children, and most bought for them. I've trusted the women of the town, and trust them still. One young woman in Shadwell took a fancy the t'other week for a pearl necklace, 'it became her so,' which it didn't; and offered to pay me 6d. a week for it if I wouldn't sell it away from her. The first week she paid 6d.; the second nothing; and next week the full tip, 'cause her Jack had come home. I never lost a halfpenny by the women. Yes, they pays you a fairish price, but nothing more. Sometimes they've beat me down 1d., and has said, 'It's all the money I has.'

"It's not very long ago that one of them offered me a fine goold watch which I could have bought at any price, for I saw she knew nothing of what it was worth. I never do anything that way. I believe a very few in my line does, for they can't give the prices the rich fences can. It's common enough for them gals to ask any street-jeweller they knows how much a watch ought to pop for, or to sell for, afore they tries it on. But it isn't they as tries it on, sir; they gets some respeckbel old lady, or old gent, to do that for them. I've had cigars and Cavendish of them; such as seamen had left behind them; you know, sir, I've never given money, only jewellery for it. Plenty of shopkeepers is glad to buy it of me, and not at a bad price. They asks no questions, and I tells them no lies. One reason why these gals buys free is that when the jewellery gets out of order or out of fashion, they can fling it away and get fresh, it's so cheap. When I've had no money on a day until I has sold to these women, I've oft enough said, 'God bless 'em!' Earrings is hardly any go now, sir; nothing to what they was; they're going out. The penny jewellery's little good; it's only children what buys, or gets it bought for them. I sell most of brooches from 3d. to 6d., very seldom higher, and bracelets— they calls them armlets now—at the same price. I buys all my goods at a swag-shop: there's no other market. Watchguards was middling sale,

both silver and goold, or washed white and washed yellow, and the swags made money in them; but instead of 1s., they're not to be sold at a Joey now, watchguards ain't, if a man patters ever so."

I am informed that there are not less than 1000 individuals who all buy their jewellery at the London swag-shops, and sell it in the streets, with or without other articles, but principally without; and that of this number 500 are generally in London and its suburbs, including such places as Gravesend, Woolwich, and Greenwich. Of these traders about one-tenth are women; and in town about three-fifths are itinerant, and the others stationary. One-half, or thereabouts, of the women, are the wives of street-sellers; the others trade on their own account. A few "swop" jewellery for old clothes, with either the mistress or the maids. Four or five, when they see a favourable opportunity, offer to tell any servant-maid her fortune. "'Buy this beautiful agate brooch, my dear,' the woman 'll say, 'and I'll only charge you 1s. 6d.'—a German thing, sir, costing her seven farthings one street-jeweller informed me,—'and I'll tell you your fortune into the bargain.'"

One "old hand" calculated, that when a street-jeweller could display 50s. worth of stock, he could clear, all the year round, 15s. a week. "People," said this man, "as far as I've known the streets, like to buy of what they think is a respectable man, and seemingly well to do; they feel safe with him." Those, however, who cannot boast so large a stock of jewellery as 50s. worth, may only clear 10s. instead of 15s. weekly. One trader thought that the average earnings of his fraternity might be taken at 12s. a week; another—and both judged from their own experience—thought 10s. 6d. was high enough. Calculating, then, at a weekly profit of 10s. 6d., and a receipt of 18s. per individual, we find 23,410l. expended in the street-trade, including the sales at Gravesend, Woolwich, and Greenwich; where—both places being resorted to by pleasure-seekers and seamen—the trade is sometimes considerable; watches, which now are almost unknown in a regular street-trade, there forming an occasional part of it.

OF THE PEDLAR-JEWELLERS.

I HAVE heard a manufacturer of Birmingham jewellery assert, that one pound of copper was sufficient to make 10l. worth of jewellery; consequently, the material to provide the unmanufactured stock in trade of a wholesale dealer in Birmingham jewellery, is not over expensive. It may be imagined then that the pedlars who hawk jewellery do not invest a very great capital in the wares they sell; there are some few, however, who have very valuable stocks of goods, pedlars though they be. This trade is principally pursued by Jews, and to a great extent (especially in a small way) by foreign Jews. The Jews are, I think, more attentive to the wants of their poorer brethren than other people; and instead of supplying them with trifling sums of money, which must necessarily soon be expended, they give them small quantities of goods, so that they may immediately commence foraging for their own support. Many of these poor Jews, when provided with their stock of merchandise, can scarcely speak a word of English, and few of them know but little respecting the value of the goods they sell; they always take care to ask a good price, leaving plenty of room for abatement. I heard one observe that they could not easily be taken in by being overcharged, for according what they paid for the article they fixed the price upon it. Some of these men, notwithstanding their scanty knowledge of the trade at starting, have eventually become excellent judges of jewellery; some of them, moreover, have acquired riches in it; indeed from the indomitable perseverance of the Hebrew race, success is generally the result of their untiring industry. If once you look at the goods of a Jew pedlar, it is not an easy matter to get out of his clutches; it is not for want of perseverance if he does not bore and tease you, until at length you are glad to purchase some trifle to get rid of him. One of my informants tells me he is acquainted with several Jews, who now hold their heads high as merchants, and are considered very excellent judges of the wares they deal in, who originally began trading with but a small stock of jewellery, and that a charitable donation. As well as Jews there are Irishmen who deal in such commodities. The pedlar generally has a mahogany box bound with brass, and which he carries with a strap hung across his shoulder; when he calls at a house, an inquiry is made whether there is any old silver or gold to dispose of. "I will give you a full price for any such articles." If the lady or gentleman accosted seems to be likely to buy, the box is immediately opened and a tempting display of gold rings, chains, scent-boxes, lockets, brooches, breast-pins, bracelets, silver thimbles, &c., &c., are exposed to view. All the eloquence the pedlar can command is now brought into play. The jewellery is arranged about the persons of his expected customers to the best advantage. The pedlar says all he can think of to enhance their sale: he will chop and change for anything they may wish to dispose of—any old clothes, books, or useless lumber may be converted into ornaments for the hair or other parts of dress. The Irish pedlar mostly confines his visits to the vicinity of large factories where there are many girls employed; these he supplies with earrings, necklaces, shawl-pins, brooches, lockets, &c., which are bought wholesale at the following prices:—Earrings and drops at from 3s. 6d. to 12s. per dozen pairs; the 3d. earring is a neat little article says my informant, and those sold at 1s. each, wholesale, are gorgeous-looking affairs; many of the latter have been disposed of by the pedlars at 1l. the pair, and even a greater price. Necklaces are from 5s. to 1l. per dozen. Lockets may be purchased wholesale at from 2s. to 10s. per dozen; guard chains (German silver) are 4s. per dozen; gilt heavy-looking waistcoat chains 6s. per dozen: and all other articles are equally low in price. The pedlar jeweller can begin busi-

ness "respectably" for two pounds. His box costs him 7s. 6d.; half-a-dozen pairs of earrings of six different sorts, 3s.; half-a-dozen lockets (various), 1s. 9d.; half-a-dozen guard chains, 2s.; half-a-dozen shawl brooches, 2s. 6d.; one dozen breast-pins (different kinds), 3s.; one dozen finger rings of various descriptions, 3s. 6d.; half-a-dozen brooches at 4d. each, 2s.; one dozen necklaces (a variety), at 6s.; three silver pencil-cases at 1s. 9d. each, 5s. 3d.; half-a-dozen waistcoat chains, 3s.; one silver toothpick, at 1s. 6d. These make altogether two pounds. If the articles are arranged with taste and seeming care (as if they were very valuable), with jeweller's wadding under each, and stuck on pink cards, &c., while the finger rings are inserted in the long narrow velvet-lined groove of the box, and the other "valuables" well spread about the little portable shop—they may be made to assume a very respectable and almost "rich" appearance. Many who now have large establishments commenced life with much less stock than is here mentioned. The Jews, I do not think, continues my informant, are the best salesmen; and the fact of their being Israelites is, in many instances, a bar to their success; country people, especially, are afraid of being taken in by them. The importunities and appeals of the Hebrew, however, are far more urgent than any other tradesman; and they always wait where they think there's the slightest chance of effecting a sale, until the door is slammed in their face. I believe there are not, at the present time, many (especially small traders) who deal exclusively in jewellery; they mostly add other small and light articles—such as fancy cutlery, side combs, &c. There may, at a rough guess, be 500 of them travelling the country; half the number are poor foreign Jews; a quarter are Jews, who have, perhaps, followed the same calling for years; and the remaining quarter, a mixture of Irish and English, with a small preponderance of Irishmen. All these "swop" their goods for old gold and silver, and frequently realize a large sum, by changing the base metal for the sterling article. Their goods are always sold as being gold or silver—If asked whether a particular article be gold, they reply "It's jewellers' gold;" "Is this ring gold?" inquires the customer, taking one from the box—"No, ma'am, I wouldn't deceive you!" is the answer, "that is not gold; but here is one," adds the pedlar (taking up one exactly of the same description, and which cost the same price) "which is of a similar shape and fashion, and the best jeweller's gold that is made." The profits of the pedlar-jewellers it is almost impossible to calculate, for they will sell at any price upon which the smallest amount of profit can be realized. The foreign Jews, especially, will do this, and it is not an unusual circumstance for one of these men to ask 5s. for an article which originally cost them 3d., and which they will eventually sell for 4d.

In London there are about 200 hawkers of jewellery, who visit the public-houses; but few of these have boxes—they invite customers by displaying some chains in their hands, or having one or two arranged in front of their waistcoats, while the smaller articles are carried in their waistcoat pockets. The class of persons who patronize the public-house hawkers are those who visit the tap-rooms of taverns, and countrymen in the vicinity of Smithfield upon market days, (one of the hawkers tells me, that they succeed better upon the hay-market days than at the cattle sales, for the butchers, they say, are too "fly" for them. Sailors are among their best customers, but the coster-girls are very fond of drop earrings and coral beads; the sailors, however, give the best prices of all. I am told that the quantity of old gold and silver which the country pedlars obtain in exchange for their goods is "astonishing;" and there have been occasions on which a pedlar has been enriched for life by one single transaction of barter; some old and unfashionable piece of jewellery, that they received for their goods, has been composed of costly stones, which had lain by for years, and of which the pedlar's customer was unacquainted with the value. The more respectable jewellery pedlars put up at the better class of public-houses, and, even after their day's travels are over, they still have an eye to business; they open the box upon the table of the tap-room where they are lodging, and, under the pretence of cleaning or arranging their goods, temptingly display their glittering stock. The bar-maid, kitchen-maid, the landlady's daughter, or perhaps the landlady herself, admires some ornaments, which the pedlar declares would become them vastly. He hangs a necklace upon the neck of one of them; holds a showy earring and drop to the ear of another; facetiously inquires of the girls whether they are not likely to want some-thing of this sort shortly—as he holds up first a wedding-ring, and then a baby's coral; or else he exhibits a ring set with Turquoise, or pearls and small diamonds in a cluster, to the landlady, and tries it on her finger; and by such arts a sale that will cover his expenses is generally effected. There is one peculiarity these men have when bartering their goods. A worn-out ornament of jewellery is brought to them, and, although it be brass, the pedlar never attempts to undeceive the possessor, if he finds it is considered to be genuine. Of course he never gives cash for such articles; but he offers a large price in barter. "I will take 10s. for this ring, and allow you 5s. for the old one," says the pedlar. It would never do to say the ornament was not gold; the customer bought it years ago for such, and no one ever disputed its being the precious metal; should our pedlar do so, he might as well shut up shop immediately. The lady would be angry and suspicious; neither would she believe him, but rather suspect that he wanted only to cheat her; consequently the pedlar barters, obtains the old ring, or some other article, and 5s., for his commodity; and though the article he has taken in exchange is worth only a few pence, he very likely profits to the amount of 200 per cent. upon the cash received. The pedlars of lesser consequence put up at humble private or public-houses, and some of them at the common lodging-houses. Those who have only small stocks confine their visits to farm-houses and villages.

OF THE STREET-SELLERS OF CARD-COUNTERS, MEDALS, ETC.

THE "card-counters," or, as I have heard them sometimes called by street-sellers, the "small coins," are now of a very limited sale. The slang name for these articles is "Jacks" and "Half Jacks." They are sold to the street-people at only two places in London; one in Holborn, and the other at Black Tom's (himself formerly a street-seller, now "a small swag"), in Clerken-well. They are all made in Birmingham, and are of the size and colour of the genuine sovereigns and half sovereigns; but it is hardly possible that any one who had ever received a sovereign in payment, could be deceived by the substitution of a Jack. Those now sold in the streets are much thinner, and very much lighter. Each presents a profile of the Queen; but instead of the super-scription "Victoria Dei Gratiâ" of the true sove-reign, the Jack has "Victoria Regina." On the reverse, in the place of the "Britanniarum Regina Fid. Def." surrounding the royal arms and crown, is a device (intended for an imitation of St. George and the Dragon) representing a soldier on horse-back—the horse having three legs elevated from the ground, while a drawn sword fills the right hand of the equestrian, and a crown adorns his head. The superscription is, "to Hanover," and the rider seems to be sociably accompanied by a dragon. Round the Queen's head on the half Jack is "Victoria, Queen of Great Britain," and on the reverse the Prince of Wales's feather, with the legend, "The Prince of Wales's Model Half Sovereign."

Until within these five or six years the gilt card-counters had generally the portraiture of the monarch, and on the reverse the legend "Keep your temper," as a seasonable admonition to whist players. Occasionally the card-counter was a gilt coin, closely resembling a sovereign; but the magistracy, eight or nine years back, "put down" the sale of these imitations.

Under another head will be found an account of the use made of these sovereigns, in pretended wagers. A further use of them was to add to the heaps of apparent gold at the back of the table-keeper in a race booth, when gambling was allowed at Epsom, and the "great meetings."

There are now only two men regularly selling Jacks in the streets. There have been as many as twelve. One of these street-sellers is often found in Holborn, announcing "30s. for 1d.! 30s. for 1d.! cheapest bargain ever offered; 30s. for 1d.!"

The Jacks cost, wholesale, 4s. 6d. the gross; the half Jacks 2s. 9d. The two are sold for 1d. If the sale be not brisk, the street-seller will give a ring into the bargain. These rings cost 1s. the gross, or the third part of a farthing each.

If there be, on the year's average, only two street-sellers disposing of the Jacks, and earning 9s. a week—to earn which the receipts will be about 20s.—we find 104l. expended in the streets on these trifles.

Of medals the street sale is sometimes con-siderable, at others a mere nothing. When a popular subject is before the public, many of the general patterers "go to medals." I could not learn that any of the present street-people vended medals in the time of the war; I believe there are none at present among the street folk who did so. I am told that the street sale in war medals was smaller than might reasonably have been expected. The manufacture of those articles in the Salamanca, Vittoria, and even Waterloo days, was greatly inferior to what it is at present, and the street price demanded was as often 6*d.* as a smaller sum. These medals in a little time presented a dull, leaden look, and the knowledge that they were "poor things" seems to have prevented the public buying them to any extent in the streets, and perhaps deterred the street-sellers from offering them. Those who were the most successful of the medal-sellers had been, or assumed to have been, soldiers or seamen.

Within the last eighteen years, or more, there has hardly been any public occurrence without a comparatively well-executed medal being sold in the streets in commemoration of it. That sold at the opening of London-bridge was, I am told, considered "a superior thing," and the improvement in this art or manufacture has progressed to the present time. Within the last three years the most saleable medals, an experienced man told me, were of Hungerford Suspension (bridge), the New Houses of Parliament, the Chinese Junk, and Sir Robert Peel. The Thames Tunnel medals were at one time "very tidy," as were those of the New Royal Exchange. The great sale is at present of the Crystal Palace; and one man had heard that there were a great many persons coming to London to sell them at the opening of the Great Exhibition. "The great eggs and bacon, I call it," he said; "for I hope it will bring us that sort of grub. But I don't know; I'm afraid there'll be too many of us. Besides, they say we shan't be let sell in the park."

The exhibition medal is as follows:—

What the street medal-sellers call the "right-side"—I speak of the "penny" medal, which commands by far the greatest sale—presents the Crystal Palace, raised from the surface of the medal, and whitened by the application of aqua fortis. The superscription is "THE BUILDING FOR THE INTERNATIONAL EXHIBITION, LONDON, 1851." On the "wrong side" (so called) is the following inscription, occupying the whole face of the medal:

> THE CONSTRUCTION IS OF
> IRON AND OF GLASS,
> 1848 FEET LONG.
> ABOUT HALF IS 456 WIDE.
> THE REMAINDER 408 FEET WIDE,
> AND 66 FEET HIGH;
> SITE, UPWARDS OF 20 ACRES.
> COST £150,000.
> JOSH. PAXTON, ARCHT.

The size of this medal is between that of a shilling and a half-crown.

A patterer, who used to sell medals on Sunday mornings in the park, informed me that he told his customers the Crystal Palace part was dead silver, by a new discovery making silver cheap; but for all that he would risk changing it for a four-penny bit!

The two-penny medal is after the same style, but the letters are more distinct. On my stating, to a medal-seller, that it was difficult to read the inscription on his "pennies," he said, "Not at all, sir; but it's your eyes is dazzled." This was said quietly, and with a touch of slyness, and I have no doubt was the man's "cut-and-dried" answer.

The patterer whom I have mentioned, told me, that encouraged by a tolerably sale and "a gathering of the aristocrats," on a very fine Sunday in January or February—he could not remember which—he ventured upon 6 "sixpenny medals," costing him 1*s.* 9*d.* He sold them all but one, which he showed me. It was exactly the size of a crown-piece. The Crystal Palace was "raised," and of "dead silver," as in the smaller medals. The superscription was the same as on the penny medal; but underneath the representation of the palace were raised figures of Mercury and of a naked personage, with a quill as long as himself, a cornucopia, and a bee-hive: this I presume was Industry. These twin figures are supporters to a medallion, crown-surmounted, of the Queen and Prince Albert: being also in "dead silver." On the reverse was an inscription, giving the dimensions, &c., of the building.

The medals in demand for street-sale in London seem to be those commemorative of local events only. None, for instance, were sold relating to the opening of the Britannia Bridge.

The wholesale price of the medals retailed in the street at 1*d.* is 7*s.* the gross; those retailed at 2*d.* are 12*s.* the gross, but more than three-fourths of those sold are penny medals. They are all bought at the swag-shops, and are all made in Birmingham. It is difficult to compute how many persons are engaged in this street trade, for many resort to it only on occasions. There are, however, from 12 to 20 generally selling medals, and at the present time about 30 are so occupied: they, however, do not sell medals exclusively, but along with a few articles of jewellery, or occasionally of such street stationery as letter stamps and "fancy" pens, with coloured glass or china handles. A fourth of the number are women. The weather greatly influences the street medal trade, as rain or damp dims their brightness. One seller told me that the day before I saw him he had sold only four medals. "I've known the trade, off and on," he said, "for about six years, and the greatest number as ever I sold was half-a-gross one Saturday. I cleared rather better than 3*s.* I sold them in Whitehall and by Westminster-bridge. There was nothing new among them, but I had a good stock, and it was a fine day, and I was lucky in meeting parties, and had a run for sets." By a "run for sets," my informant meant that he had met with customers who bought a medal of each of the kinds he displayed; this is called "a set."

An intelligent man, familiar with the trade, and who was in the habit of clubbing his stock-money with two others, that they might buy a gross at a time, calculated that 15 medal sellers were engaged in the traffic the year through, and earned, in medals alone, 6*d.* a day each, to clear which they would take 6s. 6d. weekly, giving a yearly outlay of 253l. 10s. It must be remembered, to account for the smallness of the earnings, that the trade in medals is irregular, and the calculation embraces all the seasons of the trade.

On occasions when medals are the sole or chief articles of traffic, they are displayed on a tray, which is a box with a lid, and thus look bright as silver on the faded brown velvet, with which the box is often lined. Among the favourite pitches are Oxford-street, the approaches to London, Blackfriars, Westminster, and Waterloo-bridges, the railway stations, and the City-road.

Of small coins (proper) there is now no sale in the streets. When there was an issue of half-farthings, about seven years ago, the street-sellers drove a brisk trade, in vending them at four a penny, urging on the sale before the coins got into circulation, which they never did. "It's not often," said one patterer to me, "that we has anything to thank the Government for, but we may thank them for the half-farthings. I dare say at least 30 of us made a tidy living on them for a week or more; and if they wasn't coined just to give us a spirt, I should like to know what they was coined for! I once myself, sir, for a lark, gave one to a man that swept a capital crossing, and he was in a thundering passion, and wanted to fight me, when I told him they was coined to pay the likes of him!"

There was afterwards a tolerable sale of the "new silver pennies, just issued from the Mint, three ha'pence each, or 7 for 6d.;" also of "genuine models of the new English florin, only 1d.:" both of these were fictitious.

OF THE STREET-SELLERS OF RINGS AND SOVEREIGNS FOR WAGERS.

THIS class is hardly known in the streets of London at present. Country fairs and races are a more fitting ground for the ring-seller's operations. One man of this class told me that he had been selling rings, and occasionally medals, for wagers for this last fifteen years. "It's only a so-so game just now," he said; "the people get so fly to it. A many hold out their penny for a ring, and just as I suppose I'm a going to receive it, they put the penny into their pockets, and their thumb upon their nose. I wish I had some other game, for this is a very dickey one. I gives 3d. a-dozen for the rings at the swag shop; and sometimes sells a couple of dozen in a day, but seldom more. Saturday is no better day than any other. Country people are my best customers. I know them by their appearance. Sometimes a person in the crowd whispers to others that he bought one the other day and went and pawned it for 5s., and he'd buy another, but he's got no money. I don't ask for such assistance; I suppose it's done for a lark, and to laugh at others if they buy. Women buy more frequently than any one else. Several times since I have been on this dodge, women have come back and abused me because the ring they bought for a penny was not gold. Some had been to the pawn shop, and was quite astonished that the pawn-

broker wouldn't take the ring in. I do best in the summer at races: people think it more likely that two sporting gents would lay an out of the way wager (as you know I always make out) then than at any other time. I have been interfered with at races before now for being an impostor, and yet at the same time the gamblers was allowed to keep their tables; but of course theirs was all fair—no imposition about them—oh no! I am considered about one of the best patterers among our lot. I dare say there may be twenty on us all together, in town and country, on rings and sovereigns. Sometimes, when travelling on foot to a race or fair, I do a little in the *Fawney dropping* line;" (fawneys are rings;) "but that is a dangerous game, I never did it but two or three times. There were some got lagged for it, and that frightened me. In ring-dropping we pretend to have found a ring, and ask some simple-looking fellow if it's good gold, as it's only just picked up. Sometimes it is immediately pronounced *gold*: 'Well it's no use to me,' we'll say, 'will you buy it?' Often they are foolish enough to buy, and it's some satisfaction to one's conscience to know that they think they are a taking you in, for they give you only a shilling or two for an article which if really gold would be worth eight or ten. Some ring-droppers write out an account and make a little parcel of jewellery, and when they pick out their man, they say, 'If you please, sir, will you read this for me, and tell me what I should do with these things, as I've just found them?' Some people advise they should be taken to the police office—but very few say that; some, that they should be taken to the address; others, that they should be sold, and the money shared; others offer a price for them, stating that they're not gold, they're only trumpery they say, but they'll give half-a-crown for them. It's pleasant to take such people in. Sometimes the finder says he's in haste, and will sell them for anything to attend to other business, and he then transfers his interest at perhaps 200 per cent. profit. This game won't friz now, sir, it's very dangerous. I've left it off long since. I don't like the idea of quod. I've been there once." Another plan of dropping rings is to write a letter. This is the style :—

"My dear Anne,
"I have sent you the ring, and hope it will fit.— Excuse my not bringing it. John will leave it with you. —You know I have so much to attend to.—I shall think every minute a year until the happy day arrives.
"Yours devotedly,
"JAMES BROWN."

This love epistle containing the wedding-ring was most successful when it first came up, but the public now are too wide awake. According to another informant, the ring-dropping "lurk" is now carried on this way, for the old style is "coopered." "A woman," he says, "is made up so as to appear in the family-way—pretty far gone—and generally with a face as long as a boy's kite. Up she goes to any likely ken, where she knows there are women that are married or expect to get married, and commences begging. Then comes the tale of woe, if she can get them to listen—' I 'm in the family-way,' she says, ' as you can plainly see *young ladies* (this she says to the *servants,* and that prides them you know). My husband has left me after serving me in this way. I don't know where he is, and am forced to solicit the ladies' charity.' Well, the servants will bring broken victuals and make a little collection among themselves for the 'unprotected female;' for which in return, with many thanks for their kindness, she offers her gold wedding-ring for sale, as she wants to get back to her suffering kids to give them something to eat, poor things, and they shall have the gold ring, she says, for half what it 's worth ; or if they won 't buy it, will they lend 2s. or 3s. on it till she can redeem it, as she hasn't been in the habit of pledging ! The girls are taken off their guard (she not being in the habit of pledging is a choker for them) by the woman's seeming simplicity, and there 's a consultation. One says to the other—' Oh, you 'll want it, Mary, for John;' and another, ' No, you 'll want it first, Sally, for William.' But the woman has her eye on the one as says the least, as the likeliest of all to want it, and so she says to the John and William girls, ' Oh, you don't want it ; but *here* (touching the silent one), here's a *young lady* as does,' (that sweetens the servant girl up directly.) She says, ' I don't want it, bless you (with a giggle), but I 'll lend you a trifle, as you are in this state, and have a family, and are left like this by your husband—aint he cruel, Sally (she adds to her fellow-servant)?' The money the ring-woman gets, sir, depends upon the servant's funds ; if it is just after quarter-day, she generally gets a tidy tip—if not, 4 or 5 bob. I 've known one woman get 10s. and even 12s. this way. The ring is made out of brass gilt buttons, and stunning well : it 's faked up to rights, and takes a good judge even at this day to detect it without a test."

" The best sort of rings for *fawney dropping* is the Belchers. They are a good thick looking ring, and have the crown and V. R. stamped upon them. They are 7d. a dozen. I takes my stand now, in my ring-selling, as if I was in a great hurry, and pulls out my watch. I used to have a real one, but now it 's a dummy. ' Now, ladies and gentlemen,' says I, ' I am not permitted to remain more than ten minutes in one spot. I have rings to sell to decide a wager recently made between two sporting noblemen, to the effect that I do not sell a certain quantity of these rings in a given time, at a penny a piece. I can recommend the article as being well worth the money I ask for it, perhaps something more. I do not say they are gold ; in fact, I must not say too much, as there is a person in this company watching my proceedings, and seeing that I do not remain more than ten minutes in this spot,'—here I always looks very hard at the most respectable and gentlemanly-looking person among my hearers, and sometimes gives him a wink, and sometimes· a nod,—' but if you should hear anything more about these rings, and you want to purchase, don't be vexed if I am gone when you want me. The ten minutes has nearly expired; three minutes

more ; any more buyers ? It makes no difference to me whether I sell or not—I get my pay all the same ; but, if you take my advice, buy ; and perhaps if you was to call at the sign of the Three Balls, as you go home, you may be agreeably surprised, and hear something to your advantage. Perhaps I have said too much. I have one minute more, before I close the establishment. After shutting the box, I dare not sell another in this spot, if you were to offer me 5l. for it; therefore, if you wish to purchase, now is your time.' I make many a pitch, and do not sell a single ring; and the insults I receive used to aggravate me very much, but I do not mind them now, I 'm used to it. The flyest cove among all us ring-sellers is little Ikey, the Jew. There were two used to work the game. They had a real gold ring, just like the ones they were selling, and they always used to pitch near a pawnbroker's shop. Ikey's pal would buy a ring for a penny, of the street-seller, and would then say, loud enough to be heard by the bystanders, ' There's a pawn shop—I 'll go and ask them to take it in.' A crowd would follow him. He would enter the pawnbroker's—present a real gold ring—obtain a loan of 5s., and would present the ticket to the bystanders, who would then buy very fast. When the pitch was over, Ikey's pal would take the ring out of pawn, and away the two would go to work near some other pawnbroker's. I have heard Ikey say they have pawned the ring thirty-five times in a day. I tried the same caper ; but my pal cut with the gold ring the first day, and I 've never had another go at that *fake* since.

" Before I commenced the jewellery line," continued my candid informant, " a good many years ago, I used to hold horses about Bond-street. Afterwards I was taken as an errand boy at a druggist's, was out of an errand one day and got 6d. for holding a gentleman's horse, which kept me nearly an hour; when I went back to my master's I was told I wasn't wanted any more. I had been cautioned about stopping of errands two or three times before; however I didn't like the situation, it was too confining. I next got a place as pot-boy, in Brick Lane. Here I was out one day gathering in the pots. I hung the strap of pots to a railing to have a game at chances (pitch and toss), somebody prigged my strap of pots, and I cut. A few weeks after I was grabbed for this, and got a month at the mill; but I was quite innocent of prigging—I was only careless. When I came out of prison, I went to Epsom races, thinking to get a job there at something or other. A man engaged me to assist him in ' pitching the hunters.' Pitching the hunters is the three sticks a penny, with the snuffboxes stuck upon sticks; if you throw your stick, and they fall out of the hole, you are entitled to what you knock off. I came to London with my master the pitcher-hunter, he went to a swag shop in Kent-street, in the Borough, to purchase a new stock. I saw a man there purchasing rings, this was little Ikey, the Jew; some days afterwards I saw him making a pitch, and selling very fast. I had fourpence in my pocket; went to Kent-street, to the swag shops, bought a dozen rings, and commenced selling them. I sold that day three dozen; that wasn't bad considering that my toggery was very queer, and I looked anything but like one who would be trusted with ten pounds' worth of gold rings. This wager between the two sporting noblemen has been a long time settling. I've been at it more than fifteen years. The origin of it was this here: when sovereigns were first coined, the Jew boys and others used to sell medals and card-counters upon particular occasions, the same as they do now, and shove them in a saucepan lid, with silver paper under them. Captain Barclay and another of the same sort, bet a wager, that one of these Jew-boys could not dispose of a certain number of real sovereigns in a given time, supposing the Jew-boy cried out nothing more than 'here's sovereigns, only a penny a piece.' The number he was to sell was 50 within the hour, and to take his station at London Bridge. The wager was made, the Jew-boy procured, and the sovereigns put into the pot lid. 'Here are real sovereigns a penny a piece, who'll buy?' he cried; but he sold only a few. The number disposed of, within the hour, I have heard, was seventeen. Those who purchased, when they found that they had really bought sovereigns at a penny a piece, returned for more, but the salesman was gone. A good harvest was afterwards reaped among the Jews, who got up a medal something like a sovereign, and sold them in every quarter of London, for the Captain's wager soon spread about everywhere. It's a stale game now; it was so before my time, but I've heard the Jews talk about it. The second day I tried the ring dodge, I was a little more successful; indeed every day for some time exceeded the day before, for, as I improved in patter, my sales increased. My appearance, too, was improving. At one time I was a regular swell, sported white kid gloves, white choker, white waistcoat, black ribbon, and a quizzing glass. Some people used to chaff me, and cry out 'there's a swell.' I never was saving, always spent my money as fast as I got it. I might have saved a goodish bit, and I wish I had now. I never had a wife, but I have had two or three broomstick matches, though they never turned out happy. I never got hold of one but what was fond of lush. I live in Westminster, at a padding-ken. I'd rather not tell you where, not that I've anything to fear, but people might think I was a *nose*, if anybody came after me, and they would crab me. I'd rather get something else to do if I could, but I think this is the best street game I could follow. I don't believe any of the ring-sellers dispose of more than myself, except little Ikey; he now adds other articles, a silver thimble (he calls it), some conundrums, a song-book and a seal, and all for a penny. I tried the same thing, but found I could do just as well with the rings alone. We all expects to do great things during the Exhibition. I think all on us ought to be allowed to sell in the parks. Foreigners are invited to witness specimens of British Industry, and it's my opinion they should see all, from the highest to the lowest. We *did* intend petitioning the Prince on the subject, but I don't suppose it would be any go, seeing as how the slang coves" (the showmen), "have done so, and been refused."

OF THE STREET-SELLERS OF CHILDREN'S GILT WATCHES.

THESE articles were first introduced into general street sale about 10 years ago. They were then German made. The size was not much larger than that of a shilling, and to this tiny watch was appended as tiny a chain and seal. The street-price was only 1*d.*, and the wholesale price was 8*s.* the gross. They were sold at eight of the swag-shops, all "English and foreign," or "English and German" establishments. From the price it would appear that the profit was 4*d.* a dozen, but as the street-sellers had to "take the watches as they came," the profit was but 3*d.*, as a dozen watches in a gross had broken glasses, or were otherwise damaged and unsaleable. The supply of these watches was not equal to the demand, for when a case of them was received, "it could have been sold twice over." One street-seller told me that he had sold 15 and even 16 dozen of these watches on a day, and that once on a Saturday night, and early on Sunday morning, he had sold 2 gross, or 24 dozen. Such, however, was not the regular sale; a "good week" was a profit of 15*s.*

About six years ago gilt watches of a very superior kind were sold in the streets in a different way. They were French made, and were at first vended at 1*s.* each. Some were displayed in case-boxes, fitted up with divisions, in which were placed the watches with the guard-chains, about three-quarters of a yard long, coiled round them. There were also two or three keys, one in the form of a pistol. The others were hung from a small pole, sometimes a dozen, and sometimes two, being so suspended, and they had a good glittering appearance in a bright light; this street fashion still continues. The street-sellers, however, are anxious not to expose these watches too much, as they are easily injured by the weather, and any stain or injury is irreparable. The shilling sale continued prosperously for about six weeks, and then the wholesale price—owing, the street-sellers were told at the swag-shops, to "an opposition in the trade in Paris,"—was reduced to 4*s.* 6*d.* the dozen, and the retail street-price to 6*d.* each. When the trade was "at its best" there were thirty men and twenty women selling these watches, all May, June, and July, and each clearing from 12*s.* to 20*s.* (but rarely the latter sum) a week. Last "season" there were for the same period about half the number of sellers mentioned, averaging a profit of about 15*d.* a day each, or 9*s.* a week. The cry is—"Handsome present for 6*d.* Beautiful child's watch and chain, made of Peruvian metal, by working jewellers out of employ. Only 6*d.* for a handsome present."

The vendors of these watches are the regular

street-sellers, some of them being tolerably good patterers. One of these men, in the second year of the street-sale of watches, appeared one morning in an apron and sleeves, to which brass and copper.filings were made to adhere, and he announced himself as an English working jeweller unemployed, offering his own manufactures for sale, "better finished and more solider nor the French." The man's sale was greatly increased. On the following day, however, four other English working jewellers appeared in Leicester-square and its approaches, each in besprinkled apron and sleeves, and each offering the productions of his own handicraft! The apron and sleeves were therefore soon abandoned.

Among the best "pitches,"—for the watch-sellers are not itinerant, though they walk to and fro— are the Regent's-park, Leicester-square, the foot of London-bridge, and of Blackfriars-bridge, and at the several railway stations.

The principal purchasers, I was told by an intelligent patterer, who sometimes "turned his hand to the watches," were "fathers and mothers," he thought, "and them as wished to please such parties."

Calculating that twenty-five persons now vend watches for twelve weeks in the year, and—as they are 10 per cent. cheaper than they were at the swag-shops—that each clears 8s. weekly, we find 360l. yearly expended in London streets in these toy watches.

OF THE STREET-SELLERS OF TINWARE.

THE sellers of tins, who carry them under their arms, or in any way on a round, apart from the use of a vehicle, are known as hand-sellers. The word hand-seller is construed by the street-traders as meaning literally *hand-seller*, that is to say, a *seller* of things held or carried in the *hand;* but the term is clearly derived from the Scotch *hand-sell*, as in "handsell penny." Handsell, according to Jamieson, the Scotch etymologist, means, (1) "The first money that a trader receives for goods; also a gift conferred at a particular season. (2) A piece of bread given before breakfast." Ihre, the Gothic lexicographer, views the term handsell as having sprung from the Mæso-Gothic *hunsla* (sacrifice or offering). This is the same as the Anglo-Sax *husl* (the Eucharist), whence comes the English *housel* and *unhouseled;* and he considers the word to have originally meant a gift or offering of any kind. Hence, the hand-sellers of tin and other wares in the street, would mean simply those who *offered* such tin or other wares for sale. The goods they dispose of are dripping-pans (sometimes called "square pans"), sold at from 3d. to 18d., the 3d. pans being "6 inch," and the 18d. "15 inch;" cullenders, 6d. to 9d.; hand-bowls, for washerwomen, 1s. (now a very small portion of the trade); roasting-jacks, with tin bodies, 6d. to 1s. 6d. (this used to be the best article for profit and ready sale in the trade, but "they are going out of date"); and the smaller articles of graters, &c.

The hand-sellers also trade in other articles which are less portable; the principal sale, however, is at "stands," and there chiefly on a Saturday night, the great business-time of street-commerce! These less portable articles are tea-kettles, 10d. to 18d.; saucepans of all sizes, the smallest being the "open pints" at 2d. or 2½d. each (they cost them 20d. a dozen; it's a bargain to get them at 18d.), and the largest the "nine quart;" but the kinds most in demand are the "three pints" and "two quarts," sold at 6d. and 8d. There are also fish-kettles in this street-traffic, though to a very limited extent—"one fish-kettle," I was told, "to four-and-twenty saucepans;" the selling price for the fish-kettles is 5s. and 3s. 6d. each; candlesticks are sold at 4d. to 1s.; and shaving-pots, 4d. A few tin things used to be sold at the mews, but the trade is now almost entirely abandoned. These were tins for singeing horses, 2s. 6d. each when first introduced, ten or twelve years ago, but now 1s., and stable lanterns, of punched tin, which cannot be sold now for more than 1s. each, though they cost 10s. per dozen at a tin-shop.

There are other tin articles vended in the streets, but they will be more properly detailed in my account of street-artisans, as the maker and the street-seller are the same individual. Among these are Dutch ovens, which are rarely offered now by those who purchase their goods at the tin-shops, as the charge there is 6d. "Why," said a working tinman to me, "I've had 10d. many a week for making ovens, and the stuff found. It takes two plates of tin to make an oven, that's 3d. at any tin-shop, before a minute's labour is given to it, and yet the men who hawk their own goods sell their ovens regularly enough at 4d. It's the ruin of the trade." The tin-shops, I may observe, supply the artisans with the materials they require, as well as the ready-made articles, to the street-seller.

One of the largest street-stands "in tin" is in St. John-street, Clerkenwell, on Saturday evenings, but the proprietor pertains to the artisan class, though he buys some of his goods at the tin-shops.

The hand-sellers of tin are about 100 in number, and 60 of that number may be said to be wives and children of the remaining 40; as the majority of the itinerant vendors of tinware are married men with families. "Tins" are not a heavy carriage, and can very well be borne from house to house by women, while children sell such things as nutmeg-graters, pepper-boxes, extinguishers, and save-alls. Those who sell the larger tin articles in the streets are generally the makers of them. "A dozen years back or more, perhaps, there was," I was informed, "some prime block-tin tea-pots sold in the streets; there's none now. Metal's druv out tin."

Among the street tin-sellers I heard many complaints of the smallness, and the constantly diminishing rate of their earnings. "Our people has bad luck, too," said one man, "or they isn't wide awake. You may remember, sir, that a few weeks back, a new save-all came in, and was called candle-wedges, and went off well. It was a tin thing, and ought by rights to have been started by the tin-shops for us. But it was first put out by the swag-men at 3s. the gross. The first and second days the men were soon sold out. Them as could patter tidy did the best—I tried, but you see, sir, I'm no scholar. Well, they went at night to Mr. ——'s, in Houndsditch, I think it is, and he says, 'I'm out of them, but I'll have some in the morning.' They goes in the morning, and the swag says : ' O, I can't afford 'em at three shillings, you can have 'em at four.' He put 1s. exter on the gross, cause they sold, nothing else, sir; and a relation of mine heard the swag shopkeeper say, ' Why, they're cheap at four; Jim (the street-seller) there made 3s. 3d. on 'em yesterday. I ain't a going to slave, and pay rent, and rates, and taxes, to make your fortens; it ain't likely.' You see, sir, they was sold at ½d. each, and cost ¼d., which is 3d. a dozen, and so the swag got a higher profit, while the poor fellows had to sell for less profit."

From the most reliable information which I could acquire, it appears that these tin-sellers, taken altogether, do not earn above 6s. a week each, as regards the adult men, and half that as regards the children and women. To realize this amount, the adults must take 13s., and the women and children 7s., for the latter are less " priced down." Thus, if we calculate an average receipt, per individual, of 10s. weekly, reckoning 100 sellers, we find a yearly expenditure on tins, bought in the street, of 2500l. The trade is greatest in the suburbs, and some men, who have become " known on their rounds," supply houses, by order, with all the tins they require.

There is a branch of the tin-trade carried on in a way which I have shown prevailed occasionally among the costermongers, viz., the selling of goods on commission. This system is now carried on among all the parties who trade "from" swag-barrows.

The word "swag" which has been so often used in this work of late, is, like many other of the street-terms, of Scotch origin (as handseller, and busker). The Scotch word is sweg or swack, and means, according to Jamieson, a quantity, a considerable number, a large collection of any kind. (The root appears to be an ancient German term, sweig—a flock, a herd.) Hence a Swag Warehouse is a warehouse containing a large collection of miscellaneous goods; and a Swag Barrow, a barrow laden with a considerable assortment of articles. The slang term swag means booty, plunder—that is to say, the collection of goods—the "lot," the "heap" stolen.

Of these swag-barrowmen, there are not less than 150, and the barrows are mostly the property of three individuals, who are not street-sellers themselves. One of these men has 50 barrows of his own, and employs 50 men to work them. The barrow proprietor supplies not only the vehicle, but the stock, and the men's remuneration is 3s. in the 1s. on the amount of sales. Each article they sell is charged to the public 1d. The tin-wares of the swag-barrows are nutmeg-graters, bread-graters, beer-warmers, fish-slices, goblets, mugs, save-alls, extinguishers, candle-shades, money-boxes, children's plates, and rattles. In addition

to the tin-wares, the swag-barrows are stocked with brooches, rings, pot-ornaments, plates, small crockeryware, toys, &c., each article being also vended at 1d. The trade is so far stationary, that the men generally confine themselves to one neighbourhood, if not to one street. The majority of the swag-barrowmen have been costermongers, and nearly the whole have been engaged in street avocations all their lives. One man familiar with the trade thought I might state that the whole were of this description ; for though there was lately a swag barrowman who had been a tradesman in an extensive way, there was, he believed, no such exception at the present time. These barrowmen are nearly all uneducated, and are plodding and persevering men, though they make few exertions to better their condition. As the barrow and stock are supplied to them, without any outlay on their part, their faculties are not even sharpened, as among many of the costermongers, by the necessity of providing stock-money, and knowing how to bargain and buy to advantage. They have merely to sell. Their commission furnishes little or nothing more than the means of a bare subsistence. The great sale is on Saturday nights at the street-markets, and to the working people, who then crowd those places, and, as one said to me, "has a few pennies to lay out." At such times as much as 3l. has been taken by a swag-barrowman. During the other days of the week their earnings are small. It is considered a first-rate week, and there must be all the facilities for street-trade afforded by fine weather, to take 2s. a day (clearing 6d), and 3l. on a Saturday night. This gives the swag-barrowman a commission of 18s. ; but I am informed, by competent persons, that the average of the weekly profits of these street-traders does not exceed 10s. a week. This shows a yearly receipt, by the men working the barrows, of 3900l. as their profit or payment, and a gross receipt of 11,700l. Of this large amount nearly two-thirds, I am assured, is expended on tin-wares.

The prime cost, at the tin-shops, of these wares, to the barrow proprietors, are 7s. and 7s. 6d. the gross, leaving from 1½d. to 2d. profit on every shilling, over the 3d. commission paid to the salesman. The tins are all made in London. The jewellery, and other stock of the swag-barrows, are bought at the general swag-shops, of which I have before spoken.

OF THE LIFE OF A TIN-WARE SELLER.

THE following street-biography was communicated to me in writing. It is, I believe, a striking instance of the vicissitudes and privations to which a street-life is subject. It forms, moreover, a curious example of those moral contradictions which make the same individual at one time give way hopelessly to the force of circumstances, and at another resolutely control them.

" My object," says my correspondent, " for writing this, what some folks no doubt will call a nonsensical epistle, is merely to show how much human nature is capable of enduring in the shape of privations. People in easy circumstances will scarcely credit what I am about to relate; and many of the poor will smile at what I have termed hardships, and at my folly in endeavouring to paint the misery I have endured, which will appear slight when compared to what they themselves have suffered.

"I am the son of a mechanic who was accidentally drowned some weeks previous to my birth. My mother, through industry and perseverance, endeavoured to support me and my sister till we arrived at the ages of 15 and 18, I being the younger. I entered a gentleman's service as pantry-boy, where I continued until I considered myself competent to take a higher situation. Still a servant's life was not the bent of my inclinations; martial music and viewing soldiers on parade made me think that a rifle was a more graceful tool than a toasting-fork. I resolved to serve his Majesty, and for that purpose enlisted in the 60th Rifles on the route for India, but Providence ordained it otherwise. On the afternoon on which I 'listed I fell by accident and broke my leg, and as I was not sworn in I was entitled to no pension. I was six months confined to my bed, and it was three years before I could go without my crutch. Grief for my misfortunes had borne my mother to an early grave, and I was left a cripple and destitute. Whether by design or accident I do not recollect, but I met with the lady (Lady M———) in whose service I first entered as pantry-boy; she took pity on my forlorn condition, and kindly invited me to her Mansion, where I remained until completely restored to health, but still crippled. After this I was employed painting and glazing, &c., and, considering myself competent to get my living in that line, I resolved to go to London—the theatre of all my misery to come, for I was disappointed. On reaching the metropolis my paint-brush was turned into a shovel, my paint-pot into a dust sieve, for I could only get employed by a man to work in a dust-yard at 10s. a week. From thence I went to a firm belonging to a friend at Beckenham, near Croydon, as working time-keeper, or foreman; but during a fair in that village I neglected to back the time, and being discharged was cast upon the world again with only 3s. in my pocket, which I eat and drank up, having no idea of street trading. Then came my trials; but having had sufficient food during the day, I did not feel much the effects of my first night in the streets. The next day I had no food, and towards dusk began bitterly to feel my situation; that night I slept, or rather lay, in an empty house. Towards noon of the next day I felt weak, and drank large quantities of water, for I had no particular desire for food. Passing by a shop where old clothes were offered for sale, I saw a man wretched in appearance disposing of an old vest for a few pence. I caught the malady and was instantly spoiled of my coat, having received in exchange for it 2s. and an old frock—such as are generally worn by waggoners or countrymen. I more than once smiled at my novel appearance. A penny loaf, a drink of water, and a threepenny lodging was the first assault upon my

2s. I regretted, however, the 3d. paid for my lodging, and determined not to risk another, for my bedfellows were so numerous, and of such teazing propensities, that they would not allow me to sleep; truly indeed is it said that 'poverty makes us acquainted with strange bedfellows.' At this time I formed an acquaintance with a man whose condition was similar to my own; he engaged to put me 'fly to a dodge' or two; an explanation from him was necessary to make me acquainted with the sense of his words, which I soon found simply meant artful manœuvres. One of these dodges was to snooze (a term for sleeping) in the Adelphi arches; I felt grateful for such a mark of disinterested friendship, and next day my friend and me fared sumptuously on the produce of my coat, and at night we repaired to the Arches in question, and there found a comfortable lodging in a hay-loft. I lay for some time, but did not sleep. I was several times addressed by my companion in an under tone, 'Are you asleep,' he whispered, 'ain't it a stunning dos?' (which means a good bed). I was not in a mood for conversation, and made no reply; to silence him completely I affected to snore, and this had the desired effect. For a few minutes he was quite quiet, and then he commenced with great caution to unlace my boots, with a view to stealing them, I perceived his object, and immediately left my lodging and companion. I felt grieved and disappointed at the loss of one in whom I placed all confidence; but this time wisdom was purchased cheaply, inasmuch as I suffered no loss except that my money might have lasted me a little longer. The remainder of that night I strayed about the Strand and Charing cross, after a drink of water; I took a seat on a curb surrounding the pump; many wretched beings came and seated themselves beside me, and a conversation ensued respecting their several destinations during the day. One proposed going to Hungerford-market to do a feed on decayed shrimps or other offal laying about the market; another proposed going to Covent-garden to do a 'tightener' of rotten oranges, to which I was humorously invited; I accepted the invitation, and proceeded with my new companion. I fared well; I filled my hat, took a seat, and made a most delicious breakfast. I remained strolling about the Garden all day, and towards evening was invited by my companions to a 'dos' in an open shed in Islington; this I declined, alleging that I had a lodging, but that night I slept amongst a heap of stones near the pillar at Charing-cross. I continued to attend the Garden for several weeks, subsisting entirely on the offal of that market. One day I took notice of a man there selling chestnut leaves; I enquired how he obtained them: he told me he plucked them from the trees without hindrance, and directed me to where I could obtain some. I went to a grove in the vicinity of Kilburn, and lay there all night. Next morning I found no leaves, so I returned disappointed to town, and on going through the market a woman employed me to carry a bushel of pears some little distance for her for a penny. I felt quite elevated in anticipation of such a treat as a penny loaf, but alas! I fell down under the weight of the fruit and poverty; my employer, however, kindly gave me the penny, though some of her pears were injured, and I had not taken them half the required distance. With the money I purchased a loaf, and sat on a stone near the pump in Covent Garden and began my meal. Here I soon had a companion, who after rincing a lettuce at the pump, began to devour it. I shared my loaf with him. 'O God!' said he, 'what are we destined to suffer. I have escaped the bullets of the Carlists in Spain to die in the streets of London with hunger.' I felt an interest in the poor fellow, who I discovered in the course of conversation had been a gentleman's servant in his time; he assured me he had been living in the same way for several weeks as I myself had been. Towards night my companion asked me where I slept. I told him my different haunts, he told me I'd better go to the straw-yard with him; this was a place I had not yet heard of; it was the nightly refuge for the houseless poor. I accompanied him without hesitation; my confidence was not misplaced; I slept there several nights. Bread was distributed to us night and morning, and this was fortunate, for the Garden began to fail. In the course of conversation with some of the inmates of the Refuge, we found that we could obtain employment at stone-breaking; this we tried the next morning, and succeeded. We worked all day, and received 6*d.* each on leaving work. We then made up our minds to go to lodgings that we might have an opportunity of washing what were once shirts.

"Misery had not had that wasting influence on my companion as it had on me. I was at this time a complete skeleton; a puff of wind would cause me to stagger. I continued stone-breaking, but about noon of the third day I sunk exhausted on the heap of stones before me. Poverty had done its work, and I anticipated with pleasure approaching dissolution. I was assisted to my lodging by my companion, and went to bed. When the woman at the lodging-house discovered that I was ill, she ordered some of her domestics to dress me and put me in the street, alleging that she was under a penalty of 20*l.* were it discovered that she lodged a sick stranger. I was, therefore, cast into the street at 12 o'clock at night. My companion then gave me the 3*d.* he had earned that day to procure me a lodging if possible, and he slept in the streets the remainder of the night. I went to another lodging, concealing as much as possible my illness; my money was taken, and I was conducted to bed. I spent a wretched night, and next morning I was very bad. The landlady led me to the workhouse; I was admitted directly; had they detained me asking questions I should have sunk on the floor. My disorder was pronounced English cholera. I lay three weeks in a precarious state, but at the end of seven weeks was recovered sufficiently to walk about. I was then discharged; but on going towards the Abbey in Westminster I fainted, and on recovery found myself surrounded by a number of persons. I was advised to return to the

house; I did so, and was admitted for a short time, after which I was again discharged, but I received out-door relief twice a week; and for some time a small portion of bread and cheese as well. *I had now lost not only all hope, but even desire of bettering my condition;* during these trials I made none acquainted with my privations, save those situated as I was. I now altered my condition as regards sleeping; I walked about during the night, and slept a portion of the day on a heap of sand near Westminster-bridge. I then remembered to have a poor relative in Kensington; I did not plead distress, but merely asked whether she knew where I might procure employment. I had a cup of tea, the first I had tasted since I was in the workhouse, a period of five weeks. Being asked some question by my relative, I could not help making reference to some of my sufferings. At this place I found a young man of whom I had had a previous acquaintance; I told him of my inability to procure a lodging, and he allowed me without the knowledge of his parents to sleep in the stable-loft; the bed was hard, but the coal sacks kept me warm. Here I had many opportunities of earning a few pence, and I began to regain my spirits. On one occasion, seeing a lad illtreated by a young man who was much his superior in size and strength, I interposed, and it may be conjectured in what manner. This circumstance procured me a friend, for, with the assistance of the lad I had protected, I was enabled to live tolerably well, and after a short while I got a situation at a coal-shed at 10*s.* a week. I continued in this place eighteen months, but, my master giving up the business, I was again cast on the world. I then began to think seriously of some way of living, and for the first time asked for the loan of 15*s.* With this I purchased a few articles of furniture, laid out 7*s.* 6*d.* for two hundred of oranges, with which I walked and hawked about two days, taking but 4*d.* during the time. I disposed of the remainder of my stock, wholesale, for 6*s.*; with this I purchased a small tin saucepan, a piece of marble slab, and commenced sugar-boiling. I retailed my manufacture in the streets. By dint of perseverance and economy I managed to live this way through the winter and a portion of the spring; but summer being now come, people needed none of my compounds to warm their mouths, so it was necessary for me to change my hand. What should I do? Thoughts came and vanished at their births. I recollected having seen a person selling rings at a penny each; I made up my mind to try the same. I laid out 5*s.* in a tray and stock; after arranging the goods to the best advantage I sallied into the streets. The glittering baubles took for a while, but when discoloured were useless. Having once a considerable stock of these soiled rings, I was prompted to begin "lot selling." After calculating the profits, I commenced selling in that line. As this continued for seven weeks I managed to get a living. The system then became general; every street in the metropolis contained a lot seller, so I was determined to change my hand. One day in the street I saw a girl with a bundle of old umbrellas going towards a marine store shop; I asked if the umbrellas were for sale; she replied in the affirmative; the price she asked was 4*d.*; I became a purchaser. With these old umbrellas I commenced a new life. I bought some trifling tools necessary for repairing umbrellas, and, after viewing well the construction of the articles, I commenced operations. I succeeded, and in a little time could not only mend an old umbrella, but make a new one. This way of living I followed three years. In one of my walks through the streets crying old umbrellas to sell, I saw a street tinker repairing a saucepan; he seemed so very comfortable with his fire-pan before him, that I resolved from that moment to become a tinker, and for that purpose I bought a few tools, prepared a budget, and sallied into the streets with as much indifference as if I had been at the business since my birth. After a little practice I fancied I was fit for better things than mending old saucepans, and flattered myself that I was able to make a new one. This I resolved to attempt, and succeeded so well, that I at once abandoned the rainy-day system, and commenced manufacturing articles in tin-ware, such as are now sold in the streets, namely funnels, nutmeg-graters, penny mugs, extinguishers, slices, savealls, &c. I soon became known to the street-sellers and swag-shop proprietors. The prices I get are low, and I am deficient in some of the tools necessary to forward the work, with the required speed to procure returns adequate to my expenses; but thanks to the Lord I am better off than ever I expected to be, with the difference only of a somewhat shattered constitution. There are many at the present day suffering as I have done, and they may be found in and about the different markets of the metropolis."

OF THE STREET-SELLERS OF DOG-COLLARS.

OF these street-traders there are now regularly twelve; one man counted to me fourteen, but two of these only sold dog-collars occasionally, when they could not get employment in their trade as journeymen brass-founders. Of the regular hands, one, two, and sometimes three sell only dog-collars (with the usual adjuncts of locks, and sometimes chains, and key-rings), but even these, when their stock-money avails, prefer uniting to the collars some other trifling article.

Two of the most profitable pitches for the sale of these articles are in the neighbourhood of the Old Swan Pier, off Thames-street, and at a corner of the Bank. Neither of these two traders confines his stock to dog-collars, though they constitute the most valuable portion of it. The one sells, in addition to his collars, key-rings, keys and chains, dog-whistles, stamps with letters engraved upon them, printer's type, in which any name or initials may be set up, shaving-brushes, trowser-straps, razors, and a few other light articles. The other sells little more than "dog" articles, with the addition of brass padlocks and small whips. But the minor commodities are frequently varied, according to the season and to the street-seller's opinion of what may "sell."

Some of these traders hang their wares against the rails of any public or other building in a good situation, where they can obtain leave. Others have stalls, with "a back," from the corners of which hang the strings of dog-collars, one linked within another. The manner in which one street-seller displays his wares is shown in the illustration before given. Of the whole number, half are either itinerant on a round, or walk up and down a thoroughfare and an adjacent street or two. "Dog-collars," said one man, "is no good at Saturday-night markets. People has said to me—for I was flat enough to try once—'Dogs! pooh, I've hardly grub enough for the kids.' For all that, sir, some poor people has dogs, and is very fond of them too; ay, and I've sold them collars, but seldom. I think it's them as has no children has dogs."

The collars most in demand are brass. One man pointed out to me the merits of his stock, which he retailed from 6*d.* each (for the very small ones) to 3*s.*—for collars seemingly big enough for Pyrenean sheep dogs. Some of the street-sold collars have black and red rims and linings; others are of leather, often scarlet, stitched ornamentally over a sort of jointed iron or wire-work. A few are of strong compact steel chain-work; "but them's more the fashion," said one seller, "for sporting dogs, like pointers and greyhounds, and is very seldom bought in the streets. It's the pet dogs as is our best friends."

The dog-collar sellers have, as regards perhaps one-half, been connected in their youth with some mechanical occupation in metal manufacture. Four, I am told, are or were pensioners to a small amount, as soldiers or sailors.

Some further particulars of the business will be found in the following statement given me by a man in the trade. He was sickly-looking, seemed dispirited at first, but to recover his spirits as he conversed, and spoke with a provincial (I presume a Warwickshire or Staffordshire) accent.

"I served my time, sir; my relations put me —for my parents died when I was a boy—to a harness furniture maker, in Wa'sall (Walsal), who supplied Mr. Dixon, a saddler's ironmonger, in a good way. I had fair makings, and was well treated, and when I was out of my time I worked for another master, and I then found I could make my pad territs" (the round loops of the harness pad, through which the reins are passed), "my hooks, my buckles, my ornaments (some of 'em crests), as well as any man. I worked only in brass, never plated, but sometimes the body for plating, and mostly territs and hooks. Thinking I'd better myself, I came to London. I was between five and six weeks before I got a stroke of work, and my money had gone. I found that London harness makers and coachmakers' names was put on Walsal-made goods, and 'London made' and 'town made' was put too. They might be as good, but they wasn't town made no more nor I am. I can't tell what I suffered, and felt, and thought, as at last I walked the streets. I was afraid to call at any brass-worker's—for I can do many sorts of brass work—I was so shabby. I called once at

Mr. A——'s, near Smithfield, and he, or his foreman perhaps it was, says to me, 'Give that tugbuckle a file.' I'd had nothing to eat but an apple I found in the street that day, and my hand trembled, and so he told me that drunkards, with trembling hands, wouldn't do there. I was never a drinking man; and at that time hadn't tasted so much as beer for ten days. My landlady—I paid her 1*s.* a week for half a bed with a porter—trusted me my rent, 'cause I paid her when I had it; but I walked about, narvussed and trembling, and frightened at every sudden sound. No, sir, I've stood looking over a bridge, but, though I may have thought of suicide, I never once had really a notion of it. I don't know how to tell it, but I felt stupified like, as much as miserable. *I felt I could do nothing.* Perhaps I shouldn't have had power of mind to drown myself if I'd made up my resolution; besides, it's a dreadful wickedness. I always liked reading, and, before I was fairly beaten out, used to read at home, at shop-windows, and at book-stalls, as long as I dared, but latterly, when I was starving, I couldn't fix my mind to read anyhow. One night I met a Wa's'll friend, and he took me to his inn, and gave me a good beef-steak supper and some beer, and he got me a nice clean bed in the house. In the morning he gave me what did me most good of all, a good new shirt, and 5*s.* I got work two days after, and kept it near five years, with four masters, and married and saved 12*l.* We had no family to live, and my poor wife died in the cholera in 1849, and I buried her decently, thank God, for she was a good soul. When I thought the cholera was gone, I had it myself, and was ill long, and lost my work, and had the same sufferings as before, and was without soles to my shoes or a shirt to my back, 'till a gentleman I'd worked for lent me 1*l.*, and then I went into this trade, and pulled up a little. In six weeks I paid 15*s.* of my debt, and had my own time for the remaining 5*s.* Now I get an odd job with my master sometimes, and at others sell my collars, and chains, and key-rings, and locks, and such like. I'm ashamed of the dog-collar locks; I can buy them at 2*d.* a dozen, or 1*s.* 6*d.* a gross; they're sad rubbish. In two or three weeks sometimes, the wire hasp is worn through, just by the rattling of the collar, and the lock falls off. I make now, one way and another, about 10*s.* a week. My lodging's 2*s.* a week for a bed-room—it's a closet tho,' for my furniture all went. God's good, and I'll see better days yet. I have sure promise of regular work, and then I can earn 30*s.* to 40*s.* I do best with my collars about the docks. I'm sure I don't know why."

I am told that each of the street-sellers of dog-collars sell on the average a dozen a week, at a medium receipt of 12*s.* ("sometimes 20*s.*, and sometimes 6*s.*"), though some will sell three and even four dozen collars in the week. Any regular dog-collar seller will undertake to get a name engraved upon it at 1*d.* a letter. The goods are bought at a swag-shop, or an establishment carried on in the same way. The retailer's profit is 35 per cent.

Reckoning 12*s.* weekly taken by twelve men, we find 374*l.* expended yearly in the streets in dog-collars.

OF THE LIFE OF A STREET-SELLER OF DOG-COLLARS.

FROM the well-known vendor of these articles whose portrait was given in No. 10 of this work, I had the following sketch of his history:—

"I was born in Brewer-street, St. James," he said, in answer to my questions; "I am 73 years of age. My father and mother were poor people; I never went to school; my father died while I was young; my mother used to go out charing; she couldn't afford to pay for schooling, and told me, I must look out and *yearn* my own living while I was a mere chick. At ten years of age I went to sea in the merchant sarvice. While I was in the merchant sarvice, I could get good wages, for I soon knowed my duty. I was always of an industrious turn, and never liked to be idle; don't you see what I mean. In '97 I was pressed on board the INCONSTANT frigate; I was paid off six months arterwards, but hadn't much to take, and that, like all other young men who hadn't larned the dodges of life, I spent very soon; but I never got drunk—thank God!" said the old man, "I never got drunk, or I shouldn't ha been what I am now at 73 years of age. I was drafted into the Woolwich 44-gun ship; from her to the OVERISAL." I inquired how the name of the ship was spelt; "Oh I am not scholard enough for that there," he replied, "tho' I did larn to read and write when abord a man of war. I larned myself. But you must look into a *Dutch dictionary*, for it's a Dutch name. I then entered on board the AMPHINE frigate, and arter I had sarved some months in her, I entered the merchant sarvice again, and arter that I went to Greenland to the whale-fishery—they calls me here in the college" (he is now an inmate of Greenwich Hospital) "' *Whaler Ben*,' but I arnt affronted—most on 'em here have nicknames. I went three voyages besides to the West Ingees. I never got drunk even there, though I was obliged to drink rum; it wouldn't ha done to ha drunk the water NEAT, there was so many insects in it. When my sailor's life was over I comes to Liverpool and marries a wife—aye and as good a wife as any poor man ever had in England. I had saved a goodish bit o' money, nearly 300*l.*, for I was not so foolish as some of the poor sailors, who yearns their money like horses and spends it like asses, I say. Well we sets up a shop—a chandler shop—in Liverpool: me and my old 'ooman does; and I also entered into the pig-dealing line. I used to get some of my pigs from Ireland, and some I used to breed myself, but I was very misfortunate. You recollect the year when the disease was among the cattle, in course you recollects that; well, sir, I lost 24 pigs and a horse in one year, and that was a good loss for a poor man, wer'n't it? I thought it werry hard, for I'd worked hard for my money at sea, and I was always werry careful, arter I knowed what life was. My poor wife too used to trust a good deal in the shop, and by-and-by, behold you, me and my old 'ooman was on our beam ends. My wife was took ill too—and, for the purpose of getting the best adwice, I brings her to London, but her cable had run out, and she died, and I 've been a poor forlorned creatur' ever since. You wouldn't think it, but arter that I never slept on a bed for seven years. I had blankets and my clothes—but what I means is that I never had a bed to lie on. I sold most of my bits o' things to bury my wife. I didn't relish applying to the parish. I kept a few sticks tho', for I don't like them ere lodging-houses. I can't be a werry bad kerackter, for I was seven years under one landlord, and I warrant me if I wanted a room agin he would let me have one. Arter my wife died, knowing some'at about ropes I gets work at Maberley's, the great contractors—in course you knows *him*. I made rope traces for the artillery; there's a good deal of leather-work about the traces, and stitching them, you see, puts me up to the making of dogs'-collars. I was always handy with my fingers, and can make shoes or anythink. I can work now as well as ever I could in my life, only my eyes isn't so good. Ain't it curious now, sir, that wot a man larns in his fingers he never forgets ? Well being out o' work, I was knocking about for some time, and then I was adwised to apply for a board to carry at one of them cheap tailors, but I didn't get none ; so I takes to hawking link buttons and key rings, and buys some brass dog-collars ; it was them brass collars as made me bethought myself as I could make some leather ones. Altho' I had been better off I didn't think it any disgrace to get a honest living. The leather collars is harder to make than the brass ones, only the brass ones wants more implements. There are about a dozen selling in the streets as makes brass-collars—there's not much profit on the brass ones. People says there's nothing like leather, and I thinks they are right. Well, sir, as I was a telling you, I commences the leather-collar making,—in course I didn't make 'em as well at first as I do now. It was werry hard lines at the best of times. I used to get up at 4 o'clock in the morning in the summer time, and make my collars ; then I 'd turn out about 9, and keep out until 7 or 8 at night. I seldom took more than 2s. per day. What profit did I get out of 2s.? Why, lor bless you, sir ! if I hadn't made them myself, I shouldn't have got no profit at all. But as it was, if I took 2s., the profits was from 1s. to 1s. 6d.; howsomever, sometimes I didn't take 6d. Wet days too used to run me aground altogether; my rheumatics used to bore me always when the rain come down, and then I couldn't get out to sell. If I 'd any leather at them times I used to make it up ; but if I hadn't none, why I was obligated to make the best on it. Oh, sir ! you little knows what I 've suffered ; many a banyan day I 've had in my little room—upon a wet day—aye, and other days too. Why, I think I 'd a starved if it hadn't a been for the 'bus-men about Hungerford-market. They are good lads them there 'bus lads to such as me ; they used to buy my collars when they didn't want them. Ask any on 'em

if they know anything about old Tom, the collar-maker, and see if they don't flare up and respect me. They used sometimes to raffle my collars and give 'em back to me. Mr. Longstaff too, the landlord of the Hungerford Arms—I believe it 's called the Hungerford Hotel—has given me something to eat very often when I was hungry, and had nothing myself. There 's what you call a hor'nary there every day. You knows what I mean—gentlemen has their grub there at so much a head, or so much a belly it should be, I says. I used to come in for the scraps, and werry thankful I was for them I can assure you. Yes, Mr. Longstaff is what you may call a good man. He 's what you calls a odd man, and a odd man 's always a good man. All I got to say is, ' God bless him !' he 's fed me many time when I 've been hungry. I used to light upon other friends too,—landlords of public-houses, where I used to hawk my collars ; they seemed to take to me somehow ; it wer'n't for what I spent in their houses I'm sure, seeing as how I 'd nothing to spend. I had no pension for my sarvice, and so I was adwised to apply for admission to ' the house here ' (Greenwich Hospital). I goes to Somerset-House; another poor fellow was making a application at the same time ; but I didn't nothing till one very cold day, when I was standing quite miserable like with my collars. I 'd been out several hours and hadn't taken a penny, when up comes the man as wanted to get into the house, running with all his might to me. I thought he was going to tell me he had got into the house, and I was glad on it, for, poor fellow, he was werry bad oft ; howsomever he says to me, ' Tom,' says he, ' they wants you at the Admirality.' ' Does they ?' says I, and 'cordingly away I goes ; and arter telling the admiral my sarvice, and answering a good many questions as he put to me, the admiral says, says he, ' The order will be made out ; you shall go into the house.' I think the admiral knowed me or somethink about me, you see. I don't know his name, and it would'nt ha' done to have axed. God bless him, whoever he is, I says, and shall say to my dying day ; it seemed like Providence. I hadn't taken a ha'penny all that day ; I was cold and hungry, and suffering great pain from my rheumatics. Thank God," exclaimed the old man in conclusion, "I am quite comfortable now. I 've everythink I want except a little more tea and shuggar, but I 'm quite content, and thank God for all his mercies."

The old man informed me moreover that he did not think there were more than half-a-dozen street-sellers besides himself who made leather collars ; it was a poor trade, he said, and though the other makers were younger than he was, he "could lick them all at stitching." He did not believe, he told me, that any of the collar-sellers sold more than he did—if as many—for he had friends that perhaps other men had not. He makes collars now sometimes, and wishes he could get some shopkeeper to sell them for him, and then maybe, he says, he could obtain a little more tea and shuggar, and assist a sister-in-law of his whom he tells me is in great distress, and whom he has been

THE STREET-SELLER OF DOGS' COLLARS.

[From a Daguerreotype by BEARD.]

THE STREET-SELLER OF CROCKERY-WARE

BARTERING FOR OLD CLOTHES.

[*From a Daguerreotype by* BEARD.]

in the habit of assisting for many years, notwithstanding his poverty. The old man, during the recital of his troubles, was affected to tears several times—especially when he spoke of his wife, and the distress he had undergone—and with much sincerity blessed God for the comforts that he now enjoys.

OF THE STREET-SELLERS OF TOOLS.

THESE people are of the same class as the sellers of hardware articles, though so far a distinct body that they generally sell tools only.

The tools are of the commonest kind, and supplied by the cheapest swag-shops, from which establishments the majority of the street-traders derive their supplies. They are sometimes displayed on a small barrow, sometimes on a stall, and are mostly German-made.

The articles sold and the price asked—and generally obtained, as no extravagant profit is demanded—is shown by the following :—

Claw hammers, 6d. Large claw, black and glaze-faced, 1s. Pincers, 4d.; larger ones, 6d. Screw-drivers, from 2d. to 1s.! Flat-nose pliers, 6d. a pair ; squares, 6d. to 1s. Carpenters' oil-cans, from 9d. to 1s. 3d. Nests of brad-awls (for joiners, and in wooden cases), 6d. to 2s. Back saws, 1s. to 2s. 6d.

While many of the street-sellers of tools travel the several thoroughfares and suburbs of the metropolis, others vend tools of a particular kind in particular localities. These localities and sellers may be divided into four distinct classes:— (1) The street-sellers of tools in the markets; (2) The street-sellers of tools at the docks and warehouses; (3) The street-sellers of tools at mews, stable-yards, and job-masters'; and (4) The street-sellers of tools to working men at their workshops.

The markets which are usually frequented by the vendors of tools are Newgate and Leadenhall. There are, I am informed, only five or six street-sellers who at present frequent these markets on the busy days. The articles in which they deal are butchers' saws, cleavers, steels, meat-hooks, and knives; these saws they sell from 2s. to 4s. each; knives and steels, from 9d. to 1s. 3d. each; cleavers, from 1s. 6d. to 2s. each; and meat-hooks at 1d., 2d., and 3d. each, according to the size. It is very seldom, however, that cleavers are sold by the street-sellers, as they are too heavy to carry about. I am told that the trade of the tool-sellers in Newgate and Leadenhall markets is now very indifferent, owing chiefly to the butchers having been so frequently imposed upon by the street-sellers, that they are either indisposed or afraid to deal with them. When the itinerant tool-sellers are not occupied at the markets they vend their wares to tradesmen at private shops, but often without success. "It is a poor living," said one of the hawkers to me; "sometimes little better than starving. I have gone out a whole day and haven't taken a farthing." I am informed that the greater portion of these street-sellers are broken-down butchers. The tools they vend are purchased at the Brummagem warehouses. To start in this branch of the street-business 5s. or

10s. usually constitutes the amount of capital invested in stock, and the average takings of each are about 2s. or 2s. 6d. a day.

"A dozen years back twenty such men offered saws at my shop," said a butcher in a northern suburb to me; "now there's only one, and he seems half-starving, poor fellow, and looks very hungrily at the meat. Perhaps it's a way he's got to have a bit given him, as it is sometimes."

The only street-seller of tools at present frequenting Billingsgate-market is an elderly man, who is by trade a working cutler. The articles he displays upon his tray are oyster-knives, fish-knives, steels, scissors, packing-needles, and hammers. This tradesman makes his own oyster-knives and fish-knives; the scissors and hammers are second-hand ; and the packing-needles are bought at the ironmongers. Sometimes brad-awls, gimlets, nails, and screws form a part of his stock. He informed me that he had frequented Billingsgate-market upwards of ten years. "Wet or dry," he said, " I am here, and I often suffer from rheumatics in the head and limbs. Sometimes I have taken only a few pence ; on other occasions I have taken 3s. or 4s., but this is not very often. However, what with the little I take at Billingsgate, and at other places, I can just get a crust, and go on from day to day."

The itinerant saw-sellers offer their goods to any one in the street as well as at the shops, and are at the street markets on Saturday evenings with small saws for use in cookery. With the butchers they generally barter rather than sell, taking any old saw in exchange with so much money, for a new one. "I was brought up a butcher," said one of these saw-sellers, "and worked as a journeyman, off and on, between twenty and thirty year. But I grew werry delicate from rheumaticks, and my old 'ooman was bad too, so that we once had to go into Marylebone work'us. I had no family living, perhaps they're better as it is. We discharged ourselves after a time, and they gave us 5s. I then thought I'd try and sell a few saws and things. A master-butcher that's been a friend to me, lent me another 5s., and I asked a man as sold saws to butchers to put me in the way of it, and he took me to a swag-shop. I do werry badly, sir, but I'll not deny, and I can't deny—not anyhow—when you tell me Mr. —— told you about me—that there's 'elps to me. If I make a bargain, for so much ; or for old saws or cleavers, or any old butcher thing, and so much ; a man wot knows me says, 'Well, old boy, you don't look satisfied ; here's a bit of steak for you.' Sometimes it's a cut off a scrag of mutton, or weal ; that gives the old 'ooman and me a good nourishing bit of grub. I can work at times, and every Saturday a'most I'm now a porter to a butcher. I carries his meat from Newgate, when he's killed hisself, and wants no more than a man's weight from the market ; and when he 'asn't killed hisself in course he hires a cart. I makes 1s. a day the year round, I think, on saws, and my old 'ooman makes more than 'arf as much at charing, and there's the 'elps, and then I gets 18d. and my grub every Saturday. It's no use grumbling; lots isn't grubbed 'arf so well as me and my old 'ooman. My rent's 20d. a week."

The articles vended by the second class of the street-sellers of tools, or those whose purchasers are mostly connected with the docks and warehouses, consist of iron-handled claw-hammers, spanners, bed-keys, and corkscrews. Of these street-traders there are ten or twelve, and the greater portion of them are blacksmiths out of employ. Some make their own hammers, whereas others purchase the articles they vend at the swag-shops. " We sell more hammers and bed-keys than other things," said one, " and sometimes we sells a corkscrew to the landlord of a public-house, and then we have perhaps half-a-pint of beer. Our principal customers for spanners are wheelwrights. Those for hammers are egg-merchants, oilmen, wax and tallow-chandlers, and other tradesmen who receive or send out goods in wooden cases; as well as chance customers in the streets." The amount of capital required to start in the line is from 5s. to 15s.: "it is not much use," said one, "to go to shop with less than 10s."

A third class of the street-sellers of tools are the vendors of curry-combs and brushes, mane-combs, scrapers, and clipping instruments; and these articles are usually sold at the several mews, stable-yards, and jobbing-masters' in and about the metropolis. The sellers are mostly broken-down grooms, who, not being able to obtain a situation, resort to street-selling as a last shift. " It is the last coach, when a man takes to this kind of living," said one of my informants, a groom in a "good place;" "and it's getting worse and worse. The poor fellows look half-starved. Why, what do you think I gave for these scissors? I got 'em for 6d. and a pint of beer, and I should have to give perhaps half-a-crown for 'em at a shop." The trade is fast declining, and to gentlemen's carriage mews the street-sellers of such tools rarely resort, as the instruments required for stable-use are now bought, by the coachmen, of the tradesmen who supply their masters. At the " mixed mews," as I heard them called, there are two men who, along with razors, knives, and other things, occasionally offer " clipping" and " trimming" scissors. Four or five years ago there were four of these street-sellers. The trimming-scissors are, in the shops, 1s. 6d. to 2s. 6d. a pair. There is one trade still carried on in these places, although it is diminutive compared to what it was: I allude to the sale of curry-combs. Those vended by street-sellers at the mews are sold at 7d. or 6d. The best sale for these curry-combs is about Coventry-street and the Hay-market, and at the livery-stables generally. Along with curry-combs, the street-vendors sell wash-leathers, mane-combs (horn), sponges (which were like dried moss for awhile, I was told, got up by the Jews, but which are now good), dandy-brushes (whalebone-brushes, to scrape dirt from a horse's legs, before he is groomed), spoke-brushes (to clean carriage-wheels), and coach-mops. One dweller in a large West-end mews computed that 100 different street-traders resorted thither daily, and that

twenty sold the articles I have specified. In this trade, I am assured, there are no broken-down coachmen or grooms, only the regular street-sellers. A commoner curry-comb is sold at 2d. (prime cost 1s. 3d. a dozen), at Smithfield, on market-days, and to the carmen, and the owners of the rougher sort of horses; but this trade is not extensive.

There may be ten men, I am told, selling common "currys;" and they also sell other articles (often horse oil-cloths and nose-bags) along with them.

The last class of street-sellers is the beaten-out mechanic or workman, who, through blindness, age, or infirmities, is driven to obtain a livelihood by supplying his particular craft with their various implements. Of this class, as I have before stated, there are six men in London who were brought up as tailors, and are now, through some affliction or privation, incapacitated from following their calling. These men sell needles at four and five for 1d.; thimbles 1d. to 2d. each; scissors from 1s. to 2s. 6d.; and wax 1d. the lump. There are also old and blind shoemakers, who sell a few articles of grindery to their shopmates, as they term them, as well as a few decayed members of other trades, hawking the implements of the handicraft to which they formerly belonged. But as I have already given a long account of one of this class, under the head of the blind needle-seller, there is no occasion for me to speak further on the subject.

From one of the street-traders in saws I had the following account of his struggles, as well as the benefit he received from teetotalism, of which he spoke very warmly. His room was on the fourth floor of a house in a court near Holborn, and was clean and comfortable-looking. There were good-sized pictures, in frames, of the Queen, the Last Supper, and a Rural Scene, besides minor pictures: some of these had been received in exchange for saws with street-picture-sellers. A shelf was covered with china ornaments, such as are sold in the streets; the table had its oil-skin cover, and altogether I have seldom seen a more decent room. The rent, unfurnished, was 2s. a week.

" I've been eight years in this trade, sir," the saw-seller said, " but I was brought up to a very different one. When a lad I worked in a coal-pit along with my father, but his behaviour to me was so cruel, he beat me so, that I ran away, and walked every step from the north of England to London. I can't say I ever repented running away—much as I've gone through. My money was soon gone when I got to London, and my way of speaking was laughed at. [He had now very little of a provincial accent.] That's fourteen year back. Why, indeed, sir, it puzzles me to tell you how I lived then when I did live. I jobbed about the markets, and slept, when I could pay for a lodging, at the cheap lodging-houses; so I got into the way of selling a few things in the streets, as I saw others do. I sold laces and children's handkerchiefs. Sometimes I was miserable enough when I hadn't a farthing, and if I managed to make a sixpence I got tipsy on it. For six weeks I slept every night in the Peckham Union. For another five or six weeks I slept every night in the dark arches by the Strand. I've sometimes had twenty or thirty companions there. I used to lie down on the bare stones, and was asleep in a minute, and slept like a top all night, but waking was very bad. I felt stiff, and sore, and cold, and miserable. How I lived at all is a wonder to me. About eleven years ago I was persuaded to go to a Temperance Meeting in Harp Alley (Farringdon-street), and there I signed the pledge; that is, I made my mark, for I can't read or write, which has been a great hinder to me. If I'd been a scholard a teetotal gent would have got me into the police three years ago, about the time I got married. I did better, of course, when I was a teetotaller—no more dark arches. I sold a few little shawls in the streets then, but it was hardly bread and butter and coffee at times. Eight year ago I thought I would try saw-selling: a shopkeeper advised me, and I began on six salt saws, which I sold to oil-men. They're for cutting salt only, and are made of zinc, as steel would rust and dirty the salt. The trade was far better at first than it is now. In good weeks I earned 16s. to 18s. In bad weeks 10s. or 12s. Now I may earn 10s., not more, a week, pretty regular: yesterday I made only 6d. Oilmen are better customers than chance street-buyers, for I'm known to them. There's only one man besides myself selling nothing but saws. I walk, I believe, 100 miles every week, and that I couldn't do, I know, if I wasn't teetotal. I never long for a taste of liquor if I'm ever so cold or tired. It's all poisonous."

The saws sold are 8 inch, which cost at the swag-shops 8s. and 8s. 6d. a dozen; 10 inch, 9s. and 9s. 6d.; and so on, the price advancing according to the increased size, to 18 inch, 13s. 6d. the dozen. Larger sizes are seldom sold in the streets. The second man's earnings, my informant believed, were the same as his own.

The wife of my informant, when she got work as an embroideress, could earn 11s. and 12s. At present she was at work braiding dresses for a dressmaker, at 2½d. each. By hard work, and if she had not her baby to attend to, she could earn no more than 7½d. a day. As it was she did not earn 6d.

OF THE BEGGAR STREET-SELLERS.

UNDER this head I include only such of the beggar street-sellers as are neither infirm nor suffering from any severe bodily affliction or privation. I am well aware that the aged—the blind—the lame and the halt often *pretend* to sell small articles in the street—such as boot-laces, tracts, cabbage-nets, lucifer-matches, kettle-holders, and the like; and that such matters are carried by them partly to keep clear of the law, and partly to evince a disposition to the public that they are willing to do something for their livelihood. But these being really objects of charity, they belong more properly to the second main division of this book, in which the poor, or those that can't work, and their several means of living, will be treated of.

Such, though beggars, are not "lurkers"— a lurker being strictly one who loiters about for some dishonest purpose. Many modes of thieving as well as begging are termed "lurking"—the "dead lurk," for instance, is the expressive slang phrase for the art of entering dwelling-houses during divine service. The term "lurk," however, is mostly applied to the several modes of plundering by representations of sham distress.

It is of these alone that I purpose here treating —or rather of that portion of them which pretends to deal in manufactured articles.

In a few instances the street-sellers of small articles of utility are also the manufacturers. Many, however, *say* they are the producers of the things they offer for sale, thinking thus to evade the necessity of having a hawker's licence. The majority of these petty dealers know little of the manufacture of the goods they vend, being mere tradesmen. Some few profess to be the makers of their commodities, solely with the view of enlisting sympathy, and thus either selling the trifles they carry at an enormous profit, or else of obtaining alms.

An inmate of one of the low lodging-houses has supplied me with the following statement:—

"Within my recollection," says my informant, "the great branch of trade among these worthies, was the sale of sewing cotton, either in skeins or on reels. In the former case, the article cost the 'lurkers' about 8d. per pound; one pound would produce thirty skeins, which, sold at one penny each, or two for three halfpence, produced a heavy profit. The lurkers could mostly dispose of three pounds per day; the article was, of course, damaged, rotten, and worthless.

"The mode of sale consisted in the 'lurkers' calling at the several houses in a particular district, and representing themselves as Manchester cotton spinners out of employ. Long tales, of course, were told of the distresses of the operatives, and of the oppression of their employers; these tales had for the most part been taught them at the padding-ken, by some old and experienced dodger of 'the school;' and if the spokesman could patter well, a much larger sum was frequently obtained in direct alms than was reaped by the sale."

Cotton on reels was—except to the purchaser— a still better speculation; the reels were large, handsomely mounted, and displayed in bold relief such inscriptions as the following:—

PIKE'S
PATENT COTTON.
120 YARDS.

The reader, however, must divide the "120 yards," here mentioned, by 12, and then he will arrive at something like the true secret as to the quantity; for the surface only was covered by the thread.

"The 'cotton Lurk' is now 'cooper'd' (worn out); a more common dodge—and, of course, only an excuse for begging—is to envelope a packet of 'warranted' needles, or a few inches of 'real Honiton lace' in an envelope, with a few lines to the 'Lady of the House,' or a printed bill, setting forth the misery of the manufacturers, and the intention of the parties leaving the 'fakement' to presume to call for an answer in a few hours. I subjoin a copy of one of these documents.

'THE LACE-MAKERS' APPEAL.

'It is with extreme regret we thus presume to trespass on your time and attention, we are Lace Makers by trade, and òwing to the extensive improvements in Machinery, it has made hand labour completely useless.

'So that it has thrown hundreds of honest and industrious men out of employment, your petitioners are among the number. Fifteen men with their families have left their homes with the intention of emigrating to South Australia, and the only means we have of supporting ourselves till we can get away, is by the sale of some Frame Thread and Traced Lace Collars of our own manufacture, at the following low prices—Fashionable Frame Lace Collars 3d. each, warranted to wash and wear well ; Frame Thread Collars 6d. each, Traced Lace Collars 1s. each, the best that can be made, and we trust we shall meet with that encouragement from the Friends of Industry which our necessities require.

'The enclosed two 6d.

'The patry calling for this, will have an assortment of the Newest Patterns of Frame Thread Lace and Edgings for your inspection, and the smallest purchase will be thankfully received and gratefully remembered by G. DAVIS, Lace Makers.

'We beg to state that a number of the families being destitute of clothing, the bearer is authorised to receive any articles of such in exchange for Lace, Edgings or Collars.

'ALLEN, Printer, Long-row, Nottingham."

"These are left by one of 'the school' at the houses of the gentry, a mark being placed on the door post of such as are 'bone' or 'gammy,' in order to inform the rest of 'the school' where to call, and what houses to avoid. As the needles cost but a few pence per thousand, and the lace less than one halfpenny per yard— a few purchasers of the former at 1s. per packet (25 needles), or of the latter at 2s. 6d. per yard, is what these 'lurkers' term a 'fair day's work for a fair day's wages.'

"Another and very extensive branch of the pseudo-'manufacturing' fraternity is to be found among the sham street-sellers of cutlery.

"At some of the least respectable of the swag-shops may be bought all the paraphernalia requisite in order to set up as the real manufacturer of Sheffield and 'Brummagem' goods—including, beside the cutlery, chamois-leather aprons, paper caps (ready crushed, to give them the appearance of age and usage), and last, but not least, a compound of black lead and tallow, to 'take the granny' off them as has white 'ands, so as the flat's shan't 'tumble' to the 'unworkmanlike appearance of the palms of the 'lurker.'

"Thus 'got up' for the part," continues my informant, "and provided with a case of razors, which perhaps has cost him two groats, and (if he can raise as much) a noggin o' rum to 'give him cheek' and make him 'speak up' to his victims—

'Jack Beaver,' the 'king of the street-cutlers,' will sally forth, and meet, intercept, and follow any gentleman who seems a 'likely spec,' till worried perhaps by importunity, the 'swell' buys what he does not want, and, I need scarcely add, what he cannot use. Next, in importance, to ' Jack Beaver,' is the notorious ' Pat Connor.' Pat ' does nothing on the blob,' that is to say (he does not follow people and speak to them on the streets). His ' dodge'—and it has been for years a successful one—is to go round to the public offices, dressed as before described, with the exception of being in his shirt sleeves (he has every day a *clean* shirt), and teaze the clerks till they purchase a pen-knife. He has been known to sell from fifteen to twenty knives in one day, at two shillings each, the first cost being about threepence-halfpenny. Of course he is often interrupted by porters and other officials, but he always carries in one hand a roll of wire, and a small hammer in the other, and having got the name of some gentleman up stairs, he pretends that he is going to mend Mr. So-and-so's bell. This worthy, a short time ago, made free—in the Custom House—with a timepiece, belonging to one of the clerks, for which the 'Sheffield manufacturer' got twelve months in Newgate. I have not seen him since," adds my informant, "and therefore imagine that he is now taking a provincial tour. "

OF THE "HOUSE OF LORDS," A STREET-SELLER'S DEFUNCT CLUB.

I HAVE given an account of a defunct club, of which the "paper workers" were the chief members ; and I have now to do the same of a society not very dissimilar in its objects, of which the street-sellers of manufactured articles constituted the great majority. It was called the "house of lords," and was established about eight years ago, at the Roebuck-tavern, Holborn, and existed three years. Its object was to relieve its members in sickness. The subscription was 2d. a week, and the relief to a sick member was as many pennies a week as the club contained members, with, in any pressing case, an additional halfpenny, which the members paid into the fund, over and above their weekly subscription. For the greater part of its existence the club contained ninety members (a few of them honorary), and there were very few cases of "declaring on the fund" by sick members. At one period for many weeks there were no such declarations, and the "house of lords" had 30l. in hand. One of the leading members, a very intelligent man, who had "a good connection in hardware," had taken great pains to prepare a code of rules, which, having been approved by the other members, it was considered time that the "house of lords" should be enrolled. Delays, however, intervened. " To tell you the truth, sir," one of them said, " we were afraid to employ an attorney, and thought of waiting upon Mr. Tidd Pratt ourselves, but it wasn't to be."

The club was, moreover, looked upon as somewhat select. "No costers were admitted, sir," I was told by a hardware seller in the streets ;

"not but what there's many very industrious and honest men among them, but they're in a different line, and are a different sort of people to us." The members met once a week, and, though they were merry and talkative enough, drunkenness was strongly discouraged. It was common for the subscribers who were regarded as the "geniuses" of the trade, to take counsel together, and "invent any new move." They were reputed to be knowing among the most knowing, in all street arts and dodges, and the way in which the club came to an end, considering the strong claims to knowingness of its members, was curious enough.

One Saturday evening a member who was considered a respectable man, and was sufficiently regular in his payments, appeared at the weekly meeting, introducing his landlord, who, as a non-member, had to pay 1*d.* for admission. The man told how his family had suffered from illness, and how he had been ill, and got into arrears of rent, for he did not like to distress the fund; and how his landlord was then in possession of his "sticks," which must be sold in the morning if he could not pay 15*s.*; and, moreover, how his landlord—a very kind-hearted, indulgent man—was forced to do this, for he himself was in difficulties. The members voted that the 15*s.* should be advanced; but before the next meeting night it was discovered that the statement of the poor member in arrears was an imposition. The landlord was merely a confederate; the worthy couple had been drinking together, and, to prolong their tippling, had hit upon the roguish scheme I have mentioned.

This, among other things, lowered the confidence of the members. The numbers fell off until it was thought best to "wind up the concern." The small funds in hand were fairly apportioned among the remaining members, and the club ceased to exist.

Another Street-sellers' Club has recently been formed by the men themselves, of which the following is the prospectus, and it is to be hoped that this attempt on the part of the street-folk to better their condition will meet with a better fate than its predecessor:—

Our motto is "To live honestly by daily perseverance and industry."

Street Mechanics, Labourers, Hawkers, &c.

PROTECTION ASSOCIATION,

HELD AT THE LAMB TAVERN,

NEW TURNSTILE, HOLBORN,
Proprietor, Mr. White.

The above-named classes are kindly invited to attend a Meeting convened for

SUNDAY EVENING NEXT,

And every succeeding Sunday Evening, at the above house, to carry out the object unanimously agreed to by the Enrolled Members and the General Committee. Furthermore, to take into consideration the most appropriate means whereby we may be enabled to assist each other in the time of adversity.

COMMITTEE:

Mr. Taylor, Chairman,   Mr. Thoresby,
— Travers,   — Dowse,
— Cowan,   — Manly,
— Moody,   — Morris,
— Moore,   — Lawson,
— Hand,   — Lamb,
— Martin.
Mr. J. White, Treasurer. Mr. F. A. Thoresby,
                 Secretary.

The chair will be taken at Seven o'clock, and the Committee are requested to be in attendance one hour previous.

OF THE STREET-SELLERS OF CROCKERY AND GLASS-WARES.

WE now come to a new class of the street-sellers of manufactured articles—viz., the "crocks," as they are termed. I have before alluded to one characteristic of these traders—that they all strive to be barterers in preference to salesmen. They also present other varying qualities when compared with other classes of street-sellers. Of these "crocks," there are, from the best data I could obtain from men in the trade, and from the swag-shop people who supply them, 250 men and 150 women; of these, 120 couples (man and woman) "work" together; of the remainder, sometimes two men work in unison, and some women work singly. On my inquiring of one of these street folk if ever three worked together, I was told that such was never the case, as the "crocks" would quote a saying: "Two's good company, three's none at all." Of the men and women carrying on this traffic conjointly more than half are married; showing a difference of habits to the costermongers. The reason assigned to me by one of the class (himself once a costermonger) was that the interest of the man and woman in the business was closer than in costermongering, while the serviceableness of a woman helpmate in "swopping," or bartering, was much greater. This prompts the women, I am told, even if they are unmarried at the outset, to insist upon wedlock; and the man —sometimes, perhaps, to secure a valuable "help," at others, it may be, from better motives—consents to what in this rank of life, and under the circumstances of such street-traders, is more frequently the woman's offer than the man's. The trade, in its present form, has not been known more than twelve years.

The goods, which are all bought at the crock swag-shops, of which an account is given below, are carried in baskets on the head, the men having pads on the cloth caps which they wear—or sometimes a padding of hay or wool inside the cap—while the women's pads are worn outside their bonnets or caps, the bonnet being occasionally placed on the basket. The goods, though carried in baskets on the head to the locality of the traffic, are, whilst the traffic is going on, usually borne from house to house, or street to street, on the arm, or when in large baskets carried before them by the two hands. These baskets are strongly made; the principal mart is close to Spitalfields-market.

The men engaged in this trade are usually strong, robust, and red-faced. Most of them are above the middle stature; very few are beyond middle age, and the majority of them are under or little more than 30. The women, more than the men, have contracted a stoop or bend to one side, not so much by carrying weights on the head, as by carrying them on the arm. The weights they carry are from three to five stone. The dress of the men is the same as the costermongers, with the exception of shooting-cut jackets being more frequent among the "crocks" than the costers, and red plush waistcoats are very popular with them. When not at work, or on Sundays—for they never work on the Sabbath, though they do not go to church or chapel—these men are hardly ever seen to wear a hat. Both men and women wear strong boots and, unless when "hard-up," silk handkerchiefs. Their places of residence are, as regards the majority, in Spitalfields, Bethnal-green, and Shoreditch. Of the others the greater portion reside in the neighbourhood of Kent-street, in the Borough. Their abode usually consists of one room, which is in most cases more comfortable, and better furnished than those of the costers. "We pick up a tidy ornament now and then," one crock said, "such as a picture, in the way of swop, and our good women likes to keep them at home for a bit of show." They live well, in general, dining out almost every day; and I am told that, as a body, they have fewer children than any other class of street-folk.

The trade is almost entirely itinerant. Crock-sellers are to be seen at street-markets on Saturday nights, but they are not the regular crocks, who, as I have said, do not care to *sell*. The crocks go on "rounds," the great trade being in the suburbs. Sometimes a round lasts a week, the couple resting at a fresh place every night. Others have a round for each day of the week.

The long rounds are to Greenwich, Woolwich, Northfleet, Gravesend, Stroud, Rochester, Chatham, and then to Maidstone. Some will then make Maidstone the head-quarters, and work the neighbouring villages—such as East Farleigh, Town Malling, Yalding, Aylesford, and others. The return to town may be direct by railway, or by some other route, if any stock remains unsold. On these long rounds the higher priced goods are generally carried, and stock is forwarded from London to the "crock" whilst on the round, if the demand require it. Another long round is Vauxhall, Wandsworth, Kingston-on-Thames, and Guildford, with divergings to the villages. The return from Guildford is often by Richmond, Kew, &c. A third long round is Hampstead, Kilburn, Barnet, Watford, and so on to St. Alban's. The other long rounds are less frequented; but some go to Uxbridge; others to Windsor and Eton, and as far as Reading; others to Cambridge, by Tottenham, Edmonton, Ware, &c. When no trade is to be done close to London, the "crocks" often have themselves and their wares conveyed to any town by rail. The short, or town rounds, are the Dover-road, New Kent-road, Walworth, Camberwell, and back by Newington; Kennington, Brix-

ton, Clapham, and back by Vauxhall; Bayswater, Notting-hill, and back by Paddington; Camden Town, St. John's Wood, and Hampstead; Stoke Newington, Dalston, Clapton, Shacklewell, and Stamford-hill; Mile-end, Stratford, and Bow; Limehouse, Poplar, and back by the Commercial-road. It would be easy to cite other routes, but these show the character of the trade. Some occupy two days. A few crocks "work" the poor neighbourhoods, such as Hoxton, Kingsland-road, parts of Hackney, &c., and cry, "Here we are—now, ladies, bring out your old hats, old clothes, old umbrellas, old anythink; old shoes, metal, old anythink; *here* we are!"

The trade, from the best information I could acquire, is almost equally divided into what may be called "fancy" and "useful" articles. A lodging-letter, for instance, will "swop" her old gowns and boots, and drive keen bargains for plates, dishes, or wash-hand basins and jugs. A housekeeper, who may be in easier circumstances, will exchange for vases and glass wares. Servant-maids swop clothes and money for a set of china, " 'gainst they get married." Perhaps there are no more frequent collisions between buyer and seller than in the crock swag-shops. A man who had once been an assistant in one of these places, told me that some of the "crocks" were tiresome beyond measure, and every now and then a minute or two was wasted by the "crock" and the swag-shopman in swearing one at another. Some of these street traffickers insist upon testing the soundness of *every* article, by striking the middle finger nail against it. This they do to satisfy their customers also, in the course of trade, especially in poor neighbourhoods.

From the best data at my command, one quarter of the goods sold at the swag-shops are sold to the crock dealers I have described, and in about equal proportions as to amount in fancy or useful articles. There are, in addition to the crock bar-terers, perhaps 100 traders who work the poor streets, chiefly carrying their goods in barrows, but they *sell*, and though they will barter, do not clamour for it. They cry : " Free trade for ever ! Here's cup and saucer for a halfpenny ! Pick'em out at your own price ! Tea-pot for three halfpence ! Pick 'em out ! Oho ! oho ! Giving away here !" They rattle dishes and basins as they make this noise. These men are all supplied at the swag-shops, buying what is called "common lots," and selling at 30 per cent. profit. Such traders have only been known in the streets for five years, and for three or four months of the year half of these "go to costering." The barrows are about seventy in number, and there are thirty stalls. Seven-eighths of the "barrow-crocks" are men. The swag-barrowmen also sell small articles of crockery wares, and altogether one half of the trade of the crock swag-shops (which I have described) is a trade for the streets.

Of the way in which the "crock barterers" dispose of their wares, &c., I have given an account below. They are rapidly supplanting the "old clo'" trade of the Jews.

The hucksters of crockery-ware are a considerable class. One who has great experience in the business thinks there must be some hundreds employed in it throughout London. He says he meets many at the swag warehouses on the evenings that he goes there. He is often half an hour before he can be served. There are seven or eight swag warehouses frequented by the hucksters, and at the busy time my informant has often seen as many has twenty-five at each house, and he is satisfied that there must be three or four hundred hucksters of china and glass throughout the metropolis. The china and glass in which they deal are usually purchased at the east end of the town, upon the understanding that if the huckster is unable to dispose of them in the course of the day the articles will be taken back in the morning, if uninjured, and the money returned. The hucksters usually take out their goods early in the day. Their baskets are commonly deposited at the warehouse, and each warehouse has from thirty to forty baskets left there over-night, when the unsold articles are returned. The baskets are usually filled with china and glass and ornaments, to the amount of from 5s. to 15s., according to the stock-money of the huckster. A basket filled with 15s. worth of china is considered, I am told, "a very tidy stock." In the same neighbourhood as they get the crockery, are made the baskets in which it is carried. For these baskets they pay from 2s. to 6s., and they are made expressly for the hucksters; indeed, on one side of a well-known street at the east end, the baskets made in the cellars may be seen piled outside the houses up to the second-floor windows. The class of persons engaged in hawking china through the metropolis are either broken-down tradesmen or clerks out of place, or Jews, or they may be Staffordshire men, who have been regularly bred to the business. They carry different kinds of articles. The Staffordshire man may generally be known by the heavy load of china that he carries with him. He has few light or fancy articles in his basket; it is filled chiefly with plates and dishes and earthenware pans. The broken-down tradesmen carries a lighter load. He prefers tea services and vases, and rummers and cruet-stands, as they are generally of a more delicate make than the articles carried by the Staffordshire men. The Jew, however, will carry nothing of any considerable weight. He takes with him mostly light, showy, Bohemian goods—which are difficult "to be priced" by his customers, and do not require much labour to hawk about. The hucksters usually start on their rounds about nine. There are very few who take money; indeed they profess to take none at all. "But that is all flam," said my informant. "If any one was to ask me the price of an article in an artful way like, I shouldn't give him a straightforward answer. To such parties we always say, 'Have you got any old clothes?'" The hucksters *do* take money when they can get it, and they adopt the principle of exchanging their goods for old clothes merely as a means of evading the licence. Still they are compelled to do a great deal in the old clothes' line. When they take money

they usually reckon to get 4d. in the shilling, but at least three-fourths of their transactions consist of exchanges for old clothes. "A good tea-service we generally give," said my informant, "for a left-off suit of clothes, hat, and boots—they must all be in a decent condition to be worth that. We give a sugar-basin for an old coat, and a rummer for a pair of old Wellington boots. For a glass milk-jug I should expect a waistcoat and trowsers, and they must be tidy ones too. But there's nothing so saleable as a pair of old boots to us. There is always a market for old boots, when there is not for old clothes. You can any day get a dinner out of old Wellingtons; but as for coats and waistcoats—there's a fashion about them, and what pleases one don't another. I can sell a pair of old boots going along the streets if I carry them in my hand. The snobs will run after us to get them—the backs are so valuable. Old beaver hats and waistcoats are worth little or nothing. Old silk hats, however, there's a tidy market for. They are bought for the shops, and are made up into new hats for the country. The shape is what is principally wanted. We won't give a farden for the polka hats with the low crowns. If we can double an old hat up and put it in our pockets, it's more valuable to us than a stiff one. We know that the shape must be good to stand that. As soon as a hatter touches a hat he knows by the touch or the stiffness of it whether it's been 'through' the fire or not; and if so, they'll give it you back in a minute. There is one man who stands in Devonshire-street, Bishopsgate-street, waiting to buy the hats of us as we go into the market, and who purchases at least thirty dozen of us a week. There will be three or four there besides him looking out for us as we return from our rounds, and they'll either outbid one another, according as the demand is, or they'll all hold together to give one price. The same will be done by other parties wanting the old umbrellas that we bring back with us. These are valuable principally for the whalebone. Cane ribbed ones are worth only from 1d. to 2d., and that's merely the value of the stick and the supporters. Iron skewers are made principally out of the old supporters of umbrellas." The china and crockery bought by the hucksters at the warehouses are always second-rate articles. They are most of them a little damaged, and the glass won't stand hot water. Every huckster, when he starts, has a bag, and most of them two—the one for the inferior, and the other for the better kind of old clothes he buys. "We purchase gentlemen's left-off wearing apparel. This is mostly sold to us by women. They are either the wives of tradesmen or mechanics who sell them to us, or else it is the servant of a lodging-house, who has had the things given to her, and with her we can deal much easier than the others. She's come to 'em light, and of course she parts with 'em light," said the man, "and she'll take a pair of sugar basins worth about 6d., you know, for a thing that'll fetch two or three shillings sometimes. But the mistresses of the houses are she-dragons. They wants a whole dinner *chany* service for their husband's rags. As for plates and dishes, they think they can be had for picking up. Many a time they sells their husband's things unbeknown to 'em, and often the gentleman of the house coming up to the door, and seeing us make a deal—for his trowsers maybe—puts a stop to the whole transaction. Often and often I 've known a woman sell the best part of her husband's stock of clothes for *chany* ornaments for her mantelpiece. And I 'm sure the other day a lady stripped the whole of her passage, and gave me almost a new great coat, that was hanging up in the hall, for a few trumpery tea-things. But the greatest ' screws' we has to deal with are some of the ladies in the squares. They stops you on the sly in the streets, and tells you to call at their house at sitch a hour of the day, and when you goes there they smuggles you quietly into some room by yourselves, and then sets to work Jewing away as hard as they can, pricing up their own things, and downcrying yourn. Why, the other day I was told to call at a fashionable part of Pimlico, so I gave a person 3*d.* to mind the child, and me and my good woman started off at eight in the morning with a double load. But, bless you, when we got there, the lady took us both into a private room unbeknown to the servants, and wanted me to go and buy expressly for her a green and white chamber service all complete, with soap trays and brush trays, together with four breakfast cups—and all this here grand set-out she wanted for a couple of old washed-out light waistcoats, and a pair of light trowsers. She tried hard to make me believe that the buttons alone on the waistcoats was worth 6*d.* a piece, but I knowed the value of buttons afore she was borned ; at first start off I'm sure they wouldn't have cost 1*d.* each, so I couldn't make a deal of it no how, and I had to take all my things back for my trouble. I asked ¦her even for a pint of beer, but she wouldn't listen to no such thing. We generally cry as we go, ' any old clothes to sell or exchange,' and I look down the area, and sometimes knock at the door. If I go out with a 15*s.* basket of crockery, may be after a tidy day's work I shall come home with 1*s.* in my pocket (perhaps I shall have *sold* a couple of tumblers, or half a dozen plates), and a bundle of old clothes, consisting of two or three old shirts, a coat or two, a suit of left-off livery, a woman's gown may be, or a pair of old stays, a couple of pair of Wellingtons, and a waistcoat or so. These I should have at my back, and the remainder of my *chany* and glass on my head, and werry probably a humberella or two under my arm, and five or six old hats in my hand. This load altogether will weigh about three quarters of a cwt., and I shall have travelled fifteen miles with that, at least; for as fast as I gets rid on the weight of the crockery, I takes up the weight of the old clothes. The clothes I hardly know the value on till I gets to the Clothes Exchange, in Houndsditch. The usual time for the hucksters arriving there is between three and four in the winter, or between five and six in the summer. In fact, we must be at the Exchange at them hours, because there all our buyers is, and

we can't go out the next day until we 've sold our lot. We can't have our baskets stocked again until we 've got the money for our old clothes." The Exchange is a large square plot of damp ground, about an acre in extent, enclosed by a hoarding about eight feet high, on the top of which is a narrow sloping roof, projecting sufficiently forward to shelter one person from the rain. Across this ground are placed four rows of double seats, ranged back to back. Here meet all the Jew clothesmen, hucksters, dealers in second-hand shoes, left-off wardrobe keepers, hareskin dealers, umbrella dealers and menders, and indeed buyers and sellers of left-off clothes and worn-out commodities of every description. The purchasers are of all nations, and in all costumes. Some are Greeks, others Swiss, and others Germans ; some have come there to buy up old rough charity clothing and army coats for the Irish market, others have come to purchase the hareskins and old furs, or else to pick up cheap old teapots and tea-urns. The man with the long flowing beard and greasy tattered gaberdine is worth thousands, and he has come to make another sixpence out of the rags and tatters that are strewn about the ground in heaps for sale. At a little before three o'clock the stream of rag-sellers sets in in a flood towards this spot. At the gate stands " Barney Aaron," to take the half-penny admission of every one entering the ground. By his side stands his son with a leather pouch of half-pence, to give change for any silver that may be tendered. The stench of the old clothes is positively overpowering. Every one there is dressed in his *worst.* If he has any good clothes he would not put them on. Almost each one that enters has a bag at his back, and scarcely has he passed the gate before he is surrounded by some half dozen eager Jews—one feels the contents of the bundle on the huckster's back—another clamours for the first sight. A third cries, " I 'm sure you have something that 'll suit me." " You know me," says a fourth, " I 'm a buyer, and give a good price." "Have you got any breaking ?" asks this Jew, who wants an old coat or two to cut up into cloth caps—" Have you got any fustian, any old cords, or old boats ?" And such is the anxiety and greediness of the buyers, that it is as much as the seller can do to keep his bundle on his back. At length he forces his way to a seat, and as he empties the contents of his sack on the ground, each different article is snapped up and eagerly overhauled by the different Jews that have followed him to his seat. Then they all ask what sum is wanted for the several things, and they, one and all, bid one quarter of the price demanded. I am assured that it requires the greatest vigilance to prevent the things being carried off unpaid in the confusion. While this scene is going on, a Jew, perched upon a high stage in the centre of the ground, shouts aloud to the multitude, " Hot wine, a half-penny a glass, here." Beside him stands another, with smoking cans of hot eels ; and next to this one is a sweetmeat stall, with a crowd of Jew boys gathered round the keeper of it, gambling with marbles for Albert rock and hardbake. Up and down between the seats push women with baskets of sheep's trotters on their arms, and screaming, "Legs of mutton, two for a penny; who'll give me a handsel—who'll give me a handsel?" After them comes a man with a large tin can under his arm, and roaring, "Hot pea, oh! hot pea, oh!" In one corner is a coffee and beer shop. Inside this are Jews playing at draughts, or settling and wrangling about the goods they have bought of one another. In fact, in no other place is such a scene of riot, rags, and filth to be witnessed. The cause of this excitement is the great demand on the part of the poor, and the cheap clothiers as well, for those articles which are considered as worthless by the rich. The old shoes are to be cobbled up, and the cracks heel-balled over, and sold out to the working-classes as strong durable articles. The Wellingtons are to be new fronted, and disposed of to clerks who are expected to appear respectable upon the smallest salaries. The old coats and trowsers are wanted for the slop-shops; they are to be "turned," and made up into new garments. The best black suits are to be "clobbered" up—and those which are more worn in parts are to be cut up and made into new cloth caps for young gentlemen, or gaiters for poor curates; whilst others are to be transformed into the "best boys' tunics." Such as are *too* far gone are bought to be torn to pieces by the "devil," and made up into new cloth—or "shoddy" as it is termed—while such as have already done this duty are sold for manure for the ground. The old shirts, if they are past mending, are bought as "rubbish" by the marine store dealers, and sold as rags to the paper-mills, to be changed either into the bank-note, the newspaper, or the best satin note-paper.

The average earnings of the hucksters who exchange crockery, china and glass for the above articles, are from 8s. to 10s. per week. Some days, I am told, they will make 3s., and on others they will get only 6d. However, taking the good with the bad, it is thought that 10s. a week is about a fair average of the earnings of the whole class. The best times for this trade are at the turn of the winter, and at the summer season, because then people usually purchase new clothes, and are throwing off the old ones. The average price of an old hat is from 1d. to 8d.; for an old pair of shoes, from 1d. to 4d.; an old pair of Wellingtons fetch from 3d. to 1s. 6d. (those of French leather are of scarcely any value). An old coat is worth from 4d. to 1s.; waistcoats are valued from 1d. to 3d.; trowsers are worth from 4d. to 8d.; cotton gowns are of the same value; bonnets are of no value whatever; shirts fetch from 2d. to 6d.; stockings are 1d. per pair; a silk handkerchief varies in value from 3d. to 1s. The party supplying me with the above information was originally in the coal and greengrocery business, but, owing to a succession of calamities, he has been unable to carry it on. Since then he has taken to the vending of crockery in the streets. He is a man far above the average of the class to which he at present belongs.

OF THE "SWAG," CROCKERY, AND GLASS SHOPS.

IN addition to the 150 general and particular "swag-shops," or shops having a large *collection* of goods, of which I have spoken, there are twenty establishments for the sale of crockery and china, which I heard styled by persons in the trade "swag-crocks," or "crock-shops." The principle on which the trade is conducted in these places is the same as that of the swag-shops, inasmuch as the sales are wholesale, to street-sellers, shop-keepers, and shippers, but rarely to private individuals.

The crock swag-shops are to be found in the streets neighbouring Spitalfields market, and in and near to Liquorpond-street. As at the more general or miscellaneous swag-shops, the crock-swags make no display. In one of the most extensive, indeed, two large windows are filled with goods. Here are spirit-stands, with the invariable three bottles (invariable in the cheap trade), blue, green, or uncoloured; some lettered "gin," "rum," "brandy," but most of them unlabelled. Here, too, are cruet-stands, and "pot" or spar figures under glass shades; and a number of many-coloured flower-glasses, some of them profusely gilded; and small china vases; but the glass wares greatly predominate. Although there are glass and colour and gilding enough to make "an imposing display," the display is nevertheless anything but showy; the goods look dingy, and, if I may so speak of such things, faded. Some of the coloured glass seems to be losing its colour, and few of the wares have the bright look of newness.

The windows of these shops are, for the most part, literally *packed* to a certain height, so as almost to exclude the light, with pitchers, and basins, and cups, and jugs, and the sundry smaller articles of this multifarious trade, all undusted, and seemingly uncared for. In one "large concern" I saw a number of glass salt-cellars wrapped severally in paper, which had changed from white to a dusty brown, and which from age, and perhaps damp, seemed about to fall to tatters.

The "interiors" of some of these warehouses are very spacious. I saw one large and lofty shop, into which two apartments and a yard had been flung, the partitions having been taken down, and the ceilings supported by pillars, in order to "extend the premises." It was really a hall of pots. On the floor were large crates, the tops removed so that the goods might be examined, packed, one with cups, another with saucers, a third with basins, and packed as only a potter could pack them. Intermixed with them were piles of blue-and-white dishes and plates, and, beside them, washing-pans, fitted one into another like the old hats on a Jew's head. The pillars had their festoons of crockery, being hung with children's white and gold mugs "for a good boy," and with white metal-lidded and brown-bodied mustard pots, as well as other minor articles. The shelves were loaded with tea-services of many shapes and hues, while the unoccupied space was what sufficed to allow the warehousemen and the customers to thread the mazes of this labyrinth of crockerywares. Of the glass goods there was little display, as they are generally kept in cases and other packages, to preserve their freshness of appearance.

The crockery of the swag-shops is made in Staffordshire; the glass principally in Lancashire. At none of these establishments do they issue circulars of prices, such as I have cited of the general swag-shops. The articles are so very many, I was told, that to specify all the sizes and prices "would take a volume and a half." I give a statement, however, of the prices of the goods most in demand, on the occasions when the street vendors sell them without barter, and the prices at which they are purchased wholesale: Blue-edged plates sold at 1*d.* each cost 1*s.* 8*d.* the dozen; this would appear to entail a loss of 8*d.* on every dozen sold, but in this article "30 is a dozen." Dishes are bought at the "swag-crocks" in "nests," which comprise 10 dishes, or 5 pairs, of different sizes. These the street crockman sells, if possible, in pairs, but he will sell them singly, for he can always make up the complement of his "nest" at the warehouse. The prices run, chiefly according to size, from 8*d.* to 1*s.* 6*d.* (sometimes 1*s.* 8*d.*) the pair. "The 8*d.* a pair," said one street crockseller, "costs me 6*d.*, not a farthing under, and the 18*d.* a pair—it's very seldom we can 'draw' 1*s.* 8*d.*—costs 1*s.* 2*d.* That's all, sir; and the profit's so small, it makes us keen to swop. I'll swop for old clothes, or dripping, or grease, or anything. You see the profit, when you sells downright down, *must* be small, 'cause there's so many pot-shops with prices marked on the plates and other things. They can buy better than us sometimes, and they're hard to stand up against. If a woman says to me—for I very seldom deal with men—'Why, they're cheaper at D——'s, in Oxford-street,'—I answers, 'And worser. I'll tell you what it is, ma'am. The cheapest place was in two houses, painted all red, in the London-road. But one fine morning them two houses fell, and the pots was smashed as a matter of course. It was a judgment on their bad pots.' But it's a fact, sir, that these houses fell, about 7 or 8 years ago, I think, and I've seen goods, with one or two of 'em broken, offered for sale when the place was re-built, having been 'rescued from the ruins;' and at less than half price.' Of course that was gammon. I've cracked and broke a few plates, myself, and sold them in the New Kent-road, and in Walworth and Newington, at half price, from the ruins, and at a very tidy profit.' A stone china tea-service, of 32 pieces—12 cups, 12 saucers, 4 bread-and-butter plates, a tea-pot, a sugar-basin, a slop-basin, and a cream-jug—is bought for 6*s.* 9*d.* while 9*s.* is asked for it, and sometimes obtained. A "china set" costs, as the general price, 10*s.* 6*d.*, and for it 14*s.* is asked.

The glass wares are so very rarely sold—being the most attractive articles of barter—that I could hardly get any street-seller to state his prices. "Swop, sir," I was told repeatedly, "they all goes in swop." The glass goods, however, which are the most sold in the streets, I ascertained to be cream-jugs, those vended at 6*d.* each, costing 4*s.* the dozen; and flower-glasses, the most frequent price being 1*s.* a pair, the prime cost 7*d.*

I have estimated the sum turned over by the general swag-shops at 3000*l.* each. From what I can learn, the crock swag-shops, averaging the whole, turn over a larger sum, for their profits are smaller, ranging from 10 to 30 per cent., but rarely 30. Calculating, then, that each of these swag-shops turns over 4000*l.* yearly, we find 80,000*l.* expended, but this includes the sales to shopkeepers and to shippers, as well as to street-folk.

OF THE STREET-SELLERS OF SPAR AND CHINA ORNAMENTS, AND OF STORE FRUIT.

"SPARS," as spar ornaments are called by the street-sellers, are sold to the retailers at only four places in London, and two in Gravesend (where the hawkers are for the most part supplied). The London spar-houses are—two in Westminster, one in Shoreditch, and one on Battle-bridge. None of them present any display of their goods which are kept in large drawers, closets, and packages. At Gravesend the spar-shops are handsome.

These wares are principally of Derbyshire spar, and made in Matlock; a few are German. The "spars" are hawked on a round, and are on fine Saturday nights offered for sale in the street and markets. The trade was unknown as a street, or a hawking trade in London, I am informed, until about twenty-five years ago, and then was not extensive, the goods, owing to the cost of carriage, &c., being high-priced. As public conveyance became more rapid, certain and cheap, the trade in spars increased, and cheaper articles were prepared for the London market. From ten to fifteen years ago the vendors of spars "did well in swop" (as street-sellers always call barters). The articles with which they tempted housewives were just the sort of article to which it was difficult for inexperienced persons to attach a value. They were massive and handsome ornaments, and the spar-sellers did not fail to expatiate on their many beauties. "God rest Jack Moody's soul," said an Irishman, now a crock-seller, to me; "Jack Moody was only his nick-name, but that don't matter; God rist his sowl and the hivens be his bid. He was the boy to sell the spar-r's. They was from the cavrents at the bottom of the say, he towld them, or from a new island in the frozen ocean. He did well; God rist him; but he died young." The articles "swopped" were such as I have described in my account of the tradings of the crock-sellers; and if the "swop" were in favour of the spar-seller, still the customer became possessed of something solid, enduring, and generally handsome.

At the outset of the street or hawking trade, the spar-sellers carried their goods done up in paper, in strong baskets on their heads; the man's wife sometimes carrying a smaller basket, with less burdensome articles, on her arm. Men have been known to start on a round, with a basket of spars, which would weigh from 1 cwt. to 1½ cwt. (or 12 stone). This, it must be remembered, might have to be borne for three or four miles into the suburbs, before its weight was diminished by a sale. One of these traders told me that twelve years ago he had sold spar watch-stands, weighing above 15 lbs. These stands were generally of a square form; the inner portion being open, except a sort of recess for the watch. "The tick sounds well on spar, I 've often heard," said one spar-seller.

Some of the spar ornaments are plain, white, and smooth. Of these many have flowers, or rims, or insects, painted upon them, and in brilliant colours. Those which are now in demand for the street sales, or for itinerant barterings, are— Small microscopes, candlesticks, inkstands, pincushions, mugs, paper-holders, match perfumery, and shaving-boxes, etc. The general price of these articles is 6d. to the street-seller or hawker, some of the dealers being licensed hawkers. The wholesale price varies from 2s. 6d. to 5s. per dozen; or an average of 3s. 9d. or 4s. Of the larger articles the most saleable are candlesticks, at from 1s. to 2s. 6d. each; from 1s. to 1s. 6d. being the most frequent price. Watch-stands and vases are now, I am told, in small demand. "People's got stocked, I think," one man said, "and there 's so much cheap glass and chaney work, that they looks on spars as heavy and old-fashioned."

Some street-sellers have their spars in covered barrows, the goods being displayed when the top of the barrow is removed, so that the conveyance is serviceable whether the owner be stationary or itinerant. The spar-sellers, however, are reluctant to expose their goods to the weather, as the colours are easily affected.

In this trade I am informed that there are now twelve men, nine of whom are assisted by their wives, and that in the summer months there are eighteen. Their profits are about 15s. per week on an average of the whole year, including the metropolis and a wide range of the suburbs. What amount of money may be expended by the public in the street purchase of "spars" I am unable to state, so much being done in the way of barter; but assuming that there are fourteen sellers throughout the year, and that their profits are cent. per cent., there would appear to be about 1000l. per annum thus laid out.

Of stone fruit there are now usually six street sellers, and in fine weather eight. Eight or ten years ago there were twenty. The fruit is principally made at Chesterfield in Derbyshire, and is disposed of to the London street-sellers in the swag-shops in Houndsditch. Some of the articles, both as regards form and colour, are well executed; others are far too red or too green; but that, I was told, pleased children best. The most saleable fruits are apples, pears, peaches, apricots, oranges, lemons and cucumbers. The cucumbers, which are sometimes of pot as well as of stone,'are often hollow, and are sometimes made to serve for gin-bottles, holding about a quartern.

The price at the swag-shops is 4s. 3d. for a gross of fruit of all kinds in equal quantities; for a better quality the price is 7s. 6d. The street-seller endeavours to get 1d. each for the lower priced, and

2d. for the higher, but has most frequently to be content with ½d. and 1d. The stone fruitmen are itinerant during the week and stationary in the street markets on Saturday, and sometimes other evenings. They carry their stock both in baskets and barrows. One man told me that he always cried, "Pick 'em out! pick 'em out! Half-penny each! Cheapest fruit ever seen! As good to-morrow as last week! Never lose flavour! Ever-lasting fruit."

Supposing that there are six persons selling stone-fruit in the streets through the year, and that each earns—and I am assured that is the full amount—9s. weekly (one man said 7s. 6d. was the limit of his weekly profits in fruit), we find 140l. received as profit on these articles, and calculating the gains at 33 per cent., an outlay of 420l.

The trade in China ornaments somewhat differs from the others I have described under the present head. It is both a street and a public-house trade, and is carried on both in the regular way and by means of raffles. At some public-houses, indeed, the China ornament dealers are called "rafflers."

The "ornaments" now most generally sold or raffled are Joy and Grief (two figures, one laughing and the other crying); dancing Highlanders; mustard pots in the form of cottages, &c.; grotesque heads, one especially of an old man, which serves as a pepper-box, the grains being thrown through the eyes, nose, and mouth; Queen and Alberts (but not half so well as the others); and, until of late, Smith O'Briens. There are others, also, such as I have mentioned in my account of the general swag-shops, to the windows of many of which they form the principal furniture. Some of these "ornaments" sold "on the sly" can hardly be called obscene, but they are dirty, and cannot be further described.

The most lucrative part of the trade is in the raffling. A street-seller after doing what business he can, on a round or at a stand, during the day, will in the evening resort to public-houses, where he is known, and is allowed to offer his wares to the guests. The ornaments, in public-house sale, are hardly ever offered for less than 6d. each, or 6d. a pair. The raffling is carried on rapidly and simply. Dice are very rarely used now, and when used, provoke many murmurs from the landlords. The raffler of the China ornaments produces a portable roulette box or table—these tables becoming an established part of street traffic—eight or ten inches in diameter. What may be called "the board" of some of these "roulettes" is numbered to thirty-two. It is set rapidly spinning on a pivot, a pea is then slipped through a hole in the lid of the box, and, when the motion has ceased, the pea is found in one of the numbered partitions. "Now, gentlemen," a raffler told me he would say, "try your luck for this beautiful pair of ornaments; six of you at 1d. a piece. If you go home rather how came you so, show what you've bought for the old lady, and it'll be all right and peaceful." If six persons contribute 1d. each, the one "spinning" the highest number gains the prize, and is congratulated by the ornament seller on having gained for 1*d.* what was only too cheap at 6*d.* "Why, sir," said a man who had recently left the trade for another calling, and who was anxious that I should not give any particular description of him, "in case he went back to the raffling,"—"Why, sir, I remember one Monday evening four or five months back, going into a parlour, not a tap-room, mind, where was respectable mechanics. They got to play with me, and got keen, and played until my stock was all gone. If one man stopped raffling, another took his place. I can't recollect how many ornaments I raffled, but I cleared rather better than 3*s.* 6*d.* When there was no ornaments left they gave me 1*d.* a piece—there was eleven of them then—and a pint of beer to let them have the roulette till 12 o'clock; and away they went at it for beer and screws, and bets of 1*d.* and 2*d.* One young man that had been lucky in winning the ornaments got cleaned out, and staked his ornaments for 2*d.*, or for a 1*d.* rather than not play. That sort of thing only happened to me once, to the same extent. If the landlord came into the room, of course they was only playing for drink, or he might have begun about his licence."

The ornaments are bought at the swag shops I have described, and are nearly all of German make. They are retailed from 1*d.* and sometimes ½*d.* to 1*s.* each, and the profit is from 25 to 75 per cent. There are, I am informed, about thirty persons in this trade, two-thirds of them being rafflers, and their receipts being from 25*s.* to 30*s.* weekly. Most of them mix "fancy glass" goods and spars, and other articles, with their "ornament" trade, so that it is not easy to ascertain what is expended upon the china ornaments independently of other wares. If we calculate it at 10*s.* weekly (a low average considering the success of some of the raffles), we find 780*l.* expended in the streets in these ornamental productions.

Of the Street-Sellers of Textile Fabrics.

These street-folk present perhaps as great a diversity of character as any of which I have been called upon to treat.

Among them are the strong persevering men, who carry rolls of linen or cotton manufacture in packs on their backs, and trudge along holding a yard-wand by the middle, which—it is a not uncommon joke against them—is always worn down an inch or two, by being used as a walking-stick in their long pedestrian journeys. Such, however, is not the case, for the packman—when measuring is resorted to—generally shows the justice of his measure, or invites the purchaser to use her own yard-wand (for women are now their most frequent customers). Some of these men love to tell of the many hundreds of miles they have walked in their time, and in the three kingdoms. The most of those who make London, or any large town their head-quarters, and take regular journeys into the country, are licensed hawkers; those who confine their sales exclusively to London and its immediate vicinity, frequently conduct their business without

incurring the annual cost of a licence. The penalty for hawking without a licence is 10*l.*, or an imprisonment (in default of payment) not exceeding three months, with a discretionary power of mitigation to the magistrates. Some of these men may be styled hereditary hawkers, having first accompanied and then succeeded their parents on a round; some were in their youth assistants to hawkers; some had been unsuccessful as tallymen when shopkeepers, or travellers for tally-shops, and have resorted to hawking or street-trading, occasionally, in their transactions with different parties, blending the tally system with the simple rules of sale for ready money.

In striking contrast to these sturdy and often astute traders are the street-sellers of lace and millinery, the majority of whom are women. A walk through a street-market, especially on a Saturday evening, will show any one the frequent difference of the established street-milliner to the other female traders surrounding her stall. The milliner, as she is commonly called by the street-folk, wears a clean, and often tasty cap, beneath her closely-fitting bonnet, a cap in which artificial flowers are not wanting, should she sell those adornments. Her shawl is pinned beneath her collar; her gown, if it be old or of poor material, is clean; and she is rarely to be seen in boots or shoes made for men's wear. Near her stall are stout, coarse-looking Irish girls, with unstringed bonnets, half-ragged shawls, thrown loose round their shoulders, necks red from exposure to the weather, coarse and never brushed, but sometimes scraped, shoes, when shoes are worn, and a general dirtiness of apparel. The street-milliners have been ladies'-maids, working milliners and dress-makers, the wives of mechanics who have been driven to the streets, and who add to the means of the family by conducting a street-trade themselves, with a sprinkling from other classes.

The street-sellers of lace are of the same class as the milliners, but with perhaps less smartness, and carrying on an inferior trade both as regards profit and display.

The street-sellers of boot and stay-laces and of such things as sewing cotton, threads and tapes, when sold separately from more valuable articles, are children and old people, some of whom are infirm, and some blind. The children have, in some instances, been bred to the streets; the old people probably are worn out in street-trades requiring health and strength, and so adopt a less laborious calling, or else they have been driven to it, either from comparatively better circumstances, or by some privation or affliction, in order to avoid the workhouse.

The sale of belts, stockings, braces, straps and garters, is mostly in the hands of men, who, from all that I can learn, are regular street-sellers, who "turn their hands first to this and then to that," but this portion of street-traffic is often combined with the sale of dog-collars, chains, &c. The trade is more a public-house than a distinct traffic in the street. The landlord of a well-frequented inn in Lambeth told me that every day at least 100 of such street-sellers—not including match-girls and women—entered his house to offer their wares; the greatest number of such sellers was in the evening.

I have so far described what may be called the fair traders, but to them the street-sellers of textile fabrics are not confined. There are besides these, two other classes known as "Duffers" and as "Lumpers," and sometimes the same man is both "Duffer" and "Lumper." The two names are often confounded, but an intelligent street-seller, versed in all the arts and mysteries of this trade, told me that he understood by a "Duffer," a man who sold goods under false pretences, making out that they were smuggled, or even stolen, so as to enhance the idea of their cheapness; whereas a "Lumper" would sell linens, cottons, or silks, which might be really the commodities represented; but which, by some management or other, were made to appear new when they were old, or solid when they were flimsy.

OF THE HABERDASHERY SWAG-SHOPS.

BY this name the street-sellers have long distinguished the warehouses, or rather shops, where they purchase their goods. The term *Swag*, or *Swack*, or *Sweg*, is, as was before stated, a Scotch word, meaning a large collection, a "lot." The haberdashery, however, supplied by these establishments is of a very miscellaneous character; which, perhaps, can best be shown by describing a "haberdashery swag," to which a street-seller, who made his purchases there, conducted me, and which, he informed me, was one of the most frequented by his fraternity, if not *the* most frequented, in the metropolis.

The window was neither dingy, nor, as my companion expressed it, "gay." It was in size, as well as in "dressing," or "show"—for I heard the arrangement of the window goods called by both those names by street people—half-way between the quiet plainness of a really wholesale warehouse, and the gorgeousness of a retail drapery concern, when a "tremendous sacrifice" befools the public. Not a quarter of an inch of space was lost, and the announcements and prices were written many of them in a bungling school-boy-like hand, while others were the work of a professional "ticket writer," and show the eagerness of so many of this class of trade to obtain custom. In one corner was this announcement: "To bootmakers. Boot fronts cut to any size or quality." There was neither boot nor shoe visible, but how a boot front *can be* cut "to any quality," is beyond my trade knowledge. Half hidden, and read through laces, was another announcement, sufficiently told, in a window decorated with a variety of combustible commodities : "Hawkers supplied with fuzees cheaper than any house in London." On the "ledge," or the part shelving from the bottom of the window, within the shop, were paper boxes of steel purses with the price marked so loosely as to leave it an open question whether 1s. 0¾d. or 10½d. was the cost. There was also a good store of silk purses, marked 2½d.; bright-coloured ribbons, in a paper box, and done up in small rolls, 1½d.; cotton reels, four a penny; worsted balls,

three a penny; girls' night-caps, 1¾d.; women's caps, from 2¾d. to 7¾d.; (the ¾d. was always in small indistinct characters, but it was a very favourite adjunct); diamond patent mixed pins—London and Birmingham—1d. an oz. My companion directed my attention to the little packets of pins : "They're well done up, sir, as you can see, and in very good and thick and strong pink papers, with ornamental printers' borders, and plenty of paper for three ounces. The paper's weighed with the pins, and the price is 1d. an oz.; so the paper fetches 1s. 4d. a pound." There were also many papers of combs, and one tied outside the packet as a specimen, without a price marked upon them. "The price varies, sir," said my guide and informant, and I heard the same account from others; "it varies from 1d. a pair to such as me; up to 6d. or perhaps 1s. to a servant-maid what looks innocent."

From what appeared to be slender rods fitted higher up to the breadth of the window depended "black lace handkerchiefs, 4¾d.;" and cap fronts, some being a round wreath of gauze ornamented with light rose-coloured artificial flowers, and marked "only 5½d.;" together with lace (or edgings) which hung in festoons, and filled every vacancy. Higher up were braces marked 5d.; and more lace; and to the back of all was a sort of screen—for it shuts out all view of the inside of the shop—of big-figured shawls (the figures in purple, orange, and crimson) and of silk handkerchiefs : "They're regular duffers," I was told, "and very tidy duffers too—very, for it's a respectable house."

In the centre of the window ledge was a handsome wreath of artificial flowers, marked 2½d. "If a young woman was to go in to buy it at 2½d., I've seen it myself, sir," said the street-seller, "she's told that the ticket has got out of its place, for it belonged to the lace beneath, but as she'd made a mistake without thinking of the value, the flowers was 1s. 6d. to her, though they was cheap at 2s. 6d."

From this account it will be seen that the swag or wholesale haberdashers are now very general traders; and that they trade "retail" as well as "wholesale." Twenty or twenty-five years ago, I am informed, the greater part of these establishments were really haberdashery swags; but so fierce became the competition in the trade, so keen the desire "to do business," that gradually, and more especially within these four or five years, they became "all kinds of swags."

A highly respectable draper told me that he never could thoroughly understand where hosiery, haberdashery, or drapery, began or ended; for hosiers now were always glovers, and often shirtmakers; haberdashers were always hosiers (at the least), and drapers were everything; so that the change in the character of the shops from which the street-sellers of textile fabrics procure their supplies, is but in accordance with the change in the general drapery trade. The literal meaning of the word haberdashery is unknown to etymologists.

There are now about fifty haberdashery swags

resorted to by street-sellers, but only a fifth part of them make the trade to street-sellers a principal, while none make it a sole feature of their business. In the enumeration of the fifty haberdashery " swags," five are large and handsome shops carried on by "cutting" drapers. Some of these—one in the borough, especially—do not " serve " the street-sellers, except at certain hours, generally from four to six.

There is another description of shops from which a class of street traders derive their supplies of stock. These are the " print-brokers," who sell " gown-pieces" to the hawkers or street-traders. Only about a dozen of such shops, and those principally in the borough and in Wormwood-street, Bishopsgate, are frequented by the London street-sellers. One man showed me a draper's shop, at which hawkers were "supplied," but without an announcement of such a thing, as it might affect the character of the concern for gentility. The gown-pieces were rolled loosely together, and to each was attached a ticket, 2s. 11d. or 3s. 11d., with intermediate prices, but those here mentioned were the most frequent. The 11d. was in pencil, so that it could be altered at any time, without the expense of a new ticket being incurred. " That one marked 2s. 11d.," said the street-seller, " would be charged to me 2s. 2d., and the 3s. 11d. in the same way 3s. 2d., or I might get it at 3s. If those gown-pieces don't take—and they are almost as thin as silver-paper, —they'll be marked down to 2s. 2d. and 3s. 2d., just by degrees, as you see them shown in the window." The regular " print-brokers" make no display in their windows or premises.

The "duffers" and "lumpers" are supplied almost entirely at one shop in the east end. The proprietor has the sham, or inferior, silk handkerchiefs manufactured for the purpose ; and for the supply of his other silk-goods, he purchases any silk " miscoloured" in the dyeing, or faded from time. " A faded lavender," one of his customers told me, "he'll get dyed black, and made to look quite new and fresh. Sometimes it's good silk, but it's mostly very dicky." This tradesman is also a retailer.

Such things as braces and garters are sold to the street people at the general as well as the haberdashery swag-shops ; and are more frequently sold wholesale than other goods ; indeed the general swag-shop keepers sell them by no other way ; but the " wholesale haberdashers" will sell a single pair, though not, of course, at wholesale price. Some houses again supply the more petty street-sellers, solely with such articles as are known in Manchester by the name of small-ware, including thread, cotton, tapes, laces, &c.

Of Hawkers, Pedlars, and Petty Chapmen.

The machinery for the distribution of commodities has, in this and in all other " progressive " countries, necessarily undergone many changes ; but whether these changes have been beneficial to the community, or not, this is not the place for me to inquire ; all I have to do here is to set forth the order of such changes, and to show the position that the hawker and pedlar formerly occupied in the state.

The "distributor" of the produce of the country is necessarily a kind of go-between, or middleman, introduced for the convenience of bringing together the producer and consumer—the seller and the buyer of commodities. The producer of a particular commodity being generally distinct from the consumer, it follows, that either the commodity must be carried to the consumer, or the consumer go to the commodity. To save time and trouble to both parties, it seems to have been originally arranged that producer and consumer should meet, periodically, at appointed places. Such periodical meetings of buyers and sellers still exist in this and many other countries, and are termed either fairs or markets, according as they are held at long or short intervals—the fair being generally an annual meeting, and the market a weekly one. In the olden time the peculiar characteristic of these commercial congregations was, that the producer and consumer came into immediate contact, without the intervention of any middleman. The fair or market seemed to be a compromise between the two, as to the inconvenience of either finding the other when wanted. The producer brought his goods, so to speak, half way to the consumer, while the consumer travelled half way to the goods. " There would be a great waste of time and trouble," says Stewart Mill, " and an inconvenience often amounting to impracticability, if consumers could only obtain the article they want by treating directly with the producers. Both producers and consumers are too much scattered, and the latter often at too great a distance from the former."

" To diminish this loss of time and labour," continues Mr. Mill, " the contrivance of fairs and markets was early had recourse to, where consumers and producers might periodically meet, without any intermediate agency ; and this plan still answers tolerably well for many articles, especially agricultural produce—agriculturists having at some seasons a certain quantity of spare time on their hands. But even in this case, attendance is often very troublesome and inconvenient to buyers who have other occupations, and do not live in the immediate vicinity ; while, for all articles the production of which requires continuous attention from the producers, these periodical markets must be held at such considerable intervals, and the wants of the consumers must either be provided for so long beforehand, or must remain so long unsupplied, that even before the resources of society permitted the establishment of shops, the supply of those wants fell universally into the hands of *itinerant dealers*, the pedlars who might appear once a month, being preferred to the fair, which only returned once a year. In country districts, remote from towns or large villages, the vocation of the pedlar is not yet wholly superseded. But a dealer who has a fixed abode, and fixed customers," continues Mr. Mill, " is so much more to be depended on, that customers prefer resorting to him, if he is conveniently accessible ; and dealers, therefore, find their advantage in establishing themselves in every locality where there are sufficient consumers near at hand to afford them remuneration."

Thus we see that the pedlar was the original distributor of the produce of the country—the primitive middleman, as well as the prime mover in extending the markets of particular localities, or for particular commodities. He was, as it were, the first "free-trader;" increasing the facilities for the interchange of commodities, without regard to market dues or tolls, and carrying the natural advantages of particular districts to remote and less favoured places; thus enabling each locality to produce that special commodity for which it had the greatest natural convenience, and ex-changing it for the peculiar produce of other parts.

Now, this extension of the markets necessarily involved some machinery for the conveyance of the goods from one district to another. Hence, the ped-lar was not only the original merchant, but the pri-mitive carrier—to whom, perhaps, we owe both our turnpike-roads and railways. For, since the peculiar characteristic of the pedlar was the carrying the produce to the consumer, rather than troubling the consumer to go after the produce, of course it soon became necessary, as the practice increased, and in-creased quantities of goods had to be conveyed from one part of the country to another, that increased facilities of transit should be effected. The first change was from the pack-*man* to the pack-*horse*: for the former a foot-way alone was re-quired; while the latter necessitated the formation of some kind of a road. Some of these ancient pack-horse roads existed till within these few years. Hagbush-lane, which was described by William Hone only twenty years ago, but which has now vanished, was the ancient bridle or pack-horse road from London to the North, and ex-tended by the Holloway back road as far as the City-road, near Old-street. "Some parts of Hag-bush-lane," says Hone, "are much lower than the meadows on either side." At one time a terraced ridge, at another a deep rut, the pack-horse road must have been to the unaccustomed traveller a somewhat perilous pass. The historian of Craven, speaking of 1609, says, "At this time the com-munication between the north of England and the Universities was kept up by the carriers, who pur-sued their long but uniform route with trains of pack-horses. To their care were consigned pack-ages, and not unfrequently the persons ·of young scholars. It was through their medium, also, that epistolary correspondence was managed; and as they always visited London, a letter could scarcely be exchanged between Yorkshire and Oxford in less time than a month." The General Post Office was established by Act of Parliament in the year 1660, and all letters were to be sent through this office, "except such letters as shall be sent by coaches, common-known carriers of goods by carts, waggons, and pack-horses, and shall be carried along with their carts, waggons, and pack-horses respectively."

"·There is no such conveyance as a waggon in this country" (Scotland), says Roderick Random, referring to the beginning of the last century,

"and my finances were too weak to support the expense of hiring a horse. I determined therefore to set out with the carriers, who transport goods from one place to another on horseback; and this scheme I accordingly put in execution on the 1st day of November, 1739, sitting on a pack-saddle between two baskets, one of which contained my goods in a knapsack. But by the time we arrived at Newcastle-upon-Tyne, I was so fatigued with the tediousness of the carriage, and benumbed with the coldness of the weather, that I resolved to travel the rest of my journey on foot, rather than proceed in such a disagreeable manner."

The present mode of travelling, compared with that of the pack-horse means of conveyance as pursued of old, forms one of the most striking contrasts, perhaps, in all history.

Hence we see that the pedlar was originally both carrier and seller; first conveying his pack on his back, and then, as it increased in bulk, transferring it to the back of " the pack-horse." But as soon as the practice of conveying the com-modities to the buyers, instead of compelling the buyers to go to the commodities, was found to be advantageous to both consumer and producer, it was deemed expedient that the two distinct pro-cesses of carriage and sale, which are included in the distribution of commodities, should be conducted by distinct persons, and hence the carrying and selling of goods became separate vocations in the State; and such is now the machinery by which the commodities of different parts of this country, as well as of others, are at present diffused over the greater portion of this kingdom. In remote districts however, and the poorer neighbourhoods of large towns, where there are either too few consumers, or too few commodities required now to support a fixed distributor with a distinct apparatus of transit, the pedlar still continues to be the sole means of dif-fusing the produce of one locality among the in-habitants of another; and it is in this light—as the poor man's merchant—that we must here con-sider him.

Among the more ancient of the trades, then, carried on in England is that of the hawker or pedlar. It is generally considered, as I said be-fore, that hawking " is as ancient a mode of trade as that carried on in fairs and markets, towns and villages, as well as at the castles of the nobles or the cottages of their retainers." To fix the origin of fairs is impossible, for, in ancient and mediæval times, every great gathering was necessarily a fair. Men—whom it is no violence to language to call " hawkers"—resorted alike to the Olympic games and to the festivals of the early Christian saints, to sell or barter their wares. Of our English fairs Mr. Jacob says, in his " Law Dictionary "— " Various privileges have been annexed to them, and numerous facilities afforded to the disposal of property in them. To give them a greater degree of solemnity, they were originally, both in the ancient and modern world, associated with reli-gious festivals. In most places, indeed, they are still held on the same day with the wake or feast of the saint to whom the church is dedicated; and till the practice was prohibited, it was customary in England to hold them in churchyards. This practice, I may add, was not fully prohibited until the reign of Charles II., although it had long before fallen into disuse. Thus the connection between church and market is shown to be of venerable antiquity." The hawker dealt, in the old times, more in textile fabrics than in anything else. Indeed, Shakspere has dashed off a catalogue of his wares, in the song of *Autolycus:*

"Lawn as white as driven snow,
Cyprus black as e'er was crow."

In the reigns succeeding the termination of the Wars of the Roses, and down to the Commonwealth, the hawker's pack was often stocked with costly goods; for great magnificence in dress was then the custom of the wealthy, and even the burgesses on public occasions wore velvet, fine cambric ruffs, and furs. The hawker was thus often a man of substance and frequently travelled on horseback, with his wares slung in bags on his horse's side, or fitted to the crupper or pommell of his saddle. He was often, moreover, attended by a man, both for help in his sales, and protection in travelling. In process of time an established hawker became the medium of news and of gossip, and frequently the bearer of communications from town to town. His profits were often great, but no little trust seems to have been reposed in him as to the quality and price of his goods; and, until the present century or so, slop goods were little manufactured, so that he could not so well practise deceptions. Neither, during the prosperity of the trade, does it appear that any great degree of dishonesty characterized the hawker, though to this there were of course plenty of minor exceptions as well as one glaring contradiction. The wreckers of our southern coasts, who sometimes became possessed of rich silks, velvets, laces, &c.—(not unfrequently murdering all the mariners cast on shore, and there was a convenient superstition among the wreckers, that it was unlucky to offer help to a drowning man) —disposed of much of their plunder to the hawkers; and as communication was slow, even down to Mr. Palmer's improvements in the Post Office in 1784, the goods thus rescued from the deep, or obtained by the murder of the mariners, were disposed of even before the loss of the vessel was known at her destination; for we are told that there was generally a hawker awaiting a wreck on the most dangerous shores of Cornwall, Devon, Dorset, and Sussex.

During the last century, and for the first ten years of the present, the hawker's was a profitable calling. He usually in later times travelled with horse and covered cart, visiting fairs, markets, and private houses, more especially in the country. In some parts the calling was somewhat hereditary, son succeeding to father after having officiated as his assistant, and so becoming known to the customers. The most successful of the class, alike on both sides of the border, were Scotchmen.

In 1810 the prosperity of this trade experienced a check. In that year "every hawker, pedlar, or petty chapman going from town to town, or to

other men's houses, and travelling on foot, carrying to sell or exposing for sale any goods" was required to pay a yearly licence of 4*l.*, with an additional 4*l.* for every horse, ass, or mule, used in the business. Nothing, however, in the Act in question, 50 Geo. III. c. 41, as I have before intimated, "extended to prohibit" the hawking for sale of "any fish, fruit, or victuals" without licence. Neither is there any extension of the prohibition to the unlicensed workers or makers of any goods or wares, or their children or servants resident with them, hawking such goods, and selling them "in every city, borough, town corporate, or market town," but not in villages or country places. "Tinkers, coopers, glaziers, plumbers, and harness-menders," are likewise permitted to carry about with them the proper materials necessary for their business, no licence being necessary.

The passing of this Act did not materially check the fraudulent practices of which the hawkers were accused, and of which a portion of them were doubtlessly guilty; indeed some of the manufacturers, whose names were pirated by the hawkers, were of opinion that the licensing for ten or twenty years facilitated fraud, as many people, both in London and the country, thought they were safe in dealing with a "licensed" hawker, since he could not procure a licence without a certificate of his good character from the clergyman and of his place of residence, and from two "reputable inhabitants." Linen of good quality used to be extensively hawked, but from 1820 to 1825, or later in some parts, the hawkers got to deal in an inferior quality, "unions" (a mixture of linen and cotton), glazed and stiffened, and set off with gaudy labels bearing sometimes the name of a well-known firm, but altered in spelling or otherwise, and expressed so as to lead to the belief that such a firm were the manufacturers of the article. Jews, moreover, as we have seen, travelled in all parts with inferior watches and jewellery, and sometimes "did well" by persuading the possessors of old solid watches, or old seals or jewellery, that they were ridiculously out of fashion, and so inducing them to give money along with the old watch for a watch or other article of the newest fashion, which yet was intrinsically valueless compared with the other. These and other practices, such as selling inferior lace under pretence of its having been smuggled from France, and of the choicest quality, tended to bring the hawker's trade into disrepute, and the disrepute affected the honest men in the business. Some sank from the possession of a good horse and cart to travelling on foot, as of yore, forwarding goods from place to place by the common carriers, and some relinquished the itinerant trade altogether. The "cutting" and puffing shopkeepers appeared next, and at once undersold the "slop" hawker, and foiled him on his own ground of pushing off inferior wares for the best. The numbers of the hawkers fell off considerably, but notwithstanding I find, in the last census tables (1841), the following returns as to the numbers of "hawkers, hucksters, and pedlars," distributed throughout Great Britain. The Government returns, however, admit of no comparison being formed between these numbers and those of any previous time.

ENGLAND AND WALES.			
Bedford	79	Cardigan	38
Berks	160	Carmarthen	49
Bucks	129	Carnarvon	32
Cambridge	139	Denbigh	69
Chester	362	Flint	35
Cornwall	175	Glamorgan	202
Cumberland	217	Merioneth	25
Derby	427	Montgomery	31
Devon	230	Pembroke	46
Dorset	97	Radnor	20
Durham	301	Islands in the British	
Essex	339	Seas	47
Gloucester	437		—
Hereford	44		624
Hertford	137	SCOTLAND.	
Huntingdon	45	Aberdeen	105
Kent	284	Argyll	44
Lancaster	1862	Ayr	144
Leicester	292	Banff	33
Lincoln	435	Berwick	41
Middlesex	1597	Bute	17
Monmouth	163	Caithness	4
Norfolk	431	Clackmannan	18
Northampton	214	Dumbarton	29
Northumberland	426	Dumfries	72
Nottingham	267	Edinburgh	401
Oxford	94	Elgin, or Moray	37
Rutland	23	Fife	77
Salop	240	Forfar	108
Somerset	201	Haddington	54
Southampton	226	Inverness	33
Stafford	472	Kincardine	27
Suffolk	288	Kinross	9
Surrey	609	Kirkcudbright	46
Sussex	238	Lanark	677
Warwick	476	Linlithgow	33
Westmorland	44	Nairn	2
Wilts	109	Orkney and Shetland	10
Worcester	247	Peebles	13
City of York	63	Perth	119
East Riding of York	200	Renfrew	107
North Riding	187	Ross and Cromarty	11
West Riding	1039	Roxburgh	96
	—	Selkirk	18
	14,038	Stirling	95
WALES.		Sutherland	5
Anglesey	14	Wigtown	36
Brecon	63		—
			2561

Thus we find that, in 1841, there were of these trades in

England	14,038
Wales	624
British Isles	47
Scotland	2,561

Total in Great Britain 17,270

The counties in which the hawkers, hucksters, and pedlars most abound appear to be—1st, Lancaster; 2nd, Middlesex; 3rd, Yorkshire (West Riding); 4th, Lanark; and 5th, Surrey.

What rule, if any rule, was observed in classing these "hawkers, hucksters, and pedlars," or what distinction was drawn between a hawker and a huckster, I am unable to say, but it is certain that the number of "licensed hawkers" was within one-half of the 17,270; for, in 1841, the hawkers' duty realized only 32,762*l.* gross revenue, and waiving the amount paid for the employment of horses, &c., the official return, reckoning so many persons paying 4*l.* each, shows only 8190 licensed hawkers in 1841.

The hawker's business has been prosecuted far more extensively in country than in town, but he still continues to deal in London.

OF THE PACKMEN, OR HAWKERS OF SOFT WARES.

THE packman, as he is termed, derives his name from carrying his merchandise or pack upon his back. These itinerant distributors are far less numerous than they were twenty or twenty-five years since. A few years since, they were mostly Irishmen, and their principal merchandise, Irish linens—a fabric not so generally worn now as it was formerly.

The packmen are sometimes called Manchestermen. These are the men whom I have described as the sellers of shirtings, sheetings, &c. One man, who was lately an assistant in the trade, could reckon twenty men who were possessed of good stocks, good connections, and who had saved money. They traded in an honourable manner, were well known, and much respected. The majority of them were natives of the north of Ireland, and two had been linen manufacturers. It is common, indeed, for all the Irishmen in this trade to represent themselves as having been connected with the linen manufacture in Belfast.

This trade is now becoming almost entirely a country trade. There are at present, I am told, only five pursuing it in London, none of them having a very extensive connection, so that only a brief notice is necessary. Their sale is of both cottons and linens for shirts. They carry them in rolls of 36 yards, or in smaller rolls, each of a dozen yards, and purchase them at the haberdashery swag-shops, at from 9*d.* to 18*d.* a yard. I now speak of good articles. Their profits are not very large—as for the dozen yards, which cost them 9*s.*, they often have a difficulty in getting 12*s.*—while in street-sale, or in hawking from house to house, there is great delay. A well-furnished pack weighs about one cwt., and so necessitates frequent stoppages. Cotton, for sheetings, is sold in the same manner, costing the vendors from 6*d.* to 1*s.* 3*d.* a yard.

Of the tricks of the trade, and of the tally system of one of these chapmen, I had the following account from a man who had been, both as principal and assistant, a travelling packman, but was best acquainted with the trade in and about London.

" My master," he said, " was an Irishman, and told everybody he had been a manager of a linen factory in Belfast. I believe he was brought up to be a shoemaker, and was never in the north of Ireland. Anyhow, he was very shy of talking about Irish factories to Irish gentlemen. I heard one say to him, ' Don't tell me, you have the Cork brogue.' I know he 'd got some knowledge of linen weaving at Dundee, and could talk about it very clever; indeed he was a clever fellow. Sometimes, to hear him talk, you 'd think he was quite a religious man, and at others that he was a big blackguard. It wasn't drink that made the difference, for he was no drinker. It's a great thing on a round to get a man or woman into a cheerful talk, and put in a joke or two; and that he could do, to rights. I had 12*s.* a week, standing wages, from him, and bits of commissions on sales that brought me from 3s. to 5s. more. He was a buyer of damaged goods, and we used to 'doctor' them. In some there was perhaps damages by two or three threads being out all the way, so the manufacturers wouldn't send them to their regular customers. My master pretended it was a secret where he got them, but, lord, I knew; it was at a swag-shop. We used to cut up these in twelves (twelve yards), sometimes less if they was very bad, and take a Congreve, and just scorch them here and there, where the flaws was worst, and plaster over other flaws with a little flour and dust, to look like a stain from street water from the fire-engine. Then they were from the stock of Mr. Anybody, the great draper, that had his premises burnt down—in Manchester or Glasgow, or London—if there'd been a good fire at a draper's—or anywhere; we wasn't particular. They was fine or strong shirtings, he'd say—and so they was, the sound parts of them—and he'd sell as cheap as common calico. I've heard him say, 'Why, marm, sure marm, with your eyes and scissors and needle, them burns—ah! fire's a dreadful judgment on a man—isn't the least morsel of matter in life. The stains is cured in a wash-tub in no time. It's only *touched* by the fire, and you can humour it, I know, in cutting out as a shirt ought to be cut; it should be as carefully done as a coat.' Then we had an Irish linen, an imitation, you know, a kind of 'Union,' which we call double twist. It is 'made, I believe, in Manchester, and is a mixture of linen and cotton. Some of it's so good that it takes a judge to tell the difference between it and real Irish. He got some beautiful stuff at one time, and once sold to a fine-dressed young woman in Brompton, a dozen yards, at 2s. 6d. a yard, and the dozen only cost him 14s. Then we did something on tally, but he was dropping that trade. The shopkeepers undersold him. 'If you get 60l. out of 100l., in tally scores,' he often said, 'it's good money, and a fair living profit; but he got far more than that. What was worth 8s. was 18s. on tally, pay 1s. a week. He did most that way with the masters of coffee-shops and the landlords of little public-houses. Sometimes, if they couldn't pay, we'd have dinner, and that went to account, and he'd quarrel with me after it for what was my share. There's not much of this sort of trade now, sir. I believe my old master got his money together and emigrated.'

"Do you want any ginuine Irish linin, ma'am?" uttered in unmistakable brogue, seemed to authenticate the fact, that the inquirer (being an Irishman) in all likelihood possessed the legitimate article; but as to their obtaining their goods from Coleraine and other places in the Emerald Isle, famed for the manufacture of linen, it was and is as pure fiction as the Travels of Baron Munchausen.

The majority of these packmen have discontinued dealing in linens exclusively, and have added silks, ladies' dresses, shawls and various articles connected with the drapery business. The country, and small towns and villages, remote from the neighbourhood of large and showy shops,

are the likeliest markets for the sale of their goods. In London the Irish packmen have been completely driven out by the Scotch tallymen, who indeed are the only class of packmen likely to succeed in London. If the persevering Scotch tallyman can but set foot in a decent-looking residence, and be permitted to display his tempting finery to the "lady of the house," he generally manages to talk her into purchasing articles that perhaps she has no great occasion for, and which serve often to involve her in difficulties for a considerable period—causing her no little perplexity, and requiring much artifice to keep the tallyman's weekly visits a secret from her husband—to say nothing of paying an enormous price for the goods; for the many risks which the tallyman incurs, necessitates of course an exorbitant rate of profit.

"The number of packmen or hawkers of shawls, silks, &c., I think" (says one of their own body) "must have decreased full one-half within the last few years. The itinerant haberdashery trade is far from the profitable business that it used to be, and not unfrequently do I travel a whole day without taking a shilling : still, perhaps, one day's good work will make up for half a dozen bad ones. All the packmen have hawkers' licences, as they have mostly too valuable a stock to incur the risk of losing it for want of such a privilege. Some of the fraternity" (says my informant) "do not always deal 'upon the square ;' they profess to have just come from India or China, and to have invested all their capital in silks of a superior description manufactured in those countries, and to have got them on shore 'unbeknown to the Customhouse authorities.' This is told in confidence to the servant-man or woman who opens the door— 'be so good as tell the lady as much,' says the hawker, 'for really I'm afraid to carry the goods much longer, and I have already sold enough to pay me well enough for my spec—go, there's a good girl, tell your missus I have splendid goods, and am willing almost to give them away, and if we makes a deal of it, why I don't mind giving you a handsome present for yourself.'" This is a bait not to be resisted. Should the salesman succeed with the mistress, he carries out his promise to the maid by presenting her with a cap ribbon, or a cheap neckerchief.

The most primitive kind of packmen, or hawkers of soft-wares, who still form part of the distributing machinery of the country, traverse the highlands of Scotland. They have their regular rounds, and regular days of visiting their customers; their arrival is looked for with interest by the country people ; and the inmates of the farm-house where they locate for the night consider themselves fortunate in having to entertain the packman ; for he is their newsmonger, their story-teller, their friend, their acquaintance, and is always made welcome. His wares consist of hose—linsey wolsey, for making petticoats—muslins for caps—ribbons —an assortment of needles, pins, and netting-pins —and all sorts of small wares. He always travels on foot. It is suspected that he likewise does a little in the "jigger line," for many of these

Highlanders have, or are supposed to have, their illicit distilleries; and the packmen are suspected of trafficking without excise interference. Glasgow, Dundee, Galashiels, and Harwick are the principal manufacturing towns where the packman replenishes his stock. "My own opinion," says an informant of considerable experience, "is that these men seldom grow rich; but the prevailing idea in the country part of Scotland is, that the pedlar has an unco lang stockin wi' an awfu' amount o goden guineas in it, and that his pocket buik is plumped out wi' a thick roll of bank notes. Indeed there are many instances upon record of poor packmen having been murdered—the assassins, doubtlessly, expecting a rich booty." It scarcely ever costs the packman of Scotland anything for his bed and board. The Highlanders are a most hospitable people with acquaintances—although with strangers at first they are invariably shy and distant. In Ireland there is also the travelling pedlar, whose habits and style of doing business are nearly similar to that of the Scotchman. Some of the packmen of Scotland have risen to eminence and distinction. A quondam lord provost of Glasgow, a gentleman still living, and upon whom the honour of knighthood has been conferred, was, according to common report, in his earlier days a packman; and rumour also does the gentleman the credit to acknowledge that he is not ashamed to own it.

I am told by a London hawker of soft goods, or packman, that the number of his craft, hawking London and its vicinity, as far as he can judge, is about 120 (the census of 1841 makes the London hawkers, hucksters and pedlars amount to 2041). In the 120 are included the Irish linen hawkers. I am also informed that the fair trader's profits amount to about 20 per cent., while those of the not over-particular trader range from 80 to 200 per cent. In a fair way of business it is said the hawker's taking will amount, upon an average, to 7*l.* or 8*l.* per week; whereas the receipts of the "duffer," or unfair hawker, will sometimes reach to 50*l.* per week. Many, however, travel days, and do not turn a penny.

STATEMENT OF A PACKMAN.

OF the way of trading of a travelling-pedlar I had the following account from one of the body. He was well dressed, and a good but keen-looking man of about thirty-five, slim, and of rather short stature, with quick dark eyes and bushy whiskers, on which it was evident no small culture was bestowed. His manners were far from obtrusive or importunate—to those whom he sought to make customers—for I happened to witness a portion of his proceedings in that respect; but he had a quiet perseverance with him, which, along with perfect civility, and something like deference, might be the most efficient means of recommending himself to the maid-servants, among whom lay his chief customers. He showed a little of the pride of art in describing the management of his business, but he would not hear that he "pattered:" he talked to his customers, he declared, as any

draper, who knew his business well, might talk to *his.*

When I saw him, his pack, which he carried slung over one shoulder, contained a few gown-pieces of printed cotton, nearly all with pink grounds; a few shawls of different sizes; and three rolls firmly packed, each with a card-label on which was neatly written, " French Merino. Full duty paid. A.B.—L.F.—18—33—1851. French Chocolate." There were also six neat paper packages, two marked " worked collars," three, " gauze handkerchiefs," and the other " beautiful child's gros de naples." The latter consisted of 4½ yards of black silk, sufficient for a child's dress. He carried with him, moreover, 5 umbrellas, one inclosed in a bright glazed cover, while from its mother-of-pearl handle hung a card addressed—" The Lady's Maid, Victoria Lodge, 13*s.* 6*d.*"

" This is a very small stock," he said, " to what I generally carry, but I'm going on a country round to-morrow, and I want to get through it before I lay in a new one. I tell people that I want to sell off my goods cheap, as they 're too good for country sale; and that 's true, the better half of it."

On my expressing some surprise that he should be leaving London at this particular time, he answered :—

" I go into the country because I think all the hawkers will be making for town, and there 'll be plenty of customers left in the country, and fewer to sell to them at their own places. That 's my opinion."

" I sell to women of all sorts. Smart-dressing servant-maids, perhaps, are my best customers, especially if they live a good way from any grand ticketing shop. I sold one of my umbrellas to one of them just before you spoke to me. She was standing at the door, and I saw her give half a glance at the umbrellas, and so I offered them. She first agreed to buy a very nice one at 3*s.* 3*d.* (which should have been 4*s.*), but I persuaded her to take one at 3*s.* 9*d.* (which should have been 4*s.* 6*d.*). 'Look here, ma'am,' said I, ' this umbrella is much bigger you see, and will carry double, so when you 're coming from church of a wet Sunday evening, a friend can have share of it, and very grateful he 'll be, as he 's sure to have his best hat on. There 's been many a question put under an umbrella that way that's made a young lady blush, and take good care of her umbrella when she was married, and had a house of her own. I look sharp after the young and pretty ladies, Miss, and shall as long as I 'm a bachelor.' ' O,' says she, ' such ridiculous nonsense. But I 'll have the bigger umbrella, because it 's often so windy about here, and then one must have a good cover if it rains as well.'

" That 's my way, sir. I don't mind telling that, because they do the same in the shops. I 've heard them, but they can't put love and sweet-hearting so cleverly in a crowded shop as we can in a quiet house. It 's that I go for, love and sweet-hearting; and I always speak to any smart servant as if I thought she was the mistress, or as if I wasn't sure whether she was the mistress or the lady's-maid; three times out of four she's house-maid or maid of all work. I call her 'ma'am,' and 'young lady,' and sometimes 'miss.' It's no use offering to sell until a maid has tidied herself in the afternoon—not a bit. I should make a capital draper's shopman, I know, only I could never bear the confinement. I never will hear such words as 'I don't want it,' or, 'nothing more to-day,' no more than if I was behind a counter.

"The great difficulty I have is to get a chance of offering my goods. If I ring at a gate—for I always go a little way out of town—they can see who it is, and I may ring half an hour for nothing. If the door's opened it's often shut again directly, and I just hear 'bother.' I used to leave a few bills, and I do so still in some parts of the country, with a list of goods, and 'this bill to be called for' printed at the bottom. But I haven't done that in town for a long time; it's no good. People seem to think it's giving double trouble. One of the prettiest girls I ever saw where I called one evening, pointed—just as I began to say, 'I left a bill and'—to some paper round a candle in a stick, and shut the door laughing.

"In selling my gown-pieces I say they are such as will suit the complexion, and such like; and I always use my judgment in saying so. Why shouldn't I? It's the same to me what colour I sell. 'It's a genteel thing, ma'am,' I'll say to a servant-maid, 'and such as common people won't admire. It's not staring enough for them. I'm sure it would become you, ma'am, and is very cheap; cheaper than you could buy at a shop; for all these things are made by the same manufacturers, and sold to the wholesale dealers at the same price, and a shopkeeper, you know, has his young men, and taxes, and rates, and gas, and fine windows to pay for, and I haven't, so it don't want much judgment to see that I must be able to sell cheaper than shopkeepers, and I think your own taste, ma'am, will satisfy you that these here are elegant patterns.'

"That's the way I go on. No doubt there's others do the same, but I know and care little about them. I have my own way of doing business, and never trouble myself about other people's patter or nonsense.

"Now, that piece of silk I shall, most likely, sell to the landlady of a public-house, where I see there's children. I shall offer it after I've got a bit of dinner there, or when I've said I want a bit. It's no use offering it there, though, if it isn't cheap; they're too good judges. Innkeepers aren't bad customers, I think, taking it altogether, to such as me, if you can get to talk to them, as you sometimes can at their bars. They're generally wanting something, that's one step. I always tell them that they ought to buy of men, in my way, who live among them, and not of fine shop-keepers, who never came a-near their houses. I've sold them both cottons and linens, after such talk as that. I live at public-houses in the country. I sleep nowhere else.

"My trade in town is nothing to what it was ten or a dozen years back. I don't know the

reason exactly. I think so many threepenny busses is one; for they'll take any servant, when she's got an afternoon, to a thoroughfare full of ticket-shops, and bring her back, and her bundle of purchases too, for another 3d. I shall cut it altogether, I think, and stick to the country. Why, I've known the time when I should have met from half-a-dozen to a dozen people trading in my way in town, and for these three days, and dry days too, I haven't met one. My way of trading in the country is just the same as in town. I go from farm-house to farm-house, or call at gentlemen's grand seats—if a man's known to the servants there, it may be the best card he can play—and I call at every likely house in the towns or villages. I only go to a house and sell a mistress or maid the same sort of goods (a little cheaper, perhaps), and recommend them in the same way, as is done every day at many a fine city, and borough, and West-End shop. I never say they're part of a bankrupt's stock; a packfull would seem nothing for that. I never pretend that they're smuggled. Mine's a respectable trade, sir. There's been so much dodging that way, it's been a great stop to fair trading; and I like to go on the same round more than once. A person once taken-in by smuggled handkerchiefs, or anything, won't deal with a hawker again, even though there's no deception. But 'duffing,' and all that is going down fast, and I wish it was gone altogether. I do nothing in tally. I buy my goods; and I've bought all sorts, in wholesale houses, of course, and I'd rather lay out 10l. in Manchester than in London. O, as to what I make, I can't say it's enough to keep me (I've only myself), and escape the income-tax. Sometimes I make 10s. a week; sometimes 20s.; sometimes 30s.; and I have made 50s.; and one week, the best I ever did, I made as much as 74s. 6d. That's all I can say."

Perhaps it may be sufficiently accurate to compute the average weekly earnings of a smart trader like my informant, at from 21s. to 25s. in London, and from 25s. to 30s. in the country.

OF THE TALLY PACKMAN.

THE pedlar tallyman is a hawker who supplies his customers with goods, receiving payment by weekly instalments, and derives his name from the tally or score he keeps with his customers. Linen drapery—or at least the general routine of linen-draper's stock, as silk-mercery, hosiery, woollen cloths, &c.—is the most prevalent trade of the tallyman. There are a few shoemakers and some household furniture dealers who do business in the tally or "score" system; but the great majority are linen-drapers, though some of them sell household furniture as well. The system is generally condemned as a bad one; as leading to improvidence in the buyer and rapacity in the seller. There are many who have incurred a tally debt, and have never been able to "get a-head of it," but have been kept poor by it all their lives. Some few, however, may have been benefited by the system, and as an outfit for a young man or woman entering service is necessary—when the parties are too poor to pay ready money—it is an accommodation. I have never heard any of the tallyman's customers express an opinion upon the subject, other than that they wish they had done with the tallyman, or could do without him.

The system does not prevail to so great an extent as it did some years back. The pedlar or hawking tallyman travels for orders, and consequently is said not to require a hawker's licence. The great majority of the tally-packmen are Scotchmen. The children who are set to watch the arrival of the tallyman, and apprise the mother of his approach, when not convenient to pay, whisper instead of "Mother, here's the Tallyman," "Mother, here's the Scotchman." These men live in private houses, which they term their warehouse; they are many of them proprietors themselves in a small way, and conduct the whole of their business unassisted. Their mode of doing business is as follows :—they seldom knock at a door except they have a customer upon whom they call for the weekly instalment, but if a respectable-looking female happens to be standing at her door, she, in all probability, is accosted by the Scotchman, "Do you require anything in my way to-day, ma'am?" This is often spoken in broad Scotch, the speaker trying to make it sound as much like English as possible. Without waiting for a reply, he then runs over a programme of the treasures he has to dispose of, emphasising all those articles which he considers likely to suit the taste of the person he addresses. She doesn't want perhaps any—she has no money to spare then. "She may want something in his way another day, may-be," says the tallyman. "Will she grant him permission to exhibit some beautiful shawls—the last new fashion? or some new style of dress, just out, and an extraordinary bargain?" The man's importunities, and the curiosity of the lady, introduces him into the apartment,—an acquaintance is called in to pass her opinion upon the tallyman's stock. Should she still demur, he says, "O, I'm sure your husband cannot object—he will not be so unreasonable; besides, consider the easy mode of payment, you'll only have to pay 1s. 6d. a week for every pound's worth of goods you take; why it's like nothing; you possess yourself of respectable clothing and pay for them in such an easy manner that you never miss it; well, I'll call next week. I shall leave you this paper." The paper left is a blank form to be filled up by the husband, and runs thus :—"I agree on behalf of my wife to pay, by weekly instalments of 1s. 6d. upon every pound's worth of good she may purchase." This proceeding is considered necessary by the tallymen, as the judges in the Court of Requests now so frequently decide against him, where the husband is not cognisant of the transaction.

These preliminaries being settled, and the question having been asked what business the husband is—where he works—and (if it can be done without offence) what are his wages? The Scotchman takes stock of the furniture, &c. ; the value of what the room contains gives him a sufficiently correct estimate of the circumstances of his customers. His next visit is to the nearest chandler's shop, and there as blandly as possible he inquires

into the credit, &c., of Mr. ——. If he deal, however, with the chandler, the tallyman accounts it a bad omen, as people in easy circumstances seldom resort to such places. "It is unpleasant to me," he says to the chandler, "making these inquiries; "but Mrs. —— wishes to open an account with me, and I should like to oblige them if I thought my money was safe." "Do you trust them, and what sort of payers are they?" According to the reply—the tallyman determines upon his course. But he rarely stops here; he makes inquiries also at the greengrocer's, the beer shop, &c.

The persons who connect themselves with the tallyman, little know the inquisition they subject themselves to.

When the tallyman obtains a customer who pays regularly, he is as importunate for her to recommend him another customer, as he originally was to obtain her custom. Some tallymen who keep shops have "travellers" in their employ, some of whom have salaries, while others receive a percentage upon all payments, and do not suffer any loss upon bad debts. Notwithstanding the caution of the tallyman, he is frequently "victimised." Many pawn the goods directly they have obtained them, and in some instances spend the money in drink. Their many losses, as a matter of course, somebody must make good. It therefore becomes necessary for them to charge a higher price for their commodities than the regular trader.

However charitably inclined the tallyman may be at first, he soon becomes, I am told, inured to scenes of misery, while the sole feeling in his mind at length is, "I will have my money;" for he is often tricked, and in some cases most impudently victimised. I am told by a tallyman that he once supplied goods to the amount of 2l., and when he called for the first instalment, the woman said she didn't intend to pay, the goods didn't suit her, and she would return them. The tallyman expressed his willingness to receive them back, whereupon she presented him a pawnbroker's duplicate. She had pledged them an hour after obtaining them. This was done in a court in the presence of a dozen women, who all chuckled with delight at the joke.

The principal portion of the tallyman's customers are poor mechanics. When the appearance of the house, and the inquiries out of doors are approved of, no security is required; but the tallyman would at all times rather add a security, when attainable. Servant-girls who deal with tallymen must find the security of a housekeeper; and when such housekeeper agrees to be responsible for the payments, the same inquisitorial proceedings are adopted, in order to ascertain the circumstances of the surety. There are about fifty drapery shops in London where the tally-trade is carried on; and about 200 Scotchmen, besides fifty others (part English, part Irish), are engaged in the trade. A clerk of a tally-shop, at the West-end, informs me that there are ten collectors and canvassers for customers, out each day, from that one establishment; and that, until lately, they were accustomed to collect moneys on Sundays. Some collect as much as 12*l.* or 14*l.* a day; and some not more than 2*l.* or 3*l.* The average sum collected may be about 5*l.* each, or 50*l.* per day by the whole. The profits are 30 per cent., the bad debts 10 per cent., thus leaving 20 per cent. net.

The Scotchman who does not choose to extend his business beyond his own cautious superintendence, is content with smaller profits, perhaps 20 per cent., and his bad debts may be estimated at 2½ per cent. One of the body informed me that he had been in the tally-trade about five years; that he commenced with a capital of only 10*l.*, and that now his collections average 30*l.* per week. He never bought, he said, on credit; and his stock on hand is worth nearly 200*l.* cost price, while his outstanding debts are nearly 200*l.* also. "This is a flourishing state of affairs," he remarked; "I do not owe a penny in the world, and I have accomplished all this in little less than five years." This man had served his apprenticeship to a draper in Glasgow, and had originally arrived in London with 20*l.* in his pocket. After some weeks' fruitless endeavour to obtain a situation, his money dwindling away the while, he was advised, by a fellow-countryman, who was a tallyman, to try the tally-trade. For a few days previous to adopting the business, he went the "rounds" with his friend, for the purpose of getting initiated, and the week after started on his own account. Notwithstanding his having no hawker's licence, he tried to effect sales for ready money, and, to a trifling extent, succeeded. The first week he obtained three tally customers. He could have got, he said, a dozen; but he selected three whom he considered good, and he was not deceived, for they continued to be customers of his to this day. The amount of goods that each of these took of him was 20*s.*; and the three instalments of 1*s.* 6*d.* each (4*s.* 6*d.* per week) the tallyman determined to subsist upon, though his lodging and washing cost him 2*s.* per week. He lived principally upon "parritch" and skim milk, indulging now and then in the luxury of a herring and a few potatoes. In twelve weeks he had added only one more credit customer to his books. He had hawked for ready money, and had succeeded so far as to increase his stock to 15*l.* in value. His first three customers had, by this time, paid their accounts, and again patronized him. In the course of a little time his fourth customer had also paid up, and had another supply of goods; he then added two more tally customers, and commenced indulging (though very seldom) in a mutton chop. He progressed slowly, and is now in flourishing circumstances. He states that he has met with only one loss during his connection with the tally-trade, and that but a trifling one. It is those who wish to drive a very extensive business, he says, who are principally victimised. The most industrious of the packmen tallymen seldom travel less than twenty miles a day, carrying a burthen upon their backs of from 100 to 120 lbs. They used to carry merely patterns to their customers, but they find that the full-

length article is more likely to secure purchasers and customers. Those who keep shops do not carry goods with them; the would-be customer is invited to the shop.

The best day for business in the tally-trade is Monday, and most of these shops upon that day are crowded. Sometimes an unsolicited customer (mostly a female) presents herself, and wishes to be supplied with goods on tally. "Who recommended you?" inquires the tallyman. "Oh, Mrs. ——, sir, a customer of yours." "Ah! indeed, very much obliged to Mrs. ——," is the answer. The articles required are shown, selected, and cut. The new customer is treated most civilly by the tallyman, who further inquires her name and abode. The purchaser, of course, expects the next process will be to deliver up the parcel to her, when she is informed that they "will send it home for her." "Oh," she replies, "I won't trouble you, I can carry it myself." "Our rule, ma'am," returns the tallyman, "is always to send parcels home. We certainly cannot doubt your respectability, but we never deviate from our practice." The disappointed female departs, and if the inquiries do not prove satisfactory, she never hears further from the tallyman. The goods which she selected, and which were cut expressly for her, find their way to the shelves of the establishment. If, however, a good customer accompanies a friend whom she wishes to recommend, the parcels are delivered when purchased, if required. The tallyman (to good customers) often extends his civilities to a glass of wine; or, if the "Ladies" prefer it (which it must be confessed they mostly do), a glass of gin.

There is another class of tallymen who sell clocks, receiving payment by weekly instalments. These are content with an instalment of 1*s.* in the pound per week. They are principally Germans who can speak English. Their proceedings altogether are similar to the tally linendraper.

I have given the rise and progress of a Scotch tallyman, and will now relate the downfall of another—an Englishman. He commenced a tally-shop in the neighbourhood of ——, and was carrying on a prosperous and daily increasing trade. At one time, a bill in the shop window announced that an errand boy was wanted—an applicant soon presented himself—was engaged, and proved a steady lad. In the course of a few weeks, this youth was promoted to the office of serving in the shop, and afterwards became collecting clerk. "George," said his master one day, "we have three days in the week unemployed; suppose you try and form a connection around Finchley, Highgate, Hampstead, and that neighbourhood." George was quite willing to make the experiment, and succeeded beyond expectation. The country connection soon surpassed the town trade; and George, the errand boy, became a man of some consequence in the establishment. The principal of the firm was what is termed "gay." He was particularly fond of attending public entertainments. He sported a little as well, and delighted in horse-racing. His business, though an excellent one, was neglected ; the books got out of order; and he became involved in difficulties. An examination of his affairs took place ; and a Mr. R—— was engaged from a wholesale house in the city to assist in making up the accounts, &c. During this person's sojourn in the shop, he saw that George (the quondam errand boy) was the chief support of the concern. The country customers had never seen any other person, and a partnership was proposed. The proposal was accepted, and the firm R—— and W—— became one of the most prosperous tally-shops in the neighbourhood of Tottenham-court-road. George's master was made bankrupt, and is now a street-seller in Fitzroy-market—vending sandwiches, &c.

The cases are not a few where ruin has followed a connection with the tallymen. I will particularize one instance related to me on good authority. A lawyer's clerk married, when young, a milliner; his salary was a guinea per week, and he and his wife had agreed to "get on in the world." They occupied furnished lodgings at first, but soon accumulated furniture of their own, and every week added some little useful article towards their household stock. "At the end of a year," said the individual in question, "I had as comfortable a little home as any man would wish to possess; I was fond of it too, and would rather have been there than anywhere else. My wife frequently wished to obtain credit; 'it would be so easy,' said she, 'to pay a trifling instalment, and then we could obtain immediately whatever we might want.' I objected, and preferred supplying our wants gradually, knowing that for ready money I could purchase to much better advantage. Consequently we still kept progressing, and I was really happy. Judge my astonishment one day, when I came home, and found an execution was in the house. My wife had run in debt with the tallyman unknown to me. Summonses had been served, which by some means she had concealed from me. The goods which I had taken so much pains to procure were seized and sold. But this was not all. My wife grew so much alarmed at the misery she had caused that she fled from me, and I have never seen her but once since. This occurred seven years ago, and she has been for some time the companion of those who hold their virtue of little worth. For some time after this I cared not what became of me; I lost my situation, and sunk to be a supernumerary for 1s. a night at one of the theatres. Here, after being entrusted with a line to speak, I eventually rose to a 'general utility man,' at 12s. per week. With this and some copying, that I occasionally obtain from the law-stationers, I manage to live, but far from comfortably, for I never think of saving now, and only look out for copying when I stand in need of more money. I am always poor, and scarcely ever have a shilling to call my own."

Some of the principal establishments, "doing largely" in the tally-trade, are in or about Red Lion-square and street, the higher part of High Holborn, the vicinity of Tottenham-court-road, the Blackfriars, Waterloo, Westminster, St. George's, Walworth, New Kent, and Dover roads.

At some of these tally-shops horses and carts are kept to carry out the goods ordered of the "travellers," especially when furniture is supplied as well as drapery; while in others the "travellers" are resident on the premises, and are occasionally shopmen, for a "large" tally-master not unfrequently carries on a retail trade in addition to his tally-business.

The tallymen not concerned with these large establishments, but carrying on trade on their own account, reside generally in the quieter streets in the neighbourhood of the thoroughfares I have mentioned, and occupy perhaps the ground-floor, letting (for the house is generally their own) the other apartments. Sometimes a piece of cotton-print is placed in their parlour-window, and sometimes there is no indication whatever of any business being carried on within, for the hawking tallymen do not depend in any measure upon situation or display, but solely on travelling and personal solicitations at people's own residences.

OF THE "DUFFERS" OR HAWKERS OF PRETENDED SMUGGLED GOODS.

OF "duffers" and "lumpers," as regards the sale of textile fabrics, there are generally, I am informed, about twenty in London. At such times as Epsom, Ascot-heath, or Goodwood races, however, there is, perhaps, not one. All have departed to prey, if possible, upon the countrymen. Eight of them are Jews, and the majority of the others are Irishmen. They are generally dressed as sailors, and some wear either fur caps, or cloth ones, with gilt bands round them, as if they were the mates or stewards of ships. They look out for any likely victim at public-houses, and sometimes accost persons in the streets—first looking carefully about them, and hint that they are smugglers, and have the finest and cheapest "Injy" handkerchiefs ever seen. These goods are now sold in "pieces" of three handkerchiefs. When times were better, I was told, they were in pieces of four, five, and six. One street-seller said to me, "Yes, I know the 'duffers;' all of them. They do more business than you might think. Everybody likes a smuggled thing; and I should say these men, each of the 'duffers,' tops his 1l. a week, clear profit." I am assured that one of the classes most numerously victimised is a body who generally account themselves pretty sharp, viz. gentlemen's grooms, and coachmen at the several mews. Sailors are the best customers, and the vicinity of the docks the best locality for this trade; for the hawker of pretended smuggled goods always does most business among the "tars." The mock handkerchiefs are damped carefully with a fine sponge, before they are offered for sale; and they are often strongly perfumed, some of the Jews supplying cheap perfumes, or common "scents." When the "duffer" thinks he may venture upon the assertion, he assures a customer that this is "the smell the handkerchiefs brought with 'em from foreign parts, as they was smuggled in a bale of spices!"

The trade however is not without its hazards ; for I am informed that the "duffers" sometimes, on attempting their impositions imprudently, and sometimes on being discovered before they can leave the house, get soundly thrashed. They have, of course, no remedy.

The "pieces" of three handkerchiefs sold by the "duffers" are purchased by them in Houndsditch, at from 3s. to 7s. ; but 7s. is only given when there is a design to palm off the 3s. goods along with them. Cent. per cent. is a low profit in this trade.

One intelligent street-trader, to whom I am indebted for carefully-considered information, said to me very quietly : " I 've read your work, sir, at a coffee-shop ; for I can't afford to take it in. I know you're going to open the eyes of the public as to the 'duffer's' tricks, now. All right, sir, they're in honest men's ways. But, sir, when are you going to say something about the rich shopkeepers as sells, and the rich manufacturers as makes, the 'duffer's' things? Every man of them knows it 's for roguery."

There is a peculiar style among the "duffers ;" they never fold their goods neatly—the same as drapers do, but thrust them into the pack, in a confused heap, as if they did not understand their value—or their business. There are other classes of "duffers" whose calling is rather more hazardous than the licensed-hawker "duffer." " I have often thought it strange," says a correspondent, "that these men could induce any one to credit the fact of their being sailors, for, notwithstanding the showy manner in which they chew their quid, and the jack-tar like fashion in which they suffer their whiskers to grow, there is such a fresh-waterfied appearance about them, that they look no more like a regular mariner than the supernumerary seamen in a nautical drama, at the Victoria Theatre. Yet they obtain victims readily. Their mode of proceeding in the streets is to accost their intended dupes, while walking by their side; they usually speak in a half whisper, as they keep pace with them, and look mysteriously around to see if there be any of 'them ere Custom-house sharks afloat.' They address the simple-looking passers by thus: 'Shipmate' (here they take off their fur-cap and spit their quid into it)—' shipmate, I 've just come ashore arter a long voyage—and splice me but I 've something in the locker that 'll be of service to you ; and, shiver my timbers' (they are very profuse in nautical terms), ' you shall have it at your own price, for I 'm determined to have a spree, and I haven't a shot in the locker ; helm's a-lee ; just let's turn into this creek, and I 'll show you what it is' (perhaps he persuades his dupe down a court, or to a neighbouring public-house). ' Now here is a beautiful piece of *Ingy* handkerchiefs.' (They are the coarsest description of spun not *thrown* silk, well stiffened into stoutness, and cost the "duffer" perhaps 15d. each; but as business is always done on the sly, in a hurry, and to escape observation, an examination seldom or never takes place). ' I got 'em on shore in spite of those pirates, the Custom-house officers. You shall have 'em cheap, there 's half a dozen on

'em, they cost me 30s. at Madras, you shall have 'em for the same money.' (The victim, may be, is not inclined to purchase. The pretended tar, however, must have money.) 'Will you give me 25s. for them?' he says; ' d—n it, a pound? Shiver my topsails, you don't want them any cheaper than that, do you!' The 'duffer' says this to make his dupe believe that he really does want the goods, or has offered a price for them. Perhaps if the 'duffer' cannot extort more he takes 10s. for the half dozen ' Ingy ' handkerchiefs, the profit being thus about 2s. 6d. ; but more frequently he gets 100 and even 200 per cent. on his transactions according to the gullibility of his customers. The ' duffer ' deals also in cigars ; he accosts his victim in the same style as when selling handkerchiefs, and gives himself the same sailor-like airs.

"Sometimes the 'duffers' visit the obscure streets in London, where there are small chandlers' shops ; one of them enters, leaving his mate outside to give him the signal in case the enemy heaves in sight. He requests to be served with some trifling article—when if he approve of the physiognomy of the shopkeeper, and consider him or her likely to be victimised—he ventures an observation as to how enormously everything is taxed' (though to one less innocent it might appear unusual for a sailor to talk politics) ; ' even this 'ere baccy ' he says, taking out his quid, ' I can't chew, without paying a tax ; but,' he adds, chuckling—' us sailor chaps sometimes shirks the Custom-house lubbers, sharp as they are. (Here his companion outside puts his head in at the door, and, to make the scene as natural as possible, says, 'Come, Jack, don't stop there all night spinning your yarns ; come, bear a hand, or I shall part convoy.') ' Oh, heave to a bit longer, my hearty,' replies the 'duffer,' ' I will be with you in the twinkling of a marling spike. I'll tell you what we've got, marm, and if you likes to buy it you shall have it cheap, for me and my mate are both short of rhino. We've half-a-dozen pounds of tea—you can weigh it if you like—and you shall have the lot for 12s.' Perhaps there is an immediate purchase, but if 12s. is refused, then 10s. 8s. or 6s. is asked, until a sale be effected, after which the sailors make their exit as quickly as possible. Then the chandler's-shop keeper begins to exult over the bargain he or she has made, and to examine more minutely the contents of the neatly packed, and tea-like looking packet thus bought. It proves to be lined with a profuse quantity of tea lead, and though some Chinese characters are marked on the outside, it is discovered on opening to contain only half-a-pound of tea, the remainder consisting principally of chopped hay. The ' duffers ' enact the same part, and if a purchaser buy 10 lbs. of the smuggled article, then 9 lbs. at least consist of the same chopped hay.

"Sometimes the 'duffers' sell all their stock to one individual. No sooner do they dispose of the handkerchiefs to a dupe, than they introduce the smuggled tobacco to the notice of the unsuspecting customer ; then they palm off their cigars, next their tea, and lastly, as the ' duffer' is determined to raise as much money as he can ' to have his spree ;' 'why d—e,' he exclaims to his victim—'I 'll sell you my watch. It cost me 6*l.* at Portsmouth—give me 3*l.* for it and it 's yours, shipmate. Well, then, 2*l.*—— 1*l.*' The watch, I need not state, is made solely for sale.

" It is really astonishing," adds my informant, " how these men ever succeed, for their look denotes cunning and imposition, and their proceedings have been so often exposed in the newspapers that numbers are alive to their tricks, and warn others when they perceive the "duffers" endeavouring to victimise them ; but, as the thimble-men say, " There's a fool born every minute."

OF THE STREET-SELLERS OF "SMALL-WARE," OR TAPE, COTTON, ETC.

THE street-sellers of tape and cotton are usually elderly females ; and during my former inquiry I was directed to one who had been getting her living in the street by such means for nine years. I was given to understand that the poor woman was in deep distress, and that she had long been supporting a sick husband by her little trade, but I was wholly unprepared for a scene of such startling misery, sublimed by untiring affection and pious resignation, as I there discovered.

I wish the reader to understand that I do not cite this case as a type of the sufferings of this particular class, but rather as an illustration of the afflictions which frequently befall those who are solely dependent on their labour, or their little trade, for their subsistence, and who, from the smallness of their earnings, are unable to lay by even the least trifle as a fund against any physical calamity.

The poor creatures lived in one of the close alleys at the east end of London. On inquiring at the house to which I had been directed, I was told I should find them in " the two-pair back." I mounted the stairs, and on opening the door of the apartment I was terrified with the misery before me. There, on a wretched bed, lay an aged man in almost the last extremity of life. At first I thought the poor old creature was really dead, but a tremble of the eyelids as I closed the door, as noiselessly as I could, told me that he breathed. His face was as yellow as clay, and it had more the cold damp look of a corpse than that of a living man. His cheeks were hollowed in with evident want, his temples sunk, and his nostrils pinched close. On the edge of the bed sat his heroic wife, giving him drink with a spoon from a tea-cup. In one corner of the room stood the basket of tapes, cottons, combs, braces, nutmeg-graters, and shaving-glasses, with which she strove to keep her old dying husband from the workhouse. I asked her how long her good man had been ill, and she told me he had been confined to his bed five weeks last Wednesday, and that it was ten weeks since he had eaten the size of a nut in solid food. Nothing but a little beef-tea had passed his lips for months. " We have lived like children together," said the old woman, as her eyes flooded with tears, " and never had no dispute. He hated drink, and there was no cause for us to quarrel. One of my legs, you see, is shorter

than the other," said she, rising from the bed-side, and showing me that her right foot was several inches from the ground as she stood. " My hip is out. I used to go out washing, and walking in my pattens I fell down. My hip is out of the socket three-quarters of an inch, and the sinews is drawn up. I am obliged to walk with a stick." Here the man groaned and coughed so that I feared the exertion must end his life. "Ah, the heart of a stone would pity that poor fellow," said the good wife.

" After I put my hip out, I couldn't get my living as I 'd been used to do. I couldn't stand a day if I had five hundred pounds for it. I must sit down. So I got a little stall, and sat at the end of the alley here with a few laces and tapes and things. I've done so for this nine year past, and seen many a landlord come in and go out of the house that I sat at. My husband used to sell small articles in the streets—black lead and furniture paste, and blacking. We got a sort of a living by this, the two of us together. It 's very seldom though we had a bit of meat. We had 1*s.* 9*d.* rent to pay—Come, my poor fellow, will you have another little drop to wet your mouth?" said the woman, breaking off. " Come, my dearest, let me give you this," she added, as the man let his jaw fall, and she poured some warm sugar and water flavoured with cinnamon— all she had to give him—into his mouth. " He 's been an ailing man this many a year. He used to go of errands and buy my little things for me, on account of my being lame. We assisted one another, you see. He wasn't able to work for his living, and I wasn't able to go about, so he used to go about and buy for me what I sold. I am sure he never earned above 1*s.* 6*d.* in the week. He used to attend me, and many a time I 've sat for ten and fourteen hours in the cold and wet and didn't take a sixpence. Some days I'd make a shilling, and some days less ; but whatever I got I used to have to put a good part into the basket to keep my little stock." [A knock here came to the door ; it was for a halfpenny-worth of darning cotton.] " You know a shilling goes further with a poor couple that 's sober than two shillings does with a drunkard. We lived poor, you see, never had nothing but tea, or we couldn't have done anyhow. If I 'd take 18*d.* in the day I 'd think I was grandly off, and then if there was 6*d.* profit got out of that it would be almost as much as it would. You see these cotton braces here " (said the old woman, going to her tray). " Well, I gives 2*s.* 9*d.* a dozen for them here, and I sells 'em for 4½*d.*, and oftentimes 4*d.* a pair. Now, this piece of tape would cost me seven farthings in the shop, and I sells it at six yards a penny. It has the *name* of being eighteen yards. The profit out of it is five farthings. It 's beyond the power of man to wonder how there 's a bit of bread got out of such a small way. And the times is so bad, too ! I think I could say I get 8*d.* a day profit if I have any sort of custom, but I don't exceed that at the best of times. I 've often sat at the end of the alley and taken only 6*d.*, and that 's not much more than 2*d.* clear—it an't 3*d.* I 'm sure. I think I could safely state that for the last nine year me and my husband has earned together 5*s.* a week, and out of that the two of us had to live and pay rent—1*s.* 9*d.* a week. Clothes I could buy none, for the best garment is on me; but I thank the Lord still. I've paid my rent all but three weeks, and that isn't due till to-morrow. We have often reckoned it up here at the fire. Some weeks we have got 5*s.* 3*d.*, and some weeks less, so that I judge we have had about 3*s.* to 3*s.* 6*d.* a week to live upon the two of us, for this nine year past. Half-a-hundred of coals would fit me the week in the depths of winter. My husband had the kettle always boiling for me against I came in. He used to sit here reading his book—he never was fit for work at the best—while I used to be out minding the basket. He was so sober and quiet too. His neighbours will tell that of him. Within the last ten weeks he's been very ill indeed, but still I could be out with the basket. Since then he's never earnt me a penny—poor old soul, he wasn't able! All that time I still attended to my basket. He wasn't so ill then but what he could do a little here in the room for hisself; but he wanted little, God knows, for he couldn't eat. After he fell ill, I had to go all my errands myself. I had no one to help me, for I'd nothing to pay them, and I'd have to walk from here down to Sun-street with my stick, till my bad leg pained me so that I could hardly stand. You see the hip being put out has drawn all the sinews up into my groin, and it leaves me incapable of walking or standing constantly; but I thank God that I've got the use of it anyhow. Our lot's hard enough, goodness knows, but we are content. We never complain, but bless the Lord for the little he pleases to give us. When I was away on my errands, in course I couldn't be minding my basket; so I lost a good bit of money that way. Well, five weeks on Wednesday he has been totally confined to his bed, excepting when I lifted him up to make it some nights; but he can't bear *that* now. Still the first fortnight he was bad, I did manage to leave him, and earn a few pence; but, latterly, for this last three weeks, I haven't been able to go out at all, to do anything."

"She's been stopping by me, minding me here night and day all that time," mumbled the old man, who now for the first time opened his gray glassy eyes and turned towards me, to bear, as it were, a last tribute to his wife's incessant affection. "She has been most kind to me. Her tenderness and care has been such that man never knew from woman before, ever since I lay upon this sick bed. We've been married five-and-twenty years. We have always lived happily—very happily, indeed—together. Until sickness and weakness overcome me I always strove to help myself a bit, as well as I could; but since then she has done all in her power for me—worked for me—ay, she has worked for me, surely—and watched over me. My creed through life has been repentance towards God, faith in Jesus Christ, and love to all my brethren. I've made up my mind that I must soon change this

tabernacle, and my last wish is that the good people of this world will increase her little stock for her. She cannot get her living out of the little stock she has, and since I lay here it's so lessened, that neither she nor no one else can live upon it. If the kind hearts would give her but a little stock more, it would keep her old age from want, as she has kept mine. Indeed, indeed, does she deserve it. But the Lord, I know, will reward her for all she has done to me." Here the old man's eyelids dropped overcome exhausted.

"I've had a shilling and a loaf twice from the parish," continued the woman. "The overseer came to see if my old man was fit to be removed to the workhouse. The doctor gave me a certificate that he was not, and then the relieving officer gave me a shilling and a loaf of bread, and out of that shilling I bought the poor old fellow a sup of port wine. I bought a quartern of wine, which was 4*d.*, and I gave 5*d.* for a bit of tea and sugar, and I gave 2*d.* for coals; a halfpenny rushlight I bought, and a short candle, that made a penny—and that's the way I laid out the shilling. If God takes him, I know he'll sleep in heaven. I know the life he's spent, and am not afraid; but no one else shall take him from me—nothing shall part us but death in this world. Poor old soul, he can't be long with me. He's a perfect skeleton. His bones are starting through his skin."

I asked what could be done for her, and the old man thrust forth his skinny arm, and laying hold of the bed-post, he raised himself slightly in his bed, as he murmured "If she could be got into a little parlour, and away from sitting in the streets, it would be the saving of her." And, so saying, he fell back overcome with the exertion, and breathed heavily.

The woman sat down beside me, and went on. "What shocked him most was that I was obligated in his old age to go and ask for relief at the parish. You see, he was always a spiritual man, and it hurted him sorely that he should come to this at last, and for the first time in his lifetime. The only parish money that ever we had was this, and it *does* hurt him every day to think that he must be buried by the parish after all. He was always proud, you see."

I told the kind-hearted old dame that some benevolent people had placed certain funds at my disposal for the relief of such distress as hers; and I assured her that neither she nor her husband should want for anything that might ease their sufferings.

The day after the above was written, the poor old man died. He was buried out of the funds sent to the "Morning Chronicle," and his wife received some few pounds to increase her stock; but in a few months the poor old woman went mad, and is now, I believe, the inmate of one of the pauper lunatic asylums.

OF THE STREET-SELLERS OF LACE.

THIS trade is carried on both by itinerants and at stands, or "pitches." The itinerants, of whom I will first treat, are about forty in number (thirty women and ten men). They usually carry their lace in boxes, or cases. It is not uncommon for the women to represent themselves as lacemakers from Marlow, or some other place in Buckinghamshire, or from Honiton, in Devonshire, while the men assert they are from Nottingham. I am informed that there are among these itinerant lacesellers two women and one man who really have been lacemakers. They all buy their wares at the haberdashery swag-shops.

The lace, which is the principal staple of this trade, is "edgings," or the several kinds of cheap lace used for the bordering of caps and other female requirements. Among street-people the lace is called "driz," and the sellers of it "drizfencers." It gained this slang name, I was informed, many years ago, when it was sold, and often to wealthy ladies, as rare and valuable lace, smuggled from Mechlin, Brussels, Valenciennes, or any foreign place famous, or once famous, for its manufacture. The pretended smuggled lace trade is now unknown in London, and is very little practised in the country. There is, however, still some smuggling connected with laceselling. Two, and sometimes three, female lacesellers are also "jigger-workers." They carry about their persons pint bladders of "stuff," or "jigger stuff" (spirit made at an illicit still). "I used to supply them with it until lately," one street-trader told me, "from a friend that kept a 'jigger,' and a tidy sale some of them had. Indeed, I've made the stuff myself. I knew one woman, six or seven years back, that did uncommon well at first, but she got too fond of the stuff, and drank herself into the work'us. They never carried gin, for brandy was most asked for. They sold the brandy at 2s. 6d. the pint; rum at 1s. 6d.; and whiskey at 2s.; sometimes higher, and always trying for 6d. a pint profit, at least. O yes, sir; I know they got the prices I've mentioned, though they seem high; for you must remember that the jigger spirit is above proof, and a pint will make two pints of gin-palace stuff. They sold it, I've heard them say, to ladies that liked a drop on the sly; and to some as pretended they bought that way for economy; yes, and to shopkeepers and publicans too. One old lady used to give 3s. for three yards of driz, and it was well enough understood, without no words, that a pint of brandy was part of them three yards. But the trade that way is nothing to what it was, and gets less and less every year."

From a middle-aged woman selling laces I had the following account:—

"I've been in the trade about six years, sir. Ten years back or more I was in place, and saved a little money, as a servant of all work. I married a house-painter, but trade got bad, and we both had illnesses; and my husband, though he's as good a man as need be, can't stick to anything very long at a time." (A very common failing, by the bye, with the street-folk.) "It seems not in his nature. When we was reduced very low he got on a cab—for he can turn his hand to almost anything—and after that we came to street-selling. He's now on jewellery, and I think it suits him as

well or better than anything he's tried; I do my part, and we get on middling. If we're ever pushed it's no use fretting. We had one child, and he died when he wanted just a month of three years old, and after I'd lost him I said I would never fret for trifles no more. My heart was broke for a long time—it was indeed. He was the loveliest boy ever seen, and everybody said so. I went into lace, because my husband got to know all about it, and I had no tie at home then. I was very shy and ashamed at first to go into houses, but that wears off, and I met with some nice people that bought of me and was very civil, so that encourages one. I sell nothing but lace. I never cleared more than 2s. 6d. in a day, and that only once. I suppose I clear from 3s. 6d. to 4s. 6d. a week now; perhaps, take it altogether, rather more than 4s. I have a connection, and go to the houses in and about the Regent's Park, and all the small streets near it, and sometimes Maida Hill way. I once tried a little millinery made-up things, but it didn't suit somehow, and I didn't stick to it. You see, sir, I sell my lace to very few but servant maids and small shopkeepers' wives and daughters; but then they're a better sort of people than those as has to buy everything ready made like servants has. They can use their own needles to make themselves nice and smart, and they buy of such as me to do it cheap, and they're not often such beaters down as them that buys the ready-made. I can do nothing, or next to nothing, in very wet weather. If I'm in the habit of going into a nice kitchen, perhaps the housemaid flies at me for 'bringing in all that dirt.' My husband says all women is crossest in bad weather, and perhaps servants is.

"I buy my lace near Shoreditch. It's a long walk, but I think I'm best used there. I buy generally a dozen yards, from 3½d. to 1s., and sometimes up to 2s. I sell the commoner at 1d. a yard, and three yards 2d.; and the better at 2d. and 3d. a yard. It's a poor trade, but it's doing something. My husband seldom earns less than 12s. a week, for he's a good salesman, and so we pay 2s. rent regular every Monday for an unfurnished room, and has the rest to live on. I have sold in the Brill on a Saturday night, but not often, nor lately I don't like it; I haven't tongue enough."

In addition to the itinerants there are about seventy stationary lace sellers, and not less than eighty on the Saturday evenings. The best pitches are, I am told, near the Borough-market; in Clare-market; the New Cut (on Saturday nights); Walworth-road; Tooley-street; and Dockhead, Bermondsey. From the best information at my command, it appears that at least half of these traders sell only lace, or rarely anything else. The others sell also net for making caps and "cauls," which are the plain portion at the back, to be trimmed or edged according to the purchaser's taste. Some sell also, with their lace, cap ribbons—plain or worked collars—and muslin, net, or worked under-sleeves. Braid and gimp were formerly sold by them, but are now in no demand. The prices run from 2d. to 6d. for lace articles, and about the same for net, &c. per yard; the lowest priced are most sold.

In this stationary trade are as many men and
youths as women and girls. One woman, who
had known street-selling for upwards of twenty
years, said she could not do half so well now as
she could twenty years ago, for the cheaper things
got the cheaper people would have them. " Why,
twenty year ago," she exclaimed, " I bought a
lot of ' leno' cheap—it was just about going out
of fashion for caps then, I think—and one Saturday night in the Cut, I cleared 15s. on it. I don't
clear that in a fortnight now. I have sold to women of the town, as far as I've known them to be
of that sort, but very seldom. It's not often
you'll catch *them* using a needle for theirselves.
They do use their needles, I know. You can see
some of them sewing at their doors and windows
in Granby-street, Waterloo-road, or could lately—
for I haven't passed that way for some time—but
I believe it's all for money down, for the slop-
shops. It suits the slop-shops to get work cheap
anyway; and it suits the women to have some sort
of occupation, which they needn't depend upon for
their living."

The stationary lace sellers, for the most part,
display their goods on stalls, but some spread them
on a board, or on matting on the ground. Some
of the men gather an audience by shouting out,
" Three yards a penny, edging !" As at this rate
the lace-seller would only clear ¼d. in a dozen yards,
the cry is merely uttered to attract attention. A
few who patter at the trade—but far fewer than
was once the case—give short measure. One man,
who occasionally sold lace, told me, that when he
was compelled to sell for " next to no profit, and a
hungry Sunday coming," he gave good short measure, thirty full inches to a yard. His yard wand
was the correct length, " but I can do it, sir," he
said with some exultation, " by palming," and he
gave a jerk to his fingers, to show how he caught in
the lace, and " clipped it short."

Calculating that 100 persons in this trade each
take 10s. 6d. weekly, the profit being about cent.
per cent., we find 2600l. expended in the streets
in lace and similar commodities.

Of the Street-Sellers of Japanned Table-Covers.

This trade, like several others, as soon as the
new commodities became in established demand,
and sufficiently cheap, was adopted by street-
sellers. It has been a regular street-trade between
four and five years. Previously, when the covers
were dearer, the street-sellers were afraid to speculate much in them; but one man told me that he
once sold a table-cover for 8s., and at another time
for 10s.

The goods are supplied to the street-folk principally by three manufacturers—in Long-lane, Smithfield, Whitechapel-road, and Petticoat-lane. The
venders of the glazed table-covers are generally
considered among the smartest of the street-folk,
as they do not sell to the poor, or in poor neighbourhoods, but "at the better sort of houses, and
to the wealthier sort of people." Table-covers are
now frequently disposed of by raffle. " I very

seldom sell in the streets," said one man, " though
I one evening cleared 4s. by standing near the
Vinegar-works, in the City-road, and selling to
gents on their way home from the city. The
public-house trade is the best, and indeed in winter
evenings, and after dark generally, there's no
other. I get rid of more by raffling than by sale.
On Saturday evening I had raffles for two covers,
which cost me 1s. 4d. each. I had some trouble
to get 1s. 9d. for one; but I got up a raffle for
the other, and it brought me 2s.; six members at
4d. each. It's just the sort of thing to get off in
a raffle on Saturday night, or any time when mechanics have money. A man thinks—leastways
I've thought so myself, when I've been in a
public-house raffle—now I've spent more money
than I ought to, and there's the old woman to
face; but if I win the raffle, and take the thing
home, why my money has gone to buy a nice
thing, and not for drink." I may remark that in
nearly all raffles got up in this manner, the article
raffled for is generally something coveted by a
working man, but not so indispensably necessary
to him, that he feels justified in expending his
money upon it. This fact seems well enough
known to the street-sellers who frequent public-
houses with their wares. I inquired of the informant in question if he had ever tried to get up
a raffle of his table-covers in a coffee-shop as well
as a public-house. " Never, with table-covers,"
he said, " but I have with other things, and find
it's no go. In a coffee-shop people are quiet, and
reading, unless it's one of them low places for
young thieves, and such like; and they've no
money very likely, and I wouldn't like to trust
them in a raffle if they had. In public-houses
there's talk and fun, and people's more inclined
for a raffle, or anything spicy that offers."

There are now fifteen regular street-sellers, or
street-hawkers of these table-covers, in London,
four of whom are the men's wives, and they not
unfrequently go a round together. Sometimes, on
fine days, there are twenty. I heard of one
woman who had been very successful in bartering
table-covers for old clothes. " I've done a little
that way myself," said a man in the trade, " but
nothing to her, and people sees into things so now,
that there's hardly a chance for a crust. The
covers is so soft and shiny, and there's such fine
parrots and birds of paradise on them, that before
the price was known there was a chance of a good
bargain. I once got for a cover that cost me 2s. 9d.
a great coat that a Jew, after a hard bargaining,
gave me 6s. 3d. for."

The prices of the table-covers (wholesale) run
from 8s. a dozen to 30s.; but the street-sellers
rarely go to a higher price than 18s. They can
buy a dozen, or half a dozen—or even a smaller
quantity—of different sizes. Some of these street-
traders sell, with the table-covers, a few wash-
leathers, of the better kind. Calculating that
fifteen street-sellers each take 25s. weekly the
year round—one-half being the profit, including
their advantages in bartering and raffling—we
find 975l. expended yearly upon japanned table-
covers, bought in the streets.

OF THE STREET-SELLERS OF BRACES, BELTS, HOSE, TROWSER-STRAPS, AND WAISTCOATS.

THE street-sellers of braces are a numerous and a mixed class. They are nearly all men, and the majority are Irishmen; but this relates only to the itinerant or public-house brace-sellers. These wares are sold also by street-traders, who make other articles the staple of their trade—such as the dog-collar-sellers.

The braces sold thirty years ago were of a very different manufacture from those vended in the streets at present. India-rubber web was then unknown as a component part of the street braces. The braces, which in some parts of the country are called " gallowses," were, at the time specified, made of a woollen web, both washable and durable. " One pair of such braces, good ones," said an old tailor with whom I had some talk on the subject, " would last a poor man his lifetime. Now they 're in a rope or in rags in no time." These woollen braces were sold at from 1s. to 2s. the pair in the streets; the straps being of good firm leather. Not long after this period a much cheaper brace-web was introduced—a mixture of cotton with the woollen—and the cheap manufacture gradually supplanted the better article, as respects the street trade. The cheaper braces were made with sheepskin straps, which soon yielded to friction, and were little serviceable. The introduction of the India-rubber web was another change in the trade, and the manufacture has become lower and lower-priced until the present time.

The braces sold in the streets, or hawked in the public-houses, are, however, not all of the very inferior manufacture. Some are called " silk," others " buck-leather," and others " knitted cotton." The "silk" are of a silken surface, with an admixture of cotton and India-rubber; the " buck-leather " (a kind now very little known in street sale) are of strong sheepskin, dressed buck-leather fashion; and the " knitted " cotton are woven, some kinds of them being very good and strong.

The street brace-sellers, when trying to do business in the streets, carry their goods generally with a few belts, and sometimes with hose in their hands and across their arms. They stretch them from end to end, as they invite the custom of passers by, to evince the elasticity and firmness of the web. Sometimes the braces are slung from a pole carried on the shoulder. The sellers call at the public-house bars and tap-rooms; some are admitted into the parlours; and at a well-frequented gin-palace, I was informed by a manager of one, a brace-seller will call from twelve to twenty times a day, especially on a Monday; while on a Saturday evening they will remain two, three, or four hours, accosting fresh customers. At the gin-palaces, the young and strong Irishmen offering these wares—and there are many such—are frequently scoffed at for selling " braces and things a baby can carry."

The following account, which I received from a street brace-seller, shows the class who purchase such articles:—

" I was put to a carriage-lamp maker," the man said, " at Birmingham, but soon ran away. Nobody saw after me, for I had only an uncle, and he left me to to the parish. It was all my own fault. I was always after some idle end, though I can read very well. It seems as if I couldn't help it, being wild, I mean. I ran away to Worcester, *without knowing where I was going*, *or caring either*. I was half starved in Worcester, for I lived as I could. I found my way to London afterwards. I 've been in the streets ever since, at one thing or the other; how many years I can't say. Time goes so quick sometimes, and sometimes so slow, and I 'm never long in one place. I 've sold braces off and on ever since Amato won the Derby, if you know when that was. I remember it because I went to Epsom races that year to sell race cards. When I came to London after the races I laid out 12s. in braces. I hardly remember how many pairs I bought for it, but they wasn't such common things as I 'm carrying now. I could sell a few then at from 9d. to 1s. 3d. a pair, to the ' cads' and people at such places as the ' Elephant,' and the ' Flower Pot' in Bishopsgate-street, which was a great ' 'bus' place then. I used to sell, too, to the helpers in inn-yards, and a few in the mews. The helpers in the mews mostly buys knitted cotton. I 've got 1s. and sometimes 1s. 6d. for an extra article from them, but now I don't carry them; there 's no demand there. You see, many of them work in their shirts, and the head coachmen and grooms, which is often great Turks, would blow up if the men had dirty braces hanging to their buttons, so they uses what'll wash. Nearly all my business now is done at public-houses. I go from one tavern to another on my round all day long, and sell in the street when I can. I think I sell as many at 5d. and at 10d. as at all other prices together, and most at 5d.; but when I have what I call a full stock I carry 'em from 4d. to 20d. The poorer sort of people, such as wears braces—for there 's a many as does without 'em—likes the 1d. out of 6d., and the others the 2d. out of the 1s.; it tempts them. It 's a tiresome life, and not so good as costermongering, for I once did tidy well in apples. But in the brace trade you arn't troubled with hiring barrows, and it 's easy carried on in public-houses in wet weather, and there 's no stock to spoil. I sell all to working-people, I think. Sometimes an odd pair or two at 1s. 6d., or so, to a tradesman, that may happen to be in a bar, and likes the look and the price; or to a gentleman's servant. I make from 1s. to 1s. 6d. a day; full 1s. 6d. if I stick close to it. I may make 2s. or 2s. 6d. a week, too, in selling belts and stockings; but I only sometimes carry stockings. Perhaps I clear 9s. a week the year round. There 's lots in the trade don't clear 1s. a day, for they only carry low-priced things. I go for 4d. profit on every shilling's worth I sell. I 've only myself to keep. I pay 3d. a night at a lodging-house, and nothing on Sundays. I had a young woman with me when I was a coster, but we didn't agree, and parted. She was too fond of lifting her hand to her mouth (' tippling') to please me. I mean to live very near this week, and get a few shillings if I can to try something at Greenwich next Monday." This was said on the Tuesday in Passion-week.

The braces are bought by the street-sellers at the swag-shops I have described. The prices range from 1s. 6d. (for common children's) to 12s. a dozen; 3s., 3s. 6d., 6s. 6d., and 7s. being the most frequent prices. Higher-priced articles are also sold at the swags and by the street-sellers, but not one in twenty of these compared with the lower priced.

In London and its suburbs, and on "rounds," of which the metropolis forms the central point, and at stands, there are, I am assured, not fewer than 500 persons vending braces. Of these a twentieth portion may be women, and a tenth old and sometimes infirm men. There are few children in the trade. The stall-keepers, selling braces with other articles, are about 100, and of the remainder of this class, those who are not Irishmen are often impoverished mechanics, such as tailors—brace-vending being easily resorted to, and carried on quietly in public-houses, and it does not entail the necessity of bawling aloud, to which a working-man, driven to a street-life, usually feels repugnance. Calculating that 500 brace-sellers clear 5s. a week each on those articles alone, and estimating the profit at 33 per cent., it shows a street expenditure of 3900l. One brace-seller considered that 500 such sellers was too low a number; but the most intelligent I met with agreed on that estimate.

The Belts sold in the street are nearly all of stout cotton web, " with India-rubber threads," and usually of a drab colour, woollen belts being rarely ever seen now. They are procured in the same way, and sold by the same parties, as are braces. The amount expended on belts is, from the best information I can command, about an eighth of that expended on braces. The belts are sold at 1s. each, and cost 8s. the dozen, or 9d. each, if only one be purchased.

The street-sale of hose used to be far more considerable than it is now, and was, in a great measure, in the hands of a class who had personal claims to notice, independent of the goodness of their wares. These were old women, wearing, generally, large white aprons, and chintz-patterned gowns, and always scrupulously clean. They carried from door to door, in the quieter streets, and in the then suburbs, stockings of their "own knitting." Such they often were; and those which were not were still knitted stockings, although they might be the work of old women in the country, who knitted by the fireside, needing no other light on winter evenings and at the doors of their cottages in the sunshine in summer. Of these street-sellers some were blind. Between thirty and forty years ago, I am told, there were from twelve to twenty blind knitters, but my informant could not speak with certainty, as he might probably observe the same women in different parts. The blind stocking-sellers would knit at a door as they waited. The informant I have quoted thought that the last of these knitters and street-sellers disappeared upwards of twenty years ago, as he then missed her from his door, at

which she used to make her regular periodical appearance. The stockings of this trade were most frequently of white lamb's-wool, and were sold at from 3s. 6d. to 5s. 6d. They were long in the leg, and were suited "for gentle-people's winter wear." The women-sellers made in those days, I am assured, a comfortable livelihood.

The sale of stockings is now principally in the hands of the men who vend braces, &c. The kind sold is most frequently unbleached cotton. The price to a street-buyer is generally from 6d. to 9d.; but the trade is of small extent. "It 's one of the trades," a street-seller said to me, "that we can't compete with shop-keepers in. You shall go to a haberdashery swag-shop, and though they have ' wholesale haberdashers,' and ' hawkers supplied' on the door-post, you 'll see a pair of stockings in the window marked with a very big and very black 6, and a very little and not half black ¾ ; and if I was to go in, they 'd very likely ask me 6s. 6d. a dozen for an inferior thing. They retail themselves, and won't be undersold if they can help it, and so they don't care to accommodate us in things that 's always going."

A few pairs of women's stockings are hawked by women, and sold to servant-maids ; but the trade in these goods, I am informed, including all classes of sellers—of whom there may be fifty—does not exceed (notwithstanding the universality of the wear), the receipt of 6s. weekly per individual, with a profit of from 1s. 4d. to 2s., and an aggregate expenditure of about 800l. in the year. The trade is an addition to some other street trade.

The brace-sellers used to carry with their wares another article, of which India-rubber web formed the principal part. These were trowser-straps, " with leather buttonings and ingy-spring bodies." It was only, however, the better class of brace-sellers who carried them ; those who, as my informant expressed it, "had a full stock ;" and their sale was insignificant. At one time, the number of brace-sellers offering these straps was, I am informed, from 70 to 100. " It was a poor trade, sir," said one of the class. " At first I sold at 4d., as they was 6d. in middling shops, and 1s. in the toppers, if not 1s. 6d. ; but they soon came down to 3d., and then to 2d. My profit was short of 3d. in 1s. My best customers for braces didn't want such things ; plain working-men don't. My grooms, and stable-keepers generally, wears boots or knee-gaiters, and footmen sports knee-buckles and stockings. All I did sell to was, as far as I can judge, young mechanics as liked to turn out like gents on a Sunday or an evening, and real gents that wanted things cheap. I very seldom cleared more than 1s. a week on them. The trade 's over now. If you see a few at a stand, it 's the remains of an old stock, or some that a swag-shop has pushed out for next to nothing to be rid of them."

The sale of waistcoats is confined to Smithfield, as regards the class I now treat of—the sellers of articles made by others. Twelve or fourteen years back, there was a considerable sale in what was a branch of duffing. Waistcoats were sold to countrymen, generally graziers' servants, under the pretence that they were of fine silk plush, which was then rather an object of rustic Sunday finery. A drover told me that a good many years ago he saw a countryman, with whom he was conversing at the time, pay 10s. 6d. for a "silk plush waistcoat," the vendor having asked 15s., and having walked away—no doubt remarking the eagerness of his victim—when the countryman refused to give more than 10s. "He had a customer set for it," he said, "at half-a-guinea." On the first day the waistcoat was worn—the drover was afterwards told by the purchaser—it was utterly spoiled by a shower of rain; and when its possessor asked the village tailor the value of the garment, he was told that it had no value at all; the tailor could not even tell what it was made of, but he never saw anything so badly made in his life; never. Some little may be allowed for the natural glee of a village tailor on finding one of his customers, who no doubt was proud of his London bargain, completely taken in; but these waistcoats, I am assured by a tailor who had seen them, were the veriest rubbish. The trade, however, has been unknown, unless with a few rare exceptions at a very busy time—such as the market for the show and sale of the Christmas stock—since the time specified.

The waistcoats now sold in Smithfield market, or in the public-houses connected with it, are, I am told, and also by a tailor, very paltry things; but the price asked removes the trade from the imputation of duffing. These garments are sold at from 1s. to 4s. 6d. each; but very rarely 4s. 6d. The shilling waistcoats are only fit for boys—or "youths," as the slop-tailors prefer styling them—but 1s. 6d. is a common price enough; and seven-eighths of the trade, I am informed, is for prices under, or not exceeding, 2s. The trade is, moreover, very small. There are sometimes no waistcoat-sellers at all; but generally two, and not unfrequently three. The profits of these men are 1s. on a bad, and 2s. 6d. on a good day. As, at intervals, these street-sellers dispose of a sleeve-waistcoat (waiscoat with sleeves) at from 4s. 6d. to 6s., we may estimate the average earnings in the trade at 5s. per market day, or 10s. in the week. This shows an outlay of 78l. in the year, as the profits of these street traders may be taken at 33 per cent.; or, as it is almost invariably worded by such classes, "4d. in the 1s." The material is of a kind of cotton made to look as stout as possible, the back, &c., being the commonest stuff. They are supplied by a slop-house at the East End, and are made by women, or rather girls.

The sale of waistcoats in the street, markets, &c., is of second-hand goods, or otherwise in the hands of a distinct class. There are other belts, and other portions of wearing apparel, which, though not of textile fabrics, as they are often sold by the same persons as I have just treated of, may be described here. These are children's "patent leather" belts, trowser-straps, and garters. The sellers of children's and men's belts and trowser-straps are less numerous than they were, for both these things, I am told, but only on street authority, are going out of fashion. From one

elderly man who had "dropped belts, and straps, and all that, for oranges," I heard bitter complaints of the conduct of the swag shop-keepers who supplied these wares. The substance of his garrulous and not very lucid complaint was that when boys' patent leather belts came into fashion, eleven, twelve, or thirteen years back, he could not remember which, the usual price in the shops was 1s., and they were soon to be had in the streets for 6d. each. The belt-sellers "did well" for a while. But the "swags" who, according to my informant, at first supplied belts of patent horse-leather, came to substitute patent sheep-leather for them, which were softer, and looked as well. The consequence was, that whenever the sheep-leather belts were wet, or when there was any "pull" upon them, they stretched, and "the polish went to cracks." After having been wet a few times, too, they were easily torn, and so the street trade became distrusted. It was the same with trowser-straps.

The belt trade is now almost extinct in the streets, and the strap trade, which was chiefly in the hands of old and infirm, and young people, is now confined to the sellers of dog-collars, &c. The trowser-straps are not glazed or patent-leather, now, but "plain calf;" sold at 2d. a pair generally, and bought at from 1s. 2d. to 1s. 4d. the dozen pairs. Many readers will remember how often they used to hear the cry, "Three pair for sixpence! Three pair for sixpence!" A cry now, I believe, never heard.

Among the belt and strap-sellers were some blind persons. One man counted to me three blind men whom he knew selling them, and one sells them still, attached to the rails by St. Botolph's church, Bishopsgate.

The same persons who sold straps, &c., not including the present sellers, the dog-collar men, &c., had lately no small traffic in the vending of garters. The garter-sellers were, however, far more numerous than ever were the strap-sellers. At one time, I am told, there were 200 garter sellers; all old or infirm, or poor women, or children, and chiefly Irish children. As these children were often stockingless and shoeless, their cry of "Penny a pair! India-rubber garters, penny a pair!" was sometimes pitiful enough, as they were offering a cheap article, unused by themselves. The sudden influx of garters, so to speak, was owing, I am told, to a manufacturer having discovered a cheap way of "working the India-rubber threads," and having "thrown a lot into the market through the swag shops." The price was at first 8s. a gross (8d. a dozen), but as the demand increased, it was raised to 9s. and 9s. 6d. The trade continued about six weeks, but has now almost entirely ceased. The stock of garters still offered for sale is what stall-keepers have on hand, or what swag shop-keepers tempt street-sellers to buy by reducing the price. The leather garter-trade, 1d. a pair being the usual price for sheep-skin garters, is now almost unknown. It was somewhat extensive.

OF THE STREET-SELLERS OF BOOT AND STAY-LACES, &c.

LIKE many street-callings which can be started on

the smallest means, and without any previous knowledge of the article sold being necessary to the street-vendor, the boot and stay-lace trade has very many followers. I here speak of those who *sell* boot-laces, and subsist, or endeavour to subsist, by the sale, without mixing it up with begging. The majority, indeed the great majority, of these street traders are women advanced in years, and, perhaps, I may say the whole of them are very poor. An old woman said to me, "I just drag, on, sir, half-starving on a few boot-laces, rather than go into the workhouse, and I know numbers doing the same."

The laces are bought at the haberdashery swag-shops I have spoken of, and amongst these old women I found the term "swag-shop" as common as among men who buy largely at such establishments. The usual price for boot-laces to be sold in the streets is 1*d*. a dozen. Each lace is tagged at both ends, sufficing for a pair of boots. The regular retail price is three a penny, but the lace-sellers are not unfrequently compelled to give four, or lose a customer. A better quality is sold at 1½*d*. and 2*d*. a dozen, but these are seldom meddled with by the street lace-sellers. It is often a matter of strong endeavour for a poor woman to make herself mistress of 11*d*., the whole of which she can devote to the purchase of boot-laces, as for 11*d*. she can procure a gross, so saving 1*d*. in twelve dozen.

The stay-laces, which are bought at the same places, and usually sold by the same street-traders, are 2*d*. and 2½*d*. the dozen. I am told that there are as many of the higher as of the lower priced stay-laces bought for street sale, "because," one of the street-sellers told me "there's a great many servant girls, and others too, that's very particular about their stay-laces." The stay-laces are retailed at ½*d*. each.

These articles are vended at street-stalls, along with other things for female use; but the most numerous portion of the lace-sellers are itinerant, walking up and down a street market, or going on a round in the suburbs, calling at every house where they are known, or where, as one woman expressed it, "we make bold to venture." Those frequenting the street-markets, or other streets or thoroughfares, usually carry the boot-laces in their hands, and the stay-laces round their necks, and offer them to the females passing. Their principal customers are the working-classes, the wives and daughters of small shop-keepers, and servant-maids. "Ladies, of course," said one lace-seller, "won't buy of us." Another old woman whom I questioned on the subject, and who had sold laces for about fourteen years, gave me a similar account; but she added:—"I've sold to high-up people though. Only two or three weeks back, a fine-dressed servant maid stopped me and said, 'Here, I must have a dozen boot-laces for mistress, and she says, she'll only give 3*d*. for them, as it's a dozen at once. A mean cretur she is. It's grand doings before faces, and pinchings behind backs, at our house.'"

Among the lace-sellers having rounds in the suburbs are some who "have known better

days." One old woman had been companion and housekeeper to a lady, who died in her arms, and whose legacy to her companion-servant enabled her to furnish a house handsomely. This she let out in apartments at "high-figures," and anything like a regular payment by her lodgers would have supplied her with a comfortable maintenance. But fine gentlemen, and fine ladies too, went away in her debt; she became involved, her furniture was seized, and step by step she was reduced to boot-lace selling. Her appearance is still that of "the old school;" she wears a very large bonnet of faded black silk, a shawl of good material, but old and faded, and always a black gown. The poor woman told me that she never ventured to call even at the houses where she was best received if she saw any tax-gatherer go to or from the house: "I know very well what it is," she continued, "it's no use my calling; they're sure to be cross, and the servants will be cross too, because their masters or mistresses are cross with them. If the tax-gatherer's not paid, they're cross at being asked; if he is paid, they're cross at having had to part with their money. I've paid taxes myself."

The dress of the boot lace-sellers generally is that of poor elderly women, for the most part perhaps a black chip, or old straw bonnet (often broken) and a dark-coloured cotton gown. Their abodes are in the localities in all parts of the metropolis, which I have frequently specified as the abodes of the poor. They live most frequently in their own rooms, but the younger, and perhaps I may add, coarser, of the number, resort to lodging-houses. It is not very uncommon, I was told by one of the class, for two poor women, boot-lace sellers or in some similar line, "to join" in a room, so saving half the usual rent of 1*s*. 6*d*. for an unfurnished room. This arrangement, however, is often of short duration. There is always arising some question, I was told, about the use or wear of this utensil or the other, or about washing, or about wood and coals, if one street-seller returned an hour or two before her companion. This is not to be wondered at, when we bear in mind that to these people every farthing is of consequence. From all that I can learn, the boot-lace sellers (I speak of the women) are poor and honest, and that, as a body, they are little mixed up with dishonest characters and dishonest ways. The exceptions are, I understand, among some hale persons, such as I have alluded to as sojourning in the lodging-houses. Some of these traders receive a little parochial relief.

One intelligent woman could count up 100 persons depending chiefly upon the sale of boot and stay-laces, in what she called her own neighbourhood. This comprised Leather-lane, Holborn, Tottenham Court-road, the Hampstead-road, and all the adjacent streets. From the best data at my command, I believe there are not fewer than 500 individuals *selling* these wares in London. Several lace-sellers agreed in stating that they sold a dozen boot-laces a-day, and a dozen stay-laces, and 2 dozen extra on Saturday nights; but the drawbacks of bad weather, &c., reduce the average sale to not more than 6 dozen a week, or 384,400 boot-laces in a year, at an outlay to the public of 3120*l.* yearly ; from a half to three-fourths of the receipts being the profit of the street-sellers.

The same quantity of stay-laces sold at 6*d.* a dozen shows an outlay of 4680*l.*, with about an equally proportional profit to the sellers.

Most of these traders sell tapes and other articles as well as laces. The tapes cost 3*d.* and 3½*d.* the dozen, and are sold at ½*d.* a knot. A dozen in 2 days is an average sale, but I have treated more expressly of those who depend principally upon boot-lace selling for their livelihood. Their average profits are about 3*s.* a week, on laces alone. The trade, I am told, was much more remunerative a few years back, and the decline was attributed "to so many getting into the trade, and the button boots becoming as fashionable as the Adelaides."

OF A BLIND FEMALE SELLER OF "SMALL-WARES."

I NOW give an account of the street-trade, the feelings, and the life of a poor blind woman, who may be seen nearly every fine day, selling what is technically termed " small-ware," in Leather-lane, Holborn. The street "small-wares" are now understood to be cotton-tapes, pins, and sewing cotton ; sometimes with the addition of boot and stay-laces, and shirt-buttons.

I saw the blind small-ware seller enter her own apartment, which was on the first floor of a small house in a court contiguous to her " pitch." The entrance into the court was low and narrow ; a tall man would be compelled to stoop as he entered the passage leading into the court. Here were unmistakeable signs of the poverty of the inhabitants. Soapsuds stood in the choked gutter, old clothes were hung out to dry across the court, one side being a dead wall, and the windows were patched with paper, sometimes itself patched with other paper. In front of one window, however, was a rude gate-work, behind which stood a root of lavender, and a campanula, thriving not at all, but yet, with all their dinginess, presenting a relief to the eye.

The room of the blind woman is reached by a very narrow staircase, on which two slim persons could not pass each other, nor up old and worn stairs. Her apartment may be about ten feet square. The window had both small and large panes, with abundance of putty plastering. The furniture consisted of a small round deal table (on which lay the poor woman's stock of black and white tapes, of shirt-buttons, &c.), and of four broken or patched chairs. There were a few motley-looking " pot" ornaments on the mantel-shelf, in the middle of which stood a doctor's bottle. The bust of a female was also conspicuous, as was a tobacco-pipe. Above the mantel-piece hung some pictureless frames, while a pair of spectacles were suspended above a little looking-glass. Over a cupboard was a picture of the Ethiopian serenaders, and on the uncoloured walls were engravings of animals apparently from some work on natural history. There were two thin beds, on one of which was stowed a few costermonger's old baskets and old clothes (women's and boys'), as if

stowed away there to make room to stir about. All the furniture was dilapidated. An iron rod for a poker, a pair of old tongs, and a sheet-iron shovel, were by the grate, in which glimmered a mere handful of fire. All showed poverty. The rent was 1*s.* a week (it had been 1*s.* 9*d.*), and the blind woman and a lodger (paying 6*d.* of the rent) slept in one bed, while a boy occupied the other. A wiry-haired dog, neither handsome nor fat, received a stranger (for the blind woman, and her guide and lodger, left their street trade at my request for their own room) with a few querulous yelps, which subsided into a sort of whining welcome to me, when the animal saw his mistress was at ease. The pleasure with which this poor woman received and returned the caresses of her dog was expressed in her face. I may add that owing to a change of street names in that neighbourhood, I had some difficulty in finding the small-ware seller, and heard her poor neighbours speak well of her as I inquired her abode ; usually a good sign among the poor.

The blind tape-seller is a tall and somewhat strongly-formed woman, with a good-humoured and not a melancholy expression of face, though her manner was exceedingly quiet and subdued and her voice low. Her age is about 50. She wore, what I understand is called a " half-widow's cap ;" this was very clean, as indeed was her attire generally, though worn and old.

I have already given an account of a female small-ware seller (which account formerly appeared in one of my letters in the *Morning Chronicle*) strongly illustrating the vicissitudes of a street life. It was the statement, however, of one who is no longer in the streets, and the account given by the blind tape and pin seller is further interesting as furnishing other habitudes or idiosyncracies of the blind (or of an individual blind woman), in addition to those before detailed ; more especially in its narrative of the feelings of a perhaps not very sensitive woman who became " dark " (as she always called it) in mature age.

" It 's five years, sir," she said, " since I have been quite dark, but for two years before that I had lost the sight of one eye. Oh, yes, I had doctors but they couldn't save my eyesight. I lost it after illnesses and rheumatics, and from want and being miserable. I felt *very* miserable when I first found myself quite dark, as if everything was lost to me. I felt as if I 'd no more place in the world ; but one gets reconciled to most things, thank God, in time ; but I 'm often low and sad now. Living poorly and having a sickly boy to care about may be one reason, as well as my blindness and being so bad off.

" I was brought up to service, and was sent before that to St. Andrew's school. I lost my parents and friends (relatives) when I were young. I was in my first place eighteen months, and was eight or nine years in service altogether, mostly as maid of all work. I saved a little money and married. My husband was a costermonger, and we didn't do well. Oh, dear no, sir, because he was addicted to drinking. We often suffered great pinching. I can't say as he was unkind to me.

He died nine years or more since. After that I supported myself, and two sons we had, by going out to wash and 'chair.' I did that when my husband was living. I had tidy work, as I 'chaired' and washed for one family in Clerkenwell for ten years, and might again if I wasn't dark. My eldest son's now a soldier and is with his regiment at Dover. He's only eighteen, but he could get nothing to do as hard as he tried ; I couldn't help him ; he knew no trade ; and so he 'listed. Poor fellow ! perhaps I shall never see him again. Oh, *see* him ! That I couldn't if he was sitting as near me as you are, sir ; but perhaps I may never hear his voice again. Perhaps he'll have to go abroad and be killed. It's a sad thought that for a blind widow ; I think of it both up and in bed. Blind people thinks a great deal, I feel they does. My youngest son—he's now fourteen —is asthmatical ; but he's such a good lad, so easily satisfied. He likes to read if he can get hold of a penny book, and has time to read it. He's at a paper-stainer's and works on fancy satin paper, which is very obnicious" (the word she used twice for pernicious or obnoxious) " to such a delicate boy. He has 5s. a week, but, oh dear me, it takes all that for his bit of clothes, and soap for washing, and for shoes, and then he must carry his dinner with him every day, which I makes ready, and as he has to work hard, poor thing, he requires a little meat. I often frets about his being so weakly ; often, as I stands with my tapes and pins, and thinks, and thinks. But, thank God, I can still wash for him and myself, and does so regularly. No, I can't clean my room myself, but a poor woman who lives by selling boot-laces in the streets has lodged with me for many years, and she helps me."

"Lives !" interrupted the poor boot-lace woman, who was present, "starves, you mean ; for all yesterday I only took a farthing. But anything's better than the house. I 'll live on 4d. a day, and pay rent and all, and starve half my time, rather nor the great house" (the Union).

"Yes, indeed," resumed the blind woman, "for when I first went dark, I was forced to send to my parish, and had 6d. twice a week, and a half-quartern loaf, and that was only allowed for three weeks, and then there was the house for me. Oh dear, after that I didn't know what I could do to get a bit of bread. At first I was so frightened and nervous, I was afraid of every noise. That was when I was quite dark ; and I am often frightened at nothing still, and tremble as I stand in the lane. I was at first greatly distressed, and in pain, and was very down-hearted. I was so put about that I felt as if I was a burden to myself, and to everybody else. If you lose your sight as I did, sir, when you 're not young, it 's a long time *before you learns to be blind.* [So she very expressly worded it.] A friend advised me to sell tapes and cottons, and boot-laces, in the street, as better than doing nothing ; and so I did. But at first I was sure every minute I should be run on. The poor woman that lodges with me bought some things for me where she buys her own—at Albion-house, in the Borough. O, I

does very badly in my trade, very badly. I now clear only 2d., 3d., or 4d. a day ; no, I think not more than 1s. 6d. a week ; that is all. Why, one day this week I only sold a ha'porth of pins. But what I make more than pays my rent, and it 's a sort of employment ; something to do, and make one feel one 's not quite idle. I hopes to make more now that nights are getting long, for I can then go into the lane (Leather-lane) of an evening, and make 1d. or 2d. extra. I daren't go out when it 's long dark evenings, for the boys teases me, and sometimes comes and snatches my tapes and things out of my hands, and runs away, and leaves me there robbed of my little stock. I 'm sure I don't know whether it 's young thieves as does it, or for what they calls a lark. I only knows I loses my tapes. Do I complain to the police, do you say, sir ? I don't know when a policeman 's passing, in such a crowded place. Oh yes, I could get people to complain for me, but perhaps it would be no good ; and then I'm afraid of the police ; they 're so arbitry. [Her word.] It 's not very long since one of them—and I was told afterwards he was a sergeant, too—ordered me to move on. ' I can't move on, sir,' said I, ' I wish I could, but I must stand still, for I'm blind.' ' I know that,' says he, ' but you 're begging.' ' No, I 'm not,' says I, ' I 'm only a trying to sell a few little things, to keep me out of the work 'us.' ' Then what's that thing you have tied over your breast?' says he. ' If you give me any more of your nonsense, I 'll lock you up ;' and then he went away. I 'm terrified to think of being taken to the station."

The matter which called forth the officer's wrath, was a large card, tied from the poor woman's shoulders, on which was printed, in large letters, " PLEASE TO BUY OF THE POOR BLIND." " Ay," said the blind woman's companion, with a bitterness not uncommon on the part of street-sellers on such occasions, " and any shopkeeper can put what notice he likes in his window, that he can, if it 's ever such a lie, and nothing 's said if *he* collects a crowd ; oh dear, no. But *we* mus'n't say our lives is our own."

" Yes, sir," said the blind woman, as I questioned her further, "there I stands, and often feels as if I was half asleep, or half dreaming ; and I sometimes hardly knows when I dreams, and what I thinks ; and I think what it was like when I had my eyesight and was among them, and what it would be like if I had my eyesight again ; all those people making all that noise, and trying to earn a penny, seems so queer. And I often thinks if people suffered ever so much, they had something to be thankful for, if they had their eyesight. If I 'd been dark from a child, I think I shouldn't have felt it so much. It wouldn't have been like all that lost, and I should be handier, though I 'm not bad that way as it is, but I 'm afraid to go out by myself. Where I lives there 's so many brokers about, I should run against their furniture. I 'm sometimes not spoken to for an hour and more. Many a day I 've only took 1d. Then I thinks and mopes about what will become of me, and thinks about my children. I don't know who buys of me, but I'm sure I'm very thankful to all as does. They takes the things out of my hands, and puts the money into them. I think they're working-people as buys of me, but I can't be sure. Some speaks to me very kind and pleasant. I don't think they're ladies that speaks kind. My husband used to say that if ladies went to places like the Lane, it was on the sly, to get something cheap, and they did'nt want to be seen there, or they might be counted low. I'm sure he was right. And it ain't such as them as buys of a poor blind woman out of kindness. No, sir, it's very seldom indeed that I get more than the regular price. A halfpenny a knot for my tapes; and a halfpenny and a farthing for pins; and a halfpenny and a penny a dozen for shirt-buttons; and three a penny when I sells boot-laces; and a halfpenny a piece when I has stay-laces. I sells good things, I know, for the friend as gets them wouldn't deceive me, and I never has no complaints of them.

"I don't know any other blind woman in the trade besides myself. No, I don't associate with blind people. I wasn't brought up, like, to such a thing, but am in it by accident. I can't say how many blind women there may be in my line in the streets. I haven't the least notion. I took little notice of them, God forgive me, when I had my eyesight, and I haven't been thrown among them since. Whether there's many of them or not, they're all to be pitied.

"On a Sunday I never stirs out, except to chapel, with my lodger or my son. No, sir, not a Roman Catholic chapel, but a Protestant. When it's not very fine weather we goes to the nearest, but you hears nothing but what's good in any of them. Oh dear, no.

"I lives on tea and bread and butter all the week—yes, I can make it ready myself—except on Sundays, when my son has his dinner here, and we has a bit of cheap meat; not often fish; it's troublesome. If bread and things wasn't cheap I couldn't live at all, and it's hardly living as it is. What *can* any one do on all that I can earn? There's so many in the streets, I'm told, in my line, and distress drives more and more every week—everybody says so, and wages is so bad, and there's such under-selling, that I don't know whatever things will come to. I've no 'spectation of anything better in the time that has to come, nothing but misery, God help me. But I'm sure I should soon fret to death in a work'us."

The poor woman lodging with the blind street-seller is herself in the same trade, but doing most in boot and stay-laces. She has a sharp and pinched outline of countenance, as if from poverty of diet, and is indeed wretchedly poor, earning only about 6*d*. a day, if so much. She is about the same age as her landlady, or somewhat younger, and has apparently been good-looking, and has still an intelligent expression. She lodged with the blind woman during her husband's lifetime, when he rented two rooms, letting her one, and she had lived with the present widow in this way

about fourteen years. She speaks cheerfully and seems an excellent companion for a blind person. On my remarking that they could neither of them be very cross-tempered to have lived so long together, the lodger said, laughingly, " O, we have a little tiff now and then, sir, as women will, you know; but it's not often, and we soon are all right again. Poor people like us has something else to think of than tiffs and gossipping."

THE BLIND STREET-SELLER OF BOOT-LACES.

THE character, thoughts, feelings, regrets, and even the dreams, of a very interesting class of street-folk—the blind—are given in the narratives I now proceed to lay before the reader, from blind street-folk; but a few words of general introduction are necessary.

It may be that among the uneducated—among those whose feelings and whose bodies have been subjected to what may be called the wear and tear of poverty and privation—there is a tendency, even when misfortunes the most pitiable and undeserved have been encountered, to fall from misery into mendicancy. Even the educated, or, as the street people more generally describe them, those "who have seen better days," sometimes, after the ordeal of the streets and the low lodging-houses, become trading mendicants. Among such people there may be, in one capacity or other, the ability and sometimes the opportunity to labour, and yet—whether from irrepressible vagabondism, from utter repugnance to any *settled* mode of subsistence (caused either by the natural disposition of the individual, or by the utter exhaustion of mind and body driving him to beg)—yet, I say, men of this class become beggars and even "lurkers."

As this is the case with men who have the exercise of their limbs, and of the several senses of the body, there must be some mitigating plea, if not a full justification, in the conduct of those who beg directly or indirectly, because they *cannot* and perhaps *never could* labour for their daily bread— I allude to those afflicted with blindness, whether " from their youth up" or from the calamity being inflicted upon them in maturer years.

By the present law, for a blind man to beg is to be amenable to punishment, and to be subjected to perhaps the bitterest punishment which can be put upon him—imprisonment; to a deprivation of what may be his chief solace—the enjoyment of the fresh air; and to a rupture of the feeling, which cannot but be comforting to such a man, that under his infirmity he still has the sympathies of his fellow-creatures.

It appears to me, then, that the blind have a right to ask charity of those whom God has spared so terrible an affliction, and who in the terms best understood by the destitute themselves, are " well to do ;" those whom—in the canting language of a former generation of blind and other beggars—" Providence has blessed with affluence." This right to solicit aid from those to whom such aid does not even approach to the sacrifice of any idle indulgence—to say nothing of any necessary want—is based on their helplessness, but lapses if it becomes a mere business, and with all the trickiness by which a street business is sometimes characterised.

On this question of moral right, as of political expediency, I quote an authority which must command attention, that of Mr. Stuart Mill:—

Apart from any metaphysical considerations respecting the foundation of morals or of the social union, he says, "It will be admitted to be right, that human beings should help one another; and the more so, in proportion to the urgency of the need; and none needs help so urgently as one who is starving. The claim to help, therefore, created by destitution, is one of the strongest which can exist; and there is *primâ facie* the amplest reason for making the relief of so extreme an exigency as certain, to those who require it, as, by any arrangements of society, it can be made.

"On the other hand, in all cases of helping, there are two sets of consequences to be considered; the consequences of the assistance itself, and the consequences of relying on the assistance. The former are generally beneficial, but the latter for the most part injurious; so much so, in many cases, as greatly to outweigh the value of the benefit. And this is never more likely to happen than in the very cases where the need of help is the most intense. There are few things for which it is more mischievous, that people should rely on the habitual aid of others, than for the means of subsistence, and unhappily there is no lesson which they more easily learn." I may here mention, in corroboration of this statement, that I was told by an experienced parochial officer, that there was truth in the saying, "Once a pauper, and always a pauper;" which seems to show that the lesson of relying on the habitual aid of others may not only be learned with ease, but is forgotten with difficulty. "The problem to be solved," continues Mr. Mill, "is, therefore, one of peculiar nicety, as well as importance; how to give the greatest amount of needful help, with the smallest encouragement to undue reliance on it.

"Energy and self-dependence are, however," Mr. Mill proceeds to argue, and, in this respect, it seems to me, to argue to demonstration, "liable to be impaired by *the absence of help, as well as by its excess. It is even more fatal to exertion to have no hope of succeeding by it, than to be assured of succeeding without it.* When the condition of any one is so disastrous that his energies are paralyzed by discouragement, assistance is a tonic, not a sedative: it braces, instead of relaxing the active faculties: always provided that the assistance is not such as to dispense with self-help, by substituting itself for the person's own labour, skill, and prudence, but is limited to affording him a better hope of attaining success by those legitimate means. This, accordingly, is a test to which all plans of philanthropy and benevolence should be brought, whether intended for the benefit of individuals or of classes, and whether conducted on the voluntary or on the government principle.

"In so far as the subject admits of any general doctrine or maxim, it would appear to be this— *that if assistance is given in such a manner that the condition of the person helped is rendered as desirable as that of another* (in a similar grade of society) *who succeeds in maintaining himself without help, the assistance, if systematic and capable of being previously calculated upon, is* MISCHIEVOUS: *but if, while available to everybody, it leaves to all a strong motive to do without it if they can, it is then for the most part* BENEFICIAL."

That the workhouse should bring less comfort and even greater irksomeness and restraint to any able-bodied inmate, than is felt by the poorest agricultural labourer in the worst-paid parts of the country, or the most wretched slop tailor, or shoemaker, or cabinet maker in London, who supports himself by his own labour, is, I think, a sound principle. However wretched the ploughman may be in his hut, or the tailor in his garret, he is what I have heard underpaid mechanics call, still "his own man." He is supported by his labour; he has escaped the indignity of a reliance on others.

I need not now enter into the question whether or not the workhouse system has done more harm than good. Some harm it is assuredly doing, for its over-discipline drives people to beg rather than apply for parish relief; and so the public are twice mulct, by having to pay compulsorily, in the form of poor's-rate, and by being induced to give voluntarily, because they feel that the applicant for their assistance deserves to be helped.

But although the dogma I have cited, respecting the condition of those in a workhouse, may be sound in principle as regards the able-bodied, how does it apply to those who are not able-bodied? To those who *cannot* work? And above all how does it apply to those to whom nature has denied even the capacity to labour? To the blind, for instance? Yet the blind man, who dreads the injustice of such a creed applied to his misfortune, is subject to the punishment of the mendacious beggar, should he ask a passer-by to pity his afflictions. The law may not often be enforced, but sometimes it is enforced—perhaps more frequently in country than in town—and surely it is so enforced against abstract right and political morality. The blind beggar, "worried by the police," as I have heard it described, becomes the mendacious beggar, no longer asking, in honesty, for a mite to which a calamity that no prudence could have saved him gave him a fair claim, but resorting to trick in order to increase his precarious gains.

That the blind resort to deceitful representations is unquestionable. One blind man, I am informed, said to Mr. Child the oculist, when he offered to couch him, "Why, that would ruin me!" And there are many, I am assured, who live by the streets who might have their eyesight restored, but who will not.

The public, however, must be warned to distinguish between those determined beggars and the really deserving and helpless blind. To allow their sympathies to be blunted against *all*, because some are bad, is a creed most consolatory to worldly successful selfishness, and alien to every principle of pure morals, as well as to that of more than morals—the spirit of Christianity.

The feelings of the blind, apart from their mere sufferings as poor men, are well described in some of the narratives I give, and the account of a blind man's dreams is full of interest. Man is blessed with the power of seeing dreams, it should be remembered, *visionally;* but the blind man, to whose statement I invite attention, dreams, it will be seen, like the rest of his fraternity, through the sense of hearing, or of feeling, best known as "touching;" that is to say, by audible or tactile representations.

Some of the poor blind, he told me, are polishers' wheel-turners, but there is not employment for one in one hundred at this. My informant only knew two so engaged. People, he says, are glad to do it, and will work at as low wages as the blind. Some of the blind, too, blow blacksmiths' forges at foundries; others are engaged as cutlers' wheel-turners. "There was one talking to me the other day, and he said he'd get me a job that way." Others again turn mangles, but at this there is little employment to be had. Another blind acquaintance of my informant's chops chaff for horses. Many of the blind are basket-makers, learning the business at the blind school, but one-half, I am told, can't make a living at this, after leaving the school; they can't do the work so neatly, and waste more rods than the other workers. Other blind people are chair-bottomers, and others make rope mats with a frame, but all of these can scarcely make a living. Many blind people play church organs. Some blind men are shoemakers, but their work is so inferior, it is almost impossible to live by it.

The blind people are forced to the streets because, they say, they can do nothing else to get a living; at no trade, even if they know one, can they get a living, for they are not qualified to work against those who can see; and what's more, labourers' wages are so low that people can get a man with his eyesight at the same price as they could live upon. "There's many a blind basket-weaver playing music in the streets 'cause he can't get work. At the trade I know one blind basket-maker can make 15s. a-week at his trade, but then he has a good connection and works for hisself; the work all comes home. He couldn't make half that working for a shop. At turning wheels there's nothing to be done; there's so many seeing men out of employment that's glad to do the work at the same price as the blind, so that unless the blind will go into the workhouse, they must fly to the streets. The police, I am told, treat the blind very differently: some of the force are very good to them, and some has no feeling at all—they shove them about worse than dogs; but the police is just like other men, good and bad amongst them. They're very kind to me," said my blind informant, "and they have a difficult duty to perform, and some persons, like Colonel Cavendish, makes them harsher to us than they would be." I inquired whether my blind informant had received one of the Census papers to fill up, and he told me that he had heard nothing about them, and that he had certainly made no return to the government about his blindness; but what

it was to the government whether he was blind or not, he couldn't tell. His wife was blind as well as himself, and there was another blind man living in his room, and none of his blind friends, that he had heard of, had ever received any of the papers.

"Some blind people in the streets carry laces. There are some five men and one woman at the West-end do this, and three of these have dogs to lead them; one stands always on Langham-place. One carries cabbage-nets, he is an old man of seventy year, with white hair, and is likewise led by a dog. Another carries matches (he has a large family), and he is often led by one of his boys. There is a blind woman who always sits by the Polytechnic, and has indeed done so since it was built. She gets her living by sewing, making caps and things for ladies. Another blind woman obtains a livelihood by knitting garters and covers for bread trays and backs of chairs. She generally walks about in the neighbourhood of Baker-street, and Portman-square. Many recite a lamentation as they go along, but in many parts of London the police will not allow them to do so.

"It's a very jealous place, is London. The police is so busy; but many recites the lamentation for all that. It's a feeling thing — Oh, they're very touching words."

The greater part in the streets are musicians; five to one are, or ten to one. My informant thinks, last Thursday week, there were seven blind musicians all playing through the streets together in one band. There are four living in York-court; two in Grafton-court; two in Clement's-lane; one in Orchard-place; two in Gray's-buildings; two in Half-Moon-street, in the City, and two in a court hard by; one up by Ball's-pond; two in Rose-court, Whitechapel; three in Golden-lane; two at Chelsea; three in Westminster; one up at Paddington; one (woman) in Marylebone; one in Westminster; one in Gray's-inn-lane; one in Whitechapel: in all thirty-one; but my informant was satisfied there must be at least as many more, or sixty blind musicians in all.

In the course of a former inquiry into the character and condition of street performers, I received the following account from a blind musician:—

"The street blind tried, some years back, to maintain a burying and sick club of our own; but we were always too poor. We live in rooms. I don't know one blind musician who lives in a lodging-house. I myself know a dozen blind men now performing in the streets of London. The blind musicians are chiefly married men. I don't know one who lives with a woman unmarried. The loss of sight changes a man, he doesn't think of women, and women don't think of him. We are of a religious turn, too, generally.

"When we agreed to form the blind club there was not more than a dozen members. These consisted of two basket-makers; one mat-maker; four violin players; myself; and my two mates;

and this was the number when it dropped for want of funds; that's now sixteen years ago. We were to pay 1s. a month, and sick members were to have 5s. a week when they had paid two years. Our other rules were the same as other clubs. There's a good many blind who play at sailors dances, Wapping and Deptford way. We seldom hire children to lead us in the streets; we have plenty of our own generally. I have five. Our wives are generally women that have their eyesight; but some blind men marry blind women."

My informant was satisfied that there were at least 100 blind men and women getting their living in the streets, and about 500 throughout the country. There are many who stay continually in Brighton, Bristol, Liverpool, Birmingham, Manchester, Newcastle-on-Tyne, Plymouth, and indeed all large towns. "There are a great many blind people, I am told," he said, "in Cornwall. It's such a humane place for them; the people has great feeling for the blind; they're very religious there, and a many lose their sight in the mines, and that's what makes them have a feeling for others so." This man heard a calculation made some time back, that there were 5000 blind people, including those in schools and asylums, within five miles round St. Paul's. The most of the blind have lost their sight by the small-pox — nine out of every ten of the musicians have done so; since the vaccination has been discovered, I am told the cases of blindness from small-pox have been considerably increased. "Oh, that was a very clever thing—very," said the blind boot-lace seller to me. Those who have not lost their sight by the small-pox, have gone blind from accidents, such as substances thrown or thrust in the eyes, or inflammation induced from cold and other ailments. My informant was not acquainted with one blind person in the streets who had been born blind. One of his acquaintance who had been blind from birth caught the small-pox, and obtained his sight after recovery at eight years old. "The great majority have lost their sight at an early age—when mere children, indeed; they have consequently been trained to no employment; those few who have" (my informant knew two) "been educated in the blind schools as basket-makers, are unable to obtain employment at this like a seeing person. Why, the time that a blind man's feeling for the hole to have a rod through, a seeing man will have it through three or four times. The blind people in the streets mostly know one another; they say they have all a feeling of brotherly love for another, owing to their being similarly afflicted. If I was going along the street, and had a guide with me that could see, they would say, 'Here's a blind man or blind woman coming;' I would say, 'Put me up to them so as I'll speak to them;' then I should say, as I laid my hand upon them, 'Holloa, who's this?' they'd say, 'I'm blind.' I should answer, 'So am I.' 'What's your name?' would be the next question. 'Oh, I have heard tell of you,' most like, I should say. 'Do you know so and so?' I would say, 'Yes, he's coming to see me,' or perhaps, 'I'm

going to see him on Sunday:' then we say, 'Do you belong to any of the Institutions?' that's the most particular question of all; and if he's not a traveller, and we never heard tell of one another, the first thing we should ask would be, 'How did you lose your sight?' You see, the way in which the blind people in the streets gets to know one another so well, is by meeting at the houses of gentlemen when we goes for our pensions."

The boot, shoe, and stay laces, are carried by the blind, I am told "seldom for sale;" for it's very few they sell of them. "They have," they say, "to prevent the police or mendicity from interfering with them, though the police do not often show a disposition to obstruct them." "The officers of the Mendicity Society," they tell me, "are their worst enemies." These, however, have desisted from molesting them, because the magistrates object to commit a blind man to prison. The blind never ask anybody for anything, they tell me their cry is simply "Bootlace! Bootlace!" When they do sell, they charge 1½d. per pair for the leather boot-laces, 1d. per pair the silk boot-laces, and ½d. per pair for the cotton boot-laces, and ½d. each for the stay-laces. They generally carry black laces only, because the white ones are so difficult to keep clean. For the stay-laces they pay 2d. a dozen, and for the boot-laces 5d. a dozen, for the leather or for the silk ones; and 1½d. for the cotton; each of the boot-laces is double, so that a dozen makes a dozen pair. They buy them very frequently at a swag-shop in Compton-street. My informant carried only the black-cotton laces, and doesn't sell six-penny worth in a week. He did not know of a blind boot lace-seller that sold more than he did.

"Formerly the blind people in the street used to make a great deal of money; up to the beginning of the peace, and during all the war, the blind got money in handfuls. Where there was one blind man travelling then, there's ten now. If they didn't take 2l. and 2l. 10s. a day in a large town, it was reckoned a bad day's work for the musicianers. Almost all the blind people then played music. In war time there was only one traveller (tramp); there are 100 now. There was scarcely a common lodging-house then in one town out of the three; and now there's not a village hardly in the country but what there's one, and perhaps two or three. Why the lodging-houses coin money now. Look at a traveller's house where there's twenty beds (two in each bed), at 3d. each, and that's 10s. you know. There was very few blind beggars then, and what there was done well. Certainly, done well; they could get hatfuls of money almost, but then money was of no valley scarcely; you could get nothing for it most; but now if you get a little, you can buy a plenty with it. What is worth 6d. now fetched 2s. then. I wasn't in the streets then, I wish I had been, I should have made a fortin, I think I should. The blind beggars then could get 2l. a day if they went to look for it." "I myself," said one, "when I first began, have gone and sat myself down by the side of the road and got my 1l., all in half-pence. When I went to Braintree, I stood beside a public-house, the 'Orange Tree,' just by where the foot-people went on to the fair ground, and I took 15s. a day for two days only, standing there a pattering my lamentation from 1 o'clock till the dusk in the evening. This is what I said:—

> 'You feeling Christians look with pity,
> Unto my grief relate—
> Pity my misfortune,
> For my sufferings are great.

> 'I'm bound in dismal darkness—
> A prisoner I am led;
> Poor and blind, just in prime,
> Brought to beg my bread.

> 'When in my pleasant youthful days
> In learning took delight,

(and when I was in the country I used to say)

> And by the small-pox
> I lost my precious sight.

(some says by an inflammation)

> 'I've lost all earthly comforts,
> But since it is God's will,
> The more I cannot see the day,
> He'll be my comfort still.

> 'In vain I have sought doctors,
> Their learned skill did try,
> But they could not relieve me,
> Nor spare one single eye.

> 'So now in dismal darkness
> For ever more must be,
> To spend my days in silent tears,
> Till death doth set me free.

> 'But had I all the treasures
> That decks an Indian shore,
> Was all in my possession,
> I'd part with that wealthy store,

> 'If I once more could gain my sight,
> And when could gladly view
> That glorious light to get my bread,
> And work once more like you.

> 'Return you, tender Christians dear,
> And pity my distress;
> Relieve a helpless prisoner,
> That's blind and comfortless.

> 'I hope that Christ, our great Redeemer,
> Your kindness will repay,
> And reward you with a blessing
> On the judgment day.'

"Some say 'pity the poor blind,' but the lamentation is better. It's a very feeling thing. Many people stands still and hears it right through, and gives a halfpenny. I'd give one myself any day to hear it well said. I'm sure the first time I heard it the very flesh crept on my bones. I larnt it to one blind man myself last summer.

"Now just to show you the difference of things two year afterwards: I went to the very same place where I had took 1l. by the road side, as I told, and all I got was 4s., so you can see how things was falling. The day I took the 1l., there was only one blind man in the town beside me; but when I got the 4s., there was three men blind there. But things now is much worse—bless you, a hundred times worse. If I went now to Braintree fair, I don't think as I should take 3s. You see there's so many blind men now about that I should'nt wonder if there'd be eight or ten at that very fair; they don't know where to run to now to get a halfpenny; there's so many blind people that persons makes game of them. If they see two near one another, they cries out, there's opposition! See what things is come to.

Twelve year ago I should have thought the town was completely done, and people quite tired of me, If I didn't get my shilling going down only one side of a street, and now I may go up and down and not get a penny. If I get 3d. I am very well satisfied. But mind, I may perhaps sometimes meet a gentlemen who may give me a shilling, or one who may give me 2s. 6d.; a person the other day tapped me on the shoulder, near Brook-street, and said, 'Here's half-a-crown for you.' Why, even five year ago one gentleman gave me 1l. twice over within three months, and Prince Napoleon gave me a sovereign last 23rd June was two year. I know the date, because that's the day the blind people goes to the Cloth Hall to get their quarter's money, 25s., and I thought I was as good as they." My informant told me he does better than any of them. "Not one does better than me," he said, "because I sticks to it night and day. It's 12 o'clock every night before I leave the streets. You know I leaves home by ten of a morning. I will have it to get a living. Many says they don't know how I stand it to keep so long on my legs. I only has two meals a day—my breakfast, a bit of summat about five or six at a public-house—my dog though has plenty. I feeds him well, poor fellow. Many times I sleep as I go, and knock my stick just the same as if I was awake. I get a comfortable living—always a little in debt. I've got a very good kerackter, thank God—indeed all the blind men has—they can always get credit; and my dog gets me many a shilling that I wouldn't get at all. But then it's dreadful slavery. I've never no amusement—always out excepting on Sunday. Then I've got 5l. from Cloth Hall, besides a small pension of 1s., and 2s. 6d., and 5s. a year from different gentlemen, who allows us poor blind a small pension yearly. There are many gentleman do this at the West-end. Some will allow 10s. a year, and some only 1s. a year, to a stated number; and they all pay on a particular day that they may appoint. The Earl of Mansfield allows twenty-four destitute blind people 10s. 6d. a year; and his mother gives two blind 1l., and four 10s. The Baroness Rothschild gives to between seventy and eighty 5s. a piece once a year." ("Bless her," said my informant, most heartily, "she is a good woman.") "The Earl Stanhope gives to between forty and fifty the same sum every year, and he's a fine kind-hearted gentleman. The Earl of Cork's brother gives eight or nine of us a shilling a piece once a year. Lady Otway Cave, she is very good to us; she gives seventy or eighty of us 1s. each every fust of May; but the butler, like a many more, I am told, takes advantage of the blind, and puts them off with 6d., and takes a receipt from them for 1s. The Earl of Normanton gives 2s. 6d. to ten of us. Mrs. Managan, of May-fair, gives three 2s. 6d. a piece. The Hon. Miss Brande 1s. a piece to eight. Lady Clements, Grosvenor-square, 2s. a piece to fifteen. The Marchioness of Aylesbury, 5s. a piece to about thirty. The Earl of Harrowby gives twelve 5s. a piece. Lord Dudley Stuart gives to seven or eight 5s. a piece.

Mr. Gurney, 1s. a piece to forty. Mr. Ellis, Arlington-street, 2s. 6d. a piece to fourteen. The Marquis of Bute used to give 5s. a piece to sixty or seventy; but the Marchioness, since his death, has discontinued his allowance. The Dean of Westminster gives 1s. a piece to thirty on Boxing-day. Mr. Spottiswoode, 1s. a piece to about fourteen. Archbishop of Oxford, 5s. a piece to twelve. Rev. Sir Samuel Jarvis, 2s. 6d. a piece to five. Lady Dundas, 1s. a piece to about fourteen or fifteen. The Earl of Besborough, 1s. each to ten. Lord Stafford, 1s. each to about twenty; he used to give 2s. 6d., but, owing to his servant, I am told the sum has been reduced to 1s. Lady Isabella Thynne, 1s. to ten. The Countess of Carlisle, 2s. 6d. each to sixteen. Earl Fitzwilliam used to give 5s. to some, and 2s. 6d. to others, to about twenty. The Countess of Essex, 2s. 6d. each to three. Lord Hatherton, 2s. 6d. each to twelve. John Ashley Warr, Esq., 5s. each to twenty-four. Lord Tynemouth, 2s. 6d. each to forty. Miss Vaughan, 2s. 6d. each to forty (this is bequeathed for ever). Lord Saltoun, 5s. each to three. Mr. Hope, 1s. each to fifty. Mr. Warren (Bryanstone-square), 1s. each to twenty-five. Miss Howard (York-place), 1s. each to every blind person that calls on Boxing-day. Sir John Curtis, 1s. each to eighty (this is also a bequest). Lady Beresford, 1s. each to forty. Lord Robert Grosvenor gives 1l. each to some few. The Countess of Andover, 2s. 6d. a piece to ten. Lord Stanley used to give 3s. to about twelve; but two years ago the allowance was discontinued. The Marquis of Bristol gives 10s. to eighteen. The Bishop of London, 5s. to every one that can obtain a minister's signature. Mr. Mackenzie (Devonshire-place), 2s. 6d. to ten. Mr. Deacon, 2s. 6d. to ten. Miss Sheriff (Manchester-square), 1s. to twenty. Miss Morrison (Cadogan-place), 1s. each to ten. Mrs. Kittoye (Wilton-crescent), 1s. to twenty. Mrs. Ferguson, 2s. 6d. each to seven. The Earl of Haddington, 10s. each to twelve." I am assured that these are only half of the donors to the blind, and that, with the exception of Lady Liddledam, there is not one person living eastward of Tottenham Court-road, who allows the smallest pension to the blind. My informant told me that he knew of no attorneys, barristers, surgeons, physicians, soldiers or sailors, who distributed any money to the blind, nor one tradesman. I think I get 10s. a week regular," he said. "While the quality's in town I'm safe. For other times I can't count above 5s. a week at the outside—if it's the least damp in the world, the quality will not come out. The musicians, you see, have got the chance of a damp day, for then all the best people's at home; but such as me does well only when they're out. If it wasn't for the pensions that the quality gives to the blind during the winter, they couldn't do at all. The blind people who have guides pay them no wages, they find them their victuals and clothes; but the guides are mostly children, and the blind are very good to them; many that I know spoils them."

The blind people are mostly all of a religious turn of mind. They all make a point of attending divine service; and the majority of them are Catholics. My informant knew only five among his blind neighbours who were Protestants—and two of these were Presbyterians, one a Methodist, and two Churchmen; and on the other hand he numbered up fourteen Catholics, all going to the same chapel, and living within a short distance of himself. They are peculiarly distinguished by a love of music. "It's a sure bit of bread to the most; besides, it makes them independent, you see, and that's a great thing to people like us." There is not one teetotaller, I am told, among the street blind, but they are not distinguished by a love of drink. The blind musicians often, when playing at public-houses, are treated to drink, and, indeed, when performing in the streets, are taken by drunken men to play at taverns, and there supplied with liquor; but they do not any of them make a habit of drinking. There is, however, one now in prison who is repeatedly intoxicated; and this, the blind say, is a great injury to them; for people who see one of them drunk in the streets, believe that they are all alike; and there is one peculiarity among them all—being continually mistaken for one another. However different they may be in features, still, from the circumstance of their being blind, and being mostly accompanied by a dog, or a guide, few persons can distinguish one from another. They are mostly very jealous, they tell me, because they say every one takes advantage of their affliction, even their own children, and their own wives. "Some of the wives dress themselves very gaily, because they know their husbands can't see their fine clothes, particularly those that have got no children—then there's none to tell. But, pray mind I only speaking of some of them—don't blame the whole. People never took no money out of my dog's basket—two gals of the town once did try to steal a shilling out of it, that some gentleman had dropped in, but the dog barked, and they gave a scream, and run away. Many of the blind men have married blind women—they say that they don't like seeing women. If seeing men find it a hard job to take care of seeing women, how are blind men to do it?" My informant knows six blind men who have married blind wives—the blind wives, I am told, stick closer to home—and do not want to go to plays, or dances, or shows, and have no love of dress—and they are generally more sober than those who can see. "A blind person," says one, "has no reason to be as wicked as those that can see—there's not half the temptation, you know. The women do all their household duties as well as if they had their eyesight. They make puddings and pies, and boil them, or send them to the oven, as well, as quick, and as handy as a woman that can see. They sweep the floor without leaving a speck; and tidy the room, and black-lead the grate, and whiten the hearth, and dress the chimney-piece off quite handsome, I can tell you. They take great pride in their chimney-piece—they like other people to see it—and they take great pride in having their house quite clean and neat. Where I live it's the remark of all, that they who can't see have their houses the cleanest. I don't know of any blind person that has a looking-glass over the mantelpiece, though. I'm sure that many would, if they had the money, just to please their friends. And, what's more strange, the blind wives will wash their husbands' shirts quite clean." "The blind are very fond of their children, you see, sir," said one; "we owe so much to them, they're such helps to us, even from their very infancy. You'll see a little thing that can hardly walk, leading her blind father about, and then, may be, our affliction makes them loves us the more. The blind people are more comfortable at home—they are more together, and more dependent on one another, and don't like going out into company as others do. With women a love of company is mostly of a love of seeing others, and being seen themselves, so the blind wives is happy and contented at home. No man that could see, unless he was a profligate, would think of marrying a blind woman; and the blind women knows this, and that's why they love their blind husbands the more—they pity one another, and so can't help liking each other." Now, it's strange, that with so many blind couples living together, no one ever heard of any accident from fire with blind people —the fact is, their blindness makes them so careful, that there's no chance of it; besides, when there's two blind people together, they never hardly light a candle at all, except when a stranger comes in, and then they always ask him, before he leaves, to put the light out.

The blind people generally are persons of great feeling; they are very kind and charitable to persons who are in any way afflicted, or even to poor persons. Many of those who live on charity themselves are, I am assured, very generous to those that want. One told me that "a beggar had come to his house, and he had made him cry with his story; my heart" he said, "was that full I was ashamed." They're not particularly proud, though they like to be well-dressed, and they say that no one can get a wife so soon as a blind man. One assured me that he'd go into any lodging-house in the country and get two or three if he wanted—only they'd fight, he said. "You see in the lodging-houses there are many woman whose husbands (but they're not married, you know) have told them to go on and said they would follow them, which of course they don't; or there's many in such places as wants a companion. When a blind man goes into one of these houses, a woman is sure to say to him, 'Can I fetch you anything, master?' Half an ounce of tea may be, and when they've got it, of course, they're invited to have a cup, and that does the business. She becomes the blind man's guide after that. The next morning, after telling one another where to meet—'I'm going such a road,' they whisper to each other,—away they starts. I've known many a blind man run away with a seeing man's wife. The women, I think, does it for a living, and that's all.

"I can't see the least light in the world —not the brightest sun that ever shone. I have pressed my eye-balls—they are quite decayed, you see; but I have pushed them in, and they have merely hurt me, and the water has run from them faster than ever. I have never seen any colours when I did so." (This question was asked to discover whether the illusion called "peacock's feathers" could still be produced by pressure on the nerve). "I have been struck on the eye since I have been blind, and then I have seen a flash of fire like lightning. I know it's been like that, because I've seen the lightning sometimes, when it's been very vivid, even since I was stone blind. It was terrible pain when I was struck on the eye. A man one day was carrying some chairs along the street, and struck me right in the eye ball with the end of the leg of one of the chairs; and I fell to the ground with the pain. I thought my heart was coming out of my mouth; then I saw the brightest flash that ever I saw, either before or since I was blind." (I irritated the ball of the eye with the object of discovering whether the nerve was decayed, but found it impossible to produce any luminous impression—though I suspect this arose principally from the difficulty of getting him to direct his eye in the proper direction). "I know the difference of colours, because I remember them; but I can't distinguish them by my touch, nor do I think that any blind man in the world ever could. I have heard of blind people playing at cards, but it's impossible they can do so any other way than by having them marked. I know many that plays cards that way." He was given two similar substances, but of different colours, to feel, but could not distinguish between them—both were the same to him, he said, "with the exception that one felt stiffer than the other. I know hundreds of people myself—and they know hundreds more —and none of us has ever heard of one that could tell colours by the feel. There's blind people in the school can tell the colours of their rods; but they do so by putting their tongue to them, and so they can distinguish them that's been dipped in copperas from them that hasn't. I know blind people can take a clock to pieces, and put it together again, as well as any person that can see. Blind people gets angry when they hear people talk of persons seeing with their fingers. A man has told me that a blind person in St. James's workhouse could read the newspaper with his fingers, but that, the blind know, is quite impossible."

Many blind men can, I am told, distinguish between the several kinds of wood by touch alone. Mahogany, oak, ash, elm, deal, they say, have all a different feel. They declare it is quite ridiculous, the common report, that blind people can discern colours by the touch. One of my informants, who assured me that he was considered to be one of the cleverest of blind people, told me that he had made several experiments on this subject, and never could distinguish the least difference between black or red, or white, or yellow, or blue, or, indeed, any of the mixed colours. "My wife," said one, "went blind so young, that she doesn't never remember having seen the light; and I am often sorry for her that she has no idea of what a beautiful thing light or colours is. We often talk about it together, and then she goes a little bit melancholy, because I can't make her understand what the daylight is like, or the great delight that there is in seeing it. I've often asked whether she knows that the daylight and the candlelight is of different colours, and she has told me she thinks they are the same; but then she has no notion of colours at all. Now, it's such people as these I pities." I told the blind man of Sanderson's wonderful effect of imagination in conceiving that the art of seeing was similar to that of a series of threads being drawn from the distant object to the eye; and he was delighted with the explanation, saying, "he could hardly tell how a born blind man could come at such an idea." On talking with this man, he told me he remembered having seen a looking-glass once—his mother was standing putting her cap on before it, and he thought he never saw anything so pretty as the reflection of the half-mourning gown she had on, and the white feathery pattern upon it (he was five years old then). He also remembered having seen his shadow, and following it across the street; these were the only two objects he can call to mind. He told me that he knew many blind men who could not comprehend how things could be seen, round or square, *all at once;* they are obliged, they say, to pass their fingers all over them; and how it is that the shape of a thing can be known in an instant, they cannot possibly imagine. I found out that this blind man fancied the looking-glass reflected only one object at once—only the object that was immediately in front of it; and when I told him that, looking in the glass, I could see everything in the room, and even himself, with my back turned towards him, he smiled with agreeable astonishment. He said, "You see how little I have thought about the matter." There was a blind woman of his acquaintance, he informed me, who could thread the smallest needle with the finest hair in a minute, and never miss once. "She'll do it in a second. Many blind women thread their needles with their tongues; the woman who stitches by the Polytechnic always does so." My informant was very fond of music. One of the blind makes his own teeth, he told me; his front ones have all been replaced by one long bit of bone which he has fastened to the stumps of his two eye teeth : he makes them out of any old bit of bone he can pick up. He files them and drills a hole through them to fasten them into his head, and eats his food with them. He is obliged to have teeth because he plays the clarionet in the street. "Music," he said, "is our only enjoyment, we all like to listen to it and learn it." It affects them greatly, they tell me, and if a lively tune is played, they can hardly help dancing. "Many a tune I've danced to so that I could hardly walk the next day," said one. Almost all of the blind men are clever at reckoning. It seems to come natural to them after the loss of their sight. By counting they say they spend many a dull hour—it appears to be all mental arithmetic with them, for they never aid their calculations by their fingers or any signs whatever. My informant knew a blind man who could reckon on what day it was new moon for a hundred years back, or when

it will be new moon a century to come—he had never had a book read to him on the subject in his life—he was one of the blind wandering musicians. My informant told me he often sits for hours and calculates how many quarters of ounces there are in a ship-load of tea, and such like things. Many of the blind are very partial to the smell of flowers. My informant knew one blind man about the streets who always would have some kind of smelling flowers in his room.

"The blind are very ingenious; oh, very !" said one to me, "they can do anything that they can feel. One blind man who kept a lodging-house at Manchester and had a wife fond of drink, made a little chest of drawers (about two feet high), in which he used to put his money, and so cleverly did he arrange it that neither his wife nor any one else could get at the money without breaking the drawers all to pieces. Once while her blind husband was on his travels, she opened every drawer by means of false keys, and though she took each one out, she could find no means to get at the money, which she could hear jingling inside when she shook it. At last she got so excited over it that she sent for a carpenter, and even he was obliged to confess that he could not get to it without taking the drawers to pieces. The same blind man had a great fancy for white mice, and made a little house for them out of pieces of wood cut into the shape of bricks: there were doors, windows, and all," said my informant. The blind are remarkable for the quickness of their hearing—one man assured me he could hear the lamp-posts in the streets, and, indeed, any *substance* (any solid thing he said) that he passed in the street, provided it be as high as his ear; if it were below that he could not *hear* it so well.

"Do you know, I can hear any substance in the street as I pass it by, even the lamp-post or a dead wall—anything that's the height of my head, let it be ever so small, just as well, and tell what it is as well as you can see. One night I was coming home—you'll be surprised to hear this—along Burlington-gardens, between twelve and one o'clock, and a gentleman was following me. I knew he was not a poor man by his walk, but I didn't consider he was watching me. I just heerd when I got between Sackville-street and Burlington-street. Oh, I knows every inch of the street, and I can go as quick as you can, and walk four mile an hour; know where I am all the while. I can tell the difference of the streets by the sound of my ear—a wide street and a narrow street—I can't tell a long street till I get to the bottom of it. I can tell when I come to an opening or a turning just by the click on the ear, without either my touching with hand or stick. Well, as I was saying, this gentleman was noticing me, and just as I come to turn up Cork-street, which, you know, is my road to go into Bond-street, on my way home; just as I come into Cork-street, and was going to turn round the corner, the sergeant of police was coming from Bond-street, at the opposite corner of Cork-street, I heerd him, and he just stopped to notice me, but didn't know the gentleman was noticing me too. I whipped round the corner as quick as any man that had his sight, and said, 'Good night, policeman.' I can tell a policeman's foot anywhere, when he comes straight along in his regular way while on his beat, and they all know it too. I can't tell it where there's a noise, but in the stillness of the night nothing would beat me. I can't hear the lamp-posts when there's a noise. When I said, 'Good night, policeman,' the gentleman whipped across to him, and says, 'Is that man really blind?' and by this time I was half way up Cork-street, when the gentleman hallooed to me to stop; and he comes up, and says, says he, 'Are you really blind?' The sergeant of police was with him, and he says, 'Yes, he is really blind, sir;' and then he says, 'How is it that you go so cleverly along the street if you're blind?' Well, I didn't want to stop bothering with him, so I merely says, 'I do far cleverer things than that. I can hear the lamp-post as well as you that can see it.' He says, 'Yes, because you know the distance from one to another.' The sergeant stood there all the time, and he says, 'No, that can't be, for they're not a regular distance one from another.' Then the gentleman says, 'Now, could you tell if I was standing in the street when you passed me by?' I said, 'Yes; but you mustn't stand behind the lamp-post to deceive me with the sound of the substance.' Then he went away to try me, and a fine try we had. He will laugh when he sees that they're all put down. When he went away I recollected that if he didn't stand as near to the pavement as the lamp-post is, and remain still, he'd deceive me. Oh, certainly, I couldn't hear him if he was far off, and I shouldn't hear him in the same way as I can hear the lamp-posts if he didn't stand still. The policeman hallooed after him, and told him that he mustn't deceive me; but he wouldn't make no answer, for fear I should catch the sound of his voice and know where he was. I had agreed to touch every substance as I went along and round the street to look for him; we always call it looking though we are blind. Well, when he had stood still the sergeant told me to go; he's the sergeant of St. James' station-house, and has been often speaking to me since about it; and on I went at the rate of about three mile an hour, and touched every lamp-post without feeling for them, but just struck them with my stick as I went by, without stopping, and cried out, 'There's a substance.' At last I come to him. There's a mews, you know, just by the hotel in Cork-street, and the gentleman stood between the mews and Clifford-street, in Cork-street; and when I come up to him, I stopped quite suddenly, and cried out 'There's a substance.' As I was offering to touch him with my stick, he drew back very softly, just to deceive me. Then he would have another try, but I picked him out again, but that wouldn't satisfy him, and he would try me a third time; and then, when I come up to him, he kept drawing back, right into the middle of the road. I could hear the stones scrunch under his feet; so I says, 'Oh, that's not fair;' and he says, 'Well, I'm bet.' Then he made me a present, and said that he would like to spend an hour some night

with me again. I don't think he was a doctor, 'cause he never took no notice of my eyes, but he was a real gentleman—the sergeant said so.

"When I dream, it's just the same as I am now, I dream of hearing and touching. The last dream that I had was about a blind man—that's in prison just now. I went into his wife's house, I knew it was her house by the sound of my foot in it. I can tell whether a place is clean or dirty by the sound. Then I heard her say, 'Well, how do you get on?' and I said 'Very well;' and she said 'Sit down,' and after sitting there a little while, I heard a voice at the door, and I said to her, 'Bless me, wouldn't you think that was John;' she said, 'Yes, I would,' but she took no farther notice, and I heard his voice repeatedly. I thought he was speaking to a child, and I got up and went to the door, and says, 'Halloa! is this you;' I was quite surprised and took him by the arm (laying his hand on his own) and he was in his shirt sleeves. I knew that by the feel. Then I was kind of afeard of him, though I am not afeard of anything. I was rather surprised that he should come out three weeks before his time. Then I dreamt that he tried to frighten and pushed me down on the floor, that way (making the motion sideways), to make me believe he was a ghost. I felt it as plain as I should if you were to do the same to me now. I says to him 'Don't be so foolish, sit down', and I pushed him away and got up. When I got up, his wife says to him, 'Sit down, John, and don't be so foolish; sit down, and behave yourself;' and then we set down the two of us, just on the edge of the bed (here he moved his hand along the edge of the table). I thought it was turned down. He's a very resolute man and a wicked one, this blind man is, so I would like to have been out from him, but I was afeard to go, for he'd got a hold of me; after that I waked and I heerd no more. But it's my real opinion that he's dead now, it is indeed, through having such dreams of him I think so; and the same night his wife dreamt that I was killed and all knocked into about a hundred pieces; and those two dreams convince me something's come to him. Oh, I do firmly believe in dreams, that I do; they're sent for people to foresee things, I'm certain of it, if people will only take notice of 'em. I have been many times in prison myself, while I've been travelling in the country. You know in many towns they comes and takes you up without given you never no warning if they catches you begging. I was took up once in Liverpool, once in Hull, once in Exeter, and once in Biddeford, in Devonshire. Most of the times I had a month, and one of them only seven days. I think that's very unjust—never to say you mustn't do it; but to drag you off without never no warning. Every time before I was put in quod I had always dreamt that my father was starving to death for want of victuals, and at last I got to know whenever I dreamt that, I was sure of going to prison. I never dreamt about my mother; she died, you see, when I was very young, and I never remember hearing her speak but once or twice. My father never did the thing that was right to me, and I didn't care much about him. When I was at home I was very fond of pigeons, and my mind went so much upon them, that I used to dream of it the night before, always when they had eggs, and when my rabbits had young ones too. I know when I wake in the morning that I am awake by my thoughts. Sometimes I dream I've got a lot of money in my hand, and when I wake and put my hand to feel it, it's gone, there's none there, and so I know it's been only a dream. I'm much surprised at my disappointment though."

Many of the blind are very fond of keeping birds and animals ; some of them keep pigeons in one of their rooms, others have cocks and hens, and others white mice and rabbits, and almost all have dogs, though all are not led about by them. Some blind men take delight in* having nothing but bull-dogs, not to lead them, but solely for fancy. Nobody likes a dog so much as a blind man, I am told—"they can't—the blind man is so much beholden to his dog, he does him such favours and sarvices." "With my dog I can go to any part of London as independent as any one who has got his sight. Yesterday afternoon when I left your house, sir, I was ashamed of going through the street. People was a saying, 'Look'ee there, that's the man as says he's blind.' I was going so quick, it was so late you know, they couldn't make it out, but without my dog I must have crawled along, and always be in great fear. The name of my present dog is ' KEEPER ;' he is a mongrel breed ; I have had him nine years, and he is with me night and day, goes to church with me and all. If I go out without him, he misses me, and then he scampers all through the streets where I am in the habit of going, crying and howling after me, just as if he was fairly out of his mind. It's astonishing. Often, before my first blind wife died (for I've been married twice to blind women, and once to a seeing woman), I used to say I'd sooner lose my wife than my dog; but when I did lose her I was sorry that ever I did say so. I didn't know what it was. I'm sorry for it yet, and ever will be sorry for it; she was a very good woman, and had fine principles. I shall never get another that I liked so much as the first. My dog knows every word I say to him. Tell him to turn right or left, or cross over, and whip! round he goes in a moment. Where I go for my tobacco, at the shop in Piccadilly, close to the Arcade—it's down six or seven steps, straight down—and when I tells Keeper to go to the baccy shop, off he is, and drags me down the steps, with the people after me, thinking he's going to break my neck down the place, and the people stands on top the steps making all kinds of remarks, while I'm below. If he was to lose me to-night or to-morrow, he'd come back here and rise the whole neighbourhood. He knows any public-house, no matter whether he was there before or not; just whisper to him, go to the public-house, and away he scampers and drags me right into the first he comes to. Directly I whis-

per to him, go to the public-house, he begins playing away with the basket he has in his mouth, throwing it up and laying it down—throwing it and laying it down for pleasure ; he gets his rest there, and that's why he's so pleased. It's the only place I can go to in my rounds to sit down. Oh, he's a dear clever fellow. Now, only to show you how faithful he is, one night last week I was coming along Burlington-gardens, and I stopped to light my pipe as I was coming home, and I let him loose to play a bit and get a drink ; and after I had lit my pipe I walked on, for I knew the street very well without any guide. I didn't take notice of the dog, for I thought he was following me. I was just turning into Clifford-street when I heard the cries of him in Burlington-gardens. I know his cry, let him be ever so far away; the screech that he set up was really quite dreadful; it would grieve anybody to hear him. So I puts my fingers in my mouth and gives a loud whistle; and at last he heard me, and then up he comes tearing along and panting away as if his heart was in his mouth; and when he gets up to me he jumped up to me right upon my back, and screams like—as if really he wanted to speak—you can't call it panting, because it's louder than that, and he does pant when he a'n't tired at all; all I can say is, it's for all the world like his speaking, and I understands it as such. If I say a cross word to him after he's lost—such as, ah, you rascal, you —he'll just stand of one side, and give a cry just like a Christian. I've known him break the windows up two story high when I've left him behind, and down he would have been after me only he durstn't jump out. I've had Keeper nine year. The dog I had before him was Blucher ; he was a mongrel too ; he had a tail like a wolf, an ear like a fox, and a face black like a monkey. I had him thirteen year. He was as clever as Keeper, but not so much loved as he is. At last he went blind ; he was about two year losing his sight. When I found his eyes was getting bad I got Keeper. The way I first noticed him going blind was when I would come to cross a street on my way home ; at nightfall the shade of the house on the opposite side, as we was crossing, would frighten him and drive him in the middle of the road; and he wouldn't draw to the pavement till he found he was wrong; and then after that he began to run again the lamp-posts in the dark; when he did this he'd cry out just like a Christian. I was sorry for him, and he knowed that, for I used to fret. I was sorry for him on account of my own affliction. At last I was obligated to take to Keeper. I got him of another blind man, but he had no larning in him when he come to me. It was a long time teaching him, for I didn't do it all at once. I could have teached him in a week, but I used to let the old dog have a run, while I put Keeper into the collar for a bit" (here the blind man was some time before he could proceed for his tears), "and so he larnt all he knows, little by little. Now Keeper and Blucher used to agree pretty well; but I've got another dog now, named Dash, and Keeper's as jealous of him as a woman is of a man. If I say, ' Come Keeper, come and have the collar on,' I may call twenty times before he'll come; but if I say, 'Dash, come and have the collar on,' Keeper's there the first word, jumping up agin me, and doing anything but speak. At last my old Blucher went stone blind, as bad as his master; it was, poor thing; and then he used to fret so when I went out without him that I couldn't bear it, and so got at length to take him always with me, and then he used to follow the knock of my stick. He done so for about six months, and then I was one night going along Piccadilly and I stops speaking to a policeman, and Blucher misses me; he couldn't hear where I was for the noise of the carriages. He didn't catch the sound of my stick, and couldn't hear my voice for the carriages, so he went seeking me into the middle of the road, and there a buss run over him, poor thing. I heerd him scream out and I whistled to him, and he came howling dreadful on to the pavement again. I didn't think he was so much hurt then, for I puts the collar on him to take him safe back, and he led me home blind as he was. The next morning he couldn't rise up at all, his hind parts was useless to him. I took him in my arms and found he couldn't move. Well, he never eat nor drink nothing for a week, and got to be in such dreadful pain that I was forced to have him killed. I got a man to drown him in a bag. I could'nt have done it myself for all the world. It would have been as bad to me as killing a Christian. I used to grieve terribly after I'd lost him. I couldn't get him off my mind. I had had him so many years, and he had been with me night and day, my constant companion, and the most faithful friend I ever had, except Keeper: there's nothing in the world can beat Keeper for faithfulness—nothing."

OF THE LIFE OF A BLIND BOOT-LACE SELLER.

THE blind boot lace-seller who gave me the following history of his life was the original of the portrait given in No. 17. He was a tall, strongly-built man. In face he was ghastly, his cheek bones were sharp and high, his nose flat to his face, and his eyes were so deeply sunk in that he had more the appearance of a death's head than of a living man. His shirt was scrupulously clean. He wore a bright red cotton neckerchief and a plaid waistcoat of many colours. His dog accompanied him and never left his master's side one moment.

"It's very sorrowful—very sorrowful indeed to hear that," said the boot-lace seller to me, on my reading him the account of the blind needle-seller; "it touches me much to hear that. But you see I don't grieve for the loss of my sight as he do, poor man. I don't remember ever seeing any object. If there was a thing with many colours in it, I could dissarn the highest colour. I couldn't tell one from another, but only the highest.

"I was born in Northumberland," he said, "about five-and-fifty years ago. My father was a grocer and had 1,000l. worth of freehold property besides his business, which was very large for a small town; his was the principal shop, and in the general line. He had a cart of his own, in which he attended market. I was very comfortably brought up, never wanted for nothing, and had my mother lived I should have had an independent fortune. At five years old, while mother was still alive, I caught the small pox. I had four sisters and one brother, and we all six had it at once; that was before the vaccination was properly established. I've heerd said that father did not want to have us inoculated, because of the people coming backwards and forwards to the shop. I only wish vaccination had been in vogue then as it is now, and I shouldn't have lost my eyes. God bless the man who brought it up, I say; people doesn't know what they've got to thank him for. Well, all my sisters and brothers had not a mark upon them. It laid hold of only me. They couldn't lay a finger upon me, they was obligated to lift me up in one of my father's shirts, by holding the corners of it like a sheet. As soon as ever the pock began to decay it took away my eyes altogether. I didn't lose both my eyeballs till about twenty years after that, though my sight was gone for all but the shadow of daylight and any high colours. At sixteen years of age my left eye bursted; I suffered terribly then— oh terribly! yes, that I did. The black-and-white like all mixed together, the pock came right through the star of the eye the doctor said; and when I was five-and-twenty my other eye-ball bursted, and then my eyes was quite out of my head. Till that time I could see a little bit; I could tell the daylight, and I could see the moon, but not the shape of it. I never could see a star, and do you know I grieved about the loss of that little bit of sight as much as if I was losing the whole of it. As my eye-ball sloughed day by day, I could see the light going away by little, every day till the week's end. When I looked at the daylight just before it all went, I could see the light look as red as fire—as red as blood; and when it all left me, oh, I was dreadful sorrowful, I thought I was lost altogether. But, I shouldn't have been so bad off, as I said, if mother had lived, but she died when I was about six year old. I didn't care much about her, indeed I took a dreadful dislike to her. I heerd her say one day to a person in the shop, that she would sooner see me dead and buried than be as I was, but now I know that it was her fondness for me. Mother catched a cold, and died after six day's illness. When she was gone, father got to neglect his business. He had no one then to attend to it, and he took and shut up the shop. He lost heart, you see. He took and turned all the tenants out of his property, and furnished all the rooms of a large house suitable for the quality that used to come to the town to bathe. He mortgaged the place for 250l. to buy the furniture, and that was the ruin of him. Eighteen years afterwards the lawyers got the better of him, and all the family was turned out of the door without a penny. My father they'd put in jail before. He died a few years afterwards in the workhouse. When the family was turned out, there was only my eldest brother away at sea, and my eldest sister in sarvice; so me and my three sisters was sent in the wide world without the means of getting a crust or a place to put our heads in. All my sisters after that got into sarvice, and I went to drive some coal carts at North Shields. The coal carts was father's, and they was all he had left out of his property; so I used to go to Wall's End and fill the carts, then take them down to North Shields and sell them at the people's doors. We never used to sell less than the load. I did all this, blind as I was, without a person to guide, and continued at it night and day for about fifteen year. It was well known to the whole country side. I was the talk for miles round. They couldn't believe I was blind; though they see my eyes was gone, still they couldn't hardly believe. Then, after the fifteen year, me and my father had a complete fall out. He took an advantage of my sister. He had borrowed 20l. of her, and when he could he wouldn't pay her. He behaved as bad as father could, and then I broke with him." (He then went over the whole story, and was affected, even to speechlessness, at the remembrance of his family troubles. Into these there is no necessity to enter here ; suffice it, the blind man appears to have behaved very nobly.) "I came away and went to my brother, who was well off at Hull ; when I got there, I found he had gone to Russia and died there that very spring. While I was on my way to Hull, I used to go to sleep at the lodging-houses for travellers. I had never been in one before, and there I got to think, from what I heerd, that a roving life was a fine pleasant one. The very first lodging-house I went into was one in Durham, and there persons as was coming the same road persuaded me to go and beg with them, but I couldn't cheek it ; it was too near hand at home. We came on to Darlington, that was 18 miles further, that day. They still kept company with me, and wanted me to beg, but I wouldn't ; I couldn't face it. I thought people would know me. The next day we started on our way to Northallerton, and then my few shillings was all gone ; so that night we went to seek relief, and got a pennyworth of milk, and a penny loaf each and our bed. The parish gave us a ticket to a lodging-house. The next morning we started from Northallerton, and then I was very hungry ; all I had the day before was the pennyworth of bread I got from the parish. Then as we got about a mile out of the town, there was a row of houses, and the Scotchman who was with me says, ' If ye'll gang up wi' me, I'll speak for ye.' Well, we went up and got 3d., and plenty of bread and butter ; almost every house we got something at; then I was highly delighted ; thinks I, this is a business—and so I did. We shared with the other man who had come on the road with us, and after that we started once more, and then I was all eager to go on with the same business. You see I'd never had no pleasure, and it seemed to me like a new world — to be able to get victuals without doing anything— instead of slaving as I'd been with a couple

of carts and horses at the coal-pits all the time. I didn't think the country was half so big, and you couldn't credit the pleasure I felt in going about it. I felt as if I didn't care for nothing ; it was so beautiful to be away there quite free, without any care in the world, for I could see plainly I could always get the best of victuals, and the price of my lodgings. There's no part in all England like Yorkshire for living. We used to go to all the farm-houses, we wouldn't miss one if it was half a mile off the road ; if the Scotchman who was with me could only see a road he'd take me up it, and we got nice bits of pie and meat, and bread and cake, indeed as much as would serve four people, when we got to the lodging-house at night and a few shillings beside. I soon got not to care about the loss of my brother. At last we got to make so much money that I thought it was made to chuck about the streets. We got it so easy, you see. It was only 4s. or 5s., but then I was only a flatty or I could have made 14s. or 15s. at least. This was in Borough-bridge, and there at a place called, I think, Bridely-hill, there was a lodging-house without never a bed in it at all ; but only straw littered on the ground, and here I found upwards of sixty or seventy, all tramps, and living in different ways, pattering, and thieving, and singing, and all sorts ; and that night I got to think it was the finest scene I had ever known. I grew pleaseder, and pleaseder, with the life, and wondered how any one could follow any other. There was no drunkenness, but it was so new and strange, and I'd never known nothing of life before, that I was bewildered, like, with over-joy at it. Then I soon got to think I'd have the summer's pleasure out and wouldn't go near Hull till the back end of the year, for it was the month of May, that what I'm talking about took place ; and so things went on. I never thought of home, or sisters. or anything, indeed. I was so over-joyed that I could think of nothing else. Whenever I got to a new county it seemed like getting into a new nation, and when I heard we were close upon a new place I used to long and long to get into it. At last I left the Scotchman and took up with an old sailor, a man-of-warsman, who was coming up to London to get his pension, and he was a regular 'cadger' like the other who had put me 'fly to the dodge,' though none of us wer'nt 'fly' to nothing then. I can't tell you, I wanted to, how I longed to be in town, and, as I came through the streets with him, I didn't know whether I carried the streets or they carried me. You see I had heard people talk about London in North Shields, and I thought there was no poor people there at all—none but ladies and gentlemen and sailors. In London the sailor drew his pension, and he and me got robbed, and then the sailor left me, and then I started off without a penny into the country ; and at Stratford-le-Bow I began, for the first time, to say, ' Pity the poor blind.' Up to this time I had never axed no one —never spoke, indeed—the cadgers who had been with me had done this for me, and glad to have the chance of sharing with me. A blind man can get a guide at any place, because they know

THE BLIND BOOT-LACE SELLER.

[*From a Daguerreotype by* BEARD.]

he's sure to get something. I took only 5d. at Stratford-le-Bow, and then started on my way to Romford; and there, in the lodging-house, I met a blind man, who took me in partnership with him, and larnt me my business complete—that he just did, and since then I've been following it, and that's about two or three and twenty year ago. Since I've been in London, and that's fourteen year, I've lived very regular, always had a place, and attended my church. If it hadn't been for the lodging-houses I should never, may be, have been as I am; though, I must confess, I always had a desire to find out travelling, but couldn't get hold of any one to put me in the way of it. I longed for a roving life and to shake a loose leg, still I couldn't have done much else after my quarrel with my father. My sister had offered to lend me money enough to buy a horse and cart for myself, but I didn't like that, and thought I'd get it of my brother at Hull; and that and the padding kens is solely the cause of my being as I am; and since I first travelled there's more now than ever—double and treble as many."

OF THE LOW LODGING-HOUSES.

THE revelations of the Blind Boot-Lace Seller concerning the low lodging-houses make me anxious to arouse the public to a full sense of the atrocities committed and countenanced in those infamous places. It will have been noticed that the blind man frankly tells us that he was "taught his business" as a mendicant in one of these houses of call for vagabonds of all kinds—beggars, prostitutes, cheats, and thieves. Up to the time of his starting to see his brother at Hull, he appears to have had no notion of living but by his labour, and, more especially, no wish to make a trade of his affliction. Till then he seems to have been susceptible of some of the nobler impulses of humanity, and to have left his home solely because he refused to be party to a fraud on his own sister. Unfortunately, however, on his way to carry out his generous purposes, he put up for the night at the "travellers'" house in the town where he arrived, at the end of his first day's journey; from the very minute that he set foot in the place he was a lost man. Here were assembled scores of the most degraded and vicious members of society, lying in ambush, as it were, like tigers in the jungle, ready to spring upon and make a prey of any one who came within the precincts of their lair. To such as these—sworn to live on the labours of others, and knowing almost to a sixpence the value of each human affliction as a means of operating upon both the heart-strings and the purse-strings of the more benevolent of the industrious or the affluent—to such as these, I say, a blind man, unskilled in the art and system of mendicancy, was literally a God-send. A shipwreck or a colliery explosion, as they too well knew, some of the more sceptical of the public might call in question, but a real blind man, with his eye-balls gone, was beyond all doubt; and to inspire faith, as they were perfectly aware, was one of the most important and difficult processes of the beggar's craft. Besides, of all misfortunes, blindness is one which, to those who have their sight, appears not only the greatest of human privations, but a privation which wholly precludes the possibility of self-help, and so gives the sufferer the strongest claim on our charity. In such a place, therefore, as a low lodging-house, the common resort of all who are resolved not to work for their living, it was almost impossible for a blind man to pass even an hour without every virtuous principle of his nature being undermined, and overtures of the most tempting character being made to him. To be allowed to go partners in so valuable a misfortune was a privilege that many there would strive for; accordingly, as we have seen, the day after the blind man entered the low lodging-house, he who, up to that time, had been, even in his affliction, earning his living, was taken out by one of the "travellers," and taught how much better a living—how much more of the good things of this world—he could get by mendicancy than by industry; and from the very hour when the blind man learnt this, the most dangerous lesson that any human being can possibly be taught, he became, heart and soul, an ingrained beggar. His description of the delight he felt when he found that he had no longer any need to work—that he could rove about the country as he pleased—without a care, without a purpose—with a perfect sense of freedom, and a full enjoyment of the open air in the day, and the wild licence of the lodging-house society at night, satisfied that he could get as much food and drink, and even money as he needed, solely for the asking for it; his description of this is a frank confession of a few of the charms of vagabondism—charms to which the more sedate are not only strangers, but of which they can form no adequate conception. The pleasure of "shaking a loose leg," as the vagrants themselves call it, is, perhaps, known only in its intensity by those wayward spirits who object to the restraint of work or the irksomeness of any settled pursuit. The perfect *thoughtlessness* that the blind man describes as the first effect produced upon him by his vagabondism is the more remarkable, because it seems to have effaced from his mind all regard, even for the sister for whose sake he had quitted his home—though it is one of those curious inconsistencies which form the principal feature in the idiosyncrasy of the class, and which, indeed, are a necessary consequence of the very purposelessness, or want of some permanent principle or feeling, which constitutes, as it were, the mainspring of vagabondism. Indeed, the blind man was a strange compound of cunning and good feeling; at one moment he was weeping over the afflictions of others—he was deeply moved when I read to him the sufferings of the Crippled Nutmeg-Grater Seller; and yet, the next minute he was grinning behind his hand, so that his laughter might be concealed from me, in a manner that appeared almost fiendish. Still, I am convinced that at heart he was far from a bad man; there was, amid the degradation that necessarily comes of habitual

mendicancy, a fine expression of sympathy, that
the better class of poor always exhibit towards
the poor ; nor could I help wondering when I
heard *him*—the professed mendicant—tell me
how he had been moved to tears by the recital of
the sufferings of another mendicant—sufferings
that might have been as profitable a stock in
trade to the one as his blindness was to the other;
though it is by no means unusual for objects of
charity to have *their* objects of charity, and to be
imposed upon by fictitious or exaggerated tales of
distress, almost as often as they impose upon
others by the very same means.

I now invite the reader's attention to the narratives given below as to the character of the low
lodging-houses. The individuals furnishing me
with those statements, it should be observed, were
not "picked" people, but taken promiscuously
from a number belonging to the same class. I
shall reserve what else I may have to remark on
the subject till the conclusion of those statements.

Prisons, tread-mills, penal settlements, gallows,
I said, eighteen months ago, in the ' Morning
Chronicle,' are all vain and impotent as punishments—and Ragged Schools and City missions
are of no avail as preventives of crime—so long
as the wretched dens of infamy, brutality, and
vice, termed " padding-kens " continue their
daily and nightly work of demoralization. If we
would check the further spread of our criminals—
and within the last four years they have increased
from 24,000 to 30,000—we must apply ourselves
to the better regulation and conduct of these
places. At present they are not only the pre-
paratory schools, but the finishing academies for
every kind of profligacy and crime.

" The system of lodging-houses for travellers, otherwise trampers," says the Constabulary Commissioners'
Report, " requires to be altogether revised ; at present
they are in the practice of lodging all the worst characters unquestioned, and are subject to no other control
than an occasional visit of inspection from the parish
officers, accompanied by the constables, whose power of
interference—if they have a legal right of entry—does
not extend to some of the most objectionable points connected with those houses, as they can merely take into
custody such persons as they find in commission of some
offence. The state in which those houses are found on
the occasion of such visit, proves how much they require interference. The houses are small, and yet as
many as thirty travellers, or even thirty-five, have been
found in one house ; fifteen have been found sleeping in
one room, three or four in a bed—men, women, and
children, promiscuously : beds have been found occupied
in a cellar. It is not necessary to urge the many opportunities of preparing for crime which such a state of
things presents, or the actual evils arising from such a
mode of harbouring crowds of low and vicious persons."

According to the report of the Constabulary
Commissioners, there were in 1839—

	Mendicants' Lodging-houses.	Total No. of Lodgers.	Inmates.
In London	221	average 11 or	2,431
In Liverpool	176	6	1,056
Bristol	69	7	483
Bath	14	9	126
Kingston-on-Hull	11	3	33
Newcastle-on-Tyne	78	3	234
Chester (see Report, p. 35)	150	3	450
	619		4,813

Moreover, the same Report tells us, at p. 32,

that there is a low lodging-house for tramps in
every village. By the Post-office Directory there
are 3823 postal towns in England and Wales ;
and assuming that in each of these towns there
are two " travellers' " houses, and that each of
these, upon an average, harbours every night ten
tramps (in a list given at p. 311, there were in
83 towns no less than 678 low lodging-houses,
receiving 10,860 lodgers every night ; this gives,
on an average, 8 such houses to each town, and
16 lodgers to each such house), we have thus
76,460 for the total number of the inmates of
such houses.

To show the actual state of these lodging-houses
from the testimony of one who had been long
resident in them, I give the following statement.
It was made to me by a man of superior education and intelligence (as the tone of his narrative
fully shows), whom circumstances, which do not
affect the object of my present letter, and therefore need not be detailed, had reduced from affluence to beggary, so that he was compelled to be
a constant resident in those places. All the other
statements that I obtained on the subject—and
they were numerous—were corroborative of his
account to the very letter :—

" I have been familiar, unfortunately for me,
with low lodging-houses, both in town and country, for more than ten years. I consider that, as
to the conduct of those places, it is worse in London than in the country—while in the country
the character of the keeper is worse than in London, although but a small difference can be noted.
The worst I am acquainted with, though I haven't
been in it lately, is in the neighbourhood of Drury-
lane—this is the worst both for filth and for the
character of the lodgers. In the room where I
slept, which was like a barn in size, the tiles were
off the roof, and as there was no ceiling, I could
see the blue sky from where I lay. That may be
altered now. Here I slept in what was called the
single men's room, and it was confined to men.
In another part of the house was a room for
married couples, as it was called, but of such
apartments I can tell you more concerning other
houses. For the bed with the view of the blue
sky I paid 3*d.* If it rained there was no shelter.
I have slept in a room in Brick-lane, Whitechapel,
in which were fourteen beds. In the next bed to
me, on the one side, was a man, his wife, and
three children, and a man and his wife on the
other. They were Irish people, and I believe the
women were the men's wives—as the Irish women
generally are. Of all the women that resort to
these places the Irish are far the best for chastity.
All the beds were occupied, single men being
mixed with the married couples. The question is
never asked, when a man and woman go to a
lodging-house, if they are man and wife. All
must pay before they go to bed, or be turned into
the street. These beds were made—as all the
low lodging-house beds are—of the worst cotton
flocks stuffed in coarse, strong canvas. There is
a pair of sheets, a blanket, and a rug. I have
known the bedding to be unchanged for three
months ; but that is not general. The beds are an

average size. Dirt is the rule with them, and cleanliness the exception. They are all infested with vermin. I never met with an exception. No one is required to wash before going to bed in any of these places (except at a very few, where a very dirty fellow would not be admitted), unless he has been walking on a wet day without shoes or stockings, and then he must bathe his feet. The people who slept in the room I am describing were chiefly young men, almost all accompanied by young females. I have seen girls of fifteen sleep with 'their chaps'—in some places with youths of from sixteen to twenty. There is no objection to any boy and girl occupying a bed, even though the keeper knows they were previously strangers to each other. The accommodation for purposes of decency is very bad in some places. A pail in the middle of a room, to which both sexes may resort, is a frequent arrangement. No delicacy or decency is ever observed. The women are, I think, worse than the men. If any one, possessing a sense of shame, says a word of rebuke, he is at once assailed, by the women in particular, with the coarsest words in the language. The Irish women are as bad as the others with respect to language, but I have known them keep themselves covered in bed when the other women were outraging modesty or decency. The Irish will sleep anywhere to save a halfpenny a night, if they have ever so much money." [Here he stated certain gross acts common to lodging-houses, which cannot be detailed in print.] "It is not uncommon for a boy or man to take a girl out of the streets to these apartments. Some are the same as common brothels, women being taken in at all hours of the day or night. In most, however, they must stay all night as a married couple. In dressing or undressing there is no regard to decency, while disgusting blackguardism is often carried on in the conversation of the inmates. I have known decent people, those that are driven to such places from destitution, perhaps for the first time, shocked and disgusted at what they saw. I have seen a decent married pair so shocked and disgusted that they have insisted on leaving the place, and have left it. A great number of the lodging-houses are large old buildings, which were constructed for other purposes; these houses are not so ill-ventilated, but even there, where so many sleep in one room, the air is hot and foul. In smaller rooms, say twelve feet by nine, I have seen four beds placed for single men, with no ventilation whatsoever, so that no one could remain inside in warmish weather, without every door and window open; another room in the same house, a little larger, had four double beds, with as many men and women, and perhaps with children. The Board of Health last autumn compelled the keepers of these places to whitewash the walls and ceilings, and use limewash in other places; before that, the walls and ceilings looked as if they had been blackwashed, but still you could see the bugs creeping along those black walls, which were not black enough to hide that. In some houses in the summer you can hardly place your finger on a part of the wall

free from bugs. I have scraped them off by hand-fulls.

"Nothing can be worse to the health than these places, without ventilation, cleanliness, or decency, and with forty people's breaths perhaps mingling together in one foul choking steam of stench. [The man's own words.] They are the ready resort of thieves and all bad characters, and the keepers will hide them if they can from the police, or facilitate any criminal's escape. I never knew the keepers give any offender up, even when rewards were offered. If they did, they might shut up shop. These houses are but receptacles, with a few exceptions, for beggars, thieves, and prostitutes, and those in training for thieves and prostitutes—the exceptions are those who must lodge at the lowest possible cost. I consider them in every respect of the worst possible character, and think that immediate means should be adopted to improve them. Fights, and fierce fights too, are frequent in them, and I have often been afraid murder would be done. They are money-making places, very. One person will own several —as many as a dozen. In each house he has one or more 'deputies,' chiefly men. Some of these keepers are called respectable men; some live out in the country, leaving all to deputies. They are quite a separate class from the keepers of regular brothels. In one house that I know they can accommodate eighty single men; and when single men only are admitted, what is decent, or rather what is considered decent in such places, is less unfrequent. Each man in such houses pays 4d. a night, a bed to each man or boy; that is 26s. 8d. nightly, or 486l. 13s. 4d. a year, provided the beds be full every night—and they are full six nights out of seven. Besides that, some of the beds supply double turns; for many get up at two to go to Covent-garden or some other market, and their beds are then let a second time to other men; so that more than eighty are frequently accommodated, and I suppose 500l. is the nearest sum to be taken for an accurate return. The rent is very trifling; the chief expense to be deducted from the profits of the house in question is the payment of three and sometimes four deputies, receiving from 7s. to 12s. a week each—say an average of from 30s. to 40s. a week—as three or four are employed. Fire (coke being only used) and gas are the other expenses. The washing is a mere trifle. Then there are the parochial and the water-rates. The rent is always low, as the houses are useable for nothing but such lodgings. The profits of the one house I have described cannot be less than 300l. a year, and the others are in proportion. Now, the owner of this house has, I believe, 10 more such houses, which, letting only threepenny beds (some are lower than that), may realise a profit of about 200l. a year each. These altogether yield a clear profit of 2300l. for the eleven of them; but on how much vice and disease that 2300l. has been raised is a question beyond a schoolmaster. The missionaries visit these lodging-houses, but, judging from what I have heard said by the inmates in all of them, when the missionaries have left, scarcely any good effect has resulted from the visits. *I never saw a clergyman of any denomination in any one of these places, either in town or country.* In London the master or deputy of the low lodging-house does not generally meddle with the disposal of stolen property, as in the country. This is talked about, alike in the town and country houses, very openly and freely before persons known only to be beggars, and never stealing: it is sufficient that they are known as tramps. In London the keepers must all know that stolen property is nightly brought into the house, and they wink at its disposal, but they won't mix themselves up with disposing of it. If it be provisions that have been stolen, they are readily disposed of to the other inmates, and the owner or deputy of the house may know nothing about it, and certainly would not care to interfere if he did. I never heard robberies planned there, but there are generally strangers present, and this may deter. I believe more robberies are planned in low coffee-shops than in lodging-houses. The influence of the lodging-house society on boys who have run away from their parents, and have got thither, either separately or in company with lads who have joined them in the streets, is this:— Boys there, after paying their lodgings, may exercise the same freedom from every restraint as they see the persons of maturer years enjoy. This is often pleasant to a boy, especially if he has been severely treated by his parents or master; he apes, and often outdoes, all the men's ways, both in swearing and lewd talk, and so he gets a relish for that sort of life. After he has resorted to such places—the sharper boys for three, and the duller for six months—they are adepts at any thieving or vice. Drunkenness, and even moderate drinking, is very rare among them. I seldom or never see the boys drink—indeed, thieves of all ages are generally sober men. Once get to like a lodging-house life, and a boy can hardly be got out of it. I said the other day to a youth, 'I wish I could get out of these haunts and never see a lodging-house again;' and he replied, 'If I had ever so much money I would never live anywhere else.' I have seen the boys in a lodging-house sit together telling stories, but paid no attention to them."

Statement of a Young Pickpocket.

To show the class of characters usually frequenting these lodging-houses, I will now give the statement of a boy—a young pickpocket—without shoes or stockings. He wore a ragged, dirty, and very thin great coat, of some dark jean or linen, under which was another thin coat, so arranged that what appeared rents—and, indeed, were rents, but designedly made—in the outer garment, were slits through which the hand readily reached the pockets of the inner garment, and could there deposit any booty. He was a slim, agile lad, with a sharp but not vulgar expression, and small features. His hands were of singular delicacy and beauty. His fingers were very long, and no lady's could have been more taper. A burglar told me that with such a hand he ought to have made his

fortune. He was worth 20*l.* a week, he said, as a "wire," that is, a picker of ladies' pockets. When engaged "for a turn," as he told me he once was by an old pickpocket, the man looked minutely at his fingers, and approved of them highly. His hands, the boy said, were hardly serviceable to him when very cold. His feet were formed in the same symmetrical and beautiful mould as his hands. "I am 15," he said. "My father was a potter, and I can't recollect my mother" (many of the thieves are orphans or motherless). "My father has been dead about five years. I was then working at the pottery in High-street, Lambeth, earning about 4*s.* a week; in good weeks, 4*s.* 6*d.* I was in work eight months after my father died; but one day I broke three bottles by accident, and the foreman said 'I shan't want you any more;' and I took that as meant for a discharge; but I found afterwards that he did'nt so mean it. I had 2*s.* and a suit of clothes then, and tried for work at all the potteries; but I couldn't get any. It was about the time Smithfield fair was on. I went, but it was a very poor concern. I fell asleep in a pen in the afternoon, and had my shoes stolen off my feet. When I woke up, I began crying. A fellow named Gyp then came along (I knew his name afterwards), and he said, 'What are you crying for?' and I told him, and he said, 'Pull off your stockings, and come with me, and I'll show you where to sleep.' So I did, and he took me to St. Olave's workhouse, having first sold my stockings. I had never stolen anything until then. There I slept in the casual ward, and Gyp slept there too. In the morning we started together for Smithfield, where he said he had a job to sweep the pens, but he couldn't sweep them without pulling off his coat, and it would look so queer if he hadn't a shirt—and he hadn't one. He promised to teach me how to make a living in the country if I would lend him mine, and I was persuaded—for I was an innocent lad then—and went up a gateway and stripped off my shirt and gave it to him, and soon after he went into a public-house to get half a pint of beer; he went in at one door and out at another, and I didn't see him for six months afterwards. That afternoon I went into Billingsgate market and met some boys, and one said, 'Mate, how long have you been knocking about; where did you doss?' I didn't know what they meant, and when they'd told me they meant where did I sleep? I told them how I'd been served. And they said, 'Oh! you must expect that, until you learn something,' and they laughed. They all know'd Gyp; he was like the head of a Billingsgate gang once. I became a pal with these boys at Billingsgate, and we went about stealing fish and meat. Some boys have made 2*s.* in a morning, when fish is dear—those that had pluck and luck; they sold it at half-price. Billingsgate market is a good place to sell it; plenty of costermongers are there who will buy it, rather than of the salesmen. I soon grew as bad as the rest at this work. At first I sold it to other boys, who would get 3*d.* for what they bought at 1*d.* Now they can't do me. If I can get a thing cheap where I lodge, and have the money, and can sell it dear, that's the chance. I carried on this fish rig for about two years, and went begging a little, too. I used to try a little thieving sometimes in Petticoat-lane. They say the 'fliest' is easy to take in sometimes—that's the artfullest; but I could do no good there. At these two years' end, I was often as happy as could be; that is, when I had made money. Then I met B——, whom I had often heard of as an uncommon clever pickpocket; he could do it about as well as I can now, so as people won't feel it. Three of his mates were transported for stealing silver plate. He and I became pals, and started for the country with 1d. We went through Foot's Cray, and passed a farm where a man's buried at the top of a house; there's something about money while a man's above ground; I don't understand it, but it's something like that. A baker, about thirty miles from London, offended us about some bread; and B—— said 'I'll serve him out.' We watched him out, and B—— tried at his pocket, saying, 'I'll show you how to do a handkerchief;' but the baker looked round, and B—— stopped; and just after that I flared it (whisked the handkerchief out); and that's the first I did. It brought 1s. 3d. We travelled across country, and got to Maidstone, and did two handkerchiefs. One I wore round my neck, and the other the lodging-housekeeper pawned for us for 1s. 6d. In Maidstone, next morning, I was nailed, and had three months of it. I didn't mind it so much then, but Maidstone's far worse now, I've heard. I have been in prison three times in Brixton, three times in the Old Horse (Bridewell), three times in the Compter, once in the Steel, and once in Maidstone—thirteen times in all, including twice I was remanded, and got off; but I don't reckon that prison. Every time I came out harder than I went in. I've had four floggings; it was bad enough—a flogging was—while it lasted; but when I got out I soon forgot it. At a week's end I never thought again about it. If I had been better treated I should have been a better lad. I could leave off thieving now as if I had never thieved, if I could live without." [I am inclined to doubt this part of the statement.] "I have carried on this sort of life until now. I didn't often make a very good thing of it. I saw Manning and his wife hung. Mrs. Manning was dressed beautiful when she came up. She screeched when Jack Ketch pulled the bolt away. She was harder than Manning, they all said; without her there would have been no murder. It was a great deal talked about, and Manning was pitied. It was a punishment to her to come on the scaffold and see Manning with the rope about his neck, if people takes it in the right light. I did 4s. 6d. at the hanging—two handkerchiefs, and a purse with 2s. in it—the best purse I ever had; but I've only done three or four purses. The reason is, because I've never been well dressed. If I went near a lady, she would say, 'Tush, tush, you ragged fellow!' and would shrink away. But I would rather rob the rich than the poor; they miss it less. But 1s. honest goes further than 5s. stolen. Some call that only a saying, but it's true. All

the money I got soon went—most of it a-gambling. Picking pockets, when any one comes to think on it, is the daringest thing that a boy can do. It didn't in the least frighten me to see Manning and Mrs. Manning hanged. I never thought I should come to the gallows, and I never shall—I'm not high-tempered enough for that. The only thing that frightens me when I'm in prison is sleeping in a cell by myself—you do in the Old Horse and the Steel—because I think things may appear. You can't imagine how one dreams when in trouble. I've often started up in a fright from a dream. I don't know what might appear. I've heard people talk about ghosts and that. Once, in the County, a tin had been left under a tap that went drip—drip—drip. And all in the ward were shocking frightened; and weren't we glad when we found out what it was! Boys tell stories about haunted castles, and cats that are devils; and that frightens one. At the fire in Monument-yard I did 5s. 7d. —3s. in silver and 2s. 3d. in handkerchiefs, and 4d. for three pairs of gloves. I sell my handkerchiefs in the Lane (Petticoat-lane). I carry on this trade still. Most times I've got in prison is when I've been desperate from hunger, and have said to B——, 'Now I'll have money, nailed or not nailed.' I can pick a woman's pocket as easy as a man's, though you wouldn't think it. If one's in prison for begging, one's laughed at. The others say, 'Begging! Oh, you cadger!' So a boy is partly forced to steal for his character. I've lived a good deal in lodging-houses, and know the ways of them. They are very bad places for a boy to be in. Where I am now, when the place is full, there's upwards of 100 can be accommodated. I won't be there long. I'll do something to get out of it. There's people there will rob their own brother. There's people there talk backward— for one they say eno, for two owt, for three eerht, for four ruof, for five evif, for six exis. I don't know any higher. I can neither read nor write. In this lodging-house there are no women. They talk there chiefly about what they've done, or are going to do, or have set their minds upon, just as you and any other gentlemen might do. I have been in lodging-houses in Mint-street and Kent-street, where men and women and children all slept in one room. I think the men and women who slept together were generally married, or lived together; but it's not right for a big boy to sleep in the same room. Young men have had beds to themselves, and so have young women there; but there's a deputy comes into the room, every now and then, to see there's nothing wrong. There's little said in these places, the people are generally so tired. Where I am there's horrid language—swearing, and everything that's bad. They are to be pitied, because there's not work for honest people, let alone thieves. In the lodging-houses the air is very bad, enough to stifle one in bed—so many breaths together. Without such places my trade couldn't be carried on; I couldn't live. Some though would find another way out. Three or four would take a room among them. Any-body's money's good — you can always get a room. I would be glad to leave this life, and work at a pottery. As to sea, a bad captain would make me run away—sure. He can do what he likes with you when you're out at sea. I don't get more than 2s. a week, one week with the other, by thieving; some days you do nothing until hunger makes your spirits rise. I can't thieve on a full belly. I live on 2s. a week from thieving, because I understand fiddling—that means, buying a thing for a mere trifle, and selling it for double, or for more, if you're not taken in yourself. I've been put up to a few tricks in lodging-houses, and now I can put others up to it. Everybody must look after themselves, and I can't say I was very sorry when I stole that 2s. from a poor woman, but I'd rather have had 1s. 6d. from a rich one. I never drink—eating's my part. I spend chief part of my money in pudding. I don't like living in lodging-houses, but I must like it as I'm placed now—that sort of living, and those lodging-houses, or starving. They bring tracts to the lodging-houses—pipes are lighted with them; tracts won't fill your belly. Tracts is no good, except to a person that has a home; at the lodging-houses they're laughed at. They seldom are mentioned. I've heard some of them read by missionaries, but can't catch anything from them. If it had been anything bad, I should have caught it readily. If an innocent boy gets into a lodging-house, he'll not be innocent long—he can't., I know three boys who have run away, and are in the lodging-houses still, but I hope their father has caught them. Last night a little boy came to the lodging-house where I was. We all thought he had run away, by the way he spoke. He stayed all night, but was found out in two or three falsehoods. I wanted to get him back home, or he'll be as bad as I am in time, though he's nothing to me; but I couldn't find him this morning; but I'll get him home yet, perhaps. The Jews in Petticoat-lane are terrible rogues. They'll buy anything of you —they'll buy what you've stolen from their next-door neighbours—that they would, if they knew it. But they'll give you very little for it, and they threaten to give you up if you won't take a quarter of the value of it. 'Oh! I shee you do it,' they say, 'and I like to shee him robbed, but you musht take vot I give.' I wouldn't mind what harm came to those Petticoat-laners. Many of them are worth thousands, though you wouldn't think it." After this I asked him what he, as a sharp lad, thought was the cause of so many boys becoming vagrant pickpockets? He answered, " Why, sir, if boys runs away, and has to shelter in low lodging-houses—and many runs away from cruel treatment at home—they meet there with boys such as me, or as bad, and the devil soon lays his hand on them. If there wasn't so many lodging-houses there wouldn't be so many bad boys—there couldn't. Lately a boy came down to Billingsgate, and said he wouldn't stay at home to be knocked about any longer. He said it to some boys like me; and he was asked if he could get anything from his mother, and he said ' yes, he could.' So he went back, and brought a brooch and some other things with him to a place fixed on, and then he and some of the boys set off for the country; and that's the way boys is trapped. I think the fathers of such boys either ill-treat them, or neglect them; and so they run away. My father used to beat me shocking; so I hated home. I stood hard licking well, and was called ' the plucked one.'" This boy first stole flowers, currants, and gooseberries out of the clergyman's garden, more by way of bravado, and to ensure the approbation of his comrades, than for anything else. He answered readily to my inquiry, as to what he thought would become of him?—" Transportation. If a boy has great luck he may carry on for eight years. Three or four years is the common run, but transportation is what he's sure to come to in the end." This lad picked my pocket at my request, and so dexterously did he do his " work," that though I was alive to what he was trying to do, it was impossible for me to detect the least movement of my coat. To see him pick the pockets, as he did, of some of the gentlemen who were present on the occasion, was a curious sight. He crept behind much like a cat with his claws out, and while in the act held his breath with suspense; but immediately the handkerchief was safe in his hand, the change in the expression of his countenance was most marked. He then seemed almost to be convulsed with delight at the success of his perilous adventure, and, turning his back, held up the handkerchief to discover the value of his prize, with intense glee evident in every feature.

STATEMENT OF A PROSTITUTE.

THE narrative which follows—that of a prostitute, sleeping in the low-lodging houses, where boys and girls are all huddled promiscuously together, discloses a system of depravity, atrocity, and enormity, which certainly cannot be paralleled in any nation, however barbarous, nor in any age, however " dark." The facts detailed, it will be seen, are gross enough to make us all blush for the land in which such scenes can be daily perpetrated. The circumstances, which it is impossible to publish, are of the most loathsome and revolting nature.

A good-looking girl of sixteen gave me the following awful statement :—

" I am an orphan. When I was ten I was sent to service as maid of all-work, in a small tradesman's family. It was a hard place, and my mistress used me very cruelly, beating me often. When I had been in place three weeks, my mother died; my father having died twelve years before. I stood my mistress's ill-treatment for about six months. She beat me with sticks as well as with her hands. I was black and blue, and at last I ran away. I got to Mrs. ——, a low lodging-house. I didn't know before that there was such a place. I heard of it from some girls at the Glasshouse (baths and washhouses), where I went for shelter. I went with them to have a halfpenny worth of coffee, and they took me to the lodging-house. I then had three shillings, and stayed about a month, and did nothing wrong, living on the three shillings and what I pawned my clothes for, as I got some pretty good things away with me. In the lodging-house I saw nothing but what was bad, and heard nothing but what was bad. I was laughed at, and was told to swear. They said, ' Look at her for a d—— modest fool'— sometimes worse than that, until by degrees I got to be as bad as they were. During this time I used to see boys and girls from ten and twelve years old sleeping together, but understood nothing wrong. I had never heard of such places before I ran away. I can neither read nor write. My mother was a good woman, and I wish I'd had her to run away to. I saw things between almost children that I can't describe to you—very often I saw them, and that shocked me. At the month's end, when I was beat out, I met with a young man of fifteen—I myself was going on to twelve years old—and he persuaded me to take up with him. I stayed with him three months in the same lodging-house, living with him as his wife, though we were mere children, and being true to him. At the three months' end he was taken up for picking pockets, and got six months. I was sorry, for he was kind to me ; though I was made ill through him ; so I broke some windows in St. Paul's-churchyard to get into prison to get cured. I had a month in the Compter, and came out well. I was scolded very much in the Compter, on account of the state I was in, being so young. I had 2s. 6d. given to me when I came out, and was forced to go into the streets for a living. I continued walking the streets for three years, sometimes making a good deal of money, sometimes none, feasting one day and starving the next. The bigger girls could persuade me to do anything they liked with my money. I was never happy all the time, but I could get no character and could not get out of the life. I lodged all this time at a lodging-house in Kent-street. They were all thieves and bad girls. I have known between three and four dozen boys and girls sleep in one room. The beds were horrid filthy and full of vermin. There was very wicked carryings on. The boys, if any difference, was the worst. We lay packed on a full night, a dozen boys and girls squeedged into one bed. That was very often the case—some at the foot and some at the top—boys and girls all mixed. I can't go into all the particulars, but whatever could take place in words or acts between boys and girls did take place, and in the midst of the others. I am sorry to say I took part in these bad ways myself, but I wasn't so bad as some of the others. There was only a candle burning all night, but in summer it was light great part of the night. Some boys and girls slept without any clothes, and would dance about the room that way. I have seen them, and, wicked as I was, felt ashamed. I have seen two dozen capering about the room that way ; some mere children, the boys generally the youngest. * * * * There were no men or women present. There were often fights. The deputy never interfered. This is carried on just the same as ever to this day, and is the same every night. I have heard young girls shout out to one another how often they had

been obliged to go to the hospital, or the infirmary, or the workhouse. There was a great deal of boasting about what the boys and girls had stolen during the day. I have known boys and girls change their ' partners,' just for a night. At three years' end I stole a piece of beef from a butcher. I did it to get into prison. I was sick of the life I was leading, and didn't know how to get out of it. I had a month for stealing. When I got out I passed two days and a night in the streets doing nothing wrong, and then went and threatened to break Messrs. —— windows again. I did that to get into prison again ; for when I lay quiet of a night in prison I thought things over, and considered what a shocking life I was leading, and how my health might be ruined completely, and I thought I would stick to prison rather than go back to such a life. I got six months for threatening. When I got out I broke a lamp next morning for the same purpose, and had a fortnight. That was the last time I was in prison. I have since been leading the same life as I told you of for the three years, and lodging at the same houses, and seeing the same goings on. I hate such a life now more than ever. I am willing to do any work that I can in washing and cleaning. I can do a little at my needle. I could do hard work, for I have good health. I used to wash and clean in prison, and always behaved myself there. At the house where I am at is 3d. a night ; but at Mrs. ——'s it is 1d. and 2d. a night, and just the same goings on. Many a girl—nearly all of them—goes out into the streets from this penny and twopenny house, to get money for their favourite boys by prostitution. If the girl cannot get money she must steal something, or will be beaten by her ' chap' when she comes home. I have seen them beaten, often kicked and beaten until they were blind from bloodshot, and their teeth knocked out with kicks from boots as the girl lays on the ground. The boys, in their turn, are out thieving all day, and the lodging-house keeper will buy any stolen provisions of them, and sell them to the lodgers. I never saw the police in the house. If a boy comes to the house on a night without money or sawney, or something to sell to the lodgers, a handkerchief or something of that kind, he is not admitted, but told very plainly, ' Go thieve it, then.' Girls are treated just the same. Anybody may call in the daytime at this house and have a halfpennyworth of coffee and sit any length of time until evening. I have seen three dozen sitting there that way, all thieves and bad girls. There are no chairs, and only one form in front of the fire, on which a dozen can sit. The others sit on the floor all about the room, as near the fire as they can. Bad language goes on during the day, as I have told you it did during the night, and indecencies too, but nothing like so bad as at night. They talk about where there is good places to go to and thieve. The missioners call sometimes, but they're laughed at often when they're talking, and always before the door's closed on them. If a decent girl goes there to get a ha'porth of coffee, seeing the board over the door, she is always shocked. Many a poor girl has been ruined in this house since I was, and boys have boasted about it. I never knew boy or girl do good, once get used there. Get used there, indeed, and you are life-ruined. I was an only child, and haven't a friend in the world. I have heard several girls say how they would like to get out of the life, and out of the place. From those I know, I think that cruel parents and mistresses cause many to be driven there. One lodging-house keeper, Mrs. ——, goes out dressed respectable, and pawns any stolen property, or sells it at public-houses."

As a corroboration of the girl's statement, a wretched-looking boy, only thirteen years of age, gave me the following additional information. He had a few rags hanging about him, and no shirt—indeed, he was hardly covered enough for purposes of decency, his skin being exposed through the rents in his jacket and trowsers. He had a stepfather, who treated him very cruelly. The stepfather and the child's mother went "across the country," begging and stealing. Before the mother died, an elder brother ran away on account of being beaten:—

"Sometimes (I give his own words) he (the stepfather) wouldn't give us a bit to eat, telling us to go and thieve for it. My brother had been a month gone (he's now a soldier in Gibraltar) when I ran away to join him. I knew where to find him, as we met sometimes. We lived by thieving, and I do still—by pulling flesh (stealing meat). I got to lodge at Mrs. ——, and have been there this eight months. I can read and write a little." [This boy then confirmed what the young girl had told me of the grossest acts night by night among the boys and girls, the language, &c., and continued]—" I always sleep on the floor for 1d. and pay a ½d. besides for coke. At this lodging-house cats and kittens are melted down, sometimes twenty a day. A quart pot is a cat, and pints and half pints are kittens. A kitten (pint) brings 3d. from the rag shops, and a cat 6d. There's convenience to melt them down at the lodging-house. We can't sell clothes in the house, except any lodger wants them; and clothes nearly all goes to the Jews in Petticoat-lane. Mrs. —— buys the sawney of us; so much for the lump, 2d. a pound about; she sells it again for twice what she gives, and more. Perhaps 30 lb. of meat every day is sold to her. I have been in prison six times, and have had three dozen ; each time I came out harder. If I left Mrs. ——'s house I don't know how I could get my living. Lots of boys would get away if they could. I never drink, I don't like it. Very few of us boys drink. I don't like thieving, and often go about singing; but I can't live by singing, and I don't know how I could live honestly. If I had money enough to buy a stock of oranges I think I could be honest."

The above facts require no comment from me.

STATEMENT OF A BEGGAR.

A beggar decently attired, and with a simple and what some would call even a respectable look, gave me the following account :—

"I am now twenty-eight, and have known all connected with the begging trade since I was fourteen. My grandfather (mother's father) was rich, owning three parts of the accommodation houses in St. Giles's ; he allowed me 2s. a week pocket-money. My grandfather kept the great house, the old Rose and Crown, in Church-lane, opposite Carver-street, best known as the ' Beggar's Opera.' When a child of seven, I have seen the place crowded—crammed with nothing but beggars, first-rates—none else used the house. The money I saw in the hands of the beggars made a great impression upon me. My father took away my mother's money. I wish my mother had run away instead. He was kind, but she was always nagging. My father was a foreman in a foundry. I got a situation in the same foundry after my father cut. Once I was sent to a bank with a cheque for 88l. to get cashed, in silver, for wages. In coming away, I met a companion of mine, and he persuaded me to bolt with the money, and go to Ashley's. The money was too much for my head to carry. I fooled all that money away. I wasn't in bed for more than a fortnight. I bought linnets in cages for the fancy of my persuader. In fact, I didn't know what use to put the money to. I was among plenty of girls. When the money was out I was destitute. I couldn't go back to my employers, and I couldn't face my mother's temper —that was worse ; but for that nagging of hers I shouldn't have been as I am. She has thrashed me with a hand broom until I was silly; there's the bumps on my head still ; and yet that woman would have given me her heart's blood to do me a good. As soon as I found myself quite destitute, I went wandering about the City, picking up the skins of gooseberries and orange peel to eat, to live on—things my stomach would turn at now. At last my mother came to hear that I tried to destroy myself. She paid the 88l., and my former employers got me a situation in Paddington. I was there a month, and then I met him as advised me to steal the money before—he's called the ex-king of the costermongers now. Well he was crying hareskins, and advised me again to bolt, and I went with him. My mind was bent upon costermongering and a roving life. I couldn't settle to anything. I wanted to be away when I was at work, and when I was away I wanted to be back again. It was difficult for me to stick to anything for five minutes together; it is so now. What I begin I can't finish at the time—unless it's a pot of beer. Well, in four days my adviser left me ; he had no more use for me. I was a flat. He had me for a " go-along," to cry his things for him. Then, for the first time in my life, I went into a low lodging-house. There was forty men and women sleeping in one room. I had to sleep with a black man, and I slept on the floor to get away from the fellow. There were plenty of girls there ; some playing cards and dominoes. It was very dirty—old Mother ——, in Lawrence-lane—the Queen of Hell she was called. There was one tub among the lot of us. I felt altogether disgusted. Those who lived there were beggars, thieves, smashers, coiners,

purchasers of begged and stolen goods, and prostitutes. The youngest prostitute was twelve, and
so up to fifty. The beastliest language went on.
It's done to outrival one another. There I met
with a man called Tom Shallow (*shallow* is cant
for half-naked), and he took me out ballad-singing,
and when we couldn't get on at that (the songs
got dead) he left me. I made him 10s. or 12s. a
day in them days, but he only gave me my lodgings and grub (but not half enough), and two
pipes of tobacco a day to keep the hunger down,
that I mightn't be expensive. I then 'listed. I
was starving, and couldn't raise a lodging. I took
the shilling, but was rejected by the doctor. I
'listed again at Chatham afterwards, but was rejected again. I stayed jobbing among the soldiers
for some weeks, and then they gave me an old re-
gimental suit, and with that I came to London.
One gave me a jacket, and another a pair of
military trowsers, and another a pair of old am-
munition boots, and so on. About that time a
batch of invalids came from Spain, where they
had been under General Evans. On my way up
from Chatham, I met at Gravesend with seven
chaps out on ' *the Spanish lurk*' as they called it
—that is, passing themselves off as wounded men
of the Spanish Legion. Two *had been* out in Spain,
and managed the business if questions were asked;
the others were regular English beggars, who had
never been out of the country. I joined them as
a serjeant, as I had a sergeant's jacket given me
at Chatham. On our way to London—' the school'
(as the lot is called) came all together—we picked
up among us 4l. and 5l. a day—no matter where
we went. ' The school' all slept in lodging houses,
and I at last began to feel comfortable in them. We
spent our evenings in eating out-and out suppers.
Sometimes we had such things as sucking pigs,
hams, mince pies—indeed we lived on the best.
No nobleman could live better in them days. So
much wine, too ! I drank in such excess, my nose
was as big as that there letter stamp ; so that I
got a sickening of it. We gave good victuals
away that was given to us—it was a nuisance to
carry them. It cost us from 6d. to 1s. a day to
have our shoes cleaned by *poor* tramps, and for
clean dickies. The clean dodge is always the
best for begging upon. At Woolwich we were
all on the fuddle at the Dust Hole, and our two
spokesmen were drunk ; and I went to beg of
Major ——, whose brother was then in Spain—
he himself had been out previously. Meeting
the major at his own house, I said, ' I was a
sergeant in the 3rd Westminster Grenadiers, you
know, and served under your brother.' ' Oh ! yes,
that's my brother's regiment,' says he. ' Where
was you, then, on the 16th of October ?' ' Why,
sir, I was at the taking of the city of Irun,' says
I—(in fact, I was at that time with the costermonger in St. Giles's, calling cabbages, ' white
heart cabbages, oh !') Then said the major,
' What day was Ernani taken on ?' ' Why,' said
I (I was a little tipsy, and bothered at the question), ' that was the 16th of October, too.' ' Very
well, my man,' says he, tapping his boots with a
riding whip he held, ' I 'll see what I can do for

you ;' and the words were no sooner out of his
mouth than he stepped up to me and gave me a
regular pasting. He horsewhipped me up and
down stairs, and all along the passages ; my flesh
was like sassages. I managed at last, however,
to open the door myself, and get away. After
that ' the school' came to London. In a day we
used to make from 8l. to 10l. among us, by walking up Regent-street, Bond-street, Piccadilly, Pall-
mall, Oxford-street, the parks—those places were
the best beats. All the squares were good too.
It was only like a walk out for air, and your 25s.
a man for it. At night we used to go to plays,
dressed like gentlemen. At first the beaks protected us, but we got found out, and the beaks
grew rusty. The thing got so overdone, every
beggar went out as a Spanish lurksman. Well,
the beaks got up to the dodge, and all the Spanish
lurksmen in their turns got to work the universal
staircase, under the care of Lieutenant Tracy (Tothill-fields treadmill). The men that had really
been out and got disabled were sent to that staircase at last, and I thought I would try a fresh
lurk. So I went under the care and tuition of a
sailor. He had been a sailor. I became a *turnpike sailor*, as it 's called, and went out as one of
the Shallow Brigade, wearing a Guernsey shirt
and drawers, or tattered trowsers. There was a
school of four. We only got a tidy living—16s.
or 1l. a day among us. We used to call every
one that came along—coalheavers and all—sea-
fighting captains. ' Now, my noble sea-fighting
captain,' we used to say, ' fire an odd shot from
your larboard locker to us, Nelson's bull-dogs ;'
but mind we never tried that dodge on at Greenwich, for fear of the old geese, the Collegemen.
The Shallow got so grannied (known) in London,
that the supplies got queer, and I quitted the land
navy. Shipwrecks got so common in the streets,
you see, that people didn't care for them, and
I dropped getting cast away. I then took to
screeving (writing on the stones). I got my head
shaved, and a cloth tied round my jaws, and
wrote on the flags—

' *Illness and Want*,'

though I was never better in my life, and always
had a good bellyfull before I started of a morning.
I did very well at first : 3s. or 4s. a day—sometimes more—till I got grannied. There is one
man who draws Christ's heads with a crown of
thorns, and mackerel, on the pavement, in coloured
chalks (there are four or five others at the same business) ; this one, however, often makes 1l. a day
now in three hours ; indeed, I have known him
come home with 21s., besides what he drank on the
way. A gentleman who met him in Regent-street
once gave him 5l. and a suit of clothes to do
Christ's heads with a crown of thorns and mackerel
on the walls. His son does Napoleon's heads best,
but makes nothing like so much as the father.
The father draws cats' heads and salmon as well
—but the others are far the best spec. He will
often give thirteen-pence, and indeed fourteen-
pence, for a silver shilling, to get rid of the coppers. This man's pitch is Lloyd-square, not far
from Sadler's Wells. I have seen him commence

his pitch there at half-past eleven, to catch the people come from the theatre. He is very clever. In wet weather, and when I couldn't chalk, as I couldn't afford to lose time, I used to dress tidy and very clean for the '*respectable broken-down tradesman or reduced gentleman*' caper. I wore a suit of black, generally, and a clean dickey, and sometimes old black kid gloves, and I used to stand with a paper before my face, as if ashamed—

'*To a Humane Public.*
'*I have seen better days.*'

This is called standing pad with a fakement. It is a wet-weather dodge, and isn't so good as screeving, but I did middling, and can't bear being idle. After this I mixed with the street patterers (men who make speeches in the streets) on *the destitute mechanics' lurk*. We went in a school of six at first, all in clean aprons, and spoke every man in his turn. It won't do unless you're clean. Each man wanted a particular article of dress. One had no shirt—another no shoes—another no hat—and so on. No two wanted the same. We said:—

"' Kind and benevolent Christians!—It is with feelings of deep regret, and sorrow and shame, that us unfortunate tradesmen are compelled to appear before you this day, to ask charity from the hands of strangers. We are brought to it from want—I may say, actual starvation.' (We always had a good breakfast before we started, and some of us, sir, was full up to the brim of liquor.) ' But what will not hunger and the cries of children compel men to do.' (We were all single men.) ' When we left our solitary and humble homes this morning, our children were crying for food, but if a farthing would have saved their lives, we hadn't it to give them. I assure you, kind friends, me, my wife, and three children, would have been houseless wanderers all last night, but I sold the shirt from off my back as you may see (opening my jacket) to pay for a lodging. We are, kind friends, *English* mechanics. It is hard that you wont give your own countrymen a penny, when you give so much to *foreign* hurdy-gurdies and organ-grinders. Owing to the introduction of steam and machinery and foreign manufactures we have been brought to this degraded state. Fellow countrymen, there are at this moment 4000 men like ourselves, able and willing to work, but can't get it, and forced to wander the streets. I hope and trust some humane Christian within the sound of my voice will stretch out a hand with a small trifle for us, be it ever so small, or a bit of dry bread or cold potato, or anything turned from your table, it would be of the greatest benefit to us and our poor children.' (Then we would whisper to one another, ' I hope they won't bring out any scran—only coppers.') ' We have none of us tasted food this blessed day. We have been told to go to our parishes, but that we cannot brook; to be torn from our wives and families is heart-rending to think of—may God save us all from the Bastile!' (We always pattered hard at the overseers).

The next of the school that spoke would change the story somehow, and try to make it more heart-rending still. We did well at first, making about 5s. a day each, working four hours, two in the morning and two in the afternoon. We got a good deal of clothing too. The man who went without a shirt never went to a door to ask for one; he had to show himself in the middle of the road. The man that *did* go to the door would say, ' Do bestow a shirt on my poor shopmate, who hasn't had one for some days.' It's been said of me, when I had my shirt tied round my waist all the time out of sight. The man who goes without his shirt has his pick of those given; the rest are sold and shared. Whatever trade we

represented we always had one or two really of the trade in the school. These were always to be met at the lodging-houses. They were out of work, and had to go to low lodging-houses to sleep. There they met with beggars who kiddied them on to the lurk. The lodging-houses is good schools for that sort of thing, and when a mechanic once gets out on the lurk he never cares to go to work again. I never knew one return. I have been out oft and oft with weavers with a loom, and have woven a piece of ribbon in a gentleman's parlour—that was when we was Coventry ribbon weavers. I have been a stocking weaver from Leicester, and a lacemaker too from Nottingham. Distressed mechanics on their way to London get initiated into beggar's tricks in the low lodging-houses and the unions. This is the way, you see, sir. A school may be at work from the lodging-house where the mechanic goes to, and some of the school finds out what he is, and says, ' Come and work with us in a school: you'll do better than you can at your business, and you can answer any questions; we'll lurk on your trade.' I have been out with a woman and children. It's been said in the papers that children can be hired for that lurk at 4d. or 6d. a day—that's all fudge, all stuff, every bit of it —there's no children to be hired. There's many a labouring man out of work, who has a wife and three or more children, who is glad to let them go out with any patterer he knows. The woman is entitled to all the clothes and grub given, and her share of the tin—that's the way it's done; and she's treated to a drink after her day's work, into the bargain. I've been out on the *respectable family man* lurk. I was out with a woman and three kids the other day; her husband was on the pad in the country, as London was too hot to hold him. The kids draws, the younger the better, for if you vex them, and they're oldish, they'll blow you. Liverpool Joe's boy did so at Bury St. Edmund's to a patterer that he was out with, and who spoke cross to him. The lad shouted out so as the people about might hear, ' Don't you jaw me, you're not my father; my father's at home playing cards.' They had to crack the pitch (discontinue) through that. The respectable family dodge did pretty well. I've been on *the clean family* lurk too, with a woman and children. We dressed to give the notion that, however humble, at least we were clean in all our poverty. On this lurk we stand by the side of the pavement in silence, the wife in a perticler clean cap, and a milk-white apron. The kids have long clean pinafores, white as the driven snow; they're only used in clean lurk, and taken off directly they come home. The husband and father is in a white flannel jacket, an apron worn and clean, and polished shoes. To succeed in this caper there must be no rags, but plenty of darns. A pack of pawn-tickets is carried in the waistcoat pocket. (One man that I know stuck them in his hat like a carman's.) That's to show that they've parted with their little all before they came to that. They are real pawn-tickets. I have known a man pay 2s. 6d.

for the loan of a marriage certificate to go out on the clean lurk. If a question is asked, I say —'We've parted with everything, and can get no employment; to be sure, we have had a loaf from the parish, but what's that among my family?'. That takes the start out of the people, because they say, why not go to the parish? Some persons say, 'Oh, poor folks, they're brought to this, and how clean they are—a darn is better than a patch any time.' The clean lurk is a bare living now—it was good—lots of togs came in, and often the whole family were taken into a house and supplied with flannel enough to make under clothing for them all ; all this was pledged soon afterwards, and the tickets shown to prove what was parted with, through want. Those are some of the leading lurks. There's others. 'Fits,' are now bad, and 'paralytics' are no better. *The lucifer lurk* seems getting up though. I don't mean the selling, but the dropping them in the street as if by accident. It's a great thing with the children ; but no go with the old 'uns. I'll tell you of another lurk : a woman I knows sends out her child with ¼ oz. of tea and half a quarter of sugar, and the child sits on a door step crying, and saying, if questioned, that she was sent out for tea and sugar, and a boy snatched the change from her, and threw the tea and sugar in the gutter. The mother is there, like a stranger, and says to the child :—'And was that your poor mother's last shilling, and daren't you go home, poor thing?' Then there is a gathering—sometimes 18*d.* in a morning ; but it's almost getting stale, that is. I've done *the shivering dodge* too —gone out in the cold weather half naked. One man has practised it so much that he can't get off shivering now. Shaking Jemmy went on with his shivering so long that he couldn't help it at last. He shivered like a jelly—like a calf's foot with the ague—on the hottest day in summer. It's a good dodge in tidy inclement seasons. It's not so good a lurk, by two bob a day, as it once was. This is a single-handed job ; for if one man shivers less than another he shows that it isn't so cold as the good shiverer makes it out—then it's no go. Of the *maimed beggars*, some are really deserving objects, as without begging they must starve to death ; that's a fact, sir. What's a labouring man to do if he's lost any of his limbs? But some of these even are impostors. I know several blind men who have pensions ; and I know two who have not only pensions, but keep lodging houses, and are worth money, and still go out a begging—though not near where they live. There's the man with the very big leg, who sits on the pavement, and tells a long yarn about the tram carriage having gone over him in the mine. He does very well—remarkable well. He goes tatting and billy-hunting in the country (gathering rags and buying old metal), and comes only to London when he has that sort of thing to dispose of. There's Paddy in the truck too ; he makes a good thing, and sends money home to Ireland ; he has a decrepit old mother, and it's to his credit. He never drinks. There's Jerry, the collier, he has lost both arms, and does a tidy living, and

deserves it ; it's a bad misfortune. There's Jack Tiptoe, he can't put one heel to the ground—no gammon ; but Mr. Horsford and he can't agree, so Jack takes to the provinces now. He did very well indeed here. There used to be a society among us called *the Cadger's Club*; if one got into a prison there was a gathering for him when he came out, and 6*s.* a week for a sick member, and when he got out again two collections for him, the two amounting perhaps to 1*l.* We paid 3*d.* a week each—no women were members—for thirteen weeks, and then shared what was in hand, and began for the next thirteen, receiving new members and transacting the usual business of a club. This has been discontinued these five years ; the landlord cut away with the funds. We get up raffles, and help one another in the best way we can now. At one time we had forty-five members, besides the secretary, the conductor, and under-conductor. The rules were read over on meeting nights—every Wednesday evening. They were very strict ; no swearing, obscene or profane language was permitted. For the first offence a fine of 1*d.* was inflicted, for the second 2*d.*, and for the third the offender was ejected the room. There was very good order, and few fines had to be inflicted. Several respectable tradesmen used to pay a trifle to be admitted, out of curiosity, to see the proceedings, and used to be surprised at their regularity. Among the other rules were these : a fine of 1*d.* for any member refusing to sing when called on ; visitors the same. All the fines went to the fund. If a member didn't pay for five meeting nights he was scratched. Very few were scratched. The secretary was a windmill cove (sold children's windmills in the streets), and was excused contributing to the funds. He had 1*d.* from each member every sharing night, once a quarter, for his labour ; he was a very good scholar, and had been brought up well. The landlord generally gave a bob on a sharing night. The conductor managed the room, and the under-conductor kept the door, not admitting those who had no right to be there, and putting out those who behaved improperly. It was held in the Coachmakers' Arms, Rose-street, Longrave-street ; tip-top swells used to come among us, and no mistake ; real noblemen, sir. One was the nephew of the Duke of ——, and was well-known to all of us by the nick-name, Facer.

I used to smoke a very short and very black pipe, and the honourable gent has often snatched it from my mouth, and has given me a dozen cigars for it. My face has been washed in the gin by a noble lord after he'd made me drunk, and I felt as if it was vitriol about my eyes. The beggars are now dispersed and broken up. They live together now only in twos and threes, and, in plain truth, have no money to spend ; they can't get it. Upon an average, in former days a cadger could make his two or three guineas per week without working overtime ; but now he can hardly get a meal, not even at the present winter, though it's been a slap up inclement season, to be sure. The Mendicity Society has ruined us— them men took me and gave me a month, and I can say from my conscience, that I was no more guilty of begging at that time than an unborn baby. The beggars generally live in the low lodging-houses, and there of a night they tell their tales of the day, and inform each other of the good and bad places throughout London, and what 'lurks' do the best. They will also say what beats they intend to take the next day, so that those who are on the same lurk may not go over the same ground as their pals. It is no use telling a lie, but the low lodging-houses throughout London and the country are nests for beggars and thieves. I know some houses that are wholly supported by beggars. In almost every one of the padding kens, or low lodging-houses in the country, there is a list of walks written on a piece of paper, and pasted up over the kitchen mantel-piece. Now at St. Alban's, for instance, at the ———, and at other places, there is a paper stuck up in each of the kitchens. This paper is headed ' WALKS OUT OF THIS TOWN,' and underneath it is set down the names of the villages in the neighbourhood at which a beggar may call when out on his walk, and they are so arranged as to allow the cadger to make a round of about six miles, each day, and return the same night. In many of those papers there are sometimes twenty walks set down. No villages that are in any way ' gammy ' are ever mentioned in these papers, and the cadger, if he feels inclined to stop for a few days in the town, will be told by the lodging-house keeper, or the other cadgers that he may meet there, what gentleman's seats or private houses are of any account on the walk that he means to take. The names of the good houses are not set down in the paper, for fear of the police. Most of the lodging-house keepers buy the ' scran ' (broken victuals) of the cadgers ; the good food they either eat themselves or sell to the other travellers, and the bad they sell to parties to feed their dogs or pigs upon. The cadgers' talk is quite different now to what it was in the days of Billy. You see the flats got awake to it, so in course we had to alter the patter. The new style of cadgers' cant is nothing like the thieves' cant, and is done all on the rhyming principle. This way 's the caper. Suppose I want to ask a pal to come and have a *glass* of *rum* and smoke a *pipe* of *tobacco*, and have a game at cards with some *blokes* at *home* with me, I should say, if there were any flats present, ' Splodger, will you have a Jack-sur*pass* of finger-and-*thumb*, and blow your yard of *tripe* of nosey me *knacker*, and have a touch of the *broads* with me and the other heaps of *coke* at my *drum*. [In this it will be observed that every one of the 'cant words rhymes with the words ordinarily used to express the same idea.] I can assure you what little we cadgers do get we earn uncommon hard. Why, from standing shaking—that is, being out nearly naked in the hardest frosts—I lost the use of my left side for nearly three years, and wasn't able to stir outside the door. I got my living by card-playing in the low lodging-houses all that time. I worked the oracle—they were not up to it. I put the first and seconds on and the bridge also. I 'd play at cards with any

one. You see, sir, I was afeard to come to you at first because I had been ' a starving ' on the pavement only a few days ago, not a hundred yards from your very door, and I thought you might know me."

MEETING OF THIEVES.

As a further proof, however, of the demoralizing influences of the low lodging-houses, I will now conclude my investigations into the subject with a report of the meeting of vagrants, which I convened for the express purpose of consulting them generally upon several points which had come under my notice in the course of my inquiries. The Chronicle reporter's account of this meeting was as follows :—

A meeting of an unprecedented character was held at the British Union School-room, Shakspeare-walk, Shadwell, on Monday evening last. The use of the school-room was kindly granted by Mr. Fletcher, the proprietor, to whose liberality we stand indebted for many similar favours. It was convened by our Metropolitan Correspondent, for the purpose of assembling together some of the lowest class of male juvenile thieves and vagabonds who infest the metropolis and the country at large ; and although privately called, at only two days' notice, by the distribution of tickets of admission among the class in question at the various haunts and dens of infamy to which they resort, no fewer than 150 of them attended on the occasion. The only condition to entitle the parties to admission was that they should be vagrants, and under twenty years of age. They had all assembled some time before the hour for commencing the proceedings arrived, and never was witnessed a more distressing spectacle of squalor, rags, and wretchedness. Some were young men, and some mere children ; one, who styled himself a " cadger," was six years of age, and several who confessed themselves " prigs " were only ten. The countenances of the boys were of various characters. Many were not only good-looking, but had a frank, ingenuous expression that seemed in no way connected with innate roguery. Many, on the other hand, had the deep-sunk and half-averted eye which are so characteristic of natural dishonesty and cunning. Some had the regular features of lads born of parents in easy circumstances. The hair of most of the lads was cut very close to the head, showing their recent liberation from prison ; indeed, one might tell by the comparative length of the crop, the time that each boy had been out of gaol. All but a few of the elder boys were remarkable, amidst the rags, filth, and wretchedness of their external appearance, for the mirth and carelessness impressed upon their countenances. At first their behaviour was very noisy and disorderly : coarse and ribald jokes were freely cracked, exciting general bursts of laughter ; while howls, cat-calls, and all manner of unearthly and indescribable yells threatened for some time to render the object of the meeting utterly abortive. At one moment a lad would imitate the bray of a jack-ass, and immediately the whole hundred and fifty would fall to braying.

Then some ragged urchin would crow like a cock, whereupon the place would echo again with a hundred and fifty cock-crows. Then, as a black boy entered the room, one of the young vagabonds would shout out "swe-ee-op." This would be received with peals of laughter, and followed by a general repetition of the same cry. Next, a hundred and fifty cat-calls of the shrillest possible description would almost split the ears. These would be succeeded by cries of "Strike up, you catgut scrapers," "Go on with your barrow," "Flare up, my never-sweats," and a variety of other street sayings. Indeed, the uproar which went on before the meeting began will be best understood if we compare it to the scene presented by a public menagerie at feeding time. The greatest difficulty, as might be expected, was experienced in collecting the subjoined statistics of their character and condition. By a well-contrived and persevering mode of inquiry, however, the following facts were elicited:—

With respect to their *ages*, the youngest boy present was 6 years old. He styled himself a "cadger," and said that his mother, who is a widow, and suffering from ill-health, sends him into the streets to beg. There were seven of 10 years of age, three of 12, three of 13, ten of 14, ten of 15, eleven of 16, twenty of 17, twenty-six of 18, and forty-five of 19.

Nineteen had *fathers and mothers* still living; thirty-nine had only one parent, and eighty were orphans in the fullest sense of the word, having neither father nor mother alive.

Of *professed beggars* there were fifty, and sixty-six who acknowledged themselves to be *habitual thieves.* The announcement that the greater number present were thieves pleased them exceedingly, and was received with three rounds of applause.

Twelve of the youths assembled had been *in prison* once (two of these were but 10 years of age); 5 had been in prison twice; 3, thrice; 4 four times; 7, five times; 8, six times; 5, seven times; 4, eight times; 2, nine times (1 of them 13 years of age); 5, ten times; 5, twelve times; 2, thirteen times; 3, fourteen times; 2, sixteen times; 3, seventeen times; 2, eighteen times; 5, twenty times; 6, twenty-four times; 1, twenty-five times; 1, twenty-six times; and 1, twenty-nine times. The announcements in reply to the questions as to the number of times that any of them had been in prison were received with great applause, which became more and more boisterous as the number of imprisonments increased. When it was announced that one, though only 19 years of age, had been in prison as many as twenty-nine times, the clapping of hands, the cat-calls, and shouts of "bravyo!" lasted for several minutes, and the whole of the boys rose to look at the distinguished individual. Some chalked on their hats the figures which designated the sum of the several times that they had been in gaol.

As to the *causes of their vagabondism,* it was found that 22 had run away from their homes, owing to the ill-treatment of their parents; 18 confessed to having been ruined through their parents allowing them to run wild in the streets,

and to be led astray by bad companions; and 15 acknowledged that they had been first taught thieving in a lodging-house.

Concerning the vagrant habits of the youths, the following facts were elicited: 78 regularly roam through the country every year, 65 sleep regularly in the casual wards of the unions, and 52 occasionally slept in tramper's lodging-houses throughout the country.

Respecting their *education,* according to the popular meaning of the term, 63 of the 150 were able to read and write, and they were principally thieves. Fifty of this number said they had read "Jack Sheppard," and the lives of Dick Turpin, Claude du Val, and all the other popular thieves' novels, as well as the "Newgate Calendar" and "Lives of the Robbers and Pirates." Those who could not read themselves, said they'd had "Jack Sheppard" read to them at the lodging-houses. Numbers avowed that they had been induced to resort to an abandoned course of life from reading the lives of notorious thieves, and novels about highway robbers. When asked what they thought of "Jack Sheppard," several bawled out "He's a regular brick"—a sentiment which was almost universally concurred in by the deafening shouts and plaudits which followed. When asked whether they would like to be Jack Shepparts, they answered, "Yes, if the times was the same now as they were then." Thirteen confessed that they had taken to thieving in order to go to the low theatres; and one lad said he had lost a good situation on the Birmingham Railway through his love of the play.

Twenty stated they had *been flogged in prison* —many of them two, three, and four different times. A policeman in plain clothes was present; but their acute eyes were not long before they detected his real character notwithstanding his disguise. Several demanded that he should be turned out. The officer was accordingly given to understand that the meeting was a private one, and requested to withdraw. Having apologised for intruding, he proceeded to leave the room— and, no sooner did the boys see the policeman move towards the door, than they gave vent to several rounds of very hearty applause, accompanied with hisses, groans, and cries of "throw him over."

The process of interrogating them in the mass having been concluded, the next step was to call several of them separately to the platform, to narrate, in their peculiar style and phraseology, the history of their own career, together with the causes which had led them to take up a life of dishonesty. The novelty of their position as speech-makers seemed peculiarly exciting to the speakers themselves, and provoked much merriment and interest amongst the lads. Their antics and buffoonery in commencing their addresses were certainly of the most ludicrous character. The first speaker, a lad 17 years of age, ascended the platform, dressed in a torn "wide-a-awake" hat, and a dirty smock-frock. He began:—Gentlemen [immense applause and laughter], I am a Brummagem lad [laughter]. My father has been dead three years, and my mother seven. When my father died I had to go and live along with my aunt. I fell out of employment, and went round about the town, and fell into the company of a lot of chaps, and went picking ladies' pockets. Then I was in prison once or twice, and I came to London, and have been in several prisons here. I have been in London three years; but I have been out of it several times in that time. I can't get anything honest to do; and I wish I could get something at sea, or in any foreign land. I don't care what or where it is [cheers and yells].

Another lad about 16, clad in a ragged coat, with a dirty face and matted hair, next came forward and said—My father was a soldier, and when I growed up to about ten years I joined the regiment as a drummer in the Grenadier Guards. I went on and got myself into trouble, till at last I got turned away, and my father left the regiment. I then went out with some more chaps and went thieving, and have been thieving about two years now. [Several voices—" Very good ;" " that 's beautiful ;" " I hope you do it well."]

The third boy, who stated that he had been twenty-four times in prison, said he belonged to Hendon, in Middlesex, and that his father left his mother seventeen years ago, and he did not know whether he was dead or alive. He went to Christchurch school for some time, but afterwards picked up with bad companions, and went a thieving. He went to school again, but again left it to go a thieving and cadging with bad companions. He had been doing that for the last five years ; and if he could get out of it he would be very glad to leave it [cheers].

The fourth lad (who was received with loud cheering, evidently indicating that he was a well-known character) said, he came from the city of York, and was a farrier. His father died a few years ago, and then he took to work ; but " the play" led him on to be a thief, and from that time to the present he had done nothing but beg or thieve. If he could go to Australia he would be very glad ; as if he stopped in England he feared he should do nothing but thieve to the end [laughter, with cries of " well done," " very well spoken"].

The next speaker was about 18 years of age, and appeared a very sharp intelligent lad. After making a very grave but irresistibly comical prefatory bow, by placing his hand at the back of his head, and so (as it were) forcing it to give a nod, he proceeded: My father is an engineer's labourer, and the first cause of my thieving was that he kept me without grub, and wallopped me [laughter]. Well, I was at work at the same time that he was, and I kept pilfering, and at last they bowled me out [loud cheers]. I got a showing up, and at last they turned me away; and, not liking to go home to my father, I ran away. I went to Margate, where I had some friends, with a shilling in my pocket. I never stopped till I got to Ramsgate, and I had no lodging except under the trees, and had only the bits of bread I could pick up. When I got there my grandfather took me in and kept me for a twelvemonth.

My mother's brother's wife had a spite against me, and tried to get me turned away. I did not know what thieving was then; and I used to pray that her heart might be turned, because I did not know what would become of me if my grandfather turned me away. But she got other people to complain of me, and say I was a nuisance to the town; but I knowed there was no fault in me; but, however, my grandfather said he could put up with me no longer, and turned me away. So after that I came back to London, and goes to the union. The first night I went there I got tore up [cheers and laughter]. Everything was torn off my back, and the bread was taken away from me, and because I said a word I got well wallopped [renewed laughter]. They " small-ganged" me; and afterwards I went seven days to prison because others tore my clothes. When I went in there—this was the first time—a man said to me, " What are you here for?" I said, " For tearing up." The man said to another, " What are you here for?" and the other made answer, " For a handkerchief." The man then said, " Ah, that 's something like ;" and he said to me, " Why are you not a thief— you will only get to prison for that." I said, " I will." Well, after that I went pilfering small things, worth a penny or twopence at first; but I soon saw better things were as easy to be got as them, so I took them [laughter]. I picked up with one that knowed more than me. He fairly kept me for some time, and I learnt as well as him. I picked him up in a London workhouse. After that I thought I would try my friends again, and I went to my uncle at Dover, but he could do nothing for me, so I got a place at a butcher's, where I fancied myself fairly blessed, for I had 2s. a week and my board and washing. I kept a twelvemonth there honest, without thieving. At last my master and I fell out and I left again, so I was forced to come up to London, and there I found my old companions in the Smithfield pens—they were not living anywhere. I used to go to the workhouse and used to tear up and refuse to work, and used to get sent to " quod," and I used to curse the day when it was my turn to go out. The governor of the prison used to say he hoped he wouldn't see my face there again; but I used to answer, " I shall be here again to night, because it's the only place I 've got." That 's all I 've got to say.

The next lad, who said he had been fourteen times in prison, was a taller, cleaner, and more intelligent-looking youth than any that had preceded him. After making a low affected bow, over the railing, to the company below, and uttering a preliminary a-hem or two with the most ludicrous mock gravity, he began by saying:— " I am a native of London. My father is a poor labouring man, with 15s. a week—little enough, I think, to keep a home for four, and find candlelight [laughter]. I was at work looking after a boiler at a paper-stainer's in Old-street-road at 6s. a week, when one night they bowled me out. I got the sack, and a bag to take it home in [laughter]. I got my wages, and ran away from home, but in four days, being hungry, and having no money, I went back again. I got a towelling, but it did not do me much good. My father did not like to turn me out of doors, so he tied me to the leg of the bedstead [laughter]. He tied my hands and feet so that I could hardly move, but I managed somehow to turn my gob (mouth) round and gnawed it away. I run down stairs and got out at the back door and over a neighbour's wall, and never went home for nine months. I never bolted with anything. I never took anything that was too hot for me. The captain of a man-of-war about this time took me into his service, where I remained five weeks till I took a fever, and was obliged to go to the hospital. When I recovered, the captain was gone to Africa; and not liking to go home, I stepped away, and have been from home ever since. I was in Brummagem, and was seven days in the new 'stir' (prison), and nearly broke my neck. When I came out, I fell into bad company, and went cadging, and have been cadging ever since; but if I could leave off, and go to the Isle of Dogs, the Isle of Man, or the Isle of Woman [laughter], or any other foreign place, I would embrace the opportunity as soon as I could. And if so be that any gentleman would take me in hand, and send me out, I would be very thankful to him, indeed. And so good night" [cheers].

A dirty little boy, fourteen years of age, dressed in a big jacket, next stood forward. He said his father was a man-of-war's man, and when he came home from sea once his father, his mother, and all of them got drunk. The lad then stole 4*d.* from his father's pocket. After this, when he was sent for sixpenny rum he used to fetch fourpenny, and for fourpenny gin threepenny; and for fourpenny beer he used to fetch threepenny, and keep the difference to himself. His mother used to sell fruit, and when she left him at the stall he used to eat what he could not sell, and used to sell some to get marbles and buttons. Once he stole a loaf from a baker's shop. The man let him off, but his father beat him for it. The beating did him no good. After that he used to go "smugging" [running away with] other people's things. Then one day his father caught him, and tied his leg to the bedstead, and left him there till he was pretty near dead. He ran away afterwards, and has been thieving ever since.

A lad about twenty was here about to volunteer a statement concerning the lodging-houses, by which he declared he had been brought to his ruin, but he was instantly assailed with cries of "come down!" "hold your tongue!" and these became so general, and were in so menacing a tone, that he said he was afraid to make any disclosures, because he believed if he did so he would have perhaps two or three dozen of the other chaps on to him [great confusion].

MR. MAYHEW: Will it hurt any of you here if he says anything against the lodging-houses [yes, yes]? How will it do so?

A Voice: They will not allow stolen property to come into them if it is told.

MR. MAYHEW: But would you not all gladly quit your present course of life [yes, yes, yes]? Then why not have the lodging-house system, the principal cause of all your misery, exposed?

A Voice: If they shut up the lodging-houses, where are we to go? If a poor boy gets to the workhouse he catches a fever, and is starved into the bargain.

MR. MAYHEW:—Are not you all tired of the lives you now lead? [Vociferous cries of "yes, yes, we wish to better ourselves!" from all parts of the room.] However much you dread the exposure of the lodging-houses, you know, my lads, as well as I do, that it is in them you meet your companions, and ruin, if not begun there, is at least completed in such places. If a boy runs away from home he is encouraged there and kept secreted from his parents. And do not the parties who keep these places grow rich on your degradation and your peril? [Loud cries of "yes, yes!"] Then why don't you all come forward now, and, by exposing them to the public, who know nothing of the iniquities and vice practised in such places, put an end to these dens at once? There is not one of you here—not one, at least, of the elder boys, who has found out the mistake of his present life, who would not, I verily believe, become honest, and earn his living by his industry, if he could. You might have thought a roving life a pleasant thing enough at first, but you now know that a vagabond's life is full of suffering, care, peril, and privation; you are not so happy as you thought you would be, and are tired and disgusted with your present course. This is what I hear from you all. Am I not stating the fact? [Renewed cries of "yes, yes, yes!" and a voice: "The fact of it is, sir, we don't see our folly till it is too late."] Now I and many hundreds and thousands really wish you well, and would gladly do anything we could to get you to earn an honest living. All, or nearly all, your misery, I know, proceeds from the low lodging-houses ["yes, yes, it does, master! it does"]; and I am determined, with your help, to effect their utter destruction. [A voice, "I am glad of it, sir—you are quite right; and I pray God to assist you."]

The elder boys were then asked what they thought would be the best mode of effecting their deliverance from their present degraded position. Some thought emigration the best means, for if they started afresh in a new colony, they said they would leave behind them their bad characters, which closed every avenue to employment against them at home. Others thought there would be difficulties in obtaining work in the colonies in sufficient time to prevent their being driven to support themselves by their old practices. Many again thought the temptations which surrounded them in England rendered their reformation impossible; whilst many more considered that the same temptations would assail them abroad which existed at home.

MR. MAYHEW then addressed them on another point. He said he had seen many notorious thieves in the course of his investigations. Since then he had received them at all hours into his house—men of the most desperate and women of the most abandoned characters—but he had never lost a 6*d*. worth of his property by them. One thief he had entrusted with a sovereign to get changed, and the lad returned and gave him back the full amount in silver. He had since gone out to America. Now he would ask all those present whether, if he were to give them a sovereign, they would do the same? [Several voices here called out that they would, and others that they would not. Others, again, said that they would to him, but to no one else.]

Here one of the most desperate characters present, a boy who had been twenty-six times in prison, was singled out from the rest, and a sovereign given to him to get changed, in order to make the experiment whether he would have the honesty to return the change or abscond with it in his possession. He was informed, on receiving it, that if he chose to decamp with it, no proceedings should be taken against him. He left the room amid the cheers of his companions, and when he had been absent a few moments all eyes were turned towards the door each time it opened, anxiously expecting his arrival, to prove his trustworthiness. Never was such interest displayed by any body of individuals. They mounted the forms in their eagerness to obtain the first glimpse of his return. It was clear that their honour was at stake; and several said they would kill the lad in the morning if he made off with the money. Many minutes elapsed in almost painful suspense, and some of his companions began to fear that so large a sum of money had proved too great a temptation for the boy. At last, however, a tremendous burst of cheering announced the lad's return. The delight of his companions broke forth again and again, in long and loud peals of applause, and the youth advanced amidst triumphant shouts to the platform, and gave up the money in full.

The assemblage was then interrogated as to the effect of flogging as a punishment; and the general feeling appeared to be that it hardened the criminal instead of checking his depravity, and excited the deadliest enmity in his bosom at the time towards the person inflicting it. When asked whether they had seen any public executions, they almost all cried out that they had seen Manning and his wife hung; others said that they had seen Rush and Sarah Thomas executed. They stated that they liked to go a "death-hunting," after seeing one or two executed. It hardened them to it, and at last they all got to thieve under the gallows. They felt rather shocked at the sight of an execution at first; but, after a few repetitions, it soon wore off.

Before the meeting broke up several other lads expressed a strong desire to make statements.

A young man, 18 years of age, and of a miserable and ragged appearance, said he first left home from bad usage; and could not say whether it was the same with his sister or not, but she left her home about nine months ago, when he met her while he was getting his living as a costermonger. With the stock-money that he had, rather than she should be driven to prostitution and the

streets, he bought as many things as he could to furnish a room. This exhausted his stock-money, and then his furniture had to go a little at a time to support him and his sister in food. After this he was obliged to take a furnished room, which put him to greater expense. To keep her off the streets, he was compelled to thieve. His father, if he ever had the feeling of a Christian, would never have treated him as he had done. Could a father (he asked) have any feeling, who chained his son up by the leg in a shed, as *his* father had done to him, and fed him on bread and water for one entire month : and then, after chaining him up all day, still chain him in bed at night. This it was that drove him into the streets at first. It was after his mother died, and he had a stepmother, that his father treated him thus. His mother-in-law ill-treated him as well as his father. If he had been a transport he could not have been treated worse. He told his father that he was driving him on the road to transportation, but he took no notice of it; and he was obliged to leave his roof. He had been in Newgate since.

A little boy, dressed in the garb of a sailor, came up to Mr. Mayhew crying bitterly, and implored him to allow him to say a word. He stated —I am here starving all my time. Last night I was out in the cold and nearly froze to death. When I got up I was quite stiff and could hardly walk. I slept in Whitechapel under a form where they sell meat. I was an apprentice on board of a fishing smack, and ran away because I was ill-treated. After I ran away I broke into my master's house because I was hungry. He gave me twelve months, and now he is in the union himself; he failed in business and got broken up. I have been out of prison three months, starving ; and I would rather do anything than thieve. If I see a little thing I take it, because I can't get anything to eat without it. [Here the child, still weeping piteously, uncovered his breast, and showed his bones starting through his skin. He said he was anxious to get out of the country.]

The following statement respecting the lodging-houses was made, after the others had left, by another lad. He left home when about thirteen, and never thieved before that. His father was dead, and his mother was unable to keep him. He got a situation and held it for three years and nine months, until he picked up with a man from a lodging-house, and through keeping late hours he was obliged to leave his place and sleep in a lodging-house himself. The lodging-house is in Short's-gardens. This he considered to have been the commencement of his downfall. About forty thieves lived in the house, and they brought in stolen property of every description, and the deputies received it and took it to other people to sell it again, and get the price and pay the thieves. They got double as much as the thieves did, or else they would have nothing to do with it. Several housebreakers lived at the house, and he heard them there plan the robbery of Bull and Wilson, the woollen-drapers in St. Martin's-lane. One of the men secreted himself in the house in the daytime, and the other two were admitted by him at night. If he had stated this at the meeting the persons present would have killed him. He was sure that more might be done by giving proper encouragement to virtue, and by reforming the criminal, than by rigorous prosecution. He said (with tears in his eyes) that he should be very willing and happy to work for an honest living if he could only get it to do. He showed a letter of recommendation for good conduct to his former master, and a Bible; both of which had been given him by the chaplain of the gaol which he had just left, after undergoing an imprisonment of twelve months. It was useless (he said) for a young man like him to apply to the parish for relief; he might just as well stand in the street and talk to a lamp-post. Then what was a man to do after he left prison? He must go a thieving to live. He was persuaded that if there was an institution to give employment to the homeless, the friendless, and the penniless, after being liberated from prison, it would be the means of rescuing thousands.

The proceedings then terminated. The assemblage, which had become more rational and manageable towards the close, dispersed, quite peaceably it should be added, and the boys were evidently sincerely grateful for the efforts being made to bring their misfortunes before the notice of those in whose power it may be to alleviate them.

Before they were dismissed, as much money was dispensed to each as would defray his night's lodging.

Of the Country Lodging-Houses.

Concerning the lodging-houses, more especially in the country, I give the statement of a middle-aged man, familiar with them for twenty years. He was recommended to me as possessed of much humour and a great master of humourous slang:—

"I can tell you all about it, sir; but one lodging-house is so like another that I can't draw much distinction. In small country towns, especially agricultural towns, they are decent places enough, regular in their hours, and tidy enough. At these places they have what they call 'their own travellers,' persons that they know, and who are always accommodated in preference. As to the characters that frequent these places, let us begin with *the Crocuses*. They carry about a lot of worms in bottles, which they never took out of anybody, though they'll tell you different, or long pieces of tape in bottles, made to look like worms, and on that they'll *patter* in a market place as if on a real cure, and they've got the cheek to tell the people that that very worm was taken from Lady ——, near the town, and referring them to her to prove it. The one I knew best would commence with a piece of sponge in a bottle, which he styled the stomach wolf. That was his leading slum, and pretty well he sponged them too. When he'd pattered on about the wolf, he had another bottle with what he called a worm 200 inches long, he bounced it was, which the day before yesterday he had from Mrs. ——'s girl (some well-known person), and referred them to her. While he's going on, a

brother Crocus will step up, a stranger to the people, and say, 'Ah, Doctor ——, you're right. I had the pleasure of dining with Mr. —— when the worm was extracted, and never saw a child so altered in my life.' That's what the Crocus's call giving a jolly; and after that don't the first Crocus's old woman serve out the six-pennyworths? The stuff is to cure every mortal thing a man can ail—ay, or a woman either. They'd actually have the cheek to put a blister on a cork leg. Well, when they're done pattering on the worm racket, then come the wonderful pills. Them are the things. These pills, from eight to a dozen in a box, are charged 4*d.* to 6*d.* according to the flat's appearance—as the Crocus calls his customers. The pills meet with a ready sale, and they're like chip in porridge, neither good nor harm. It's chiefly the bounciful patter, the cheek they have, that gets them Crocusses on. It's amazing. They'll stare a fellow in the face, and make him believe he's ill whether he is or no. The man I speak of is a first-rate cove; he trains it and coaches it from market to market like any gentleman. He wears a stunning fawny (ring) on his finger, an out-and-out watch and guard, and not a duffer neither—no gammon; and a slap-up suit of black togs. I've seen the swell bosmen (farmers) buy the pills to give the people standing about, just to hear the Crocus patter. Why they've got the cheek to pitch their stall with their worms opposite a regular medical man's shop, and say, 'Go over the way and see what he'll do—he'll drive up in a horse and gig to your door, and make you pay for it too; but I don't—I've walked here to do you good, and I *will* do you good before I leave you. One trial is all I ask'—and quite enough too (said my informant). I'll warrant they won't come a second time; if they do, it's with a stick in their hands. If he does much business in the worm-powder way (some have it in cakes for children), the Crocus never gives them a chance to catch him. But if it's only pills, he'll show next market day, or a month after, and won't he crack about it then? He says, 'One trial is all I ask,' and one of them got it and was transported. I knew one of these Crocusses who was once so hard up from lushing and boozing about that he went into a field and collected sheep dung and floured it over, and made his pills of it, and made the people swallow it at Lutterworth market, in Leicestershire; because there they'll swallow anything. If the Crocus I have mentioned see this in the paper—as he will, for he's a reading-man—won't he come out bounceful? He'll say, 'Why am I thus attacked—why don't the proprietor and the editor of this paper come forward—if he's among you? Who made this report? let him come forward, and I'll refute him face to face.' And no doubt (my informant remarked), he'd give him a tidy dose, too, the Crocus would. For myself, I'd far rather meet him face to face than his medicine, either his blue or his pink water. There's another sort who carry on the crocussing business, but on a small scale; they're on the penny and twopenny racket, and are called hedge crocusses—men who sell corn salve, or 'four pills

LONDON LABOUR AND THE LONDON POOR.

a penny,' to cure anything, and go from house to house in the country. But as the hedge crocus is shickery togged, he makes poorly out. Respectable people won't listen to him, and it's generally the lower order that he gulls. These hedge fellows are slow and dull; they go mouching along as if they were croaking themselves. I've seen the head crocus I've mentioned at four markets in one week, and a town on a Saturday night, clear from 5l. to 7l.—all clear profit, for his fakement costs him little or nothing. For such a man's pound, the hedge fellow may make 1s. The next I'll tell you about is durynacking, or duryking. The gipsies (and they're called Romanies) are the leading mob at this racket, but they're well known, and I needn't say anything about those ladies. But there're plenty of travelling women who go about with a basket and a bit of driss (lace) in it, gammy lace, for a stall-off (a blind), in case they meet the master, who would order them off. Up at a bosken (farm-house) they'll get among the servant girls, being pretty well acquainted with the neighbourhood by inquiries on the road, as to the number of daughters and female servants. The first inquiry is for the missus or a daughter, and if they can't be got at they're on to the slaveys. Suppose they do get hold of one of the daughters, they commence by offering the driss, which, as it is queer stuff, wouldn't be picked up by an agricultural young lady, as the durynacker very well knows. Then she begins, ' Ah! my sweet young lady, my blessed looking angel'—if she's as ugly as sin, and forty; they say that, and that's the time you get them to rights, when they're old and ugly, just by sweetening them, and then they don't mind tipping the loaver (money)—'I know you dont want this stuff (she'll continue), there's something on your mind. I see you're in love; but the dear handsome gentleman—he'll not slight you, but loves you as hard as a hammer.' This is thrown out as a foeler, and the young lady is sure to be confused; then the durrynacker has hold of her mauly (hand) in a minute. It's all up with the girl, once the woman gets a grip. She's asked in directly, and of course the sisters (if she has any) and the slavey are let into the secret, and all have their fortunes told. The fortune-teller may make a week's job of it, according as the loaver comes out. She'll come away with her basket full of eggs, bacon, butter, tea and sugar, and all sorts of things. I *have* seen them bring the scran in! Every one is sure to have handsome husbands, thumping luck, and pretty children. The durrynacker, too, is not particular, if there's a couple of silver spoons—she doesn't like odd ones; and mind you, she alway carries a basket—big enough too. I know a man on this lurk, but he works the article with a small glass globe filled full of water, and in that he shows girls their future husbands, and kids them on to believe they do see them—ay, and the church they're to be married in—and they fancy they do see it as they twist the globe this way and that, while he twists the tin out of them, and no flies. He actually had the cheek, though he knew

I was fly to every fake, to try to make me believe that I could see the place where Smith O'Brien had the fight in Ireland ! ' Don't you see them cabbages, and a tall man in a green velvet cap among them, holloring out, "I'm the King of Munster?"' I don't know any other male durrynacker worth noticing; the women have all the call. Young women won't ask their fortunes of men. The way the globe man does is to go among the old women and fiddle (humbug) them, and, upon my word, three-parts of them are worse than the young ones. Now I'll tell you about the tat (rag) gatherers; buying rags they call it, but I call it bouncing people. Two men I lodged with once, one morning hadn't a farthing, regularly smashed up, not a feather to fly with, they'd knocked down all their tin lushing. Well, they didn't know what to be up to, till one hit upon a scheme. 'I've got it, Joe,' says he. He borrows two blue plates from the lodging-house keeper, a washing jug and basin. Off they goes, one with the crockery, and the other with a bag. They goes into the by-courts in Windsor, because this bouncing caper wouldn't do in the main drag. Up goes the fellow with a bag, and hollas out, ' Now, women, bring out your copper, brass, white rags, old flannel, bed-sacking, old ropes, empty bottles, umbrellas—any mortal thing—the best price is given;' and the word's hardly out, when up comes his pal, hollaring, ' Sam, holloa ! stop that horse,' as if he'd a horse and cart passing the court, and then the women bring out their umbrellas and things, and the're all to be exchanged for crockery such as he shows, and all goes into the bag, and the bagman goes off with the things, leaving the other to do the bounce, and he keeps singing out for the horse and cart with the load of crockery, gammoning there is one, that the ladies may have their choice, and he then hurries down to quicken his cart-driver's movements, and hooks it, leaving the flats completely stunned. Oh ! it does give them a ferry-cadouzer. Two other men go about on this lurk, one with an old cracked plate under his waistcoat, and the other with a bag. And one sings out, ' Now, women, fourpence a pound for your white rags. None of your truck system, your needles and thread for it. I don't do it that way; ready money, women, is the order of the day with me.' Well, one old mollesher (woman), though she must have known her rags would only bring 2d. a lb. at a fair dealer's, if there be one, brought out 8 lbs. of white rags. He weighs them with his steelyards, and in they went to the bag. The man with the bag steps it immediately, and the other whips out his flute quite carelessly, and says—' Which will you have marm, Jem Crow, or the Bunch of Roses?' The old woman says directly, ' What do you mean, 8 times 4 is 32, and 32 pence is 2s. 8d.; never mind, I won't be hard, give me half-a-crown.' Well, when she finds there's no money, out she hollars, and he plays his distracted flute to drown her voice, and backs himself manfully out of the court. I have known these men get on so that I have seen them with a good horse and cart. There's another class of rag bloaks, who have bills printed with the Queen's Arms at the top, if you please, ' By royal authority'—that 's their own authority, and they assume plenty of it. Well, this bill specifies the best prices for rags, left-off clothes, &c. One fellow goes and drops these bills at the kens (houses), the other comes after him, and as the man who drops marks every house where a bill has been taken, the second man knows where to call. Any house where he gets a call commences the caper. Well, anything to be disposed of is brought out, often in the back yard. The party of the house produces the bill, which promises a stunning tip for the old lumber. The man keeps sorting the things out, and running them down as not so good as he expected ; but at the same time he kids them on by promising three times more than the things are worth. This is a grand racket—the way he fakes them, and then he says, ' Marm (or sir, as it may be), I shall give you 15s. for the lot,' which stuns the party, for they never expected to get anything like that—and their expectations is not disappointed, for they don't. Then he turns round directly, and commences sorting more particularly than before, putting the best and the easiest to carry altogether. He starts up then, and whips a couple of bob, or half a bull (2s. 6d.) into the woman's hand, saying, ' I always like to bind a bargain, marm—one of the fairest dealing men travelling. Do save all your old lumber for me.' Of a sudden he begins searching his pockets, and exclaims, ' Dear me, I haven't enough change in my pocket, but I 'll soon settle that—my mate has it outside. I 'll just take a load out to the cart, and come back for the others with the money ;' and so he hooks it, and I 've no occasion to tell you he never comes back; and that 's what he calls having them on the knock.''

The other inmates at the lodging-houses which my informant described are of the class concerning whom full information is or will be given in other portions of this or the following letters. His description of the lodging-houses, too, was a corroboration of the statement I give to-day. All the classes described meet and mix at the lodging-houses.

I shall reserve what I have to say concerning the influence of the low lodging-houses of London and the country till the conclusion of the present volume.

OF THE STREET-SELLERS OF CHEMICAL ARTICLES OF MANUFACTURE.

THE street purveyors of blacking, of the different preparations of black lead, of plating-balls, of corn-salves, of grease-removing compositions, of china and glass cements, of rat poisons, of fly-papers, of beetle-wafers, of gutta-percha heads, of lucifer-matches, and of cigar-lights, may be classed generally under two heads. They are either very old or very young persons, or else they are men who recommend their wares by patter.

Among the first-mentioned class are the vendors of cakes of blacking, papers of black-lead, and lucifer matches. Of blacking and black-lead the street-sellers are more frequently old women ; of

lucifer matches they are usually women and children, and of all ages. It is not uncommon, in the quieter roads of the suburbs especially, to see a young woman extend her bare red arm from beneath a scanty ragged shawl, and with an imploring look, a low curtsey, and a piteous tone, proffer a box of matches for sale ; while a child in her arms, perhaps of two or three years old, extends in its little hand another box. There are also in the street sale of lucifer matches very many girls and boys, parentless or uncared for, and many old or infirm women and men.

The street-sellers of chemically-manufactured articles, who feel it necessary to recommend their wares by a little street oratory, or patter, (the paper-worker, whose humorous remarks I have before quoted, once described it to me as " advertising by word of mouth,") are the vendors of the articles which are to cure, to repair, to renovate, or to kill. Any other itinerant vendors of chemical articles are of the ordinary class of street traders.

OF THE STREET-SELLERS OF BLACKING, BLACK LEAD, ETC.

I SPECIFY these two commodities jointly, because they are frequently sold by the same individual. In Whitechapel and Spitalfields are eight establishments, where the street-sellers of blacking are principally supplied with their stock. It is sold in cakes, which are wrapped in a kind of oil paper, generally printed on the back, so as to catch the eye, with the address of some well-known blacking manufacturer. Thus some which a street-seller of blacking showed me were printed, in large type, as a sort of border, " Lewis's India Rubber Blacking," while in the middle was a very black and very predominant 30, and beneath it, in small and hardly distinguishable type, " Princess-st., Portman-market." Any shopkeeper, who " supplies the trade," if he be a regular customer of the manufacturer, can have his name and address printed on the cover of the blacking-cakes. The 30 is meant to catch the eye with the well-known flourish of " 30, Strand."

The quality of these cakes of blacking, the street-sellers whom I questioned told me was highly approved by their customers, and, as blacking is purchased by the classes who aim at a smartness and cleanliness above that of the purchasers of many street commodities, there is no reason to doubt the assertion. The sale of this blacking, indeed, is chiefly on a round, and it would be hopeless as to future custom to call a second time at any house where bad blacking had been sold on a previous visit. The article is vended wholesale, in " gross boxes," and " half-gross boxes." The half-gross boxes are 1s. 9d., and capital, even in this trifling trade, has its customary advantages, for the " gross boxes " are but 3s. It should be remembered, however, that to the buyer of two " half-gross " a couple of the plain wooden boxes, in which the blacking is sold, and often hawked, must be supplied ; but to the buyer of a " gross box " only one of these cases is furnished. I may mention, to the credit of the vendors, that of the wholesale blacking makers, two have themselves been street-sellers, and one still, but only at intervals, goes "on a blacking-round" among his old customers. There are other blacking-makers, but those I have specified, as to number, are more particularly the providers for the street trade. The poor people who sell blacking at a distance from the manufacturer's premises—as in the case of the "30, Princess-st., Portman-market"—are supplied by oilmen, chandlers, and other shopkeepers, who buy largely of the manufacturers, and can consequently supply the purchasers by the dozen, for street sale or hawking, as cheaply as they would be supplied by the manufacturer himself. A dozen is generally charged 3½d., and as the cakes are sold at ½d. each (occasionally 1d., both by the street people and more frequently the small shopkeepers) the profit is moderate enough. The cakes, however, which are regularly retailed at 1d., are larger, and cost nearly twice the amount of the others wholesale.

This trade presents the peculiarity of being almost entirely a street "door-to-door" trade, as I heard it described. Blacking is not presented for purposes of begging, as are lucifer-matches, tracts, memorandum-books, boot-laces, &c.; for the half-trading, half-begging, is carried on in the quieter parts of town, and more extensively in the suburbs, ladies being principally accosted, and to them blacking is not offered.

There are now, I learn from good authority, never fewer than 200 persons selling cake blacking, "from door to door." More than half of them are elderly women, and more than three-fourths women of all ages and girls. The other sellers are old men and boys. None of the blacking-sellers make the article they vend. To sell eight dozen cakes a week is a full average, and of these the "pennies" and the "half-pennies" are about equally divided. This gives a weekly outlay of 6s. to each individual seller, with an average profit of about 2s. 6d., and shows a yearly street-expenditure by the public of 3120l. The profit, however, is not in equal apportionment among the traders in blacking, for the "old hands" on a regular round will do double the business of the others.

In liquid blacking the trade is now small. It is occasionally sold in the street markets on Saturday nights, but the principal traffic is in the public-houses. This kind of blacking is retailed at 2d. a bottle, and, I was informed by a man who had sold it, was "rather queer stuff." It is labelled "equal to" (in very small letters) DAY AND MARTIN" in very large letters. One of the manufacturers a few years ago told my informant that he had been threatened "with being sued for piracy, but it was no use sueing a mouse." There are sometimes none, and sometimes twenty persons hawking this blacking, and they are principally, I am informed, the servants of showmen, "out of employ," or "down on their luck." Some of these men "raffle" their blacking in public-houses. They are provided with tickets, numbered from one to six, which are thrown, the

blank sides upwards on a table, and the drawer of number six wins a two-penny bottle of blacking for ½d.; for this the raffler receives 3d. Few of these traders sell more than one dozen bottles in a day, the principal trade being in the evening, and "one-and-a-half dozen is a very good day." The goods are carried in a sack, slung from the shoulder, and are a very heavy carriage, as two-and-a-half dozen, which are often carried, weigh about 100 lbs. If ten men, the year through, take each 6s. weekly (about half the amount being profit), which, I am assured, is the average extent of the trade, we find 156l. yearly expended in this liquid blacking. "Ten years ago," said one blacking seller to me, "it was three times as much as it is now." At the mews blacking is sold by men who are for the most part servants out of place, or who have become known to the denizens of the mews, from having been "helpers" in some capacity, if they have not worn a livery. Here the article vended is what it is announced to be,—"Hoby's" or "Everett's" blacking. The sellers are known to the coachmen and grooms, many of whom have to "find their own blacking," or there would be no business done in the mews, the dwellers there being great sticklers for "a good article." The profit to the vendors is 3s. in 12s. Shilling bottles are vended as numerously as "sixpennies." An old coachman, who had lived in mews in all parts of town, calculated that, take the year through, there was every day twenty men selling blacking in the mews, with an average profit of 10d. a day, or 5s. a week, so taking 15s. each. This gives a mews expenditure, yearly, of 780l.

Black-Lead, for the polishing of grates, is sold in small paper packets, the half ounce being a ½d., and the ounce a 1d. The profit is cent. per cent. Nearly all the women who sell blacking, as I have described, sell black-lead also. In addition to these elderly traders, however, there are from twenty to thirty boys and girls who vend black-lead in the street markets, but chiefly on Saturday nights, and on other days offer it through the area rails—their wretched plight, without any actual begging, occasionally procuring them custom.

The black-lead sold in the streets has often a label in imitation of that of established shop-keepers, as "Superfine Pencil Black-Lead, prepared expressly for, and sold by T. H. Jennings, Oil-Colour and Italian Warehouse, 25, Wormwood-street, City." The name and address must of course be different, but the arrangement of the lines, and often the type, is followed closely, as are the adornments of the packet, which in the instance cited are heraldic. In other parts of town, the labels of tradesmen are imitated in a similar way, but not very closely; and in nearly half the qantity sold a *bonâ fide* label is given, without imitation or sham. "There would be more sold in that way," I was told by a sharp lad, "quite the real ticket, if the dons as wholesales the black-lead, would make it up to sell in ha'porths and penn'orths, with a proper 'lowance to us as sells." This boy and a young sister went on a round; the boy with black-lead, the girl with boot-laces, in one direction, the mother going in another, and each making for their room at six in the evening, or as soon as " sold out."

There are, I am informed, 100 to 150 persons selling and hawking black-lead in the streets, and it may be estimated that they take 4s. each weekly (the adults selling other small articles with the black-lead); thus we find, averaging the number of sellers at 125, that 1250l. is yearly expended in this article, half of which sum forms the profit of the street-folk.

OF THE STREET-SELLERS OF FRENCH POLISH.

THE greater part of the French polish vended in the streets is bought at oil and varnish-shops in Bethnal-green and Whitechapel, the wholesale price being 1s. a pint. The street-vendors add turpentine to the polish, put it into small bottles, and retail it at 1d. a bottle. They thus contrive to clear 5d. on each shilling they take.

There are now five and sometimes six men selling French polish in the streets and public-houses. " But the trade 's getting stale," I was told ; " there was twice as many in it three or four years back, and there 'll be fewer still next year." When French polish first became famous there were, I was informed, several cabinet-makers who hawked it—some having prepared it themselves—and they would occasionally clear 5s. in a day. Of these street-traders there are now none, the present vendors having been in no way connected with the manufacture of furniture. These men generally carry with them pieces of " fancy wood," such as rose, or sandal wood, which they polish up in the streets to show the excellence of the varnish. The chief purchasers are working people and small tradespeople, or their wives, who require trifling quantities of such a composition when they re-polish any small article of furniture.

The French polish-sellers, I am assured by a man familiar with the business, take 2s. a day each, or rather in an evening, for the sales are then the most frequent : the 2s. leaves a profit of 10d. The street expenditure is, therefore (reckoning five regular sellers), 156l. yearly. None of the French polish-sellers confine themselves entirely to the sale of it.

OF THE STREET-SELLERS OF GREASE-REMOVING COMPOSITIONS.

THE persons engaged in this trade carry it on with a regular patter. One man's street announcement is in the following words : " Here you have a composition to remove stains from silks, muslins, bombazeens, cords, or tabarets of any kind or colour. It will never injure nor fade the finest silk or satin, but restore it to its original colour. For grease on silks, &c., only rub the composition on dry, let it remain five minutes, then take a clothes' brush and brush it off, and it will be found to have removed the stains. For grease in woollen cloths spread the composition on the place with a piece of woollen cloth and cold water ; when dry rub it off, and it will remove the grease or stain. For pitch or tar use hot water instead of cold, as that prevents the nap coming off the cloth. Here

it is. Squares of grease-removing composition, never known to fail, only 1d. each."

This street-traffic, I was informed, was far more extensively carried on when silks and woollen cloths, and textile manufactures generally, were more costly and more durable than at present, and when to dye, and scour, and " turn" a garment, was accounted good housewiveship. The sellers then told wonders of their making old silk gowns, or old coats, as good as new, by removing every discolouration, no matter from what cause. Now a silk dress is rarely, if ever, subjected to the experiment of being renovated by the virtues of grease-removing compositions sold in the streets. The trade, at present, is almost confined to the removing of the grease from coat-collars, or of stains from contact with paint, &c., with which boys (principally) have damaged their garments.

The grease-remover generally carries his wares on a tray slung in front of him, and often illustrates the efficacy of his composition, by showing its application to the very greasy collar of a boy's old jacket, which is removed with admirable facility. The man patters as he carries on this work. " You would have thought now that jacket was done for, and only fit for the rag-bag, or to go to make up a lot for a Jew ; but with my composition—only 1d. a cake—it has acquired a new nap and a new gloss, and you 've escaped a tailor's bill for awhile for 1d. You can use your own eyes. You 've seen me do it, and here 's the very same stuff as I have proved to you is so useful and was never known to fail. No mother, or wife, or mistress, or maid, that wishes to be careful and not waste money, should be without it in the house. It removes stains from silks, &c., &c."

Notwithstanding these many recommendations, the street trade in grease-removing cakes is a very poor one. It cannot be carried on in bad weather, for an audience cannot then be collected, and to clear 1s. 6d. in a day is accounted fair work. No grease-remover confines his trade to that commodity. One of the best known sells also plate balls, and occasionally works conundrums and comic exhibitions. The two brothers, who were formerly Grecians at the Blue Coat School, are also in this line. There are now seven men who sell grease-removing compositions, which they prepare themselves. The usual ingredients are pipe clay, two pennyworth of which is beat up and " worked with two colours," generally red lead and stone blue. This gives the composition a streaky look, and takes away the appearance of pipe clay.

The purchasers of this article are, I am told, women and servants, but the trade is one which is declining. One of the best localities for sale is Ratcliff Highway and the purchasers there are sailors. One man told me that he once made a pound's worth for a sailor, who took it to sea with him. The street-seller did not know for what purpose, but he conjectured that it was as a matter of speculation to a foreign country.

Calculating that the seven grease-removers carry on the sale of the article 3 days each week, and clear 1s. 6d. per day, we find 78 guineas yearly expended in the streets for the removal of grease. Nearly the whole is profit.

Plating Balls are generally sold by the grease-removers, but sometimes they are proffered for sale alone. There are four men whose principal dependance is on the sale of plating balls. One announces his wares as "making plate as good as silver, and all inferior metals equal to the best plated. No tarnish can stand against my plate balls," he goes on, "and if, in this respectable company, there should chance to be any lady or genl'man that has no plate, then let him make an old brass candlestick shine like gold, or his tin candlestick, extinguisher and all, shine like silver. Here are the balls that can do it, and only 4 a penny. You have only to rub the ball on your wash-leather, or dry woollen cloth, and rub it on what has to be restored. Four a penny!"

These balls, which are prepared by the street-sellers, are usually made of a halfpennyworth of whitening, a farthing'sworth of red-lead, and an ounce of quicksilver, costing 7*d.* A gross of balls costs 7¾*d.*, as regards the materials. The receipts of the plating ball sellers are the same as those of the grease-removers, but with a somewhat smaller profit.

OF THE STREET-SELLERS OF CORN-SALVE.

THE street purveyors of corn-salve, or corn-plaster, for I heard both words used, are not more than a dozen in number; but, perhaps, none depend *entirely* upon the sale of corn-salve for a living. As is the wont of the pattering class to which they belong, these men make rounds into the country and into the suburbs, but there are sometimes, on one day, a dozen "working the main drags" (chief thoroughfares) of London: there are no women in the trade. The salve is most frequently carried on a small tray, slung in front of the street professional; but sometimes it is sold at a small stall or stand. Oxford-street, Holborn, Tottenham-court-road, and Whitechapel, are favourite localities for these traders; as are Black-friars-road and Newington-causeway on the Surrey side of the Thames. On the Saturday evening the corn-salve sellers resort to the street markets.

The patter of these traders is always to the same purport (however differently expressed)—the long-tested efficacy and the unquestionable cheapness of their remedies. The vendors are glib and unhesitating; but some, owing, I imagine, to a repetition of the same words, as they move from one part of a thoroughfare to another, or occupy a pitch, have acquired a monotonous tone, little calculated to impress a street audience—to effect which a man must be, or appear to be, in earnest. The patter of one of these dealers, who sells corn-salve on fine evenings, and works the public-houses, "with anything likely," on wet evenings, is, from his own account, in the following words:—

"Here you have a speedy remedy for every sort of corn! Your hard corn, soft corn, blood corn, black corn, old corn, new corn, wart, or bunion, can be safely cured in three days! Nothing further to do but spread this salve on a piece of glove-leather, or wash-leather, and apply it to the place. Art and nature does the rest. Either corns, warts, or bunions, cured for one penny."

This, however, is but as the announcement of the article on sale, and is followed by a recapitulation of the many virtues of that peculiar recipe; but, as regards the major part of these street-traders, the recapitulation is little more than a change of words, if that. There are, however, one and sometimes two patterers, of acknowledged powers, who every now and then sell corn-salve—for the restlessness of this class of people drives them to incessant changes in their pursuits—and their oratory is of a higher order. One of the men in question speaks to the following purport:—

"Here you are! here you are! all that has to complain of corns. As fast as the shoemaker lames you, I'll cure you. If it wasn't for me he dursn't sing at his work; bless you, but he knows I'll make his pinching easy to you. Hard corn, soft corn, any corn—sold again! Thank you, sir, you'll not have to take a 'bus home when you've used my corn-salve, and you can wear your boots out then; you can't when you've corns. Now, in this little box you see a large corn which was drawn by this very salve from the honourable foot of the late lamented Sir Robert Peel. It's been in my possession three years and four months, and though I'm a poor man—hard corn, soft corn, or any corn—though I'm a poor man, the more's the pity, I wouldn't sell that corn for the newest sovereign coined. I call it the free-trade corn, gen'l'men and leddis. No cutting and paring, and sharpening penknives, and venturing on razors to level your corns; this salve draws them out—only one penny—and without pain. But wonders can't be done in a moment. To draw out such a corn as I've shown you, the foot, the whole foot, must be soaked five minutes in warm soap and water. That makes the salve penetrate, and draw the corn, which then falls out, in three days, like a seed from a flower. Hard corn, soft corn, &c., &c."

The corn from "the honourable foot" of Sir Robert Peel, or from the foot of any one likely to interest the audience, has been scraped and trimmed from a cow's heel, and may safely be submitted to the inspection and handling of the incredulous. "There it is," the corn-seller will reiterate—"it speaks for itself."

One practice—less common than it was, however,—of the corn-salve street-seller, is to get a friend to post a letter—expressive of delighted astonishment at the excellence and rapidity of the corn-cure—at some post-office not very contiguous. If the salve-seller be anxious to remove the corns of the citizens, he displays this letter, with the genuine post-mark of Piccadilly, St. James's-street, Pall-mall, or any such quarter, to show how the fashionable world avails itself of his wares, cheap as they are, and fastidious as are the fashionable! If the street-professional be offering his corn-cures in a fashionable locality, he produces a letter from Cheapside, or Cornhill—"there it is, it speaks for itself"—to show how the shrewd city-people, who were never taken in

THE STREET-SELLER OF GREASE-REMOVING COMPOSITION, etc.

[*From a Daguerreotype by* BEARD.]

THE LUCIFER MATCH GIRL.

From a Daguerreotype by BEARD

by street-sellers in their lives, and couldn't be, appreciated that particular corn-salve ! Occasionally, as the salve-seller is pattering, a man comes impetuously forward, and says loudly, " Here, doctor, let me have a shilling's-worth. I bought a penn'orth, and it cured one corn by bringing it right out—here the d——d thing is, it troubled me seven year—and I've got other corns, and I'm determined I'll root out the whole family of them. Come, now, look sharp, and put up a shilling's-worth." The shilling's-worth is gravely handed to the applicant as if it were not only a *bona fide*, but an ordinary occurrence in the way of business.

One corn-salve seller—who was not in town at the time of my inquiry into this curious matter—had, I was assured, "and others might have" full faith in the efficacy of the salve he vended. One of his fellow-traders said to me, " Ay, sir, and he has good reason for trusting to it for a cure ; he cured *me* of my corns, that I'm sure of ; so there can be no nonsense about it. He has a secret." On my asking this informant if he had tried his own corn-salve, he laughed, and said " No ! I'm like the regular doctors that way, never tries my own things." The same man, who had no great faith in what he sold being of any use in the cure of " corn, wart, or bunion," assured me—and I have no doubt with truth—that he had sold his remedy to persons utter strangers to him, who had told him afterwards that it had cured their corns. " False relics," says a Spanish proverb, " have wrought true miracles," and to what cause these corn-cures were attributable, it is not my business to inquire.

I had no difficulty in acquiring a knowledge of the ingredients of a street corn-salve. " Anybody," said one man, " that understands how to set about it, can get the recipe for 2*d*." Resin, 1 lb., (costing 2*d*.) ; tallow, ¼ lb. (1½*d*.) ; emerald green (1*d*.) ; all boiled together. The emerald green, I was told, was to " give it a colour." The colour is varied, but I have cited the most usual mode of preparation. Attempts have been made to give an aromatic odour to the salve, but all the perfumes within the knowledge, or rather the means, of the street-sellers, were overpowered by the resin and the tallow, " and it has," remarked one dealer, " a physicky sort of smell as it is, which answers." The quantity I have cited would supply a sufficiency of the composition for the taking of " a sovereign in penn'orths." In a week or so the stuff becomes discoloured, often from dust, and has to be re-boiled. Some of the traders illustrate the mode of applying the salve by carrying a lighted candle, and a few pieces of leather, and showing how to soften the composition and spread it on the leather. " After all, sir," said the man, who had faith in the virtues of his fellow street-trader's salve, " the regular thing, such as I sell, may do good ; I cannot say ; but it is very likely that the resin will draw the corn, just as people apply cobbler's wax, which has resin in it. The chemists will sell you something of the same sort as I do."

The principal purchasers are working men, who buy in the streets, and occasionally in the public-houses. The trade, however, becomes less and less remunerative. To take 15*s*. in a week is a good week, and to take 10*s*. is more usual ; the higher receipt is no doubt attributable to a superior patter being used, as men will give 1*d*. to be amused by this street work, without caring about the nostrum. Calculating that eight of these traders take 10*s*. weekly—so allowing for the frequent resort of the patterers to anything more attractive—we find 208*l*. expended in the streets on this salve. The profits of the seller are about the same as his receipts, for 240 pennyworths can be made out of materials costing only 4½*d*. The further outlay necessary to this street profession is a tray worth 1*s*. or 1*s*. 6*d*., but a large old backgammon board, which may be bought at the second-hand shops for 1*s*. and sometimes for 6*d*., is more frequently used by the street purveyors of corn-salve.

OF THE STREET-SELLERS OF GLASS AND CHINA CEMENT, AND OF RAZOR PASTE.

THE sale of glass and china cement is an old trade in the streets, but one which becomes less and less followed. Before the finer articles of crockeryware became cheap as they are now, it was of importance to mend, if possible, a broken dish of better quality, and of more importance to mend a china punch-bowl. Dishes, however, are now much cheaper, and china punch-bowls are no longer an indispensable part of even tavern festivity.

The sellers of this cement proclaim it as one which will " cure any china, stone, or earthenware, and make the broken parts adhere so firmly, that if you let it fall again, it will break, not at the part where it has been cemented, but at some other. Only a halfpenny, or a penny a stick." These traders sometimes illustrate the adhesive strength of the composition by producing a plate or dish which has been cemented in different places, and letting it fall, to break in some hitherto sound part. This they usually succeed in doing. For the cementing of glass the street article is now perhaps never sold, and was but scantily sold, I am informed, at any time, as the junction was always unsightly.

There are now four men who sell this cement in the streets, one usually to be found in Wilderness-row, Goswell-street, being, perhaps, the one who carries on the trade most regularly. They all make their own cement ; one of the receipts being—1 lb. shellac (5*d*.), ¼ lb. brimstone (½*d*.), blended together until it forms a thick sort of glue. This quantity makes half-a-crown's-worth of the cement for the purposes of retail. The sellers do not confine themselves to one locality, but are usually to be found in one or other of the street-markets on a Saturday night. If each seller take 5*s*. weekly (of which 4*s*. may be profit), we find 52*l*. expended yearly by street customers in this cement.

I include razor paste under this head, as sometimes, and at one time more frequently than now, the same individual sold both articles, though not at the same time.

There are twelve street-sellers of razor-paste, but they seem to prefer "working" the distant suburbs, or going on country rounds, as there are often only three in London. It is still vended, I am told, to clerks, who use it to sharpen their pen-knives, but the paste, owing to the prevalence of the use of steel pens, is now almost a superfluity, compared to what it was. It is bought also, and frequently enough in public-houses, by working men, as a means of "setting" their razors. The vendors make the paste themselves, except two, who purchase of a street-seller. The ingredients are generally fuller's earth (1*d.*), hog's lard (1*d.*), and emery powder (2*d.*). The paste is sold in boxes carried on a tray, which will close and form a sort of case, like a backgammon board. The quantity I have given will make a dozen boxes (each sold at 1*d.*), so that the profit is 7*d.* in the 1*s.*, for to the 4*d.* paid for ingredients must be added 1*d.*, for the cost of a dozen boxes. The paste is announced as "warranted to put an edge to a razor or pen-knife superior to anything ever before offered to the public." The street-sellers offer to prove this by sharpening any gentleman's pen-knife on the paste spread on a piece of soldier's old belt, which sharpening, when required, they accomplish readily enough. One of these paste-sellers, I was told, had been apprenticed to a barber; another had been a cutler, the remainder are of the ordinary class of street-sellers.

Calculating that 6 men "work" the metropolis daily, taking 2*s.* each per day (with 1*s.* 2*d.* profit), we find 187*l.* the amount of the street outlay.

OF THE STREET-SELLER OF CRACKERS AND DETONATING BALLS.

This trade, I am informed by persons familiar with it, would be much more frequently carried on by street-folk, and in much greater numbers, were it not the one which of all street callings finds the least toleration from the police. "You must keep your eyes on both corners of the street," said one man, "when you sell crackers; and what good is it the police stopping us? The boys have only to go to a shop, and then it's all right." The trade is only known in the streets at holiday seasons, and is principally carried on for a few days before and after the 5th of November, and again at Christmas-tide. "Last November was good for crackers," said one man; "it was either Guy Faux day, or the day before, I'm not sure which now, that I took 15*s.*, and nearly all of boys, for waterloo crackers and ball crackers (the common trade names), 'waterloo' being the 'pulling crackers.' At least three parts was ball crackers. I sold them from a barrow, wheeling it about as if it was hearthstone, and just saying quietly when I could, 'Six a penny crackers.' The boys soon tell one another. All sorts bought of me; doctors' boys, school boys, pages, boys as was dressed beautiful, and boys as hadn't neither shoes nor stockings. It's sport for them all." The same man told me he did well at what

he called "last Poram fair," clearing 13*s.* 6*d.* in three days, or rather evenings or nights. "Poram fair, sir," he said, "is a sort of feast among the Jews, always three weeks I've heard, afore their Passover, and I then work Whitechapel and all that way."

I inquired of a man who had carried on this street trade for a good many years, it might be ten or twelve, if he had noticed the uses to which his boy-customers put his not very innocent wares, and he entered readily into the subject.

"Why, sir," he said, "they're not all boy-customers, as you call them, but they're far the most. I've sold to men, and often to drunken men. What larks there is with the ball-crackers! One man lost his eye at Stepney Fair, but that's 6 or 7 years ago, from a lark with crackers. The rights of it I never exactly understood, but I know he lost his eye, from the dry gravel into the ball-cracker bouncing into it. But it's the boys as is fondest of crackers. I sold 'em all last Christmas, and made my 5*s.* on Boxing-day. I was sold out before 6 o'clock, as I had a regular run at last—just altogether. After that, I saw one lad go quietly behind a poor lame old woman and pull a Waterloo close behind her ear; he was a biggish boy and tidily dressed; and the old body screamed, 'I'm shot.' She turned about, and the boy says, says he, 'Does your grand-mother know you're out? It's an improper thing, so it is, for you to be walking out by yourself.' You should have seen her passion! But as she was screaming out, 'You saucy wagabone! You boys is all wagabones. People can't pass for you. I'll give you in charge, I will,' the lad was off like a shot.

"But one of the primest larks I ever saw that way was last winter, in a street by Shoreditch. An old snob that had a bulk was making it all right for the night, and a lad goes up. I don't know what he said to the old boy, but I saw him poke something, a last I think it was, against the candle, put it out, and then run off. In a minute, three or four lads that was ready, let fly at the bulk with their ball-crackers, and there was a clatter as if the old snob had tumbled down, and knocked his lasts down; but he soon had his head out— he was Irish—and he first set up a roar like a Smithfield bull, and he shouts, 'I'm kilt intirely wid the murthering pistols! Po—lice! Po—o—lice!' He seemed taken quite by surprise —for they was capital crackers—I think he couldn't have been used to bulks, or he would have been used to pelting; but how he did bellow, surely.

"I think it was that same night too, I saw a large old man, buttoned up, but seeming as if he was fine-dressed for a party, in a terrible way in the Commercial-road. I lived near there then. There was three boys afore me—and very well they did it —one of 'em throws a ball-cracker bang at the old gent's feet, just behind him, and makes him jump stunning, and the boy walks on with his hands in his pocket, as if he know'd nothing about it. Just after that another boy does the same, and then the t'other boy; and the old gent—Lord, how he swore! It was shocking in such a re-spectable man, as I told him, when he said, *I'd crackered him!* 'Me cracker you,' says I ; 'it 'ud look better if you 'd have offered to treat a poor fellow to a pint of beer with ginger in it, and the chill off, than talk such nonsense.' As we was having this jaw, one of the boys comes back and lets fly again ; and the old gent saw how it was, and he says, 'Now, if you 'll run after that lad, and give him a d——d good hiding, you shall have the beer.' 'Money down, sir,' says I, 'if you mean honour bright;' but he grumbled some-thing, and walked away. I saw him soon after, talking to a Bobby, so I made a short cut home."

At the fairs near London there is a consider-able sale of these combustibles; and they are often displayed on large stalls in the fair. They furnish the means of practical jokes to the people on their return. "After last Whitsun Greenwich Fair," said a street-seller to me, I saw a gent in a white choker, like a parson, look in at a pastry-cook's shop, as is jist by the Elephant (and Castle), a-waiting for a 'bus, I s'pose. There was an old 'oman with a red face standing near him; and I saw a lad, very quick, pin something to one's coat and the t'other's gown. They turned jist arter, and bang goes a Waterloo, and they looks savage one at another; and hup comes that in-dentical boy, and he says to the red faced 'oman, a pointing to the white choker, 'Marm, I seed him a twiddling with your gown. He done it for a lark arter the fair, and ought to stand some-thing.' So the parson, if he were a parson, walked away."

There are eight makers, I am told, who supply the street-sellers and the small shops with these crackers. The wholesale price is 4*d.* to 6*d.* a gross, the "cracker-balls" being the dearest. The retail price in the streets is from six to twelve a penny, according to the appearance and eagerness of the purchaser. Some street traders carry these com-modities on trays, and very few are stationary, except at fairs. I am assured, that for a few days last November, from 50 to 60 men and women were selling crackers in the streets, of course "on the sly." In so irregular and sur-reptitious a trade, it is not possible even to ap-proximate to statistics. The most intelligent man that I met with, acquainted, as he called it, "with all the ins and outs of the trade," calcu-lated that in November and Christmas, 100*l.* at least was expended in the streets in these com-bustibles, and another 100*l.* in the other parts of the year. About Tower-hill, Ratcliff-highway (or "the Highway," as street-sellers often call it), and in Wapping and Shadwell, the sale of crackers is the best. The sellers are the ordinary street-sellers, and no patter is required.

OF THE STREET-SELLERS OF LUCIFER-MATCHES.

UNDER this head I shall speak only of those who *sell* the matches, apart from those who, in proffer-ing lucifer boxes, mix up trade with mendicancy. The latter class I have spoken of, and shall treat of them more fully under the head of "the Lon-don Poor."

Until "lucifers" became cheap and in general use, the matches sold by the street-folks, and there were numbers in the trade, were usually prepared by themselves. The manufactures were simple enough. Wooden splints, twice or thrice the length of the lucifer matches now in use, were prepared, and dipped into brimstone, melted in an iron ladle. The matches were never, as now, self-igniting, or rather ignitable by rapid friction ; but it was necessary to "strike a light" by the concussion of a flint and steel, the sparks from which were communicated to tinder kept in a "box."

The brimstone match-sellers were of all ages, but principally, I am told, old people. Many of them during, and for some years after the war, wore tattered regimentals, or some remains of military paraphernalia, and had been, or assumed to have been, soldiers, but not entitled to a pen-sion; the same with seamen. I inquired of some of the present race of match-sellers what became of the "old brimstones," as I heard them called, but from them I could gain little inform-ation. An old groundsel-gatherer told me that some went into his trade. Others, I learned, "took to pins," and others to song or tract selling. Indeed the brimstone match-sellers not unfre-quently carried a few songs to vend with their matches. It must be borne in mind that, 15 years ago, those street trades, into which any one who is master of a few pence can now embark, were less numerous. Others of the match-sellers, with rounds, or being known men, displaced their "brimstones" for "lucifers," and traded on as usual. I heard of one old man, now dead, who made a living on brimstone-matches by selling a good quantity in Hackney, Stoke Newington, and Islington, and who long refused to sell lucifer-matches; "they was new-fangled rubbish," he said, "and would soon have their day." He found his customers, however, fall off, and in apprehension of losing them all, he was compelled to move with the times.

"I believe, sir," said one man, still a street-seller, but not having sold matches of any kind for years,—"I believe I was the first who hawked 'Congreves,' or 'instantaneous lights;' they weren't called 'lucifers' for a good while after. I bought them at Mr. Jones's light-house in the Strand, and if I remember right, for it must be more than 20 years ago, between 1820 and 1830, Mr. Jones had a patent somehow about them. I bought them at 7*s.* a dozen boxes, and sold them at 1*s.* a box. I'm not sure how many matches was in a box, but I think it was 100. You 'll get as much for a farthing now, as you would for a shilling then. The matches were lighted by being drawn quickly through sand-paper. I sold them for a twelvemonth, and had the trade all to myself. As far as I know, I had ; for I never met with or heard of anybody else in it all that time. I did decent at it. I suppose I cleared my 15*s.* a week. The price kept the same while I was in the business. I sold them at city offices. I supplied the Phœnix in Lombard-street, I remember, and the better sort of shops.

People liked them when they wanted to light a candle in a hurry, in places where there was no fire to seal a letter, or such like. There was no envelopes in them days. The penny-postage brought *them* in. I was sometimes told not to carry such things there again, as they didn't want the house set on fire by keeping such dangerous things in it. Now, I suppose, lucifers are in every house, and that there's not a tinder-box used in all London." Such appears to have been the beginning of the extensive street-trade in these chemical preparations now carried on. At the twelvemonth's end, my informant went into another line of business.

The "German Congreves" were soon after introduced, and were at first sold wholesale at the "English and German" swag-shops in Houndsditch, at 2*s.* the dozen boxes, and were retailed at 3*d.*, 4*d.*, and sometimes as high as 6*d.* the box. These matches, I am told, "kept their hold" about five years, when they ceased to be a portion of the street trade. The German Congreves were ignited by being drawn along a slip of sandpaper, at the bottom of the box, as is done at present; with some, however, a double piece of sand-paper was sold for purposes of igniting.

After this time cheaper and cheaper matches were introduced, and were sold in the streets immediately on their introduction. At first, the cheaper matches had an unpleasant smell, and could hardly be kept in a bed-room, but that was obviated, and the trade progressed to its present extent.

The lucifer-match boxes, the most frequent in the street-trade, are bought by the poor persons selling them in the streets, at the manufacturers, or at oil-shops, for a number of oilmen buy largely of the manufacturers, and can "supply the trade" at the same rate as the manufacturer. The price is 2¼*d.* the dozen boxes, each box containing 150 matches. Some of the boxes (German made) are round, and many used to be of tin, but these are rarely seen now. The prices are proportionate. The common price of a lucifer box in the streets is ½*d.*, but many buyers, I am told, insist upon and obtain three a penny, which they do generally of some one who supplies them regularly. The trade is chiefly itinerant.

One feeble old man gave me the following account of his customers. He had been in the employ of market-gardeners, carmen, and others, whose business necessitated the use of carts and horses. In his old age he was unable to do any hard work; he was assisted, however, by his family, especially by one son living in the country; he had a room in the house of a daughter, who was a widow, but his children were only working people, with families, he said, and so he sold a few lucifers "as a help," and to have the comfort of a bit of tobacco, and buy an old thing in the way of clothing without troubling any one. Out of his earnings, too, he paid 6*d.* a week for the schooling of one of his daughter's children.

"I *sell* these lucifers, sir," he said, in answer to my inquiries, "I never beg with them: I'd scorn it. My children help me, as I've told you; I did my best for them when I was able, and so I have a just sort of claim on them. Well, indeed, then, sir, as you ask me, if I had only myself to depend upon, why I couldn't live. I must beg or go into the house, and I don't know which I should take to worst at 72. I've been selling lucifers about five years, for I was worn out with hard work and rheumatics when I was 65 or 66. I go regular rounds, about 2 miles in a day, or 2½, or if it's fine 3 miles or more from where I live, and the same distance back, for I can sometimes walk middling if I can do nothing else. I carry my boxes tied up in a handkerchief, and hold 2 or 3 in my hand. I'm ashamed to hold them out on any rail where I aint known; and never do if there isn't a good-humoured looking person to be seen below, or through the kitchen window. But my eyesight aint good, and I make mistakes, and get snapped up very short at times. Yesterday, now, I was lucky in my small way. There's a gentleman, that if I can see him, I can always sell boxes to at 1*d.* a piece. That's his price, he says, and he takes no change if I offer it. I saw him yesterday at his own door, and says he, 'Well, old greybeard, I haven't seen you for a long time. Here's 1*s.*, leave a dozen boxes.' I told him I had only 11 left; but he said, 'O, it's all the same,' and he told a boy that was crossing the hall to take them into the kitchen, and we soon could hear the housekeeper grumbling quite loud—perhaps she didn't know her master could hear—about being bothered with rubbish that people took in master with; and the gentleman shouts out, 'Can't you stop that old —— mouth, will you? She wants a profit out of them in her bills.' All was quiet then, and he says to me quite friendly, 'If she wasn't the best cook in London I'd have quitted her long since, by G——.'" The old man chuckled no little as he related this; he then went on, "He's a swearing man, but a good man, I'm sure, and I don't know why he's so kind to me. Perhaps he is to others. I'm ashamed to hold my boxes to the ary rails, 'cause so many does that to beg. I sell lucifers both to mistresses and maids. Some will have 3 for a 1*d.*, and though it's a poor profit, I do it, for they say, 'O, if you come this way constant, we'll buy of you whenever we want. If you won't give 3 a penny, there's plenty will.' I sell, too, in some small streets, Lisson-grove way, to women that see me from their windows, and come down to the door. They're needle-workers I think. They say sometimes, 'I'm glad I've seen you, for it saves me the trouble of running out.'

"Well, sir, I'm sure I hardly know how many boxes I sell. On a middling good day I sell 2 dozen, on a good day 3 dozen, on a bad day not a dozen, sometimes not half-a-dozen, and sometimes, but not often, not more than a couple. Then in bad weather I don't go out, and time hangs very heavy if it isn't a Monday; for every Monday I buy a threepenny paper of a newsman for 2*d.*, and read it as well as I can with my old eyes and glasses, and get my daughter to read a bit to me in the evening, and next day I send the paper to my son in the country, and so save him buying one. As well as I can tell I sell about 9 dozen boxes a week, one week with another, and clear from 2s. to 2s. 6d. It's employment for me as well as a help."

It is not easy to estimate the precise number of persons who really sell lucifer matches as a means of subsistence, or as a principal means. There are many, especially girls and women, the majority being Irishwomen, who do not directly solicit charity, and do not even say, " Buy a box of lucifers from a poor creature, to get her a ha'porth of bread ;" or, " please a bit of broken victuals, if it 's only cold potatoes, for a box of the best lucifers." Yet these match-sellers look so imploringly down an area, or through a window, some " shouldering" a young child the while, and remain there so pertinaciously that a box is bought, or a halfpenny given, often merely to get rid of the applicant.

An intelligent man, a street-seller, and familiar with street-trading generally, whom I questioned on the subject, said : " It 's really hard to tell, sir, but I should calculate this way. It 's the real sellers you ask about ; them as tries to live on their selling lucifers, or as their main support. I have worked London and the outside places—yes, I mean the suburbs—in ten rounds, or districts, but six is better, for you can then go the same round the same day next week, and so get known. The real sellers, in my opinion, is old men and women out of employ, or past work, and to beg they are ashamed. I 've read the Bible you see, sir, though I 've had too much to do with gay persons even to go to church. I should say that in each of those ten rounds, or at any rate, splicing one with another, was twenty persons really selling lucifers. Yes, and depending a good deal upon them, for they 're an easy carriage for an infirm body, and as ready a sale as most things. I don't reckon them as begs, or whines, or sticks to a house for an hour, but them as sells ; in my opinion, they 're 200, and no more. All the others dodges, in one way or other, on pity and charity. There 's one lurk that 's getting common now. A man well dressed, and very clean, and wearing gloves, knocks at a door, and asks to speak to the master or mistress. If he succeeds, he looks about him as if he was ashamed, and then he pulls out of his coat-pocket a lucifer box or two, and asks, as a favour, to be allowed to sell one, as reduced circumstances drive him to do so. He doesn't beg, but I don't reckon him a seller, for he has always some story or other to tell, that 's all a fakement." Most dwellers in a suburb will have met with one of these well-dressed match-sellers.

Adopting my informant's calculation, and supposing that each of these traders take, on lucifers alone, but 4s. weekly, selling nine dozen (with a profit to the seller of from 1s. 9d. to 2s. 6d.), we find 2080l. expended in this way. The matches are sold also at stalls, with other articles, in the street markets, and elsewhere ; but this traffic, I am told, becomes smaller, and only amounts to one-

tenth of the amount I have specified as taken by itinerants. These street-sellers reside in all parts of town which I have before specified as the quarters of the poor.

OF THE STREET-SELLERS OF CIGAR LIGHTS, OR FUZEES.

THIS is one of the employments to which boys, whom neglect, ill-treatment, destitution, or a vagrant disposition, have driven or lured to a street life, seem to resort to almost as readily as to the offers," " Old your 'os, sir ? " Shall I carry your passel, marm ?"

The trifling capital required to enter into the business is one cause of its numbering many followers. The " fuzees," as I most frequently heard them called, are sold at the " Congreve shops," and are chiefly German made. At one time, indeed, they were announced as " German tinder." The wholesale charge is 4½d. per 1000 " lights." The 1000 lights are apportioned into fifty rows, each of twenty self-igniting matches ; and these " rows" are sold in the streets, one or two for ½d., and two, three, or four 1d. It is common enough for a juvenile fuzee-seller to buy only 500 ; so that 2¼d. supplies his stock in trade.

The boys (for the majority of the street-traders who sell *only* fuzees, are boys) frequent the approaches to the steam-boat piers, the omnibus stands, and whatever places are resorted to by persons who love to smoke in the open air. Some of these young traders have neither shoes nor stockings, more especially the Irish lads, who are at least half the number, and their apology for a cap fully displays the large red ears, and flat features, which seem to distinguish a class of the Irish children in the streets of London. Some Irish boys hold out their red-tipped fuzees with an appealing look, meant to be plaintive, and say, in a whining tone, " Spend a halfpenny on a poor boy, your honour." Others offer them, without any appealing look or tone, either in silence, or saying—" Buy a fuzee to light your pipe or cigar, sir ; a row of lights for a ½d."

I met with one Irish boy, of thirteen or fourteen years of age, who was offering fuzees to the persons going to Chalk Farm fair on Easter Tuesday, but the rain kept away many visitors, and the lad could hardly find a customer. He was literally drenched, for his skin, shining with the rain, could be seen about his arms and knees through the slits of his thin corduroy jacket and trowsers, and he wore no shirt.

" It 's oranges I sell in ginral, your honour," he said, " and it 's on oranges I hopes to be next week, plaze God. But mother—it 's orange-selling she is too—wanted to make a grand show for Aister wake, and tuk the money to do it, and put me on the fuzees. It 's the thruth I'm telling your honour. She thought I might be after making a male's mate" (meal's meat) " out of them, intirely ; but the sorra a male I 'll make to day if it cost me a fardin, for I haven't tuk one. I niver remimber any fader ; mother and me lives together somehow, glory be to God ; but it 's often knowin' what it is to be hungry we are. I 've sould fuzees before, when ingans, and nuts, and oranges was dear and not for the poor to buy, but I niver did so bad as to-day. A gintleman once said to me : ' Here, Pat, yer sowl, you look hungry. Here's a thirteener for yez; go and get drunk wid it.' Och, no, your honour, he wasn't an Irish gintleman ; it was afther mocking me he was, God save him." On my asking the boy if he felt hurt at this mockery, he answered, slily, with all his air of simplicity, "Sure, thin, wasn't there the shillin' ? For it was a shillin' he gave me, glory be to God. No, I niver heard it called a thirteener before, but mother has. Och, thin, sir, indeed, and it's could and wet I am. I have a new shirt, as was giv to mother for me by a lady, but I wouldn't put it on sich a day as this, your honour, sir. I'll go to mass in it ivery Sunday. I've made 6*d.* a day and sometimes more a sellin' fuzees, wid luck, God be praised, but the bad wither's put me out intirely this time."

The fuzee-sellers frequently offer their wares at the bars of public-houses in the daytime, and sometimes dispose of them to those landlords who sell cigars. From the best information I can command there are now upwards of 200 persons selling fuzees in the streets of the metropolis. But the trade is often collateral. The cigar-seller offers fuzees, play-bill sellers (boys) do so sometimes at the doors of the theatres to persons coming out, the pipe-sellers also carry them ; they are sometimes sold along with lucifer matches, and at miscellaneous stalls. It will, I believe, be accurate to state that in the streets there are generally 100 persons subsisting, or endeavouring to subsist, on the sale of fuzees alone. It may be estimated also that each of these traders averages a receipt of 10*d.* a day (with a profit exceeding 6*d.*), so that 1300*l.* is yearly laid out in the streets in this way.

Of the fuzee-selling lads, those who are parentless, or runaway, sleep in the lodging-houses, in the better conducted of which the master or deputy takes charge of the stock of fuzees or lucifer-matches during the night to avert the risk of fire; in others these combustibles are stowed anywhere at the discretion, or indiscretion, of the lodgers.

Of the Street-Sellers of Gutta-Percha Heads.

There are many articles which, having become cheap in the shops, find their way to the street-traders, and after a brief, or comparatively brief, and prosperous trade has been carried on in them, gradually disappear. These are usually things which are grotesque or amusing, but of no utility, and they are supplanted by some more attractive novelty—a main attraction being that it is a novelty.

Among such matters of street-trade are the elastic toys called "gutta-percha heads ;" these, however, have no gutta-percha in their composition, but consist solely of a composition made of glue and treacle—the same as is used for printer's rollers. The heads are small coloured models of the human face, usually with projecting nose and chin, and wide or distorted mouth, which admit of being squeezed into a different form of features, their elasticity causing them to return to the original caste. The trade carried on in the streets in these toys was at one time extensive, but it seems now to be gradually disappearing. On a fine day a little after noon, last week, there was not one " head" exposed for sale in any of the four great street markets of Leather-lane, the Brill, Tottenham-court-road including the Hampstead-road, and High-street, Camden-town.

The trade became established in the streets upwards of two years ago. At first, I am told by a street-seller, himself one of the first, there were six " head-sellers," who " worked" the parks and their vicinity. My informant one day sold a gross of heads in and about Hyde-park, and a more fortunate fellow-trader on the same day sold 1½ gross. The heads were recommended, whenever opportunity offered, by a little patter. " Here," one man used to say, " here's the Duke of Wellington's head for 1*d.* It's modelled from the statty on horseback, but is a improvement. His nose speaks for itself. Sir Robert Peel's only 1*d.* Anybody you please is 1*d.* ; a free choice and no favour. The Queen and all the Royal Family 1*d.* apiece." As the street-seller offered to dispose of the model of any eminent man's head and face, he held up some one of the most grotesque of the number. Another man on Saturday evening sold five or six dozen to costermongers and others in the street markets " pattering" them off as the likenesses of any policeman who might be obnoxious to the street-traders ! This was when the trade was new. The number of sellers was a dozen in the second week ; it was soon twenty-five, all confining themselves to the sale of the heads; besides these the heads were offered to the street-buying public by many of the stationary street-folk, whose stock partook of a miscellaneous character. The men carrying on this traffic were of the class of general street-sellers.

" The trade was spoiled, sir," said an informant, " by so many going into it, but I 've heard that it's not bad in parts of the country now. The sale was always best in the parks, I believe, and Sundays was the best days. I don't pretend to be learned about religion, but I know that many a time after I'd earned next to nothing in a wet week, it came a fine Sunday morning, and I took as much as got me and my wife and children a good dinner of meat and potatoes, and sometimes, when we could depend on it, smoking hot from the baker's oven ; and I then felt I had something to thank God for. You see, sir, when a man's been out all the week, and often with nothing to call half a dinner, and his wife's earnings only a few pence by sewing at home, with three young children to take care of, you 're nourished and comforted, and your strength keeps up, by a meat dinner on a Sunday, quietly in your own room. But them as eats their dinner without having to earn it, can't understand that, and as the Sunday park trade was stopped, the police drive us about like dogs, not gentlemen's dogs, but stray or mad dogs. And it seems there's some sort of a new police. I can't understand a bit of it, and I don't want to, for the old police is trouble enough."

The gutta-percha heads are mostly bought at the "English and German" swag-shops. A few are made by the men who sell them in the streets. The "swag" price is 1s. the gross; at one time the swag man demurred to sell less than half a gross, but now when the demand is diminished, a dozen is readily supplied for 8d. The street price retail, is and always was 1d. a head. The principal purchasers in the street are boys and young men, with a few tradesmen or working people, "such as can afford a penny or two," who buy the "gutta percha" heads for their children. There used to be a tolerable trade in public houses, where persons enjoying themselves bought them "for a lark," but this trade has now dwindled to a mere nothing. One of the "larks," an informant knew to be practised, was to attach the head to a piece of paper or card, write upon it some one's name, make it up into a parcel, and send it to the flattered invidual. The same man had sold heads to young women, not servant-maids he thought, but in some not very ill paid employment, and he believed, from their manner when buying, for some similar purpose of "larking." When the heads were a novelty, he sold a good many to women of the town.

There are now no street-folks who depend upon the sale of these gutta-percha heads, but they sell them occasionally. The usual mode is to display them on a tray, and now, generally with other things. One man showed me his box, which, when the lid was raised, he carried as a tray slung round his neck, and it contained gutta-percha heads, exhibition medals, and rings and other penny articles of jewellery.

There are at present, I am informed, 30 persons selling gutta-percha heads in the streets, some of them confining their business solely to those articles. In this number, however, I do not include those who are both makers and sellers. Their average receipts, I am assured, do not exceed 5s. a week each, for, though some may take 15s. a week, others, and generally the stationary head-sellers, do not take 1s. The profit to the street retailer is one third of his receipts. From this calculation it appears, that if the present rate of sale continue, 390l. is spent yearly in these street toys. At one time it was far more than twice the amount.

OF THE STREET-SELLERS OF FLY-PAPERS AND BEETLE-WAFERS.

FLY-PAPERS came, generally, into street-traffic, I am informed, in the summer of 1848.

The fly-papers are sold wholesale at many of the oil-shops, but the principal shop for the supply of the street-traders is in Whitechapel. The wholesale price is 2¼d. a dozen, and the (street) retail charge ½d. a paper, or three 1d. A young man, to whom I was referred, and whom I found selling, or rather bartering, crockery, gave me the following account of his experience of the fly-paper trade. He was a rosy-cheeked, strong-built young fellow, and said he thought he was "getting

on" in his present trade. He spoke merrily of his troubles, as I have found common among his class, when they are over.

"My father had a milk-walk," he said, "and when he died I was without money and had nothing to do, but I soon got a place with a single gentleman. He had a small house, and kept only me and a old housekeeper. I was to make myself generally useful, but when I first went, the most I had to do was to look after a horse that master had. Master never was on horseback in his life, but he took Skipjack—that was the horse's name, he was rising six—for a debt, and kept him two months, till he could sell him to his mind. Master took a largeish garden—for he was fond of growing flowers and vegetables, and made presents of them—just before poor Skipjack went, and I was set to work in it, besides do my house-work. It was a easy place, and I was wery comfable. But master, who was a good master and a friend to a poor man, as I know, got into difficulties; he was something in the City; I never understood what; and one night, when I'd been above a year and a-half with him, he told me I must go, for he couldn't afford to keep me any longer. Next day he was arrested, quite sudden I believe, and sent to prison for debt. I had a good character, but nobody cared for one from a man in prison, and in a month my money was out, and my last 3s. 6d. went for an advertisement, what was no good to me. I then took to holding horses or anything that way, and used to sleep in the parks or by the road-sides where it was quiet. I did that for a month and more. I've sometimes never tasted food all day, and used to quench myself (so he worded it) with cold water from the pumps. It took off the hunger for a time. I got to know other boys that was living as I was, and when I could afford it I slept at lodging-houses, the boys took me to or told me about. One evening a gentleman gave me 1s. for catching his horse that he'd left standing, but it had got frightened, and run off. Next morning I went into the fly-paper trade,—it's nearly two years ago, I think—because a boy I slept with did tidy in it. We bought the papers at the first shop as was open, and then got leave of the deputy of the lodging-house to catch all the flies we could, and we stuck them thick on the paper, and fastened the paper to our hats. I used to think, when I was in service, how a smart livery hat, with a cockade to it, would look, but instead of that I turned out, the first time in my life that ever I sold anything, with my hat stuck round with flies. I felt so ashamed I could have cried. I was miserable, I felt so awkerd. But I spent my last 2d. in some gin and milk to give me courage, and that brightened me up a bit, and I set to work. I went Mile-end way, and got out of the main streets, and I suppose I'd gone into streets and places where there hadn't often been fly-papers before, and I soon had a lot of boys following me, and I felt, almost, as if I'd picked a pocket, or done something to be 'shamed of. I could hardly cry 'Catch 'em alive, only a halfpenny!' But I found I could sell my papers to public-houses and shopkeepers, such as grocers and confectioners, and that gave me pluck. The boys caught flies, and then came up to me, and threw them against my hat, and if they stuck the lads set up a shout. I stuck to the trade, however, and took 2s. 6d. to 3s. every day that week, more than half of it profit, and on Saturday I took 5s. 6d. The trade is all to housekeepers. I called at open shops and looked up at the windows, or held up my hat at private houses, and was sometimes beckoned to go in and sell my papers. Women bought most, I think. 'Nasty things,' they used to say, 'there's no keeping nothing clean for them.' I stuck to the trade for near two months, and then I was worth 13s. 6d., and had got a pair of good shoes, and a good second-hand shirt, with one to change it; and next I did a little in tins and hardware, at the places where I used to go my fly rounds, and in the winter I got into the crock-trade, with another young fellow for a mate, and I'm in it yet, and getting a tidy connection, I think."

Some of the fly-paper sellers make their stock-in-trade, but three-fourths of the number buy them ready-made. The street-sellers make them of old newspapers or other waste-paper, no matter how dirty. To the paper they apply turpentine and common coach varnish, some using resin instead of varnish, and occasionally they dash a few grains of sugar over the composition when spread upon the paper.

Last summer, I was informed, there were fifty or sixty persons selling fly-papers and beetle wafers in the streets; some of them boys, and all of them of the general class of street-sellers, who "take" to any trade for which 1s. suffices as capital. Their average earnings may be estimated at 2s. 6d. a day, about one-half being profit. This gives a street outlay, say for a "season" of ten weeks, of 375l., calculating fifty sellers.

A few of these street traders carried a side of a newspaper, black with flies, attached to a stick, waving it like a flag. The cries were "Catch 'em alive! Catch 'em alive for ½d!" "New method of destroying thousands!"

Of the Street-Sellers of Miscellaneous Manufactured Articles.

In addition to the more staple wares which form the street trade in manufactured articles of a miscellaneous character, are many, as I said before, which have been popular for a while and are now entirely disused. In the course of my inquiry it was remarkable how oblivious I found many of the street-sellers as to what they had sold at various periods. "O dear, yes sir, I've sold all sorts of things in the streets besides what I'm on now; first one and then another as promised a few pence," was the substance of a remark I frequently heard; but *what* was meant by the one and the other thing thus sold they had a difficulty to call to mind, but on a hint being thrown out they could usually give the necessary details. From the information I acquired I select the following curious matter.

Six or seven years ago *Galvanic Rings* were sold extensively by the street-folk. These were clumsy lead-coloured things, which were described by the puffing shop-keepers, and in due course by the street-sellers, as a perfect amulet; a thing which by its mere contact with the finger would not only cure but prevent "fits, rheumatics, and cramps." On my asking a man who had sold them if these were all the ailments of which he and the others proclaimed the galvanic rings an infallible cure, he answered: "Like the quack medicines you read about, sir, in 'vertisements, we said they was good for anything anybody complained of or was afraid was coming on them, but we went mostly for rheumatics. A sight of tin some of the shopkeepers must have made, for what we sold at 1d. they got 6d. a piece for. Then for gold galvanics—and I've been told they was gilt—they had 10s. 6d. each. The streets is nothing to the shops on a dodge. I've been told by people as I'd sold galvanics to, that they'd had benefit from them. I suppose that was just superstitious. I think Hyams did the most of any house in galvanics."

The men selling these rings—for the business was carried on almost entirely by men—were the regular street-traders, who sell "first one thing and then another." They were carried in boxes, as I have shown medals are now, and they generally formed a portion of the street-jeweller's stock, whether he were itinerant or stationary. The purchasers were labourers in the open air, such as those employed about buildings, whose exposure to the alternations of heat and cold render them desirous of a cure for, or preventive against rheumatism. The costermongers were also purchasers, and in the course of my inquiries among that numerous body, I occasionally saw a galvanic ring still worn by a few, and those chiefly, I think, fish-sellers.

Nor was the street or shop trade in these galvanic rings confined to amulets for the finger. I heard of one elderly woman, then a prosperous street-seller in the New Cut, who slept with a galvanic ring on every toe, she suffered so much from cramp and rheumatism! There were also galvanic shields, which were to be tied round the waist, and warranted "to cure all over." They were retailed at 6d. each. Galvanic earrings were likewise a portion of this manufacture. They were not "drops" from the ear, but filled behind and around it as regards the back of the skull, and were to avert rheumatic attacks, and even aching from the head. The street price was 1s. the pair. Galvanic bracelets, handsomely gilt, were 2s. 6d. the pair. But the sale of all these highter-priced charms was a mere nonentity compared to that of the penny rings.

Another trade—if it may be classed under this head—carried on by great numbers and with great success for a while, was that of *cards with the Lord's Prayer in the compass of a sixpence*. This was an engraving—now and then offered in the streets still—strictly fulfilling the announcement as to the compass in which the Prayer was contained, with the addition of a drawing of the Bible, as part of the engraving, "within the sixpence." This trade was at first, I am told, chiefly in the hands of the patterers : " Grand novelty !" they said ; "splendid engraving ! The Lord's Prayer, with a beautiful picture of the Bible, all legible to the naked eye, in the compass of a six-pence. Five hundred letters, all clear, on a six-pence." One man said to me: "I knew very well there wasn't 500, but it was a neat number to cry. A schoolmaster said to me once—' Why, there isn't above half that number of letters.' He was wrong though ; for I believe there 's 280." This card was published six or seven years ago, and the success attending the sale of the Lord's Prayer, led to the publication of the Belief in the same form. " When the trade was new," said one man, " I could sell a gross in a day without any very great trouble ; but in a little time there was hundreds in the trade, and one might patter hard to sell four dozen."

The wholesale price was 8s. the gross, and as thirteen cards went to the dozen, the day's profit when a gross was sold was 5s. When the sale did not extend to beyond four dozen the profit was 1s. 8d. A few cards " in letters of gold " were vended in the streets at 6d. each. They had large margins and presented a handsome appearance. The wholesale price was 3s. 6d. the dozen. When this trade was at its height, there were, I am told, from 500 to 700 men, women and children engaged in it ; selling the cards both with and without other articles. The cards had also a very extensive sale in the country.

Pen-holders with glass or china handles are another commodity which appeared suddenly, about six months ago, in street commerce, and at once became the staple of a considerable traffic. These pens are eight or nine inches long, the " body," so to speak, being of solid round glass, of almost all colours, green, blue, and black predominating, with a seal (lacquered white or yellow) at the top, and a holder of the usual kind, with a steel pen at the bottom. Some are made of white pot and called " China pens," and of these some are ornamented with small paintings of flowers and leaves. These wares are German, and were first charged 9s. 6d. the gross, without pens, which were an additional 3d. at the swag-shops. The price is now 5s. the gross, the pens being the same. The street-sellers who were fortunate enough to " get a good start " with these articles did exceedingly well. The pen-holders, when new, are handsome-looking, and at 1d. each were cheap ; some few were at first retailed at 2d. One man, I am told, sold two-and-a-half gross in one day in the neighbourhood of the Bank, purchasers not seldom taking a dozen or more. As the demand continued, some men connected with the supply of goods for street sale, purchased all the stock in the swag-shops, expending about 170l., and at once raised the price to 10s. 6d. the gross. This amount the poorer street-sellers demurred to give, as they could rarely obtain a higher price than 1d. each, and 2d. for the ornamented holders, but the street-stationers (who bought, however, very sparingly) and the small shopkeepers gave the advance " as they found the glass-holders asked for." On the

whole, I am told, this forestalling was not very profitable to the speculators, as when fresh supplies were received at the " swags," the price fell.

At first this street business was carried on by men, but it was soon resorted to by numbers of poor women and children. One gentleman informed me that in consequence of reading " London Labour and the London Poor," he usually had a little talk with the street-sellers of whom he purchased any trifle ; he bought these pen-holders of ten or twelve different women and girls ; all of them could answer correctly his inquiry as to the uses of the pens; but only one girl, of fifteen or sixteen, and she hesitatingly, ventured to assert that she could write her own name with the pen she offered for sale. The street-trade still continues, but instead of being in the hands of 400 individuals—as it was, at the very least, I am assured, at one period—there are now only about fifty carrying it on itinerantly, while with the " pitched " sales-people, the glass-holders are merely a portion of the stock, and with the itinerants ten dozen a week (a receipt of 10s., and a profit of 4s. 9d.) is now an average sale. The former glass-holder sellers of the poorer sort are now vending oranges.

Shirt Buttons form another of the articles— (generally either " useful things " or with such recommendation to street-buyers as the galvanic amulets possessed)—which every now and then are disposed of in great quantities in the streets. If an attempt be made by a manufacturer to establish a cheaper shirt button, for instance, of horn, or pot, or glass, and if it prove unsuccessful, or if an improvement be effected and the old stock becomes a sort of dead stock, the superseded goods have to be disposed of, and I am informed by a person familiar with those establishments, that the swag-shopkeepers can always find customers, " for anything likely," with the indispensable proviso that it be cheap. In this way shirt buttons have lately been sold in the streets, not only by the vendors of small wares in their regular trade, but by men, lads, and girls, some of the males shirtless themselves, who sell them solely, with a continuous and monotonous cry of " Half-penny a dozen ; halfpenny a dozen." The wholesale price of the last " street lot," was 3d. the gross, or ¼d. the dozen. To clear 6d. a day in shirt buttons is " good work ;" it is more frequently 4d.

OF THE STREET-SELLERS OF WALKING-STICKS.

THE walking-sticks sold in the streets of London are principally purchased at wholesale houses in Mint-street and Union-street, Borough, and their neighbourhoods. " There 's no street-trade," said an intelligent man, " and I 've tried most that 's been, or promised to be, a living in the streets, that is so tiresome as the walking-stick trade. There is nothing in which people are so particular. The stick 's sure to be either too short or too long, or too thick or too thin, or too limp or too stiff. You would think it was a simple thing for a man to choose a stick out of a lot, but if you were with me a selling on a fine Sunday at Battersea Fields, you'd see it wasn't. O, it's a tiresome job." The trade is a summer and a Sunday trade. The best localities are the several parks, and the approaches to them, Greenwich-park included ; Hampstead Heath, Kennington Common, and, indeed, wherever persons congregate for pedestrian purposes, Battersea Fields being, perhaps, the place where the greatest Sunday trade is carried on. Some of the greater thoroughfares too, such as Oxford-street and the City-road, are a good deal frequented by the stick-sellers.

This trade—like others where the article sold is not of general consumption or primary usefulness—affords, what I once heard a street-seller call, "a good range." There is no generally recognised price or value, so that a smart trader in sticks can apportion his offers, or his charges, to what he may think to be the extent of endurance in a customer. What might be 2d. to a man who "looked knowing," might be 6d. to a man who "looked green." The common sticks, which are the "cripples," I was told, of all the sorts of sticks (the spoiled or inferior sticks) mixed with "common pines," are 15d. the dozen. From this price there is a gradual scale up to 8s. the dozen for "good polished ;" beyond that price the street-seller rarely ventures, and seldom buys even at that (for street-trade) high rate, as fourpenny and sixpenny sticks go off the best ; these saleable sticks are generally polished hazel or pine. "I've sold to all sorts of people, sir," said a stick-seller. "I once had some very pretty sticks, very cheap, only 2d. a piece, and I sold a good many to boys. They bought them, I suppose, to look like men, and daren't carry them home ; for I once saw a boy I'd sold a stick to, break it and throw it away just before he knocked at the door of a respectable house one Sunday evening. I've sold shilling sticks to gentlemen, sometimes, that had lost or broken or forgot their own. Canes there's nothing done in now in the streets; nor in 'vines,' which is the little switchy things that used to be a sort of a plaything. There's only one stickman in the streets, as far as I know—and if there was, I should be sure to know, I think—that has what you may call a capital in sticks. Only the other day I saw him sell a registered stick near Charing-cross. It was a beauty. A Bath cane, with a splendid ivory head, and a compass let into the ivory. The head screwed off, and beneath was a map of London and a Guide to the Great Exhibition. O, but he has a beautiful stock, and aint he aristocratic ! 'Ash twigs,' with the light-coloured bark on them, not polished, but just trimmed, was a very good sale, but they're not now. Why, as to what I take, it's such an uncertain trade that it's hard to say. Some days I haven't taken 6d., and the most money I ever took was one Derby day at Epsom—I wish there was more Derby days, for poor people's sakes — and then I took 30s. The most money as ever I took in London was 14s. —one Sunday, in Battersea Fields, when I had a prime cheap stock of bamboos. When I keep entirely to the stick trade, and during the sum-

mer, I may take 35s. in a week, with a profit of 15s.

The street stick-sellers are, I am assured, sometimes about 200 in number, on a fine Sunday in the summer. Of these, some are dock-labourers, who thus add to their daily earnings by a seventh day's labour ; others, and a smarter class, are the "supers" (supernumeraries) of theatres, who also eke out their pittance by Sunday toil ; porters, irregularly employed, and consequently "hard pushed to live," also sell walking-sticks on the Sundays; as do others who "cannot afford."—as a well-educated man, a patterer on paper, once said to me—"to lose a day if they were d——d for it." The usual mode of this street-trade is to carry the bundle of sticks strapped together, under the arm, and deposit the ends on the ground when a sale is to be effected. A few, however, and principally Jews, have "stands," with the walking-sticks inclosed in a sort of frame. On the Mondays there are not above a third of the number of stick-sellers there are on the Sundays ; and on the other days of the week not above a seventh, or an eighth. Calculating that for 12 weeks of the year there are every day 35 stick-sellers, each taking, on an average, 30s. a week (with a profit, individually, of about 12s.), we find 630l. expended in walking-sticks in the streets.

On clear winter days a stick-seller occasionally plies his trade, but on frosty days they are occupied in letting out skates in the parks, or wherever ponds are frozen.

OF THE STREET-SELLERS OF WHIPS, ETC.

THESE traders are a distinct class from the stick-sellers, and have a distinct class of customers. The sale is considerable; for to many the possession of a whip is a matter of importance. If one be lost or stolen, for instance, from a butcher's cart at Newgate-market, the need of a whip to proceed with the cart and horse to its destination, prompts the purchase in the quickest manner, and this is usually effected of the street-seller who offers his wares to the carters at every established resort.

The commonest of the whips sold to cart-drivers is sometimes represented as whalebone covered with gut; but the whalebone is a stick, and the flexible part is a piece of leather, while the gut is a sort of canvas, made to resemble the worked gut of the better sort of whips, and is pasted to the stock; the thong—which in the common sort is called "four-strands," or plaits—being attached to the flexible part. Some of these whips are old stocks recovered, and many are sad rubbish; but for any deceit the street-seller can hardly be considered responsible, as he always purchases at the shop of a wholesale whipmaker, who is in some cases a retailer at the same price and under the same representations as the street-seller. The retail price is 1s. each; the wholesale, 8s. and 9s. a dozen. Some of the street whip-sellers represent themselves as the makers, but the whips are almost all made in Birmingham and Walsall.

Of these traders very few are the ordinary street-sellers. Most of them have been in some

THE STREET-SELLER OF WALKING-STICKS.

[From a Daguerreotype by BEARD.]

way or other connected with the care of horses, and some were described to me as "beaten-out countrymen," who had come up to town in the hope of obtaining employment, and had failed. One man, of the last-mentioned class, told me that he had come to London from a village in Cambridgeshire, bringing with him testimonials of good character, and some letters from parties whose recommendation he expected would be serviceable to him; but he had in vain endeavoured for some months to obtain work with a carrier, omnibus proprietor, or job-master, either as driver or in charge of horses. His prospects thus failing him, he was now selling whips to earn his livelihood. A friend advised him to do this, as better than starving, and as being a trade that he understood:—

"I often thought I'd be forced to go back home, sir," he said, "and I'd have been ashamed to do't, for I *would* come to try my luck in London, and would leave a place I had. All my friends—and they're not badly off—tried to 'suade me to stop at home another year or two, but come I would, as if I must and couldn't help it. I brought good clothes with me, and they're a'most all gone; and I'd be ashamed to go back so shabby, like the prodigal's son; you know, sir. I'll have another try yet, for I get on to a cab next Monday, with a very respectable cab-master. As I've only myself, I know I can do. I was on one, but not with the same master, after I'd been six weeks here; but in two days I was forced to give it up, for I didn't know my way enough, and I didn't know the distances, and couldn't make the money I paid for my cab. If I asked another cabman, he was as likely to tell me wrong as right. Then the fares used to be shouting out, 'I say, cabby, where the h—— are you going? I told you Mark-lane, and here we are at the Minories. Drive back, sir.' I know my way now well enough, sir. I've walked the streets too long not to know it. I notice them on purpose now, and know the distances. I've written home for a few things for my new trade, and I'm sure to get them. They don't know I'm selling whips. There would be such a laugh against me among all t' young fellows if they did. Me as was so sure to do well in London!

"It's a poor trade. A carman'll bid me 6*d.* for such a whip as this, which is 4*s.* 3*d.* the half dozen wholesale. 'I have to find my own whips,' my last customer said, 'though I drives for a stunning grocer, and be d——d to him.' They're great swearers some of them. I make 7*s.* or 8*s.* in a week, for I can walk all day without tiring. I one week cleared 14*s.* Next week I made 3*s.* I *have* slept in cheap lodging-houses—but only in three: one was very decent, though out of the way; one was middling; and the t'other was a pig-sty. I've seen very poor places in the country, but nothing to it. I now pay 2*s.* a week for a sort of closet, with a bed in it, at the top of a house, but it's clean and sweet; and my landlord's a greengrocer and coal-merchant and firewood-seller;—he's a good man—and I can always earn a little against the rent with him, by

cleaning his harness, and grooming his pony—he calls it a pony, but it's over 15 hands—and greasing his cart-wheels, and mucking out his stable, and such like. I shall live there when I'm on my cab."

Other carmen's whips are 1*s.* 6*d.*, and as high as 2*s.* 6*d.*, but the great sale is of those at 1*s.* The principal localities for the trade are at the meat-markets, the "green markets," Smithfield, the streets leading to Billingsgate when crowded in the morning, the neighbourhood of the docks and wharfs, and the thoroughfares generally.

The trade in the other kind of whips is again in the hands of another class, in that of cabmen who have lost their licence, who have been maimed, and the numerous "hands" who job about stables—especially cab-horse stables—when without other employment. The price of the inferior sort of "gig-whips" is 1*s.* to 1*s.* 6*d.*, the wholesale price being from 9*s.* 6*d.* to 14*s.* 6*d.* the dozen. Some are lower than 9*s.* 6*d.*, but the cabmen, I am told, "will hardly look at them; they know what they're a-buying of, and is wide awake, and that's one reason why the profit's so small." Occasionally, one whip-seller told me, he had sold gig-whips at 2*s.* or 2*s.* 6*d.* to gentlemen who had broken their "valuable lance-wood," or "beautiful thorn," and who made a temporary purchase until they could buy at their accustomed shops. "A military gent, with mustachers, once called to me in Piccadilly," the same man stated, "and he said, 'Here, give me the best you can for half-a-crown, I've snapped my own. I never use the whip when I drive, for my horse is skittish and won't stand it, but I can't drive without one.'"

In the height of the season, two, and sometimes three men, sell handsome gig-whips at the fashionable drives or the approaches. "I have taken as much as 30*s.* in a day, for three whips," said one man, "each 10*s.*; but they were silver-mounted thorn, and very cheap indeed; that's 8 or 9 years back; people looks oftener at 10*s.* now. I've sold horse-dealers' whips too, with loaded ends. Oh, all prices. I've bought them, wholesale, at 8*s.*, a dozen, and 7*s.* 6*d.* a piece. Hunting whips are never sold in the streets now. I have sold them, but it's a good while ago, as riding whips for park gentlemen. The stocks were of fine strong lancewood—such a close grain! with buck horn handles, and a close-worked thong, fastened to the stock by an 'eye' (loop), which it's slipped through. You could hear its crack half a mile off. 'Threshing machines,' I called them."

All the whip-sellers in a large way visit the races, fairs, and large markets within 50 miles of London. Some go as far as Goodwood at the race-time, which is between 60 and 70 miles distant. On a well-thronged race-ground these men will take 3*l.* or 4*l.* in a day, and from a half to three-fourths as much at a country fair. They sell riding-whips in the country, but seldom in town.

An experienced man knew 40 whip-sellers, as nearly as he could call them to mind, by sight, and 20 by name. He was certain that on no day were there fewer than 30 in the streets, and sometimes—though rarely—there were 100. The most prosperous of the body, including their profits at races, &c., make 1*l.* a week the year through; the poorer sort from 5*s.* to 10*s.*, and the latter are three times as numerous as the others. Averaging that only 30 whip-sellers take 25*s.* each weekly (with profits of from 5*s.* to 10*s.*) in London alone, we find 2340*l.* expended in the streets in whips.

Some of the whip-sellers vend whipcord, also, to those cabmen and carters who "cord" their own whips. The whipcord is bought wholesale at 2*s.* the pound (sometimes lower), and sold at ½*d.* the knot, there being generally six dozen knots in a pound.

Another class "mend" cabmen's whips, re-thonging, or "new-springing" them, but these are street-artisans.

Of the Street-Sellers of Pipes, and of Snuff and Tobacco Boxes.

The pipes now sold in the streets and public-houses are the "china bowls" and the "comic heads." The "china-bowl" pipe has a bowl of white stone china, which unscrews, from a flexible tube or "stem," as it is sometimes called, about a foot long, with an imitation-amber mouth-piece. They are retailed at 6*d.* each, and cost 4*s.* a dozen at the swag-shops. The "comic heads" are of the clay ordinarily used in the making of pipes, and cost 16*d.* the dozen, or 15*s.* the gross. They are usually retailed at 2*d.* Some of the "comic heads" may be considered as hardly well described by the name, as among them are death's-heads and faces of grinning devils. "The best sale of the comic heads," said one man, "was when the Duke put the soldiers' pipes out at the barracks; wouldn't allow them to smoke there. It was a Wellington's head with his thumb to his nose, taking a sight, you know, sir. They went off capital. Lots of people that liked their pipe bought 'em, in the public-houses especial, 'cause, as I heerd one man —he was a boot-closer—say, ' it made the old boy a-ridiculing of hisself.' At that time—well, really, then, I can't say how long it's since—I sold little bone ' tobacco-stoppers'—they're seldom asked for now, stoppers is quite out of fashion—and one of them was a figure of ' old Nosey,' the Duke you know—it was intended as a joke, you see, sir; a tobacco-*stopper.*"

There are now nine men selling pipes, which they frequently raffle at the public-houses; it is not unusual for four persons to raffle at ½*d.* each, for a "comic head." The most costly pipes are not now offered in the streets, but a few are sold on race-courses. I am informed that none of the pipe-sellers depend entirely upon their traffic in those wares, but occasionally sell (and raffle) such things as china ornaments or table-covers, or tobacco or snuff-boxes. If, therefore, we calculate that four persons sell pipes daily the year through, taking each 25*s.* (and clearing 10*s.*), we find 260*l.* yearly expended upon the hawkers' pipes.

The snuff and tobacco-boxes disposed of by street-traders, for they are usually sold by the same individual, are bought at the swag-shops. In a matter of traffic, such as snuff-boxes, in which the "fancy" (or taste) of the purchaser is freely exercised, there are of course many varieties. The exterior of some presents a series of transverse lines, coloured, and looking neat enough. Others have a staring portrait of the Queen, or of " a young lady," or a brigand, or a man inhaling the pungent dust with evident delight; occasionally the adornment is a ruin, a farm-house, or a hunting scene. The retail price is from 4*d.* to 1*s.*, and the wholesale 3*s.* to 7*s.* 6*d.* the dozen. The Scotch boxes, called " Holyroods " in the trade, are also sold in the streets and public-houses. These are generally the "self-colour" of the wood; the better sort are lined with horn, and are, or should be, remarkable for the closeness and nice adjustment of the hinges or joints. They are sold —some I was told being German-made—at the swag-shops at 3*s.* the dozen, or 4*d.* each, to 6*s.* the dozen, or 8*d.* each. " Why, I calc'lated," said one box-seller, " that one week when I was short of tin, and had to buy single boxes, or twos, at a time, to keep up a fair show of stock, the swags got 2*s.* more out of me than if I could have gone and bought by the dozen. I once ventured to buy a very fine Holyrood; it 'll take a man three hours to find out the way to open it, if he doesn't know the trick, the joints is so contrived. But I have it yet. I never could get an offer for what it cost me, 5*s.*"

The tobacco-boxes are of brass and iron (though often called "steel"). There are three sizes: the " quarter-ounce," costing 3*s.* the dozen; the " half-ounce," 4*s.* 3*d.*; and " the ounce," 5*s.* 6*d.* the dozen, or 6½*d.* each. These are the prices of the brass. The iron, which are "sized " in the same way, are from 2*s.* to 3*s.* 6*d.* the dozen, wholesale. They are retailed at from 3*d.* to 6*d.* each, the brass being retailed at from 4*d.* to 1*s.* All these boxes are opened and shut by pressure on a spring; they are partly flat (but rounded), so as to fit in any pocket. The cigar-cases are of the same quality as the snuff-boxes (not the Holyroods), and cost, at the German swag-shops, 3*s.* 6*d.* the dozen, or 4½*d.* each. They are usually retailed, or raffled for on Saturday and Monday nights, at 6*d.* each, but the trade is a small one.

One branch of this trade, concerning which I heard many street-sellers very freely express their opinions, is the sale of "indecent snuff-boxes." Most of these traders insisted, with a not unnatural bitterness, that it would be as easy to stop the traffic as it was to stop Sunday selling in the park, but then " gentlemen was accommodated by it," they added. These boxes and cigar-cases are, for the most part, I am told, French, the lowest price being 2*s.* 6*d.* a box. One man, whose information was confirmed to me by others, gave me the following account of what had come within his own knowledge :—

" There's eight and sometimes nine persons carrying on the indecent trade in snuff-boxes and cigar-cases. They make a good bit of money, but they 're drunken characters, and often hard up. They 've neither shame nor decency; they 'll tempt lads or anybody. They go to public-houses which they know is used by fast gents that has money to spare. And they watch old and very young gents in the streets, or any gents indeed, and when they see them loitering and looking after the girls, they take an opportunity to offer a 'spicy snuff-box, very cheap.' It's a trade only among rich people, for I believe the indecent sellers can't afford to sell at all under 2s. 6d., and they ask high prices when they get hold of a green 'un; perhaps one up on a spree from Oxford or Cambridge. Well, I can't say where they get their goods, nor at what price. That's their secret. They carry them in a box, with proper snuff-boxes to be seen when its opened, and the others in a secret drawer beneath; or in their pockets. You may have seen a stylish shop in Oxford-street, and in the big window is large pipe heads of a fine quality, and on them is painted, quite beautiful, naked figures of women, and there's snuff-boxes and cigar-cases of much the same sort, but they're nothing to what these men sell. I must know, for it's not very long since I was forced, through distress, to colour a lot of the figures. I could colour 50 a day. I hadn't a week's work at it. I don't know what they make; perhaps twice as much in a day, as in the regular trade can be made in a week. I was told by one of them that one race day he took 15l. It's not every day they do a good business, for sometimes they may hawk without ever showing their boxes; but gentlemen will have them if they pay ever so much for them. There's a risk in the trade, certainly. Sometimes the police gets hold of them, but very very seldom, and it's 3 months. Or if the Vice Society takes it up, it may be 12 months. The two as does best in the trade are women; they carry great lots. They've never been apprehended, and they've been in the trade for years. No, I should say they was not women of the town. They're both living with men, but the men's not in the same trade, and I think is in no trade; just fancy men. So I've understood."

I may observe that the generality of the hawkers of indecent prints and cards are women.

There are about 35 persons selling snuff and tobacco-boxes—the greatest sale being of tobacco-boxes—and cigar-cases, generally with the other things I have mentioned. Of these 35, however, not one-half sell snuff-boxes constantly, but resort to any traffic of temporary interest in the public or street-public estimation. Some sell only in the evenings. Reckoning that 15 persons on snuff and tobacco and cigar boxes alone take 18s. weekly (clearing 7s. or 8s.), we find 692l. thus expended.

OF THE STREET-SELLERS OF CIGARS.

CIGARS, I am informed, have constituted a portion of the street-trade for upwards of 20 years, having been introduced not long after the removal of the prohibition on their importation from Cuba. It was not, however, until five or six years later that they were at all extensively sold in the streets; but the street-trade in cigars is no longer extensive, and in some respects has ceased to exist altogether.

I am told by experienced persons that the cigars first vended in the streets and public-houses were really smuggled. I say "really" smuggled, as many now vended under that pretence never came from the smuggler's hands. "Well, now, sir," said one man, "the last time I sold Pickwicks and Cubers a penny apiece with lights for nothing, was at Greenwich Fair, on the sly rather, and them as I could make believe was buying a smuggled thing, bought far freer. Everybody likes a smuggled thing." [This remark is only in consonance with what I have heard from others of the same class.] "In my time I've sold what was smuggled, or made to appear as sich, but far more in the country than town, to all sorts—to gentlemen, and ladies, and shopkeepers, and parsons, and doctors, and lawyers. Why no, sir, I can't say as how I ever sold anything in that way to an exciseman. But smuggling'll always be liked; it's sich a satisfaction to any man to think he's done the tax-gatherer."

The price of a cigar, in the earlier stages of the street-traffic, was 2d. and 3d. One of the boxes in which these wares are ordinarily packed was divided by a partition, the one side containing the higher, and the other the lower priced article. The division was often a mere trick of trade—in justification of which any street-seller would be sure to cite the precedent of shopkeepers' practices—for the cigars might be the same price (wholesale) but the bigger and better-looking were selected as "threepennies," the "werry choicest and realest Hawanners, as mild as milk, and as strong as gunpowder," for such, I am told, was the cry of a then well-known street-trader. The great sale was of the "twopennies." As the fuzees, now so common, were unknown, and lucifer matches were higher-priced, and much inferior to what they are at present, the cigar seller in most instances carried tow with him, a portion of which he kept ignited in a sort of tinder-box, and at this the smokers lighted their cigars; or the vender twisted together a little tow and handed it, ignited, to a customer, that if he were walking on he might renew his "light," if the cigar "wouldn't draw."

A cheaper cigar soon found its way into street commerce, "only a penny apiece, prime cigars;" and on its first introduction, a straw was fitted into it, as a mouth-piece. "Cigar tubes" were also sold in the streets; they were generally of bone, and charged from 2d. to 1s. each. The cigar was fitted into the tube, and they were strongly recommended on the score of economy, as "by means of this tube, any gen'l'man can smoke his cigar to half a quarter of an inch, instead of being forced to throw it away with an inch and a half left." These tubes have not for a long time been vended in the streets. I am told by a person, who himself was then engaged in the sale, that the greatest number of penny cigars ever sold in the streets in one day was on that of her Majesty's coronation (June 28, 1838). Of this he was quite positive from what he had experienced, seen, and heard.

"In my opinion," said another street-seller, "the greatest injury the street-trade in such things had was when the publicans took to selling cigars. They didn't at first, at least not generally; I 've sold cigars myself, at the bars of respectable houses, to gentlemen that was having their glass of ale with a friend, and one has said to another, 'Come, we 'll have a smoke,' and has bought a couple. O, no; I never was admitted to offer them in a parlour or tap-room; that would have interfered with the order for 'screws' (penny papers of tobacco), which is a rattling good profit, I can tell you. Indeed, I was looked shy at, from behind the bar; but if customers chose to buy, a landlord could hardly interfere. Now, it 's no go at all in such places."

One common practice among the smarter street-seller, when "on cigars," was, until of late years, and still is, occasionally at races and fairs, to possess themselves of a few really choice "weeds," as like as they could procure them to their stock-in-trade, and to smoke one of them, as they urged their traffic.

The aroma was full and delicate, and this was appealed to if necessary, or, as one man worded it, the smell was "left to speak for itself." The street-folk who prefer the sale of what is more or less a luxury, become, by the mere necessities of their calling, physiognomists and quick observers, and I have no reason to doubt the assertion of one cigar-vendor, when he declared that in the earlier stages of this traffic he could always, and most unerringly in the country, pick out the man on whose judgment others seemed to rely, and by selling him one of his choice reserve, procure a really impartial opinion as to its excellence, and so influence other purchasers. When the town trade "grew stale"—the usual term for its falling-off—the cigar-sellers had a remunerative field in many parts of the country.

In London, before railways became the sole means of locomotion to a distance, the cigar-sellers frequented the coaching-yards; and the "outsides" frequently "bought a cigar to warm their noses of a cold night," and sometimes filled their cases, if the cigar-seller chanced to have the good word of the coachman or guard.

The cigar street-trade was started by two Jews, brothers, named Benasses, who were "licensed to deal in tobacco," and vended good articles. When they relinquished the open-air business, they supplied the other street-sellers, whose numbers increased very rapidly. The itinerant cigar-vending was always principally in the hands of the Jews, but the general street-traders resorted to the traffic on all occasions of public resort,—"such times," observed one, "as fairs and races, and crownations, and Queen's weddings; I wish they came a bit oftener for the sake of trade." The manufacture of the cigars sold at the lowest rates, is now almost entirely in the hands of the Jews, and I am informed by a distinguished member of that ancient faith, that when I treat of the Hebrew children, employed in *making* cigars, there

will be much to be detailed of which the public have little cognisance and little suspicion.

The cigars in question are bought (wholesale) in Petticoat-lane, Rosemary-lane, Ailie-street, Tenter-ground, in Goodman's-fields, and similar localities. The kinds in chief demand are Pickwicks, 7s. and 8s. per lb.; Cubas, 8s. 6d.; common Havannahs and Bengal Cheroots, the same price; but the Bengal Cheroots are not uncommonly smuggled.

"The best places for cigar-selling," one man stated, "I 've always found to be out of town; about Greenwich and Shooter's Hill, and to the gents going to Kensington Gardens, and such like places. About the Eagle Tavern, too, as well as the streets leading to the Surrey Zoological —one could whisper, 'cheap cigar, sir, half what they 'll charge you inside.' I 've known young women treat their young men to cigars as they were going to Cremorne, or other public places; but there 's next to no trade that way now, and hasn't been these five or six years. I don't know what stopped it exactly. I 've heard it was shop-keepers that had licences, complaining of street people as hadn't, and so the police stopped the trade as much as they could."

At all the neighbouring races and fairs, and at any great gathering of people in town, cigars are sold, more with the affectation than the reality of its being done, "quite on the sly." The retail price is 1d. each, and three for 2d. Some of the cheap cigars are made to run 200, and even as high as 230 to the pound. A fuzee is often given into the bargain.

I am told that, on all favourable opportunities, there are still 100 persons who vend cigars in the streets of London, while a greater number of "London hands" carry on the trade at Epsom and Ascot races. At other periods the business is all but a nonentity. To clear 1l. a week is considered "good work." At one period, on every fine Sunday, there were not, I was assured, fewer than 500 persons selling cigars in the open air in London and its suburbs.

OF THE STREET-SELLERS OF SPONGE.

THIS is one of the street-trades which has been long in the hands of the Jews, and, unlike the traffic in pencils, sealing-wax, and other articles of which I have treated, it remains so principally still.

In perhaps no article which is a regular branch of the street-trade, is there a greater diversity in the price and quality than in sponge. The street-sellers buy it at 1s. (occasionally 6d.), and as high as 21s. the pound. At one time, I believe about 20 years back, when fine sponge in large pieces was scarce and dear, some street-sellers gave 28s. the pound, or, in buying a smaller quantity, 2s. an ounce.

"I have sold sponge of all sorts," said an experienced street-seller, "both 'fine toilet,' fit for any lady or gentleman, and coarse stuff not fit to groom a ass with. That very common sponge is mostly 1s. the lb. wholesale, but it 's no manner of use, it 's so sandy and gritty. It weighs heavy, or there might be a better profit on it. It has to be trimmed up and damped for showing it, and then it always feels hask (harsh) to the hand. It rubs to bits in no time. There was a old gent what I served with sponges, and he was very perticler, and the best customer I ever had, for his housekeeper bought her leathers of me. Like a deal of old coves that has nothing to do and doesn't often stir out, but hidles away time in reading or pottering about a garden, he was fond of a talk, and he'd give me a glass of something short, as if to make me listen to him, for I used to get fidgety, and he'd talk away stunning. He's dead now. He's told me, and more nor once, that sponges was more of a animal than a wegetable," continued the incredulous street-seller, " I do believe people reads theirselves silly. Such —— nonsense ! Does it look like a animal ? Where's its head and its nose? He'd better have said it was a fish. And it's not a wegetable neither. But I'll tell you what it is, sir, and from them as has seen it where its got with their own eyes. I have some relations as is seafarin'-men, and I went a woyage once myself when a lad—one of my relations has seen it gathered by divers, I forget where, from the rocks at the bottom and shores of the sea, and he says it 's just seamoss—stuff as grows there, as moss does to old walls in England. That's what it is, sir. As it's grown in the water, it holds water you see. I've made 15s. on sponge alone, in a good week, when I had a good stock; but oftener I've made only 10s., and sometimes not 5s. My best trade is at private houses a little ways out of town. I've heard gents say, ' A good sponging 's as good as a bath,' and when I could get good things cheap they'd be sure to sell. No, I never did much at the mews."

Another man told me that he once bought a large quantity of sponge at 6d. the lb., trimmed it up as well as he could, and got a man to help him, and the two " worked it off" in barrows ; there was six barrows full, and as one was empted it was replenished. It was sold at 1d. and 2d. a lump; about twenty lumps, or pieces, going to a pound, so that there was 14d. profit on what cost 6d., even on the penny lumps. He had forgotten the exact amount he cleared, and he and his mate sold it all in one summer's evening, but it was somewhere about 10s. This happened some years ago, when the common sponge, which I heard called also "honeycomb" sponge, was not so " blown upon," as my informant expressed it, as it is now. On my asking this man as to the proportion of Jews in this trade, he answered : " Well, many a day I 'm satisfied there 's 100 people selling sponge, and I should say that for every ten or twelve Jews is one Christian, and half of them, or more, has been in some sort of service, I mean the Christians has, most likely stable-helpers, and they supplies the mews and the job and livery stables, such of them as requires men to find their own sponges, but that's only a few ; sponges is mostly bought for such places at the saddlers' and other shops. In my opinion, sir, Jews is better Christians than

Christians themselves, for *they* help one another, and we don't. I've been helped by a Jew myself, without any connection with them. They 're terrible keen hands at a bargain, though."

The sponge in the street-trade is purchased, wholesale, chiefly in Houndsditch. The wholesale trade in sponge, I may add, is also in the hands of the Jews. The great mart is Smyrna, the best qualities being gathered in the islands of the Greek Archipelago. The sponge is carried by the street-traders in baskets, the bearer holding a specimen piece or two in his hand. Smaller pieces are sometimes carried in nets, and nets were more frequently in use for this purpose than at present. It is nearly all sold by itinerants, in the business parts as well as the suburbs, the purchasers being "shopkeepers, innkeepers, gentlemen, and gentlemen's servants." Sometimes low-priced sponge is offered in a street-market on a Saturday or Monday night, but very rarely, as it is a thing little used by the poor. A little is sold to the cabmen at their stands. The sponge-sellers, I may add, when going a regular round, offer their wares to any passer-by. A little is done by the Jews in bartering sponge for old clothes. There are five or six women in the trade.

I have reason to believe that the estimate of my informant, as to the number of sponge-sellers, is correct. But some sell sponge only occasionally, some make it only a portion of their business, and others vend it only when they " have it a bargain." Calculating, then, that only fifty persons (so allowing for the irregularities in the trade) vend sponge daily, and that each takes 15s. weekly,— some taking 25s., and others but 5s.—with about half profit on the whole (the common sponge is often from 200 to 300 per cent. profit), we find the outlay to be 1850l.

OF THE STREET-SELLERS OF WASH-LEATHERS.

THE wash-leathers, sometimes called " shammys " (chamois), now sold extensively in the streets, are for the most part the half of a sheep-skin, or of a larger lamb-skin. The skin is " split " by machinery, and to a perfect nicety, into two portions. That known as the " grain " (the part to which the fleece of the animal is attached) is very thin, and is dressed into a " skiver," a kind of leather used in the commoner requirements of bookbinding, and for such purposes as the lining of hats. The other portion, the " flesh," is dressed as wash-leather. These skins are bought at the leather-sellers and the leather-dressers, at from 2s. to 20s. the dozen. The higher priced, or those from 12s. are often entire, and not " split " skins. The great majority of the street-sellers of wash-leathers are women, and principally Irishwomen. They offer their wash-leathers in all parts of town, calling at shops and inns ; and at private houses offering them through the area rails, or knocking at the door when it is accessible. Many of these street-sellers are the wives of Irish labourers, employed by bricklayers and others, who are either childless, or able to leave their younger children under the care of an older brother or sister, or when the poverty of the parents, or their culpable neglect, is extreme, allow them to run at large in the court or street, untended. The wives by this street-trade add to the husbands' earnings. In the respects of honesty and chastity, these women bear good characters.

The wash-leathers are sold for the cleaning of windows, and of plate and metal goods. Sixpence is a common price for a leather, the higher priced being sold at the mews and at gentlemen's houses. The "chamois" sold at the mews, however, are not often sold by the Irishwomen, but by the class I have described as selling scissors, &c., there. The leathers are also cut into pennyworths, and these pennyworths are sometimes sold on Saturday evenings in the street-markets.

There are, I am assured, 100 individuals selling little or nothing else but wash-leathers (for these traders are found in all the suburbs) in London, and that they take 10s. weekly, with a profit of from 4s. to 5s. There are, also, 100 other persons selling them occasionally, along with other goods, and as they vend the higher-priced articles, they probably receive nearly an equal amount. Hence it would appear that upwards of 5000l. is annually expended in the streets in this purchase.

OF THE STREET-SELLERS OF SPECTACLES AND EYE-GLASSES.

TWENTY-FIVE years ago the street-trade in spectacles was almost entirely in the hands of the Jews, who hawked them in their boxes of jewellery, and sold them in the streets and public-houses, carrying them in their hands, as is done still. The trade was then far more remunerative that it is at the present time to the street-folk carrying it on. "People had more money then," one old spectacle-seller, now vending sponges, said, "and there wasn't so many forced to take to the streets, Irish particularly, and opticians' charges were higher than they are now, and those who wanted glasses thought they were a take-in if they wasn't charged a fair price. O, times was very different then."

The spectacles in the street-trade are bought at swag-shops in Houndsditch. The "common metal frames," with or without slides, are 2s. 6d. to 3s. 6d. the dozen wholesale, and are retailed from 4d. to 1s. The "horn frames" are 6s. to 7s. 6d. the dozen, and are retailed from 9d. to 18d., and even 2s. The "thin steel" are from 10s. 6d. to 21s. the dozen, and are retailed from 1s. 6d. to 3s. There are higher and lower prices, but those I have cited are what are usually paid by the street-traders. The inequality of the retail prices is accounted for by there being some difference in the spectacles in a dozen, some being of a better-looking material in horn or metal; others better finished. Then there is the chance of which street-sellers are not slow to avail themselves— ("no more nor is shopkeepers," one man said) —I mean, the chance of obtaining an enhanced price for an article, with whose precise value the buyer is unacquainted.

"The patter," said the street-trader I have before quoted, "is nothing now, to what I've known it. You call it patter, but I don't. I think it's more in the way of persuasion, and is mostly said in public-houses, and not in the streets. Why, I've persuaded people, when I was in the trade and doing well at it—for that always gives you spirits—I've persuaded them in spite of their eyes that they wanted glasses. I knew a man who used to brag that he could talk people blind, and then they bought! It wasn't old people I so much sold to as young and middle-aged. I think perhaps I sold as many because people thought they looked better, or more knowing in them, than to help their eyesight. I've known my customers try my glasses, one pair after another, in the chimney glass of a public-house parlour. 'They're real Scotch pebbles,' I used to say sometimes—and I always had a fair article,—' and was intended for a solid silver frame but the frame was made too small for them, and so I got them and put them into this frame myself, for I'm an optician, out of work, by trade. They're worth 15s., but you may have them, framed and all, for 7s. 6d.' I got 5s. for one pair once that way but they were a superior thing; I had them a particular bargain." One man told me that not long ago he asked 10d. for a pair of spectacles, and a journeyman slop-tailor said to him, "Why I only gave 1s. for this pair I'm wearing a few years back, and they ought to be less than 10d. now, for the duty's off glass."

The eye-glasses sold in the streets are "framed" in horn. They are bought at the same places as the spectacles, and cost, wholesale, for "single eyes" 4s. 6d. to 7s. 6d. the dozen. The retail price is from 6d. to 1s. The "double eyes," which are jointed in the middle so that the frame can be fitted to the bridge of the nose, are 10s. 6d. to 15s. the dozen, and are retailed by the street-folk from 1s. 3d. to 2s. each.

The spectacles are sold principally to working men, and are rarely hawked in the suburbs. The chief sale is in public-houses, but they are offered in all the busier thoroughfares and wherever a crowd is assembled. "The eye-glasses," said a man who vended them, "is sold to what I calls counter-hoppers and black-legs. You'll see most of the young swells that's mixed up with gaming concerns at races—for there's gaming still, though the booths is put down in many places—sport their eye-glasses; and so did them as used to be concerned in getting up Derby and St. Leger 'sweeps' at public-houses; least-ways I've sold to them, where sweeps was held, and they was busy about them, and offered me a chance, sometimes, for a handsome eye-glass. But they're going out of fashion, is eye-glasses, I think. The other day I stood and offered them for nearly five hours at the foot of London-bridge, which used to be a tidy pitch for them, and I couldn't sell one. All that day I didn't take a halfpenny."

There are sometimes 100 men, the half of whom are Jews and Irishmen in equal proportions, now selling spectacles and eye-glasses. Some of these traders are feeble from age, accident, continued sickness, or constitution, and represent that they must carry on a "light trade," being incapable of hard work, even if they could get it. Two women sell spectacles along with Dutch drops. As in other "light trades," the spectacle sellers do not, as a body, confine themselves to those wares, but resort, as one told me, "to any-thing that's up at the time and promises better," for a love of change is common among those who pursue a street life. It may be estimated, I am assured, that there are thirty-five men (so allowing for the breaks in regular spectacle selling) who vend them daily, taking 15s. a week (with a profit of 10s.), the yearly expenditure being thus 1365l.

OF THE STREET-SELLERS OF DOLLS.

THE making of dolls, like that of many a thing required for a mere recreation, a toy, a pastime, is often carried on amidst squalor, wretchedness, or privation, or—to use the word I have frequently heard among the poor—"pinching." Of this matter, I shall have to treat when I proceed to consider the manufacture of and trade in dolls generally, not merely as respects street-sale.

Dolls are now so cheap, and so generally sold by open-air traders whose wares are of a miscel-laneous character, as among the "swag-barrow" or "penny-a-piece" men of whom I have treated separately, that the sale of what are among the most ancient of all toys, as a "business of itself," is far smaller, numerically, than it was.

The dolls are most usually carried in baskets by street-sellers (who are not makers) and gene-rally by women who are very poor. Here and there in the streets most frequented by the patrons of the open-air trade may be seen a handsome stall of dolls of all sizes and fashions, but these are generally the property of makers, although those makers may buy a portion of their stock. There are also smaller stalls which may present the stock of the mere seller.

The dolls for street traffic may be bought at the swag-shops or of the makers. For the little armless 1d. dolls the maker charges the street-seller 8s., and to the swag-shop keeper who may buy largely, 7s. 6d. the dozen. Some little stalls are composed entirely of penny dolls; on others the prices run from 1d. to 6d. The chief trade, how-ever, among the class I now describe, is carried on by the display of dolls in baskets. If the vendor can only attract the notice of children—and more especially in a private suburban residence, where children are not used to the sight of dolls on stalls or barrows, or in shops—and can shower a few blessings and compliments, "God be wid your bhutiful faces thin—and yours too, my lady, ma'am (with a curtsey to mistress or maid). Buy one of these dolls of a poor woman : shure they 're bhutiful dolls and shuted for them angels o' the worruld ;" under such circumstances, I say, a sale is almost certain. I may add that the words I have given I myself heard a poor Irishwoman, whom I had seen before selling large pincushions

in the same neighbourhood (that of the Regent's Park), address to a lady who was walking round her garden accompanied by two children.

A vendor of dolls expresses an opinion that as long as ever there are children from two years old to ten, there will always be purchasers of dolls ; " but for all that," said he, " somehow or another 't is nothing of a trade to what it used to be. I 've seen the time when I could turn out in the morn-ing and earn a pound afore night ; but it 's dif-ferent now there 's so many bazaars, and so many toy shops that the doll hawker hasn't half the chance he used to have. Sartinly we gets a chance now and then—fine days is the best—and if we can get into the squares or where the children walks with their nurses, we can do tidy ; but the police are so very particular there's not much of a livelihood to be got. Spoiled children are our best customers. Whenever we sees a likely customer approaching—we, that is, those who know their business—always throw ourselves in the way, and spread out our dolls to the best advantage. If we hears young miss say *she will* have one, and cries for it, we are almost sure of a customer, and if we see her kick and fight a bit with the nuss-maid we are sure of a good price. If a child *cries well* we never baits our price. Most of the doll-sellers are the manufacturers of the dolls—that is, I mean, they puts 'em together. The heads are made in Hamburgh ; the principal places for buying them in London are at Alfred Davis's, in Houndsditch ; White's, in Houndsditch ; and Joseph's, in Leadenhall-street. They are sold as thus :—The heads that we sell for 3d. each, when made up, cost us 7s. 6d. per gross, or 7½d. per dozen ; these are called 1—O's. No. 2— O's., are 8s. 6d. per gross, and No. 3—O's. 10s. per gross. One yard and half of calico will make a dozen bodies, small size. These we get sewn for three halfpence, and we stuffs and finishes them ourselves.

"When our 3d. dolls are made up, they cost about 1s. per dozen—so there is 2d. profit on every doll, which I thinks is little enough ; but we often sells 'em at 2d. ; we lays 'em out to the best advantage in a deep basket, all standing up, as it were, or leaning against the sides of the basket. The legs and bodies is carefully wrapped in tissue paper, not exactly to preserve the lower part of the doll, for that isn't so very valuable, but in reality to conceal the legs and body, which is rather the reverse of symmetrical ; for, to tell the truth, every doll looks as if it were labouring under an attack of the gout. There are, however, some very neat articles exported from Germany, especially the jointed dolls, but they are too dear for the street-hawker, and would not show to such advantage. There is also the plaster dolls, with the match legs. I wonder how they keep their stand, for they are very old-fashioned ; but they sell, for you never see a chandler's shop window without seeing one of these sticking in it, and a falling down as if it was drunk. Then there 's the wax dolls. Some of 'em are made of wax, and others of '*pappy mashy*,' and afterwards dipped in wax. The cheapest and best mart for these is in Barbican; it would astonish many if they knew exactly what was laid out in the course of a year in dolls. It would be impossible, I think, to ascertain exactly; but I think I could guess something near the mark. There are, at least, at this time of year, when the fairs are coming on, fifty doll-hawkers, who sell nothing else. Say each of these sells one dozen dolls per day, and that their average price is 4d. each. That is just 10l. a day, and 60l. per week. In the winter time so many are not sold; but I have no doubt that 50l.'s worth of dolls are sold each week throughout the year by London hawkers alone, or just upon 3000l. per annum. The shops sell as many as the hawkers, and the stalls attending fairs half the amount; and you may safely say that the sum taken for dolls in and around London in one year amounts to 7500l. A doll-merchant can begin business with a trifle," continued my informant; "a shilling will obtain a dozen 3d. dolls. If you have no basket, carry them in your arms, although they don't show off to such advantage there as they do when nicely basketed; however, if you 've luck, you may soon raise a basket; for 3s. 6d. you can get a very nice one; and although the doll trade is not what it used to be, there are," said my informant, "worse games than that yet, I know. One man, who is now in a very respectable way of business —' a *regular gentleman'*—was a very few years ago only a doll-hawker. Another man, who had two hands and only one arm—poor fellow! he was born with one arm, and had two hands, one appended to his arm in the usual way, and the other attached to his shoulder—a freak of nature, I think, they called it. However, my one-armed friend keeps now a very respectable little swag-shop at North Shields, in Northumberland."

I inquired of my informant whether he objected to relate a little of his history? He replied, "not the least," and recounted as follows:—

"They call me *Dick the Dollman.* I was, I believe, the first as ever cried dolls three a shilling in the streets. Afore I began they al'ays stood still with 'em; but I cried 'em out same as they do mackrel; that is twenty years ago. I wasn't originally a doll-seller. My father was a pensioner in Greenwich College. My mother used to hawk, and had a licence. I was put to school in St. Patrick's-school, Lanark's-passage, where I remained six years, but I didn't learn much. At thirteen years of age I was apprenticed to a brush and broom maker's, corner of C—— Street, Spitalfields. My master was not the honestest chap in the world, for he bought hair illegal, was found out, and got transported for seven years. A man who worked for my master took me to finish my apprenticeship; this man and his wife were very old people. I used to work four days in the week, two for them and two for myself; the other two days I went out hawking brooms and brushes, and very often would earn 7s. or 8s. on a Saturday, but times was better then than they are now. Arter that, for sake of gain, I left the old people, and I was offered 20s. to make and hawk; and in course I took it. I remained with this master five months; he was afflicted with rheumatic fever—

went into the hospital—and I was left to shift for myself. When my master went to the hospital I had 7s. 6d. in my pocket; I knew I *must* do something, and, to tell you the truth, I didn't like the brush-making; I would rather have hawked something without the trouble of making it. I think *now* I was a little afflicted with laziness. I was passing London-bridge and saw a man selling Marshall's pocket-books; I knowed him afore; I thought I should like to try the pocket-book selling, and communicated my wishes to the man; he told me they cost eight shillings a dozen, if I liked we would purchase a dozen a'twixt us; we did so; I received half a dozen, but I afterwards learned that my friend obtained seven for his share, as they were sold thirteen to the dozen. I went to Chancery-lane with my lot and was very lucky; I sold the six books to one gentleman for six shillings: in course I soon obtained another supply; that day I sold four dozen, and earned 20s. I was such a good seller that Marshall let me have 3l. or 4l.'s worth on credit—*and I never paid him.* I know that was wrong now; but I was such a foolish chap, and used to spend my money as fast as I got it. I would have given Marshall a shilling the other day if I had had one, for I see him selling penny books in the street. I thought it was hard lines, and had been such a gentleman too. Somerset-house corner was a capital stand for selling pocket-books. The way I took to the dolls was this; I met a girl with a doll basket one day as I was standing at Somerset-house corner; she and I got a talking. 'Will you go to the ' Delphy to night?' says I; she consented. They was a playing Tom and Jerry at this time, all the street-sellers went to see it, and other people; and nice and crabbed some on 'em was. Well, we goes to the 'Delphy—and I sees her often arter that, and at last gets married. She used to buy her dolls ready made; I soon finds out where to get the heads—and the profits when we made them ourselves was much greater. We began to serve hawkers and shops; went to Bristol—saved 47l.—comes to London and spends it all; walks back to Bristol, and by the time we got there we had cleared more than 20l. We were about a month on the journey, and visited Cheltenham and other towns. We used to spend our money very foolishly; we were too fond of what was called getting on the spree. You see we might have done well if we had liked, but we hadn't the sense. My wife got very clever at the dolls and so did I. Then I tried my hand at the wax dolls, and got to make them very well. I paid a guinea to learn.

"I was selling wax-dolls one day in London, and a gentleman asked me if I could mend a wax figure whose face was broken. I replied, yes, for I had made a few wax heads, large size, for some showmen. I had made some murderers who was hung; lately I made Rush and Mr. and Mrs. Manning; but the showmen can't afford to get new heads now-a-days, so they generally makes one head do for all; sometimes they changes the dress. Well, as I was telling you, I went with this gentleman, and proposed that he should have a new head cast, for the face of the figure was so much broken. It was Androcles pulling the thorn out of the lion's foot, and was to be exhibited. I got 20s. for making the new head. The gentleman asked me if I knew the story about Androcles. Now I had never heard on him afore, but I didn't like to confess my ignorance, so I says 'yes;' then he offers me 30s. a week to describe it in the Flora Gardens, where it was to be exhibited. I at once accepted the engagement; but I was in a bit of a fix, for I didn't know what to say. I inquired of a good many people, but none on 'em could tell me; at last I was advised to go to Mr. Charles Sloman—you know who I mean—him as makes a song and sings it directly; I was told he writes things for people. I went, and he wrote me out a patter. I asked him how much he charged; he said, ' Nothing my man.' Sartinly he wasn't long a-doing it, but it was very kind of him. I got what Mr. Sloman wrote out for me printed, and this I stuck inside my hat; the people couldn't see it, though I dare say they wondered what I was looking in my hat about. However, in a week or so, I got it by heart, and could speak it well enough. After exhibiting Androcles I got an engagement with another waxwork show—named Biancis—and afterwards at other shows. I was considered a very good doorsman in time, but there's very little to be got by that now; so we keeps to the dolly business, and finds we can get a better living at that than anything else. Me and the old woman can earn 1l. a week, bad and all as things are; but we're obliged to hawk."

OF THE "SWAG-BARROWMEN," AND "LOT-SELLERS."

THE "swag" (miscellaneous) barrow is one of the objects in the streets which attracts, perhaps more readily than any other, the regards of the passer-by. There are so many articles and of such various uses; they are often so closely packed, so new and clean looking, and every here and there so tastefully arranged, that this street-trader's barrow really repays an examination. Here are spread on the flat part of the barrow, pepper-cruets or boxes, tea-caddies, nutmeg-graters, vinegar-cruets, pen-cases, glass or china-handled pens, pot ornaments, beads, ear-rings, finger-rings (plain or with "stones"), cases of scent-bottles, dolls, needle-cases, pincushions, Exhibition medals and "frames" (framed pictures), watches, shawl-pins, extinguishers, trumpets and other toys, kaleidoscopes, seals, combs, lockets, thimbles, bone tooth-picks, small playing-cards, teetotums, shuttle-cocks, key-rings, shirt-studs or buttons, hooks and eyes, coat-studs, money-boxes, spoons, boxes of toys, earthenware-mugs, and glass articles, such as salt-cellars and smelling-bottles. On one barrow were 225 articles.

At the back and sides of the swag-barrow are generally articles which are best displayed in an erect position. These are children's wooden swords, whips, climbing monkeys, and tumblers, jointed snakes twisting to the wind from the top of a stick, kites, and such things as tin egg-holders.

Perhaps on very few barrows or stalls are to be seen *all* the articles I have enumerated, but they are all "in the trade," and, if not found in this man's stock, may be found in his neighbour's. Things which attain only a temporary sale, such as galvanic rings, the Lord's Prayer in the compass of a sixpence, gutta-percha heads, &c., are also to be found, during the popular demand, in the miscellaneous trader's stock.

Each of the articles enumerated is retailed at 1d. "Only a penny!" is the cry, "pick 'em out anywhere; wherever your taste lies; only a penny, a penny, a penny!" But on a few other barrows are goods, mixed with the "penny" wares, of a higher price; such as knives and forks, mustard pots, sham beer glasses (the glasses which appear to hold beer frothing to the brim), higher-priced articles of jewellery, skipping-ropes, drums, china ornaments, &c. At these barrows the prices run from 1d. to 1s.

The practice of selling by commission, the same as I have shown to prevail among the costers, exists among the miscellaneous dealers of whom I am treating, who are known among street-folk as "swag-barrowmen," or, in the popular ellipsis, "penny swags;" the word "swag" meaning, as I before showed, a collection—a lot.

The "swag-men" are often confounded with the "lot-sellers"; so that I proceed to show the difference.

The *Lot-Sellers* proper, are those who vend a variety of small articles, or "a lot," all for 1d. A "lot" frequently consists of a sheet of songs, a Chinese puzzle, a 5l. note (Bank of Elegance), an Exhibition snuff-box (containing 6 spoons), a half jack (half sovereign), a gold ring, a silver ring, and a chased keeper with rose, thistle, and shamrock on it. The lots are diversified with packs of a few cards, little pewter ornaments, boxes of small wooden toys, shirt-buttons, baby thimbles, beads, tiny scent bottles, and such like.

The "penny apiece" or "swag" trade, as contradistinguished from the "penny lots" vended by the lot-sellers, was originated by a man who, some 19 years ago, sold a variety of trifles from a tea-tray in Petticoat-lane. My informant had heard him say—for the original "penny apiece" died four years ago—that he did it to get rid of the odds and ends of his stock. The system, however, at once attracted popularity, and the fortunate street-seller prospered and "died worth money." At that period penny goods (excepting such things as sweet-stuffs, pastry, &c.) were far less numerous in the streets, and yet I have never met with an old street-trader (a statement fully borne out by old and intelligent mechanics) who did not pronounce spare pennies to be far more abundant in those days among the poorer and even middle classes. There were, moreover, far fewer street chapmen, so that this novel mode of business had every chance to thrive.

The origin of "lot-selling," or selling "penny lots" instead of penny articles, was more curious. It was commenced by an ingenious Swiss (?)

(about a year after the "penny apiece" trade), known in the street circles as "Swede." He was a refugee, a Roman Catholic, and¹ a hot politician. He spoke and understood English well, but had no sympathy with the liberal parties in this country. "He was a republican," he would say, "and the Chartists were only milk and water." When he established his lot-selling he used to place to his mouth an instrument, which was described to me as "like a doubled card," and play upon it very finely. This would attract a crowd, and he would then address them in good English, but with a slight foreign accent : " My frents ; come to me, and I will show you my musical instruments, which will play Italian, Swiss, French, Scotch, Irish, or any tunes. And here you see beautiful cheap lots of useful tings, and elegant tings. A penny a lot, a penny a lot !" The arrangement of the "lots" was similar to what it is at present, but the components of the pennyworth were far less numerous. This man carried on a good trade in London for two or three years, and then applied his industry to a country more than a town career. He died about five or six years ago, at his abode in Fashion-street, Spitalfields, "worth money." At the time of his decease he was the proprietor of two lodging-houses; one in Spitalfields, the other in Birmingham, both I am told, well conducted ; the charge was 4*d.* a night. He did not reside in either, but employed "deputies." I may observe that he sold his " musical instruments," also, at 1*d.* each, but the sale was insignificant. " Only himself seemed master of 'em," said one man ; "with other people they were no better nor a Jew's-harp."

Of the " penny apiece " street-vendors, there are about 300 in London ; 250 having barrows, and 50 stalls or pitches on the ground. Some even sell at "a halfpenny apiece," but chiefly to get rid of inferior wares, or when "cracked up," and unable to "spring" a better stock. The barrows are 7 feet by 3 ; are well built in general, and cost 50*s.* each. These barrows, when fully stocked, are very heavy (about 4 cwt.), so that it requires a strong man to propel one any distance, and though occasionally the man's wife officiates as the saleswoman, there is always a man connected with the business. In my description of a stock of penny goods, I have mentioned that there were 225 articles ; these were counted on a barrow in a street near the Brill—but probably on another occasion (when there appeared a better chance of selling) there might be 500 articles, such things as rings and the like admitting of being stowed by the hundred in very small compass. The great display, however, is only on the occasion of holidays, or "when a man starts and wants to stun you with a show." At Maidstone Fair the other day, a London street-seller, rather well to do, sold his entire stock of penny articles to a shopkeeper of the town, and when counted there were exactly fifteen gross, or 2160 "pieces" as they are sometimes called. These, vended at 1*d.* each, would realize just 9*l.*, and would cost, wholesale, about 6*l.*, or for ready money, at the swag-shops, where they may be bought, from 10*s.*

to 20*s.* less, according to the bargaining powers of the buyer. The man's reason for selling was that the Fair was "no good ;" that is to say, the farmers had no money, and their labourers received only 7*s.* a week, so there was no demand ; the swag-seller, therefore, rather than incur the trouble and expense of having to carry his wares back to London, sold at a loss to a shopkeeper in Maidstone, who wanted a stock.

The swag-barrowmen selling on commission have 3*s.* in every 20*s.* worth of goods that they sell. The commission may average from 9*s.* to 12*s.* a week in tolerable weather, but as in bad, and especially in foggy weather, the trade cannot be prosecuted at all, 7*s.* 6*d.* may be the highest average, or 10*s.* the year through.

The character of the penny swag-men belongs more to that of the costermongers than to any other class of street-folk. Many of them drink as freely as their means will permit. I was told of a match between a teetotaller and a beer-drinker, about nine years ago. It was for 5*s.* a side, and the "Championship." Each man started with an equal stock, alike in all respects, but my informant had forgotten the precise number of articles. They pattered, twenty-five yards apart one from another, three hours in James-street, Covent-garden ; three hours in the Blackfriars-road ; and three hours in Deptford. The teetotaller was " sold out " in seven-and-a-half hours ; while his opponent—and the contest seems to have been carried on very good-humouredly—at the nine hours' end, had four dozen articles left, and was rather exhausted, or, as it was described to me, " told out." The result, albeit, was not looked upon, I was assured, as anything very decisive of the relative merits of beer or water, as the source of strength or inspiration of "patter." The teetotaller was the smarter, though he did not appear the stronger, man ; he abandoned the championship, and went into another trade four years ago. The patter of the swag-men has nothing of the humour of the paper-workers; it is merely declaratory that the extensive stock offered on such liberal terms to the public would furnish a wholesale shop ; that such another opportunity for cheap pennyworths could never by any possibility occur again, and that it was a duty on all who heard the patterer to buy at once.

The men having their own barrows or stalls (but the stall-trade is small) buy their goods as they find their stock needs replenishment at the swag-shops. " It was a good trade at first, sir," said one man, "and for its not being a good trade now, we may partly blame one another. There was a cutting down trade among us. Black earrings were bought at 14*d.* the dozen, and sold at a loss at 1*d.* each. So were children's trap-bats, and monkeys up sticks, but they are now 9*d.* a dozen. Sometimes, sir, as I know, the master of a swag-barrow gets served out. You see, a man may once on a time have a good day, and take as much as 2*l.* Well, next day he'll use part of that money, and go as a penny swag on his own account ; or else he'll buy things he is sold out of, and work them on his own account on his master's barrow. All right, sir; his master makes him a convenience for his own pocket, and so his master may be made a convenience for the man's. When he takes the barrow back at the week's end, if he's been doing a little on his own dodge, there's the stock, and there's the money. It's all right between a rich man and a poor man that way; turn and turn about's fair play."

The lot-sellers are, when the whole body are in London, about 200 in number; but they are three times as itinerant into the country as are the traders in the heavier and little portable swag-barrows. The lot-sellers nearly all vend their goods from trays slung from their shoulders. The best localities for the lot-sellers are Ratcliffe-highway, Commercial-road, Whitechapel, Minories, Tower-hill, Tooley-street, Newington-causeway, Walworth, Blackfriars and Westminster-roads, Long-acre, Holborn, and Oxford-street. To this list may be added the Brill, Tottenham-court-road, and the other street-markets, on Saturday evenings, when some of these places are almost impassable. The best places for the swag-barrow trade are also those I have specified. Their customers, alike for the useful and fancy articles, are the working-classes, and the chief sale is on Saturdays and Mondays. One swag-man told me that he thought he could sell better if he had a less crowded barrow, but his master was so keen of money that he *would* make him try everything. It made selling more tiresome, too, he said, for a poor couple who had a penny or two to lay out would fix on half the things they saw, and change them for others, before they parted with their money.

Of the penny-a-piece sellers trading on their own account, the receipts may be smaller than those of the men who work the huge swag-barrows on commission, but their profits are greater. Calculating that 100 of these traders are, the year round, in London (some are absent all the summer at country fairs, and on any favourable opportunity, while a number of swag-barrowmen leave that employment for costermongering on their own account), and that each takes 2*l.* weekly, we find no less than 10,400*l.* thus expended in the streets of London in a year.

The lot-sellers also resort largely to the country, and frequently try other callings, such as the sale of fruit, medals, &c. Some also sell lots only on Saturday and Monday nights. Taking these deductions into consideration, it may be estimated that only fifty men (there is but one female lot-seller on her own account) carry on the trade, presuming it to be spread over the six days of the week. Each of them may take 13*s.* weekly (with a profit of 7*s.* 6*d.*), so showing the street outlay to be 1190*l.* The "lots" are bought at the German and English swag-shops; the principal supply, however, is procured from Black Tom in Clerkenwell.

OF THE STREET-SELLERS OF ROULETTE BOXES.

IN my account of the street-trade in "China ornaments" I had occasion to mention a use to which a roulette box, or portable roulette table,

was put. I need only repeat in this place that the box (usually of mahogany) contains a board, with numbered partitions, which is set spinning, by means of a central knob, on a pivot; the lid is then placed on the box, a pea is slipped through a hole in the lid, and on the number of the partition in which the pea is found deposited, when the motion has ceased, depends the result. The table, or board, is thus adapted for the determination of that mode of raising money, popular among costermongers and other street-folk, who in their very charities crave some excitement; I mean a "raffle;" or it may be used for play, by one or more persons, the highest number "spun" determining the winner. These street-sold tables may still be put to another use: In the smaller sort, "going no higher than fourteen," one division is blank. Thus any one may play against another, or several others spinning in turns, the "blank" being a chance in the "banker's" favour. Some of the tables, however, are as high as 36, or as a seller of them described it, "single and double zero, bang; a French game."

This curious street-trade has been carried on for seven years, but with frequent interruptions, by one man, who, until within these few weeks, was the sole trader in the article. There are now but two selling roulette-boxes at all regularly. The long-established salesman wears mustachios, and has a good deal the look of a foreigner. During his seven years' experience he has sold, he calculates, 12,000 roulette-boxes, at a profit of from 175*l.* to 200*l.* The prices (retail) are from 1*s.* to 2*l.*, at which high amount my informant once disposed of "a roulette" in the street. He has sold, however, more at 1*s.* than at all other rates together. The "shilling roulette" is about three inches in diameter; the others proportionately larger. These wares are German made, bought at a swag-shop, and retailed at a profit of from 15 to 33 per cent. They are carried in a basket, one being held for public examination in the vendor's hand.

"My best customers," said the experienced man in the business, "are stock-brokers, travellers, and parsons; people that have spare time on their hands. O, I mean by 'travellers,' gentlemen going on a railway who pass the time away at roulette. Now and then a regular 'leg,' when he's travelling to Chester, York, or Doncaster, to the races, may draw other passengers into play, and make a trifle, or not a trifle, by it; or he will play with other legs; but it's generally for amusement, I've reason to believe. Friends travelling together play for a trifle to pass away time, or who shall pay for breakfasts for two, or such like. I supplied one gaming-house with a large roulette-table made of a substance that if you throw it into water—and there's always a pail of 'tepid' ready—would dissolve very quickly. When it's not used it's hung against the wall and is so made that it looks to be an oil-painting framed. It cost them 10*l.* I suppose I have the 'knock' of almost every gaming-house in London. There's plenty of them still. The police can drive such as me about in the streets or out of the streets to starve, but lords, and gentlemen, and some parsons, I know, go to the gaming-houses, and when one's broke into by the officers—it's really funny —John Smith, and Thomas Jones, and William Brown are pulled up, but as no gaming implements are found, there's nothing against them. Some of these houses are never noticed for a long time. The ' Great Nick' hasn't been, nor the ' Little Nick.' I don't know why they're called ' Nicks,' those two ; but so they are. Perhaps after Old Nick. At the Great Nick I dare say there's often 1000*l.* depending. But the Little Nick is what we call only ' brown papermen,' low gamblers—playing for pence, and 1*s.* being a great go. I wonder the police allow *that.*"

OF THE STREET-SELLERS OF POISON FOR RATS.

THE number of Vermin-Destroyers and Rat-Catchers who ply their avocation in London has of late years become greatly diminished. One cause which I heard assigned for this was that many ruinous old buildings and old streets had been removed, and whole colonies of rats had been thereby extirpated. Another was that the race of rat-catchers had become distrusted, and had either sought some other mode of subsistence, or had resorted to other fields for the exercise of their professional labours.

The rat-catcher's dress is usually a velveteen jacket, strong corduroy trowsers, and laced boots. Round his shoulder he wears an oil-skin belt, on which are painted the figures of huge rats, with fierce-looking eyes and formidable whiskers. His hat is usually glazed and sometimes painted after the manner of his belt. Occasionally—and in the country far more than in town—he carries in his hand an iron cage in which are ferrets, while two or three crop-eared rough terriers dog his footsteps. Sometimes a tamed rat runs about his shoulders and arms, or nestles in his bosom or in the large pockets of his coat. When a rat-catcher is thus accompanied, there is generally a strong aromatic odour about him, far from agreeable ; this is owing to his clothes being rubbed with oil of thyme and oil of aniseed, mixed together. This composition is said to be so attractive to the sense of the rats (when used by a man who understands its due apportionment and proper application) that the vermin have left their holes and crawled to the master of the powerful spell. I heard of one man (not a rat-catcher professionally) who had in this way tamed a rat so effectually that the animal would eat out of his mouth, crawl upon his shoulder to be fed, and then " smuggle into his bosom" (the words of my informant) " and sleep there for hours." The rat-catchers have many wonderful stories of the sagacity of the rat, and though in reciting their own feats, these men may not be the most trustworthy of narrators, any work on natural history will avouch that rats *are* sagacious, may be trained to be very docile, and are naturally animals of great resources in all straits and difficulties.

One great source of the rat-catcher's employment and emolument thirty years ago, or even to a later period, is now comparatively a nonentity. At that time the rat-catcher or killer sometimes received a yearly or quarterly stipend to keep a London granary clear of rats. I was told by a man who has for twenty-eight years been employed about London granaries, that he had never known a rat-catcher employed in one except about twenty or twenty-two years ago, and that was in a granary by the river-side. The professional man, he told me, certainly poisoned many rats, " which stunk so," continued my informant—but then all evil odours in old buildings are attributed to dead rats—" that it was enough to infect the corn. He poisoned two fine cats as well. But I believe he was a young hand and a bungler." The rats, after these measures had been taken, seem to have deserted the place for three weeks or a month, when they returned in as great numbers as ever ; nor were their ravages and annoyances checked until the drains were altered and rebuilt. It is in the better disposition of the drains of a corn-magazine, I am assured, that the great check upon the inroads of these " varmint " is attained—by strong mason work and by such a series and arrangement of grates, as defy even the perseverance of a rat. Otherwise the hordes which prey upon the garbage in the common sewers, are certain to find their way into the granary along the drains and channels communicating with those sewers, and will increase rapidly despite the measures of the rat-catcher.

The same man told me that he had been five or six times applied to by rat-catchers, and with liberal offers of beer, to allow them to try and capture the black rats in the granary. One of these traders declared that he wanted them " for a gent as vas curous in them there hinteresting warmint ;" But from the representations of the other applicants, my informant was convinced that they were wanted for rat-hunts, the Dog Billy being backed for 100*l.* to kill so many rats in so many minutes. " You see, sir," the corn merchant's man continued, " ours is an old concern, and there's black rats in it, great big fellows ; some of 'em must be old, for they 're as white about the muzzle as is the Duke of Wellington, and they have the character of being very strong and very fierce. One of the catchers asked me if I knew what a stunning big black rat would weigh, as if I weighed rats ! I always told them that I cared nothing about rat-hunts and that I knew our people wouldn't like to be bothered ; and they was gentlemen that didn't admire sporting characters."

The black rat, I may observe, or the English rat, is now comparatively scarce, while the brown, or Hanoverian, rat is abundant. This brown rat seems to have become largely domiciled in England about the period of the establishment of the Hanoverian dynasty ; whence its name. " A Hanover rat" was a term of reproach applied by the Jacobites to the successful party.

The rat-catchers are also rat-killers. They destroy the animals sometimes by giving them what is called in the trade " an alluring poison." Every professional destroyer, or capturer, of rats will pretend that as to poison he has his own particular method—his secret—his discovery. But there is no doubt that arsenic is the basis of all their poisons. Its being inodorous, and easily reducible to a soft fine powder, renders it the best adapted for mixing with anything of which rats are fond—toasted cheese, or bacon, or fried liver, or tallow, or oatmeal. Much as the poisoner may be able to tempt the animal's appetite, he must, and does, proceed cautiously. If the bait be placed in an unwonted spot, it is often untouched. If it be placed where rats have been accustomed to find their food, it is often devoured. But even then it is frequently accounted best to leave the bait un-poisoned for the first night; so that a hungry animal may attack it greedily the second. With oatmeal it is usual to mix for the first and even second nights a portion of pounded white sugar. If this be eaten it accustoms the jealous pest to the degree of sweetness communicated by arsenic. The "oatmeal poison" is, I am told, the most effectual; but even when mixed only with sugar it is often refused; as "rats is often better up to a dodge nor Kirstians" (Christians).

Another mode of killing rats is for the professional destroyer to slip a ferret into the rats' haunts wherever it is practicable. The ferret soon dislodges them, and as they emerge for safety they are seized by terriers, who, after watching the holes often a long time, and very patiently, and almost breathlessly, throttle them silently, excepting the short squeak, or half-squeak, of the rat, who, by a "good dog," is seized un-erringly by the part of the back where the terrier's gripe and shake is speedy death; if the rat still move, or shows signs of life, the well-trained rat-killer's dog cracks the vermin's skull between his teeth.

If the rats have to be taken alive, they are either trapped, so as not to injure them for a rat-hunt (or the procedure in the pit would be accounted "foul"), or if driven out of their holes by ferrets, they can only run into some cask, or other contrivance, where they can be secured for the "sportsman's" purposes. Although any visible injury to the body of the rat will prevent its reception into a pit, the creatures' teeth are often drawn, and with all the cruelty of a rough awkwardness, by means of pinchers, so that they may be unable to bite the puppies being trained for the pit on the rats. If the vermin be not truly seized by the dog, the victim will twist round and inflict a tremendous bite on his worrier, generally on the lip. This often causes the terrier to drop his prey with a yell, and if a puppy he may not forget the lesson from the sharp nip of the rat. To prevent this it is that the rat-catchers play the dentist on their unfortunate captives.

I heard many accounts of the "dodges" practised by, or imputed to, the rat-catchers: that it was not a very unusual thing to deposit here and there a dead rat, when those vermin were to be poisoned on any premises; it is then concluded that the good poison has done its good work, and the dead animal supplies an ocular demonstration of professional skill. These men, also, I am informed, let loose live rats in buildings adapted for

the purpose, and afterwards apply for employment to destroy them.

I am informed that the principal scene of the rat-catcher's labours in London is at the mews, and in private stables, coach-houses, and out-buildings. It is probable that the gentlemen's servants connected with such places like the excitement of rat-hunting, and so encourage the profession which supplies them with that gratification. In these places such labours are often necessary as well as popular; for I was informed by a coachman, then living with his family in a West End mews, and long acquainted with the mews in different parts of town, that the drainage was often very defective, and sanitary regulations —except, perhaps, as regarded the horses—little cared for. Hence rats abounded, and were with difficulty dislodged from their secure retreats in the ill-constructed drains and kennels.

The great sale of the rat-catchers is to the shops supplying "private parties" with rats for the amusement of seeing them killed by dogs. With some "fast" men, one of these shopkeepers told me, it was a favourite pastime in their own rooms on the Sunday mornings. It is, however, somewhat costly if carried on extensively, as the retail charge from the shops is 6d. per rat. The price from the catcher to the dealer is from 2s. 6d. to 7s. the dozen. Rats, it appears, are sometimes scarce, and then the shopkeeper must buy, "to keep up his connection," at enhanced cost. One large bird-seller, who sold also plain and fancy rats, white mice, and live hedgehogs, told me that he had, last winter, been compelled to give 7s. a dozen for his vermin and sell them at 6d. each.

The grand consumption of rats, however, is in Bunhill-row, at a public-house kept by a pugilist. A rat-seller told me that from 200 to 500 rats were killed there weekly, the weekly average being, however, only the former number; while at Easter and other holidays, it is not uncommon to see bills posted announcing the destruction of 500 rats on the same day and in a given time, admittance 6d. Dogs are matched at these and similar places, as to which kills the greatest number of these animals in the shortest time. I am told that there are forty such places in London, but in some only the holiday times are celebrated in this small imitation of the beast combats of the ancients. There is, too, a frequent abandonment of the trade in consequence of its "not paying," and perhaps it may be fair to estimate that the average consumption of this vermin-game does not exceed, in each of these places, 20 a week, or 1040 in a year; giving an aggregate—over and above those consumed in private sport —of 52,000 rats in a year, or 1000 a week in public amusement alone.

To show the nature of the sport of rat-catching, I print the following bill, of which I procured two copies. The words and type are precisely the same in each, but one bill is printed on good and the other on very indifferent paper, as if for distribution among distinct classes. The concluding announcement, as to the precise moment at which killing will commence, reads supremely business-like :—

RATTING FOR THE MILLION!

A SPORTING GENTLEMAN, Who is a Staunch Supporter of the destruction of these VERMIN

WILL GIVE A

GOLD REPEATER

WATCH,

TO BE KILLED FOR BY

DOGS *Under* 13¾ *lbs. Wt.*

15 *RATS EACH!*

TO COME OFF AT JEMMY MASSEY'S,
KING'S HEAD,
COMPTON ST., SOHO,
On *Tuesday, May* 20, 1851.

☞ To be Killed in a Large Wire Pit. A chalk Circle to be drawn in the centre for the Second.— Any Man touching Dog or Rats, or acting in any way unfair his dog will be disqualified.

TO GO TO SCALE AT Half past 7 KILLING TO COMMENCE At Half past 8 PRECISELY.

A dealer in live animals told me that there were several men who brought a few dozens of rats, or even a single dozen, from the country; men who were not professionally rat-catchers, but worked in gardens, or on farms, and at their leisure caught rats. Even some of the London professional rat-catchers work sometimes as country labourers, and their business is far greater, in merely rat-catching or killing, in the country than in town. From the best information I could command, there are not fewer than 2000 rats killed, for sport, in London weekly, or 104,000 a year, including private and public sport, for private sport in this pursuit goes on uninterruptedly; the public delectation therein is but periodical.

This calculation is of course exclusive of the number of rats *killed* by the profession, "on the premises," when these men are employed to "clear the premises of vermin."

There are, I am told, 100 rat-catchers resorting, at intervals, to London, but only a fourth of that number can be estimated as carrying on their labours regularly in town, and their average earnings, I am assured, do not exceed 15s. a week; being 975l. a year for London merely.

These men have about them much of the affected mystery of men who are engaged on the turf. They have their "secrets," make or pretend to "make their books" on rat fights and other sporting events; are not averse to drinking, and lead in general irregular lives. They are usually on intimate terms with the street dog-sellers (who are much of the same class). Many of the rat-catchers have been brought up in stables, and there is little education among them. When in London, they are chiefly to be found in White-chapel, Westminster, and Kent-street, Borough;

the more established having their own rooms; the others living in the low lodging-houses. None of them remain in London the entire year.

These men also sell rat-poison (baked flour or oatmeal sometimes) in cakes, arsenic being the ingredient. The charge is from 2d. to 1s., "according to the circumstances of the customer." In like manner the charge for "clearing a house of vermin" varies from 2s. to 1l.: a very frequent charge is 2s. 6d.

OF THE STREET-SELLERS OF RHUBARB AND SPICE.

FROM the street-seller whose portrait has already been given I received the following history. He appeared to be a very truthful and kindly-disposed old man :—

"I am one native of Mogadore in Morocco. I am an Arab. I left my countree when I was sixteen or eighteen year of age. I forget, sir. I don't know which, about eighteen, I tink it was. My fader was like market man, make de people pay de toll—he rent de whole market, you see, from de governemen, and make de people pay so much for deir stands. I can't tell you what dey call dem dere. I couldn't recollect what my fader pay for de market; but I know some of de people pay him a penny, some a ha'penny, for de stands. Dere everyting sheap, not what dey are here in England. Dey may stop all day for de toll or go when de market is over. My fader was not very rish—not very poor—he keep a family. We have bread, meat, shicken, apples, grapes, all de good tings to eat, not like here—tis de sheapest countree in de world. My fader have two wifes, not at once you know, he bury de first and marry anoder. I was by second wife. He have seven shildren by her, four sons and tree daughters. By de first I tink dere was five, two sons and tree daughters. Bless you, by de time I was born dere was great many of 'em married and away in de world. I don't know where dey are now. Only one broder I got live for what I know, wheder de oders are dead or where dey are I can't tell. De one broder I speak of is in Algiers now; he is dealer dere. What led me to come away, you say? Like good many I was young and foolish; like all de rest of young people, I like to see foreign countries, but you see in my countree de governemen don't like de people to come away, not widout you pay so mush, so Gibraltar was de only port I could go to, it was only one twenty miles across de water—close to us. You see you go to Gibraltar like smuggling —you smuggle yourself—you talk wid de Captain and he do it for you.

"My fader been dead years and years before I come away, I suppose I was about ten year old when he die. I had been at school till time I was grown up, and after dat I was shoemaker. I make de slippers. Oh yes! my moder was alive den—she was dead when I was here in England. I get about one penny a pair for de slippers in my countree; penny dere as good as shilling here amost. I could make tree, four, five pair in one day. I could live on my gains den better dan what I could do here wid twelve times as mush—

THE STREET RHUBARB AND SPICE SELLER.

[*From a Daguerreotype by* BEARD.]

dat time I could. I don't know what it is now.
Yes, my moder give me leave to go where I like.
She never see me since " (sighing). " Oh yes, I
love her very mush. I am old man now, but I never
forgot her yet ;" here the old man burst into tears
and buried his face in his handkerchief for several
minutes. "No, no! she don't know when I come
away dat she never see me again, nor me neider.
I tell I go Gibraltar, and den I tell her I go to
Lisbon to see my broder, who was spirit merchant
dere. I didn't say noting not at all about coming
back to her, but I tought I should come back
soon. If I had tought I never see no more, not
all de gold in de world take me from her. She
was good moder to me. I was de youngest but
one. My broders kept my moder, you see. Where
I came from it is not like here, if only one in de
family well off, de oders never want for noting.
In my country, you see, de law is you must maintain your fader and moder before you maintain
your own family. You must keep dem in de
house." Here he repeated the law in Hebrew.
" De people were Mahomedans in Mogadore, but
we were Jews, just like here, you see. De first
ting de Jews teesh de shildren is deir duty to deir
faders and deir moders. And dey love one anoder
more than de gold ; but dey love de gold more
dan most people, for you see gold is more to dem.
In my countree de governemen treat de Jews very
badly, so de money all de Jews have to help dem.
Often de government in my country take all deir
money from de Jews, and kill dem after, so de
Jews all keep deir money in secret places, put de
gold in jars and dig dem in de ground, and de
men worths hundreds go about wid no better
clothes dan mine.
" Well, you see I leave my poor moder, we kissed
one anoder, and cry for half an hour, and come
away to Gibraltar. When I get dere, my broder
come away from Lisbon to Gibraltar ; dat time it
was war time, and de French was coming to Lisbon, so everybody run. When I come away
from Mogadore, I have about one hundred dollars
—some my moder give me, and some I had save.
When I got to Gibraltar, I begin to have a little
stand in de street wid silk handkershiefs, cotton
handkershiefs, shop goods you know. I do
very well wid dat, so after I get licence to hawk
de town, and after dat I keep shop. Altogeder,
I stop in Gibraltar about six year. I had den
about five or six hundred dollars. I live very
well all de time I dere. I was wid my broder
all de time. After I am six year in Gibraltar,
I begin to tink I do better in England. I tink,
like good many people, if I go to anoder part dat
is risher—'t is de rishest countree in de world
—I do better still. So I start off, and get I
here I tink in 1811, when de tree shilling pieces
first come out. I have about one hundred and
tirty pound at dat time. I stop in London a
good bit, and eat my money ; it was most done
before I start to look for my living. I try to
look what I could do, but I was quite stranger
you see. I am about fourteen or fifteen month
before I begin to do anyting. I go to de play
house ; I see never such tings as I see here before

I come. When I come here, I tink I am in heaven
altogether—God a'mighty forgive me—such sops
(shops) and such beautiful tings. I live in Mary
Axe Parish when I first come; same parish where
I live now. Well, you see some of my countreemen den getting good living by selling de
rhubarb and spices in de street. I get to know
dem all ; and dat time you see was de good
time, money was plenty, like de dirt here.
Dat time dere was about six or seven Arabians in
de street selling rhubarb and spices, five of 'em
was from Mogadore, and two from not far off ;
and dere is about five more going troo de country.
Dey all sell de same tings, merely rhubarb and
spice, dat time; before den was good for tem tings—
after dat dey get de silks and tings beside. I can't
tell what first make dem sell de rhubarb and de
spice ; but I tink it is because people like to buy
de Turkey rhubarb of de men in de turbans.
When I was little shild, I hear talk in Mogadore
of de people of my country sell de rhubarb in
de streets of London, and make plenty money
by it.
" Dere was one very old Arabian in de streets
wen I first come; dey call him Sole ; he been
forty year at de same business. He wear de long
beard and Turkish dress. He used to stand by
Bow Shursh, Sheapside. Everybody in de street
know him. He was de old establish one. He
been dead now, let me see—how long he been
dead—oh, dis six or seven and twenty year. He
die in Gibraltar very poor and very old—most
ninety year of age. All de rhubarb-sellers was
Jews. Dere was anoder called Ben Aforiat, and
two broders ; and anoder, his name was Azuli.
One of Aforiat's broders use to stand in St. Paul's
Shurshyard. He was very well know ; all de
oders hawk about de town like I do myself. Now
dey all gone dead, and dere only four of us now
in England ; dey all in London, and none in de
country. Two of us live in Mary Axe, anoder
live in, what dey call dat—Spitalfield, and de
oder in Petticoat-lane. De one wat live in
Spitalfield is old man, I dare say going for 70.
De one in Petticoat-lane not mush above 30. I
am little better dan 73, and de oder wat live in
Mary Axe about 40. I been de longest of all in
de streets, about tirty-eight or tirty-nine year.
All dat was here when I first come, die in
London, except dat old man Sole wat I was
telling you of, dat die in Gibraltar. About
tirteen or fourteen die since I come to England ;
some die in de Hospital of de Jews at Mile End ;
some die at home—not one of dem die worth
no money. Six of dem was very old people,
between 60 and 70 ; dere was some tirty, some
forty. Some of dem die by inshes. Dere was
one fine fellow, he was six foot two, and strong
man, he take to his bed and fall away so ; at last
you see troo his hand ; he was noting but de car-
case ; oders die of what you call de yellow jaun-
dice ; some have de fever, but deir time was come ;
de death we must be.
" When I first come to dis countree me make
plenty money by selling de rhubarb in de street.
Five-and-twenty year ago I make a pound a day

some time. Take one week wid another, I dare say I clear, after I pay all de cost of my living, tirty shillings; and now, God help me, I don't make not twelve shilling a week, and all my food to pay out of dat. One week wid anoder, when I go out I clear about twelve shilling. Everyting is so sheep now, and dere is so many sops (shops), people has no money to buy tings with. I could do better when everyting was dear. I could live better, get more money, and have more for it. I have better food, better lodging, and better clothes. I don't know wat is de cause, as you say. I only know dat I am worse, and everybody is worse; dat is all I know. Bread is sheeper, but when it was one and nine-pence de loaf I could get plenty to buy it wid, but now it is five pence, I can't no five pence to have it. If de cow is de penny in de market what is de use of dat, if you can't get no penny to buy him? After I been selling my rhubarb for two years, when I fust come here, I save about a hundred and fifty pound, and den you see I agree wid tree oder of my countrymen to take a sop (shop) in Exeter. De oder tree was rhubarb-sellers, like myself, and have save good bit of money as well. One have seven hundred pound; but he have brought tree or four hundred pound wid him to dis countree. Anoder of de tree have about two hundred, and de oder about one hundred; dey have all save deir money out of de rhubarb. We keep our sop, you see, about five year, and den we fall in pieces altogeder. We take and trust, and lose all our money. T'oders never keep a sop before, and not one of us was English scholar; we was forced to keep a man, and dat way we lose all our money, so we was force to part, and every one go look for hisself. Den we all go selling rhubarb again about de country, and in London; and I never able to hold up my head since. When I come back to de rhubarb times is getting bad, and I not able to save no more money. All I am worth in de world is all I got in my box, and dat altogether is not more dan ten shilling. Last week I havn't a pound of meat in de house, and I am obliged to pawn my waistcoat and handkerchief to get me some stock. It easy to put dem in, but very hard to get dem out.

"I had two wives. After two or tree year when I come I marry my first. I had two shildren by my first, but both of dem die very young; one was about five year old and de oder about tree. When I travel the countree, my first wife she go wid me everywhere. I been to all parts — to Scotland, to Wales, but not Ireland. I see enough of dem Irish in dis countree, I do no want no more of dem dere. Not one of my countree I tink ever been to Ireland, and only one beside myself been to Scotland; but dat no use, de Scotsh don't know wat de spice is. All de time I am in Scotland I can't get no bread, only barley and pea meal, and dat as sour as de winegar—and I can't get no flour to make none too—so I begin to say, by God I come to wrong countree here. When I go across de countree of England I never live in no lodging-houses—always in de public—because you see I do business dere; de missus perhaps dere buy my spices of me. I lodge once in Taunton, at a house where a woman keep a lodging-house for de Jewish people wat go about wid de gold tings—de jewellery. At oder towns I stop at de public, for dere is de company, and I sell my tings.

"I buy my rhubarb and my spice of de large warehouse for de drugs; sometime I buy it of my countreemen. We all of us know de good spice from de bad. You look! I will show you how to tell de good nutmeg from de bad. Here is some in de shell: you see, I put de strong pin in one and de oil run out; dat is because dey has not been put in de spirit to take away de oil for to make de extract. Now, in de bad nutmeg all de oil been took out by de spirit, and den dere is no flavour, like dose you buy in de sheep sops (cheap shops). I sell de Rhubarb, East Indy and Turkey, de Cloves, Cinnamons, Mace, Cayenne Pepper, White Pepper—a little of all sorts when I get de money to buy it wid. I take my solemn oat I never sheat in scales nor weight; because de law is, 'take weight and give weight,' dat is judge and justice. Dere is no luck in de sort weight—no luck at all. Never in my life I put no tings wid my goods. I tell you de troot, I grind my white pepper wid my own hands, but I buy me ginger ground, and dat is mixed I know. I tink it is pea flour dey put wid it, dere is no smell in dat, but it is de same colour—two ounces of ginger will give de smell to one pound of pea flour. De public-houses will have de sheap ginger and dat I buy. I tell you de troot. How am I tell what will become of me. Dat is de Almighty's work" (here he pointed to Heaven). "De Jews is very good to deir old people. If it was not for my old woman I be like a gentleman now in de hospital at Mile End; but you see, I marry de Christian woman, and dat is against our people—and I would never leave her—no not for all de good in de world to come to myself. If I am poor, I not de only one. In de holiday times I send a petition, and perhaps dere is five shillings for me from de hospital. In de Jews' Hospital dere is only ten—what you call de Portuguese Jews. We have hospital to our ownselves. Dere de old people — dey are all above sixty—are all like noblemen, wid good clothes, plenty to eat, go where you like, and pipe of tobacco when you want. But I wont go in no hospital away from my old woman. I will get a bit of crust for her as long as I can stand—but I can hardly do that now. Every one got his feeling, and I will feel for her as long as I live. When dere is de weather I have de rheumatis— oh! very bad—sometime I can scarcely stand or walk. I am seventy-tree, and it is a sad time for me now. I am merry sometime tho'. Everyting wid de pocket. When de pocket is merry, den I am merry too. Sometime I go home wid one shilling, and den I tink all gets worse and worse, and what will become of me I say—but dat is de Almighty's work, and I trust in him. Can I trust any better one? Sometime I say I wish I was back in my countree—and I tink of my poor moder wat is dead now, and den I am very sad. Oh yes, bless your heart, very sad indeed!"

The old man appears to sell excellent articles, and to be a very truthful, fair-dealing man.

OF THE HAWKING OF TEA.

"PERSONS hawking tea without a licence" (*see* Chitty's Edition of "Burn's Justice," vol. ii. p. 1113) "are liable to a penalty, under 50 Geo. III., cap. 41.; and, even though they had a licence, they would be liable to a penalty for selling tea in an unentered place." The penalty under this act is 10*l.*, but the prohibition in question has long been commonly, if not very directly, evaded.

The hawking of tea in London cannot be considered as immediately a street-trade, but it is in some respects blended with street callings and street traffic, so that a brief account is necessary.

I will first give a short history of what is, or was, more intimately a portion of the street-trade.

Until about eight or ten years ago, tea was extensively hawked—from house to house almost— "on tally." The tally system is, that wherein "weekly payments" are taken in liquidation of the cost of the article purchased, and the trade is one embodying much of evil and much of trickery. At the present time the tallymen are very numerous in London, and in the tally trade there are now not less than 1000 hawkers of, or travellers in, tea; but they carry on their business principally in the suburbs. When I come to treat of the class whom I have called "distributors," I shall devote an especial inquiry to the tally trade, including, of course, the tea trade. Mr. M'Culloch mentions that a Scotchman's "tally-walk"—and the majority of the tallymen are Scotchmen—is worth 15 per cent. more than an Englishman's.

The branch of the tea trade closely connected with the street business is that in tea-leaves. The exhausted leaves of the tea-pot are purchased of servants or of poor women, and they are made into "new" tea. One gentleman—to whose information, and to the care he took to test the accuracy of his every statement, I am bound to express my acknowledgments—told me that it would be fair to reckon that in London 1500 lbs. of tea-leaves were weekly converted into new tea, or 78,000 lbs. in the year! One house is known to be very extensively and profitably concerned in this trade, or rather *manufacture*, and on my asking the gentleman who gave me the information if the house in question (he told me the name) was accounted respectable by their fellow-citizens, the answer was at once, "*Highly* respectable."

The *old* tea-leaves, to be converted into *new*, are placed by the manufacturers on hot plates, and are re-dried and *re-dyed*. To give the "green" hue, a preparation of copper is used. For the "black" no dye is necessary in the generality of cases. This tea-manufacture is sold to "cheap" or "slop" shopkeepers, both in town and country, and especially for hawking in the country, and is almost always sold ready mixed.

The admixture of sloe-leaves, &c., which used to be gathered for the adulteration of tea, is now unknown, and has been unknown since tea became cheaper, but the old tea-leaf trade is, I am assured, carried on so quietly and cleverly that the most vigilant excise-officers are completely in the dark; a smaller "tea-maker" was, however, fined for tea-leaf conversion last year.

Into this curious question, concerning the purposes for which the old tea-leaves are now purchased by parties in the street, I shall enter searchingly when I treat of the *street-buyers*. The information I have already received is of great curiosity and importance, nor shall I suppress the names of those dishonest traders who purchase the old dried tea-leaves, as a means of cheating their customers.

Into the statistics of this strange trade I will not now enter, but I am informed that great quantities of tea-leaves are sent from the country to London. Perhaps of the 1500 lbs. weekly manufactured in the metropolis, three quarters may be collected in the metropolis.

I may here add, that the great bulk of the tea *now* hawked throughout the metropolis is supplied from the handsome cars, or vans, of well-known grocers and tea-dealers. Of these—it was computed for me—there are, on no day, fewer than 100 in the streets of London, and of its contiguous and its more remote suburbs, such as Woolwich, and even Barnet. One tradesman has six such cars. The tea is put up in bags of 7, 14, and 21 lbs., duly apportioned in quarter, half, and whole pounds; a quarter of a pound being the smallest quantity vended in this manner. The van and its contents are then entrusted to a driver, who has his regular round, and very often his regular customers. The customers purchase the tea from their faith in the respectability of the firm—generally well known through extensive advertising. The teas *are* supplied by the house which is pronounced to supply them; for the tradesman is the capitalist in the matter, his carman is the labourer, and the house is responsible for the quality of the article. When a new connection has to be formed, or an "old connection" to be extended, circulars (*bonâ fide*) are sent round, and the carman afterwards calls: and, "in some genteel streets," I was told, "calls, oft enough, at every house, and, in many districts, at every decent-looking house in every street." So far, then, even this part of the traffic may be considered one of the streets. The remuneration of the street-traveller in, or hawker of, tea, is usually 1*d.* per lb. on the lower-priced kinds, 2*d.* on the higher (but more often 1*d.*) and, very rarely indeed, 3*d.* on the highest. The trade is one peculiar to great cities—and most peculiar, I am assured, to London—for the tradesman does not know so much as the name of his customer; nor, perhaps, does the carman, but merely as "Number such-an-one." The supply is for ready money, or, if credit be given, it is at the risk of the carman, who has a weekly wage in addition to his perquisites. Every evening, when the vehicle is driven back to the premises of its owner, "stock is taken," and the money taken by the carman—

minus what may be called the " poundage"—is paid over to the proper party.

A man who had driven, or, as he called it, "managed," one of these vans, told me that he made this way, 2s. to 2s 6d. a day ; " but," he added, " if you make a good thing of it that way, you have all the less salary." These carmen are men of good character and good address, and were described to me, by a gentleman familiar with the trade, as " of the very best class of porters."

As this vehicular-itinerant business has now become an integral part of the general tea-trade, I need not further dwell upon it, but reserve it until I come to treat of the shopmen of grocers and tea-dealers, and thence of the tea-trade in general. I may add, however, that the tea thus hawked is, as regards, perhaps, three-fourths of the quantity sold, known as "mixed," and sold at 4s. per lb.—costing, at a tea-broker's, from 2s. 11d. to 3s. 3d. It is announced, as to its staple or entire compound, to be " congou," but is in reality a tea known as " pouchong." Some old ladies are still anxious, I was told, for a cup of good strong bohea ; and though bohea has been unknown to the tea-trade since the expiration of the East India Company's Charter in 1834, the accommodating street-traveller will undertake to supply the genuine leaf to which the old lady had been so long accustomed. The green teas thus sold (and they are not above a fiftieth part of the other) are common twankays and common young hysons, neither of them—I can state on excellent authority—accounted in the trade to be "true teas," but, as in the case of some other green teas, " Canton made." The "green" is sold from the vans generally at 4s. 6d. ; sometimes, but rarely, as high as 5s. 6d. What is sold at 4s. 6d. may cost, on the average, 3s. 5d. I may add, also, that when a *good* article is supplied, such profits in the tea-trade are not accounted at all excessive.

But the more usual mode of tea hawking is by itinerant dealers who have a less direct connection with the shop whereat they purchase their goods. To this mode of obtaining a livelihood, the hawkers are invited by all the persuasive powers of advertising eloquence : " To persons in want of a genteel and lucrative employment"—" To Gentlemen of good address and business habits," &c., &c. The genteel and lucrative employment is to hawk tea under the auspices of this "company " or the other. The nature of this business, and of the street tea-trade generally, is shown in the following statement :—"About twelve years ago I came to London in expectation of a situation as tidewaiter ; I did not succeed, however, and not being able to obtain any other employment, and trusting to the promises of gentlemen M.P.s for too long a time, my means were exhausted, and I was at length induced to embark in the tea business. To this I was persuaded by a few friends who advanced me some money, considering that it would suit me well, while my friends would endeavour to get me a connection, that is, procure me customers. I accordingly went to a well-known Tea Company in the City, a firm bearing a great name. Their advertisements put forth extraordinary statements, of so many persons realizing independencies from selling their teas, and in very short spaces of time. I was quite pleased at the prospect presented to me in such glowing terms, and, depending not a little on my own industry and perseverance, I embraced the opportunity and introduced myself forthwith to the Company. They advised me in the first place to take out a licence for selling teas, to secure me against any risk of fines or forfeitures. The cost of a licence, after payment of 2s. 11½d. preliminary expenses, is 11s. per annum, to be paid quarterly, as it becomes due, and it is paid by the Company for their agents. The licence is granted for the place of abode of the ' traveller,' and strictly prohibits him from hawking or exposing his wares for sale at places other than at such place of abode, but he may of course supply his customers where he will, and serve them at their places of abode respectively. Everything thus prepared, I commenced operations, but soon found that this tea dealing was not so advantageous as I had anticipated. I found that the commission allowed by the Company on cheap teas was very low. For those generally used by the working people, ' 4s. tea,' for instance, or that at 4s. per pound, I had to pay to the Company 3s. 6d. per pound, thus allowing the travelling dealer or agent for commission only 6d. in the pound, or 1½d. per quarter. Now 80 or 100 customers is considered a fair connection for a dealer, and allowing each customer to take a quarter of a pound at an average, 80 good customers at that rate would bring him in 10s., or 100 customers 12s. 6d. clear profit weekly. But many customers do not require so much as a quarter of a pound weekly, while others require more, so that I find it rather awkward to subdivide it in portions to suit each customer, as the smallest quantity made at the warehouse is a quarter of a pound, and every quarter is done up in a labelled wrapper, with the price marked on it. So that to break or disturb the package in any way might cause some customers to suspect that it had been meddled with unfairly.

" Another disadvantage is in dealing with the ' Tea Company.' No sugars are supplied by them, which makes it more inconvenient for the travelling dealer, as his customers find it difficult to get sugars, most retail grocers having an objection to sell sugars to any but those who are purchasers of teas as well. However, I was not confined to deal with this Company, and so I tried other places, and found a City house, whose terms were preferable. Here I could get tea for 3s. 3d., as good as that for which the Company charged 3s. 6d., besides getting it done up to order in plain paper, and in quantities to suit every variety of customer. There were also sugars, which must be had to accommodate the customers, at whatever trouble or inconvenience to the traveller ; for it is very lumbersome to carry about, and leaves scarcely any profit at all.

" The trade is anything but agreeable, and the customers are often exacting. They seem to fancy, however cheaply and well they may be supplied, that the tea-seller is under obligations to them; that their custom will be the making of him, and, therefore, they expect some compliment in return. The consequence is, that very often, unless he be willing to be accounted a ' shabby man,' the tea-dealer is obliged, of a Saturday night, to treat his customers, to ensure a continuance of their custom. Other customers take care to be absent at the time he calls. Those who are anxious to run up bills, perhaps, keep out of the way purposely for two or more successive nights of the dealer's calling, who, notwithstanding, cannot very well avoid serving such customers. This is another evil, and if the tea-man's capital be not sufficient to enable him to carry on the business in this manner, giving credit (for it is unavoidable), he is very soon insolvent, and compelled to give up the business. I had to give it up at last, after having carried it on for four years, leaving 8*l.* or 9*l.* due to me, in small sums, varying from 1*s.* to 10*s.*, one shilling of which I never expect to be paid. I could not have continued it so long, for my means would not allow me to give credit; but getting partial employment at the last-mentioned house, where I dealt, enabled me to do so. When, however, I got permanently employed, I grew tired of tea-dealing, and gave it up.

" In my opinion the business would best suit persons casually employed, such as dockmen and others, who might have leisure to go about; those

also who get other commissions and hawk about other commodities, such as soft wares, might do very well by it; otherwise, in most cases, 't is only resorted to as a make-shift where no other employment can be obtained.

" I do not know how many persons are in the trade. I have, however, heard it asserted, that there were between 4000 and 5000 persons in London engaged in the business, who are, with but few exceptions, Scotchmen; they, of all others, manage to do the best *in this* line.

" A man, to undertake the tea business, requires a double capital, because in the first place, he has to purchase the tea, then he must give credit, and be able to support himself till such time as he can get in his money. Some of the tea-dealers manage to eke out their profits by mixing tea-leaves, which have been used, with the genuine commodity. They spread the old tea-leaves on tins which they have for the purpose, and, by exposing them either to the action of the air or the heat of the fire, the leaves crisp up as they had been before they were used, and are not distinguishable from the rest. I never vended such an article, and that may be one reason why I could not succeed in the business."

I believe the career thus detailed is a common one among the hawkers of tea, or rather the " travellers" in the tea trade. Many sell it on tally.

OF THE WOMEN STREET-SELLERS.

As the volume is now fast drawing to a close, and a specific account has been furnished of almost every description of street-*seller* (with the exception of those who are the *makers* of the articles they vend), I purpose giving a more full and general history and classification than I have yet done of the feminine portion of the traders in the streets.

The women engaged in street-sale are of all ages and of nearly all classes. They are, however, chiefly of two countries, England and Ireland. There are (comparatively) a few Jewesses, and a very few Scotchwomen and Welchwomen who are street-traders; and they are so, as it were, accidentally, from their connection, by marriage or otherwise, with male street-sellers. Of foreigners there are German broom-women, and a few Italians with musical instruments.

The first broad and distinctive view of the female street-sellers, is regarding them *nationally*, that is to say, either English or Irish women— two classes separated by definite characteristics from each other.

The Irishwomen — to avoid burthening the reader with an excess of subdivisions—I shall speak of generally; that is to say, as one homogeneous class, referring those who require a more specific account to the description before given of the street-sellers.

The Englishwomen selling in the streets appear to admit of being arranged into four distinct groups, viz. :—

1. The Wives of Street-Sellers.
2. Mechanics' or Labourers' Wives, who go out Street-Selling (while their husbands are at work) as a means of helping out the family income.
3. Widows of former Street-Sellers.
4. Single Women.

I do not know of any street-trade carried on *exclusively* by women. The sales in which they are principally concerned are in fish (including shrimps and oysters), fruit and vegetables (widows selling on their own account), fire-screens and ornaments, laces, millinery, artificial flowers (but not in any great majority over the male traders), cut flowers, boot and stay-laces and small wares, wash-leathers, towels, burnt linen, combs, bonnets, pin-cushions, tea and coffee, rice-milk, curds and whey, sheeps'-trotters, and dressed and undressed dolls.

What may be called the "heavier " trades, those necessitating the carrying of heavy weights, or the pushing of heavily-laden barrows, are in the hands of men; and so are, even these exclusively, what may be classed as the more skilled trades of the streets, viz. the sale of stationery, of books, of the most popular eatables and drinkables (the coffee-stalls excepted), and in every branch dependent upon the use of patter. In such callings as root-selling, crock-bartering, table-cover selling, mats, game, and poultry, the wife is the helpmate of her husband; if she trade separately in these things, it is because there is a full stock to dispose of, which requires the exertions of two persons, perhaps with some hired help just for the occasion.

The difference in the street-traffic, as carried on by Englishwomen and Irishwomen, is marked enough. The Irishwoman's avocations are the least skilled, and the least remunerative, but as regards mere toil, such as the carrying of a heavy burthen, are by far the most laborious. An Irishwoman, though not reared to the streets, will carry heavy baskets of oranges or apples, principally when those fruits are cheap, along the streets while her English co-trader (if not a costermonger) may be vending laces, millinery, artificial flowers, or other commodities of a "light," and in some degree of street estimation a "genteel" trade. Some of the less laborious callings, however, such as that in wash-leathers, are principally in the hands of young and middle-aged Irishwomen, while that in sheeps'-trotters, which does not entail heavy labour, are in the hands mostly of elderly Irishwomen. The sale of such things as lucifer-matches and watercresses, and any "stock" of general use, and attainable for a few pence, is resorted to by the very poor of every class. The Irishwoman more readily unites begging with selling than the Englishwoman, and is far more fluent and even eloquent; perhaps she pays less regard to truth, but she unquestionably pays a greater regard to chastity. When the uneducated Irishwoman, however, has fallen into licentious ways, she is, as I once heard it expressed, the most "savagely wicked" of any. After these broad distinctions I proceed to details.

1. From the best information at my command it may be affirmed that about one-half of the women employed in the diverse trades of the streets, are the wives or concubines (permanently or temporarily) of the men who pursue a similar mode of livelihood—the male street-sellers. I may here observe that I was informed by an experienced police-officer—who judged from his personal observation, without any official or even systematic investigation—that the women of the town, who survived their youth or their middle age, did not resort to the sale of any commodity in the streets, but sought the shelter of the workhouse, or died, he could not tell where or under what circumstances. Of the verity of this statement I have no doubt, as a street-sale entails some degree of industry or of exertion, for which the life of those wretched women may have altogether unfitted them.

In the course of the narratives and statements I have given, it is shown that some wives pursue one (itinerant or stationary) calling, while the husband pursues another. The trades in which the husband and wife (and I may here remark that when I speak of "wives," I include all, so regarded in street life, whether legally united or not)—the trades in which the woman is,

more than in any others, literally the help-mate of the man, are the costermonger's (including the flower, or root, sellers) and the crockeryware people. To the costermonger some help is often indispensable, and that of a wife is the cheapest and the most honest (to say nothing of the considerations connected with a home) which can be obtained. Among the more prosperous costermongers too, especially those who deal in fish, the wife attends to the stall while the husband goes "a round," and thus a greater extent of business is transacted. In the root and crockery-trades the woman's assistance is necessary when barter takes place instead of sale, as the husband may be ignorant of the value of the old female attire which even "high-hip ladies," as they were described to me, loved to exchange for a fuchsia or a geranium; for a glass cream-jug or a china ornament. Of the married women engaged in any street trade, I believe nineteen-twentieths are the wives of men also pursuing some street avocation.

2. There are, however, large classes of female street-sellers who may be looked upon as exceptions, the wife selling in the streets while the husband is engaged in some manual labour, but they are only partially exceptions. In the sale of wash-leathers, for instance, are the wives of many Irish bricklayers' labourers; the woman may be constantly occupied in disposing of her wares in the streets or suburbs, and the man labouring at any building; but in case of the deprivation of work, such a man will at once become a street-seller, and in the winter many burly Irish labourers sell a few nuts or "baked taties," or a few pairs of braces, or some article which seems little suitable for the employment of men of thews and muscle. In the course of my present inquiry I have, in only very rare instances, met with a poor Irishman, who had not a reason always at his tongue's end to justify anything he was doing. Ask a bricklayer's labourer why, in his youth and strength, he is selling nuts, and he will at once reply: "Sure thin, your honnur, isn't it better than doin' nothing? I must thry and make a pinny, 'til I'm in worruk again, and glory be to God, I hope that'll be soon."

An experienced man, who knows all the street-folk trading in Whitechapel and its neighbourhood, and about Spitalfields, told me that he could count up 100 married women, in different branches of open-air commerce, and of them only two had husbands who worked regularly in-doors. The husband of one woman works for a slop-tailor, the other is a bobbin turner; the tailor's wife sells water-cresses every morning and afternoon; the turner's wife is a "small-ware woman." The tailor, however, told my informant that his eye-sight was failing him, that his earnings became less and less, that he was treated like dirt, and would go into some street-trade himself before long. When the man and his wife are both in the street-trade, it is the case in three instances out of four (excluding of course the costermongers, root-sellers, and crock-man's pursuits) that the couple carry on different callings.

THE STREET COMB SELLER.

[From a Daguerreotype by BEARD.]

In the full and specific accounts I gave of the largest body of street-sellers, viz., the coster-mongers, I showed that concubinage among persons of all ages was the rule, and marriage the exception. It was computed that, taking the mass of coster-mongers, only one couple in twenty, living together, were married, except in Clerkenwell, where the costers are very numerous, and where the respected incumbent at certain seasons marries poor persons gratuitously; there one couple in ten were really man and wife.

Of the other classes of women street-sellers, directly the reverse is the case; of those living as man and wife, one couple in twenty may be *unmarried.* An intelligent informant thought this average too high, and that it was more probably one in sixteen. But I incline to the opinion of one in twenty, considering how many of the street-traders have " seen better days," and were married before they apprehended being driven to a street career. In this enumeration I include only street-*traders.* Among such people as ballad singers, concubinage, though its wrong-fulness is far better understood than among ignorant costermongers, is practised even more fully; and there is often among such classes even worse than concubinage—a dependance, more or less, on the wages of a woman's prostitution, and often a savage punishment to the wretched woman, if those wages of sin are scant or wanting.

3. The widows in the street-trades are very generally the widows of street-sellers. I believe that very few of the widows of mechanics, when left unprovided for on their husbands' demise, resort to street traffic. If they have been needle-women before marriage, they again seek for em-ployment at needle-work; if they have been ser-vants, they become charwomen, or washerwomen, or again endeavour to obtain a livelihood in domestic service.

There are some to whom those resources are but starvation, or a step from starvation, or whom they fail entirely, and then they "*must* try the streets," as they will describe it. If they are young and reckless, they become prostitutes; if in more advanced years, or with good principles, they turn street-sellers; but this is only when desti-tution presses sharply.

4. The single women in the street-callings are generally the daughters of street-sellers, but their number is not a twentieth of the others, excepting they are the daughters of Irish parents. The coster-mongers' daughters either help their parents, with whom they reside, or carry on some similar trade; or they soon form connections with the other sex, and easily sever the parental tie, which very pro-bably has been far too lax or far too severe. I made many inquiries, but I did not hear of any unmar-ried young woman, not connected with street-folk by birth or rearing, such as a servant maid,—en-deavouring to support herself when out of work or place by a street avocation. Such a person will starve on slop millinery or slop shirt-making; or will, as much or more from desperation than from viciousness, go upon the town. With the

Irish girls the case is different: brought up to a street-life, used to whine and blarney, they grow up to womanhood in street-selling, and as they rarely form impure connections, and as no one may be induced to offer them marriage, their life is often one of street celibacy. A young Irishwoman, to whom I was referred in the course of my inquiry among fruit-sellers, had come to London in the hopes of meeting her brother, with whom she was to emigrate; but she could learn nothing of him, and, concluding that he was dead, be-came an apple-seller. She sat, when I saw her, on cold wintry days, at the corner of a street in the Commercial-road, seemingly as much dead as alive, and slept with an aunt, also a single wo-man, who was somewhat similarly circumstanced; and thus these two women lived on about 6*d.* a day each. Their joint bed was 1*s.* a week, and they contrived to subsist on what remained when this shilling was paid. The niece referred me, not without a sense of pride, to her priest, as to her observance of her religious duties, and de-clared that where she lodged there were none but women lodgers, and those chiefly her own coun-trywomen. I believe such cases are not un-common. A few, who have had the education of ladies (as in the case of an envelope-seller whose statement I gave), are driven to street-trading, but it is as a desperate grasp at something to supply less bitter bread, however little of it, than is sup-plied in the workhouse. I have many a time heard poor women say: " God knows, sir, I should live far better, and be better lodged and better cared for in the house (they seldom call it work-house), but I 'd rather live on 2*d.* a day." Into the question of out and in-door relief I need not now enter, but the prevalent feeling I have indi-cated is one highly honourable to the English poor. I have heard it stated that the utter repugnance to a workhouse existence was weaker than it used to be among the poor, but I have not met with anything to uphold such an opinion.

Such constitute the several classes of women street-sellers. I shall now proceed to speak of the habits and characters of this peculiar portion of the street-folk.

As regards the religion of the women in street-trades, it is not difficult to describe it. The Irish-women are Roman Catholics. Perhaps I am justi-fied in stating that they are *all* of that faith. The truth of this assertion is proved, moreover, to as full a demonstration as it very well can be proved without actual enumeration, by the fact that the great majority of the Irishwomen in the streets are from the Catholic provinces of Connaught, Lein-ster, and Munster; there are very few from Ulster, and not one-twentieth of the whole from any one of the other provinces. Perhaps, again, it is not extravagant to estimate that three-fourths of the women and girls from the sister island, now selling things in the streets, have been, when in their own country, connected through their husbands or parents with the cultivation of the land. It is not so easy to speak of what the remaining fourth were before they became immigrants. Some were the wives of mechanics, who, when their husbands failing to obtain work in London became street-traders, had adopted the same pursuits. I met with one intelligent man having a stall of very excellent fruit in Battle-bridge, who had been a brogue-maker. He had been in business on his own account in Tralee, but mended the indifferent profits of brogue-making by a little trade in "dry goods." This, he told me with a cautious glance around him and in a half whisper, though it was twenty-eight years since he left his country, meant smuggled tobacco. He found it advisable, on account of being "wanted" by the revenue officers, to leave Tralee in great haste. He arrived in London, got employment as a bricklayer's labourer, and sent for his wife to join him. This she did, and from her first arrival, sold fruit in the streets. In two or three years the husband's work among the builders grew slack, and he then took to the streets. Another man, a shoemaker, who came from Dublin to obtain work in London, as he was considered "a good hand," could not obtain it, but became a street-seller, and *his* wife, previously to himself, had resorted to a street-trade in fruit. He became a widower and married as "his second," the daughter of an Irish carpenter who had been disappointed in emigrating from London, and whose whole family had become fruit-sellers. A third man, who had worked at his trade of a tailor in Cork, Waterford, Wicklow, and Dublin (he "tramped" from Cork to Dublin) had come to London and been for many years a street-seller in different capacities. His wife and daughter now assist him, or trade independently, in selling "roots." "Rayther," this man said, "than put up wid the wages and the *ter-ratement* (said very emphatically) o' thim slop masters at the Aist Ind, I'd sill myself as a slave. The sthraits doesn't degrade a man like thim thieves o' the worruld." This man knew, personally, ten Irish mechanics who were street-sellers in London, as were their wives and families, including some five-and-twenty females.

I adduce these and the following details somewhat minutely, as they tend to show by what class of Irish immigrants the streets of the imperial metropolis are stocked with so large a body of open-air traders.

There is also another class of women who, I am informed on good authority, sometimes become street-sellers, though I met with no instance myself. The orphan children of poor Irish parents are, on the demise of their father and mother sometimes taken into a workhouse and placed out as domestic servants. So, as regards domestic servants, are the daughters of Irish labourers, by their friends or the charitable. As the wages of these young girls are small and sometimes nominal, the work generally hard, and in no few instances the food scanty and the treatment severe, domestic service becomes distasteful, and a street life "on a few oranges and limmons" is preferred. There is, moreover, with some of this class another cause which almost compels the young Irish girl into the adoption of some street calling. A peevish mistress, whose numerous family renders a servant necessary, but whose means are small or precarious,

becomes bitterly dissatisfied with the awkwardness or stupidity of her Irish handmaiden; the girl's going, or "teasing to go," every Sunday morning to mass is annoying, and the girl is often discharged, or discharges herself "in a huff." The mistress, perhaps, with the low tyranny dear to vulgar minds, refuses her servant a character, or, in giving one, suppresses any good qualities, and exaggerates the failings of impudence, laziness, lying, and dirtiness. Thus the girl cannot obtain another situation, and perforce perhaps she becomes a street-seller.

The readiness with which young Irish people thus adapt themselves to all the uncertainties and hardships of a street life is less to be wondered at when we consider that the Irish live together, or at any rate associate with one another, in this country, preserving their native tastes, habits, and modes of speech. Among their tastes and habits, a dislike to a street life does not exist as it does among English girls.

The poor Irish females in London are for the most part regular in their attendance at mass, and this constant association in their chapels is one of the links which keeps the street-Irish women so much distinct from the street-English. In the going to and returning from the Roman Catholic chapels, there is among these people—I was told by one of the most intelligent of them—a talk of family and secular matters,—of the present too high price of oranges to leave full 6*d.* a day at two a penny, and the probable time when cherries would be "in" and cheap, "plaze God to prosper them." In these colloquies there is an absence of any interference by English street-sellers, and an unity of conversation and interest peculiarly Irish. It is thus that the tie of religion, working with the other causes, keeps the Irish in the London streets knitted to their own ways, and is likely to keep them so, and, perhaps, to add to their number.

It was necessary to write somewhat at length of so large a class of women who *are* professors of a religion, but of the others the details may be brief; for, as to the great majority, religion is almost a nonentity. For this absence of religious observances, the women street-sellers make many, and sometimes, I must confess, valiant excuses. They must work on a Sunday morning, they will say, or they can't eat; or else they tell you, they are so tired by knocking about all the week that they must rest on a Sunday; or else they have no clothes to go to church in, and ar'n't a-going there just to be looked down upon and put in any queer place as if they had a fever, and for ladies to hold their grand dresses away from them as they walked in to their grand pews. Then, again, some assert they are not used to sit still for so long a time, and so fall asleep. I have heard all these causes assigned as reasons for not attending church or chapel.

A few women street-sellers, however, *do* attend the Sunday service of the Church of England. One lace-seller told me that she did so because it obliged Mrs. ———, who was the best friend and customer she had, and who always looked from her pew in the gallery to see who were on the poor seats. A few others, perhaps about an equal number, attend dissenting places of worship of the various denominations—the Methodist chapels comprising more than a half. If I may venture upon a calculation founded on the result of my inquiries, and on the information of others who felt an interest in the matter, I should say that about five female street-sellers attended Protestant places of worship, in the ratio of a hundred attending the Roman Catholic chapels.

The localities in which the female street-sellers reside are those (generally) which I have often had occasion to specify as the abodes of the poor. They congregate principally, however, in the neighbourhood of some street-market. The many courts in Ray-street, Turnmill-street. Cow-cross, and other parts of Clerkenwell, are full of street-sellers, especially costermongers, some of those costermongers being also drovers. Their places of sale are in Clerkenwell-green, Aylesbury-street, and St. John-street. Others reside in Vine-street (late Mutton-hill), Saffron-hill, Portpool Lane, Baldwin's-gardens, and the many streets or alleys stretching from Leather-lane to Gray's-inn-lane, with a few of the better sort in Cromer-street. Their chief mart is Leather-lane, now one of the most crowded markets in London. The many who use the Brill as their place of street-traffic, reside in Brill-row, in Ossulston-street, Wilstead-street, Chapel-street, and in the many small intersecting lanes and alleys connected with those streets, and in other parts of Somers-town. The saleswomen in the Cripplegate street-markets, such as Whitecross-street, Fore-street, Golden-lane, &c., reside in Play-house-yard, and in the thick congregation of courts and alleys, approximating to Aldersgate-street, Fore-street, Bunhill-row, Chiswell-street, Barbican, &c., &c. Advancing eastward, the female street-sellers in Shoreditch (including the divisions of the Bishopsgate-streets Within and Without, Norton Folgate, and Holywell-street) reside in and about Artillery-lane, Half-moon-street, and the many narrow " clefts " (as they are called in one of Leigh Hunt's essays) stretching on the right hand as you proceed along Bishopsgate-street, from its junction with Cornhill ; "clefts" which, on my several visits, have appeared to me as among the foulest places in London. On the left-hand side, proceeding in the same direction, the street-sellers reside in Long-alley, and the many yards connected with that, perhaps narrowest, in proportion to its length, of any merely pedestrian thoroughfare in London. Mixed with the poor street-sellers about Long-alley, I may observe, are a mass of the tailors and shoemakers employed by the east-end slop-masters ; they are principally Irish workmen, carrying on their crafts many in one room, to economise the rent, while some of their wives are street-sellers.

The street-sellers in Spitalfields and Bethnal-green are so mixed up as to their abodes with the wretchedly underpaid cabinet-makers who supply the "slaughter-houses;" with slop-employed tailors and shoemakers (in the employ of a class, as respects shoemakers, known as "garret-

masters" or middle-men, between the workman and the wholesale warehouse-man), bobbin-turners, needle-women, slop-milliners, &c., that I might tediously enumerate almost every one of the many streets known, emphatically enough, as the "poor streets." These poor streets are very numerous, running eastward from Shoreditch to the Cambridge-road, and southward from the Bethnal-green-road to Whitechapel and the Mile End-road. The female street-sellers in Whitechapel live in Wentworth-street, Thrawl-street, Osborne-street, George-yard, and in several of their intermingle-ments with courts and narrow streets. The Petticoat-lane street-dealers are generally Jews, and live in the poorer Jewish quarters, in Petticoat-lane and its courts, and in the streets running on thence to Houndsditch. Rosemary-lane has many street-sellers, but in the lane itself and its many yards and blind alleys they find their domiciles. Westward in the metropolis one of the largest street-markets is in Tottenham-court-road ; and in the courts between Fitzroy-market and Tottenham-court-road are the rooms of the women vending their street goods. Those occupying the Hampstead-road with their stalls—which is but a continuation of the Tottenham-court-road market—live in the same quarters. In what is generally called the St. George's-market, meaning the stalls at the western extremity of Oxford-street, the women who own those stalls reside in and about Thomas-street, Tom's-court, and the wretched places—the very existence of which is perhaps unknown to their aristocratic neighbourhood—about Grosvenor-square ; some of them lamentably wretched places. It might be wearisome to carry on this enumeration further. It may suffice to observe, that in the populous parts of Southwark, Lambeth, and Newington, wherever there is a street-market, are small or old streets inhabited by the street-sellers, and at no great distance. From the Obelisk at the junction, or approximate junction, of the Westminster, Waterloo, Blackfriars, Borough, and London-roads, in pretty well every direction to the banks of the Thames, are a mass of private-looking streets—as far as the absence of shops constitutes the privacy of a street—old and half-ruinous, or modern and trim, in all of which perhaps may be found street-sellers, and in some of which are pickpockets, thieves, and prostitutes.

Of course it must be understood that these specified localities are the residence of the male, as well as the female street-sellers, both adults and children.

The proportion of female street-traders who reside in lodging-houses may be estimated at one-tenth of the entire number. This may appear a small proportion, but it must be remembered that the costermongering women do not reside in lodging-houses—so removing the largest class of street-folk from the calculation of the numbers thus accommodated—and that the Irish who pursue street callings with any regularity generally prefer living, if it be two or three families in a room, in a place of their own. The female street-folk sleeping in lodging-houses, and occasionally taking their meals there, are usually those who are itinerant; the women who have a settled trade, especially a "pitch," reside in preference in some "place of their own." Of the number in lodging-houses one half may be regular inmates, some having a portion of a particular room to themselves; the others are casual sojourners, changing their night's shelter as convenience prompts.

Of the female street-sellers residing in houses of ill-fame there are not many; perhaps not many more than 100. I was told by a gentleman whose connection with parochial matters enabled him to form an opinion, that about Whitecross-street, and some similar streets near the Cornwall-road, and stretching away to the Blackfriars and Borough-roads—(the locality which if any in London is perhaps the most rank with prostitution and its attendant evils)—there might be 600 of those wretched women and of all ages, from 15 to upwards of 40; and that among them he believed there were barely a score who occupied themselves with street-sale. Of women, and more especially of girl, street-sellers, such as flower-girls, those pursuing immoral courses are far more numerous than 100, but they do not often reside in houses notoriously of ill-fame, but in their own rooms (and too often with their parents) and in low lodging-houses. For women who are street-sellers, without the practice of prostitution, to reside in a house of ill-fame, would be a reckless waste of money; as I am told that in so wretched a street as White-horse-street, the rent of a front kitchen is 4s. 6d. a week; of a back kitchen, 3s. 6d.; of a front parlour, 6s.; and of a back parlour, 4s. 6d.; all being meagrely furnished and very small. This is also accounted one of the cheapest of all such streets. The rent of a street-seller's unfurnished room is generally 1s. 6d. or even 1s. a week; a furnished room is 3s. or 2s. 6d.

The state of education among the female street-sellers is very defective. Perhaps it may be said that among the English costers not one female in twenty can read, and not one in forty can write. But they are fond of listening to any one who reads the newspaper or any exciting story. Among the street-selling Irish, also, education is very defective. As regards the adults, who have been of woman's estate before they left Ireland, a knowledge of reading and writing may be as rare as among the English costerwomen; but with those who have come to this country sufficiently young, or have been born here, education is far more diffused than among the often more prosperous English street children. This is owing to the establishment of late years of many Roman Catholic schools, at charges suited to the poor, or sometimes free, and of the Irish parents having availed themselves (probably on the recommendation of the priest) of such opportunities for the tuition of their daughters, which the English costers have neglected to do with equal chances. Of the other classes whom I have specified as street-sellers, I believe I may say that the educa-

tion of the females is about the average of that of "servants of all work" who have been brought up amidst struggles and poverty; they can read, but with little appreciation of what they read, and have therefore little taste for books, and often little leisure even if they have taste. As to writing, a woman told me that at one time, when she was "in place," and kept weekly accounts, she had been complimented by her mistress on her neat hand, but that she and her husband (a man of indifferent character) had been street-sellers for seven or eight years, and during all that time she had only once had a pen in her hand; this was a few weeks back, in signing a petition—something about Sundays, she said—she wrote her name with great pain and difficulty, and feared that she had not even spelled it aright! I may here repeat that I found the uneducated always ready to attribute their want of success in life to their want of education; while the equally poor street-sellers, who were "scholars," are as apt to say, "It's been of no manner of use to me." In all these matters I can but speak generally. The male street-sellers who have seen better days have of course been better educated, but the most intelligent of the street class are the patterers, and of them the females form no portion.

The diet of the class I am describing is, as regards its poorest members, tea and bread or bread and grease; a meal composed of nothing else is their fare twice or thrice a day. Sometimes there is the addition of a herring—or a plaice, when plaice are two a penny—but the consumption of cheap fish, with a few potatoes, is more common among the poor Irish than the poor English female street-sellers. "Indeed, sir," said an elderly woman, who sold cakes of blacking and small wares, "I could make a meal on fish and potatoes, cheaper than on tea and bread and butter, though I don't take milk with my tea—I've got to like it better without milk than with it—but if you're a long time on your legs in the streets and get to your bit of a home for a cup of tea, you want a bit of rest over it, and if you have to cook fish it's such a trouble. O, no, indeed, this time of year there's no 'casion to light a fire for your tea—and tea 'livens you far more nor a herring—because there's always some neighbour to give a poor woman a jug of boiling water." Married women, who may carry on a trade distinct from that of their husbands, live as well as their earnings and the means of the couple will permit: what they consider good living is a dinner daily off "good block ornaments" (small pieces of meat, discoloured and dirty, but not tainted, usually set for sale on the butcher's block), tripe, cow-heel, beef-sausages, or soup from a cheap cook-shop, "at 2d. a pint." To this there is the usual accompaniment of beer, which, in all populous neighbourhoods, is "3d. a pot (quart) in your own jugs." From what I could learn, it seems to me that an inordinate or extravagant indulgence of the palate, under any circumstances, is far less common among the female than the male street-sellers.

During the summer and the fine months of the spring and autumn, there are, I am assured, one-third of the London street-sellers—male and female—

"tramping" the country. At Maidstone Fair the other day, I was told by an intelligent itinerant dealer, there were 300 women, all of whose faces he believed he had seen at one time or other in London. The Irish, however, tramp very little into the country for purposes of trade, but they travel in great numbers from one place to another for purposes of mendicancy; or, if they have a desire to emigrate, they will tramp from London to Liverpool, literally begging their way, no matter whether they have or have not any money. The female street-sellers are thus a fluctuating body.

The beggars among the women who profess to be street-traders are chiefly Irishwomen, some of whom, though otherwise well-conducted, sober and chaste, beg shamelessly and with any mendacious representation. It is remarkable enough, too, that of the Irishwomen who will thus beg, many if employed in any agricultural work, or in the rougher household labours, such as scouring or washing, will work exceedingly hard. To any feeling of self-respect or self-dependence, however, they seem dead; their great merit is their chastity, their great shame their lying and mendicancy.

The female street-sellers are again a fluctuating body, as in the summer and autumn months. A large proportion go off to work in market-gardens, in the gathering of peas, beans, and the several fruits; in weeding, in hay-making, in the corn-harvest (when they will endeavour to obtain leave to glean if they are unemployed more profitably), and afterwards in the hopping. The women, however, thus seeking change of employment, are the ruder street-sellers, those who merely buy oranges at 4*d.* to sell at 6*d.*, and who do not meddle with any calling mixed up with the necessity of skill in selection, or address in recommending. Of this half-vagrant class, many are not street-sellers usually, but are half prostitutes and half thieves, not unfrequently drinking all their earnings, while of the habitual female street-sellers, I do not think that drunkenness is now a very prevalent vice. Their earnings are small, and if they become habituated to an indulgence in drink, their means are soon dissipated; in which case they are unable to obtain stock-money, and they cease to be street-sellers.

If I may venture upon an estimation, I should say that the women engaged in street sale—wives, widows, and single persons—number from 25,000 to 30,000, and that their average earnings run from 2*s.* 6*d.* to 4*s.* a week.

I shall now proceed to give the histories of individuals belonging to each of the above class of female street-sellers, with the view of illustrating what has been said respecting them generally.

OF A SINGLE WOMAN, AS A STREET-SELLER.

I HAD some difficulty, for the reasons I have stated, in finding a single woman who, by her unaided industry, supported herself on the sale of street merchandise. There were plenty of single young women so engaged, but they lived, or lodged, with their parents or with one parent, or they had some support, however trifling, from some quarter or other. Among the street Irish I could have obtained statements from many single women who depended on their daily sale for their daily bread, but I have already given instances of their street life. One Irishwoman, a spinster of about 50, for I had some conversation with her in the course of a former inquiry, had supported herself alone, by street sale, for many years. She sat, literally packed in a sort of hamper-basket, at the corner of Charles-street, Leather-lane. She seemed to fit herself cross-legged, like a Turk, or a tailor on his shopboard, into her hamper; her fruit stall was close by her, and there she seemed to doze away life day by day—for she usually appeared to be wrapped in slumber. If any one approached her stall, however, she seemed to awake, as it were, mechanically. I have missed this poor woman of late, and I believe she only packed herself up in the way described when the weather was cold.

A woman of about 26 or 27—I may again remark that the regular street-sellers rarely know their age—made the following statement. She was spare and sickly looking, but said that her health was tolerably good.

"I used to mind my mother's stall," she stated, "when I was a girl, when mother wasn't well or had a little work at pea-shelling or such like. She sold sweet-stuff. No, she didn't make it, but bought it. I never cared for it, and when I was quite young I've sold sweet-stuffs as I never tasted. I never had a father. I can't read or write, but I like to hear people read. I go to Zion Chapel sometimes of a Sunday night, the singing's so nice. I don't know what religion you may call it of, but it's a Zion Chapel. Mother's been dead these—well I don't know how long, but it's a long time. I've lived by myself ever since, and kept myself, and I have half a room with another young woman who lives by making little boxes. I don't know what sort of boxes. Pill-boxes? Very likely, sir, but I can't say I ever saw any. She goes out to work on another box-maker's premises. She's no better off nor me. We pays 1*s.* 6*d.* a-week between us; it's my bed, and the other sticks is her'n. We 'gree well enough. I haven't sold sweet stuff for a great bit. I've sold small wares in the streets, and artificials (artificial flowers), and lace, and penny dolls, and penny boxes (of toys). No, I never hear anything improper from young men. Boys has sometimes said, when I've been selling sweets, 'Don't look so hard at 'em, or they'll turn sour.' I never minded such nonsense. I has very few amusements. I goes once or twice a month, or so, to the gallery at the Wick (Victoria Theatre), for I live near. It's beautiful there. O, it's really grand. I don't know what they call what's played, because I can't read the bills.

"I hear what they're called, but I forgets. I knows Miss Vincent and John Herbert when they come on. I likes them the best. I'm a going to leave the streets. I have an aunt a laundress, because she was mother's sister, and I always helped her, and she taught me laundressing. I work for her three and sometimes four days a-week now, because she's lost her daughter Ann, and I'm known as a good ironer. Another laundress will employ me next week, so I'm dropping the streets, as I can do far better. I'm not likely to be married and I don't want to."

OF A MECHANIC'S WIFE, AS A STREET-SELLER.

A MIDDLE-aged woman, presenting what may be best understood as a decency of appearance, for there was nothing remarkable in her face or dress, gave me the following account of her experience as a street-seller, and of her feelings when she first became one :—

"I went into service very young in the country," she said, "but mistress brought me up to London with her, where master had got a situation : the children was so fond of me. I saved a little money in that and other places as girls often does, and they seems not to save it so much for themselves as for others. Father got the first bit of money I saved, or he would have been seized for rent—he was only a working man (agricultural labourer)—and all the rest I scraped went before I'd been married a fortnight, for I got married when I was 24. O no, indeed, I don't mean that my money was wasted by my husband. It was every farthing laid out in the house, besides what he had, for we took a small house in a little street near the Commercial-road, and let out furnished rooms. We did very well at first with lodgings, but the lodgers were mates of vessels, or people about the river and the docks, and they were always coming and going, and the rooms was often empty, and some went away in debt. My husband is a smith, and was in middling work for a good while. Then he got a job to go with some horses to France, for he can groom a horse as well as shoe it, and he was a long time away, three or four months, for he was sent into another country when he got to France, but I don't understand the particulars of it. The rooms was empty and the last lodger went away without paying, and I had nothing to meet the quarter's rent, and the landlord, all of a sudden almost, put in the brokers, for he said my husband would never come back, and perhaps I should be selling the furniture and be off to join him, for he told me it was all a planned thing he knew. And so the furniture was sold for next to nothing, and 1*l.* 6*s.* was given to me after the sale; I suppose that was over when all was paid, but I'd been forced to part with some linen and things to live upon and pay the rates, that came very heavy. My husband came back to an empty house three days after, and he'd been unlucky, for he brought home only 4*l.* instead of 10*l.* at least, as he expected, but he'd been cheated by the man he went into the other country with. Yes, the man that cheated him was an Englishman, and my poor John was put to great trouble and expense, and was in a strange place without knowing a word of the language. But the foreigners was very kind to him, he said, and didn't laugh at him when he tried to make hisself understood, as I've seen people do here many a time. The

landlord gave us 1*l.* to give up the house, as he had a good offer for it, and so we had to start again in the world like.

"Our money was almost all gone before John got regular work, tho' he had some odd jobs, and then he had for a good many months the care of a horse and cart for a tradesman in the City. Shortly after that he was laid up a week with a crushed leg, but his master wouldn't wait a week for him, so he hired another : 'I have nothing to say against John,' says he, when I told his master of the accident, 'and I'm sorry, very sorry, but my business can't be hindered by waiting for people getting better of accidents.' John got work at his own business next, but there was always some stopper. He was ill, or I was ill, and if there was 10*s.* in the house, then it went and wasn't enough. And so we went on for a good many years, I don't know how many. John kept working among horses and carts, or at his own business, but what with travelling abroad, I suppose, and such like, he got to like best to be in the streets, and he has his health best that way." (The husband, it is evident, was afflicted with the restlessness of the tribe.) "About seven years ago we were very badly off—no work, and no money, and neither of us well. Then I used to make a few women's plain night-caps and plain morning caps for servants, and sell them to a shopkeeper, but latterly I couldn't sell them at all, or get no more than the stuff cost me, without any profit for labour. So at last— and it was on a Friday evening of all unlucky times—my gold wedding-ring that cost 8*s.* 6*d.*, and that I'd stuck to all along, had to be pawned for 4*s.* 6*d.* for rent and bread. That *was* a shocking time, sir. We've sat in the dark of an evening, for we could get neither coals nor a candle as we was a little in debt, and John said, it was a blessing after all perhaps that we hadn't no family, for he often, both joking and serious, wished for children, but it wasn't God's will you see that we should have any. One morning when I woke very early I found my husband just going out, and when I asked him what sent him out so soon, he says : 'It's for nothing bad, so don't fret yourself, old gal.' That day he walked all over London and called on all the masters as had employed him, or knowed him, and told them how he was situated, and said that if he could borrow 20*s.* up and down, he could do a little, he knew—the thought of it came into his mind all of a sudden—in going about with a horse and cart, that he could hire, and sell coals to poor people. He raised 8*s.* 6*d.*, I think it was, and started with a quarter of a ton of coals, and then another quarter when the first was sold, and he carried it on for three or four weeks. But the hire of the horse and cart took all the profit, and the poor people wanted credit, besides people must cheat to thrive as sells coals in the street. All this time I could do nothing —though I tried for washing and charing, but I'm slow at washing—but starve at home, and be afraid every knock was the landlord. After that John was employed to carry a very heavy board over his shoulder, and so as to have it read on both sides. It was about an eating-house, and I went with him to give little bills about it to all we met, for it was as much as a man could do to carry the board. He had 1*s.* a day, and I had 6*d.* That was my first time in the streets and I felt so 'shamed to come to that. I thought if I met any people I knew in Essex, or any of my old mistresses, what would they think. Then we had all sorts of jokes to stand. We both looked pinched, and young gents used to say, 'Do you dine there yourselves?' and the boys—O, of all the torments!—they've shouted out, 'Excellent Dining-rooms' that was on the board, sir, 'and two jolly specimens of the style of grub!' I could have knocked their saucy heads together. We was resting in the shade one day—and we were anxious to do our best, for 1*s.* 6*d.* a day was a great thing then—and an old gentleman came up and said he was glad to get out of the sun. He looked like a parson, but was a joky man, and he'd been having some wine, I think, he smelled of it so. He began to talk to us and ask us questions, such as you have, sir, and we told him how we was situated. 'God bless you,' says he, 'for I think you're honest folks. People that lie don't talk like you; here's some loose silver I have,' and he gave John 5*s.* 6*d.* and went away. We could hardly think it was real; it seemed such a lot of money just then, to be got clear all at once. I've never seen him since, and never saw him, as I knows of, before, but may God Almighty bless him wherever he is, for I think that 5*s.* 6*d.* put new life into us, and brought a blessing. A relation of John's came to London not long after and gave him a sovereign and sent him some old clothes, and very good ones, when he went back. Then John hired a barrow—it's his own now—and started as a costermonger. A neighbour of ourn told him how to do it, and he's done very well at it since.

"Well, you know, sir, I could'nt like to stay at home by myself doing of a nothing, and I couldn't get any charing; besides John says, 'Why, can't *you* sell something?' So I made some plain women's caps, and as we lived in Ann's-place, Waterloo-road, then, I went into the New Cut with them on a Saturday night. But there was such crowding, and shoving, and shouting, that I was kept under and sold only one cap. I was very much nervoused before I went and thought again—it was very foolish, I know—'if I saw anybody from Essex,' for country people seem to think all their friends in London are making fortunes! Before I went my landlady *would* treat me to a little drop of gin to give me spirits, and 'for luck,' but I think it made me more nervoused. I very seldom taste any. And John's very good that way. He takes his pint or two every now and then, but I know where he uses, and if it gets late I go for him and he comes home. The next time I went to sell in the Cut I got bold, for I knew I was doing nothing but what was honest; I've sold caps, and millinery, and laces, and artificial flowers, and such like ever since. We've saved a little money now, which is in the bank, thank God, but that's not done by costering, or by my trade. But my husband buys

a poney every now and then, and grooms and fattens it up well, and makes it quite another thing, and so clears a pound or two; he once cleared 3*l.* 15*s.* on it. We don't go to church or chapel on a Sunday, we're so tired out after the week's work. But John reads a tract that a young lady leaves 'till he falls asleep over it."

Of an Irishwoman, as a Street-Seller.

I HAVE before had occasion to remark the aptitude of the poor Irish in the streets of London not so much to lie, which may be too harsh a word when motives and idiosyncrasy are considered, but to exaggerate, and misrepresent, and colour in such a way that the truth becomes a mere incident in the narrative, instead of being the animating principle throughout. I speak here not as regards any direct question or answer on one specific point, but as regards a connected statement. Presuming that a poor Irishwoman, for instance, had saved up a few shillings, very likely for some laudable purpose, and had them hidden about her person, and was asked if she had a farthing in the world, she would reply with a look of most stolid innocence, "Sorra a fardin, sir." This of course is an unmitigated lie. Then ask her *why* she is so poor and what are her hopes for the future, and a very slender substratum of truth will suffice for the putting together of a very ingenious history, if she think the occasion requires it.

It is the same when these poor persons are questioned as to their former life. They have heard of societies to promote emigration, and if they fancy that any inquiries are made of them with a view to emigration, they will ingeniously shape their replies so as to promote or divert that object, according to their wishes. If they think the inquiries are for some charitable purpose, their tale of woe and starvation is heart-rending. The probability is that they may have suffered much, and long and bravely, but they will still exaggerate. In one thing, however, I have found them understate the fact, and that I believe principally, or wholly, when they had been previously used to the most wretched of the Irish hovels. I mean as to their rooms. "Where do you live," may be asked. "Will, thin, in Paraker-street (Parker-street) Derwry-lane?" "Have you a decent room?" "Shure, thin, and it is dacint for a poor woman." On a visit, perhaps the room will be found smoky, filthy, half-ruinous, and wretched in every respect. I believe, however, that if these poor people could be made to comprehend the motives which caused their being questioned for the purposes of this work, the elucidation of the truth—motives which they cannot be made to understand—they would speak with a far greater regard to veracity. But they *will* suspect an ulterior object, involving some design on the part of the querist, and they will speak accordingly. To what causes, social or political, national, long-rooted, or otherwise, this spirit may be owing, it is not now my business to inquire.

At the outset of my inquiries amongst the poor

Irish, whose civility and often native politeness, where there is a better degree of intelligence, makes it almost impossible to be angry with them even when you listen to a story of which you believe not one-sixth—at the outset of my inquiries, I say, I was told by an Irish gentleman that I was sure to hear the truth if I had authority to use the name of their priest. I readily obtained the consent of reverend gentlemen to use their names and for any purpose of inquiry, a courtesy which I thankfully acknowledge. I mention this more especially, that it may not be thought that there has been exaggeration in my foregoing or in the following statement, where the Irish are the narrators. I have little doubt of their truth.

It may be but proper to remark, in order that one class of poor people may not be unduly *depreciated,* while another class is, perhaps, unduly *appreciated,* that the poor Irishman is much more imaginative, is readier of wit and far readier of speech, than an Englishman of a corresponding grade; and were the untaught Englishman equally gifted in those respects, who will avouch that *his* regard for the truth would be much more severe?

Of the causes which induced a good-looking Irish woman to become a street-seller I had the following account, which I give in its curious details:—

"'Deed thin, sir, it's more than 20 long years since I came from Dublin to Liverpool wid my father and mother, and brother William that's dead and gone, rest his soul. He died when he was fourteen. They was masons in Ireland. Was both father and mother masons, sir? Well, then, in any quiet job mother helped father, for she was a strong woman. They came away sudden. They was in some thrubble, but I never knew what, for they wouldn't talk to me about it. We thravelled from Liverpool to London, for there was no worruk at Liverpool; and he got worruk on buildings in London, and had 18s. a week; and mother cleaned and worruked for a greengrocer, as they called them—he sold coals more than anything—where we lodged, and it wasn't much, she got, but she airned what is such a thrubble to poor people, the rint. We was well off, and I was sent to school; and we should have been better off, but father took too much to the dhrop, God save him. He fell onste and broke his leg; and though the hospital gintlemen, God bless them for good Christians, got him through it, he got little worruk when he came out again, and died in less than a year. Mother wasn't long afther him; and on her death-bed she said, so low I could hardly hear her, 'Mary, my darlint, if you starruve, be vartuous. Rimimber poor Illen's funeral.' When I was quite a child, sir, I went wid mother to a funeral—she was a relation—and it was of a young woman that died after her child had been borrun a fortnight, and she wasn't married; that was Illen. Her body was brought out of the lying-in hospital—I've often heard spake of it since—and was in the churchyard to be buried; and her brother, that hadn't seen her for a long time, came and wanted to see her in her

coffin, and they took the lid off, and then he currused her in her coffin afore him; she'd been so wicked. But he wasn't a good man hisself, and was in dhrink too; still nobody said anything, and he walked away. It made me ill to see Illen in her coffin, and hear him curruse, and I've remimbered it ever since.

"I was thin fifteen, I believe, and hadn't any friends that had any tie to me. I was lone, sir. But the neebours said, 'Poor thing, she's left on the shuckrawn' (homeless); and they helped me, and I got a place. Mistress was very kind at first, that's my first mistress was, and I had the care of a child of three years old; they had only one, because mistress was busy making waistcoats. Master was a hatter, and away all day, and they was well off. But some women called on mistress once, and they had a deal of talkin', and bladherin', and laughin', and I don't know how often I was sent out for quarterns of gin. Then they all went out together; and mistress came home quite tipsy just afore master, and went up-stairs, and had just time to get into bed; she told me to tell master she had one of her sick head-aches and was forced to go to bed; she went on that way for three or four days, and master and she used to quarrel of a night, for I could hear them. One night he came home sooner than common, and he'd been drinking, or perhaps it might be thrubble, and he sent me to bed wid the child; and sometime in the night, I don't know what time, but I could only see from a gas-lamp that shined into the room, he came in, for there was no fastenin' inside the door, it was only like a closet, and he began to ask me about mistress. When he larned she'd been drinking wid other women, he used dreadful language, and pulled me out of bed, and struck me with a stick that he snatched up, he could see it in the gas-light, it was little Frank's horse, and swore at me for not telling him afore. He only struck me onste, but I screamed ever so often, I was so frightened. I dressed myself, and lay down in my clothes, and got up as soon as it was light—it was summer time—and thought I would go away and complain to some one. I would ask the neebours who to complain to. When I was going out there was master walking up and down the kitchen. He'd never been to bed, and he says, says he, 'Mary, where are you going?' So I told him, and he begged my pardon, and said he was ashamed of what he'd done, but he was half mad; then he began to cry, and so I cried, and mistress came home just then, and when she saw us both crying together, *she* cried, and said she wasn't wanted, as we was man and wife already. Master just gave her a push and down she fell, and he ran out. She seemed so bad, and the child began to cry, that I couldn't lave thin; and master came home drunk that night, but he wasn't cross, for he'd made out that mistress had been drinking with some neebours, and had got to her mother's, and that she was so tipsy she fell asleep, they let her stay till morning, and then some woman set her home, but she'd been there all night. They made it up at last, but I wouldn't stay. They was very kind to me when I left, and paid me all that was owing, and gave me a good pair of shoes, too; for they was well off.

"I had a many places for seven years; after that, and when I was out of a place, I stayed wid a widder, and a very dacint woman, she was wid a daughter working for a bookbinder, and the old woman had a good pitch with fruit. Some of my places was very harrud, but shure, again, I met some as was very kind. I left one because they was always wanting me to go to a Methodist chapel, and was always running down my religion, and did all they could to hinder my ever going to mass. They would hardly pay me when I left, because I wouldn't listen to them, they said —the haythens!—when they would have saved my soul. *They* save my soul, indeed! The likes o' thim! Yes, indeed, thin, I had wicked offers sometimes, and from masters that should have known better. I kept no company wid young men. One mistress refused me a karackter, because I was so unhandy, she said; but she thought better of it. At last, I had a faver (fever), and wasn't expected for long (not expected to live); when I was getting well, everything went to keep me. What wasn't good enough for the pawn went to the dolly (dollyshop, generally a rag and bottle shop, or a marine store). When I could get about, I was so shabby, and my clothes hung about me so, that the shops I went to said, ' Very sorry, but can't recommend you anywhere;' and mistresses looked strange at me, and I didn't know what to do and was miserable. I'd been miserable sometimes in place, and had many a cry, and thought how ' lone' I was, but I never was so miserable as this. At last, the old woman I stayed along wid —O, yes, she was an Irishwoman—advised me to sill fruit in the streets, and I began on strawberries, and borrowed 2s. 6d. to do it wid. I had my hilth better than ever thin; and after I'd sold fruit of all kinds for two years, I got married. My husband had a potato can thin. I knew him because he lived near, and I saw him go in and out, and go to mass. After that he got a porter's place and dropped his can, and he porters when he has a chance still, and has a little work in sewing sacks for the corn-merchants. Whin he's at home at his sacks, as he is now, he can mind the children —we have two—and I sells a few oranges to make a thrifle. Whin there's nothing ilse for him to do, he sills fruit in the sthreets, and thin I'm at home. We do middlin, God be praised."

There is no doubt my informant was a modest, and, in her way, a worthy woman. But it may be doubted if any English girl, after seven years of domestic service, would have so readily adapted herself to a street calling. Had an English girl been living among, and used to the society of women who supported themselves by street labour, her repugnance to such a life might have been lessened; but even then, I doubt if she, who had the virtue to resist the offers told of by my Irish informant, could have made the attempt to live by selling fruit. I do not mean that she would rather have fallen into immoral courses than honestly live upon the sale of strawberries, but that she would have struggled on and striven to obtain any domestic labour in preference to a street occupation.

Of a Widow, a Street-Seller.

A woman, apparently about 50, strong-built and red-faced, speaking in a loud tone, and what people of her class account a *hearty* manner, gave me the following account. I can readily condense it, for in her street career there there was nothing very novel. She was the daughter of a costermonger, and she married a costermonger before she was 20. On my hinting that sometimes the marriage ceremony was not considered indispensable, the good woman laughed and said, " married, or as good, it's hall as one—but we was married." The marriage was not one of unalloyed happiness, for the couple often wrangled and occasionally fought. This was told to me with some laughter, and with perfect good humour ; for the widow seemed interested to have a listener. She did not, I feel confident, exaggerate the merits of the deceased, nor, perhaps, his failings. He was the best judge of fish in the streets, she said, and was the neatest hand in cutting it up, or showing it off; he was not "a bad sort," and was very fond of his children. When sober and at work he was a quiet fellow, without a cross word for a whole morning, but when drunk, which was far too often (unless *very* drunk, and then he was silly), he went about tearing and swearing " like one o'clock." But if he saw his wife take but a glass or two, to do her good, he went on like a madman, and as if he never touched it himself. He never had nothing to say to other women—if he had she would have clawed their eyes out, and his'n too—he was as good that way as any nobleman could be, and he was a fine man to look at ; and on a Sunday, when he dressed hisself, he was beautiful. He was never in a church in his life, and didn't trouble hisself about such things ; they was no concern of his'n.

It may be thought that I have treated this matter too lightly, but the foregoing is really the substance, and certainly it is the tone, of the widow's talk, which she poured forth freely, without expressing wonder why any one, a perfect stranger, cared to listen to such a history. She needed but a few hints and leading questions to make her talk on. Nor is this an uncommon quality even among classes who would be shocked to be classed, in any respect, with the Widowed Street-Seller. Their own career, their own sayings and doings, hopes and disappointments, alone interest masses of people, and with the simplicity which not seldom pertains to selfishness, they will readily talk of all that interests themselves, as if it must necessarily interest others. On the whole, though the departed costermonger was greatly deplored by his widow and family, they did very well without him, and carry on the business to this day. He died four or five years back.

I have no doubt this widow is a shrewd saleswoman enough. I have heard her cry " mack'rel, live mack'rel, eight a shilling, mack'rel ! " and at other times, " Eight a bob, fine mack'rel, mack'rel, eight a bob, eight a bob ! " On my inquiring as to the cause of this difference in her cries, the fish-seller laughed and said, " I cries eight a bob when I sees people as I thinks is likely to like slang ; to others I cries eight a shilling, which no doubt is the right way of talking."

Of the Children Street-Sellers of London.

When we consider the spirit of emulation, of imitation, of bravado, of opposition, of just or idle resentment, among boys, according to their training, companionship, natural disposition, and, above all, home treatment, it seems most important to ascertain how these feelings and inclinations are fostered or stimulated by the examples of the free street-life of other lads to be seen on every side. There is no doubt that to a large class of boys, whose parents are not in poverty, the young street ruffian is a hero.

If this inquiry be important, as it unquestionably is, concerning boys, how much more important is it, when it includes the female children of the streets ; when it relates to the sex who, in all relations of life, and in all grades of society, are really the guardians of a people's virtue.

The investigation is, again, rendered more interesting and more important, when it includes those children who have known no guidance from parent, master, or relative, but have been flung into the streets through neglect, through viciousness, or as outcasts from utter destitution. Mixed with the children who really *sell* in the streets, are the class who assume to sell that they may have the better chance to steal, or the greater facility to beg.

Before I classify what I consider to be the causes which have driven children to a street career, with all its hardening consequences, I may point out that culpability cannot be imputed to them at the commencement of their course of life. They have been either untaught, mistaught, maltreated, neglected, regularly trained to vice, or fairly turned into the streets to shift for themselves. The censure, then, is attributable to parents, or those who should fill the place of parents—the State, or society. The exceptions to this culpability as regards parents are to be found in the instances where a costermonger employs his children to aid him in his business occupation, which the parents, in their ignorance or prejudices, may account as good as any other, and the youths thus become unfit, perhaps, for any other than a scrambling street life. A second exception may be where the children in a poor family (as continually happens among the Irish in London) *must* sell in the streets, that they may eat in any place.

In the following details I shall consider all to be children who are under fifteen years of age. It is just beyond that age (or the age of puberty) that, as our prison statistics and other returns show, criminal dispositions are developed, " self-

will " becomes more imperious and headstrong, that destructive propensity, or taste, which we term the ruling passion or character of the individual is educed, and the destiny of the human being, especially when apart from the moulding and well-directed care of parents or friends, is influenced perhaps for life.

The Causes, then, which fill our streets with children who either manifest. the keen and sometimes roguish propensity of a precocious trader, the daring and adroitness of the thief, or the loutish indifference of the mere dull vagabond, content if he can only eat and sleep, I consider to be these :—

1. The conduct of parents, masters, and mistresses.

2. The companionship and associations formed in tender years.

3. The employment of children by costermongers and others who live by street traffic, and the training of costermongers' children to a street life.

4. Orphanhood, friendlessness, and utter destitution.

5. Vagrant dispositions and tastes on the part of children, which cause them to be runaways.

After this I shall treat of (*a*) the pursuits of the street-trading children ; (*b*) their earnings ; (*c*) the causes or influences which have induced children to adopt some especial branch of a street life ; (*d*) their state of education ; (*e*) their morals, religion, opinions, and conduct ; (*f*) places and character of dwellings ; (*g*) diet ; (*h*) amusements ; (*i*) clothing ; (*j*) propensities.

Concerning cause 1, viz., " The conduct of parents, masters, and mistresses," I should have more to say were I treating of the juvenile criminals, instead of sellers in the streets. The brute tyranny of parents, manifested in the wreaking of any annoyances or disappointments they may have endured, in the passionate beating and cursing of their children, for trifling or for no causes, is among the worst symptoms of a depraved nature. This conduct may be the most common among the poor, for among them are fewer conventional restraints; but it exists among and debases other classes. Some parents only exercise this tyranny in their fits of drunkenness, and make that their plea in mitigation ; but their dispositions are then only the more undisguisedly developed, and they would be equally unjust or tyrannical when sober, but for some selfish fear which checks them. A boy perhaps endures this course of tyranny some time, and then finding it increase he feels its further endurance intolerable, and runs away. If he have no friends with whom he can hope to find a shelter, the streets only are open to him. He soon meets with comrades, some of whom perhaps had been circumstanced like himself, and, if not strongly disposed to idleness and vicious indulgencies, goes through a course of horse-holding, errand-running, parcel-carrying, and such like, and so becomes, if honestly or prudently inclined, a street-seller, beginning with fuzees, or nuts, or some unexpensive stock. The where to buy and the how to sell he will find plenty to teach him at the lodging-houses, where he *must* sleep when he can pay for a bed.

When I was collecting information concerning brace-selling I met with a youth of sixteen who about two years previously had run away from Birmingham, and made his way to London, with 2*s.* 6*d.* Although he earned something weekly, he was so pinched and beaten by a step-mother (his father was seldom at home except on Sunday) that his life was miserable. This went on for nearly a year, until the boy began to resist, and one Saturday evening, when beaten as usual, he struck in return, drawing blood from his step-mother's face. The father came home before the fray was well ended ; listened to his wife's statement, and would not listen to the boy's, and in his turn chastised the lad mercilessly. In five minutes after the boy, with aching bones and a bitter spirit, left his father's house and made his way to London, where he was then vending cheap braces. This youth could neither read nor write, and seemed to possess no quickness or intelligence. The only thing of which he cared to talk was his step-mother's treatment of him ; all else was a blank with him, in comparison ; this was the one burning recollection.

I may here observe, that I heard of several instances of children having run away and adopted a street life in consequence of the violence of step-mothers far more than of step-fathers.

I cite the foregoing instance, as the boy's career was exactly that I have described ; but the reader will remember, that in the many and curious narratives I have collected, how often the adult street-seller has begun such a life by being a runaway from domestic tyranny. Had this Birmingham boy been less honest, or perhaps less dull, it would have been far easier for him to have become a thief than a street-trader. To the gangs of young thieves, a new boy, who is not known to the police is often (as a smart young pickpocket, then known as the Cocksparrow, described it to me) "a God-send."

My readers will remember that in the collected statements of the street-folk, there are several accounts of runaways, but they were generally older than the age I have fixed, and it was necessary to give an account of one who comes within my classification of a child.

I did not hear of any girls who had run away from their homes having become street-sellers merely. They more generally fall into a course of prostitution, or sometimes may be ostensibly street-sellers as a means of accosting men, and, perhaps, for an attractive pretence to the depraved, that they are poor, innocent girls, struggling for an honest penny. If they resort to the low lodging-houses, where the sexes are lodged indiscriminately, their ruin seems inevitable.

2. That the companionship and associations formed in tender years lead many children to a street life is so evident, that I may be brief on the subject. There are few who are in the habit of noting what they may observe of poor children in the streets and quieter localities, who have not seen little boys playing at marbles,

or gambling with halfpennies, farthings, or buttons, with other lads, and who have laid down their basket of nuts or oranges to take part in the play. The young street-seller has probably more halfpence at his command, or, at any rate, in his possession, than his non-dealing playmates ; he is also in the undoubted possession of what appears a large store of things for which poor boys have generally a craving and a relish. Thus the little itinerant trader is envied and imitated.

This attraction to a street career is very strong, I have ascertained, among the neglected children of the poor, when the parents are absent at their work. On a Saturday morning, some little time since, I was in a flagged court near Drury-lane, a wretched place, which was full of children of all ages. The parents were nearly all, I believe, then at work, or "on the look out for a job," as porters in Covent Garden-market, and the children played in the court until their return. In one corner was a group of four or five little boys gambling and squabbling for nuts, of which one of the number was a vendor. A sharp-looking lad was gazing enviously on, and I asked him to guide me to the room of a man whom I wished to see. He did so, and I gave him a penny. On my leaving the court I found this boy the most eager of the players, gambling with the penny I had given him. I had occasion to return there a few hours after, and the same lad was leaning against the wall, with his hands in his pockets, as if suffering from listlessness. He had had no luck with the nut covey, he told me, but he hoped before long to sell nuts himself. He did not know his age, but he appeared to be about eleven. Only last week I saw this same lad hawking a basket, very indifferently stocked with oranges. He had raised a shilling, he said, and the "Early Bird" (the nickname of a young street-seller) had put him up to the way to lay it out. On my asking if his father (a journeyman butcher) knew what he was doing, he replied that so long as he didn't bother his father he could do what he pleased, and the more he kept out of his (the father's) way the better he would be liked and treated.

The association of poor boys and girls with the children of the costermongers, and of the Irish fruit-sellers, who are employed in itinerant vending, is often productive of a strong degree of envy on the part of unemployed little ones, who look upon having the charge of a basket of fruit, to be carried in any direction, as a species of independence.

3. "The employment of children by costermongers, and others who live by street traffic ; and the training of costermongers' children to a street life, is the ordinary means of increase among the street-folk."

The children of the costermongers become necessarily, as I have already intimated, street-dealers, and perhaps more innocently than in any other manner, by being required, as soon as their strength enables them, to assist their parents in their work, or sell trifles, single-handed, for the behoof of their parents. The child does but obey his father, and the father does but rear the child to the calling by which his daily bread is won. This is the case particularly with the Irish, who often have large families, and bring them with them to London.

There are, moreover, a great number of boys, "anybody's children," as I heard them called, who are tempted and trained to pursue an open-air traffic, through being engaged by costermongers or small tradesmen to sell upon commission, or, as it is termed, for "bunse." In the curious, and almost in every instance novel, information which I gave to the public concerning the largest body of the street-sellers, the costermongers, this word "bunse" (probably a corruption of *bonus*, *bone* being the slang for good) first appeared in print. The mode is this: a certain quantity of saleable, and sometimes of not very saleable, commodities is given to a boy whom a costermonger knows and perhaps employs, and it is arranged that the young commission-agent is to get a particular sum for them, which must be paid to the costermonger; I will say 3s., that being somewhere about the maximum. For these articles the lad may ask and obtain any price he can, and whatever he obtains beyond the stipulated 3s. is his own profit or "bunse." The remuneration thus accruing to the boy-vendor of course varies very materially, according to the season of the year, the nature of the article, and the neighbourhood in which it is hawked. Much also depends upon whether the boy has a regular market for his commodities; whether he has certain parties to whom he is known and upon whom he can call to solicit custom; if he has, of course his facilities for disposing of his stock in trade are much greater than in the case of one who has only the chance of attracting attention and obtaining custom by mere crying and bawling "Penny a piece, Col-ly-flowers," "Five bunches a penny, Red-dish-es," and such like. The Irish boys call this "having a back," an old Hibernian phrase formerly applied to a very different subject and purpose.

Another cause of the abundance of street-dealers among the boyish fraternity, whose parents are unable or unwilling to support them, is that some costers keep a lad as a regular assistant, whose duty it is to pull the barrow of his master about the streets, and assist him in "crying" his wares. Sometimes the man and the boy call out together, sometimes separately and alternately, but mostly the boy alone has to do this part of the work, the coster's voice being generally rough and hoarse, while the shrill sound of that of the boy re-echoes throughout the street along which they slowly move, and is far more likely to strike the ear, and consequently to attract attention, than that of the man. This mode of "practising the voice" is, however, perfectly ruinous to it, as in almost every case of this description we find the natural tone completely annihilated at a very early age, and a harsh, hoarse, guttural, disagreeable mode of speaking acquired. In addition to the costers there are others who thus employ boys in the streets: the hawkers of coal do so invariably, and the milkmen—especially those who drive cows or have

a cart to carry the milk-pails in. Once in the streets and surrounded with street-associates, the boy soon becomes inured to this kind of life, and when he leaves his first master, will frequently start in some branch of costermongering for himself, without seeking to obtain another constant employment.

This mode of employing lads, and on the whole perhaps they are fairly enough used by the costermongers, and generally treated with great kindness by the costers' wives or concubines, is, I am inclined to think, the chief cause of the abundance and even increase of the street-sellers of fish, fruit, and vegetables.

4. To "orphanhood, friendlessness, and utter destitution," the commerce of the streets owes a considerable portion of its merchants. A child finds himself or herself an orphan; the parents having been miserably poor, he or she lives in a place where street-folk abound; it seems the only road to a meal or a bed, and the orphan "starts" with a few lucifer-matches, boot-laces, nuts, or onions. It is the same when a child, without being an orphan, is abandoned or neglected by the parents, and, perhaps without any injunctions either for or against such a course, is left to his or her own will to sell or steal in the streets.

5. The vagrant dispositions and tastes of lads, and, it may be, now and then somewhat of a reckless spirit of adventure, which in our days has far fewer fields than it once had, is another cause why a street-life is embraced. Lads have been known to run away from even comfortable homes through the mere spirit of restlessness; and sometimes they have done so, but not perhaps under the age of fifteen, for the unrestrained indulgence of licentious passions. As this class of runaways, however, do not ordinarily settle into regular street-sellers, but become pickpockets, or trade only with a view to cloak their designs of theft, I need not further allude to them under this head.

I now come to the second part of my subject, the *Pursuits*, &c., of the children in street avocations.

As I have shown in my account of the women street-sellers, there is no calling which this body of juveniles monopolize, none of which they are the *sole* possessors; but some are principally in their hands, and there are others, again, to which they rarely incline.

Among the wares sold by the boys and girls of the streets are:—money-bags, lucifer-match boxes, leather straps, belts, firewood (common, and also "patent," that is, dipped into an inflammable composition), fly-papers, a variety of fruits, especially nuts, oranges, and apples; onions, radishes, water-cresses, cut flowers and lavender (mostly sold by girls), sweet-briar, India rubber, garters, and other little articles of the same material, including elastic rings to encircle rolls of paper-music, toys of the smaller kinds, cakes, steel pens and penholders with glass handles, exhibition medals and cards, gelatine cards, glass and other cheap seals, brass watch-guards, chains, and rings; small tin ware, nutmeg-graters, and other articles of a similar description, such as are easily portable ; iron skewers, fuzees, shirt buttons, boot and stay-laces, pins (and more rarely needles), cotton bobbins, Christmasing (holly and other evergreens at Christmas-tide), May-flowers, coat-studs, toy-pottery, blackberries, groundsel and chickweed, and clothes'-pegs.

There are also other things which children sell temporarily, or rather in the season. This year I saw lads selling wild birds'-nests with their eggs, such as hedge-sparrows, minnows in small glass globes, roots of the wild Early Orchis (*Orchis mascula*), and such like things found only out of town.

Independently of the vending of these articles, there are many other ways of earning a penny among the street boys : among them are found —tumblers, mud-larks, water-jacks, Ethiopians, ballad-singers, bagpipe boys, the variety of street musicians (especially Italian boys with organs), Billingsgate boys or young " roughs," Covent Garden boys, porters, and shoeblacks (a class recently increased by the Ragged School Brigade). A great many lads are employed also in giving away the cards and placards of advertising and puffing tradesmen, and around the theatres are children of both sexes (along with a few old people) offering play-bills for sale, but this is an occupation less pursued than formerly, as some managers sell their own bills inside the house and do not allow any to pass from the hands of the printer into those of the former vendors. Again : amid the employments of this class may be mentioned—the going on errands and carrying parcels for persons accidentally met with ; holding horses ; sweeping crossings (but the best crossings are usually in the possession of adults) ; carrying trunks for any railway traveller to or from the terminus, and carrying them from an omnibus when the passenger is not put down at his exact destination. During the frosty days of the winter and early spring, some of these little fellows used to run along the foot-path— Baker-street was a favourite place for this display—and keep pace with the omnibuses, not merely by-using their legs briskly, but by throwing themselves every now and then on their hands and progressing a few steps (so to speak) with their feet in the air. This was done to attract attention and obtain the preference if a job were in prospect ; done, too, in hopes of a halfpenny being given the urchin for his agility. I looked at the hands of one of these little fellows and the fleshy parts of the palm were as hard as soling-leather, as hard, indeed, as the soles of the child's feet, for he was bare-footed. At the doors of the theatres, and of public places generally, boys are always in waiting to secure a cab from the stand, their best harvest being when the night has "turned out wet" after a fine day. Boys wait for the same purpose, lounging all night, and until the place closes, about the night-houses, casinos, saloons, &c., and sometimes without receiving a penny. There are, again, the very many ways in which street boys employed to "help" other people, when temporary help is needed, as when a cabman must finish the cleaning of his vehicle in a hurry, or when a porter finds himself over-weighted in his truck. Boys are, moreover, the common custodians of the donkeys on which young ladies take invigorating exercise in such places as Hampstead-heath and Blackheath. At pigeon-shooting matches they are in readiness to pick up the dead birds, and secure the poor fluttering things which are "hard hit" by the adventurous sportsman, without having been killed. They have their share again in the picking of currants and gooseberries, the pottling of strawberries, in weeding, &c., &c., and though the younger children may be little employed in haymaking, or in the more important labours of the corn harvest, they have their shares, both with and without the company of their parents, in the "hopping." In fine there is no business carried on to any extent in the streets, or in the open air, but it will be found that boys have their portion. Thus they are brought into contact with all classes ; another proof of what I have advanced touching the importance of this subject.

It will be perceived that, under this head, I have had to speak far more frequently of boys than of girls, for the boy is far more the child of the streets than is the girl. The female child can do little but *sell* (when a livelihood is to be gained without a recourse to immorality) ; the boy can not only sell, but *work.*

The many ramifications of child-life and of child-work in our teeming streets, which I have just enumerated, render it difficult to arrive at a very nice estimation of the *earnings of the street boys and girls.* The gains of this week are not necessarily the gains of the next ; there is the influence of the weather ; there may be a larger or a smaller number of hands "taking a turn" at any particular calling this week than in its predecessor ; and, above all, there is that concatenation of circumstances, which street-sellers include in one expressive word—"luck." I mean the opportunities to earn a few pence, which on some occasions present themselves freely, and at others do not occur at all. Such "luck," however, is more felt by the holders of horses, and the class'of waiters upon opportunity (so to speak), than by those who depend upon trade.

I believe, however, both in consequence of what I have observed, and from the concurrent testimony of persons familiar with the child-life of London streets, that the earnings of the children, when they are healthful and active, are about the same in the several capacities they exercise. The waiter on opportunity, the lad "on the look-out for a job," may wait and look out all day bootlessly, but in the evening some fortunate chance may realize him "a whole tanner all in a lump." In like manner, the water-cress girl may drudge on from early morning until "cresses" are wanted for tea, and, with "a connection," and a tolerably regular demand, earn no more than the boy's 6*d.,* and probably not so much.

One of the most profitable callings of the street-child is in the sale of Christmasing, but that is only for a very brief season; the most regular returns in the child's trade, are in the sale of such things as water-cresses, or any low-priced article of daily consumption, wherever the youthful vendor may be known.

I find it necessary to place the earnings of the street-children higher than those of the aged and infirm. The children are more active, more persevering, and perhaps more impudent. They are less deterred by the weather, and can endure more fatigue in walking long distances than old people. This, however, relates to the boys more especially, some of whom are very sturdy fellows.

The oranges which the street-children now vend at two a-penny, leave them a profit of 4d. in the shilling. To take 1s. 6d. with a profit of 6d. is a fair day's work; to take 1s. with a profit of 4d. is a poor day's work. The dozen bunches of cut-flowers which a girl will sell on an average day at 1d. a bunch, cost her 6d., that sum being also her profit. These things supply, I think, a fair criterion. The children's profits may be 6d. a day, and including Sunday trade, 3s. 6d. a week; but with the drawbacks of bad weather, they cannot be computed at more than 2s. 6d. a week the year through. The boys may earn 2d. or 3d. a week on an average more than the girls, except in such things (which I shall specify under the next head) as seem more particularly suited for female traffic.

Of the causes which influence children to follow this or that course of business when a street career has been their choice or their lot, I have little to say. It seems quite a matter of chance, even where a preference may exist. A runaway lad meets with a comrade who perhaps sells fuzees, and he accordingly begins on fuzees. One youth, of whom I have given an account (but he was not of child's estate), began his street career on fly-papers. When children are sent into the streets to sell on account of their parents, they, of course, vend just what their parents have supplied to them. If "on their own hook," they usually commence their street career on what it is easiest to buy and easiest to sell; a few nuts or oranges bought in Duke's-place, lucifer-boxes, or small wares. As their experience increases they may become general street-sellers. The duller sort will continue to carry on the trades that any one with ordinary lungs and muscles can pursue. "All a fellow wants to know to sell potatoes," said a master street-seller to me, "is to tell how many tanners make a bob, and how many yenaps a tanner." [How many sixpences make a shilling, and how many pence a sixpence.] The smarter and bolder lads ripen into patterers, or street-performers, or fall into theft. For the class of adventurous runaways, the patterer's, or, rather, the paper-working patterer's life, with its alternations of town and country, fairs and hangings, the bustle of race-grounds and the stillness of a village, has great attractions. To a pattering and chaunting career, moreover, there is the stimulus of that love of approbation and of admiration, as strong among the often penniless professionals of the streets as on the boards of the opera house.

Perhaps there is not a child of either sex, now a street-seller, who would not to-morrow, if they thought they could clear a penny or two a day more by it, quit their baskets of oranges and sell candle-ends, or old bones, or anything. In a street career, and most especially when united with a lodging-house existence, there is no daintiness of the senses and no exercise of the tastes: the question is not "What do I like best to sell?" but "What is likely to pay me best?" This cannot be wondered at; for if a child earn but 5d. a day on apples, and can make 6d. on onions, its income is increased by 20 per cent.

The trades which I have specified as in the hands of street-children are carried on by both sexes. I do not know that even the stock in trade which most taxes the strength is more a boy's than a girl's pursuit. A basket of oranges or of apples is among the heaviest of all the stocks hawked by children; and in those pursuits there are certainly as many, or rather more, girls than boys. Such articles as fly-papers, money-bags, tins, fuzees, and Christmasing, are chiefly the boys' sale; cut-flowers, lavender, water-cresses, and small wares, are more within the trading of the girls.

The callings with which children do not meddle are those which require "patter." Some of the boys very glibly announce their wares, and may be profuse now and then in commendations of their quality, cheapness, and superiority, but it requires a longer experience to patter according to the appreciation of a perhaps critical street audience. No child, for instance, ventures upon the sale of grease-removing compositions, corn-salve, or the "Trial and Execution of Thomas Drory," with an "Affecting Copy of Werses."

A gentleman remarked to me that it was rather curious that boys' playthings, such as marbles and tops, were not hawked by street juveniles, who might be very well able to recommend them. I do not remember to have seen any such things vended by children.

Education is, as far as I have been able to ascertain, more widely extended among street children than it was twelve or fifteen years ago. The difficulty in arriving at any conclusion on such a subject is owing to the inability to find any one who knew, or could even form a tolerably accurate judgment of what was the state of education among these juveniles even twelve years back.

Perhaps it may be sufficiently correct to say that among a given number of street children, where, a dozen years ago, you met twenty who could read, you will now meet upwards of thirty. Of sixteen children, none apparently fifteen years of age, whom I questioned on the subject, nine admitted that they could not read; the other seven declared that they could, but three annexed to the avowal the qualifying words—"a little." Ten were boys and six were girls, and I spoke to them promiscuously as I met them in the street. Two were Irish lads, who were "working" oranges in company, and the bigger answered—"Shure, thin, we *can* rade, your honour, sir." I have little doubt that they could, but in all probability, had either of those urchins thought he would be a penny the better by it, he would have professed, to a perfect stranger, that he had a knowledge of algebra. " Yis, sir, I do, thin," would very likely be his response to any such inquiry; and when told he could not possibly know anything about it, he would answer, " Arrah, thin, but I didn't understand your honour."

To the Ragged Schools is, in all probability, owing this extension of the ability to read. It appears that the attendance of the street children at the Ragged School is most uncertain ; as, indeed, must necessarily be the case where the whole time of the lad is devoted to obtaining a subsistence. From the best information I can collect, it appears that the average attendance of these boys at these schools does not exceed two hours per week, so that the amount of education thus acquired, if education it may be called, must necessarily be scanty in the extreme ; and is frequently forgotten as soon as learned.

With many of these little traders a natural shrewdness compensates in some measure for the deficiency of education, and enables them to carry on their variety of trades with readiness and dexterity, and sometimes with exactness. One boy with whom I had a conversation, told me that he never made any mistake about the "coppers," although, as I subsequently discovered, he had no notion at all of arithmetic beyond the capability of counting how many pieces of coin he had, and how much copper money was required to make a " tanner" or a " bob." This boy vended coatstuds : he had also some metal collars for dogs, or as he said, " for cats aither." These articles he purchased at the same shop in Houndsditch, where " there was a wonderful lot of other things to be had, on'y some on'em cost more money."

In speaking of money, the slang phrases are constantly used by the street lads ; thus a sixpence is a "tanner;" a shilling a "bob," or a hog ;" a crown is "a bull ;" a half-crown "a half bull," &c. Little, as a modern writer has remarked, do the persons using these phrases know of their remote and somewhat classical origin, which may, indeed, be traced to the period antecedent to that when monarchs monopolized the surface of coined money with their own images and superscriptions. They are identical with the very name of money among the early Romans, which was *pecunia*, from *pecus*, a flock. The collections of coin dealers amply show, that the figure of a hog was anciently placed on a small silver coin, and that that of a bull decorated larger ones of the same metal : these coins were frequently deeply crossed on the reverse : this was for the convenience of easily breaking them into two or more pieces, should the bargain for which they were employed require it, and the parties making it had no smaller change handy to complete the transaction. Thus we find that the "half-bull" of the itinerant street-seller or " traveller," so far from being a phrase of modern invention, as is generally supposed, is in point of

fact referable to an era extremely remote. Numerous other instances might be given of the classical origin of many of the flash or slang words used by these people.

I now give the answers I received from two boys. The first, his mother told me, was the best scholar at his school when he was there, and before he had to help her in street sale. He was a pale, and not at all forward boy, of thirteen or fourteen, and did not appear much to admire being questioned. He had not been to a Ragged School, but to an "academy" kept by an old man. He did not know what the weekly charge was, but when father was living (he died last autumn) the schoolmaster used to take it out in vegetables. Father was a costermonger ; mother minded all about his schooling, and master often said she behaved to him like a lady. " God," this child told me, " was our Heavenly Father, and the maker of all things ; he knew everything and everybody ; he knew people's thoughts and every sin they committed if no one else knew it. His was the kingdom and the power, and the glory, for ever and ever, Amen. Jesus Christ was our Lord and Saviour ; he was the son of God, and was crucified for our sins. He was a God himself." [The child understood next to nothing of the doctrine of the Trinity, and I did not press him.] " The Scriptures, which were the Bible and Testament, were the Word of God, and contained nothing but what was good and true. If a boy lied, or stole, or committed sins," he said, " he would be punished in the next world, which endured for ever and ever, Amen. It was only after death, when it was too late to repent, that people went to the next world. He attended chapel, sometimes."

As to mundane matters, the boy told me that Victoria was Queen of Great Britain and Ireland. She was born May 24, 1819, and succeeded his late Majesty, King William IV., July 20, 1837. She was married to his Royal Highness Prince Albert, &c., &c. France was a different country to this : he had heard there was no king or queen there, but didn't understand about it. You couldn't go to France by land, no more than you could to Ireland. Didn't know anything of the old times in history ; hadn't been told. Had heard of the battle of Waterloo ; the English licked. Had heard of the battle of Trafalgar, and of Lord Nelson ; didn't know much about him ; but there was his pillar at Charing-cross, just by the candlesticks (fountains). When I spoke of astronomy, the boy at once told me he knew nothing about it. He had heard the earth went round the sun, but from what he'd noticed, shouldn't have thought it. He didn't think that the sun went round the earth, it seemed to go more sideways. Would like to read more, if he had time, but he had a few books, and there was hundreds not so well off as he was.

I am far from undervaluing, indeed I would not indulge in an approach to a scoff, at the extent of this boy's knowledge. Many a man who piques himself on the plenitude of his breeches' pocket, and who attributes his success in life to the fulness of his knowledge, knows no more of Nature, Man, and God, than this poor street child.

Another boy, perhaps a few months older, gave me his notions of men and things. He was a thick-limbed, red-cheeked fellow; answered very freely, and sometimes, when I could not help laughing at his replies, laughed loudly himself, as if he entered into the joke.

Yes, he had heer'd of God who made the world. Couldn't exactly recollec' when he'd heer'd on him, but he had, most sarten-ly. Didn't know when the world was made, or how anybody could do it. It must have taken a long time. It was afore his time, "or yourn either, sir." Knew there was a book called the Bible; didn't know what it was about; didn't mind to know; knew of such a book to a sartinty, because a young 'oman took one to pop (pawn) for an old 'oman what was on the spree—a bran new 'un—but the cove wouldn't have it, and the old 'oman said he might be d——d. Never heer'd tell on the deluge; of the world having been drownded; it couldn't, for there wasn't water enough to do it. He weren't a going to fret hisself for such things as that. Didn't know what happened to people after death, only that they was buried. Had seen a dead body laid out; was a little afeared at first; poor Dick looked so different, and when you touched his face, he was so cold! oh, so cold! Had heer'd on another world; wouldn't mind if he was there hisself, if he could do better, for things was often queer here. Had heered on it from a tailor—such a clever cove, a stunner—as went to 'Straliar (Australia), and heer'd him say he was going into another world. Had never heer'd of France, but had heer'd of Frenchmen; there wasn't half a quarter so many on 'em as of Italians, with their earrings like flash gals. Didn't dislike foreigners, for he never saw none. What was they? Had heer'd of Ireland. Didn't know where it was, but it couldn't be very far, or such lots wouldn't come from there to London. Should say they walked it, aye, every bit of the way, for he'd seen them come in, all covered with dust. Had heer'd of people going to sea, and had seen the ships in the river, but didn't know nothing about it, for he was very seldom that way. The sun was made of fire, or it wouldn't make you feel so warm. The stars was fire, too, or they wouldn't shine. They didn't make it warm, they was too small. Didn't know any use they was of. Didn't know how far they was off; a jolly lot higher than the gas lights some on 'em was. Was never in a church; had heer'd they worshipped God there; didn't know how it was done; had heer'd singing and playing inside when he'd passed; never was there, for he had'nt no togs to go in, and wouldn't be let in among such swells as he had seen coming out. Was a ignorant chap, for he'd never been to school, but was up to many a move, and didn't do bad. Mother said he would make his fortin yet.

Had heer'd of the Duke of Wellington; he was Old Nosey; didn't think he ever seed him, but had seed his statty. Hadn't heer'd of the battle of Waterloo, nor who it was atween; once

lived in Webber-row, Waterloo-road. Thought he had heerd speak of Buonaparte; didn't know what he was; thought he had heer'd of Shakespeare, but didn't know whether he was alive or dead, and didn't care. A man with something like that name kept a dolly and did stunning; but he was sich a hard cove that if *he* was dead it wouldn't matter. Had seen the Queen, but didn't recollec' her name just at the minute; oh! yes, Wictoria and Albert. Had no notion what the Queen had to do. Should think she hadn't such power [he had first to ask me what 'power' was] as the Lord Mayor, or as Mr. Norton as was the Lambeth beak, and perhaps is still. Was never once before a beak and didn't want to. Hated the crushers; what business had they to interfere with him if he was only resting his basket in a street? Had been once to the Wick, and once to the Bower: liked tumbling better; he meant to have a little pleasure when the peas came in.

The knowledge and the ignorance of these two striplings represent that of street children generally. Those who may have run away from a good school, or a better sort of home as far as means constitute such betterness, of course form exceptions. So do the utterly stupid.

The Morals, Religion, and Opinions of the street-trading children are the next topic. Their business morals have been indicated in the course of my former statements, and in the general tone of the remarks and conversation of street-sellers.

As traders their morals may be lax enough. They give short weight, and they give short measure; they prick the juice out of oranges; and brush up old figs to declare they're new. Their silk braces are cotton, their buck-leather braces are wash-leather, their sponge is often rotten, and their salves and cures quackeries.

Speak to any one of the quicker-witted street-sellers on the subject, and though he may be unable to deny that his brother traders are guilty of these short-comings, he will justify them all by the example of shopkeepers. One man, especially, with whom I have more than once conversed on the subject, broadly asserts that as a whole the streets are in all matters of business honester than the shops. "It ain't *we*," runs the purport of his remarks, "as makes coffee out of sham chickory; it ain't *we* as makes cigars out of rhubarb leaves; *we* don't make duffers handkerchiefs, nor weave cotton things and call them silk. If we quacks a bit, does *we* make fortins by it as shopkeepers does with their ointments and pills! If we give slang weights, how many rich shopkeepers is fined for that there? And how many 's never found out? And when one on 'em 's fined, why he calculates how much he's into pocket, between what he's made by slanging, and what he's been fined, and on he goes again. *He* didn't know that there ever was short weight given in his shop: not *he!* No more do *we* at our stalls or barrows! Who 'dulterates the beer? Who makes old tea-leaves into new? Who grinds rice among pepper? And as for smuggling—but nobody thinks there's any harm in buying smuggled things. What *we* does is like that pencil you're writing with to a great tree, compared to what the rich people does. O, don't tell me, sir, a gentleman like you that sees so much of what's going on, must know *we're* better than the shopkeepers are."

To remarks such as these I have nothing to answer. It would be idle to point out to such casuists, that the commission of one wrong can never justify another. The ignorant reverse the doctrine of right, and live, not by rule, but by example. I have unsparingly exposed the rogueries and trickeries of the street people, and it is but fair that one of them should be heard in explanation, if not in justification. The trade ethics of the adult street-folk are also those of the juveniles, so on this subject I need dwell no longer.

What I have said of the religion of the women street-sellers applies with equal truth to the children. Their religious feelings are generally formed for them by their parents, especially their mothers. If the children have no such direction, then they have no religion. I did not question the street-seller before quoted on this subject of the want of the Christian spirit among his fraternity, old or young, or he would at once have asked me, in substance, to tell him in what class of society the real Christian spirit was to be found?

As to the opinions of the street-children I can say little. For the most part they have formed no opinions of anything beyond what affects their daily struggles for bread. Of politics such children can know nothing. If they are anything, they are Chartists in feeling, and are in general honest haters of the police and of most constituted authorities, whom they often confound with the police officer. As to their opinions of the claims of friendship, and of the duty of assisting one another, I believe these children feel and understand nothing about such matters. The hard struggles of their lives, and the little sympathy they meet with, make them selfish. There may be companionship among them, but no friendship, and this applies, I think, alike to boys and girls. The boy's opinion of the girl seems to be that she is made to help *him*, or to supply gratification to his passions.

There is yet a difficult inquiry,—as to the opinions which are formed by the young females reared to a street-life. I fear that those opinions are not, and cannot be powerfully swayed in favour of chastity, especially if the street-girl have the quickness to perceive that marriage is not much honoured among the most numerous body of street-folk. If she have not the quickness to understand this, then her ignorance is in itself most dangerous to her virtue. She may hear, too, expressions of an opinion that "going to church to be wed" is only to put money into the clergyman's, or as these people say the "parson's," pocket. Without the watchful care of the mother, the poor girl may form an illicit connection, with little or no knowledge that she is doing wrong; and perhaps a kind and indulgent mother may be herself but a concubine, feeling little respect for a ceremony she did not scruple to dispense with. To such opinions, however, the Irish furnish the exception.

The Dwelling-places of the street-children are in the same localities as I specified regarding the women. Those who reside with their parents or employers sleep usually in the same room with them, and sometimes in the same bed. Nearly the whole of those, however, who support themselves by street-trade live, or rather sleep, in the lodging-houses. It is the same with those who live by street-vagrancy or begging, or by street-theft; and for this lazy or dishonest class of children the worst description of lodging-houses have the strongest attractions, as they meet continually with "tramps" from the country, and keep up a constant current of scheming and excitement.

It seems somewhat curious that, considering the filth and noisomeness of some of these lodging-houses, the children who are inmates suffer only the average extent of sickness and mortality common to the districts crammed with the poor. Perhaps it may be accounted for by the circumstance of their being early risers, and their being in the open air all day, so that they are fatigued at the close of the day, and their sleep is deep and unbroken. I was assured by a well-educated man, who was compelled to resort to such places, that he has seen children sleep most profoundly in a lodging-house throughout a loud and long-continued disturbance. Many street-children who are either "alone in the world," or afraid to return home after a bad day's sale, sleep in the markets or under the dry arches.

There are many other lads who, being unable to pay the 1*d*., 2*d*., or 3*d*. demanded, in prepayment, by the lodging-house keepers, pass the night in the streets, wherever shelter may be attainable. The number of outcast boys and girls who sleep in and about the purlieus of Covent Garden-market each night, especially during the summer months, has been computed variously, and no doubt differs according to circumstances; but those with whom I have spoken upon the subject, and who of all others are most likely to know, consider the average to be upwards of 200.

The Diet of the street-children is in some cases an alternation of surfeit and inanition, more especially that of the stripling who is "on his own hook." If money be unexpectedly attained, a boy will gorge himself with such dainties as he loves; if he earn no money, he will fast all day patiently enough, perhaps drinking profusely of water. A cake-seller told me that a little while before I saw him a lad of twelve or so had consumed a shilling's worth of cakes and pastry, as he had got a shilling by "fiddling;" not, be it understood, by the exercise of any musical skill, for "fiddling," among the initiated, means the holding of horses, or the performing of any odd jobs.

Of these cakes and pastry—the cakes being from two to twelve a penny, and the pastry, tarts, and "Coventrys" (three-cornered tarts) two a penny—the street-urchins are very fond. To me they seemed to possess no recommendation either to the nose or the palate. The "strong" flavour of these preparations is in all probability as grateful to the palate of an itinerant youth, as is the high *gout* of the grouse or the woodcock to the fashionable epicure. In this respect, as in others which I have pointed out, the "extremes" of society "meet."

These remarks apply far more to the male than to the female children. Some of the street-boys will walk a considerable distance, when they are in funds, to buy pastry of the Jew-boys in the Minories, Houndsditch, and Whitechapel; those keen traders being reputed, and no doubt with truth, to supply the best cakes and pastry of any. A more staple article of diet, which yet partakes of the character of a dainty, is in great demand by the class I treat of—pudding. A halfpenny or a penny-worth of baked plum, boiled plum (or plum dough), currant or plum batter (batter-pudding studded with raisins), is often a dinner. This pudding is almost always bought in the shops; indeed, in a street apparatus there could hardly be the necessary heat diffused over the surface required; and as I have told of a distance being travelled to buy pastry of the Jew-boys, so is it traversed to buy pudding at the best shops. The proprietor of one of those shops, upon whom I called to make inquiries, told me that he sold about 300 pennyworths of pudding in a day. Two-thirds of this quantity he sold to juveniles under fifteen years of age; but he hadn't noticed particularly, and so could only guess. This man, when he understood the object of my inquiry, insisted upon my tasting his "batter," which really was very good, and tasted—I do not know how otherwise to describe it—honest. His profits were not large, he said, and judging from the size and quality of his oblong halfpenny and pennyworth's of batter pudding, I have no doubt he stated the fact. "There's many a poor man and woman," he said, "aye, sir, and some that you would think from their appearance might go to an eating-house to dine, make a meal off my pudding, as well as the street little ones. The boys are often tiresome: 'Master,' they'll say, 'can't you give us a plummier bit than this?' or, 'Is it just up? I likes it 'ot, all 'ot.'"

The "baked tatur," from the street-dealer's can more frequently than from the shops, is another enjoyable portion of the street child's diet. Of the sale to the juvenile population of pickled whelks, stewed eels, oysters, boiled meat puddings, and other articles of street traffic, I have spoken under their respective heads.

The Irish children who live with their parents fare as the parents fare. If very poor, or if bent upon saving for some purpose, their diet is tea and bread and butter, or bread without butter. If not so *very* poor, still tea, &c., but sometimes with a little fish, and sometimes with a piece of meat on Sundays; but the Sunday's meat is more common among the poor English than the poor Irish street-traders; indeed the English street-sellers generally "live better" than the Irish. The coster-boys often fare well and abundantly.

The children living in the lodging-houses, I am informed, generally, partake only of such meals as they can procure abroad. Sometimes of a night they may partake of the cheap beef or mutton, purveyed by some inmate who has been "lifting flesh" (stealing meat) or "sawney" (bacon). Vegetables, excepting the baked potato, they rarely taste. Of animal food, perhaps, they partake more of bacon, and relish it the most.

Drinking is not, from what I can learn, common among the street boys. The thieves are generally sober fellows, and of the others, when they are "in luck," a half-pint of beer, to relish the bread and saveloy of the dinner, and a pennyworth of gin "to keep the cold out," are often the extent of the potations. The exceptions are among the ignorant coster-lads, who when they have been prosperous in their "bunse," drink, and ape the vices of men. The girls, I am told, are generally fonder of gin than the boys. Elderwine and gingerbeer are less popular among children than they used to be. Many of the lads smoke.

The Amusements of the street-children are such as I have described in my account of the costermongers, but in a moderate degree, as those who partake with the greatest zest of such amusements as the Penny Gaff (penny theatre) and the Two-penny Hop (dance) are more advanced in years. Many of the Penny Gaffs, however, since I last wrote on the subject, have been suppressed, and the Twopenny Hops are not half so frequent as they were five or six years back. The Jew-boys of the streets play at draughts or dominoes in coffee-shops which they frequent; in one in the London-road at which I had occasion to call were eight of these urchins thus occupied; and they play for money or its equivalent, but these sedentary games obtain little among the other and more restless street-lads. I believe that not one-half of them "know the cards," but they are fond of gambling at pitch and toss, for halfpennies or farthings.

The Clothing of the street-children, however it may vary in texture, fashion, and colour, has one pervading characteristic—it is never made for the wearers. The exceptions to this rule seem to be those, when a child has run away and retains, through good fortune or natural acuteness, the superior attire he wore before he made the choice—if choice he had—of a street life; and where the pride of a mother whose costermonger husband is "getting on," clothes little Jack or Bill in a new Sunday suit. Even then the suit is more likely to be bought ready-made than "made to measure," nor is it worn in business hours until the gloss of novelty has departed.

The boys and girls wear every variety of clothing; it is often begged, but if bought is bought from the fusty stocks of old clothes in Petticoat and Rosemary-lanes. These rags are worn by the children as long as they will hold, or can be tied or pinned together, and when they drop off from continued wear, from dirt, and from the ravages of vermin, the child sets his wits to work to procure more. One mode of obtaining a fresh supply is far less available than it was three or four years back. This was for the lads to denude themselves of their rags, and tearing them up in the casual-ward of a workhouse, as it were compel the parish-officers to provide them with fresh apparel.

This mode may be successful in parts of the country still, but it is not so, or to a very limited extent, in town. The largest, and what was accounted by the vagrants the most liberal, of all the casual wards of the metropolitan workhouses, that of Marylebone, has been closed above two years. So numerous were the applicants for admission, and so popular among the vagrants was Marylebone workhouse, that a fever resulted, and attacked that large establishment. It was not uncommon for the Irish who trudged up from Liverpool, to be advised by some London vagrant whom they met, to go at once, when they reached the capital, to Marylebone workhouse, and that the Irishman might not forget a name that was new to him, his friendly adviser would write it down for him, and a troop of poor wretched Irish children, with parents as wretched, would go to Marylebone workhouse, and in their ignorance or simplicity, present the address which had been given to them, as if it were a regular order for admission! Boys have sometimes committed offences that they might get into prison, and as they contrived that their apparel should be unfit for purposes of decency, or perhaps their rags had become unfit to wear, they could not be sent naked into the streets again, and so had clothing given to them. A shirt will be worn by one of those wretched urchins, without washing, until it falls asunder, and many have no shirts. The girls are on the whole less ragged than the boys, the most disgusting parts of their persons or apparel—I speak here more of the vagrant or the mixed vagrant trading and selling girl (often a child prostitute) than of the regular street-seller—the worst particular of these girls' appearance, I repeat, is in their foul and matted hair, which looks as if it would defy sponge, comb, and brush to purify it, and in the broken and filthy boots and stockings, which they seem never to button or to garter.

The Propensities of the street-children are the last division of my inquiry, and an ample field is presented, alike for wonder, disgust, pity, hope, and regret.

Perhaps the most remarkable characteristic of these wretched children is their extraordinary licentiousness. Nothing can well exceed the extreme animal fondness for the opposite sex which prevails amongst them; some rather singular circumstances connected with this subject have come to my knowledge, and from these facts it would appear that the age of puberty, or something closely resembling it, may be attained at a much less numerical amount of years than that at which most writers upon the human species have hitherto fixed it. Probably such circumstances as the promiscuous sleeping together of both sexes, the example of the older persons indulging in the grossest immorality in the presence of the young, and the use of obscene expressions, may tend to

produce or force an unnatural precocity, a precocity sure to undermine health and shorten life. Jealousy is another characteristic of these children, and perhaps less among the girls than the boys. Upon the most trivial offence in this respect, or on the suspicion of an offence, the "gals" are sure to be beaten cruelly and savagely by their "chaps." This appears to be a very common case.

The details of filthiness and of all uncleanness which I gave in a recent number as things of course in certain lodging-houses, render it unnecessary to dwell longer upon the subject, and it is one from which I willingly turn to other matters.

In addition to the licentious, the vagabond propensities of this class are very striking. As soon as the warm weather commences, boys and girls, but more especially boys, leave the town in shoals, traversing the country in every direction; some furnished with trifling articles (such as I have already enumerated) to sell, and others to begging, lurking, or thieving. It is not the street-sellers who so much resort to the tramp, as those who are devoid of the commonest notions of honesty; a quality these young vagrants sometimes respect when in fear of a gaol, and the hard work with which such a place is identified in their minds—and to which, with the peculiar idiosyncrasy of a roving race, they have an insuperable objection.

I have met with boys and girls, however, to whom a gaol had no terrors, and to whom, when in prison, there was only one dread, and that a common one among the ignorant, whether with or without any sense of religion—superstition. "I lay in prison of a night, sir," said a boy who was generally among the briskest of his class, "and think I shall see things." The "things" represent the vague fears which many, not naturally stupid, but untaught or ill-taught persons, entertain in the dark. A girl, a perfect termagant in the breaking of windows and such like offences, told me something of the same kind. She spoke well of the treatment she experienced in prison, and seemed to have a liking for the matron and officials; her conduct there was quiet and respectful. I believe she was not addicted to drink.

Many of the girls, as well as the boys, of course trade as they "tramp." They often sell, both in the country and in town, little necklaces, composed of red berries strung together upon thick thread, for dolls and children : but although I have asked several of them, I have never yet found one who collected the berries and made the necklaces themselves ; neither have I met with a single instance in which the girl vendors knew the name of the berries thus used, nor indeed even that they *were* berries. The invariable reply to my questions upon this point has been that they "are called necklaces ;" that " they are just as they sells 'em to us ;" that they " don't know whether they are made or whether they grow ;" and in most cases, that they "gets them in London, by Shoreditch ;" although in one case a little brown-complexioned girl, with bright sparkling eyes, said that "she got them from the gipsies."

At first I fancied, from this child's appearance, that she was rather superior in intellect to most of her class; but I soon found that she was not a whit above the others, unless, indeed, it were in the possession of the quality of cunning.

Some of the boys, on their country excursions, trade in dominoes. They carry a variety of boxes, each differing in size and varying accordingly in price: the lowest-priced boxes are mostly 6*d.* each (sometimes 4*d.*, or even 3*d.*), the highest 1*s.* An informant told me that these boxes are charged to him at the rate of 20 to 25 per cent. less; but if, as is commonly the case, he could take a number at a time, he would have them at a smaller price still. They are very rudely made, and soon fall to pieces, unless handled with extreme care. Most of the boys who vend this article play at the game themselves, and some with skill; but in every case, I believe, there is a willingness to cheat, or take advantage, which is hardly disguised; one boy told me candidly that those who make the most money are considered to be the cleverest, whether by selling or cheating, or both, at the game; nor can it be said that this estimation of cleverness is peculiar to these children.

At this season of the year great numbers of the street-children attend the races in different parts of the country, more especially at those in the vicinity of a large town. The race-course of Wolverhampton, for instance, is usually thronged with them during the period of the sport. While taking these perigrinations they sometimes sleep in the low lodging-houses with which most of our provincial towns abound: frequently "skipper it" in the open air, when the weather is fine and warm, and occasionally in barns or outhouses attached to farms and cottages. Sometimes they travel in couples—a boy and a girl, or two boys or two girls; but the latter is not so common a case as either of the former. It is rare that more than two may be met in company with each other, except, indeed, of a night, and then they usually herd together in numbers. The boys who carry dominoes sometimes, also, have a sheet of paper for sale, on which is rudely printed a representation of a draught-board and men—the latter of which are of two colours (black and white) and may be cut out with a pair of scissors; thus forming a ready means of playing a game so popular in rustic places. These sheets of paper are sold (if no more can be got for them) at a penny each. The boy who showed them to me said he gave a halfpenny a piece for them, or 6*d.* for fifteen. He said he always bought them in London, and that he did not know any other place to get them at, nor had "ever heard any talk of their being bought nowhere else."

The extraordinary lasciviousness of this class which I have already mentioned, appears to continue to mark their character during their vagabondizing career in the country as fully as in town; indeed, an informant, upon whom I think I may rely, says, that the nightly scenes of youthful or even childish profligacy in the low lodging-houses of the small provincial towns quite equal —even if they do not exceed—those which may be witnessed in the metropolis itself. Towards the approach of winter these children (like the vagrants of an older growth) advance towards London; some remain in the larger towns, such as Liverpool, Manchester, Birmingham, Sheffield, &c., but the greater proportion appear to return to the metropolis, where they resume the life they had previously led, anything but improved in education, morals, manners, or social position generally, by their summer's excursion.

The language spoken by this rambling class is peculiar in its construction: it consists of an odd medley of cockneyfied English, rude provincialisms, and a large proportion of the slang commonly used by gipsies and other "travellers," in conveying their ideas to those whom they wish to purchase their commodities.

Among the propensities of the street-boys I do not think that pugnacity, or a fondness, or even a great readiness, for fighting, is a predominant element. Gambling and thieving may be rife among a class of these poor wretches; and it may not unfrequently happen that force is resorted to by one boy bigger than another to obtain the halfpence of which the smaller child is known to be possessed. Thus quarrels among them are very frequent, but they rarely lead to fighting. Even in the full swing and fury of their jealousy, it does not appear that these boys attack the object of their suspicions, but prefer the less hazardous course of chastising the delinquent or unjustly suspected girl. The girls in the low lodging-houses, I was told a little time since, by a woman who used to frequent them, sometimes, not often, scratched one another until the two had bloody faces; and they tried to bite one another now and then, but they seldom fought. What was this poor woman's notion of a fight between two girls, it may not be very easy to comprehend.

The number of children out daily in the streets of London, employed in the various occupations I have named, together with others which may possibly have been overlooked—including those who beg without offering any article for sale—those who will work as light porters, as errand boys and the like, for chance passengers, has been variously calculated; probably nothing like exactitude can be hoped for, much less expected, in such a speculation, for when a government census has been so frequently found to fail in correctness of detail, it appears highly improbable that the number of those so uncertain in their places of resort and so migratory in their habits, can be ascertained with anything like a definite amount of certainty by a private individual. Taking the returns of accommodation afforded to these children in the casual wards of workhouses, refuges for the destitute and homeless poor; of the mendicity and other societies of a similar description, and those of our hospitals and gaols,—and these sources of information upon this subject can alone be confidently relied upon,—and then taking into the calculation the additional numbers, who pass the night in the variety of ways I have already enumerated, I think it will be found that the number of boys and girls selling in the streets of this city, and often dependent upon their own exertions for the commonest necessaries of life, may be estimated at some thousands, but nearer 10,000 than 20,000.

The consideration which I have devoted to this branch of my subject has been considerable, but still not, in my own opinion, commensurate to the importance of its nature. Steps ought most unquestionably to be taken to palliate the evils and miseries I have pointed out, even if a positive remedy be indeed impossible.

Each year sees an increase of the numbers of street-children to a very considerable extent, and the exact nature of their position may be thus briefly depicted: what little *information* they receive is obtained from the worst class—from cheats, vagabonds, and rogues ; what little *amusement* they indulge in, springs from sources the most poisonous—the most fatal to happiness and welfare; what little they know of a *home* is necessarily associated with much that is vile and base ; their very means of existence, uncertain and precarious as it is, is to a great extent identified with petty chicanery, which is quickly communicated by one to the other ; while their physical sufferings from cold, hunger, exposure to the weather, and other causes of a similar nature, are constant, and at times extremely severe. Thus every means by which a proper intelligence may be conveyed to their minds is either closed or at the least tainted, while every duct by which a bad description of knowledge may be infused is sedulously cultivated and enlarged. Parental instruction ; the comforts of a home, however humble—the great moral truths upon which society itself rests ;—the influence of proper example ; the power of education ; the effect of useful amusement ; are all denied to them, or come to them so greatly vitiated, that they rather tend to increase, than to repress, the very evils they were intended to remedy.

The costers invariably say that no persons under the age of fifteen should be allowed by law to vend articles in the streets ; the reason they give for this is—that the children under that period of life having fewer wants and requiring less money to live than those who are older, will sell at a less profit than it is fair to expect the articles sold should yield, and thus they tersely conclude, "they prevents others living, and ruins theirselves."

There probably is truth in this remark, and I must confess that, for the sake of the children themselves, I should have no objection to see the suggestion acted upon ; and yet there immediately rises the plain yet startling question—in such a case, what is to become of the children?

I now cite the histories of street-lads belonging to the several classes above specified, as illustrations of the truth of the statements advanced concerning the children street-sellers generally.

OF CHILDREN SENT OUT AS STREET-SELLERS BY THEIR PARENTS.

OF the boys and girls who are sent out to sell in the streets by parents who are themselves street-traders, I need say but little under this head. I

have spoken of them, and given some of their statements in other divisions of this work (see the accounts of the coster boys and girls). When, as is the case with many of the costermongers, and with the Irish fruit-sellers, the parents and children follow the same calling, they form one household, and work, as it were, "into one another's hands." The father can buy a larger, and consequently a cheaper quantity, when he can avail himself of a subdivision of labour as inexpensive as that of his own family—whom he must maintain whether employed or unemployed—in order to vend such extra quantity. I have already noticed that in some families (as is common with rude tribes) costermongering seems an hereditary pursuit, and the frequent and constant employment of children in street traffic is one reason why this hereditary pursuit is perpetuated, for street commerce is thus at a very early age made part and parcel of the young coster's existence, and he very probably acquires a distaste for any other occupation, which may entail more of *restraint* and *irksomeness*. It is very rarely that a costermonger apprentices his son to any handicraft business, although a daughter may sometimes be placed in domestic service. The child is usually "sent out to sell."

There is another class of children who are "sent out" as are the children of the costers, and sometimes with the same cheap and readily attained articles—oranges and lemons, nuts, chestnuts, onions, salt (or fresh) herrings, winks, or shrimps, and, more rarely, with water-cresses or cut-flowers. Sometimes the young vendors offer small wares—leather boot-laces, coat-studs, steel pens, or such like. These are often the children, not of street sales-people, but of persons in a measure connected with a street life, or some open-air pursuit ; the children of cabmen deprived of their licences, or of the hangers-on of cabmen ; of the "supers" (supernumeraries) of the theatres who have irregular or no employment, or, as they would call it, "engagement," with the unhappy consequence of irregular or no "salary :" the children, again, of street performers, or Ethiopians, or street-musicians, are "sent out to sell," as well as those of the poorer class of labourers connected with the river—ballast-heavers, lumpers, &c.; of (Irish) bricklayers' labourers and paviours' assistants ; of market-porters and dock-labourers; of coal-heavers out of work, and of the helpers at coal-wharfs, and at the other wharfs ; of the Billingsgate "roughs ;" and of the many classes of the labouring, rather than the artisan poor, whose earnings are uncertain, or insufficient, or have failed them altogether.

With such classes as these (and more especially with the Irish), as soon as Pat or Biddy is big enough to carry a basket, and is of sufficiently ripened intellect to understand the relative value of coins, from a farthing to a shilling, he or she *must* do something "to help," and that something is generally to sell in the streets. One poor woman who made a scanty living in working on corn sacks and bags—her infirmities sometimes preventing her working at all—sent out three children, together or separately, to sell lucifer-matches or small wares. "*They like it,*" she said, "*and always want to be off into the streets;* and when my husband (a labourer) was ill in the hospital, the few pence they brought in was very useful; but now he's well and at work again and we want to send the eldest—she's nine—to school; *but they all* will *go out to sell if they can get hold of any stock.* I would never have sent them at all if I could have helped it, but if they made 6*d.* a day among the three of them, perhaps it saved their lives when things were at the worst." If a poor woman, as in this instance, has not been used to street-selling herself, there is always some neighbour to advise her what to purchase for her children's hawking, and instruct her where.

From one little girl I had the following account. She was then selling boot-laces and offered them most perseveringly. She was turned nine, she said, and had sold things in the streets for two years past, but not regularly. The father got his living in the streets by "playing;" she seemed reluctant to talk about his avocation, but I found that he was sometimes a street-musician, or street-performer, and sometimes sung or recited in public houses, and having "seen better days," had it appears communicated some feeling of dislike for his present pursuits to his daughter, so that I discontinued any allusion to the subject. The mother earned 2*s.* or 2*s.* 6*d.* weekly, in shoe-binding, when she had employment, which was three weeks out of four, and a son of thirteen earned what was sufficient to maintain him as an (occasional) assistant in a wholesale pottery, or rather pot-shop.

"It's in the winter, sir, when things are far worst with us. Father can make very little then—but I don't know what he earns exactly at any time—and though mother has more work then, there's fire and candle to pay for. We were very badly off last winter, and worse, I think, the winter before. Father sometimes came home and had made nothing, and if mother had no work in hand we went to bed to save fire and candle, if it was ever so soon. Father would die afore he would let mother take as much as a loaf from the parish. I was sent out to sell nuts first : 'If it's only 1*d.* you make,' mother said, 'it's a good piece of bread.' I didn't mind being sent out. I knew children that sold things in the streets. Perhaps I liked it better than staying at home without a fire and with nothing to do, and if I went out I saw other children busy. No, I wasn't a bit frightened when I first started, not a bit. Some children—but they was such little things—said : ' O, Liz, I wish I was you.' I had twelve ha'porths and sold them all. I don't know what it made ; 2*d.* most likely. I didn't crack a single nut myself. I was fond of them then, but I don't care for them now. I could do better if I went into public-houses, but I'm only let go to Mr. Smith's, because he knows father, and Mrs. Smith and him recommends me and wouldn't let anybody mislest me. Nobody ever offered to. I hear people swear there sometimes, but it's not at me. I sell nuts to children in the streets, and laces to young women. I have

sold nuts and oranges to soldiers. They never say anything rude to me, never. I was once in a great crowd, and was getting crushed, and there was a very tall soldier close by me, and he lifted me, basket and all, right up to his shoulder, and carried me clean out of the crowd. He had stripes on his arm. ' I shouldn't like you to be in such a trade,' says he, ' if you was my child.' He didn't say why he wouldn't like it. Perhaps because it was beginning to rain. Yes, we are far better off now. Father makes money. I don't go out in bad weather in the summer ; in the winter, though, I must. I don't know what I make. I don't know what I shall be when I grow up. I can read a little. I've been to church five or six times in my life. I should *go* oftener and so would mother, if we had clothes."

I have no reason to suppose that in this case the father was an intemperate man, though some of the parents who thus send their children out *are* intemperate, and, loving to indulge in the idleness to which intemperance inclines them, are forced to live on the labour of their wives and children.

OF A " NEGLECTED " CHILD, A STREET-SELLER.

OF this class perhaps there is less to be said than of others. Drunken parents allow their children to run about the streets, and often to shift for themselves. If such parents have any sense of shame, unextinguished by their continued besottedness, they may feel relieved by not having their children before their eyes, for the very sight of them is a reproach, and every rag about such helpless beings must carry its accusation to a mind not utterly callous.

Among such children there is not, perhaps, that extreme pressure of wretchedness or of privation that there is among the orphans, or the utterly deserted. If a "neglected child" have to shift, wholly or partly, for itself, it is perhaps with the advantage of a shelter ; for even the bare room of the drunkard is in some degree a shelter or roof. There is not the nightly need of 2*d.* for a bed, or the alternative of the Adelphi arches for nothing.

I met with one little girl ten or eleven years of age, whom some of the street-sellers described to me as looking out for a job every now and then. She was small-featured and dark-eyed, and seemed intelligent. Her face and hands were brown as if from exposure to the weather, and a lack of soap ; but her dress was not dirty. Her father she described as a builder, probably a bricklayer's labourer, but he could work, she said, at drains or such like. "Mother's been dead a long time," the child continued, "and father brought another woman home and told me to call her mother, but she soon went away. I works about the streets, but only when there's nothing to eat at home. Father gets drunk sometimes, but I think not so oft as he did, and then he lies in bed. No, sir, not all day, but he gets up and goes out and gets more drink, and comes back and goes to bed again. He never uses me badly. When he's drinking and has money, he gives me some now and then to get bread and butter with, or a halfpenny pudding ; he never eats anything in the house when he's drinking, and he's a very quiet man. Sometimes he's laid in bed two or three days and nights at a time. I goes to school when father has money. We lives very well then. I've kept myself for a whole week. I mind people's stalls, if they're away a bit, and run for them if they're wanted; and I go errands. I've carried home flower-pots for a lady. I've got a halfpenny on a day, and a penny, and some bread perhaps, and I've lived on that. I should like very well to have a pitch of my own. *I think I should like that better than place.* But I have a sister who has a place in the country; she's far older than I am, and perhaps I shall get one. But father's at work now, and he says he'll take the pledge. Five or six times I've sold oranges, and ingans as well, and carried the money to Mrs. ——, who gave me all I took above 4*d.* for myself."

It could surprise no one if a child so neglected became so habituated to a street life, that she could not adapt herself to any other. I heard of other children thus or similarly neglected, but boys far more frequently than girls, who traded regularly in apples, oranges, &c., on their own account. Some have become regular street-sellers, and even in childhood have abandoned their homes and supported themselves.

OF A HIRED COSTER BOY.

ONE shell-fish seller, who has known street-commerce and street-folk for many years, thought, although he only hazarded an opinion, that there was less drinking among the young costers, and less swearing, than he had known in a preceding generation.

A young coster boy living with his parents, who had a good business, told me that he would never be nothing but a "general dealer," (which among some of these people is the "genteel" designation for a costermonger,) as long as he lived, unless, indeed, he rose to a coal shed and a horse and cart; a consummation, perhaps with the addition of a green-grocery, a fried fish, and a gingerbeer trade, not unfrequently arrived at by the more prudent costermongers. This boy could neither read nor write; he had been sent to school, and flogged to school (he grinned as he told me) by his mother, who said his father wouldn't have been "done" so often by fine folks, when he sold "grass" (asparagus) and such things as cost money, if he could have kept 'count. But his father only laughed, and said nothing, when the boy "cut away" from school, which he did so continuously, that the schoolmaster at length declined the charge of the young coster's further education. This stripling, who was about fourteen, seemed very proud of a pair of good half-boots which his mother had bought him, and which he admired continually as he glanced at his feet. His parents, from his account, were indulgent, and when they got farthings in change or in any manner, kept them for him; and so he got treats, and smart things to wear now and then. "We expects to do well," he said, for he used the "we" when he spoke of

his parents' business, "when it's peas and new potatoes, cheap enough to cry. It's my dodge to cry. I know a man as says, 'May month ought to be ashamed on itself, or things 'ud a been herlier.' Last week I sung out, it was the same man's dodge, he put me up to it—'Here's your Great Exhibition mackarel.' People laughed, but it weren't no great good. I've been to Penny Gaffs, but not this goodish bit. I likes the singing best as has a stunnin chorus. There's been a deal of hard up lately among people as is general dealers. Things is getting better, I think, and they must. It wouldn't do at all if they didn't. It's no use your a-asking me about what I thinks of the Queen or them sort of people, for I knows nothing about them, and never goes among them."

The Hired boys, for the service of the costermongers, whether hired for the day, or more permanently, are very generally of the classes I have spoken of. When the New Cut, Lambeth, was a great street-market, every morning, during the height of the vegetable and fruit seasons, lads used to assemble in Hooper-street, Short-street, York-street, and, indeed, in all the smaller streets or courts, which run right and left from the "two Cuts." When the costermonger started thence, perhaps "by the first light," to market, these boys used to run up to his barrow, "D' you want me, Jack?" or, "Want a boy, Bill?" being their constant request. It is now the same, in the localities where the costermongers live, or where they keep their ponies, donkeys, and barrows, and whence they emerge to market. It is the same at Billingsgate and the other markets at which these traders make their wholesale purchases. Boys wait about these marts "to be hired," or, as they may style it, to "see if they're wanted." When hired, there is seldom any "wage" specified, the lads seeming always willing to depend upon the liberality of the costermonger, and often no doubt with an eye to the chances of "bunse." A sharp lad thus engaged, who may acquit himself to a costermonger's liking, perhaps continues some time in the same man's employ. I may observe, that in this gathering, and for such a purpose, there is a resemblance to the simple proceedings of the old times, when around the market cross of the nearest town assembled the population who sought employment, whether in agricultural or household labour. In some parts of the north of England these gatherings are still held at the two half-yearly terms of May-day and Martinmas.

A lad of thirteen or fourteen, who did not look very strong, gave me the following account: "I helps, you see, sir, where I can, for mother (who sells sheep's-trotters) depends a deal on her trotters, but they're not great bread for an old 'oman, and there's me and Neddy to keep. Father's abroad and a soger. Do I know he is? Mother says so, sir. I looks out every morning when the costermongers starts for the markets, and wants boys for their barrows. I cried roots last: 'Here's your musks, ha'penny each. Here's yer all agro'in' and all a blo'in'.' I got my grub and 3*d.* I takes the tin home. If there's a cabbage or two left,

I 've had it guv to me. *I likes that work better
nor school. I should think so. One sees life.*
Well, I don't know wot one sees perticler; but
it 's wot people calls life. I was a week at
school once. I has a toss up sometimes when
I has a odd copper for it. I' aven't 'ad any rig'lar
work as yet. I shall p'raps when it 's real
summer." [Said, May 24th.] "This is the Queen's
birthday, is it, sir? Werry likely, but she 's
nothing to me. I can't read, in coorse not, after a
week's schooling. Yes, I likes a show. Punch is
stunnin', but they might make more on the dog. I
would if I was a Punch. O, I has tea, and bread
and butter with mother, and gets grub as I jobs
besides. I makes no bargain. If a cove 's scaly,
we gets to know him. I hopes to have a barrer
of my own some day, and p'raps a hass. Can I
manage a hass? *In* coorse, and he don't want no
groomin'. I'd go to Hepsom then; I 've never been
yet, but I 've been to Grinnage fairs. I don't
know how I can get a barrer and a hass, but I
may have luck."

OF AN ORPHAN BOY, A STREET-SELLER.

FROM one of this class I had the following account.
It may be observed that the lad's statement contains little of incident, or of novelty, but this is
characteristic of many of his class. With many
of them, it may indeed be said, " one day certifieth
another." It is often the same tale of labour and
of poverty, day after day, so that the mere
uniformity makes a youth half oblivious of the
past; the months, or perhaps years, seem all
alike.

This boy seemed healthy, wore a suit of corduroy, evidently not made for him, and but little
patched, although old; he was in good spirits.

"I believe I 'm between fifteen and sixteen,"
he said, "and mother died more than two year
ago, nearer three, perhaps. Father had gone dead
a long time afore; I don't remember him." [I am
inclined to think that this story of the death of the
father is often told by the mother of an illegitimate
child to her offspring, through a natural repugnance
to reveal her shame to her child. I do not
know, however, that it was the case in this
instance.] "I don't remember about mother's
funeral, for I was ill myself at the time. She
worked with her needle; sometimes for a dressmaker, on "skirts," and sometimes for a tailor, on
flannels. She sometimes worked all night, but
we was wery badly off—we was so. She had
only me. When mother died there was nothing
left for me, but there was a good woman—she
was a laundress and kept a mangle—and she said,
' well, here 's a old basket and a few odd things;
give the kid the basket and turn the bits of old
traps into money, and let him start on muffins, and
then he must shift for hisself.' So she tuk me to a
shop and I was started in the muffin line. I didn't
do so bad, but it 's on'y a winter trade, isn't
muffins. I sold creases next—no, not creases,
cherries; yes, it was creases, and then cherries,
for I remembers as 'ow 'Ungerford was the first
market I ever was at; it was so. Since then, I 've
sold apples, and oranges, and nuts, and chestnuts

—but *they* was dear the last time as I had 'em—
and spring garters a penny a pair, and glass pens;
yes, and other things. I goes to market, mostly to
Common Gard'n, and there 's a man goes there
what buys bushels and bushels, and he 'll let me
have any little lot reas'nable; he will so. There 's
another will, but he ain't so good to a poor kid.
Well, I doesn't know as 'ow one trade 's better
nor another; I think I 've done as much in
one as in another. But I 've done better lately;
I 've sold more oranges, and I had a few
sticks of rhubarb. I think times is mending,
but others says that 's on'y my luck. I sleeps
with a boy as is younger nor I am, and pays 9d.
a week. Tom's father and mother—he 's a coalheaver, but he 's sometimes out of work—sleeps in
the same room, but we has a good bed to ourselves. Tom's father knew my mother. There 's
on'y us four. Tom's father says sometimes if his
rheumatics continues, he and all on 'em must go
into the house. Most likely I should then go to
a lodging-house. I don't know that some on 'em's
bad places. I 've heer'd they was jolly. I has no
amusements. Last year I helped a man one day,
and he did so well on fruit, he did so, for he got
such a early start, and so cheap, that he gave me
3d. hextra to go to the play with. I didn't go.
I'd rather go to bed at seven every night than
anywhere else. I'm fond of sleep. I never wakes
all night. I dreams now and then, but I never
remembers a dream. I can't read or write; I
wish I could, if it would help me on. I'm
making 3s. 6d. a week now, I think. Some weeks
in winter I didn't make 2s."

This boy, although an orphan at a tender age,
was yet assisted to the commencement of a business by a friend. I met with another lad who
was left under somewhat similar circumstances.
The persons in the house where his mother had
died were about to take him to the parish officers,
and there seemed to be no other course to be
pursued to save the child, then nearly twelve,
from starvation. The lad knew this and ran away.
It was summer time, about three years ago, and
the little runaway slept in the open air whenever
he could find a quiet place. Want drove him
to beg, and several days he subsisted on one penny
which he begged. One day he did not find any
one to give him even a halfpenny—and towards
the evening of the second he became bold, or even
desperate, from hunger. As if by a sudden impulse he went up to an old gentleman, walking
slowly in Hyde-park, and said to him, " Sir, I 've
lived three weeks by begging, and I 'm hungering
now; give me sixpence, or I 'll go and steal." The
gentleman stopped and looked at the boy, in whose
tones there must have been truthfulness, and in
whose face was no doubt starvation, for without
uttering a word he gave the young applicant a
shilling. The boy began a street-seller's life on
lucifer-matches. I had to see him for another
purpose a little while ago, and in the course of
some conversation he told me of his start in the
streets. I have no doubt he told the truth, and I
should have given a more detailed account of him,
but when I inquired for him, I found that he had

gone to Epsom races to sell cards, and had not returned, having probably left London on a country tour. But for the old gentleman's bounty he would have stolen something, he declared, had it been only for the shelter of a prison.

OF THE LIFE OF AN ORPHAN GIRL, A STREET-SELLER.

"FATHER was a whitesmith," she said, "and mother used to go out a-washing and a-cleaning, and me and my sister (but she is dead now) did nothing; we was sent to a day school, both of us. We lived very comfortable; we had two rooms and our own furniture; we didn't want for nothing when father was alive; he was very fond on us both, and was a kind man to everybody. He was took bad first when I was very young—it was consumption he had, and he was ill many years, about five years, I think it was, afore he died. When he was gone mother kept us both; she had plenty of work; she couldn't a-bear the thought of our going into the streets for a living, and we was both too young to get a place anywhere, so we stayed at home and went to school just as when father was alive. My sister died about two year and a half ago; she had the scarlet-fever dreadful, she lay ill seven weeks. We was both very fond of her, me and mother. I often wish she had been spared, I should not be alone in the world as I am now. We might have gone on together, but it is dreadful to be quite alone, and I often think now how well we could have done if she was alive.

"Mother has been dead just a year this month; she took cold at the washing and it went to her chest; she was only bad a fortnight; she suffered great pain, and, poor thing, she used to fret dreadful, as she lay ill, about me, for she knew she was going to leave me. She used to plan how I was to do when she was gone. She made me promise to try to get a place and keep from the streets if I could, for she seemed to dread them so much. When she was gone I was left in the world without a friend. I am quite alone, I have no relation at all, not a soul belonging to me. For three months I went about looking for a place, as long as my money lasted, for mother told me to sell our furniture to keep me and get me clothes. I could have got a place, but nobody would have me without a character, and I knew nobody to give me one. I tried very hard to get one, indeed I did; for I thought of all mother had said to me about going into the streets. At last, when my money was just gone, I met a young woman in the street, and I asked her to tell me where I could get a lodging. She told me to come with her, she would show me a respectable lodging-house for women and girls. I went, and I have been there ever since. The women in the house advised me to take to flower-selling, as I could get nothing else to do. One of the young women took me to market with her, and showed me how to bargain with the salesman for my flowers. At first, when I went out to sell, I felt so ashamed I could not ask anybody to buy of me; and many times went back at night with all my stock, with-

out selling one bunch. The woman at the lodging-house is very good to me; and when I have a bad day she will let my lodging go until I can pay her. She always gives me my dinner, and a good dinner it is, of a Sunday; and she will often give me a breakfast, when she knows I have no money to buy any. She is very kind, indeed, for she knows I am alone. I feel very thankful to her, I am sure, for all her goodness to me. During the summer months I take 1s. 6d. per day, which is 6d. profit. But I can only sell my flowers five days in the week—Mondays there is no flowers in the market; a day I pay 3d. for lodging. I get a halfpenny-worth of tea; a halfpenny-worth of sugar; one pound of bread, 1½d.; butter, ½d. I never tastes meat but on Sunday. What I shall do in the winter I don't know. In the cold weather last year, when I could get no flowers, I was forced to live on my clothes, I have none left now but what I have on. What I shall do I don't know —I can't bear to think on it."

OF TWO RUNAWAY STREET-BOYS.

I ENDEAVOURED to find a boy or girl who belonged to the *well*-educated classes, had run away, and was now a street-seller. I heard of boys of this class—one man thought he knew five, and was sure of four—who now lived by street-selling, my informant believed without having any recourse to theft, but all these boys were absent; they had not returned from Epsom, or had not returned to their usual haunts, or else they had started for their summer's excursion into the country. Many a street-seller becomes as weary of town after the winter as a member of parliament who sits out a very long session; and the moment the weather is warm, and "seems settled," they are off into the country. In this change of scene there is the feeling of independence, of freedom; *they* are not "tied to their work;" and this feeling has perhaps even greater charms for the child than the adult.

The number of lads of a *well-educated class*, who support themselves by street-selling, is not large. I speak of those whom I have classed as children under fifteen years of age. If a boy run away, scared and terrified by the violence of a parent, or maddened by continuous and sometimes excessive severity, the parent often feels compunction, and I heard of persons being sent to every lodging-house in London, and told to search every dry arch, to bring back a runaway. On these occasions the street-sellers willingly give their aid; I have even heard of women, whose degradation was of the lowest, exerting themselves in the recovery of a runaway child, and that often unsolicited and as often unrecompensed.

The children who are truants through their own vicious or reckless propensities, or through the inducements of their seniors, become far more frequently, thieves or lurkers, rather than street-sellers. As to runaway girls of a well-educated class, and under fifteen, I heard of none who were street-sellers.

I now give instances of two runaway lads, who have been dishonest, and honest.

The one, when he told me his history, was a slim and rather tall young man of 23 or 24, with a look, speech, and air, anything but vulgar. He was the son of a wealthy jeweller, in a town in the West of England, and ran away from home with an adult member of his father's establishment, who first suggested such a course, taking with them money and valuables. They came to London, and the elder thief, retaining all the stolen property, at once abandoned the child, then only ten, and little and young-looking for his age. He fell into the hands of some members of the swell-mob, and became extremely serviceable to them. He was dressed like a gentleman's son, and was innocent-looking and handsome. His appearance, when I saw him, showed that this must have been the case as regards his looks. He lived with some of the swell-mobsmen—then a more prosperous people than they are now—in a good house in the Southwark-Bridge-road. The women who resided with the mobsmen were especially kind to him. He was well fed, well lodged, well clad, and petted in everything. He was called " the kid," a common slang name for a child, but he was *the* kid. He " went to work " in Regent-street, or wherever there were most ladies, and his appearance disarmed suspicion. He was, moreover, highly successful in church and chapel practice. At length he became " spotted." The police got to know him, and he was apprehended, tried, and convicted. He was, however—he believed through the interest of his friends, of whose inquiries concerning him he had heard, but of that I know nothing—sent to the Philanthropic Asylum, then in St. George's-road. Here he remained the usual time, then left the place well clothed, and with a sum of money, and endeavoured to obtain some permanent employment. In this endeavour he failed. Whether he exerted himself strenuously or not I cannot say, but he told me that the very circumstance of his having been " in the Philanthropic " was fatal to his success. His "character" and "recommendations" necessarily showed where he had come from, and the young man, as he then was, became a beggar. His chief practice was in " screeving," or writing on the pavement. Perhaps some of my readers may remember having noticed a wretched-looking youth who hung over the words "I AM STARVING," chalked on the footway on the Surrey side of Waterloo Bridge. He lay huddled in a heap, and appeared half dead with cold and want, his shirtless neck and shoulders being visible through the rents in his thin jean jacket; shoe or stocking he did not wear. This was the rich jeweller's son. Until he himself told me of it—and he seemed to do so with some sense of shame—I could not have believed that the well-spoken and well-looking youth before me was the piteous object I had observed by the bridge. What he is doing now I am unable to state.

Another boy, who thought he was not yet fifteen, though he looked older, gave me the following account. He was short but seemed strong, and his career, so far, is chiefly remarkable for his perseverance, exercised as much, perhaps, from insensibility as from any other quality. He was sufficiently stupid. If he had parents living, he said, he didn't know nothing about them ; he had lived and slept with an old woman who said she was his grandmother, and he'd been told that she weren't no relation ; he didn't trouble himself about it. She sold lucifer-boxes or any trifle in the streets, and had an allowance of 2s. weekly, but from what quarter he did not know. About four years ago he was run over by a cab, and was carried to the workhouse or the hospital ; he believed it was Clerkenwell Workhouse, but he weren't sure. When he recovered and was discharged he found the old woman was dead, and a neighbour went with him to the parish officers, by whom—as well as I could understand him—he was sent to the workhouse, after some inquiry. He was soon removed to Nor'ud. On my asking if he meant Norwood, he replied, " no, Nor'ud," and there he was with a number of other children with a Mr. Horbyn. He did not know how long he was there, and he didn't know as he had anything much to complain of, but he ran away. He ran away because he thought he would ; and he believed he could get work at paper-staining. He made his way to Smithfield, near where there was a great paper-stainer's, but he could not get any work, and he was threatened to be sent back, as they knew from his dress that he had run away. He slept in Smithfield courts and alleys, fitting himself into any covered corner he could find. The poor women about were kind to him, and gave him pieces of bread ; some knew that he had run away from a workhouse and was all the kinder. "The fust browns as ivver I yarned," he said, " was from a drover. He was a going into the country to meet some beasts, and had to carry some passels for somebody down there. They wasn't 'evvy, but they was orkerd to grip. His old 'oman luk out for a young cove to 'elp her old man, and saw me fust, so she calls me, and I gets the job. I gived the greatest of satisfaction, and had sixpence giv me, for Jim (the drover) was well paid, as they was vallyble passels, and he said he'd taken the greatest of care on 'em, and had engaged a poor lad to 'elp him." On his return the child slept in a bed, in a house near Gray's-inn-lane, for the first time since he had run away, he believed about a fortnight. He persevered in looking out for odd jobs, without ever stealing, though he met some boys who told him he was a fool not to prig. " I used to carry his tea from his old 'oman," he went on, " to a old cove as had a stunnin' pitch of fruit in the City-road. But my best friend was Stumpy ; he had a beautiful crossin' (as a sweeper) then, but he's dead now and berried as well. I used to talk to him and whistle—I *can* just whistle " [here he whistled loud and shrill, to convince me of his perfection in that street accomplishment] "—and to dance him the double-shuffle" [he favoured me with a specimen of that dance], " and he said I hinterested him. Well, he meant he liked it, I s'pose. When he went to rest hisself, for he soon got tired, over his drop of beer to his grub, I had his crossin' and his broom for nuff'n. One boy used to say to Stumpy, 'I'll give you 1*d.* for your crossin' while you's grubbin.' But I had it for nuff'n, and had all I yarned ; sometimes 1*d.*, sometimes 2*d.*, but only once 3½*d.* I've been 'elping Old Bill with his summer cabbages and flowers (cauli-flowers), and now he's on live heels. I can sing 'em out prime, but you 'eared me. I has my bit o' grub with him, and a few browns, and Old Bill and Young Bill, too, says I shall have better to do, but I can't until peas. I sleeps in a loft with 'ampers, which is Old Bill's ; a stunnin' good bed. I've cried for and 'elped other costers. Stumpy sent me to 'em. I think he'd been one hisself, but I was always on the look-out. I'll go for some

bunse soon. I don't know what I shall do time to come, I nivver thinks on it. I could read mid-dlin', and can a little now, but I'm out of practice."

I have given this little fellow's statement some-what fully, for I believe he is a type of the most numerous class of runaway urchins who ripen, so to speak, into costermongers, after "helping" that large body of street-traders.

I heard of one boy who had been discharged from Brixton, and had received 6*d.* to begin the world with, as it was his first offence, on his way back to London, being called upon suddenly as soon as he had reached the New Cut (then the greatest of all the street-markets) to help a coster-monger. This gave the boy a start, and he had since lived honestly.

OF THE CAPITAL AND INCOME OF THE STREET-SELLERS OF MANUFACTURED ARTICLES.

BEFORE giving a Summary of the Capital and Income of the above-mentioned class, I shall en-deavour to arrive at some notion as to the number of persons belonging to this division of the London Street-sellers.

As far as I am able to ascertain, the following estimate may be taken as an approximation to the truth. There are in the metropolis 100 hard ware-sellers, 6 cheap Johns, 30 sellers of cutlery, 6 sellers of tailors' needles, 20 sellers of metal spoons, 500 sellers of jewellery, 2 sellers of card counters, 15 sellers of medals, 6 sellers of rings and sovereigns for a wager, 25 sellers of children's gilt watches, 100 sellers of tin-ware, 100 swag-barrowmen, 12 sellers of dog-collars, &c., 40 sellers of tools, 380 sellers of crockery and glass-wares, 12 sellers of spar-ornaments, 30 sellers of China-ornaments, 6 sellers of stone-fruit, 120 packmen and duffers or hawkers of soft wares, 500 sellers of tapes, cottons, &c.. 100 sellers of lace, 15 sellers of japanned table covers, 500 brace and belt-sellers, 50 sellers of hose, 3 sellers of waist-coats, 230 sellers of blacking, 125 sellers of black-lead, 5 sellers of French polish, 7 sellers of grease-removing composition, 4 sellers of plating-balls, 8 sellers of corn-salve, 4 sellers of China and glass cement, 6 sellers of razor paste, 55 sellers of crackers and detonating-balls, 200 sellers of Lucifer matches, 100 sellers of cigar-lights, 30 sellers of gutta-percha heads, 50 sellers of fly-papers and beetle-wafers, 25 sellers of poison for rats, 35 sellers of walking-sticks, 30 sellers of whips, 4 sellers of clay and Meerschaum pipes, 15 sellers of tobacco-boxes, snuff-boxes, and cigar-cases, 100 sellers of cigars, 50 sellers of sponge, 200 sellers of wash-leathers, 35 sellers of specta-cles, and eye-glasses, 50 sellers of dolls, 50 lot-sellers, 2 sellers of Roulette tables, 4 sellers of rhubarb, 100 rat-catchers, 50 sellers of combs, 50 sellers of money-bags, 70 sellers of coat-studs ; making altogether a total of 4272.

Some few of the above trades are, however, of only a temporary character ; as, for instance, such as are engaged in the street-sale of crackers and detonating-balls—the month of November and the Christmas week being the only regular periods, with

the exception of fairs and races, for the vending of those articles. The fly-papers and beetle-wafers are other instances of the same kind—summer being the only season in which there is a demand for such things. Making due allowance therefore for the temporary character of some of the callings, as well as for the itinerancy and unsettledness of other trades or traders, we may, I think, safely as-sume that the street-sellers connected with this class are about 4000 in number.

Concerning the amount of capital invested in this branch of the street-traffic as well as the income derived therefrom, the following tables are given as being somewhat near the truth.

METAL.

Street-Sellers of Hardware.

	£	s.	d.
Stock-money for 100 vendors at 10*s.* each	50	0	0

Cheap Johns.

6 carts 30*l.* each, and stock-money for the same, 50*l.* each	480	0	0

Street-Sellers of Cutlery.

Stock-money for 30 vendors at 1*s.* 6*d.* each	2	5	0

Blind Street-Sellers of Tailors' Needles.

6 boxes at 1*s.* 6*d.* each; stock-money for 6 vendors at 2*s.*	1	1	0

Street-Sellers of Metal Spoons, &c., at Public-Houses.

Stock-money for 20 vendors at 2*s.* 6*d.* each	2	10	0

Street-Sellers of Jewellery.

500 boxes at 3*s.* 6*d.* each; stock-money for 500 vendors at 15*s.* each	462	10	0

Street-Sellers of Card-Counters, Medals, &c.

17 boxes at 3*s.* each; stock-money for 17 vendors at 2*s.* 6*d.* each	4	13	6

Street-Sellers of Rings and Sovereigns for Wagers.

Stock-money for 6 vendors at 2*s.* 6*d.* each	0	15	0

Street-Sellers of Children's Gilt Watches.

Stock-money for 25 vendors at 5*s.* each	6	5	0

Street-Sellers of Tin-Ware.	£	s.	d.
50 stalls, at 3s. each; stock-money for 100 vendors, averaging 6s. each	37	10	0

Street Swag-barrowmen.
100 barrows, at 1l. each; stock-money for 150 swag-barrowmen, at 10s. each 175 0 0

Street-Sellers of Dog-collars, Key-rings, &c.
6 stalls, at 3s. each; stock-money for 12 vendors, at 5s. each . . . 3 18 0

Street-Sellers of Tools.
6 stalls, at 3s. each; stock-money for 40 vendors, at 10s. each . . . 20 18 0

CROCKERY AND GLASS.
Street-Sellers of Crockery and Glass-Wares.
100 barrows, at 1l. each; 280 baskets, at 2s. 6d. each; 280 linen bags, at 1s. 6d. each; stock-money for 380 vendors, at 10s. each 346 0 0

Street-Sellers of Spar and China-Ornaments, and Stone-Fruit.
16 barrows, at 1l. each; stock-money for 12 vendors of spar-ornaments, at 15s. each; 16 baskets, at 2s. 6d. each; 16 stalls, at 3s. each; stock-money for 6 vendors of stone-fruit, at 10s. each; and 20 roulette tables, at 2s. 6d. each; stock-money for 30 sellers of China-ornaments, at 5s. each 42 8 0

TEXTILE.
Packmen and Duffers, or Hawkers of Soft Wares.
120 wrappers, at 2s. each; stock-money for 120 hawkers, at 5l. each 612 0 0

Street-Sellers of Small Ware, or Tapes, Cottons, &c.
500 boxes, at 1s. 6d. each; stock-money for 500 vendors, at 1s. each 62 10 0

Street-Sellers of Lace.
20 baskets, at 2s. 6d. each; 20 boxes, at 3s. each; 60 stalls, at 3s. each; stock-money for 100 vendors, averaging 2s. 6d. each 27 0 0

Street-Sellers of Japan Table-Covers.
Stock-money for 15 sellers, at 10s. each 7 10 0

Street-Sellers of Braces and Belts, Hose, Trowser-straps, and Waistcoats.
100 stalls, at 4s. each; 300 rods, with hooks to hang the braces upon, at 3d. each; stock-money for 500 brace-sellers, at 5s. each . . . 148 15 0

Street-Sellers of Hose.
Stock-money for 50 vendors, at 10s. each 25 0 0

Street-Sellers of Waistcoats.
Stock-money for 3 vendors, at 15s. each 2 5 0

CHEMICALS.
Street-Sellers of Blacking.
200 boxes, at 6d. each; 30 bags,

at 1s. each; stock-money for 230 vendors, averaging 2s. each . . . 29 10 0

Street-Sellers of Black-Lead.
Stock-money for 125 vendors, at 1s. each 6 5 0

Street-Sellers of French Polish.
5 boxes, at 1s. 6d. each; stock-money for 5 vendors, at 2s. 6d. each 1 0 0

Street-Sellers of Grease-removing Composition.
7 boxes, at 1s. 6d. each; stock-money for 7 vendors, at 1s. 6d. each 1 1 0

Street-Sellers of Plating-Balls.
4 boxes, at 1s. 6d. each; stock-money for 4 vendors, at 1s. each . 0 10 0

Street-Sellers of Corn-Salve.
8 boxes, at 1s. 6d. each; stock-money for 8 vendors, at 6d. each . 0 16 0

Street-Sellers of Glass and China-Cement.
4 boxes, at 1s. 6d. each; stock-money for 4 vendors, at 6d. each . 0 8 0

Street-Sellers of Razor-Paste.
6 trays, at 2s. each; stock-money for 6 vendors, at 1s. each 0 18 0

Street-Sellers of Crackers and Detonating-Balls.
55 trays, at 2s. each; stock-money for 55 vendors, at 1s. 6d. each . . 9 12 6

Street-Sellers of Lucifer Matches.
200 boxes, at 6d. each; stock-money for 200 vendors, at 6d. each . 10 0 0

Street-Sellers of Cigar-Lights.
Stock-money for 100 vendors, at 6d. each 2 10 0

Street-Sellers of Gutta-Percha Heads.
30 boxes, at 1s. 6d. each; stock-money for 30 vendors, at 1s. each . 3 15 0

Street-Sellers of Fly-Papers and Beetle-Wafers.
Stock-money for 50 vendors, at 1s. each 2 10 0

Street-Sellers of Poison for Rats.
Stock-money for 25 vendors, at 2s. 6d. each 3 2 6

MISCELLANEOUS.
Street-Sellers of Walking-sticks.
Stock-money for 35 vendors, at 5s. each 8 15 0

Street-Sellers of Whips.
Stock-money for 30 vendors, at 15s. each 22 10 0

Street-Sellers of Pipes (Tobacco).
Stock-money for 4 vendors, at 5s. each 1 0 0

Street-Sellers of Snuff-Boxes, Tobacco-Boxes, &c.
15 stalls, at 4s. each; stock-money for 15 vendors, at 10s. each . . . 10 10 0

Street-Sellers of Cigars.
Stock-money for 100 vendors, at 10s. each 50 0 0

Street-Sellers of Sponge.
50 baskets, at 1s. each; stock-money for 50 vendors, at 5s. each . 15 0 0

Street-Sellers of Wash-Leathers.
Stock-money for 200 vendors, at 2s. 6d. each 25 0 0

Street-Sellers of Spectacles and Eye-Glasses.

	£	s.	d.
Stock-money for 35 vendors, at 5s. each	8	15	0

Street-Sellers of Dolls.

	£	s.	d.
20 stalls, at 4s. each; 30 baskets, at 3s. 6d. each; stock-money for 50 vendors, at 10s. each	34	5	0

Street Lot-Sellers.

	£	s.	d.
50 boxes, at 1s. 6d. each; stock-money for 50 sellers, at 2s. 6d. each	10	0	0

Street-Sellers of Roulette Boxes.

	£	s.	d.
2 baskets, at 3s. 6d.; stock-money for 2 vendors, at 1l. each	2	7	0

Street-Sellers of Rhubarb and Spice.

	£	s.	d.
4 boxes, at 6s. each; stock-money for 4 vendors, at 10s. each	3	4	0

Rat-Catchers.

	£	s.	d.
20 belts, at 3s. 6d. each; 25 cages, at 1s. each; 25 pair of ferrets, at 2s. 6d. per pair; keep for 25 pair of ferrets, at 4d. per pair weekly	8	5	10

Street-Sellers of Combs.

	£	s.	d.
50 stalls, at 3s. each; 50 boxes, at 3s. 6d. each; stock-money for 50 vendors, at 2s. 6d. each	22	10	0

Street-Sellers of Money-Bags.

	£	s.	d.
Stock-money for 50 vendors, at 2s. each	5	0	0

Street-Sellers of Coat-Studs.

	£	s.	d.
70 boxes, at 1s. 6d. each, stock-money for 70 vendors, at 2s. 6d. each	14	0	0

	£	s.	d.
Total amount of capital	2,833	13	4

INCOME OF THE STREET-SELLERS OF MANUFAC-
TURED ARTICLES.

METAL.

Street-Sellers of Hardware.

There are at present 100 hardware sellers, trading in London, &c.; half of them, I am assured, may be said to take on an average from 20s. to 25s., weekly on the year through; a quarter take 15s., and the remaining quarter from 7s. 6d. to 10s. Calculating an average receipt of 15s. each per week, throughout the entire class, men, women, and children, we find there is annually expended in street-sold hardwares 3,900 0 0

Cheap Johns.

If we calculate that there are 6 "Cheap Johns" in London throughout the year, and that they each take 4l. per day for nine months in the year, or 24l. per week; this amounts to about 5,000l. in nine months. Say that during the winter or the remaining 13 weeks of the year, their receipts are 15l. each per week, this amounts to upwards of 1000l. additional, thus making a gross annual outlay with these dealers of 6,000 0 0

Street-Sellers of Cutlery.

Reckoning there are 30 men who are engaged regularly in the sale of cutlery, and that the average takings of each are about 15s. weekly, this gives a yearly expenditure in the street-trade of cutlery 1,170 0 0

Blind Street-Sellers of Tailors' Needles.

There are now 6 men engaged in selling needles at the several tailors' shops, and calculating their average daily receipts to be 2s. 6d. or 15s. a week each, we find that the annual takings of the whole are 234 0 0

Street-Sellers of Metal-Spoons in Publichouses.

From the best information I can arrive at, the number of metal-spoon hawkers is 20, each of whom take upon an average 16s. weekly, thus showing a yearly expenditure in the street-sale of spoons of 832 0 0

Street-Sellers of Jewellery.

I am informed that there are at present 500 persons engaged in the street sale of jewellery, and calculating a weekly profit of 10s. 6d., and a receipt of 18s. per individual, we find expended in the street-trade . . 23,400

Street-Sellers of Card-Counters.

If there be, on the year's average, only two street-sellers disposing of "Jacks" and earning 9s. a week, — to earn which the receipts will be about 20s., — we find expended in the streets on these trifles annually 104 0 0

Street-Sellers of Medals.

An intelligent man, familiar with the trade, and who was in the habit of clubbing his stock-money with two others, so that they might buy a gross of medals at a time, calculated that 15 medal-sellers were engaged in the traffic the year through, and earned, upon medals alone, 6d. a day each, to clear which they must take 6s. 6d. weekly, giving a yearly outlay of 253 10 0

Street-Sellers of Rings and Sovereigns for a Wager.

One of this class, who is "up to all the dodges of the trade," informed me that there were only 6 men working the rings and sovereigns now in the streets, and that the average takings of each might be about 12s. weekly, thus showing a yearly expenditure of 187 4 0

Street-Sellers of Children's Gilt Watches.

Calculating that 25 persons now vend watches for twelve weeks in the year and that each clears 8s. weekly, taking 24s., we find yearly expended in London streets on these toy watches 360 0 0

Street-Sellers of Tin-Ware.

If we calculate an average receipt, per individual, of 10s. weekly: we find, reckoning 100 sellers, a yearly expenditure on tins, bought in the street, of 2,600 0 0

Swag-Barrowmen. £ s. d.

Calculating that 100 of these traders are, the year round, in London (some are absent all the summer at country fairs, and on any favourable opportunity), and that each takes 2*l.* weekly, we find thus expended in the streets of London, in a year, no less than 10,400 0 0

Sellers of Dog-Collars, Key-Rings, &c.

Reckoning 12*s.* weekly taken by 12 men, there is expended yearly in the streets upon dog-collars . . . 374 0 0

Street-Sellers of Tools.

There are at present 40 men engaged in selling tools throughout the metropolis and they each average about 15*s.* weekly. This gives a yearly outlay of 1,560 0 0

Street-Sellers of Crockery and Glass-Wares.

According to the best calculation there are 380 vendors of crockery and glass-wares, and the average takings of each may be said to amount to 10*s.* weekly, so giving an annual expenditure in the streets of 9,880 0 0

Street-Sellers of Spar-Ornaments.

In this trade I am informed that there are now 12 men, 9 of whom are assisted by their wives, and that in the summer months there are 18. Their profits are about 15*s.* per week on an average of the whole year. What amount of money may be expended by the public in the street-purchase of " spars " I am unable definitely to state, so much being done in the way of barter ; but assuming that there are 14 sellers throughout the year, and that their profits are cent. per cent., there would appear to be laid out in the streets every year on these articles, about 1,000 0 0

Street-Sellers of China-Ornaments.

There are, I am informed, about 30 persons in this trade. If we calculate the receipts at 10*s.* weekly (a low average considering the success of some of the raffles), we find yearly expended in the streets in these ornamental productions 780 0 0

Street-Sellers of Stone-Fruit.

Supposing that there are 6 persons selling stone-fruit in the streets through the year, and that each earns 9*s.* weekly (one man said 7*s.* 6*d.* was the limit of his weekly profits), we find 140*l.* received as profit on these articles, and calculating the gains at 33 per cent., an outlay of 420 0 0

TEXTILE.

Packmen and Duffers, or Hawkers of Soft Wares.

I am told by a London hawker of soft goods that the number of his craft, hawking London and its vicinity, as far as he can judge, is about 120.

In this number are included the Irish £ s. d. linen hawkers. I am also informed that the fair trader's profits amount to about 20 per cent., while those of the not over-particular trader range from 80 to 200 per cent. In a fair way of business it is said the hawker's takings will amount, upon an average, to 7*l.* or 8*l.* per week ; whereas the receipts of the "duffer," or unfair hawker, will sometimes reach to 50*l.* per week ; at 7*l.* per week each, the gross takings will amount to 43,680 0 0

Street-Sellers of Small Ware, or Tapes, Cottons, Laces, &c.

From the best data at my command, I believe there are not fewer than 500 individuals selling these wares in London. Their weekly receipts do not appear to average more than 6*s.* each, hence the expenditure on these articles will amount to 7800 0 0

Street-Sellers of Lace.

100 persons in this trade may be said each to take 10*s.* 6*d.* weekly, the profit being about cent. per cent. ; hence the annual sum expended in the streets in lace and similar commodities is 2730 0 0

Street-Sellers of Japanned Table-Covers.

Calculating that 15 street-sellers each take 25*s.* weekly the year round — one-half being the profit, including their advantages in bartering and raffling—we find there is expended yearly upon japanned table-covers, bought in the streets 975 0 0

Street-Sellers of Braces and Belts.

500 brace-sellers are said to clear 5*s.* a week each on those articles alone, and estimating the profit at 33 per cent., it shows a street expenditure of 26,196*l.*, and calculating one-eighth less for belts, we find that the annual outlay in the streets on braces and belts is 29,470 0 0

Street-Sellers of Hose.

A few pairs of women's stockings are hawked by women, and sold to servant-maids ; but the trade in these goods, I am informed, including all classes of sellers—of whom there may be fifty—does not exceed (notwithstanding the universality of the wear) the receipt of 6*s.* weekly per individual, with a profit of from 1*s.* 4*d.* to 2*s.* ; thus there is an aggregate expenditure yearly of 800 0 0

Street-Sellers of Waistcoats.

There are sometimes no waistcoat-sellers at all ; but generally two, and not unfrequently three. The profits of these men are 1*s.* on a bad, and 2*s.* 6*d.* on a good day. As, at intervals, the street-sellers dispose of a sleeve-waistcoat (waistcoat with sleeves) at from 4s. 6d. to 6s., we may estimate the average earnings in the trade at 5s. per market day, or 10s. in the week; assuming their profits to be 33 per cent., this shows an annual outlay of 312 0 0

CHEMICAL.
Street-Sellers of Blacking.

There are at present 230 vendors of blacking in the London streets. 210 of these sell cake and liquid blacking, each taking 6s. weekly, while the 20 others "work" the Mews with a superior kind of blacking, taking 15s. each; thus there is a yearly expenditure in the sale of blacking in the streets of . . . 4,056 0 0

Street-Sellers of Black-Lead.

There are, I am informed, 100 to 150 persons selling and hawking black-lead in the streets; it may be estimated that they take 4s. each weekly (the adults selling other small articles with the black-lead); thus we find—averaging the number of sellers at 125—that there is expended yearly in the street-sale of this article 1,300 0 0

Street-Sellers of French Polish.

The French-polish-Sellers, I am assured by a man familiar with the business, take 2s. a day each; the 2s. leaves a profit of 10d. The street expenditure is, therefore (reckoning five regular sellers) annually . . 156 0 0

Street-Sellers of Grease-removing Composition.

Calculating that 7 grease-removers carry on the sale of the article 3 days each week, and clear 1s. 6d. per day, we find a yearly expenditure on this commodity equal to 81 18 0

Street-Sellers of Plating-Balls.

Reckoning that 4 men are engaged in selling plating-balls 3 days in each week, and that each take 2s. a day, we find there is an annual outlay on the sale of this article of 62 8 0

Street-Sellers of Corn Salve.

Calculating that 8 of these traders take 10s. weekly, we find there is expended in the streets on this salve 208 0 0

Street-Sellers of Glass and China-Cement.

There are at present 4 men vending this article in the streets of London, and if each seller take 5s. weekly (of which 4s. may be profit), we find there is expended yearly by street customers in this cement . . . 52 0 0

Street-Sellers of Razor Paste.

Calculating that 6 men "work" the metropolis daily, taking 2s. each per day (with 1s. 2d. profit), we find the amount of the street outlay to be upwards of 187 0 0

Street-Sellers of Crackers and Detonating-Balls.

I am assured that for a few days

last November, from 50 to 60 men and women were selling crackers in the streets. The most intelligent man that I met with, acquainted, as he called it, "with all the ins and outs of the trade," calculated that during the month of November and at Christmas, 100l. at least was expended in the streets in these combustibles, and another 100l. at other times of the year, thus giving altogether a yearly outlay of 200 0 0

Street-Sellers of Lucifer-Matches.

Supposing that each of the 200 traders take, on lucifers alone, but 4s. weekly, selling nine dozen (with a profit to the seller of from 1s. 9d. to 2s. 6d.), we find on lucifer-matches bought in the streets an annual outlay of 2,080 0 0

Street-Sellers of Cigar-Lights or Fuzees.

It will, I believe, be accurate to state that in the streets there are generally 100 persons subsisting, or endeavouring to subsist, on the sale of fuzees alone. It may be estimated also that each of these traders averages a receipt of 10d. a day (with a profit exceeding 6d.), so that the sum yearly laid out in the streets in this way amounts to 1,300 0 0

Street-Sellers of Gutta-Percha Heads, &c.

There are at present, I am informed, 30 persons selling gutta-percha heads in the streets, some of them confining their business solely to those articles. Their average receipts, I am assured, do not exceed 5s. a week each, for, though some may take 15s. a week, others, and generally the stationary head-sellers, do not take 1s. The profit to the street retailer is one-third of his receipts. From this calculation it appears, that if the present rate of sale continue, the sum spent yearly in these street toys is 390 0 0

Street-Sellers of Fly-Papers and Beetle-Wafers.

Last summer, I was informed, there were 50 or 60 persons selling fly-papers and beetle-wafers in the streets; some of them boys, and all of them of the general class of street-sellers, who "take" to any trade for which 1s. suffices as capital. Their average earnings may be estimated at 2s. 6d. a day, about one-half being profit. This gives a street outlay, for a "season" of ten weeks, of . . 375 0 0

Street-Sellers of Poison for Rats.

Calculating 25 sellers of rat-poison, and each taking on an average 1s. daily for the sale of their article, we find that the sum annually expended upon this commodity amounts to . 390 0 0

MISCELLANEOUS.   £ *s.* *d.*

Street-Sellers of Walking-Sticks.

For 12 weeks of the year there are, I am told, every day 35 stick-sellers, each taking, on an average, 30*s.* a week (with a profit, individually, of about 12*s.*); we find thus that the sum expended yearly in walking-sticks in the streets is 630 0 0

Street-Sellers of Whips, &c.

Averaging that 30 whip-sellers take 25*s.* each weekly (with profits of from 5*s.* to 10*s.*) in London alone, we find that the yearly sum expended in the streets in whips amounts to . 1,950 0 0

Street-Sellers of Pipes (Tobacco).

If we calculate that 4 persons sell pipes daily the year through, taking each 25*s.* (and clearing 10*s.*), we find the yearly sum expended upon the hawkers' pipes amounts to . . . 260 0 0

Street-Sellers of Snuff-Boxes, Tobacco-Boxes, &c.

Reckoning that 15 persons trading on snuff and tobacco and cigar-boxes take 18*s.* weekly (clearing 7*s.* or 8*s.*), we find the sum thus expended annually amounts to 702 0 0

Street-Sellers of Cigars.

Reckoning the number of vendors of cigars at 100, and the average takings of each to be 20*s.* weekly, we have a yearly outlay of 5,200 0 0

Street-Sellers of Sponge.

Calculating, then, that only 50 persons (and so allowing for the irregularities in the trade) vend sponge daily, and that each takes 15*s.* weekly, —some taking 25*s.*, and others but 5*s.*—with about half profit on the whole (the common sponge is often from 200 to 300 per cent. profit), we find the outlay to be 1,950 0 0

Street-Sellers of Wash-Leather.

There are, I am assured, 100 individuals selling little or nothing else but wash-leather in London (for these traders are found in all the suburbs), and that they respectively take 10*s.* weekly, with a profit of from 4*s.* to 5*s.* There are, also, 100 other persons selling them occasionally, along with other goods, and as they vend the higher-priced articles, they probably receive nearly an equal amount, Hence it would appear that there is annually expended in the streets in this purchase, upwards of 5,000 0 0

Street-Sellers of Spectacles and Eye-glasses.

It may be estimated, I am assured, that there are 35 men who vend these articles daily, taking 15*s.* a week (with a profit of 10*s.*), the yearly expenditure being thus . . 1,365 0 0

Street-Sellers of Dolls.   £ *s.* *d.*

There are, at least, at this time of year, when the fairs are coming on, 50 doll-hawkers, who vend nothing else. Say that each of these sell one dozen dolls per day, and that their average price is 4*d.* each ; that is just 10*l.* a day, and 60*l.* per week. In the winter time so many are not sold ; but I have no doubt that 50*l.*'s worth of dolls are sold each week throughout the year by London hawkers alone, hence the annual outlay on street-dolls would be close upon 3,000 0 0

Street Lot-sellers.

It may be estimated that 50 men carry on this trade. Each of these may take 13*s.* weekly (with a profit of 7*s.* 6*d.*), so showing the annual street outlay to be 1,690 0 0

Street-Sellers of Roulette Tables.

Calculating that 2 sellers of Roulette tables take 30*s.* each weekly, we find the annual outlay amounts to . . . 156 0 0

Street-Sellers of Rhubarb.

Reckoning 4 street-sellers of rhubarb and spice each taking 18*s.* weekly, we find the sum annually spent in the sale of these articles to be upwards of 187 0 0

Rat-Catchers.

There are, I am told, 100 rat-catchers resorting, at intervals, to London, but only a fourth of that number can be estimated as carrying on their labours regularly in town ; their average earnings, I am assured, do not exceed 15*s.* a week ; thus there is a yearly expenditure of 975 0 0

Street-Sellers of Combs.

From the best information I have gained, there are 50 persons who sell nothing but combs, the average takings of each are 9*s.* a week, showing the yearly outlay in the streets on these articles to be 1,170 0 0

Street-Sellers of Money-Bags.

There are at present 50 persons consisting of men, women, and children vending money-bags in the streets of London, each taking on an average 1*s.* 6*d.* daily, or 9*s.* per week, and so giving a yearly expenditure of . 1,170 0 0

Street-Sellers of Coat-Studs.

There are, I am informed, no less than 70 persons, consisting of men, women, and children. These, I am told, take upon an average 15*s.* a week each, their usual profits being cent. per cent. ; thus we find a yearly outlay on studs bought in the streets of . . 2.730 0 0

Total amount of income. . £188,189 0 0

ERRATA.

PAGE 5, line 45, second column, *for* 9,350 *read* 8,850.

6, line 39, first column, *for* 34,209 *read* 28,506.

line 43, *for* between thirty and forty thousand *read* between twenty-five and thirty thousand.

11, number of markets Surrey side, *for* 664 *read* 764.

number of markets Middlesex side, *for* 3,137 *read* 3,147.

first line, second column, *for* 3801 *read* 3,911, and *for* 102 *read* 105.

26, line 50, first column, *for* 75*l*. *read* 67*l*. 10*s*.; line 53, *for* 5,25*l*. *read* 405*l*.; line 57, *for* 6,300*l*. *read* 4,860*l*.

30, line 25, *for* 2*l*. each *read* 2*l*.

56, line 27, *for* 24,135*l*. *read* 23,775*l*.

line 28, *for* upwards *read* very nearly.

line 50, *for* 14,000*l*. *read* 9,750*l*.

line 54, *for* 6,500*l*. *read* 130*l*.

line 58, *for* 22,550*l*. *read* 17,400*l*.

line 36, second column, *for* between 1,250,000*l*. and 1,500,000*l*. *read* 1,040,000*l*.

63, line 13, *for* 5,040,000 lbs. *read* 4,940,000 lbs.

line 27, *for* 147,000,000 *read* 49,750,000.

line 36, *for* 24,300 *read* 22,067.

line 38, *for* 32,400 *read* 33,696.

69, line 38, *for* 263,281,000 *read* 263,261,000.

80, line 11, *for* 16,450 *read* 37,650.

line 14, *for* 171,000 *read* 175,000.

line 15, *for* 108,000 *read* 112,000.

line 16, *for* 24,000 *read* 26,800.

line 28, *for* 16,817,000 *read* 18,017,000

line 31, *for* 221,100 *read* 221,200.

line 39, *for* 94,000 *read* 104,400.|

line 41, *for* 32,900 *read* 37,900.

95, line 37, first column, *for* 6,270 *read* 6,240.

line 43, first column, *for* 1,960 *read* 1,950.

line 48, first column, *for* 15,300 *read* 15,200.

line 16, second column, *for* 333,420 *read* 332,400.

96, line 3, first column, *for* 333,420 *read* 332,400.

line 5, first column, *for* 292,000 *read* 292,240.

line 6, first column, *for* 626,420 *read* 625,640.

line 6, second column, *for* 2,087,270 *read* 2,086,490.

122, table, middle column, line 12, *for* 524,000 *read* 525,000.

table, middle column, line 21, *for* 524,000 *read* 525,000.

table, middle column, line 22, *for* 1,464,000 *read* 1,465,000.

130, line 4, second column, *for* 160 *read* 166.

139, line 12, second column, *for* 123,360 *read* 129,360.

142, line 46, second column, *for* 575 read 525.

144, line 7, first column, *for* 150,000 *read* 150,768.

line 33, first column, *for* 50 *read* 60.

last line, first column, *for* 2,867*l*. *read* 2,877*l*.

line 9, second column, *for* 1,183*l*. *read* 1,883*l*.

line 11, second column, *for* 2,774*l*. *read* 2,474*l*.

line 32, second column, *for* 210 *read* 160.

line 33, second column, *for* 1,667*l*. *read* 1,617*l*.

158, line 17, second column, *for* 13,949*l*. *read* 13,950*l*.

line 20, second column, *for* 520 *read* 572.

line 21, second column, *for* 28,504 *read* 28,557.

163, line 4, second column, *for* 19,448 *read* 21,910.

line 24, second column, *for* 12,102 *read* 14,586.

171, line 13, second column, *for* 3,031*l*. 11*s*. *read* 3,033*l*. 6*s*. 8*d*.

195, line 39, first column, *for* 1,452*l*. *read* 780*l*.

197, line 13, first column, *for* 3,000*l*. *read* 1,040*l*.

PAGE 203, line 12, first column, *for* 300 *read* 100.
218, line 61, first column, *for* because *read* although.
line 63, first column, *for* no *read* an utter want of.
line 51, second column, *for* flummut *read* flummuxed.
325, line 48, second column, *for* 780*l. read* 3,900*l.*
329, line 43, second column, *for* 3,500 *read* 13,500.
line 45, second column, *for* 700 *read* 2,700.
line 46, second column, *for* 25,000 *read* 20,700.
line 47, second column, *for* 250 *read* 207.
340, line 57, second column, *for* vicapicated *read* incapacitated.
347, line 41, second column, *for* 23,410 *read* 23,400.
370, line 15, second column, *for* store *read* stone.
377, In the table of Hawkers and Pedlars for England, Wales, and Scotland, the Total for Wales
is placed below the Islands in the British Seas, but should stand above it.
388, line 43, first column, *for* 2,600 *read* 2,730.
392, last line, second column, *for* 384,400 *read* 1,872,000.
393, line 2, first column, *for* 3,120 *read* 3,900.
line 5, first column, *for* 4,680 *read* 3,900.
427, line 9, first column, *for* 1,250 *read* 1,300.
440, line 9, first column, *for* 2,340 *read* 1,950.
441, line 55, first column, *for* 692 *read* 702.
443, line 39, second column, *for* 1,850 *read* 1,950.
449, line 58, first column, *for* 1,190 *read* 1,690.

INDEX.

INDEX.

CPSIA information can be obtained at www.ICGtesting.com
Printed in the USA
LVOW101808270513

335591LV00001B/138/P